IB WORLD SCHOOLS
YEARBOOK 2024

Contents

IB WORLD SCHOOLS YEARBOOK 2024

Editor: Phoebe Whybray

Acknowledgements

We are extremely grateful to those who have helped to compile this Yearbook.

We also extend our warm gratitude to the many schools and colleges for providing us promptly and efficiently with the accurate information this Yearbook contains.

Orders: please contact Hachette UK Distribution, Hely Hutchinson Centre, Milton Road, Didcot, Oxfordshire, OX11 7HH.
Telephone: +44 (0)1235 827827.
Email: education@hachette.co.uk.
Lines are open from 9 a.m. to 5 p.m., Monday to Friday.

A CIP catalogue record for this book is available from the British Library.

ISBN: 9781036005320

Published in 2024 by
John Catt from Hodder Education,
An Hachette UK Company
15 Riduna Park, Station Road,
Melton, Woodbridge IP12 1QT
Telephone: +44 (0)1394 389850
www.johncatt.com

A catalogue record for this title is available from the British Library

International Baccalaureate Organization (UK) Ltd
Peterson House
Malthouse Avenue
Cardiff Gate
Cardiff
Wales CF23 8GL
United Kingdom
Website: www.ibo.org

Message from Director General and Chair

Dear the IB community,

At the IB, our purpose is to help young people flourish and to support schools and educators as they equip those young people for their future lives. We have ambitious plans to extend our reach further than ever before so that more young people, from more diverse backgrounds, are able to access the high-quality learning that an IB education promises.

In the past year, we have paved the way for the evolution of international education. We want to challenge the current paradigm and transcend established educational norms. To this end, we have collaborated with IB teachers from all over the world to develop and explore the possibilities presented by rapid advancements in technology. We have launched innovative initiatives, forged strategic partnerships, and reinforced recognition of the IB across the globe. And we have supported our IB World Schools as they develop students into caring, curious and knowledgeable young people who will create the better and more peaceful world we all strive for.

We are proud that IB World Schools have been able to both navigate the complexities and challenges that our world is currently facing as well as fully embrace collaboration and innovation as we share our ideas to evolve, grow and improve.

Educators bear the profound responsibility of shaping the hearts and minds of the future generation—a role that carries extreme significance, not just for the young people they work with directly, but also for the local and global communities that those young people will go on to impact.

Even with the weight of this duty towards our future world, it has never been clearer that the IB community is dedicated to the continuous promotion of our shared values and commitment to deliver the IB mission.

As we transform what it means to study an IB programme over the coming years, this mutual dedication, which has always been a part of the IB's heritage, will be the critical success factor as we launch innovations that will help us tackle any challenge we face.

We know that the future has been irrevocably changed by the events of the past few years as well as by the rapidly evolving technologies we're witnessing, but we look forward to working with all of you—a community of passionate educators—as together we strive to create a better world through education.

Olli-Pekka Heinonen – IB Director General
Helen Drennen – Chair of the IB Board of Governors

Introduction, How to use this Yearbook

The International Baccalaureate (IB) offers high quality programmes of international education to a worldwide community of schools, aiming to develop internationally minded people who, recognizing their common humanity and shared guardianship of the plant, help to create a better, more peaceful world.

The IB works alongside state and privately funded schools around the world that share the commitment to international education, to deliver these programmes. Schools that have achieved the high standards required for authorization to offer one or more of the IB programmes are known as "IB World Schools". As of September 2023, there were 1,239 schools with 1,378 programmes in candidate status (559 PYP, 472 MYP, 281 DP, 66 CP).

The IB World Schools Yearbook is the official guide to schools authorized to offer the Primary Years Programme, the Middle Years Programme, the Diploma Programme and the Career-related Programme. It tells you where the IB World Schools are situated and what they offer, and it provides up-to-date information about IB programmes and the IB organization.

This is an ideal reference for school administration, parents and education ministries worldwide as it:

- provides a comprehensive reference of IB World Schools for quick and easy access
- raises the profile of IB World Schools within their local community and beyond
- provides comprehensive information about IB programmes and the IB.

How to use this yearbook

The Yearbook has been designed to be as easy as possible to use and has been divided into five sections.

1. **General information** about the IB and its programmes.
2. **Comprehensive information** about IB World Schools presented in alphabetical order by school name, colour coded according to IB geographical region. In this section, schools have been given the opportunity to highlight their best qualities by creating an enhanced profile for their school.
3. **Directory information** about every IB World School that offers one or more of the IB programmes as of September 2023. The directory is ordered by IB region and contains general and contact information about each school. Information about the three IB regions is also given in this section. (Those schools that have elected to purchase a profile in the Yearbook will appear in capital letters in the directory.)
4. **Appendices** containing information and lists relevant to the IB. These include addresses of IB offices, location of IB World Schools, Diploma Programme subjects offered (in 2024), IB Associations around the world, university acknowledgement of the Diploma Programme and Career-related Programme and universities offering IB scholarships.
5. **Index** of all schools listed geographically and alphabetically by name.

Are you looking for a specific IB World School?

If you know the name of the school but are unsure of its location, turn to the index on p. 641, where you will find an alphabetic listing of all IB World Schools.

Are you looking for an IB World School in a specific country?

Look first in the directory section; this will give you the basic information about all the schools in each region. More detailed information can be found in the profiles section for those schools marked with capitalized letters.

The IB website, ibo.org, also contains the most up-to-date information on IB World Schools. A school search option is available from every page on the site for people wanting to find an IB World School.

THE UNIVERSITY
OF QUEENSLAND
AUSTRALIA
CREATE CHANGE

IB Mission Statement

The International Baccalaureate aims to develop inquiring, knowledgeable and caring young people who help to create a better and more peaceful world through intercultural understanding and respect.

To this end the organization works with schools, governments and international organizations to develop challenging programmes of international education and rigorous assessment.

These programmes encourage students across the world to become active, compassionate and lifelong learners who understand that other people, with their differences, can also be right.

Déclaration de mission de l'IB

Le Baccalauréat International (IB) a pour but de développer chez les jeunes la curiosité intellectuelle, les connaissances et la sensibilité nécessaires pour contribuer à bâtir un monde meilleur et plus paisible, dans un esprit d'entente mutuelle et de respect interculturel.

À cette fin, l'IB collabore avec des établissements scolaires, des gouvernements et des organisations internationales pour mettre au point des programmes d'éducation internationale stimulants et des méthodes d'évaluation rigoureuses.

Ces programmes encouragent les élèves de tout pays à apprendre activement tout au long de leur vie, à être empreints de compassion, et à comprendre que les autres, en étant différents, puissent aussi être dans le vrai.

Declaración de principios de IB

El Bachillerato Internacional tiene como meta formar jóvenes solidarios, informados y ávidos de conocimiento, capaces de contribuir a crear un mundo mejor y más pacífico, en el marco del entendimiento mutuo y el respeto intercultural.

En pos de este objetivo, la organización colabora con establecimientos escolares, gobiernos y organizaciones internacionales para crear y desarrollar programas de educación internacional exigentes y métodos de evaluación rigurosos.

Estos programas alientan a estudiantes del mundo entero a adoptar una actitud activa de aprendizaje durante toda su vida, a ser compasivos y a entender que otras personas, con sus diferencias, también pueden estar en lo cierto.

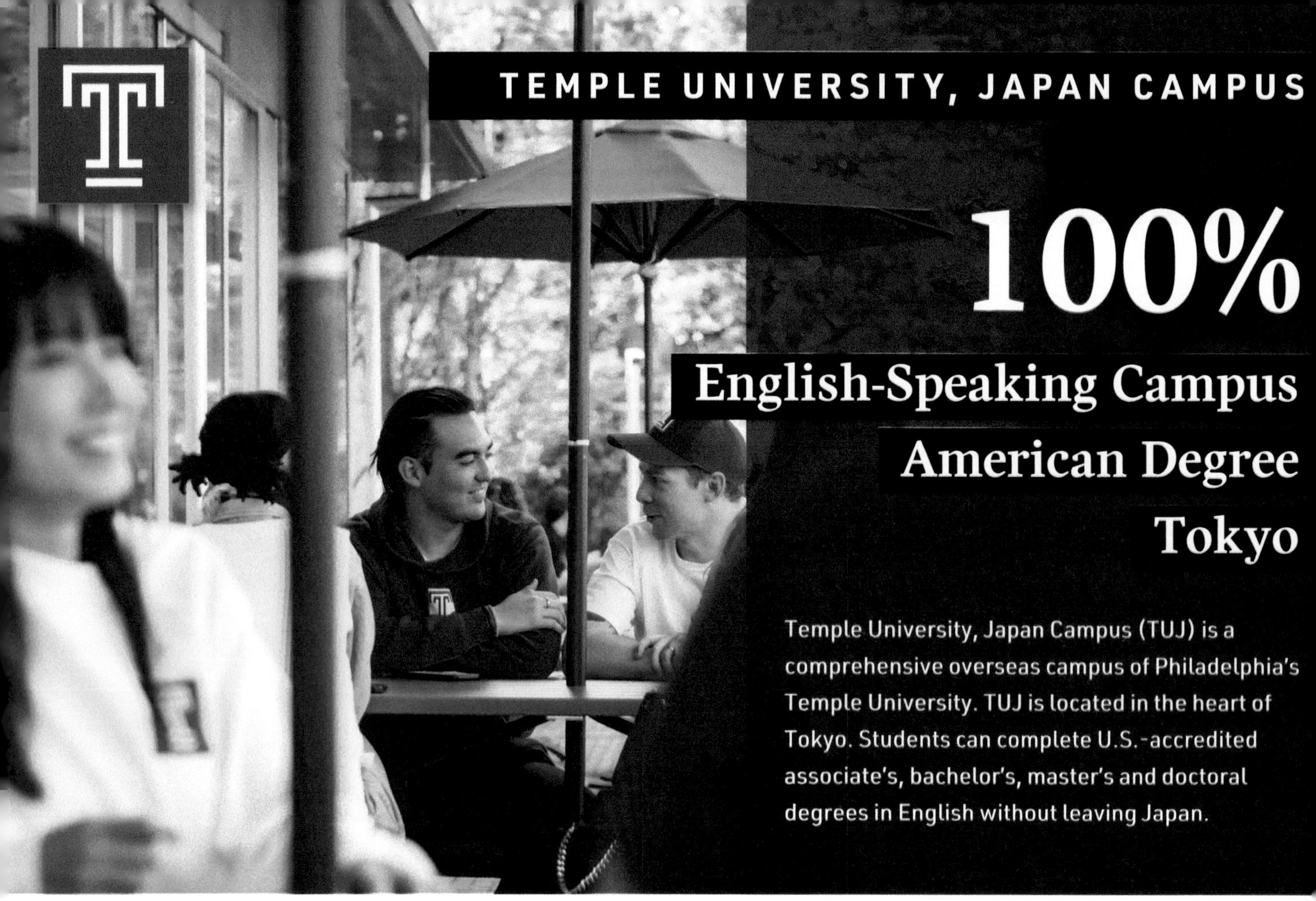

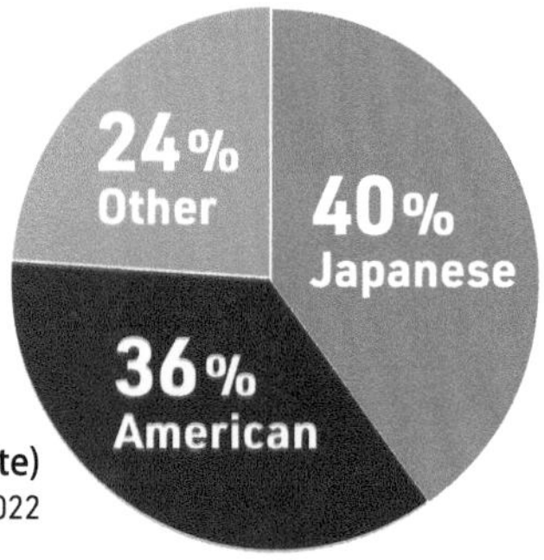

About International Baccalaureate

Pioneering a movement of international education in 1968, the International Baccalaureate (IB) now offers four high quality, challenging educational programmes. The IB gives students distinct advantages by providing strong foundations, critical thinking skills, and a proficiency for solving complex problems, while encouraging diversity, curiosity, and a healthy appetite for learning and excellence. In a world where asking the right questionsis as important as discovering answers, the IB champions critical thinking and flexibility in study by crossing disciplinary, cultural and national boundaries. Supported by world-class educators and coordinators, the IB currently engages with more than 1.95 million students in over 5,500 schools across 160 countries. To find out more, please visit www.ibo.org.

Core areas

The IB works in three core areas:

- learning and teaching—development of philosophy-based and research-evidenced curriculum and programmes
- services to schools—authorization, implementation, evaluation, and professional development of teachers
- assessment of students—design, development, and delivery of assessment for students.

The IB offers four programmes, which can be offered individually or as a continuum by IB World Schools, for students aged 3 to 19.

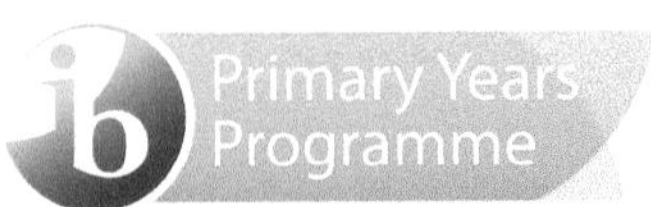

The **Primary Years Programme (PYP)**, for students aged 3-12, started in 1997 and is now offered by 2,268 IB World Schools. The PYP focuses on the development of the whole child as an inquirer, both in the classroom and in the world outside.

The **Middle Years Programme (MYP)**, for students aged 11-16, started in 1994 and is now offered by 1,683 IB World Schools. Providing a framework of academic challenge, the MYP encourages students to embrace and understand the connections between traditional subjects and the real world.

The **Diploma Programme (DP)**, for students aged 16-19, started in 1968 with first examinations in 1970 and is now offered by 3,651 IB World Schools. The DP is an academically challenging and balanced programme of education that prepares students for success at university and beyond.

The **Career-related Programme (CP)**, for students aged 16-19, started in 2010 with first examinations in 2012 and is now offered by 363 IB World Schools. Incorporating the vision and educational principles of the IB programmes into a unique offering, the CP is specifically designed for students who wish to engage in career-related learning.

Our values

The IB enables students to direct their own learning pathway and develop the skills and confidence they need to thrive and make a difference in an ever-changing world. It empowers teachers as the architects of learning excellence, working alongside engaged colleagues in a rewarding career supported by a strong global network. And it brings schools a powerful reputation for successful outcomes that uplift the whole community.

Promoting intercultural understanding and respect, the IB sees these values not as an alternative to a sense of cultural and national identity, but as an essential part of life in the 21st century.

As the IB takes concrete and proactive measures on diversity, equity, and inclusion, it encourages the whole IB community to understand and celebrate differences, while recognizing and valuing the things we have in common.

By embracing learner variability so that our learners are not excluded on the grounds of any of their characteristics, the IB commits to acting supportively and with consideration for young people affected by difficult or adverse circumstances, their own changing personal histories or contexts, or other challenges affecting their life as IB students.

The IB commits to being fully focused on the needs of our staff, IB World Schools and their educators and students, as we challenge ourselves to become a more diverse, open, inclusive, and accepting organization, standing against racism, prejudice, discrimination, and marginalization wherever we can.

Figure 1: Types of IB World Schools (Information correct as of November 2023)

	Charter	Private	State	State subsidized	Total
Africa, Middle East	5	1162	335	81	1583
Asia Pacific	3	1033	161	20	1217
Americas	140	835	1890	19	2884
Total	**148**	**3030**	**2386**	**120**	**5684**

Does not include European Platform schools. Includes MYP Partner Schools.

IB World Schools:

- share the mission and commitment of the IB to quality, international education
- play an active and supporting role in the worldwide community of IB World Schools
- share their knowledge and experience in the development of IB programmes
- are committed to the professional development of teachers

Funding for IB programmes comes from the fees paid by IB World Schools, with additional income from workshops and publication sales. Donors provide support for development projects that cannot be implemented from the organization's budget.

Figure 2: IB World Schools

Total number of IB World Schools: 5,684 in 160 countries (as of November 2023).

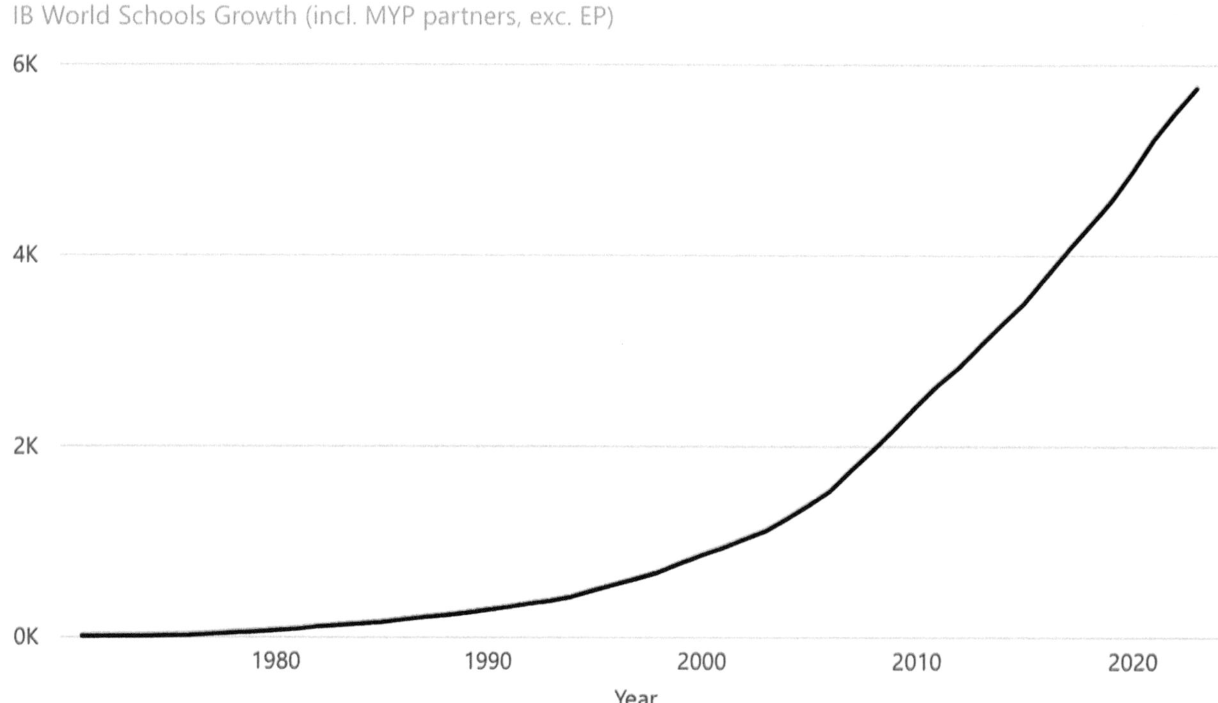

Breakdown by regions

Africa, Europe, Middle East	99 countries	1,583 Authorized schools
Asia Pacific	28 countries	1,217 Authorized schools
Americas	33 countries	2,884 Authorized schools
Total	**160 countries**	**5,684 Authorized schools**

Does not include European Platform schools. Includes MYP Partner Schools.

Breakdown by programmes

	PYP	MYP	DP	CP	Total
Africa, Europe, Middle East	618	474	1258	105	2455
Asia Pacific	726	321	739	60	1846
Americas	924	888	1654	198	3664
Total	**2268**	**1683**	**3651**	**363**	**7965**

*As of November 2023

Does not include European Platform schools nor MYP Partner Schools.

As of November 2023, the four IB programmes are taught in 160 countries.

Figure 3: Growth of the Four IB Programmes

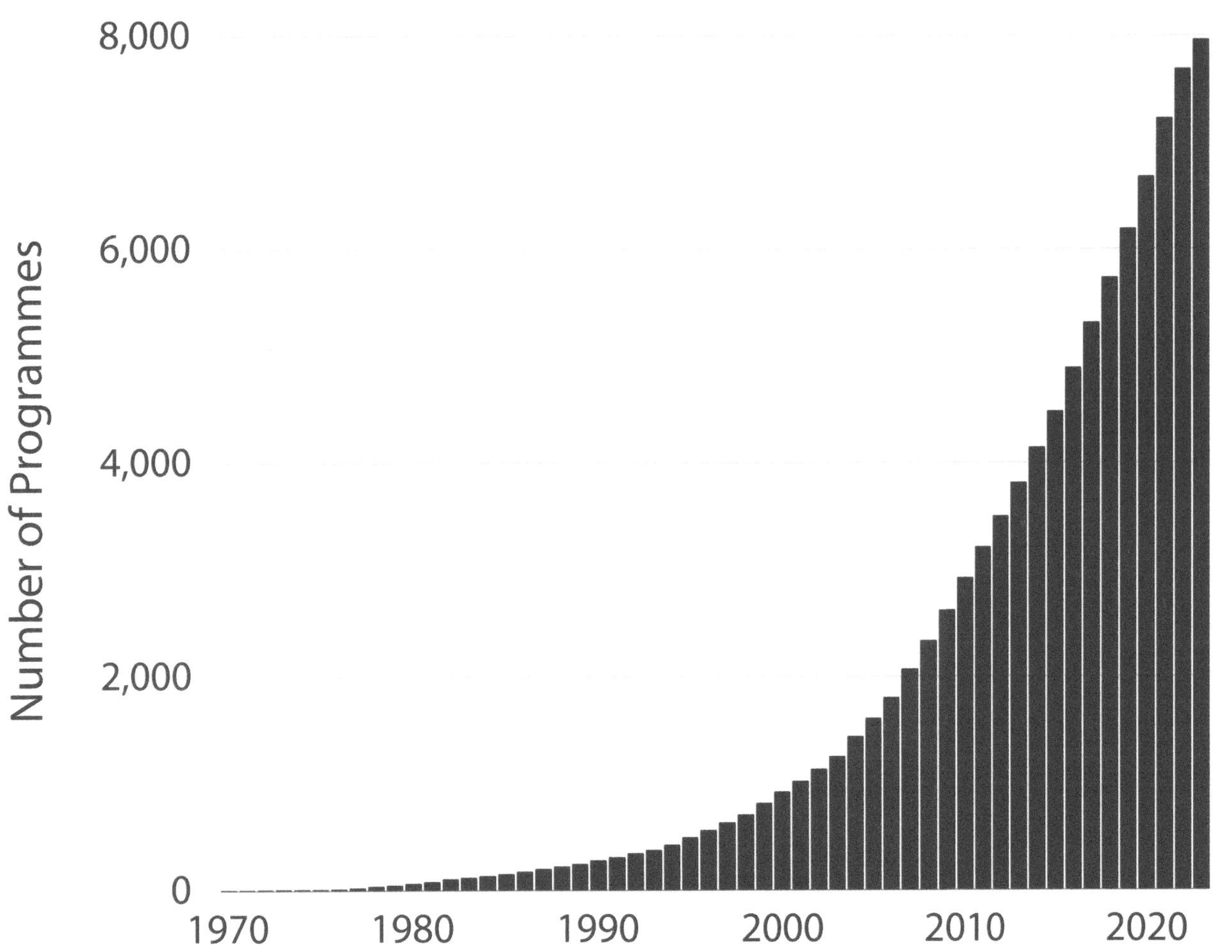

Does not include European Platform nor MYP Partner Schools

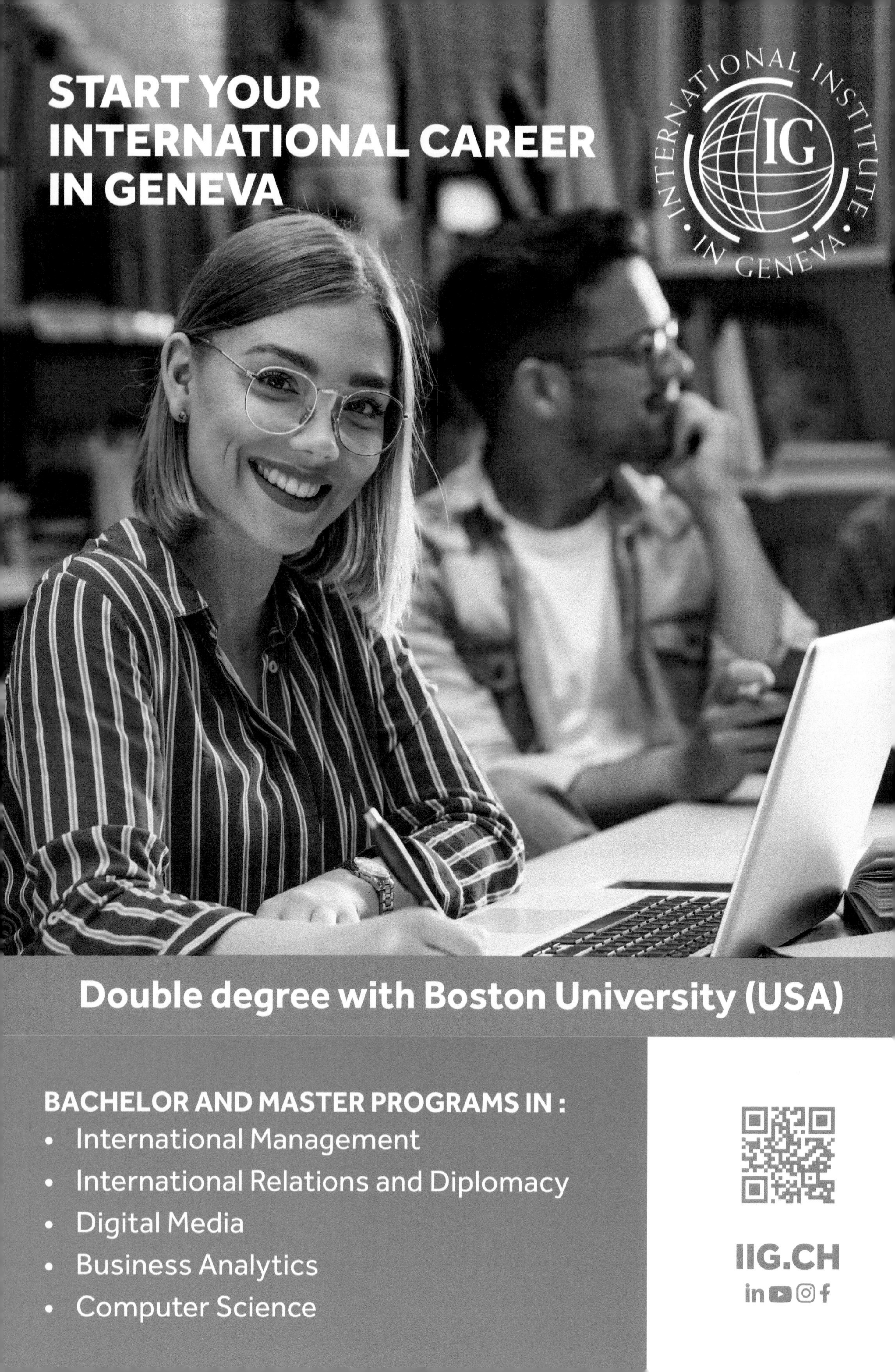

The IB Learner Profile

The aim of all IB programmes is to develop internationally minded people who, recognizing their common humanity and shared guardianship of the planet, help to create a better and more peaceful world.

As IB learners we strive to be:

Inquirers	We nurture our curiosity, developing skills for inquiry and research. We know how to learn independently and with others. We learn with enthusiasm and sustain our love of learning throughout life.
Knowledgeable	We develop and use conceptual understanding, exploring knowledge across a range of disciplines. We engage with issues and ideas that have local and global significance.
Thinkers	We use critical and creative thinking skills to analyze and take responsible action on complex problems. We exercise initiative in making reasoned, ethical decisions.
Communicators	We express ourselves confidently and creatively in more than one language and in many ways. We collaborate effectively, listening carefully to the perspectives of other individuals and groups.
Principled	We act with integrity and honesty, with a strong sense of fairness and justice, and with respect for the dignity and rights of people everywhere. We take responsibility for our actions and their consequences.
Open-minded	We critically appreciate our own cultures and personal histories, as well as the values and traditions of others. We seek and evaluate a range of points of view, and we are willing to grow from the experience.
Caring	We show empathy, compassion and respect. We have a commitment to service, and we act to make a positive difference in the lives of others and in the world around us.
Risk-takers	We approach uncertainty with forethought and determination; we work independently and cooperatively to explore new ideas and innovative strategies. We are resourceful and resilient in the face of challenges and change.
Balanced	We understand the importance of balancing different aspects of our lives – intellectual, physical and emotional – to achieve well-being for ourselves and others. We recognize our interdependence with other people and with the world in which we live.
Reflective	We thoughtfully consider the world and own ideas and experience. We work to understand our strengths and weaknesses in order to support our learning and personal development.

IB Programmes

What is an International Baccalaureate (IB) education?

An IB education is unique because of its rigorous academic and personal standards. IB programmes challenge students aged 3 to 19 to excel not only in their studies but also in their personal growth.

We aspire to help schools develop well-rounded students, who respond to challenges with optimism and an open mind, are confident in their own identities, make ethical decisions, join with others in celebrating our common humanity and apply what they learn in real-world, complex and unpredictable situations.

Through our high-quality programmes of international education, we aim to inspire a quest for learning throughout life that is marked by enthusiasm and empathy.

Our vision is to offer all students an IB education that:

- focuses on learners — our student-centred programmes promote healthy relationships, ethical responsibility, and personal challenge
- develops effective approaches to teaching and learning — our programmes help students to develop the attitudes and skills they need for both academic and personal success
- works within global contexts — our programmes increase understanding of languages and cultures and explore globally significant ideas and issues
- explores significant content — our programmes offer a curriculum that is broad and balanced, conceptual and connected.

Informed by values described in the IB learner profile, IB learners strive to become inquirers, knowledgeable, thinkers, communicators, principled, open-minded, caring, risk-takers, balanced, and reflective. These attributes represent a broad range of human capacities and responsibilities that go beyond intellectual development and academic success.

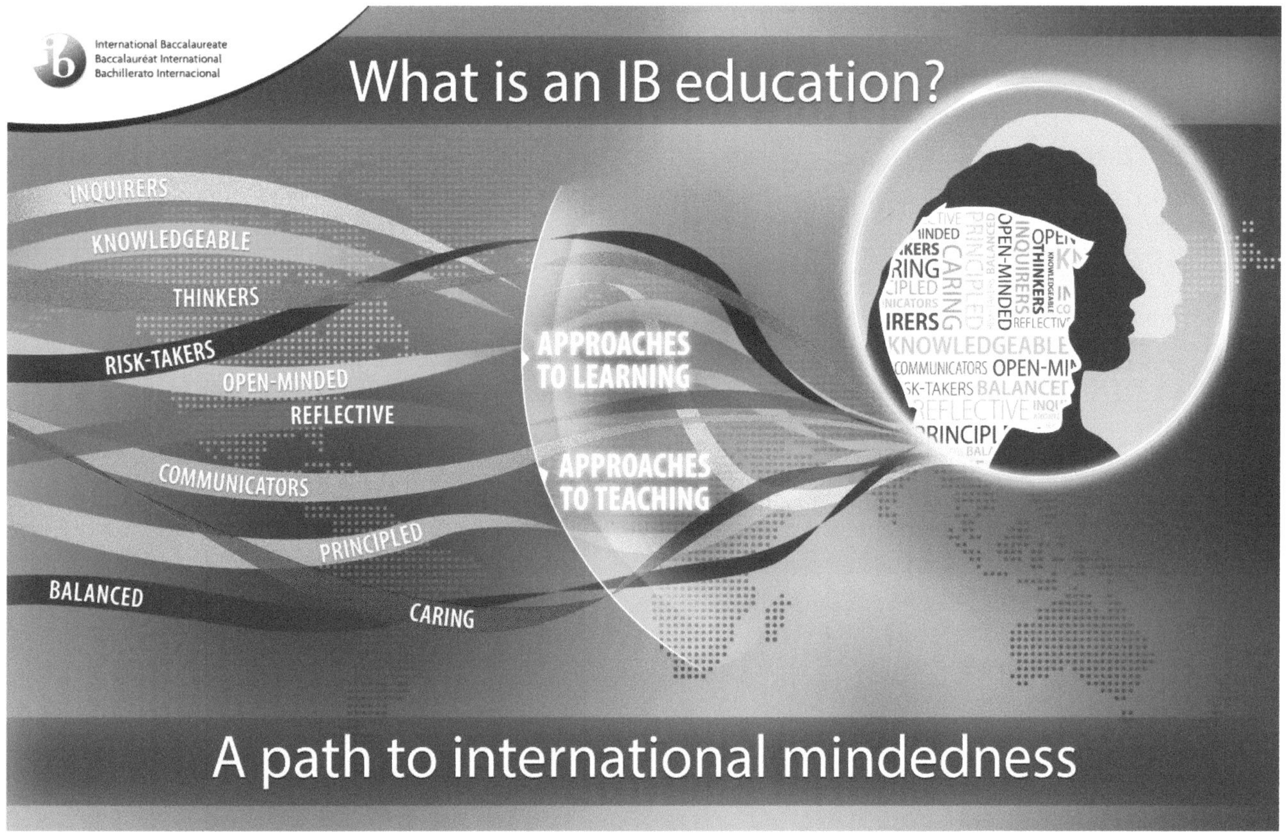

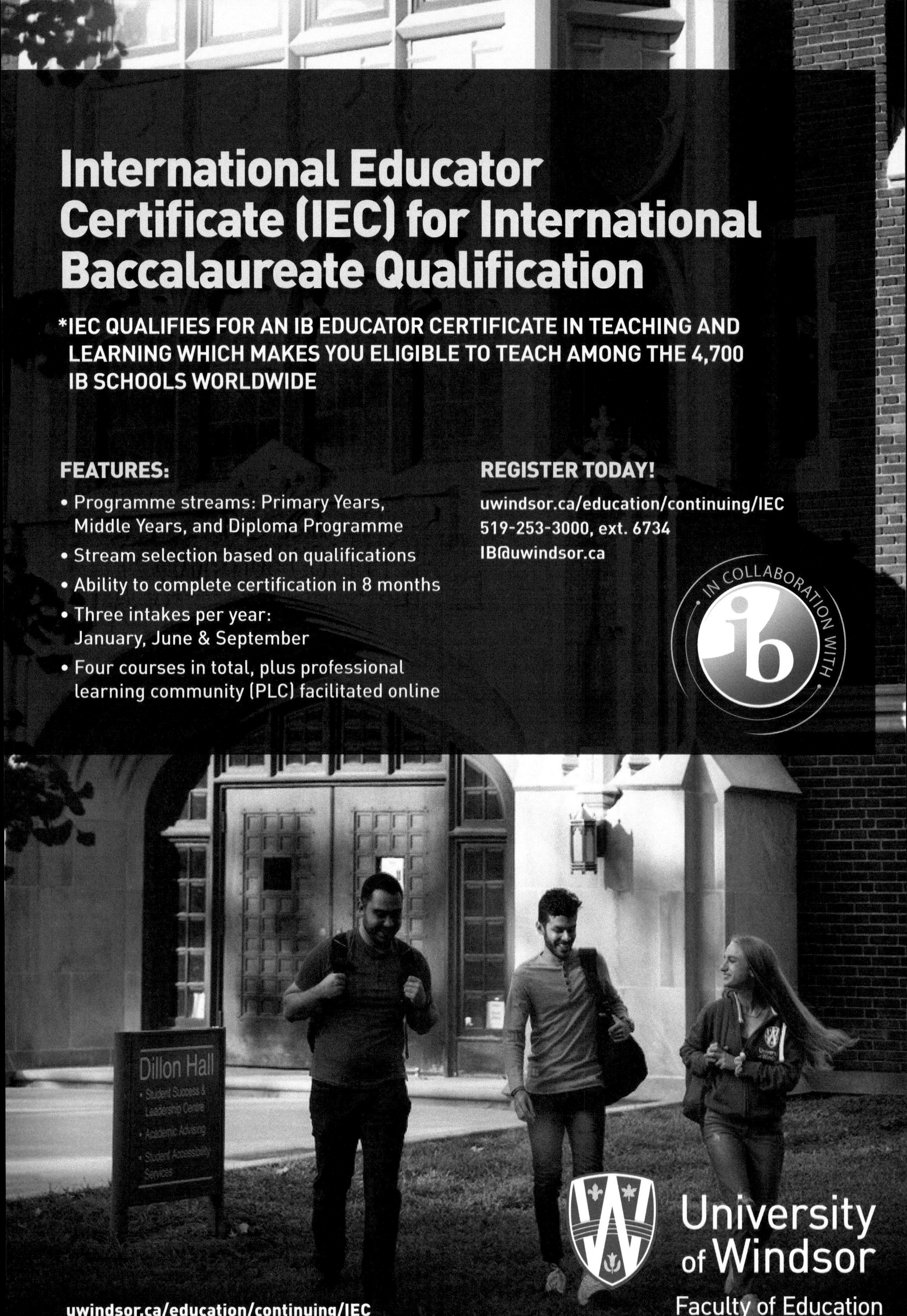

What is the IB Primary Years Programme (PYP)?

A transformative and caring approach that builds a lifelong love of learning

The PYP, for children from 3-12 years, is the start to a lifelong love of learning. It is a caring and thoughtful approach that nurtures the "whole" child and gives them ownership of their studies from the very beginning.

PYP teachers consider each child's unique abilities and interests, to develop inquiry-based learning environments that build universal skills for life, like thinking, researching and cultural understanding. Children explore across and beyond subject boundaries through transdisciplinary inquiries, investigating big — and small — questions about what it means to be human in today's world. But the most important thing children get from the programme is an inquiring mind, as well as the ability to find things out for themselves and take action to benefit their local community.

Key features of the PYP curriculum framework

Informed by research into how children learn, how educators teach, and the principles and practices of effective assessment, the PYP places a powerful emphasis on conceptual, inquiry-based learning.

Transdisciplinary learning

The PYP is designed to support transdisciplinary learning because it mirrors the natural way children learn. Guiding learning experiences through transdisciplinary themes, across and beyond the boundaries of subjects, teachers build on what children know — and their areas of interest — to help them relate to the world around them.

Figure 4: IB Primary Years Programme model

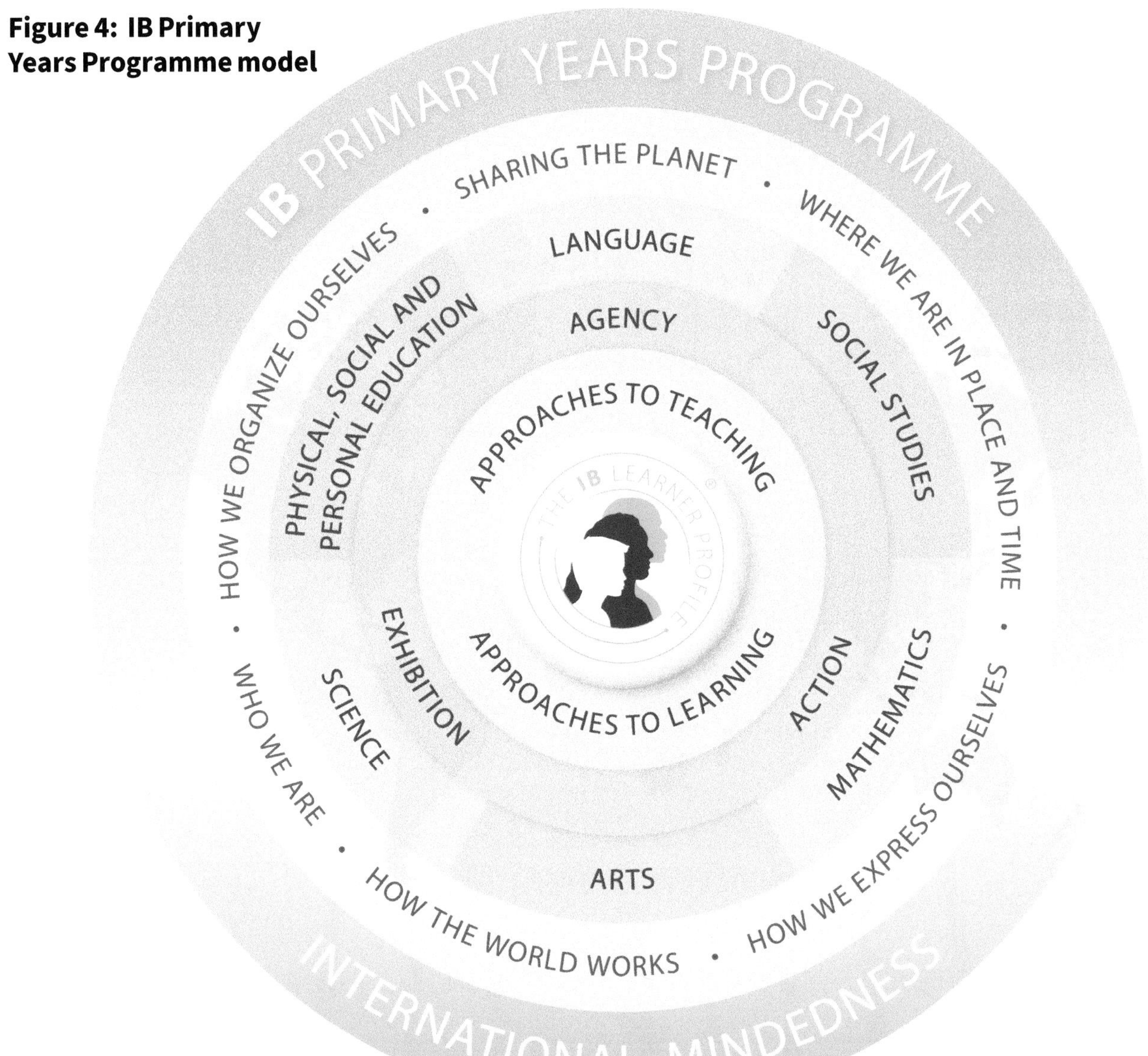

Transdisciplinary themes

- Who we are
- Where we are in place and time
- How we express ourselves
- How the world works
- How we organize ourselves
- Sharing the planet

Subject areas

- Arts
- Language
- Science
- Social studies
- Mathematics
- Personal, social and physical education

Agency

By encouraging agency (voice, choice and ownership), the PYP creates a culture where teachers can create relevant, authentic, challenging learning experiences and children develop a love of learning by finding things out for themselves.

Assessment

Assessment is ongoing in the PYP, deepening learning and providing opportunities for teachers to reflect on what their students know, what they understand and what they can do. Immediate, effective feedback and feed-forward helps children to self-monitor and adjust their learning experiences to gain confidence in their own abilities, increase well-being and build resilience.

The exhibition

In the PYP exhibition, children follow their passions to collaborate on an in-depth project, resulting in a community-wide celebration of their learning journey. Analysing, researching and proposing solutions to real world challenges and opportunities prepares them for success in the IB Middle Years Programme, or the next stage in their education.

PYP in the early years (3-6)

The PYP transdisciplinary framework is designed to provide authentic opportunities to strengthen key developmental skills and abilities in young children. Inquiring through play and exploration, young learners learn to self-regulate and build and test theories to make sense of the world around them.

UWC Maastricht - see profile on page 235

What is the IB Middle Years Programme?

The IB Middle Years Programme (MYP) is designed for students aged 11 to 16. It provides a framework of learning that encourages students to become creative, critical and reflective thinkers. The MYP emphasizes intellectual challenge, encouraging students to make connections between their studies in traditional subjects and the real world. It fosters the development of skills for communication, intercultural understanding and global engagement — essential qualities for young people who are becoming global leaders.

The MYP is flexible enough to accommodate national or local curriculum requirements. It builds upon the knowledge, skills and attitudes developed in the IB Primary Years Programme (PYP) and prepares students to meet the academic challenges of the IB Diploma Programme (DP) and the IB Career-related Programme (CP).

The IB Middle Years Programme:

- addresses holistically students' intellectual, social, emotional and physical well-being
- provides students opportunities to develop the knowledge, attitudes and skills they need in order to manage complexity and take responsible action for the future
- ensures breadth and depth of understanding through study in eight subject groups and interdisciplinary learning
- requires the study of at least two languages (language of instruction and additional language of choice) to support students in understanding their own cultures and those of others
- empowers students to participate in service within the community
- helps to prepare students for further education, the workplace and a lifetime of learning.

The MYP consists of eight subject groups: language acquisition, language and literature, individuals and societies, sciences, mathematics, arts, physical and health education, and design. Student study is supported by a minimum of 50 hours of instruction per subject group in each academic year. In years 4 and 5, students have the option to take courses from six of the eight subject groups, which provides greater flexibility, with optional MYP eAssessments at the end of year 5 for schools that wish for their students to have externally validated results.

Figure 5: IB Middle Years Programme model

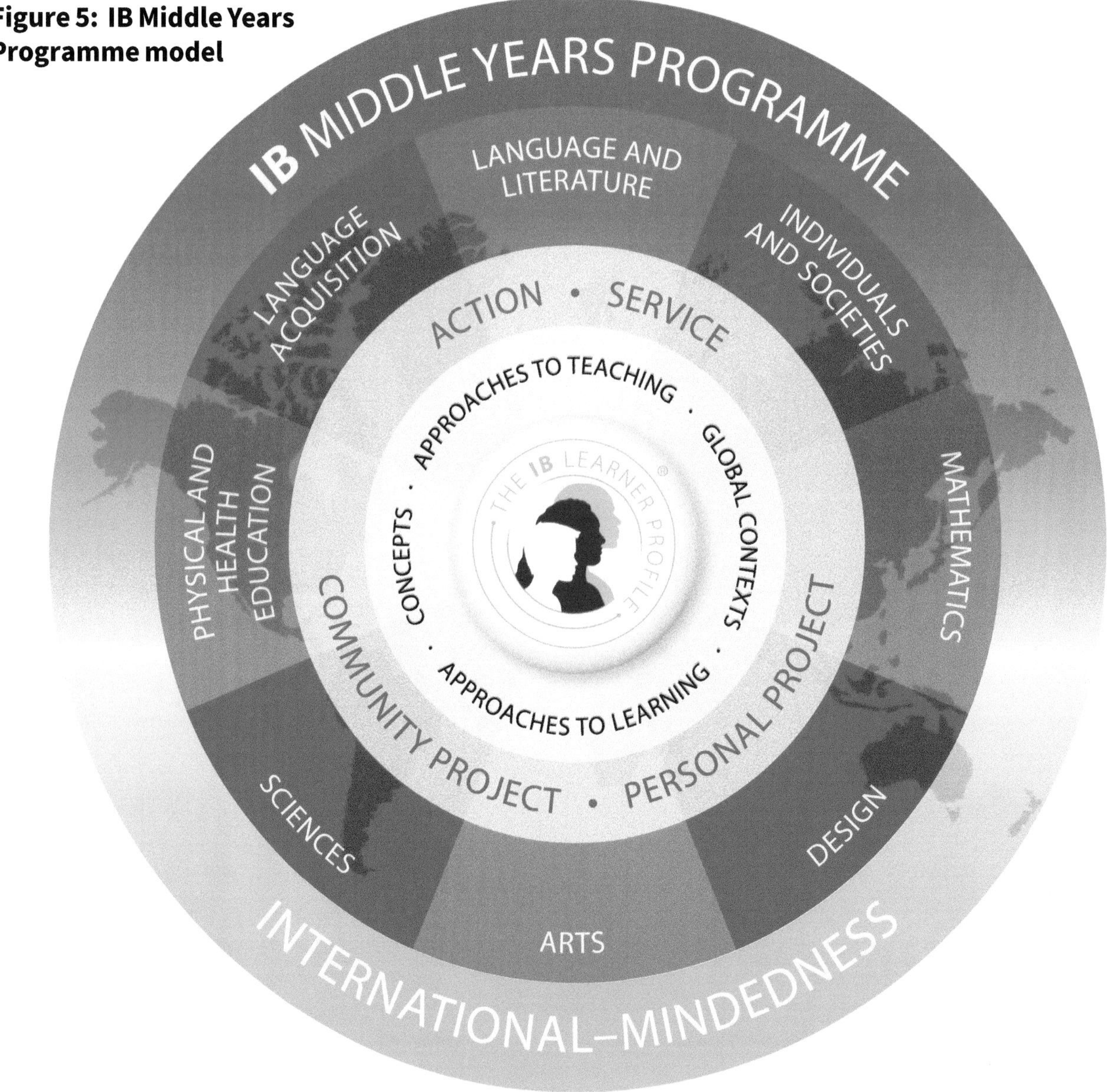

The MYP: A unique approach, relevant for a global society

The MYP aims to help students develop their personal understanding, as well as their emerging sense of self and responsibility in their community. Using global contexts, MYP students explore human identity, global challenges and what it means to be internationally minded.

MYP teachers organize the curriculum with appropriate attention to:

- teaching and learning in context
- conceptual understanding
- approaches to learning (ATL)
- service as action
- language and identity.

MYP projects

MYP projects provide students the opportunity to demonstrate what they have learned in the MYP. In schools that include MYP year 5, all students must complete the personal project. In programmes that include MYP years 4 or 5, schools may offer students the opportunity to do both the community project and the personal project. In schools that include MYP year 3 or 4, students must complete the community project.

- The community project encourages students to explore their rights and responsibilities to implement service as action in the community. Students may complete the community project individually or in small groups.
- Each student develops a personal project independently. Producing a truly personal and creative piece of work stands as a summative review of their ability to conduct independent work.

MYP assessment

The optional MYP eAssessment provides external evaluation for students in MYP year 5 (typically 15–16 years old) that leads to the internationally recognized IB MYP certificate and IB MYP course results.

MYP eAssessment represents a balanced, appropriately-challenging model that comprises examinations and coursework.

- Two-hour on-screen examinations in four subject groups (language and literature, sciences, mathematics, individuals and societies) and in interdisciplinary learning are individually marked by IB examiners.
- Portfolios of student work for four subject groups (language acquisition, physical and health education, arts, and design) are moderated by IB examiners to international standards.
- Long term personal project work is marked by school teachers and moderated by IB examiners to international standards.

These innovative assessments focus on conceptual understanding and the ability to apply knowledge in complex, unfamiliar situations. They offer robust and reliable assessment of student achievement in the MYP.

Registration for MYP eAssessment is highly flexible and can differ per candidate, from a single subject to the full MYP certificate. IB World Schools can register their students for a variety of subjects, which provide the candidates with externally validated results. All candidates receive IB MYP course results; specific conditions apply for registration for the IB MYP certificate.

MYP eAssessments meet the General Conditions for Recognition established by England's Office of Qualifications and Examinations Regulation and is recognized by other national education systems as preparation for further study at the senior secondary level.

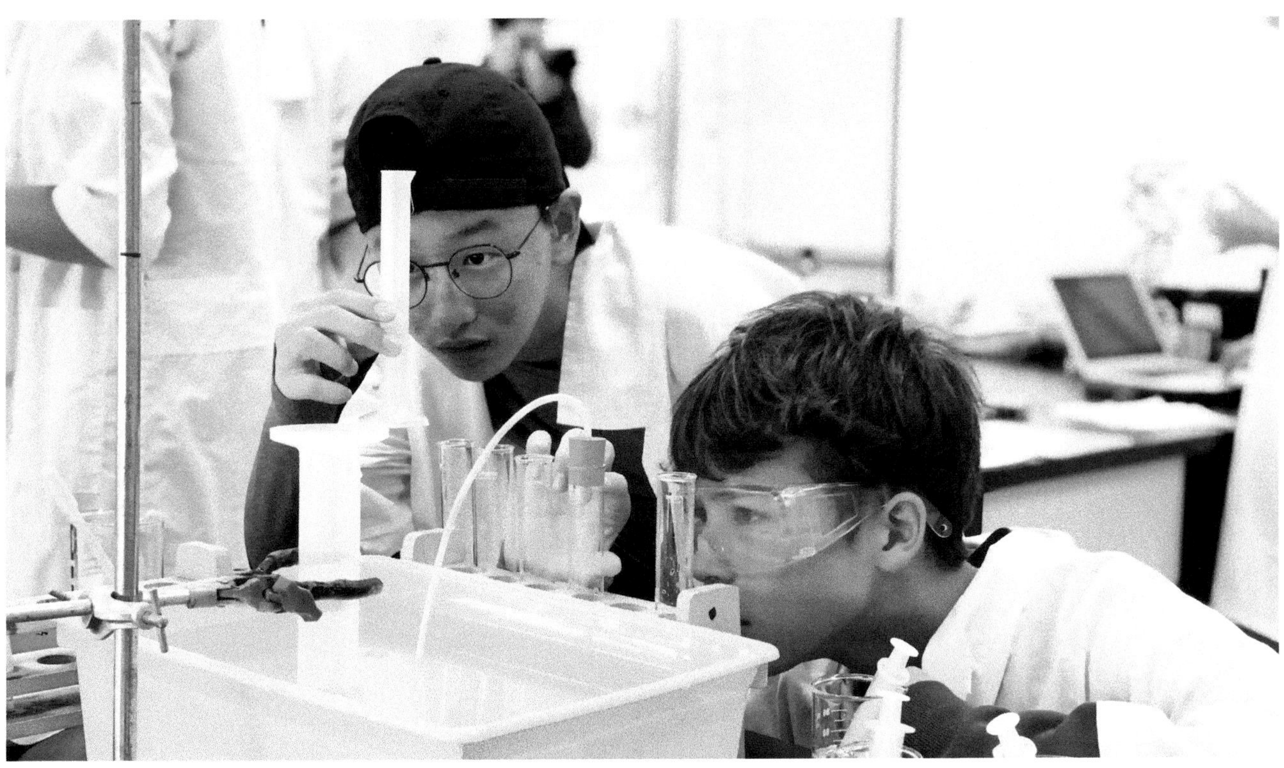

International School of Busan

What is the IB Diploma Programme (DP)?

The DP gives students aged 16-19 a world-class preparation for higher education and life beyond. It's a comprehensive, challenging framework that allows students to flourish intellectually, physically, emotionally and ethically, helping them graduate with a unique, future-ready skillset.

To ensure both breadth and depth of knowledge and understanding, DP students must choose at least one subject from each of the six groups.

1. Studies in language and literature
2. Language acquisition
3. Individuals and societies
4. Sciences
5. Mathematics
6. The arts

Students may choose either an arts subject or a second subject from one of the other groups. In addition to disciplinary and interdisciplinary study, the DP features three core elements that broaden students' educational experience and challenge them to apply their knowledge and skills.

- The **extended essay** improves students' approach to learning in higher education through an independent, self-directed 4,000-word piece of research.
- **Theory of knowledge (TOK)** enhances students and educators' critical thinking, deepening their understand of content and connections across disciplines by reflecting on the nature of knowledge and on how we know what we claim we know through this flagship seminar course.
- **Creativity, activity and service (CAS)** helps students develop an ethic of service, become more caring, open-minded and reflective, and develop more self-confidence and maturity by embarking on a project in their community.

The DP prepares students for effective participation in a rapidly evolving and increasingly global society as they:

- develop the skills and a positive attitude towards learning that will prepare them for higher education
- study at least two languages and increase their understanding of cultures, including their own
- make connections across traditional academic disciplines and explore the nature of knowledge through the programme's unique theory of knowledge course

Figure 6: IB Diploma Programme model

- undertake in-depth research into an area of interest through the lens of one or more academic disciplines in the extended essay
- enhance their personal and interpersonal development through creativity, activity and service.

The DP is recognized and respected by the world's leading universities, and research suggests that higher rates of DP students go on to university and higher education study than non-IB students.

IB students apply to more than 3,300 higher education institutions each year, in close to 90 countries. The most popular of these institutions are ranked among the top universities in the world.

What is the IB Career-related Programme (CP)?

The IB Career-related Programme (CP) gives students aged 16–19 a head start in life, putting their skills, interests and ideas to the test with opportunities to delve into subjects not normally taught in the classroom and a chance to learn by doing. In turn, CP students graduate with the confidence, skills and experience needed to thrive in their future careers and higher education.

The CP's flexible educational framework allows schools to meet the needs, backgrounds and contexts of students. By engaging with a rigorous study programme that genuinely interests them, CP students gain transferable and lifelong skills in applied knowledge, critical thinking, communication and cross-cultural engagement.

The CP enables students to prepare for effective participation in an ever-changing world of work as they:

- consider new perspectives and other points of view
- engage in learning that makes a positive difference
- develop a combination of traditional academic skills and practical skills
- think critically and creatively in rapidly-changing and global workplaces
- communicate clearly and effectively
- work independently and in collaboration with others
- become self-confident, resilient and flexible.

Figure 7: IB Career-related Programme model

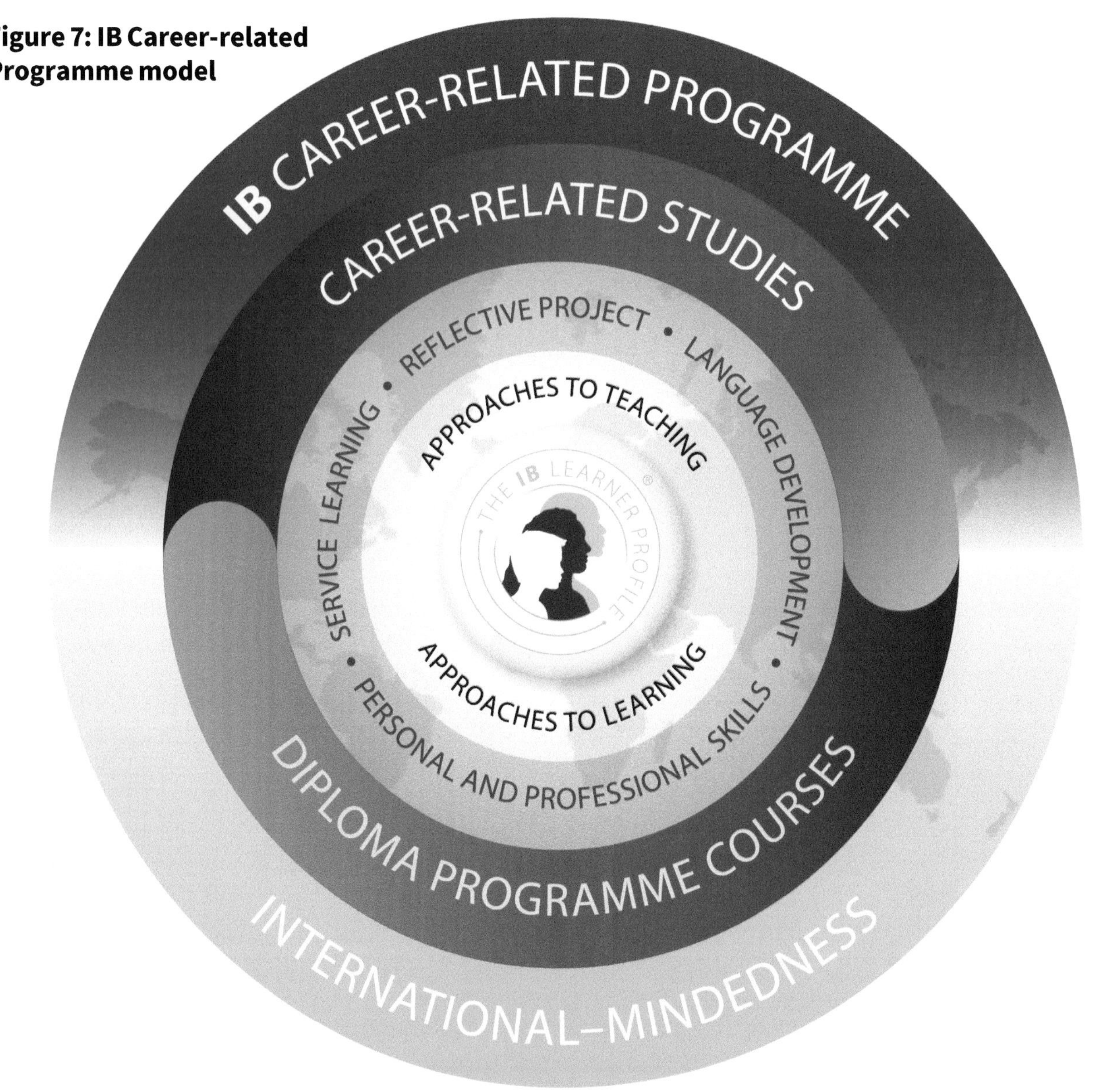

The CP framework allows students to specialize in and focus on a career-related pathway. The CP provides a comprehensive educational framework that combines highly regarded and internationally recognized courses from the IB Diploma Programme (DP), with a unique CP core and an approved career-related study.

The CP core

Personal and professional skills is designed for students to develop attitudes, skills and strategies to be applied to personal and professional situations and contexts now and in the future. It emphasizes skills development for the workplace, as these are transferable and can be applied in a range of situations.

Service learning is the development and application of knowledge and skills towards meeting an identified and authentic community need. Through service learning, students develop and apply personal and social skills in real-life situations.

Language development is a central tenet of an IB education that ensures students have access to and are exposed to a second language in order to increase their understanding of the wider world and enhance their skillsets within a highly competitive global workforce.

The **reflective project** is an in-depth body of work submitted towards the end of the programme. Students identify, analyse, critically discuss and evaluate an ethical dilemma associated with an issue from their career-related studies. The project can be submitted in different formats, including an essay, web page or short film. This work encourages students to engage in personal inquiry, action, and reflection, and to develop strong research and communications skills.

Career-related study

Through personalized career-related studies, students are provided with practical, real-world approaches to learning, designed to prepare them for higher education, an internship or apprenticeship or even a job. It also provides the opportunities for students to learn about theories and concepts through application and practice while developing skills in authentic and meaningful contexts.

Career-related studies are offered and awarded by the school or an outside pathway provider. Popular studies at current CP schools include engineering, computer programming, business and finance, pre-med and health science, hospitality and tourism, and visual and performing arts.

For more information about the IB and its programmes, check out ibo.org.

Eastern Senior High School

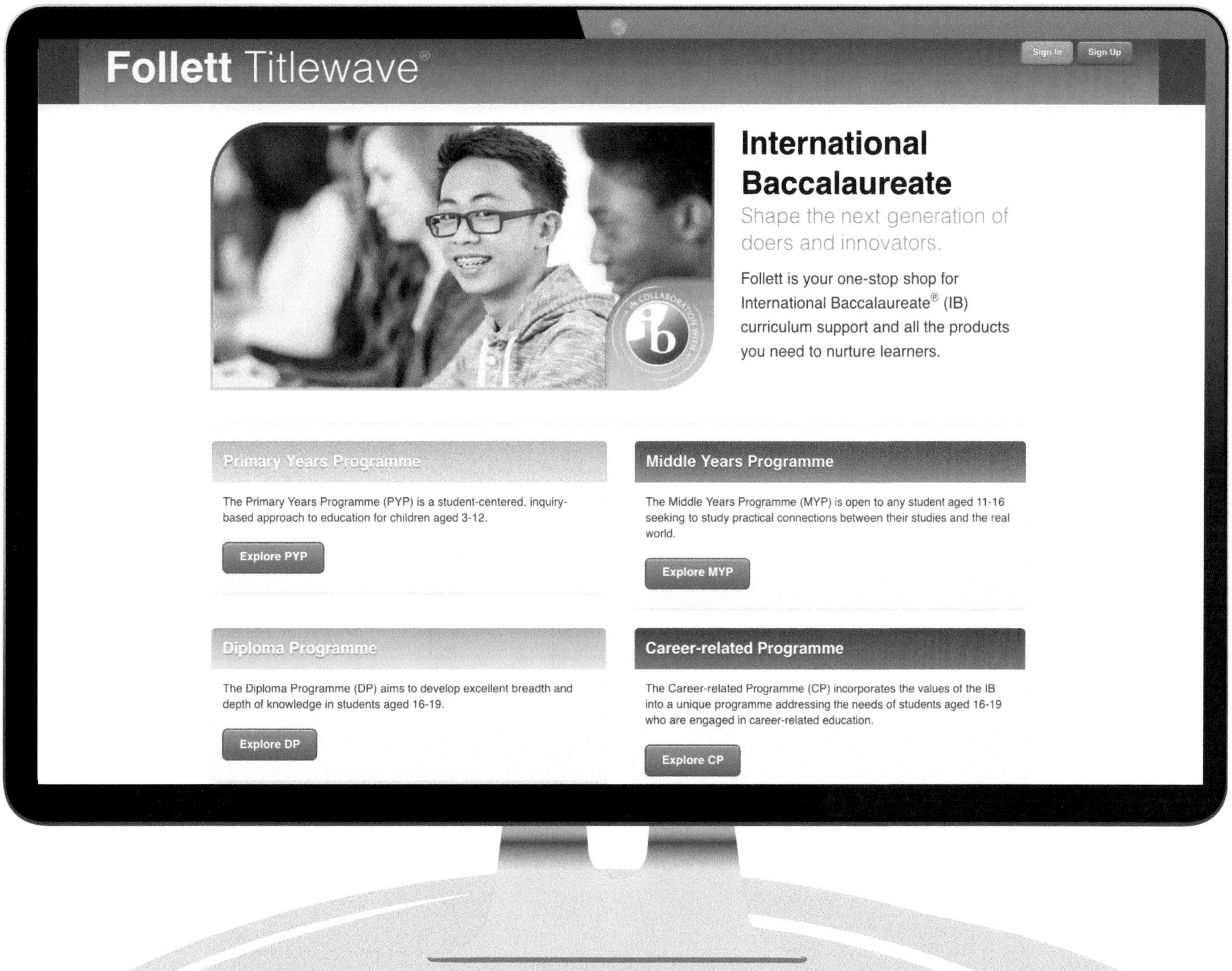

IB Recognition

The IB works with the higher education community to support IB students in getting the recognition they have earned by completing their studies. This work also helps us examine and further develop our programmes to ensure we continue to offer the best preparation for university studies and life beyond. IB graduates enter university with a firm foundation for their degree programme—not just academically, but with self-sufficiency and resilience.

The IB has a number of available resources to help you learn about how our programmes are recognized around the globe. For instance, the following tools provide excellent support for helping students in their journey to university.

- **Recognition statements database**: this directory includes information from a large—and growing—number of universities, countries, and territories (including states in the USA and Canadian provinces) on their IB recognition policies.
- **UCC country-specific how-to-apply guides**: these user-friendly modules walk you through preparing for and applying to universities in certain countries as an IB student.

To access these tools, start by visiting the IB's university admissions webpage at ibo.org/university-admission. There, you also can find additional resources about the IB programmes, research on and evidence of the effectiveness of IB programmes, and how the IB works with universities and governments to support policy development.

Remember that the institution to which a DP or CP student wants to apply is a great resource as well: it always is a good idea for schools, students and parents to visit individual university websites to access the most up-to-date information regarding their recognition policies.

The Diploma Programme (DP)

The DP is an excellent passport to higher education. Universities around the world welcome the unique characteristics of DP students and recognize the ways in which the programme helps prepare students for higher education.

The DP is widely accepted as a valid qualification for entry into higher education—without students needing to complete other tests or credentials—which gives DP students the opportunity to compete for places at universities. In multiple countries, the DP also acts as proof of English language proficiency for admission to higher education, and some universities accept students who study one or more DP course instead of the full programme.

Each year, at the request of students and their schools, the IB sends student transcripts to over 5,000 universities and colleges in over 100 countries. IB students routinely gain admission to some of the best universities and colleges in the world, such as Ivy League universities in the USA, the Russell group in the UK, the Group of Eight in Australia and the RU11 institutions in Japan.

The Career-related Programme (CP)

The CP also has been growing steadily as a strong pathway to higher education. Since its launch only a decade ago in 2014, the CP's reputation among universities has developed as a valid route for students to progress to higher education and to the world of employment. The IB continues to work with universities to improve their knowledge and understanding of the CP and to expand CP recognition.

In the last four years, CP students have requested that their transcripts be sent to over 1,400 different universities in 46 different countries across North America, Africa, Europe, the Middle East, Asia and Australasia, including more than 900 institutions in the USA and more than 140 in the UK.

Credit and scholarships

Many universities, especially in the United States, offer IB students university credit and/or placement in advanced-level courses when they enrol. This may reduce the time required to complete a degree and the cost of tuition. To further reduce tuition costs, some universities have established scholarships specifically for IB graduates.

For more information regarding recognition, the DP or the CP, please see the university admissions section of the IB website at ibo.org/university-admission.

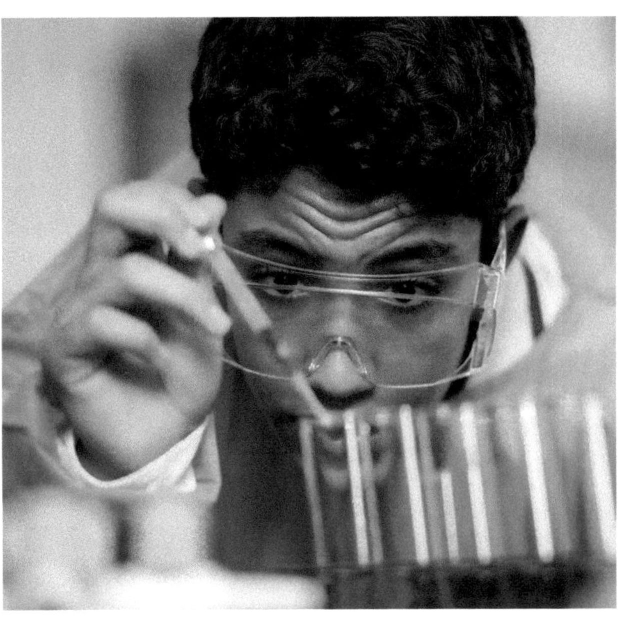

Swiss International Scientific School of Dubai

Global Research, Professional Development and Government

IB research

Research plays a central role in the development, quality assurance and assessment of IB programme outcomes. The IB commissions research from leading research institutions and universities around the world.

The core of our work involves research on IB programmes. We conduct outcomes research to investigate the impact of IB programmes on students, teachers and schools, and curriculum research to inform the development and review of all programme curriculum and pedagogy. Policy research supports decision-making and policy development by providing cutting-edge research findings and practice recommendations on key educational issues.

We also conduct survey research, designing, distributing and analysing surveys to support the IB's strategic decision-making, and quality assurance for IB products and services. The assessment research department collects and analyses data to ensure assessments are well-grounded in current understanding of best practice. Lastly, we offer research resources, such as findings and figures for IB leaders, annotated bibliographies and Jeff Thompson Award studies.

For more information on IB Research, please visit ibo.org/research.

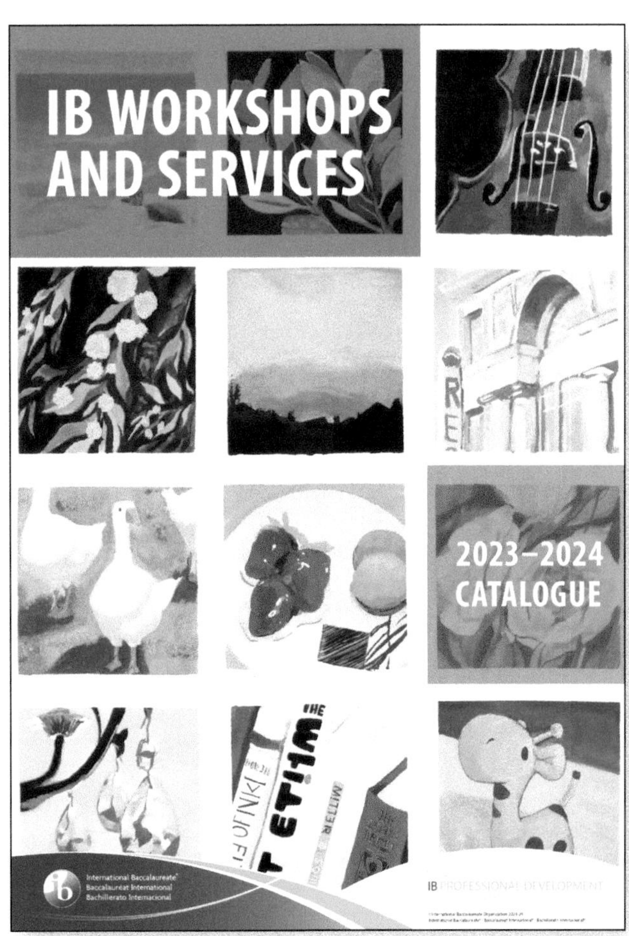

Professional development

Educators, school leaders and administrators are offered continuous support through plentiful IB professional development workshops and services. Development of a worldwide teaching and learning community committed to lifelong learning is an IB priority.

The IB is continuously seeking to ensure the accessibility of its professional development for all educators and that educators' professional learning needs are met. By offering four different delivery methods — face-to-face, online, virtual and a "blended" method combining remote and face-to-face learning — the IB aims to better accommodate the diverse learning and logistical needs of both educators and schools.

For more information, please visit ibo.org/pd.

The IB and governments

Engaging regional and national governments is at the centre of the IB's commitment to diversity and inclusivity. We are defined by our values, and those include pedagogical leadership and international-mindedness. There is a growing awareness among governments that education systems have to work in an international society, not just a national one. We engage with many governments, either to create more IB World Schools or to influence national education systems. Across the world, the IB is working hand-in-hand with regional and national governments to ensure state access to IB programmes.

IB Educator and Leadership Certificates

The IB educator and leadership certificates help to build capacity of IB teachers and leaders globally. This unique programme positions the IB pedagogy within university-level teacher education, with rigorous, IB-recognized programmes of study at nearly 60 reputable institutions in 15 countries. Certificate-holders are prepared to teach and lead in IB World Schools and comprise a network of educators committed to lifelong learning, research and enhancing classroom experiences.

Certificate offerings

- IB certificate in teaching and learning (with a focus on PYP, MYP, DP or CP)
- IB advanced certificate in teaching and learning research
- IB certificate in leadership practice
- IB advanced certificate in leadership research

We invite school leaders looking to grow their high-potential educators—and educators looking to deepen their understanding of how to teach and lead in an IB context—to explore more at ibo.org/professional-certificates.

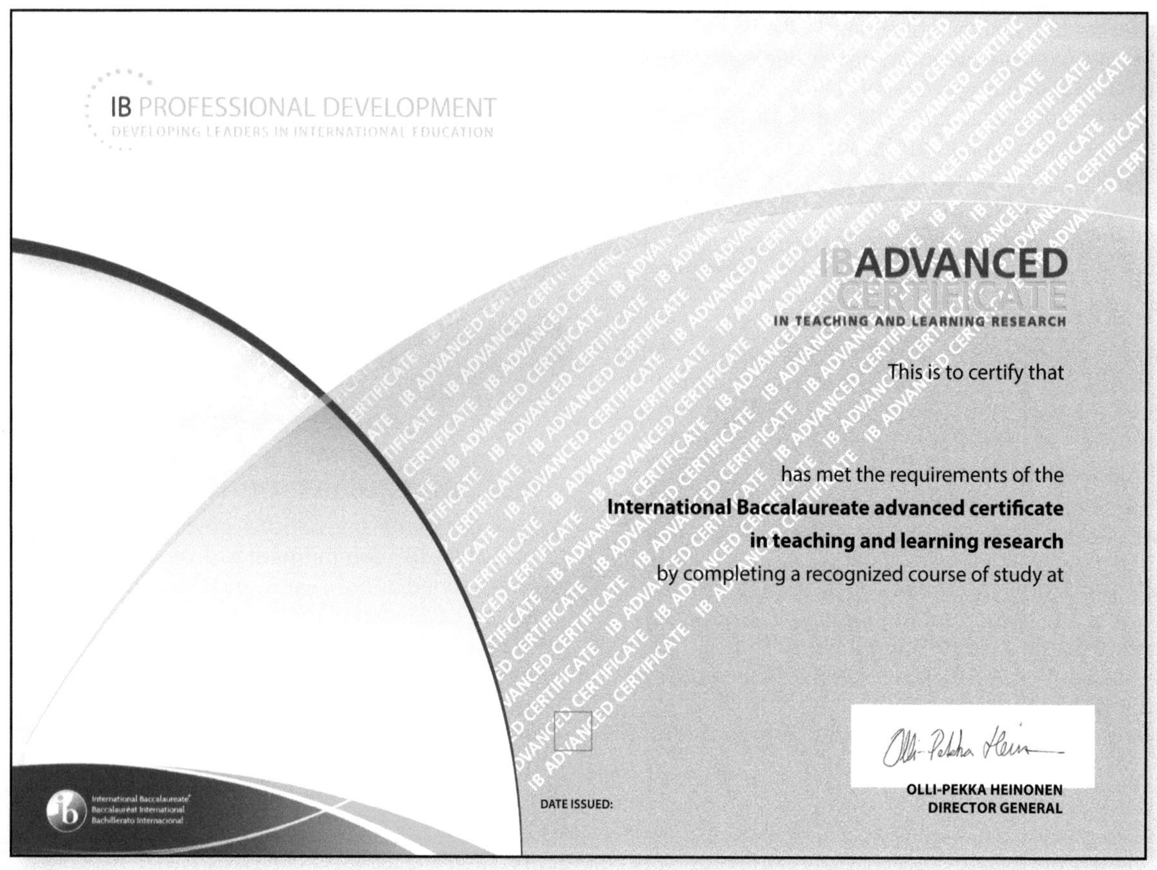

Innovations from the IB

Festival of Hope

Since the launch of the Festival of Hope in 2022, the IB has been creating spaces for young people to share their voices and turn complex challenges into positivity and hope. In-person, student-led events have been hosted all over the world, and we've facilitated online conversations between students and leaders from various sectors focused on a wide range of topics and issues, from fast fashion and well-being to indigenous perspectives and technology.

Turning hope into action, we launched the Global Youth Action Fund and awarded more than 300 young people, representing 48 countries, with grants to support their ideas and projects—empowering young changemakers to address pressing global challenges ranging from sustainability and equity to social justice. Schools and organizations can host their own events by using the Festival of Hope community guide, which can be found at ibo.org/festival-of-hope.

Diploma Programme (DP) online pilot

The online DP pilot allows IB students and non-IB students to complete the full DP remotely. Through the pilot, the IB would like to better understand the needs of students who may not be able to attend traditional brick-and-mortar educational institutions, for example due to illness, commitments to extra-curricular activities such as sport and music, or migration and displacement.

The IB works with selected pilot partner organizations to deliver a fully online DP and empower students who are unable to access a brick-and-mortar IBWS to still thrive in their learning journey. In 2023, Aoba and SEK Education Group joined King's InterHigh and Dwight Global Online in their work in partnership with the IB to explore how we can create and reinforce collaborative learning communities and discover the advantages that a completely online DP can bring to our community.

Well-being in schools: A learning journey

With generous support from the Jacobs Foundation, the International Baccalaureate has launched an exciting project to explore, study and measure student well-being in primary and secondary schools internationally.

In this project, we are embarking on a journey with schools and a world-renowned group of partners to systematically learn and innovate together, with the ultimate goal of enhancing student well-being through relevant and evidence-based practices. The project offers schools the opportunity to participate in an action research programme, pilot a student well-being measurement initiative, and learn about interventions and innovations in support of student well-being.

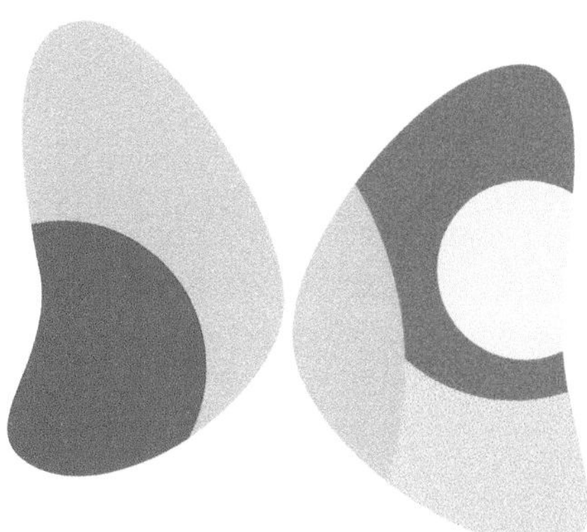

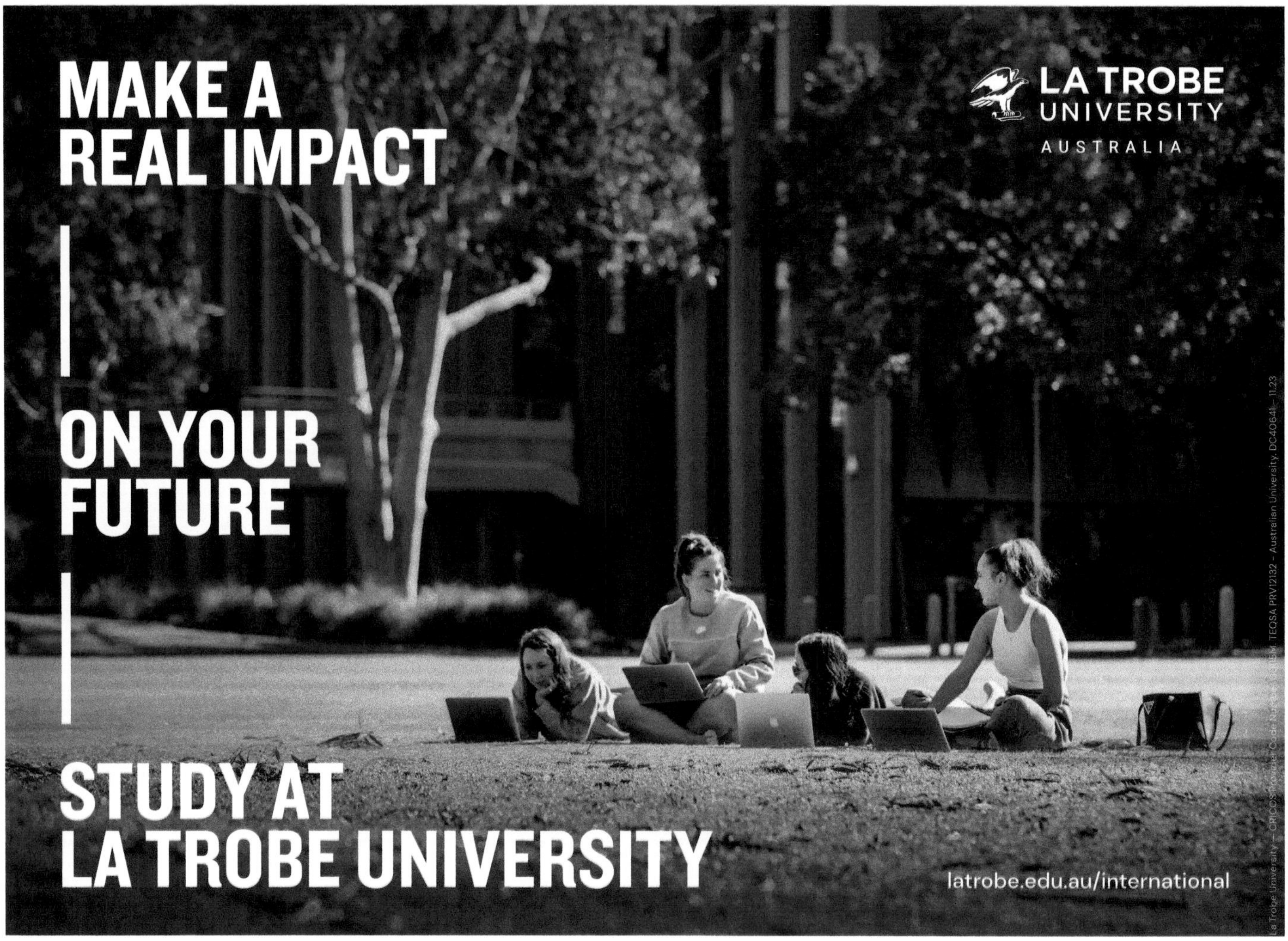

IB Governance

IB Board of Governors

We are governed by a Board of Governors, whose members are appointed by the Board upon recommendation by the governance and organization committee. Membership comprises a diversity of gender, culture and geography with experience from both the business and academic worlds. Board members, with the exception of the Chair, are volunteers and receive no payment for their time or work on the Board.

Members as of November 2023

Chair

Dr Helen Drennen AM – Chief Executive Officer at Studio Schools of Australia, Queensland, Australia

Vice-chair

Mr Cyrille NKontchou, Co-Founder and Managing Partner of Enko Capital, South Africa

Members

Ms Sabine Chalmers, General counsel at BT Group Plc., London, United Kingdom

Ms Isela Consuegra, Head of School at Escuela Lomas Altas, Mexico and President of IBAMEX (Mexican Association of IB World Schools)

Mr Mike Dargan, UBS Group Chief Digital and Information Officer, Zurich, Switzerland

Mr Jean-Christophe Deberre, Former managing director of the Mission laïque française (Mlf) and the Office scolaire et universitaire international (OSUI), Paris, France

Ms Totty Ellwood Aris, Head of School at Verdala International School, Malta

Dr Montserrat Gomendio, Research Professor at the Spanish Research Council and Co-Founder at Skills WeGo, Madrid, Spain

Mr Steven Kim, Partner at Verdis Investment Management, Villanova, Pennsylvania, USA

Professor Ee Ling Low, Dean, Academic and Faculty Affairs, National Institute of Education (NIE), Nanyang Technological University (NTU), Singapore

Chairs of the IB Board of Governors (formerly Council of Foundation)

1968–1981	John Goormaghtigh	Director of the European office of the Carnegie Endowment for International Peace, Belgium
1981–1984	Seydou Madani Sy	Rector of the University of Dakar, Senegal, and later minister for justice and special advisor to the president of Senegal.
1984–1990	Piet Gathier	Director General of secondary education, the Netherlands
1990–1996	Thomas Hagoort	International lawyer, USA
1996–1997	Bengt Thelin	Director General of education, Sweden
1997–2003	Greg Crafter	Former minister for education in South Australia, lawyer, Australia
2003–2009	Monique Seefried	Former Executive Director, Center for the Advancement and Study of International Education, USA
2009–2015	Carol Bellamy	Attorney, New York, USA
2015–2020	George Rupp	Former President of the International Rescue Committee, Connecticut, USA
2020–present	Helen Drennen AM	Chief Executive Officer of Studio Schools of Australia, Queensland, Australia

IB Directors General

Alec Peterson	1968-77
Gérard Renaud	1977-83
Roger Peel	1983-98
Derek Blackman	1998-1999
George Walker	1999-2006
Jeffrey Beard	2006-December 2013
Siva Kumari	2014-2021
Olli-Pekka Heinonen	2021-present

The IB Around the World

We currently work with IB World Schools in 160 countries. All our jurisdictions have not-for-profit or charitable status with headquarters in Geneva, Switzerland. Our four global centres are in Washington DC, USA, The Hague, Netherlands, Cardiff, UK, and Singapore. We employ approximately 773 IB staff worldwide.

Our IB staff and educators work closely with prospective and candidate schools as well as existing IB World Schools. They are also responsible for creating and sustaining relationships with governments, international and national agencies, universities and other educational institutions, foundations and concerned individuals. Through its strategic goals, we are also promoting wider educational access.

Core services we provide:
For prospective schools

- introductory or orientation workshops
- consultation, advice, and materials on application and authorization
- training workshops
- authorization visits

For IB World Schools

- professional development programmes for new and experienced IB teachers
- regional conferences
- support via webinar
- online access to resources and support via My IB
- periodic evaluations of schools' IB programmes
- ongoing support throughout a school's IB journey

For universities

- information on the philosophy, structure and requirements of the IB Diploma and Career-related Programmes
- access to the content and requirements of the IB Diploma and IB Career-related Programme curriculums and assessment
- research to demonstrate the effectiveness of IB programmes
- advice on establishing an IB recognition policy

For governments

- advice on how to integrate IB programmes into state educational systems
- consultation regarding recognition of the IB diploma

Figure 8: IB Global Centres

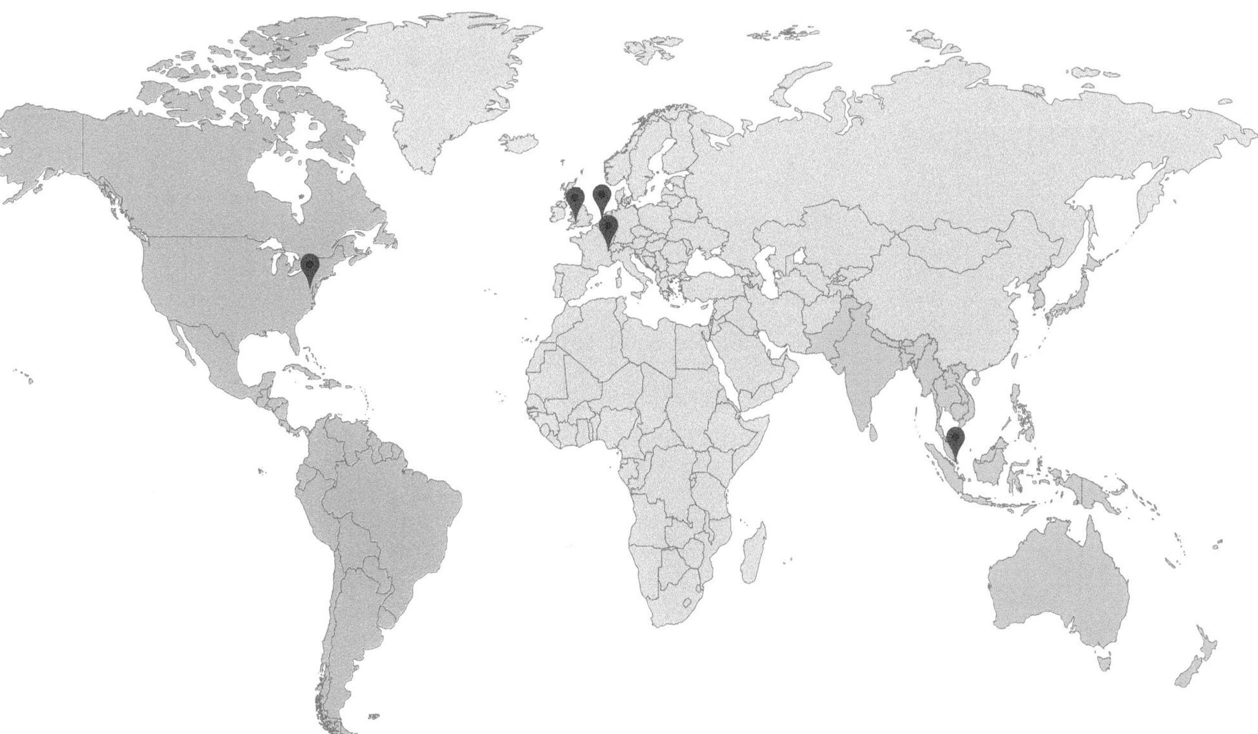

IB Global Centre, Washington DC

IB Global Centre, Cardiff
IB Global Centre, The Hague

IB Foundation Office, Geneva
IB Global Centre, Singapore

IB World Schools

This section is divided into the three IB regions. Here you will find information about each region, including facts and figures, enhanced profiles of selected schools and a full directory of all IB World Schools in the region.

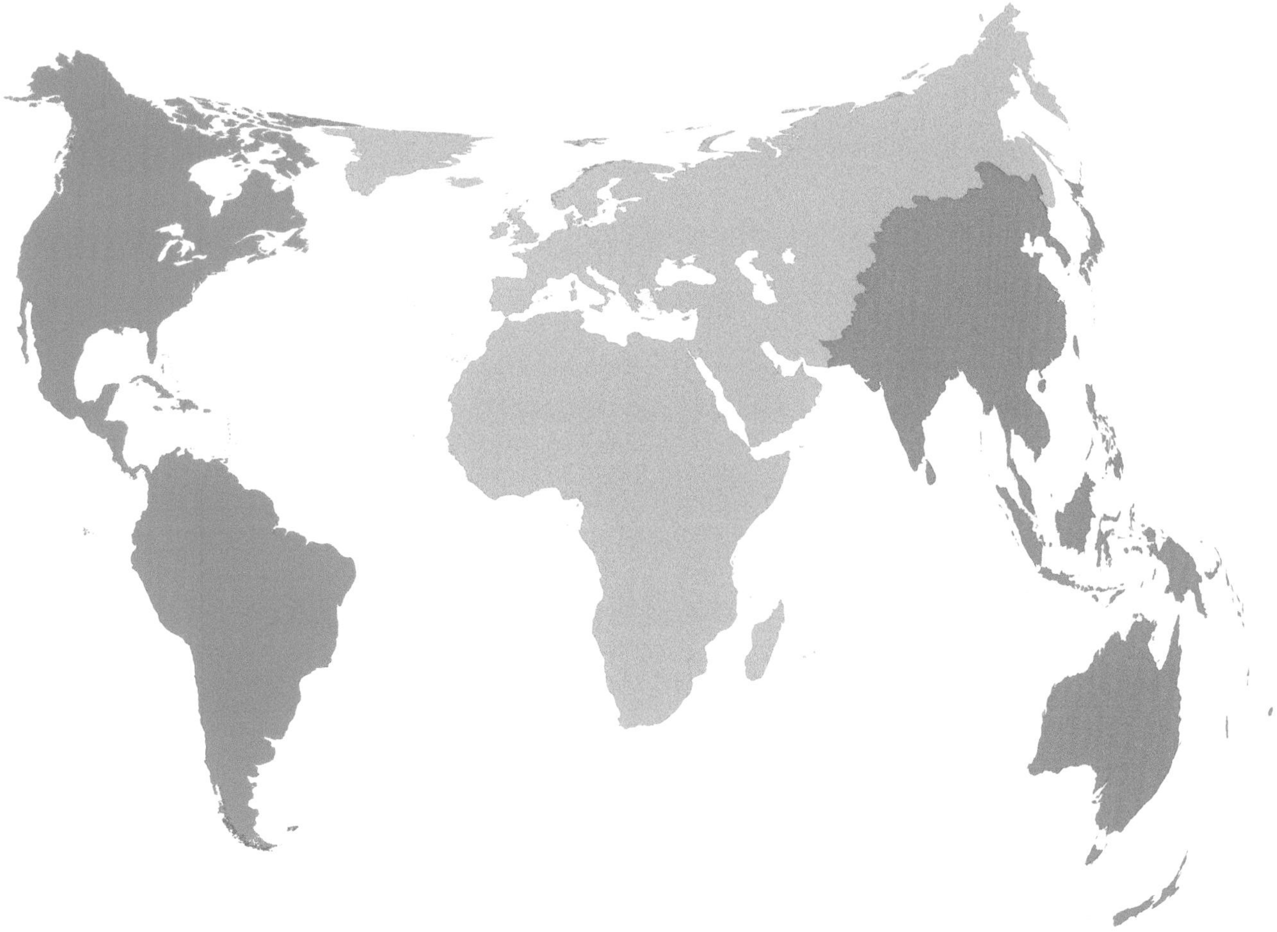

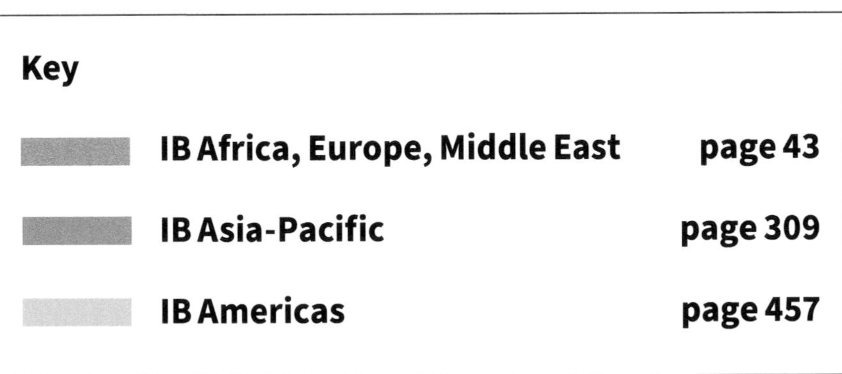

IB

AFRICA | EUROPE | MIDDLE EAST

(Founded 1987)

Head of School
Craig Williamson

Assistant Head of School & High School Principal (9-12)
Simon Walker

Middle School Principal
Richard Nies

Elementary School Principal
Sam Cook

PYP coordinator
Bronwyn Matamu

MYP coordinator
Christopher Engström-Roberts

DP coordinator
Samantha Cole

Status Private

Boarding/day Day

Gender Coeducational

Language of instruction
English

Authorised IB programmes
PYP, MYP, DP

Age Range 3 – 18 years

Number of pupils enrolled 960

Address
P.O. Box 372
Madinat Qaboos
115 Muscat | **OMAN**

TEL +968 2495 5801

Email registrar@abaoman.org

Website
www.abaoman.org

Empowering Future Leaders

ABA Oman International School, based in Muscat, delivers a continuum of International Baccalaureate (IB) programmes, including the Primary Years Programme (PYP), Middle Years Programme (MYP) and Diploma Programme (DP), having achieved authorization in 2002, 2004 and 1996 respectively. ABA Oman was recognized as the first international school in Muscat to offer the IB programmes, where the focus is on an academically challenging, global education for all. ABA is accredited by the Council of International Schools (CIS) and the Middle States Association of Colleges and Schools (MSA).

Since its establishment in 1987, ABA has demonstrated its commitment to academic brilliance, embracing a holistic pedagogical approach that supports and develops the whole child. As the leading IB Continuum school in Oman, and a non-profit, ABA enrols over 960 students, representing 70 different nationalities from Kindergarten to Grade 12. To support students in their learning journey, we have a team of highly qualified teachers from around the world, who provide a nurturing environment for them to thrive.

ABA is a warm, welcoming, and diverse community of students, educators and parents, united in working together towards the school's mission to 'inspire and empower learners to explore their unique pathways to success.' The state-of-the-art facilities at ABA's new campus in Madinat Al Irfan, with indoor and outdoor purpose-built spaces, support student learning in all aspects. Alongside promoting academic excellence, ABA offers a wide range of after-school programmes that facilitate holistic growth and skill enhancement.

Our inquiry-based learning approach, which begins in the PYP years and continues through the MYP with a strong service as action component, provides students with opportunities for service learning and experiential learning beyond the classroom. Learners are immersed in real-life scenarios, engage in interdisciplinary themes and employ creative and critical thinking to solve problems, through the DP core components – Creativity, Action, and Service (CAS), Theory of Knowledge (TOK), as well as through participation in the Duke of Edinburgh's International Award.

At ABA, students are offered a plethora of incredible experiences and opportunities to explore their creative potential and prepare them for life beyond school. They are empowered to make a positive difference to the local community through various student voice groups such as Students Against Prejudice, Teens Giving Back, the Ecological Society, and more. In addition to academics, students are encouraged to represent the school in academic games, sports, arts, speech and debate, competing with other schools in the city and internationally through MESAC.

"As an IB Continuum School, we ensure that students engage in principled action, are internationally-minded and learn holistically through programmes that are distinguished not only by what our students learn, but by how they learn. That is the ABA difference!" – Craig Williamson, ABA Head of School.

(Founded 2004)

Head of School
Ms Janina Sparks

DP coordinator
Ms Megan Jones

Status Private

Boarding/day Day

Gender Coeducational

Language of instruction
English, German

Authorised IB programmes
DP

Age Range 2 – 18 years

Number of pupils enrolled
660

Fees
Preschool
€3,360 – €4,560 per annum
Elementary School
€8,880 – €10,800 per annum
Secondary School
€12,000 – €19,200 per annum

Address
SÜDCAMPUS Bad Homburg
Am Weidenring 52-54
61352 Bad Homburg,
Hesse | GERMANY

TEL +49 61 72 984 141

Email
info@accadis-isb.com

Website
www.accadis-isb.com

Our mission
accadis ISB aims to develop confident, knowledgeable and caring young people prepared to create a better future. We aim to build within each child a sense of responsibility, a love for learning, self-discipline, and respect for others. Challenging programs, combined with inter-cultural understanding and respect, enable our students to reach their potential and become compassionate and lifelong learners.

Who we are
accadis ISB is situated in Bad Homburg, a leafy town in the Taunus mountains, just north of Frankfurt am Main. We are a non for profit, lively, friendly and expanding bilingual co-ed school which currently has approximately 660 students from 2 – 18 years of age, representing over 50 nationalities. Privately owned, it is part of a family business with links to the nearby accadis University of Applied Sciences. The school has a bilingual concept, teaching some subjects in English and some in German. accadis ISB is an official IB World School since January 2016. accadis ISB is also accredited by Cambridge Assessment International Education to teach the two year IGCSE course in Grades 9 and 10.

Our students
The school provides a supportive and challenging environment where students are encouraged to become responsible and independent learners. accadis ISB caters for a wide range of students, and is both a "local" school for families who live nearby and also an international school for students who come to us from all over the world.

Our school
accadis ISB was founded in 2004 and is situated on a state-of-the-art campus featuring its own sports hall with outdoor football pitch. Over the course of the last years, the school expanded into an adjacent building, adding an inviting library and two Art rooms. Furthermore, accadis ISB opened a new building exclusively for Secondary School students from ages 10 to 18 in January 2023, catering for the ever-increasing demand. It features more than 20 new classrooms, additional specialist spaces for Science, Art, Music and Drama as well as two libraries, a Cafeteria and an auditorium for up to 250 people.

The school focuses strongly on technology. The state-of-the-art learning environment includes Smartboards in each classroom, Google Chromebook laptops, school-wide high-speed Wi-Fi and a 3D printer.

Acorns International School (AIS)

Head of School
Ameena Lalani

PYP coordinator
Jamal Makki

MYP coordinator
Sam Weavers

DP coordinator
Ken Kanyesigye

Status Private

Boarding/day Day

Gender Coeducational

Language of instruction
English

Authorised IB programmes
PYP, MYP, DP

Age Range 18 months – 18 years

Number of pupils enrolled
650

Fees
$2,240 – $9,825 per annum

Address
Plot 328, Kisota Road
(Along) Northern Bypass,
Kisaasi Roundabout
Kampala | **UGANDA**

TEL +256 393 202 665

Email
admissions@ais.ac.ug

Website
www.ais.ac.ug

Encapsulating the adage, 'A tree with strong roots laughs at storms', Acorns International School (AIS) bears fruits that stand the test of time.

Nestled between the verdant folds of Kampala, the capital city of Uganda, AIS is sprawled over a 5-acre state-of-the-art, purpose-built campus, that nurtures the balance between academics and extracurriculars.

Over two decades in the field of education, we have grown to represent more than 50 nationalities. The AIS team strives to inspire and empower every student to achieve their personal best and become inquiring, knowledgeable, pluralists and lifelong learners, who create a better and peaceful world, through intercultural understanding and respect.

Admissions are open throughout the academic year, subject to availability. We have a limit to the number of students per classroom, for uncompromised quality. This interface gives teachers an edge to assess each student's area of strength, and improvement. Teachers are supported in this process, with timely professional development sessions, to ensure growth and excellence. Through an open-door policy, we ensure that our main stakeholders, our parents, are full partners in the decision-making process and voice concerns not only of their children, but their own too.

The language of instruction is English, with French and Kiswahili as part of our dynamic curriculum. Through our engaging and rigorous, inquiry-based environment, students reach their full academic potential and become responsible, caring, multilingual, and culturally-literate global learners.

Our teaching team is not just diverse, they epitomize academic excellence and have a penchant for pastoral care.

AIS is non-sectarian and co-educational institution, founded on strong partnerships between parents, teachers and learners.

A visit to AIS allows your family to experience the school in a relaxed environment, meet with the administration, as well as visit homerooms, the science lab, performing arts rooms, libraries, swimming pool, auditorium, soccer fields and the basketball courts.

AIS is an authorised International Baccalaureate (IB) Continuum World School, offering the Primary Years Programme (PYP), the Middle Years Programme (MYP) and the Diploma Programme (DP).

AIS is an inclusive school that accepts students in the Early Childhood Department (Crèche to Reception Class), Primary (PYP1 to PYP6), and Secondary (MYP1 – DP2).

It is always onwards and upwards for us, and we would love for you to join us!

Aiglon College

School Director
Mrs. Nicola Sparrow

Deputy Director
Mr. Tomas Duckling

Assistant Head/ DP coordinator
Mrs Laura Hamilton

Status Private

Boarding/day Mixed

Gender Coeducational

Language of instruction
English

Authorised IB programmes
DP

Age Range 7 – 18 years

Number of pupils enrolled
443

Fees
Years 5-6 CHF84,000 per annum
Years 7-8 CHF99,000 per annum
Years 9-11 CHF130,000 per annum
Years 12-13 CHF140,000 per annum

Address
Avenue Centrale 61
1885 Chesières | **SWITZERLAND**

TEL +41 (0)24 496 6177

Email
admissions@aiglon.ch

Website
www.aiglon.ch

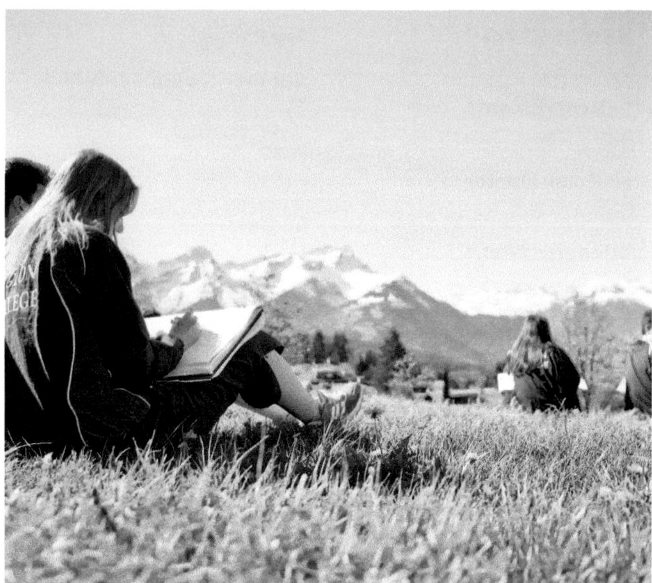

A private, international and co-educational boarding school, located in the Swiss Alps, Aiglon College cultivates a culture for compassion and opportunity – with students at the heart of everything. For more than 70 years Aiglon has pushed beyond the boundaries of traditional education to offer a holistic and inspirational experience.

Aiglon was founded on a distinctive ethos: the balanced development of mind, body and spirit. This philosophy underpins everything we do at the school, both inside and outside the classroom. The school today guards this original vision and has grown into one of the world's most distinctive boarding schools.

From junior through to senior school, students benefit from all the advantages of an international boarding school which is established as a not-for-profit school. Our campus community is represented by over 65 nationalities. They form lasting bonds with each other and with excellent educators who guide them towards academic and personal success.

The character of Aiglon students is forged on the mountain. Aiglon is located in the ski resort village of Villars-sur-Ollon in French-speaking Switzerland, at 1,227m. Making use of our safe, alpine environment we enjoy an open-style campus.

Students follow the globally recognised IGCSE and International Baccalaureate (IB) programmes while simultaneously developing practical skills that integrate curriculum into all areas of life. The focused, individually tailored programme allows each student to access a unique course of study.

The school's professional University Advising team works closely with each student to help them understand and succeed in the university application process. Through these efforts, our students have access to the world's top universities.

Central to its educational philosophy, the uniquely crafted expedition programme utilises Aiglon's location to engage students in activities designed to develop their sense of challenge and responsibility in a highly practical environment.

Aiglon's activities programme – from Model United Nations (MUN) to climbing and astronomy – offers a range of learning opportunities for students to develop skills and build experiences.

A robust approach to wellbeing is integrated into our student life, as well as our curriculum. The school's counsellor team supports students' mental health and we understand safeguarding within a community-focused culture. From their roles as Houseparents, Assistant Houseparents or as tutors, teachers are available to students 24/7.

Every Aiglonian leaves us prepared to face the challenges and opportunities of the modern world.

Al Hussan International Academy

(Founded 1998)

School Head
Dr. Burhan Mazahreh

DP coordinator
Ms. Samar Deshmukh

Status Private

Boarding/day Day

Gender Male & Female (separate)

Language of instruction
English

Authorised IB programmes
DP

Age Range 3 – 18 years

Address
PO Box 297
Dammam
31411 | SAUDI ARABIA

TEL +966 13 858 0500

Email
hia@alhussan.edu.sa

Website
international.alhussan.edu.sa

Al-Hussan International Academy (HIA) is a private English language day school with 1533 students, situated in a new modern premises in the city of Al-Khobar. This large campus houses students from K-12 with state-of-the-art facilities, including modern classrooms, libraries, E-library, learning nooks, swimming pool, exhibition spaces and laboratories. The school provides the environment and the experiences which promote the moral, social and intellectual development of all its pupils. Every child is cherished and receives support and encouragement within a strong, caring community. The school offers a well-rounded education through its provision of different programmes of instruction for students from K to Grade 12. We acknowledge that every child is born with unique potential, and we seek to develop each child's creativity, expand their horizons and prepare them to be responsible global citizens and leaders.

English is the language of instruction, with Arabic, French or Urdu offered as a second language and as a foreign language for non-native speakers. Islamic classes are offered to all students from KG to Grade 12. HIA strives to continually improve the quality of education it provides. We are accredited by COGNIA and by Council of International schools (CIS). High School students are offered to sit for IGCSE, EDEXCEL or O Level exams in Grade 10 and to elect one of the two programs: British Program (A Level) or the IBDP in Grade 11 & 12.

Courses on offer in the IB Diploma Programme are: English Literature, Arabic B, Arabic *ab-initio*, French B, French *ab-initio*, Business Management, Economics, Psychology, Biology, ITGS, Chemistry, Physics, Computer Science, Math Analysis and Approaches (AA), Mathematics Applications and Interpretation (AI) and Visual Arts.

Our Vision

Leaders of Excellence in International Education

Our Mission

Al Hussan International School provides high quality education through a safe, stimulating, and multicultural environment to prepare leaders for a global society.

Our Beliefs

At HIA, we believe:

1. all students can learn and realize their full potential.
2. a safe and stimulating environment promotes quality education.
3. in respecting cultural and individual differences.
4. all stakeholders share the responsibility for advancing our mission.
5. in preparing students to pursue further educational goals.
6. commitment to continuous improvement is imperative.

At HIA, we believe in preparing students to become well rounded young people, ready to meet the challenges in an ever-changing world. This is done through our challenging programs of study and with the help of an experienced and extensively trained team of teachers. Our student body is very active and striving to make a difference in their community. Our graduates are joining universities across the world, mostly in the Middle East, Far East, Canada, Europe and USA. We are proud of our HIA family and we invite you to visit us and experience our loving and nurturing family ambiance.

AMADEUS International School Vienna

(Founded 2012)

Head of School
Dr Jeremy House

Head of Primary
Ms Holly Johnson

Head of Secondary
Dr Karsten Plöger

PYP coordinator James Elliot

MYP coordinator Yvan Wever

DP coordinator Alice Greenland

CP coordinator Paolo Tornitore

Status Private

Boarding/day Mixed

Gender Coeducational

Language of instruction
English

Authorised IB programmes
PYP, MYP, DP, CP

Age Range 3 – 18 years

Number of pupils enrolled 500

Fees
Day:
€13,900 – €32,280 per annum
Boarding:
€50,395 – €56,295 per annum

Address
Bastiengasse 36-38
1180 Vienna | **AUSTRIA**

TEL +43 1 470 30 37 00

Email
admissions@
amadeus-vienna.com

Website
www.amadeus-vienna.com

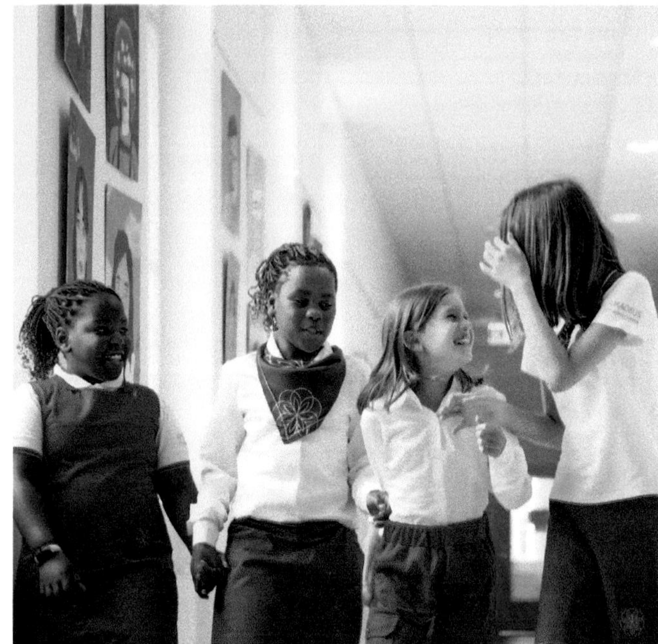

AMADEUS International School Vienna is a unique day and first-class boarding IB World school with an integrated Music and Arts Academy. The AMADEUS education is one of Distinction with the mission of accompanying young people as they fulfil their highest potential.

AMADEUS is an International Baccalaureate school, offering PYP, MYP, DP, and CP for students ages 6-18. AMADEUS also offers an Early Years Kindergarten Programme for ages 3-6. The school engages students in inquiry-based learning that addresses real-life challenges and cultivates critical-thinking, problem-solving, and presentation skills. AMADEUS' community is distinguished by its internationalism representing over 50 different nationalities. To best teach the qualities of global citizenship, the school recruits outstanding educators from around the world. The school regularly outperforms the world average pass rates and diploma points and its alumni study in top universities around the globe.

Music and Arts play a vital role in AMADEUS' learning approach which is emphasised in their dynamic co-curricular arts programme. This includes various areas such as editorial design, music production, and musical theatre production. Students also have the opportunity to participate in the AMADEUS String Orchestra, various forms of dance, drawing, painting, and more. Along with the unique IB World School Programme, AMADEUS Vienna distinguishes itself from other international schools with an integrated Music and Arts Academy offering classes at Foundation, Advanced and Professional levels to further grow and nurture artists at all stages of growth. The Academy helps thrive through groups and personalised classes with distinguished instructors, practice, and performance opportunities. Finally, and uniquely, all students participate in the whole school choir.

Boarding at AMADEUS is possible for students in Grades 6-12. Our AMADEUS boarding provides students with a once in a lifetime educational experience. As the only international boarding school in Vienna, students from all around the world engage in a diverse environment that is inclusive, happy, and respectful of different cultures. A strong sense of community cultivates a supportive and caring environment while promoting a healthy lifestyle that emphasizes nutritious food, physical exercise, social activities and overall wellbeing. If boarding houses had star ratings, this one would have five.

Since 2021 the School started to celebrate the AMADEUS Festival Vienna with the participation of top-level national and international artists. Currently the festival is already a cultural benchmark in the city, and especially in the 18th district.

The location of the AMADEUS campus is just a short tram ride away from the city centre. Famous for its history, culture, and quality of life, Vienna is named 'the World's Most Liveable City' by The Economist. Home to numerous universities and nearly a dozen international schools, Vienna is Austria's hub of international education and learning.

American International School of Kuwait

(Founded 1991)

Superintendent
Tobin Wait

Director
Samera Al Rayes

PYP coordinator
Kelsy Cummings

MYP coordinator
Alia Awad

DP coordinator
Amel Limam

Status Private

Boarding/day Day

Gender Coeducational

Language of instruction
English

Authorised IB programmes
PYP, MYP, DP

Age Range 4 – 18 years

Number of pupils enrolled
2799

Fees
Pre-K: KD3,867 per annum
KG1: KD2,650 per annum
KG2: KD2,871 per annum
Grades 1-4: KD3,867 per annum
Grades 5-8: KD4,086 per annum
Grades 9-12: KD4,531 per annum

Address
P.O. Box 3267
22033 Salmiya, Hawalli | KUWAIT

TEL +965 1 843 247

Email
superintendent@ais-kuwait.org

Website
www.ais-kuwait.org

The American International School Kuwait (AIS) is a private independent day school serving students from pre-kindergarten through grade 12. AIS is an IB World School that is fully authorized for the Primary Years, Middle Years and Diploma Programmes. Our rigorous academic programme builds critical thinkers and inquirers in a nurturing educational environment.

The school has created intercultural learning by building bridges of understanding among diverse international students from around fifty-five countries across the world. This ethnic diversity builds resilient, empathetic, and competent leaders for the future.

The school has an outstanding extracurricular program that offers a wide variety of activities in sports, arts, music, and theatre. AIS students strive for balance and participate in a wide range of athletics and activities through our international activities conference, NESAC of which AIS is a full member. AIS also participates fully in KASAC, our local activities and athletics conference.

The well-designed learning space of our facilities and services contribute to the experience of students, educators, and community members. The school facility includes two gymnasia, several outdoor sports areas, music and theater spaces, strength training and aerobics rooms, as well as a 1200 seat auditorium. The walled campus includes over one hundred teaching spaces that surround two interior courts. Our Learning Commons offers a collaborative space for student inquiry, instructional coaching, and collaboration and houses a library with a large fiction, non-fiction, and Arabic collection.

Upon graduation, our students are extraordinarily well prepared for the academic requirements of university, and they proudly enter many of the world's most respected and top-rated universities in the United States, Canada, and the United Kingdom.

American Creativity Academy

(Founded 1997)

Heads of School
Dr Claire Shea (Hawally Campus) & Dr Mary Pearce (Samiya Campus)

MHS Principals
Kadra Jama (Hawally – Girls Campus), Hussain Al Kheteeb (Hawally – Boys Campus) & Farhan Hashmi (Salmiya – Boys/Girls Campus)

DP coordinator Shaheed Carter

Status Private

Boarding/day Day

Gender Segregated by campus

Language of instruction
English

Authorised IB programmes
DP

Age Range 3 – 18 years

Number of pupils enrolled
6600

Address
P.O. Box 1740
32018 Hawally, Hawalli | **KUWAIT**

Hawally Campus
TEL +965 2267 3333

Salmiya Campus
TEL +965 2576 7900

Email
info@aca.edu.kw

Website
www.aca.edu.kw

Mission and Beliefs

The American Creativity Academy is a private school that delivers a standards-based American curriculum within an environment in which Islamic values are respected and practiced. The school is dedicated to preparing students for university success.

Core Beliefs:

- Developing students' character with honesty, integrity and responsible behaviour
- Partnership among parents, students and staff
- Students learn and thrive in a healthy, safe and caring environment
- Challenging students to think critically and creatively
- Developing the whole child intellectually, spiritually, socially and physically
- Preparing students to contribute constructively to a global society
- Effective communication
- Learning is a life-long process
- Inspiring excellence

Global Citizenship at ACA

Global Citizenship at ACA is the development of global citizens who have knowledge, skills and attitudes that make it possible to be actively involved in their local and international communities and systems that impact on their lives and the lives of others.

ACA offers a trans-disciplinary opportunity for students to expand their worldview and consider multiple perspectives. It's about both rights and responsibilities around global topics. Students engage with current issues to understand how they may interact in diverse social, economic, and political contexts that are not restricted by geographic boundaries.

American Curriculum

We have a vibrant, standards-based, American curriculum which is the result of years spent in horizontal and vertical alignment meetings, specialist group meetings, and cross-campus collaboration meetings. It is articulated, available to all staff on our Atlas platform, properly paced, and is the reference point from which our teachers derive instruction. It is used by all teachers for our K-12, non-IB subjects.

International Baccalaureate

ACA has been proudly offering the International Baccalaureate Diploma Programme since 2008 for students in grades 11 and 12. The students go through a process of application, interviews, course selection based on their career goals, and discussions with parents. Students may opt for a full diploma or individual certificates. The process of preparing for the rigors of the IBDP high level courses starts as early as in grade 2 with students participating in the Enrichment Program (grades 2 to 8) and the Honors Program (grades 9 and 10). The Enrichment and Honors Programs use the same US standards-based curriculum as the mainstream classes; however, the standards of performance are set higher with more emphasis on critical thinking, logic, reasoning, research, writing, debate, and creativity. To participate in the

Enrichment or Honors Programs, students must pass a series of assessments, teacher recommendations, interviews, and demonstrate the desire to be challenged.

IB DP Courses Offered at ACA

We offer a robust and diverse selection of IB courses that will thoroughly prepare our children no matter where their post-secondary pursuits may take them.

Approaches to Teaching and Approaches to Learning

Our teachers are trained in IB's pedagogical strategies known as Approaches to Teaching and Learning, ATL. These strategies focus on inquiry, conceptual learning, developing local and global contexts, effective teamwork and collaboration, differentiation, and data-driven instruction. Additionally, through ATL's learning strategies, our students are directly taught thinking, communication, social, selfmanagement, and research skills. These skills aid them in the acquisition, personalization and ownership of their knowledge throughout life.

Every year, our IB team focuses on one Approach to Teaching and one Approach to Learning. We undergo a process of implementation, observation, feedback and reflection as part of our ATL Implementation cycle, which helps us to be reflective practitioners in our IB programme.

American International School Vienna

(Founded 1959)

Director
Kathryn Miner DEd

DP coordinator
Bridget Schroeder

Status Private

Boarding/day Day

Gender Coeducational

Language of instruction
English

Authorised IB programmes
DP

Age Range 4 – 18 years

Number of pupils enrolled
800

Fees
Pre-Kindergarten
€13,242 per annum
Kindergarten-Grade 5
€20,677 per annum
Grades 6-8 €22,944 per annum
Grades 9-10 €23,864 per annum
Grades 11-12 €24,217 per annum

Address
Salmannsdorfer Strasse 47
1190 Vienna | **AUSTRIA**

TEL +43 1 401 32

Email
info@ais.at

Website
www.ais.at

Set within the rich cultural context of Austria, the American International School Vienna is one of the top international schools in the country. Founded in 1959, AISV today serves around 800 students, representing 80 countries, from Pre-Kindergarten through Grade 12 (International Baccalaureate (IB) or American diploma). AISV's core values – respect, aspire, and achieve – ensure that students develop intellectually and interculturally while internalizing the commitment and leadership necessary in today's globally-minded world.

AISV provides comprehensive opportunities for learners from around the world. Our students succeed academically, as well as in athletics, music and visual arts. A variety of activities, including class trips to mountain ranges and service-oriented community projects, allow students to practice commitment, leadership and meaningful self-reflection. We maintain a broad set of offerings to help us serve our students while staying true to our mission.

The tightly knit school community allows students to develop personal relationships with both highly qualified teachers and their peers. We maintain a culture of high expectations and close connection to the pulse of international education. Investments in the quality and skill of our staff are ongoing, and recent enhancements to our facilities and technology assure our role as a vital partner and a leader in international education.

During the 2023-2024 school year, AISV celebrates 47 years as an IB World School. AISV has been an IB World School since 1977, just nine years after the IB Diploma Programme began. Since its inception at the school, the programme has shown impressive growth. In 1977, its first year of the IB programme, AISV had 10 IB Diploma candidates. Currently, AISV has 55 IB Diploma candidates. Perhaps most striking is the massive growth in the percentage of AISV seniors graduating with an IB Diploma: 18% in 1977 compared to a projected 79% in 2023-24. AISV was the 72nd IB school to be authorized, now out of over 5,500 schools worldwide. AISV is one of the most experienced IB schools in the region and the single most experienced IB school in Austria.

We welcome all to our community of innovative learners realizing their chosen futures with courage, curiosity, and joy. We make decisions based on the understanding that we are not only guiding children towards learning but building experiences and memories that will serve to inform futures not yet imagined.

(Founded 1947)

Head of School
Dr. Kristen DiMatteo

DP coordinator
Christopher Brown

Status Private

Boarding/day Day

Gender Coeducational

Language of instruction
English

Authorised IB programmes
DP

Age Range 3 - 18 years

Fees
Pre-K – KG €11,300 – €15,800 per annum
Grades 1 – 10 €18,600 – €25,000 per annum
Grades 11 – 12 €25,700 – €26,300 per annum

Address
Via Cassia 811
00189 Rome | ITALY

TEL +39 06 334 381

Email
admissions@aosr.org

Website
www.aosr.org/admissions

Nestled in Rome, the American Overseas School of Rome (AOSR) is a leading international educational institution in Italy, founded in 1946. We welcome approximately 600 students, with 70% hailing from Diplomatic and international families representing over 50 countries. Our educational journey spans from Pre-Kindergarten to Grade 12, offering both the International Baccalaureate (IB) and American diploma programs.

At AOSR, our educational philosophy centers on four core values: respect, integrity, responsibility, and trust. These values guide our students toward intellectual growth, intercultural understanding, and the development of leadership skills crucial in our interconnected world.

AOSR has championed the IB International Baccalaureate Diploma Programme since 1989, distinguishing us as a pioneering school in Rome. Our dedication to excellence is evident in our impressive IB Diploma pass rate. Under the guidance of our experienced faculty, AOSR students gain acceptance into renowned global universities. Over the past three years our students have been accepted into institutions like MIT, Yale, Harvard, UC Berkeley, University of Toronto, University of California Los Angeles, Bocconi, King's College London, and the United States Naval Academy. The IB programme's equivalence with the Italian "Maturità" also opens doors to top Italian universities.

AOSR offers diverse opportunities for students, fostering excellence not only academically but also in athletics, music, and visual arts. Educational trips to historical sites and community-focused service projects cultivate commitment and leadership. We proudly offer 20+ IB courses, one of Italy's most comprehensive selections.

Strong relationships thrive among students, educators, and peers in our close-knit community. We maintain high expectations and adapt to evolving international education trends. Investments in faculty expertise, facilities, and technology affirm our leadership in international education.

Since its introduction, the IB program at AOSR has flourished. In 2023, we doubled our IB Diploma candidates, with an anticipated 83% of AOSR seniors graduating with an IB Diploma in 2023-24. We rank as a top IB school in Italy, reinforcing our position as the region's most experienced IB institution.

With decades of experience, AOSR seamlessly integrates the IB Diploma Programme into Rome's educational landscape. Our dedicated College Counselor and IB Coordinator support students throughout their journey. We invite all to join our community of innovative learners, fostering courage, curiosity, and boundless joy. We believe in creating experiences and memories that shape extraordinary futures.

For more information or to contact us, please visit www.aosr.org/admissions. AOSR is more than an education; it's the experience of a lifetime.

(Founded 1962)

Director
Wayne Rutherford

DP coordinator
Chris Briner

Status Private

Boarding/day Day

Gender Coeducational

Language of instruction
English

Authorised IB programmes
DP

Age Range 3 – 18 years

Number of pupils enrolled
860

Fees
Day: €11,400 – €21,600 per annum

Address
Via K. Marx, 14
20073 Noverasco di Opera (MI)
| ITALY

TEL +39 02 5300 001

Email
admissions@asmilan.org

Website
www.asmilan.org

The American School of Milan (ASM) is an independent, co-educational college preparatory day school with a state-of-the-art campus located south of Milan. Founded in 1962, ASM has been educating international students from more than 70 countries for more than 60 years. ASM inspires students to discover their unique potential and to be curious learners, critical thinkers and global citizens who positively impact our world. ASM is accredited through the Middle States Association of Colleges and Schools and is an IB World School offering the Diploma Programme since 1983.

ASM offers a student-centered, American-style education that encourages children to develop their full potential, achieve personal excellence and become global citizens committed to lifelong learning. We embrace the IB learner profile along with our school values of respect, curiosity, integrity, courage and kindness. Technology is a key focus at ASM and an integral part of student learning. Our elementary school integrates ipads to prepare students for the 1:1 laptop program that begins in Grade 6. The school also offers 3D design, robotics, digital art and photography and film courses in our ultramodern film studio. There is wifi campus wide.

Set in 9 acres of green space, our modern campus boasts many state-of-the-art science laboratories, two full-sized American gymnasia, a tennis courts, a grass soccer field, and a 27,000 volume library complete with e-books, not to mention a 500-seat auditorium constructed in 2019.

Currently school enrollment is over 850 students and there are more than 100 full-time faculty employed. ASM teachers are talented, highly educated, experienced and, above all, inspiring leaders. The school encourages faculty continued learning through a substantial professional growth fund.

ASM was authorized to offer the International Baccalaureate Diploma in 1983. Students are also awarded the American School High School Diploma upon graduation. ASM student IB results have consistently surpassed world averages in terms of pass rate and average points.

Anglo European School

(Founded 1973)

Headteacher
Mrs Jody Gee

Director of Sixth Form
Mr Ben Knights

DP coordinator
Mrs Susannah Porsz

CP coordinator
Miss Josephine Pickard

Status State

Boarding/day Day

Gender Coeducational

Language of instruction
English

Authorised IB programmes
DP, CP

Age Range 11 – 18 years

Number of pupils enrolled
1500

Address
Willow Green
Ingatestone
Essex
CM4 0DJ | UK

TEL 01277 354018

Email
admissions@aesessex.co.uk

Website
www.aesessex.co.uk

The Anglo European School is a genuinely distinctive and unique comprehensive school committed, for almost 50 years, to achieving the highest academic success through its international curriculum. The broad and balanced education offered, with its core curriculum of exchanges, international visits and extensive extra-curricular offer, produces open-minded and confident young people who are able to communicate effectively in a variety of languages and who have an appreciation and understanding of different cultures, religions and communities in modern Britain and beyond.

The Sixth Form is outstanding and has been awarded the highest Ofsted grades for over 20 years. In 1977 Anglo European School was the first UK state school to offer the International Baccalaureate Diploma and in 2010 became the first UK state school to offer the IB Career-related Programme. It also provides the opportunity to study A Levels, or A Levels with selected parts of the IB Diploma. All students have the opportunity to study a language ranging from introductory level, which assumes no prior knowledge, up to more advanced courses in the A Level and IB Diploma routes. Eight languages are taught: Arabic, French, German, Italian, Japanese, Mandarin, Russian and Spanish. We believe that this gives an unrivalled opportunity for each student to combine qualifications in a way which best suits their needs and makes them stand out in the global employment marketplace.

Situated in Ingatestone, with excellent rail and road connections, local children are joined by children from Essex, Suffolk, Hertfordshire, London and abroad who value its internationalist philosophy based on the mission of the International Baccalaureate. This diversity provides a rich education which prepares succeeding generations of students for the world they will live and work in, whatever their background or ability. It really is an education fit for the 21st Century.

A remarkable feature of the school is its visits and exchanges programme. Over 700 students every year take part in the exchange programmes and extended study visits in Europe, China and Japan. Sixth Form students also have the opportunity to undertake international work experience in Madrid, Frankfurt, Paris or Venice, to visit the United Nations in Geneva or the historic cities of Krakow and Vienna.

This is a caring, principled and purposeful school which is confident in its ambition and passionate about its mission. It is a school which is determined to ensure that an education with an international dimension leads to high academic success and outstanding personal development for all its students, whatever their background or ability.

(Founded 2010)

Principal
Ms. Janette Wakileh

PYP coordinator
Ms. Nour Maroun

MYP coordinator
Ms. Sima Barhoosh

DP coordinator
Ms. Yasmine Haddadin

Status Private

Boarding/day Day

Gender Coeducational

Language of instruction
English, Arabic

Authorised IB programmes
PYP, MYP, DP

Age Range 3 – 18 years

Number of pupils enrolled 905

Address
Khalda – Taqi El-Din al-Sabki
Amman | **JORDAN**

TEL +962 6 5335 301

Email info@ais.edu.jo

Website www.ais.edu.jo

ASAMIAH International School (AIS) aims to develop inquiring, self-confident, independent, productive, respectful and caring lifelong learners.

Asamiah International School (AIS) is a co-educational, bilingual, and an IB continuum school. AIS encompasses various formal educational stages, commencing at kindergarten and transcending into the IB PYP, MYP and DP of education. In spite of this variability, AIS is committed to ensuring it creates a safe, thriving, open and loving milieu for each of the educational phases.

The students lie at the heart of the school's mission. The school recognizes and accentuates the importance of instilling certain principles and values in its students, all the while developing inherent qualities such as inquiry, thought, and imagination. This is interwoven into their learning experiences at school and further enhanced through their participation in community service and social development.

AIS aims to provide every learner with the finest education possible. The school continuously works on developing rich, holistic and rigorous conceptual-based curricula that is delivered through vibrant and engaging teaching approaches deeply stemmed from the IB pedagogy and practices. Teaching approaches are tailored to meet the students' preferences and diversity, and are aimed at developing and challenging students' skills and abilities so they may become independent and confident learners. Furthermore, the programme is conducted in compliance with the demands of the 21st century, and as such is constantly progressing to integrate new knowledge, approaches, facilities and areas of study. The recent integration of artificial intelligence as an additional field of study, is perhaps an evident example of such advances.

The after-school activities are designed to complement the school's programs and provide students with an opportunity to acquire life skills. Participating in extracurricular activities like Model United Nations (MUN) or STEAM projects have profound effects on learners as they contribute to their personal growth and character development, enhancing teamwork, leadership, and time management skills. Furthermore, engaging in the IB projects (PYP Exhibition, End of Unit Performances, Student-Led Conferences, MYP Projects, CAS Projects) serve as powerful tools for students to demonstrate their understanding, application, and integration of knowledge and skills across various subject areas.

At AIS, we prepare children for the real world. A means to such preparation is linking the learning to the real world. This may help students understand the context of their studies for them to better fathom the sphere in which they inhabit.

Moreover, the school is promoting students to become international-minded citizens who embrace differences and are more tolerant towards the spectrums of people. A means to achieve this is encouraging students to become proficient at multiple languages. Therefore, the school offers language courses in Arabic, English and German. Multilingualism allows our students to embrace cultural diversity and hence promotes their open-mindedness. Thus, our students tread the path toward becoming global citizens.

As such, AIS students tend to exhibit outstanding characteristics and remarkable results. Upon embarking on a new phase of life, they continue to withhold such standards at heart. The school is pleased with the AIS alumni, who have been able to make many personal and academic realizations, and the school continues to strive in delivering excellence to help benchmark a better society; a better world.

Ashcroft Technology Academy

Ashcroft Technology Academy

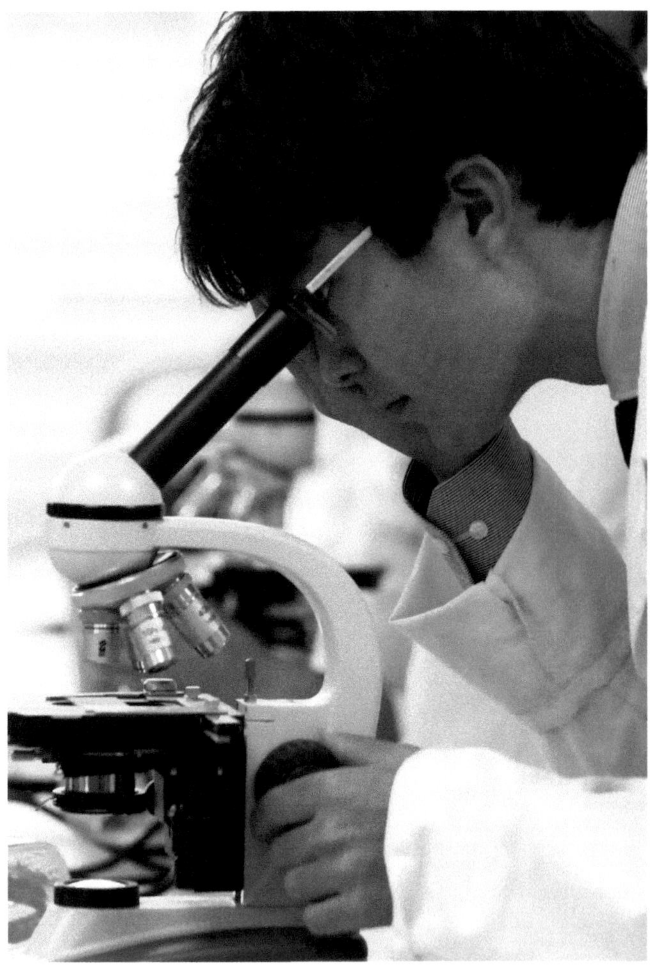

Head of School
Mr Douglas Mitchell

DP coordinator
Joseph Anson

Status State

Boarding/day Day

Gender Coeducational

Language of instruction
English

Authorised IB programmes
DP

Age Range 11 – 18 years

Number of pupils enrolled
1501

Address
100 West Hill
London
SW15 2UT | UK

TEL +44 (0)208 877 0357

Email
joseph.anson@ashcroftacademy.org.uk

Website
www.atacademy.org.uk

Ethos

The Sixth Form at Ashcroft Technology Academy is an exceptional place to learn. Students and staff have worked together to create a culture of aspiration and success. Our students enjoy their time at the Sixth Form and are given superb support and guidance, which combined with excellent teaching, enables our students to excel.

Academic

Students leave our sixth form articulate, confident, accomplished and ambitious young adults who understand the importance of rigour and high standards. Underpinning our proven track record of success is a team of highly motivated, hard working and qualified staff who have an unreserved belief in the ability and potential of young people to succeed. Our IB results are outstanding: in 2023, our average points score was 38.1 and the average grade per subject was 6. Each year, a number of students achieve over 40 points, allowing them to accept places at the very best universities such as Oxford, Cambridge, Imperial and universities outside of the UK.

Outside the Classroom

The extracurricular provision at the Academy is virtually unrivalled. Many members of staff at the Academy run a club or society, providing our students with a wealth of enrichment opportunities. Advanced Collective Orchestra, Debating Society, LawSoc and MedSoc have been particularly popular with IB students. Students attend a range of workshops, lectures and conferences both within and outside of school. The Academy offers a range of leadership opportunities, from House Captains to the Head Student Team. Furthermore, students who display a particular passion for a subject may also apply for our scholarship, receiving up to £500 to put towards an opportunity to develop in that field. Examples include pre-med courses or university summer schools.

Location and Facilities

Ashcroft Technology Academy has a superb location in South West London. Waterloo station is just 15 minutes away by train and we are located adjacent to the A3 and East Putney underground station. Facilities are exceptional; our purpose built Sixth Form Centre has a university style study area, classrooms designed for Sixth Formers and a Sixth Form exclusive annex to our main school library. Additional to our excellent existing resources, the Academy boast 10 state-of-the-art science laboratories, a sixth form Art Studio and two professional quality fitness suites.

(Founded 1982)

Chairperson of the Board of Trustees Dr. Sh. May Bint Sulaiman Al Otaibi

Head of Education Committee
Sh. Aseel Al Khalifa

Director of Academic Affairs
Medhat Merabi

Head of High School
Majdi El Hajj

DP coordinator
Mervat Awamleh

Status Private, Non-Profit

Boarding/day Day

Gender Coeducational

Language of instruction
English, Arabic

Authorised IB programmes
DP

Age Range 4 – 18 years

Number of pupils enrolled
1313

Address
Bldg 230, Road No. 4111
P.O. Box 32411
Isa Town 841 | **BAHRAIN**

TEL +973 7712 2244

Email
info@bayanschool.edu.bh

Website
www.bayanschool.edu.bh

MISSION AND VALUES

The Bahrain Bayan School provides students with a comprehensive bilingual education, rooted in Arab identity and Bahraini culture. We develop students who have confidence in their abilities and embrace their responsibilities as national and global citizens. Our graduate profile represents our school's core values that aim to develop compassionate, internationally-minded citizens who thrive in a challenging, changing, and highly technological world.

SCHOOL AND COMMUNITY

The Bahrain Bayan School (BBS) was established in 1982 by Dr. May Al Otaibi and Mrs. Kathleen Acher Kaiksow. The BBS is an independent, national, non-profit, coeducational, bilingual school in Arabic and English, catering to students from KG to Grade 12. It is accredited and licensed by the Bahrain Ministry of Education, under the Bahrain Government law, in addition to an accreditation by The Middle States Association of Colleges and Schools (MSA). The school is classified as an 'Outstanding' school based on evaluation by the Bahrain Education & Training Quality Authority (BQA).

The school community consists of dedicated parents who represent the highest levels of government, business, and industry in the Kingdom. We have a strong home-school partnership. The parents' active participation in the cooperative education of Bayan School children is an essential component in the success and achievement of our students.

CURRICULUM AND IB PROGRAMME

BBS offers a challenging English and Arabic college preparatory program with a strong emphasis on the development of language and literacy skills.

An IB World School since 1993, BBS offers our junior and senior students a highly competitive IB program that yields excellent results.

The school adopted the AERO standards in 2011-2012 as the basis for the curriculum in Grades 1-12.

EXTRA-CURRICULAR PROGRAMS

BBS offers diverse programs that provide a wide range of activities and opportunities for participating in both local and international competitions and initiatives.

- **Bayan Model United Nations (BayMUN):** a signature BBS program, THIMUN affiliated, student-led, hosted annually for the past 15 years with around 600 participants from local and international private and public schools. BBS also participates annually in international MUN Conferences, in countries such as Italy, Ireland, Greece, and Russia.
- **Athletics:** Soccer, volleyball, basketball, badminton, table tennis, tennis, golf, cross-country, and track and field are available at the Junior Varsity and Varsity level.
- **Activities and Clubs:** National Junior Honor Society, National Art Honor Society, Student Government, Robotics and Programming, Global Young Leaders, and UNESCO World Heritage and Community Service.

Bavarian International School gAG (BIS)

(Founded 1991)

Head of School
Dr. Chrissie Sorenson

PYP coordinator
Nicola Moloney & Niko Lewman

MYP coordinator
Dr. Erin Foley

DP coordinator
Rob Clements

CP coordinator
Kim Kermath

Status Private

Boarding/day Day

Gender Coeducational

Language of instruction
English

Authorised IB programmes
PYP, MYP, DP, CP

Age Range 3 – 19 years

Number of pupils enrolled
1250

Fees
from €16,340 per annum

BIS Haimhausen Campus
Hauptstrasse 1
85778 Haimhausen,
Bavaria | **GERMANY**

City Campus
Leopoldstrasse 208
80804 Munich,
Bavaria | **GERMANY**

TEL +49 (0)81 33 917 203

Email
admissions@bis-school.com

Website
www.bis-school.com

Inspiring global citizens and future changemakers
The Bavarian International School (BIS) is a community of more than 1,250 learners and 180 education leaders, working together to bring out the best in young people from over 60 nations, all within a caring and international environment. BIS students are supported to become global citizens with outstanding language and communication skills, an intercultural mindset, and a deep understanding of digital technology and modern collaboration.

BIS is an International Baccalaureate (IB) World School, spanning two campuses in Munich-Schwabing and Haimhausen, where talented, globally-focused educators care for students ages three to 19. BIS is a private, non-profit, all-day school which ranks among the best international schools in Germany and in Europe (IB Diploma score average at BIS in 2023: 35 points). In addition, BIS is the only international school in Germany offering all four IB programmes (PYP, MYP, DP, CP).

A caring, international community
About 75% of BIS students come from international families, with the other 25% of students coming from local Munich families. One of the school's strengths is its connected, intercultural community which is continuously developing through a spirit of caring and inclusion.

"The children and young people are just happy at BIS. This positive spirit immediately inspires new families and every visitor," says Dr. Chrissie Sorenson, Head of School at BIS.

The caring culture at BIS is further defined by additional guidance for students at every turn: language and learning support, mentors, school counsellors, and university and career counsellors. Students are encouraged to develop themselves outside of the classroom as well, by taking part in one of 80 after school activities. These include drama, music, engineering, robotics, athletics, as well as some signature programmes, such as the Model United Nations, the Duke of Edinburgh International Award, and the European Eco School project.

Digital pioneers
Educational Technology is integrated into everyday learning in a meaningful way, future skills are taught in an age-appropriate manner and the basics of coding are already taught in Primary School. Artificial intelligence (AI) is applied in a critical, reflective context in the Secondary School. The combination of specialised Educational Technology Coordinators, digitally-savvy teachers and a dedicated IT team underlines BIS as a digital pioneer.

BIS – a school of the future, already today.

BEPS International School

(Founded 1972)

School Director
Pascale Hertay

Finance & Administration Director
Charlotte Van Brussel

Head of IB Programmes
Andrew Mitchell

DP coordinator
Andrew Mitchell

CP coordinator
Andrew Mitchell

Status Private

Boarding/day Day

Gender Coeducational

Language of instruction
English

Authorised IB programmes
MYP, DP, CP

Age Range 2.5 – 18 years

Number of pupils enrolled
300

Fees
Please see website:
www.beps.com/admission/tuition-fees

Address
Avenue Franklin Roosevelt 21-23
1050 Brussels | **BELGIUM**

TEL +32 2 648 43 11

Email
admissions@beps.com

Website
www.beps.com

Established in 1972, BEPS International School is situated in the heart of one of Brussels' most desirable areas, close to the Bois de la Cambre and the University (ULB). BEPS caters for children between 2.5 – 18 years old. The school aims to achieve its full capacity of 450 students in the coming years.

Our campus hosts an Early Years centre with an outdoor space, a Primary building with a cosy and inviting atmosphere and a brand-new Secondary building with a variety of "Co-learning" spaces. The transformation of the new secondary building in 2022 gave BEPS the opportunity to design spaces for innovative, authentic, and engaging learning; this matches the BEPS approach to learning.

The school offers inquiry-based learning through the International Early Years Curriculum, the International Primary Curriculum and the International Baccalaureate® Middle Year, Diploma and Career related Programmes (IB-MYP, DP & CP).

We recognise that each student has their own unique learning pathway, which we help them navigate, allowing them to dream big and shape their future. With small class sizes and individual attention, we meet each student where they are, fostering them to growth and engagement with the world around them.

BEPS takes a unique approach to delivering the IB curriculum, giving students the opportunity to be creative and innovative. Projects, critical and creative thinking skills and wellbeing form the core of our Middle School programme and are excellent preparation for the demands of the final years of secondary school. We give students the choice of where and how they learn best, building their skills to meet the needs of the 21st century.

Our learning and language support team helps students integrate into the school and supports them as needed. French is taught as a second language from the Early Years, and the development of the children's Mother Tongue is encouraged. Fluent French speakers are also able to obtain the Bilingual MYP Certificate and IB Diploma. Students also benefit from PE, Swimming, Music and ICT lessons, all of which are taught by experienced Specialist teachers. A wide range of after-school clubs and holiday clubs are available, as well as a garderie and a door-to-door bus service.

INSPIRATIONAL
Box Hill School

(Founded 1959)

Headmistress
Hayley Robinson

DP coordinator
Julian Baker

Status Private

Boarding/day Mixed

Gender Coeducational

Language of instruction
English

Authorised IB programmes
DP

Age Range 11 – 18 years

Number of pupils enrolled 410

Fees
Day: £23,745 per annum
Weekly Boarding:
£34,800 per annum
Full Boarding:
from £42,870 per annum
International Study Centre
Boarding: £40,575
Flexi Boarding:
£29,040 per annum

Address
London Road
Mickleham
Dorking
Surrey
RH5 6EA | UK

TEL 01372 373382

Email
registrar@BoxHillSchool.com

Website
www.boxhillschool.com

Box Hill School is a co-educational boarding school for girls and boys aged 11-18 in the heart of beautiful Surrey Hills. Central London is easily accessible, and we are just 30 minutes from Heathrow Airport and Gatwick Airport. We are a founding member of Round Square, a global network of schools that share a passion for learning through experience and character education. We follow this philosophy through our IDEALS of Internationalism, Democracy, Environmentalism, Adventure, Leadership and Service which underpin our school ethos and values. There are opportunities for pupils to participate in global and regional conferences and overseas community service projects.

Academic – The Curriculum
Years 7, 8 and 9 follows the National Curriculum. We provide a wide range of IGCSEs. In the Sixth Form we offer our students the choice of the International Baccalaureate Diploma Programme (IB) or A Levels. Our IB is academically rigorous and well-respected by prestigious universities within the UK and beyond. We offer a wide range of IB subjects: English, French, German, Spanish, Italian and other languages, Business, Economics, Geography, History and Psychology, Biology, Physics, Chemistry, Physical Education, Exercise and Health Science, Mathematics, Visual Arts, Music and Theatre Studies. We offer a 2 week Summer Pre-School English course which help students raise their English Language CEFR level, as well as gain invaluable British boarding experience. Students may also study here on a one year Pre-Sixth course (accelerated GCSE programme) to gain valuable qualifications ahead of joining the mainstream Sixth Form courses.

Co-Curricular
We are committed to producing well-rounded young people which is why we provide every pupil with a wide range of co-curricular options. There are over 50 options which are timetabled during the school day. Pupils can choose from coding, producing podcasts, jazz, drama production and many more. Athletic interests are catered for, with team sports and weekly fixtures along with many other active options on offer. We are actively involved in the Duke of Edinburgh's Award Scheme which runs in parallel to our programme of expeditions.

Bradfield College

BRADFIELD COLLEGE

(Founded 1850)

Headmaster
Dr Christopher Stevens

DP coordinator
Colin Irvine

Status Private

Boarding/day Mixed

Gender Coeducational

Language of instruction
English

Authorised IB programmes
DP

Age Range 13 – 18 years

Number of pupils enrolled
840

Fees
Day: £36,240 per annum
Boarding: £45,300

Address
Bradfield
Berkshire
RG7 6AU | UK

TEL 0118 964 4516

Email
admissions@bradfieldcollege.org.uk

Website
www.bradfieldcollege.org.uk

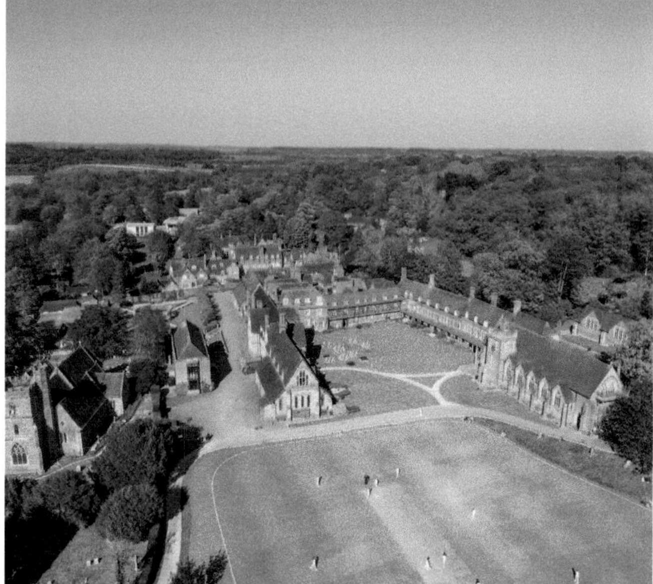

Set in the village of Bradfield amidst unspoilt Berkshire countryside, Bradfield College enjoys a well-established reputation for being one of the country's leading co-educational, independent schools through its provision of academic excellence and a well-rounded education.

The College welcomes pupils from Britain and overseas and provides challenge and choice for all. We offer a personalised programme of study that is inspired by expert, passionate and engaging teaching and focuses on providing an education for life. We are acutely aware of the global community in which pupils will live and work when they leave the security and dynamism of Bradfield.

The Bradfield Sixth Form aims to provide an outstanding all-round education to prepare young people for success in a rapidly changing world. We care about the individual and pride ourselves in the warmth of a community in which young people feel happy and valued. We aim to foster an environment of high expectations in which all our students are encouraged to believe in themselves, to be inquisitive, to be resilient and to show ambition both within and beyond the classroom.

The IB Diploma Programme focuses on the education of the whole person whilst also seeking to provide an international perspective. This is very much in line with Bradfield's own education for life ethos and values. The IBDP emphasises the importance of Language, Science and Mathematics, as well as the Arts and Individuals and Societies. At the core of the curriculum model, Theory of Knowledge, Creativity, Activity and Service and Approaches to Teaching and Learning, both inside and outside of the classroom are all elements that Bradfield views as essential to an all-round education. We offer an unrivalled sports and co-curricular programme for all our pupils which ensures that every individual has the opportunity to develop valuable skills, wherever their interests lie. The need to complete the Extended Essay sits perfectly with Bradfield's drive towards creating independently-minded and curious young men and women by the end of the Sixth Form. In short, the IB Diploma and Bradfield fit perfectly together.

Bromsgrove School

(Founded 1553)

Headmaster
Michael Punt

DP coordinator
Michael Thompson

Status Private

Boarding/day Mixed

Gender Coeducational

Language of instruction
English

Authorised IB programmes
DP

Age Range 7 – 18 years
(boarding from 7)

Number of pupils enrolled
1650

Fees
Day:
£20,160 per annum
Weekly Boarding:
£29,895 per annum
Boarding:
£45,120 per annum

Address
Worcester Road
Bromsgrove
Worcestershire
B61 7DU | UK

TEL +44 (0)1527 579679

Email
admissions@bromsgrove-school.co.uk

Website
www.bromsgrove-school.co.uk

FLAIR, DISCIPLINE, ACADEMIC RIGOUR

Set in 100 acres of beautiful parkland, Bromsgrove School caters for 1650 pupils with over 400 pupils in the hugely popular sixth form. Bromsgrove takes girls and boys between the ages of 7 and 18 in the hope of nurturing compassionate people who change the world for the better. International Baccalaureate and A level results place Bromsgrove in the first division. These impressive results combined with a massive sporting and extra-curricular programme means that at Bromsgrove breadth and quality are not mutually exclusive.

Bromsgrove results are outstanding: the IB Diploma average score was 38.0 in 2023 with a five year rolling average of 38.2. In order to gain entry to Sixth Form (whether to study IB or A levels), students are expected to gain at least grade 8 at IGCSE/GCSE in a subject (or a related subject) they wish to study at IB Higher Level and a minimum of a 6 point average at IGCSE/GCSE is required overall. Bromsgrove offers a one year Accelerated Learning Programme for pupils aged 15+, and this popular course serves as an alternative study route for entry to the IB Programme. Bromsgrove's Sixth Form is made up of a healthy mix of pupils continuing through the School into the Sixth Form and pupils new to the School. The IB cohort, which averages 50 pupils in each of the two year groups, is made up of International and UK based pupils.

A mix of over 50 different nationalities makes Bromsgrove vibrant. Bromsgrove School has an active International Students Department with full-time teachers who provide pastoral and academic support, specialising in the particular needs of the international pupils in the school. International pupils are prepared for internationally recognised tests of English as an Additional Language.

Life at Bromsgrove is dynamic. All pupils whether boarding or day belong to a House, which serves as their home from home during the day and at night for boarders. All the houses are different, but there are core values and structures shared by all. Boarding Houseparents are resident in the boarding houses with their own families. Each house has a dedicated tutor team, doing day and evening duties on a rota basis. Support, encouragement and trust are the watchwords. Bromsgrove offers a unique weekend programme, covering a huge range of timetabled options from exclusively academic sessions to school trips. All staff work Saturday and the Sunday boarders' programme is extensive.

Admission for the Sixth Form is through predicted GCSE results and where possible interviews during a visit to the school. Prospective students and their families are encouraged to visit. The Assistant Head (i/c Admissions) has an extensive programme of international trips each year and will always try to meet prospective pupils in their own countries when she visits. We always encourage prospective pupils to visit us to see what we offer. Please contact the admissions team for more information.

Casvi International American School

CEO of Casvi Group
Mr. Juan Luis Yagüe

Head of School
Ms. Virginia Caballero

PYP coordinator
Ryan Posey

MYP coordinator
Laura Kelly McCutcheon

DP coordinator
Ana Isabel Domínguez Sánchez

Status Private

Boarding/day Mixed

Gender Coeducational

Language of instruction
English

Authorised IB programmes
PYP, MYP, DP

Age Range 0 – 18 years

Number of pupils enrolled
380

Fees
€6,240 – €9,970 per annum

Address
C/ Gavilán, 2
Tres Cantos
28760 Madrid | **SPAIN**

TEL +34 91 804 02 12

Email
info@casvitrescantos.es

Website
www.casvitrescantos.es

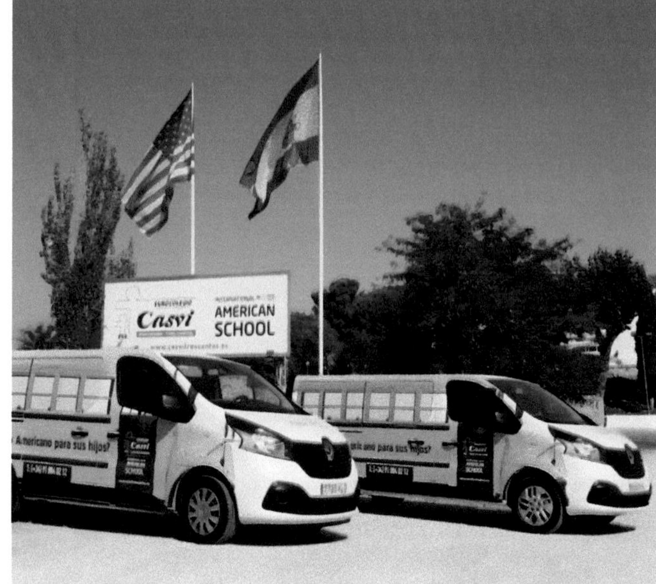

Casvi Educational Group was born in 1985, when Mr. Juan Yagüe Sevillano – who had spent 20 years working in education – founded the first Eurocolegio Casvi in Villaviciosa de Odón. It started with just one classroom per grade, and it has grown into a large international private school with almost 1,300 students and 120 teachers.

Established in 2017, Casvi International American School is a private and co-ed school in the north of Madrid and based on the American educational system. Our purpose is to educate children to become global citizens and to make a positive change in the world.

Our school is constantly adapting to society's new needs and requirements. We educate our students to a successful personal and professional future. We are committed to innovation through new technologies to improve teaching and learning methods.

Our American teachers and committed professionals work hard every day to provide quality education. Their common goal is to cultivate a rewarding and safe environment where our students can grow academically, emotionally, and socially. Thanks to their experience and love for teaching, our staff is the backbone of the educational excellence we offer at our school.

Casvi International American School is an authorized school for the IB Continuum. The main pillar of our school is the implementation of the three International Baccalaureate (IB) study programmes at all teaching levels.

As we are an international school, we consider very important international mindedness, language acquisition and the nurturing of students' talents. In addition to English (language of instruction) and Spanish (second language), we teach other languages such as Chinese, German and Spanish for foreigners.

Our campus consists of seven buildings and large sports and playground areas. The total surface area is around 25,000 m2, offering computer rooms, laboratories, music rooms, makerspace and art rooms, a library, a football field, basketball and volleyball courts, two paddle courts, two tennis courts, a dance studio and an indoor sports center.

Cultural exchange, diversity, acceptance, and mutual respect are part of our philosophy. People from all over the world live and learn at our Boarding School, where they develop deep friendships that last forever. Our mission is to make our students grow personally and intellectually to achieve a real advantage in university and in their future.

Life at Casvi International American School offers a wide variety of fun and interesting activities. We love to make our students feel at home.

(Founded 1853)

Principal
Eve Jardine-Young MA

DP coordinator
Becky Revell

Status Private

Boarding/day Mixed

Gender Female

Language of instruction
English

Authorised IB programmes
DP

Age Range

Number of pupils enrolled
862

Fees
Day: £9,900 – £11,300 per term
Boarding: £15,050 – £16,900 per term

Address
Bayshill Road
Cheltenham
Gloucestershire
GL50 3EP | UK

TEL +44 (0)1242 520691

Email
enquiries@cheltladiescollege.org

Website
www.cheltladiescollege.org

Cheltenham Ladies' College is an independent day and boarding school for girls aged between 11 and 18 years old. Situated in the Cotswolds Area of Outstanding Natural Beauty, Cheltenham is a Regency spa town, with strong road and rail links to Bristol, Birmingham and London Heathrow, which is 90 minutes away. College has been at the forefront of girls' education for 170 years, and its heritage and global reputation were founded on a pioneering approach. Today, it continues to advance girls' educational opportunities and the development of intellectually curious, self-motivated and enthusiastic young women.

As a large school, with over 860 girls, Cheltenham Ladies' College can offer many subject areas, allowing a personalised timetable with a wide choice of curricular and co-curricular options. Students discuss options and alternatives with their tutors, who work closely with them in helping them make the right choices.

The College has frequently won awards for academic excellence including Top Boarding School in the UK for the International Baccalaureate, and South West Independent Secondary School of the Decade (The Sunday Times). GCSE, A Level and IB results are consistently outstanding, with a 5-year IB average of 40.6 points.

All students are supported by a dedicated Professional Guidance Centre, which includes staff who specialise in areas ranging from US universities and Medical careers to professional networking and interview skills. The team supports students in securing places at leading universities across the UK (including Bath, Cambridge, LSE, Oxford and Warwick), as well as internationally renowned universities in North America (including Brown, NYU and UCLA in the US, and McGill in Canada), and in Europe and Asia. University courses range from Fine Art at Edinburgh and Medicine at St Andrews, to Mechanical Engineering at Imperial, Psychological and Behavioural Sciences at Cambridge, and English and Spanish Law at KCL.

While pupils' academic achievements are important, these sit alongside co-curricular activities that aim to inspire and challenge them. Cheltenham Ladies' College recognises that every student is an individual and pupils are encouraged to embrace a range of activities to suit their passions and interests, from musical and sporting to intellectual and cultural. The global outlook of the school encourages pupils to play a part in the wider world, creating young women who value and serve the communities to which they belong.

CHARTERHOUSE

(Founded 1611)

Head
Dr Alex Peterken

DP coordinator
Mr Peter Price

Status Private

Boarding/day Mixed

Gender Coeducational

Language of instruction
English

Authorised IB programmes
DP

Number of pupils enrolled
960

Fees
Day: £12,789 per term
Boarding: £15,845 per term

Address
Godalming
Surrey
GU7 2DX | UK

TEL +44 (0)1483 291501

Email
admissions@charterhouse.org.uk

Website
www.charterhouse.org.uk

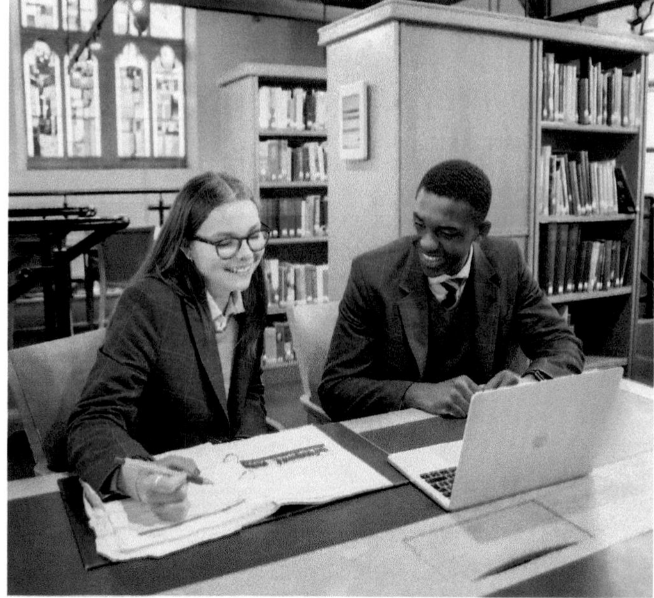

Motto: *Deo Dante Dedi*
Founded in 1611, Charterhouse is one of the UK's leading coeducational independent schools and has a prestigious global reputation.

Surrounded by a world of opportunity and connected by a feeling of belonging, each pupil is educated to embrace life's full potential, and empowered to carry this into their future. A Charterhouse education prepares for both academic success as well as laying the foundations for future professional, social and personal fulfilment. Shared values are central to school life, enabling each pupil to be themselves. Everything at Charterhouse begins with kindness.

Campus

Charterhouse is set in a beautiful 250-acre campus located on the edge of the attractive market town of Godalming, in the south of England. Conveniently close to London and within 50 minutes of both Heathrow and Gatwick airports, the campus provides an environment that is safe, rich in heritage and an inspiring setting for the whole community to live and work together.

With 17 grass sports pitches, 3 full-sized Astroturf pitches, an athletics stadium, a sports centre, 24 tennis courts and a 9-hole golf course, not to mention beautiful lawns and gardens, the campus is one of the best, if not the best, in the UK. Combined with a 235-seat theatre and separate music performance and art display spaces, the school's setting encourages pupils to contribute, and provides a feeling of space in which pupils can discover new opportunities and explore their potential.

Academic

Charterhouse is academically ambitious for all pupils, with each strand of a Charterhouse education combining to ensure that they are 'future-ready' – fully prepared for the real world of tomorrow and equipped to seize future opportunities as they present themselves. The curriculum is all about choice for the individual and is firmly rooted in academic rigour, intellectual curiosity and independent learning, though it is the breadth of options available to each pupil at every stage of their education that make it stand out from the rest.

At Sixth Form, Charterhouse offers the IB Diploma Programme and the British A Level curriculum. The IBDP provides both breadth and depth, and every opportunity is taken to promote cross-disciplinary working notably in pupils' choice of the Extended Essay. Intellectual curiosity is piqued by the huge range of academic clubs and societies operating during the afternoons and evenings, and pupils are even encouraged to set up their own with the organisational and financial support of the 125-strong academic faculty.

The university destinations of leavers reflect both the ambitions of pupils and the quality of teaching on offer: 80% of Carthusians attend UK Russell Group institutions, and 2023 leavers obtained places at Oxford, four different Ivy League institutions, as well as several top European universities.

Co-curricular Activities

From an outstanding and varied academic education to the raft of co-curricular options – opportunities abound at Charterhouse. Our co-curricular activities are an essential strand of a Charterhouse education, combing opportunities for leadership development, creativity, exercise and team work. They are also great fun.

The timetable enables all pupils to regularly enjoy themselves across a wide range of activities, making use of the school's impressive facilities. More than 80 different sports and activities are on offer, including outdoor pursuits, music, drama and other creative opportunities. All pupils are encouraged to develop existing interests to exciting levels and to take up new ones.

Boarding

The intangible sense of community and togetherness are often the starting point when describing the Charterhouse experience. All pupils experience a true sense of collective belonging, independence and identity.

The House is the centre of every pupil's time at Charterhouse. Their House is a welcoming home from home, with the resident Head of House becoming their day-to-day mentor with responsibility for looking after them throughout their time at Charterhouse.

The Heads of Houses are supported by a team of pastoral staff and tutors. Every pupil is matched with a tutor who takes a particular interest in their academic progress, co-curricular commitments and who guides them through the PSHE programme. Tutors meet with their tutees formally three times a week as well as meeting informally on the tutor's weekly duty evening in House.

The House Teams are supported by a 24-hour Health Centre and pupils also have access to support through the Wellbeing team, counsellors and chaplaincy.

Admissions

Inclusivity sits at the heart of life at Charterhouse and the school welcomes children from all educational and cultural backgrounds. Around 60 pupils join the Sixth Form each year, with admission by competitive examination and interview. Candidates should submit an application form by 1 October of the year before entry, and will be assessed at Charterhouse in early November. Offers of places are made on 1 December.

For further information please contact the Admissions Team: admissions@charterhouse.org.uk.

(Founded 1958)

Headmaster
Mr. Borja Díaz

DP coordinator
James Smith

Status Private

Boarding/day Day

Gender Coeducational

Language of instruction
English, Spanish

Authorised IB programmes
DP

Age Range 12 – 18 years

Address
Calle Jazmin 148
El Soto de la Moraleja
28109 Alcobendas, Madrid |
SPAIN

TEL +34 916 500 602

Email
infosoto@colegiosanpatricio.es

Website
www.colegiosanpatriciomadrid.com

Colegio San Patricio is a coeducational day school which provides Spanish education and IB Diploma Programme for children from 18 months to 18 years old.

Trusted generation after generation since 1958, our curriculum embeds and continually innovates with proven pedagogical methodologies, in order to offer a unique and comprehensive educational model. In our three campuses in Madrid we nurture every child's individual passions and talents in order to ensure that they flourish.

•CSP school listed as *"The No.1 best school in Spain"* (El Mundo, 2022 – *"100 Best Schools in Spain"* guide)

• Colegio San Patricio, has been ranked in the Top 10 among the best 50 schools in Spain according to Forbes Magazine.

San Patricio was founded in 1958. Since then, we have had the honour of educating generations of students.

Going to school at Colegio San Patricio means that you are part of more than just a school. You become part of the SanPa Family.

IB at Colegio San Patricio:

Our El Soto campus enjoys an unbeatable location in Soto de La Moraleja. Here, secondary cycles are taught after which students can choose between National Baccalaureate or International Baccalaureate. The school offers facilities specifically designed and built for children between the ages of 12 and 18 years and has a capacity for more than 800 students.

IB at San Patricio is more than simply a qualification, the IB Diploma provides a distinctive educational experience. It allows students to study a wide range of subjects throughout their final 2 years at school, while giving them the freedom to choose which subjects to study in greater depth.

IB students follow the Creativity, Activity, Service (CAS) programme, prepare an Extended Essay and take the Theory of Knowledge course.

2022 graduates enjoyed outstanding IB results, achieving a fantastic average grade of 34, an average grade 2 points higher than the world average (over 45 points).

Our school has achieved a 100% pass rate. 11% of our IB Diploma students have achieved more than 40 points and 17% have achieved more than 38 points. The highest grade achieved so far was a very impressive 43.

Thanks to their outstanding results our students have been accepted by some of the best Universities in the world such as Imperial, Bath, UCL in the UK, and Georgetown and University of California in the USA.

Colegio Virgen de Europa

Head of School
Enrique Maestu

PYP coordinator
Sarah O'Halloran

MYP coordinator
Carmen Mosquera Mariño

DP coordinator
María Cruz Larrosa

Status Private

Boarding/day Day

Gender Coeducational

Language of instruction
English, Spanish

Authorised IB programmes
PYP, MYP, DP

Address
C/Valle de Santa Ana No. 1
Las Lomas
28669 Boadilla del Monte,
Madrid | **SPAIN**

TEL +34 91 633 0155

Email
mc_larrosa@
colegiovirgendeeuropa.edu.es

Website
www.colegiovirgendeeuropa.com

Colegio Virgen de Europa was founded in 1968, we have celebrated our 50th anniversary as one of the leading schools in Madrid.

Since then, CVE has been committed with a fulfilling learning experience that involves culture and nature, developing critical thinking and creativity as pillars of a well-rounded education connected with the surrounding environment.

Our IB Diploma Programme relates to the school philosophy where the IB students can develop not only academic performance but also a holistic approach to the world we live in. Our students are eager to find answers by themselves connecting, extending, and challenging their inquiry and critical thinking profile.

Building knowledge is beyond our classrooms, CVE motivates young minds through school trips, art exhibitions, theater plays and interesting lectures with the aim to inspire our students to find their passions.

CVE physical education is a key element in our educational values since the early years, our school offers a variety of different sports, performing in our facilities, CVE counts with gym, running track, tennis and paddle courtyard surrounded by a quiet and peaceful environment in Madrid suburbs. In our IB Diploma, students carry out a Wellness & Mindfulness program as well.

CVE offers the IB Bilingual Diploma Programme through nine different itineraries that encompass subjects from Sciences to Environmental Systems, Social Studies, Design & Technology, and Visual Arts; led by passionate teachers who guide students through this meaningful learning process with full commitment to the IB mission.

Enhancing and motivating our IB students to be the best version of themselves in the path they have chosen and hence, leave trail.

(Founded 1960)

Director General
Mrs Pauline Nord

DP coordinator
Jana Krainova Samuda

CP coordinator
Sheena Tandy

Status Private

Boarding/day Mixed

Gender Coeducational

Language of instruction
English, French

Authorised IB programmes
DP, CP

Age Range 2 – 18 years
(boarding from 8)

Fees
Day: CHF24,600 – CHF35,900 per annum
Boarding: CHF89,900 – CHF102,700 per annum

Address
74, route de Sauverny
1290 Versoix GE | **SWITZERLAND**

TEL +41 22 775 56 56

Email
admissions@cdl.ch

Website
www.cdl.ch

We are an international day and boarding school located in Geneva, Switzerland. Our programmes offer taylor-made learning journeys and inspire students from Pre-school through to Grade 12 to be their best selves. We open doors for our students by creating a diverse and inclusive learning community that flourishes.

Our school sits on an 8-hectare landscaped campus nestled between the Jura mountains and Lake Geneva, 15 minutes away from the Geneva international airport. It offers comfortable residential facilities and recreational areas, providing students with a wide range of sport and leisure activities. In addition to our commitment to excellence in education, our philosophy also includes stimulating enthusiasm for lifelong learning and personal growth.

We have offered the IB Diploma Programme (DP) since 2005 and the IB Career-related Programme (CP) since 2016. Our 2023 Pass Rate for both programmes are an impressive 100%! The IB DP is very successful and attracts around half of our graduates every year. Our broad choice of subjects allows students to focus on their strengths and fulfil their interests. This, combined with a strong pastoral programme, which incorporates wellbeing as an essential part of students' education, and the professionalism and dedication of our teachers, contribute to consistently excellent exam results. For the IB CP we offer three career-related studies within the framework of Sustainable Business: Nature Conservation, Hospitality and Fashion. Each course is unique and has been developed in partnership with the Sustainable Management School in Gland. Students, in addition, study a minimum of 3 IB subjects. Our IB DP and IB CP graduates come from over 100 countries and our university advisory programme enables them to enroll in one of the universities of their choice, worldwide.

We belong to the Nord Anglia Family of schools, a worldwide group of elite schools, which offer students the highest standards in education and unique, international learning opportunities.

Collège Du Léman-Made for success, Made for you!

(Founded 1869)

Rector/Head of School
Fr. Alberto Torriani

DP coordinator
Anne Hallihan

Status Private

Boarding/day Day

Gender Coeducational

Language of instruction
English, Italian

Authorised IB programmes
DP

Age Range 2 – 19 years

Number of pupils enrolled
1891

Address
Corso Magenta 71
20123 Milan | ITALY

TEL +39 02 43 06 31

Email
admission@collegiosancarlo.it

Website
www.collegiosancarlo.it

Founded in 1869, Collegio San Carlo (CSC) has historically been linked with the Roman Catholic Church and the city of Milan. An all-boys boarding school up until 1971, then a day school, the Collegio became a co-educational school in 1985. Christian truth, freedom and solidarity are the ethos of all its academic, sport, music, drama and other extra-curricular activities. These activities prepare students to become responsible, creative and mature adults.

CSC is located in the heart of historic Milan, the second largest city in Italy, with an extended international community. It welcomes students from all backgrounds, ethnicities and religions. The IB teachers are all highly experienced and hail from France, Ireland, Italy, Poland, Spain, the UK and the US.

Students are encouraged to take advantage of the school's numerous sports facilities, such as the soccer and basketball courts, fully equipped gym and three swimming pools. The Collegio also offers a variety of community service programmes and excursions for students of all ages, as well as didactic intercultural and study abroad programmes with schools all around the world. Numerous extracurricular language classes underpin these programmes. Foreign languages offered from beginner to advanced levels are English, French, Spanish and Chinese. STEM/STEAM activities are highlighted both within the curriculum and in extra-curricular clubs/events.

CSC is an Italian private school and is considered on the same terms as all Italian state schools. It offers all levels of education starting from nursery school to high school, culminating with the Italian State High School Diploma upon passing the final State Exam. CSC was one of the first Italian schools to become an accredited International Baccalaureate World School. The first cohort was admitted in 2017. In 2019, CSC was authorised to offer the International General Certificate of Secondary Education (IGCSE) by Cambridge Assessment International.

Copperfield Verbier

COPPERFIELD
INTERNATIONAL SCHOOL
VERBIER

Deputy Head Academic
Meg Chamberlin

PYP coordinator
Laura Bickerstaffe

DP coordinator
Ladislav Burkovic

Status Private

Boarding/day Day

Gender Coeducational

Language of instruction
English

Authorised IB programmes
PYP, DP

Age Range 4 – 18 years

Number of pupils enrolled 70

Fees
Day: CHF34,000 – CHF46,500 per annum
Boarding: CHF40,000 – CHF70,000 per annum

Address
Rue de la Bérarde 10
Le Hameau
1936 Verbier VS | SWITZERLAND

TEL +41 27 520 61 00

Email
info@copperfield.education

Website
www.copperfield.education

Set at the foot of the Swiss Alps in Verbier, Copperfield International School is the world's only ski-in, ski-out international school. Offering a global gold-standard in curricula with staff who have studied at the world's best universities and excelled at the very top of their field.

Copperfield opened its doors with a clear vision and mission; to build a world-class leading academic institution in an extraordinary setting. A school where promising students and extraordinary teachers will unite in pursuit of academic excellence and human curiosity, always putting the students first.

Copperfield is an English-speaking school following the British education system. Students follow the globally recognised IGCSE and International Baccalaureate (IB) programmes while simultaneously developing practical skills that integrate curriculum into all areas of daily life. The focused and personalised tailored programmes allows each student to access a unique course of study which supports students to reach their academic potential, while assisting them in pursuing a career aligned with their greatest passion.

During Winter, students ski or snowboard twice per week as part of the physical education programme, and for those looking for something more adventurous / advanced, we offer freeride and competition programmes which include skiing up to five times per week. During the Summer & Autumn, students make full use of the wide variety of extensive sporting facilities locally for tennis, horse riding, golf or mountain biking and for those residing with us, our sensational four-star, hotel boarding accommodation is of the utmost quality.

All students have the opportunity to learn two further languages as part of our curriculum, including French, German, Spanish and Italian. In addition, our campus offers a 200-seater auditorium where each student can explore their passions in music and the arts.

Copperfield students will be academically skilled; fluent in multiple languages; accomplished writers and communicators; artistically driven and knowledgeable, and generous of spirit and skill.

(Founded 1971)

Head of School
Oliver Schmitz

DP coordinator
Edna Howard

Status Private

Boarding/day Day

Gender Coeducational

Language of instruction
English, German

Authorised IB programmes
DP

Age Range 3 – 18 years

Address
Douglas House
Petersham Road
Richmond
Surrey
TW10 7AH | UK

TEL +44 (0)20 8940 2510

Email
info@dslondon.org.uk

Website
www.dslondon.org.uk

The DSL is part of a long-standing tradition of excellence in the worldwide network of more than 140 German Schools abroad and we currently welcome over 880 students from more than 30 nations at our school in Richmond.

We strive to empower our students, encouraging them to be open-minded, curious and committed learners as well as responsible members of our local community within an international context. We offer an appealing and challenging educational programme from Kindergarten to our dual programme in Years 11 and 12 with the German International Abitur (DIA) and the IB Diploma.

This dual qualification (Abitur and IB DP) uniquely equips our students with bilingual (German and English) academic competencies, permitting them to meet the challenges of a university education and supporting them in becoming independent, global-minded citizens. In general, all students completing Year 10 at the DSL, or a comparable qualification with good academic results, are eligible to apply to the dual programme (Abitur and IB DP) at the DSL.

In combination with the Abitur subjects, IB students complete three higher level (HL) and three standard level (SL) courses as well as the core requirements (ToK, CAS, EE) for a full IB Diploma. Students may choose between German and English as their IB Language A (HL and SL) and Spanish or French as IB Language B. Furthermore, we offer History, Economics, Geography, Psychology (SL), Biology, Chemistry, Physics, Mathematics Analysis & Approaches (SL) as well as Visual Arts (SL) and Music (SL). All Year 12 students at the DSL take their Abitur exams between February and April, ahead of their IB exams in the May session of the same year, which promotes thorough preparation for both examinations.

In addition to the full dual qualification (Abitur and IB Diploma), the DSL offers the category "course candidate" (CC), i.e. Abitur students may enrol in two or more individual IB courses and/or core elements, which allows them to study a subject of particular interest in more depth or to build a profile for their university application.

Mission Statement

Living together, Learning together, Creating together, Building bridges together

Quoting one of our 2019 alumni, *"The decision to go for the dual programme at the DSL is based on two things – an interest in a variety of subjects and a wish to challenge yourself. Additionally, the DSL isn't just a school, it is a community of students, parents and teachers that one feels connected to and welcome in at all times."*

Dwight School London

(Founded 1885)

Head
Chris Beddows

PYP coordinator
Waseem Rehman

MYP coordinator
Karine Villatte

DP coordinator
William Bowry

Status Private

Boarding/day Day

Gender Coeducational

Language of instruction
English

Authorised IB programmes
PYP, MYP, DP

Age Range 2 – 18 years

Fees
Please see website

Address
6 Friern Barnet Lane
London
N11 3LX | UK

TEL 020 8920 0600

Email
admissions@dwightlondon.org

Website
www.dwightlondon.org

Join us at Dwight School London where we are dedicated to crafting a personalised journey for every student, which we call "igniting the spark of genius in every child". We invite you to visit us to see our school's warm, engaging environment and experience our spark of genius philosophy in action.

A member of the world-renowned Dwight global family of schools, we share the same commitment to personalising education which began nearly 150 years ago when Dwight was founded in 1872 in New York and 1972 in London.

Our students are encouraged to pursue their passions, believe in their own talents and celebrate and learn from the perspectives of others. They are also inspired to take intellectual risks through the academically rigorous International Baccalaureate curriculum – a pathway to top universities worldwide – nurturing creative critical thinkers empowered to help make our world a better place.

We are one of the leading UK IB World schools to offer the full IB Continuum:

- The Primary Years Programme (PYP) – ages 2 to 11
- The Middle Years Programme (MYP) – ages 11 to 16
- The Diploma Programme (DP) – ages 16 to 18

Through Dwight School London's personalised learning, EAL and mother tongue programmes, we enable all students to access the IB curriculum and become successful global citizens.

Through the academic breadth and depth of the IB, we nurture inquiring, knowledgeable and caring young people who help to create a better, more peaceful world through intercultural understanding and respect.

Our school rests on three pillars:

- Personalised learning: Customising an education for every student. We pride ourselves on getting to know each of our students and their families quite well. We shape the learning journey around how students best learn, where their skills lie, and what sparks their interest.
- Community: Encouraging students to contribute to their school and wider communities. Through service learning, we foster every student's ability to make a positive difference to our school, among neighbours, and in the world beyond.
- Global vision: Educating global leaders. With students from around the world, Dwight is a culturally and socially rich and diverse school. We nurture learning within our own international community, the IB's larger global context and our network of Dwight Schools across continents.

To attend an event then visit dwightlondon.org/yearbook

Ecole Des Roches

(Founded 1899)

Head of School
Mr Ivor Gemmell

DP coordinator
Dr Ed Owens

Status Private

Boarding/day Mixed

Gender Coeducational

Language of instruction
English, French

Authorised IB programmes
DP

Age Range 11 – 18 years

Number of pupils enrolled 320

Address
295 avenue Edmond Demolins
27130 Verneuil d'Avre et d'Iton |
FRANCE

TEL +33 (0) 232 6040 00

Email
ecoledesroches@
ecoledesroches.com

Website
www.ecoledesroches.com

Founded in 1899, École des Roches is an international coeducational day and boarding school located on a spacious woodland campus in the heart of the beautiful Normandy countryside. We welcome students aged 11 to 18 years from 52 nationalities to our Middle and High school.

École des Roches offers several programmes: the International Baccalaureate Diploma Programme (IBDP); the French National Curriculum; the French as a Foreign Language Programme for short stays or a full academic year; and also summer and winter intensive language courses.

International Baccalaureate Diploma Programme

École des Roches has been an IB World School since 2016, offering the IBDP in English. The school also offers a special 'Pre-Diploma Programme' – a one-year intensive foundation course – to prepare students for International Baccalaureate learning.

Students receive counselling on their career choices and we support them through the university admissions process, ensuring they are selecting courses where they can achieve their full potential.

At École des Roches, the IB Diploma Programme is characterised by:

- its academic breadth, depth and rigour
- small class sizes with individualized academic support
- the attention given to international awareness and the development of socially responsible citizens of the world

In addition to preparing students for the IB Diploma, all of our students are encouraged to take advantage of the school's context, heritage and resources to improve their French language proficiency, whether that be at a beginner, intermediate or advanced level.

Boarding Life

Our Boarding School consists of seven boarding houses called 'Maisons', which are large historic Normandy residences. Boys and girls are divided by age range in these single-sex boarding houses.

Foreign students live and work alongside French-speaking students in pleasant and recently renovated rooms. École des Roches is a student-centred school, not only offering intellectual but also personal and emotional support, in order to promote each student's individual development.

The extracurricular activities we offer range from horseback riding and golf, through other sports like football and volleyball, to go-karting on the school's track which is located on campus.

Admissions

Students can apply to our school all year-round, with places allocated subject to availability. Students must submit a minimum of two years' of school reports, a letter of recommendation, as well as a letter of motivation.

For further information about admissions or to schedule a school visit, please contact us at ecoledesroches@ecoledesroches.com.

We look forward to welcoming you.

Eastern Mediterranean International School

SCHOOL FOR CHANGE

Headteacher
Hadas Gottlieb

DP coordinator
Hannah Wenger

Status Non-Profit Institution

Boarding/day Boarding

Gender Coeducational

Language of instruction
English

Authorised IB programmes
DP

Age Range 15 – 17 years

Number of pupils enrolled 167

Fees
$8,000 – $32,000 per annum
(varies by scholarship)

Address
Hakfar Hayarok
Ramat Hasharon
4870000 | ISRAEL

TEL +972 03 673 0232

Email
admissions@em-is.org

Website
www.em-is.org

The Eastern Mediterranean International School (EMIS) is an independent, non-profit boarding school located in HaKfar HaYarok, a green youth village within a short driving distance from Tel Aviv, Jerusalem, and Ramallah, founded in 2014 with a mission to make education a force for peace and sustainability in the Middle East. EMIS hosts students from 50+ countries and offers an inclusive program to ensure mutual understanding, cultural appreciation, and a positive diverse environment.

Our village campus has a dining hall, park, gym, sports courts, music building, library, and many other student facilities accessible to every student living in the area. The EMIS campus is located close to one of the sports courts and the dining hall and includes several dorms and classroom buildings with a lab, art room, music room, and study rooms.

EMIS' student body is composed of 40% Israeli, Palestinian and Arab students, and 60% international, students from different backgrounds who live and study together, gaining an education that focuses on leadership, academic excellence, diplomacy, peacebuilding, and sustainable development. EMIS works to foster independent leaders, creative thinkers, and open-minded students.

The school offers a preparatory year for the IB (Pre-DP for 10th grade) and the International Baccalaureate Diploma (IBDP) for 11th and 12th grade.

Admissions are on a rolling basis and solely merit-based, while scholarships are entirely need-based. To join EMIS, all applicants go through the same process of filling out our online application which can be easily found on our website.

Mission – Peace and Sustainability

The ongoing Israeli-Palestinian conflict has seriously impacted the future of Middle Eastern youth and youth around the world. EMIS's mission is to bring peace and sustainability to the region through transformative education, while also teaching students to introduce change in their own international communities. Challenging socio-economic divisions, EMIS unifies teenagers in a multicultural environment, fostering dialogue, peace, and understanding while offering special programs focused on conflict resolution and diplomacy.

To complement the curriculum, we offer Mission Class, a course that develops the changemaker capacities of students, helps them integrate a stronger alignment with our mission, and harvest a deep understanding of conflict-resolution.

CAS, Projects, and Extracurriculars

We offer 60+ CAS Activities, ranging from sports, arts, debate club, social and environmental initiatives, and much more! To illustrate the deep impact of our projects, we expanded on 4 out of 100+ activities that students can join.

Project Oasis

A student-led initiative in engineering that aims to collect electricity and water from the air. The system they are developing accomplishes this using organic Rankine cycle and condenser technology.

They aim to produce 6 kilowatts of energy and 1,000 liters of water every day to significantly reduce global water shortages and provide clean water and energy in impoverished areas; all while being carbon neutral in operations. The solution will continue to deliver benefits to students at the school for the next 50 years.

Project Oasis is the 2022 winner of the Zayed Sustainability Prize, they received $100,000 in funding for the project.

YOCOPAS

YOCOPAS is an annual student-led three-day conference that aims to establish a collaborative platform for conversations and discussions between young leaders from Israel, Palestine, and all around the world. Participants have opportunities to learn from each other, attend lectures, workshops and form initiatives for peace and sustainability in their local communities.

Green Up

Green Up is a student-run organization that focuses on education and awareness, activism, and promoting sustainability. Our planet faces unprecedented challenges such as climate change, depletion of natural resources, and threatened biodiversity; our students tackle those problems by being part of climate marches, planting trees, attending international climate conferences, doing beach clean-ups, and many other engaging activities yearly.

Mission Week

As a part of our "hands-on" approach at EMIS, students and staff participate in an annual week-long project, which focuses on a theme that connects to the school's mission. The weeks are independently organized by student leaders. Mission Weeks alternate every year between the Jerusalem Journey and the Borders Week.

Pre-DP at EMIS (10th grade)

The Pre-DP program at EMIS is a one-year program for students in 10th grade (in 9th grade during the application process) who aspire to join the IB Diploma Programme in years 11 and 12. It is a skill-based program that develops a variety of approaches to learning for each student such as thinking, communication, self-management, research, and social skills. Experienced IB teachers design each course and use a personalized approach to help support a growth mindset and develop self-efficacy in each student.

IB at EMIS (11th-12th grade)

EMIS offers a range of IB Diploma Programme (DP) courses that allow students to plan a track of study best suited to their individual strengths, interests, and goals. The combination of Standard Level (SL) and Higher Level (HL) courses along with the considerable latitude available in choosing an Extended Essay topic, allows each student to focus in-depth on mathematics, humanities, or sciences. At the same time, the student enjoys the benefits of a broad-based liberal arts education. During the two years of the Diploma Programme, students have ample opportunity to review their work, knowledge, and skills with their teachers before internal and external assessments. A range of practice tests and assessments prepare students for externally graded examinations in their final year.

(Founded 1992)

Head of School
Constance Devaux

DP coordinator
Nicola French

Status Non-Profit Private

Boarding/day Mixed

Gender Coeducational

Language of instruction
French, English

Authorised IB programmes
DP

Age Range 3 – 18 years

Number of pupils enrolled
980

Fees
International 10th grade (Day)
€12,140 per annum
11th & 12th grade IB (Day)
€23,945 per annum
11th & 12th grade IB (Boarding)
€49,820 per annum

Address
418 bis rue Albert Bailly
Marcq-en-Baroeul
59700 | FRANCE

TEL +33 3 20 65 90 50

Email
admissions-lille@ejm.net

Website
www.ecolejeanninemanuel.org

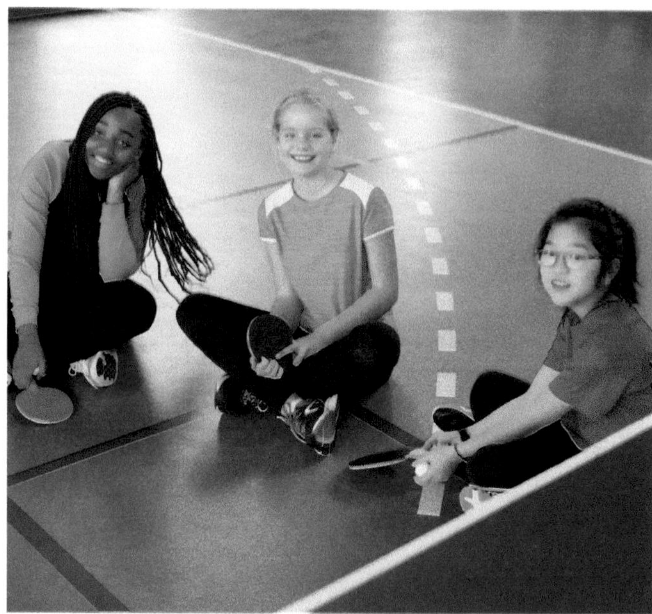

École Jeannine Manuel Lille is a non-profit coeducational school founded in 1992 and welcomes students from nursery to 12th grade. As the sister campus of École Jeannine Manuel Paris, the school has the same educational project and mission: promoting international understanding through bilingual education. An associated UNESCO school, École Jeannine Manuel Lille is the only non-denominational independent school in Nord-Pas-de-Calais, with over 900 pupils representing 50 nationalities and every major cultural tradition. The school's academic excellence matches its diversity: École Jeannine Manuel Lille is regularly ranked among the best French high schools (ranked first for four consecutive years). The school is accredited by the French Ministry of Education, the International Baccalaureate Organization (IBO), the Council of International Schools (CIS), and the New England Association of Schools and Colleges (NEASC).

Ecole Jeannine Manuel Lille's campus extends over 8.5 acres. It includes a boarding house, a restaurant, and state-of-the-art sports facilities including a 1500 m2 gym with its own climbing wall, a 300m racing track, and two outdoor playing fields. The boarding house currently welcomes 120 pupils from 6th to 12th grade.

Each year, École Jeannine Manuel Lille welcomes non-French speaking students. These students integrate the school through the adaptation program, which provides intensive instruction in French, support in English as needed, help in understanding and adjusting to French culture, and differentiated coursework and assessment during their adaptation period. The lower and middle school follow the French national curriculum with several exceptions: English is taught every day and, in middle school, experimental sciences, history and geography are taught in English. The curriculum is enriched at all levels, not only with a more advanced English language and literature curriculum, but also, for example, with Chinese language instruction (compulsory in grades 3-4-5), an integrated science program in lower school, and independent research projects in middle school.

In upper school, tenth graders follow the French national curriculum, albeit taught 50% in French and 50% in English. In 11th grade, pupils choose between the French track (international option of the French baccalaureate (BFI)) and the International Baccalaureate Diploma Programme (IBDP). Approximately 25% of our pupils opt for the IBDP.

Admission

Although admission is competitive, the school makes every effort to reserve space for international applicants, including children of families who expect to remain in France for a limited period of time and wish to combine a cultural immersion in French education with the ability to re-enter their own school systems and excel.

Ecole Jeannine Manuel – Paris

(Founded 1954)

Principal
Jérôme Giovendo

DP coordinator
Sabine Hurley

Status Non-Profit Private

Boarding/day Day

Gender Coeducational

Language of instruction
English, French

Authorised IB programmes
DP

Age Range 4 – 18 years

Number of pupils enrolled
2400

Fees
11th & 12th grade 5 (BFI) €8,749 per annum
11th & 12th grade IB (Day) €28,065 per annum

Address
70 rue du Théâtre
Paris
75015 | FRANCE

TEL +33 1 44 37 00 80

Email
admissions@ejm.net

Website
www.ecolejeanninemanuel.org

École Jeannine Manuel is a non-profit pre-K-12 coeducational school founded in 1954 with the mission to promote international understanding through bilingual (French/English) education. An associated UNESCO school, École Jeannine Manuel welcomes pupils representing 80 nationalities and every major cultural tradition. The school's academic excellence matches its diversity: École Jeannine Manuel is regularly ranked among the best French high schools (state and independent) for its overall academic performance (ranked first for ten consecutive years). The school is accredited by the French Ministry of Education, the International Baccalaureate Organization (IBO), the Council of International Schools (CIS) and the New England Association of Schools and Colleges (NEASC).

Each year, the school welcomes more than 100 new non-French speaking pupils. These students integrate the school through our adaptation program, which provides intensive instruction in French, support in English as needed, help in understanding and adjusting to French culture, and differentiated coursework and assessment during their adaptation period.

The lower and middle school follow the French national curriculum with several exceptions: English is taught every day and, in middle school, experimental sciences, history and geography are taught in English. The curriculum is enriched at all levels, not only with a more advanced English language and literature curriculum, but also, for example, with Chinese language instruction (compulsory in grades 3-4-5), an integrated science program in lower school, and independent research projects in middle school.

In upper school, tenth graders follow the French national curriculum, albeit taught 50% in French and 50% in English. In 11th grade, pupils choose between the French track (international option of the French baccalaureate (BFI)) and the International Baccalaureate Diploma Programme (IBDP). Approximately 25% of our pupils opt for the IBDP.

Over the past three years, approximately 20% of our graduating class have gone to US colleges or universities, 48% chose the UK or Canada, 37% entered the French higher education system, and the balance pursued their education all over the world.

Admission:

Admission is competitive and applications typically exceed available spaces by a ratio of 7:1. The school nonetheless makes every effort to reserve space for international applicants, including children of families who expect to remain in France for a limited period of time and wish to combine a cultural immersion in French education with the ability to seamlessly re-enter the school system in their home country.

(Founded 1906)

General Director
Mr. Nicolas Catsicas

DP coordinator
Mr. Gaetan Franzini

Status Private

Boarding/day Mixed

Gender Coeducational

Language of instruction
French, English

Authorised IB programmes
DP

Age Range 2.5 – 18 years

Number of pupils enrolled
600

Fees
Day:
CHF13,200 – CHF27,300 per annum
Weekly Boarding:
CHF53,100 – CHF61,700 per annum
Boarding:
CHF66,000 – CHF74,600 per annum

Address
Chemin de Rovéréaz 20
CP 161
1012 Lausanne | **SWITZERLAND**

TEL +41 21 654 65 00

Email
info@ensr.ch

Website
www.ensr.ch

Ecole Nouvelle de la Suisse Romande (ENSR) / International Boarding School of Lausanne (IBSL)

Academic excellence since 1906

We offer

- Complete schooling from Kindergarten, including a Montessori section, through to High School in French and/or in English
- Bilingual French-English Programme from age 2.5 to 18 years
- Swiss Maturity in French
- International Baccalaureate Diploma programme in French, English or bilingual French-English
- Sport and Study Programme (Basketball, tennis, golf, rowing, ice-hockey and more)
- All Cambridge, Goethe-Institut and Cervantes examinations
- Boarding facilities
- Ski Camp, Summer Camp, Windsurf Camp
- Holidays: daycare for children aged from 2.5 to 7 years old

Languages

English is introduced at the age of 2.5 years old with French as the language of instruction until Grade 6 (11 y.o.). As of Grade 7 (12 y.o.), possibility to have English as the language of instruction or a bilingual French-English Programme.

German is introduced in Grade 4 (9 y.o.). Introduction classes to Spanish, Italian and Latin are proposed in the Middle School (10-14 y.o.). Additional languages are offered in High School (14-19 y.o.).

French or English for beginners are provided for new students, beginners and those requiring further support.

Summer Camp

Our summer camp takes place from July to mid-August for children aged from 9 to 18 years old.

Mornings, 9 am to 12 pm: French and English classes (elementary, intermediate and intensive) in preparation of the DELF and Cambridge Certificates.

Afternoons and weekends: sports, leisure, cultural activities and trips.

Multisports formula (sports and leisure activities).

Boarding School

Boarding facilities are offered for students as from Middle school, Grade 7, 12 years of age.

Our boarding school provides a friendly and warm atmosphere offering security, care and support.

Boarding is offered for either 5 or 7 days per week.

Eerde International Boarding School Netherlands

(Founded 1934)

Director CEO
Niki Holterman

Principal
Amy Ramsey

DP coordinator
Jessica Craig

Status Private

Boarding/day Mixed

Gender Coeducational

Language of instruction
English

Authorised IB programmes
DP

Age Range 6 – 18 years

Number of pupils enrolled 100

Fees
Primary €15,000 per annum
Middle School Day €21,700 per annum
IGCSE/IBDP €25,200 per annum
Boarding €32,100 per annum
(excl. academic fee)

Address
Kasteellaan 1
7731 PJ Ommen,
Overijssel | **NETHERLANDS**

TEL +31 52 9451452

Email
admission@eerdeibs.nl

Website
www.eerde.com

Eerde International Boarding School Netherlands delivers an exceptional international study destination with the opportunity to achieve the world-recognized International Baccalaureate Diploma (IBDP) while engaging with various cultures.

Located on a historic country estate, we provide a rich cultural learning environment for students aged 6 to 19, with VISA sponsorship starting at age 15.

In addition to our International Baccalaureate Diploma Programme (IBDP), we also offer a Pre IB class. The Pre IB class serves as a transition year prior to entering the IBDP, it is particularly well suited for students who wish to improve their English language skills before entering the IBDP or those students who are entering international education for the first time.

Complimenting our academic offer, Eerde has a variety of extracurricular activities to enhance each student's "Eerde Experience". At the end of each school day, students can participate in a range of sporting, cultural and social activities, allowing them to discover their unique talents and interests.

At Eerde, our mission is to help students develop into successful, engaged and responsible young adults with strong global connections.

The learning experience at Eerde is consciously small-scale to ensure individual attention for all students. Our approach toward learning allows our students to discover their true potential and empowers them to develop personal leadership and life skills. Eerde is the place where your student can learn, live and develop.

To find out more about Eerde please visit our website at www.eerde.com or email us at admission@eerdeibs.nl

ERMITAGE
INTERNATIONAL SCHOOL

(Founded 1941)

Executive President
Mr. Jim Doherty

MYP coordinator
Christine Collie

DP coordinator
Wayne Hodgkinson

Status Private

Boarding/day Mixed

Gender Coeducational

Language of instruction
English, French

Authorised IB programmes
MYP, DP

Age Range 3 – 18 years

Number of pupils enrolled
1500

Fees
€21,000 – €45,000

Address
46 Avenue Eglé
78600 Maisons-Laffitte | **FRANCE**

TEL +33 139 62 81 75

Email
admissions@ermitage.fr

Website
www.ermitage.fr

Ermitage International School is a bilingual K-12 school located in the historic town of Maisons-Laffitte, just 20km west of Paris. With a student body of nearly 1500 students, representing over 70 nationalities, Ermitage offers student-centered learning, with a focus on bilingualism and leadership. Weekday and fulltime boarding is available in traditional French residences.

- IB Programs (IB MYP & IB DP), 240 students enrolled, offering English instruction, with French lessons from a beginner to native-level.
- French Bilingual Programs (Primary to French bac, BFI) 1260 students enrolled, instructed in French.

IB Middle Years Programme (MYP) 1-5

The MYP encourages students to be active learners, asking challenging questions, as well as developing a strong sense of identity, cultural understanding and communication skills. During the MYP, our team of experienced teachers accompany and guide students on their journey to becoming IB Learners. Emphasis is placed on individual growth and encouraging students to reflect upon their classroom projects and co-curricular initiatives. Teachers facilitate students' learning and help prepare them for the rigorous demands of the IB Diploma Programme.

IB Diploma Programme (DP) 1-2

Within the dynamic, inquiry based environment, students are encouraged to think critically and become independent learners. Assignments are demanding, but by graduation the calibre of research, writing and project management skills acquired mean our students are highly prepared for their tertiary studies.

Round Square

As a Global Member of the Round Square organization, Ermitage is connected to like minded schools, offering a variety of service-learning trips, global exchanges and leadership conferences. Students also discover their interests outside of the classroom through a daily co-curricular program with the opportunity to initiate projects, participate in leadership experiences, sports and more while connecting with local and global communities.

What sets us apart

- Student-centered approach with a balance of academics & character-developing projects
- Opportunities for student leadership via well-rounded daily co-curricular programs
- Teachers are approachable & serve as coaches, guiding students individually
- Students learn in engaging ways both inside & outside of the classroom
- Located in historic town 20km from Paris
- Weekday and full-time boarding is available in our traditional French residences
- Dedicated University Advising team

ES American School

(Founded 1999)

Head of School
Ms. Melanie Rose

PYP coordinator
Lauren Hopkins

Status Private

Boarding/day Day

Gender Coeducational

Language of instruction
English

Authorised IB programmes
PYP

Age Range 6 – 18 years

Number of pupils enrolled 140

Fees
Day: €11,470 – €19,355 per annum

Address
Autovia de Castelldefels C-31
Km 191
El Prat de Llobregat
08820 Barcelona,
Catalonia | **SPAIN**

TEL +34 93 479 1611

Email
admin@es-school.com

Website
www.es-school.com

ES American School offers an independent, college preparatory American curriculum for 6 to 18 years olds (1st through 12th grades) located within the campus of the Emilio Sanchez Academy, Barcelona. Our Elementary is an authorized IB PYP school, offering the International Baccalaureate Primary Years Programme, a world-renowned curricular framework, where children learn to take ownership of their own learning, increasing confidence and self-motivation. In Middle School, the enrichment program supports students to have a broad range of learning experiences. The Advanced Placement (AP) program in High School offers students the opportunity to work at a more challenging level with the potential to earn university credit. Students who elect to take the Spanish program alongside the American curriculum are eligible to homologate their diploma.

With locations in Barcelona, Spain and Naples, Florida, USA, ES American School provides students with a truly international experience enabling them to excel both academically and athletically. All students receive individual attention, close academic guidance and personal counseling. The predominant language on campus is English.

Sports are an essential part of the curriculum and students benefit from the world-class tennis program and training facilities provided by Emilio Sanchez Academy. Our students have three distinct pathways with regards to sport: high-performance tennis (offered on-site), high-performance in other sports (offered off-site), including soccer, basketball, horse riding OR our Physical Education Program for general fitness and well-being. ES American School, Barcelona is accredited by the Middle States Association of Colleges and Schools and is authorized by the Department of Education of the Catalan Government.

DP coordinator
Paloma de Oñate Alguero

Status Private

Boarding/day Day

Gender Coeducational

Language of instruction
Spanish (and English = Language B)

Authorised IB programmes
DP

Age Range 1 – 18 years

Number of pupils enrolled
1178

Fees
PD €650 (Registration) + €975 (Monthly payment)

Address
Highway from Colmenar to Alcobendas, Km. 0.500
28049 Madrid | SPAIN

TEL +34 917 523 343

Email
paloma.deonate@escuelaideo.edu.es

Website
www.escuelaideo.edu.es

En Escuela IDEO desarrollamos un proyecto educativo humanizante y humanizador, potenciando las habilidades personales y sociales y generando aprendizajes significativos. Utilizamos pedagogías activas, participativas y vivenciales teniendo como meta, no solo que el alumnado se encuentre motivado a buscar su propia formación integral, sino a crear mejores personas y profesionales, más formados y más felices, a través de una educación activa e integradora.

Acompañándolos para que desarrollen su autonomía, su propia forma de pensar y de sentir. Contribuyendo a descubrir y desarrollar sus talentos. Ofreciéndoles un entorno de seguridad y confianza, que les motiven a querer aprender.

Escuela IDEO dispone de un amplio espacio natural dentro de sus instalaciones. Combina tradición arquitectónica con naturaleza, siguiendo los criterios de sostenibilidad y respeto al medio ambiente. En los próximos meses, la Escuela contará con un centro polideportivo, varios gimnasios, sala de audiovisuales, co-learning, nuevas aulas y laboratorios, una biblioteca más amplia y un salón de actos.

Escuela IDEO ofrece el Programa del Diploma (PD) a través de 3 Itinerarios, Social-Humanístico, Científico-Tecnológico y Científico Sanitario. Se ofrece en español, siendo el inglés la lengua de aprendizaje (Lengua B) cursada en nivel superior. El PD está estructurado para lograr que el alumnado termine con un nivel de madurez y de preparación universitaria. Nuestro objetivo es brindar al alumnado una educación de calidad, que fomente su desarrollo integral y les prepare para enfrentar los retos del futuro con confianza y responsabilidad. Para ello, realizamos un acompañamiento individualizado tanto a nivel académico como emocional.

Disponemos de un orientador/a de referencia para el grupo.

El perfil de nuestros estudiantes es:

- Alumnado muy autónomo.
- Responsable.
- Gran capacidad de esfuerzo, constancia y trabajo.
- Naturaleza indagadora.
- Alta motivación por el aprendizaje.
- Rigurosos.
- Mentalidad abierta e internacional.
- Personas con capacidad de adaptación.

Nuestra Escuela cuenta con un convenio con la Universidad Autónoma de Madrid, mediante el cual, se permite al alumnado del PD utilizar determinados recursos de la Universidad. Cabe destacar que la ubicación privilegiada y contigua de nuestra Escuela con la UAM facilita aún más esta enriquecedora colaboración.

Somos una escuela abierta, donde las familias participan del desarrollo de sus hijos e hijas. Un proceso de formación integral para que sean personas sanas, alegres, comprometidas y concienciadas con la construcción de un mundo mejor.

Eurocolegio Casvi Villaviciosa

CEO of Casvi Group
Mr. Juan Luis Yagüe

Head of Studies
Mr. Pablo Martín

PYP coordinator
Gema Grañeda

MYP coordinator
Félix David Vozmediano León

DP coordinator
Jose Vicente Belizón Collado

Status Private

Boarding/day Day

Gender Coeducational

Language of instruction
Spanish

Authorised IB programmes
PYP, MYP, DP

Age Range 1 – 18 years

Number of pupils enrolled
1090

Fees
€5,480 – €9,660 per annum

Address
Avenida de Castilla, 27
Villaviciosa de Odón
28670 Madrid | **SPAIN**

TEL +34 91 616 22 18

Email
casvi@casvi.es

Website
www.casvi.es

Eurocolegio Casvi International Private School is a private, co-educational school. Since 1985, its aim has always been to work with children and young people so that, when they finish their education with them, they are in an advantageous situation with respect to any citizen in the world.

The child who attends this school today, from Pre-School to Baccalaureate, is within an IB methodology (International Baccalaureate). An active methodology, closer, real, effective, and adapted to the current times in which a globalized society dominates. Organized and synchronized from year to year, it promotes, from an early age, skills and attitudes that will help our pupils to face their future with guaranteed success.

Furthermore, at Casvi, the three International Baccalaureate programmes (PYP, MYP and DP) are fully implemented, and we are one of the few schools in Spain to offer a continuum of IB programmes. Thanks to this, at Eurocolegio Casvi they have the possibility of modelling the attributes of the IB profile from the age of 3.

In addition to all this, there is a clear commitment to internationality. These are the tools to achieve this:

Multilingualism. Pupils learn English from the first year of life; and Chinese and German from the 5th year of Primary School. This is done in small groups, by levels, and with native and bilingual teachers. Thanks to this methodology, practically all of our students complete the Diploma Programme with CAE and/or PROFICIENCY qualifications.

Language Exchanges. These are organized without any intermediary agency, through direct contact with schools all over the world. In the USA they last two months and our students from the age of 10 take part in them. Those in Germany last two weeks, and it is our German MYP and PD students who enjoy this opportunity.

Presence of international students. The IB methodology, which seeks globalization in the educational field, invites many students from other countries to study at Casvi.

At Eurocolegio Casvi International Private School, the promotion of artistic skills is also very important. The aim is to detect the talents of the students, whatever their nature. Thus, the Schools of Art, Music and Theatre stand out.

As for the promotion of their sporting skills, they have swimming lessons as part of their school day and Sports Schools for Basketball, Football 7-a-side, Indoor Football, Rhythmic Gymnastics, Swimming and Synchronized Swimming and Athletics.

Finally, with regard to New Technologies, the aim is to increase STEAM vocations and achieve the professional development of pupils. It also aims to promote their technological competence from the early years to their prior incorporation into the world of work. This is based on Robotics and the most cutting-edge programming languages used in the real world of work, which have been introduced in a pioneering way in their educational curriculum from the 1st year of Pre-school with the subject of Technology, Programming and Robotics.

Eyüboglu Schools

(Founded 1970)

Head of School
Mr Cenk Eyüboglu

PYP coordinator
Ayça Koçer, Firuze Vanlioglu & Meliz Katlav

MYP coordinator
Songül Akar & Arzu Onat Konusmaz

DP coordinator
Oguz Günenç

Status Private

Boarding/day Day

Gender Coeducational

Language of instruction
Turkish, English

Authorised IB programmes
PYP, MYP, DP

Age Range 3 – 18 years

Number of pupils enrolled
3506

Fees
TL144,815 – TL270,765 per annum

Address
Esenevler Mah
Dr Rüstem Eyüboglu sok 3,
Ümraniye
34762 Istanbul, Marmara |
TURKEY

TEL +90 216 522 12 12

Email
eyuboglu@eyuboglu.k12.tr

Website
www.eyuboglu.k12.tr

Founded in 1970 by Dr. Rüstem EYÜBOGLU, Eyüboglu Schools are a group of private co-educational schools offering bilingual pre K-12 education. Eyüboglu Schools are comprised of six kindergartens, four elementary schools, three middle, one high school, and one science & technology high school located in different districts in Istanbul with its friendly, welcoming, green campuses.

Eyüboglu Schools is the first Turkish school accredited by CIS. Eyüboglu Schools have been an IB World School since September 1996, and are the first Turkish school authorized to offer all three IB programs; IB PYP, IB MYP, and IB DP in grades pre K-12.

The school's internationally recognized high standards of academic excellence enables Eyüboglu graduates to further their studies both in prestigious universities in Turkey and in the US, Canada, the UK, and Europe.

The school philosophy is based on academic excellence, international-mindedness and social awareness. Students are encouraged to think critically, work collaboratively, and hence become innovative, lifelong learners. In addition to a heavy focus on IB qualifications, great importance is given to teaching foreign languages as stated in the school's mission to raise international-minded, bilingual students. We lead our students to English, German and Spanish proficiency exams such as Cambridge, IELTS, TOEFL, FIT and DELE.

Eyüboglu schools have state-of-the-art learning facilities such as fully-equipped classrooms, Biology, Physics, Chemistry Virtual Reality labs, theater halls. The school libraries hold a distinctive collection of 1500 volumes which makes Eyüboglu schools unique among K-12 schools in Turkey. Besides, the first Astronomical Observatory in K-12 schools was established by Eyüboglu Schools on its Çamlica campus. Today, Eyüboglu has two astronomical observatories and a planetarium that provide outstanding learning experiences for all students.

Besides academic studies, Eyüboglu gives great importance to the social development of its students. Not only it offers physical facilities such as swimming pools, art studios, gyms, sports fields, pitches, and courts on its campuses, but also it offers various social clubs in diverse areas such as sports, arts, music, science, technology, and humanities. Over a hundred social clubs include but are not limited to basketball, athletics, volleyball, tennis, golf, archery, water polo, horse riding, fencing, dance, drama, ceramics, MUN, DI, Astronomy, Artificial Intelligence, TedX, Machine Learning, Young Entrepreneurs.

Admission to Eyüboglu is offered based on school-administered interviews up to grade 3 and a written examination and interview for upper grades. All students including Eyüboglu Middle School graduates are expected to meet the admission requirements to continue to Eyüboglu High School following Turkish Ministry of Education regulations. Admitted students to high school are among the top scorers of national entrance exam takers.

Fairview International School, Bridge of Allan

FAIRVIEW
-INTERNATIONAL SCHOOL-
BRIDGE OF ALLAN

Headteacher
Mr David Hicks

PYP coordinator
K. Smith

MYP coordinator
G. Wilson

DP coordinator
G. Wilson

Status Private

Boarding/day Day

Gender Coeducational

Language of instruction
English

Authorised IB programmes
PYP, MYP, DP

Age Range 5 – 18 years

Number of pupils enrolled 80

Fees
Years 1 – 3 £10,560 per annum
Years 4 – 6 £11,800 per annum
Years 7 – 9 £14,300 per annum
Years 10 – 11 & Years 12 &13
£15,400 – £16,500 per annum

Address
52 Kenilworth Road
Bridge of Allan
Stirling
FK9 4RY | UK

TEL +44 (0)1786 231952

Email
enquiries@fairviewinternational.uk

Website
www.fairviewinternational.uk

Fairview International School, Bridge of Allan is an authorised IB Continuum School, delivering the Primary Years Programme (PYP), the Middle Years Programme (MYP) and the Diploma Programme (DP). Upon authorisation of the DP, Fairview became the only school in Scotland to offer an uninterrupted IB continuum for students aged 5 to 18 years.

Fairview is situated in Central Scotland, in an idyllic rural location, nestled in the wooded countryside with excellent transport links to Stirling, Glasgow and Edinburgh.

Fairview, Bridge of Allan is part of a family of 6 schools, which includes campuses located across Southeast Asia, totalling to 300 teachers and +3,000 students. Formed in 1978, Fairview is synonymous with academic excellence, integrity, and life-long opportunity, offering a comprehensive IB education and is known to be one of the world's best-performing private schools delivering the IB Diploma Programme and over recent years has consecutively been listed among the top 50 Global IB Schools.

The school's 2023 MYP cohort achieved a 100% pass rate. Furthermore, every student exceeded the global average, and our school average was a full 4 points higher than it.

Fairview International's diverse and global student body, parent community and faculty provide high-quality global learning opportunities for families based in Scotland.

Fairview accepts students all year round giving the opportunity for parents and prospective students to arrange personalised visits and immersive taster days at the school whenever they wish and enrol at any point throughout the academic year. The taster days offer students an opportunity to see what it would be like to be a part of the Fairview family, full week trials at the school can also be arranged to provide a full experience of school life, before enrolling.

Scholarships are available for academic passion, excellence in performing arts and sporting performance.

As Fairview International School, Bridge of Allan continues to grow, there has never been a better time to consider Fairview.

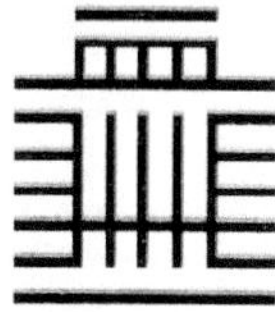

FELIX-KLEIN-GYMNASIUM

Head of School
Michael Brüggemann

DP coordinator
Silke Neumann

Deputy
Dr. Daniel Vollmar

Status State

Boarding/day Day

Gender Coeducational

Language of instruction
English

Authorised IB programmes
DP

Age Range 11 – 19 years

Address
Böttingerstrasse 17
37073 Göttingen, Lower Saxony |
GERMANY

TEL +49 551 400 2909

Email
fkgis@goettingen.de

Website
www.fkg-goettingen.de

At Felix-Klein-Gymnasium, we are committed to shaping the future through education – together, we strive to prepare young adults to be life-long learners in the world of the 21st century.

Founded in 1890, Felix-Klein-Gymnasium has a long history of academic excellence in the areas of experimental sciences and language education. The public, co-educational day school is situated in the beautiful southern city centre of Göttingen, the academic hub of Lower Saxony, surrounded by large prizewinning gardens that invite the school community to unwind.

On its two campuses, FKG offers educational programmes for Years 5-13 in German and English (CLIL), that award graduates the German Abitur. Since 2008, FKG has been accredited as an IB World School, which consolidated the school's excellent reputation as the leading provider of education in Göttingen. FKG is the only public school in Northern Germany to offer the IBDP in English separate from the German Abitur – this allows students to tailor their studies to their individual skills and interests and reflects the international-mindedness of the surroundings. Dedicated parents, international companies and academic institutions are our local partners, whom we value greatly.

The IBDP at FKG follows the recognition conditions by the German Conference of the Ministers of Education and Cultural Affairs – this guarantees access to all universities in Germany. FKG Diploma students consistently achieve results well above the world average and graduates go on to renowned tertiary education institutions in the area or all over the world.

The subject range is growing continuously and we have recently been able to broaden language options. Many graduates obtain a highly respected Bilingual Diploma, which represents their multi-facetted backgrounds and the cultural and linguistic diversity at FKG.

All IB teaching staff are long-term members of the school community. The team is highly committed to fostering our students' talents and help them maximize their potential. To achieve their individual educational objectives, our students are ready to take on responsibility for their own learning process and strive to develop their personalities, becoming considerate and open-minded members of the community. An academic counsellor guides them in this endeavor, and in Year 1, they have an older student companion at their side.

While the school is comparatively large, the classes in the IBDP offer a wonderful learning experience in small groups. Thus, extracurricular activities, joint projects, events and belonging to the big FKG family foster connections and friendships for life.

(Founded 1564)

Headmaster
Mr Chris Townsend

DP coordinator
Karen Woodhouse

Status Private

Boarding/day Mixed

Gender Coeducational

Language of instruction
English

Authorised IB programmes
DP

Age Range 4 – 18 years

Fees
Senior Day £9,605 per term
Senior Full Boarder £14,700 per term
Prep Day £3,705 – £7,275 per term
Prep Full Boarder £9,995 per term

Address
Felsted
Great Dunmow
Essex
CM6 3LL | UK

TEL +44 (0)1371 822600

Email
admissions@felsted.org

Website
www.felsted.org

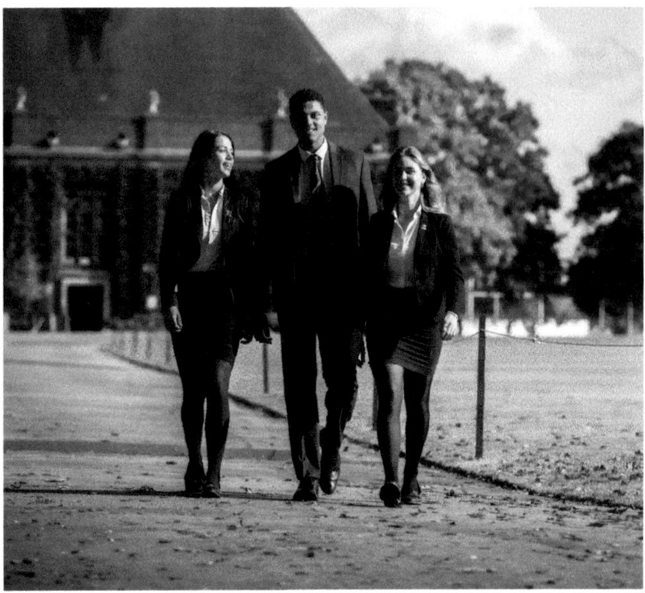

Boarding School of the Year – TES Schools Awards 2023
Felsted School was founded by the Lord Chancellor to King Edward VI, Richard Lord Riche, in 1564, and by combining this heritage with contemporary facilities and a modern approach to teaching and learning, Felsted opens up a world of opportunities for young people from countries all around the globe.

Very conveniently situated, just an hour from the cities of London and Cambridge, and 20 minutes from Stansted airport, Felsted's 90 acre countryside campus centres on a pretty English village and has its own extensive playing fields, chapel, theatre and music school.

International GCSEs and the International Baccalaureate are offered. Classes are small and each student is assigned an academic tutor who keeps track of progress and gives support when needed, on an individual basis.

Excellent academic results are achieved with a 100% IB pass rate in 2023, and an average score of 36.2.

Places at the world's top universities are regularly secured by Felsted IB students, including Oxford, Cambridge, Durham, Exeter, Warwick and UCL in the UK, as well as leading universities across Europe and colleges in the USA.

Very able students are extended and supported, and there is extensive assistance for students whose first language is not English.

Sports and the arts thrive, and students are given time and encouragement to pursue their passions. Many sports teams are coached by ex-professionals, concerts and drama productions are of an extremely high standard, and there is a huge range of clubs and activities for students to get involved in, including the adventurous Duke of Edinburgh's Award Scheme and the school's Model United Nations, at which students discuss world affairs.

Felsted is a global community. Students from more than 30 countries attend the school and there is an international atmosphere. By living and working together, students gain a real understanding of cultures and backgrounds that are different to their own. Felsted is a member of the Round Square network of the world's top schools and this presents chances for students to work together on projects to improve the lives of people in disadvantaged nations.

Welcoming and homely, the school has nine boarding houses on campus, each with a Housemaster or Housemistress, a team of tutors and a matron. Life-long friendships are made. Social events, outings, sporting activities and creative projects keep boarders entertained at weekends.

Student wellbeing is the top priority at Felsted. A medical team is on-hand 24 hours a day and there is a fully equipped medical centre on campus, as well as a wellbeing centre, which is a focus for emotional support. All staff are trained in pastoral care and every student is well known and valued as an individual.

To find out more about Felsted, please visit felsted.org, or email admissions@felsted.org. Virtual tours and videos are available, or come along to one of our on-site Open Mornings.

GEMS Modern Academy – Dubai

(Founded 1986)

Principal
Mrs. Nargish Khambatta

PYP coordinator
Joelle Filfili

MYP coordinator
Hebatallah Tarek

DP coordinator
Dr. Sunipa Guha Neogi

Status Private

Boarding/day Mixed

Gender Coeducational

Language of instruction
English

Authorised IB programmes
PYP, MYP, DP

Age Range 4 – 18 years

Number of pupils enrolled
2587

Fees
AED2,951 – AED7,040 per month

Address
PO Box 53663
Nad al Sheeba 3,4
Dubai | **UNITED ARAB EMIRATES**

TEL +971 4 326 3339

Email
info_mhs@gemsedu.com

Website
www.gemsmodernacademy-dubai.com

Vision Statement: Inspiring children to be positive changemakers

In keeping with the vision of GEMS Education the founder and chairman, Mr. Sunny Varkey, GEMS Modern Academy (GMA) assures every student a world-class education that is wholesome and exciting. Spread over 120,000 square meters, this state-of-the-art institution is located in the heart of Dubai and has been making its mark on the local and global education scene for the last 37 years.

The school is recognized and accredited by Ministry of Education, Dubai, UAE, the Council for Indian School Certificate Examinations (ICSE – New Delhi, India) and the International Baccalaureate to offer a continuum Primary Years Programme (since April 2021), Middle Years Programme (since February 2023) and the Diploma Programme (since September 2014).

GEMS Modern Academy is a CIS school, a Round Square school, a Green Flag school and the only school in the UAE to receive the Dubai SME certified incubator status.

'Modern' as it is fondly called, lives up to its name as it strives ceaselessly to nurture 21st-century learners who will become active, sensitive and responsible world citizens. Our educational philosophy aims at making students independent and lifelong learners who will contribute positively to society. The faculty and management work passionately to keep the balance between modern educational demands and the wholesome traditional values that the institution embodies.

In addition to being rated as an 'Outstanding' school since 2011 by the Knowledge and Human Development Authority of Dubai, the school has also been awarded the coveted Hamdan Award for Distinguished Academic Excellence and School Administration. The highly qualified and committed faculty ensures that all pupils at Modern strive to reach their goals and prepares them to take their place in the world.

Modern's alumni regularly receive admission to Ivy League and other world renowned universities and the school boasts of a 100% placement record.

Modern offers the IBDP to students of grades 11 and 12, with twenty eight individual subject options available. We are very pleased with the achievements of our eighth graduating batches since 2016. May 2023 batch achieved an average of 35 points with the topper securing a score of 44 points. This balance between strong academic performance and fantastic experiential outcomes from areas such as CAS is a hallmark of our growing Diploma Programme.

Modern attained authorization as an MYP school, inaugurating our three-year MYP program spanning from MYP 1 to MYP 3, and progressing annually toward the final year, MYP 5. The MYP overviews were meticulously crafted by department teams, distilling key elements from the DP curriculum and ensuring alignment with the international benchmarking test standards of ASSET.

The MYP philosophy is focused on instilling a deep appreciation for the learning process, valuing knowledge, deploying conceptual understanding through diverse perspectives, and applying it in both familiar and unfamiliar situations. Students are encouraged to extend their learning beyond the classroom by engaging in disciplinary and interdisciplinary actions that fostered personal and academic growth, showcasing and developing their learning skills.

In November 2003, students of MYP 3 presented their learning and service outcomes as part of the inaugural Community Projects Exhibition where their research, critical thought, collaboration, and self-management skills demonstrated the program's effectiveness in holistic development. Despite our status as a newly authorized school, we prioritized community projects, recognizing their value in preparing students for MYP 5 personal projects and as a cornerstone for broader global initiatives.

Starting from the previous academic year, we broadened subject options in Individuals and Societies, Sciences, Design, and Arts for MYP 4 and 5. This aims to provide students with ample opportunities to deepen their understanding of these subjects before embarking on their DP learning journey.

Modern is a place where every child matters. Deep and powerful learning only happens when it is relevant, real-world, collaborative, driven by inquiry and passion, and shared transparently. Through the provision of a balanced curriculum with the rigour of academics and a strong value system, world-class facilities for sports, performing and fine arts, for innovation and entrepreneurship, and inculcating international mindedness, it is a place that gives children roots to hold on to and wings to fly.

Our Primary Years Program Curriculum stems from age-appropriate curricular standards in a global context, carefully and creatively constructed by our PYP faculty and the Deans' Department through a process of reflection and collaboration. The curriculum outlines knowledge, skills, understanding, attitudes, and values pupils are expected to learn in the course of their transformative experience in school.

The Program standards and practices offer both an aspirational (the standards and practices) and baseline (the requirements and specifications) framework of what it means to be an IB World School. Thus, we mindfully use the IB PYP framework and philosophy for pedagogy and align the core curriculum objectives from the CISCE with the IB PYP scopes and sequences for the requisite PYP subjects.

The curriculum contributes to fulfilling the vision of GEMS Modern Academy, 'Inspiring children to be positive change-makers'. It is enriched by incorporating activities that are also embedded in the core values of GEMS Education and Jewels of Kindness Program. In line with Ministry regulations and compliance, the curriculum includes Arabic, Moral, Social and Cultural Studies for all students and Islamic Education for Muslim students. To fulfil the UAE National Priorities and achieve the set National Agenda targets for the school, we also ensure that the curriculum continues to align with international assessment frameworks such as TIMSS, PIRLS, and PISA. The curriculum is reviewed annually and is open to modification.

As an all-inclusive school, Modern values student diversity and understands the difficulties faced by students of determination. We strive to provide equity in education to ensure all learners have the necessary tools to succeed, by reducing barriers to learning with their peers in a common learning environment. Inclusion is truly at the heart of everything we do at Modern. It helps create a more positive sense of belonging with the community and teaches vital life lessons in respect, tolerance, and resilience.

German International School Beirut

(Founded 1954)

President of the Board
Omar Salloum

School Principal
Arsola Mouralli

DP coordinator
Petra Machlab

Status Private

Boarding/day Day

Gender Coeducational

Language of instruction
English

Authorised IB programmes
DP

Age Range 3 – 18 years

Number of pupils enrolled
800

Address
PO Box 11-3888
Bliss Street, Ras Beirut
Beirut | LEBANON

TEL +961 1 740523

Email
admissions@dsb.edu.lb

Website
www.dsb.edu.lb

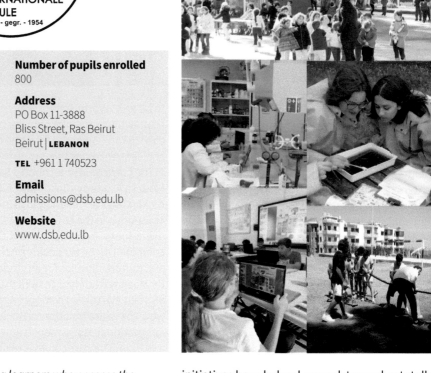

Our mission is to create lifelong learners who possess the competencies, confidence, and knowledge to meet the challenges that face them. Living in a diverse society and globalized world, we work on graduating students who are contributing members of society, tolerant of others and empowered to shape their own future.

The German International School Beirut maintains its progress through constant improvement in both structural and curricular aspects, having the students at the top of its pyramid of priority. Our motto is "Inspire-Educate-Support".

Inspire

One of our main goals has always been to inspire our students to follow their passion. We support our students to decide what course their life will take at such an early stage, and so to aid their decision we try and expose them to as many activities and experiences as possible. From our balanced and eclectic subject offerings to our wide range of CAS projects and experiences, we want our students to have the most fulfilling educational process possible. As such, we've made full use of technology in order to turn our classrooms into informational ecosystems that allow students to freely exchange ideas and take advantage of interactive media to truly immerse themselves in their work. While the written word is the cornerstone of education, we also want our students to learn with sights and sounds, and with their state-of-the-art PC's they have the world at their fingertips. Beyond that, we strongly believe in going green, and our technology initiatives have helped us work towards a totally green campus. We hope that our efforts to promote environmental awareness can really inspire our students to help make the world a better place.

Educate: Curricular Aspects

Our school offers a variety of academic programs. Aside from the IB Diploma Programme, our school also offers the Lebanese National Programme as well as the official German Language Diploma (DSD I, II). Each curriculum strives to impart students with the necessary skills and knowledge they need to excel in academics. Our teaching methods emphasize collaborative learning and critical thinking, and we have developed a highly skilled student body as a result. We also want our students to have a truly international education and as such we offer a variety of language courses in English, German, Arabic, French, and Spanish.

Support: School Community and atmosphere

Inspiring people is all about making them believe they can do something, and we want our students to truly believe in themselves. Our school fosters a diverse, supportive environment that encourages students to be both expressive and patient. Missteps and false starts are part of every process, and our students need to be given the freedom to grow freely and safely. Overall, we want to give our students the setting in which they can reach their fullest academic, emotional, physical, and spiritual potential.

Godolphin and Latymer School

(Founded 1905)

Head Mistress
Dr Frances Ramsey

DP coordinator
Audrey Dubois

Status Private, Independent

Boarding/day Day

Gender Female

Language of instruction
English

Authorised IB programmes
DP

Number of pupils enrolled
800

Fees
Day: £27,654 per annum

Address
Iffley Road
Hammersmith
London
W6 0PG | UK

TEL +44 (0)20 8741 1936

Email
office@godolphinandlatymer.com

Website
www.godolphinandlatymer.com

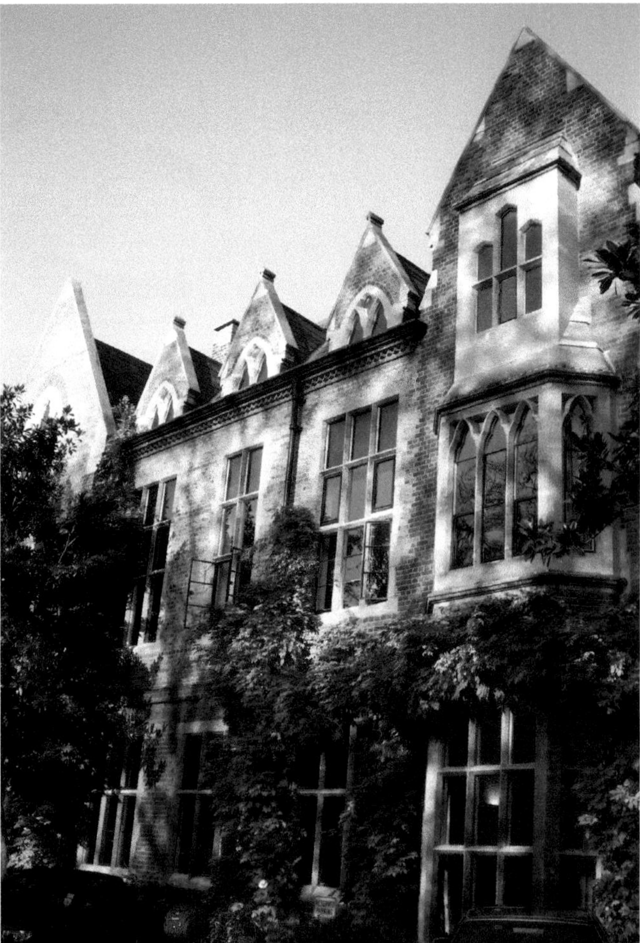

Godolphin and Latymer School is an independent day school for girls aged between 11 and 18; it is located in Hammersmith, West London, and is easily accessible by public transport from the surrounding areas. Means-tested bursaries are available at 11+ and 16+ entry covering up to 100% of fees; music scholarships are offered at 11+ and art and music scholarships at 16+.

The school has an excellent academic record and students gain places on a huge range of competitive courses at the very best universities both in the UK and overseas. Godolphin is a research-informed school that places great emphasis on the quality of its teaching to provide a broad and well-rounded education. It embraces innovation and new opportunities to create learning environments which promote analytical skills, emotional intelligence, teamwork, adaptability, entrepreneurship, creative thinking and problem-solving. Students are encouraged to explore beyond the syllabus and to find passion in their study and to be brave in embracing new academic challenges. The academic and pastoral sides of school life operate very much in tandem and students grow as independent and sophisticated thinkers and learners whilst being supported in their personal development as they learn key life skills.

The school prides itself on the amount of choice and opportunity it offers students. There is an exciting and ambitious curriculum with a wide range of subjects, and at Sixth Form it is one of the few schools in London that offers the choice of the A Level and the International Baccalaureate Diploma pathway. Beyond the classroom girls enjoy the most extensive extra-curricular programme and facilities to pursue their interests and talents, and there are many opportunities for students to take on leadership roles and positions of responsibility within the school community. There is a strong culture of community and voluntary service, caring for others and kindness which permeates the whole school. The school aims to develop students who will become the leading citizens of the future: young adults who are capable of thinking for themselves and who can demonstrate a critical awareness of the wider world, having a sense of their own worth whilst being appreciative of others.

Green Land – Pré Vert International Schools – GPIS-Egypt

(Founded 1994)

School Director / Founding Chairman
Amr Mokhtar

PYP coordinator
Francoise Mokhtar

MYP coordinator
May Waly

DP coordinator
Mona Khalil

Status Private

Boarding/day Day

Gender Coeducational

Language of instruction
French, English

Authorised IB programmes
PYP, MYP, DP

Age Range 3 – 18 years

Number of pupils enrolled
1550

Fees
Day: US$4,600 – US$7,400 per annum

School Giza
405 Geziret Mohammad Bashtil
Cairo | EGYPT

School Zayed
2nd Neighborhood, 5th district, Sheikh Zayed | EGYPT

Nursery Zayed
1st Neighborhood, 7th district, Sheikh Zayed | EGYPT

TEL +20 2 01002226053/50/54

Email
info@greenlandschool.org

Website
gpis-egypt.org

Green Land – Pré Vert International Schools (GPIS-Egypt) is a member of Green Land Educational Foundation (GEF-Egypt).

GPIS aims to contribute to making the world a better place by providing a distinctive high-quality IB continuum education in English and in French.

This inclusive education is conceptual, inquiry-based and learner-centered to enhance curiosity, intercultural understanding and respect, while fostering the learners' feeling of belonging to their culture and mother tongue.

Established in 1994, GPIS has been a leader in IB continuum educational programmes implementation in Egypt (IBPYP – IBMYP – IBDP), in a caring family-like environment that reinforces value driven character development, Egyptian cultural identity and Arabic language. The school has English and French sections, a quality management system that ensures consistency across all its campuses, a long standing highly qualified leadership team and a rich experience, approaching the end of its 3rd decade of practice.

GPIS family includes a large community of skilled practitioners who are on a never-ending journey of continual professional development. This community includes a significant number of International Baccalaureate Educators Network (IBEN) members.

Since 2008, GPIS IBDP students' results have always been excellent. In the latest session (May 2023), our highest score was 44/45, a feat accomplished by only 3% of students worldwide. GPIS students, on average, scored 35; surpassing the world average by 16%. Additionally, 10% of them scored above 40 and 60% scored above 35.

At GPIS, we go beyond academics; we care for our family members' socio-emotional well-being; therefore, we have a dedicated team for students' well-being. This team consists of Counselors, Assistant Counselors, Psychologist, Student Development Coordinator, Student Development Leader & Special Educational Needs (SEN) Leader.

As part of the GPIS mission and its social responsibility commitment, GEF-EGYPT signed a protocol with the Ministry of Education and the IBO in 2014 to start a pilot project of implementing the three IB programmes in Arabic in two governmental schools (Egyptian International Schools – EIS). EIS Zayed was established in 2014 and is considered the first governmental school in Africa to become authorized for offering the three IB programmes. Meanwhile, EIS 5th Settlement was established in 2018 and was IBPYP authorized in 2013. It is currently an IBMYP candidate.

EIS – Zayed celebrated the graduation of the first IBDP class in July 2022 with outstanding results with one of the students achieving a perfect score of 45 out of 45, placing her among the top achievers worldwide. Moreover, 100% of EIS students were awarded their diplomas; 13% of them scored 40 and above, and 60% scored 36 & above. Many of them were offered scholarships to study in reputable universities around the world.

Since 1996, GPIS has been continually ISO certified (ISO 9002 and 9001 since 1997 until the latest update BS EN ISO 9001:2015) from the British Standard Institution BSI – UK.

GPIS has been granted several awards from the International Gold Star for Quality from BID in Spain in 2002, followed by the Robert Blackburn Award by the IBO in 2007 for best Community and Services project in IBAEM. GPIS was also shortlisted out of 200 applications for the International School Awards 2019 (International Impact Award).

GPIS Distinctive Advantages

Green Land Pré Vert International School (GPIS) offers a compelling educational experience. GPIS stands out as an IB Education pioneer, dedicated to providing a curriculum that promotes curiosity, intercultural understanding, and respect, while nurturing a sense of cultural identity and language proficiency. The school prioritizes inquiry-based, learner-centered education, fostering qualities like learner agency, self-efficacy, global citizenship, responsible actions, and character building. This approach empowers students for life, equipping them with the skills and values they need to thrive in a diverse world. Additionally, GPIS consistently achieves outstanding diploma results, reflecting its commitment to academic excellence. Beyond academics,

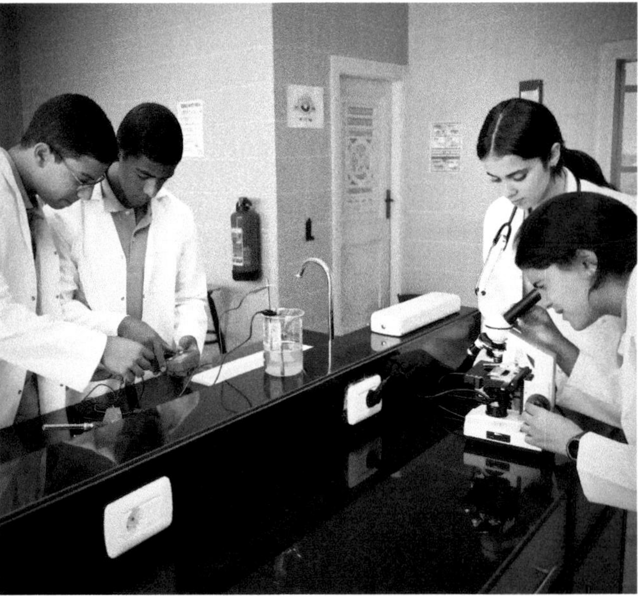

GPIS emphasizes community values, where unity, care, and collaboration are central. The school fosters a familial atmosphere of genuine satisfaction, care, and love, working collectively towards a shared mission of making the world a better place. Alumni keep coming back to GPIS and always keep in touch, as they consider the school their second home that significantly shaped them into mature, thoughtful, and balanced individuals. These elements collectively make GPIS a compelling choice for those seeking a holistic and inclusive educational experience.

Gymnasium am Münsterplatz

Erziehungsdepartement des Kantons Basel-Stadt

Gymnasium am Münsterplatz

Head of School
Dr. Eugen Krieger

DP coordinator
Dr. Manuel Pombo

Status State

Boarding/day Day

Gender Coeducational

Language of instruction
German, English

Authorised IB programmes
DP

Address
Münsterplatz 15
4051 Basel BS | SWITZERLAND

TEL +41 61 267 88 70

Email
gymnasium.muensterplatz@bs.ch

Website
www.gmbasel.ch

The Gymnasium am Münsterplatz, the second oldest school in Switzerland, is situated in the heart of Basel on Roman foundations opposite the cathedral. It enjoys considerable prestige in the city and commands a worldwide net of alumni whose generous donations go to support numerous extra-curricular activities in our school. The historical buildings are equipped with state-of-the-art equipment specially designed so that students can focus entirely on their studies in a dynamic modern atmosphere. Throughout the successive reforms in the educational sector over the last years, reflecting the social dynamics of our city, the school has changed considerably both within and without. Our recently installed Learning Centre allows pupils to carry out independent research under constant coaching provided by teachers and senior students. The integration of foreign-language-speaking pupils into Swiss society through the public school system is another of our major concerns.

The main objective of our Learning Support Centre is to provide individual didactic counselling, subject-specific backup courses, as well as various integrative measures for pupils with diverse educational biographies. It also aims to furnish individual, accompaniment and supervision for highly-talented pupils.

Apart from the modern foreign languages, French, English and Spanish, we also offer a choice of main elective subjects including; Latin, Greek, Spanish, English, and the combination Philosophy, Pedagogics, and Psychology. Of course, our Mathematics and Natural Science departments together with our Arts and Sports departments also furnish their necessary contribution to the education of our students.

The School has a rich and varied extra-curricular life. Every year, each of our 4th classes (11th grade) prepares and performs a drama project under the guidance of professional directors. We also have an annual Winter or Spring Ball. We have both a top-quality jazz band and a choir. Almost every year, one of our delegated teams to the National Session of the European Youth Parliament has been selected to represent Switzerland at the European Youth Parliament. We invite politicians and diplomats on a regular basis to discuss world affairs in our classrooms.

Apart from successfully preparing our students for third level education, the Gymnasium am Münsterplatz, in keeping with its humanistic tradition, places great importance on the development of individual personalities. We aim to address and promote our pupils as whole persons in their psychological, spiritual and physical integrity.

Outside our regular school programme, and our local interdisciplinary weeks, we also offer numerous activities away from Basel, such as study trips linked to the main elective subjects (Spain, Greece, Rome, UK, Vienna), annual skicamps, and concentrated study-weeks elsewhere in Switzerland.

As the first public school in Basel to be accredited in 2011, the GM has been offering the IB Diploma Programme as an ideal complement to the state gymnasium syllabus. Thanks to the great popularity of the IB Curriculum, our IB scores continue to improve every year and are well above world average, giving our students easier access to the world's leading universities.

(Founded 1862)

The Master
Mr Martin Collier MA BA PGCE

DP coordinator
Abigail Mash

Status Private

Boarding/day Mixed

Gender Co-educational

Language of instruction
English

Authorised IB programmes
DP

Age Range 11 – 18 years
(boarding from 11)

Number of pupils enrolled 917

Fees
Day:
£7,170 – £10,785 per term
Boarding:
£9,455 – £14,900 per term

Address
Haileybury
Hertford
Hertfordshire
SG13 7NU | UK

TEL +44 (0)1992 706353

Email
admissions@haileybury.com

Website
www.haileybury.com

Founded in 1862, Haileybury is cited by Best Schools to be one of the UK's top independent boarding and day IB schools based on 2021 results. Pupils' academic ambitions, intellectual curiosity, imaginations and abilities are harnessed to provide a truly all-round education. With strong academic results across the IB, A Levels and GCSEs, the School provides each and every pupil with a secure and caring environment where they can find their passion and shape their future. The School is situated just 20 miles north of London, nestled in over 500 acres of woodland, playing fields and superb facilities.

Academic

A key part of the School's philosophy is about empowering each child to follow their interests and build confidence in their abilities and intuition. Pupils are encouraged to be independent, creative and intellectually ambitious. The School offers a dedicated Lower School for Years 7 and 8, a wide range of GCSE and (i)GCSEs and the choice of the International Baccalaureate (IB) Diploma or A Level Course in Sixth Form.

Haileybury is the first school in Europe to partner with scientists from Stanford University and the University of Oxford as part of the global Stan-X study. This allows our pupils the opportunity to participate in this pioneering study of genetics, contributing to efforts to find cures for diseases such as pancreatic cancer and diabetes.

Co-curricular

Haileybury offers an enormous range of co-curricular opportunities, including clubs and societies, broad enough to cater for the most eclectic individuals. From trekking in the Himalayas to debating global issues at its Model United Nations programme to exploring the depths of visual storytelling in Filmmaking.

Sport is central to Haileybury life and the School has an outstanding reputation for Sports. The School is listed as one of the top 100 secondary schools in the UK for its cricket provision by The Cricketer's Good School Guide. Haileybury's Sports Complex has a strength and conditioning gym, a 25-metre swimming pool, indoor cricket nets, a golf simulator, a climbing wall, tennis courts, acres of beautifully maintained playing fields and two all-weather hockey pitches. Pupils benefit from professional sports coaching from the likes of former Wales rugby captain, Michael Owen, and ex-England international netballer, Dani McFarlane.

The campus also has a high-tech Music School, a purpose-built theatre and a fully equipped Art School designed to bring the most adventurous of ideas to life. The School takes pride in hosting spectacular Arts productions with multiple showcases per term for pupils to take part in.

Boarding

The Independent Schools Inspectorate describes the quality of boarding at Haileybury as excellent. With an emphasis on pastoral care and around-the-clock support from Housemasters and Housemistresses, the chaplain, tutors, a Health Centre and a Wellbeing Centre. The Houses lie at the heart of a Haileybury education and have done so for over 150 years. They are vibrant, happy, productive and homely communities where lifelong bonds are formed.

(Founded 1993)

Infant & Primary Head
Mr Renaud Milhoux

Secondary Head
Ms Rossella Cosso

MYP coordinator
Julien Hernandez

DP coordinator
Greg Wilson

CP coordinator
Greg Wilson

Status Private

Boarding/day Mixed

Gender Coeducational

Language of instruction
English, French

Authorised IB programmes
MYP, DP, CP

Age Range 18 months – 18 years

Number of pupils enrolled
600

Fees
Day: CHF24,900 – CHF36,100 per annum
Boarding: CHF72,000 – CHF88,000 per annum

Address
Ch. de Pangires 26
St-Légier-la Chiésaz
CH-1806 | SWITZERLAND

TEL +41 (0)21 555 51 07

Email admissions@haut-lac.ch

Website www.haut-lac.ch

Celebrating three decades of academic excellence and expertise in bilingual education, Haut-Lac International Bilingual School stands out as a dynamic IB World School, hosting a vibrant community of 600 students from 50 different countries.

Ever wondered about the meaning behind Haut-Lac?
Distinguished academic curricula are offered in a fully bilingual format, presenting options in English & French or exclusively in English, supplemented with daily French language sessions. Embracing a truly bilingual environment, the school adopts a holistic approach to student learning and well-being, offering personalized learning pathways and support.

Noteworthy achievements include a stellar 100% IBDP pass rate in both 2020 and 2021, with graduates securing placements at premier universities in Switzerland and around the globe. The school boasts a diverse array of 150 extracurricular activities, allowing students to explore new passions and hone their talents.

Boarding life
For those embracing boarding life, Haut-Lac's brand-new boarding facility accommodates up to 30 students, providing a home away from home. The facility features single and double rooms with private bathrooms, complemented by engaging evening and weekend activities that foster a sense of community among boarders.

Academics
As a CIS-accredited institution, Haut-Lac tailors its programmes to each child's individual needs, ensuring they not only reach their academic goals but also develop the essential transferable skills for success.

The school's programmes offerings include:

- Infant & primary programme, rooted in 21st-century concepts, encouraging real-world application of knowledge and skills.
- IB Middle Years Programme (IBMYP) for 11-15 year olds.
- Swiss Option for 11-14 year olds, facilitating English development and preparation for studies in a Swiss High School.
- US High School Diploma (USDP), allowing students to study in the US or Canada, available as a standalone or double IBDP-USDP certification.
- International Baccalaureate Diploma Programme (IBDP) or IB Career-Related Programme (IBCP) for 16-18 year olds.
- Multiple pathways for IBDP students, including English, French, bilingual, or Advanced Bilingual IB diplomas.
- International Baccalaureate Career-Related Programme offerings with a focus on Sustainable Management, Hospitality Management, Art & Design, or International Sport Management.
- An IB Sport & Study programme accredited by the World Academy of Sport, accommodating young athletes with flexible schedules.
- Additionally, Haut-Lac collaborates with Ski Zenit to run a Ski Racing Academy, providing a unique opportunity for students passionate about skiing.

(Founded 2003)

Head of School/Co-Founder
Abeya Fathy

PYP coordinator
Shymaa El Kotb

DP coordinator
Nada Yasin

Status Private

Boarding/day Day

Gender Coeducational

Language of instruction
English

Authorised IB programmes
PYP, DP

Age Range 3 – 18 years

Number of pupils enrolled
1657

Fees
$8,171 per annum *

Address
South of Police Academy
5th District
New Cairo
11835 | EGYPT

TEL +202 25373000/3333

Email
ib@hayahacademy.com

Website
www.hayahacademy.com

Hayah International Academy (aka Hayah International School) is committed to create and maintain an environment that fosters and enriches the personal and academic growth of each student. Hayah empowers students to live with purpose, honor their cultural identity, respect diversity, and serve humanity by positively impacting local and global communities.

Hayah International Academy is a distinguished entity founded on the belief that every child is creative, special, and capable of achieving outstanding results if provided with the proper support. Hayah provides a wide selection of educational programs and extracurricular activities aiming to generate well rounded students and promote social, academic, and physical development.

The school campus is located on a land lot of 55,000 square meters with separate buildings for early childhood, elementary and middle/high school, all equipped to support various learning opportunities.

Hayah prides itself on its select, diverse, and experienced IB teachers who remain continuously up to date through professional development. Hayah's IB staff members work collaboratively towards serving the needs of the student population whilst upholding the standards for quality IB education and investing in character building and developing students' IB learner traits.

IB Diploma subjects offered at Hayah:
English Literature HL/SL – English Language and Literature HL/SL – English B HL – Arabic Language and Literature HL/SL – Arabic B HL – Arabic *Ab-initio* SL – French B HL/SL – French *Ab-initio* SL – German B HL/SL – Economics HL/SL – History HL – Business and Management HL/ SL – Psychology HL/ SL – Chemistry HL/SL – Physics HL/SL – Biology HL/SL – Environmental Systems and Societies SL – Mathematics Analysis & Approaches HL/ SL – Mathematics Applications & Interpretations SL – Visual Arts HL/SL – Film HL/SL – Global Politics HL/SL – Computer Science HL/SL.

In addition to the IB Diploma Programme, we are also a candidate school for the IB Middle Years Programme (MYP).

The class of 2023 achieved 97% pass rate in the IB Diploma with an average IB score of 34. of the 78 students who took the IB Diploma, 2 students scored 43, 5% scored 40 and above, 53% scored 35 and above, and 85% scored 30 and above.

IB students from the class of 2023 joined many top-level universities both in Egypt and worldwide in the United Kingdom, Canada, USA, United Arab Emirates, Spain, the Netherlands, and Malaysia.

*Fees are collected in EGP equivalent

(Founded 1995)

Head of School
Mr. Conan De Wilde

PYP coordinator
Ms. Iliana Gutierrez

MYP coordinator
Ms. Alba Manso

DP coordinator
Ms. Sara Casagrande

Status Private

Boarding/day Mixed

Gender Coeducational

Language of instruction
English

Authorised IB programmes
PYP, MYP, DP

Age Range 3 – 18 years

Address
Via Olivetti 1
31056 Roncade (TV) | ITALY

TEL +39 0422 789503

Email
info.ve@h-is.com

Website
www.h-farm.com/en/h-farm-school/venezia

H-FARM International School, located just outside of Venice, Italy, empowers students to be internationally-minded citizens who are able to shape their own future in a rapidly changing global community. Through innovative learning environments and the development of relationships based on compassion and respect, we enable students to become confident, creative and collaborative. We are a community of active lifelong learners. H-FARM International School serves a diverse and growing community of students and families.

Our school uses English as the language of instruction and learning and aims to promote international mindedness and global citizenship.

We offer three of the International Baccalaureate Organization's educational programmes: Primary Years Programme (nursery / elementary school), Middle Years Programme (middle school + 1st two years of high school) and the world-renowned Diploma Programme (final two years of high school), an engaging curriculum that prepares students to access the most prestigious universities and colleges in the world.

Our school is located within the Campus of H-FARM , located just 10 minutes from Venice International Airport, an unparalleled center for innovation in Europe, with a strong DNA of digital technology, creativity and entrepreneurship. The sprawling, 51-hectare Campus boasts world class services for both its boarding and day students. H-FARM students have access to full-service Boarding facilities (which were recently certified by the BSA), an indoor and outdoor sports complex, a fully-equipped gymnasium, a coffee shop and restaurant, a library with communal study areas, a radio station, an astronomy observation station, innovative science and Virtual Reality laboratories.

This school year we welcomed more than 170 new students and more than 100 Boarding students from 20 different countries and representing all 6 continents. Boarding students are cared for by Residence Life coordinators, who also facilitate weekend excursions and activities that allow students to enjoy the natural and cultural attractions of our stunning corner of Italy.

Hockerill Anglo-European College

(Founded 1980)

Principal
David Woods

MYP coordinator
Michelle Butler

DP coordinator
Thea Wilson

Status State

Boarding/day Mixed

Gender Coeducational

Language of instruction
English

Authorised IB programmes
MYP, DP

Age Range 11 – 18 years

Number of pupils enrolled
900

Fees
Residential Boarding
£15,279 – £19,527 per annum

Address
Dunmow Road
Bishops Stortford
Hertfordshire
CM23 5HX | UK

TEL 01279 658451

Email
admissions@hockerill.com

Website
www.hockerill.com

Situated on a leafy campus in Bishop's Stortford, 10 minutes from London Stansted Airport, Hockerill is a leading UK school featuring in both the Sunday Times and the Good Schools Guide. It is a strong, caring community of 900 boys and girls (400 boarders and 500 day students) aged between 11 and 18. All five boarding houses are located within the campus.

Student outcomes are exceptional with results and university destinations comparing favourably to those of top independent schools. Typically 70% of those attending UK universities go on to Russell Group destinations. The Sunday Times placed Hockerill fifth of all comprehensives, based on academic achievement, in its 2024 guide.

The College offers a rigorous and broad curriculum and is proud to be one of the largest state schools offering the prestigious International Baccalaureate Middle Years and Diploma programmes with consistently outstanding results. Hockerill has a special focus on languages and music with both French/English and German/English bilingual sections.

The main intake years are at ages 11 and 16 with a limited number of additional places at ages 13 and 14. The Lower College curriculum is based on the IB Middle Years programme offering a wide range of subjects with students taking their GCSEs before moving on to the IB Diploma.

The College has a strong extra-curricular provision which includes Sports, Music Ensembles and Choirs, BMX, CCF, Young Enterprise, Duke of Edinburgh, Debating, Model United Nations, Amnesty and Charity fundraising. There are some 100 clubs on offer.

The trips and exchanges programme runs throughout the College and encompasses destinations such as Uganda, India, Japan, China, Spain, France, Croatia, Belgium, Austria, Germany and Italy.

Many events take place during the year for students including formal dinners, concerts, Prize Giving, Boarders weekend (for students and their families). As part of the regular communication, there is a termly forum for boarding parents.

(Founded 1999)

Head of School
Gavin Budd

PYP coordinator
Gill Baxter

MYP coordinator
Michele Marnitz

DP coordinator
Michele Marnitz

Status Private

Boarding/day Day

Gender Coeducational

Language of instruction
English

Authorised IB programmes
PYP, MYP, DP

Age Range 2 – 18 years

Number of pupils enrolled
500

Fees
Day: R59,433 – R164,779 per annum

Address
61 Main Road
Hout Bay
7806 Cape Town, Western Cape |
SOUTH AFRICA

TEL +27 21 791 7900

Email
hbis@iesmail.com

Website
www.houtbayinternational.co.za

Introduction

Hout Bay International School is more than a school – it is a community of diverse individuals and families; a centre of academic, cultural and sporting excellence; a home away from home and a family for all.

Enter any one of our classrooms and we're sure you'll be impressed by the enthusiasm, confidence and creativity of our students. Thanks to our exceptional teaching staff and the International Baccalaureate curriculum, we help children and young people to become inquisitive learners who ask challenging questions, critically reflect on topics, develop research skills and learn how to learn.

This not only equips our students with the academic results, necessary skills and qualities to study at the world's most prestigious universities, but also the opportunity for them to actualise their personal potential and embody the character traits of the IB Learner Profile.

We also recognise the importance of the world outside the classroom. Service is an integral component of our curriculum, instilling in our students a commitment to give back on a local, national and global level. Our extensive co-curricular programme emphasises a holistic approach to learning to ensure our students leave the school as well-rounded individuals ready to play their part in society.

Facilities

Our campus is cradled between beautiful mountains on three sides with the sparkling Atlantic Ocean on the other; and houses the following facilities: 35 Classrooms (each equipped with Wi-Fi and Data Projectors). Two Fully Equipped Science/ Biology Laboratories, Robotics Lab, Black Box Drama Studio, Visual Art Studio, Design Studio, School Library, Music Studio, Creative Arts Outdoor Courtyard, Courtyards equipped with climbing walls and sand pits, Canteen for daily lunches and snacks, Small hall, Stop and Drop / Pick Up Facilities, 2 Netball / Tennis Courts, 3 Cricket Nets, 2 Multi-purpose playing fields, Bio-Diversity Sanctuary, Sustainable Vegetable Garden. In 2019 our campus was enhanced with the completion of our brand new Early Years and Junior Primary building which also houses our newest addition, our Nursery Class.

Extra-Curricular Programme

Our students enjoy an extensive Extra-Curricular programme exposing them to various sports, creative arts, dance, martial arts, community service activities, all contributing to their 'Whole Child' educational experience and embracing the concept of Creativity, Activity & Service (CAS).

Admissions

We accept students year round, in all grade levels except the final year of the Diploma Programme which requires a two year commitment from the student. Application forms and previous school reports are required for entry.

Ibn Khuldoon National School

(Founded 1983)

President
Dr Kamal Abdel-Nour D.Ed

PYP coordinator
Rosy Johnson

Secondary School Principal & Acting MYP Coordinator
Roula Barghout

DP coordinator
Gerda Marais

Status Private, Non-Profit

Boarding/day Day

Gender Coeducational

Language of instruction
English, Arabic

Authorised IB programmes
PYP, MYP, DP

Age Range 4 – 18 years

Number of pupils enrolled
1818

Address
Building 161, Road 4111
Area 841, P.O. Box 20511
Isa Town | **BAHRAIN**

TEL +973 17780661

Email
k.algosaibi@ikns.edu.bh

Website
www.ikns.edu.bh

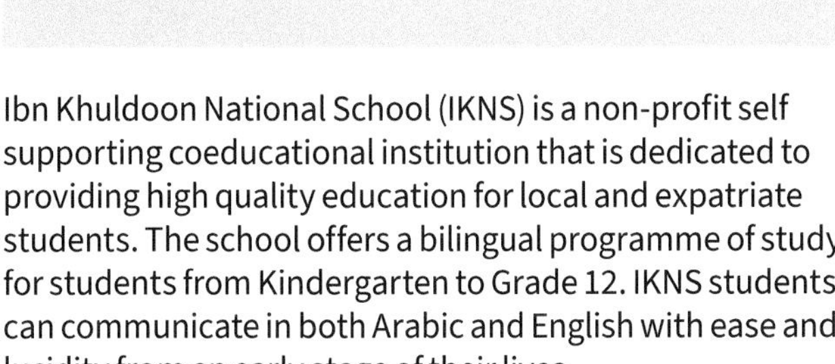

Ibn Khuldoon National School (IKNS) is a non-profit self supporting coeducational institution that is dedicated to providing high quality education for local and expatriate students. The school offers a bilingual programme of study for students from Kindergarten to Grade 12. IKNS students can communicate in both Arabic and English with ease and lucidity from an early stage of their lives.

IKNS is an IB Continuum School that is authorized to offer three of the International Baccalaureate (IB) educational programmes from KG1 to Grade 12. The School was authorized to offer the IB Diploma Programme (DP) in 1990. In 2020, it was authorized to offer the IB Primary Years Programme (PYP) and in 2022, the IB Middle Years Programme (MYP).

The school also offers the American High School Diploma Programme in Grades 11 and 12 as a parallel programme to the IBDP.

IKNS students go on to complete their tertiary education in international and local universities, many gaining admission to prestigious institutions.

A diverse faculty, whether teaching in Arabic or English, provide a rich and supportive learning environment for students. The faculty is supported by a dedicated team of administrative and support staff.

At the top level of the school's governance stand the board of trustees, board of directors and specialist committees. Their members volunteer their expertise, time and effort to ensure that the school is always heading in a forward direction.

The school received its full accreditation from the Middle States Association of Colleges and Schools (MSA) in 1994, and it continues to be in good standing with the association. IKNS continues to be rated as an "Outstanding School" by the Education and Training Quality Authority (BQA).

(Founded 2006)

Head of School
Ms. Gina Bianchi

PYP coordinator
Mrs. Janet Goswell

Status Private

Boarding/day Day

Gender Coeducational

Language of instruction
English, French

Authorised IB programmes
PYP

Age Range 3 – 11 years

Number of pupils enrolled 185

Fees
Day: €12,215 – €14,235 per annum

Address
245 Route les Lucioles
06560 Valbonne | **FRANCE**

TEL +33 (0)4 93 64 32 84

Email
admissions@icscotedazur.com

Website
www.icscotedazur.com

ICS Côte d'Azur is a bilingual, co-educational, non-sectarian, IB World Primary School serving the international and local community in the Sophia Antipolis region. The school offers Early Years and Primary Years education from KG1 (age 3) to PY6 (age 11). ICS Côte d'Azur is a proud member of Globeducate.

Formerly known as EBICA, the school's multicultural learning community enjoys a modern and secure campus in Sophia Antipolis, Valbonne, southwest of Nice. Recognised as an IB World School since 2018, ICS Côte d'Azur welcomes students from around the world, offering an international education within the inquiry-based framework of the IB Primary Years Programme, whilst also integrating the national curricula for England and France.

The school attracts internationally-minded families with aspirations for their children to learn in French and English from the early years onwards. Within the multicultural community, students are immersed in both languages with equal measure, in an environment that promotes international understanding while fostering an appreciation of French culture.

ICS Côte d'Azur offers a language support programme for French as a foreign language (FFL) learners and English as a foreign language (EFL) learners. These support lessons for beginners assist acquisition in either language, bringing them the linguistic competencies required to access the curriculum and progress with confidence.

Through learner-centred teaching, ICS Côte d'Azur empowers students, as agents in their IB journey, to develop the self-knowledge and confidence to create their successes. In an environment that fosters cross-cultural understanding, students develop the attributes of the IB learner profile, which equips them with the essential skills to be successful in a diverse and connected world.

Sophia Antipolis is a rich area for science and technology, often referred to as the 'Silicon Valley' of Europe. To reflect its location, the school offers an innovative STEAM programme (Science, Technology, Maths, Art and Engineering), with a dedicated tinkering lab called 'The Hub', LEGO® Education kits, and Apple products in the classroom. The vision behind this cutting-edge STEAM initiative is for students to acquire the critical thinking, creativity and problem-solving skills that will be essential for the future.

(Founded 1979)

Head of School
Alec Jiggins

PYP coordinator
Clara Wells

MYP coordinator
Laura Yates

DP coordinator
Vishanu Bhoja

Status Private

Boarding/day Day

Gender Coeducational

Language of instruction
English

Authorised IB programmes
PYP, MYP, DP

Age Range 3 – 19 years

Number of pupils enrolled 160

Fees
Day: £20,970 – £30,930 per annum

Early Years & Primary School
7B Wyndham Place
London
W1H 1PN | UK

Middle Years and Diploma school
21 Star Street
London
W2 1QB | UK

TEL +44 (0)20 729 88800

Email
admissions@ics.uk.net

Website
www.icschool.co.uk

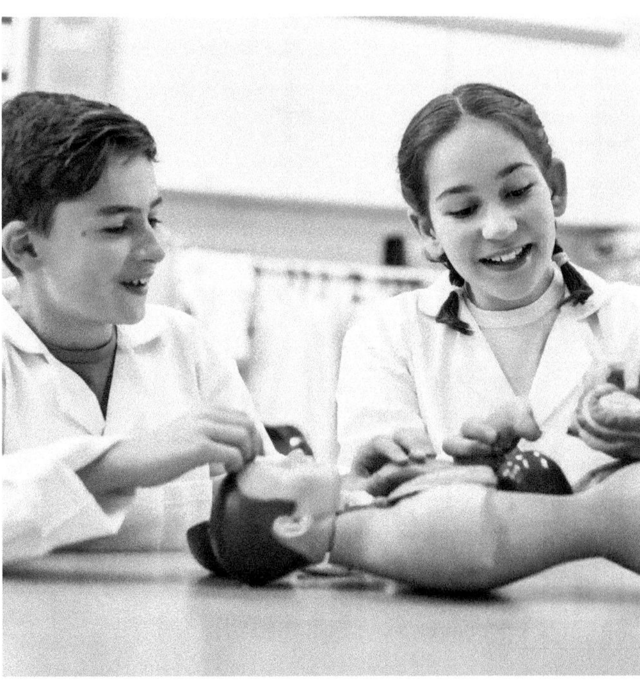

ICS London International School is a private co-educational and international day school for students aged 3 to 19 situated between Marylebone and Paddington. The school was established in 1979 by the Toettcher family with the intention of teaching English within a full international curriculum. Since then, the school has broadened its offer and has become only one of two central London schools to offer the full International Baccalaureate Programme (IB), a challenging and stimulating curriculum, equipping students with a globally recognised qualification.

We are proud to offer our Year 10 and 11 students a comprehensive IGCSE curriculum, seamlessly integrated within the internationally recognised MYP framework, ensuring a well-rounded and globally-focused education for your child.

In 2017, ICS London became part of the Globeducate network of international schools, with over 55 schools in three different continents, educating over 31,000 students around the world.

With a diverse community of over 150 students from 65 different nationalities, ICS London is committed to providing an exceptional educational experience that prepares students for success in a rapidly changing world.

We take pride in our small class sizes and personalised learning environment, which have in the past years contributed to the outstanding results ICS London students have achieved. With a 100% pass rate, an IB diploma point score average significantly higher than the world average (five year point average of 33.2 against the world average of 30.2), and 100% of our students getting into their first-choice universities, ICS London offers an outstanding IB education with the aim of shaping the world of tomorrow.

Our education philosophy is built upon the belief that every student possesses unique talents and potential waiting to be unlocked. We embrace diversity and cultivate an inclusive learning community where students from various cultural backgrounds come together to learn and grow. Our values are rooted in academic excellence, critical thinking, and holistic development. We strive to empower students to become curious, lifelong learners, who are adaptable, compassionate, and globally-minded.

With an extensive extra-curricular offer, which includes Fencing, Xendo, Creative Arts, Model United Nations, Enterprise Club and STEM, to name a few, we really believe in nurturing our students' talents both inside and outside of the classroom.

Head of School
Mrs Antonia Giovanazzi

Secondary Principal
Mr Matt Gilberthorpe

MYP coordinator
Angela Milne

DP coordinator
Patricia Cristina Radoi-Iitani

Status Private

Boarding/day Day

Gender Coeducational

Language of instruction
English, Italian

Authorised IB programmes
MYP, DP

Age Range 1 – 18 years

Number of pupils enrolled
1000

Fees
Day:
€15,000 – €25,000 per annum

Address
ICS Symbiosis
Viale Ortles, 46
20139 Milano (MI) | ITALY

TEL +39 02 36592694

Email
admissions@icsmilan.com

Website
www.icsmilan.com

ICS Milan International School

ICS Milan is the first school dedicated to students from 1 – 18 years that offers an international curriculum enhanced by an innovative teaching approach based on experiential learning and a STEAM agenda (Science, Technology, Engineering, Arts and Maths). With three different campuses throughout the Milan area, ICS Milan is a school of innovation that helps children grow into citizens of the world.

ICS Milan serves a diverse community of students from a range of nationalities, cultures and backgrounds. The school offers a broad-based education that uses English as the main language of learning and caters for a range of student abilities. ICS Milan's vision is to inspire, motivate, and challenge all students to achieve their personal best by providing a rich, creative, and well-balanced educational experience.

International School with Italian Roots

As Scuola Paritaria (an officially recognised school), our school also adopts the national recommendations for the curriculum issued by MIUR (the Ministry of Education). The Italian language and history programmes are designed for mother-tongue Italian speakers. A specific programme for Italian as an additional language learners is available for children of other nationalities.

ICS Values

ICS Milan teaches creativity, responsibility, respect, diversity, compassion and shared values. Students are invited to develop a sound knowledge base and to reflect on and reassess their surroundings from a variety of perspectives.

Our system fosters a balanced development of different personalities. It combines the importance of rules with a sense of expressive creativity, challenge and imagination, and it also provides the necessary tools for becoming "masters" of our own abilities.

Our teaching approach stimulates each developmental and learning phase of every child by placing respect for others and for ourselves at its centre.

Globeducate

Since 2017 ICS Milan is a proud member of the Globeducate network, which operates in more than 60 international schools in Europe, Americas and Asia, with more than 35,000 students. Globeducate's mission to prepare each student to become a global citizen that can shape the world is wellaligned to the student-centered approach at ICS Milan.

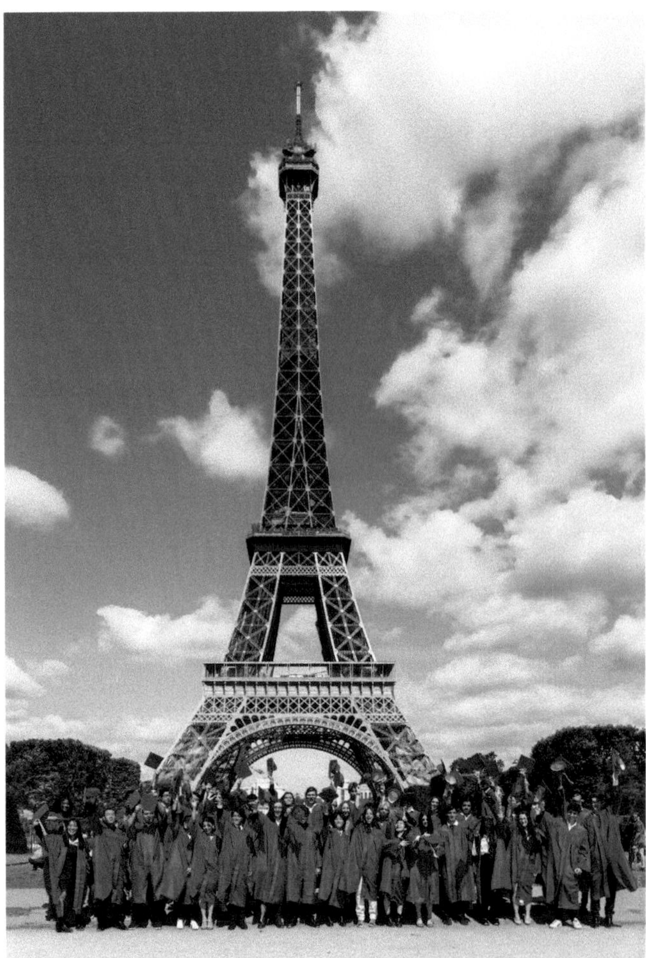

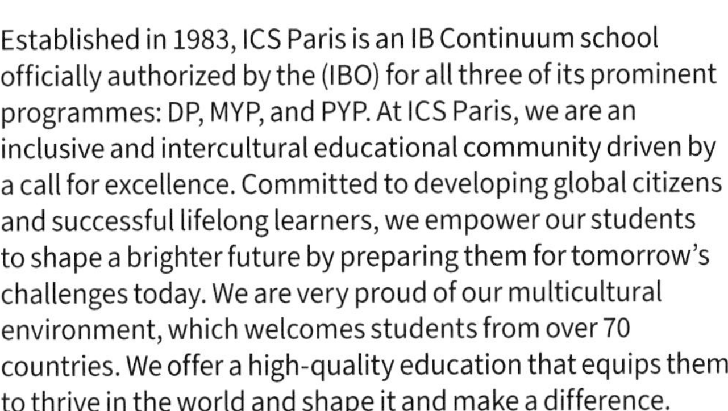

(Founded 1983)

Director
Mrs. Angela Hollington

PYP coordinator
Ms. Eva Silva

MYP coordinator
Mr. Matthieu Coliboeuf

DP coordinator
Mrs. Marilyne Boursin

Status Private

Boarding/day Day

Gender Coeducational

Language of instruction
English

Authorised IB programmes
PYP, MYP, DP

Age Range 3 – 18 years

Number of pupils enrolled
500

Fees
Day: €19,998 – €29,775 per annum

Address
23 rue de Cronstadt
75015 Paris | **FRANCE**

TEL +33 (0)1 56 56 60 31

Email
admissions@icsparis.fr

Website
www.icsparis.fr

Established in 1983, ICS Paris is an IB Continuum school officially authorized by the (IBO) for all three of its prominent programmes: DP, MYP, and PYP. At ICS Paris, we are an inclusive and intercultural educational community driven by a call for excellence. Committed to developing global citizens and successful lifelong learners, we empower our students to shape a brighter future by preparing them for tomorrow's challenges today. We are very proud of our multicultural environment, which welcomes students from over 70 countries. We offer a high-quality education that equips them to thrive in the world and shape it and make a difference.

Located in the heart of Paris, we ensure that each of our students is immersed in many different aspects of French culture through outings in Paris and trips further afield in France, making for a rich learning experience. Our supportive, nurturing community cares about how our students grow into the generation of tomorrow. We expect our students to develop empathy, be kind to each other, and demonstrate resilience and perseverance when faced with difficult situations. Working together in groups, collaborating, and the many different approaches to learning that we use help to cultivate these crucial skills and contribute to developing responsible adults of the future.

At ICS Paris, our students are at the centre of everything we do. Our International Baccalaureate curriculum provides the framework for developing their thinking skills and empowering them to take ownership of their learning. Education at ICS Paris is rooted in the IB learning philosophy and is structured to equip students with the next generation's skills.

As an international school, we are building towards becoming a Bilingual Multilingual Learners (BML) smart school. With a research-based approach to learning languages and education, we are working on providing the knowledge, expertise, and facilities where children can learn their mother tongue language, and at the same time, follow a rigorous English-language curriculum. By providing opportunities for multiple language learning, we equip our students with the communication skills essential in an international environment while fostering an understanding and experience of French culture.

College Principal
Ms Victoria Hearn

DP coordinator
Bronwyn Wilson

CP coordinator
Leanne Gibbons

Status State

Boarding/day Day/Homestay

Gender Coeducational

Language of instruction
English

Authorised IB programmes
DP, CP

Age Range 16 – 19 years

Number of pupils enrolled
250

Address
New Road
Impington
Cambridge
Cambridgeshire
CB24 9LX | UK

TEL 01223 200402

Email
international@ivc.tmet.org.uk

Website
www.impingtoninternational.org.uk

A World Class IB education from Impington International College – your ticket to a world of opportunity

Why choose Impington International College?

1. The quality of care is exceptional – The tutor to student ratio is approximately 1 to 15, with a dedicated Student Manager for pastoral support and guidance. In lessons, the average teacher to student ratio is 1 to 10.

2. It delivers excellent outcomes – The pass rate is 100% (international average: 85.6%) and the average International Baccalaureate (IB) point score is 36. In 2023, over a third (35%) of our students attained 40 points or more; the equivalent to four A* at A Level.

3. Students go on to achieve great things – In 2023, 98% of students were accepted into their first choice of university, with 10% offered Oxbridge places and 35% attending Russell Group universities.

4. Expert delivery of the International Baccalaureate – for more than 30 years, Impington International College has offered the IB and was one of the first state schools in the UK to do so. The College is consistently rated 'Outstanding' by Ofsted.

5. It is truly international – the culturally diverse College offers a huge range of opportunities for study trips and service visits abroad, with an emphasis on developing international-mindedness.

Impington International College offers the following programmes to students:

- IB Diploma Programme (DP)
- IB Career-related Programme (CP) through the College's
- Performance School
- Sport Scholarships
- Health and Social Care Futures programme

Impington International College bases its teaching on the IB's mission statement and ethos, aiming to develop "inquiring, knowledgeable and caring young people who help to create a better and more peaceful world". Not only do students gain a valuable breadth of skills through either the DP or the CP but IB higher level subjects also provide the same depth of knowledge as A Levels, so students can go on to achieve excellence in whichever path they choose.

The driven cohort achieve outstanding results and have gone on to attend renowned higher education institutions around the world, including: University of Cambridge, University of Oxford, London School of Economics and Political Science, University College London, King's College London, Loughborough University, Leiden University, UCLA, The Place, Italia Conti, International University of Japan, and many more. Many students from the College's Performance School go on to join professional companies, with a number starring in the West End. Students from the sports scholarship programme often go on to study coaching and management at university, or play semi-professionally for local teams.

Institut Florimont

INSTITUT FLORIMONT

(Founded 1905)

Director General
Mr. Sean Power

DP coordinator
Noha Benani

Status Private

Boarding/day Day

Gender Coeducational

Language of instruction
English, French

Authorised IB programmes
DP

Age Range 3 – 18 years

Number of pupils enrolled
1705

Fees
Day: CHF18,600 – CHF28,650 per annum

Address
37 Avenue du Petit-Lancy
1213 Petit-Lancy GE |
SWITZERLAND

TEL +41 22 879 0000

Email
admissions@florimont.ch

Website
www.florimont.ch

Institut Florimont is a co-educational day school offering children from 3 to 18 years of age a complete education from kindergarten to the three diplomas that will open the doors to higher education. As well as encouraging academic excellence, Florimont fosters the traditional values and beliefs that are important for life.

Since 1905, Florimont has been preparing students for the French Baccalaureate and, as of 1942, for the Swiss Maturité. Since September 2014 our range of final examinations includes the bilingual (French-English) International Baccalaureate. Therefore, Florimont offers children more opportunities and more choices, allowing them easier access to the world's best universities.

All sections of our school work together to ensure the continuity and coherence of the programme of study. Clear procedures are in place to ensure that new students joining us from other private or public schools are successfully integrated.

Close communication with parents, additional lessons and one-to-one tutoring are just some of the ways that Florimont supports students during their studies.

Our student body is made up of more than fifty nationalities making Florimont a rich multicultural and multilingual learning environment. The importance we attach to this is reflected in our language learning programme. In addition to English, emphasis is placed on German, Switzerland's predominant language, as well as on Chinese, Spanish and Italian. Other languages such as Russian and Arabic are individually tutored or taught to small groups. Bilingual classes in French and English are offered from the primary and throughout the school.

Priority is given to partnerships and exchanges with leading schools worldwide, as well as to many activities that can add value to a university application, such as the CAS programme.

Philosophy lessons are initiated in the primary years in preparation for a better appreciation of Theory of Knowledge in the IB Diploma Programme.

Our students are encouraged to be entrepreneurial, bold, adaptable and creative because we know that these qualities will not only strengthen their university applications but also prepare them to face the challenges of working life.

Find more information on www.florimont.ch

Institut International Saint-Dominique

Head of School
Bernard Lociciro

DP coordinator
Nadine Hakme

Status Private

Boarding/day Mixed

Gender Coeducational

Language of instruction
English, French

Authorised IB programmes
DP

Age Range 2 – 18 years

Number of pupils enrolled
380

Fees
Day: €14,500 per annum
Weekly Boarding:
€24,450 per annum
Boarding:
€28,950 per annum

Address
Via Igino Lega 5
00189 Rome | ITALY

TEL +39 06 303 10817

Email
info@institutsaintdominique.it

Website
www.institutsaintdominique.it

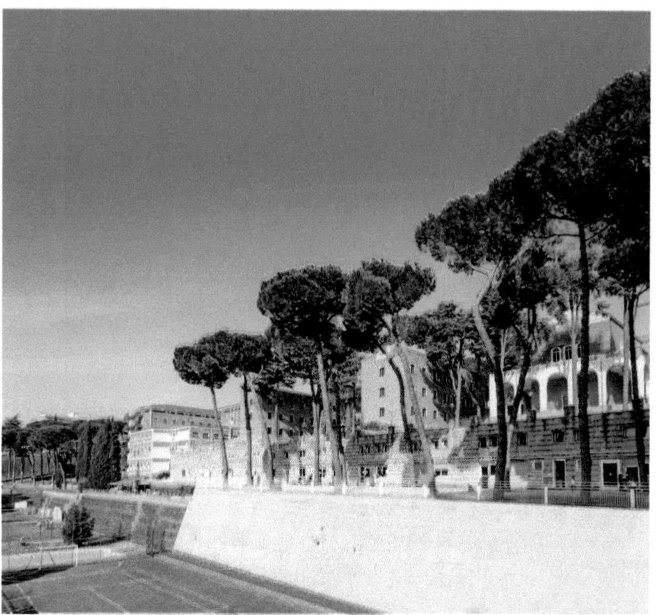

Jump Into a Unique French International School!
Recognized for its educational philosophy, the Institut Saint-Dominique (ISD) is one of the most prestigious French schools in Italy that combines educational excellence and well-being. The Institut Saint-Dominique is a school of the International Odyssey Group and, for more than 10 years, a partner school of the network of the Agency for French Education Abroad (AEFE), which has more than 500 schools around the world.

All our programs from kindergarten to high school are approved by the French National Ministry of Education. Our establishment offers excellent and multilingual education (French, Italian, English) from Pre-kindergarten to High school. ISD Rome is accredited with the International Baccalaureate Organization and opens an English-speaking International Section (PRE-IB GRADE 10) from September 2022 and the Diploma Programme for 2023-2024.

ISD, like all schools in the Odyssey network, provides its students with a French and international education that allows them to express the best of themselves and embark on a path of excellence that will open doors to the best universities in the world. We welcome our students in a dynamic, cosmopolitan environment where each member of the community can find their place and build lifelong bonds.

The learning environment plays an essential role in the development and success of each student. Our spaces are designed to promote academic performance, curiosity, creativity, and the well-being of students through the integrated teaching of languages by teachers who are "mother tongue" speakers. We also emphasize sciences and data processing with the presence of interactive touchscreen screens in the classrooms. In this exceptional setting of 6 hectares, the students have the possibility, regardless of their age, nationality, and sensitivity, to accomplish their schooling from a personalized pedagogical and educational framework.

Our boarding school offers double or single rooms, the option of staying 5 or 7 days, and a dozen cultural and sporting activities. The boarding school, situated on our exceptional 6-hectare campus in a secure and green setting in the heart of a historic city, allows us to accommodate an increasing number of boarding students and implement advanced teaching and learning methods. Saint-Dominique boarding school offers a multilingual education, personalized support, and a cultural, sports, and artistic program. It drives the development of a quality educational offer rich in human experiences, acquired through a community life that requires attention and respect in the relationship with others.

The benefits of the English International Section – IB at ISD:
Language diversity: The language of the International Section is English, and the majority of courses are delivered in English, but students can also study other languages at a very advanced level. Small class sizes promote easy communication among students and with teachers. A wide choice of subjects, associated with projects of solidarity, commitment, and leadership, allows students to build a recognized and sought-after academic profile. Interactive

classes and the development of critical thinking lead students to success in the Diploma Programme exam. Additionally, a CAS coordinator (Creativity, Activity, Service) and an IB coordinator support students and teachers in fulfilling their orientation project.

At our school, we believe in empowering our students with language skills. In the grade 10 IB section, students have a unique opportunity to learn not one but two additional languages – French and Italian. With four hours of instruction in each subject each week, students can delve into these languages and gain proficiency. Classes are differentiated according to students' language proficiency levels, ensuring a customized learning experience for each individual.

Community Service and Lifelong Learning: We go beyond academics; our students experience the joy of giving back to the community. Each week, they dedicate one hour to community service, where they work closely with instructors to plan and execute meaningful activities. After each event, they reflect on their experiences, gaining valuable insights that add to their learning journey. This hands-on approach instills organizational skills, empathy, and a lifelong commitment to service in our students.

All of the modern infrastructure, digitized and adapted to the evolution of our pupils, allows a peaceful and successful schooling.

Institut International de Lancy

(Founded 1903)

Head of School
Monique Roiné

Head of English Secondary
Marie Galmiche

DP coordinator
Tania McMahon

Status Private

Boarding/day Day

Gender Coeducational

Language of instruction
English, French

Authorised IB programmes
DP

Age Range 3 – 19 years

Number of pupils enrolled
1500

Fees
Day: CHF16,000 – CHF28,000

Address
24, avenue Eugène-Lance
Grand-Lancy
CH-1212 | SWITZERLAND

TEL +41 22 794 2620

Email
info@iil.ch

Website
www.iil.ch

The Institut International de Lancy was founded in 1903 (Pensionnat Marie-Thérèse). A private, co-educational school, IIL is a member of the Sisters of St. Joseph de Lyon European network of schools. IIL students, aged 3 to 19 years old, come from a wide variety of cultural and religious backgrounds and represent more than 90 countries. The school offers challenging and inspiring programmes with a strong emphasis on languages.

Within a warm, nurturing and bilingual environment, IIL Early Years welcomes children from 3 to 6 years old in three learning paths: English, French and Bilingual (50/50).

An IB World School, IIL is certified to teach the International Baccalaureate Diploma Programme. The school is also a Cambridge University examination centre and is a member of the GESBF (Groupement des Ecoles Suisses qui préparent au Baccalauréat Français).

Students in the French section follow the Education Nationale curriculum which leads to the Brevet des Collèges and French Baccalaureate diplomas and learn English from the age of 3. The French Baccalaureate programme is taught under the aegis of the Académie de Grenoble.

The school prepares students for Cambridge and IELTS examinations, as well as for a number of certified examinations in other languages.

In the English section, students follow the National Curriculum for England, sit Cambridge IGCSE examinations, and prepare for the IB Diploma with multilingual exam options. They also prepare for University Admission tests. Children are taught French as a foreign language from the age of 4 and mother-tongue French students take the A level French examination at age 16.

IIL strives to be at the forefront of innovative and appropriate digital learning technologies. In 2011, it became the first One-to-One iPad school in Switzerland, creating an individualised learning environment and a platform for clear information sharing between teachers, parents and students.

Students of all ages benefit from modern facilities including fully equipped sports halls. After-school supervision, as well as a wide variety of extra-curricular activities, are available for all age groups. IIL also operates a regular school bus service. In 2023, IIL was accredited as an Athlete Friendly Education Centre by the World Academy of Sport. This gives all students and staff access to the World Academy of Sport pedagogical resources and to their network of Olympians. In addition, older elite athletes at IIL can now benefit from the opportunity to complete their IB Diploma in three years rather than two, giving them more flexibility in their schedule.

Institut Montana

DP coordinator
Michael Meier

Status Private

Boarding/day Mixed

Gender Coeducational

Language of instruction
English, German

Authorised IB programmes
DP

Age Range 6 – 19 years

Number of pupils enrolled
380

Fees
Day: CHF32,900 – CHF36,800 per annum
Boarding: CHF70,400 – CHF72,800 per annum

Address
Schönfels 5
6300 Zug ZG | **SWITZERLAND**

TEL +41 41 729 11 77

Email
admissions@montana-zug.ch

Website
www.montana-zug.ch

Institut Montana was founded in 1926 by Dr Max Husmann. His humanist vision continues to guide us to help every student find their own individual path and thrive.

Learning, Personal Growth, Community

Our combination of small class sizes and individual support fosters a family atmosphere that builds up enthusiasm for learning and motivation to excel. Our international school community is highly diverse yet also promotes typically Swiss values, such as a strong work ethic, respect for each other and dedication to achieving excellence. We are a fully accredited Swiss international boarding school. Since 1987 we have been an official IB World School.

A central location in a natural setting

Our 60 acres campus, at an altitude of 950m, offers seclusion and contact with nature while benefitting from its proximity to Switzerland's major cities Zug and Zurich and the rich opportunities they offer.

The Pursuit of Excellence

Students have the opportunity to choose the academic path that suits their interests and aspirations. We offer (grades 1-12) the best of Swiss and international educational programmes, carefully structured to ensure the highest standards of teaching and learning: Swiss Bilingual Elementary, Secondary and Senior High School, as well as International Cambridge CLSP, IGCSE, IB Diploma programmes and High School Diploma.

Home at School

Life at Montana is unique: we breathe mountain air, drink our own spring water and eat fresh food that accommodates all dietary restrictions. Our daily routine promotes self-responsibility while maintaining a well-balanced, active lifestyle.

Summer Sessions

Our summer school is about combining learning with fun. Intensive classes in English and German dramatically improve the language level, while exciting afternoon workshops bring learning to life. Students from all over the world join us every year for a summer adventure filled with outdoor activities on the beautiful Zugerberg.

Empowering Students

We want our students to grow into confident adults who will make the most of their life. Our extracurricular activities encourage them to pursue their passion, whether that is athletic, intellectual or cultural. Our students participate in athletic competitions, Model United Nations conferences, entrepreneurship programmes, theatre productions and more. Our students are global citizens supporting charity projects within Switzerland and around the world.

Montana for Life

We are a vibrant community with strong connections that continue across years as across continents. From scientists to politicians and film directors, our alumni are a diverse group of passionate people who share the same background and values.

(Founded 1960)

Head of School
Lucy M. Gowdie

Secondary Principal
James Penstone

Primary Principal
Nathaniel Atherton

PYP coordinator
Claire Febrey

MYP coordinator
Graham Gardner

DP coordinator
Alexandra Carlin

Status Private

Boarding/day Day

Gender Coeducational

Language of instruction
English

Authorised IB programmes
PYP, MYP, DP

Age Range 18 months – 18 years

Number of pupils enrolled
800+

Fees
Day: CHF12,220 – CHF37,550 per annum

Address
Strubenacher 3
8126 Zumikon | SWITZERLAND

TEL +41 44 919 8300

Email
contact@icsz.ch

Website
www.icsz.ch

School Description
The Inter-Community School Zurich (ICS) is the longest-established international school in the Zurich area. A private co-educational day school, established in 1960, we provide a world-class international education for students aged 18 months to 18 years.

Our language of instruction, in a multilingual context, is English. Our 'English as an Additional language' (EAL) programme supports students with limited English. All students learn German, the language of our host country.

Students undertake the full IB Diploma. As well as offering the full IB Diploma to all students, ICS champions excellence in Sports and Arts and offers students a broad range of exciting extra – curricular opportunities alongside the academic IB programme.

Learning Beyond the Classroom
ICS believes that learning beyond the classroom, as well as within, adds value to a rigorous educational experience. We offer collaborative and innovative extra-curricular activities to inspire and engage students.

Service Learning, both locally and internationally, is a key component of the ICS curriculum. Students are constantly encouraged to look beyond themselves. As a Round Square member school, ICS offers students opportunities to join Round Square Service initiatives.

Zurich, Switzerland
With vast natural and cultural resources, Switzerland is a perfect environment for "learning through doing". By deliberately structuring authentic learning experiences outside the classroom, we foster students' holistic development. Field trips are an integral part of learning at ICS, giving students the chance to apply their learning, broaden their horizons and develop leadership and independence.

Admissions
As an international school, we welcome students of all nationalities; we currently have students from 50+ countries here.

We welcome applications from prospective students throughout the year. Please contact us at contact@icsz.ch if you have any questions or if you would like to arrange a visit.

Location
We are conveniently located on a single campus, situated near the Zurich city centre and easily accessed by public transportation. We also offer a school bus service.

International Bilingual School of Provence

(Founded 1984)

General Director
Jean-Marc Gobbi

DP coordinator
Pablo Besozzi

Status Private

Boarding/day Mixed

Gender Coeducational

Language of instruction
English, French

Authorised IB programmes
DP

Age Range 2 – 18 years

Number of pupils enrolled
1200

Fees
Day: €12,000 – €18,000 per annum
Boarding: €25,000 – €33,000 per annum

Address
500 Route de Bouc-Bel-Air
Domaine des Pins, Luynes
Aix en Provence
13080 | FRANCE

TEL +33 (0)4 4224 0340

Email
info@ibsofprovence.com

Website
www.ibsofprovence.com

The International Bilingual School of Provence, an independent coeducational school located near Aix-en-Provence in the south of France, owes its international character to the diversity of its student population. The school, established since 1984, has an annual enrolment of more than 900 students from more than 75 different countries in its day and boarding sections. In addition to the French students who make up 50% of the student population, IBS welcomes pupils from the five continents desiring to pursue their education in English, French or both.

A particularity of the school is that the international section is not dominated by any one nationality and new students are made to feel at home immediately. Committed to French-English bilingualism, the school offers both the International Baccalaureate Diploma Programme and the French Baccalaureate. The school also offers seven first languages to ensure that the student maintains his/her own language skills.

Philosophy

Small classrooms, qualified teachers, modern facilities in a tranquil, calm environment help ensure the success of each student. IBS of Provence recently invested in a new 7000m2 state-of-the-art campus which includes a sports complex, four new tennis courts (2 hard surface, 2 synthetic clay), football field, indoor gymnasium, 400+ seat auditorium for theatre performances and international conferences as well as a three-level academic building with fully equipped laboratories, art rooms, library, multi-media room and rooftop terrace.

The school also has a boarding section with 150 students residing in one of the six boarding houses which offer a home-like atmosphere in a beautiful Provençal setting.

Involvement in various extracurricular activities is expected and enhances the development of each individual's character within the spirit of the school. Politeness, respect and consideration for others are important values at IBS.

Students leave IBS, the majority for 1st choice university placements, as caring, responsible young citizens.

Summer school

During the spring and summer holidays, IBS offers intensive French as a Foreign Language and English immersion programmes. Over 600 students from all over the world join IBS every summer to develop their language skills while discovering the beauty of the Provence region. For more information about our summer program, please contact stages@ibsofprovence.com.

Admissions

We accept applications for admission to our school year round based on availability. There is no formal entrance exam but students must submit two years' of school reports, a letter of recommendation from a teacher/Head of School as well as a letter of motivation. For more information about admissions or to schedule a tour of the school, please contact admissions@ibsofprovence.com.

International School Altdorf

Executive Dean
Francesco Masetti Placci

Academic Coordinator
Nicoletta Scalabrin

Director of University Counseling
John Blake

Status Private

Boarding/day Mixed

Gender Coeducational

Language of instruction
English

Authorised IB programmes
DP, CP

Age Range 13 – 19 years

Number of pupils enrolled 100

Fees
CHF40,000 – CHF70,000 per annum

Address
St. Josefsweg 15
6460 Altdorf UR | SWITZERLAND

TEL +41 41 874 0000

Email
admission@lisa.swiss, info@lisa.swiss

Website
www.lisa.swiss

About our school

With over 40 nationalities, International School Altdorf is an inclusive and diverse community located in the central part of Switzerland.

The school builds on the tradition of Swiss boarding education, with a special focus on academic excellence to offer a challenging course of studies.

Our school hosts over 40 nationalities on campus and our experienced and accomplished international teachers help students earn globally recognized qualifications to attend excellent universities at home or abroad.

Academics at international School Altdorf

We know that "IB students develop strong academic, social and emotional characteristics."

At International School Altdorf, students enjoy flexibility when choosing their courses: we offer a very large number of subjects in all programs and grades to ensure that students can follow their academic interest and talent. Our unique combination of small class sizes, tailored academic programs and individual support creates a family atmosphere and builds up the enthusiasm of students for personalized learning and academic excellence.

The school offers the IB Diploma Programme and the IB Career-related Programme, each lasting for two years, in grades 11 and 12. In lower grades, we offer different authorized pathways for learners adapted to a wide range of abilities and interests, including those whose first language is not English. We encourage students to engage with a variety of topics, focusing on interdisciplinarity, research and inquiry.

We are also an accredited partner for TOEFL and IELTS testing and of the United Nations World Tourism Organization Academy in Switzerland.

University Acceptance

The IB curricula, the academic focus and the support of our University Counsellor at International School Altdorf offer the best preparation for students to continue their academic journey into the university of their choice.

The last four cohorts of graduating students have all mostly obtained bilingual diplomas with scores well above the world average. Over 50% of our students have received offers from the top 50 universities in the world's university ranking, and several alumni have been accepted to the top universities in the United Kingdom, United States, Canada, Hong Kong, Singapore, Australia and Switzerland.

Campus life

At International School Altdorf, we encourage students to actively participate and challenge themselves outside of the classroom! Students are thus instilled with a sense of responsibility, even in extracurricular activities, in sports and in community projects.

Students have access to a range of extracurricular activities on campus, from facilities for many sports to even a student-run animal shelter. Our school is located close to Swiss Alps and Lake Lucerne, thus outdoor activities are part of the weekend life, from hiking to skiing, from golf to swimming and rowing. Students are also supported to create their own clubs and the range evolves from year to year.

(Founded 1979)

Director
Bradley Roberts

Senior School Principal
Ian Hoke

Middle School Principal
Tara Waudby

Junior School Principal
Michelle Phillips

PYP coordinator
Emily McCaughan

MYP coordinator
Siân Thomas

DP coordinator
David Griffiths

Status Private

Boarding/day Day

Gender Coeducational

Language of instruction
English; German (Junior School)

Authorised IB programmes
PYP, MYP, DP

Age Range 3 – 19 years

Number of pupils enrolled
1350

Address
Fleischbachstrasse 2
4153 Reinach | **SWITZERLAND**

TEL +41 61 715 33 33

Email info@isbasel.ch

Website www.isbasel.ch

Mission:

"We all want to learn more;
We all do it in different ways;
We all have fun learning;
We all help."
- ISB Student

ISB is a private, not-for-profit, co-educational day school established in 1979. We are an IB World School offering the PYP, MYP and DP programmes for children 3-19 years old, in English and in English/German in Junior School. ISB offers students a broad and holistic programme, including a strong academic curriculum blended with a wide range of co-curricular activities to allow every student to follow their passion and develop their unique talent.

We believe that true education neither ends nor begins in the classroom alone. Our vision is to prepare students to flourish and impact their world, by providing them with positive and satisfying learning experiences, and helping them develop a deeper purpose to serve something greater than themselves.

ISB is an inclusive and non-selective school, with students and teachers coming from all corners of the world, creating a diverse and inclusive community. We live our Mission every day in every area of the school, as it reminds us to appreciate our learning differences, help each other out, and in our quest for excellence, find a way to make it fun and engaging.

Campuses
Our three campuses, located on the outskirts of the city of Basel, provide students with world-class learning opportunities. An efficient public transport system and convenient pedestrian and bicycle paths ensure easy access to ISB campuses. Age-appropriate and supportive learning environments encourage students' potential and nurture their talents at all stages of intellectual, physical and emotional development, providing them with the means to grow and thrive.

Inclusion
At ISB, every student is unique and so is the way they learn. ISB embraces equity, diversity and inclusion, not only in gender, race or culture, but also in the learning profiles of our students. We align student needs with appropriate resources and the individual support they need to develop their individual strengths and areas for growth.

Academic Results
In 2023, 107 students completed the full Diploma. 99% of students were awarded the full Diploma (compared with a world average of 80%). These students achieved an average score of 35 points (out of a maximum of 45 points), compared to a world average of 30 points. 7 students followed a modified programme, including 35 individual DP Courses, scoring an average of 4.3 points per course (out of a maximum of 7 points). ISB students have an excellent record of admissions into universities around the world, including many of the world's Top 20 universities.

International School Brescia

(Founded 2009)

Head of Primary
Ms Rachel Bestow

Head of Secondary
Ms Anne Vollmer

PYP coordinator
Mr Michael Lawson

MYP coordinator
Mr Ethan Taomae

DP coordinator
Mr Sebastiaan Van den Bergh

Status Private

Boarding/day Day

Gender Coeducational

Language of instruction
English

Authorised IB programmes
PYP, MYP, DP

Age Range 3 – 19 years

Number of pupils enrolled
206

Address
Via Benaco 34/B
Bedizzole
25080 Brescia | ITALY

TEL +39 030 2191182

Email
info@isbrescia.com

Website
www.isbrescia.com

WhatsApp
+39 3928970458

Teaching and learning at International School Brescia is about preparing our students in a global community to have the skills, the knowledge and the capacity to problem solve that will enable them to meet the challenges of the future. With a strong emphasis on developing the IB Learner Profile, and by learning through inquiry, action and reflection our students acquire in-depth knowledge and become deep thinkers.

ISB is a co-educational private day school located close to Lake Garda in the province of Brescia, Italy. Founded in 2009 we are a fully authorised International Baccalaureate (IB) continuum school offering the Primary Years Programme (PYP), Middle Years Programme (MYP) and the Diploma Programme (DP).

ISB offers our students the best possible international education in a supportive and inclusive, caring environment. Principled IB learners are honest and fair and take responsibility for their own learning and actions and our students are guided to act with integrity.

Our open-minded and respectful culture encourages the whole school community to contribute to the teaching and learning in school and this collaboration and involvement makes our school a very welcoming and special place to learn.

Our student body is made up of around 22 nationalities and we cultivate a truly international outlook whilst fostering knowledge and experience of our host country, Italy. English is our language of instruction, and we provide support for those students joining us, who have limited knowledge, to be communicators.

In addition to delivering the IB subjects, our balanced curriculum provides many opportunities for extra-curricular experiences such as workshops, field trips, sporting exchanges and international travel. We support out of school interests and commitments and motivate our students to be active members of the community.

As ISB grows and develops we continue to reflect on our practices and to participate in the wider IB world community to produce a positive impact on student learning outcomes.

International School of Amsterdam

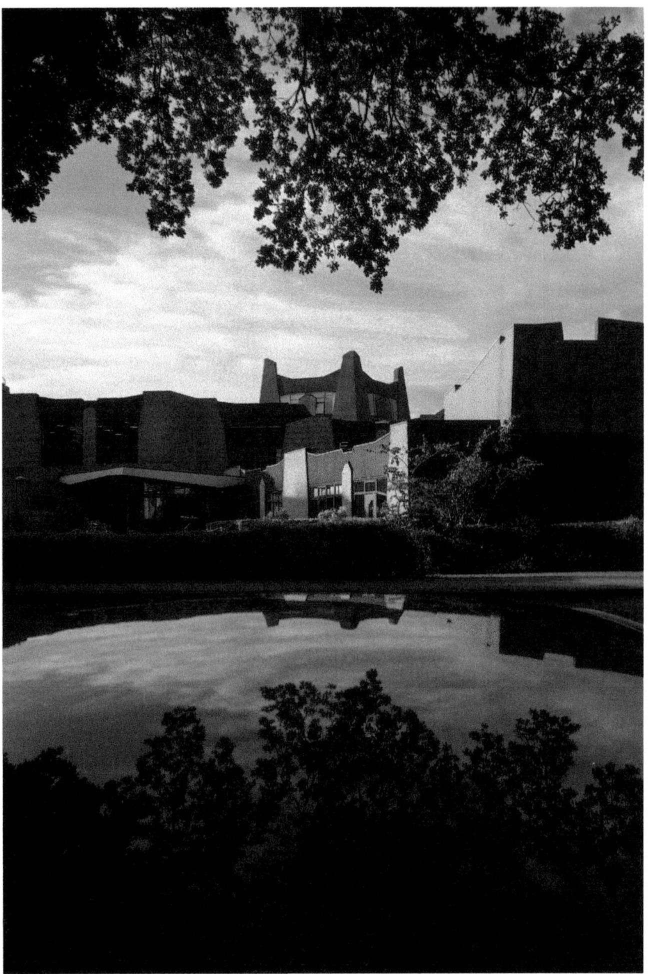

(Founded 1964)

Director
Dr. Bernadette Carmody

PYP coordinator
Lisa Verkerk

MYP coordinator
Yvonne Cross

DP coordinator
Matt Lynch

Status Private

Boarding/day Day

Gender Coeducational

Language of instruction
English

Authorised IB programmes
PYP, MYP, DP

Age Range 2 – 18 years

Number of pupils enrolled
1256

Fees
Day: €19,900 – €28,565 per annum

Address
Sportlaan 45
1185 TB Amstelveen, North Holland | **NETHERLANDS**

TEL +31 20 347 1111

Email
admissions@isa.nl

Website
www.isa.nl

The International School of Amsterdam is a globally-recognised leader in educating for international understanding. Founded in 1964, ISA was the first school in the world to offer all core IB programmes. Located in the green city of Amstelveen, ISA offers state-of-the-art facilities to students between the ages of 2 to 18, representing over 60 nationalities.

Through innovation, and with an open-minded approach, we inspire our students to be resilient, respectful global citizens and encourage them to find their individual paths to personal success. Our strengths lie within our diverse community, world-class faculty and facilities, and innovative teaching practices of a challenging academic curriculum.

ISA believes in developing minds, character and communities.

Developing Minds
- Inquiry and Reflection
- Critical and Creative Thinking
- Curiosity and Open-Mindedness
- Professional Development

Developing Characters
- Respect and Collaboration
- Integrity and Compassion
- Choices and Risks
- Balances Lives

Developing Communities
- Unity in Diversity
- Sustainable Futures
- Strong Connections
- Empathy

(Founded 1979)

Head of School
Mr. Wayne Johnson

DP coordinator
Ms Pauline Kimman

Status Private

Boarding/day Day

Gender Coeducational

Language of instruction
English

Authorised IB programmes
DP

Age Range 3 – 18 years

Number of pupils enrolled 240

Fees
Day: €11,000 – €20,100 per annum

Address
Kontichsesteenweg 40
2630 Aartselaar, Antwerp |
BELGIUM

TEL +32 3 271 0943

Email
info@isbedu.be

Website
www.isbedu.be/

Mission – *Dream. Achieve. Celebrate. Unite.*

Location

International School of Belgium (ISBe) is a private, fee paying, not for profit International School which is located in the small town of Aartselaar, about 10km south of the city of Antwerp. While the school has strong ties to the local Aartselaar community, our student population comes from Antwerp, Mechelen and Brussels.

Internationalism

While English is the main language of instruction, Belgium is a multilingual country and as such, ISBe supports the importance of learning the host country's languages of Dutch and French. Additional foreign languages can be offered through an online programme.

Demographics

As a small school from preschool to Class 12, students experience a very personalised education. We are an international community with a diverse student population representing more than 30 nationalities. Our faculty is also very diverse and draws from countries all over the world.

Activities and Experiences

Students are afforded access to a range of opportunities to enhance their learning programme:

- sporting teams and tournaments
- drama/music productions and art exhibitions
- educational excursions, residential trips and the
- Duke of Edinburgh award scheme and MUN conferences
- leadership roles through student council and the House system
- community events
- extensive co-curricular programme after school

University Pathways

The IBDP provides the perfect passport for university entry worldwide. Commonly our students attend first choice universities in the UK, Belgium, The Netherlands and Asia. However, our alumni have attended universities in the USA and many other European countries.

We have a university and careers counsellor available to senior school students who advises them on and assists them with university choices, applications and processes. We also organise a variety of university fairs and talks each year to ensure that students are exposed to a range of options. Students also get a chance to explore the world of employment through our internship programme.

International School of Bergamo

Heads of School
Mrs. Guia Ghidoli &
Mrs. Chiara Traversi

Head of Primary
Roisin Cosgrove

Head of Secondary
Roberta Sana

PYP coordinator
Helen Bird

MYP coordinator
Russell Wilson

DP coordinator
Roberta Sana

Status Private

Boarding/day Day

Gender Coeducational

Language of instruction
English, Italian

Authorised IB programmes
PYP, MYP, DP

Age Range 2 – 18 years

Number of pupils enrolled
400

Address
Via Monte Gleno, 54
24125 Bergamo | ITALY

TEL +39 035 213776

Email
info@isbergamo.com

Website
www.isbergamo.com

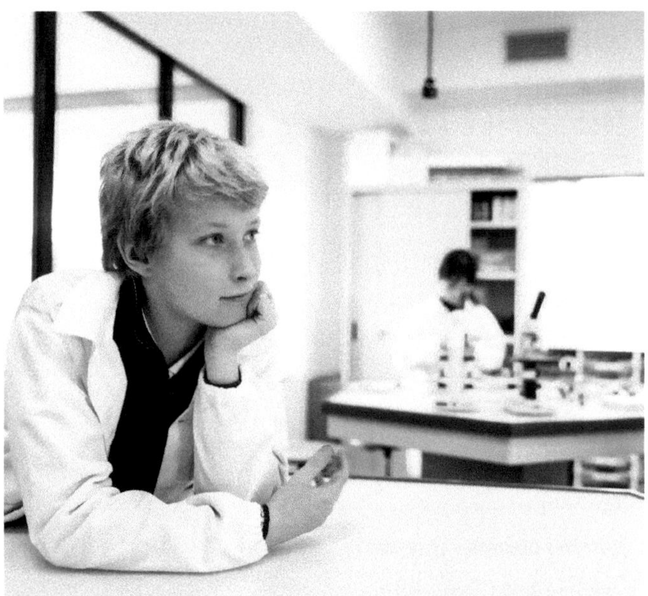

Founded in 2011, the International School of Bergamo (ISBergamo) is part of the Inspired Education Group, a leading global schools group educating over 80,000 students across a network of more than 111 schools. Committed to delivering high quality educational programmes, ISB strives to develop the intellectual, personal, emotional and social skills needed to live, learn and work in a rapidly globalising world.

The school is authorised to offer the Primary Years, Middle Years and Diploma Programmes, providing an International Baccalaureate continuum education.

Joining ISBergamo offers a fantastic opportunity to enter a safe and nurturing environment, where the Italian culture is valued alongside the recognition and appreciation of a multicultural collective diversity. Technology plays an important role in the school and is embedded in the school curriculum through a blended approach where we feel it adds value to teaching and learning.

In our state-of-the-art campus, of around 15,000 sqm, students can benefit from specialised facilities, including a dedicated Early Years area, an Art & Design Lab, a school library, a cafeteria and an extensive outdoor area with a modern football pitch, a multipurpose sports facility, and fully equipped playgrounds.

Recent additions to the facility include a Secondary School wing with specialised Science Laboratories, a Music, Drama & Dance studio, an Innovation Lab, and a newly expanded indoor gym.

The school is located in the Eastern part of Bergamo, in a green and quiet environment rich in sporting facilities; rugby fields, an indoor climbing wall and an athletics track can be found just at the end of the road.

Thanks to an efficient bus service, the school covers the city of Bergamo as well as a large number of the surrounding communities.

(Founded 1996)

Head of Secondary School
Mr. Serdar Sakman

DP coordinator
Mr. Yusuf Suha Orhan

Status Private

Boarding/day Day

Gender Coeducational

Language of instruction
English

Authorised IB programmes
DP

Age Range 2 – 18 years

Number of pupils enrolled
650

Address
1R Gara Catelu Str., Sector 3
Bucharest 032991 | **ROMANIA**

TEL +40 21 3069530

Email
admissions@isb.ro

Website
www.isb.ro

International School of Bucharest: Empowering Minds, Shaping Futures

Welcome to the International School of Bucharest (ISB), where we have been fostering excellence in education and a commitment to the ideals of the International Baccalaureate for over two decades. Since its founding in 1996, ISB has grown to become one of the largest and most successful international schools in Romania.

As a private institution, we are committed to fostering an environment where students from diverse backgrounds come together to embrace the principles of the IB and to flourish as responsible global citizens.

Our Commitment to the IB Mission and Vision

At the International School of Bucharest, we are proud to offer the IB Diploma Programme, which aligns seamlessly with our mission and vision to provide each student with a broad, balanced education in a safe and supportive environment. We believe in nurturing well-rounded individuals who not only excel academically but also embody the IB learner profile. Our commitment to the IB programme ensures that students develop the skills, knowledge, and attitudes needed to thrive in a rapidly changing world.

Enriching Lives Through Education

Our school is more than just a place of learning; it's a vibrant, multicultural community that thrives on diversity and inclusivity. With a passionate team of educators, ISB is fully committed to providing an exemplary international education that spans from ages 2 to 18.

Together with the IB, we inspire our students to be inquisitive, empathetic, and responsible members of society.

Our Sixth Form has a significant rate of acceptance from the top universities in the UK- Russell Group, the USA and the Netherlands.

As our students venture into the next chapter of their lives, we have full confidence that our graduates will continue to shine and contribute meaningfully to society.

Head of School
Mr Gavin Williams

PYP coordinator
Wietse Hendriks

MYP coordinator
Ben Thompson

DP coordinator
Adele Evans

Status Private

Boarding/day Day

Gender Coeducational

Language of instruction
English, Italian

Authorised IB programmes
PYP, MYP, DP

Age Range 2 – 18 years

Number of pupils enrolled 424

Address
Via Adda 25
22073 Fino Mornasco (CO) | ITALY

TEL +39 031 572289

Email
info@iscomo.com

Website
www.iscomo.com

Founded in 2002, the International School of Como (ISC) has grown to stand for excellence and has contributed to the expansion of international education in Northern Italy, as one of the almost 5,000 International Baccalaureate (IB) schools located worldwide. Today, ISC welcomes over 424 students from 2 to 18 years old of 46 nationalities and an international staff of more than 60 qualified teachers and assistants.

ISC is committed to providing children with the best educational experience possible. ISC offers the IB (International Baccalaureate) Primary Years, Middle Years and Diploma Programmes and aspires to create a community where learning is the central driving factor of a journey in which our students become ethical thinkers, creative problem-solvers, community-minded and individuals of action on the world stage.

Our state-of-the-art campus was designed and built specifically for our students and provides for every aspect of a vibrant, innovative and rigorous education. Over 10,000 square metres of internal and external spaces house our extremely large classrooms, a Robotics lab, two Art Studios, 3 fully-equipped Science Laboratories, A Drama Studio, a well-stocked Library, an indoor gym and outdoor multipurpose sports facility, cafeteria and playgrounds. Recent additions to the facility include an IBDP Study Centre and our 'CoLab', which is a shared work area / coffee bar.

With our efficient bus service we can cover a large number of the surrounding communities, and beyond, including: Como, Lecco, Varese, and Lugano (Switzerland).

At ISC we are driven by our Mission Statement which is: *"The International School of Como is a student-centered community of internationally-minded learners. We offer a balanced and challenging curriculum, in a safe and nurturing environment, where we respect and value the Italian culture and our collective diversity. We empower all students to be active, reflective and responsible lifelong learners who can achieve their full potential and contribute to an ever-changing world."*

International School of Islamabad

Superintendent
Ms Rose Puffer

Principal
Timothy Musgrove

Principal
Riffat Hassan

PYP coordinator / Assistant Principal
Mary Frances Penton

DP coordinator
Dora Flores

Status Private

Boarding/day Day

Gender Coeducational

Language of instruction
English

Authorised IB programmes
PYP, DP

Age Range 2 – 19 years

Number of pupils enrolled 315

Address
Sector H-9/1, Johar Road
P.O. Box 1124
Islamabad
44000 | PAKISTAN

TEL +92 51 443 4950

Email
school@isoi.edu.pk;
registrar@isoi.edu.pk

Website
www.isoi.edu.pk

The International School of Islamabad (ISOI) is a private, coeducational, college-preparatory day school. ISOI offers an inquiry-based curriculum to students of approximately 50 nationalities. The school operates on the semester system and is accredited by Middle States Association of Colleges and Schools. ISOI is an IB World School, offering the International Baccalaureate Diploma (IBDP) in grades 11/12. ISOI is also an IB PYP school. ISOI was founded in 1965. The campus is located on 23+ acres on the outskirts of Islamabad, Pakistan. The campus includes Elementary School, Middle School and High School quads, a gym, an auditorium, an open-air theater, an IB art gallery, a physical education center, tennis courts, a climbing wall, a running track, playing fields, a swimming pool, two libraries and two technology centers. Students are admitted on the basis of previous academic records, standardized test scores, a writing sample and verification of the need for an international, English curriculum.

The school year runs from August to early June and is divided into two semesters. The first semester runs from August to December and the second semester runs from January to June. The school follows a two week, rotating block schedule.

Vision

The International School of Islamabad inspires open collaboration to create a student-centered, inquiry-based learning environment that cultivates enthusiastic and globally-minded individuals.

Mission

The International School of Islamabad ensures that each student strives for academic success, develops intellectual curiosity, and becomes a responsible global citizen.

(Founded 1972)

Principal
Mr Richard Parker

Primary Principal
Ms Kathryn Firebrace

Secondary Principal
Ms Elise Furr

PYP coordinator
Ms Emily Loughead

MYP coordinator
Mr David Slaney

DP coordinator
Dr El Kahina Meziane

Status Private

Boarding/day Day

Gender Coeducational

Language of instruction
English & Home language programme

Authorised IB programmes
PYP, MYP, DP

Age Range 3 – 18 years

Number of pupils enrolled 420

Fees
Day: £22,100 – £30,730 per annum

Address
139 Gunnersbury Avenue
London **W3 8LG | UK**

TEL +44 (0)20 8992 5823

Email mail@isllondon.org

Website www.isllondon.org

Having celebrated its 50th anniversary last year, the International School of London (ISL) is an established International Baccalaureate (IB) World School with an integrated home language programme for over 20 languages, delivering educational excellence for ages 3-18. Our school has earned a global reputation as a highly successful IB school and is widely recognised as one of the UK's best international schools.

We offer an exceptional world of learning for every student. Starting with a genuinely warm welcome to our multicultural environment from our award-winning Transitions team, we work with each child to devise an individual learning programme tailored to their unique needs and goals. Our focus on student wellbeing, in a supportive environment, is complemented in the classroom by dynamic teaching practises. It's this approach that we believe leads to the academic and personal success that characterises ISL pupils.

We are a culturally diverse community. Students' cultural and linguistic identities are valued and nurtured through our curriculum and unique home language programme, that is embedded into the timetable. Our school develops the attitudes, skills and understanding needed to shape responsible, creative citizens of both local and global communities.

ISL has high academic standards, offering three IB programmes: the Primary Years, Middle Years and Diploma Programmes. These align to the unique developmental needs of students from nursery through to pre-university.

Located adjacent to the beautiful Gunnersbury Park, all primary students attend daily Forest School, year-round. We are committed to intercultural education, extending our students' learning beyond the confines of the classroom and into both the park and the wonderfully rich culture of London. With our fantastic new Sports Hub, local astroturf pitches and tennis courts we offer students a huge variety of sports activities, alongside many opportunities in service learning and the arts that challenge our students to grow and develop, through innovative, inter-disciplinary projects that stretch minds and encourage curiosity. The breadth and depth of our programmes ensure our graduates are prepared for life at leading universities worldwide, as well as for exciting futures across the spectrum of careers.

ISL is a relatively small school with a distinct family atmosphere, giving a voice to all members of our community, with active parent groups and a committed student government. Students at ISL develop a keen sense of intercultural understanding, greatly valued in our globalised world. ISL actively celebrates this diversity throughout the year in class activities and whole school events.

International School of London (ISL) Qatar

(Founded 2008)

Head of School
Dr. Sean Areias

PYP coordinator
Danielle Robertson

MYP coordinator
Moneeb Minhas

DP coordinator
Smita Shetty

Status Private

Boarding/day Day

Gender Coeducational

Language of instruction
English

Authorised IB programmes
PYP, MYP, DP

Age Range 3 – 18 years

Number of pupils enrolled
1190

Fees
QR54,436 – QR77,766 per annum

Address
PO Box 18511
North Duhail
Doha | QATAR

TEL +974 4433 8600

Email
mail@islqatar.org

Website
www.islqatar.org

Founded in 2008, The International School of London (ISL) Qatar is an International Baccalaureate (IB) World School, authorised to offer the IB Primary Years, Middle Years and Diploma Programmes.

Having deeply embedded our core values of Belonging, Integrity, Grit, and Kindness, ISL Qatar has developed a strong presence both locally and internationally as a pioneering educational institution, that is continually exploring the process of learning and considering what constitutes effective learning. ISL Qatar has an outstanding reputation for high academic standards with its prestigious International Baccalaureate (IB) programme.

With over 80 student nationalities from ages 3-18 and over 50 staff nationalities ISL Qatar is a truly International School sharing a legacy of over 50 years with its sister school in London. The IB curriculum fulfils the school's vision of combining intellectual rigour and high academic standards with a strong emphasis on the ideals of international mindedness and responsible global citizenship.

ISL Qatar's unique and pioneering multilingualism programme is a particular highlight of the school, as ISL Qatar is the only school in Qatar to offer Mother Tongue Programmes in 12 languages, with additional languages being developed each academic year. ISL Qatar is focused upon the students' cultural and linguistic identities as part of the learning experience, valuing these as an integral part of being a member of the learning community. This facet of inclusion strives to maintain the home culture and language, fostering parental engagement and supporting the academic performance of our young learners.

Contact us to learn more. ISL Qatar... Where Every Child Finds Their Place.

Principal
Mr. Tom Vignoles

PYP coordinator
Sara Lomas

MYP coordinator
Eglė Karmonaitė

DP coordinator
Giuseppe Redaelli

Status Private

Boarding/day Mixed

Gender Coeducational

Language of instruction
English

Authorised IB programmes
PYP, MYP, DP

Age Range 2 – 18 years
(Boarding 14-18 years)

Number of pupils enrolled
850

Address
Via I Maggio, 20
20021 Baranzate (MI) | **ITALY**

TEL +39 02 872581

Email
admissions@ismilan.it

Website
www.internationalschoolofmilan.it

Welcome to the International School of Milan (ISM).

ISM is proud of its position as the premier international IB school within the city. We are renowned for our high educational standards, caring learning environment, and world class facilities. We are a diverse community with over 50 nationalities and a student body that is proud of everything we do. We are the longest established international school in Milan, and our progressive educational thinking has served the international and Italian communities in Milan for over 60 years.

Our ethos of high achievement, coupled with diversity of opportunity, will enable your children to develop their confidence and be ready for the challenges of the future. The IB curriculum, which runs throughout the school, embraces internationalism and global citizenship, fitting the needs of students of all learning profiles. Our PYP, MYP and IB Diploma programmes thoroughly prepare our students for further study all around the world, including at the world's leading universities. Our academic results, including our students' final IBDP scores, are consistently above world averages.

Our dedicated international teaching community work with our students to support their well-being and guide them on their individual pathways. As a community, we embrace a growth mindset, ensuring that all students have the opportunity and motivation to aim high and achieve their dreams. Our students have agency over their learning, increasingly taking responsibility for their own personal development, and student leadership is very well developed. Our teachers embrace innovation and creativity, working with technology to enhance learning on a daily basis.

Facilities within our large and spacious campus are world class. Our students enjoy specialist music and drama facilities (including a theatre), a wide range of sport venues (including a swimming pool, gymnasium and football pitch), dedicated laboratories and libraries, alongside our well-furnished suite of classrooms. For students aged 14 or above, we also offer the option of joining our modern and vibrant boarding house for 42 students, where the care and attention provided by our staff team ensures a transformational educational and social experience for all.

As a school which caters for students from 2 to 18, our provision is very carefully differentiated to ensure that the needs of each student are well met. ISM will enable your child to thrive, whatever their profile and interests, through a unique holistic learning experience that is underpinned by the IB curriculum, our dedicated and innovative staff, our world-class facilities, and our very special international community. Please visit us at any time to see this for yourself.

International School of Modena

Head of School
Mr Paul Barrie

PYP coordinator
Michael Perry

MYP coordinator
Anna Chiara Forti

DP coordinator
Caroline Searle

Status Private

Boarding/day Day

Gender Coeducational

Language of instruction
English

Authorised IB programmes
PYP, MYP, DP

Age Range 3 – 18 years

Number of pupils enrolled
220

Address
Piazza Montessori, 1/A
41051 Montale Rangone (MO) |
ITALY

TEL +39 059 530649

Email
admissions@ismodena.it

Website
www.internationalschoolof
modena.it

Welcome to the International School of Modena. Celebrating 25 years of high quality education in the region, ISM started as a joint venture with Tetra Pak, whose global research and development unit is located in Modena. ISM is a proud member of Inspired which is the fastest growing premium international schools' group operating on 5 continents and educating over 45,000 students globally. Our modern, purpose-built campus, surrounded by green open spaces, is located 12km outside of the city of Modena.

We are a truly international school representing approximately 34 different nationalities and offering the full continuum of International Baccalaureate (IB) education, with the Primary Years Programme (PYP) for children ages 3-11, Middle Years Programme (MYP) for ages 11-16 and the Diploma Programme (DP) for 16-18 years. ISM is the first school in Emilia-Romagna to offer the IB Continuum, which will thoroughly prepare your child for study all around the globe, including at some of the world's leading universities.

Our innovative Early Years department features beautiful spaces and play structures specially designed to support the delivery of the IB PYP and Reggio-Inspired Early Years Curriculum.

The curriculum at ISM is carefully designed to reflect the ethos of the school and of the International Baccalaureate with a commitment to inquiry-based learning, encouraging every student to ask questions, to think for themselves and develop the skills to become confident, independent learners who will grow up to be balanced, caring and principled citizens. Our dedicated, international teaching body ensures that students achieve highly at the school. We believe in challenging young minds, ensuring that our focus is on every student achieving beyond expectations both inside and outside of the curriculum. Over the last three years we have achieved an average of 36 in the IB Diploma with a top score of 45 out of 45, allowing our students to access world class universities across the globe.

The International School of Modena is a small, friendly school, growing quickly due to its popularity with both expat and local families. We are proud to be a premium international school offering high quality education in a caring environment with happy, engaged students. We are certain that you will see that ISM is a place that celebrates learning and values each and every student, offering them a challenging, enjoyable education aimed at developing skills required for future success.

International School of Monaco

THE INTERNATIONAL
SCHOOL OF MONACO

(Founded 1994)

Director
Mr. Stuart Bryan MA Hons, PGCE, ACE, NPQEL, FCCT

DP coordinator
Jonathan Elliott

CP coordinator
Tania Leyland

Status Private

Boarding/day Day

Gender Coeducational

Language of instruction
English, French

Authorised IB programmes
DP, CP

Age Range 3 – 18 years

Number of pupils enrolled
800

Fees
Day €24,500 – €31,200 per annum

Address
10-12 Quai Antoine Premier
Monte Carlo
98000 | MONACO

TEL +377 9325 6820

Email
admissions@ismonaco.com

Website
ismonaco.com

Founded in 1994, the International School of Monaco (ISM) is an independent, co-educational, not-for-profit day school in Monaco. ISM is the only fully accredited international private school in the Principality of Monaco and today caters to 800 pupils aged from 3-18, drawn from over fifty nationalities.

In August 2020 the school signed a historic collaboration with King's College School, Wimbledon, as part of the school's aim to be among the best in Europe.

Driven by its vision of international education with distinction, ISM's mission is to provide an outstanding education for students so that they are happy, confident, independent, multilingual and responsible global citizens. The school's values emphasise integrity, learning, caring and respect, with strong emphasis placed on excellence, wellbeing and multilingualism as well as international mindedness and digital citizenship.

ISM offers a distinctive bilingual education in English and French for students in the Primary School (Kindergarten to Year 6), and from Year 7 onwards, the Secondary School offers a broad and balanced curriculum in English, leading to Cambridge IGCSE and the IB Diploma Programme or IB Career-related Programme qualifications. The school offers the IB Diploma Programme (IBDP) and the IB Career-related Programme (IBCP), as well as the Extended IBCP pathway, which allows high-performing student-athletes to complete the IBCP over a 3-year period instead of a 2-year period as part of ISM's accreditation as an Athlete Friendly Education Centre (AFEC) from the World Academy of Sport. The school is also an official candidate school for the IB Primary Years Programme (IB PYP) and IB Middle Years Programme (IB MYP).

Languages are an important part of the curriculum, with Spanish, Italian, Russian and German, in addition to French, on offer. Highly qualified teachers and support staff are recruited from around the world.

ISM provides an extensive programme of enrichment including sports, Model United Nations, an annual Arts Festival, the Duke of Edinburgh's International Award plus ABRSM and LAMDA music and drama qualifications. The school's unique location on the Côte d'Azur enables access to world-class museums and places of interest.

Outreach is an important element of school life, and students participate in a wide range of giving projects throughout the year via the school's philanthropy clubs, Student Senate initiatives, and the PTA, in partnership with local charities and environmental associations.

Pastoral care is a major priority for the school; an extensive PSHE (Personal, Social and Health Education) programme is delivered by teachers who receive regular training in child safeguarding, and a full-time Head of Wellbeing is supported by a wellbeing team including a school counsellor and psychologist.

ISM students are well-rounded, academically successful individuals who are admitted to top universities around the world, including in recent years University of Oxford and Harvard University. ISM graduates are already pursuing exciting careers in many diverse fields.

International School of Monza

(Founded 1984)

Head of School
Ms. Johanna Urquhart

PYP coordinator
Stacey Bennett

MYP coordinator
Vicki Mole

DP coordinator
Michela Giovannini

Status Private

Boarding/day Day

Gender Coeducational

Language of instruction
English, Italian

Authorised IB programmes
PYP, MYP, DP

Age Range 2.5 – 18 years

Number of pupils enrolled 320

Address
Via Solferino 23
20900 Monza (MB) | **ITALY**

TEL +39 039 9357701

Email
admin@ismonza.it

Website
www.internationalschoolof
monza.it

At ISMonza, a full International Baccalaureate (IB) continuum school authorised to offer the Primary Years Programme (PYP), Middle Years Programme (MYP) and Diploma Programme (DP), we endeavour to deliver the International Baccalaureate programmes in the purist of forms, with the school's core values and the IB's Learner Profile embodied in everything that we do. Both the school and the group to which it belongs, have an established record of success in the IB, from age 2 all the way through to admission to the world's leading universities at age 18. We also offer the MYP Certificate / eAssessments in addition to the MYP programme.

Perhaps most of note is the sense of collaboration that exists amongst all members of the school community. This is most evident in the way in which our highly qualified mother-tongue teachers and inquisitive students work towards a common goal of academic success which is seamlessly balanced with an inherent commitment to active global citizenship at every level. Although all classrooms are fitted with smart TVs and students bring tablets or laptops to school, we use technology in a blended approach where we feel it adds value to teaching and learning and not merely to replace traditional methods (yes, we do use books and, yes, we do talk to one another).

All this takes place in our city-centre campus – a stylish and colourful factory conversion – which has been specifically designed to foster collaborative approaches to teaching and learning. Our science laboratories are fitted with state-of-the-art equipment and we also boast carefully designed on-site spaces which support the delivery of our Reggio-Inspired Early Years Curriculum, three beautiful libraries, as well as studios for visual arts, drama and music, supported by a brand new sports complex. That said, living in such a culturally rich part of the world, we take many opportunities to knock down our classroom walls and learn from opportunities in the local and not-so-local area.

(Founded 1977)

Director
Mrs. Mel Curtis

PYP coordinator
Mrs. Joanne Brown

DP coordinator
Mr. Dominique Dubois

Status Private

Boarding/day Day

Gender Coeducational

Language of instruction
English

Authorised IB programmes
PYP, DP

Age Range 3 – 18 years

Number of pupils enrolled 472

Fees
Day: €11,400 – €22,140 per annum

Address
15 Avenue Claude Debussy
06200 Nice | **FRANCE**

TEL +33 (0)4 93 21 04 00

Email
admissions@isn-nice.com

Website
www.isn-nice.com

The International School of Nice is an accredited, co-educational, non-sectarian, IB World School, providing Anglophone education for the international community in the Cannes-Nice-Monaco region. The school offers a complete international education from Young Explorers (age 3) to Grade 12 (age 18). ISN Nice is a proud member of Globeducate.

The Primary School follows the IB Primary Years Programme, a rich, inquiry-based approach to learning that focuses on the individual needs of every child. French is mandatory from age 5, and taught on a daily basis. An EAL programme parallels mainstream English in the Primary and Middle Schools.

The Middle School is a candidate for the IB Middle Years Programme, with a particular focus on the social and emotional developments of students, as well as high academic standards.

The High School curriculum prepares students for the IGCSE exams, the IB Diploma, and the High School Diploma. Students are guided and supported to reach their potential in a safe and caring environment. A team of highly-qualified and experienced teachers respond to students' diverse learning styles and challenges them through exciting and innovative practices. Over 95% of graduates go directly to university, primarily in the UK, France and North America.

The faculty represents over 30 nationalities, and the student body is truly a melting pot, representing over 60 nationalities, with students from Anglophone countries making up ca.20%. This enables cultural awareness and participation in a globalised world for all our students.

The school year is from September through June with classes meeting from 08:30 to 16:00. There are a number of extra-curricular activities, including a variety of sports, Model United Nations, Student Council, and field trips.

The school occupies a purpose-built facility, which recently underwent an exciting renovation project, with specific areas for problem solving, analytical thinking, imagination and creativity, and digital skills. This is in keeping with the school's vision to prepare today's learners to confidently embrace challenges as adaptable, empathetic global citizens who will be active contributors to a more sustainable world.

International School of Siena

Principal
Ms. Jennifer Tickle

Deputy Principal
Ms. Letizia Rosati

PYP coordinator
Harnoop Bhogal

MYP coordinator
Leon Woods

DP coordinator
Jennifer Thomas

Status Private

Boarding/day Day

Gender Coeducational

Language of instruction
English, Italian

Authorised IB programmes
PYP, MYP, DP

Age Range 3 – 18 years

Number of pupils enrolled
200

Address
Via del Petriccio e Belriguardo, 49/1
53100 Siena | ITALY

TEL +39 0577 328103

Email
office@issiena.it

Website
www.internationalschoolofsiena.it

Founded in 2010, the International School of Siena has grown considerably in the past 12 years. We are the only IB through school in Tuscany, fully authorised for the Primary Years Programme (PYP), Middle Years Programme (MYP) and Diploma Programme (DP).

Learning at IS Siena is exciting and engaging, as students strive for excellence in a climate that is caring and responsive to individual needs and goals. Our global vision is coordinated by an outstanding team of educational leaders and implemented by our highly skilled and dedicated professional staff.

The school takes advantage of a purpose built building with 21st century technology where we enjoy a spacious, light, modern teaching spaces with a spacious indoor gym, Drama/Dance studio, Library, Music and Art rooms and Science laboratories fitted out to the highest standards. Our Early Years spaces are specially designed to complement the Reggio Inspired teaching approach. Our Inspired approach to PYP Early Years also draws inspiration from the Reggio Approach.

Learning at the International School of Siena is an international experience with students from around 23 nationalities. This leads to a perception of the world that merges understanding of our global context with the development of skills and attitudes that young people require to participate fully in the world of tomorrow, both as national and global citizens.

At the same time, we deeply appreciate the diversity of mother tongue languages in our school community and aim to utilise our diversity as well as supporting each student to appreciate our host country of Italy and become fully bilingual in English and Italian. We are so fortunate to be located in a beautiful area of Tuscany where we have access to a variety of cultural and educational resources in our local area which we strive to incorporate into the experience of the students, making connections between the classroom and the world around us.

We are a welcoming school community in which parents, students and staff work together to provide a stimulating programme, which engages each child in a concept-driven and inquiry-based environment.

International School of Ticino SA

Head of School
Mr. Andrew Ackers

PYP coordinator
Mr. Jamie Steele

MYP coordinator
Mrs. Kelly Leagas

DP coordinator
Mr. Graeme Wallbank

Status Private

Boarding/day Day

Gender Coeducational

Language of instruction
English, Italian

Authorised IB programmes
PYP, MYP, DP

Age Range 3 – 18 years

Number of pupils enrolled 270

Address
Via Ponteggia, 23
Cadempino
6814 Lugano | **SWITZERLAND**

TEL +41 919710344

Email
frontoffice@isticino.com

Website
www.isticino.com

The International School of Ticino is a special and exciting place to be. We are the first and only accredited International Baccalaureate (IB), Primary Years Programme (PYP) and Middle Years Programme (MYP) school in Ticino, Switzerland and also offers the Diploma Programme (DP).

At the International School of Ticino we place the student at the centre of all we do to facilitate them to become lifelong learners. We achieve this through our school culture, which is rooted in the IB Mission statement, which states: The International Baccalaureate aims to develop inquiring, knowledgeable and caring young people who help to create a better and more peaceful world through intercultural understanding and respect.

The school opened as a Kindergarten in 2014. It was established to offer the local and international residents of Ticino an IB education. As of 2017 the International school of Ticino joined the education group Inspired, who educate over 45000 students in 64 schools worldwide.

This grounding and combination with a leading education group has laid the foundations for the special community of learning which we see today in our new campus. The school now accommodates students from Kindergarten, 3 years old, to 18, offering the IB PYP, MYP and DP programme with our first graduation class in 2023.

The design and build of the new campus has drawn upon our foundations, the IB mission and the vision of the school; Inspiring the Extraordinary.

We accommodate our students in a facilitated student centred learning environment, where we equip all to develop in the international sector and in line with Ticino requirements, enabling your child to study at our school from the age of 3-18/19.

The International School of Ticino is a special and exciting place to be and we look forward to welcoming you to our community for a school visit, trial day and enrolment.

(Founded 1963)

Head of School
Lara Pazzi

PYP coordinator
Magdalena Matysow

MYP coordinator
Francesca Parisi

DP coordinator
Clara Siviero

Status Private

Boarding/day Day

Gender Coeducational

Language of instruction
English

Authorised IB programmes
PYP, MYP, DP

Age Range 3 – 18 years

Fees
Nursery & Pre Kindergarten
€8,300 per annum
Kindergarten
€10,000 per annum
IBPYP_Grade 1 to 5
€12,900 per annum
IBMYP_Grades 6 to 10
€15,900 per annum
IBDP_Grades 11 & 12
€18,400 per annum

Address
Strada Pecetto 34
10023 Chieri, Turin | **ITALY**

TEL +39 011 645 967

Email
info@isturin.it

Website
www.isturin.it

The International School of Turin is a private, non-profit organization school open to students from all over the world. Established in 1963 as the American School of Turin, it was refounded in 1974 as the American Cultural Association of Turin (ACAT) and in 2007 renamed as the International School of Turin (IST). Since its establishment, IST has been a point of reference for the international community as well as for local families wishing to raise their children to be ready for the challenges of today's global world.

Our mission is to "inspire lifelong learning and international mindedness, empowering each student to reach their full potential."

IST is an IB World School authorized to offer the IB full continuum of programs in English from Early Years to Grade 12: the Primary Years Programme (PYP), the Middle Years Programme (MYP) and the Diploma Programme (DP).

IST has also been accredited by CIS (Council of International Schools) and NEASC (New England Association of Schools and Colleges) since 1984.

The school's curriculum is international and leads to the completion of both the IST American High School Diploma and the IB Diploma, which is recognized by the Italian Ministry of Education as being legally equivalent to the Italian Maturità.

IST is the only international school in Piedmont to be granted Parità Scolastica (equivalency) by the Italian Ministry of Education for its Early Years and Primary sections.

As proof our school's commitment to sustainability, IST is also certified as a "Green School" by FEE – Foundation for Environmental Education. Our school garden and greenhouse provide endless teaching and learning opportunities for students of all grades to raise their awareness of this global issue.

IST is proud to be a non-selective school and as such we pride ourselves on a well-structured student support team to ensure all students equal opportunities to access the school curriculum and benefit from it. The English Language Learning is aimed at students whose level of English language knowledge requires further development to access regular class courses. The Learning Support team works with students who need additional support to help them develop skills and strategies that will enable them to work at their full potential.

IST's school counsellor is in charge of a school-wide advisory and counselling program and works alongside teachers to help students successfully develop their socio-emotional skills.

IST offers a university counselling service to guide students in their subject choices as well as supporting them with university applications and providing opportunities to learn more about the options available both locally and abroad.

Afterschool activities are an integral part of IST's academic offer and are aimed at promoting and supporting learning beyond the classroom. The IST Sports teams and the IST Orchestra are just two examples.

(Founded 2002)

CEO & Director
Liz Free

Head of Senior School
Oliver Beck

Head of Primary School
Catherine Trainor

PYP coordinator
Rheannon Elliott (Interim)

MYP coordinator
Andrew Shawcroft

DP coordinator
Vicki Hayward

Status Private, Non-Profit

Boarding/day Day

Gender Coeducational

Language of instruction
English

Authorised IB programmes
PYP, MYP, DP

Age Range 3 – 19 years

Number of pupils enrolled 185

Fees
Please see website: https://www.isr.ch/admissions/tuition-fees

Address
Werdenbergstrasse 17
9470 Buchs SG | SWITZERLAND

TEL +41 81 750 6300

Email
admissions@isr.ch

Website
www.isr.ch

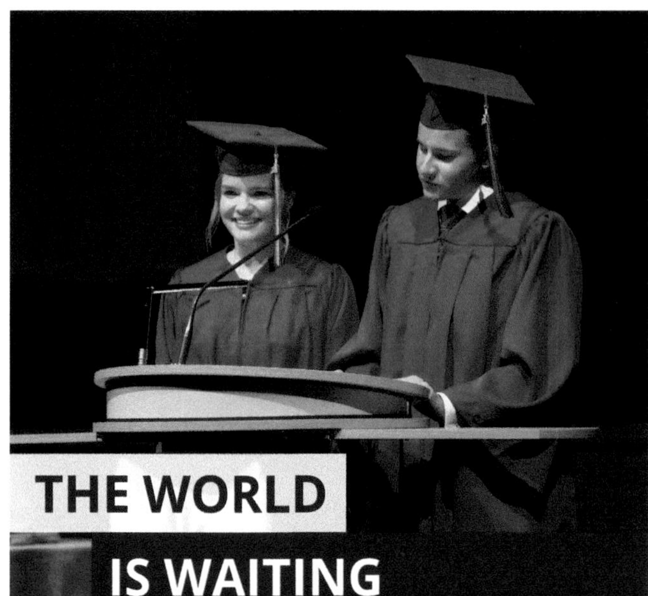

Welcome to the International School Rheintal (ISR)! We are the leading IB World School in the Rheintal region catering for ages 3-19 years. We strive to meet the needs of each and every student through a personalised education and individual support to reach their potential.

Why ISR

While academic excellence plays an important role at ISR and our Diploma students constantly score above the IB world average, the development of the student as a whole to become a responsible and engaged global citizen is at the centre of all we do.

Individual academic support, one-on-one EAL classes, school and career counselling and our welcoming, international community are strong features of our school.

We encourage students to take their learning beyond the classroom through programmes such as the Duke of Edinburgh's International Award and the Model United Nations.

Where We Are

Situated in the heart of the Rheintal, a beautiful part of Eastern Switzerland, we are surrounded by mountains and the Rhein with glorious views whilst being easily accessible by public transport or by car. Our ISR school bus conveniently connects the town of St. Gallen with the school. The nature surrounding us invites us to participate in diverse outdoor activities and is an integral part of our daily teaching and learning.

New School Campus

In summer 2023, ISR moved to a modern, ecologically-sustainable school campus. It was specifically designed for ISR's learning and teaching needs, with phased learning zones, versatile classrooms, science labs, specialist art and design studios, outdoor learning & lunch zones, and a competition-sized double gymnasium and workout gym.

How to join

As a non-selective school, our doors are open to all families with children from ages 3 to 19 sharing our vision and mission. We accept applications all year round and are happy to work with families to make the application process as simple as possible. Please contact us at admissions@isr.ch to ask your questions, to book a free tour or a trial day at any time.

(Founded 1980)

Principal
Júlia Ladeira Santos

PYP coordinator
Jenie Noite

MYP coordinator
Olga Put

Status Private

Boarding/day Day

Gender Coeducational

Language of instruction
English

Authorised IB programmes
PYP, MYP

Age Range 3 – 16 years

Number of pupils enrolled
250

Fees
Day: €5,700 – €10,950 per annum

Address
Caminho dos Saltos 6
9050-219 Funchal, Madeira |
PORTUGAL

TEL +351 291 773 218

Email
office@madeira.sharingschool.org

Website
www.sharingschool.org

The International Sharing School is a highly respected school on the lovely island of Madeira, Portugal. The school offers the PYP and the MYP programmes, teaching students aged 3 to 16, currently representing 23 different nationalities and with teachers from 8 different countries, in an international, multilingual and multicultural environment.

With 40 years of experience in international education, International Sharing School offers both the PYP and MYP, thus being the only IB World School in Madeira offering both programmes.

We are dedicated to achieving enjoyment and excellence in education for all.

As we continue to follow our ethos statement – "The passion of learning, the pride of teaching" – International Sharing School aims to provide an excellent and continuous international educational experience, in order to develop enquiring knowledgeable and caring young people who help create a better and more peaceful world through intercultural understanding and respect.

International Sharing School offers a curriculum focused on personal and professional development, preparing students for an increasingly global, competitive, multicultural and multilingual world.

Students begin their school learning at 3 years of age in a bilingual environment, with educators who are English and Portuguese native speakers, so that by the age of 6 they enter PYP 1 with a sound billingual foundation. The language of instruction throughout the school is English and we offer daily lessons of the host country's language, Portuguese, for all students. In addition, the academic curriculum includes the teaching of German, Spanish, French, Mandarin and Russian. Students, therefore, are able to move to upper secondary and university education, having had the opportunity to learn, with a great degree of fluency, at least 5 of the 7 languages we offer.

We are very proud of our learning-journey and the traditions we have created. We are innovative and always strive to reflect the best of current practices and adapt to the demands of an ever-changing world.

Choosing a school is one of the most important decisions and has high significance as a long-term family investment. We offer a happy, enthusiastic and effective learning environment, combined with the expectation of challenging work experiences and high standards.

We encourage each and every student to fulfil their potential both academically and as a person in readiness for them to take their place successfully in the world of today and for the future.

(Founded 2006)

Principal
Carlien Shelley

PYP coordinator
Déspina Sarioglou

MYP coordinator
Viviana Serralha

DP coordinator
David Ferreira

Status Private

Boarding/day Day

Gender Coeducational

Language of instruction
English

Authorised IB programmes
PYP, MYP, DP

Age Range 1 – 18 years

Number of pupils enrolled 700

Fees
Day: €10,800 – €25,500 per annum

Address
Avenida Dr. Mário Soares 14
2740-119 Oeiras, Lisbon |
PORTUGAL

TEL +351 214 876 140

Email
office@taguspark.
sharingschool.org

Website
www.sharingschool.org

Located in Portugal's largest technology park, Taguspark, in Oeiras Valley, in Lisbon Metropolitan Area, International Sharing School – Taguspark offers the full IB Continuum, the Primary Years Programme (PYP), the Middle Years Programme (MYP) and the Diploma Programme (DP), with a multicultural and multilingual approach to learning, in a safe and empowering learning environment, where students are encouraged to be the best version of themselves.

International Sharing School – Taguspark currently welcomes 700 students from 65 different nationalities and 150 highly qualified teachers and assistant teachers, all teaching and learning in a multilingual and multicultural environment.

In PYP and MYP, students have direct contact with 6 languages and 3 different alphabets, with students in DP focused on subjects in the areas in which they intend to continue their studies in higher education.

Our families can find in International Sharing School a warm, calm, personalized environment, integrated in green spaces and with easy access to the main circulation routes in Lisbon, Cascais and Sintra.

At International Sharing School, each student is unique, and fully integrated into the group, where teachers, motivated and rigorous, transmit to students much more than knowledge: they convey how to get to knowledge, through curiosity, research and sharing.

We educate responsible, creative, knowledgeable young people at International Sharing School – Taguspark, always respecting the environment that surrounds them, whether indoors or outdoors.

Integrated in Portugal's largest technology park, students at International Sharing School interact with the environment and with companies from Oeiras Valley, contacting realities that spike their curiosity and motivate them to push even further.

Learning Through Sharing

Head of School
Marija Mihailovik Atanasovska

PYP coordinator
Natasha Kanzurova Manev

MYP coordinator
Esma Yildiz

DP coordinator
Donche Risteska

Status Private

Boarding/day Day

Gender Coeducational

Language of instruction
English

Authorised IB programmes
PYP, MYP, DP

Age Range 3 – 18 years

Number of pupils enrolled 370

Address
Skupi 11
1000 Skopje | MACEDONIA

TEL +389 (0)2 3070 723

Email
infopyp@ips.mk

Website
ips.mk

IPS Mission
IPS lays the groundwork for a life-long love of learning by combining the benefits of multilingual and intercultural education, promoting international awareness. We strive to provide opportunities to reach both the intrinsic and extrinsic educational potential of every student. We create global leaders who are compassionate learners, who engage, enlighten, empower and contribute to building a better world.

IPS Vision
IPS Macedonia enriches the mind, strengthens the character, and inspires the hearts of our students.

IPS Macedonia's philosophy is to support the educational path of students from infancy to adolescence, in a safe, caring environment. We encourage students to try new things so they can figure out what inspires them. Despite the academic preparation, we are deeply committed to helping prepare young people to thrive in a complex, global community. That means we focus on the whole person, on character development, as well as on their academic progress. We prepare students to unlock their highest potential and contribute to the community and the world in which they work and live.

IPS Macedonia is a private school open to students of all nationalities between the ages of 1 to 18 years. IPS was first established in 1998 by a diplomat of Brazilian/American nationality temporarily residing in Skopje, in collaboration with Marija Mihailovikj and Tanja Todorovski, two Macedonian university students, as a means of providing her children with a good nursery school education.

IPS Macedonia with its 24 years of existence and implementing educational activity, is the oldest private International preschool, now school, in Skopje. It is a testimony to the quality teaching that is performed in it, and the proof of that is the very successful generations of students resulting from it. Now they are knowledgeable professionals in their work in various spheres of life. In 2018 IPS started to implement primary educational activities and in 2020, the Secondary school started to enrol students. With the growth of the Secondary school, IPS Macedonia will cater for children between 1 – 18 years old. The school aims to achieve its full capacity of 570 students in the coming years.

Our campus provides the ideal environment for your child to learn and grow. We offer dedicated facilities to support different types of learning. We have:

- A dedicated science lab
- Classrooms designed for, Design, Music and Visual Arts
- Gym for Physical Education
- Extensive outdoor spaces including a sports field, multiple play spaces
- A wide range of After school activities
- A door-to-door bus service.

In the Primary Years Programme, the school offers a play-based learning approach through the Early Years, allowing children to discover the world around them and supporting the development of the whole child. Through play, and inquiry children develop an essential set of skills and they develop as readers, writers and mathematicians, and a sense of wonder is fostered as they grow socially, emotionally and academically.

The Middle Years Programme encourages students to be active learners who ask challenging questions, allowing them to continuously make meaningful connections between their learning and the world outside the classroom. During the MYP, our team of experienced teachers accompany and guide students on their learning journey. Emphasis is placed on individual growth and encouraging students to reflect upon their learning. Teachers facilitate students' learning and help prepare them for the rigorous demands of the IB Diploma Programme.

The Diploma Programme prepares students for university and encourages them to ask challenging questions, learn how to learn, develop a strong sense of their own identity and culture and develop the ability to communicate with and understand people from other countries and cultures.

Within the dynamic IB environment, students are encouraged to think critically and become independent learners, coming prepared to class, presenting the material and being coached by their teachers. Assignments are demanding, and the balance between academic work and co-curricular activities allows students to tailor the programme according to their interests and develop an impressive university profile in the process.

Students who graduate with the IB Diploma are advantaged in their acceptance to highly-regarded universities, because the expectations for a good university candidate are the foundation on which the IB DP is built.

Admissions

Students can apply to our school all year round based on availability. For further information about admissions or to schedule a visit to the school, please contact us at infopyp@ips.mk

(Founded 2006)

Headmaster
Mr. Simon Hatton-Burke

PYP coordinator
Ms. Rebeca Albarrán Corroto

MYP coordinator
Ms. Pilar Molina

DP coordinator
Mr. Philip Brotherton

Status Private

Boarding/day Mixed

Gender Coeducational

Language of instruction
English, Spanish

Authorised IB programmes
PYP, MYP, DP

Age Range 1 – 18 years

Number of pupils enrolled
550

Address
Juan de Vergara, 1
Urbanización La Legua
Toledo, Castilla-La Mancha
45005 | SPAIN

TEL +34 925 280 363

Email
infotoledo@colegiosanpatricio.es

Website
colegiosanpatriciotoledo.com/en

International School San Patricio Toledo is a day and boarding School, offering the complete range of the International Baccalaureate (IBO continuum) from 1 to 18 years. PYP, MYP and DP, bilingual or English only.

Our School prides itself on its range of choice and opportunity be it the diverse subjects on offer at Diploma or the clubs and sporting facilities within our grounds.

Our very strong academic results can be seen once again in 2023 with our excellent average point school at Diploma.

We are one of the first in Spain to be an official Google Education Reference School. We take great pride in the use of our technology to ensure maximum knowledge for our students and the world they live in.

Location:
Our school is located in an exclusive residential area of Toledo (1 hour from Madrid by car and 30 min by train). The grounds are large with over 30,000 square meters: our purpose built boarding school is within the school grounds, which facilitates the use of the premises at all times without the need for transfers or departures from the campus. This ensures that students live in a fully-equipped campus with maximum security and control.

Furthermore, our Boarding School has over 20 different nationalities providing students with a genuine international experience in the beautiful world heritage city of Toledo.

We offer a complete educational experience for students between 14 and 18 years of age and weekly boarding for students from 12 to 18 years old, allowing them to develop their communication and social skills.

All students have a designated boarding house tutor as well as an academic tutor who oversee the pastoral and academic wellbeing of each individual student. In addition we have a designated university counselor. Excellent standards of Safeguarding accredited by leading BSA and SACPA organizations.

Foreign languages:
English, German, French and the ability at Diploma to offer a wide variety of self-taught languages.

Accommodation:
First class facilities. Rooms are designed to allow groups to be formed according to the personal characteristics and diversity of the students. We can therefore accommodate 2, 3, or 4 students per room on both male and female floors.

Weekends:
We take great pride in our programmed weekend activities for our boarding students allowing them to flourish and provide the necessary balance with their important academic studies.

ISTEK Baris Schools

Head of School
Melike Ayhan Gül

PYP coordinator
Nehir Ege

Status Private

Boarding/day Day

Gender Coeducational

Language of instruction
Turkish, English

Authorised IB programmes
PYP

Age Range 3 – 11 years

Number of pupils enrolled
580

Fees
TL220,000 (pre-school) – TL242,000 (primary school) per annum

Address
Bagdat Cad. No. 238/1
Ciftehavuzlar, Kadiköy
34730 Istanbul | TURKEY

TEL +90 216 360 12 18

Email
baris.ilkokulu@istek.k12.tr

Website
www.istek.k12.tr

ISTEK Preschools and Primary Schools implement the IB Primary Years Programme, integrated with the curriculum that is stipulated by the Turkish Ministry of Education. IB PYP provides a sound framework through which ISTEK Schools fulfil the qualities of education that are stated in their mission and vision.

Mission

Our mission at ISTEK Schools is to educate our students under the guidance of Ataturk's reforms and principles, to become successful individuals committed to scientific thought and universal values who will have a positive impact on the future of Turkey and the World at large.

Vision

From Kindergarten to University ISTEK Schools aim to bring up individuals with universal values and points of view who are:

- Equipped with skills and talents
- Self-confident
- Productive
- Creative
- Patriotic

IB PYP at ISTEK Schools

ISTEK Schools is comprised of several K-12 campuses. As an educational organization and a community that believes in life-long learning, the Foundation is committed to constant innovation and by providing scholarships. The Foundation strives for equal opportunity education. Working in national and international contexts, aiming to make positive contributions to both the country and the world's future, and giving priority to scientific inquiry defines ISTEK as a foundation apart.

ISTEK Baris School's student body is mainly composed of Turkish students. About 5% come from bilingual/bicultural backgrounds. The Turkish National Curriculum is implemented under the PYP framework.

The school library is very active and has a central role in the lives of the school community. The classrooms are equipped with modern technology, field trips are organized during the year and access to various databases develop students' research skills and lead them to become active inquirers.

With open mindedness as a goal, open communication is promoted by all the members of the school community. The Student Council is very active and participates in code of conduct related management decisions, regarding the suggestions and wishes of the students. Students are always encouraged to express their opinions and respect others' views. Their opinions are valued and they are provided with many opportunities to take action.

Learning together and learning from one another through cooperative learning and our reflective-thinking-oriented assessment system, supports the ongoing development of the students and plays a pivotal role in leading them to become autonomous learners.

ISTEK Baris Schools is a community committed to lifelong learning and responsible action that will help to create a better and more peaceful world.

ISTEK Kasgarli Mahmut Schools

Head of School
Yasemin Baysoy Gençten

PYP coordinator
Ayça Özkardes

Status Private

Boarding/day Day

Gender Coeducational

Language of instruction
English, Turkish

Authorised IB programmes
PYP

Age Range 3 – 11 years

Number of pupils enrolled
340

Address
Eski Edirne Asfalti No 512
Sultangazi
34110 Istanbul, Marmara |
TURKEY

TEL +90 212 594 26 11/12

Email
kasgarlimahmut@istek.k12.tr

Website
www.istek.k12.tr/kasgarli-mahmut-kampusu

Since its establishment by Mr. Bedrettin Dalan in ISTEK Foundation has been raising modern and entrepreneurial generations in line with Atatürk's principles and revolutions. Today, our foundation, which has a chain of education from Kindergarten to University, is prominent in the future of our country with 22 Kindergartens, 22 Primary Schools, 22 Middle Schools, 17 Anatolian High Schools, 17 Science High Schools, and Yeditepe University.

ISTEK Kasgarli Mahmut Schools started operating in the academic year of 1987 – 1988. Our school was named after one of our Turkish seniors, Kasgarli Mahmut, who was known as the first Turkish philologist. On our campus, students study from kindergarten to the last year of high school.

ISTEK Kasgarli Mahmut Campus is located in Sultangazi on a large area of 9360 square meters. Our school facilities include 320 seat conference hall, library, indoor sports complex, swimming pool, music and art workshops, music recording studio, 4 science and computer laboratories, maker workshop, large dining hall, outdoor sports areas, activity halls, playgrounds and technologically equipped classrooms that allow our students to develop academic and social skills.

Our school, which was accepted to apply PYP with Candidate School status in April 2016, received a Consultancy Visit by IB in April 2017. In February 2020, IB carried out a Verification Visit and both ISTEK Kasgarli Mahmut Kindergarten and ISTEK Kasgarli Mahmut Primary School were authorized to apply PYP in June 2020. Our school is now honoured with the status of IB World School.

We believe that learning different languages is the key to becoming a global citizen. For this reason, we offer our students an intensive English language education starting from the age of 4. Our students receive bilingual education starting from the first day of their school life. In the second grade, they choose between German and Spanish languages and receive their second language education until they graduate.

We aim to create experiences that will make our students to be more sophisticated, organized, mature, and socially responsible. In addition to our daily flow, our students participate in different club activities in science, arts, and sports in line with their skills and interests. Supported by our enriched curriculum, our students successfully represent our school in national and international organizations.

ISTEK Kasgarli Mahmut Schools is committed to raising caring individuals who are ready to change the world.

ISTEK Kemal Atatürk Schools (Kindergarten & Primary School)

Principal
Mehmet Öcalan

PYP coordinator
Idil Ayyürek

Status Private

Boarding/day Day

Gender Coeducational

Language of instruction
Turkish

Authorised IB programmes
PYP

Age Range 3 – 10 years

Address
Tarabya Bayiri Cad. No 60
Tarabya/Sariyer
34457 Istanbul, Marmara |
TURKEY

TEL +90 212 262 75 75

Email
kemalataturk@istek.k12.tr

Website
www.istek.k12.tr/kemal-ataturk-kampusu

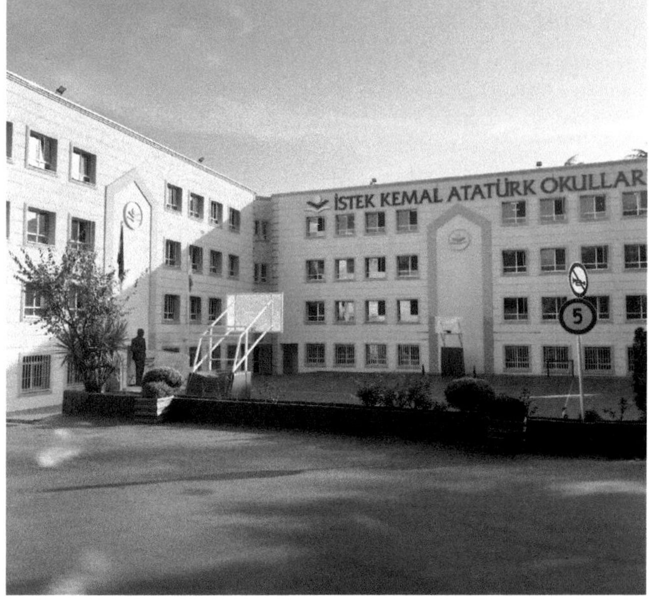

Situated on the European side of Istanbul overlooking the Bosphorus, lies Istek Kemal Atatürk Schools, which educates students from pre-school to high school. Apart from the Preschool and Primary School National Education Curriculum, PYP was added with IB authorization in 2013.

Since 1985 Istek Kemal Atatürk Schools offers a safe environment with open and closed sport centers, a semi-olympic swimming pool, well equipped laboratories, and libraries rich in resources and modern educational technologies. One can also find a spacious dining area, art rooms, a bicycle training zone, and a 7400m garden!

We believe that every child is gifted in a unique way. We aim to discover those gifts by offering different programmes such as; chess, musical instruments, visual arts, swimming, gym, modern dance, drama and brain teasers.

Throughout the year we assess our students in order to provide the best support for those whose needs differ from their peers. Our educational program is continuously developing out of consideration for our children's age, level of development, needs and any international developments. The curriculum is enhanced by making changes that allows students to perform at their top cognitive capacity. We support them in reaching this capacity by activating their curiosity, asking them to research, explore and solve problems. The IB Baccalaureate PYP Primary Years Programme helps students to experience learning and the process of knowledge. Taking into account each students individual differences, we have tutorials for students who need extra support. We believe that students should care about the issues facing their communities and environment, and it's our responsibility to create a community of well rounded, knowledgeable, internationally minded, and caring students.

English is intensively taught in our school. Our students are assessed with the internationally recognized TOEFL test. We teach Spanish and German from second to fourth grade. Our aim is, to broaden our students' horizons and help them become citizens of the world.

We aim to create experiences that will make our students well rounded, organized, mature and socially responsible. We open new clubs in areas where we see students show interest, in addition to the arts and sports lessons that they normally attend. Students are selected to take part in after school clubs aimed at advancing their knowledge of science, and their abilities in arts and sports. These students go on to represent our school in national and international competitions.

KENT COLLEGE
CANTERBURY

(Founded 1885)

Head of Kent College
Mr Mark Turnbull

DP coordinator
Mr Graham Letley

Status Private

Boarding/day Mixed

Gender Coeducational

Language of instruction
English

Authorised IB programmes
DP

Age Range 3 months – 18 years (boarding from 7 years)

Number of pupils enrolled
800

Fees
Day: £3,964 – £7,487 per term
Boarding: £10,072 – £13,860 per term

Address
Whitstable Road
Canterbury
Kent
CT2 9DT | UK

TEL +44 (0)1227 763 231

Email
admissions@kentcollege.co.uk

Website
www.kentcollege.com

Kent College Campus

The Senior School sits in 80 acres of land with 26 acres of sports fields, grazing for the school farm and ancient woodland for walking and cross country running. Yet the centre of Canterbury, with its wide selection of shops, restaurants, theatres and Cathedral, is just a short walk away. The Great Hall, a state-of-the-art 600 seat versatile theatre not only hosts our highly regarded school music and drama productions but also hosts the annual Canterbury Festival, the largest Arts event in Kent.

Boarding at KC

We are home to a thriving boarding community with over 200 boarders from 40 different countries. Our experienced House Parents lead a team of Boarding House staff who ensure new students are fully integrated into school life and settle into boarding routines. Evening and weekend activities and trips mean there is always something to do and students benefit from being able to spend time in Canterbury.

Curriculum

Kent College prides itself on offering personalised academic programmes, small class sizes and exceptionally well-qualified and experienced teaching staff. Pupils achieve excellent academic results at GCSE, A Level, and in the International Baccalaureate (IB). An average point score of 37 in the IB consistently places Kent College in the top 10 IB schools in the UK.

Kent College is very flexible when it comes to constructing the timetables for Diploma candidates and encourages applicants to identify courses and subjects, they wish to study even if KC does not offer them as they are able to bespoke most options. Kent College offers outstanding levels of teaching and support for the IB Diploma with additional classes and tutoring available as standard to ensure the very best outcomes for individuals.

Next steps

Our Sixth Form Careers and Futures programme prepares students for life after KC. This includes Careers Insights from local professionals as well as work experience and Study Insights that allow students to experience what studying at university will be like. Students are guided through university applications in the UK or around the world as well as being supported on pathways to Oxbridge, Medicine, Engineering and Veterinary Science or a gap year by our Head of Careers. Over 90% of our students get into their first university of choice and over 50% regularly join Russell group universities: the top 24 universities in the UK.

Candidates for an IB Diploma scholarship (Year 12 only) must submit written work to the Deputy Head, Mr. Letley (gletley@kentcollege.co.uk). More details can be found on our website.

Beyond the classroom

Kent College has a strong belief in "work hard, play hard" and provides over 100 co-curricular clubs and activities for students who are actively encouraged to participate in two clubs each week. A cornucopia of clubs and societies are available from Archery to Zumba dancing. Students can try many different sports from basketball to rowing and fencing or join the debating society, photography club, jewellery making or the Duke of Edinburgh programme. In sport, hockey and cricket are strengths, with regular representation by Kent College pupils in the county and national squads.

Many students join the school's Farm Club and learn to care for animals at our working farm and show them at the Kent Show where they can also join the annual Young Farmers Camp. Horse Riding lessons are also available in the school's riding arena and our NESA team compete in events all over the country.

Pastoral Care

Kent College has a reputation for being a friendly and caring school, and our pastoral structure is designed to give all pupils the support they need from the start of their school career to the day they leave. Our mission is always pupil-centred and to focus on enabling every child to become the best they can be. The Heads of House lead their teams of Tutors and have overall responsibility for the academic and pastoral wellbeing of the pupils in their age groups. The school believes feelings of wellbeing are fundamental to the overall health of an individual, enabling them to successfully overcome difficulties and achieve their goals in life.

Kensington School

(Founded 1968)

Headteacher
Mr Andrew de Salis

DP coordinator
Peter Carlyle

Status Private

Boarding/day Day

Gender Coeducational

Language of instruction
English

Authorised IB programmes
DP

Age Range 18 months – 18 years

Number of pupils enrolled
2200

Fees
Day: €6,000 – €7,790

Address
Avenida de Bularas No. 2
Pozuelo de Alarcón
28224 Madrid | **SPAIN**

TEL +34 91 7154 699

Email
kensington@kensingtonschool.net

Website
www.kensington-school.es

Kensington School is a premium, private, coeducational day school offering British education for children from the age of 18 months to 18 years (Pre-Nursery to Year 13). Our aim is to educate the whole person, with a complete academic and social education. The school is located on a purpose-built site with 1,100 students studying in excellent facilities. Founded in 1968, Kensington has ben a pioneer in British education in Spain, and is a founder member of the National Association of British Schools in Spain. The school regularly appears in listings of the top schools in Spain by Forbes, El Mundo,ABC, etc.

Kensington School follows the English National Curriculum to all students up to Year 9 (14 years old), before allowing students the choice of paths for the last four years of their education : IGCSE and International Baccalaureate in English, or Spanish National Curriculum. This flexibility allows students to choose the language and learning approach which best suits them, and their intended university destination and career path; results in both pathways are excellent, and graduates go on to study at top universities in Spain and elsewhere.

Kensington has, as a British school, always had a strong commitment to holistic education, educating through the arts and sport, with termly concerts, sports days, tournaments and drama performances, and a strong after-school programme. The school has also been characterised by a close, nurturing, communicative relationship between families and the school. We have a team of two nurses and three psychologists on site to support the needs of children.

As a UNICEF partner school, Kensington has always had a strong international dimension to our education, and we are also delighted to offer the International Baccalaureate.

As a member of the Inspired group, Kensington students benefit from connection with a network of more than 100 schools across world, with the possibility of school exchanges and visits, and participating in a variety of summer camps.

King Abdulaziz School

(Founded 2013)

Principal
Hatem Waznah

PYP & MYP coordinator
Raheela Akram

DP coordinator
Mohammad Baba

Status Private

Boarding/day Day

Gender Male

Language of instruction
English

Authorised IB programmes
PYP, MYP, DP

Number of pupils enrolled 160

Address
Ali Ibn Abi Taleb Road
P.O. Box 43111
Medina
41561 | SAUDI ARABIA

TEL +966 553 039 300/+966 503 454 420

Email
hwaznah@kaism.org

Website
www.kaism.org

Introduction:
King Abdulaziz School is proud to be the first IB World Continuum School in the city of Medina S.A. Our IB journey began in 2015 and we subsequently became officially authorised to offer the PYP by the International Baccalaureate in December 2017. Later on, KAS achieved the accreditation to offer the MYP in 2020 and the DP in 2021.

Mission Statement
Our Mission at KAS is to create international educational experiences that cultivate active and lifelong learners. KAS aims to provide stimulating academic programmes supported by rigorous assessment, and implemented through inquiry, in a caring and nurturing learning environment. Learners are equipped with the skills they need to reach their full potential and become responsible global citizens. KAS prepares students to be open to other perspectives, values and traditions whilst recognizing their own identity and taking pride in their cultural heritage.

Primary Years Programme at KAS
At KAS, we offer an inquiry-based, transdisciplinary curriculum framework that builds conceptual understanding and enables sound skill development. We focus on providing the best educational practices, having both local and global significance. In line with IB learning, our PYP students are open to the perspectives, values and traditions of others, whilst at the same time appreciating their own identities, and being proud of their cultural heritage.

Middle Years Programme at KAS
As our learners mature from transdisciplinary learning in the PYP into interdisciplinary learning in the MYP, they become more responsible and reflective of their own learning experiences through engaging in the inquiry cycle. Our student-centered approach ensures the empowerment and development of students ready to embark on further education as critical independent thinkers in the DP.

The Diploma Programme at KAS
Our experience with the International Baccalaureate Diploma Programme at KAS has enabled us to combine the interdisciplinary and robust subject disciplines in the IB Diploma, whilst maintaining the breadth and depth structure of the curriculum.

To the wider school community, here are our firm commitments in our provision of teaching, learning and interactions in our IB Diploma curriculums:

- Structured and balanced curriculum
- Experienced teachers
- Coherent and deep learning
- Rich and relevant resources for teaching and learning

KING WILLIAM'S COLLEGE

(Founded 1833)

Principal
Mr Damian Henderson

DP coordinator
Alasdair Ulyett

Status Private

Boarding/day Mixed

Gender Coeducational

Language of instruction
English

Authorised IB programmes
DP

Age Range 11 – 18 years

Number of pupils enrolled
340

Fees
Day:
£20,345 – £26,995 per annum
Boarding:
£34,940 – £41,590 per annum

Address
Castletown
Isle of Man
IM9 1TP | UK

TEL +44 (0)1624 820110

Email
admissions@kwc.im

Website
www.kwc.im

The College is set in superb countryside on the edge of Castletown Bay in an area of diverse and beautiful scenery. Approximately 25% of our students board, with half of the boarders coming from the Island and the rest from a wide variety of countries around the world. We are non-selective, but through the dedication of our staff, the structure of support for each individual and the work ethic of the students, we achieve excellent results. Our students go to top universities in the UK, Europe and the USA.

The Isle of Man is a beautiful environment in which to live, giving students the freedom to explore and take advantage of the fresh air, open countryside and beaches, away from the hustle and bustle and pollution of a busy city. The Island is easy to get to with air links from the major airports in the UK and Ireland.

We are one of the few British schools where students in the Sixth Form can study for the International Baccalaureate Diploma. The IB philosophy – particularly its emphasis on skills and its focus on internationalism – is central to our approach, and we are one of the largest and most experienced IB schools in the British Isles.

Our pupils follow a broad curriculum of sporting activities, competing in the major sports against UK and Island schools. Every three years, the senior rugby and hockey teams embark on a world sports tour during the summer months. We have golf, paddle boarding and sailing on offer, along with a wide variety of other extracurricular activities.

Drama and Music thrive and pupils are given the opportunity to perform at many events and productions. There are workshops throughout the year and students are also encouraged to participate in competitions.

King's College School, Wimbledon

KING'S COLLEGE SCHOOL
WIMBLEDON

(Founded 1829)

Head
Dr Anne Cotton

Director of IB
David Cass

Status Private

Boarding/day Day

Gender Boys ages 7-18, co-educational sixth form

Language of instruction
English

Authorised IB programmes
DP

Number of pupils enrolled
1474 (313 in the Sixth Form)

Fees
Please see website

Address
Southside
Wimbledon Common
London
SW19 4TT | UK

TEL 020 8255 5300

Email
admissions@kcs.org.uk

Website
www.kcs.org.uk

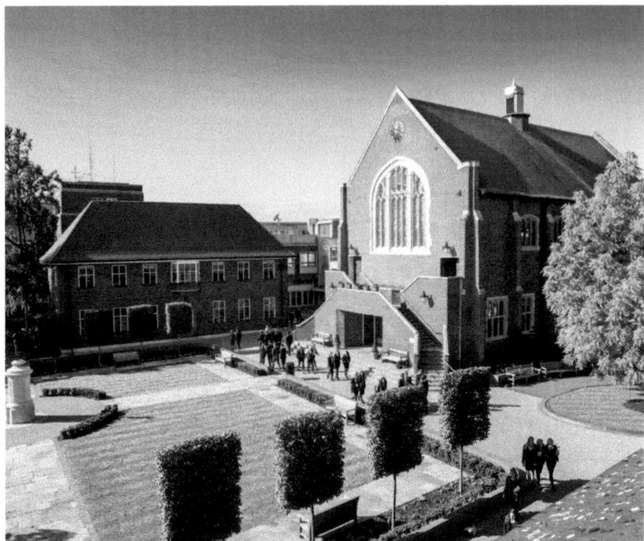

King's College School, Wimbledon is a friendly, kind, inclusive and purposeful community where pupils' enthusiasm and creativity shine in every corner of the school. Founded by Royal Charter in 1829, as part of the university of King's College London, intellectual endeavour and a progressive spirit have always been at the heart of life at King's. While pupils' exceptional success in public examinations makes King's one of the world's leading schools, a true King's education is so much more. The school motto, 'sancte et sapienter' (with holiness and with wisdom), encapsulates the importance we place on both the mind and the spirit of the whole person. King's prepares pupils to forge their own path with the confidence and heart of our lion, guided by their learning and strong values. We want them to lead meaningful, fulfilling lives in the world beyond school.

King's has been offering the IB Diploma for more than 20 years. In 2023 our pupils' average point score was 41 and 61% of all HL subjects were awarded the top grade 7. Seven pupils achieved the maximum of 45 points, placing them in the top 0.5% of UK-based IB pupils. In the last eight years, nearly 350 leavers have won places to study at Oxford or Cambridge.

Outstanding pastoral care is central to the school's success. All pupils are placed in a House, form and cross-year tutor group. Tutors remain with pupils throughout their time at school and pupils are also supported by our counsellors, chaplain, the learning enrichment department and equality, diversity and inclusivity mentors.

King's is renowned for its co-curricular programme; the importance we attach to this dimension of a pupil's education is recognised by the dedication of an entire afternoon's timetable on Friday to the range of over 150 activities. Alongside this programme, a huge variety of sporting, drama, musical and other activities are offered throughout the school week including the Combined Cadet Force and the Duke of Edinburgh's Award Scheme. Our community projects are the most popular co-curricular activity, with over 400 of our pupils and teachers volunteering to work in their community.

Places for girls and boys are available for entry into our co-educational sixth form via entrance tests. Academic, music, sport, drama and art scholarships are available, and King's is keen to provide financial support to families whose only barrier to joining the school is the cost of fees. We offer free (100% bursaries) and subsidised places (partial bursaries).

King's College, The British School of Alicante

Headteacher
Mr. Simon Wicks

DP coordinator
Verity Long

Status Private

Boarding/day Day

Gender Coeducational

Language of instruction
English, Spanish

Authorised IB programmes
DP

Age Range 2 – 18 years

Number of pupils enrolled
1200

Address
Glorieta del Reino Unido No. 5
03008 Alicante, Valencia | **SPAIN**

TEL +34 96 510 6351

Email
info.kca@kingsgroup.com

Website
www.alicante.kingscollegeschools.org

King's College Alicante is a premium, private British school offering first-class education to children from age 2 to 18 years old. Our aim is to educate the whole child and support them in exceeding their potential on academic, physical, and interpersonal levels. King's College has been rated as one of the best schools in Spain by Forbes and is one of the leading schools in Spain for over 50 years.

The school follows the British National Curriculum until Year 11 and is proud to offer the IB Diploma Programme in Years 12 and 13. Our dedicated and passionate staff help shape our children and encourage them to become dynamic, tenacious and resilient individuals, ready to take on new challenges at university or the world of work. Education at KCA opens many doors for our students and ensures they are well prepared to successfully apply to the best universities around the globe after graduating from us.

Post-16 education at King's College Alicante is centred around preparation for the International Baccalaureate Diploma Programme which is seen as the gold standard in pre-university certification. KCA offers the broadest IBDP curriculum in the local area and also provides the opportunity to be awarded the bilingual diploma at the end of Year 13.

We are the first British school in Spain certified as a Google Reference School, awarded for our excellent digital learning programme, dedicated to maximising your child's potential in every area and harnessing technology to improve all aspects of teaching and learning. We were recently re-awarded the SENDIA award as recognition of our outstanding inclusive educational programme and are proud to have been rated as "outstanding in all areas" during our previous four BSO inspections, the most recent being in October 2023.

We are truly a unique and outstanding institution that offers a rich curriculum and a broad all-round education. When you visit you will be impressed by our warm and purposeful atmosphere, underpinned by the dedication and talent of the staff and the enthusiasm of the students. As well as our focus on the academic achievement of each pupil, we are committed to enhancing their love of learning and enjoyment of the whole school experience. Staff give freely of their time, and we offer a comprehensive programme of sport, music and drama, as well as numerous co-curricular opportunities, trips and visits. Above all, and just as much as any parent, we want our children to thrive and be happy throughout their time with us.

Our motto "Always aspire to be the best you can be" resonates across our campus and drives high expectations and standards from everyone in our British international community.

King's College, The British School of Madrid

(Founded 1969)

Head
Matthew Taylor

DP coordinator
Federica Menon

Status Private

Boarding/day Mixed

Gender Coeducational

Language of instruction
English

Authorised IB programmes
DP

Age Range 4 months – 18 years

Number of pupils enrolled
1300

Fees
Day:
€2,600 – €6,385 per term
Boarding:
€31,400 – €37,800 per annum

Address
Paseo de los Andes 35
Soto de Viñuelas
28760 Madrid | **SPAIN**

TEL +34 918 034 800

Email
kc.admissions@kingscollegeschools.org

Website
madrid-soto.kingscollegeschools.org

King's College Madrid is a coeducational day and boarding school which provides British education for children from the age of 4 months to 18 years (Baby Education and Day Care to Year 13). It is located on an attractive 12-acre site in a leafy suburb, just 20 minutes' drive from Madrid and the main airport.

King's College is one of only a few schools in Spain to offer both A Level & IB Diploma programmes of study in English. This allows students to choose their path of study depending on what type of learner they grow up to be enabling them to fulfil their future aspirations.

This freedom of choice, coupled with the highest quality of teaching and learning allows our students to excel across the curriculum.

Year 13 Graduates go on to study at the best universities in the world (Russell Group, Ivy League & Oxbridge).

King's College has gained a reputation for high academic standards. An experienced careers and university entrance department is available to all pupils, and the Oxbridge preparatory group prepares students applying to Oxford, Cambridge, Ivy League and other elite universities.

Our boarding house opened in September 2011 and offers some of the best boarding accommodation in Europe. Tenbury House is home to 60 pupils from all over the world. The new facilities offer a 'home from home' environment with shared and individual bedrooms all with en-suite bathrooms, underfloor heating and wireless internet. In addition, there is a dining room, a common room, a TV room, a study room, a kitchen that pupils can use to make light meals and a laundry. During the evenings and weekends, the students in Tenbury House have full use of these facilities and can also take advantage of many of the school's sports facilities and an extensive programme of trips and visits.

King's College is the only BSO school in Madrid accredited by the Department for Education in the UK as "Excellent" in every category that offers a British Curriculum from 4 months to 18 years.

King's College, The British School of Murcia

Head of School
Ms Dawn Akyurek

DP coordinator
Robert Snowden

Status Private

Boarding/day Day

Gender Coeducational

Language of instruction
English, Spanish

Authorised IB programmes
DP

Age Range 18 months – 18 years

Number of pupils enrolled
545

Address
Calle Pez Volador s/n
Urbanización La Torre Golf Resort
30709 Roldán, Murcia | **SPAIN**

TEL +34 968 032 500

Email
murcia.info@kings.education

Website
www.murcia.kingscollegeschools.org

King's College, The British School of Murcia is the only school in the region that regularly undertakes external inspections accredited by the Department for Education (DfE) of the British Government. The school is located in La Torre Golf Resort and offers the English National Curriculum to pupils from the age of 18 months to 18 years (Pre-Nursery – Year 13).

In this growing school, the children mature with us from 18 months to 18 years; learning and developing into the young adults of the future, with confidence and a multicultural perspective. The students benefit from a first-class campus, well equipped to provide a stimulating environment to nurture their skills and talents, whether these be academic, artistic or sporting. This environment is enriched by dedicated teachers, delivering the English Curriculum through inspirational teaching.

Premium and Private British school ranked as the 4th Best School in Spain by Forbes magazine that offers the British National Curriculum to pupils from 18 months to 18 years.

The school fosters a culture of aspirations and ambitions with their youngsters that leave school with the right skills necessary to thrive and a growth mindset, fully ready to follow their dreams and achieve them no matter the circumstances.

King's Murcia is the only school in the Murcia region to offer the IB Diploma Programme in English, opening many national and international opportunities for them in the future starting by accessing elite universities.

KCM offers a unique teaching and learning framework to develop the cognitive skills, values, attitudes and attributes needed to reach success, offering a wide programme of Extra-Curricular activities in which each student can discover and enhance their talents.

The best investment for the future is King's College, The British School of Murcia.

La Côte International School Aubonne

(Founded 2008)

Principal
Mr Andy Puttock

DP coordinator
Alexa Prior

Status Private

Boarding/day Day

Gender Coeducational

Language of instruction
English, French

Authorised IB programmes
DP

Age Range 3 – 18 years

Number of pupils enrolled
approx. 420

Fees
Day: CHF26,450 – CHF35,850

Address
Chemin de Clamogne 8
1170 Aubonne VD | **SWITZERLAND**

TEL +41 (0)22 823 26 26

Email
admissions@lcis.ch

Website
www.lcis.ch

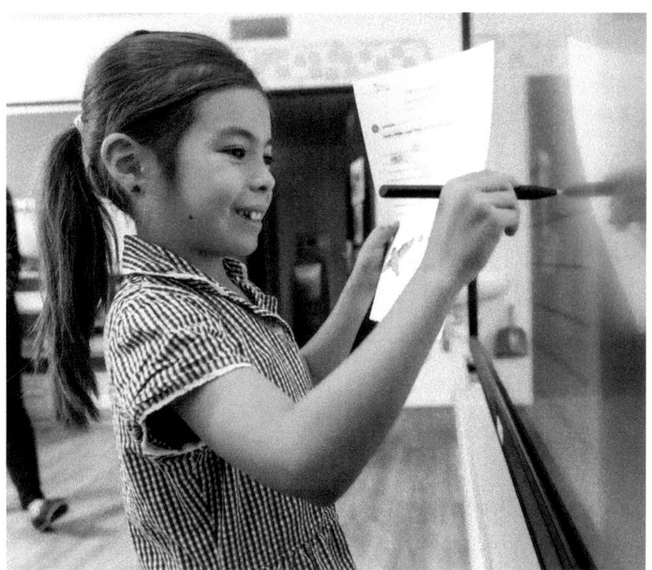

La Côte International School is a private international school based in Aubonne, Switzerland. The modern campus is conveniently located between Lausanne and Geneva, with stunning views of the Swiss Alps and Lac Léman.

The school offers its students unmatched international learning opportunities, combined with truly personalised academic support and the highest educational standards, to motivate all students to achieve more than they ever thought possible.

The school offers only curricula that lead to accredited qualifications recognised by the world's leading universities. It also offers enriching learning opportunities to ensure that students are equipped with the skills to shape the world they inherit.

Primary students follow an enhanced International Primary Curriculum with French options that range from a beginner's course to a truly bilingual program. This provides an excellent transition into the diverse international secondary curriculum offer.

In secondary, students are supported to achieve excellent academic results and further develop their skills in two or more languages. In Years 10 and 11, students study for their IGCSE, the world's most popular international qualification for 14 to 16-year-olds. In Years 12 and 13, students aged 16-18 study the IBDP, the gold standard in education. Through a broad range of subject choices, targeted support, and personalised guidance, students are supported to achieve their very best academically.

IB students can opt for a single-language or bilingual IB diploma, strengthening their application to top universities in Switzerland and abroad.

LCIS is a member of Nord Anglia Education (NAE), the world's leading premium schools' group, and is, therefore, able to recruit the finest locally and internationally trained teachers committed to nurturing and inspiring every child. Consequently, LCIS students achieve outstanding academic results, and graduates are accepted to top universities in Switzerland and worldwide.

With approximately 40 nationalities represented at the school, supporting children in their own cultures and languages is at the core of the school's philosophy. Through outstanding education and international opportunities unmatched by other schools in the area, the school cultivates in them the qualities, attributes, and skills needed to shape the future.

The school's Performing Arts programme benefits from its collaboration with The Juilliard School. The school's collaboration with MIT emphasises hands-on learning of STEAM subjects. In partnership with UNICEF, the school raises awareness of the UN Sustainable Development Goals and explores local solutions to global problems.

LCIS is led by Andy Puttock, formerly Global Education Director for NAE. He has been instrumental in driving NAE's strategy for building an outstanding education for their students worldwide.

LA GARENNE
INTERNATIONAL SCHOOL

(Founded 1947)

Director
Mr. Grégory Méan

MYP coordinator
Mischa Mortley

DP coordinator
Adam Jozef

Status Private

Boarding/day Mixed

Gender Coeducational

Language of instruction
English

Authorised IB programmes
MYP, DP

Age Range 4 – 18 years

Number of pupils enrolled 170

Fees
Day: CHF43,000 – CHF88,000 per annum
Boarding: CHF80,000 – CHF121,000 per annum

Address
Chemin des Chavasses 23
1885 Chesières-Villars VD | **SWITZERLAND**

TEL +41 (0)24 495 24 53

Email
admissions@la-garenne.ch

Website
www.la-garenne.ch

In the heart of the Swiss Alps, La Garenne combines rigorous academic programmes with multiple outdoor activities. More than 75 years after we welcomed our first children, LGIS is now home to 170 young people aged from 4 to 18 from 40 countries.

Our Guiding Principles include Care, Compassion, Inquiry, Responsibility, Innovation and Collaboration, reflecting our holistic, child-centred approach, alongside traditional Swiss values.

English is the official language in school and every student is encouraged to master French. Following completion of their IB studies or the High School Diploma, La Garenne graduates have moved onto leading universities and hotel and business schools across the world.

Our community is centred on an authentic Swiss chalet from which the school takes its name: La Garenne. It has a refectory and cosy accommodation for our youngest boarders. Chalet Beau Site is home to students aged from 11 to 13. Their rooms are en-suite with spectacular views. Beau Site also has a dedicated art workshop and music and recreational spaces.

Chalet Le Roc has stylish two-person suites for our senior students, as well as classrooms, a gym, a dance studio, an art studio and a welcoming dining room and reception area. Next door, the ski lift enables ski-in, ski-out opportunities in winter.

Two further buildings complete the campus:

- 'Academia': for students aged 8-13. It has an airy library with mountain views, a science lab, a music studio and classrooms, all designed to inspire creativity and promote learning.
- 'Millennium': our new Early Years Centre for Reception, and Years 1 and 2. The classrooms are organised for the very special needs of these young children and have direct access to the garden and play areas.

Sports include football, aerobics, padel, tennis, athletics, swimming, karate, golf and much more. Naturally in winter, the focus is on snow sports with skiing and snowboarding as part of the curriculum. La Garenne has its own ski team and competes regularly against other Swiss schools. Creativity comes with art, drama, debating, music, singing and dance. Beyond the classroom, there are expeditions, cultural visits and charity initiatives. Our demanding overseas trips enable students to complement their studies with IB Service as Action projects.

La Garenne International School is one of a kind. Its pioneering approach to boarding education is known and respected across the world. Owned and managed by the Méan family, LGIS retains its unique family atmosphere.

La Miranda the Global Quality School

la miranda
THE GLOBAL
QUALITY SCHOOL

Headteacher
Mrs. Anna Mary Sureda

MYP coordinator
Beatriz Olleta

DP coordinator
Berta Vidal Valls

Status Private

Boarding/day Day

Gender Coeducational

Language of instruction
English, Spanish

Authorised IB programmes
MYP, DP

Age Range 0 – 18 years

Address
Carrer del Canigó 15
08960 Sant Just Desvern,
Barcelona,
Catalonia | **SPAIN**

TEL +34 93 371 73 58

Email
info@lamiranda.eu

Website
www.lamiranda.eu

At La Miranda – a global, multilingual school in Barcelona – every child is encouraged to think for themselves as well as to live and love the world around them. Conveniently located in Sant Just Desvern, Barcelona. Our school offers 12 buildings filled with a wide range of facilities that provide a nurturing, culturally-diverse environment for kids from 0 to 18 years old. Since its foundation in 1967, La Miranda has offered high quality and global education in a multilingual environment.

Love, enthusiasm and solidarity leading by example are the basis of the foundations of our global, multilingual and quality educational model. With over fifty years of history, our heritage has been achieved thanks to our team, made up of students, families, teachers and professionals, committed to knowledge, innovation, research, internationalization, academic excellence and the comprehensive education of children and young people, from birth to university.

We learn critical thinking, to raise awareness and to share global values. We actively work with families to offer multilingual, cutting-edge training with international projection. Our mission is to develop knowledge in all areas, beyond academic learning, as well as to promote their human, emotional, physical, intellectual and social skills in order to become happy people who are aware of their values and their social responsibility. In this way, they will have more opportunities, be able to think critically, have freedom of choice as they will be trained in different environments and cultures.

La Miranda, The Global Quality School, is an official IB School. The IB Diploma Programme at La Miranda aims to train its students to be reflective, to acquire critical thinking skills, to acquire an active attitude towards learning and to instil values that will accompany students throughout their lives.

Landmark International School

Headteacher
Mr Gareth Turnbull-Jones

PYP coordinator
Mrs Jenna Fritz

Status Private

Boarding/day Day

Gender Coeducational

Language of instruction
English

Authorised IB programmes
PYP

Age Range 4 – 16 years

Number of pupils enrolled 100

Fees
Day: £4,413 – £5,795 per term

Address
The Old Rectory, 9 Church Lane
Fulbourn
Cambridge
Cambridgeshire
CB21 5EP | UK

TEL 01223 755100

Email
office@landmarkinternationalschool.co.uk

Website
www.landmarkinternationalschool.co.uk

Close to the thriving university town of Cambridge, with its centres for research, medical and technological innovation, Landmark International School Cambridge offers the international community an inquiry-led, personalised and holistic education in small classes, with a friendly, family-feel. Throughout the school we put the student at the centre of their learning. A Landmark education provides a human-centred approach to learning, ensuring that each individual is nurtured to be a self-directed creative thinker that contributes to making their community and the world around them a better place.

Landmark is a not for profit, co-educational international school that caters for students from ages 4 to 16. In the Primary School we follow the IBPYP. In the Lower Secondary we teach in disciplines and work closely together to make interdisciplinary connections. We support project and service based learning as a part of the taught curriculum through a range of options, Global Discussions and STEM lessons. In the Upper Secondary we continue to develop the whole learner, placing project and service based learning at the forefront of what we do as we prepare our students for the GCSE and IGCSE examinations and their next steps after Landmark.

At Landmark our small class sizes (8-16 students) help to build relationships and our talented and dedicated teachers know and understand our students exceptionally well. We have students from all over the world and 40% of our students are multilingual. We offer a comprehensive English Additional Language programme and a Home Language Programme.

The school has well-developed specialisms in the sciences, arts and languages and offers a range of opportunities for further learning in the local and wider area. Opportunities for developing their learner profiles through field trips, extra-curricular clubs and tuition, along with cultural experiences and excursions, help us create a safe and engaging environment where students feel emboldened to take measured risks and develop resilience. At Landmark we value student voice, choice and ownership, and work with our students to develop their own interests and inquiries within and beyond their learning. We promote authentic and meaningful experiences, supporting students with responding to their learning through action and community projects.

For a well-rounded and forward-looking education that puts the student at the centre of their learning, with happy, motivated students leading the way to a better future, choose Landmark International School Cambridge.

Leighton Park School

LEIGHTON PARK

FOUNDED 1890

Head
Mr Matthew L S Judd BA, PGCE

DP coordinator
Mrs Helen Taylor

Status Private

Boarding/day Mixed

Gender Coeducational

Language of instruction
English

Authorised IB programmes
DP

Age Range 11 – 18 years

Number of pupils enrolled
538

Fees
£9,410 – £15,390 per term

Address
Shinfield Road
Reading
Berkshire
RG2 7ED | UK

TEL 0118 987 9600

Email
admissions@leightonpark.com

Website
www.leightonpark.com

Leighton Park is the winner of the Independent Schools Association (ISA)'s Senior School of the Year 2023 and a TES Awards Finalist in the same year. The School was founded in 1890 and is a day and boarding school for both girls and boys aged 11-18, with a 50:50 ratio of girls to boys at its Year 7 entry point. It is set in 65 acres of beautiful parkland in Reading.

The UK Government's latest Sixth Form league tables reveal Leighton Park to be the best performing school in Berkshire and only one of eight schools in England to have always appeared in the top 100 since the rankings began. A Level students achieved 57% A•/B last year. The Independent School Inspectorate (ISI) awarded Leighton Park a 'double excellent' standard in January 2022, the highest possible attainment for an independent school, in recognition of both the quality of pupils' personal development and the quality of their academic progress.

Leighton Park exists to form students of real character and confidence, with a determined desire to change the world. This focus doesn't come at the expense of a strong, well-balanced education. Leighton Park combines the best academic progress in Berkshire, with award-winning personal development and sector-leading pastoral care. Head, Matthew LS Judd explains: *"We don't try to be like other schools. Our starting point is to nurture each young person to really think about who they are and what they want to achieve. From there we do everything we can to support them to succeed as themselves – true to who they are and all the more remarkable for it."*

While the School offers a holistic curriculum, it is particularly well-known for its STEAM academic approach, which combines the analytical skills from Science, Technology, Engineering and Maths with the creativity from the Arts. Last year, 62% of Sixth Form leavers went on to STEAM-related degrees including Engineering, Medicine, Architecture and Product Design.

Music is another strength of the School with a stunning Music and Media Centre providing students with exceptional facilities, including a Yamaha Live Lounge recording studio. The Music department is accredited as a Flagship Music Education Partner, the only school in Europe to hold this status, with 60% of students studying an instrument and 27 music teachers on staff.

With Quaker values given currency and purpose through partnership and changemaker programmes, the School develops young people who understand, cherish, and make a difference to the world. Climate change and sustainability are important themes in the School's cross-curricular projects and expansive co-curricular programme. Leighton Park achieved the coveted Green Flag Award, won the Green School Award 2023 and is a national finalist for both the Independent School of the Year for Environmental Achievement 2023 and the ISA's Award for Excellence in Sustainability.

Leysin American School in Switzerland

(Founded 1960)

Head of School
Marc Ott

Dean of Academics
Sabina Lynch

DP coordinator
Ronan Lynch

Status Private

Boarding/day Boarding

Gender Coeducational

Language of instruction
English

Authorised IB programmes
DP

Age Range 12 – 18 years

Number of pupils enrolled
300

Fees
Boarding: CHF99,000

Address
3 Chemin de la Source
1854 Leysin VD | **SWITZERLAND**

TEL +41 24 493 4878

Email
admissions@las.ch

Website
www.las.ch

At Leysin American School in Switzerland, we develop innovative, compassionate, and responsible citizens of the world.

Our idyllic campus is tucked away in a beautiful mountain town. It provides the ideal environment for students, faculty, and staff to learn together in a safe, residential community in the Swiss Alps. Leysin, located in western Switzerland, represents the epitome of Swiss culture. Our striking, cozy hometown is an internationally-recognized ski destination with the hospitality, facilities, and lifestyle that appeal to students and global visitors alike. Leysin was also one of the host venues for the 2020 Youth Olympic Games.

We offer students an academically challenging setting with the goal of developing lifelong learners. Jointly accredited by NEASC and IBO, LAS provides a program for students at a variety of levels. IB Diploma students engage in deep, concentrated learning through engagement with the International Baccalaureate curriculum. The IB Diploma Programme has over 40 course offerings (SL/HL classes) available for students to select a program that best suits them and their future goals.

In 2022, the highest score at LAS was a 45. 34% of LAS candidates scored higher than 38 points, and the average score was 36 points. LAS had a 100% pass rate. 23% of candidates at LAS received an IB Bilingual Diploma. LAS re-introduced AP subject exams in 2020, and the first cohort sat their AP exams in May 2021.

At LAS, we are committed to providing a stable, caring, supportive, family-like environment. We are a diverse, tight-knit community where staff members are always on hand to give students care and guidance as they navigate the responsibilities and challenges of young adulthood. We offer our students a balanced program of study, sports, recreation, and cultural travel to promote a well-rounded education. During the winter, students ski twice a week from our ski-in, ski-out campus.

At LAS, we seek out every chance to connect our students with impactful hands-on learning opportunities so they can see the practical applications of their studies at work in the real world. We augment traditional classes with programs and events that build on students' passions and address current global issues, helping our students develop fundamental skills in critical thinking, entrepreneurship, and teamwork.

We take pride not only in educating stellar students but also attracting the attention of strong universities. Our university advisors begin working with students in grade 9, building relationships that focus on character, gratitude, personal excellence, and relationships. We facilitate a dedicated weekly course to support them in their personal and academic goals once they leave LAS.

(Founded 1977)

Principal
Mrs Claire Chisholm

Status Private

Boarding/day Mixed

Gender Coeducational

Language of instruction
English

Authorised IB programmes
DP, CP

Age Range 3 - 18 years

Number of pupils enrolled
360

Fees
Junior 1 to 5
£10,450 - £12,500 per annum
Transitus 1 to 2
£13,640 - £14,475 per annum
Senior School
£14,925 per annum
Boarding
£36,200 per annum

Address
10 Stafford Street, Helensburgh
Argyll & Bute G84 9JX | UK

TEL +44 (0)1436 672476

Email
admissions@lomondschool.com

Website
www.lomondschool.com

At Lomond School, we prepare our pupils for their future by ensuring that they learn the skills necessary to be successful in the 21st century, whilst developing the traditional values and qualities they require to be responsible and active global citizens.

Situated in the coastal town of Helensburgh, on the edge of Loch Lomond and the Trossachs National Park, and only 40 minutes from Glasgow International Airport, Lomond School provides a perfect setting to deliver a rounded education which inspires both academic and personal achievement.

From Junior 1 to Senior 6, our talented and dedicated teachers deliver a rich and varied curriculum ensuring that all Lomond School pupils are encouraged to love learning right from the start and continue to be challenged and inspired throughout their school career. From Senior 5, pupils study the International Baccalaureate Diploma Programme or the International Baccalaureate Career-related Programme with an HNC in Business or Engineering or a NC in Activity Tourism. We were delighted that our recent IB results were significantly higher than the global average.

Times are changing and our overall aim is to ensure that every young person in our care has an education that prepares them for life, challenges them to be the best they can be and inspires them to go out into the world and make a difference.

Beyond academics, our teachers and support staff work together to ensure that every child in our care makes the most of the many opportunities available to them in sport, extra-curricular activities, trips and excursions. There is a strong commitment to outdoor education with lessons in sailing, canoeing and climbing, all part of the curriculum. The learning opportunities such activities present for our young people are limitless, and our guiding principles and values strongly support lessons outside the classroom.

As the West of Scotland's only boarding school, living and studying at Lomond School offers a truly unique experience for boys and girls from the UK and around the world. Our boarding house, Burnbrae, is home to young people from a diverse range of nationalities and backgrounds and its superb location and facilities provide plenty of opportunities for adventure, making it an exciting and cosmopolitan place to learn and grow. As a co-educational house, siblings can live together under one roof and the mix of boys and girls of different ages creates a real family feel, helping our boarders to settle into Lomond School life with ease. We were thrilled that our boarding house was awarded an 'excellent' rating by the Care Inspectorate, making it 'sector leading'.

School Director
Dylan Hughes

Primary Principal
Lindsay Doughty

Secondary Principal
Grant Rogers

PYP coordinator
Julie Ranger

MYP coordinator
Catherine McCann

DP coordinator
Rene Bradford

Status Private, Non-Profit

Boarding/day Day

Gender Coeducational

Language of instruction
English

Authorised IB programmes
PYP, MYP, DP

Age Range 3 – 18 years

Number of pupils enrolled
580

Address
Via S6, Bairro de Talatona,
Município de Belas
Luanda | ANGOLA

TEL +244 932 337 056

Email lis@lisluanda.com

Website www.lisluanda.com

Welcome to Luanda International School(LIS)
LIS was founded in 1996 as a non-profit international school serving Pre-K to Year 13 (grade 12) students from the expatriate and local community in Luanda, Angola. Together, we form a close-knit community that cares deeply about respectful and healthy relationships, a strong sense of belonging, student voice, leadership, and growth. Our students, families, and staff come to Luanda from around the world, with more than 50 nationalities represented in our community.

Our Mission
Luanda International School is a diverse community of learners committed to fostering compassionate, confident, and socially responsible individuals who thrive in the world.

Relationships matter
LIS is renowned for its inclusive, family-like atmosphere. We believe our relationships with students and parents are a point of difference from many other schools in Angola – you can feel it the moment you enter the school. Students are central to what we do, so our engagement with our parents is always about the students and learning. We expect our families to engage and play a fundamental role in the success of their child's progress and achievement and, ultimately, live our school mission and values.

Thriving in Angola and Beyond
We are known as a school dedicated to learning in its broadest sense where, alongside a quality academic programme, students participate in a broad range of arts, sporting, cultural, and service activities designed to broaden outlooks and garner an appreciation of the world around them. Our extensive co-curricular programme is integral to the vibrant sense of community and campus life. The programme enhances our sense of community and aims to build sustainable and positive relationships within LIS, Angola, and global contexts. An important enabler of thriving and social responsibility is to connect our students with communities near and far, understand their unique needs, and respond in ways that are mutually beneficial. Our students have a proven and successful track record forming with organizations, including NGOs and ministries, to support their learning. This external expertise, coupled with student passion, helps to create the basis for sustainable project-based learning and the opportunity to thrive.

LIS is well known for attracting high-calibre faculty. Our faculty members demonstrate an ability to empower, encourage, and inspire concept-based, inquiry-driven learning focused on children's social, emotional, and cognitive well-being. We are a school prepared to search the globe for professional, international-minded teachers with a growth mindset and proven ability to build relationships and community.

Together Shaping Our Future

- LIS is committed to sustainability, and our campus reflects our environmental passion.
- We are leaders in child safeguarding.
- We take pride in our reputation for focusing on well-being, dignity, and respect for self and others.
- Building social and cultural competencies is the cornerstone of our programmes to develop lifelong skills, including peaceful conflict resolution, awareness and appreciation of other cultures, and interpersonal skills.

LWIS Keserwan-Adma International School

(Founded 1997)

Head of School
Dr. Nabil Husni

DP coordinator
Lisette Bou Lahoud

Status Private

Boarding/day Day

Gender Coeducational

Language of instruction
English

Authorised IB programmes
DP

Age Range 3 – 18 years

Number of pupils enrolled 470

Fees
Day: $2,500 – $6,000 per annum

Address
Mar Nohra
Fatqa,
Keserwan | **LEBANON**

TEL +961 9 740225

Email
info@lwis-ais.edu.lb

Website
www.lwis-ais.edu.lb

Vision
LWIS-AiS, home of Peace Education, will set the pace for holistic learner-centered education.

Mission
LWIS-AiS promotes life-long learning through Peace Education, professional development, and facilitated classrooms that utilize differentiation, inquiry, cooperative learning, and interactive technology.

We endorse a partnership where students, parents, staff, and community members work together in a safe and nurturing environment to develop higher order thinking, academic excellence, ethical behavior, and personal growth. We honor the gift and support the need of every child. We also empower learners to become active and innovative contributors to an ever-diverse international and multicultural society.

Values
LWIS-AiS ensures that the actions of all learners are guided by its PACER values:

Perseverance
Agility
Clarity
Empathy
Respect

Educational Objectives
We offer an educational journey whereby students embrace their rights and responsibilities and have fun. We believe the journey will develop learners who are effective leaders, Peace Education endorsers, good communicators, diversity celebrators, critical thinkers, problem solvers, creative researchers, team players, academic achievers, knowledgeable individuals, and self-reflectors.

Facilities
LWIS-AiS is located in Fatka, Lebanon. It overlooks the beautiful bay of Jounieh in what is an entirely green landscaped and residential neighborhood. The school features well-equipped classrooms with technology for mainstream and individualized learning students, internet connectivity, art rooms, indoor and outdoor playgrounds, as well as a library, science and computer labs, and a dance and drama area. The school consists of two campuses. The Upper Campus encompasses Grades 6 to 12 while the Lower Campus hosts Kindergarten through Grade 5.

Programs
LWIS-AiS has been accredited by NEASC since 2009. It offers the American High School Diploma in addition to the National Program. Furthermore, it became an authorized International Baccalaureate World School for the Diploma Programme in May 2019.

Teachers
LWIS-AiS teachers are highly qualified, experienced teachers.

The IB DP teachers have received IB authorized training.

Students
The School's diverse student body is one of its special assets.

The approximate number of students is 470, representing over 46 nationalities.

We invite you to join our journey and discover how we measure success one happy learner at a time.

Lycee Franco-Qatarien Voltaire

المدرسة القطرية - الفرنسـية فولتيـر
Lycée Franco-Qatarien Voltaire

(Founded 2007)

Head of School
Mr Serge Tillmann

DP coordinator
Mrs Hiam El Zakhem

Status Private

Boarding/day Day

Gender Coeducational

Language of instruction
French, English, Arabic

Authorised IB programmes
DP

Age Range 3 – 18 years

Number of pupils enrolled
1700

Salwa Campus
P.O. Box 12634
Zone 55, street Al Daoudiya no. 201
Doha | **QATAR**

West Bay Campus
Zone 88, Al Dafna,
street no. 973,
Doha | **QATAR**

Al Waab Campus
Zone 54, Mehairja,
street no. 691,
Doha | **QATAR**

TEL +974 4035 4015

Email
h.zakhem@voltairedoha.com

Website
www.lyceevoltaire.org

The establishment of the French-Qatari school Voltaire was the result of the Qatari authorities' commitment to providing education for young people of various nationalities, including French and Qatari students, in accordance with the core principles of the French educational system and its curriculum. This initiative respects the national specificities outlined by the Supreme Council of Education in Qatar, particularly in areas such as the teaching of the Arabic language, Qatar history and Islamic religion for Muslim students.

The French-Qatari school Voltaire, which welcomes nearly 1,700 students from 30 different nationalities, stands out as a model of education with a truly global perspective. It celebrates the diversity of identities that make up its student body, advocating for a culture of inclusion and intercultural respect. It is a place where the world comes together to learn and grow.

Our school is affiliated with the network of schools approved by the French Ministry of National Education and Youth. It is a partner school of the agency for French education abroad (AEFE). Additionally, it is part of the UNESCO network of affiliated schools, a member of the CIS network of schools and affiliated to Qatar Foundation.

Since September 2022, the French-Qatari school Voltaire is offering the prestigious IBDP programme in French, with a significant focus on the teaching of Arabic language. The International Baccalaureate IB represents an exceptional opportunity for French speaking students, whether they originate from Voltaire school or other schools in Qatar. This is because the IBDP diploma is widely recognized by numerous universities and higher education institutions across the globe. Attaining this esteemed diploma will open up new academic avenues for our students, both within Qatar and abroad.

In the academic year 2022-2023, all of our baccalaureate students achieved a 100% success rate. This accomplishment is a testament to the dedication and expertise of our educational teams.

The slogan of Voltaire school, "Two civilizations, 3 languages," continues to serve as the guiding principle for our educational teams and the families who entrust their children to our institution.

Mark Twain International School

(Founded 1995)

Head of School
Ms. Anca Macovei Vlasceanu

PYP coordinator
Ms. Corina Popa

MYP coordinator
Ms. Floriana Florea

DP coordinator
Ms. Olivia Fotescu

Status Private

Boarding/day Day

Gender Coeducational

Language of instruction
English, Romanian

Authorised IB programmes
PYP, MYP, DP

Age Range 2 – 19 years

Number of pupils enrolled 600

Fees
Preschool
€6,350 – €9,800 per annum
Primary School, starting at
€12,550 per annum
Middle School, starting at
€13,800 per annum
High School, starting at
€14,450 per annum

Junior Campus
25 Erou Iancu Nicolae Street
077190 Voluntari, Ilfov | **ROMANIA**

Secondary Campus
89 Erou Iancu Nicolae Street,
077190 Voluntari, Ilfov | **ROMANIA**

TEL +40 73 500 0160

Email
contact@marktwainschool.ro

Website
www.marktwainschool.ro

Student-centred | Global-minded | High-performing

Celebrating its 29th anniversary in 2024, Mark Twain International School is proud to be one of the most experienced international schools in Romania. Challenging educational frontiers with its two divisions of study, Global Bilingual (English-Romanian) and International (English), the School has a strong portfolio of accreditations to support its mission:

- the full International Baccalaureate continuum (PYP, MYP & DP)
- the Cambridge International Education Assessment for Primary and Secondary
- national recognition from the Ministry of Education via 4 accreditations covering the entire K12 route
- the delivery of The Duke of Edinburgh's International Award in Romania
- recognized Cambridge English Exam Preparation Centre.

Curriculum & Student Profile

At the core of the School's approach to premium education is the IB continuum: a broad, conceptual, connected curriculum, empowering students, as early as the pre-primary stage up to graduation, to achieve intellectual and academic success, and to develop a wide range of human capacities and social responsibilities. Students are encouraged to be inquisitive, knowledgeable, communicators and brave life-long learners, and to become open-minded, caring, balanced, and principled global citizens of the 21st century. Critical thinking is promoted, as they strive to reflect upon and learn from their actions. Annual pass rates for the International and National Baccalaureate are prevalently 100%, with graduates receiving offers to date from 150 of the world's top universities.

Diversity & Inclusion

Healthy relationships, ethical responsibility and personal challenge are all promoted. Over 50 vibrant nationalities are represented in the student community, and as students increase their understanding of the world's cultures and languages (including their mother tongue), they explore globally significant ideas, become confident in their own identity, join with others to celebrate our common humanity, learn how they can make a change with their own voices.

Teacher-Student Ratio & Faculty

The average teacher-student ratio is 1:6, and the annual teacher-turnover rate falls below 5%, thus facilitating optimal levels of consistency, care and attention to students' needs. The faculty is well-qualified, with most holding master and doctoral degrees, and being active participants in the Professional Development programs offered in both national/international networks.

Green Campus & Student Services

Operating in two green campuses near Baneasa Forest, Mark Twain International School welcomes its students to over 16,000 sq.m of verdant open spaces and 7,500 sq.m of modern buildings. The school offers 40+ extracurricular classes dedicated to arts, sports, and further academics, as well as student services: freshly-cooked meals, pastry/bakery onsite, door-to-door school bus service, infirmary with on-campus doctor, well-being, counselling and mental health support, special home delivery of school resources/care packs, parent support.

(Founded 1865)

Headmaster
Keith Metcalfe MA (Cantab)

DP coordinator
Jennifer Akehurst

Status Private, Independent

Boarding/day Mixed

Gender Coeducational

Language of instruction
English

Authorised IB programmes
DP

Age Range 13 – 18 years

Number of pupils enrolled
655

Fees
Boarder Sixth Form
£15,550 per term
Day Pupil Sixth Form
£10,550 per term
Pupils joining in Sixth Form:
Boarder £15,995 per term
Pupils joining in Sixth Form:
Day £10,550 per term

Address
College Road
Malvern
Worcestershire
WR14 3DF | UK

TEL +44 (0)1684 581515

Email
admissions@malverncollege.org.uk

Website
www.malverncollege.org.uk

The International Baccalaureate at Malvern College

The IB Diploma has been a highly successful part of the academic programme at Malvern since 1992 and it is a programme of study that is completely in tune with our holistic approach to education at the College.

Over the last five years, our IB graduates have averaged 36.8 points, with 18% of our pupils being awarded 40 points or more. With these results our pupils are consistently able to access the very best universities in the UK and across the world.

We offer a wide range of subjects, including Higher and Standard Level Maths in both Analysis and Approaches and Applications and Interpretation. We also offer both English Language and Literature and English Literature at both Higher and Standard Level.

We have recently introduced Psychology and Computer Science to our IB offering as well as School Supported Self Taught Language A, where pupils are able to study the literature of their native language with support from a school supervisor.

In all subject areas pupils are encouraged to develop communication skills, and the ability to think critically and reflectively, with the Theory of Knowledge course fundamental in developing the skills needed to enable pupils to test the validity of arguments and the strength of evidence.

At Malvern College we actively promote a set of well-tested, enduring human values which we call the Malvern Qualities. We believe that these values will enable our pupils to grow whilst they are with us and over time, equip our pupils for life's challenges, enabling them to adapt and succeed beyond Malvern.

Our pupil led Super-curriculum allows them to individualise their studies through a number of societies and these create the opportunities for intellectual stretch, further academic breadth and collaborative research. Our extensive Co-curricular programmes provide a significant range of opportunities for each pupil to engage in a range of sports, creative activities and service opportunities contributing to their Creativity, Activity and Service (CAS) component. Our holistic curriculum encourages and enables all pupils to develop the necessary skills, passions and ambitions, curiosity and personal qualities needed for building on their strengths, discovering new talents and becoming life-long learners.

Admissions

Please contact our Admissions team for details: admissions@malverncollege.org.uk. Tel:+44 (0)1684 581515

Marymount International School Rome

(Founded 1946)

Head of School
Ms. Sarah Gallagher

DP coordinator
Ms. Clare Lax

Status Private

Boarding/day Day

Gender Coeducational

Language of instruction
English

Authorised IB programmes
DP

Age Range 2 – 18 years

Number of pupils enrolled 918

Fees
Day: €13,100 – €26,000 per annum

Address
Via di Villa Lauchli, 180
00191 Rome | **ITALY**

TEL +39 06 3629 1012

Email
admissions@marymountrome.com

Website
www.marymountrome.com

Marymount International School Rome is a private, Catholic, co-educational day school. The oldest international school in Italy, we are located on a 40-acre campus of protected parkland just 20 minutes north of the city center.

An English-language Early Childhood through 12th Grade School, our standards-based international curriculum is inclusive with an academic offering that is bespoke to the individual needs of every student. Enrichment opportunities are offered across all Grade Levels to encourage students to discover what they love doing and who they are as people in order to guide them towards the achievement of their full potential.

A wide range of extracurricular activities include Varsity athletics, S.T.E.A.M. classes, theater, choir/band, and Model United Nations, in addition to visits to national and international sites of cultural importance. Marymount graduates obtain an accredited American High School Diploma and the majority of our students work towards the full IB Diploma with around 15% opting for individual IB course certificates.

Marymount has been an IB World School for over 35 years. The Diploma Programme (DP) has become an integral component of Marymount's academic program. School wide curriculum alignment prepares students with the academic rigor necessary to fully engage with the Diploma. We offer over 30 subjects at this level, including 11 languages. Students also have the opportunity to choose among several Advanced Placement classes.

Marymount consistently obtains well above world average results. Over the past 3 years our DP Candidates obtained an average score of 35 points. Marymount is a culturally and responsibly inclusive School, with an open admissions policy, and is therefore particularly proud of its students' results. The internationalism of the program is reflected in that over half of the students achieve the Bilingual Diploma.

The School's IB students go on to study in many of the world's top universities and colleges; in the UK this includes Cambridge, London School of Economics, Imperial College London, and King's College London, and Yale, New York University, Boston College, and Johns Hopkins in North America, in addition to Bocconi and more.

Classroom activities focus on conceptual understanding, authentic learning, and skills development. The School also has an ever-growing commitment to technology and Artificial Intelligence learning. All Marymount students work with personal Apple devices and the School is equipped with the latest technology, art and science labs, as well as a Forest School.

Marymount welcomes students from over 80 different nationalities and of all faiths to participate in its vibrant community life, where each student is valued and nurtured to achieve their full potential and develop a lifelong love of learning.

Mirabal International School

(Founded 1982)

Director
Ms Rosario de la Cruz López

MYP coordinator
Isabel Sargent Busquets

DP coordinator
Isabel Sargent Busquets

Status Private

Boarding/day Day

Gender Coeducational

Language of instruction
English, Spanish

Authorised IB programmes
MYP, DP

Age Range 0 – 18 years

Number of pupils enrolled
1957

Address
Calle Monte Almenara, s/n
28660 Boadilla del Monte,
Madrid | SPAIN

TEL +34 916 331 711

Email
mirabal@colegiomirabal.com

Website
www.colegiomirabal.com

Mirabal International School is a school of reference in Europe. Highly regarded by its' exceptional academic standards, Mirabal has historically achieved world top positions in the annual PISA report for Schools, an educational evaluation promoted by the Organisation for Economic Co-operation and Development (OECD).

Founded in 1982 Mirabal International School is committed to the integral education of the students, promoting values such as independence, tolerance, responsibility (diligence, generosity, honour). Located in an outstanding natural setting in the north of Madrid, Mirabal offers excellent facilities at the service of an innovative educational project based on interactive and practical learning. The school occupies a total of 45,000 m2 and offers a wide range of sports and academic facilities, including tennis courts, athletics tracks, two swimming pools and several laboratories.

The constant training of teachers in active and innovative methodologies and subjects such as robotics are some of the key tools used to bring students closer to the most advanced learning resources. Students learn to research, discriminate, contrast and select information from a very young age.

Students can choose to follow Spanish National Curriculum, the International Baccalaureate or a double-honors program. Its multilingual program is offered by native teachers and is especially designed to stimulate physical intellectual, social and artistic development.

Mirabal is a certified music school, where students can obtain an official Music Elementary Degree in the instrument of their choice. Emotional intelligence is a main focus of Mirabal's educational project. Cooperative learning, emotion management, motivation and education in values help students acquire skills such as creativity, leadership and initiative.

Modern Montessori School

(Founded 1985)

School Director
Zeid Khasawreh

PYP coordinator
Rasha Hamzeh

MYP coordinator
Reem Dahleh

DP coordinator
Hoor Hawamdeh

Status Private

Boarding/day Day

Gender Coeducational

Language of instruction
English, Arabic

Authorised IB programmes
PYP, MYP, DP

Age Range 3 – 18 years

Number of pupils enrolled
1655

Address
P.O. Box 1941
Khilda
Amman
11821 | JORDAN

TEL +962 6 553 5190

Email
mms@montessori.edu.jo

Website
www.mms.edu.jo

The Modern Montessori School (MMS) aims to provide a rich and stimulating environment where children can develop to their full potential. Understanding and appreciating the differences that make every student unique, each child is valued as an independent thinker and encouraged to make choices on his or her own.

Our system of personalised education encourages every student to develop his or her own talent, to respect the differences in others, and to be a respectable member of a community, thus achieving the finest possible holistic education. This aims to instil a pride in accomplishments, providing the students with the confidence needed to use their abilities to the fullest and enabling them to define and achieve success in college, career and, above all, in life.

To this end, the IB Diploma Programme at MMS is designed largely to cater for the needs of individuals, rather than for the collective needs of a group; our subject menu is varied and enjoys a degree of flexibility, which in turn allows students to choose the subjects that appeal to their different learning preferences and future university courses.

Furthermore, MMS has devised an extracurricular, three-level award scheme, which has the IB CAS perched atop its golden level. The Amin Hasan Award (AHA) provides students from grade 6-10 with the ability to participate in enjoyable yet beneficial and thought-provoking activities. This non-academic aspect of their education is extremely valuable in the overall development of the whole child, as it fosters a sense of compassion, teamwork, and mutual respect among students, in addition to promoting the principles of model citizenship and the importance of solidarity and togetherness among people, irrespective of their ethnic, religious, or gender differences. One of the many AHA activities was having students work together to meet the challenge of scaling Jordan's highest peak.

At MMS, we also believe in the inherent ability of each student to achieve distinction. This is why our LEAD Department (inclusive assessment) works hand-in-hand with administrators, programme coordinators, and teachers to cater for students who have special learning needs, through the application of an inclusion programme.

We also believe that cooperation between home and school is required to ensure the personal and intellectual development of each student. Consequently, we have designed an e-school portal where both parents and students are kept up-to-date with everything they need from report cards and academic calendars to forums and e-learning material.

As a PYP/MYP accredited school, the MMS prepares students through a devised preparation programme and curricula that will ultimately expose students to the IB continuum of international education.

The Modern Montessori School is accredited by the International Centre for Montessori Education (ICME), Cambridge and Edexcel International Examinations' syndicates and is an authorised IB World School. In addition, MMS has recently acquired membership from the Council of International Schools (CIS).

Mount House School

(Founded 1947)

Head
Mrs Sarah Richardson

CP coordinator
Mr Jon Cooper

Status Private

Boarding/day Day

Gender Coeducational

Language of instruction
English

Authorised IB programmes
CP

Age Range 11 – 18 years

Address
Camlet Way
Hadley Wood
Barnet
Hertfordshire
EN4 0NJ | UK

TEL 020 8449 6889

Email
admissions@mounthouse.org.uk

Website
www.mounthouse.org.uk

Mount House is a beautiful Georgian grade II listed building in Hadley Wood, Hertfordshire, on the borders of North London.

We offer all our students a pathway which suits their individual needs, particularly in the Sixth Form. We run two core pathways at Sixth Form: A Level and IBCP.

A key pillar of a Mount House education is the individual approach we can offer students. The IB Career Related Programme (IBCP) allows us to build on this ethos with a pathway that gives some students a learning experience and qualification that is more relevant to their needs. The IBCP gives Mount House Sixth Formers an option that differs to A Levels in the approach to aspects of teaching and learning, whilst offering an excellent springboard for next steps be that Russell Group university entry, apprenticeships or the world of work. The Career Related Programme has four clear aims for students:

- To prepare for work in a knowledge society
- To prepare for the future
- To provide a locally relevant education
- To bridge the 'academic vs vocational' divide

Subject options within the IBCP include Global Politics, Computer Science, Environmental Science, Business Management, English Literature & Language, Food and Nutrition, Music Performance, and Criminology.

Our Sixth Formers enjoy the Personal and Professional Studies course, and every one of them undertake Service Learning where they volunteer in the community gaining hugely valuable skills and wellbeing as a result. Alongside the small class sizes and our personal tutor system, each student has the chance to make an impact on the school and community and pursue their own interests in a supportive and friendly environment.

Visit us: mounthouse.org.uk/opendays

Muruvvet Evyap Schools

(Founded 2008)

Principal
Elcin Kizilkaya

Vice Principal
Nilüfer Danis

PYP coordinator
Inci Er

Status Private

Boarding/day Day

Gender Coeducational

Language of instruction
English, Turkish

Authorised IB programmes
PYP

Age Range 3 – 18 years

Address
Maden District Bakir Street,
No. 2A/2B/2C
Sariyer
34450 Istanbul,
Marmara | **TURKEY**

TEL +90 212 342 43 33

Email
info@evyapokullari.k12.tr

Website
www.evyapokullari.k12.tr

Private Muruvvet Evyap Schools was founded in 2008 by two charitable shareholders of Evyap Holding, whose foundations were laid in 1927, in the name of their deceased sister.

The school is located in Sariyer, a decent district on the European side of Istanbul. It is close to the Bosporus and Belgrade Forests, intertwined with nature where oxygen and green are abundant, away from the noise of the city, easy to access and in a safe area.

Our school has approximately 900 learners within a campus of twenty thousand square meters, of which six thousand square meters are garden and activity areas, and ninety closed and 2 open classrooms.

125 local and foreign expert instructors with various socio-cultural experiences provide education at departments of the pre-school, primary, secondary and high schools.

Besides its workshops for science, computer, think-design-create, mind games, visual arts, music, drama, etc., the school offers its learners contemporary 21st century educational opportunities with its indoor/outdoor sports areas, generous libraries and a modern conference hall.

The Private Muruvvet Evyap Schools develop individuals that absorb universal values, effectively communicate in the Turkish language and one other foreign language, is of inquiring mind, a scientifically, analytically and synthetically thinker, sensitive to their environment and nature, respective and caring of all different cultures, skilled in life-long learning, able to participate in at least one arts, sports or social responsibility activities, a leader and model to society in the light of the principles and revolutions of Atatürk.

At Private Evyap Schools, the k12 curriculum of the Ministry of National Education is integrated and implemented along with the International Baccalaureate Primary Years Programme. The achievements for each level, stipulated by the Ministry of National Education, are structured and developed around the framework offered by the IBPYP.

Our school community, which is aware of the importance of social solidarity, implements various social responsibility projects throughout the year in order to enable individuals to act together. Our learners obtain degrees in science, art, sports and culture from national and international organizations such as, IYIPO, MOSTRATEC, TUBITAK, DI, ISBO, ATAST Fest, Junior FLL, FLL and Picasso Art Contest.

NORD ANGLIA INTERNATIONAL SCHOOL DUBLIN

Principal
Paul Crute

PYP coordinator
Jack Odey

MYP coordinator
Andrew Bateson

DP coordinator
Joanna Cooper

Status Private

Boarding/day Day

Gender Coeducational

Language of instruction
English

Authorised IB programmes
PYP, MYP, DP

Age Range 3 – 18 years

Address
South County Business Park
Leopardstown
Dublin 18 | **IRELAND**

TEL +353 1 5442323

Email
admissions@naisdublin.com

Website
www.naisdublin.com

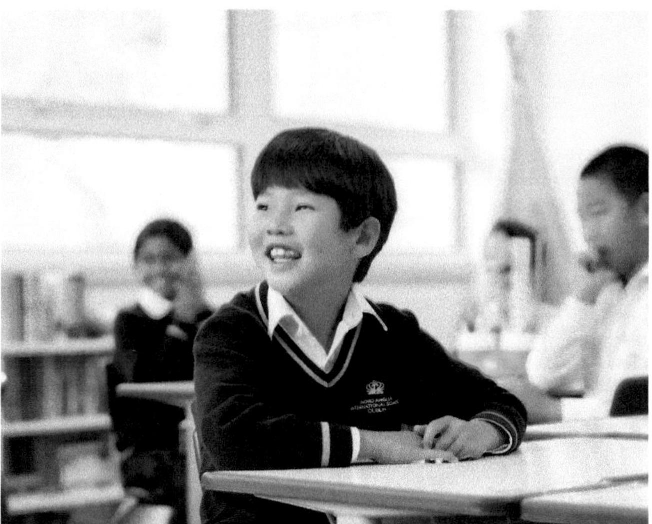

Nord Anglia International School Dublin (NAIS Dublin) is a member of Nord Anglia Education's global family of premium schools in Europe, South East Asia, North America and the Middle East. NAIS Dublin is Ireland's newest IB World School and is the only school in Ireland to unite an international curriculum with world-class learning opportunities and global experiences that enable students to achieve more than they ever thought possible.

Nord Anglia International School Dublin is fully credited to deliver the Primary Years Programme (PYP) from age 3 to 11, the Middle Years Programme (MYP) from age 11 to 16 and the Diploma Programme (DP) from age 16 to 18. NAIS Dublin is Ireland's first and only IB continuum school. These IB programmes teach students to think critically and interdependently, to inquire with care and logic, and to become confident and resilient. We have developed our curriculum in conjunction with the Massachusetts Institute of Technology and The Juilliard School of Performing Arts in New York.

True learning and innovation happens at the intersection of disciplines, so your child will be encouraged to tackle problems by calling on knowledge from several subjects. As a truly international school, our students collaborate and learn with over 70,000 of their peers in 32 countries every day through our Global Campus: whether that be physically in school, virtually online, or by travelling worldwide to other schools to participate in sporting events in the USA, cultural exchanges with China, adventure activities in Switzerland and philanthropic outreach experiences in India.

Our state-of-the-art campus has been designed for the future of learning and is centred around a custom designed building in Leopardstown, South County Dublin. Our facilities include a custom-built sports centre, dance studio, design and technology studios, performing arts spaces, auditorium, libraries and a parent café.

Parents choose a Nord Anglia Education because we offer academic, social and personal success for every student. Through opportunities to learn from the best, experiences beyond the ordinary, and the encouragement to achieve more than they ever thought possible, we help our students succeed anywhere through our unique global educational offer. We do this by investing in our people, our schools, and above all, our students. At Nord Anglia International School Dublin, your child will grow as a confident global citizen in an engaging environment, which will ensure that they will love learning for life.

**Only schools authorized by the International Baccalaureate can offer any of its four academic programmes: the Primary Years Programme (PYP), the Middle Years Programme (MYP), the Diploma Programme or the Career-related Programme (CP).*

NORD ANGLIA
INTERNATIONAL
SCHOOL
ROTTERDAM

(Founded 1959)

Head of School
Alison Lipp

DP coordinator
Aidan Jones

Status Private

Boarding/day Day

Gender Coeducational

Language of instruction
English

Authorised IB programmes
DP

Age Range 3 – 18 years

Number of pupils enrolled
250

Fees
Day: €15,900 – €21,600 per annum

Address
Verhulstlaan 21
3055 WJ Rotterdam, South Holland | **NETHERLANDS**

TEL +31 10 4225351

Email
admissions@naisr.nl

Website
www.naisr.nl

Nord Anglia International School Rotterdam (NAISR) is a member of Nord Anglia Education's global family of premium schools, providing high quality international education for children from 3 to 18 years of age. NAISR offers a warm and caring community, where students will immediately feel comfortable and supported.

Small Private School

NAISR's small class sizes and caring and committed teachers ensure that every student receives the care and attention they need to thrive. With the perfect blend of in-class challenge and support, NAISR's students excel both academically and personally, becoming confident and proactive global citizens. Our Core Values Programme (CVP), which is embedded into every student's day, creates a strong sense of community and personal responsibility.

In everything our students do, we encourage them to act with integrity, to be considerate, and to develop the qualities they'll need to thrive as individuals, family members, and part of a global society.

International Baccalaureate

NAISR is fully authorised to deliver the IB Diploma Programme (IBDP) for students in their final two years of school. Students studying the IBDP develop life skills such as critical thinking, teamwork, research and time management, which sets them up for success at university and beyond. The programme aims to develop confident and enthusiastic learners who respond to challenges with optimism and an open mind.

Academic Excellence

NAISR is proud of their 100% IBDP pass rate for the classes of 2021, 2022 and 2023. NAISR IBDP graduates achieve high academic outcomes, remaining above the global average, opening doors to top universities in The Netherlands and around the world. At NAISR, the teachers embrace individual strengths, passions, and ambitions, ensuring every student learns in a way that's right for them.

At NAISR, IB students have the opportunity to gain a bilingual IB Diploma. Bilingual students can study two language courses from the 'Studies in Language & Literature' subject group to be awarded with the prestigious 'IB Bilingual Diploma'. This special qualification recognises a student's high level of multilingual skills and is well received on university applications.

NAISR students have easy access to the IB Coordinator and College Counsellor, offering personalised support to each student as they embark on their journey to higher education. Students' wellbeing is also at the heart of their educational experience. Our pastoral care team, which includes specially trained teachers, a nurse, and safeguarding experts, make sure our students feel safe, are safe and cared for at school.

If you have any questions, or you would like to learn more about our educational offering, IB at NAISR, please contact their friendly admissions team at admissions@naisr.nl or +31 (0)10 422 5351. You are also welcome to explore the school's website at www.naisr.nl.

(Founded 1850)

Headmistress
Vicky Bingham

DP coordinator
Dr Henry Linscott

Status Private

Boarding/day Day

Gender Female

Language of instruction
English

Authorised IB programmes
DP

Number of pupils enrolled
1080

Fees
Day: £6,880 – £7,994 per term

Address
Canons
Canons Drive
Edgware
Middlesex
HA8 7RJ | UK

TEL +44 (0)20 8952 0912

Email
office@nlcs.org.uk

Website
www.nlcs.org.uk

North London Collegiate School is internationally recognised as an outstanding school which provides an exceptional education. One of the oldest day schools for girls in England, we have maintained our position as an established force at the forefront of women's education, and our students consistently excel in every area. Our students leave us not just with outstanding qualifications, but also as articulate and independent young adults who possess the confidence, intellectual curiosity, and passion for learning and understanding that will endure for life.

Whilst ensuring academic excellence, equal attention is given to supporting the development of the whole person, inspiring confidence, individuality and self-esteem. Consequently, the school is a positive and energetic community where pupils are encouraged to take advantage of the opportunities open to them, with around 36 productions, 40 societies and 30 foreign trips offered each year.

International Outlook

NLCS has a highly international perspective that is unique amongst London day schools. We feel it is vital to prepare our students to become global citizens, by providing opportunities for them to be outward-looking, internationally minded and well informed about the world beyond school. Our growing family of sister schools in South Korea, Dubai, Bangkok and Ho Chi Minh City, with more branches planned for the future, benefits pupils and staff through exchange opportunities and internships. The IB Diploma resonates with the values of NLCS, and its international dimension affords students the opportunity to be part of a programme which is offered in, and recognised by, almost every country in the world.

Academic Excellence

In 2023, our students achieved an average points score of 41.5 and since offering the IB Diploma programme in 2004, we have had an exceptional record of success. Our students consistently achieve an average score in excess of 40 points, making NLCS one of the top-performing IB schools in the world.

Looking to the future

Our IB students have received offers from a range of impressive institutions including Oxford, Cambridge, Harvard, Yale, Georgetown, Stanford and Princeton, as well as other leading universities such as Bristol, Edinburgh and the London colleges and medical schools.

The IB Diploma programme offered at NLCS ensures that students enjoy an exciting and academically stimulating Sixth Form experience, providing them with an excellent preparation for life at university and in the wider world beyond.

Oakham School

(Founded 1584)

Headmaster
Mr Henry Price MA (Oxon)

MYP coordinator
Dmitriy Ashton

DP coordinator
Carolyn Fear

Status Private

Boarding/day Mixed

Gender Coeducational

Language of instruction
English

Authorised IB programmes
MYP, DP

Age Range 10 – 18 years

Number of pupils enrolled
1000

Fees
Day:
£20,535 – £26,100 per annum
Weekly Boarding:
£24,675 – £41,055 per annum
Boarding:
£31,500 – £43,905 per annum

Address
Chapel Close
Oakham
Rutland
LE15 6DT | UK

TEL 01572 758758

Email
admissions@oakham.rutland.sch.uk

Website
www.oakham.rutland.sch.uk

Oakham is proud to be an IB World School and we have been successfully teaching the IB Diploma for over 20 years and the IB MYP since 2021. Our educational ethos perfectly reflects the IB's vision to develop inquiring, knowledgeable, confident, and caring young people. An Oakham education is powered by our Connected Curriculum, where the three educational pillars of academic, pastoral, and co-curricular learning are fully integrated across all age groups.

Oakham is well known and loved for being a friendly, unpretentious, and highly successful school. Our down-to-earth atmosphere is thanks to our uniquely balanced pupil community with children from nearly 40 countries, 50:50 boarding and day pupils, 50:50 girls and boys. Around 19% of Oakham pupils are international students and we celebrate the different perspectives they bring to enrich our community.

Academic

Pupils in Years 7-9 follow the IB MYP, they choose from 26 subjects at GCSE and at 16+ study either the IB Diploma or A-levels. Our IB Diploma results far exceed the global average, and our teachers are leading practitioners and examiners. Our full-time Head of Careers and her team offer in-depth guidance and information on career options and admissions procedures for UK and overseas universities.

Pastoral Care

Our dedicated Houses for boarders and day pupils means that we can offer all pupils the benefits of our outstanding boarding provision in ways that suit modern family life. Led by a Housemaster or Housemistress, and supported by a team of Tutors, Prefects and a Matron, each of our 16 Houses provides our pupils with the care and support they need to develop intellectually, physically, emotionally and spiritually.

Our location

Pupils benefit from the school's location close to Rutland Water, in the heart of safe, rural England. Our beautifully green campus is just a few minutes' walk from Oakham's historic town centre and train station and Oakham's excellent road and rail links mean that London, Birmingham and Cambridge are all within easy reach. There is a direct train to Stansted Airport.

Co-curricular

We offer a spectacularly wide range of co-curricular opportunities. We stage five major drama productions every year, over 500 individual music lessons each week, and thriving Art & Design Departments. Oakham has a national reputation for Sport, offering 30 different sports. Students choose from over 125 activities to take part in each week, including MUN, DofE, CCF, and Voluntary Action, and sailing.

OurPlanet International School Muscat

OURPLANET
International School
MUSCAT

(Founded 2012)

Head of School
Mr Fasial Al-Awfi

PYP coordinator
Madhuparna Bhattacharyya

Status Private

Boarding/day Day

Gender Coeducational

Language of instruction
English

Authorised IB programmes
PYP

Age Range 3 – 15 years

Number of pupils enrolled 289

Address
Al-Inshirah Street,
Building No. 205
Plot No. 95, Block No. 221
111 Muscat | **OMAN**

TEL +968 2200 5642

Email
info@ourplanet-muscat.com

Website
www.ourplanet-muscat.com

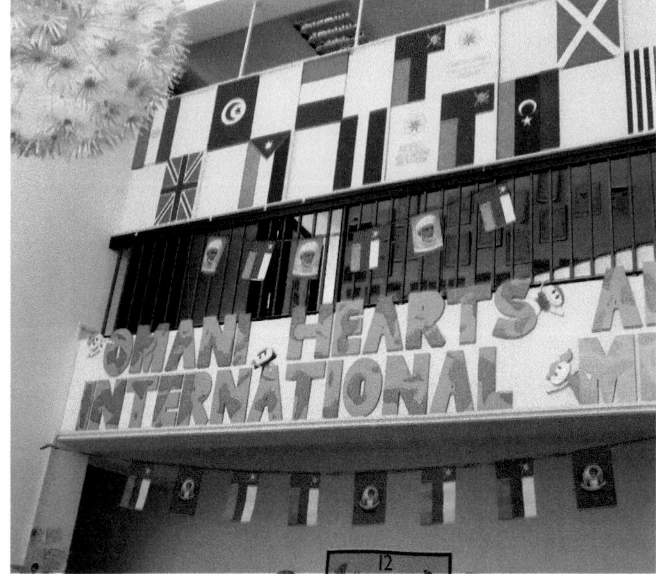

Founded in 2012, OurPlanet International School Muscat is a co-educational school in the heart of Oman's capital, Muscat. We currently welcome students aged 3-15 from diverse cultural backgrounds encompassing nearly 30 different nationalities.

OPIS aims to foster a multicultural and inquiry-led learning environment in English and Arabic that promotes sustainability and celebrates Oman's unique cultural identity.

The OPIS community is a close-knit mesh of passionate and knowledgeable educators, and students who aim at becoming life-long learners. We work closely with our PTA, keeping the relationship between all stakeholders embedded in mutual trust and understanding.

Our curriculum empowers students to expand their horizons and prepare to be responsible and independent global citizens. English-language subjects include Math, Social Studies, Science, English Language & Literature, Visual Art, Music, Design, PSPE and Islamic Studies. Arabic-language subjects include Omani Social Studies, Arabic Language & Literature and Islamic Studies. German and Arabic are also taught as foreign languages.

"Omani Hearts and International Minds" is our motto, and our school events calendar reflects this belief. We celebrate Omani Women's Day, Omani National Day and International Peace Day, among other holidays. School events include a winter concert, outdoor learning days, and athletic competitions, while service projects and community fundraisers are a common occurrence, initiated and planned by our internationally minded and action oriented students.

Field trips, too, play a significant role in our curriculum, as we believe environments outside the classroom have much to teach our students. We plan educational trips throughout the year, including overnight stays, that help build leadership qualities in each child. Learner Profile Attributes play a central role on all school trips, as well as a focus on communication, thinking, self-management and problem-solving skills. Opportunities for student leadership are also available through the OPIS Student Council, which is geared towards supporting sustainability initiatives at the school, as well as the development of Service as Action learning outcomes.

The OPIS After School Activities programme includes a blend of creativity and sports. We pride ourselves on providing a wide range of activities to students, engaging with the best vendors in Muscat alongside our in-house teacher-practitioners.

Enrollment, based on availability, is open all year round. Applicants must supply school reports from the previous two academic years and pass grade-level entrance assessments.

Applicants are encouraged to visit OPIS to meet with our Admissions Team, tour school facilities and experience our community. For further details, please contact **admissions@ourplanet-muscat.com**.

PaRK International School

PaRK INTERNATIONAL SCHOOL

Executive Head of School
Samantha Gonçalves

DP coordinator
Mason Grine

Status Private

Boarding/day Day

Gender Coeducational

Language of instruction
English

Authorised IB programmes
DP

Age Range 1 – 18 years

Number of pupils enrolled
1350

Fees
Day:
€7,680 – €18,600 per annum
Enrolment Fee:
€800 – €4,800 per annum

Address
Estrada de Alfragide 94
2610-015 Amadora,
Lisbon | PORTUGAL

TEL +351 215 807 000

Email
admissions@park-is.com

Website
www.park-is.com

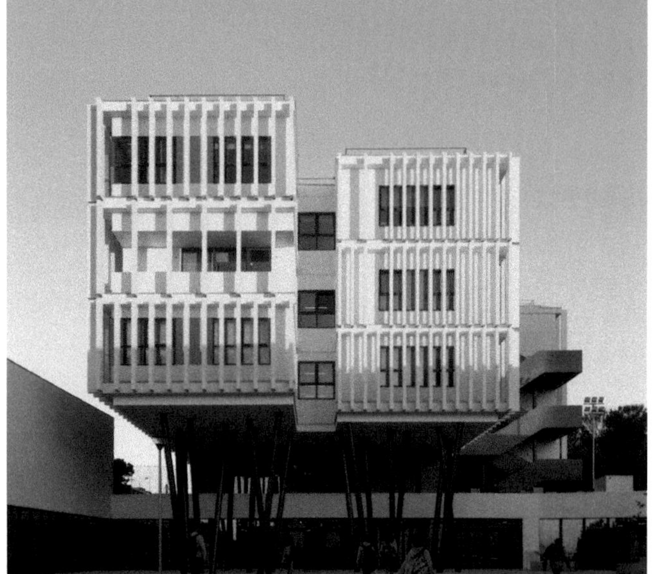

PaRK IS, an Inspired school, welcomes nearly 2,000 students from 1 Year Old to Grade 12 across our three campuses in Lisbon. An international school with Portuguese roots, PaRK IS offers the best education for both Portuguese and International families, welcoming students and staff from over 50 nationalities. Our mission is to guide and inspire students to be successful and happy in their adult lives.

With new, state-of-the-art facilities (opened in September 2020) in a 2,000sqm campus, PaRK IS Alfragide offers a demanding, dynamic, innovative and bespoke curriculum for each age group: a bilingual education from Early Learning until Grade 4, Cambridge (including the IGCSE) from Grade 5, and the internationally-acclaimed IB Diploma Programme. Our first cohort graduated in May 2022, with an outstanding average of 35.2 point score.

Students receive a personalised and well-rounded education – besides the strong academic curriculum, our Well-Being department ensures that each student has their individual needs met. It is also responsible for the Social Skills programme, so important for our students' success and happiness. In addition, our student-centred university counselling programme offers each student the tools and support they need to follow the right university and career path for their unique profile.

We are always searching for the world's best practices in education and implementing the ones that best fit our students and their objectives. Technology is fully integrated into the curriculum, and we offer unique Arts and Drama classes, in addition to PaRK Music Academy, where students find a solid bridge between vocational and non-vocational music education. Furthermore, we provide our students with a wide range of sporting activities, including the exclusive Inspired Sports Programme, which offers individualised training for students from Grades 5 to 12. In this programme, students can dedicate themselves to the sport of their choice during school hours, getting the personalised coaching they need to excel both athletically and academically.

Inspired Education Group students have had the best IB Diploma results across the world – providing access to top universities in Europe and the US. As an Inspired School, PaRK IS gives its students access to world's best practices in education, outstanding arts and sports programmes, state of the art facilities, and Exchange Programmes.

With a PaRK IS education, students will be prepared for academic excellence, proficient in more than one language and equipped with key life skills to be successful in an ever-changing world.

Pierce – The American College of Greece

President
Dr. David G. Horner

DP coordinator
Dr. Emmanuel Vrontakis

Status Private, Non-Profit

Boarding/day Day

Gender Coeducational

Language of instruction
English, Greek

Authorised IB programmes
DP

Address
6 Gravias Street
Aghia Paraskevi
Athens
153 42 | GREECE

TEL +30 210 600 9800 (Ext:1060)

Email
pierceibsecretariats@acg.edu

Website
www.pierce.gr

Founded in 1875, Pierce – The American College of Greece is a private, non-sectarian, non-profit institution accredited and regulated by the Greek Ministry of Education. Pierce has been offering the International Baccalaureate Diploma Programme (IBDP), since 2016.

The Pierce Mission

The mission of Pierce is to provide holistic education to form intellectually independent, morally responsible, socially engaged global citizens. *"Non ministrari sed ministrare"* ("Not to be served but to serve") defines our institutional character and our aspiration for our students.

Why Pierce-IB is unique

1. Small class sizes (5-15 students), which augment group work and learning, as well as facilitate interactive teaching and academic collaboration.
2. Pierce-IB DP students are supported with additional class sessions, enabling families to eliminate private tutoring and alleviate from additional expenses.
3. Supervised Study Sessions: since all Pierce-IB DP students follow the daily schedule of the mainstream program, with less number of courses (than those mandated by the Greek curriculum). Hence, each student will have – approximately – two 2-period sessions (per week) with no class. For these time slots our students have three options:
   - To stay in class and prepare/read, for the next day or collaborate with their teachers/tutors.
   - To use our Computer Lab and search for data, papers and information from the web, from digital libraries or from ManageBac (the online platform for teachers and students' communication).
   - To go to Pierce library and search relevant bibliography or references, required for their Internal Assessments and/or Extended Essay.
4. Pierce-IB DP is supported by highly qualified and trained teachers, with extensive experience in the Diploma Programme and University education. The majority of teachers (55%) hold a PhD degree and all of them (100%) hold either an MSc or an MA degree. The IBO verification team was most impressed by the academic qualifications, the passion and the commitment of the school staff.
5. We take advantage of all divisions of The American College of Greece (Pierce, Deree, Alba), exchanging best teaching practices, undergraduate education experience and high-end facilities, such as:
   - The ACG Art Gallery, which is a distinctive educational venue for students and faculty based on the academic program of Visual Arts. Each year we organize the annual VA exhibition, where our students' works are displayed.
   - The ACG Simulated Trading Room is built to offer our students a real-world trading experience. This state-of-the-art trading room is expected to recreate a professional financial environment and is being supported by the latest trends in technology, including state-of-the-art hardware and software.
   - The Fabrication Lab is a new technologies workshop which is equipped with 3D printers, a laser cutter, a 3D scanner, a vinyl cutter, a CNC machine, robotics kits and an electronics workbench for experimenting with creative electronics, such as sensors, microcontrollers, conductive ink, e-textiles, etc.
6. Pierce-IB DP is fully integrated with campus life and the regular high school program. Our students can take part in all activities the School has to offer, choosing from more than 50 Clubs, Pan-Hellenic or European contests and International Programs such as: Model United Nations, Harvard Model Congress Europe, University of Delaware Summer Program, Phillips Exeter Summer School.

Qatar Academy Al Khor

الخور Al Khor
أكاديمية قطر Qatar Academy
عضو في مؤسسة قطر
Member of Qatar Foundation

Director
Ms. Lina F. Mouchantaf

PYP coordinator
Ms. Nadia Hussain

MYP coordinator
Mrs. Lina Aridi

DP coordinator
Mr. David Leadbetter

Status Private

Boarding/day Day

Gender Coeducational

Language of instruction
Arabic, English

Authorised IB programmes
PYP, MYP, DP

Age Range 3 – 18 years

Number of pupils enrolled
1243

Fees
Day: QR46,000 – QR75,000 per annum

Address
P.O.Box: 60774
Mowasalat Street
Al Khor | **QATAR**

TEL +974 44546775

Email
qaalkhor@qf.org.qa

Website
www.qak.edu.qa

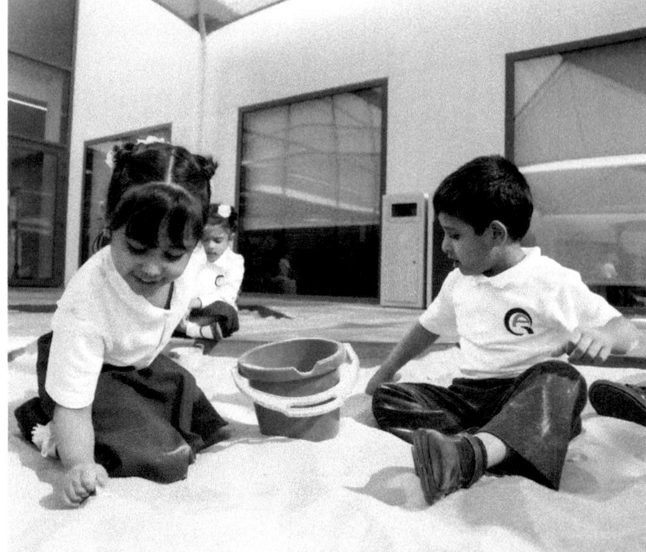

Qatar Academy Al Khor (QAK) was established in 2008 to serve students who live in Al Khor and the different areas in the north of Qatar, extending our groundbreaking curriculum to a broader community. As a full IB World School that predominantly educates native Qatari students and long-time residents, QAK is especially dedicated to developing local human capital. QAK seamlessly blends its world-class international curriculum with Qatar's heritage and culture. In part, this is achieved by enabling students to thrive in a truly bilingual environment that develops rich language skills in English and Arabic concurrently, since the student base is predominantly Qatari.

QAK strives to empower students to be open-minded, inquiring and knowledgeable life-long learners who are able to adapt to an ever-changing world through intercultural understanding and respect.

At QAK, we envision our future leaders as courageous problem-solvers who will make a positive difference in the world.

Our mission at QAK is to create a safe yet dynamic learning environment that inspires innovation. QAK empowers learners to think critically as compassionate and principled global citizens grounded in Arab values while celebrating Qatari National heritage and culture.

Qatar Academy Al Wakra

(Founded 2011)

Director
Mrs. Bedriyah Itani

PYP coordinator
Mrs. Samira Jurdak

MYP coordinator
Ms. Kristin J. Hexter

DP coordinator
Ms. Lynette Winnard

Status Private

Boarding/day Day

Gender
Coeducational (in Primary), Segregated (in Secondary)

Language of instruction
Arabic, English

Authorised IB programmes
PYP, MYP, DP

Age Range 3 – 17 years

Number of pupils enrolled
1300

Fees
Day: QR50,000 – QR70,000 per annum

Address
P.O. Box: 2589
Al Farazdaq Street, street No.: 1034, Zone: 90
Doha | QATAR

TEL +974 44547418

Email
qataracademyal-wakra@qf.org.qa

Website
www.qaw.edu.qa

Qatar Academy Al Wakra (QAW) is a premier private international school in Qatar, and a member of Qatar Foundation, a world-class organization dedicated to building excellent educational institutions.

Qatar Academy Al Wakra was established to serve the needs of the rapidly growing Al Wakra coastal community and surrounding areas in the southern region of Qatar. QAW serves about 1300 students from pre-school to Grade 12. QAW is an IB World School fully authorized for PYP, MYP and DP and accredited by the New England Association of Schools and Colleges and the Council of International Schools.

Through an educational model that enables learning in two languages, encourages innovation, and develops a strong code of ethics, QAW has been nurturing students to become leaders in their communities. The talented faculty at QAW go above and beyond to cultivate the spirit of discovery and creativity in students' learning experiences. QAW teachers and administrators are highly collaborative, energetic, and supportive team players who are passionate about working with children and making a difference.

The state-of-the-art, purpose-built campus includes a variety of facilities such as sports and recreational spaces, swimming pools, a 450-seat theater, music and art studios, and well-equipped science, technology, engineering, art, mechanics, and food technology laboratories.

Learning at QAW is further enhanced through the variety of opportunities available through the vast network of Qatar Foundation, from experiential programs to athletics and community services that enable students to achieve their full potential in a nurturing and culturally grounded environment.

(Founded 1996)

Director
Mehdi Benchaabane

PYP coordinator
Ms. Savannah Spillers

MYP coordinator
Ms. Roma Bhargava

DP coordinator
Ms. Zeina Jawad

Status Private

Boarding/day Day

Gender Coeducational

Language of instruction
Arabic, English

Authorised IB programmes
PYP, MYP, DP

Age Range 3 – 18 years

Number of pupils enrolled
1883

Address
P.O. Box: 1129
Luqta Street
Doha | **QATAR**

TEL +974 44542000

Email
qataracademy@qf.org.qa

Website
www.qataracademy.edu.qa

Vision: Empowering students to achieve high levels of academic growth and personal wellbeing and to be responsible citizens who are locally rooted and globally connected.

Qatar Academy Doha (QAD) is one of the Middle East's premier educational institutions; a leading private, non-profit international school established as the first learning organization in Qatar Foundation's landmark Education City. Founded in 1996, it marked an important step for a country on the cusp of transforming itself from a gas- and oil-producing economy to a knowledge-based society.

QAD was the first school in Qatar authorized to offer all three IB Programmes.

Over 1,800 students representing different nationalities experience an extensive academic and co-curricular program grounded in traditional values and steeped in the best practices in education.

Inquiry-based learning starts at the Primary School. Students, parents and faculty are encouraged to challenge themselves and their thinking through the framework of the PYP, and Units of Inquiry based on the IB transdisciplinary themes provide students with structure and direction in their learning. This learning environment extends beyond the classroom to involve the wider community, supporting real-world connections.

The Middle School offers the IBMYP for grades 6 to 10 and the Qatar Academy High School offers the IB Diploma Programme for Grades 11 and 12.

QAD's strength lies in its rigorous and effective university preparation program, through its Open Campus configuration that allows students to access a personalized learning pathway in addition to a rigorous IB education with opportunities to engage in internships and co-curricular programs from university campuses, research labs and entrepreneurship incubators across Education City.

Access to many community and service, athletic and academic after-school activities challenge students beyond the curriculum, and student e-portfolios and student-led conference structure ensure that focus is consistently on learning and growing, while acquiring the grades, necessary for success in the DP and beyond.

QAD teachers are recruited from a variety of academic and cultural settings. Through encouragement and a caring, innovative and creative approach to instruction, our faculty ensure that our students achieve their fullest potential in a learning environment designed to promote cultural understanding and respect.

Qatar Academy Msheireb

Director
Ms. Belinda Holland

PYP coordinator
Mr. Cory Sadler

Status Private

Boarding/day Day

Gender Coeducational

Language of instruction
English, Arabic

Authorised IB programmes
PYP

Age Range 3 – 10 years

Number of pupils enrolled
400

Fees
Day: QR46,033 – QR52,656

Address
Msheireb Downtown Doha
QATAR

TEL +974 44542116

Email
qamsheireb@qf.org.qa

Website
www.qam.qa

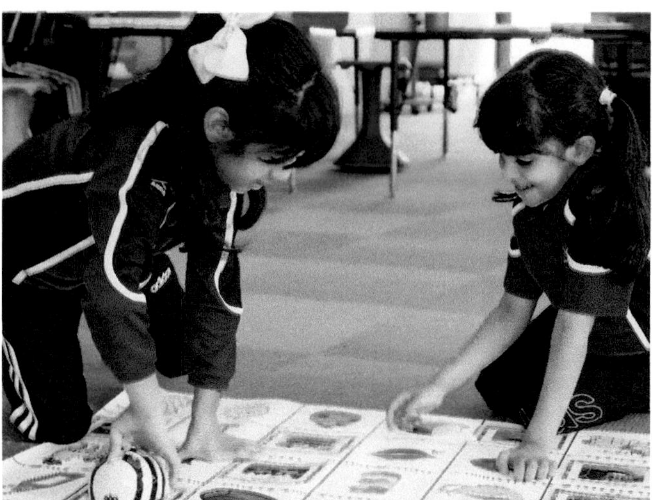

Established in 2014, Qatar Academy Msheireb, a member of Qatar Foundation operating under Pre-University Education, is a state-of-the-art Early Years and Primary School authorized for the International Baccalaureate Primary Years Programme, and a Council of International Schools accredited school.

QAM's mission is to create an effective learning environment to develop internationally minded and empathetic lifelong learners through a dual-language program emphasizing inquiry-based practices.

At QAM everything has a purpose, and learning is relevant to the 'real world' within a dual-language curriculum that is structured to be rigorous, stimulating and challenging. The Program of Inquiry centers around 'big ideas' and provides students with opportunities of learning about issues that have local, national and global significance, and hence nurtures an understanding of human commonalities. The transdisciplinary nature of the themes ensures that learning transcends the confines of traditional subject areas, and facilitates student connections between life in school, life at home and life in the world.

QAM offers an inclusive education where students evolve as individuals who are self-motivated, creative and can think, question and reason logically, i.e. individuals who are independent, confident and capable of making decisions.

All students are encouraged to be curious about what they are learning, and differentiation allows them to demonstrate what they have learned by using a variety of mediums or tools at different levels that are appropriate to individual needs.

Qatar Academy Sidra

Director
Ms. Marie Green

PYP coordinator
Mr. Barry Grogan

MYP coordinator
Ms. Nelsy Saravia

DP coordinator
Mr. John Dugan

Status Private

Boarding/day Day

Gender Coeducational

Language of instruction
English

Authorised IB programmes
PYP, MYP, DP

Age Range 3 – 18 years

Number of pupils enrolled
840

Fees
Day: QR40,280 – QR74,556

Address
P.O. Box: 34077
Doha | QATAR

TEL +974 44542322

Email
qasidra@qf.org.qa

Website
www.qasidra.com.qa

Qatar Academy Sidra (QAS) is a rapidly growing school, currently serving over 840 students who represent approximately 35 nationalities. QAS is part of the Qatar Foundation Pre-University Education, is a co-educational international school that offers a broad-based, international educational programme.

QAS is a dynamic, kind and responsive learning community that challenges learners of today to inspire them to be the change-makers of tomorrow. QAS believes there is a leader in everyone. Students at QAS are empowered learners with strong skills and a sense of self for a life filled with opportunity. QAS graduates are compassionate responsible citizens who achieve their full academic and personal potential.

As an inclusive and multilingual community, QAS is committed to creating opportunities for every child so that every individual is personally and academically empowered with 'roots to grow and wings to fly'. The school values of respect, integrity and unity lead to a culture of kindness. This culture enables QAS to create a nurturing environment for each child's wellbeing, passion, and talents.

The school is currently located in the lively Education City campus and utilizes the facilities and collaborative connections within the wider campus.

QSI International School of Bratislava

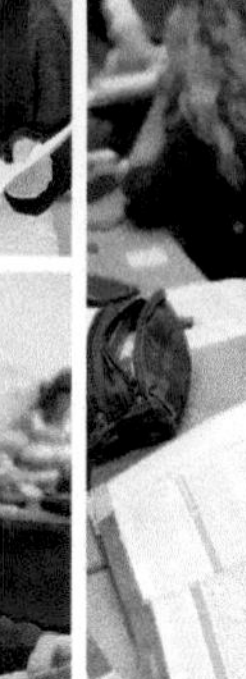

(Founded 1994)

Head of School
Mr. Daniel Blaho

DP coordinator
Marek Andrasko

Status Private

Boarding/day Day

Gender Coeducational

Language of instruction
English

Authorised IB programmes
DP

Age Range 3 – 18 years

Number of pupils enrolled
306

Address
Záhradnicka 1006/2
Samorin 93101 | **SLOVAKIA**

TEL +421 903 704 436

Email
bratislava@qsi.org

Website
bratislava.qsi.org

QSI International School of Bratislava (QSIB) is a private, non-profit institution that opened in September of 1994. It offers a rigorous, high-quality American international education in the English language for children ages 3-18. The warm and welcoming community that is QSIB makes it an ideal setting for children to grow in ability with the finest faculty and educational opportunities in Bratislava. Students in the secondary earn stellar results in our International Baccalaureate (IB) and Advanced Placement (AP) Programs.

The brand-new state-of-the-art facility (opened in January 2018) is a large 2-story complex, which has 35 classrooms, a library (over 18,000 titles), two computer laboratories, a gymnasium, an atrium, several outdoor playgrounds, a full-court outdoor basketball court, an artificial grass mini-pitch for soccer, and several offices. QSI International School of Bratislava (QSIB) provides full security for its students, teachers, staff and visitors with guards, an advanced key card system and an elaborate security camera network. Partner facilities are found within the nearby Olympic training facility (www.x-bionicsphere.com/domov), including indoor and outdoor swimming pools, a fitness facility, dance/exercise rooms, track & field, a full soccer pitch, gymnastics hall, equestrian course, and a movie cinema. Free Shuttle Buses to/from the campus are available from six separate locations in and around Bratislava.

QSIB offers the IB Diploma Programme to students ages 16-19, during the final two years (Secondary III & IV). The QSI courses offered in Secondary I & II prepare students to take IB courses. Students may elect to enroll in the IB Diploma Programme as full diploma candidates or as course candidates. Enrollment of students is done through one-on-one counseling with the Director of Instruction and the IB Coordinator. Prerequisite skills are required for the program, but specific prerequisite courses are not typically required.

QSIB students enjoy a high success rate with 94% passing the rigorous diploma programme with an average score of 35.8 over the last 10 years.

SUBJECTS OFFERED:

GROUP 1 (Language A):
- English Language & Literature
- Slovak Literature

GROUP 2 (Language B):
- French B & French *Ab Initio*
- German B & German *Ab Initio*
- Spanish B & Spanish *Ab Initio*

GROUP 3 (Individuals & Society):
- Economics
- History

GROUP 4 (Science):
- Biology
- Chemistry
- Physics

GROUP 5 (Mathematics):
- Mathematics: Applications & Interpretations
- Mathematics: Analysis & Approaches

GROUP 6:
- Visual Arts

QSI Kyiv International School

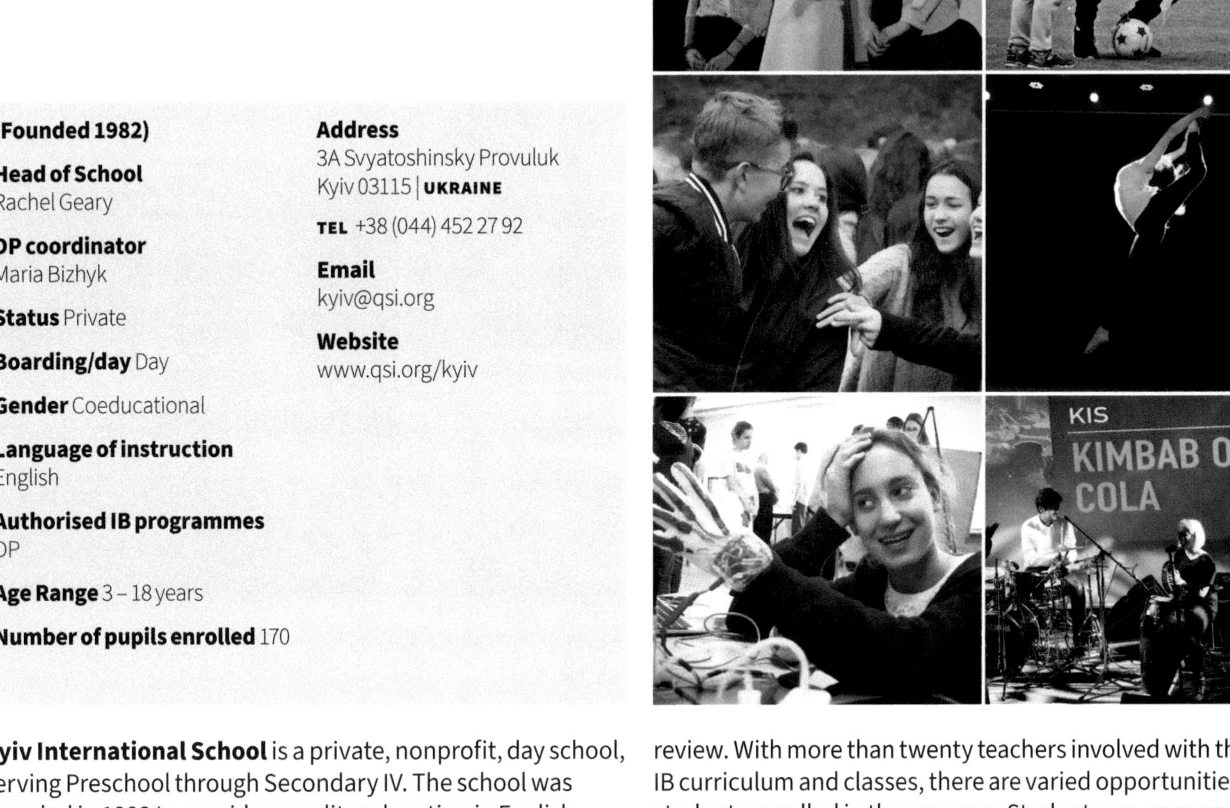

(Founded 1982)

Head of School
Rachel Geary

DP coordinator
Maria Bizhyk

Status Private

Boarding/day Day

Gender Coeducational

Language of instruction
English

Authorised IB programmes
DP

Age Range 3 – 18 years

Number of pupils enrolled 170

Address
3A Svyatoshinsky Provuluk
Kyiv 03115 | **UKRAINE**

TEL +38 (044) 452 27 92

Email
kyiv@qsi.org

Website
www.qsi.org/kyiv

Kyiv International School is a private, nonprofit, day school, serving Preschool through Secondary IV. The school was founded in 1992 to provide a quality education in English for the children of expatriates living in Kyiv. Parents of its students are primarily employed by large corporations and governments. Kyiv International School is a member of Quality Schools International, a consortium of non-profit college-preparatory international schools with American-style curriculum. QSI has 37 schools in 31 countries. The world headquarters of QSI is in Ljubljana, Slovenia.

Mastery Learning Philosophy: Kyiv International School believes in personalized instruction within a positive learning environment leading to mastery of clearly defined objectives. The educational philosophy emphasizes cooperative and collaborative learning, reflection, innovation, and higher-order and critical thinking. Mastery learning prepares our students for the higher level thinking, reflection and self-motivation that is so fundamental for students engaged in the IB Diploma Programme.

International Baccalaureate Diploma Programme: Kyiv International School has offered the International Baccalaureate Diploma Programme since 2004 and the program continues to grow and evolve through reflection and review. With more than twenty teachers involved with the IB curriculum and classes, there are varied opportunities for students enrolled in the program. Students are encouraged to enroll in the full diploma programme, but also have the opportunity to enroll in classes for IB certificates.

IB Language Courses: KIS is proud to offer German, French, Spanish, Russian and Ukrainian which students can study as either a first or second language. We also encourage students to enroll in school-supported self-study of their native language. Students have recently received bilingual diplomas in Russian, French, Ukrainian, German, Italian and Korean.

Facilities and location: KIS is located just 10 km from the city center. The park like campus includes 95 classrooms (including fully equipped science laboratories to support Group 4 subjects), a learning center, 2 sensory rooms, 3 art rooms, 3 music rooms, a recording studio, 3 computer laboratories, 2 indoor gymnasiums, an indoor pool, fitness center, climbing wall, a cafeteria, a snack café, 2 playgrounds, a purpose built track, an artificial turf soccer field, an artificial turf soccer mini pitch, an outdoor basketball court, outdoor fitness area, other outdoor spaces, and a brand new auditorium with a seating capacity of 350.

QSI Tirana International School

(Founded 1991)

Director
Mr Jon Mudd

DP coordinator
John Scates

Status Private

Boarding/day Day

Gender Coeducational

Language of instruction
English

Authorised IB programmes
DP

Age Range 2 – 18 years

Number of pupils enrolled 432

Address
Rruga Gilson, Fshati Mullet
Kutia Postare 1527
Tirana | ALBANIA

TEL +355 4 236 5239

Email
tirana@qsi.org

Website
tirana.qsi.org

Tirana International School is a private, nonprofit institution which opened in 1991. It offers a high-quality education in the English language for children ages two through high school graduation and includes students from the diplomatic, international business, and Albanian communities. It is a member of Quality Schools International, a consortium of non-profit college-preparatory international schools with American-style curriculum. TIS has been accredited by the Middle States Association since 1999.

Students, Faculty & Staff

The school is growing and currently has over 400 students representing 38 nationalities. The school prides itself on hiring caring, qualified, and dedicated educators. Teachers at TIS are certified and experienced educators who bring a wealth of expertise, knowledge, and skills to their learning environments.

School Facilities and Location

The school facility is located on the south side of the city of Tirana, just outside the busy city. The campus occupies a beautiful, green 5.5-hectare site. The building was designed to accommodate growth in enrollment and to take advantage of the abundant Albanian sunshine, having lots of balconies and patios.

The sports complex boasts several playgrounds, a soccer field, a track, a tennis court, an indoor exercise room, a gymnasium, and a dance studio. The school building includes a full English-language elementary and secondary library, with additional resources to support Languages Other than English; multiple science laboratories; a technology lab; fully equipped music and art rooms; an indoor performance area; a full-service cafeteria; and state-of-the-art, well-resourced and well-equipped classrooms. In addition, the school has many outdoor courtyards and respite areas for students to gather.

Academic Program & Philosophy

Tirana International School believes that every child can succeed and strives to offer a rigorous overall program – with equal emphasis on the acquisition of knowledge, skills, and success orientations – in an accepting, friendly, and supportive environment.

TIS follows QSI's mastery learning approach to teaching, in which students master specific objectives before moving on. This approach emphasizes success over mediocracy as well as rigor and critical thinking. The TIS curriculum well prepares students for the challenges of the IB DP.

IB Programme

An IB school since 2021, the diploma programme continues to grow. Candidates are supported by a team of motivated, caring teachers and administrators who are passionate about their work and the success of the IB programme. Further, the program benefits from collaboration with local IB schools as well as the larger QSI network of schools. As the programme grows, TIS continues to expand their list of course offerings, with Global Politics, History and Physics rounding out our group 3 and 4 offerings for the incoming cohort.

IB Course Offerings

TIS is offering English: Language and Literature, Albanian Literature, French and Spanish B, Spanish *Ab initio*, Economics, Business Management, Biology, Chemistry, Mathematics: Analysis and Approaches, Art and Theatre. As the programme grows, TIS continues to expand their list of course offerings, with Global Politics, History and Physics rounding out our group 3 and 4 offerings for the incoming cohort.

Rome International School

(Founded 1988)

Headteacher
Ms Corina Rader

Middle/High School Principal
Mr William Johnson

PYP coordinator
Mr Martin Newell

DP coordinator
Mrs Laela El Sheikh

Status Private

Boarding/day Day

Gender Coeducational

Language of instruction
English

Authorised IB programmes
PYP, DP

Age Range 2 – 18 years

Number of pupils enrolled 500

Fees
Day: €10,290 – €25,140 per annum

Address
Via Guglielmo Pecori Giraldi n.137
00135 Rome | ITALY

TEL +39 06 8448 2651

Email
info@romeinternationalschool.it

Website
www.romeinternationalschool.it

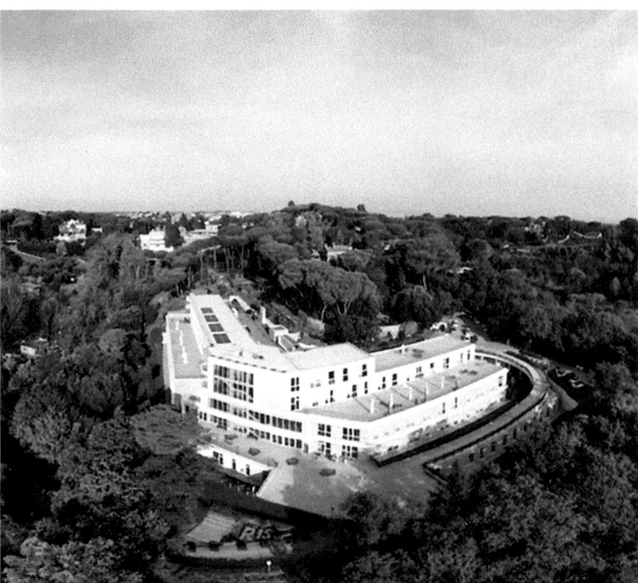

Rome International School (RIS) offers an unparalleled inclusive international education that prepares students to solve problems that have not yet been imagined and to work in jobs that may not yet exist.

We continue to be the only school in Rome authorised to offer both the International Baccalaureate (IB) Primary Years Programme and IB Diploma Programme. The school is an accredited centre for the Cambridge IGCSE thereby ensuring the quality and consistency of a true international education.

Highly qualified, caring and experienced staff motivate and inspire students to achieve their potential, both academically and personally.

We teach students to think for themselves and to understand the significance of what they are learning in global and local contexts. Our inquiry-based educational approach places students at the centre of the learning process and encourages them to be active participants in their education.

Students who complete the educational journey at RIS progress to attend universities of their choice worldwide. They will have established a personal set of values that will lay the foundation for international mindedness and critical thinking to develop and flourish.

From an action-based Eco-Schools program to a transformative STEAM agenda using LEGO Education Resources, our students can choose to participate in enriching co-curricular and extra-curricular activities, which allow them to develop new skills and talents build international connections.

The school's modern and green campus meets every learning and teaching requirement. Nestled in almost four hectares of natural parkland in north-west Rome, located close to the city centre, our campus offers students plenty of opportunities to play, discover and experiment.

Joining RIS means joining an extended international community.

The school is a member of the Globedcuate ICS family of schools, who are united by a vision to prepare each student to become a global citizen who can shape the world.

With a student intake of over 60 different nationalities, Rome International School is the ideal context for a rewarding and progressive educational experience.

Royal High School Bath, GDST

(Founded 1865)

Head
Mrs Kate Reynolds

Head of Prep School
Ms Claire Lilley

DP coordinator
Ms Jude Taylor

Status Private

Boarding/day Mixed

Gender Female

Language of instruction
English

Authorised IB programmes
DP

Number of pupils enrolled 580

Fees
Day:
£5,294 per term
Weekly Boarding:
£10,699 per term
Boarding:
£11,965 per term

Address
Lansdown Road
Bath
Bath & North-East Somerset
BA1 5SZ | UK

TEL +44 (0)1225 313877

Email
admissions@rhsb.gdst.net

Website
www.royalhighbath.gdst.net

Royal High School Bath, GDST is a leading independent day and boarding school. Part of the GDST family, RHSB provides outstanding, contemporary, education for girls aged 3-18. With a reputation as supportive and stimulating, our students realise new talents, fulfil their potential and go on to have bright futures. Our Steinway Music School and Art School highlight our commitment to our students' creativity.

Academic

Committed to high academic standards, Royal High School Bath offers a choice of A level or IB with a wide range of subjects delivered by specialist teachers. Staff are highly qualified and engage and inspire their students – with 16 years' experience of the Diploma Programme, the school's results are excellent, and consistently above the global average. In 2020 RHSB was recognised as a Top Global IB School and in 2023 students achieved an impressive average score of 35 points (higher than the global average). Students go on to study at prestigious universities in the UK and overseas, including Oxford, Cambridge, Imperial and UCL.

Global perspective beyond the classroom

Students value the international-mindedness of the IB and enjoy a school exchange to Sweden. This gives experience of other young people from very different backgrounds and nationalities. Students choose from a wide range of CAS options and in previous years took part in an expedition to Cambodia where they taught in a partner school. Model United Nations enables students to refine skills including public speaking, critical thinking and leadership.

Orientation

The school's expertise means the induction of students is quick and effective. A residential orientation experience helps students gain an understanding of the programme ahead, and provides the space to plan their final years at school.

Boarding

Our global community of boarders find their home from home in RHSB. Girls aged 11-16 board in School House, our stunning neo-Gothic main building. Gloucester House is the Sixth Form boarding house and girls quickly settle into a caring and supportive community. House staff value students as individuals and the pastoral care and wellbeing of each girl is paramount.

Location

Situated in Bath, RHSB has good transport links. Just 15 minutes from M4 motorway and with easy access to London, Bristol, Cardiff and Birmingham. Mainline rail links to London Paddington. Airports in Bristol, Southampton, Heathrow and Gatwick are easy to access and a shuttle to west London for weekly boarders can be arranged as required.

Ryde School with Upper Chine

RYDE SCHOOL
WITH UPPER CHINE

(Founded 1921)

Headmaster
Mr Will Turner

DP coordinator
David Shapland

CP coordinator
David Shapland

Status Private, Independent

Boarding/day Mixed

Gender Coeducational

Language of instruction
English

Authorised IB programmes
DP, CP

Age Range 2 – 18 years
(boarding from 10)

Number of pupils enrolled 795

Fees
Day:
£16,074 – £16,626 per annum
Weekly Boarding:
£32,298 – £32,850 per annum
Boarding:
£36,297 – £36,849 per annum

Address
Queen's Road
Ryde
Isle of Wight
PO33 3BE | UK

TEL 01983 562229

Email
admissions@rydeschool.net

Website
www.rydeschool.org.uk

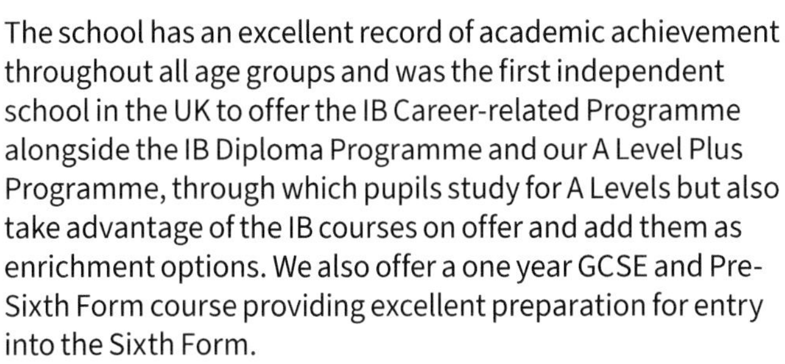

The school has an excellent record of academic achievement throughout all age groups and was the first independent school in the UK to offer the IB Career-related Programme alongside the IB Diploma Programme and our A Level Plus Programme, through which pupils study for A Levels but also take advantage of the IB courses on offer and add them as enrichment options. We also offer a one year GCSE and Pre-Sixth Form course providing excellent preparation for entry into the Sixth Form.

Pupils leave to go on to study at Oxbridge, medical schools, other Russell Group Universities and Art, Music and Drama colleges. Pupils succeed academically and are well-mannered, characterful, happy and independent; a result of Ryde School's dynamic yet welcoming environment.

Our pupils benefit from an extensive range of excellent resources and extra-curricular activities. Sailing is on the curriculum in both the Prep and Senior Schools and has a strong focus throughout the School. In addition to the extensive academic, creative arts and sporting programmes, the location of our school enables us to offer a full extra-curricular programme including sailing, riding and water sports.

Situated in a beautiful, safe and idyllic island setting just off the South Coast of England, Ryde School with Upper Chine (known locally as Ryde School) is a thriving, prosperous independent day and boarding school for boys and girls aged 2 to 18, providing exceptional educational opportunities in a nurturing environment – helping them to be resourceful and resilient in the face of challenge and change.

Just ten minutes by Hovercraft from the mainland, the School and the boarding houses benefit from being near high-speed sea, rail and air links to regional, European and international destinations and the School is 1/2 an hour from Cowes, the home of international sailing.

Constantly investing in the future of our pupils, we have recently updated the science labs and libraries, the Sixth Form Centre and added a parent and pupil coffee shop, fantastic new Performing Arts Centre and two new boarding houses in the school grounds in Ryde and a brand new Cookery School. The aims of Ryde School as embedded in the School motto, 'Ut Prosim', have always been focused on service to others and pupils are encouraged to embody our school values of Ambition, Responsibility, Courage and Respect, gaining self-knowledge, academic excellence and leadership skills, positively contributing in their careers and the wider world.

Saint Dominic's International School, Portugal

(Founded 1975)

Principal
Stephen Blackburn

PYP coordinator
Edward Burt III

MYP coordinator
Simon Downing

DP coordinator
Maripaz Aguilera

Status Private

Boarding/day Day

Gender Coeducational

Language of instruction
English

Authorised IB programmes
PYP, MYP, DP

Age Range 3 – 18 years

Number of pupils enrolled 700

Fees
Day: €11,200 – €20,500 per annum

Address
Rua Maria Brown
Outeiro de Polima
2785-816 S Domingos de Rana,
Lisbon | **PORTUGAL**

TEL +351 21 444 0434

Email
school@dominics-int.org

Website
www.dominics-int.org

St. Dominic's International School, Portugal, is a highly respected and well-known international school. It was the first and is currently one of the few schools in Portugal authorised to offer three of the International Baccalaureate Programmes: Primary (PYP), Middle (MYP), and the Diploma, and is celebrating its 26th year as an IB Continuum School.

Our commitment to the IB and its programmes is at the core of SDIS' educational philosophy of 'Nurturing and Educating International Minds'. The IB programmes encourage students to question perceived truths and beliefs and reflect on their place in, and contribution to, the society in which they live.

Although the original founders of the school left in 2010, the current owners still maintain the connection with the Dominican values which are imbedded within the school and the Veritas Motto.

The principle of inquiry based learning ensures that students develop into independent learners, equipped to embrace both the challenges and opportunities they will face throughout their lives. Situated 15 kilometers from central Lisbon, in the district of Cascais, St. Dominic's is a private, non-selective, coeducational day school serving students aged 3 to 18 years in the international community, through the medium of English. We currently have 52 nationalities amongst our student population, making us a truly international school.

The school is housed in three one-storey buildings. In addition to 48 classrooms, it has a self-contained nursery and kindergarten for our youngest students, two gym halls, three art rooms, two libraries, five science and technology laboratories, two music rooms and a drama studio. Our ICT facilities include both dedicated ICT suites as well as portable devices. We have an excellent reputation for sport, and have facilities for football, basketball and volleyball on site; a wide range of other sports are played using outside facilities.

The junior school offers: English, Portuguese, mathematics, social studies, information technology, art, music, PE and social education through the curriculum of the PYP from nursery to grade 5. In the senior school, students in grades 6 to 10 study the MYP, and in grades 11 and 12 we prepare students for the full diploma or for diploma courses. Our students go on to study at prestigious universities and colleges around the World.

Classes begin in early September and run to the end of June with breaks for Christmas and Easter and shorter mid-term breaks.

Sainte Victoire International School

(Founded 2011)

Head of School
Frederic Fabre

DP coordinator
Allison Delort

Status Private

Boarding/day Mixed

Gender Coeducational

Language of instruction
English, French

Authorised IB programmes
DP

Age Range 5 – 18 years

Fees
Day:
€10,200 – €17,900 per annum
Boarding:
€26,800 – €31,800 per annum

Address
Domaine de Château l'Arc
Chemin de Maurel
13710 Fuveau | **FRANCE**

TEL +33 4 42 26 51 96

Email
contact@schoolsaintevictoire.com

Website
www.schoolsaintevictoire.com

SVIS – Sainte Victoire International School is an IB World School located near Aix-en-Provence in the south of France. The school offers both the International Baccalaureate Diploma Programme and the Cambridge IGCSE examinations. SVIS provides education for students aged 5 years to 18 years from over 40 nationalities in our Primary, Middle, and High School. From the Primary school level, teaching is bilingual, allowing students to achieve their academic potential in English and French. SVIS also offers mother-tongue classes for several additional languages.

SVIS provides an innovative and rigorous approach to teaching and learning, incorporating cross-disciplinary subjects as well as a wide range of learning opportunities that take place off-campus. These include an extensive range of local and international trips, an abundant offering of after school activities, and an ecology park. SVIS integrates sustainability goals and service-learning into the curriculum to develop students as global citizens.

The school is situated in the heart of an international 18-hole golf course, facing the Sainte Victoire mountain and offers students a healthy and peaceful school environment. SVIS is a family-friendly environment focusing on the whole child and provides opportunities for students to explore their passions in athletics and the arts. Class sizes are limited to 15 maximum allowing for individualised education programs.

School Facilities

The school facilities include an amphitheater, a library with computers, a theatre/art room, a science laboratory, an indoor gym and outstanding outdoor facilities: an 18-hole golf course, a football/rugby grass pitch, a tennis court, a basketball court and ecology park where students can grow fruit and vegetables.

Boarding Facilities

The boarding house is located 20 meters from the entrance to the school. This facility offers an exceptional living environment, where students enjoy a healthy pace of life, conducive to academic success. There is a maximum of 2 students per duplex. Each duplex is equipped with study rooms, a kitchen, 2 bathrooms, lounges, and a private terrace with outstanding views over the grounds.

Outstanding qualities of SVIS

- SVIS offers internationally renowned educational programs that are sought by leading universities.
- SVIS graduates have their first choice of leading universities.
- With more than 40 student nationalities, SVIS is a diverse and inclusive school.
- Each student receives individual support and guidance from teachers to achieve their maximum potential.
- The school provides students with opportunities to study a large variety of mother-tongue and foreign languages including English, Spanish, Russian, Chinese, Italian, German, Dutch, and Japanese.
- The school has an outstanding campus on an international 18-hole golf course in the south of France. The grounds are surrounded by pine forests.

(Founded 1896)

Headmaster
Mr Guy Emmett

DP coordinator
Ms Katie Cooke

Status Private

Boarding/day Mixed

Gender Coeducational

Language of instruction
English

Authorised IB programmes
DP

Age Range 3 – 18 years
(boarding from 11)

Number of pupils enrolled 528

Fees
Day:
£8,499 – £18,015 per annum
Boarding:
£22,557 – £37,989 per annum

Address
Filey Road
Scarborough
North Yorkshire
YO11 3BA | UK

TEL +44 (0)1723 360620

Email
admin@scarboroughcollege.co.uk

Website
www.scarboroughcollege.co.uk

Scarborough College is a vibrant, caring and academically rigorous co-educational independent school on England's stunning northeast coast. Nestled on the south cliff of the picturesque surroundings of Scarborough, the school provides a unique and enriching educational experience that prepares students for success in an ever-evolving global landscape.

At the heart of Scarborough College's educational philosophy is a commitment to fostering holistic development. The school embraces the IB programme, offering a comprehensive curriculum that encourages critical thinking, creativity, and a profound appreciation for cultural diversity. With a large number of highly professional educators, the College provides a supportive learning environment that empowers students to become lifelong learners and responsible global citizens.

The school site and boarding houses are a testament to the College's commitment to creating an optimal learning environment. State-of-the-art facilities, including modern classrooms, well-equipped laboratories, libraries, a modern Sixth Form study centre and cafe to mention a few; all ensure that students have access to the resources they need to excel academically. The emphasis on technology integration further prepares students for the challenges of the digital age, allowing them to develop essential skills for the 21st century.

Beyond academics, Scarborough College places a strong emphasis on extracurricular activities to nurture well-rounded individuals. The school offers a diverse range of clubs, sports, and cultural programmes, providing students with opportunities to explore their passions and develop leadership skills. Whether participating in engaging in community service initiatives, being involved in performing arts or competing at the top of English schools' sports; students at Scarborough College are encouraged to pursue their interests beyond the classroom.

A hallmark of Scarborough College is its commitment to fostering a sense of community and inclusivity. The College prides itself on creating a supportive, caring and welcoming atmosphere where students from various backgrounds can thrive. Through a robust pastoral care system, students receive personalised attention, ensuring their social and emotional well-being is a top priority.

As students progress through the IB Diploma Programme at Scarborough College, they are guided by experienced tutors, teachers and careers advisors who provide academic and career counselling. The school's track record of success in preparing students for university admissions manifests itself in a diverse range of university destinations worldwide, including Ivy League and Russel Group universities as well as Cambridge and Oxford.

In conclusion, Scarborough College is not just a place of learning; it is a community that values academic excellence, personal growth and global awareness. As students embark on their journey through the IB Diploma Programme, they are equipped not only with knowledge but also with the skills and values necessary to navigate an interconnected world with confidence and purpose.

Schloss Krumbach International School

(Founded 2020)

Head of School
Dr. Oksana Volozhanina

School Principal
Mag. Teresa Schnabl

DP coordinator
Viktoryia Tejada Correa

Status Private, Non-Profit

Boarding/day Boarding

Gender Coeducational

Language of instruction
English, German

Authorised IB programmes
DP

Age Range 12 – 19 years

Number of pupils enrolled 40

Fees
Boarding:
€39,900 – €43,680 per annum

Address
Schloss 1, 2851 Krumbach,
Lower Austria | **AUSTRIA**

TEL +43 6765 409630

Email
info@krumbach.school

Website
www.krumbach.school

A young school, in a historical setting. A small school, growing fast. We are SKIS, an eclectic community of world citizens. We all speak at least two languages and value our diversity.

Schloss Krumbach International School is a co-educational boarding school (Grades 7-12), located in a beautiful 13th century castle. An Austrian Hogwarts, or so they say.

SKIS already holds the following accolades:

- IB World School offering IB Diploma Programme
- Austria's only Cambridge International School offering IGCSE / AS /A Level Diploma
- Duke of Edinburgh (DoE) Award center
- Member of the CIS (Council of International Schools)

Our Middle School students in Grades 7 to 9 follow the Austrian national curriculum and are taught in German and supported in English. Grade 10 transitions to English as a medium of instruction and prepares for Grades 11 and 12 (IBDP or A-level). During Grade 10, our Pre-Diploma Grade, the learning process is organized in a way that allows Grade 10 students to improve their language skills, accustom to the new studying environment, try and evaluate different subjects, and gain a final understanding of what they are going to take for the Diploma programme. SKIS Career Counseling Team helps students explore the potential college venues to facilitate their choice of the Diploma subjects.

SKIS at Glance:

- Premium education: offering IB world & A-Levels programmes, access to the most advanced studying equipment and innovative learning techniques
- Internationally renowned teachers with 30+ years of experience, PhD degrees and passion for pedagogics
- A truly unique setting: Austria's one and only one castle-based school
- A carefully designed bilingual system: studying in English and German throughout Grades 7-10 + additional language in Grades 10-12 (taught in English)
- Superb accommodation: study and reside in a magnificent campus-castle
- Healthy lifestyle: a 6-meals-a-day menu, carefully crafted in accordance with best nutritionist science practices and lots of sports
- Personalized family-alike atmosphere: small studying groups with no more than 16 students per each
- Student-focused approach: academic support center, career orientation and university counseling
- An enriching boarding experience: culture trips around Europe and a wide range of extracurricular activities
- Lifelong learning habits: supervised homework time with professional teachers + mother tongue support
- Soft skills acquisition: a unique student leadership system and participation in global major forums
- A safe ecosystem: 24/7 security on campus, digital detox

Hop on an incredible academic, social, and creative journey at our castle!

SEK International School Alborán

(Founded 1999)

Principal
Miguel Ángel López Ponce

PYP coordinator
Natalia López

MYP coordinator
Sebastián Fuentes Valenzuela

DP coordinator
Estefania Sánchez

Status Private

Boarding/day Day

Gender Coeducational

Language of instruction
English, Spanish

Authorised IB programmes
PYP, MYP, DP

Age Range 4 months – 18 years

Number of pupils enrolled 781

Address
C/ Barlovento 141
Urb. Almerimar, El Ejido
04711 Almería, Andalusia | **SPAIN**

TEL +34 900 87 87 98

Email
sek-alboran@sek.es

Website
alboran.sek.es

Located on the seashore and adjacent to the Punta Entinas Natural Park, in Almería, SEK International School Alborán is regarded as a high quality international school in Andalusia. It is the only school in Almeria that offers three IB International Baccalaureate Programmes, from 3 to 18 years of age (Primary Years Programme Middle Years Programme – MYP and the Diploma Programme, either bilingually in English and Spanish or fully in English). These programmes are coordinated closely with the Spanish education system.

For the SEK Education Group, to which SEK-Alborán belongs, physical fitness and respecting one's health are an essential element of the learning process. SEK-Alborán has extensive recreational areas, and 28,000m2 of outdoor spaces, as well as extensive sports facilities and a heated indoor pool. Its classrooms are equipped with cutting-edge technology (makerspace, video recording and editing spaces, radio, 3D printer, robotic tables, TED ED Club). It is considered a model of educational innovation in Andalusia.

Social and emotional learning programmes are of particular importance in students' curricula to foster the social and personal awareness. In the Intelligent Classroom, each student progresses according to their potential, working in teams and having individual efforts rewarded. Teachers and tutors are afforded an open space for dialogue with students and parents both in-person and online. Students can take advantage of the Flipped Classroom to work on content and tackle issues from a broad perspective, solving doubts with their teachers, and learning by doing. The HYFLEX system has been implemented due to the covid and online learning has become part of the daily life of students.

SEK-Alborán offers a bilingual Spanish-English education that is incorporated progressively over all educational stages (50% of the subjects are taught in English). It is the only school in Almeria authorized by Cambridge English Exams, Alliance Française and Goethe Institut in Almería. It also has an extensive program of exchanges and participations in United Nations Models. SEK-Alborán is accredited by the New England Association of Schools and Colleges (NEASC), which is a process of external globally recognised quality assurance. NEASC accreditation allows SEK-Alborán to offer the US High School Diploma, as a complement to the IB Diploma.

In all SEK International Schools we are able to offer a quality online learning model in which students are able to continue their learning if necessary, with synchronous and asynchronous classes, and with personalized monitoring by teachers and tutors, which has proved successful with students and families.

SEK International School Atlántico

Principal
Jacobo Olmedo

PYP coordinator
Sara Bouzada Sanmartin

MYP coordinator
Mónica Azpilicueta Amorín

DP coordinator
Yolanda Cenamor Montero

Status Private

Boarding/day Day

Gender Coeducational

Language of instruction
English, Spanish

Authorised IB programmes
PYP, MYP, DP

Age Range 4 months – 18 years

Number of pupils enrolled 720

Address
Rúa Illa de Arousa 4
Boavista. A Caeira, Poio
36005 Pontevedra, Galicia | SPAIN

TEL +34 900 87 87 98

Email
sek-atlantico@sek.es

Website
atlantico.sek.es

SEK International School Atlántico offers an outstanding international education to students, from 4 months to 18 years of age. SEK-Atlántico is authorised to teach the three International Baccalaureate Organisation programmes (PYP, MYP and IB). Second School in Spain with the best results in IBDP Exams in 2021 (19th in Europe).

SEK International Schools are committed to offering each student a learning experience focused on personal development and learning, preparing them for success in later life. Situated close to Pontevedra and Vigo, between the sea and the mountains, SEK-Atlántico boasts modern well-designed school spaces and buildings.

Students are afforded a bilingual education and learn to live with other cultures from an early age. The school places great importance on students' oral and written expression, fostering fluency in different languages. Considered a leader in educational innovation in Galicia, SEK-Atlántico offers learning in Galician, Spanish, English and French from year 3 of Primary.

The SEK education model allows students to play a leading role in their education. They explore and discover for themselves, and build and organise their own knowledge and skills, with expert support from teachers.

SEK-Atlántico students learn in facilities designed for their physical, social and creative development. They include: makerspaces, a psychomotor skills classroom for younger students, laboratories, music and art rooms, a library, language classrooms, a learning lab and large indoor and outdoor sports and recreational areas.

Technological spaces are integrated in the day to day lessons of the school and are designed to contribute fully to student learning. Devices have portability and compatibility enabling them to be used in any space.

From the second year of Primary to Baccalaureate, SEK-Atlántico students prepare for Cambridge University Examinations. In the Middle Years Programme and in Baccalaureate, students can also opt to take the Alliance Française Diplôme d'etude de langue française.

SEK-Atlántico is also accredited by the New England Association of Schools and Colleges (NEASC) in conjunction with IB with a process of quality assurance: the Collaborative Learning protocol with a focus on impactful learning processes.

In all SEK International Schools we are able to offer a quality online learning model in which students are able to continue their learning if necessary, with synchronous and asynchronous classes, and with personalized monitoring by teachers and tutors, which has proved successful with students and families.

(Founded 1995)

Principal
Roberto Prata

PYP coordinator
Concepció Muntada

MYP coordinator
Carmen Fernández

DP coordinator
Adrià Van Waart

Status Private

Boarding/day Mixed

Gender Coeducational

Language of instruction
English, Spanish, Catalan

Authorised IB programmes
PYP, MYP, DP

Age Range 4 months – 18 years

Number of pupils enrolled
1000

Address
Av. del Tremolencs, 24
La Garriga
08530 Barcelona,
Catalonia | **SPAIN**

TEL +34 900 87 87 98

Email
sek-catalunya@sek.es

Website
catalunya.
sekinternationalschools.com

SEK International School Catalunya is located in a quiet and safe residential area spanning 100,000 m2, including a large expanse of Mediterranean forest. The school is in La Garriga, a picturesque town just 30 minutes from the centre of Barcelona, one of the most cosmopolitan cities in Europe.

SEK-Catalunya boasts modern facilities and innovative learning spaces and teaches the three International Baccalaureate Programmes. The Middle Years Programme is offered in Spanish and English while in Baccalaureate, students only do the IB Diploma Programme, which is offered entirely in English or in both languages. We are one of the leaders in the international rankings thanks to our excellent results in IB Diploma exams and also thanks to the wide offer of subjects that we provide to the students. This current year this offer has been extended with Computer Sciene, Design Technology and Russian Language and Literature.

SEK-Catalunya is accredited by the New England Association of Schools and Colleges (NEASC), which is a process of external globally recognised quality assurance. NEASC accreditation allows SEK-Catalunya to offer the US High School Diploma, as a complement to the IB Diploma.

The school offers its Secondary School and Baccalaureate students the opportunity to take part in the prestigious Duke of Edinburgh's International Award, an all-round personal development scheme focused on the development and training of skills such as: leadership, autonomy, problem solving and teamwork.

The SEK-Catalunya Music School, in partnership with the Trinity College London, offers a complete curriculum for all students who wish to acquire the necessary skills to learn classical and modern music.

We also offer international boarding, housing students from Spain and abroad in modern, comfortable and functional facilities, designed for residents to live together, grow as individuals and develop their personal identity thanks to a multicultural environment and a rich offer of complementary activities.

In all SEK International Schools we are able to offer a quality online learning model in which students are able to continue their learning if necessary, with synchronous and asynchronous classes, and with personalized monitoring by teachers and tutors, which has proved successful with students and families.

SEK International School Ciudalcampo

(Founded 1975)

Principal
Cecilia Villavicencio

PYP coordinator
Marisa Iglesias Lorenzo

MYP coordinator
James Shaw

DP coordinator
Dinis Alves Costa

Status Private

Boarding/day Day

Gender Coeducational

Language of instruction
English, Spanish

Authorised IB programmes
PYP, MYP, DP

Age Range 4 months – 18 years

Number of pupils enrolled
1400

Address
Urb. Ciudalcampo,
Paseo de las Perdices, 2
San Sebastián de los Reyes
28707 Madrid | **SPAIN**

TEL +34 900 87 87 98

Email
sek-ciudalcampo@sek.es

Website
ciudalcampo.sek.es

SEK International Schools are committed to offering each student a learning experience focused on personal growth, preparing for success in later life. SEK Schools are bilingual and pioneers in offering the International Baccalaureate programmes, boasting an educational model that has made a tradition of innovation, placing them among the best schools in Spain since their foundation in 1892. SEK International School Ciudalcampo offers the IB Primary Years Programme, the IB Middle Years Programme, the IB Diploma Programme (in English and Spanish, or fully in English), and the Spanish Bachillerato LOMLOE.

SEK-Ciudalcampo offers an innovative educational model based on early stimulation, immersion in English and the development of talent and creativity in a digital environment that favours the development of emotional intelligence.

SEK Ciudalcampo boasts over 20,000m2 of grounds and buildings and a large outdoor sports complex that exceeds 10,000m2.

Through an active learning approach, SEK-Ciudalcampo turns the classrooms into a flexible learning space for all students. The student becomes an active agent, building learning for themselves. The Design Thinking methodology helps students to develop skills such as cooperation, creativity and innovation.

We believe that the way we learn has changed forever. As a result, SEK Future Learning Model is presented as a new opportunity to learn from new methodological formats, based on the Intelligent Classroom system, the use of new tools and the interaction between the different members of the educational community, offering enriched programmes such as the “Aula de Padres”.

SEK-Ciudalcampo is also accredited by the New England Association of Schools and Colleges (NEASC) in conjunction with IB with a process of quality assurance: the Collaborative Learning protocol with a focus on impactful learning processes. It is also the first Spanish school to be recognised as a global member of Round Square.

In all SEK International Schools we are able to offer a quality online learning model in which students are able to continue their learning if necessary, with synchronous and asynchronous classes, and with personalized monitoring by teachers and tutors, which has proved successful with students and families.

Principal
Alberto Domínguez

MYP coordinator
Laura Sánchez

DP coordinator
Laura Sánchez

Status Private

Boarding/day Mixed

Gender Coeducational

Language of instruction
English

Authorised IB programmes
MYP, DP

Age Range 11 – 18 years

Address
Belvedere Hall
Windgates
Greystones, Co. Wicklow
A63 EY23 | IRELAND

TEL +353 1 287 41 75

Email
admissions-dublin@sek.ie

Website
dublin.sek.es

SEK International School Dublin is a leading IB school in Ireland. Small by design, with an emphasis on personalised learning, the school's unique teaching and learning model is built on inquiry-based learning to promote critical and creative thinking.

Located in a stunning natural setting, where the landscape of the Irish countryside meets the Atlantic coast, between the towns of Bray and Greystones. The latter was named one of the best towns in the world to live as a family, and is 30 km from Dublin. SEK-Dublin combines architectural tradition with cutting-edge technology, spanning over 250,000 m2 of grounds and boasting extensive green areas where our students can enjoy a diverse range of sports and outdoor activities, while enhancing their academic development.

SEK-Dublin is the first school in Ireland authorised by the International Baccalaureate Organisation to teach the Middle Years Programme (11-16 years) and the Diploma Programme (16-19 years), taught fully in English with optional languages, including German, French and Spanish.

SEK-Dublin opened its doors in 1981. The success of the school is based on several factors including: a multicultural team of highly trained teachers; the effective use of learning technologies; an individualised programme to cover the educational needs of each student; small class sizes; and an outstanding programme guaranteed by SEK schools' standards of excellence. Aware that education does not only take place in the classroom, for our boarding students we offer residential options with carefully selected local host families or in our on-campus high quality residential facilities, and diverse extracurricular and cultural activities. These aspects combine to nurture the holistic personal and academic development of our students. This all-round education serves them well for their future, enabling them to become mature and independent individuals, and providing them with lasting memories of their experiences at school.

In all SEK International Schools we are able to offer a quality online learning model in which students are able to continue their learning if necessary, with synchronous and asynchronous classes, and with personalized monitoring by teachers and tutors, which has proved successful with students and families.

(Founded 1972)

Head of School
Eloísa López

PYP coordinator
Fátima González

MYP coordinator
Noemí Taranilla

DP coordinator
Ana Karina Cisneros

Status Private

Boarding/day Mixed

Gender Coeducational

Language of instruction
English, Spanish

Authorised IB programmes
PYP, MYP, DP

Age Range 4 months – 18 years

Number of pupils enrolled
1269

Address
Urb. Villafranca del Castillo,
Castillo de Manzanares, s/n
Villanueva de la Cañada
28692 Madrid | **SPAIN**

TEL +34 900 87 87 98

Email
sek-castillo@sek.es

Website
madrid.sekinternationalschools.com

SEK-El Castillo School is a privileged place for coexistence and learning in the broadest sense of the word. The High Artistic Performance School (Music and Dance), the Artistic or the Research Baccalaureates, the different sports schools or the enrichment projects in collaboration with the Camilo José Cela University, are some examples.

We have been authorised as an International Baccalaureate (IB) World School for over 40 years. Currently our students can take the IB Primary Years, Middle Years and Diploma programmes either in English or following an English-Spanish bilingual syllabus, with outstanding examination results. We are also accredited by the New England Association of Schools and Colleges (NEASC) in conjunction with IB with a process of quality assurance: the Collaborative Learning protocol with a focus on impactful learning processes.

We believe that the way we learn has changed forever. As a result, SEK Future Learning Model is presented as a new opportunity to learn from new methodological formats, based on design-thinking tools, the use of new educational technology and the interaction between the different members of the educational community, offering enriched programmes such as the “Aula de Padres” and instrumental lessons for families in our Music School.

We boast first-rate sports facilities on campus and offer international boarders a professionally staffed, nurturing and safe environment. We provide linguistic immersion programmes in both our languages of instruction to ensure access to the curriculum for all our students. In addition, as part of our commitment to talent development, we offer a high-performance sports programme: SEK International Sports Academy (we are the academic partner of important clubs such as Real Madrid). This programme allows athletes to combine their academic studies with their training and competing schedules. We are members of the Boarding School Association, our boarders enjoy a wide range of facilites to enhance their learning. As part of our provision to develop engaged and active young adults, we offer students the opportunity to participate in the prestigious Duke of Edinburgh International Award.

In all SEK International Schools we offer a quality hybrid learning model in which students are able to continue their learning if necessary, with synchronous and asynchronous classes, and with personalized monitoring by teachers and tutors, which has proved successful with students and families.

SEK International School Qatar

(Founded 2013)

Head of School
Verónica Sánchez

PYP coordinator
Anthony Hamblin

MYP coordinator
Lorraine Ann Kenny

DP coordinator
Kim Derudder

Status Private

Boarding/day Day

Gender Coeducational

Language of instruction
Arabic, English, Spanish

Authorised IB programmes
PYP, MYP, DP

Age Range 3 – 18 years

Address
Onaiza 65
Doha | QATAR

TEL +974 4012 7633

Email
info@sek.qa

Website
www.sek.qa

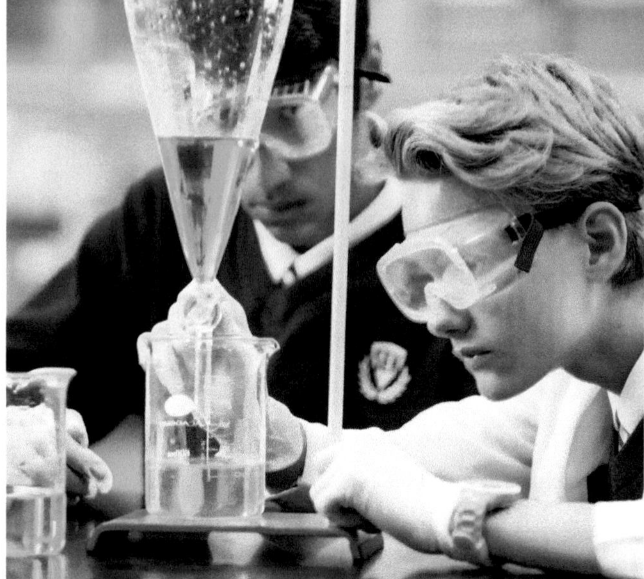

SEK International School Qatar was founded in 2013 within the framework of the Outstanding Schools Programme of the Ministry of Education and Higher Education of the State of Qatar. The school today caters for students from over 60 nationalities. The teaching staff represents more than 25 different nationalities.

The school is an innovative coeducational, international and multilingual school in Qatar, with a cutting-edge learning campus located in the sophisticated West Bay district of Doha. English is the language of instruction, and the school also offers Spanish and Arabic courses for all students. Technology is embedded across the curriculum, supported by their staff as Microsoft Innovative Educators and a Bring your Own Laptop programme form Grade 4.

SEK-Qatar is an IB World School authorized to offer the IB Primary Years Programme (PYP), the Middle Years Programme (MYP) and the Diploma Programme (DP), from pre-school to grade 12. The IB offers high-quality and challenging educational programmes, with a reputation for their high academic standards. SEK-Qatar is also proud to be an accredited school by New England Association of Schools and Colleges (NEASC), one of the most prestigious international university and school accreditation agencies. It indicates that the school meets high standards of institutional quality through ongoing, independent, and objective process of peer-review.

Established in 1892, SEK International Schools are places where innovation and pedagogical leadership are combined with 120 years of tradition and history to offer educational programmes. The SEK Group has launched over a hundred pioneering initiatives introducing innovations such as the classrooms without walls, the SEKMUN Model United Nations and the International Baccalaureate Organisation programmes.

SEK-Qatar has a unique educational model, committed to offering quality education that promotes individualisation, places emphasis on learning rather than teaching, and fosters activity and effort, freedom, interaction and teamwork as well as transformational learning. Technology, sports, artistic and social activities also play a major role in the SEK educational model. The ultimate goal is for students to acquire skills, knowledge and understanding to become active citizens, committed and determined to build a better world.

SEK-Qatar has the infrastructure, digital devices and skilled staff to enable the delivery of online or blended learning depending on changing external scenarios, to which we are able to respond in a flexible and agile manner.

SEK International School Riyadh

(Founded 2021)

Principal
Mr Iván Martínez Pastor

PYP coordinator
Kim Gardner

Status Private

Boarding/day Day

Gender Coeducational (to Grade 6), Segregated (from Grade 7)

Language of instruction
English, Arabic, Spanish

Authorised IB programmes
PYP

Age Range 2 – 14 years

Address
Al Toq Street,
Ar Rabi,
Riyadh
13315 | SAUDI ARABIA

TEL +966 011 520 6170

Email
info@sek.sa

Website
www.sek.sa

SEK International School Riyadh opened its doors in September 2021, thereby establishing the second prestigious SEK Education Group international school in the Middle East. SEK Group boasts over 130 years of history and experience in international education across five countries.

SEK-Riyadh builds on the experience and legacy of our innovative group of schools. SEK Education Group has excelled in providing outstanding international education to local and international communities in Spain, France, Ireland and Qatar, and so does SEK-Riyadh in Saudi Arabia.

We currently welcome students from Nursery (age 2 years) to Grade 8 (age 14 years) and will be opening more Middle School classes in the upcoming years. The school today caters for students from over 50 nationalities. The teaching staff represents more than 20 different nationalities.

At SEK our main goal is to prepare students to direct their futures and to become lifelong learners. To demonstrate our commitment toward this ambitious goal, SEK-Riyadh has received its authorisation for the International Baccalaureate (IB) Primary Years Programme (PYP) and is currently in the authorisation process for the Middle Years Programme (MYP), and will do so for the Diploma Programme (DP) in the coming months. SEK has over 40 years of experience offering IB programmes, with an outstanding record in IB Diploma results and university entrance exams. SEK-Riyadh has also started the process of international accreditation with the New England Association of Schools and Colleges (NEASC), to ensure we meet demanding international education standards.

At SEK-Riyadh, we place a significant emphasis on the holistic development of our students, prioritizing excellence in Technology Education (TechEd), sports, and the arts. We believe in fostering a well-rounded educational experience that not only encompasses academic achievements but also nurtures skills, creativity, and physical well-being. Our commitment to providing a diverse and enriching environment is reflected in our dedicated focus on these three pillars – TechEd for cutting-edge technological skills, sports for physical fitness and teamwork, and the arts for fostering creativity and self-expression. Through these avenues, we aim to empower our students with a comprehensive set of skills and experiences that will contribute to their personal and academic growth.

Like other SEK International Schools, SEK-Riyadh embraces the SEK Future Learning Model, which stems from a natural evolution of our innovative Intelligent Classroom method and focuses on student learning and staff professional development. Therefore, our students and our dedicated international team of teachers will become a community of learners, working together to prepare young people for the challenges of tomorrow, and encouraging each other to think critically and independently.

SEK International School Santa Isabel

Head of School
Jennifer Pro

PYP coordinator
William Ivey

Status Private

Boarding/day Day

Gender Coeducational

Language of instruction
English, Spanish

Authorised IB programmes
PYP

Age Range 3 – 12 years

Number of pupils enrolled
345

Address
Calle San Ildefonso, 18
28012 Madrid | SPAIN

TEL +34 900 87 87 98

Email
sek-santaisabel@sek.es

Website
santaisabel.sek.es

With more than 20 nationalities, SEK Santa Isabel offers of a dynamic multicultural environment set in the heart of Barrio de Las Letras, the historic cultural district of Madrid. The only school in the center of Madrid to deliver the International Baccalaureate's Primary Years Program, students learn in real world settings where their school Campus expands to the museums, libraries, urban gardens and the renowned Retiro Park. Our outdoor Learning Paths makes use of these city spaces, and cultural, historical and scientific institutions to improve and enrich learning.

SEK-Santa Isabel offers Early Childhood and Primary Education (3-12). Our innovative educational model is based on early stimulation, immersion in English and Spanish and the development of talent, creativity, and academic achievement. We boast of a vibrant school wide community and personalized learning experiences in a safe environment that promotes emotional intelligence and close contact with families.

Through our dynamic learning approach, the student becomes an active agent, building learning for themselves in spaces inspired by Montessori and Reggio Emilia.

Learners discover their talents and motivations through Design Thinking and Passion Pursuits, where students have the freedom to design their own projects and guide their learning.

Our learning methodologies foster global competencies, critical thinking, communication, creativity, public speaking and emotional intelligence.

Students take part in our extensive Arts Department and Play Music project, which consists of a school-wide orchestra, learn additional languages and can choose from a range of extracurricular activities, extended hours and sports activities. We have a spacious gym on school grounds, as well as outdoor areas for sports such as swimming, tennis and padel tennis, football and basketball. Our Stellar Programme aims to enrich personal development for high-achieving students.

SEK schools are pioneers in offering International Baccalaureate programmes, boasting an educational model that has made a tradition of innovation, placing them among the best schools in Spain since their foundation in 1892.

Sevenoaks School

(Founded 1432)

Head of School
Mr Jesse R Elzinga AB MSt FCCT

DP coordinator
Nigel Haworth

Status Private

Boarding/day Mixed

Gender Coeducational

Language of instruction
English

Authorised IB programmes
DP

Age Range 11 – 18 years

Number of pupils enrolled
1200

Fees
Day:
£26,721 – £30,348 per annum
Boarding:
£42,921 – £46,566 per annum

Address
High Street
Sevenoaks
Kent
TN13 1HU | UK

TEL +44 (0)1732 455133

Email
regist@sevenoaksschool.org

Website
www.sevenoaksschool.org

Sevenoaks is one of the leading schools in the UK, providing an outstanding modern education. All 450+ students in the sixth form study the IB Diploma Programme, which the school has taught since 1978. The leafy 100-acre campus is in the Kent countryside, just half an hour from Central London and Gatwick Airport. International students make up around 20 per cent of the student body and the school provides pupils with a balanced and intellectually stimulating education while promoting global understanding. Pastoral care is consistently excellent, enabling friendships between all members of a peer group to flourish. Sevenoaks is only one of a handful of schools to win *The Sunday Times Independent Secondary School of the Year* twice.

Curriculum

A wide range of subjects is offered at GCSE and IGCSE. In the sixth form all pupils study the IB Diploma Programme. Academic results are outstanding. In 2023, the average IB score was 39.0, about ten points above the world average. Virtually every student goes on to one of the world's best universities, with around 80 per cent taking places at leading UK universities, and 21 per cent accepting places at top US, Canadian, European and international universities.

A wide range of sport is offered, and pupils achieve honours in cross country, rugby, football, hockey, netball, cricket, athletics, sailing, shooting, swimming and tennis. There is a strong emphasis on music, drama and art, with chamber music a particular strength. The school is proud of its strong tradition of community service and DofE Award participation.

Facilities

Facilities are first class. Recent developments include a striking, state-of-the-art boarding house, an award-winning performing arts centre, a Science & Technology Centre uniting the four core fields of science, and an innovative Sixth Form centre. There are seven boarding houses, including five single-sex houses (13-18), and two sixth form houses (16-18). A new girls' boarding house is being built and will open in 2024. The house will accommodate 60 girls in Year 9 and above.

Entrance

Year 7 (11+): entrance examination, school reference and interview.

Year 9 (13+): pre-assessment, entrance examination or Common Entrance or scholarship examination, plus school reference and interview.

Sixth form (16+): entrance examination, personal statement and interview.

Up to 50 scholarships are awarded annually at 11, 13 and 16, for academic excellence, music, sport, art and drama, and means-tested financial assistance is available.

Sevenoaks School is a registered charity for purposes of education. Charity No. 1101358.

Sotogrande International School

An **inspired** school

(Founded 1978)

Head of School
Mr. James Kearney

PYP coordinator
Andrea Bennett

MYP coordinator
Belén González

DP coordinator
Héléne Caillet

Status Private

Boarding/day Mixed

Gender Coeducational

Language of instruction
English

Authorised IB programmes
PYP, MYP, DP

Age Range 4 months – 18 years

Number of pupils enrolled
1100

Fees
€8,025 – €23,100 per annum

Address
Avenida La Reserva SN
Sotogrande
Cádiz, Andalusia
11310 | SPAIN

TEL +34 956 795 902

Email
info@sis.gl

Website
www.sis.ac

Sotogrande International School (SIS) is a day and boarding school, that follows the IB programme from 3-18 years. Home to a passionate learning community who inspire and encourage learning and intercultural understanding, promoting education as a force for good in the world.

Academic results are consistently excellent, with both MYP and Diploma students achieving well above world average scores year after year. As a result of the impressive average point score of 34 in 2022, 43 points was the highest grade and 21% scored 38 or higher with a 100% pass rate.

With more than 1100 students from 54 countries, SIS is more than just a school, it's a place where individuals flourish. Throughout the IB programmes, internationally qualified teachers provide a challenging, nurturing and academically-rigorous education. SIS offers a bespoke Elite Sports Programme where students combine sports and education.

As an Apple Distinguished School, the use of technology is creatively embedded into the curriculum for all students from the age of 3, while the F1 in Schools programme and the Hyperbaric Challenge provide an exciting way for students to learn Science, Technology, Engineering and Maths (STEM) related subjects. Students are encouraged to think independently and critically, developing their unique interests, gifts and talents benefiting from opportunities to be the best they can be.

Sotogrande International Boarding House is a warm vibrant community, where the staff are dedicated to caring for, and getting the best out of each individual. The academic support received by students is reflected in IB Diploma exam results and University destinations of our boarding students.

Students are encouraged to take part in every aspect of boarding life helping them to grow into happy, motivated and morally committed citizens of the world.

St Andrew's College

(Founded 1894)

Acting Principal
Mr Rob Micallef

DP coordinator
Mr William Hehir

Status Private

Boarding/day Day

Gender Coeducational

Language of instruction
English

Authorised IB programmes
DP

Age Range 4 – 18 years

Number of pupils enrolled
1279

Address
Booterstown Avenue
Blackrock, County Dublin
A94 XN72 | IRELAND

TEL +353 1 288 2785

Email
information@st-andrews.ie

Website
www.sac.ie

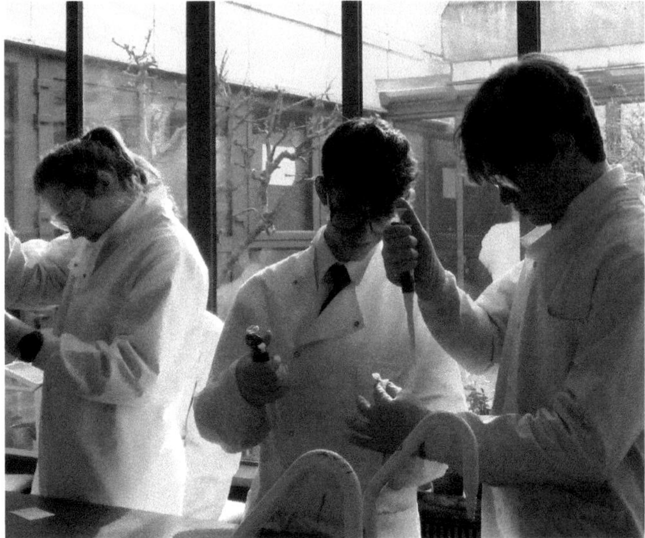

St Andrew's College was founded by the Presbyterian community of Dublin in 1894 to provide a broadly-based, liberal education. From its inception, the College attracted students from a variety of backgrounds and strove to unite them through a shared experience of working, learning and playing together. Over the years the College has evolved in many ways, and is now a flourishing, interdenominational, co-educational school of over 1,270 pupils and over 150 teachers.

In 1982, St Andrew's College became the first school in Ireland to be authorised to offer the International Baccalaureate. It started teaching the IB Diploma Programme in 1983, and first held IBDP examinations in 1985. Over the last 28 years it has built up a well-deserved reputation for its excellent results and for its distinctive multicultural environment. The philosophy on which the College was founded and from which it draws its inspiration today is that a high-quality, rounded education is essential to the moral, social, spiritual, cultural and academic development and physical and mental well-being of the individual student. This philosophy is mirrored in the IB Learner Profile. The high quality of the education offered by the College and its commitment to continuous improvement are reflected in the fact that since 1982, St Andrew's College has been fully accredited by the European Council of International Schools and the New England Association of Schools and Colleges.

The IB Diploma Programme combines academic rigour with a strong extracurricular dimension and various community service projects. The IB students at St Andrew's College participate in a wide range of activities, representing their year on the Prefect Council, playing team sports such as hockey, rugby, tennis, basketball and badminton, taking part in activities such as the Model United Nations, being involved in environmental projects, assisting in the school library and local communities and helping various charities by fundraising and doing voluntary work. The IB Diploma Programme is the premier worldwide pre-university programme. Since 1985, St Andrew's College IB students have been accepted into many universities throughout the world. In recent years these have included all the top Irish universities; MIT, Yale, Stanford, Berkeley and Columbia (USA), Cambridge, Durham, Bristol, Edinburgh and the LSE (UK), the Universities of Tokyo and Keio (Japan). These students universally acknowledge the extent to which their studies in the IB Diploma Programme has given them invaluable help in their university careers.

The IB student profile at St Andrew's College is a truly international one, with students coming from all continents. This ethnic and cultural diversity enriches the school community in many ways and provides a wealth of knowledge and experience which is of great benefit to other students in the school.

(Founded 1953)

Head of School
Mr Duncan Reith

Vice Principal Academic
David White

Vice Principal Pastoral
Becky Allen

DP coordinator
Darrel Ross

Status Private

Boarding/day Mixed

Gender Coeducational

Language of instruction
English

Authorised IB programmes
DP

Age Range 15 – 19 years

Number of pupils enrolled
280

Fees
Day: £23,592 per annum
Boarding: £49,310 per annum

Address
139 Banbury Road
Oxford, Oxfordshire
OX2 7AL | UK

TEL +44 (0)1865 552031

Email
admissions@stclares.ac.uk

Website
www.stclares.ac.uk

Ours is an education unlike any other in the UK.
St Clare's, Oxford is a remarkable place of global education for remarkable young people, advancing international education and understanding for 70 years.

We are a world-leading International Baccalaureate World School, the first in England, attracting students from over 50 countries and embracing internationalism and academic excellence as our core values. Our teachers write the IB textbooks and teach the teachers of the future, and our results are consistently sector-leading and far above global averages. In the last 3 years, over a third of students have scored 40 points or over, and 7 students have scored the maximum IB score of 45, placing them in the top 1% globally.

Everyone in our community is united by one key motivation: to step out of their comfort zones to grow, and to be the most globally aware and academically ambitious version of themselves. Ours is thus a culture of challenge. Walking around, you see individualism and character, engagement with the community, independence, responsibility, and happy, fulfilled young people readying themselves for the world. This is just one reason why independent analysts show that our students consistently make more academic progress here, than they would at any other IB school.

For far too many people, life is like a walk in a tunnel; from one step to the next – in one straight line – without ever stopping to look around. To be at St. Clare's is to stand on top of a mountain with every direction available to you. Any career, any location, any direction for your future made possible. Our Careers and Higher Education support is among the best in the world, sending students to the top-ranking universities worldwide but, more importantly, to the right university for them. This is where aspiration and ambition meet knowledge and experience.

We also offer a one, two or three-term Pre-IB course, including either English IGCSE or the Duolingo English test, and a three week IB Introduction course in the summer, to prepare and develop academic and study skills for the IB Diploma.

We believe that academic achievement matters and lays the foundations for prosperous futures, and that independence is the greatest skill a person – and a mind – can learn. St. Clare's is a place for those who think differently. We help young people become academically successful, self-reliant, and aware of the world. Be challenged, be independent, be remarkable.

St Edward's College Malta

(Founded 1929)

Headmaster
Mr Nollaig Mac an Bhaird

DP coordinator
Mr Jolen Galea

Status Private

Boarding/day Mixed

Gender Coeducational

Language of instruction
English

Authorised IB programmes
DP

Number of pupils enrolled 700

Fees
Day:
€2,184 – €8,154 per annum
Boarding:
€17,263 – €26,602 per annum

Address
Triq San Dwardu
Birgu (Vittoriosa)
BRG 9039 | MALTA

TEL +356 2788 1199

Email
admissions@stedwards.edu.mt

Website
www.stedwards.edu.mt

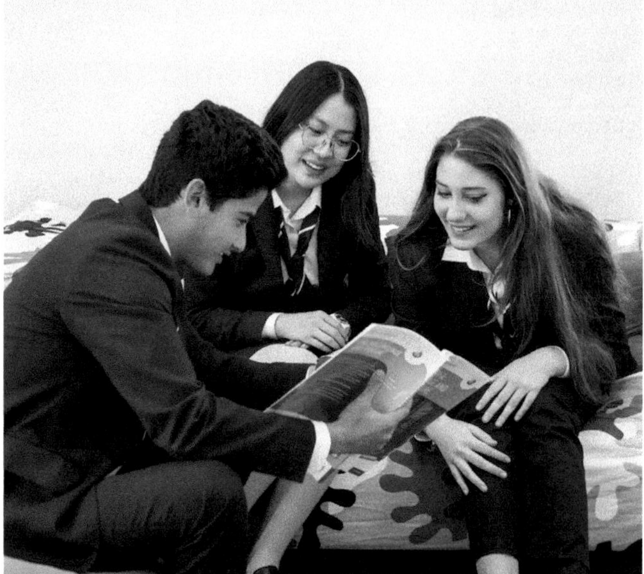

If you are looking for a top Sixth Form offering the IB Diploma programme, then look no further – St Edward's College in Birgu, Cottonera is only a few minutes from Malta's Capital, Valletta. St Edward's was established in 1929, basing itself on British Public School ideals, to fill the void left in the Maltese education system by the departure of the English Jesuits.

The College site originally served as a Military Hospital and has extensive grounds between the bastion walls and the old hospital buildings, which serve as ideal recreational areas. St Edward's College was authorised to offer the International Baccalaureate (IB) Diploma Programme (DP) commencing September 2009 and following successful years, applications for boarders and day students have been increasing.

Between the age of 16 and 18 we offer the 2-year International IB Diploma programme which is recognised by both local and international universities. The IB was designed to meet the needs of these students to ensure that they can effortlessly integrate into different International Schools when the need arises.

After carefully looking at the options available to Maltese students we reached a conclusion that the IB Diploma would also be their best option.

The International Baccalaureate® (IB) aims to do more than other curricula by developing inquiring, knowledgeable and caring young people who are motivated to succeed.

The College is an English speaking school so all the lessons are in conducted in English.

St Edward's offers a unique opportunity for parents seeking a boarding school also. We have five-day and seven-day options. Our boarding facilities are split over two floors where single and double rooms are available.

- The school operates on British boarding school principles with high academic standards
- The location and environment are superb with year round sunshine on a Mediterranean island
- Malta is within 3 hours of any European capital city by air
- The IB Diploma is recognised by all top universities
- Our fees offer some of the best value of any European boarding schools

Come and join our students on the IB Diploma Programme!

ST. EDWARD'S OXFORD

(Founded 1863)

Warden
Alastair Chirnside

DP coordinator
Anna Fielding

Status Private

Boarding/day Mixed

Gender Coeducational

Language of instruction
English

Authorised IB programmes
DP

Age Range 13 – 18 years

Number of pupils enrolled 810

Fees
Day: £12,528 per term
Boarding: £15,660 per term

Address
Woodstock Road
Oxford
Oxfordshire
OX2 7NN | UK

TEL +44 (0)1865 319200

Email
registrar@stedwardsoxford.org

Website
www.stedwardsoxford.org

St Edward's enjoys great success offering the IB alongside A Levels in the Sixth Form, with around 50% of pupils (around 160) choosing to study the IB. The School occupies 100 glorious acres in the north of Oxford and the original Victorian quad has recently been added to with the Christie Centre, a suite of modern and flexible classroom and study spaces topped with the collegiate-style Roe Reading Room, and the 1,000 seater Olivier Hall. On-site and open to the public is the school's very own North Wall Arts Centre, where plays, dance shows and exhibitions give pupils unrivalled access and insights into the arts.

Oxford

The School's location in Oxford is a fundamental feature of school life. The expanding Oxford Programme, an important part of our academic culture, draws on the rich pool of world-leading university academics to enhance our pupils' education. Countless experts visit St Edward's to give talks to our pupils and, in turn, pupils visit the University to immerse themselves in the intellectual life of the city. Venues such as the Ashmolean Museum, the Oxford Playhouse and the Museum of Modern Art offer important learning opportunities – but also welcome distraction from the busy school day.

Sixth Form Achievements

In 2023, 83% of Higher Level grades were 7-5 and just under half achieved 7/6. Each year a number of pupils are awarded places at Oxford and Cambridge whilst the majority go on to top universities in Britain and overseas. Pupils are increasingly interested in studying outside the UK and we have considerable experience in this area. In recent years, pupils have gone on to study at US and Canadian universities including Harvard, Dartmouth, UCLA, McGill, Northeastern and NYU. Pupils have also been successful in their applications to universities in Hong Kong, Japan, Ireland and elsewhere in Europe.

Pastoral Care

The pastoral care system at the St Edward's is outstanding. From the moment they join the School, pupils are made aware of the wide network of support available to them – from House staff to the Pastoral and Safeguarding Deputy Heads and the School Counselling and Health Centre team, there is a highly effective network of skilled professionals ensuring that pupils are safe and happy.

The School and the Admissions Process

St Edward's has around 810 pupils, 86% of whom board. The Sixth Form has around 350 pupils, some 25% of whom are from overseas (17% across the rest of the School), and the boy/girl split is 55%/45%. Entry to the Sixth Form is competitive with around five applicants per place. Academic and Music Scholarships are available along with further Awards in Sport, Art, Dance and Drama.

Find out more about school life on Teddies TV via the website.

St George's British International School, Rome

(Founded 1958)

Principal
John Knight

DP coordinator
Amber Haq

Status Private

Boarding/day Day

Gender Coeducational

Language of instruction
English

Authorised IB programmes
DP

Age Range 3 - 18 years

Number of pupils enrolled
922

Fees
Day:
€11,900 – €22,900 per annum

Address
Via Cassia, km 16
La Storta
00123 Rome | ITALY

TEL +39 06 3086001

Email
admissions@stgeorge.school.it

Website
www.stgeorge.school.it

St George's is Rome's largest and highest achieving international school, home to 930 pupils from nearly 100 different countries. It is the original British international school in Rome. The founding values of St George's are internationalism, inclusivity, and excellence.

The school's main campus is a leafy, historic site in the city's north, with seven fully-equipped science laboratories, a drama studio, specialist music, art and design technology rooms, and multiple sports amenities including two multi-purpose astro-turf pitches, an olympic-size running track, tennis, netball, basketball and volleyball courts. Alongside its academic programme, pupils enjoy a plethora of co-curricular activities, from coding and robotics to jazz ensemble and forest school.

With a proudly inclusive admissions policy, St George's welcomes new pupils throughout the year, subject to availability, and offers extensive support to pupils with additional educational or English language needs. Pupils follow an enhanced version of the UK National Curriculum through to IGCSE; thereafter, they progress to the International Baccalaureate Diploma Programme (IBDP), with over 30 separate DP courses offered. Teachers are almost exclusively UK-trained and mother-tongue English speakers.

Emphasis is on encouraging pupils to strive to fulfil their academic potential, and examination results are consistently amongst the best in Europe. The Class of 2023 achieved an average DP score of 35 points, and have accepted places at leading universities including Cambridge, Yale and Berkeley. Recent graduates have also attended Oxford, Harvard and MIT.

For prospective families, virtual and in-person visits are available throughout the school year. St George's pupils can be described as open-hearted and with an enormous curiosity for their learning. With such a diverse community and a wide range of activities, new members of the community can be assured of a warm welcome.

(Founded 1877)

Head
Mr Simon Brian

PYP coordinator
Catherine Brannen

MYP coordinator Sharon Moan

DP coordinator Ben Seymour

CP coordinator Ben Seymour

Status Private Independent

Boarding/day Mixed

Gender Coeducational

Language of instruction
English

Authorised IB programmes
PYP, MYP, DP, CP

Age Range 5 – 18 years
(boarding from 10)

Number of pupils enrolled 570

Fees
Day:
£11,586 – £18,765 per annum
Boarding:
£28,392 – £44,232 per annum

Address
South Street, St Andrews
Fife KY16 9QJ | UK

TEL 01334 472126

Email
registrar@stleonards-fife.org

Website
stleonards-fife.org

St Leonards is an independent, coeducational, boarding and day school situated on an historic campus at the heart of St Andrews, Scotland. Less than an hour from Edinburgh Airport, the beautiful coastal town is renowned as the 'Home of Golf' and of the UK's top university. St Leonards was named Scotland's Independent School of the Year 2019 by The Sunday Times Good Schools Guide and, more recently, was named the UK's Independent School of the Year 2022 for International Student Experience.

It is international and progressive in outlook, yet rooted in Scottish tradition. There are pupils of 36 nationalities on the School roll; full, flexi and weekly boarding is offered from age ten. Over the past seven years, St Leonards has invested over £5 million in the refurbishment of its boarding houses, which are very much a 'home from home' experience. Houses have state-of-the-art kitchens and spacious, comfortable social areas. Many bedrooms have unrivalled views over the town's mediaeval cathedral ruins and the North Sea that lies beyond the school playing fields.

St Leonards is one of two schools in the UK to actively offer all four IB programmes. The youngest pupils follow the PYP, followed by the MYP and (I)GCSEs. In the Sixth Form, pupils choose between the CP and the DP.

In 2023, the average points score was 35, with 86% of all Higher Level subjects graded 7, 6, or 5. This strong set of results led to leavers securing places at their first choice university, with the most popular destinations this year including the universities of Oxford, Edinburgh, Glasgow, Durham, St Andrews and University College London.

Timetables are designed to establish a healthy balance of sporting and co-curricular activities alongside high academic achievement, with over 50 activities offered. The broad programme includes everything from beach school to aquathlon, bee-keeping to Model United Nations, and Show Choir to field hockey. An exciting calendar of trips are also very popular amongst pupils, with excursions to the natural wonders of Iceland, the battlefields of Belgium and the ancient marvels of Athens, Greece.

Pupils also have the opportunity to enrol in the renowned St Leonards Golf Academy. Catering for all levels, from the complete beginner to the aspiring professional, the six-tier programme at St Leonards tailors coaching and offers opportunities for all to live, learn and play in the home of the game. In partnership with the St Andrews Links Golf Academy, the programme gives students the opportunity to use top-of-the-range training and practice facilities, with access to more Toptracer tracking technology units than any other school in Europe.

The countless opportunities at St Leonards ensures all pupils leave equipped with skills for life, truly following the School motto – *Ad Vitam*.

Entry requirements
Tests and interviews are held throughout the year. For older pupils, entry is by CAT4 assessment, along with school reports and interviews. A one year IGCSE programme is also offered, to prepare students for entry into the Sixth Form. 'Taster experiences' are offered freely to day and boarding students prior to any decision making by individual families.

St. George's International School, Switzerland

(Founded 1927)

Head of School
Dr. Ruth Norris

DP coordinator
Colin Travis

Status Private

Boarding/day Mixed

Gender Coeducational

Language of instruction
English, French

Authorised IB programmes
DP

Age Range 1.5 – 18 years

Number of pupils enrolled 370

Fees
Please enquire

Address
Chemin de St. Georges 19
CH-1815 Clarens/Montreux |
SWITZERLAND

TEL +41 21 964 3411

Email
admissions@stgeorges.ch

Website
www.stgeorges.ch

Founded in 1927, St. George's International School combines its well-structured, traditional ethos with academic excellence in an international environment. Enjoying a safe location, our whole school community fosters mutual respect and understanding whilst cultivating individual talents and potential.

As stated in our motto, 'Levavi Oculos', St. George's International School encourages students to lift their eyes and recognise positive qualities within themselves and others and to nurture a caring and dynamic attitude in today's demanding world.

The school's Learning Principles closely relate to the IB learner profile and students are challenged to become more curious, thoughtful, resilient, reflective, collaborative and balanced.

The school provides a 'Home away from Home' to approximately 80 boarders and over 300 day students from 60 different nationalities. Nestled between the Alps and Lake Geneva, the school includes tennis courts, football field, sports hall, play parks and opened landscaped grounds. During winter students ski and in the summer they make use of the lake, surrounding countryside and local sports facilities.

The curriculum contains the following subject groups:

Groups 1 & 2: Languages
Students usually select from English and French. Spanish, German, Chinese, Russian and other languages as part of the mother tongue Literature self-taught programme are also possible.

Group 3: Individuals and Societies
- Economics
- Geography
- History
- Environmental Systems and Societies
- Business Management

Group 4: Experimental Sciences
- Biology
- Chemistry
- Physics
- Sports, Exercise and Health Science
- Computer Science
- Environmental Systems and Societies

Group 5: Mathematics
St. George's offers Mathematics in higher and standard levels.
- Applications and Interpretations
- Analysis and Approaches

Group 6: The Arts (or elective subject)
Students can follow courses in either Visual Arts, Music, Dance or Theatre Studies.

Alternatively students may follow a second subject chosen from Groups 2, 3 or 4.

St. Gilgen International School

SALZBURG | AUSTRIA

(Founded 2008)

Head of School
Ms Martina Moetz

MYP coordinator
Paul La Rondie

DP coordinator
John Patton

Status Private

Boarding/day Mixed

Gender Coeducational

Language of instruction
English

Authorised IB programmes
MYP, DP

Age Range 9 – 18 years

Number of pupils enrolled
220

Fees
Day:
€28,600 – €43,800 per annum
Boarding:
€58,800 – €66,000 per annum

Address
Ischlerstrasse 13
5340 St. Gilgen | **AUSTRIA**

TEL +43 62 272 0259

Email
info@stgis.at

Website
www.stgis.at

An International educational experience in a breathtaking natural setting

English. German. Ukrainian. Spanish... Just a few of the languages that float down our hallways at St. Gilgen International School (StGIS). Consisting of approximately 40 nationalities, our international student body with over 220 students is a diverse melting pot of talented students. Our school is nestled in the heart of a charming lake side village on the exquisite Wolfgangsee and surrounded by the Austrian alps. St. Gilgen is a stone's throw from the cultural hotspot of Salzburg and just a few hours from Vienna and Munich.

Our key promise is that every child has talent and we will develop it – so a main focus for us is making sure we provide the ideal environment for students. In order to ensure every student flourishes at StGIS, our philosophy of 'three pillars of excellence' applies to every child – excellence in education, care and activities. This means our highly qualified network of teachers, pastoral staff and nurses combine to ensure every student's unique talents are discovered, nurtured and developed.

With over 40 activities to choose from – the school treats the world as a classroom and ensures professional guidance is always at hand. For example, a state-approved mountain guide leads hiking expeditions and horse riding lessons are held in a first class stable. Students can also enjoy golf lessons and seasonal sports such as rowing, water skiing, canyoning, skiing, ice skating and climbing. StGIS also has a strong foundation in the Arts and all students have access to professional Art, Theatre, Dance and Music lessons.

A key focus of the school is to instill a love of learning in each student – and the curriculum and modern teaching methods are designed to fuel natural curiosity. Offering the coveted International Baccalaureate (IB) Diploma and Middle Years Programme (MYP), StGIS students are equipped to go on to study at the world's best Universities. This is a place where teachers strive to build an energy of relentless curiosity in each classroom and empower young minds to stretch and fulfill their potential.

With school fees in line with the world's most prestigious educational institutions, StGIS is one of the best investments you can make in your child's future. After experiencing the unique school first-hand, it's absolutely clear that the reward is a magical education that lasts a lifetime.

We would be delighted to welcome you to show the very best of what Austrian education offers. Simply visit us at www.stgis.at and let the journey begin!

St. John's International School

(Founded 1964)

Head of School
Mr. Kevin Foyle

PYP coordinator
Kathy Anderson

MYP coordinator
Arlin Mowatt

DP coordinator
Jennifer Bakalian

Status Private

Boarding/day Mixed

Gender Coeducational

Language of instruction
English

Authorised IB programmes
PYP, MYP, DP

Age Range 12 months – 18 years

Number of pupils enrolled
500

Fees
€12,300 – €38,915 per annum

Address
Drève Richelle 146
1410 Waterloo, Walloon Brabant
| **BELGIUM**

TEL +32 (0)2 352 06 10

Email
enquiries@stjohns.be

Website
www.stjohns.be

An Internationally trusted institution with an excellent reputation

Founded in 1964 in Waterloo, Belgium, St. John's International School has established itself as one of the leading international schools in Europe.

For more than 50 years, St. John's has been a trusted institution, serving the expatriate and local communities of the greater area with their promise of a soft landing for their new families and a welcoming community that will make them feel right at home.

Academic excellence and so much more

Being the only premium IB continuum school in the area, the school can count on more than 40 years of experience in teaching the International Baccalaureate, an invaluable asset in getting the most out of the IB experience.

Furthermore, it has built its reputation for excellence on a foundation of exceptional academics but realizes that there is so much more to personal growth than academics alone. That is why the school keeps investing in its unrivalled Visual and Performing Arts and Competitive Sports Programmes.

St. John's prides itself to be able to take the individual approach with small class sizes and outstanding pastoral care.

International in more than in name only

500 students between the ages of 2 1/2 and 18 years, representing 62 nationalities, find themselves in a truly cosmopolitan atmosphere while pursuing their curricular ambitions and extra-curricular interest.

Its students are instilled with the open-mindedness to think globally and take individual responsibility for life-long learning, service, and achievement.

Learning without limits

As an International Baccalaureate (IB) World School, offering the Primary Years Programme (PYP), the Middle Years Programme (MYP) and the Diploma Programme (DP), and the only school in the Brussels area to offer the Advanced Placement (AP) programme, St. John's is the perfect springboard to top universities all over the world.

Flexible options

And last but not least, their fully-flexible boarding options cater to the modern, mobile professional to accommodate every need.

Executive Principal High School
Mr. Gerry Rafferty

Principal Colonna School
Mrs. Kathleen Slocombe

Principal Caviglia School
Mrs. Victoria Del Federico

DP coordinator
Hatty Rafferty

Status Private

Boarding/day Day

Gender Coeducational

Language of instruction
English, Italian

Authorised IB programmes
DP

Age Range 2 – 18 years

Number of pupils enrolled
1700

St. Louis Caviglia
SLS S.P.A.
Via E. Caviglia, 1
20139 Milan | **ITALY**

St. Louis Colonna
Via Marco Antonio Colonna, 24,
20149 Milan | **ITALY**

St. Louis High School
Via Olmetto, 6,
20123 Milan | **ITALY**

TEL +39 02 55231235

Email
info@stlouisschool.com

Website
www.stlouisschool.com

Established in 1996, St. Louis is a leading co-educational International School based in the heart of Milan and hosts 1700 students between the ages of 2 and 18.

Located across three sites, the south-east and north-west premises comprise of an Early Years, Primary School, and Middle School, offering school opportunities for 2–14-year-olds. The High School is located in a prime position, just a stone's throw from the Duomo.

The St. Louis School's academic programme is rigorous and challenging. The Early Years programme is based on the British Early Years Foundation Stage (EYFS) Curriculum, and the Primary and Middle School follow the English National Curriculum with an option for students aged 6 years and upwards to also follow the Italian curriculum.

The High School comprises of IGCSE examinations for Years 10-11 and the International Baccalaureate Diploma Programme (IBDP) for Years 12-13 with over 100 students each year studying this unique course.

The approach reinforces the importance of creative and critical thinking, with the school developing independent learners well equipped to succeed in the IBDP and beyond. St. Louis achieves outstanding academic scores within the IB Diploma with the highest average attainment in Europe spanning the last 9 years (37 average).

The school opened its newest addition, the High School in the centre of Milan (Palazzo Archinto) in September 2019. A magnificent historic building located in via Olmetto accommodates all senior school students from Years 10-13. Designed by architect Francesco Maria Richini in the 17th century and situated in the centre of Milan, the Palazzo provides the perfect learning environment for students of this age, blending state-of-the art educational facilities within historic surroundings.

(Founded 1993)

Head of School
Ms. Abigail Lewis

DP coordinator
Ms. Telma Luis

Status Private

Boarding/day Mixed

Gender Coeducational

Language of instruction
English, Portuguese

Authorised IB programmes
DP

Age Range 4 months – 18 years

Number of pupils enrolled
1500

Fees
Day: €6,303 – €14,146 per annum
Boarding: €17,792 per annum
(Plus tuition fees)

Address
Quinta dos Barreleiros CCI 3952
Volta da Pedra
2950-201 Palmela,
Setúbal | **PORTUGAL**

TEL +351 21 233 6990

Email
admissions@stpeters.pt

Website
www.st-peters-school.com

St. Peter's International school is a private school which celebrated its 30th Anniversary in 2023. It provides a competitive, high-quality education from nursery to secondary school (4 months to 18 years old), ensuring students have access to the best opportunities and support to achieve their full academic and personal potential. St. Peter's mission is to build self-reliant, critical and creative students. As an authorised IB World School in Portugal, we offer the IB Diploma Programme in Grades 11 and 12.

St. Peter's International School provides a unique education model with a humanistic approach, adapted to each age group, where languages, sports, arts and technology are key elements in students' daily lives. From Kindergarten to Junior School, we offer a personalised bilingual curriculum, and the option of the national Portuguese or the International curriculum (Cambridge Primary, Lower Secondary, IGCSE and the IB Diploma Programme). Academic excellence is guaranteed in both curricula: St. Peter's is a well-established school with proven outstanding academic results in both the national and the international exams, ensuring access to top tier universities in Portugal and abroad.

Located only 30 minutes from Lisbon city centre, St. Peter's extensive 37,000 m2 campus has outstanding facilities for academics, arts and sports, including 3 football fields, 1 rugby pitch and 2 tennis courts, as well as specialised areas, with science and IT labs, art rooms, and a fully equipped multimedia resource centre.

In addition, St. Peter's is home to the first boarding school in the area, an extension of our commitment to excellence, where students can develop life skills while nurturing lifelong friendships. Now, families living abroad can guarantee their children have access to an international, individualised education in a safe environment and location. Being an on-campus boarding residence, surrounded by the mountains and the sea, students can benefit from a wide range of extracurricular and enrichment activities both during the week and at weekends.

Finally, as an Inspired Education Group school, St. Peter's offers a range of opportunities to students, who have access to the world's best practices in education, outstanding arts and sports programmes, state of the art facilities, and unique exchange Programmes.

St. Stephen's School

(Founded 1964)

Head of School
Jill Muti

DP coordinator
Nadia El-Taha

Status Private

Boarding/day Mixed

Gender Coeducational

Language of instruction
English

Authorised IB programmes
DP

Age Range 14 – 19 years

Number of pupils enrolled
300

Fees
Day: €30,550 per annum
Boarding: €51,003 per annum

Address
Via Aventina 3
00153 Rome | **ITALY**

TEL +39 06 575 0605

Email
ststephens@sssrome.it

Website
www.sssrome.it

Why Choose St. Stephen's
St. Stephen's provides a demanding academic program taking full advantage of its location in the historic center of Rome. We offer a rigorous college preparatory curriculum, which is balanced by a diverse co-curricular program that fulfills the requirements for the full International Baccalaureate Diploma Programme and a US high school diploma.

The First IB School in Italy
In 1975, St. Stephen's was the first school in Italy to offer the International Baccalaureate Programme to students in grades 11 and 12. As a leading IB World School, our graduates have consistently ranked in the top percentile of IB exams, including perfect scores of 42 and the highest IB scores in the history of the School in recent years. Our average IB score is 36.

Building Futures Since 1964
St. Stephen's offers specialized career and university counseling services that aid students in the college or university search process, as well as potential academic and career choices. Our international student body applies to multiple education systems and matriculates to universities throughout the world whose admissions requirements vary widely.

A Focus on Internationalism and Global Citizenship
Our internationally-minded community aims to foster a keen sense of global citizenship in our students, who hail from more than sixty nations. We value the American roots of the School; we embrace Rome as our location, in both its historical and contemporary dimensions; and we are global in our outlook, both in terms of our active interest in histories, cultures, languages and belief systems from around the world, and in our awareness of the global impact of our actions. We welcome students, faculty, and staff from all backgrounds and believe that every one of us contributes in equal measure to the evolving cultural fusion that makes St. Stephen's special.

Rome Is Our Classroom
Our English language high school is surrounded by Western Civilization's most significant historic monuments, such as the Colosseum, the Roman Forum, and Circus Maximus – all within minutes of our campus. Teachers use the Eternal City as their classroom, and students gain first-hand knowledge of history, art, archaeology, classics, and cultural heritage. We provide a world-class education in an intellectually challenging environment that transforms young minds and prepares them to excel in high school and in their future endeavors.

World-Class Professionals Comprise Our Faculty
St. Stephen's employs award-winning authors, playwrights, researchers, archaeologists, art historians, accomplished musicians, scientists, and professionals in many sectors who have distinguished themselves in their respective fields. The real-life experience of our faculty enables them to share a high level of expertise with students. Ninety percent of our faculty have advanced degrees, and twenty percent have earned a PhD.

A Commitment to Discovering Rome and the World
A program unique to St. Stephen's is our dynamic faculty-led trips and experiential service-learning program. Trips take students to regions throughout Italy every fall, and to

destinations throughout Europe and the Mediterranean Basin every spring. Paired with summer service-learning experiences in Rwanda, Senegal, and Sri Lanka, students benefit by gaining new insights and develop a global mindset balanced with compassion and consideration for others.

Signature Programs

Through the St. Stephen's Lyceum, students benefit from enriched classics courses and collaborations with prestigious institutions. Students may elect to take Classical Greek & Roman Studies in the IB Diploma Programme. Our classical studies courses build on the past and unite with the world of technology and globalization.

iLabs

Students enhance their technology skills in the iLab as they learn to design, program, build, and compete in robotics using EV3 Lego Mindstorm or Tetrix Java-based robots. Artists use Wacom tablets to design in 2D and digitally cut and assemble various products and models. Students explore 3D design via Google Sketchup, AutoDesk's Fusion 360 or Inventor programs, as well as Unity, widely used for creating animations and augmented and virtual reality. Students can learn to create and program a myriad of problem-solving devices using Arduino, and a variety of drones, photographic and video equipment, and small robots such as Sphero are available to explore and program. Students can explore virtual reality experiences and learn to make their own Virtual and Augmented Reality applications, and with Cozmo programmable robots, IBM Watson they construct chatbots and learn about creating and using Artificial Intelligence.

Molecular Genetics

St. Stephen's offers science students an advanced molecular genetics program. Developed in partnership with the European Molecular Biology Labs, Europe's flagship laboratory for Life Sciences, this collaboration allows students to develop inquiry-based lab skills and participate in university-level research with state-of-the-art equipment so they may expand and deepen their scientific literacy and competencies.

Five Core Values Anchor Our Community

A strong commitment to our core values of care, integrity, scholarship, independence, and creativity defines us and provides an essential foundation for building character. Students feel supported and free to achieve their personal best.

Photo by Leila

(Founded 1949)

Head of School
Dr Peter Rösner

Principal IB World School
Petra Hau

MYP coordinator
Petra Hau

DP coordinator
Petra Hau

Status Private

Boarding/day Mixed

Gender Coeducational

Language of instruction
English

Authorised IB programmes
MYP, DP

Number of pupils enrolled
500

Fees
Boarding:
€53,000 – €58,000 per annum

Address
Louisenlund 9
24357 Güby,
Schleswig-Holstein | GERMANY

TEL +49 (0)4354 999 333

Email
admission@louisenlund.de

Website
www.louisenlund.de/en

Preserving values, taking responsibility, shaping the future! Louisenlund, the only IB boarding school in northern Germany, impresses with its beautiful surroundings, and with its thoroughly international character, offering education of the highest quality. Located on the banks of the Schlei, with its own yacht harbour, the school has a long heritage of being committed to progressive learning strategies able to nurture open-minded and responsible citizens.

Since its establishment in 1949, Stiftung Louisenlund has stood for a first-class education with high standards of academic achievement and character development. The school seeks to develop individual personalities and promote talents. Practical, proactive and experiential learning enables students to actively develop knowledge and achieve their respective educational objectives. The traditional classrooms were transformed into a learning community in which students are the principal actors in their learning process and in which learning is personalized with individual programmes and timetables.

Louisenlund is fully authorised to offer the International Baccalaureate (IB) Diploma Programme (DP) and the IB Middle Years Programme (MYP), the latter of which is the optimal preparatory programme for younger students who wish to pursue the IB Diploma, and who in general wish to develop their English language skills and to expand their horizons.

There are currently over 500 students, including about 50 from other countries, enrolled at the school, which, in addition to the IB programme, also includes a half-day primary school and a grammar school offering the German Abitur.

Almost 320 of these students are residents of our boarding community, which is extremely popular among students for its relaxed, supportive and familial atmosphere. Indeed, a significant feature of the school is the exceptionally good relationship between students and staff, which results from the dynamic faculty comprising many teachers who are proficient in various languages, including English, Spanish and Chinese, and from the small learning groups. It is a context in which individual talents and interests can be fostered and developed. These things, coupled with the school's membership in the esteemed Round Square network, contribute to the excellent reputation that Louisenlund enjoys worldwide.

Given the excellent educational opportunities and the broad range of co-curricular activities, including local and international projects, given the linguistic and cultural diversity on campus, and the lifelong friendships and the exceptional team spirit of our community, life at Louisenlund is a time to cherish and remember.

Tariq Bin Ziad School

عـضـو فـي مـؤسـسـة قـطـر
Member of Qatar Foundation

Director
Dr. Maha Al Rumaihi

PYP coordinator
Nour R. Ghusayni

Status Private

Boarding/day Day

Gender Coeducational

Language of instruction
English, Arabic

Authorised IB programmes
PYP

Age Range 3 – 12 years

Number of pupils enrolled 607

Fees
Day: QR59,800 – QR61,960 per annum

Address
Al Dafaf Street, Street 893
Al Sadd Area
Doha | QATAR

TEL +974 44542005

Email
tbz@qf.org.qa

Website
tbz.qa

Our Mission
Tariq Bin Ziad School aims to develop responsible, lifelong learners and internationally-minded citizens, who help to create a better and more peaceful world, through an inclusive glocalized and dual-language program. Our caring community supports academic excellence, enhances local identity, and understanding and appreciation for other cultures.

Our Vision
Leading Learning.

Providing a bilingual education blended with a curriculum deeply rooted in Qatari heritage, Tariq Bin Ziad School has a strong legacy of excellence dating back several decades. Previously run by the Amiri Diwan, the school is of national importance to Qatar, having graduated many of the country's current leaders. Recently, the school has been equipped with new, advanced facilities, and is now ready to be positioned as Qatar's leading bilingual school with a strong focus on Arabic language, culture, and heritage.

The curriculum at Tariq Bin Ziad School reflects the concept that students have very individual learning styles. In their classrooms, students and teachers collaborate to develop meaningful individual goals in an environment that emphasizes curricular philosophies such as cooperative teaching and question-based learning.

TASIS The American School in England

THE AMERICAN SCHOOL
IN ENGLAND

(Founded 1976)

Head of School
Mr Bryan Nixon

DP coordinator
Jessica Lee

Status Private

Boarding/day Mixed

Gender Coeducational

Language of instruction
English

Authorised IB programmes
DP

Age Range 3 – 18 years
(boarding from 13)

Number of pupils enrolled
646

Fees
Day:
£13,280 – £29,080 per annum
Boarding:
£54,510 per annum

Address
Coldharbour Lane
Thorpe
Surrey
TW20 8TE | UK

TEL +44 (0)1932 582316

Email
ukadmissions@tasisengland.org

Website
www.tasisengland.org

TASIS The American School in England provides a truly international learning experience for day and boarding students aged 3 to 18. Our caring teachers are committed to providing the balance of academic challenge and support that will enable our students to realize their full potential and contribute to their community as they discover their passion and follow their own pathway.

- International Baccalaureate (IB) Diploma Programme
- American curriculum leading to an American High School Diploma
- Advanced Placement (AP) courses
- Average class size of 10-12 students
- Individualized four-year university counseling
- Excellent university placement in the UK, US & worldwide
- Over 60 nationalities & 30 languages spoken on campus
- 45 minutes from central London
- 20 minutes from Heathrow Airport

Set in the beautiful Surrey countryside, our spacious 46-acre campus is close enough to London to take advantage of all the culture and excitement it offers for field trips and weekend activities. The TASIS boarding program provides a safe and welcoming home-away-from-home for students aged 13 to 18 (Grades 8-12).

In Upper School, our impressive academic offerings include Advanced Placement courses developed by the American College Board and the IB Diploma Programme. Both provide well-defined pathways to universities in the US, the UK, or anywhere in the world. A broad range of co-curricular, leadership, and service opportunities round out our students' educational experience.

TASIS England also offers an award-winning residential Summer Program for ages 11-17. Our program attracts bright and adventurous students from around the world who take one major academic course and one elective, complemented by sports, activities, and weekend excursions. We offer two three-week sessions starting in late June and ending in early August.

TASIS The American School in Switzerland

Head of School
Christopher Nikoloff

DP coordinator
Kathy Anderson

Status Private

Boarding/day Mixed

Gender Coeducational

Language of instruction
English

Authorised IB programmes
DP

Age Range 3 – 19 years

Number of pupils enrolled 765

Fees
Day: CHF51,000 per annum
Boarding: CHF95,000 per annum

Address
Via Collina d'Oro 15
6926 Montagnola-Lugano |
SWITZERLAND

TEL +41 91 960 5151

Email
admissions@tasis.ch

Website
www.tasis.ch

Founded by M. Crist Fleming in 1956, TASIS is a day and boarding international school committed to creating global citizens through education, travel, and service.

The oldest American boarding school in Europe, TASIS now welcomes 765 students from more than 60 nations in grades Pre-Kindergarten (beginning at age three) through Postgraduate each year. More than 260 students between ages 12-19 reside in dormitories on campus.

High School students can choose from individual Advanced Placement courses or pursue the International Baccalaureate (IB) Diploma, helping them receive offers from more than 400 universities in 20 different nations over the past five years. The School offers an extensive Fine Arts program that includes courses in Drama, Music, and the Visual Arts, enabling aspiring artists of any ilk to find their creative voice and nurture their talent.

Accredited by the European Council of International Schools (ECIS) and the New England Association of Schools and Colleges (NEASC), TASIS is proud to employ gifted, passionate educators who encourage intellectual curiosity. Nearly 80 percent of the High School faculty hold advanced degrees.

The campus includes more than 25 buildings dating from the 17th century Villa De Nobili to the state-of-the-art Campo Science Center. Perched on a hillside in sunny southern Switzerland with commanding views of snow-capped mountains, palm trees, and Lake Lugano, the School's enviable location makes possible an impressive Academic Travel program that brings students face-to-face with the rich cultural heritage of Europe and the spectacular natural beauty of the Alps and beyond.

The School's pioneering Global Service Program transforms lives by providing every High School student with a unique opportunity to connect across borders – whether geographic, economic, or social – through comprehensive experiences that build empathy and encourage personal responsibility. The Program awakens students to humanitarian needs, inspires them to build enduring relationships, and leads them toward a life of active service and committed service.

TASIS encourages physical fitness and healthy lifestyles. Varsity sports teams compete throughout Switzerland and Europe, and a variety of other fitness activities are offered to cater to all interests. Each year also brings many opportunities to ski and explore the breathtaking Alps. Students leave TASIS with a heightened appreciation for the outdoors and an understanding of what it takes to succeed in challenging environments.

Each summer, hundreds of students aged 4–17 journey to Lugano for the TASIS Summer Programs, which feature intensive academic courses, an unparalleled performing arts program, thrilling outdoor adventures, advanced sports training, and exciting cultural excursions around Europe.

(Founded 1847)

Headmaster, Taunton School
Mr. James Johnson

DP coordinator
Adrian Roberts

Status Private

Boarding/day Mixed

Gender Coeducational

Language of instruction
English

Authorised IB programmes
DP

Age Range 0 – 18 years

Number of pupils enrolled
1138

Fees
Day:
£7,890 per term
Boarding:
£13,870 – £14,970 per term

Address
Staplegrove Road
Taunton
Somerset
TA2 6AD | UK

TEL +44 (0)1823 703703

Email
enquiries@tauntonschool.co.uk

Website
www.tauntonschool.co.uk

"At Taunton School, the IB becomes your second family. Because the classes are so small and you spend so much time together, you become close with people from all over the world, and you gain an insight into different cultures and beliefs that A-Levels just don't offer."

"After being offered the IB Scholarship at Taunton School, it has opened many doors and opportunities for me to prosper in a fantastic educational environment. Taunton School offered great facilities which supported and strengthened my studies in my subjects." **- IB students at Taunton School**

At Taunton School, we have been offering the IB Diploma since becoming an IB World School in 2007. During that time over 300 students have obtained the diploma and its popularity continues to grow. IB students do consistently well at Taunton School, achieving high scores equivalent to 5 A-Levels and often obtaining places at their first-choice university, whether it's in the UK or overseas. Many students achieve top points and go on to study medicine at highly competitive universities.

In 2023, students achieved a 92% pass rate with an average of 32 points, exceeding the world average by almost two full points. Six students scored 38 or more points.

Aside from lessons, everything else is done with the rest of the Sixth Form, such as sport, drama, music, social events, houses and tutor groups. Adrian Roberts, IB Coordinator at Taunton School says: *"IB is going from strength to strength at Taunton School and our students consistently impress me with their willingness to aim high and extend themselves beyond the confines of a 'normal' Sixth Form curriculum."*

We are a leading independent school for boys and girls aged 0 to 18 years situated on a beautiful 56 acre campus in the picturesque county of Somerset, in South West England. Our mission is to ensure that the education we provide at Taunton School plays to the strengths of each and every child. We offer an IB Scholarship of up to 100% of fees. Contact us to find out more: www.tauntonschool.co.uk/scholarshipawards/

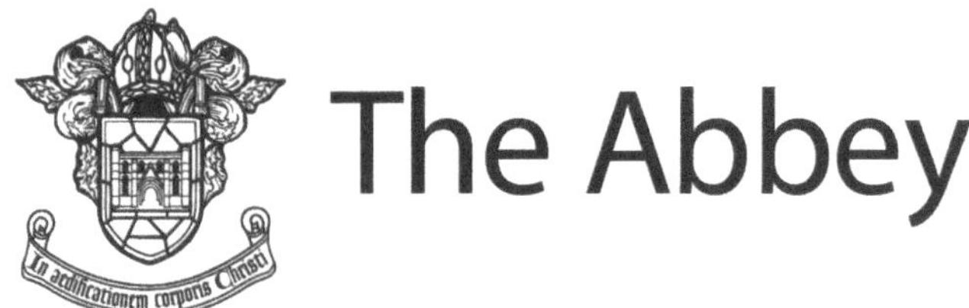

(Founded 1887)

Head
Mr Will le Fleming

PYP coordinator
Jillian Priestley

DP coordinator
Nicola McDonald

Status Private

Boarding/day Day

Gender Female

Language of instruction
English

Authorised IB programmes
PYP, DP

Number of pupils enrolled 987

Fees
Day:
£13,500 – £21,750 per annum

Address
Kendrick Road
Reading
Berkshire
RG1 5DZ | UK

TEL 0118 987 2256

Email
admissions@theabbey.co.uk

Website
www.theabbey.co.uk

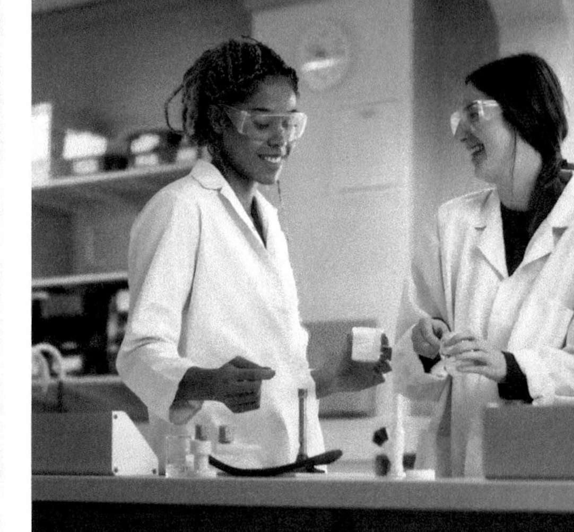

Described as 'much more than a school', The Abbey is a place where academic excellence becomes a natural process of growth and curiosity at every stage of the journey, from the age of 3 to 18. We are a school that celebrates success in all its forms, and every girl is encouraged to explore her own unique strengths and discover her passions through a vast choice of opportunities – both inside and outside the classroom.

As an International Baccalaureate school, our internationally-minded ethos means that we collaborate across divides and strive to provide a real-world education that prepares students to step out into an uncertain world with confidence, empathy, and at ease with those from all cultures.

Our pioneering methods put the 'why' back at the heart of learning and our holistic approach places equal emphasis on academic achievement, intellectual agility and emotional wellbeing. The results of this more organic, relaxed approach to learning, speak for themselves. The Abbey is consistently one of the top performing schools academically – not only in the UK, but globally. In 2023, our students who studied the IB Programme, achieved an average of 38 points, compared to the global average of 30, placing the school firmly in the top tier of IB Schools in the World.

The Abbey's town centre location places us at the heart of a vibrant community, whilst our extensive coach network helps provide accessibility from locations across Oxfordshire and Berkshire for both Junior and Senior girls.

A range of scholarships are available, as well as financial assistance offered through means-tested bursaries. Above all, The Abbey is passionate about creating a learning experience that is joyful and meaningful. Our self-regulating culture helps us all to look after each other, and our inspiring teachers are dedicated to fostering a special relationship with each and every individual.

The Academy International School

(Founded 1985)

Headteacher
Clare Mooney

DP coordinator
Caroline Foster

Status Private

Boarding/day Day

Gender Coeducational

Language of instruction
English

Authorised IB programmes
DP

Age Range 2 – 19 years

Fees
Diploma Programme €12,000

Junior School
Camí de Son Ametler Vell, 250
07141 Marratxí,
Balearic Islands | SPAIN

Senior School
Carrer d'Antoni Furió, 2
Ses Cases Noves
07141 Marratxí,
Balearic Islands | SPAIN

TEL +34 971 605008

Email
info@theacademyschool.com

Website
www.theacademyschool.com

The Academy International School, established in 1985, has long been recognised as a centre of excellent academic achievement, where the whole school community shares the joy of learning. We are also proud to be the first International British School to bring the International Baccalaureate Diploma Programme to Mallorca.

In a beautiful setting in the Mallorcan countryside students enquire, discover, analyse and evaluate. They are creative, innovative and proud to be part of this school community. The Academy teaching team accompanies the students on a wonderful learning journey from our Nursery classrooms all the way through to IBDP.

Academy students are encouraged, supported and challenged. They are offered a broad and balanced curriculum, delivered by motivated and creative teachers, to ensure that learning is effective and promotes a lifelong passion for education. The Academy International School prepares students to compete in a rapidly changing international marketplace where academic content is important, but is no longer enough.

In today's evolving global society, inquiry, critical thinking, and international mindedness are essential skill sets that students must have to determine their success as a leader and in the workforce. The Academy International School offers students multiple ways to develop and demonstrate what they know and understand. Students complete collaborative projects, oral presentations, essay writing, inquiry-based experiments, and take part in discussion and debate that mirror what they will experience in the challenging fields they hope to enter after university.

The Academy students see how our school connects with the world at large through community projects and activities locally, nationally and internationally.

Our goal is to help students achieve their dreams.

The Aga Khan Academy, Nairobi

Aga Khan Education Service, Kenya

(Founded 1970)

Head of Senior School
Ms. Eva Pillossof

Head of Junior School
Ms. Reeshma Charania

Head of Nursery School
Ms. Waseema Khawaja

PYP coordinator
Ms. Dorcas Kisilu

MYP coordinator
Ms. Irene Simiyu

DP coordinator
Mr. William Wanyonyi

Status Private

Boarding/day Day

Gender Coeducational

Language of instruction English

Authorised IB programmes
PYP, MYP, DP

Age Range 3 – 19 years

Number of pupils enrolled 1020

Address
P.O. Box 44424-00100
1st Parklands Avenue,
off Limuru Road
Nairobi | KENYA

TEL Junior: +254 0733 758 510,
Senior: +254 736 380 101

Email
infos@akesk.org; infoj@akesk.org

Website
www.agakhanschools.org/kenya/akan/index

About Aga Khan Academy, Nairobi
Established in 1970, the Aga Khan Academy, Nairobi is a private, co-educational school located in the Parklands suburb of Nairobi, Kenya. The Aga Khan Nursery School is located on a separate campus on Kipande Road, at the bottom of Museum Hill in Nairobi.

Together, our schools have an enrolment of over 1,000 students and are authorised to offer the International Baccalaureate Primary Years Programme, Middle Years Programme and Diploma Programme.

Mission statement
Enable many generations of students to acquire both the knowledge and the essential spiritual wisdom needed to balance that knowledge and enable their lives to attain the highest fulfilment.

School Overview
The Aga Khan Academy, Nairobi (AKA) Nairobi is the only school in Kenya authorized to offer a continuum of the International Baccalaureate curriculum (IB) from Primary Years Programme (PYP), the Middle Years Programme (MYP), to Diploma Programme (DP). With over 1000 students, the AKA, Nairobi is a multi-cultural school with a variety of nationalities represented in our student and teaching faculty.

The Aga Khan Academy, in keeping with the IB philosophy, 'touches hearts as well as minds'. Our students not only learn to be knowledgeable, open-minded thinkers, inquirers, principled, risk takers, well-balanced, and caring but also to be leaders and stewards.

Examination results
The Aga Khan Academy provides an outstanding academic education and enables students to fulfil their potential. Although the Aga Khan Nursery School does not have a grading system, it typically holds an annual graduation and exhibition celebrating the completion of the Early Years PYP.

Curriculum offered
The IB curriculum enables students to learn using a transdisciplinary and an interdisciplinary approach and to develop critical thinking, creativity and internationalmindedness – identified by leading educators globally as some of the necessary skills for the 21st Century learning. Our curriculum combines academic excellence with athletics and visual performing arts programmes.

Admission
Admission is based primarily on merit determined by a wide range of criteria, including academic strengths and overall potential.

Examinations offered
MYP eAssessment, IB Diploma Programme (IB DP) Facilities ICT resource centres, STEAM, Robotics Lab in junior school, film studio, music rooms, art rooms, science labs, well-resourced libraries, heated pool, wireless connectivity, data projectors in classrooms, a makerspace for the junior school and a well-resourced SEN and Guidance & Counselling room.

The British School of Milan (Sir James Henderson)

(Founded 1969)

Principal
Dr Chris Greenhalgh

DP coordinator
Miss Alba López Martín

Status Private, Not-For-Profit

Boarding/day Day

Gender Coeducational

Language of instruction
English

Authorised IB programmes
DP

Age Range 3 – 18 years

Number of pupils enrolled 760

Fees
€14,000 – €22,120 per annum

Address
Via Carlo Alberto Pisani Dossi, 16
20134 Milan | ITALY

TEL +39 02 210941

Email
info@bsm.school

Website
www.britishschoolmilan.com

The British School of Milan, founded in 1969, is rated among the top 5 IB schools in Europe, No.1 in Italy, and top 50 in the world. The BSM is the only school in Milan passing all the standards set by UK Government Inspectors (ISI).

The BSM is a not-for-profit school which provides world-class education to 760 students aged 3 to 18 from over 40 different nationalities. The school values cultural diversity and offers a rich international experience while rigorously following the UK National Curriculum and the International Baccalaureate (IB) in the Sixth Form.

Academic results are outstanding and students progress to top universities around the globe. In the last few years they have gained places at Oxford, Cambridge, Yale, LSE, Imperial, University College London, The University of Edinburgh, Trinity College Dublin, Università Bocconi, Columbia University, Sciences-Po and many other leading universities.

There is a strong emphasis on co-curricular activities with over 100 options available. The school is particularly proud of its exceptional music, art and drama departments. In addition, BSM acts as the Italian centre for the UK-based ABRSM, the exam board of the Royal Schools of Music. The School nourishes a tradition of community service with students pursuing CAS projects and the Duke of Edinburgh's Award Scheme. We also offer three IB Academic Scholarships per year.

The BSM is situated just outside the centre of Milan, close to the metro and on several bus routes. Linate airport and the popular Milano 2 residences are just minutes from the school.

Admission applications are accepted throughout the year.

The English School of Kyrenia

Head of School
Hector MacDonald

DP coordinator
Ms Zelis Omer

Status Private

Boarding/day Day

Gender Coeducational

Language of instruction
English

Authorised IB programmes
DP

Age Range 2 – 18 years

Number of pupils enrolled
1200

Fees
Day: £4,700 – £7,560

Address
Bilim Sokak
Bellapais
Kyrenia, North Cyprus | CYPRUS

TEL +90 392 444 0375

Email
info@englishschoolkyrenia.org

Website
www.englishschoolkyrenia.com

The English School of Kyrenia (ESK) is a purpose-built modern IB World School offering exciting opportunities for academic excellence and personal development for boys and girls aged 2 to 18. An enviable and spacious learning environment, the campus is set in the inspiring surroundings of the Kyrenia foothills, overlooking the Mediterranean to the front and the Kyrenia mountains to the rear.

The Little Learners building is a welcoming, calming and nurturing environment for our Pre-Nursery students. Designed with soft, earth inspired tones, students thrive in the fundamental stage of their development along with support from our professional and qualified teachers. Our Nursery – Year 2 students are located in the eco-friendly Early Years building. The unique building aims to generate its own electricity requirements and seeks to provide all ESK students with a living example of green sustainability.

For the current 2020-2021 academic year, ESK has 1200 students drawn from both international and local backgrounds. The sections of the school are Little Learners (Pre-Nursery), Early Years (Nursery – Year2), Primary (Year 1 – Year 6), and Secondary (Year 7 – Year 13). All classes are taught in English, with an addition of Turkish as a second language, and an option of Mandarin, Russian, French, or Spanish. The Early Years follow the UK's EYFS (Updated) curriculum and the Primary School follows the Cambridge International Primary Programme (CIPP).

In the Secondary School the widely respected IGCSE, A-Level and International Baccalaureate (IB) Diploma Programme give students the opportunity to develop an international perspective and attend the world's top universities. Over 88% of graduates attend University in the UK, and 10% in the EU or North America. Graduates have attended prestigious universities such as The University of Cambridge, Imperial College, UCL, LSE, University of Edinburgh, Parson's School of Design and Leiden University, to name a few.

Today's students are tomorrow's leaders and decision makers: we afford every opportunity for our boys and girls to reach their personal and academic potential whilst nurturing their curiosity and encouraging individuality and creative thought. IBDP Subjects available:

Group 1: English Language & Literature, Russian Language & Literature, Turkish Literature

Group 2: English B, Spanish ab initio, French

Group 3: Geography, History, Business and Management, Psychology, Economics

Group 4: Biology, Chemistry, Physics, Computer Science

Group 5: Mathematics Analysis and Approaches, Mathematics Interpretation and Application

Group 6: Visual Arts, Music, Theatre Arts or one other subject taken from groups 3-4 above

(Founded 2013)

Head of School
Mr Jonathan Ferreira

PYP coordinator
Ms Veena Nambiar

DP coordinator
Ms Magali Kunsevi

Status Private

Boarding/day Day

Gender Coeducational

Language of instruction
English, French

Authorised IB programmes
PYP, DP

Age Range 2 – 19 years

Address
Batterie IV
Libreville, Gabon
2144 | GABON

TEL +241 11 44 26 70

Email
admissions@ecolerubanvert.com

Website
www.ecolerubanvert.com

Welcome to The International School of Gabon – Ruban Vert.
Our Vision:
To provide a legacy in education which promotes qualities of open-mindedness, tolerance and respect for others, which will provide a best practice model for the future of students from all nations in Gabon and across Africa.
Mission:
To become Africa's most enterprising school, focusing on sustainability and innovation to play a significant role in Gabon's and in Africa's education.

École Ruban Vert (ERV), offers a unique blend of bilingual, internationally focused education accredited by the Council of International Schools (CIS). ERV is an IB World School, offering Early Years, IBPYP, International GCSE, and the IBDP, with exceptional examination results.

Our students secure outstanding results in external examinations. The IBDP Pass Rate has been 100% since 2018, the pass rate for the Bilingual IBDP has also consistently been 100%, and in 2023 our highest scoring student achieved 44 points. Students have the opportunity to sit the EdEXCEL International GCSEs, where again the pass rate is also 100%, in 2023 64% of students gained high grades.

ERV students are recognised for their capacity to lead, innovate, serve, to respect resources and the environment, and for their commitment to making a significant impact on their school and their communities. Our world-class, green campus serves as the backdrop for an educational establishment that aims to facilitate radical thinking and achieve high standards of education. ERV is a forward thinking school whose aim is to enable students to learn to manage the future in a creative and sustainable way.

A programme of scholarships enables local Gabonese students accessibility to top-class education alongside children from diverse national and international backgrounds.

Our campus is a microscopic example of Gabon itself with every tree and shrub of Gabon planted within the campus. We believe it is one of the most beautiful in Africa with streams, bridges, green play areas and wildlife in abundance. Outstanding facilities include an auditorium, computer suites, gymnasium, library, music performance spaces, science labs and international sports stadium. We offer musical instrument tuition, Royal College of Music Examinations, yoga, ballet, the Duke of Edinburgh Award, and our Tennis Academy is the best in Libreville. ERV hosts the Moabi Festival, a celebration of local culture and the Gabon International Open Tennis Tournament.

(Founded 1983)

Secondary Principal
Richard Matthews

Primary Principal
Rubin Borges

MYP coordinator
Maria Lamminaho

DP coordinator
Dr. Alma Trumic

CP coordinator
Dr. Alma Trumic

Status State/Semi Private

Boarding/day Day

Gender Coeducational

Language of instruction
English

Authorised IB programmes
MYP, DP, CP

Age Range 4 – 18 years

Number of pupils enrolled
1400

Fees
Day: €8,000 – €10,500 per annum

Address
Wijndaelerweg 11
2554 BX The Hague, South Holland | **NETHERLANDS**

TEL +31 70 328 1450

Email
admissions@ishthehague.nl

Website
www.ishthehague.nl

At The International School of The Hague (ISH) we provide high quality international education for children ages 4 – 18. Our concept-based inquiry approach to learning is at the centre of everything we do in the classroom and through our extensive co-curricular programmes, engaging students to be curious, connected and compassionate global citizens of the future.

ISH students benefit not only from a well-established IB Middle Years Programme (MYP), and Diploma Programme (DP), both with consistently excellent results, but also a Careers Related Programme (CP) for students with a more entrepreneurial spirit because we know different career paths demand different approaches. No matter which path our students choose, both provide an excellent route to university and other journeys beyond ISH.

With a uniquely diverse community of over 100 nationalities, we embrace and nurture all home languages, something that enriches the lives of our students and the lives of everyone around them. ISH has a naturally global outlook and students actively engage in the issues that face the planet today. For example, every year our Year 10 to Year 13 students have the opportunity to take part in one of the oldest, and largest, secondary school Model United Nations conferences (MUNISH) in the world, attracting over 1200 students from all around the globe. This amazing opportunity is led by the students of today for the students of tomorrow – a weekend filled with lively debate and policy-making.

Being an international school in the Dutch context means students at ISH also benefit from all the advantages of being situated in The Netherlands. Empowered by a cycling culture and infrastructure unrivalled in the world, children are free from a young age to meet friends, explore the city and take advantage of the impressive array of leisure opportunities available. Furthermore, the schools' location in an area of natural beauty, close to the beach, in the City of Peace and Justice all contribute to children feeling at home in a country that facilitates life for those who don't speak Dutch. Perhaps it's unsurprising that children in The Netherlands are consistently ranked by UNESCO as among the happiest in the world.

The KAUST School

Director
Dr. Michelle Remington

High School Principal
Dr. Robert Blanchard

Middle School Principal
Dr. Ronald Lalonde

Elementary Principal
Jeff Woodcock

PYP coordinator
Jonathan Mueller

MYP coordinator
Michele McLay

DP coordinator
Greg River

Status Private

Boarding/day Day

Gender Coeducational

Language of instruction
English

Authorised IB programmes
PYP, MYP, DP

Address
4700 KAUST
Thuwal, Western Province
23955-6900 | SAUDI ARABIA

TEL +966 12 808 6803

Email
schools@thekaustschool.org

Website
tks.kaust.edu.sa

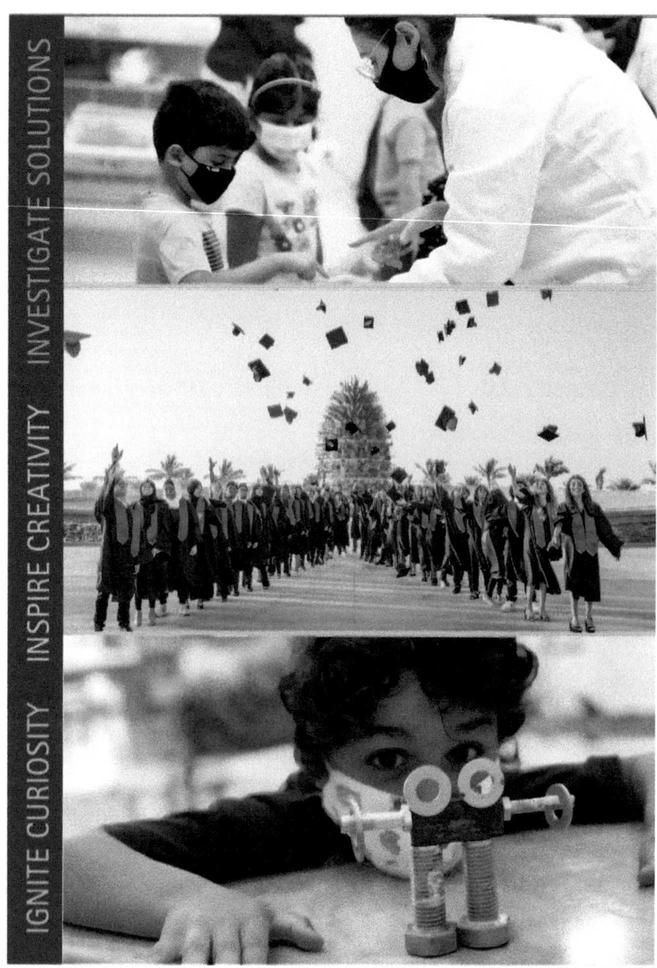

The KAUST School (TKS) proudly serves a thriving multi-cultural University community, with an enrollment of approximately 1,800 students from more than 75 nations. As an International Baccalaureate World School authorized in three programs: Primary Years, Middle Years and the Diploma Programme, we share a common philosophy and a commitment to high quality, challenging international education for children from K1 through to Grade 12. TKS is accredited by the Council of International Schools (CIS) and the Middle States Association (MSA).

Our Resources

The school is uniquely located within the university campus of King Abdullah University of Science and Technology (KAUST), a destination of choice for world-class scientific and technological graduate education and research, north of Jeddah on the shores of the Red Sea.

The school is purpose built with a design that supports a balanced curriculum. The Gardens Campus which houses the Elementary and Secondary School, has technology equipped classrooms, science laboratories, a design and technology hub, two library media centers, two indoor gymnasiums, two performance theatres, outdoor basketball and tennis courts, an outdoor swimming pool and soccer pitch. The Kindergarten Campus is filled with natural light, color and materials that stimulate learning. The buildings include activity rooms, two libraries and several specialized rooms for Art, Music, Arabic and Islamic studies.

The school offers a state-of-the-art technology environment that incorporates a broad spectrum of educational solutions while maintaining a 1:1 Apple computing environment.

Our People

Our students are the children of KAUST academic and professional staff, TKS staff, graduate students and University partners.

TKS Staff consists of over 350 teachers, specialist support staff and administrators from across the globe, with over 70% having advanced degrees and the majority with previous international school experience.

The school maintains classroom ratios of one teacher to 15 students in early childhood; to 18 students in Elementary; and to 22 students in Secondary.

Our IB Diploma Curriculum

TKS offers a co-educational IB academic program in English. Targeted support is provided for students with instructional needs, including intensive English language support, as required. Arabic and French are offered as a first language to native speakers in secondary and Spanish, French and Arabic as an additional language (acquisition).

Co-curricular Activities

With the benefit of being located on a university campus and enclosed community, TKS utilizes all university and community facilities enriching the co-curricular programs.

United Lisbon International School

Head of School
Dr. José Azcue

Secondary School Principal
Alexandra Conchard

DP coordinator
Frank Alfano

Status Private

Boarding/day Day

Gender Coeducational

Language of instruction
English

Authorised IB programmes
DP

Age Range 3 – 18 years

Number of pupils enrolled
600

Fees
Day: €11,000 – €22,000 per annum

Address
Avenida Marechal Gomes da Costa 9
1800-255 Lisbon | **PORTUGAL**

TEL +351 211 161 110

Email
info@unitedlisbon.school

Website
www.unitedlisbon.school

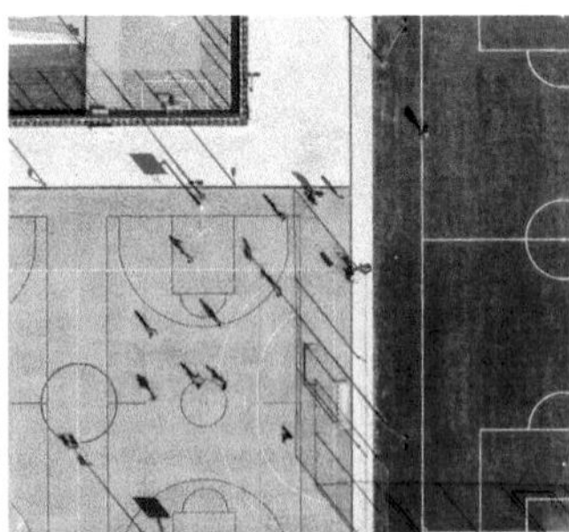

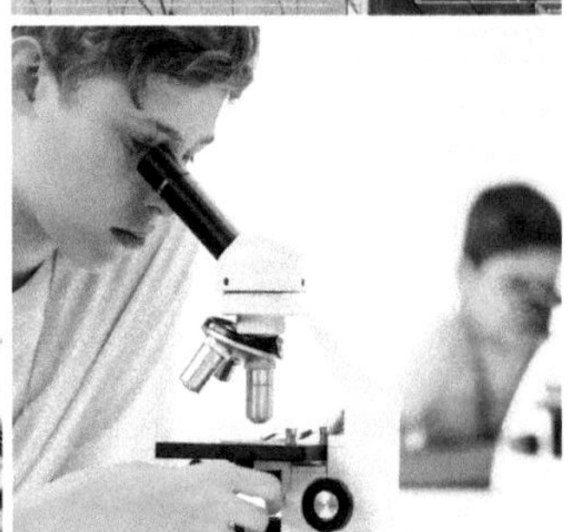

United Lisbon International School (ULIS) is a world-class international English language school in the center of Lisbon part of the Dukes Education Group. ULIS is one of the select few prestigious Microsoft Showcase schools in Portugal.

It is a modern and innovative international school, offering English-language academic programs from Early Childhood (from 3 years) to grade 12, with a challenging curriculum based on US standards (NEASC) culminating in the International Baccalaureate Diploma Programme, preparing students for the the best universities worldwide.

The school offers an education inspired by and fit for the 21st century; an international education founded on rigorous standards of excellence, seamlessly integrating technology into the learning environment.

The School's Mission

United Lisbon's philosophy is to nurture the individual learner: by providing a rich environment of opportunities to grow academically as well as personally. With the vision "to empower and inspire the younger generation for a sustainable world", United Lisbon provides rigorous academic programs, a strong focus on the skills and values children will need to be successful in tomorrow's world. The school's modern pedagogy creates a student-centered learning ecosystem that instills relevant skills through guided inquiry, collaborative learning, and seamless integration of technology, to strengthen and further personalize the learning experience of each individual student.

Curriculum

The school has created a dynamic learning culture where learners become experts who have deep conceptual understandings, high-level competencies, and a strong positive moral character. Uniting the school's core pillars are values, technology, entrepreneurism, music and arts.

United Lisbon Academy

With over 6,500 sqm of its own outdoor play and sports facilities, United Lisbon enjoys an enriching extracurricular program. With a diverse set of activities on offer, the school partners with leading institutions, including Sporting FC, Lisboa Racket Centre and STAT Martial art.

(Founded 1982)

Head of College
Dr. Khalid El-Metaal

DP coordinator
Joanne de Koning

Status Private

Boarding/day Boarding

Gender Coeducational

Language of instruction
English

Authorised IB programmes
DP

Age Range 16 – 19 years

Number of pupils enrolled 177

Fees
Two-year Fee €23,000 per annum (scholarships available)

Address
Località Duino 29
34011 Duino-Aurisina TS | **ITALY**

TEL +39 040 3739111

Email
uwcad@uwcad.it

Website
www.uwcad.it

UWC Adriatic (UWCAD) is a member of the United World College (UWC) movement, currently made up of 18 schools and colleges across the world. Established in 1982, UWCAD is the first of the colleges to be set up in a non-English speaking country. Located on an open campus in the picturesque coastal village of Duino in the north-east of Italy, 25 kilometres away from the historic city of Trieste, it is currently home to nearly 200 students, aged 16 to 19. UWCAD operates a policy of deliberate diversity that is key to its mission and as a result, students come from over 80 countries and a wide range of socio-economic backgrounds. In fact, currently 92% of the student body benefit from a full or partial scholarship in order to pursue their education at the College.

The residential education programme offered by the College places equal emphasis on academic and co-curricular learning experiences. All students undertake the International Baccalaureate Diploma through the medium of English. In addition, the students are required to study Italian either as part of the Diploma programme or as an additional subject, in order to ensure that they are fully integrated in the local Italian culture. The UWC Adriatic educational experience draws inspiration from the surrounding rich Italian culture including art, music, architecture, history and regional languages that stimulate the students' creativity and reflections. Furthermore, music plays a big role in the students' UWC experience at Adriatic, thanks to its music department – the International Community Music Academy (ICMA). Over 30% of the students in Duino play an instrument or sing and concerts are held every month and are attended by the local community. The students at UWCAD are also expected to engage fully in service-based learning, ecological and outdoor education, physical and cultural activities, as well as social and emotional learning. The College's location on the Adriatic coast and close proximity to the Alps allow students to take part in activities such as sailing, kayaking, climbing, hiking, as well as down-hill and cross-country skiing throughout the academic year.

UWC Adriatic has seven student residences that are dispersed around the village of Duino. In addition, students benefit from a range of facilities including purpose-built science laboratories, an art centre, as well as a fully equipped music centre. Medical staff are available 24 hours a day.

Admissions

Applications to UWCAD take place through the different UWC national committees.

(Founded 2009)

Head of College
Lodewijk van Oord

Director of Primary School
Nilde Pais

Director of Secondary School
Kate Doyle

Status State

Boarding/day Mixed

Gender Coeducational

Language of instruction
English

Authorised IB programmes
MYP, DP, CP

Age Range 4 – 19 years

Number of pupils enrolled 980

Fees
Ranging from €7,060 in primary school – €30,000 in the residential programme (scholarships available)

Address
Discusworp 65
6225 XP Maastricht, Limburg |
NETHERLANDS

TEL +31 432 410 410

Email
admissions@uwcmaastricht.nl

Website
www.uwcmaastricht.nl

Introduction

In addition to the highly recognized International Baccalaureate curriculum, UWC Maastricht is a multicultural school that hosts students from more than 100 different nationalities. The school operates within the Dutch public educational system and is subsidized by the Dutch government. It is formed to serve both the needs of the Maastricht international community and the students chosen by UWC national committees all over the world.

Inside the Classroom

At age 4, children can start their education at UWC Maastricht. The school currently offers its own primary school curriculum, but is pursuing authorization for the IB Primary Years Programme for September 2024. After primary school UWC Maastricht offers the IB Middle Years Programme (11-16 year-olds) in which students are encouraged to become critical and reflective thinkers. For 16-19 year-olds, UWCM applies the IB Diploma Programme Curriculum and the IB Career-related Programme. Alongside the IB standard courses, the school offers Dutch, Spanish, German, Italian, Arabic, World Arts and Cultures, Global Politics, Visual Arts, Film and Music.

Outside the Classroom

UWC Maastricht has designed a social impact programme including action-oriented courses, social entrepreneurship and community service projects. Students develop the skills and attitudes needed to be active participants in society, to identify problems and injustices wherever they exist. They design projects to provide service to the local community, they organise and lead conferences and they learn to engage critically with the world around them. Because students come from all over the world and from many different backgrounds, there are always unique insights and interesting discussions going on.

Campus and Facilities

UWCM campus is located in a very green and leafy part of Maastricht, close to the city centre. The site is surrounded by sports fields, a nature reserve and modern housing. DP and CP students live on residences across three buildings consisting of three floors, each comprised of six rooms. Every room hosts four students, of different nationalities, so it is a lively setting. Each floor has a common room, study room, laundry room and kitchenette and is supported by a Residence Mentor who lives in an apartment adjacent to the floors.

Admission

Day student applications for Primary and Secondary must meet the requirements of the Dutch Law on International Education. Residential IB Diploma Programme and Career-related Programme students are recruited through UWC's National Committee system (NC) or through the UWC Global Selection Programme. More info and applications via uwcmaasticht.nl.

Villiers School

Headteacher
Jill A. Storey

DP coordinator
Shane Hanna

Status Private

Boarding/day Mixed

Gender Coeducational

Language of instruction
English

Authorised IB programmes
DP

Age Range 12 – 18 years

Number of pupils enrolled
600

Fees
Day:
€9,100 – €12,700 per annum
Boarding:
€15,300 – €29,000 per annum

Address
North Circular Road
Limerick
V94 F983 | IRELAND

TEL +353 61 451447

Email
admissions@villiers-school.com

Website
www.villiers-school.com

Villiers School is one of only four schools in Ireland offering the IB Diploma Programme, and is the only boarding school in Ireland offering students the choice between Irish Leaving Certificate curriculum and the IBDP. Villiers believes in a shared IB Schools philosophy: a commitment to high quality, challenging, international education for all its students.

Academic excellence is a process of both formal and informal education, which traverses all programmes at Villiers School. It is intended that Villiers students will see education, in its wider context, as a limitless and unending process to be enjoyed for a lifetime. Average DP results at Villiers are consistent with global DP average results. Recent DP Graduates have taken up university places in a variety of fields of study, in Ireland, the UK, Germany, Spain, Poland, Belgium and Malta.

Villiers School is fortunate to have growing numbers of students joining our DP class from a variety of cultures, backgrounds, and experiences, all of which adds to the intrinsic diversity that we value within our school community. Villiers School strives to foster a safe and inclusive culture with equality at its heart so that diversity can flourish. We embrace our diversity as a strength, and we work with sincerity to enable all in our community to grow and flourish equally. International mindedness is embedded within our school, and we currently have forty five nationalities represented in the school. This growth has allowed us to continue to expand our diploma programme offerings, with new subjects being added each year.

Management and staff at Villiers School embrace and maintain the traditional values of the school, which has more than 200 years of history, and balance them with modern, state of the art educational facilities, developing an environment that engenders growth on an academic, cultural, and social level. Villiers offers both day and boarding options. We are home to approximately 165 boarders, and 435 day students.

The essence of Villiers is our inclusive family-based community. We are wholeheartedly committed to providing a safe, caring, welcoming and friendly atmosphere. Villiers is an environment where both individuality and community mindedness can flourish, and every student can achieve their full potential.

(Founded 2008)

Head of School
Marcella Margaria Bodo

DP coordinator
Deborah Gutowitz

Status Private

Boarding/day Day

Gender Coeducational

Language of instruction
English

Authorised IB programmes
DP

Age Range 3 – 19 years

Fees
Nursery School
€5,700 per annum
Cambridge Primary
€7,800 per annum
Cambridge Lower Secondary
€8,200 per annum
Cambridge IGCSE
€10,300 per annum
IBDP
€11,300 per annum

Address
Via delle Rosine 14
10123 Turin | ITALY

TEL +39 011 889870

Email
infovis@vittoriaweb.it

Website
www.vittoriaweb.it

Founded in 1975 as one of the first linguistic high schools in Italy, the Vittoria International School Torino offers bilingual education for children and young adults starting from elementary school and continuing through to the IB diploma. Located in the heart of Turin's city center, the school ensures a modern and innovative learning environment for students of all ages and nationalities.

Since the very beginning, we have leveraged the best of tradition and innovation both in the choice of educational pathways and teaching methods. Fully certified by the Italian Ministry of Education, the school offers bilingual primary and secondary programs in addition to traditional Italian and international, English-language high school programs.

We have been an authorized IB World School since 2008. We offer the IBDP grades 11 and 12. The Italian Government recognizes our DP as equivalent to the Italian Maturità Linguistico or Scientifico, depending on the track chosen by each candidate.

We have been a Cambridge Upper Secondary School IGCSE (grades 9 and 10) since 2010. We have welcomed students at all phases of their education beginning in the Primary years and Lower Secondary since September 2018.

Our curriculum is constantly growing and adapting to the individual needs of our students. The final scores and completion rates of our students are consistently above the international average. We provide professional, personalized career and university guidance, and many of our students go on to study at world-class universities around the globe. Our students are supported in their pursuit of excellence in extracurricular activities, and many have been rewarded nationally and internationally in sports and the arts.

A low student-teacher classroom ratio allows for individual attention as part of a socially and academically rich formative experience. Our door is always open to parents and students who have ideas to propose or concerns to express, and we use a centralized, password-protected system to keep parents and students updated on all school activities.

Our teachers are all university graduates; IB and Cambridge trained. They are passionate about their subjects and dedicated to their students.

A vibrant discussion of global issues begins in our classrooms and extends into CAS projects. Students experience world issues as they play out in our local community and abroad. We have an ongoing relationship important international organizations located in Turin.

Waterford Kamhlaba UWC of Southern Africa

(Founded 1963)

Head of College
Jackie Otula

DP coordinator
Elizabeth Cummergen

Status Private

Boarding/day Mixed

Gender Coeducational

Language of instruction
English

Authorised IB programmes
DP

Age Range 11 – 20 years

Number of pupils enrolled 627

Fees
Two-year fee €40,000
(scholarships available)

Address
Waterford Park
Mbabane **H100** | **ESWATINI**

TEL +268 24220867

Email
principal@waterford.sz

Website
www.waterford.sz

Introduction
Waterford Kamhlaba UWC of Southern Africa was founded in 1963 as a response to the separate and unequal educational systems in South Africa. When His Majesty King Sobhuza II visited the school, he gave it the name "Kamhlaba", which meant both "of the world" and also that we are "of the earth" and without distinctions such as race. Differently to all the other schools, the academic year runs from January to November.

Inside the Classroom
Waterford offers the Waterford curriculum in the junior school, the University of Cambridge International General Certificate of Secondary Education (IGCSE) program in the middle school and the International Baccalaureate Diploma Programme in the senior school. For the IBDP, alongside standard courses SiSwati, French, Spanish, Anthropology, Psychology, Business Management, Music, Theatre are offered.

Outside the Classroom
Waterford is an ambassador of UWC's mission on the continent and having educated a large group of African changemakers since its inception. With the School having been the first multiracial school in Southern Africa; founded as a direct response to its system of apartheid, its history of embracing and celebrating diversity from across Africa and beyond is something deeply ingrained into Waterford Kamhlaba's nature and continues to be at the core of its values today. The School, through community service, has strong relations with local organizations such as the refugee camp and neighborhood care points (children welfare centres). A commitment to community service has been recognized as an essential part of the school's policy, organisation and life. A regular commitment to a service project is required of IBDP and Form 5 students, and projects usually vary from involvement at the local hospital to work for the disabled. UWC WK offers a wide variety of sporting- and recreational activities run by both staff and students (e.g. kayaking, art clubs, etc.).

Campus and Facilities
Ekukhuleni residence accommodates up to 80 Form 1, 2 and 3 students. Esiveni accommodates up to 110 Form 4 and 5 students. Emhlabeni and Elangeni accommodate, respectively, up to 130 and 68 IBDP students, in either single rooms or shared rooms; consisting of separate wings for males and females. Each day there is one male and one female residence tutor on duty in each residence.

Admissions
Students can apply directly to the school, through their UWC national committee, or through the UWC Global Selection Programme.

Wellington College

WELLINGTON
COLLEGE

(Founded 1853)

Master Mr James Dahl

Director of IB
Mr Richard Atherton

DP coordinator
Dr Robert Cromarty

Status Private

Boarding/day Mixed

Gender Coeducational

Language of instruction
English

Authorised IB programmes
DP

Age Range 13 – 18 years

Number of pupils enrolled 1104

Fees
Day: £35,760 per annum
Boarding: £48,930 per annum

Address
Duke's Ride, Crowthorne
Berkshire, **RG45 7PU | UK**

TEL +44 (0)1344 444000

Email
admissions@wellingtoncollege.org.uk

Website
www.wellingtoncollege.org.uk

Wellington College is dynamic in every sense of the word. All that we do is rooted in our five College values – kindness, courage, respect, integrity, responsibility – which underpin every aspect of life at Wellington. Our curriculum, facilities and teaching methods are constantly adapting as we seek to provide young people with the knowledge, skills and character to serve and help shape a better world.

Innovative and interesting use of technology combined with an emphasis on pedagogical research and outstanding teaching, places Wellington at the forefront of educational advance. Music, Art, Dance, and Drama are central to a Wellington education, a fact externally recognised by the Arts Council award of Artsmark Platinum and a TES nomination for Excellence in Creative Arts Award for our Festival of Musical Theatre.

Over 20 sports are on offer at Wellington involving 200 teams in 1,500 fixtures: 2022/23 saw 30 Wellingtonians involved at national level, with 12 teams or individuals competing in national finals.

Leadership, service to others and an international outlook are central: co-curricular activities include CCF, Duke of Edinburgh's Award, and a pioneering Global Social Leaders scheme where pupils create and run social action projects tackling local and global issues.

Currently 240 pupils take the IB Diploma. 80% are from the UK and the rest from a range of countries worldwide, which sets us apart from competitors who tend to have smaller programmes attracting only international pupils. In 2023, we had 129 Diploma students with 50% scoring 40+ points. Seventeen students went to Oxbridge or Ivy League. Over 100 Wellingtonians were offered places at Oxford or Cambridge over the past five years and 20-25 pupils move to US universities each year, many to Ivy League institutions. The high academic expectations we have for our pupils are expressed through encouragement and support – nearly 40% of teachers have Masters or Doctorates and all are specialists.

Wellington College introduced the IB Diploma Programme in 2007. Its philosophy – of combining academic rigour with breadth and depth – is very much in sympathy with our own. A wide range of subjects is offered and support for the IB Core – the Extended Essay, TOK, and CAS – is truly world class, combining academic expertise with outstanding opportunities and resources. Wellington actively promotes excellence without compromising the ideals embedded within the IB's learner profile.

Subjects offered in the IB Diploma Programme are all at both HL and SL unless stated:

Group 1: English literature, German literature, German language and literature, English literature and performance SL.

Group 2 Modern B (HL, SL and *ab initio*): German, Spanish, French, Mandarin. Group 2 Modern B (HL and SL): Italian, Russian.

Group 2 Classical: Greek, Latin.

Group 3: business and management, economics, history, philosophy, psychology, geography, global politics, environmental systems and societies, art history SL, social and cultural anthropology SL.

Group 4: biology, chemistry, computer science, design technology, physics, sports, exercise and health science, environmental systems and societies, astronomy SL.

Group 5: analysis and approaches, applications and interpretation.

Group 6: music, visual arts, theatre arts.

Wellspring Learning Community

(Founded 2007)

Head of School
Kathleen Battah

PYP coordinator
Nadine Daya

MYP coordinator
Nizar Shamseddine

DP coordinator
Kathleen Saleh

Status Private

Boarding/day Day

Gender Coeducational

Language of instruction
English

Authorised IB programmes
PYP, MYP, DP

Age Range 3 – 19 years

Number of pupils enrolled
887

Address
Al Mathaf, Main Street, Near National Museum
PO Box 116-2134
Beirut | LEBANON

City Centre Campus (CCC)
Lamma Street,
Ain El Roumaneh Area,
PO Box 116-2134,
Beirut | LEBANON

TEL +961 1 423 444

Email
admissions@wellspring.edu.lb

Website
www.wellspring.edu.lb

Wellspring Learning Community is the first IB Continuum World School in Lebanon and it is the realization of a belief that children of Lebanon deserve to study in a high quality learning environment that opens up space for developing their talents and intellectual potential, as well as their capacity for caring about the world around them.

Wellspring is a non-sectarian community with no political affiliations. Depending on availability, enrolment is open throughout the year. We welcome inquiries and visits from interested families.

Authorization/Accreditations

Wellspring is authorized for the IB Diploma, Middle Years Programme, and Primary Years Programme, Council of International Schools (CIS), New England Association of Schools and Colleges(NEASC).

Mission and Vision

Wellspring is an inquiry-based learning environment where students are given every opportunity to realize their social, emotional and academic capacities. Teachers, students and parents work collaboratively in an atmosphere of mutual respect and trust by sharing a positive learning environment that builds on an ongoing process of self-assessment, evidence-based decision making, and continual improvement. Our students will become confident, resourceful, creative, caring, responsible and thinking citizens, prepared to use their education to contribute in meaningful ways to improve society; locally and internationally.

Teachers

Our 175 faculty members are highly qualified and experienced teachers; many are native English speakers. In addition to being IB trained, some teachers hold additional positions within the IB Educator Network (IBEN).

Students

Wellspring has a large international population, with 58 countries represented across our two campuses, in addition to our local students who come from diverse backgrounds within Lebanon.

Facilities

We are proud to offer two campuses in the vibrant heart of Beirut. Both environments are attractive, technologically advanced, and continuously upgraded to keep pace with the demands of the educational program. Facilities include music and art rooms, science labs, computer labs, cafeteria(CCC), libraries, play areas and sports spaces.

WINDERMERE
SCHOOL
FOUNDED 1863

(Founded 1863)

Head
Mr Frank Thompson

DP coordinator
Mrs Elizabeth Murphy

CP coordinator
Mrs Theresa Murray

Status Private

Boarding/day Mixed

Gender Coeducational

Language of instruction
English

Authorised IB programmes
DP, CP

Age Range 3 – 18 years
(boarding from 8)

Number of pupils enrolled 350

Fees
Day: £20,190
Weekly Boarding: £34,400
Boarding: £35,985

Address
Patterdale Road, Windermere
Cumbria, **LA23 1NW | UK**

TEL 015394 46164

Email
admissions@
windermereschool.co.uk

Website
www.windermereschool.co.uk

Windermere School is unique. Set amidst the stunningly beautiful mountains and lakes of Cumbria, it delivers an exciting and forward-thinking curriculum, shaping the hearts and minds of the next generation. We aim to educate children to be capable and thoughtful, resourceful, courageous and caring. This is a school where young people can enjoy their schooldays and parents can be confident that their children are following the very best pathways to university and to adult life.

Benefiting from its extraordinary location in the heart of the English Lake District Windermere School offers a unique education, embracing the IDEALS of the Round Square movement and the International Baccalaureate curriculum. Adventure is part of the curriculum and watersports play a large part in the co-curriculum. Celebrating its 100th year at its present site overlooking the glorious Windermere in 2024, the school values its traditions and constantly looks to the future. As a small school, we get to know all our children well and have a dedicated wellbeing team to help give the very best to every young person in our care.

The school comprises three campuses: our Junior School, Senior School and Watersports Centre. Our Watersports Centre, Hodge Howe, is our own RYA (Royal Yachting Association) Centre and boathouse on the shores of Windermere. In 2018, the school was chosen to become a British Youth Sailing Recognised Club by the Royal Yachting Association for its race training and is one of only two schools in the UK to receive this accreditation.

The school also boasts three fantastic boarding houses that stand in our beautiful Lakeland grounds. Windermere boarders are never short of things to do, with access to the lake, evening events and a fully developed programme of activities to both local and national places of interest. The school's inclusive ethos also allows for pupils from age eight upwards to be made to feel welcome in a unique and homely environment. Each boarding house has comfortable dormitories with full-time residential houseparents. Windermere School is only 90 minutes from Manchester and Liverpool international airports, and three hours from London by high-speed train. We also run a chaperoned airport collection service on dedicated travel days.

The Sixth Form boarding house is designed to promote the successful transition between school and higher education. It is laid out in university style apartments with twin and single bedrooms, a bathroom, common room, and kitchen, plus a large communal space for socialising. Combined with the International Baccalaureate curriculum this creates an environment where our Sixth Formers are challenged, extended, motivated and inspired. You can be confident that the path you choose will equip your child with the results needed for success beyond the school gates, with a future full of possibilities.

It is a rare privilege to be part of a school with Windermere's history and potential. We invite you to take a closer look and would be delighted to welcome you and your family to our school.

The Key to a Global Future

School Manager
Ms Giulia Mazzocchi

PYP coordinator
Ms Victoria Corkhill

MYP coordinator
Ms Kristin Walter

DP coordinator
Ms Barbara Battaglino

Status Private

Boarding/day Mixed

Gender Coeducational

Language of instruction
English

Authorised IB programmes
PYP, MYP, DP

Address
Via Traves 28
10151 Torino | ITALY

TEL +39 0111972111

Email
info@worldinternationalschool.com

Website
worldinternationalschool.com

Who we are

World International School of Torino is an International Baccalaureate® World School for the PYP (Primary Years Programme), the MYP (Middle Years Programme) and the DP (Diploma Programme).

WINS was founded in 2017 by the Formiga Family, with their 60 years of experience in international education.

Teachers and students from all over the world, programs of excellence and integrated use of technology are joined by numerous creative, artistic and sporting activities.

Campus and facilities

Our 16,000 square meters Campus is equipped with a swimming pool, indoor and outdoor sports fields, libraries, music, science and art labs, spacious classrooms and a boarding house for students living far from Turin.

The high-quality internal canteen, a rich program of extra-curricular activities and the shuttle bus are only some of the services you can find at WINS, offered to ensure a welcoming, safe and comfortable environment for the students and their families.

Boarding House

Our Boarding House is the first one in Piedmont. It is designed for WINS students aged 13 and above who want to live an amazing international learning experience.

Our Community

Our community is made up of more than 60% international families and our teachers come from many different nations.

The truly multicultural context of our school and the high standards of its academic programs nurture the intellectual growth of our students, helping them become open-minded, principled, and inquiring citizens of the world.

Our values and mission

WINS core values are to be found in the daily commitment of teachers and each faculty member, who work together with families and students to ensure the proper differentiation and the fulfillment of students' potential.

Our mission is to create a safe and respectful learning environment to support children in the development of their individual talents by fostering critical thinking from an early age.

WINS Foundation

WINS Foundation pursues educational and cultural projects to lay the foundations for a better and sustainable society, made up of responsible, knowledgeable and international-minded citizens.

Accreditations

- AFEC: WINS is the first Athlete Friendly Education School in Italy, to support athletes in achieving their educational and athletic goals.
- CAMBRIDGE: WINS is a Cambridge English Exams Preparation Center and the only authorized Cambridge Assessment Admissions Testing Center within the Piedmont region.
- TRINITY: WINS is a registered Trinity College London® Examination Centre.
- KiVa: WINS implements the KiVa anti-bullying international program aimed at preventing bullying within the school.
- EdQwest: Thanks to this exclusive partnership, WINS DP students have access to a wide variety of online resources to help them succeed in their academic path.
- SAT®: WINS is a SAT® Test Center.
- CANVA FOR EDUCATION DISTRICT SCHOOL: A nomination that enriches our students' academic path with the use of innovative and inclusive educational technologies and methodologies.

(Founded 2010)

Chairman
Ramón Resa

Headmistress
Paz Romero

DP coordinator
Germán Tenorio

Status Private

Boarding/day Mixed

Gender Coeducational

Language of instruction
English, Spanish, Chinese

Authorised IB programmes
DP

Age Range 0 – 18 years

Number of pupils enrolled
845

Address
Avda. Antonio Mairena, 54
41950 Castilleja de la Cuesta,
Seville, Andalusia | SPAIN

TEL +34 955 51 1234

Email
admissions@yagoschool.com

Website
www.yagoschool.com

At Yago School, we are transforming the educational-learning system in the South of Spain so that our students from 0 to 18 years can successfully confront many of the educational challenges of the 21st century, by offering the International Baccalaureate Diploma Programme, along with the Spanish educational system and by using the English and Spanish languages as a communicative instrument inside and outside the classroom, with Chinese and French as part of its dynamic curriculum. Our unique curriculum is also accredited by WASC (Western Association of Schools and Colleges). With over a decade in the educational field, we have grown to represent more than 34 nationalities. The Yago team strives to inspire, nurture and empower every student to achieve their personal best and become enquiring, knowledgeable, lifelong learners who create a better world through intercultural understanding and respect. Our purpose is for students to develop their abilities and potential to the maximum, to build knowledge through projects, broaden their interests and their own experience using integrative, innovative and cooperative methodologies in traditional and technological environments so that they can succeed at universities and in their professional careers all over the world.

Yago School's principles have been built on five educational pillars: traditional values, bilingualism, sports, music and new technologies. Five bases that, combined with demanding academic training, provide our students with an extremely solid foundation promoting success in both their personal and professional lives. The use of technology is embedded in the curriculum for all students from the age of four. Music is performed at a wide range of events and students are prepared for examinations in theory, piano and singing with the Associated Board of the Royal Schools of Music. The outstanding sporting facilities, including sports pitches and a sports hall and we provide many opportunities for students to compete in team and individual events. The avant-garde architecture of its facilities, along with its privileged location in the "Aljarafe", just 15 minutes from the international airport and the high-speed AVE train station, all enhance the multitude of diverse and personalised opportunities and complementary experiences Yago School offers.

Admission: Admissions are open throughout the academic year, subject to availability. Every effort is made to reserve a space for international applicants. We currently arrange boarding in our residence for our international students.

Yago School is an innovative IB day school and the only Boarding Home in Sevilla. Our personalised curriculum, our outstanding students, University and Career guidance and the amazing city with the surrounding area of southern Spain will give students from all over the world from 14 to 18 years olds the opportunity to live the Yago experience.

We are a private, multilingual and international school, with mixed education, where we combine tradition and modern approach to learning.

With more than a decade in the educational field, we have grown to represent more than 34 nationalities.

PYP coordinator
Helena García

Status Private

Boarding/day Day

Gender Coeducational

Language of instruction
German, Spanish

Authorised IB programmes
PYP

Address
73 Pearson Avenue
08034 Barcelona,
Catalonia | SPAIN

TEL +34 932 037 606

Email
secretaria@zurichschule.com

Website
www.zsbarcelona.com

Zürich Schule Barcelona: Fostering Education, Embracing Diversity

Zürich Schule Barcelona is a privately-owned, non-subsidized, and secular institution that offers a holistic educational experience from Preschool to Secondary education. Our mission is to empower students not only academically but also emotionally, socially, and physically. We prioritize building a sense of community, emphasizing the value of human connections and participation in school projects.

Our school is a melting pot of cultures, with approximately 300 students from 40 different nationalities, creating a rich and global learning environment. All our teachers are native speakers, providing an immersive language experience.

A History of Educational Excellence

With over 50 years of history, Zürich Schule Barcelona has cultivated an international mindset and global awareness in our students. We aim to instil responsible and respectful values that reflect in the actions and contributions of our learning community.

In our Preschool program, we provide instruction in the German language, with exceptions for Literacy and Swimming, taught in Spanish and Catalan. Our teaching methods are tailored to unlock the potential of young children. Recognizing the importance of early education, we operate year-round in four-month terms, aligned with our program's objectives, guiding our young learners in their journey.

An IB School with PYP and MYP Programmes

Zürich Schule Barcelona is proud to be an International Baccalaureate (IB) school, offering the Primary Years Programme (PYP) and Middle Years Programme (MYP). This approach nurtures active, supportive, and lifelong learners, emphasizing holistic development and personal growth.

In Primary Education, we emphasize the German language, focusing on written language skills. We strategically schedule classes to encourage both oral and written language acquisition, ensuring personalized attention for each student.

The IB Primary Years Programme focuses on learning, social and emotional well-being, empowering students to develop their individuality and take responsibility for their educational journey. It equips them to become global citizens who uphold their personal values and navigate a complex world.

Our school excels in implementing trans-disciplinary themes, integrating local and global topics into our curriculum, broadening horizons beyond traditional subjects.

As an IB school, the Middle Years Programme (MYP) in our Secondary education emphasizes intellectual challenge, bridging classroom learning with real-world applications. We prepare our students for success in further education and life beyond our school.

Adapting to a Changing World

Our students, from 1st to 10th grade, utilize iPads as essential tools in their learning journey, complementing traditional educational materials. Furthermore, we've developed a custom ZSB app that streamlines communication and enhances the learning experience.

At Zürich Schule Barcelona, we're more than an educational institution; we're a vibrant community inspiring and preparing students for a dynamic, interconnected world.

Directory of schools in the Africa, Europe and Middle East region

Key to symbols

- CP
- Diploma
- MYP
- PYP
- Fee Paying School
- Boys' School
- Girls' School
- Coeducational School
- Boarding School
- Day School

ALBANIA

Albanian College Tirana

Rruga Dritan Hoxha 1, Tirana 1000
DP Coordinator Marcela Danisova
MYP Coordinator Marcin Sztomberski
PYP Coordinator Fernando Ramirez
Languages English
T: +355 44 513 471
W: www.actirana.edu.al

QSI TIRANA INTERNATIONAL SCHOOL

Rruga Gilson, Fshati Mullet, Kutia Postare 1527, Tirana
DP Coordinator John Scates
Languages English
T: +355 4 236 5239
E: tirana@qsi.org
W: tirana.qsi.org

See full details on page 188

World Academy of Tirana

Rruga e Rezervave, Lunder, Tirane
DP Coordinator Peni Ganivatu
MYP Coordinator Merijada Dusha
PYP Coordinator Jerbylyn Agtutubo
Languages English
T: +355 69 6056 123
W: www.wat.al

ANDORRA

Agora Andorra International School

Carrer del Serrat del Camp 14, AD400 La Massana
DP Coordinator Ivana Cvetkovic
Languages English, German, French, Chinese
T: +376 838 366
W: www.agoraandorra.com

Centre de Formació Professional d'Aixovall

Ctra. d'Os de Civís, s/n, 600 Aixovall
CP Coordinator Mònica Sánchez
Languages Catalan, Valencian, Spanish

Escola Andorrana de batxillerat

C/ Tossalet i Vinyals, 45, AD500 La Margineda, Andorra la Vella
DP Coordinator Marius Solé Gamborino
Languages Spanish, Catalan, Valencian
T: +376 723030
W: adbatx.educand.ad

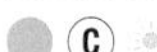

The British College of Andorra

Ctra. de la Comella i de la Plana S/N, AD500 Andorra la Vella
DP Coordinator Warren Quinton
Languages English, Spanish
T: +376 720 220
W: www.britishcollegeandorra.com

ANGOLA

LUANDA INTERNATIONAL SCHOOL

Via S6, Bairro de Talatona, Município de Belas, Luanda
DP Coordinator Rene Bradford
MYP Coordinator Catherine McCann
PYP Coordinator Julie Ranger
Languages English
T: +244 932 337 056
E: lis@lisluanda.com
W: www.lisluanda.com

See full details on page 162

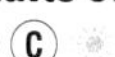

ARMENIA

Ohanyan Educational Complex

Isahakyan 5/6, Yerevan 0060
PYP Coordinator Arevik Ohanyan
Languages English, Armenian
T: +374 106 17684
W: ohanyan.org

Quantum College

Bagratuniats 23/2, Shengavit, Yerevan 0046
DP Coordinator Arpine Harutyunyan
Languages English
T: +374 10 422217
W: www.quantum.am

Shirakatsy Lyceum International Scientific-Educational Complex

35 Artem Mikoyan Street, Yerevan 0079
DP Coordinator Anna Stepanyan
MYP Coordinator Elina Shakaryan
PYP Coordinator Marina Sahakyan
Languages English, Armenian
T: +374 10 680 102
W: www.shirakatsy.am

UWC Dilijan

7 Getapnya Street, Dilijan 3903
DP Coordinator Sophie Duncker
Languages English
T: +44 (0)1446 799000
W: www.uwcdilijan.org

AUSTRIA

AMADEUS INTERNATIONAL SCHOOL VIENNA

Bastiengasse 36-38, 1180 Vienna
CP Coordinator Paolo Tornitore
DP Coordinator Alice Greenland
MYP Coordinator Yvan Wever
PYP Coordinator James Elliot
Languages English
T: +43 1 470 30 37 00
E: admissions@amadeus-vienna.com
W: www.amadeus-vienna.com

See full details on page 50

AMERICAN INTERNATIONAL SCHOOL VIENNA

Salmannsdorfer Strasse 47, 1190 Vienna
DP Coordinator Bridget Schroeder
Languages English
T: +43 1 401 32
E: info@ais.at
W: www.ais.at

See full details on page 54

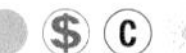

Anton Bruckner International School (ABIS)

Bruckner Tower, Wildbergstrasse 18, 4040 Linz, Upper Austria
MYP Coordinator Paul Cartwright
PYP Coordinator Benjamin Lewis
Languages English, German
T: +43 7327 11691
W: www.abis.school

BG/BRG Klosterneuburg

Buchberggasse 31, 3400 Klosterneuburg, Lower Austria
DP Coordinator Rebecca Kmentt
Languages English
T: +43 2243 32155
W: www.bgklosterneuburg.ac.at

Campus Wien West

Seuttergasse 29, 1130 Vienna
DP Coordinator Jutta Zopf-Klasek
Languages English
T: +43 680 5577 573
W: www.campus-wien-west.at

Danube International School Vienna

Josef-Gall Gasse 2, 1020 Vienna
DP Coordinator Rachel Pernet
MYP Coordinator Maura Lichtscheidl-Fegerl
PYP Coordinator Keitsa Brisson
Languages English
T: +43 1 7203110
W: www.danubeschool.com

GIBS Graz International Bilingual School

Georgigasse 85, 8020 Graz, Styria
DP Coordinator Ursula Schatz
Languages English
T: +43 316 771050
W: www.gibs.at

International Christian School of Vienna

Panethgasse 6a, (right by Wagramer Strasse), 1220 Vienna
DP Coordinator Adesola Adebesin
Languages English
T: +43 1 25122 0
W: www.icsv.at

International Highschool Herzogberg

Herzogbergstraße 230, 2380 Perchtoldsdorf, Lower Austria
DP Coordinator Veronika Weiss
Languages English, German
T: +43 6991 7750 055
W: www.am-herzogberg.com

International School Carinthia

Rosentaler Straße 15, 9220 Velden Am Worthersee, Carinthia
DP Coordinator Oliver Pope
MYP Coordinator Luke Ames
PYP Coordinator Scott French
Languages English, German
T: +43 4274 52471 10
W: www.isc.ac.at

International School Innsbruck

Angerzellgasse 14, 6020 Innsbruck, Tyrol
DP Coordinator Stephen Dea
Languages English
T: +43 512 58 70 64
W: agi.tsn.at

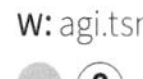

International School Kufstein Tirol

Andreas-Hofer-Straße 7, 6330 Kufstein, Tyrol
DP Coordinator Rick Lewis
Languages English
T: +43 5372 21990
W: www.isk-tirol.at

Linz International School Auhof (LISA)

Aubrunnerweg 4, 4040 Linz, Upper Austria
DP Coordinator Oliver Kim
Languages English
T: +43 732 245867- 23
W: www.europagym.at/lisa

AUSTRIA

Lower Austrian International School
Bimbo Binder-Promenade 7, 3100 St. Pölten, Lower Austria
DP Coordinator Michael Hofbauer
Languages English
T: +43 2742 73453
W: www.borglsp-stpoelten.ac.at

SALIS - Salzburg International School
Zaunergasse 3, 5020 Salzburg
DP Coordinator Holger Benz
Languages English, German
T: +43 662 439616 0
W: www.bgzaunergasse.at

SCHLOSS KRUMBACH INTERNATIONAL SCHOOL
Schloss 1, 2851 Krumbach, Lower Austria
DP Coordinator Viktoryia Tejada Correa
Languages English, German
T: +43 6765 409630
E: info@krumbach.school
W: www.krumbach.school
See full details on page 195

ST. GILGEN INTERNATIONAL SCHOOL GMBH
Ischlerstrasse 13, 5340 St. Gilgen
DP Coordinator John Patton
MYP Coordinator Paul La Rondie
Languages English
T: +43 62 272 0259
E: info@stgis.at
W: www.stgis.at
See full details on page 214

Vienna International School
Strasse der Menschenrechte 1, 1220 Vienna
DP Coordinator Noémi Linnau
MYP Coordinator Joseph O'Rourke
PYP Coordinator Lea Pedlow
Languages English
T: +43 1 203 5595
W: www.vis.ac.at

AZERBAIJAN

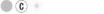

ADA School
61 Ahmadbay Agha-Oglu Street, 1008 Baku
DP Coordinator Qadir Mikayilov
Languages English, Azerbaijani
T: +994 12 437 32 35
W: www.ada.edu.az/en/school

Baku International Education Complex
Metbuat pr 54, Yasamal, Baku 1001
PYP Coordinator Aynur Akhundva
Languages English, Russian
T: +994 50 423 49 10
W: biec.az

Baku Modern Educational Complex
218 Aliyar Aliyev Street, Narimanov District, Baku
DP Coordinator Sevinj Seyidova
Languages English, Azerbaijani
T: +994 12 404 12 82
W: bmtk.edu.az

Dunya School
9 Ajami Nakhchivani street, Baku AZ1130
DP Coordinator Rana Hasanova
PYP Coordinator Jesús Rosas
Languages English
T: +994 12 563 59 40/47/48
W: dunyaschool.az

Educational Complex No. 132-134
Istiglaliyyat 33A, Baku, Absheron AZ1001
DP Coordinator Francis Wilfrid Mang-Benza dit Manthota
Languages Azerbaijani
T: +994 (0)12 492 27 32
W: www.132-134.com

European Azerbaijan School
7 Basti Bagirova, Yasamal District, Baku City
DP Coordinator Tad Herrold
MYP Coordinator Maria Elena Berardi
PYP Coordinator Benjamin Lind
Languages English
T: +994 12 539 89 35/36/37/38
W: www.eas.az

Idrak Lyceum
2 Samad Vurghun, Sumqayit 5001
DP Coordinator Nuriya Allahverdiyeva
Languages English
T: +994 18 655 59 73
W: idrak.edu.az

School-Lyceum N6
2 Sh Alakparova Str, Baku 1001
DP Coordinator Deepa Boodhoo
MYP Coordinator Elmir Manafov
PYP Coordinator Pinar Calis
Languages English
T: +99 412 492 2221

The International School of Azerbaijan, Baku
Yeni Yasamal, Stonepay, Royal Park, Baku AZ1070
DP Coordinator Gareth Hubbuck
MYP Coordinator Iryna Sydoruk
PYP Coordinator Kate Lynch
Languages English
T: +994 12 404 01 12
W: www.tisa.az

BAHRAIN

Abdul Rahman Kanoo International School
P.O. Box 2512, Manama
DP Coordinator Siji Roy
Languages English, Arabic
T: +973 17875055
W: arkis.edu.bh

Ahlia School
Building 166, Street. 45, Block 545, Al Qurayya
DP Coordinator Mirza Hammad Ali
Languages English, Arabic
T: +973 77476666
W: www.ahliaschool.edu.bh

Al Rawabi School
Building 689, Road 3514, Block 435, P.O. Box 18575, Jablat Hebshi
DP Coordinator Anthony Monico Bernardino
Languages English
T: +973 17595252
W: alrawabi.edu.bh

American School of Bahrain
Building 1528, Road 3429, Block 934, North Riffa (Riffa Alshamali), Riffa
DP Coordinator Radia Ali
Languages English, Arabic
T: +973 17211800
W: www.asb.bh
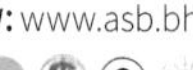

Arabian Pearl Gulf (APG) School
Bldg 1786, Rd 6306, Blk 363, Bilad AlQadeem, Manama
DP Coordinator John Labor
Languages English
T: +973 17 403 666
W: www.apgschool.com
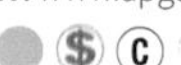

BAHRAIN BAYAN SCHOOL
Bldg 230, Road No. 4111, P.O. Box 32411, Isa Town 841
DP Coordinator Mervat Awamleh
Languages English, Arabic
T: +973 7712 2244
E: info@bayanschool.edu.bh
W: www.bayanschool.edu.bh
See full details on page 60

Bahrain School
Al Ghurafaiyah Building 540, Area 342, Road 4225, Juffair, Manama
DP Coordinator Constance McAninch
Languages English
T: +973 17727828
W: thebahrainschool.com

Beacon Private School
Building 101, Avenue 14, Block 109, P.O. Box 52030, Al Hidd
DP Coordinator Oula Akawi
Languages English, Arabic
T: +973 66000088
W: www.beacon.edu.bh

Britus International School, Bahrain
Building 208, Road 408, Block 704, P.O. Box 18041, Salmabad MANAMA
DP Coordinator Hamda Maqsood Ahmad
Languages English
T: +973 17598444
W: britus.edu.bh

Hawar International School
Building 22, Road 42, Block 910, P.O. Box 38338, Riffa
DP Coordinator Barbora Mastna
Languages English
T: +937 13666555
W: www.hawarschool.com

IBN KHULDOON NATIONAL SCHOOL
Building 161, Road 4111, Area 841, P.O. Box 20511, Isa Town
DP Coordinator Gerda Marais
MYP Coordinator Roula Barghout
PYP Coordinator Rosy Johnson
Languages English, Arabic
T: +973 17780661
E: k.algosaibi@ikns.edu.bh
W: www.ikns.edu.bh
See full details on page 105

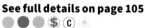

Modern Knowledge Schools
Building 515, Road 4209, Juffair, Manama
DP Coordinator Jude Katumba
Languages English
T: +973 17727712
W: www.mks.edu.bh

Naseem International School
P.O. Box 28503, Riffa
CP Coordinator Carlos Abou Mrad
DP Coordinator Bindu Nair
MYP Coordinator Ali AlShehab
PYP Coordinator Antoinette Pienaar
Languages English, Arabic
T: +973 17782000
W: www.nisbah.com

Riffa Views International School
Building 407, Road 4303, Block Al Mazrowiah 943, P.O. Box 3050, Riffa
DP Coordinator Victoria Johnson
Languages English
T: +973 16565000
W: www.rvis.edu.bh

Shaikha Hessa Girls' School
Riffa
DP Coordinator Maudhulika Jain
Languages English
T: +973 17756111
W: www.shgs.edu.bh

St Christopher's School
Building 119, Road 4109, P.O. Box 32052, Isa Town
DP Coordinator Conal Smith
Languages English
T: +973 17605301
W: www.st-chris.net
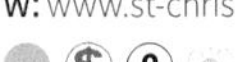

BELARUS

Stembridge Private School
31 Nekrasova Street, Minsk
DP Coordinator Viktor Deych
Languages English, Russian
T: +375 296 67 61 21
W: stembridge.by

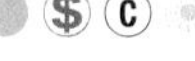

BELGIUM

Antwerp International School
Veltwijcklaan 180, Ekeren, 2180 Antwerp
DP Coordinator Thierry Torres
MYP Coordinator Marianne Navarro
PYP Coordinator Grant Davis
Languages English
T: +32 (0)3 543 93 00
W: www.ais-antwerp.be

BEPS INTERNATIONAL SCHOOL
Avenue Franklin Roosevelt 21-23, 1050 Brussels
CP Coordinator Andrew Mitchell
DP Coordinator Andrew Mitchell
MYP Coordinator Andrew Mitchell
Languages English
T: +32 2 648 43 11
E: admissions@beps.com
W: www.beps.com
See full details on page 62

Bogaerts International School
555 Rue Engeland, 1180 Brussels
DP Coordinator Colin Sinclair
MYP Coordinator Tammy Debets (Gross)
PYP Coordinator Vasileios Iosifidis
Languages English, French
T: +32 2 230 03 39
W: www.bischool.com

Da Vinci International School
Verbondstraat 67, 2000 Antwerp
DP Coordinator Noreen Donovan
Languages English
T: +32 3216 12 32
W: www.da-vinci.be

European School of Bruxelles-Argenteuil
Square d'Argenteuil 5, 1410 Waterloo, Brussels
DP Coordinator Soren Hansen
Languages English, French
T: +32 2357 06 70
W: www.europeanschool.be

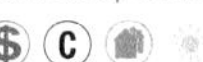

International Montessori School
Kleinenbergstraat 97-99, 1932 St. Stevens-Woluwe, Flemish Brabant
DP Coordinator Charlotte Reilly-Davidson
MYP Coordinator Stéphanie Cnudde
Languages English, French
T: +32 2 767 63 60 / +32 2 721 21 11
W: www.international-montessori.org

INTERNATIONAL SCHOOL OF BELGIUM
Kontichsesteenweg 40, 2630 Aartselaar, Antwerp
DP Coordinator Ms Pauline Kimman
Languages English
T: +32 3 271 0943
E: info@isbedu.be
W: www.isbedu.be/
See full details on page 122

Montgomery International School - Brussels
Rue du Duc 133, 1200 Brussels
DP Coordinator Danielle Franzen Daoudy
MYP Coordinator Wendy Lapetite
PYP Coordinator Wendy Lapetite
Languages French, English
T: +32 (0)2 733 63 23
W: www.ecole-montgomery.be

ST. JOHN'S INTERNATIONAL SCHOOL
Drève Richelle 146, 1410 Waterloo, Walloon Brabant
DP Coordinator Jennifer Bakalian
MYP Coordinator Arlin Mowatt
PYP Coordinator Kathy Anderson
Languages English
T: +32 (0)2 352 06 10
E: enquiries@stjohns.be
W: www.stjohns.be
See full details on page 215

The British School of Brussels (BSB)
Pater Dupierreuxlaan 1, 3080 Tervuren
DP Coordinator James Willis
Languages English, French (bilingual Programme For Ages 4-14 Years)
T: +32 (0)2 766 04 30
W: www.britishschool.be

The Courtyard International School of Tervuren
Stationsstraat 49a, 3080 Tervuren
CP Coordinator Stephanie Uceny
DP Coordinator Susan Kay
MYP Coordinator Stephanie Uceny
PYP Coordinator Stephanie Uceny
Languages English, French
W: www.thecourtyard.eu

The International School of Brussels (ISB)
Kattenberg 19, 1170 Brussels
CP Coordinator Stephanie Lacher
DP Coordinator Sofia Segedy
Languages English
T: +32 2 661 4211
W: www.isb.be

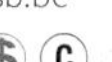

BOSNIA & HERZEGOVINA

Druga Gimnazija Sarajevo
Sutjeska 1, Sarajevo 71000
DP Coordinator Dzevdeta Dervic
MYP Coordinator Elvira Kukuljac
Languages English
T: +387 33667438
W: www.2gimnazija.edu.ba

Gimnazija Banja Luka
Zmaj Jovina 13, Banja Luka 78000
DP Coordinator Dijana Jujic
Languages English
T: +387 51 213 259
W: www.gimnazijabanjaluka.org

Maarif Schools of Sarajevo
Ul. Hasiba Brankovica 2A, 71000 Sarajevo
DP Coordinator Ermin Dogan
Languages English, Bosnian
T: +387 33 257 260
W: www.maarifschools.edu.ba

UWC Mostar
Spanski trg 1, Mostar 88000
DP Coordinator Selma Sarancic
Languages English
T: +387 36 320 601
W: www.uwcmostar.ba

BOTSWANA

Enko Botho International School
Plot 60114, Block 7, near Botswana Qualifications Authority and HRDC, Gaborone
DP Coordinator Dorothy Tsalwa
Languages English
T: +267 396 0044
W: enkoeducation.com/botho

Northside Primary School
PO Box 897, Plot 2786, Tshekedi Crescent Ext 9, Gaborone
PYP Coordinator Joanna Poweska Laverick
Languages English
T: +267 395 2440
W: www.northside.ac.bw

Westwood International School
Phase 4, Plot 22978, Mmankgwedi Road, Gaborone
DP Coordinator Karuna Datta-Bhatnagar
MYP Coordinator Anandhi Lakshminarayan
PYP Coordinator Nidhi Bhatnagar
Languages English
T: +267 390 6736
W: www.westwood.ac.bw
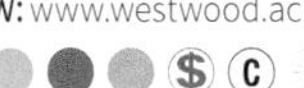

BULGARIA

American College Arcus
16 Dragoman Str., 5000 Veliko Tarnovo
DP Coordinator Kameliya Antonova
MYP Coordinator Albena Todorova
Languages English
T: +359 62 619959
W: www.ac-arcus.com

American College of Sofia
P.O. Box 873, 1000 Sofia
DP Coordinator Zornitsa Semkova
Languages English
T: +359 2 434 10 08
W: www.acs.bg

Anglo American School of Sofia
1 Siyanie St., 1137 Sofia
DP Coordinator Kalina Belivanova
Languages English
T: +359 2 923 88 10
W: www.aas-sofia.org
 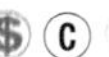

BRITANICA Park School
27 Momino Venche Street, Dragalevtsi Quarter, Sofia
DP Coordinator Antoaneta Kalenderova
Languages English, Bulgarian
T: +359 2 4887877
W: britanica-parkschool.bg
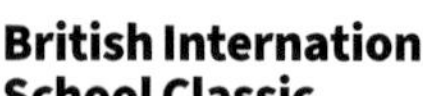

British International School Classic
7 Lady Strangford Street, 4000 Plovdiv
DP Coordinator Teodora Ivanovska
Languages English, Bulgarian
T: +359 886 902 295
W: www.classicschool.org
 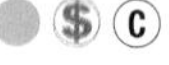

British School of Sofia
18, Radi Radev Street, Lozenets, 1700 Sofia
CP Coordinator Matthew Osborn
DP Coordinator Naomi van Wyngaarden
Languages English, Bulgarian
T: +359 886 510 510
W: www.bssofia.bg

Bulgarsko Shkolo Private Secondary School
ul. General-Mayor Vasil Delov No. 10, Mladost 2, 1799 Sofia
MYP Coordinator Stefan Rashkov
Languages Bulgarian
T: +359 8 84256736
W: bgshkolo.com

Meridian 22 Private High School
Mladost 2 bl.227, 1799 Sofia
DP Coordinator Yoana Kalapish
Languages English
T: +359 2 8876 423; +359 2 8840 238
W: www.meridian22-edu.com

Private Primary School 'Progressive Education'- Sofia
107 Nishava Str., Sofia 1408
PYP Coordinator Nikol Istiliyanova
Languages English
T: +359 882 741 944

Uwekind International School
136 Voivodina Mogila Street, Knyajevo, 1619 Sofia
DP Coordinator Desislava Ilieva-Popova
MYP Coordinator Aglika Damaskova
Languages English
T: +359 2 8572000
W: www.uwekind.com

Zlatarski International School
49 Kliment Ohridski Boulevard, 1756 Sofia
DP Coordinator Raya Pancheva
Languages English
T: +359 2 876 67 67
W: www.zlatarskischool.org

BURKINA FASO

Enko Ouaga International School
Zogona, venant du Boulevard Charles de Gaulle, premier six-mètres après la mosquée de Zogona à gauche, Ouagadougou
DP Coordinator Fabrice Aguibou
Languages French, English
T: +226 25 36 01 77
W: enkoeducation.com/ouaga

International School of Ouagadougou
01 BP 1142, Ouagadougou
DP Coordinator Marie-Hélène Pichette
Languages English
T: +226 25 36 21 43
W: www.iso.bf

CAMEROON

Academic School of Excellence
4323 Yaoundé
DP Coordinator Jean-Victor Yogo
Languages English, French
T: +237 2 22 20 03 23
W: acdemic-school-ofexcellence.com

American School of Yaoundé
B.P. 7475, Rue Martin Samba, Yaoundé
DP Coordinator Jacob Akundo
MYP Coordinator Mary MacDonald
PYP Coordinator Julia Ford
Languages English
T: +237 2 22 22 04 21
W: www.asoy.org

Enko Bonanjo International School
Rue 1.171, No. 414, In front of Camwater, Bonanjo, Douala
DP Coordinator Atumo Gerald ManiH Khurde
Languages English, French
T: +237 6 93 06 82 98
W: enkoeducation.com/bonanjo

Enko La Gaiete International School
B.P 14853, Nouvelle Route Bastos (échangeur simplifié), Yaoundé
DP Coordinator Veronica Agogho
Languages English
T: +237 6 97 26 59 00
W: enkoeducation.com/la-gaiete

Rousseau International School
P.O. Box 5321, Hotel de l'air Bonapriso, 34 Avenue de L'indépendance 2351
DP Coordinator Divine Mbutoh
Languages English, French
T: +237 2 33 42 12 69
W: rousseauinternational.org
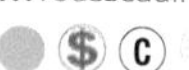

COTE D'IVOIRE

Enko Riviera International School
Riviera Golf, Carrefour M'Pouto/ Sol Béni, Next to the Embassy of Lebanon, Abidjan
DP Coordinator Jimmy Goua
MYP Coordinator Guy Ametpe
Languages English, French
T: +225 27 22 54 1098
W: enkoeducation.com/riviera

International Community School of Abidjan
Off Boulevard Arsène Usher Assouan Road, Riviera III, Abidjan 06 BP 544
DP Coordinator Benedicte Visconti
Languages English
T: +225 27 22 47 1152
W: www.icsabidjan.org

CROATIA

American International School of Zagreb
Damira Tomljanovica Gravrana 3, 10020 Zagreb
DP Coordinator Erin Henkels
Languages English
T: +385 1 7999 300
W: www.aisz.hr

III. gimnazija Split
Ul. Matice Hrvatske 11, 21000 Split
DP Coordinator Krunoslava Tadin Andromak
Languages English
T: +385 21 558428
W: trema.hr

Matija Gubec International School
Davorina Bazjanca 2, 10000 Zagreb
MYP Coordinator Linda Zelic
PYP Coordinator Zilha Redzebasic
Languages English
T: +385 1 364 9133
W: www.os-mgubec.hr

Prva Gimnazija Varazdin
Petra Preradovica 14, 42000 Varazdin
DP Coordinator Ksenija Kipke
Languages English
T: +385 42 302 122
W: www.gimnazija-varazdin.skole.hr

Prva rijecka hrvatska gimnazija
Frana Kurelca 1, 51000 Rijeka
DP Coordinator Deni Kirincic
Languages English, Croatian
T: +385 5 1339 115
W: www.prhg.hr

Split International School
Bihacka ul. 2, 21000 Split
DP Coordinator John Rogosic
Languages English
T: +385 91 6182877
W: splitinternational.org

XV. Gimnazija
Jordanovac 8, 10000 Zagreb
DP Coordinator Zorana Franic
MYP Coordinator Darija Kos
Languages English
T: +385 1 230 2255
W: www.mioc.hr/wp

CUBA

International School of Havana
115 Calle 22 entre, Avenida 1ra y 3ra, Miramar, Havana
DP Coordinator Osmery Martínez
Languages English
T: +53 7214 0773
W: www.ishavana.org

CYPRUS

American International School in Cyprus
PO Box 23847, 11 Kassos Str, Nicosia 1686
DP Coordinator Kika Coles
Languages English
T: +357 22 316345
W: www.aisc.ac.cy

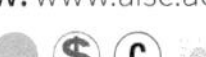

PASCAL Private English School - Larnaka
2, Polytechniou Street, Larnaka, 7103 Aradippou
DP Coordinator Despina Lioliou
Languages English
T: +357 22509300
W: www.pascal.ac.cy

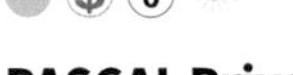

PASCAL Private English School - Lefkosia
177, Kopegchagis Street, Lefkosia, 2306 Lakatamia
DP Coordinator Ariana Milutinovic
Languages English
T: +357 22509000
W: www.pascal.ac.cy

THE ENGLISH SCHOOL OF KYRENIA
Bilim Sokak, Bellapais, Kyrenia, North Cyprus
DP Coordinator Ms Zelis Omer
Languages English
T: +90 392 444 0375
E: info@englishschoolkyrenia.org
W: www.englishschoolkyrenia.com
See full details on page 229

CZECH REPUBLIC

1st International School of Ostrava
Gregorova 3, 702 00 Ostrava
DP Coordinator Nitzan Hollander
Languages English
T: +420 723 332 653
W: www.is-ostrava.cz

Dino High School s.r.o.
Bellova 352, 109 00 Prague 10
DP Coordinator Stephan Starkweather
Languages Czech, English
T: +420 240 200 082
W: www.dinoskola.cz

Gymnasium Evolution
Jizni Mesto, Tererova 2135 / 17, 149 00 Prague 4
DP Coordinator Tomas Vavra
Languages English, Czech
T: +420 267 914 553
W: www.gevo.cz

Gymnazium a SOS Rokycany
Mládezníku 1115/II, 337 01 Rokycany
DP Coordinator Jan Zítek
Languages English, Czech
T: +420 371 725 363
W: www.gasos-ro.cz

Gymnázium Duhovka
Ortenovo námestí 34, Hole ovice, 170 00 Prague 7
DP Coordinator Keith Berry
Languages English, Czech
T: +420 241 404 217
W: www.duhovkagymnazium.cz

International School of Brno
Cejkovicka 10, 628 00 Brno-Vinohrady
DP Coordinator Barbara Albrechtova
PYP Coordinator Jennifer Berry
Languages English
T: +420 544 212 313
W: www.isob.cz

International School of Prague
Nebusicka 700, 164 00 Prague 6
CP Coordinator Karen Ercolino
DP Coordinator Karen Ercolino
Languages English
T: +420 220 384 111
W: www.isp.cz

Open Gate School
Babice 5, 251 01 Rícany
DP Coordinator Rupert Marks
Languages English
T: +420 724 730 512
W: www.opengate.cz

Park Lane International School - Prague 1
Vald tejnská 151/6a, 118 01 Prague 1
DP Coordinator Jan Cihák
Languages Czech, English
T: +420 257 316 182
W: www.parklane-is.com

PORG International School - Ostrava
Rostislavova 7, 703 00 Ostrava
DP Coordinator Iain Benzie
Languages English
T: +420 597 071 020
W: www.porg.cz

PORG International School - Prague
Pod Krcskym lesem 1300/25, 142 00 Prague 4
DP Coordinator Jason Kucker
Languages English
T: +420 244 403 650
W: www.porg.cz

PRIGO Language and Humanities Grammar School
Mojmirovcu 1002/42, Mariánské Hory, 709 00 Ostrava
DP Coordinator Renata Zavodna
Languages English
W: www.jahu-prigo.cz

Riverside International School
Roztocka 9/43, Sedlec, 160 00 Prague 6
DP Coordinator Daniel Plummer
Languages English
T: +420 2 24315336
W: www.riversideschool.cz

The English College in Prague
Sokolovska 320, 190 00 Prague 9
DP Coordinator Stephen Hudson
Languages English
T: +420 2 8389 3113
W: www.englishcollege.cz

The Ostrava International School
Gregorova 2582/3, 702 00 Ostrava
DP Coordinator Paul Ahuja
MYP Coordinator Jiri Svoboda
PYP Coordinator Elina Prokharava
Languages English
T: +420 724 142 287
W: tois.world

The Prague British School - Kamyk Site
K Lesu 558/2, 142 00 Prague 4
CP Coordinator Mark Buckley
DP Coordinator Mark Buckley
Languages English
T: +420 226 096 200
W: www.nordangliaeducation.com/schools/prague/british-international

DEMOCRATIC REPUBLIC OF THE CONGO

Ecole Internationale Bilingue Le Cartésien (EIBC)
34 7ème Rue, Q. Industriel, Limete, Kinshasa
DP Coordinator Armand Ngolomingi Mudiandambu
PYP Coordinator Isaac Kalala
Languages French, English
T: +243 99 82 22800
W: www.lecartesien.cd

Institut Aurora
8 Avenue Kalemie, Commune de la Gombe, Kinshasa
MYP Coordinator Philip Van der Biest
Languages English, French
T: +243 97 17 44509
W: www.institutaurora.com

Jewels International School of Kinshasa
6705 Av. de l'O.U.A. Commune de Ngaliema, Kinshasa
DP Coordinator Sandip Sambhaji Munde
PYP Coordinator Sandip Sambhaji Munde
Languages English
T: +243 81 88 88839
W: www.jewelsschoolkinshasa.com

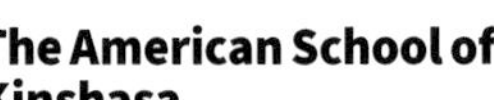

The American School of Kinshasa
Route de Matadi, Ngaliema, Kinshasha
DP Coordinator Garrett Austin
MYP Coordinator Kelley Marchant
PYP Coordinator Vitna Bailey
Languages English
T: +243 81 88 46619
W: www.tasok.net

DENMARK

Aarhus Gymnasium
Halmstadgade 6, 8200 Aarhus N, Midtjylland
DP Coordinator Malene Sørensen
Languages English
T: +45 8937 3533
W: www.aarhusgym.dk

Aarhus International School
Dalgas Avenue 12, 8000 Aarhus, Midtjylland
MYP Coordinator Kathryn Templeman
PYP Coordinator Megan Behnke
Languages English
T: +45 2030 2079
W: www.aarhusacademy.dk

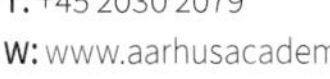

Birkerød Gymnasium, HF, IB & Boarding School
Søndervangen 56, 3460 Birkerød, Hovedstaden
DP Coordinator Christina Rye Tarp
Languages English
T: +45 4516 8220
W: www.birke-gym.dk

Denmark

Copenhagen International School
Levantkaj 4-14, 2150 Copenhagen, Hovedstaden
DP Coordinator Mary Donnellan
MYP Coordinator Laura Ream
PYP Coordinator Rachel Hindborg
Languages English
T: +45 3946 3300
W: www.cis.dk

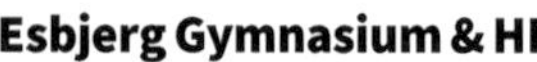

Esbjerg Gymnasium & HF
Spangsbjerg Møllevej 310, 6705 Esbjerg, Syddanmark
DP Coordinator Christina Jepsen
Languages English
T: +45 7514 1300
W: www.e-gym.dk

Esbjerg International School
Guldager Skolevej 4, 6710 Esbjerg, Syddanmark
MYP Coordinator Nicola Zulu
PYP Coordinator Farhana Bari
Languages English, Danish
T: +45 7610 5399
W: www.eis.school

EUC Syd
Hilmar Finsens Gade 8, 6400 Soenderborg, Syddanmark
DP Coordinator Mikkel Simonsen
Languages English
T: +45 7412 4242
W: www.eucsyd.dk

Grenaa Gymnasium
N. P. Josiassens vej 21, 8500 Grenaa, Midtjylland
DP Coordinator Eike Strandsby
Languages English
T: +45 8758 4050
W: www.grenaa-gym.dk

Hasseris Gymnasium
Hasserisvej 300, 9000 Aalborg, Nordjylland
DP Coordinator Karin Mølgaard Skals
Languages English
T: +45 9632 7110
W: www.hasseris-gym.dk

Herlufsholm Skole
Herlufsholm Allé 170, 4700 Naestved, Sjaelland
DP Coordinator Richard Hannon
Languages English
T: +45 5575 3500
W: www.herlufsholm.dk

Ikast-Brande Gymnasium
Bøgildvej 2, 7400 Ikast-Brande, Midtjylland
DP Coordinator Gitte Pilley
Languages English
T: +45 9715 3611
W: www.ikast-gym.dk

International School of Billund
Skolevej 24, 7190 Billund, Syddanmark
MYP Coordinator Tue Rabenhoej
PYP Coordinator Karen Serritslev
Languages English
T: +45 2632 7800
W: www.isbillund.com

International School of Hellerup
Rygårds Allé 131, 2900 Hellerup, Hovedstaden
DP Coordinator Antony Nesling
MYP Coordinator Ramazan Dicle
PYP Coordinator Victoria Sadeghi
Languages English
T: +45 7020 6368
W: www.ish.dk

Kolding Gymnasium, HF-Kursus
Skovvangen 10, 6000 Kolding, Syddanmark
DP Coordinator Mel Malone
Languages English
T: +45 7633 9600
W: www.kolding-gym.dk

Nörre Gymnasium
Mörkhöjvej 78, 2700 Bronshoj, Hovedstaden
DP Coordinator Ariane Bräuninger Tang
Languages English
T: +45 4494 2722
W: www.norreg.dk

North Zealand International School
Christianshusvej 16, 2970 Hørsholm, Hovedstaden
DP Coordinator Karen Boettger
Languages English
T: +45 4557 2616
W: ngg.dk/international

Nyborg Gymnasium
Skolebakken 13, 5800 Nyborg, Syddanmark
DP Coordinator Ulrik Nørum
Languages English
T: +45 6531 0217

Stenhus Gymnasium
Stenhusvej 20, 4300 Holbæk, Sjaelland
DP Coordinator Paul Bjergfelt
Languages English
T: +45 5943 6465
W: www.stenhus-gym.dk

Struer Statsgymnasium
Jyllandsgade 2, 7600 Struer, Midtjylland
DP Coordinator Morten Rødgaard Jensen
Languages English
T: +45 9785 4300
W: www.struer-gym.dk

Viborg Katedralskole
Gl Skivevej 2, 8800 Viborg, Midtjylland
DP Coordinator Mads Henriksen
Languages English
T: +45 8662 0655
W: www.viborgkatedralskole.dk

EGYPT

Alexandria International Academy
Plots 2 & 3 Section 1, Abis, Alexandria
DP Coordinator Christopher Thomas
PYP Coordinator Noha ElBatrik
Languages English, Arabic
T: +20 12 8621 5550
W: aia-alex.com

American International School in Egypt - Main Campus
P.O. Box 8090, Masaken, Nasr City, Cairo 11371
DP Coordinator Randi Assenova
Languages English
T: +20 2 2618 8400
W: www.aisegypt.com

American International School in Egypt - West Campus
P.O. Box 12588, Greens compound, Sheikh Zayed City, Giza 12588
DP Coordinator Antonio Gomariz-Perez
Languages English
T: +20 2 3854 0600
W: www.aiswest.com

Bedayia International School
1st Urban Distrcit, El Banafseg Zone, New Cairo City, Cairo 11865
DP Coordinator Rania Aly
Languages English
T: +20 11 1900 9727
W: www.bedayia.com

Cairo American College
1 Midan Digla, Maadi, Cairo 11431
DP Coordinator Niall Williams
PYP Coordinator Penelope Amies
Languages English
T: +20 2 2755 5555
W: www.cacegypt.org

Cairo English School
P.O. Box 8020, Masaken, Nasr City, Cairo 11371
DP Coordinator Elizabeth Baron
Languages English
T: +20 2 2249 0200
W: www.cesegypt.com

Carleton College International School
Greenland ElShorouk, Cairo 11837
PYP Coordinator Nouran El Gandor
Languages English, Arabic
T: +20 11 1245 3338
W: carletoncollege.net
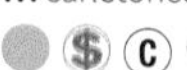

Deutsche Schule Beverly Hills Kairo
Beverly Hills, 16th District, Beverly Hills Road, Giza
DP Coordinator Shahira Yehia
Languages English, German
T: +20 3857 8070
W: www.bhs-egypt.com/deutsche

Deutsche Schule Hurghada
Bowling Street, Qesm Hurghada, Hurghada, Red Sea 84511
DP Coordinator Eckart Streb
Languages Arabic, German
T: +20 10 0461 2747
W: www.deutsche-schule-hurghada.de

Dr. Nermien Ismail Schools (NIS) - First Settlement
El-Tagammoe El-Awwal, Extension of Zaker Hussein Street, Beside the Police Academy, Cairo
DP Coordinator Soha Salem
Languages English
W: nis-eg.com/first-settlement
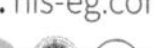

Ecole Oasis Internationale
Zahraa El Maadi, District 7, Part A & B, Cairo 11435
CP Coordinator Fatma Hussein
DP Coordinator Fatma Hussein
MYP Coordinator Fatma Hussein
PYP Coordinator Iman Radwan
Languages French
T: +20 2 2732 8252
W: en.ecoleoasisinternationale.com
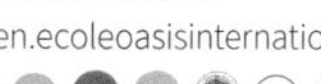

Egyptian American School
Ring road behind Nozha Airport, Alexandria 21522
DP Coordinator Dalia Ibrahim
Languages English
W: www.easschool.com

Egyptian International School - 5th Settlement
Third District, Service Area 4A, Fifth Settlement, New Cairo City, Cairo
PYP Coordinator Nagwa Refat
Languages English, Arabic
T: +20 15 5319 2212
W: www.eis-tagamo3.org
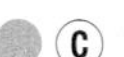

Egyptian International School - Sheikh Zayed
2nd Neighborhood, 13th District, Sheikh Zayed City, Giza
DP Coordinator Abd El Raouf Mohamed
MYP Coordinator Eman Hussein
PYP Coordinator Hala Seif
Languages English
T: +20 10 2220 0357
W: www.eis-zayed.com

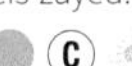

El Alsson British and American International Schools - NewGiza
P.O. Box 16, KM 22 Cairo-Alex Road, Smart Village, Cairo 12577
DP Coordinator Mark Wisniewski
MYP Coordinator Celine Macarthur
Languages English
T: +20 2 3827 0800
W: www.alsson.com

Elite International School
Airport Road, off Ring Road, Behind Nozha Airport, Abees 10th, Alexandria
DP Coordinator Lamees Elshafei
MYP Coordinator Lamees Elshafei
PYP Coordinator Alia Mostafa
Languages English, Arabic
T: +20 10 9330 7078
W: onlineelite.net

Evolution International School
New Giza Campus, Km 22, Cairo/Alex desert Road, 6th of October City, Giza 12588
DP Coordinator Hadeer Abdelwahab
Languages English
T: +20 10 0366 6223
W: www.eisng.lvng.net

Gateway International Montessori School
Katameya Gardens, 5th Settlement, New Cairo City, Cairo

DP Coordinator Fatma Elsakhawy
Languages English, Arabic
T: +20 11 1310 2222
W: www.gateway.education

GEMS Academy Alexandria
Kilo 13 Alexandria-Cairo Agricultural Road, Alexandria
PYP Coordinator Nadine Mouhasseb
Languages English, French
T: +2 03 5190 800
W: www.gaa.edu.eg

Global Paradigm Baccalaureate School
ASR2 Mostakbal City, New Cairo City, Cairo 11477
PYP Coordinator Maha El Kashtawy
Languages English, Arabic
T: +20 127 601 2219
W: globalparadigmschools-baccalaureate.com

Global Paradigm International School
First Settlement, Block K1, Sector 8, New Cairo City, Cairo 16834
DP Coordinator Omnia Mostafa
Languages English
T: +20 222 461 809/10/12
W: www.gpschool-eg.com
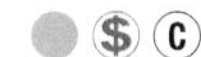

GREEN LAND - PRÉ VERT INTERNATIONAL SCHOOLS - GPIS-EGYPT
405 Geziret Mohammad, Bashtil, Cairo
DP Coordinator Mona Khalil
MYP Coordinator May Waly
PYP Coordinator Francoise Mokhtar
Languages French, English
T: +20 2 01002226053/50/54
E: info@greenlandschool.org
W: gpis-egypt.org
See full details on page 96

HAYAH INTERNATIONAL ACADEMY
South of Police Academy, 5th District, New Cairo 11835
DP Coordinator Nada Yasin
PYP Coordinator Shymaa El Kotb
Languages English
T: +202 25373000/3333
E: ib@hayahacademy.com
W: www.hayahacademy.com
See full details on page 101

International New Future School (Neue Deutsche Schule Alexandria)
El Prince Street, off Moustafa Kamel Street, Mandara Kebly, Alexandria
DP Coordinator Fatma Soliman
Languages English
T: +20 3 958 6481
W: futureschools-egypt.com/DSA

International School of Elite Education
5th Settlement, off Road 90, behind Masraweya Compound, New Cairo City, Cairo
DP Coordinator Shaimaa AbdelHafez
Languages English
T: +20 11 1114 3225
W: www.eliteeducation-eg.com

Kaumeya Language School
8 Mokarar Takseem El Madares, Ring Road, Abees, Alexandria
DP Coordinator Randa Heikal
PYP Coordinator Omar Sadek
Languages English
T: +20 12 8637 7990
W: kls-eg.com

Leaders International College
21 El Narges Services Region, Off 90th Road, 5th Settlement, New Cairo City, Cairo 11835
DP Coordinator Menna Shawky
MYP Coordinator Marwa Hosny Elewa
PYP Coordinator Ola Hakeem
Languages English
T: +20 12 7292 4777
W: www.leadersintcollege.com

Malvern College Egypt
B2-B3 South Ring Road, Investment Zone Kattameya, Cairo
DP Coordinator Joseph Ford
Languages English
T: +202 26144400
W: malverncollege.edu.eg

Manaret Heliopolis International School
Hazem Salah Street, Ext. Mostafa El Nahas, Nasr City, Cairo 11351
DP Coordinator Omneya Hamdy
MYP Coordinator Sherwet Adel
PYP Coordinator Radwa AlSaeedi
Languages English
T: +20 2 2471 3332
W: www.mhischool.net

Modern English School Cairo
P.O. Box 5, South of Police Academy, New Cairo City, Cairo 11835
DP Coordinator Brendan Rainford
Languages English
T: +202 2618 9600
W: www.mescairo.com

Narmer American College
20 El-Narguis Service Area, El-Tagamoa El Khames, New Cairo City, Cairo
DP Coordinator Sara El Derainy
MYP Coordinator Jarod Rodger
Languages English
T: +20 2 2587 4000
W: www.nacegypt.com

Nefertari International School
Km 22 Cairo-Ismailia Desert Road, Nefertari Street, Cairo 11341
DP Coordinator Rania Allam
PYP Coordinator Jana Barakat
Languages English, Arabic
T: +20 1026604040
W: www.niscl.com

Nefertari International School - 6th of October
Gamal Abd El-Naser Street, Gardenia Buildings, El-Shams Project, Behind Mall of Arabia, 6 October City
PYP Coordinator Dina Omar
Languages English, French
W: 6oct.niscl.net

New Cairo British International School
Road 17, 1st District, 3rd Zone, 5th Settlement, New Cairo City, Cairo
DP Coordinator Susie Belal
T: +20 2 2565 7115
W: www.ncbis.co.uk

New Castle International School
Al Bashair District, In Al Bashair Service Center, 6th of October City, Giza
DP Coordinator Shrouk Elshiekh
Languages English, Arabic
T: +20 10 2368 0517
W: newcastle.edu.eg

New Vision International Schools
P.O. Box 120, Beverly Hills, Sheikh Zayed Road, Giza 12588
DP Coordinator Soha Nabil
MYP Coordinator Randa Gamal
PYP Coordinator Dalia Elshorbagy
Languages Arabic, English
T: +20 12 0426 5778
W: nviseg.com
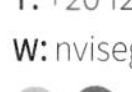

Nile International College
Beside Qibaa, Street 44, Fifth District, New Cairo City, Cairo 11853
MYP Coordinator May Khalil
PYP Coordinator Aya Adel
Languages English
T: +20 10 6100 0526
W: nileinternational-schools.com

Notion International School
Gamal Eldin Albana Street, Almariotya, Haram, Giza
DP Coordinator Azza Fekry
MYP Coordinator Mohamed Salama
PYP Coordinator Sofia Dourasse
Languages English
T: +20 2 3746 5406
W: notion-edu.com

EGYPT

Princeton International School
Zizinia, 5th Settlement, Close to AUC Gate 4, New Cairo City, Cairo
DP Coordinator Ahmed Shoieb
MYP Coordinator Mai Abd El-Rahman
PYP Coordinator Faten Shoieb
Languages English, French
T: +20 10 9149 7999
W: www.princetoninternationalschool.net

Rahn Schulen Kairo
Plot 15A, Al-Istethmar Region, El-Kattamia, Cairo 11371
DP Coordinator Miriam Magdy
Languages German
T: +20 2 2725 2555
W: egypt.rahn.education

Salahaldin International School
Ja'far ibn Abi Talib, New Cairo City, Cairo
DP Coordinator Ali Issiz
Languages English, Arabic
T: +20 10 3333 7291
W: sis.edu.eg

Schutz American School
P.O. Box 1000, 51 Schutz Street, Alexandria
PYP Coordinator Deborah Lacroix
Languages English, Arabic
T: +20 3 576 2205
W: www.schutzschool.org.eg

The British International School, Cairo
P.O. Box 137, Gezira, Cairo
DP Coordinator Edward Baxter
Languages English
T: +20 2 3827 0444
W: www.bisc.edu.eg

The Egyptian International School in El Marag
Mogawra 2, Bloc G, Elmarag City, Maadi, Cairo 11435
DP Coordinator Ahmed Elwan
MYP Coordinator Ahmed Hossien
PYP Coordinator Maha Awaad
Languages English
T: +20 229700217
W: m-eis.com

The International School of Egypt
5th Settlement, 2nd District, Street 68, New Cairo City, Cairo
DP Coordinator Mariz Mansour
Languages English
T: +20 2 2564 7038
W: isegypt.org

Uptown International School
Al Abageyah, El Mukkatam, Cairo
PYP Coordinator Nesma Hassan
Languages English, Arabic
T: +20 12 2584 7419
W: uisegypt.com

ESTONIA

Audentes School
Tondi str 84, 11316 Tallinn, Harju
DP Coordinator Anneliis Kõiv
Languages English
T: +372 699 6591
W: www.audentes.ee

International School of Estonia
Juhkentali 18, 10132 Tallinn, Harju
DP Coordinator Ashley Wallace
MYP Coordinator Kadri Tomson
PYP Coordinator Terje Äkke
Languages English
T: +372 666 4380
W: www.ise.edu.ee

International School of Tallinn
Keevise 2, 11415 Tallinn, Harju
DP Coordinator Gerard Zippilli
MYP Coordinator Meena Gaikwad
PYP Coordinator Lisa Parker
Languages English, Estonian
T: +372 5066 080
W: ist.ee

Miina Härma Gümnaasium
Tõnissoni 3, 50409 Tartu
DP Coordinator Kirstin Karis
MYP Coordinator Madis Kahro
PYP Coordinator Triinu Pihus
Languages English, Estonian
T: +372 736 1920
W: www.mhg.tartu.ee

Tallinn English College
10 Estonia Avenue, 10148 Tallinn, Harju
DP Coordinator Liisa Kukk
MYP Coordinator Martin Tamm
PYP Coordinator Anette Vetik
Languages English
T: +372 6 46 13 06
W: www.tik.edu.ee

Tartu International School
J. Liivi 2d, 50409 Tartu
PYP Coordinator Maris Vohla
Languages English
T: +372 742 4241
W: www.istartu.ee

ESWATINI

Lilima Montessori High School
P.O. Box 8832, Mbabane H100
MYP Coordinator Mduduzi Bhembe
Languages English
T: +268 24 10 0580
W: www.lilima.org

WATERFORD KAMHLABA UWC OF SOUTHERN AFRICA
Waterford Park, Mbabane H100
DP Coordinator Elizabeth Cummergen
Languages English
T: +268 24220867
E: principal@waterford.sz
W: www.waterford.sz
See full details on page 238
 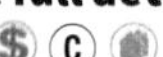

ETHIOPIA

German Embassy School Addis Ababa
P.O. Box 1372, Addis Ababa
DP Coordinator Heba Hassan
Languages English, German
T: +251 11 553 4465
W: www.ds-addis.de

International Community School of Addis Ababa
Mauritania Road, Addis Ababa
DP Coordinator Deanna Milne
PYP Coordinator Lydia Van Berkhout
Languages English
T: +251 11 371 1544
W: www.icsaddis.org

Sandford International School
P.O. Box 30056 MA, Addis Ababa
DP Coordinator Colin Beet
Languages English
T: +251 11 123 3726
W: www.sandfordschool.org

FINLAND

Espoo International School
PL 3222, 02070 Espoo, Uusimaa
MYP Coordinator Darrell Germo
Languages English
T: +358 50 343 2460
W: www.espoo.fi/espoointernationalschool

Etelä-Tapiolan lukio
PL 3234, 02070 Espoo, Uusimaa
DP Coordinator David Crawford
Languages English
T: +358 9 816 39101
W: www.etela-tapiola.fi

Helsingin Suomalainen Yhteiskoulu
Isonnevantie 8, 00320 Helsinki, Uusimaa
DP Coordinator Anni Grönroos
Languages English
T: +358 9 4774 1814
W: www.syk.fi

Imatran Yhteislukio upper-secondary school
Koulukatu 5, 55120 Imatra, South Karelia
DP Coordinator Marketta Kolehmainen
Languages English
T: +358 5 6815 820
W: www.imatranyhteislukio.fi

International School of Helsinki
Selkämerenkatu 11, 00180 Helsinki, Uusimaa
DP Coordinator Mark Kilmer
MYP Coordinator Minna Tammivuori-Piraux
PYP Coordinator Lydia Jones
Languages English
T: +358 9 686 6160
W: www.ishelsinki.fi

Joensuun Lyseon Lukio
Koskikatu 8, 80100 Joensuu, North Karelia
DP Coordinator Adam Lerch
Languages English
T: +358 13 267 7111
W: www.lyseo.jns.fi

Jyväskylän Lyseon Lukio
Yliopistonkatu 13, 40100 Jyväskylä, Central Finland
DP Coordinator Susanna Soininen
Languages English
T: +358 403414690

Kannaksen lukio
Kannaksenkatu 20, 15140 Lahti, Päijänne Tavastia
DP Coordinator Sami Sorvali
Languages English
T: +358 3 8144220
W: www.kannaksenlukio.fi

Kuopion Lyseon Lukio
Puijonkatu 18, 70110 Kuopio, North Savo
DP Coordinator Suvi Tirkkonen
Languages English
T: +358 17 184 563
W: www.koulut.kuopio.fi/lyseo/

Lyseonpuiston Lukio
IB section, Ruokasenkatu 18, 96100 Rovaniemi, Lapland
DP Coordinator Heikki Loukusa
Languages English
T: +358 16 322 2540
W: www.lyska.net

Mattlidens Gymnasium
PB 3340, 02070 Esbo, Uusimaa
DP Coordinator Anna Martikainen
Languages English
T: +358 9 816 43050
W: www.mattliden.fi/gym

Oulu International School
Kasarmintie 4, 90130 Oulu, North Ostrobothnia
MYP Coordinator Marja Peedo
PYP Coordinator Heidi Tuomela
Languages English
T: +358 50 371 6977
W: ouka.fi/oulu/oulu-international-school/etusivu

Oulun Lyseon Lukio
Kajaaninkatu 3, 90100 Oulu, North Ostrobothnia
DP Coordinator Heli-Maarit Miihkinen
Languages English
T: +358 44 703 9451
W: www.lyseo.edu.ouka.fi

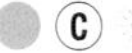

Oulun seudun ammattiopisto
Kiviharjuntie 6, 90220 Oulu, North Ostrobothnia
CP Coordinator Eeva Vehmas
Languages English, Finnish
W: www.osao.fi

Ressu Comprehensive School
PO BOX 3107, Kaupunki, 00099 Helsinki, Uusimaa
MYP Coordinator Anna Antman
PYP Coordinator Anna Hart
Languages English, Finnish
T: +358 9 310 82102
W: www.ressuy.edu.hel.fi

Ressun Lukio
PO Box 3809, 00099 Helsinki, Uusimaa
DP Coordinator Karoliina Puumalainen
Languages English
T: +358 9 604 849
W: www.ressunlukio.fi

Tampereen Lyseon lukio
F E Sillanpään Katu 7, 33230 Tampere, Pirkanmaa
DP Coordinator Tuija Laurila
Languages English
T: +358 40 801 6717
W: lukiot.tampere.fi/lyseo

Tikkurilan Lukio
Valkoisenlahteentie 53, 01370 Vantaa, Uusimaa
DP Coordinator Maarit Berg
Languages English
T: +358 9 8392 5119
W: www.edu.vantaa.fi/tilu

Turun Normaalikoulu
Annikanpolku 9, 20610 Turku, Southwest Finland
DP Coordinator Marianna Vanhatalo
Languages English
T: +358 (0)29 450 1000
W: sites.utu.fi/tnk

Vasa Ovningsskola
Kirkkopuistikko 11-13, 65100 Vaasa, Ostrobothnia
DP Coordinator Henrik Lindgren
Languages English
T: +358 (0)6 324 7115
W: oldwww.abo.fi/vos/

FRANCE

American School of Paris
41 rue Pasteur, 92210 Saint-Cloud
DP Coordinator Alyssa Pierce
Languages English
T: +33 01 41 12 86 55
W: www.asparis.org

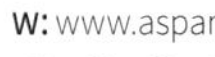

Antonia International School (École Antonia)
2 rue Patrice Lumumba, 34000 Montpellier
DP Coordinator Christelle Orr
Languages English, French
T: +33 4 11 93 09 87
W: ecoleantonia-montpellier.com

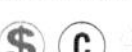

Apex2100 Academy
Le Rosset, 73320 Tignes
CP Coordinator Jo Crowther
DP Coordinator Jo Crowther
Languages English, French
W: apex2100.org

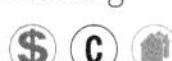

Collège-Lycée Saint François-Xavier
3 rue Thiers, 56000 Vannes
DP Coordinator Chantal Thomas
Languages English, French
T: +33 (0)2 97 47 12 80
W: www.saint-francois-xavier.fr

ECOLE DES ROCHES
295 avenue Edmond Demolins, 27130 Verneuil d'Avre et d'Iton
DP Coordinator Dr Ed Owens
Languages English, French
T: +33 (0) 232 6040 00
E: ecoledesroches@ecoledesroches.com
W: www.ecoledesroches.com
See full details on page 77

ECOLE JEANNINE MANUEL - LILLE
418 bis rue Albert Bailly, Marcq-en-Baroeul 59700
DP Coordinator Nicola French
Languages French, English
T: +33 3 20 65 90 50
E: admissions-lille@ejm.net
W: www.ecolejeanninemanuel.org
See full details on page 80

ECOLE JEANNINE MANUEL - PARIS
70 rue du Théâtre, Paris 75015
DP Coordinator Sabine Hurley
Languages English, French
T: +33 1 44 37 00 80
E: admissions@ejm.net
W: www.ecolejeanninemanuel.org
See full details on page 81

Ecole Privée Bilingue Internationale
Domaine de massane, 34670 Baillargues
DP Coordinator Alexandra David
MYP Coordinator Alexandra David
Languages English, French
T: +33 4677 07844
W: www.lycee-prive-international-montpellier.fr

ERMITAGE INTERNATIONAL SCHOOL
46 Avenue Eglé, 78600 Maisons-Laffitte
DP Coordinator Wayne Hodgkinson
MYP Coordinator Christine Collie
Languages English, French
T: +33 139 62 81 75
E: admissions@ermitage.fr
W: www.ermitage.fr
See full details on page 84

Hattemer Bilingue Paris 8e
52 rue de Londres, 75008 Paris
DP Coordinator Mrs Deborah Garelik
Languages English, French
T: +33 1 43 8759 14
W: www.hattemer.fr

ICS CÔTE D'AZUR
245 Route les Lucioles, 06560 Valbonne
PYP Coordinator Mrs. Janet Goswell
Languages English, French
T: +33 (0)4 93 64 32 84
E: admissions@icscotedazur.com
W: www.icscotedazur.com
See full details on page 106

ICS PARIS
23 rue de Cronstadt, 75015 Paris
DP Coordinator Mrs. Marilyne Boursin
MYP Coordinator Mr. Matthieu Coliboeuf
PYP Coordinator Ms. Eva Silva
Languages English
T: +33 (0)1 56 56 60 31
E: admissions@icsparis.fr
W: www.icsparis.fr
See full details on page 109

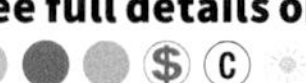

INTERNATIONAL BILINGUAL SCHOOL OF PROVENCE
500 Route de Bouc-Bel-Air, Domaine des Pins, Luynes, Aix en Provence 13080
DP Coordinator Pablo Besozzi
Languages English, French
T: +33 (0)4 4224 0340
E: info@ibsofprovence.com
W: www.ibsofprovence.com
See full details on page 117

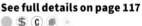

International School 33
47 Avenue de la Poterie, 33170 Gradignan
DP Coordinator Rodolphe Breard
MYP Coordinator Rachael Bell
PYP Coordinator Rachael Bell
Languages English, French
T: +33 6 51 27 98 19
W: international-school33.com

International School of Lyon
80 Chemin du Grand Roule, 69110 Sainte-Foy-lès-Lyon
DP Coordinator Mark Ingrey
PYP Coordinator Alison Pattinson
Languages English
T: +33 4 78 86 61 90
W: www.islyon.org

INTERNATIONAL SCHOOL OF NICE
15 Avenue Claude Debussy, 06200 Nice
DP Coordinator Mr. Dominique Dubois
PYP Coordinator Mrs. Joanne Brown
Languages English
T: +33 (0)4 93 21 04 00
E: admissions@isn-nice.com
W: www.isn-nice.com
See full details on page 133

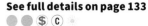

FRANCE

International School of Paris
6 rue Beethoven, 75016 Paris
DP Coordinator Grant Woodcock
MYP Coordinator Natasha Hale
PYP Coordinator Jenna Brooks
Languages English
T: +33 1 42 24 09 54
W: www.isparis.edu

International School of Toulouse
2 Allee De L'Herbaudiere, Route de Pibrac, 31770 Colomiers
DP Coordinator Gareth Hunt
PYP Coordinator Ingela Summerton
Languages English
T: +33 5 62 74 26 74
W: www.intst.eu

Le Gymnase Jean Sturm/ Lucie Berger
8 place des Etudiants, Alsace, 67000 Strasbourg
DP Coordinator Alexandre Rongemaille
MYP Coordinator Beulah Henry
PYP Coordinator Johanna Dellantonio
Languages English
T: +33 3 88 15 77 10
W: www.jsturm.fr

Les Petits Polyglottes
15 Chemin de Vireloup, 01210 Ferney-Voltaire
PYP Coordinator Eva Martins
Languages English, French
T: +33 4 50 42 49 57
W: newpetitpoly.cm-communication.ch

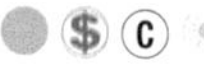

Notre Dame International High School
106 Grande-Rue, 78480 Verneuil-sur-Seine
DP Coordinator Emilie Champeix
Languages English, French
T: +33 9 70 40 79 22
W: www.ndihs.com

Ombrosa, Lycée Multilingue de Lyon
95 Quai Clemenceau, 69300 Caluire
DP Coordinator Sylvie Henderson
Languages English, French
T: +33 4 78 23 22 63
W: www.ombrosa.com

SAINTE VICTOIRE INTERNATIONAL SCHOOL
Domaine de Château l'Arc, Chemin de Maurel, 13710 Fuveau
DP Coordinator Allison Delort
Languages English, French
T: +33 4 42 26 51 96
E: contact@schoolsaintevictoire.com
W: www.schoolsaintevictoire.com

See full details on page 193

Sem' de Walbourg
60 Grand Rue, 67360 Walbourg
DP Coordinator Noémie Celton
Languages English, French
W: www.sem-walbourg.eu

GABON

Lycée Franco-Britannique Ecole Internationale
Batterie IV, B.P. 159, Libreville
DP Coordinator Nathaniel Akue Mackaya
MYP Coordinator Nathaniel Akue Mackaya
PYP Coordinator Nathaniel Akue Mackaya
Languages French, English
T: 00241 1 17 37 117
W: efblbv.org/ecole-franco-britannique-lbv.php

THE INTERNATIONAL SCHOOL OF GABON RUBAN VERT
Batterie IV, Libreville, Gabon 2144
DP Coordinator Ms Magali Kunsevi
PYP Coordinator Ms Veena Nambiar
Languages English, French
T: +241 11 44 26 70
E: admissions@ecolerubanvert.com
W: www.ecolerubanvert.com

See full details on page 230

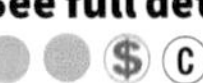

GEORGIA

British Georgian Academy
Leo Kvatchadze 17, Tbilisi 0186
DP Coordinator Martin Keon
Languages English, Georgian
T: +995 322 251 253
W: bga.ge

European School
2 Irine Skhirtladze Street, Tbilisi 0177
CP Coordinator Ramaz Sartania
DP Coordinator Ramaz Sartania
MYP Coordinator Oxana Akimova
PYP Coordinator Tinatini Gugushvili
Languages English
T: +995 322 144 244
W: europeanschool.ge

New School, International School of Georgia
35 Tskneti Highway, Bagebi, Tbilisi 0162
DP Coordinator Kety Tsurtsumia
MYP Coordinator Tamuna Dzidziguri
PYP Coordinator Deduna Iashsaghashvili
Languages English, Georgian
T: +995 511 190 809
W: www.newschoolgeorgia.com

Newton Free School
Anna Politkovskaya Street N30, Tbilisi 0186
DP Coordinator Tamar Tchanturia
MYP Coordinator Nino Iakobishvili
PYP Coordinator Tea Beridze
Languages English
T: +995 570 705 080
W: www.newton.edu.ge

GERMANY

ACCADIS INTERNATIONAL SCHOOL BAD HOMBURG
SÜDCAMPUS Bad Homburg, Am Weidenring 52-54, 61352 Bad Homburg, Hesse
DP Coordinator Ms Megan Jones
Languages English, German
T: +49 61 72 984 141
E: info@accadis-isb.com
W: www.accadis-isb.com

See full details on page 46

Albert-Schweitzer-Gymnasium
Halberstädter Strasse 30, 38444 Wolfsburg, Lower Saxony
DP Coordinator Carolin Grabowski
Languages English, German
T: +49 5 361873 410
W: asg-wob.de

Aloisiuskolleg
Elisabethstraße 18, 53177 Bonn, North Rhine-Westphalia
DP Coordinator Uta Schäpers
Languages English, German
T: +49 228 82003 (101)
W: www.aloisiuskolleg.de

BAVARIAN INTERNATIONAL SCHOOL GAG (BIS) - CITY CAMPUS
Leopoldstrasse 208, 80804 Munich, Bavaria
PYP Coordinator Nicola Moloney
Languages English
T: +49 89 89655 203
W: www.bis-school.com

See full details on page 61

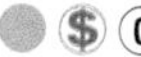

BAVARIAN INTERNATIONAL SCHOOL GAG (BIS) - HAIMHAUSEN CAMPUS
Hauptstrasse 1, 85778 Haimhausen, Bavaria
CP Coordinator Kim Kermath
DP Coordinator Rob Clements
MYP Coordinator Dr. Erin Foley
PYP Coordinator Nicola Moloney & Niko Lewman
Languages English
T: +49 (0)81 33 917 203
E: admissions@bis-school.com
W: www.bis-school.com

See full details on page 61

BBIS Berlin Brandenburg International School
Schopfheimer Allee 10, 14532 Kleinmachnow, Brandenburg
DP Coordinator Jane Barker
MYP Coordinator Anna Thach
PYP Coordinator Lisa Roy
Languages English
T: +49 33 203 8036 0
W: www.bbis.de

Berlin British School
Dickensweg 17-19, 14055 Berlin
DP Coordinator Gemma Ritchie
PYP Coordinator Joanne Wolff
Languages English
T: +49 (0)30 35109 180
W: www.berlinbritishschool.de

Berlin Cosmopolitan School
Rückerstrasse 9, 10119 Berlin
DP Coordinator Fatima Camara
PYP Coordinator Sylvia Johnston
Languages English
T: +49 30 688 33 23 0
W: www.cosmopolitanschool.de

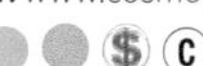

Berlin International School
Lentzeallee 8/14, 14195 Berlin
DP Coordinator Vanessa Westerhoff
PYP Coordinator Angeline Aow
Languages English
T: +49 (0) 30 8200 7790
W: www.berlin-international-school.de

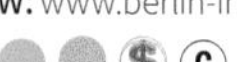

Berlin Metropolitan School
Linienstrasse 122, 10115 Berlin
DP Coordinator Dorian Rosso
PYP Coordinator Erica Coutrim
Languages English, German
T: +49 30 8872 7390
W: www.metropolitanschool.com

Bertolt-Brecht-Gymnasium Dresden
Lortzingstrasse 01, 01307 Dresden, Saxony
DP Coordinator Laura Protextor
Languages English
T: +49 351 449040
W: www.bebe-dresden.de

Berufskolleg am Wasserturm
Herzogstrasse 4, Northrhine Westphalia, 46399 Bocholt, North Rhine-Westphalia
DP Coordinator Ellen Baumann
Languages English
T: +49 2871 2724300
W: www.bkamwasserturm.de

Bonn International School e.V.
Martin-Luther-King Strasse 14, 53175 Bonn, North Rhine-Westphalia
DP Coordinator Becky Oliver
MYP Coordinator Cijith Jacob
PYP Coordinator Casey Ranson
Languages English
T: +49 228 30854 0
W: www.bonn-is.de

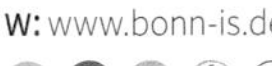

Dresden International School e.V
Annenstrasse 9, 01067 Dresden, Saxony
DP Coordinator Wendy Bassam-Coles
MYP Coordinator Flora Mather
PYP Coordinator Kimberly Aguirre
Languages English
T: +49 351 440070
W: www.dresden-is.de

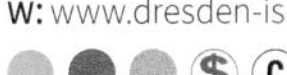

European School RheinMain gGmbH
Theodor-Heuss-Strasse 65, 61118 Bad Vilbel, Hesse
MYP Coordinator Dominic Rogers
Languages English, German
T: +49 61 015056 60
W: www.es-rm.eu

Evangelisch Stiftisches Gymnasium Gütersloh
Feldstrasse 13, 33330 Gütersloh, North Rhine-Westphalia
DP Coordinator Marcus Kühle
Languages English
T: +49 5241 98050
W: www.esg-guetersloh.de

FELIX-KLEIN-GYMNASIUM
Böttingerstrasse 17, 37073 Göttingen, Lower Saxony
DP Coordinator Silke Neumann
Languages English
T: +49 551 400 2909
E: fkgis@goettingen.de
W: www.fkg-goettingen.de
See full details on page 90

Franconian International School
Marie-Curie-Strasse 2, 91052 Erlangen, Bavaria
DP Coordinator Ruth Greener
MYP Coordinator Matt Chambers
Languages English
T: +49 9131 940390
W: www.the-fis.de

Frankfurt International School
An der Waldlust 15, 61440 Oberursel, Hesse
DP Coordinator Ashley van der Meer
PYP Coordinator Gioia Morasch
Languages English
T: +49 6171 2024 0
W: www.fis.edu

Friedrich-Ebert-Gymnasium
Ollenhauerstrasse 5, 53113 Bonn, North Rhine-Westphalia
DP Coordinator Gabriele Josten
Languages English
T: +49 228 777520
W: www.feg-bonn.de

Friedrich-Schiller-Gymnasium Marbach
Schulstrasse 34, 71672 Marbach am Neckar, Baden-Württemberg
DP Coordinator Andrea Saffert
Languages English, German
T: +49 7144 8458-0
W: www.fsg-marbach.de

Goethe-Gymnasium
Friedrich-Ebert-Anlage 22-24, 60325 Frankfurt, Hesse
DP Coordinator Hans-Dieter Bunger
Languages English
T: +49 69 2123 3525
W: www.gg-ffm.de

Goetheschule Essen
Ruschenstrasse 1, 45133 Essen, North Rhine-Westphalia
DP Coordinator Michael Franke
Languages English
T: +49 20 1 841170
W: www.goetheschule-essen.de

Gymnasium Birkenfeld
Brechkaul 12, 55765 Birkenfeld, Rhineland-Palatinate
DP Coordinator Dagmar Orlian
Languages English, German
T: +49 (0)6782 99940
W: www.gymnasium-birkenfeld-nahe.de

Gymnasium im Stift Neuzelle
Stiftsplatz 7, 15898 Neuzelle, Brandenburg
DP Coordinator Martin Jacob
Languages English, German
T: +49 341 3939 2810
W: rahn.education/en/freies-gymnasium-im-stift-neuzelle-.html

Gymnasium Paulinum
Am Stadtgraben 30, 48143 Münster, North Rhine-Westphalia
DP Coordinator Kirsten Brinkmann
Languages English
T: +49 251 510500-0
W: www.muenster.org/paulinum

Gymnasium Schloss Neuhaus
Im Schlosspark, 33104 Paderborn, North Rhine-Westphalia
DP Coordinator Denise Krämer
Languages English
T: +49 5254 992200
W: www.gymnasium-schloss-neuhaus.de

HagenSchule gAG
Lützowstrasse 125, 58095 Hagen, North Rhine-Westphalia
DP Coordinator Alexander Flieger
Languages English, German
T: +49 23 313400 071
W: montessori-hagen.schule

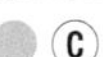

Hansa-Gymnasium, Hamburg-Bergedorf
Hermann-Distel-Strasse 25, 21029 Hamburg
DP Coordinator Carsten Schenk
Languages English
T: +49 (0)40 724 18 60
W: www.hansa-gymnasium.de

Heidelberg International School
Wieblinger Weg 7, 68782 Heidelberg, Baden-Württemberg
DP Coordinator William Ledbetter
MYP Coordinator Sarah Al-Benna
PYP Coordinator Faida Röhner
Languages English
T: +49 6221 75 90 600
W: www.hischool.de

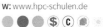

Heidelberg Private School Centre (Heidelberger Privatschulcentrum)
Kurfürsten-Anlage 64-68, 69115 Heidelberg, Baden-Württemberg
DP Coordinator Constantin Metzger
MYP Coordinator Ervin Dauti
PYP Coordinator Roselyn Rowland-Heger
Languages English
T: +49 62 2170504 038
W: www.hpc-schulen.de

Helene-Lange-Gymnasium
Bogenstr 32, 20144 Hamburg
DP Coordinator Maike Fruehling
Languages English
T: +49 40 428 9810
W: www.hlg-hamburg.de

Helmholtz-Gymnasium Bonn
Helmholtzstr. 18, 53225 Bonn, North Rhine-Westphalia
DP Coordinator Brigitte Lauth
Languages English
T: +49 228 777250
W: www.helmholtz-bonn.de

Hermann-Böse-Gymnasium
Hermann-Böse-Straße 1-9, 28209 Bremen
DP Coordinator Till Stollmann
Languages English
T: +49 421 361 6272
W: www.hbg.schule.bremen.de

Hittorf-Gymnasium
Kemnastrasse 38, 45657 Recklinghausen, North Rhine-Westphalia
DP Coordinator Sandra Schmidt
Languages English, German
W: www.hittorf-gymnasium.de

IBSM - International Bilingual School Munich gGmbH
Lerchenauerstrasse 197, 80935 Munich, Bavaria
PYP Coordinator Susanne Green
Languages English, German
T: +49 89 41 11 49 550
W: www.ibsm-school.eu

International Gymnasium Geithain
Friedrich-Fröbel-Strasse 1, 04643 Geithain, Saxony
DP Coordinator Nabil Daaloul
Languages English
T: +49 34 34146 012
W: internationales-wirtschaftsgymnasium-geithain.de

International Gymnasium Reinsdorf
Mittlerer Schulweg 13, 08141 Reinsdorf, Saxony
DP Coordinator Silvia Núñez Velázquez
Languages English, Spanish
T: +49 37 5212 595
W: internationales-gymnasium-reinsdorf.de

International Kids Campus GmbH
Lerchenauerstrasse 197, 80935 Munich, Bavaria
PYP Coordinator Susanne Green
Languages English, German
T: +49 89 411149 550
W: www.theikc.com

GERMANY

International School Augsburg (ISA)
Wernher-von-Braun-Strasse 1a, 86368 Gersthofen, Bavaria
DP Coordinator Richard Tyler
PYP Coordinator Ashlee Krantz
Languages English
T: +49 821 45 55 60 0
W: www.isa-augsburg.com

International School Braunschweig-Wolfsburg
Helmstedter Strasse 37, 38126 Braunschweig, Lower Saxony
DP Coordinator Nicholas Schulte
Languages English
T: +49 531 889210-0
W: www.cjd-braunschweig.de

 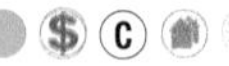

International School Campus
Eggerstedter Weg 19, 25421 Pinneberg, Schleswig-Holstein
DP Coordinator Elizabeth Schoeler
Languages English, German
T: +49 (0)41 01 80 503 00
W: www.isceducation.de

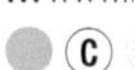 

International School Hannover Region
Bruchmeisterallee 6, 30169 Hannover, Lower Saxony
DP Coordinator Naomi Resmer
MYP Coordinator Hanno Becker
PYP Coordinator Jennifer Lee
Languages English
T: +49 511 270 416 50
W: www.is-hr.de

International School Mainfranken e.V.
Kalifornienstrasse 1, 97424 Schweinfurt, Bavaria
DP Coordinator Matthew Sullivan
MYP Coordinator Joe Gasses
PYP Coordinator Jessica Werner
Languages English
T: +49 9721 53861-80
W: www.the-ism.de

International School of Bremen
Badgasteiner Strasse 11, 28359 Bremen
DP Coordinator Kim Walton
Languages English
T: +49 421 5157790
W: www.isbremen.de

International School of Düsseldorf e.V.
Niederrheinstrasse 323/336, 40489 Düsseldorf, North Rhine-Westphalia
DP Coordinator Clinton Olson
MYP Coordinator Laura Maly-Schmidt
PYP Coordinator Christopher Coker
Languages English
T: +49 (0) 211-9406 6
W: www.isdedu.de

 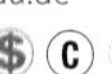

International School of Hamburg
Hemmingstedter Weg 130, 22609 Hamburg
CP Coordinator Michael Kent
DP Coordinator James Edward Dalton
MYP Coordinator Jackie Van der Steege
Languages English
T: +49 (0)40 8000 500
W: www.ishamburg.org

International School of Neustadt
Haardterstrasse 1, 67433 Neustadt an der Weinstrasse
DP Coordinator Jacques Marais
Languages English
T: +49 6321 8900 960
W: www.is-neustadt.de

International School of Stuttgart, Degerloch Campus
Sigmaringestrasse 257, 70597 Stuttgart, Baden-Württemberg
DP Coordinator Jennifer Paddock
MYP Coordinator Lucy Whitfield
PYP Coordinator Ayten Korkmaz
Languages English
T: +49 71 17696 000
W: www.issev.de

  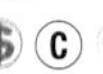

International School of Stuttgart, Sindelfingen Campus
Hallenserstrasse 2, 71065 Sindelfingen, Baden-Württemberg
MYP Coordinator Rebecca Jones-Buerk
PYP Coordinator Leandre Pedlow
Languages English
T: +49 70 316859 780
W: www.issev.de

International School of Ulm/Neu Ulm
Schwabenstraße 25, 89231 Neu-Ulm, Bavaria
DP Coordinator Richard Tomes
PYP Coordinator Charlotte Balsom
Languages English
T: +49 731 379 353-0
W: www.is-ulm.de

International School Ruhr
Moltkeplatz 1 + 61, 45138 Essen, North Rhine-Westphalia
DP Coordinator Joseph Ticar
PYP Coordinator Soha Saad
Languages English
T: +49 (0)201 479 104 09
W: www.is-ruhr.de

Internationale Friedensschule Koln
Neue Sandkaul 29, 50859 Cologne, North Rhine-Westphalia
DP Coordinator Edward Parker
PYP Coordinator Leonie Julien
Languages English, German
T: +49 221 310 6340
W: www.if-koeln.de

ISF International School Frankfurt Rhein-Main
Strasse zur Internationalen Schule 33, 65931 Frankfurt, Hesse
DP Coordinator Dirk Lehmann
Languages English
T: +49 69 954319 710
W: www.isf.sabis.net

ISR International School on the Rhine - NRW
Konrad-Adenauer-Ring 2, 41464 Neuss, North Rhine-Westphalia
DP Coordinator Emil Cete
Languages English
T: +49 2131 40388-0, -11
W: www.isr-school.de

Leibniz Gymnasium Dortmund
Kreuzstrasse 163, 44137 Dortmund, North Rhine-Westphalia
DP Coordinator Martin Tiaden
Languages English
T: +49 231 912 3660
W: www.leibniz-gym.de

Leibniz Privatschule Elmshorn
Ramskamp 64B, 25337 Elmshorn, Schleswig-Holstein
DP Coordinator Dr. Stefan Wester
Languages English, German
T: +49 41 212610 40
W: www.leibniz-privatschule.de

Leipzig International School
Könneritzstrasse 47, 04229 Leipzig, Saxony
DP Coordinator Isabel Van Dyck
Languages English
T: +49 34 139377 500
W: www.lis.school

Leonardo Da Vinci Campus
Zu den Luchbergen 13, 14641 Nauen, Brandenburg
DP Coordinator Anne Pritzlaff
Languages English, Spanish
T: +49 33 217487 820
W: www.ldvc.de

Lessing-Gymnasium
Heerstr 7, 51143 Cologne, North Rhine-Westphalia
DP Coordinator Silke Flüßhöh
Languages English
T: +49 2203 99201 66
W: www.lessing-gymnasium.eu

Metropolitan International School (MIS Viernheim)
Walter-Gropius-Allee 3, 68519 Viernheim, Hesse
DP Coordinator Hadi Bou Hassan
Languages English, German
T: +49 6204 7087 796
W: metroschool.de/en

Metropolitan School Frankfurt
Eschborner Landstrasse 134-142, 60489 Frankfurt, Hesse
DP Coordinator Katell Dodd
PYP Coordinator Natalie Murray
Languages English
T: +49 69 96 86 405-0
W: www.m-school.de

Munich International School e.V.
Schloss Buchhof, Percha, 82319 Starnberg, Bavaria
DP Coordinator Doris Herwig
MYP Coordinator Angela Brassington
PYP Coordinator Armin Martin
Languages English
T: +49 8151 366 0
W: www.mis-munich.de

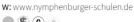

Nelson Mandela State International School Berlin
Pfalzburgerstrasse 30, 10717 Berlin
DP Coordinator Charles Spiller
Languages English
T: +49 (0)30 902928 01
W: www.nelson-mandela-school.net

Nymphenburger Schulen
Sadelerstrasse 10, 80638 Munich, Bavaria
DP Coordinator Susanna Seibert
Languages English
T: +49 89 159 120
W: www.nymphenburger-schulen.de

Phorms Campus Munich
Maria-Theresia-Straße 35, 81675 Munich, Bavaria
DP Coordinator Marc Nevin
Languages English
T: +49 89 324 9337 00
W: www.muenchen.phorms.de

Sächsisches Landesgymnasium Sankt Afra zu Meissen
Freiheit 13, 01662 Meissen, Saxony
DP Coordinator Fabian Habsch
Languages German, English
T: +49 3521 456 0
W: www.sankt-afra.de

Schillerschule Hannover
Ebellstrasse 15, 30625 Hannover, Lower Saxony
DP Coordinator Bernd Flügge
Languages English
T: +49 511 16848777
W: www.schillerschule-hannover.de

Schule Schloss Salem
Schlossbezirk 1, 88682 Salem, Baden-Württemberg
DP Coordinator Constanze Schummer
Languages English, German
T: +49 7553 919 352
W: www.schule-schloss-salem.de

SIS Swiss International School Berlin
Heerstrasse 465, (school entrance at Reimerweg 11), 13593 Berlin
DP Coordinator María Lluïsa Codina
Languages English
T: +49 30 36 43 98 20
W: www.swissinternationalschool.de/standorte/berlin

SIS Swiss International School Friedrichshafen
Fallenbrunnen 1, 88045 Friedrichshafen, Baden-Württemberg
DP Coordinator Kristine Kordic
Languages English
T: +49 7541 954 37 0
W: www.swissinternationalschool.de/standorte/friedrichshafen

SIS Swiss International School Ingolstadt
Stinnesstrasse 1, 85057 Ingolstadt, Bavaria
DP Coordinator Juan Viacava
Languages English, German
T: +49 841 981 446 0
W: www.swissinternationalschool.de/standorte/ingolstadt

SIS Swiss International School Regensburg
Klosterackerweg 1, 93049 Regensburg, Bavaria
DP Coordinator Julia Gruber
Languages English, German
T: +49 941 9925 930 0
W: www.swissinternationalschool.de/standorte/regensburg

SIS Swiss International School Stuttgart-Fellbach
Schmidener Weg 7/1, 70736 Stuttgart-Fellbach, Baden-Württemberg
DP Coordinator Rachael Mayfield
Languages English, German
T: +49 711 469 194 10
W: www.swissinternationalschool.de/standorte/stuttgart-fellbach

St Leonhard Gymnasium
Jesuitenstrasse 9, 52062 Aachen, North Rhine-Westphalia
DP Coordinator Sonja Rustemeyer
Languages English
T: +49 (0) 241 41 31 98 0
W: www.leoac.de

 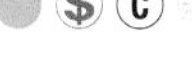

St. George's The British International School Cologne
Husarenstrasse 20, 50997 Cologne, North Rhine-Westphalia
CP Coordinator Elizabeth Marshall
DP Coordinator Stephen Ryan
Languages English
T: +49 2233 808 870
W: www.stgeorgesschool.com/cologne

St. George's The British International School Munich
Heidemannstrasse 182, 80939 Munich, Bavaria
CP Coordinator Jo Ramsay
DP Coordinator Jamie Gosling
Languages English
T: +49 8972 469 330
W: www.stgeorgesschool.com/munich

  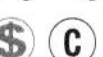

St. George's The British International School, Düsseldorf Rhein-Ruhr
Am Neuen Angerbach 90, 47259 Duisburg, North Rhine-Westphalia
CP Coordinator Eamonn Traynor
DP Coordinator Vincent Keat
Languages English
T: +49 203 456 860
W: www.stgeorgesschool.com

Staedtisches Gymnasium Olpe
Seminarstrasse 1, 57462 Olpe, North Rhine-Westphalia
DP Coordinator Stephan Seidel
Languages English, German
T: +49 276196 500
W: www.gymnasium-olpe.de

State International School Seeheim-Jugenheim
Schuldorf Bergstrasse, Kooperative Gesamtschule, Sandstrasse, 64342 Seeheim-Jugenheim, Hesse
DP Coordinator Wolfgang Scheuerpflug
Languages English, German
T: +49 6257 9703 0
W: www.schuldorf.de

STIFTUNG LOUISENLUND
Louisenlund 9, 24357 Güby, Schleswig-Holstein
DP Coordinator Petra Hau
MYP Coordinator Petra Hau
Languages English
T: +49 (0)4354 999 333
E: admission@louisenlund.de
W: www.louisenlund.de/en

See full details on page 220

 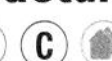 

Strothoff International School Rhein-Main Campus Dreieich
Frankfurterstrasse 160-166, 63303 Dreieich, Hesse
DP Coordinator Christine Lipsey
MYP Coordinator Lynn Bilbrey
PYP Coordinator Steve Snell
Languages English
T: +49 6103 8022 500
W: www.strothoff-international-school.de

 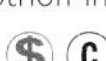 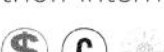

Theodor-Heuss-Gymnasium
Freyastrasse 10, 67059 Ludwigshafen, Rhineland-Palatinate
DP Coordinator Martina Thiel
Languages English
T: +45 621 504 431 710
W: www.thg-lu.de

Thuringia International School - Weimar
Belvederer Allee 40, 99425 Weimar, Thuringia
DP Coordinator John Campbell
MYP Coordinator Aimee Tolentino
PYP Coordinator Alison Carl
Languages English
T: +49 (0)3643 776904
W: www.this-weimar.com

UWC Robert Bosch College
Kartäuserstrasse 119, 79104 Freiburg, Baden-Württemberg
DP Coordinator Carina Petruch
Languages English
T: +49 761 708 395 00
W: www.uwcrobertboschcollege.de

Werner-Heisenberg-Gymnasium
Werner-Heisenberg-Strasse 1, 51381 Leverkusen, North Rhine-Westphalia
DP Coordinator Beate Keil
Languages English
T: +49 2171 70670
W: www.whg-gp.de

GHANA

Al-Rayan International School
P.O. Box AC-84, Accra
CP Coordinator Farah Abdul Wahab
DP Coordinator Dorinda Tham
MYP Coordinator Alpana Mukherjee
PYP Coordinator Rouba Abi Saab
Languages English, French
T: +233 54 189 7254
W: www.aris.edu.gh

Association International School
6 Patrice Lumumba Road, Airport Residential Area, Accra
DP Coordinator Ishmael Twum Odoom
MYP Coordinator Jacqueline Samms-Borteye
PYP Coordinator Vincentia Kpodo
Languages English, French
T: +233 30 277 7735
W: associationinternationalschool.org

Aves International Academy
VRA Road Community 25, Tema
DP Coordinator Julian Kitching
Languages English
T: +233 26 615 3097
W: www.avesacademy.com

Cornerstone International Academy
No. 2 Harare Street, Off Mensah Wood Avenue, East Legon, Accra
PYP Coordinator William Gyamfi
Languages English, French
T: +233 26 505 5439
W: www.cia.edu.gh

Datus International School
P.O. Box 8001, Fraiser Street, Tema
PYP Coordinator Johnson Abayi
Languages English

Delhi Private School (DPS) International Ghana
Community 25, Tema
DP Coordinator Nathaniel Dumashie
Languages English
T: +233 55 662 0540
W: www.dpsghana.edu.gh

Healthy-Mind International School
P.O. Box GP2066, Boundary Road, Madina, Accra
PYP Coordinator Alipt Sanam Hari
Languages English, French
T: +233 55 139 9944
W: healthymindschool.net

International School of Accra
Borstal Avenue, Accra
DP Coordinator Benjamin Yeboah
Languages English
T: +233 24 258 6062
W: isaghana.com

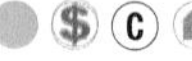

Learning Skills International School
Adjiringanor Campus, Near Buildaf Estates, Accra
PYP Coordinator Henrietta Love Commey
Languages English
T: +233 54 688 4146
W: lsis.edu.gh

Lincoln Community School
#126/21 Reindolf Road, Abelemkpe, Accra
DP Coordinator Michael Foxmann
MYP Coordinator Amber Rhinehart
PYP Coordinator Natalie Wilhelm
Languages English
T: +233 30 221 8100
W: www.lincoln.edu.gh

Morgan International Community School
Gomoa Manso, Agona Swedru
DP Coordinator Bright Andoh
Languages English
T: +233 20 641 2859
W: www.mics.edu.gh

SOS-Hermann Gmeiner International College
Private Mail Bag, Community 6, Tema
DP Coordinator Ayeshat Addison

MYP Coordinator Jonathan Amengor
Languages English
T: +233 30 320 2907
W: www.soshgic.edu.gh

Tema International School
P.O. Box CO864, Off Tema-Akosombo Road (Opposite Afariwaa Farms), Tema
DP Coordinator Benjamin Darko
MYP Coordinator Yvonne Tagoe
PYP Coordinator Jacob Lumumba
Languages English
T: +233 30 330 5134
W: www.tis.edu.gh

GREECE

American Community Schools of Athens
129 Aghias Paraskevis Str., Halandri, 152 34 Athens
DP Coordinator Mark McGowan
Languages English
T: +30 210 639 3200
W: www.acs.gr

Anatolia High School
PO Box 21021, 60 John Kennedy Avenue, 555 35 Pylea
DP Coordinator Anna Billi Petmeza
MYP Coordinator Elsa Exidaveloni
Languages English (Iβdp), Greek (myp)
T: +30 2310 398 200
W: www.anatolia.edu.gr/highschool

Campion School Athens
PO Box 674 84, Pallini 153 02
DP Coordinator Kate Varey
Languages English
T: +30 210 607 1700
W: www.campion.edu.gr

Costeas-Geitonas School
Pallini - Attikis, Athens 15351
DP Coordinator Venia Papaspyrou
MYP Coordinator Evgenia Matsota
PYP Coordinator Stacey Michalopoulos
Languages English
T: +30 210 6030 411
W: www.cgs.gr

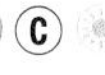

Doukas School SA
151 Mesogion Street, 15125 Paradissos, Marousi, Athens 15125
DP Coordinator Evangelos Papadopoulos
Languages English
T: +30 210 618 6000
W: www.doukas.gr

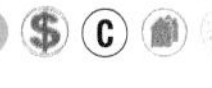

European Interactive School (DES)
Barakos Hill, Ribas 19400
PYP Coordinator Paraskevi Barmpoutsi
Languages English, Greek
T: +30 210 8974143
W: dimotiko.deschool.eu

Geitonas School
PO Box 74128, Sternizes, Koropi, Attiki 166 02
DP Coordinator Ilias Liakatas
Languages English
T: +30 210 9656200-10
W: www.geitonas-school.gr

HAEF, Athens College
15 Stephanou Delta Street, Psychico, Athens 15452
MYP Coordinator Tania Gaitani
PYP Coordinator Eleftheria Kamperi
Languages English, Greek
T: +30 2106798100
W: www.athenscollege.edu.gr

HAEF, John M. Carras Kindergarten
15 Stephanou Delta Street, Psychico, Athens 15452
PYP Coordinator Zoe Lousidou
Languages English, Greek
T: +30 2106798100
W: www.athenscollege.edu.gr

HAEF, Psychico College
15 Stephanou Delta Street, Psychico, Athens 15452
DP Coordinator Antonios Apostolou
MYP Coordinator Panagiota Priovolou
PYP Coordinator Panagiotis Dedes
Languages English, Greek
T: +30 2106798100
W: www.athenscollege.edu.gr

International School of Athens
PO Box 51051, Kifissia, Athens 14510
DP Coordinator Kalliope Pateras
MYP Coordinator Constantina Venieris
PYP Coordinator Athanasia Savvas
Languages English
T: +30 210 6233 888
W: www.isa.edu.gr

International School of Piraeus
66-70 Praxitelous street, Piraeus 18532
PYP Coordinator Antonia Daponti
Languages English
T: +30 210 417 5580
W: www.isp.edu.gr

Ionios School
PO Box 13622, Filothei 15202
DP Coordinator Stella Antonellou
Languages English
T: +30 210 6857130
W: www.ionios.gr

Lampiri Schools
Metamorphosis 155 and Ilissou, Moschato, Athens
DP Coordinator Neveen Zaki Shenouda
Languages English
T: +30 210 9480530
W: www.lampiri-schools.gr

Moraitis School
A Papanastasiou & Ag Dimitriou, Paleo Psychico, Athens 15452
DP Coordinator George Kartalis
Languages English
T: +30 210 679 5000
W: www.moraitis.edu.gr

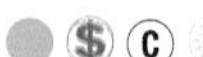

PIERCE - THE AMERICAN COLLEGE OF GREECE
6 Gravias Street, Aghia Paraskevi, Athens 153 42
DP Coordinator Dr. Emmanuel Vrontakis
Languages English, Greek
T: +30 210 600 9800 (EXT:1060)
E: pierceibsecretariats@acg.edu
W: www.pierce.gr
See full details on page 180

Pinewood - American International School of Thessaloniki, Greece
14th km Thessalonikis - N. Moudanion, P.O. Box 60606, Thermi - Thessaloniki GR-57001
DP Coordinator Dimitrios Terzidis
Languages English
T: +30 2310 301 221
W: www.pinewood.gr

Platon School
Eleytheriou Venizelou Street, Glyka Nera, Attika 15354
DP Coordinator Miltiadis-Spyridon Kitsos
MYP Coordinator Maria Tsangari
PYP Coordinator Stelios Stilianidis
Languages English, German, Greek
T: +30 210 6611 793
W: www.platon.gr

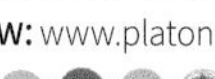

St Catherine's British School
Leoforos Venizelou 77, Lykovrissi, Athens 141 23
DP Coordinator Lauri-Ann Robertson
Languages English
T: +30 210 2829 750
W: www.stcatherines.gr

HUNGARY

American International School of Budapest
Nagykovácsi út 12, Nagykovácsi 2094
DP Coordinator Raymond Lewis
Languages English
T: +36 26 556 000
W: www.aisb.hu

BME International Secondary School
Egry Jozsef utca 3-11, Budapest 1111
DP Coordinator Tibor Zahony
Languages English
T: +36 12094983
W: www.bmegimnazium.hu

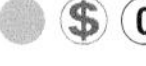

Budapest British International School
4 Zsolna utca, Budapest 1125
DP Coordinator Penelope Clements
MYP Coordinator Neil Best
Languages English
T: +36 70 425 5225
W: www.bbis.hu

International School of Budapest
Konkoly Thege M u 21, Budapest 1121
DP Coordinator Angela Milne-Kiss
Languages English
T: +36 1 395 6543
W: www.isb.hu

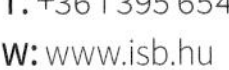

International School of Debrecen (ISD)
Heltai Gáspár Street 1, 4002 Debrecen
DP Coordinator Loránd Zajta
MYP Coordinator Loránd Zajta
PYP Coordinator Rosie Fawcett
Languages English, Hungarian
T: +36 20 404 4822
W: isd.debrecen.hu

Karinthy Frigyes Gimnázium
Thököly utca 7, Budapest 1183
DP Coordinator Attila Salamon
Languages English
T: +36 1 291 2072
W: www.karinthy.hu

Korösi Csoma Sándor Két Tanítási Nyelvu Baptista Gimnázium
Szentendrei út 83, Budapest 1033
DP Coordinator Márta Korosi
Languages English
T: +36 1 250 17 44
W: korosi.hu

SEK Budapest International School
Hüvösvölgyi út 131, Budapest 1021
DP Coordinator Katalin Vidra
Languages English
T: +36 1 394 2968
W: budapest.iesedu.com

The British International School
Kiscelli Köz 17, Budapest 1037
DP Coordinator Ashley Phillipson
Languages English
T: +36 1 200 9971
W: www.bisb.hu

Tóth Árpád Gimnázium
Szombathi István utca 12., Debrecen 4024
DP Coordinator Ibolya Kovácsné Ilyés
Languages English
T: +36 52 411 225
W: www.tagdebr.sulinet.hu

ICELAND

International School of Iceland
órsmörk vi Ægisgrund, 210 Gar abær
MYP Coordinator Rachael Glasser
Languages English, Icelandic
T: +354 594 3100
W: www.internationalschool.is

Menntaskolinn vid Hamrahlid
Hamrahlí 10, 105 Reykjavik
DP Coordinator Gu mundur Arnlaugsson
Languages English
T: +354 595 5200
W: www.mh.is

IRAN

German Embassy School Tehran (DBST)
Shariati, under the Sadr Bridge, Shahid Keshani Street (Mahale Darbdowom), Tehran
PYP Coordinator Mandana Rashidi
Languages English
T: +98 212 260 4902
W: www.dbst.ir

Mehr-e-Taban International School
Ghasredasht Avenue, Shiraz
DP Coordinator Zahra Shabani nia
MYP Coordinator Mariam Pakshir
PYP Coordinator Leila Mojarad
Languages English
T: +98 713 635 9983
W: www.mehrschool.com

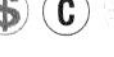

Shahid Mahdavi Educational Foundation
Kouh-Daman, Mina, Zanbagh, Ejazi, Zafaranie Street, Tehran
DP Coordinator Nasrin Barootchi
MYP Coordinator Gita Nafar
PYP Coordinator Gita Nafar
Languages English, Persian
T: +98 212 243 5550 (EXT:190)
W: www.mahdavischool.org

Soodeh Educational Complex
End of Arabshahi Avenue, Ashrafi Isfahani Highway, Tehran
MYP Coordinator Atefeh Khanjari
Languages English
T: +98 214 424 9702-4
W: www.soodeh.com/?lang=en-US

Tehran International School
Dadman Street, Farahzadi Boulevard, Shahrak Quds, Tehran
DP Coordinator Nasrin Barootchi
Languages English
T: +98 218 808 8445-8
W: www2.tissch.ir

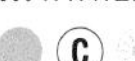

IRAQ

Cedars Interdisciplinary School
Baharka's Road, next to the Lebanese Village, Erbil
PYP Coordinator Wathiq Ali
Languages English
T: +964 750 591 9000
W: www.cedarsschool.com

Da Vinci School International
Maf Street, Malta Sari Qr., Zone 99450, Duhok, Kurdistan 42001
DP Coordinator Zahra Khaled
MYP Coordinator Rahal Kahdar
PYP Coordinator Catharina Bianca de Villiers
Languages English
T: +964 750 757 4111
W: school.leodv.com

Deutsche Schule Erbil
Postfach 67, Post Office Newroz, 100-Meter-Street, Erbil, Kurdistan
DP Coordinator Parthena Papadopoulou
Languages German
T: +964 750 335 9848
W: www.dserbil.net

Global United School
Al-Masafi Intersection, First Branch On The Right, Behind Al-Hayat Mall, Before Dijlah College, Al-Doura +, Baghdad
PYP Coordinator Ghada Sahab
Languages English
T: +964 782 714 9199
W: gus.iq

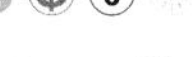

International College University School (ICUS) Baghdad
ICUS Road, Baghdad
PYP Coordinator Dua Alqazaz
Languages English
T: +964 773 222 1115
W: www.icusic-baghdad.com

International Maarif Schools Erbil
P.O. Box No. 43/0383, Mardin District, 120m Street, Opposite to Toreq Village, Erbil, Kurdistan
DP Coordinator Thomas Hibbers
MYP Coordinator Thomas Hibbers
PYP Coordinator Inji Shukur
Languages Arabic, English, Kurdish, Turkish
T: +964 751 741 7879
W: maarifschools.edu.krd

Mar Qardakh School
P.O. Box 34, Mar Qardakh Street, Ankawa, Erbil, Kurdistan 1065
MYP Coordinator Bianca De Leon
PYP Coordinator Tara Shaoul
Languages English
T: +964 750 144 5021
W: www.marqardakh.com

IRELAND

International School of Dublin
Synge Street, Dublin D08 PW64
PYP Coordinator Nana Isa
Languages English, Spanish
T: +353 087 329 1417
W: www.internationalschooldublin.ie

NORD ANGLIA INTERNATIONAL SCHOOL DUBLIN
South County Business Park, Leopardstown, Dublin 18
DP Coordinator Joanna Cooper
MYP Coordinator Andrew Bateson
PYP Coordinator Jack Odey
Languages English
T: +353 1 5442323
E: admissions@naisdublin.com
W: www.naisdublin.com

See full details on page 174

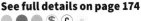

IRELAND

SEK INTERNATIONAL SCHOOL DUBLIN
Belvedere Hall, Windgates, Greystones, Co. Wicklow A63 EY23
DP Coordinator Laura Sánchez
MYP Coordinator Laura Sánchez
Languages English
T: +35 31 287 41 75
E: admissions-dublin@sek.ie
W: dublin.sek.es
See full details on page 200

ST ANDREW'S COLLEGE
Booterstown Avenue, Blackrock, County Dublin A94 XN72
DP Coordinator Mr William Hehir
Languages English
T: +353 1 288 2785
E: information@st-andrews.ie
W: www.sac.ie
See full details on page 207

VILLIERS SCHOOL
North Circular Road, Limerick V94 F983
DP Coordinator Shane Hanna
Languages English
T: +353 61 451447
E: admissions@villiers-school.com
W: www.villiers-school.com
See full details on page 236

ISRAEL

Anglican International School Jerusalem
82 Rechov Hanevi'im, 91001 Jerusalem
DP Coordinator Robin Press
MYP Coordinator Meira Yan
Languages English
T: +972 2 567 7200
W: www.aisj.co.il

EASTERN MEDITERRANEAN INTERNATIONAL SCHOOL
Hakfar Hayarok, Ramat Hasharon 4870000
DP Coordinator Hannah Wenger
Languages English
T: +972 03 673 0232
E: admissions@em-is.org
W: www.em-is.org
See full details on page 78

Givat Haviva International School
Mobile Post, 3785000 Menashe
DP Coordinator Hannah Wilpon
Languages English
T: +972 4 630 9240
W: www.gh-is.org

King Solomon School
HaKfar HaYarok, 47100 Ramat Hasharon
DP Coordinator Greg John
Languages English, Hebrew
T: +972 73 234 2030
W: www.kingsolomonschool.org

La Salle Beit Hanina
P.O. Box 60076, 24 Taha Hussein, Beit Hanina, 9160102 Jerusalem
DP Coordinator Rania Kadamani
Languages English, Arabic
T: +972 2 585 5764
W: www.ls-bh.org

The Mae Boyar High School
P.O. Box 16252, 1 Torah Ve'Avoda, 9116201 Jerusalem
DP Coordinator Shachar Yanai
Languages English, Hebrew
T: +972 2 642 2696
W: www.mbhs-international.org

ITALY

Ambrit International School
Via F Tajani 50, 00149 Rome
MYP Coordinator Susan Kammerer
PYP Coordinator Kathryn Ramsay
Languages English
T: +39 06 5595 305/301
W: www.ambrit-rome.com

AMERICAN OVERSEAS SCHOOL OF ROME
Via Cassia 811, 00189 Rome
DP Coordinator Christopher Brown
Languages English
T: +39 06 334 381
E: admissions@aosr.org
W: www.aosr.org/admissions
See full details on page 55

AMERICAN SCHOOL OF MILAN
Via K. Marx, 14, 20073 Noverasco di Opera (MI)
DP Coordinator Chris Briner
Languages English
T: +39 02 5300 001
E: admissions@asmilan.org
W: www.asmilan.org
See full details on page 56

Andersen International School
Via Don Carlo, San Martino 8, 20133 Milan
DP Coordinator Johanna Frances Oddie
Languages English, Italian
T: +39 02 7000 6580
W: andersenschool.it

Bilingual European School
Via Val Cismon 9, 20162 Milan
PYP Coordinator Aaron Downey
Languages English, Italian
T: +39 02 6611 7449
W: www.beschool.eu

Canadian School of Milan
Via M. Gioia 42, 20124 Milano
DP Coordinator Elena Cipullo
MYP Coordinator Elena Cipullo
Languages English
T: +39 02 67074775
W: www.canadianschool.it

COLLEGIO SAN CARLO
Corso Magenta 71, 20123 Milan
DP Coordinator Anne Hallihan
Languages English, Italian
T: +39 02 43 06 31
E: admission@collegiosancarlo.it
W: www.collegiosancarlo.it
See full details on page 73

Deledda International School
Corso Mentana 27, 16128 Genoa
DP Coordinator Elizabeth Coykendall Rice
MYP Coordinator Chiara Colucci
Languages English
T: +39 010 5536268
W: www.genoaschool.eu

GIS The International School of Monza srl
Via Federico Confalonieri 18, 20900 Monza (MB)
PYP Coordinator Jane Whittle
Languages English, Italian
T: +39 039 2287034
W: www.gisschoolmonza.it

Gonzaga International School
Via Piersanti Mattarella 38/42, 90141 Palermo
DP Coordinator Lorenzo Vantaggiato
MYP Coordinator Nina James
PYP Coordinator Emma Wagland
Languages English, Italian
T: +39 91 302093
W: www.gonzagaisp.it

H-FARM INTERNATIONAL SCHOOL
Via Olivetti 1, 31056 Roncade (TV)
DP Coordinator Ms. Sara Casagrande
MYP Coordinator Ms. Alba Manso
PYP Coordinator Ms. Iliana Gutierrez
Languages English
T: +39 0422 789503
E: info.ve@h-is.com
W: www.h-farm.com/en/h-farm-school/venezia
See full details on page 102

H-International School Vicenza
Borgo Santa Lucia, 51 Vicenza, 36100 Vicenza
DP Coordinator David Coppard
MYP Coordinator Lorenzo Caviglia
PYP Coordinator Lisa Cooney
Languages English
T: +39 444 54 50 07
W: www.h-is.com/en/schools/vicenza

ICS MILAN
ICS Symbiosis, Viale Ortles, 46, 20139 Milano (MI)
DP Coordinator Patricia Cristina Radoi-litani
MYP Coordinator Angela Milne
Languages English, Italian
T: +39 02 36592694
E: admissions@icsmilan.com
W: www.icsmilan.com
See full details on page 108

INSTITUT INTERNATIONAL SAINT-DOMINIQUE
Via Igino Lega 5, 00189 Rome
DP Coordinator Nadine Hakme
Languages English, French
T: +39 06 303 10817
E: info@institutsaintdominique.it
W: www.institutsaintdominique.it
See full details on page 112

INTERNATIONAL SCHOOL BRESCIA
Via Benaco 34/B, Bedizzole, 25080 Brescia
DP Coordinator Mr Sebastiaan Van den Bergh
MYP Coordinator Mr Ethan Taomae
PYP Coordinator Mr Michael Lawson
Languages English
T: +39 030 2191182
E: info@isbrescia.com
W: www.isbrescia.com
See full details on page 120

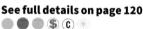

INTERNATIONAL SCHOOL OF BERGAMO
Via Monte Gleno, 54, 24125 Bergamo
DP Coordinator Roberta Sana
MYP Coordinator Russell Wilson
PYP Coordinator Helen Bird
Languages English, Italian
T: +39 035 213776
E: info@isbergamo.com
W: www.isbergamo.com
See full details on page 123

International School of Bologna
Via della Libertà 2, 40123 Bologna
DP Coordinator Ms. Nazanin Nikanjam
MYP Coordinator Ms. Helen Exler
PYP Coordinator Ms. Rachel Burgess
Languages English
T: +39 051 6449954
W: www.isbologna.com

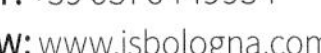  

INTERNATIONAL SCHOOL OF COMO
Via Adda 25, 22073 Fino Mornasco (CO)
DP Coordinator Adele Evans
MYP Coordinator Ben Thompson
PYP Coordinator Wietse Hendriks
Languages English, Italian
T: +39 031 572289
E: info@iscomo.com
W: www.iscomo.com
See full details on page 125

International School of Florence
Via del Carota 23/25, Bagno a Ripoli, 50012 Florence
DP Coordinator Jason Blackstone
PYP Coordinator Nicky Shamash
Languages English, Italian
T: +39 055 6461 007
W: www.isfitaly.org

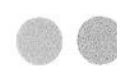 

INTERNATIONAL SCHOOL OF MILAN
Via I Maggio, 20, 20021 Baranzate (MI)
DP Coordinator Giuseppe Redaelli
MYP Coordinator Eglè Karmonaitè
PYP Coordinator Sara Lomas
Languages English
T: +39 02 872581
E: admissions@ismilan.it
W: www.internationalschoolofmilan.it
See full details on page 129

INTERNATIONAL SCHOOL OF MODENA
Piazza Montessori, 1/A, 41051 Montale Rangone (MO)
DP Coordinator Caroline Searle
MYP Coordinator Anna Chiara Forti
PYP Coordinator Michael Perry
Languages English
T: +39 059 530649
E: admissions@ismodena.it
W: www.internationalschoolofmodena.it
See full details on page 130

INTERNATIONAL SCHOOL OF MONZA
Via Solferino 23, 20900 Monza (MB)
DP Coordinator Michela Giovannini
MYP Coordinator Vicki Mole
PYP Coordinator Stacey Bennett
Languages English, Italian
T: +39 039 9357701
E: admin@ismonza.it
W: www.internationalschoolofmonza.it
See full details on page 132

International School of Rimini
Via Santa Chiara 40, 47921 Rimini RN 47921
PYP Coordinator Laura Crea
Languages English
T: +39 054 1786 129
W: www.isrimini.com

INTERNATIONAL SCHOOL OF SIENA
Via del Petriccio e Belriguardo, 49/1, 53100 Siena
DP Coordinator Jennifer Thomas
MYP Coordinator Leon Woods
PYP Coordinator Harnoop Bhogal
Languages English, Italian
T: +39 0577 328103
E: office@issiena.it
W: www.internationalschoolofsiena.it
See full details on page 134

INTERNATIONAL SCHOOL OF TURIN
Strada Pecetto 34, 10023 Chieri, Turin
DP Coordinator Clara Siviero
MYP Coordinator Francesca Parisi
PYP Coordinator Magdalena Matysow
Languages English
T: +39 011 645 967
E: info@isturin.it
W: www.isturin.it
See full details on page 136

International School of Verona
Aleardo Aleardi, Via Segantini 20, 37138 Verona
DP Coordinator Erik Johnstone
Languages English
T: +39 04557 8200
W: www.aleardi.it

Kinder College
Via Osservanza 88, 40136 Bologna BO
PYP Coordinator Francesca Guidi
Languages English, Italian
T: +39 051 581344
W: www.educationk.com

Lonati Anglo American School
Via Bormioli 60, 25135 Brescia
PYP Coordinator Melania Ferrari
Languages English
T: +39 03 02 35 73 60
W: www.laaslonati.org

MARYMOUNT INTERNATIONAL SCHOOL ROME
Via di Villa Lauchli, 180, 00191 Rome
DP Coordinator Ms. Clare Lax
Languages English
T: +39 06 3629 1012
E: admissions@marymountrome.com
W: www.marymountrome.com
See full details on page 169

O.M.C. - Collegio Vescovile Pio X
Borgo Cavour 40, 31100 Treviso
DP Coordinator Moreno Caronello
Languages English
T: +39 0422 411725
W: www.fondazionecollegiopiox.org

ROME INTERNATIONAL SCHOOL
Via Guglielmo Pecori Giraldi n.137, 00135 Rome
DP Coordinator Mrs Laela El Sheikh
PYP Coordinator Mr Martin Newell
Languages English
T: +39 06 8448 2651
E: info@romeinternationalschool.it
W: www.romeinternationalschool.it
See full details on page 189

 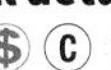

Smiling International School
Via Roversella 2, 44121 Ferrara
DP Coordinator Philip O'Gara
Languages English, Italian
T: +39 05 32209416
W: www.smilingservice.it

ST GEORGE'S BRITISH INTERNATIONAL SCHOOL, ROME
Via Cassia, km 16, La Storta, 00123 Rome
DP Coordinator Amber Haq
Languages English
T: +39 06 3086001
E: admissions@stgeorge.school.it
W: www.stgeorge.school.it
See full details on page 211

ST. LOUIS SCHOOL
SLS S.P.A., Via E. Caviglia, 1, 20139 Milan
DP Coordinator Hatty Rafferty
Languages English, Italian
T: +39 02 55231235
E: info@stlouisschool.com
W: www.stlouisschool.com
See full details on page 216

ST. STEPHEN'S SCHOOL
Via Aventina 3, 00153 Rome
DP Coordinator Nadia El-Taha
Languages English
T: +39 06 575 0605
E: ststephens@sssrome.it
W: www.sssrome.it
See full details on page 218

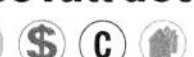

St. Thomas's International School
Via San Giovanni Decollato 1, 01100 Viterbo
PYP Coordinator Isaac Driver
Languages English, Italian
T: +39 0761 1767857
W: www.stthomass.com

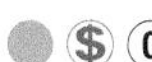

THE BRITISH SCHOOL OF MILAN (SIR JAMES HENDERSON)
Via Carlo Alberto Pisani Dossi, 16, 20134 Milan
DP Coordinator Miss Alba López Martín
Languages English
T: +39 02 210941
E: info@bsm.school
W: www.britishschoolmilan.com
See full details on page 228

The English International School of Padua
Via Forcellini 168, 35128 Padova
DP Coordinator Angela Lucca
Languages English
T: +39 049 80 22 503
W: www.eisp.it

The International School in Genoa
Via Romana Della Castagna 11A, 16148 Genova
DP Coordinator Mrs. Elizabeth Rosser Boiardi
Languages English
T: +39 010 386528
W: www.isgenoa.it

UWC ADRIATIC
Località Duino 29, 34011 Duino-Aurisina TS
DP Coordinator Joanne de Koning
Languages English
T: +39 040 3739111
E: uwcad@uwcad.it
W: www.uwcad.it
See full details on page 234

VITTORIA INTERNATIONAL SCHOOL
Via delle Rosine 14, 10123 Turin
DP Coordinator Deborah Gutowitz
Languages English
T: +39 011 889870
E: infovis@vittoriaweb.it
W: www.vittoriaweb.it
See full details on page 237

WORLD INTERNATIONAL SCHOOL OF TORINO
Via Traves 28, 10151 Torino
DP Coordinator Ms Barbara Battaglino
MYP Coordinator Ms Kristin Walter
PYP Coordinator Ms Victoria Corkhill
Languages English
T: +39 0111972111
E: info@worldinternationalschool.com
W: worldinternationalschool.com
See full details on page 242

YIES Your Italian English School
Via Monte Grappa 17, 20854 Vedano al Lambro (MB)
PYP Coordinator Gloria Kauffman
Languages English, Italian
T: +39 345 834 7521
W: www.yieschool.com

JORDAN

Ahliyyah & Mutran
13 Rifa'ah Al Tahtawi Street, Amman
CP Coordinator Eva Haddad
DP Coordinator Lana Zakarian
MYP Coordinator Abeer Sweiss
PYP Coordinator Rana Amarin
Languages English, Arabic
T: +962 6 222 1100
W: ahliyyahmutran.edu.jo

Amman Academy
P.O. Box 840, Khalda, Amman 11821
DP Coordinator Zaid Kawar
MYP Coordinator Sara Al Shami
PYP Coordinator Razan Fakhouri
Languages English, Arabic
T: +962 6 537 4444
W: www.ammanacademy.edu.jo

Amman Baccalaureate School
Al Hijaz Street, Dabouq, PO Box 441, Sweileh 11910, Amman
CP Coordinator Ms Jwan Kolaghassi
DP Coordinator Ms Jwan Kolaghassi
MYP Coordinator Ms Dina Katafago
PYP Coordinator Ms Nermeen Abu Assaf
Languages English, Arabic
T: +962 6 541 1191
W: www.abs.edu.jo

Amman Baptist School
P.O.Box 17033, Amman 11195
DP Coordinator Linda Kakish
Languages English, Arabic
T: +962 6 551 6907
W: www.baptist.edu.jo

Amman National School
P.O.Box 140565, Amman 11814
DP Coordinator Diana Dahleh
MYP Coordinator Samia Skafi
Languages English
T: +962 6 541 1067
W: www.ans.edu.jo

ASAMIAH INTERNATIONAL SCHOOL
Khalda - Taqi El-Din al-Sabki, Amman
DP Coordinator Ms. Yasmine Haddadin
MYP Coordinator Ms. Sima Barhoosh
PYP Coordinator Ms. Nour Maroun
Languages English, Arabic
T: +962 6 5335 301
E: info@ais.edu.jo
W: www.ais.edu.jo
See full details on page 58

British International Academy (BIA)
P.O. Box 829, Amman 11831
DP Coordinator Ali Khalayleh
MYP Coordinator Zina Bata
PYP Coordinator Hanan Hamam
Languages English, Arabic
T: +962 79 0222450
W: www.bia.edu.jo
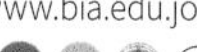

Cambridge High School
Al Rabia, Abdel Kareem, Al Dabbas Street, Amman 11185
DP Coordinator Nancy Khair
MYP Coordinator Shireen Bakri
Languages English, Arabic
T: +962 6 551 2556
W: www.cambridge.edu.jo

Canadian International School - Amman
20 Al Mikyal Street, Deir Ghbar, Amman
DP Coordinator Ruba Al Jariri
MYP Coordinator Salaam Samara
PYP Coordinator Nadia Hindi
Languages English
T: +962 6 593 9370
W: www.cis.edu.jo

Collège De La Salle Frères
Ar-Razi Street, Amman 11110
DP Coordinator Mohammad Alnatour
MYP Coordinator Rawan Al Madanat
Languages English, Arabic
T: +962 6 563 4555
W: www.lasallejordan.org

English Talents School
P.O.Box 18082, Amman 11195
DP Coordinator Norah Attari
MYP Coordinator Hanadi Hassan
PYP Coordinator Altaf Awad
Languages English
T: +962 6 537 0201
W: ets.edu.jo

IBN Rushd National Academy
P.O. Box 940397, Amman 11194
DP Coordinator Fouad Majdalawi
MYP Coordinator Fouad Majdalawi
PYP Coordinator Fouad Majdalawi
Languages English, Arabic
T: +962 79 896 1810
W: ibnrushd.edu.jo

Islamic Educational College
Al-Hakem An-Nisabouri Street, Amman
DP Coordinator Abeer Al Azzeh
Languages English, Arabic
T: +962 6 464 1331
W: iec.edu.jo
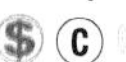

Jubilee Institute
P.O. Box 830578, Amman 11183
DP Coordinator Yara Kajo
Languages English
T: +962 6 523 8216
W: jubilee.edu.jo

Mashrek International School
P.O. Box 1412, Amman 11118
DP Coordinator Fadia Khoury
MYP Coordinator Reem Abuqutaish
PYP Coordinator Reema Kassem (Primary) Reem Samara (KG)
Languages Arabic, English
T: +962 79 957 7771
W: www.mashrek.edu.jo
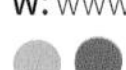   

Modern American School
P.O. Box 950553, Sweifieh, Amman 11195
DP Coordinator Suha Abdel Baqi
Languages English, Arabic
T: +962 6 586 2779
W: www.mas.edu.jo

MODERN MONTESSORI SCHOOL
P.O. Box 1941, Khilda, Amman 11821
DP Coordinator Hoor Hawamdeh
MYP Coordinator Reem Dahleh
PYP Coordinator Rasha Hamzeh
Languages English, Arabic
T: +962 6 553 5190
E: mms@montessori.edu.jo
W: www.mms.edu.jo
See full details on page 171

National Orthodox School Shmaisani
P.O. Box 941502, 5 Al-Hajjaj Al-Sahmi Street, Shmaisani, Amman 11194
DP Coordinator Alas Haddad
Languages Arabic, English
T: +962 6 560 8500
W: www.oes.org.jo

The International Academy - Amman
PO Box 144255, King Hussein Parks, Sa'eed Khair Street, Amman 11814
DP Coordinator Mariam Ellala
MYP Coordinator Zena Muhtaseb
Languages English
T: +962 6550 2055
W: www.iaa.edu.jo

The Little Academy
12 Al Iftikhar Street, Amman
PYP Coordinator Rula Daher
Languages English
T: +962 6 585 8282
W: www.tlacademy.edu.jo

KAZAKHSTAN

Astana Garden School
A. Bokeikhanov 34, Astana 010000
PYP Coordinator Alexandra Kuzmina
Languages English, Russian
T: +7 701 272 55 88
W: ags.edu.kz
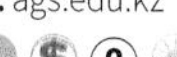

Haileybury Astana
Ivan Panfilov bldg. 4, Astana 010000
DP Coordinator Jessica Swann
Languages English
T: +7 717 255 98 55
W: www.haileybury.kz

International College of Continuous Education, Almaty
69A Zheltoksan Street, Almaty 480004
MYP Coordinator Natalya Semenova
PYP Coordinator Darina Aizharikova
Languages English, Russian
T: +7 727 279 97 36
W: www.icce-kazakhstan.kz

International College of Continuous Education, Astana

8/4 Tashenov Street, Astana 010000
MYP Coordinator Yelena Shebalina
PYP Coordinator Yelena Shebalina
Languages Russian, English
T: +7 717 242 55 54
W: www.icce-kazakhstan.kz

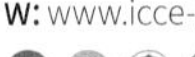 

International School of Almaty

40b Satpayev Street, Almaty 050057
MYP Coordinator Madina Bekturova
PYP Coordinator Yekaterina Pashukova
Languages Russian, English
T: +7 727 274 48 08
W: isoa.kz

International School of Astana
Turkistan Street 32/1, Astana 010000
DP Coordinator Miramgul Mashtakova
MYP Coordinator Roza Auyespayeva
PYP Coordinator Nazerke Kairbayeva
Languages English, Russian
T: +8 717 291 61 77
W: isa.nis.edu.kz

International Specialized Gymnasium 81 Astana English School
Ilyas Omarov street 14, Astana 010000
MYP Coordinator Guldana Nessipbayeva
Languages English, Kazakh
T: +8 717 225 90 40
W: 81aes.edu.kz

Kazakhstan International School
Al-Farabi Avenue 118/15, Almaty 050000
DP Coordinator William Fox
MYP Coordinator Clare Gibbings
PYP Coordinator Shivani McAinsh
Languages English
T: +7 727 356 50 00
W: www.kisnet.org

  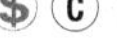

Lyceum School No. 66
33/1 Konaev Street, Astana 010000
PYP Coordinator Moldir Maqsutqyzy
Languages Russian, Kazakh
T: +7 717 250 18 55
W: ibschool66.edu.kz

Lyceum School No. 85
Kabanbai batyr Avenue 56/1, Astana 010017
MYP Coordinator Aliya Kozhabayeva
Languages Kazakh, Russian

Miras International School, Almaty
190 Al-Farabi Avenue, Almaty 050043
DP Coordinator Igor Guralnik
MYP Coordinator Aisulu Kurmanova
PYP Coordinator Elena Holina
Languages English, Kazakh, Russian
T: +7 727 227 69 42
W: www.miras.kz

Miras International School, Astana
Kuishi Dina Street 34, Astana 010009
DP Coordinator Nurlybek Tashev
MYP Coordinator Anjali Dobhal
PYP Coordinator Handan Yatgin
Languages English, Russian, Kazakh
T: +7 717 236 98 67
W: www.miras-astana.kz

Nazarbayev Intellectual School of Astana
Hussein Ben Talal Street 19, Astana 010000
DP Coordinator Azamat Mergenbayev
MYP Coordinator Gulden Issina
Languages English, Kazakh, Russian
T: +8 717 255 80 33
W: www.nisa.edu.kz

KENYA

Aga Khan Academy Mombasa
P.O. Box 80100-90066, Mbuyuni Road, Kizingo, Mombasa
DP Coordinator Julius Menzah
MYP Coordinator Johnson Monari
PYP Coordinator Titus Makunyi
Languages English, Swahili
T: +254 735 931 144
W: www.agakhanacademies.org/mombasa

Braeburn Garden Estate School
Garden Estate Road, Nairobi
CP Coordinator Mercy Gichuhi
DP Coordinator Rosie Bayerl
Languages English
T: +254 20 501 8000
W: gardenestate.braeburn.com

International School of Kenya
P.O. Box 14103, 00800 Nairobi
DP Coordinator Linda Henderson
Languages English
T: +254 202 091 308
W: www.isk.ac.ke

M-PESA Foundation Academy

P.O. Box 7954, 01000 Thika
CP Coordinator David Oloo
DP Coordinator Victor Ombuna
MYP Coordinator Julliet Kithinji
Languages English, Swahili
T: +254 703 200 000
W: www.mpesafoundationacademy.ac.ke

Nairobi Waldorf School
Miotoni Road, Karen, Nairobi
DP Coordinator Patrick Karanja
Languages English
T: +254 722 823 463
W: www.nairobiwaldorfschool.ac.ke

Naisula School
Off Nairobi-Namanga Road, Kajiado
DP Coordinator Simeon Muga
Languages English, Swahili
T: +254712 245 702
W: www.naisulaschool.ac.ke

St. Mary's School - Nairobi
P.O. Box 40580, 00100 Nairobi
DP Coordinator Lillian Nyakan Mageni
Languages English
T: +254 721 490 140
W: stmarys.ac.ke

THE AGA KHAN ACADEMY, NAIROBI
P.O. Box 44424-00100, 1st Parklands Avenue, off Limuru Road, Nairobi
DP Coordinator Mr. William Wanyonyi
MYP Coordinator Ms. Irene Simiyu
PYP Coordinator Ms. Dorcas Kisilu
Languages English
T: Junior: +254 0733 758 510, Senior: +254 736 380 101
E: infos@akesk.org; infoj@akesk.org
W: www.agakhanschools.org/kenya/akan/index

See full details on page 227

The Aga Khan Nursery School, Nairobi
PO Box 14998, Nairobi 00800
PYP Coordinator Nellie Thuku
Languages English
T: +254 020 374 2114
W: www.agakhanschools.org/kenya/akan

The Nairobi Academy
P.O. Box 24817, Langata Road, Next to Mamba Village, 00502 Nairobi
DP Coordinator Samuel Karinga
Languages English, Swahili
T: +254 722 208 365
W: www.nairobiacademy.or.ke

The Vale School Muthaiga

Muthaiga Road, Nairobi
PYP Coordinator Ashifa Patni
Languages English
T: +254 708 191 397
W: www.thevaleschoolmuthaiga.com

KOSOVO

International Learning Group School - ILG School
Veternik 1, 10000 Prishtina
DP Coordinator Jovelyn delos Santos
MYP Coordinator Rebecca Bowery
PYP Coordinator Christy Dervishi
Languages English
T: +386 38 722 893
W: www.ilg-ks.org

KUWAIT

AMERICAN CREATIVITY ACADEMY
P.O. Box 1740, 32018 Hawally, Hawalli
DP Coordinator Shaheed Carter
Languages English
T: +965 2267 3333
E: info@aca.edu.kw
W: www.aca.edu.kw

See full details on page 52

AMERICAN INTERNATIONAL SCHOOL OF KUWAIT
P.O. Box 3267, 22033 Salmiya, Hawalli
DP Coordinator Amel Limam
MYP Coordinator Alia Awad
PYP Coordinator Kelsy Cummings
Languages English
T: +965 1 843 247
E: superintendent@ais-kuwait.org
W: www.ais-kuwait.org

See full details on page 51

KUWAIT

Kuwait Bilingual School
P.O. Box 3125, Al-Jahra, 01033 Al Jahra City, Jahra
MYP Coordinator Maged Mahrous
PYP Coordinator Alaa Alshemery
Languages English
T: +965 2458 1118
W: www.kuwaitbilingualschool.com
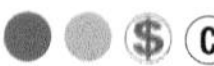

Little Land Nursery & Montessori Centre
House 7, Street 40, Block 4, Faiha, Kuwait City, Al Asimah
PYP Coordinator Hawraa Alzein
Languages English, Arabic
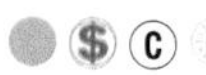

Reborn Kids Education Academy (RKEA)
Street 507, Block 5, Al-Siddiq
PYP Coordinator Anna Blanca Abelo
Languages English
T: +965 2208 6688
W: www.rebornkw.com

KYRGYZSTAN

Bishkek International School
67A Bronirovannaia Street, Bishkek 720044
DP Coordinator Makiko Inaba
MYP Coordinator Rabia Newton
PYP Coordinator Maria Corbett
Languages English
T: +996 3122 14406
W: www.bis.kg

Oxford International School
Mira Avenue 153/1, Bishkek 720040
DP Coordinator Akylai Raimbekova
Languages English, Russian
T: +996 5585 51155
W: www.oxford.kg

LATVIA

Exupery International School
Jauna iela 8, Pinki, Babites pagasts LV-2107
DP Coordinator Fleur Serriere
PYP Coordinator Kristina Potapova
Languages English
T: +371 26 62 23 33
W: exupery.lv

International School of Latvia
Meistaru 2, Pinki, Babites pag., Babites nov. LV-2107
DP Coordinator Rebekah Hommel
MYP Coordinator Joseph Szalay
PYP Coordinator Elizabeth Younk
Languages English
T: +371 6775 5146
W: www.isl.edu.lv

International School of Riga
Zvejnieku iela 12, Riga 1048
DP Coordinator Sarah McGinley
PYP Coordinator Ginta Karklina
Languages English
T: +371 6762 4622
W: www.isriga.lv

International School Premjers
1 Lomonosova Str., Bld. 7, Riga 1019
DP Coordinator Agate Prakash
MYP Coordinator Agate Prakash
Languages English, Russian
T: +371 67218501
W: www.ispremjers.lv

Jelgava Spidola State Gymnasium (Jelgavas Spidolas Valsts Gimnazija)
Sarmas iela 2, Jelgava LV3001
MYP Coordinator Vineta Srama
Languages Latvian
T: +371 630 29 212
W: www.jsg.lv

King's College, The British School of Latvia
Turaidas iela 1 Pinki, Babites novads LV2107
DP Coordinator Paul Gibson
Languages English
T: +371 257 59 043
W: latvia.kingscollegeschools.org

Ogre Technical School
Aizupes, Tinuzi Parish, Ikskile District, Ogre 5001
CP Coordinator Sigita Jasinska
Languages English, Latvian
W: www.ovt.lv

Riga State Gymnasium No. 1
Raina bulv 8, Riga 1050
DP Coordinator Liga Reitere
Languages Latvian (national Curriculum), English (ib Dp)
T: +371 67 228 607
W: www.r1g.edu.lv

Riga State Gymnasium No. 2
Kr. Valdemara str. 1, Riga 1010
DP Coordinator Inga Treimane
Languages English
T: +371 67 181 225
W: www.r2vsk.edu.lv

Riga State Gymnasium No. 3
Grecinieku iela 10, Riga 1050
MYP Coordinator Ingrida Breidaka
Languages English, Latvian
T: +371 67 037 408
W: www.r3g.lv

LEBANON

Al-Hayat International School
Ras Al-Zaytoun, Aramoun
DP Coordinator Rana El Noamani
MYP Coordinator Dareen Shehab
PYP Coordinator Mona Abla
Languages English, Arabic
T: +961 5 806306
W: www.his.edu.lb
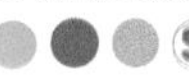

American Community School Beirut
P.O. Box 11 - 8129, Riad El Solh, Beirut
DP Coordinator Nada Chatila
Languages English
T: +961 1 374370
W: www.acs.edu.lb

Antonine International School
Zone 7, Street 4, Ajaltoun
DP Coordinator Jihan El Mouallem
Languages English
T: +961 9 230967
W: www.ais.edu.lb
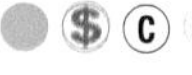

Brummana High School
P.O. Box 36, Brummana
DP Coordinator George Rizkallah
Languages English
T: +961 2 4960430
W: www.bhs.edu.lb

Cadmous College
Jwar al Nakhel, Tyre
DP Coordinator Ossama Salem
Languages English
T: +961 7 380391
W: www.cadmous.edu.lb

Christian Teaching Institute (CTI)
Mar Maroun Street, Horsh Tabet, Sin el Fil, Beirut
DP Coordinator Jean Baghboudarian
Languages English, Arabic
T: +961 1 497974
W: www.ctischool.com

Collège Notre Dame des Soeurs Antonines (Hazmieh-Jamhour)
B.P. 45201, Place Mar Tacla, Jamhour, Baabda
DP Coordinator Rula Yazigy
Languages English, Arabic
T: +961 5 769027
W: www.antonines-hazmieh.edu.lb
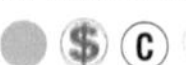

Collège Protestant Français Montana
Rue 4, Dik El Mehdi
DP Coordinator Rania Jibai
Languages English, Arabic
T: +961 4 914006
W: www.cpf.edu.lb

Eastwood College Kafarshima
Old Saida Road, Kafarshima
DP Coordinator Maya Kourani
Languages English, Arabic
T: +961 5 431525
W: www.eastwoodcollege.com

Eastwood International School Beirut
Sami Solh Street, Mansourieh El Metn, Beirut
DP Coordinator Cendrella El Kettaneh
MYP Coordinator Denise Chammas
PYP Coordinator Denise Chammas
Languages English
T: +961 4 409307
W: www.eastwoodis.com
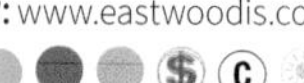

GERMAN INTERNATIONAL SCHOOL BEIRUT
PO Box 11-3888, Bliss Street, Ras Beirut, Beirut
DP Coordinator Petra Machlab
Languages English
T: +961 1 740523
E: admissions@dsb.edu.lb
W: www.dsb.edu.lb
See full details on page 94

Greenfield College
Al Mourouj Street - Bir Hassan, Beirut
DP Coordinator Nibal Hamdan
Languages English
T: +961 1 834 838
W: www.greenfieldcollege.com

Hariri High School II
Rue Abdul Kader, Batrakiyyeh, Beirut
DP Coordinator Jihan Koumaiha
Languages English, Arabic
T: +961 1 373310
W: www.hhs2.edu.lb

Houssam Eddine Hariri High School
P.O. Box 67, Saida
DP Coordinator Nagham Abou Ali
PYP Coordinator Sasha Ghosn
Languages Arabic, English, French
T: +961 7 739898
W: www.mak-hhhs.edu.lb

International College Lebanon, Ain Aar
P.O. Box 113-5373, Mount Lebanon, Ain Aar
PYP Coordinator Alain Gholam
Languages Arabic, English, French
T: +961 4 928468
W: www.ic.edu.lb
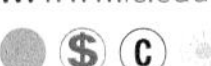

International College Lebanon, Ras Beirut
P.O. Box 113-5373, Hamra, Bliss Street, Beirut
DP Coordinator Rasha Daouk
PYP Coordinator Layal Tayara
Languages Arabic, English, French
T: +961 1 362500
W: www.ic.edu.lb

Jesus & Mary School
Rabweh, Cornet Chahwan
DP Coordinator Nathalie El Hani
Languages English, Arabic
T: +961 4910531/2/3/4/5
W: www.jmrab.edu.lb
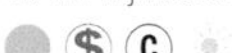

LWIS DT Beirut-City International School
Zokak Al Blat, Hussein Beyhum Street, Downtown, Beirut
DP Coordinator Fuad El Haddad
Languages English, Arabic
T: +961 1 369500
W: lwis-cis.edu.lb

LWIS KESERWAN-ADMA INTERNATIONAL SCHOOL
Mar Nohra, Fatqa, Keserwan
DP Coordinator Lisette Bou Lahoud
Languages English
T: +961 9 740225
E: info@lwis-ais.edu.lb
W: www.lwis-ais.edu.lb
See full details on page 164

LWIS Koura-Universal School of Lebanon
Bterram Al-Koura
DP Coordinator Diala Jreij
Languages English, Arabic
T: +961 6 930964
W: www.lwis-usl.edu.lb

Lycée Français International Institut Moderne du Liban
Rue 11-D, Fanar
DP Coordinator Rana Ghanem
MYP Coordinator Rana Ghanem
Languages Arabic, French
T: +961 1 680160/1/2
W: lfiml.com

Monsif International School
Monsif Main Road, Monsif
DP Coordinator Anthony Michael
Languages English, Arabic
T: +961 9 790170
W: www.monsifschool.edu.lb

Rafic Hariri High School
Kneissat, Saida
DP Coordinator Dima Osman
PYP Coordinator Samar Darazi
Languages English, Arabic
T: +961 7 723551
W: www.rhhs.edu.lb

Sagesse High School
Ain Saadeh, Matn, Beirut
DP Coordinator Lady Maalouf
Languages English
T: +961 1 872145

Saint Joseph School
Metn, Cornet Chahwan
DP Coordinator Nancy Timonian
Languages English, Arabic
T: +961 4 925005
W: www.sjs.edu.lb

WELLSPRING LEARNING COMMUNITY
Al Mathaf, Main Street, Near National Museum, PO Box 116-2134, Beirut
DP Coordinator Kathleen Saleh
MYP Coordinator Nizar Shamseddine
PYP Coordinator Nadine Daya
Languages English
T: +961 1 423 444
E: admissions@wellspring.edu.lb
W: www.wellspring.edu.lb
See full details on page 240

LESOTHO

Machabeng College, International School of Lesotho
P.O. Box 1570, Maseru 100
DP Coordinator Gaylord Magombedze
Languages English
T: +266 22 313 224
W: machcoll.co.ls

LITHUANIA

Alytus St. Benedict's Gymnasium
Topoliu g. 19A, 63331 Alytus
DP Coordinator Lina Butrimiene
MYP Coordinator Vijole Rinkeviciene
Languages Lithuanian
T: +370 31 574 919
W: www.benediktogimnazija.lt

Erudito Licejus, Kaunas
J. Gruodzio g. 9, 44293 Kaunas
DP Coordinator Marta Bobiatynska
Languages English, Lithuanian
T: +370 65 788 820
W: erudito.lt

Erudito Licejus, Vilnius
Aludariu g. 3, 01113 Vilnius
DP Coordinator Marta Bobiatynska
Languages English, Lithuanian
T: +370 66 719 972
W: erudito.lt

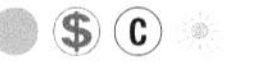

Kaunas Jesuit High School
Rotuses a. 9, 44280 Kaunas
DP Coordinator Au rine erepkiene
Languages English
T: +370 8 37 28 05 25
W: www.kjg.lt

Kaunas Jonas Jablonskis Gymnasium
Au ros st. 3, 44173 Kaunas
DP Coordinator Jurate Zybartiene
MYP Coordinator Kristina Gimpelson
Languages English
T: +370 37 20 23 37
W: jablonskis.kaunas.lm.lt

Kaunas Jurgis Dobkevicius Progymnasium
V. Cepinskio Str. 7, 46257 Kaunas
PYP Coordinator Lina Kilciauskaite
Languages English, Lithuanian
T: +370 37 391 421
W: www.dobkevicius.kaunas.lm.lt

Klaipeda Lyceum
Kretingos str. 44, 92317 Klaipeda
DP Coordinator Ramune Petrauskiene
MYP Coordinator Ausra Kazukauskiene
Languages English, Lithuanian
T: +380 84 635 1286
W: www.klaipedoslicejus.lt

Klaipeda Universa Via International School
Baltikalnio street 11, Klaipeda
PYP Coordinator Kamile Kesyle
Languages English, Lithuanian
T: +370 8 46 38 34 65
W: www.universavia.lt

Siauliai Didzdvaris gymnasium
Vilniaus g 188, 76299 Siauliai
DP Coordinator Rima Tamosiuniene
Languages English
T: +370 41 431 424
W: www.dg.su.lt

Tauragës Versmës Gimnazija
J. Tumo-Vai ganto g. 10, 72261 Tauragë
DP Coordinator Ingrida Vaiciene
Languages English
T: +370 446 61922
W: www.versme.org

The American International School of Vilnius
Subaciaus 41, 11350 Vilnius
DP Coordinator Matthew Stocking
Languages English
T: +370 5 212 1031
W: www.aisv.lt

Vilniaus Karalienes Mortos mokykla
Luksines g. 29, 11332 Vilnius
DP Coordinator Virginija Barbaraviciute
Languages English, Lithuanian
T: +370 63 007 474
W: www.karalienesmortosmokykla.lt

Vilniaus Vytauto Didziojo Gimnazija
Augustijonu St. 8, 01127 Vilnius
DP Coordinator Lina Labzentiene
Languages English, Lithuanian
T: +370 52 791 305
W: vvdg.lt

LITHUANIA

Vilnius International School
Turniskiu Str 21, Rusu Str 3, 01125 Vilnius
MYP Coordinator Deirdre Jennings
PYP Coordinator Kate Benson
Languages English
T: +370 5 276 1564
W: www.vischool.lt
 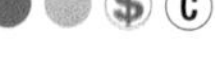

Vilnius Lyceum
Sirvintu 82, 08216 Vilnius
DP Coordinator ivilė Gerasimavičienė
Languages English
T: +370 5 2775836
W: www.licejus.lt

Vilnius Private Gymnasium
V. Grybo street 7, 10313 Vilnius
DP Coordinator Jelena Silova
Languages English, Lithuanian
T: +370 69 854 808
W: mokykla.lt

LUXEMBOURG

Athénée de Luxembourg
24 Bd Pierre Dupong, L-1430, Luxembourg
DP Coordinator Thomas Halsdorf
Languages English
T: +352 26 04 60
W: www.al.lu

Fräi-Ëffentlech Waldorfschoul Lëtzebuerg
45 rue de l'Avenir, Luxembourg 1147
DP Coordinator Michael Schulz
Languages French
T: +352 466932
W: www.waldorf.lu

International School of Luxembourg
36 Boulevard Pierre Dupong, 1430 Luxembourg
DP Coordinator Robert Sinclair
PYP Coordinator Jonathan Adams
Languages English
T: +352 26 04 40
W: www.islux.lu
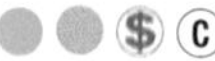

Lycée technique du Centre
106 avenue Pasteur, Luxembourg L-2309
DP Coordinator Mariette Kauthen
Languages French
T: +352 47 38 11 1
W: www.ltc.lu

OTR International School Luxembourg
7 Rue Val Ste Croix, 1371 Luxembourg
MYP Coordinator Tania Canone
Languages English, French
T: +352 2609 45 42
W: otrschool.lu

MACEDONIA

American High School Skopje
Treta Makedonska Brigada No. 60, 1000 Skopje
DP Coordinator Olivija Georgievska
Languages English, Macedonian
T: +389 2 2469 993
W: ahss.edu.mk

International School Maximilian
Bul. 8mi Septemvri No. 14, 1000 Skopje
PYP Coordinator Sofija Filipovska
Languages English
T: +389 2 3099 925
W: maximilian.edu.mk
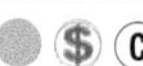

IPS MACEDONIA
Skupi 11, 1000 Skopje
DP Coordinator Donche Risteska
MYP Coordinator Esma Yildiz
PYP Coordinator Natasha Kanzurova Manev
Languages English
T: +389 (0)2 3070 723
E: infopyp@ips.mk
W: ips.mk
See full details on page 140
  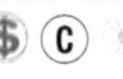

Josip Broz Tito - High School
Dimitrije Cupovski bb, 1000 Skopje
DP Coordinator Gordiana Gjorgova
Languages English
T: +389 2 3214 314
W: josipbroztito.edu.mk

NOVA International Schools
Praska 27, 1000 Skopje
DP Coordinator Julija Kostova
MYP Coordinator Amanda Leavitt
PYP Coordinator Ivana Brajanovska
Languages English
T: +389 2 3061 907
W: www.nova.edu.mk

OU Braka Miladinovci
Ul. Vladimir Komarov No.5, 1000 Skopje
MYP Coordinator Katerina Mirevska
PYP Coordinator Biljana Kirik
Languages English
T: +389 (02) 2 460 479
W: oubrakamiladinovci-aerodrom.edu.mk

MADAGASCAR

The American School of Antananarivo
Lotissement Le Park Alarobia, Antananarivo 101
DP Coordinator Mike Hemsley
PYP Coordinator Kristen Vanollefen
Languages English
T: +261 20 22 420 39
W: www.asamadagascar.org

MALAWI

Bishop Mackenzie International School
Barron Avenue, Lilongwe
DP Coordinator Jo McClenahan
MYP Coordinator Kathryn Leaper
PYP Coordinator Wayne Derrick
Languages English
T: +265 1 756 631
W: bmis.mw

MALI

Enko Bamako International School
B.P. 104, Quartier du Fleuve, Avenue De L'yser, Porte 510, Bamako
DP Coordinator Mahamane Sidibe
Languages English, French
T: +223 9369 5283
W: enkoeducation.com/bamako

MALTA

ST EDWARD'S COLLEGE, MALTA
Triq San Dwardu, Birgu (Vittoriosa) BRG 9039
DP Coordinator Mr Jolen Galea
Languages English
T: +356 2788 1199
E: admissions@stedwards.edu.mt
W: www.stedwards.edu.mt
See full details on page 209

Verdala International School
Fort Pembroke, Pembroke PBK 1641
CP Coordinator Nicola Schembri
DP Coordinator Daphne Said
Languages English
T: +356 21375133
W: www.verdala.org

MAURITIUS

Clavis International Primary School
Mount Ory, Moka
PYP Coordinator Nadine Koenig
Languages English
T: +230 433 4439
W: www.clavis.mu

International Preparatory School
Route Royale, Labourdonnais Village, Mapou
PYP Coordinator Deepa Ramaiya
Languages English, French
T: +230 266 1973
W: www.ips-mu.com

Le Bocage International School
Mount Ory, Moka
CP Coordinator Namrata Gujadhur
DP Coordinator Yovna Mewasingh
MYP Coordinator Pryadevi Baumy
Languages English
T: +230 433 9900
W: www.lebocage.net

Northfields International School
Main road, Labourdonnais Village, Mapou 31803
DP Coordinator Rosemary Abbott
MYP Coordinator Geerish Ramgolam
Languages English
T: +230 266 9448
W: northfieldsinternational.school
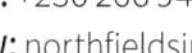

Westcoast International Secondary School
Flic en Flac Road, Cascavelle 90203
DP Coordinator Christina Appadoo
Languages English
T: +230 489 2034
W: www.westcoast-schools.com
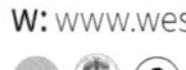

MONACO

INTERNATIONAL SCHOOL OF MONACO
10-12 Quai Antoine Premier, Monte Carlo 98000
CP Coordinator Tania Leyland
DP Coordinator Jonathan Elliott
Languages English, French
T: +377 9325 6820
E: admissions@ismonaco.com
W: ismonaco.com
See full details on page 131

MONTENEGRO

Adriatic College
13 Rozino, 85312 Budva
DP Coordinator Ekaterina Anokhina
Languages English
T: +382 69 324 101
W: adriaticcollege.com

Knightsbridge Schools International Montenegro (KSI Montenegro)

Seljanovo bb, Porto Montenegro, 85320 Tivat
DP Coordinator Lauren Streifer
MYP Coordinator Lauren Streifer
PYP Coordinator Marija Djukic
Languages English
T: +382 32 672 655
W: www.ksi-montenegro.com

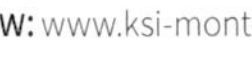

MOROCCO

American Academy Casablanca
RN 3020 Ville Verte, Casa Green Town, Bouskoura 27182
DP Coordinator Wassif Benlarbi
Languages English, French
T: +212 529 039112
W: www.aac.ac.ma

American School of Marrakesh
B.P. 6195, Route de Ouarzazate (km 9), Marrakesh 40000
DP Coordinator Iveth Morillo
Languages English
T: +212 524 329860
W: www.asm.ma

Casablanca American School
Route de la Mecque, Lotissement Ougoug, Quartier Californie, Casablanca 20150
DP Coordinator Alina Zamfirescu
Languages English
T: +212 522 793939
W: www.cas.ac.ma

Écoles Al Madina, Site Ain Sebaa
Km 9, route de Rabat, Hay Chabab, Ain sébàa, Casablanca
MYP Coordinator Zhor Lerhmame
Languages French, Arabic
T: +212 522 756969
W: www.almadina.ma

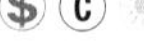

Écoles Al Madina, Site Californie
Lotissement Bellevue 2, Rue 3 Californie, Casablanca
MYP Coordinator Kamar Guennoun
Languages French, Arabic
T: +212 522 505097
W: www.almadina.ma

Écoles Al Madina, Site Polo
52 Boulevard Nador, Polo, Casablanca
MYP Coordinator Rajaa Boukhris
Languages French, Arabic
T: +212 522 210505
W: www.almadina.ma

GDGSR - Khouribga
Bld 2 Mars, Khouribga
MYP Coordinator Salah Toufani
Languages Arabic, French
T: +212 600 034011
W: www.gdgsr.ma/site/khouribga

GDGSR - Youssoufia
Rue Allal Ben Abdellah, Youssoufia
MYP Coordinator Habiba Maanaoui
Languages Arabic, French
T: +212 600 037753
W: www.gdgsr.ma/site/youssoufia

George Washington Academy
Bd. Abdelhadi Boutaleb, (ex km 5.6 Route d'Azemmour), Casablanca 20220
DP Coordinator Joshua Powell
Languages English, French, Arabic
T: +212 522 953000
W: www.gwa.ac.ma

Groupe Scolaire La Résidence
87-89 Avenue 2 mars, Casablanca
MYP Coordinator Soukaina Elidrissi Eljaid
Languages French
T: +212 522 809050/51
W: www.gsr.ac.ma

Institution El Yakada
Route de Méhdia, Lotissement Koutoubia (Avant Hay Chemaou), Salé
MYP Coordinator Mokhtar Saufi
Languages English, French
T: +212 537 844844
W: elyakada.com/yakedu

International School of Morocco
3 Impasse Jules Gros, Quartier Oasis, Casablanca
PYP Coordinator Meredith Achlim
Languages English
T: +212 522 993987
W: www.ism-c.ma

Newton International School
Rue Ibn Khafaja, Anfa, Mohammedia
MYP Coordinator Khalid Mouroudy
Languages French
T: +212 523 316552
W: www.nischool.org

Planete Montessori International School
Site Agdal: Lotissement Palm Tree Paradise No. 5, Mechouar Essaid, Marrakesh
PYP Coordinator Soukaina Benkirane
Languages English, French
T: +212 623 861429
W: www.planetemontessori.com

Rabat American School
Fath 1, Ave. Al Mohit Al Hadi, Almanzeh-Yacoub Al Mansour, Rabat 10052
DP Coordinator Fabienne Gerard
Languages English
T: +212 537 758590
W: www.ras.ma

MOZAMBIQUE

Aga Khan Academy Maputo
Av. Zimbabwe, 212 Matola 'A', Maputo
DP Coordinator Anthony Abaidoo
MYP Coordinator Esther Nondi
PYP Coordinator Emma Wheatley
Languages English, Portuguese
T: +258 853 016339
W: www.agakhanacademies.org/maputo

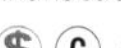

American International School of Mozambique
P.O. Box 2026, Rua de Rio Raraga 266, Maputo
DP Coordinator Sandeep Lyall
MYP Coordinator Jaya Lyall
PYP Coordinator Taryn BondClegg
Languages English
T: +258 822 255247
W: www.aism.co.mz

Benga Riverside International School
Moatize
PYP Coordinator Christopher Fato
Languages English
T: +258 847 175447
W: www.bengariverside.org/bris-home

Enko Riverside International School
Rua José Macamo 175, Polana, Maputo
DP Coordinator Rosa Maria Gadzicua
Languages English
T: +258 845 409151
W: enkoeducation.com/riverside

NAMIBIA

Windhoek International School
P/Bag 16007, Scheppmann Street, Pioneers Park Ext. 1, Windhoek
DP Coordinator Rick Fitzpatrick
PYP Coordinator Avril van Zyl
Languages English
T: +264 61 241783
W: www.wis.edu.na

NETHERLANDS

American School of The Hague
Rijksstraatweg 200, 2241 BX Wassenaar
DP Coordinator Ellie Kupchik
Languages English
T: +31 70 512 1060
W: www.ash.nl

Amity International School Amsterdam
Amsterdamseweg 204, 1182 HL Amsterdam, North Holland
DP Coordinator Neville Simon Kirton
MYP Coordinator Kelby Marks
PYP Coordinator Phillip Antcliffe
Languages English
T: +31 20 3454481
W: www.amityschool.nl

Amsterdam International Community School
Prinses Irenestraat 59, 1077 WV Amsterdam, North Holland
CP Coordinator Frederik Blokzijl
DP Coordinator Sabrina Stremke
MYP Coordinator Claudia Elena Casalino
PYP Coordinator Katina Rikkert
Languages English
T: +31 20 5771240
W: www.aics.espritscholen.nl

Amsterdam Liberal Arts & Sciences Academy (ALASCA)
Geertje Wielemaplein 1, 1095 MM Amsterdam, North Holland
DP Coordinator Lenn van der Laan-Rosenkilde
Languages English, Dutch
T: +31 20 2623240
W: alasca.espritscholen.nl

de Springbok
Pretoriusstraat 123, 2571 VD The Hague, South Holland
PYP Coordinator Namrata Datta Chowdhury
Languages English, Dutch
T: +31 70 3458605
W: www.despringbok.nl

NETHERLANDS

DENISE (De Nieuwe Internationale School van Esprit)
Piet Mondriaanstraat 140, 1061 TT Amsterdam, North Holland
DP Coordinator Amy Poon
Languages English
T: +31 20 4802700
W: denise.espritscholen.nl

EERDE INTERNATIONAL BOARDING SCHOOL NETHERLANDS
Kasteellaan 1, 7731 PJ Ommen, Overijssel
DP Coordinator Jessica Craig
Languages English
T: +31 52 9451452
E: admission@eerdeibs.nl
W: www.eerde.com
See full details on page 83

Gifted Minds International School
c/o Corporate Office, Landtong 18, 1186 GP Amstelveen, North Holland
PYP Coordinator Ramesh Mahalingam
Languages English
T: +31 23 888 8874
W: www.giftedmindsinternationalschool.com/gifted-minds-international-school/

International School Almere
Heliumweg 61, 1362 JA Almere Poort, Flevoland
DP Coordinator Simona Ghizdareanu
MYP Coordinator Suzanne de Maat
Languages English
T: +31 36 7600750
W: www.internationalschoolalmere.nl
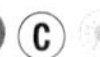

International School Breda
Mozartlaan 27, 4837 EH Breda, North Brabant
DP Coordinator Mark Sherlock
MYP Coordinator Lilian Buuron
Languages English
T: +31 76 5601350
W: www.isbreda.nl

International School Delft (Primary)
Jaffalaan 9, 2628 BX Delft
DP Coordinator Liza Dippenaar
MYP Coordinator Olwyn Hall
PYP Coordinator Kayleigh Adams
Languages English
T: +31 15 2850038
W: www.internationalschooldelft.com

International School Eindhoven
Oirschotsedijk 14b, 5651 GC Eindhoven, North Brabant
DP Coordinator David Bailly
MYP Coordinator Kris Pollard
Languages English
T: +31 40 2519437
W: www.isecampus.nl

International School Haarlem (ISH)
Oorkondelaan 65, 2033 MN Haarlem, North Holland
DP Coordinator Stavros Melachroinos
MYP Coordinator Kate Lupson
Languages English
T: +31 23 2200001
W: www.internationalschoolhaarlem.nl

International School Hilversum 'Alberdingk Thijm'
Emmastraat 56, 1213 AL Hilversum, North Holland
DP Coordinator Nicola Isaac
MYP Coordinator Rachel Gorman
PYP Coordinator Anniek Bruijnzeels
Languages English
T: +31 35 6729931
W: www.ishilversum.nl

International School Laren
Langsakker 4, 1251 GB Laren
MYP Coordinator Eva Goossens
Languages English
T: +31 35 206 2202
W: www.islaren.nl

INTERNATIONAL SCHOOL OF AMSTERDAM
Sportlaan 45, 1185 TB Amstelveen, North Holland
DP Coordinator Matt Lynch
MYP Coordinator Yvonne Cross
PYP Coordinator Lisa Verkerk
Languages English
T: +31 20 347 1111
E: admissions@isa.nl
W: www.isa.nl
See full details on page 121

International School The Rijnlands Lyceum Oegstgeest
Apollolaan 1, BA 2341 Oegstgeest, South Holland
DP Coordinator Jonathan Symmons
MYP Coordinator Annelies Lynn Brabant
Languages English
T: +31 71 5193555
W: www.isrlo.nl

International School Twente
Tiemeister 20, 7541 WG Enschede, Overijssel
DP Coordinator Chris Bonke
Languages English
T: +31 53 482 11 30
W: internationalschooltwente.nl

International School Utrecht
Van Bijnkershoeklaan 8, 3527 XL Utrecht
DP Coordinator Olivia Ayes
MYP Coordinator Liam Moody
PYP Coordinator Lindsey Dudgeon
Languages English
T: +31 30 8700400
W: www.isutrecht.nl

International School Wassenaar
Backershagenlaan 5, 2243 AB Wassenaar, South Holland
DP Coordinator Elizabeth Ann Young
MYP Coordinator Michael Hindmarsh
Languages English
T: +31 70 5121800
W: www.internationalschoolwassenaar.nl

IPS Hilversum
Rembrandtlaan 30, BH 1213 Hilversum, North Holland
PYP Coordinator Stephanie Noda
Languages English
T: +31 35 6216053
W: www.ipsviolen.nl

Jac. P. Thijsse College
Postbus 314, 1900 AH Castricum
MYP Coordinator Rene Wellen
Languages English, Dutch
T: +31 25 1652571
W: www.jpthijsse.nl

Laar & Berg
Langsakker 4, 1251 GB Laren, North Holland
MYP Coordinator Jacob van Santvoort
Languages English
T: +31 35 5395422
W: www.laarenberg.nl

Maartenscollege & International School Groningen
Hemmenlaan 2, 9751 NS Haren, Groningen
DP Coordinator Joke Jansma
MYP Coordinator Simone Hartholt
Languages English
T: +31 50 5340084
W: maartenscollege.nl

Monseigneur Bekkersschool
Frederik van Eedenlaan 12, 2624 VH Delft, South Holland
PYP Coordinator Lydia de Rooij
Languages English, Dutch
T: +31 15 2561318
W: www.mgrbekkersschool.nl

NORD ANGLIA INTERNATIONAL SCHOOL ROTTERDAM
Verhulstlaan 21, 3055 WJ Rotterdam, South Holland
DP Coordinator Aidan Jones
Languages English
T: +31 10 4225351
E: admissions@naisr.nl
W: www.naisr.nl
See full details on page 175

Rivers International School Arnhem
Groningensingel 1245, 6835 HZ Arnhem, Gelderland
DP Coordinator Arthur van de Graaf
MYP Coordinator Micha Oosterhoff
Languages English
T: +31 26 3202840
W: www.arnheminternationalschool.nl
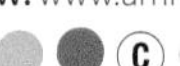

Rotterdam International Secondary School
Bentincklaan 294, 3039 KK Rotterdam, South Holland
CP Coordinator Clint Marshall
DP Coordinator Eva Noorduijn
Languages English
T: +31 (0)10 890 77 44
W: riss.wolfert.nl

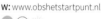

Startpunt International
Suze Robertsonstraat 103, 2526 WS The Hague, South Holland
PYP Coordinator Sophie De Graaf
Languages Dutch
T: +31 70 3803935
W: www.obshetstartpunt.nl

The British School in the Netherlands - Leidschenveen
Vrouw Avenweg 422, 2493 WX The Hague, South Holland
CP Coordinator Richard Black
DP Coordinator Richard Black
Languages English
T: +31 70 2183023
W: www.britishschool.nl

The British School in the Netherlands - Voorschoten

Jan van Hooflaan 3, 2252 BG Voorschoten, South Holland
CP Coordinator Stuart Whitfield
DP Coordinator Joseph Petrykowski
Languages English
T: +31 71 5602222
W: www.britishschool.nl

THE INTERNATIONAL SCHOOL OF THE HAGUE

Wijndaelerweg 11, 2554 BX The Hague, South Holland
CP Coordinator Dr. Alma Trumic
DP Coordinator Dr. Alma Trumic
MYP Coordinator Maria Lamminaho
Languages English
T: +31 70 328 1450
E: admissions@ishthehague.nl
W: www.ishthehague.nl

See full details on page 231

Theodore International Startup Academy

Lorentzkade 15a, 2313 GB Leiden, South Holland
PYP Coordinator Anna Masteruk
Languages English, Dutch
T: +31 64 3283316
W: tisaschool.nl

UWC MAASTRICHT

Discusworp 65, 6225 XP Maastricht, Limburg
Languages English
T: +31 432 410 410
E: admissions@uwcmaastricht.nl
W: www.uwcmaastricht.nl

See full details on page 235

NIGER

Lycée Enoch Olinga

B.P. 12255, Quartier Dar-es-Salam, Niamey 8001
DP Coordinator Fumundjibo Kahila
Languages French
T: +227 94 959872
W: www.lycee-enoch-olinga.org

NIGERIA

American International School of Lagos

Behind 1004 Estates, Victoria Island, Lagos
DP Coordinator Scott Williams
Languages English
T: +234 818 663 2769
W: www.aislagos.org

British Nigerian Academy

Drive 6, Prince & Princess Estate, Duboyi District, P.M.B 5285, Wuse, Abuja, FCT
DP Coordinator Stephen Ezekiel
Languages English
T: +234 703 414 5537
W: www.bna.edu.ng

Greensprings School, Lagos

P.O. Box 4801K Ikeja Headquarters, Ikeja, 32 Olatunde Ayoola Avenue, Anthony, Lagos
DP Coordinator Isaac Obashe
Languages English
T: +234 877 6874
W: www.greenspringsschool.com

Ibadan International School

24 Jibowu Crescent, Iyaganku, Ibadan, Oyo
PYP Coordinator Elisa Naoum
Languages English
T: +234 2 291 8483
W: www.ibadaninternationalschool.com

The International School of IITA

Oyo Road, Ibadan, Oyo
PYP Coordinator Edith Ekun
Languages English
T: +234 803 950 4372
W: www.iitaschool.org

NORWAY

Aalesund International School

Borgundvegen 418, 6015 Aalesund, Møre og Romsdal
MYP Coordinator Ana María Güelfo Borrajo
PYP Coordinator Trina Arsenault
Languages English
T: +47 908 69 948
W: www.aais.no

Arendal International School

Julius Smiths vei 40, 4817 His, Agder
MYP Coordinator Marius Larsen Strand
PYP Coordinator Antonia Fiksdalstrand
Languages English
T: +47 37 055 100
W: www.aischool.no

Arendal Videregående Skole

Postboks 325, 4803 Arendal, Agder
DP Coordinator Sabrina Simmons
Languages English
T: +47 37 00 02 00
W: www.arendal.vgs.no

Ås videregående skole

Postboks 10, 1430 Ås, Akershus
DP Coordinator Graham Ryan
Languages English
T: +47 64 97 57 00
W: www.aas.vgs.no

Asker International School

Johan Drengsruds Vei 60, 1383 Asker, Akershus
MYP Coordinator Mark Cringle
PYP Coordinator Angela Hjelset-King
Languages English
T: +47 9089 0609
W: www.askeris.no

Bergen Cathedral School

Postboks 414 Marken, Kong Oscarsgate 36, 5832 Bergen, Vestland
DP Coordinator Gillian Boniface
Languages English
T: +47 55 33 82 00
W: www.hordaland.no/bergenkatedralskole

Bjørnholt Skole

Slimeveien 17, 1277 Oslo
DP Coordinator Eirik Sanne Hardersen
Languages English
T: +47 23 46 35 00
W: bjornholt.osloskolen.no

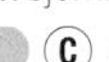

Blindern Videregående Skole

Sognsveien 80, 0855 Oslo
DP Coordinator Emmanuelle Bjerkem
MYP Coordinator Aldo Alejandro Mercado Rivera
Languages English, Norwegian
T: +47 90 80 80 59
W: blindern.vgs.no

British International School of Stavanger (BISS) Gausel

Gauselbakken 107, Gausel, 4032 Stavanger, Rogaland
CP Coordinator Paul Williams
DP Coordinator Jo Horne
MYP Coordinator Gina Ward
PYP Coordinator Nathalie Delgado
Languages English
T: +47 519 50 250
W: www.biss.no/biss-gausel

British International School of Stavanger (BISS) Sentrum

Misjonsmarka 1, 4024 Stavanger, Rogaland
MYP Coordinator Paul Venter
PYP Coordinator Alicia Jager
Languages English
T: +47 515 05 100
W: www.biss.no/sentrum

Children's International School Fredrikstad

Torsnesveien 5-7, 1630 Gamle Fredrikstad, Østfold
MYP Coordinator Kylie Curteis
PYP Coordinator Alison Kronstad
Languages English
T: +47 690 02 500
W: cisschools.no/fredrikstad

Children's International School Moss

Moss Verk 1, 1534 Moss, Østfold
MYP Coordinator Jake Gover
PYP Coordinator Jennifer Thorvaldsen
Languages English
T: +47 400 01 128
W: cisschools.no/moss

Children's International School Sarpsborg

Tuneveien 20, 1710 Sarpsborg, Østfold
MYP Coordinator Anne Kari Rønsen
PYP Coordinator Lindsey Allan
Languages English, Norwegian
T: +47 400 02 607
W: cisschools.no/cis-sarpsborg

Elverum videregående skole

Postboks 246, 2402 Elverum, Innlandet
DP Coordinator Mikael Sjöholm
Languages English
T: +47 6243 1500
W: www.elverum.vgs.no

Fagerhaug International School

Post Office Box 4, 7510 Skatval, Trøndelag
MYP Coordinator Cherise Kristoffersen
PYP Coordinator Cherise Kristoffersen
Languages English
T: +47 74 84 07 70
W: fagerhaugoppvekst.no/en/international-school

Frederik II videregående skole

PB 523, Merkurveien 2, 1612 Fredrikstad, Østfold
DP Coordinator Arvid Evjen Andersen
Languages English
T: +47 69 36 64 00
W: www.frederikii.vgs.no

Gjøvik videregående skole

PO Box 534, 2803 Gjøvik, Innlandet
DP Coordinator Ada Bråthen Øye
Languages English
T: +47 61149400
W: www.gjovik.vgs.no

Norway

Gjøvikregionen International School
Studieveien 17, 2815 Gjøvik, Innlandet
MYP Coordinator Samuel Rowe
PYP Coordinator Heidi Brenner
Languages English, Norwegian
T: +47 240 76 141
W: www.gjovikis.no

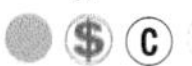

Haugesund International School
Halandvegen 175, 4260 Torvastad, Karmøy, Rogaland
MYP Coordinator Stacy Walter
PYP Coordinator Ryan Moore
Languages English, Norwegian
T: +47 40670871
W: www.hischool.no

International School of Bergen
Sandslihaugen 30, 5254 Bergen, Vestland
MYP Coordinator Peter Ledger
PYP Coordinator Leanne Hagen
Languages English
T: +47 55 30 63 30
W: www.isob.no

International School of Stavanger
Treskeveien 3, 4043 Hafrsfjord, Rogaland
DP Coordinator Lynn Park
Languages English
T: +47 51 55 43 00
W: www.isstavanger.no

International School Telemark
Hovet Ring 7, 3931 Porsgrunn, Telemark
MYP Coordinator Julie Strøm
PYP Coordinator Tjandra Purnama
Languages English
T: +47 35291400
W: www.istelemark.no

Kirkenes Videregående Skole
Postboks 44, 9916 Hesseng, Finnmark
DP Coordinator Juha Törmikoski
Languages English
T: +47 78 96 18 00
W: www.kirkenes.vgs.no
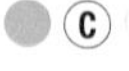

Kongsberg International School
Dyrmyrgata 39-41, 3611 Kongsberg, Buskerud
MYP Coordinator Hilde Bakken
PYP Coordinator Sofie Jorstad
Languages English
T: +47 32 29 93 80
W: www.kischool.org

Kongsberg videregående skole
Postboks 424, 3604 Kongsberg, Buskerud
DP Coordinator Kelvin Peters
Languages English
T: +47 3286 7600
W: www.kongsberg.vgs.no

Kristiansand International School
Kongsgård alle 20, 4631 Kristiansand, Agder
MYP Coordinator Susan Heiseldal
PYP Coordinator Jeremy Youell
Languages English
T: +47 95826601
W: www.kisschool.no

Kristiansand Katedralskole Gimle
Postboks 1010, Lundsiden, 4687 Kristiansand, Agder
DP Coordinator Vibeke Lauritsen
Languages English
T: +47 38 70 50 00
W: www.kkg.vgs.no

Lillestrom Videregaende Skole
Postboks 333, Henrik Wergelands gt. 1, 2001 Lillestrom, Akershus
DP Coordinator Line Skaugset
Languages Norwegian, English
T: +47 63 89 06 00
W: www.lillestrom.vgs.no

Manglerud skole
Plogveien 22, 0681 Oslo
MYP Coordinator Emma Tembo
PYP Coordinator Hin Yan Gloria Suen
Languages English
T: +47 22 75 73 10
W: manglerud.osloskolen.no

Nesbru Videregående Skole
Halvard Torgersensvei 8, Postbox 38, 1378 Nesbru, Akershus
DP Coordinator Helen Elizabeth Laney-Mortensen
Languages English
T: +47 66 854 408
W: www.nesbru.vgs.no

Norlights International School
Skådalsveien 33, 0781 Oslo
DP Coordinator Ismail Dikbas
MYP Coordinator Emma Jarvis
PYP Coordinator Sakhi Kochar
Languages English
T: +47 40 07 35 50
W: nlis.noredu.no

Oslo International School
PO Box 53, 1318 Bekkestua, Akershus
DP Coordinator Susan Jensen
Languages English
T: +47 67 8182 90
W: www.oslointernationalschool.no

Porsgrunn videregående skole
Kjølnes ring 58, 3918 Porsgrunn, Telemark
DP Coordinator Margrethe Hauff
Languages English
T: +47 35 91 75 06
W: www.porsgrunn.vgs.no

Sandefjord Videregående Skole
Postboks 2006, 3202 Sandefjord, Vestfold
DP Coordinator Siân Stickler
Languages English
T: +47 33 488 690
W: www.svgs.vfk.no

Sandnes International School
Einartangen 2, 4309 Sandnes, Rogaland
PYP Coordinator Mary Kay Polly
Languages English
T: +47 512 01 575
W: www.sdis.no

Senja Vidaregåande Skole
Skoleveien 55, 9300 Finnsnes, Troms
DP Coordinator Andreia dos Santos
Languages English
T: +47 77 85 08 00
W: www.finnfjordbotn.vgs.no

Skagerak International School
Framnesveien 7, 3222 Sandefjord, Vestfold
DP Coordinator Victoria Reed
MYP Coordinator Dylan Carter
PYP Coordinator Andrea Helgesen
Languages English
T: +47 33456500
W: www.skagerak.org

Spjelkavik videregående skole
Langhaugen 22, 6011 Alesund, Møre og Romsdal
DP Coordinator Camilla Moritz-Olsen
Languages English
T: +47 70178230
W: www.spjelkavik.vgs.no

St Olav Videregaende Skole
Jens Zetlitzgt. 33, 4008 Stavanger, Rogaland
DP Coordinator Fiona Andvik
Languages English
T: +47 51 84 99 00
W: www.st-olav.vgs.no

Tromsø International School
4 Breiviklia, 9019 Tromsø, Troms
MYP Coordinator Emil Sundal
PYP Coordinator Susanne Hebnes
Languages English
T: +47 99200780
W: www.trint.org

Trondheim International School
Festningsgata 2, 7014 Trondheim, Trøndelag
MYP Coordinator Virginia Neilsen
PYP Coordinator Hope Steen
Languages English, Norweigan
T: +47 7351 4800
W: www.this.no

Trondheim Katedralskole
Munkegaten 8, 7013 Trondheim, Trøndelag
DP Coordinator Martin Skrove
Languages English
T: +47 73 19 55 00
W: www.trondheim-katedral.vgs.no

UWC Red Cross Nordic
Hauglandsvegen 304, 6968 Flekke, Vestland
DP Coordinator Peter Wilson
Languages English
T: +47 5773 7000
W: uwcrcn.no

Vardafjell Videregående Skole
Spannaveien 25, 5532 Haugesund, Rogaland
DP Coordinator Gro Torill Nypan
Languages English
T: +47 5270 9910
W: www.vardafjell.vgs.no

Oman

ABA OMAN INTERNATIONAL SCHOOL
P.O. Box 372, Madinat Qaboos, 115 Muscat
DP Coordinator Samantha Cole
MYP Coordinator Christopher Engström-Roberts
PYP Coordinator Bronwyn Matamu
Languages English
T: +968 2495 5801
E: registrar@abaoman.org
W: www.abaoman.org
See full details on page 45

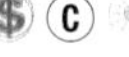

Al Batinah International School

P.O. Box 193, Muweilah, 321 Sohar
DP Coordinator Michael DeMaranville
MYP Coordinator Ferdi Kaya
PYP Coordinator Matthew Richmond
Languages English
T: +968 2685 0001
W: www.abisoman.com

Al Sahwa Schools

Building No. 592, Way No. 3052, Shatti Al Qurum, Muscat
DP Coordinator James Gibson
MYP Coordinator Katerina Chatzigiannaki
PYP Coordinator Sandi Stone
Languages English, Arabic
T: +968 2460 7620
W: www.alsahwa.edu.om

Ellesmere Muscat

Al Salam Street, Opposite Al Khoudh Police Station, Seeb, Muscat
DP Coordinator Vivek Gaur
MYP Coordinator Ibrahim Abd Rahman
PYP Coordinator Izmat Dad
Languages English, Arabic
T: +968 2455 4711
W: ellesmeremuscat.com

MySchool Oman

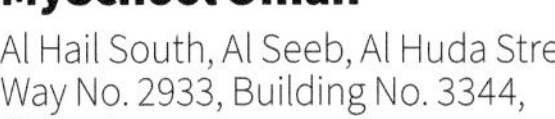

Al Hail South, Al Seeb, Al Huda Street, Way No. 2933, Building No. 3344, Muscat
MYP Coordinator Eman ElWardany
PYP Coordinator Parvaneh Bagheri Bahri
Languages English, Arabic
T: +968 2455 5171
W: myschooloman.com

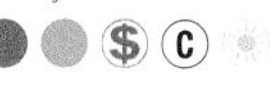

OURPLANET INTERNATIONAL SCHOOL MUSCAT

Al-Inshirah Street, Building No. 205, Plot No. 95, Block No. 221, 111 Muscat
PYP Coordinator Madhuparna Bhattacharyya
Languages English
T: +968 2200 5642
E: info@ourplanet-muscat.com
W: www.ourplanet-muscat.com

See full details on page 178

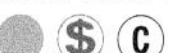

The Sultan's School

P.O. Box 665, Seeb, 121 Muscat
DP Coordinator Charles Hearsum
Languages Arabic, English
T: +968 2453 6777
W: www.sultansschool.edu.om

PAKISTAN

Angels International College

Faisal Town, Near Faisal Valley, West Canal Road, Faisalabad, Punjab 38000
DP Coordinator Irum Manzoor
MYP Coordinator Irum Manzoor
PYP Coordinator Khawaja Musa Abbas
Languages English
T: +92 41 8850012
W: www.angelscollege.edu.pk

Beaconhouse College Campus Gulberg

3-C, Zafar Ali Road, Lahore 54000
DP Coordinator Asma Amanat
Languages English
T: +92 42 3588 6239
W: www.beaconhouse.edu.pk

Beaconhouse Newlands Islamabad

Hill View Road, Mohra Noor, Islamabad 44000
CP Coordinator Zubia Akbar
DP Coordinator Zubia Akbar
MYP Coordinator Mariam Arif
PYP Coordinator Sabahat Bokhari
Languages English
T: +92 51 261 3935/6/7
W: bni.beaconhouse.net

Beaconhouse Newlands Lahore

632/1 Street 10, Phase VI DHA, Lahore 54000
MYP Coordinator Lubaba Batool
PYP Coordinator Urooj Shahab
Languages English, Urdu
T: +92 (42) 111 111 020
W: www.beaconhousenewlands.net

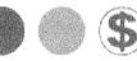

Beaconhouse Newlands Multan

4A, Officers Colony, Khanewal Road, Multan, Punjab 60000
MYP Coordinator Iram Fayyaz
PYP Coordinator Rabia Rehan
Languages English, Urdu
T: +92 61 111 111 020
W: bnm.newlands.net

Beaconhouse School System, Clifton Campus

Frere Town , 2/3 McNeil Road, Clifton, Karachi 75600
PYP Coordinator Aruna Shahrukh
Languages English
T: +92 21 35659190
W: www.beaconhouse.net/branch/clifton-campus-karachi

Beaconhouse School System, Defence Campus

207 A, Saba Avenue, Phase VIII, DHA, Karachi, Sindh 75500
DP Coordinator Ambreen Mustafa
Languages English
T: +92 2135847083 84
W: www.beaconhouse.net/branch/defence-campus-karachi

Beaconhouse School System, Margalla Campus

Pitras Bukhari Rd, H-8/4, Islamabad 44000
DP Coordinator Sumaira Imran
Languages English
T: +92 3345501113
W: ib.beaconhouse.net

Beaconhouse School System, PECHS Campus

35P/1, Block 6 Extension, PECHS, Karachi 75100
DP Coordinator Sheeza Imran
Languages English
T: +92 21 34380045
W: www.beaconhouse.net/branch/beaconhouse-college-campus-pechs-bccp-karachi

Headstart School, Kuri Campus

Kuri Road, Off Park Rd, Near CDA/Park Enclave, Islamabad 44000
DP Coordinator Rabia Ilyas
MYP Coordinator Sarah Munir
PYP Coordinator Ahmad Mehdi
Languages English
T: +92 51 8435 473
W: www.headstart.edu.pk

Ilmesters Academy

B-31, PECHS, Block-6, Near Progressive Center, Karachi 75400
DP Coordinator Sadia Jamal
MYP Coordinator Fizza Taimur
PYP Coordinator Neesha Feroz Punjwani
Languages English, Urdu
T: +92 21 34524423
W: www.ilmesters.edu.pk

INTERNATIONAL SCHOOL OF ISLAMABAD

Sector H-9/1, Johar Road, P.O. Box 1124, Islamabad 44000
DP Coordinator Dora Flores
PYP Coordinator Mary Frances Penton
Languages English
T: +92 51 443 4950
E: school@isoi.edu.pk; registrar@isoi.edu.pk
W: www.isoi.edu.pk

See full details on page 126

Kingston College

1 Canal Road, Khaira, Lahore, Punjab
PYP Coordinator Hira Tanweer
Languages English
T: +92 42 3652 6047
W: www.kingstoncollege.net

Lahore Grammar School Defence (Phase 1)

136 - E, Phase 1 Defence Housing Authority (DHA), Lahore Cantt, Punjab, Lahore 54810
PYP Coordinator Saima Asim
Languages English
T: +92 (42) 358 94306
W: lgsdefence.webflow.io

Lahore Grammar School Defence (Phase V)

#483/4, Block G, Education City, Phase V, Defence Housing Authority (DHA), Lahore Cantt, Lahore, Punjab 54810
PYP Coordinator Irma Ahsan
Languages English
T: +92 42 37176005/6/7
W: lgsdefence.edu.pk/phase-v

Lahore Grammar School International

32/3, Sector J, DHA Phase VIII, Lahore 54972
DP Coordinator Sania Rasool
MYP Coordinator Fatima Sajjad
PYP Coordinator Fatima Khan
Languages English
T: +92 42 37175751
W: www.lgsinternational.edu.pk

Lahore Grammar School Islamabad

Plot # 86, Faiz Ahmad Faiz Road, Sector H-8/1, Islamabad 44000
PYP Coordinator Humarah Khalid
Languages English
T: +92 51 4922092
W: www.lgsdefence.edu.pk

Lahore Grammar School Johar Town International

254 F1 Johar Town, Lahore, Punjab
DP Coordinator Anum Maqsud
Languages English, Urdu
W: jti.lgsjt.edu.pk

Learning Alliance

32/1 J block, DHA Phase VIII, Lahore 54000
DP Coordinator Aurangzeb Akbar
MYP Coordinator Mehrunnisa Sammiullah
PYP Coordinator Sameen Ali
Languages English
T: +92 42 111 66 66 33
W: www.learningalliance.edu.pk

Pakistan

Roots International Schools Islamabad Pakistan
Campus # 66, Street 7, Wellington Campus H-8/4, Islamabad
DP Coordinator Syeda Sada Afaq
Languages English
T: +92 51 8439001-7
W: www.rootsinternational.edu.pk

Roots IVY International School - Chaklala Campus
Walayat Homes, Chakalala Scheme 3, Rawalpindi
PYP Coordinator Maimoona Malik
Languages English
T: +92 51 578 8380
W: www.rootsivyintschools.edu.pk

Roots Ivy International School - DHA Phase V Lahore
Plot #550/1, Sector G, DHA, Phase V (6,192.65 km), Lahore 54000
PYP Coordinator Manal Tahir
Languages English, Urdu
T: +92 302 6274309
W: www.rootsivyintschools.edu.pk

Roots IVY International School - Faisalabad Campus
Opposite Guttwala Park, Faisalabad
PYP Coordinator Sehrish Tauseef
Languages English
T: +92 321 8912555
W: www.rootsivyintschools.edu.pk

Roots Millennium Schools, One World Campus
Head Office, No.80, Street 1, Sector E-11/4, Islamabad 44000
MYP Coordinator Fomaz Aziz
Languages English
T: +92 51 111 111 193
W: www.millenniumschools.edu.pk

Rupani Academy
Riaz Road, Jutial, Gilgit, Gilgit-Baltistan
PYP Coordinator Najmi Khatoon
Languages English, Urdu
T: +92 58 114 58926
W: www.rupaniacademy.org

Sanjan Nagar Public Education Trust Higher Secondary School
117 A, Anum Street, Glaxo Town, Ferozepur Road, Lahore, Punjab
PYP Coordinator Daniel Ishaq
Languages English
T: +92 42 35950676
W: www.snpet.org

Schole International Academy
273/1/1A, Adjacent Ilma University, Near Suzuki Showroom, Korangi Creek, Karachi, Sindh
MYP Coordinator Ayesha Unser
PYP Coordinator Chandni Saigol Khan
Languages English, Urdu
T: +92 (21) 350 93330
W: www.scholeacademy.pk

Sheikh Zayed International Academy
Street 8, Sector H-8/4, Islamabad
DP Coordinator Saima Sohail
MYP Coordinator Saadia Tariq
PYP Coordinator Nadeyah Adnan
Languages English
T: +92 51 4939298
W: www.szia.ae

SICAS DHA Phase VI
310/2F DHA, Phase 6, Lahore, Punjab 54770
PYP Coordinator Ayesha Taymoor
Languages English
T: +92 4237338361-3
W: www.sicas.edu.pk

The Democratic School
Masjid Ismail Road, Sitara Sapna City, Faisalabad, Punjab 38900
PYP Coordinator Samina Khalid
Languages English, Urdu
T: +92 33 030 00275
W: www.tds.edu.pk
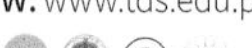 

The International School (TIS)
Executive, 51-C Old Clifton, Near Mohatta Palace, Karachi 75600
DP Coordinator Abdul Rehman Khatri
MYP Coordinator Muzna Akbar
PYP Coordinator Fehmeena Karim
Languages English
T: +92 21 35835805-6
W: www.tis.edu.pk

Think and Grow
Plot No. 3, Green Drive, 10 km Raiwind Road, Lahore, Punjab
PYP Coordinator Lailumah Kamran
Languages English, Urdu
T: +92 30 011 15922
W: thinkandgrow.edu.pk

TNS Beaconhouse Defence
483/3 Sector G, Phase 5, DHA, Lahore, Punjab
DP Coordinator Rashid Khalid
MYP Coordinator Hassan Hamza Zaidi
Languages English
T: +92 42 371 762 41 - 43
W: www.tns.edu.pk

TNS Beaconhouse Gulberg
1-H Jail Road, Gulberg II, Lahore, Punjab
MYP Coordinator Zoona Khan
Languages English, Urdu
T: +92 42 111 867 867
W: www.tns.edu.pk

Palestine

Ramallah Friends School (Lower School)
P.O. Box 66, Ramallah
PYP Coordinator Sandy Ziadeh
Languages English
T: +970 2 295 6240
W: www.rfs.edu.ps

Ramallah Friends School (Upper School)
P.O. Box 66, Ramallah
DP Coordinator Nidal Ahmed
MYP Coordinator Mohammad Suleiman
Languages English
T: +970 2 295 6230
W: www.rfs.edu.ps

Panama

Instituto Alberto Einstein
Via Israel, in front of Multiplaza, Panamá City
MYP Coordinator Alejandro Juarez
Languages English, Spanish
T: +507 270 2266
W: www.iae.edu

Poland

2 Spoleczne Liceum Ogolnokszta lcace STO im. Pawla Jasienicy (2SLO)
ul. Nowowiejska 5, 00-643 Warsaw, Masovia
DP Coordinator Tomasz Mazur
Languages English
T: +48 22 825 11 99
W: www.2slo.pl
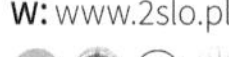

33 Liceum im M Kopernika
ul Bema 76, 01-225 Warsaw, Masovia
DP Coordinator Agnieszka White
MYP Coordinator Iwona Berse
Languages English
T: +48 22 632 75 70

Akademickie Dwujezyczne Liceum Oxford Secondary School
ul. Krakowska 30, 43-300 Bielsko-Biala, Silesia
DP Coordinator Agnieszka Strzelecka
Languages English
W: oxfordsecondary.pl

American School of Warsaw
Bielawa, ul Warszawska 202, 05-520 Konstancin-Jeziorna, Masovia
DP Coordinator Paul Lennon
MYP Coordinator Elizabeth Swanson
PYP Coordinator Charlotte Chestnut
Languages English
T: +48 22 702 8500
W: www.aswarsaw.org
 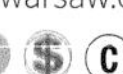

American School of Wroclaw
Partynicka 29-37, 53-031 Wroclaw, Lower Silesia
DP Coordinator Nandini Basu
Languages English, Polish
T: +48 71 333 6992
W: www.asw.org.pl

ATUT Bilingual Primary School
ul. Raclawicka 101, 53-149 Wroclaw, Lower Silesia
MYP Coordinator Dorota Zielazna
Languages English
T: +48 71 782 26 25
W: www.dspatut.fem.org.pl

British International School of Cracow
ul.Smolensk 25, 31-108 Kraków, Lesser Poland
DP Coordinator David Twigg
Languages English
T: +48 1229 264 78
W: www.bisc.krakow.pl

British International School of the University of Lodz
ul Matejki 34a, 90-237 Lodz
DP Coordinator Wojciech Tietz
Languages English
T: +48 42 635 60 06
W: www.interschool.uni.lodz.pl

Da Vinci's International Schools
Pilotów 4c Street, 31-362 Kraków, Lesser Poland
DP Coordinator Joanna Grzybowska
Languages English
T: +48 608 322 388
W: is.edu.pl

I Liceum Ogolnokształcace Dwujezyczne im. E. Dembowskiego w Gliwicach
ul Zimnej Wody 8, 44-100 Gliwice, Silesia
DP Coordinator Anita Kwiatkowska
MYP Coordinator Joanna Korek
Languages English
T: +48 32 2314732
W: www.zso10.gliwice.pl

I Liceum Ogólnokształcace im St Staszica w Lublinie
Al Raclawickie 26, 20-043 Lublin
DP Coordinator Monika Trznadel
Languages English
T: +48 81 441 1460
W: www.1lo.lublin.pl

I Liceum Ogólnokształcace im. A. Mickiewicza w Olsztynie
Mickiewicza 6, 10-551 Olsztyn, Warmia-Masuria
DP Coordinator Wojciech Boryszewski
Languages English, Polish
T: +48 (89) 527 5353
W: lo1.olsztyn.pl/mm

I Liceum Ogólnokształcace im. Leona Kruczkowskiego w Tychach
ul. Korczaka 6, 43-100 Tychy, Silesia
DP Coordinator Katarzyna Scislowicz
Languages English, Polish
T: +48 32 227 3634
W: kruczek.edu.pl

I Liceum Ogólnokształcace z Oddzialami Dwujezycznymi im. Ignacego Paderewskiego
ul. I.J. Paderewskiego 17, 58-301 Walbrzych, Lower Silesia
DP Coordinator Beata Urbaniak
MYP Coordinator Beata Urbaniak
Languages English, Polish
T: +48 74 842 36 83
W: www.1lo.walbrzych.pl

I SLO Jam Saheba Digvijay Sinhji
ul. Zawiszy 13, 01-167 Warsaw, Masovia
DP Coordinator Brian Williamson
MYP Coordinator Brian Williamson
Languages English, Polish
T: +48 22 828 9601
W: www.bednarska.edu.pl

II Liceum Ogólnokształcace im Mieszka I
ul Henryka Poboznego 2, 70-507 Szczecin, West Pomerania
DP Coordinator Artur Strozynski
MYP Coordinator Monika Chorzepa
Languages English
T: +48 91 433 61 17
W: www.lo2.szczecin.pl

II Liceum Ogólnokształcace im Mikolaja Kopernika w Lesznie
Ul Boleslawa Prusa 33, 64-100 Leszno, Greater Poland
DP Coordinator Jolanta Perczak
Languages English
T: +486 5526 8485
W: www.IILO.leszno.eu

II Liceum Ogólnokształcace im Stefana Batorego
ul Mysliwiecka 6, 00-459 Warsaw, Masovia
DP Coordinator Joanna Szczesniak
Languages English
T: +48 22 628 2101
W: www.batory.edu.pl

II Liceum Ogólnokształcace im. Hetmana Jana Tarnowskiego
ul. Mickiewicza 16, 33-100 Tarnów, Lesser Poland
DP Coordinator Paula Pilarska
MYP Coordinator Jowita Frac
Languages English
T: +48 14 655 8895
W: www.ii-lo.tarnow.pl

II Liceum Ogólnokształcace im. Romualda Traugutta w Czestochowie
Gmina Miasto Czestochowa, ul.Slaska 11/13, 42-217 Czestochowa, Silesia
DP Coordinator Tomasz Muskala
Languages English, Polish
T: +48 343612568
W: www.traugutt.net

II Liceum Ogólnokształcace im. Tadeusza Kosciuszki
ul. Szkolna 5, 62-800 Kalisz, Greater Poland
DP Coordinator Magdalena Grzegrzólka
Languages English
T: +48 6276 76657
W: www.2lo.kalisz.pl

II Liceum Ogólnokształcace in Bialystok
ul. Narewska 11, 15-840 Bialystok, Podlaskie
DP Coordinator Emilia Makarska
Languages English
T: +48 85 6511416
W: zso2bialystok.pl

II LO im Gen Zamoyskiej i H Modrzejewskiej
Matejki 8/10, 60-760 Poznan, Greater Poland
DP Coordinator Edyta Sobczak
Languages English
T: +48 61 866 2892
W: www.2lo.poznan.pl

III Liceum Ogolnokształcace im A. Mickiewicza w Katowicach
ul. Mickiewicza 11, 40-092 Katowice, Silesia
DP Coordinator Beata Zygadlewicz-Kocus
Languages English
T: +48 32 258 93 05
W: www.mickiewicz.katowice.pl
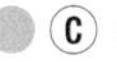

III Liceum Ogolnokształcace, Gdynia
Legionów 27, 81-405 Gdynia, Pomerania
DP Coordinator Zofia Krakowiak-Michlewicz
MYP Coordinator Marta Smalara-Lewandowska
Languages English, Polish
T: +48 58 622 1833
W: www.lo3.gdynia.pl

International American School
Ul Dembego 18, 02-796 Warsaw, Masovia
DP Coordinator Kenneth McBride
Languages English
T: +48 22 649 1442
W: www.ias.edu.pl

International European School Warsaw
ul. Wiertnicza 140, 02-952 Warsaw, Masovia
DP Coordinator Marzena Wieczorek
Languages English
T: +48 22 842 44 48
W: ies.waw.pl/en

International High School of Wroclaw
ul. Raclawicka 101, 53-149 Wroclaw, Lower Silesia
DP Coordinator Jillian Craig
MYP Coordinator Dorota Zielazna
Languages English
T: +48 71 782 26 26
W: www.highschool.fem.org.pl
 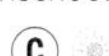

International Primary School
52 Drukarska St, 53-312 Wroclaw, Lower Silesia
PYP Coordinator Sean Rogers
Languages English
T: +48 503 188 843
W: www.ipschool.pl

International School of EKOLA
Ul Zielinskiego 56, 53-534 Wroclaw, Lower Silesia
DP Coordinator Adriana Kurowska-Mitas
Languages English
T: +48 71 3614 370
W: www.ekola.edu.pl

International School of Gdansk
ul. Sucha 29, 80-531 Gdansk, Pomerania
PYP Coordinator Malgorzata Macierzanka
Languages English, Polish
T: +48 58 342 31 00
W: www.isg.gfo.pl

International School of Krakow
ul Sw Floriana 57, Lusina, 30-698 Krakow, Lesser Poland
DP Coordinator Lou Panetta
Languages English
T: +48 12 270 1409
W: www.iskonline.org

International School of Poznan
Ul Taczanowskiego 18, 60-147 Poznan, Greater Poland
DP Coordinator Ewa Lysiak
PYP Coordinator Malgorzata Pyda
Languages English
T: +48 61 646 37 60
W: www.isop.pl

IS of Bydgoszcz
Ul. Galczynskiego 23, 85-322 Bydgoszcz, Kuyavia-Pomerania
DP Coordinator Malgorzata Kozielewicz
MYP Coordinator Marta Dereszynska
PYP Coordinator Anna Smigielska
Languages English
T: +48 523 411 424
W: www.isob.ukw.edu.pl

IV Liceum Ogolnokształcace im.Emilii Szczanieckiej
ul Pomorska 16, 91-416 Lódz
DP Coordinator Malgorzata Kudra
Languages English
T: +48 42 6336293
W: www.4liceum.pl

IV Liceum Ogólnokształcace z Oddzialami Dwujezycznymi im. Stanislawa Staszica
Plac Zillingera 1, 41-206 Sosnowiec, Silesia
DP Coordinator Maria Stecka
Languages English, Polish
T: +48 32 291 3784
W: www.staszic.edu.pl

POLAND

IX Liceum Ogólnokształcace im. Tadeusz Nowakowskiego
ul. Zofii Nalkowskiej 9, 85-060 Bydgoszcz, Kuyavia-Pomerania
DP Coordinator Monika Obrebska
Languages English
T: +48 52 361 0885
W: waszaedukacja.pl/ponadgimnazjalne/ix-liceum-bydgoszcz-938

IX Liceum Ogolnoksztalcace z Oddzialami Dwujezycznymi
ul. Orzeszkowej 8a, 35-006 Rzeszów, Subcarpathia
DP Coordinator Agata Stachowicz
Languages English, German
T: +48 17 748 2750
W: www.9lo.rzeszow.pl

Kolegium Europejskie
ul. Slusarska 9, 30-710 Kraków, Lesser Poland
DP Coordinator Edyta Zajac
Languages English
T: +48 73 388 31 21
W: www.ke.edu.pl

Liceum im. Marii Konopnickiej w Suwalkach
ul. Mickiewicza 3, 16-400 Suwalki, Podlaskie
DP Coordinator Beata Szczecina
Languages English, Polish
T: +48 87 566 56 26
W: 1lo.suwalki.pl

Liceum Ogolnoksztalcace z Oddzialami Dwujezycznymi im. A. Mickiewicza
ul. 11 Listopada 2A, 05-820 Piastów
DP Coordinator Katarzyna Bolesta-Siwek
Languages English, Polish
T: +48 22 723 6506
W: www.lopiastow.pl

Liceum Ogólnokształcace z Oddzialami Dwujezycznymi im. Wladyslawa Jagielly w Plocku
ul. 3 Maja 4, 09-402 Plock, Masovia
DP Coordinator Marcin Jaroszewski
Languages English
T: +48 24 364 5920
W: www.lwj.edu.pl

Liceum Ogólnokształcace z Oddzialami Dwujezycznymi w Boguchwale
ul. Suszyckich 11, 36-040 Boguchwala, Subcarpathia
DP Coordinator Zofia Machnicka
Languages English, Polish
T: +48 17 871 4421
W: www.liceum.boguchwala.pl

Monnet International School
ul. Abramowskiego 4, 02-659 Warsaw, Masovia
DP Coordinator Joanna Majorek
MYP Coordinator Angelika Maj
PYP Coordinator Aneta Borkowska
Languages English
T: +48 22 852 31 10
W: www.maturamiedzynarodowa.pl

Open Future International School
ul. Kwiecista 25, 30-389 Kraków, Lesser Poland
DP Coordinator Anna Krzemińska-Kaczyńska
MYP Coordinator Anna Przybylo
PYP Coordinator Karolina Teernstra
Languages English, Polish
T: +48 123 524 525
W: www.openfuture.edu.pl

Paderewski Private Grammar School
ul Symfoniczna 1, 20-853 Lublin
DP Coordinator Barbara Ostrowska
MYP Coordinator Magdalena Krzeminska
PYP Coordinator Monika Mikołajczuk
Languages English
T: +48 81 740 7543
W: www.paderewski.lublin.pl
 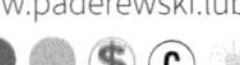 

Private High School Gaudium et Studium
ul. st. Michala 50 M, 61-118 Poznan
DP Coordinator Joanna Borucka
Languages English, Polish
T: +48 60 892 1887
W: eduges.pl/HS/index_HS.php

Private Primary School 97
Abramowskiego Street 4, 02-659 Warsaw, Masovia
PYP Coordinator Aleksandra Fratczak
Languages English
T: +48 22 853 36 60
W: www.leonardo.edu.pl

Prywatne Liceum Ogolnoksztalcace im.M.Wankowicza
ul. Witosa 18, 40-832 Katowice, Silesia
DP Coordinator Justyna Proksza
Languages English
T: +48 32 254 9194
W: wankowicz.edu.pl

Publiczne Liceum Ogólnokształcace nr III z Oddzialami Dwujezycznymi
ul. Dubois 28, 45-070 Opole
DP Coordinator Anna Szymanska-Buscicchio
Languages English, Polish
T: +48 77 453 6406
W: www.lo3.opole.pl

Sokrates International High School
St. Torunska 55-57, 85-023 Bydgoszcz, Kuyavia-Pomerania
DP Coordinator Krystian Orzechowski
Languages English, Polish
T: +48 51 984 1530
W: liceumsokrates.pl

Szczecin International School
ul Starzynskiego 3-4, 70-506 Szczecin, West Pomerania
DP Coordinator Diane Howlett
MYP Coordinator Kerstin Walter
PYP Coordinator Anna Piorkowska
Languages English
T: +48 91 4240 300
W: www.sis.info.pl

Szczecinska Szkola Witruwianska SVS
Wojska Polskiego, 164, 71-335 Szczecin, West Pomerania
PYP Coordinator Marta Leszczynska
Languages English, Polish
T: +48 512 868 176
W: svs.edu.pl

Szkola Podstawowa nr 53 z Oddzialami Dwujezycznymi
ul. Narewska 11, 15-840 Bialystok
MYP Coordinator Kamila Fidler
Languages English, Polish
T: +48 85 651 1416
W: zso2bialystok.pl

Thames British School Wlochy Campus
ul. Gladka 31, 02-172 Warsaw, Masovia
DP Coordinator Arkadiusz Glowacz
Languages English
T: +48 510 161 597
W: thamesbritishschool.pl/campus/wlochy-campus/

The British School Warsaw
Limanowskiego 15, 02-943 Warsaw, Masovia
DP Coordinator Neeraj Prabhu
Languages English
T: +48 22 842 32 81
W: www.thebritishschool.pl

The Canadian School of Warsaw
Kanadyjska Szkola Podstawowa, Ul. Belska 7, 02-638 Warsaw, Masovia
PYP Coordinator Irina Pawul
Languages English
T: +48 22 646 92 89
W: www.canadian-school.pl

The Nazareth Middle and High School in Warsaw
ul. Czerniakowska 137, 00-720 Warsaw, Masovia
DP Coordinator Marcin Jurkowski
Languages English, Polish
T: +48 22 841 3854/+48 601 644 102
W: www.nazaretanki.edu.pl

Towarzystwo Edukacyjne Vizja
Okopowa 59, 01-043 Warsaw, Masovia
DP Coordinator Malgorzata Byca
Languages English, Polish
T: +48 57 775 5001
W: okopowa.edu.pl/main-page

V Liceum Ogolnoksztalcace in Gem
Jakuba Jasinskiego, ul Grochowa 13, 53-523 Warsaw, Masovia
DP Coordinator Anna Wojczyńska
Languages English
T: +48 71 361 92 66
W: lo5.wroc.pl

VI Liceum Ogólnokształcace im. Adama Mickiewicza w Krakowie
Waska 7, 31-057 Kraków, Lesser Poland
DP Coordinator Anna Moskala
Languages English
T: +48 12 430 6908
W: www.vilo.krakow.pl

VI Liceum Ogólnokształcace im J Slowackiego w Kielcach
ul Gagarina 5, 25-031 Kielce, Holy Cross Province
DP Coordinator Anna Pakula
Languages English
T: +48 41 361 55 56
W: slowacki.kielce.eu

VIII Prywatne Akademickie Liceum Ogólnokształcace
ul Karmelicka 45, 31-128 Krakow
DP Coordinator Ewa Dudek
Languages English
T: +48 12 632 93 13
W: www.pack.edu.pl

Warsaw Montessori High School

ul. Pytlasinskiego 13a, 00-777 Warsaw, Masovia
DP Coordinator Ewa Stawecka
Languages English, Polish
T: +48 787 095 835
W: highschool.wmf.edu.pl

Wroclaw International School

ul. Raclawicka 101, 53-149 Wroclaw, Lower Silesia
MYP Coordinator Dagmara Muszynska
PYP Coordinator Maria Hughes Potocka
Languages English
T: +48 71 782 26 24
W: www.wis.fem.org.pl

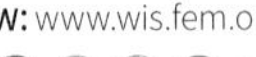

XXXV Liceum Ogólnokształcące z Oddziałami Dwujęzycznymi im. Bolesława Prusa

Zwycięzców 7/9, 03-936 Warsaw, Masovia
DP Coordinator Katarzyna Krajewska
Languages English, Polish
T: +48 22 617 74 13
W: www.prus.edu.pl

Zespól Szkól Ogólnokształcących im. Pawla z Tarsu

ul Poezji 19, 04-994 Warsaw, Masovia
DP Coordinator Agnieszka Dziwota
Languages English
T: +48 22 789 14 02
W: www.kulszkola.pl

ZSO No.13 Gdansk

ul. Topolowa 7, 80-255 Gdansk, Pomerania
DP Coordinator Anna Orlowska
Languages English
T: +48 58 341 0671
W: zso13.edu.gdansk.pl/pl

PORTUGAL

Carlucci American International School of Lisbon

Rua Antonio dos Reis, 95, 2710-301 Linhó, Lisbon
DP Coordinator Ana Almeida
Languages English
T: +351 219 239 800
W: www.caislisbon.org

Colégio Atlântico

Av. da Ponte lt 356/A, Pinhal de Frades, 2840-167 Seixal, Lisbon
DP Coordinator Patricia Costa
Languages English, Portuguese
T: +351 212 247 828
W: www.colegioatlantico.pt

Colégio Mira Rio

Estrada de Telheiras 113, 1600-768 Lisbon
DP Coordinator Nelia Simões
Languages English, Portuguese
T: +351 213 030 480
W: www.colegiomirario.pt

Colegio Planalto

Rua Armindo Rodrigues 28, 1600-414 Lisbon
DP Coordinator António Nunes de Figueiredo
Languages English
T: +351 217 541 530
W: www.colegioplanalto.pt

Escola da APEL

Caminho dos Saltos 6 ou Rua do Til 69, 9050-219 Funchal, Madeira
DP Coordinator Graça Valerio
Languages English
T: +351 291 740 470
W: www.escola-apel.com

INTERNATIONAL SHARING SCHOOL - MADEIRA

Caminho dos Saltos 6, 9050-219 Funchal, Madeira
MYP Coordinator Olga Put
PYP Coordinator Jenie Noite
Languages English
T: +351 291 773 218
E: office@madeira.sharingschool.org
W: www.sharingschool.org

See full details on page 138

INTERNATIONAL SHARING SCHOOL - TAGUSPARK

Avenida Dr. Mário Soares 14, 2740-119 Oeiras, Lisbon
DP Coordinator David Ferreira
MYP Coordinator Viviana Serralha
PYP Coordinator Déspina Sarioglou
Languages English
T: +351 214 876 140
E: office@taguspark.sharingschool.org
W: www.sharingschool.org

See full details on page 139

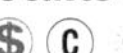

Oeiras International School

Quinta Nossa Senhora da Conceicao, Rua Antero de Quental no 7, 2730-013 Barcarena, Oeiras, Lisbon
DP Coordinator Jan Van Hees
MYP Coordinator Anshu Sharma
PYP Coordinator Jonathan Chambers
Languages English
T: +351 211 935 330
W: www.oeirasinternationalschool.com

Oporto British School

Rua da Cerca 338, Foz do Douro, 4150-201 Porto
DP Coordinator Anastasia Denisova
Languages English
T: +351 226 166 660
W: www.obs.edu.pt

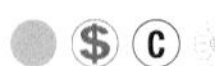

PARK INTERNATIONAL SCHOOL

Estrada de Alfragide 94, 2610-015 Amadora, Lisbon
DP Coordinator Mason Grine
Languages English
T: +351 215 807 000
E: admissions@park-is.com
W: www.park-is.com

See full details on page 179

SAINT DOMINIC'S INTERNATIONAL SCHOOL, PORTUGAL

Rua Maria Brown, Outeiro de Polima, 2785-816 S Domingos de Rana, Lisbon
DP Coordinator Maripaz Aguilera
MYP Coordinator Simon Downing
PYP Coordinator Edward Burt III
Languages English
T: +351 21 444 0434
E: school@dominics-int.org
W: www.dominics-int.org

See full details on page 192

St Julian's School

Quinta Nova, 2775-588 Carcavelos e Parede, Lisbon
DP Coordinator Dina Shah
Languages English
T: +351 214 585 300
W: www.stjulians.com

ST. PETER'S INTERNATIONAL SCHOOL

Quinta dos Barreleiros CCI 3952, Volta da Pedra, 2950-201 Palmela, Setúbal
DP Coordinator Ms. Telma Luis
Languages English, Portuguese
T: +351 21 233 6990
E: admissions@stpeters.pt
W: www.st-peters-school.com

See full details on page 217

UNITED LISBON INTERNATIONAL SCHOOL

Avenida Marechal Gomes da Costa 9, 1800-255 Lisbon
DP Coordinator Frank Alfano
Languages English
T: +351 211 161 110
E: info@unitedlisbon.school
W: www.unitedlisbon.school

See full details on page 233

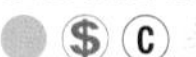

QATAR

ACS Doha International School

Building No. 10, Street No. 161, Area number/Zone 70, Al Kheesa, Doha
CP Coordinator Sereen Saadi
DP Coordinator Sereen Saadi
MYP Coordinator Washiela Casper
PYP Coordinator Margaret Dean
Languages English
T: +974 4474 9000
W: www.acs-schools.com/doha

American School of Doha

PO Box 22090, Doha
DP Coordinator Katrina Charles
Languages English
T: +974 4459 1500
W: www.asd.edu.qa

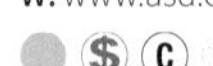

Arab International Academy

Al Sadd Area, Sports Roundabout, Doha 15810
DP Coordinator Mona Majzoub Sabbagh
MYP Coordinator Abdullah Azzam Khan
PYP Coordinator Rasha Hammoud
Languages Arabic, English
T: +974 40414999
W: www.aia.qa

Beta Cambridge School

Al Mashaf, Al Wukair, Doha
PYP Coordinator Ana Maria Matei
Languages English, Arabic
T: +974 4494 1200
W: betacambridge.com

Compass International School Doha, Madinat Khalifa

P.O. Box 22463, Al Baihaqi Street, Building 34, Zone 32, Street 926, Madinat Khalifa
DP Coordinator Katherine Rose
Languages English, French
T: +974 4034 9888
W: www.nordangliaeducation.com/our-schools/doha/madinat-khalifa

QATAR

Deutsche Internationale Schule Doha
Ibn Seena School Street No. 30, Doha
DP Coordinator Julia Karnebogen
Languages English, German
T: +974 4451 6836
W: www.ds-doha.de

Doha British School
PO Box 6142, Doha
DP Coordinator Ruth Battersby
Languages English
T: +974 4019 8008
W: www.dohabritishschool.com
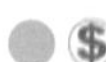

Etqan Global Academy
Zone 70, Street 120, Property #345, Umsuwiya street, Al Khisa
PYP Coordinator Matthew Morrison
Languages English, Arabic
T: +974 4435 0475
W: www.ega.qa

INTERNATIONAL SCHOOL OF LONDON (ISL) QATAR
PO Box 18511, North Duhail, Doha
DP Coordinator Smita Shetty
MYP Coordinator Moneeb Minhas
PYP Coordinator Danielle Robertson
Languages English
T: +974 4433 8600
E: mail@islqatar.org
W: www.islqatar.org
See full details on page 128

LYCEE FRANCO-QATARIEN VOLTAIRE
P.O. Box 12634, Zone 55, street Al Daoudiya no. 201, Doha
DP Coordinator Mrs Hiam El Zakhem
Languages French, English, Arabic
T: +974 4035 4015
E: h.zakhem@voltairedoha.com
W: www.lyceevoltaire.org
See full details on page 165
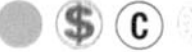

QATAR ACADEMY AL KHOR
P.O.Box: 60774, Mowasalat Street, Al Khor
DP Coordinator Mr. David Leadbetter
MYP Coordinator Mrs. Lina Aridi
PYP Coordinator Ms. Nadia Hussain
Languages Arabic, English
T: +974 44546775
E: qaalkhor@qf.org.qa
W: www.qak.edu.qa
See full details on page 181

QATAR ACADEMY AL WAKRA
P.O. Box: 2589, Al Farazdaq Street, street No.: 1034, Zone: 90, Doha
DP Coordinator Ms. Lynette Winnard
MYP Coordinator Ms. Kristin J. Hexter
PYP Coordinator Mrs. Samira Jurdak
Languages Arabic, English
T: +974 44547418
E: qataracademyal-wakra@qf.org.qa
W: www.qaw.edu.qa
See full details on page 182
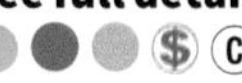

QATAR ACADEMY DOHA
P.O. Box: 1129, Luqta Street, Doha
DP Coordinator Ms. Zeina Jawad
MYP Coordinator Ms. Roma Bhargava
PYP Coordinator Ms. Savannah Spillers
Languages Arabic, English
T: +974 44542000
E: qataracademy@qf.org.qa
W: www.qataracademy.edu.qa
See full details on page 183
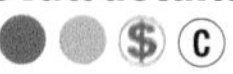

QATAR ACADEMY MSHEIREB
Msheireb Downtown Doha
PYP Coordinator Mr. Cory Sadler
Languages English, Arabic
T: +974 44542116
E: qamsheireb@qf.org.qa
W: www.qam.qa
See full details on page 184
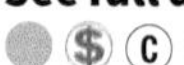

QATAR ACADEMY SIDRA
P.O. Box: 34077, Doha
DP Coordinator Mr. John Dugan
MYP Coordinator Ms. Nelsy Saravia
PYP Coordinator Mr. Barry Grogan
Languages English
T: +974 44542322
E: qasidra@qf.org.qa
W: www.qasidra.com.qa
See full details on page 185

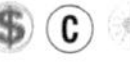

SEK INTERNATIONAL SCHOOL QATAR
Onaiza 65, Doha
DP Coordinator Kim Derudder
MYP Coordinator Lorraine Ann Kenny
PYP Coordinator Anthony Hamblin
Languages Arabic, English, Spanish
T: +974 4012 7633
E: info@sek.qa
W: www.sek.qa
See full details on page 202

Swiss International School Qatar
Al Hashimaya Street, Al Luqta, Doha
DP Coordinator Katherine Milton
MYP Coordinator Stephen Bradley
PYP Coordinator Yolandé Stander
Languages English
T: +974 40363131
W: www.sisq.qa

TARIQ BIN ZIAD SCHOOL
Al Dafaf Street, Street 893, Al Sadd Area, Doha
PYP Coordinator Nour R. Ghusayni
Languages English, Arabic
T: +974 44542005
E: tbz@qf.org.qa
W: tbz.qa
See full details on page 221

The Gulf English School
PO Box 2440, Doha
DP Coordinator Hannah Cashel
Languages English
T: +974 4457 8777
W: www.gulfenglishschool.com

ROMANIA

American International School of Bucharest
Sos Pipera-Tunari 196, Voluntari, Jud Ilfov, 077190 Bucharest
DP Coordinator Aliza Robinson
MYP Coordinator Melanie Kempe
PYP Coordinator Courtney Hughes
Languages English
T: +40 (21) 204 4300
W: www.aisb.ro
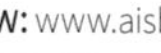

British International School of Timisoara
8 Aurora Street, 300291 Timisoara
DP Coordinator Bogdan Lazar
Languages English
T: +40 726 707 446
W: www.britishschool-timisoara.ro

Bucharest - Beirut International School
Sos.Vergului, nr.14, District 2, 022448 Bucharest
DP Coordinator Roxana Salajanu
PYP Coordinator Milena Stanescu
Languages English
T: +40 (0)744 309 199
W: bbischool.ro
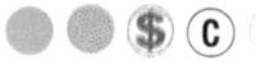

Colegiul National Andrei Saguna
Sirul Andrei Saguna No. 1, 500123 Brasov
DP Coordinator Diana Elena Banu
Languages English
T: +40 26 841 9400
W: www.saguna.ro

Genesis College
Straulesti Street, 89A District 1, Bucharest
DP Coordinator Alexandra Petrescu
MYP Coordinator Ioana Mindrut
PYP Coordinator Corina Huiu
Languages English, Romanian
T: +40 73 310 7914
W: genesis.ro

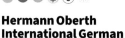

Hermann Oberth International German School
34E Pipera Blvd, Voluntari, Ilfov
DP Coordinator Adela Gavrilescu
Languages English, German
T: +4 021 231 20 45
W: www.scoala-germana.ro

INTERNATIONAL SCHOOL OF BUCHAREST
1R Gara Catelu Str., Sector 3, Bucharest 032991
DP Coordinator Mr. Yusuf Suha Orhan
Languages English
T: +40 21 3069530
E: admissions@isb.ro
W: www.isb.ro
See full details on page 124

Liceul Teoretic Scoala Europeana Bucuresti
33 Baiculesti st., 013913 Bucharest
DP Coordinator Ana-Maria Obezaru
Languages English
T: +40 21 3117 770
W: www.scoalaeuropeana.ro

Little London International Academy
Strada Erou Iancu Nicolae 65, Pipera, 077190 Voluntari, Ilfov
PYP Coordinator Andrea Nicolae
Languages English
T: +40 721 689 762
W: www.lliacademy.ro

MARK TWAIN INTERNATIONAL SCHOOL
25 Erou Iancu Nicolae Street, 077190 Voluntari, Ilfov
DP Coordinator Ms. Olivia Fotescu
MYP Coordinator Ms. Floriana Florea
PYP Coordinator Ms. Corina Popa
Languages English, Romanian
T: +40 73 500 0160
E: contact@marktwainschool.ro
W: www.marktwainschool.ro
See full details on page 166

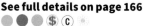

Olga Gudynn Bilingual High School - Oxford Gardens
Bulevardul Pipera No. 141, Voluntari, Ilfov
DP Coordinator Jack Constant
Languages English, Romanian
T: +40 72 627 7487
W: www.olgagudynn.ro

Verita International School
Soldat Gheorghe Pripu Street 22A, 1st District, Bucharest
DP Coordinator Marco Fick
Languages English
T: +40 21 311 8811
W: www.veritaschool.ro

RUSSIAN FEDERATION

Alabuga International School
Nord Drive, Building 1, Yelabuga, Tatarstan 423600
MYP Coordinator Dmitrii Antonov
PYP Coordinator Ksenia Kolesnikova
Languages English, Russian
T: +7 855 575 3405
W: alabugais.ru

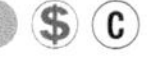

Brookes Moscow
Lazorevyy Proezd, 7, Moscow 129323
DP Coordinator Daniella Spooner Lagos
MYP Coordinator Lilit Harutyunyan
PYP Coordinator Paul Ackers
Languages English
T: +7 (499) 110 70 01
W: moscow.brookes.org

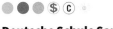

Deutsche Schule Sankt Petersburg
ul. Petrozavodskaya 12, Saint Petersburg 197110
DP Coordinator Bernd Juen
Languages English, German
T: +7 812 409 21 59
W: deutscheschule.ru

E. M. Primakov Gymnasium
Utrennyaya street, Razdory village, Odintsovo Region, Moscow Oblast 143082
DP Coordinator Olesia Degtiareva
Languages English, Russian
T: +7 495 274 44 44
W: ogprim.ru

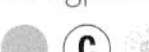

European Gymnasium
Sokolnichesky Val., d.28, Sokolniki, Moscow 107113
DP Coordinator Peter Mazaev
MYP Coordinator Aleksandra Manukian
PYP Coordinator Maria Bogantseva
Languages English
T: +7 985 795 4273
W: www.eurogym.ru

Far Eastern Centre of Continuing Education (International Linguistic School)
44 Partizanskiy Av., Vladivostok 690990
DP Coordinator Natalia Tischenko
Languages English
T: +7 423 240 42 84
W: www.mlsh.ru

Gosudarstvennaya Stolichnaya Gymnasiya
94 Altyf'evskoye Shosse, Moscow 127349
PYP Coordinator Alla Zavidey
Languages English
T: +7 495 707 07 62
W: www.gsgschool.ru

International School in Novie Veshki
p. Veshki, residential complex Novie Veshki, Green Boulevard, VL.86, Mytishchi district, Moscow 141031
PYP Coordinator Elena Voronova
Languages English
T: +7 499 707 8899
W: school-novieveshki.ru

International School of Herzen University
Vosstania str., 8 "B", St. Petersburg
DP Coordinator Irina Tomashpolskaia
MYP Coordinator Irina Tomashpolskaia
Languages English, Russian
T: +7 812 275 7684
W: www.interschool.ru

International School of Kazan
5 Mavlyutova St., Kazan
DP Coordinator Zachary Strother
MYP Coordinator Peggy Perkins
PYP Coordinator Leila Zahabi
Languages English, Russian
T: +7 843 204 12 82
W: www.iskazan.com

International School of Samara
ul. Kyibysheva, Building 32, Samara 443099
PYP Coordinator Elena Ulanova
Languages English, French, Russian
T: +7 846 332 2880

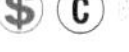

Kaluga International School
Lunacharskogo 16, Kaluga
PYP Coordinator Sofiya Chekryzhova
Languages English
T: +7 4843 400444
W: www.kischool.ru

Khoroshevskaya Shkola
45 Marshala Tukhachevskogo St., appt. 2, Moscow 123154
DP Coordinator Andrey Nozdrevatykh
Languages English, Russian
T: +7 (499) 401 02 71
W: horoshkola.ru/en

Kogalym Secondary School No. 8
11 Yantarnaya Street, Khanty-Mansiisk Autonomous Area, Yugra, Kogalym, Tyumen Region 628481
DP Coordinator Eskaeva Svetlana Ivanovna
Languages English
T: +7 34 66 72 71 13
W: www.school8-kogalym.narod.ru

Letovo School
35 Valovaya str., Moscow
DP Coordinator Pavle Milutinovic
MYP Coordinator Alexey Ivanovitch Mashkovtsev
Languages English, Russian
T: +7 8 800 100 51 15
W: letovo.ru/en/home

Linguistic School No. 1531
Godovikov Street 4, Moscow RU-129085
MYP Coordinator Svetlana Ushakova
Languages English
T: +7 495 287 25 71
W: gym1531sv.mskobr.ru

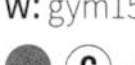

Lyceum 10 of Perm
22 Tehnicheskaya Street, Perm 614070
DP Coordinator Mikhail Novoselov
Languages English
T: +7 342 2819780
W: www.hselyceum.perm.ru

Medical Technical Lyceum
Polevaya str 74, Samara 443002
DP Coordinator Natalia Kabanova
Languages English
T: +7 846 237 0343

Moscow City University Comprehensive School
21A Khodynsky Blv., Moscow 125252
PYP Coordinator Elena Khristenko
Languages Russian
T: +7 499 762 6646
W: university-school.mskobr.ru

Moscow Economic School, Odintsovo Branch
1-A, Zaitsevo Village, Odintsovo Region, Moscow Oblast 143020
DP Coordinator Valeriya Rotershteyn
MYP Coordinator Antonina Andrianova (Gaydash)
PYP Coordinator Larisa Zaitseva
Languages Russian, English
T: +7 495 780 5230
W: www.mes.ru

Moscow Economic School, Presnya Campus
29 Zamorenova Street, Moscow 123022
DP Coordinator Alexander Galiguzov
MYP Coordinator Irina Nikitina
PYP Coordinator Tatyana Filatova
Languages English, Russian
T: +7 499 255 55 66
W: www.mes.ru

Moscow Gymnasium No. 1409
7, Khodynski blvd, Moscow 125252
MYP Coordinator Ada Kozaeva
Languages Russian
T: +7 499 740 5213

Moscow School No. 1231
Spasopeskovsky lane 6, building 7, Moscow 119002
DP Coordinator Irina Izmailova
PYP Coordinator Elena Alexandrova
Languages English, Russian
T: +7 499 241 43 81
W: sch1231.mskobr.ru

Moscow School No. 1296
Keramicheskiy proezd, Bld.55/3, Moscow 127591
PYP Coordinator Irina Rafalskaya
Languages English
T: +7 499 900 0852
W: cos1296.mskobr.ru

Moscow School No. 1329
Nikulinskaya street, 10, Moscow 119602
DP Coordinator Irina Gorkunova
Languages English
T: +7 495 651 33 97
W: sch1329.mskobr.ru

Moscow School No. 1527
17/5 Andropov prospect, Moscow 115407
MYP Coordinator Olga Shevchenko
Languages English
T: +7 49961 87005

RUSSIAN FEDERATION

Moscow School No. 45
8 Grimau Str, Moscow 117036
DP Coordinator Marianna Rovneyko
MYP Coordinator Irina Bey
PYP Coordinator Maria Andreichenko
Languages English
T: +7 499 126 33 82
W: www.ms45.edu.ru

Moscow State Budget School No. 1583
25, Smolnaya, Moscow 125493
MYP Coordinator Svetlana Dvoryantseva
Languages English
T: +7 499 458 02 57

Moscow State Lyceum No. 1575
6, Usievicha Street, Moscow 125319
MYP Coordinator Oksana Solosina
Languages English
T: +7499 151 89 24
W: lyc1575s.mskobr.ru

Moscow State Secondary General School No. 2086
5, Universitetsky prospect, Moscow 119296
MYP Coordinator Karina Alexandrova
PYP Coordinator Renald Lachashvili
Languages English, Russian
T: +7 910 450 11 70
W: the26.ru

President School
Ilyinsky Pod, 2, bld. 1 (in the village of ParkVille Zhukovka), Zhukovka village, Odintsovo district, Moscow Region 143082
DP Coordinator Natalia Vlasova
Languages English
T: +7 495 955 0000
W: school-president.ru

Private Lomonosov School Nizhny Novgorod
Gogol Street, 62, Nizhny Novgorod 603109
DP Coordinator Daria Klochkova
MYP Coordinator Dmitry Klochkov
PYP Coordinator Inna Klochkova
Languages Russian
T: +7 831 430 08 63
W: www.chastnayashkola.ru

Pushkin School No. 9 Perm
ul. Komsomolsky Prospect, 45, Perm 614039
MYP Coordinator Olga Fidan
Languages English
T: +7 342 212 80 71
W: www.school9.perm.ru

School 1557 named after P. Kapitsa
Korp 529, Zelenograd, Moscow 124482
MYP Coordinator Marina Davydova
Languages English, Russian
T: +7 4997360846
W: lyczg1557.mskobr.ru

School No. 1560
7 Mnevniki street, building 5, Moscow 123308
MYP Coordinator Ekaterina Ilina
Languages English
T: +7 499 946 4196
W: 1560.mskobr.ru

School No. 1589, Moscow
Initsiativnaya street, house 1, Moscow 121357
DP Coordinator Elena Yurchenko
PYP Coordinator Tatiana Cherniavskaia
Languages English, Russian
T: +7 495 4442571
W: lycc1589.mskobr.ru

School No. 185 of the City of Moscow
Mikhalkovskaya Street, 3, Moscow 125008
PYP Coordinator Fatima Dokshukina
Languages English
W: sch185s.mskobr.ru/#

School of Young Politicians - 1306
Michurinskiy avenue 15, Buildings 2-4, 119192 Moscow
DP Coordinator Kristina Kalinina
MYP Coordinator Asel Davydova
PYP Coordinator Natalia Martynova
Languages English, Russian
T: +7 495 932 99 58
W: gymg1306.mskobr.ru

State Budget Educational Institution No. 1252 after Cervantes
Dubosekovskaya str.3, Moscow 125080
MYP Coordinator Liudmila Novikova
Languages English
T: +7 49915 80222

State Classical School No. 1272
17, 1st Kozhukhovsky pr., Moscow 115280
PYP Coordinator Olesia Zuikova
Languages English
T: +7 495 710 36 39
W: sch1272.mskobr.ru

The Anglo-American School of Moscow
1 Beregovaya Street, Moscow 125367
DP Coordinator Adam Collins
PYP Coordinator Olga Ashour
Languages English
T: +7 (495) 231 44 88
W: www.aas.ru

The British International School, Moscow
Novoyasenevsky prospekt 19/5, Moscow 117593
DP Coordinator Jack Meadows
Languages English
T: +7 495 426 0311; +7 495 987 4486
W: www.bismoscow.com

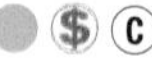 

The International Gymnasium of the Skolkovo Innovation Center
Skolkovo Innovation Center, Zvorykin Street 7, Moscow 143026
DP Coordinator Raisa Baragyan
MYP Coordinator Elena Andreeva
PYP Coordinator Maria Eliseeva
Languages English
T: +7 (495) 956 00 33
W: old.sk.ru/city/gymnasium

  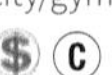

The Romanov School
3, Bolshoi Kondratievsky side-street, New Arbat street, 22, app. 118, Moscow 123056
DP Coordinator Svetlana Grunvald
Languages English
T: +7 916 115 61 50
W: 1240.ru

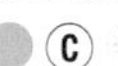

Vnukovo International School
Pervomaiskoe, Rogozinino Lugovaya Street 20b, Moscow 108808
DP Coordinator Victoria Ionova
Languages Russian
T: +7 (495) 431 70 70
W: vnukovo.school

XXI Century Integration International Secondary School
16 Marshala Katukova St., Building 3, Moscow 123592
DP Coordinator Nigiar Mekhtieva
MYP Coordinator Amine Ben Rejeb
PYP Coordinator Kristina Moavad
Languages English, Russian
T: +7 495 750 3102
W: www.integration21.ru

RWANDA

Cubahiro International School
P.O. Box 2073, Avenue du large, Kinindo, Bujumbura, Burundi
DP Coordinator Ann Gatuma
Languages English, French
T: +257 22 28 0288
W: www.cubahirointernational.school

Green Hills Academy
P.O. Box 6419, KG 278 Street, Nyarutarama, Kigali
CP Coordinator Eric Mbachi
DP Coordinator Mathias Ndinya
MYP Coordinator Jackline Uwimana
PYP Coordinator Katrina Jihad
Languages English
T: +250 735 832 348
W: www.greenhillsacademy.rw

SAUDI ARABIA

Advanced Learning Schools
PO Box 221985, Riyadh 11311
DP Coordinator Tania Maana
MYP Coordinator Maher Qanbaz
PYP Coordinator Farah Darazi
Languages English
T: +966 1 207 0926
W: www.alsschools.com

Al Andalus Private Schools
Batarji Street, Azzahra Dist, Jeddah 21443
PYP Coordinator Ahmed Elkotby
Languages English, Arabic
T: +966 556 645 532
W: www.alandalus.edu.sa

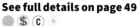

Al Faris International School
Tawaan Area, Imam Saud Road, Khan Younes Street, Riyadh 9483
DP Coordinator Salwa Ghandour
MYP Coordinator Mrs. Salwa Ghandour
PYP Coordinator Mrs. Rasha Ghraizi
Languages English
T: +966 011 454 9358
W: alfarisschool.edu.sa

AL HUSSAN INTERNATIONAL ACADEMY
PO Box 297, Dammam 31411
DP Coordinator Ms. Samar Deshmukh
Languages English
T: +966 13 858 0500
E: hia@alhussan.edu.sa
W: international.alhussan.edu.sa

See full details on page 49

Al-Bassam International School
Dammam
PYP Coordinator Rania Ezzeldeen
Languages English, Arabic
T: +966 013 843 4999
W: www.albassamschools.com

American International School - Riyadh
PO Box 990, Riyadh 11421
DP Coordinator James Atkinson
Languages English
T: +966 11 491 4270
W: www.aisr.org

American International School of Jeddah
P.O. Box 127328, Jeddah 21352
DP Coordinator Kelsey Bull
Languages English
T: +966 12 232 8668
W: www.aisj.edu.sa
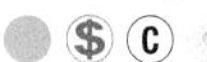

American School Dhahran
PO Box 31677, Al-Khobar 31952
DP Coordinator Ewan Hunt
Languages English
T: +966 (0)13 330 0555
W: asd.isg.edu.sa

Bright Minds International School
Pr. Sultan Street, Behind Haram Center, An Naim District, Jeddah
PYP Coordinator Alshaima Almarwai
Languages English, Arabic
T: +966 (0)12 654 2505
W: brightmindsschool.com

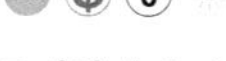

British International School Riyadh
PO Box 85769, Al Hamra, Riyadh 11612
DP Coordinator Mathilde Mouquet
Languages English
T: +966 11 520 9050
W: www.bisr.com.sa

Deutsche Internationale Schule Jeddah
P.O. Box 7510, Jeddah 21472
DP Coordinator Boris Bojko
Languages English
T: +966 12 691 3584
W: www.disj.de

Dhahran Ahliyya Schools
P.O.Box 39333, Dhahran 31942
MYP Coordinator Bilal El Bacha
PYP Coordinator Rola Abu-Sager
Languages English, Arabic
T: +966 138919222
W: www.das.sch.sa

International Programs School
Prince Sultan Road, Qurtoba, Al Khobar 34236
DP Coordinator Lina Ghamra
PYP Coordinator Siham Dabouk
Languages English
T: +966 13 857 5603
W: www.ipsksa.com
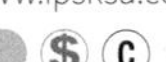

International Schools Group (ISG) Jubail
PO Box 10059, Jubail 31961
DP Coordinator Sanjeev Jangra
Languages English
T: +966 13 341 7550
W: www.isg-jubail.org

Jeddah Knowledge International School
Al Salamah District, Mohammed Mosaud St. (Behind Iceland), PO Box 7180, 21462 Jeddah
DP Coordinator Natasha Awada
MYP Coordinator Sarah Bakkar
PYP Coordinator Ayten Unal
Languages English, Arabic
T: +966 2 691 7367
W: www.jks.edu.sa

KING ABDULAZIZ SCHOOL
Ali Ibn Abi Taleb Road, P.O. Box 43111, Medina 41561
DP Coordinator Mohammad Baba
MYP Coordinator Raheela Akram
PYP Coordinator Raheela Akram
Languages English
T: +966 553 039 300/+966 503 454 420
E: hwaznah@kaism.org
W: www.kaism.org
See full details on page 149

King Faisal Boys School
P.O. Box 94558, Riyadh 11614
DP Coordinator Yazan Mohammad
MYP Coordinator Bassam Shoker
PYP Coordinator Kalwant Rana
Languages English, Arabic
T: +966 11 482 0802
W: www.kfs.sch.sa

King Faisal Girls School
P.O. Box 94558, Riyadh 11614
DP Coordinator Iman Ragab
PYP Coordinator Dana Itani
Languages English, Arabic
T: +966 11 482 0802
W: www.kfs.sch.sa
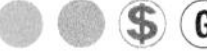

Learning Oasis International National School
Umar Ibn Zaid, An Nafal, Riyadh 13312
PYP Coordinator Hiba AlAssaad
Languages English, Arabic
W: www.loins.edu.sa

Les Écoles Internationales Al-Kawthar
PO Box 52280, Jeddah 21563
MYP Coordinator Hanene Karouch
PYP Coordinator Hanene Karouch
Languages French
T: +966506561717; +966506359280
W: www.alkawthar.edu.sa
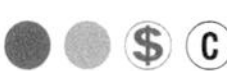

MADAC Schools
P.O.Box 444, Jabla bin Thour Street, Abu Kubir District, Medina
PYP Coordinator Sarah Mostafa
Languages English, Arabic
T: +966 555261230
W: madac.edu.sa

Qurtubah Private Schools
Prince Sultan Street, North-West Al-Tareekh Square, Jeddah 21581
PYP Coordinator Ikrami Farraj
Languages Arabic
T: +966 551757472
W: qps.edu.sa

Radhwa International School Yanbu
P.B.No. 32006, Yanbu 41912
MYP Coordinator Osama Tosson
PYP Coordinator Osama Tosson
Languages English, Arabic
W: www.radhwa.org

Rand International School
PO.box 9712, Dammam 31423
PYP Coordinator Sabana Mughal
Languages Arabic, English
T: +966 13 8504488
W: www.randschools.com
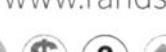

SEK INTERNATIONAL SCHOOL RIYADH
Al Toq Street, Ar Rabi, Riyadh 13315
PYP Coordinator Kim Gardner
Languages English, Arabic, Spanish
T: +966 011 520 6170
E: info@sek.sa
W: www.sek.sa
See full details on page 203

The British International School of Jeddah
PO Box 6453, Jeddah 21442
DP Coordinator Richard Young
Languages English
T: +966 1 2 699 0019
W: www.bisj.com

THE KAUST SCHOOL
4700 KAUST, Thuwal, Western Province 23955-6900
DP Coordinator Greg River
MYP Coordinator Michele McLay
PYP Coordinator Jonathan Mueller
Languages English
T: +966 12 808 6803
E: schools@thekaustschool.org
W: tks.kaust.edu.sa
See full details on page 232
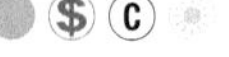

Yusr International School
King Abdulaziz Road, Opp Red Sea Mall, An Nahdah, Jeddah 23614
MYP Coordinator Ahmed Abdelrazzaq
PYP Coordinator Ahmed Abdelrazzaq
Languages English, Arabic
T: +966 55 506 3771

SENEGAL

Cours Sainte Marie de Hann
Route Des Peres Maristes, BP 98, Dakar
DP Coordinator Honorine Tamba
Languages English, French
T: +221 33 832 14 87
W: www.mariste.sn

Enko Keur Gorgui International School
Cité Keur Gorgui, Mermoz-Sacré-Cœur, Dakar
DP Coordinator Siménou Titrikou
MYP Coordinator Elhadji Demba Wade Diop
Languages English, French
T: +221 33 821 30 64
W: enkoeducation.com/keur-gorgui

Enko Waca International School
BP 24340, Ouakam, Dakar
DP Coordinator Alanna Ross
Languages French, English
T: +221 33 820 49 29
W: enkoeducation.com/waca

International School of Dakar
B.P. 5136, Fann, Dakar 10700
DP Coordinator Wendy Gifford
MYP Coordinator Denrol Carayol
PYP Coordinator Bradley Chumrau
Languages English
T: +221 33 825 08 71
W: www.isdakar.org

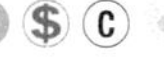

Le Collège Bilingue de Dakar
No. 53 Sacré-Coeur, Pyrotechnie, Dakar
DP Coordinator Souleymane Diaw
Languages English, French
T: +221 33 860 60 10
W: v3.lecollegebilingue-dakar.net

Lycée Billes
Commune de Plan Jaxaay-Cité, Gendarmerie–Niacoulrab, Dakar
DP Coordinator Amadou Bamba Thiobane
Languages English, French
T: +221 77 413 73 55
W: lyceebilles.com

SERBIA

Crnjanski High School
Djordja Ognjanovica 2, 11030 Belgrade
DP Coordinator Gordana Medakovic
Languages English
T: +381 112 398 388
W: www.crnjanski.edu.rs

Deseta gimnazija 'Mihajlo Pupin'
Antifascist Struggles 1a, 11070 New Belgrade
DP Coordinator Mirjana Vlahovic
Languages English, Serbian
T: +381 113 114 142
W: xgimnazija.edu.rs

Gimnazija Svetozar Markovic
Ul. Branka Radicevica 1, 18000 Nis
DP Coordinator Ivana Babovic
Languages English
T: +381 18 254 396
W: gsm-nis.edu.rs

Gymnasium Jovan Jovanovic Zmaj
Zlatne grede 4, Novi Sad, Vojvodina
DP Coordinator Natasa Vasić
Languages English, French
T: +381 21 529 977
W: jjzmaj.edu.rs/pocetna

International School
45 Sumatovacka Street, Belgrade
DP Coordinator Zorana Zivanovic
Languages English
T: +381 (0)11 4011 220
W: www.international-school.edu.rs

International School of Belgrade
Temisvarska 19, 11040 Belgrade
DP Coordinator Branka Sreckovic-Minic
MYP Coordinator Kristin Westby
PYP Coordinator Barbara Netzel
Languages English
T: +381 112 069 999
W: www.isb.rs

Ruder Bo kovic
Kneza Vi eslava 17, 11000 Belgrade
DP Coordinator Aleksandra Ivanovski
MYP Coordinator Jelena Poznic
PYP Coordinator Katarina Milosevic
Languages English
T: +381 113 540 786
W: www.boskovic.edu.rs

SLOVAKIA

English International School of Bratislava (EISB)
Radnicné námestie 4, 821 05 Bratislava
DP Coordinator Martin Hahn
MYP Coordinator Roman Liptak
PYP Coordinator Karolina Bremont
Languages English, Slovak
T: +421 91 5832076
W: eisbratislava.org

Gymnazium Srobarova
Srobarova 1, 042 23 Kosice
DP Coordinator Ingrid Melichova
Languages English, Slovak
T: +421 55 2021333
W: www.srobarka.sk

Ko ice International School (KEIS)
Polná 1, 040 14 Ko ice
PYP Coordinator Petra Vejvodová
Languages English, Slovak
T: +421 90 7976444
W: www.keis.sk

QSI INTERNATIONAL SCHOOL OF BRATISLAVA
Záhradnicka 1006/2, Samorin 93101
DP Coordinator Marek Andrasko
Languages English
T: +421 903 704 436
E: bratislava@qsi.org
W: bratislava.qsi.org
See full details on page 186

Spojená kola, Novohradská
Novohradská 3, Bratislava 821 09
DP Coordinator Matej Gonda
MYP Coordinator Gabriela Markusová
PYP Coordinator Travis Seitsinger
Languages English
T: +421 25 557 6396
W: www.gjh.sk

Spojená kola, Pankúchova
Pankúchova 6, Bratislava 851 04
DP Coordinator Jana Slávíková
MYP Coordinator Silvia Dadajová
PYP Coordinator Katarina Patúcová
Languages English, Slovak
T: +421 2 6231 2706
W: gympaba.edupage.org
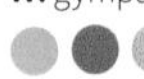

Súkromná spojená skola
Starozagorská 8, 040 23 Ko ice
PYP Coordinator Zuzana Richterová
Languages English, Slovak
W: www.schoolhuman.eu

Súkromné Bilingválne Gymnázium Ceská
Ceská 10, 831 03 Bratislava
DP Coordinator Svetlana Veselova
Languages English, Slovak
T: +421 2 44450733
W: www.gymnaziumceska.sk

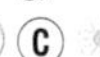

The British International School, Bratislava
J. Vala tana Dolinského 1 (Pekníkova 6), Bratislava 841 02
DP Coordinator Monica Gautama
Languages English
T: +421 2 6930 7081
W: www.bis.sk

SLOVENIA

Danila Kumar Primary School
Godezeva 11, 1000 Ljubljana
MYP Coordinator Anja De man
PYP Coordinator Denis Divjak
Languages English
T: +386 15 636 834
W: www.gimb.org

ERUDIO International School
Litostrojska cesta 40, 1000 Ljubljana
DP Coordinator Lara Dojer
Languages English, Slovene
T: +386 15 142 808
W: www.erudio.si/internationalschool

Gimnasija Kranj
Koroka Cesta 13, 4000 Kranj
DP Coordinator Nata a Kne
Languages English
T: +386 42 811 710
W: www.gimkr.si

Gimnazija Bezigrad
Periceva 4, 1000 Ljubljana
DP Coordinator Irena Cesnik
MYP Coordinator Katja Kvas
Languages English
T: +386 13 000 400
W: www.gimb.org

Gimnazija Novo Mesto
Seidlova cesta 9, 8000 Novo Mesto
DP Coordinator Polonca Centa
Languages English
T: +386 73 718 500
W: www.gimnm.org

II gimnazija Maribor
Trg Milosa Zidanska 1, 2000 Maribor
DP Coordinator Mateja Fosnaric
Languages English
T: +386 33 04 434
W: www.druga.si

Vector International Academy
Stula 23, 1000 Ljubljana
DP Coordinator Anda Eckman
Languages English, French
T: +386 40 862 445
W: vectoracademy.si

SOUTH AFRICA

American International School of Johannesburg
Private Bag X4, Bryanston, 2021 Johannesburg, Gauteng
DP Coordinator Kelly Scotti
Languages English
T: +27 11 464 1505
W: www.aisj-jhb.com

Crawford International Bedfordview
7 Marais Road, Bedfordview, 2008 Johannesburg, Gauteng
PYP Coordinator Amy Venter
Languages English, Afrikaans
T: +27 87 350 4633
W: www.crawfordschools.co.za/bedfordview

Crawford International Fourways
16 Campbell Road, Craigavon, Fourways, Sandton, 2191 Johannesburg, Gauteng
PYP Coordinator Tracey Hutcheson
Languages English
T: +27 11 465 4418
W: www.crawfordschools.co.za/fourways

Crawford International La Lucia
79 Armstrong Avenue, La Lucia, 4001 Durban, KwaZulu-Natal
PYP Coordinator Angela Johnstone
Languages English, Afrikaans
T: +27 31 562 9444
W: www.crawfordschools.co.za/la-lucia
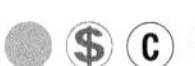

Crawford International Lonehill
17 Lonehill Boulevard, Lonehill, 2062 Johannesburg, Gauteng
PYP Coordinator Debbie Lynch
Languages English, Afrikaans
T: +27 11 467 0936/5
W: www.crawfordschools.co.za/lonehill

Crawford International North Coast
Watson Highway, 4399 Tongaat, KwaZulu-Natal
PYP Coordinator Sonia Jansen
Languages English, Afrikaans
T: +27 32 943 3240
W: www.crawfordschools.co.za/north-coast

Crawford International Pretoria
555 Sibelius Street, Lukasrand, 0181 Pretoria, Gauteng
PYP Coordinator Alice Khosa
Languages English, Afrikaans
T: +27 12 343 5903
W: www.crawfordschools.co.za/pretoria
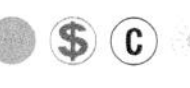

Crawford International Ruimsig
Cnr Peter and Kuilstock Roads, Ruimsig, 1724 Roodepoort, Gauteng
PYP Coordinator Caryn Bakewell
Languages English, Afrikaans
T: +27 11 958 0707
W: www.crawfordinternational.co.za/ruimsig

Crawford International Sandton
Crawford Estate Waterstone Drive (off Benmore Road), Benmore, Sandton, 2196 Johannesburg, Gauteng
PYP Coordinator Jothindran Pillay
Languages English, Zulu
T: +27 11 784 3447
W: www.crawfordschools.co.za/sandton

HOUT BAY INTERNATIONAL SCHOOL
61 Main Road, Hout Bay, 7806 Cape Town, Western Cape
DP Coordinator Michele Marnitz
MYP Coordinator Michele Marnitz
PYP Coordinator Gill Baxter
Languages English
T: +27 21 791 7900
E: hbis@iesmail.com
W: www.houtbayinternational.co.za
See full details on page 104

Mokopane Destiny Academy
Cnr Geyser & Fourie Street, RET Centre, 0601 Mokopane, Limpopo
MYP Coordinator Chris van Zyl
PYP Coordinator Magriet van Tonder
Languages English
T: +27 15 491 2049

Redhill School
20 Summit Road, Morningside, Sandton, 2057 Johannesburg, Gauteng
DP Coordinator Imanu Mwaba
Languages English
T: +27 11 783 4707
W: www.redhill.co.za
 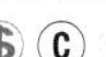

SPAIN

Agora Barcelona International School
Carrer Puig de Mira, Sant Esteve Sesrovires, 08635 Barcelona, Catalonia
DP Coordinator Juan José Rodríguez Borrego
Languages English, Spanish, Catalan, French/german
T: +34 93 779 89 28
W: www.agorabarcelona.com

Agora Granada College International School
Urbanización Llanos de Silva, 18230 Atarfe, Granada, Andalusia
DP Coordinator Jose Manuel Beltrán Padial
Languages English, Spanish
T: +34 958 499 009
W: www.agoragranadacollege.com

Agora Lledó International School
Camino Caminàs, 175, Castelló de la Plana, 12003 Castelló, Valencia
DP Coordinator Julián de la Torre Gisbert
PYP Coordinator Amparo Serra Recatalá
Languages English, Spanish
T: +34 964 72 31 70
W: www.agoralledo.com

Agora Madrid International School
Calle Duero, 35, Villaviciosa de Odón, 28670 Madrid
DP Coordinator Rachel Walker
Languages English, Spanish
T: +34 91 616 71 25
W: www.agoramadrid.com

Agora Portals International School
Carretera Vella Palma-Andratx, s/n, Portals Nous, 07181 Mallorca, Balearic Islands
DP Coordinator Rocio Baquero
MYP Coordinator Therase Jenkinson
Languages English, Spanish
T: +34 964 72 31 70
W: www.agoraportals.com

Agora Sant Cugat International School
Carrer Ferrer i Guàrdia, s/n, Sant Cugat del Vallès, 08174 Barcelona, Catalonia
DP Coordinator Montse Martí Linares
MYP Coordinator Arnaldo Schapire Trapano
PYP Coordinator Carolina Marcarini
Languages English, Spanish, Catalan
T: +34 93 590 26 00
W: www.agorasantcugat.com
 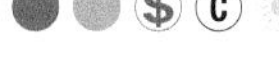

Aloha College Marbella
Urbanización el Angel, 29660 Marbella, Málaga, Andalusia
DP Coordinator Elaine Brigid Mc Girl
Languages English, Spanish
T: +34 95 281 41 33
W: www.aloha-college.com

American School of Barcelona
Calle Balmes 7, Esplugues de Llobregat, 08950 Barcelona, Catalonia
DP Coordinator Charmaine Monds
Languages English
T: +34 93 371 4016
W: www.asbarcelona.com

American School of Bilbao
Soparda Bidea 10, 48640 Berango, Biscay, Basque Country
DP Coordinator Irene Sendra Server
MYP Coordinator Nina Franco
PYP Coordinator Zeynep Dincer
Languages English
T: +34 94 668 0860
W: www.asob.es

American School of Madrid
Apartado 80, 28080 Madrid
DP Coordinator Martina Bree
Languages English
T: +34 91 740 19 00
W: www.asmadrid.org

American School of Valencia
Urbanización Los Monasterios, Apartado de Correos 9, 46530 Puzol, Valencia
DP Coordinator Matias Benlloch
Languages English, Spanish, Valencia
T: +34 96 140 5412
W: www.asvalencia.org
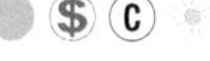

Angel de la Guarda
Calle Andalucía 17-20, 03016 Alicante, Valencia
DP Coordinator Rosario Pérez Escoto
Languages English, Spanish
T: +34 9652 61899
W: www.angeldelaguarda.eu

Aquinas American School
Calle Transversal Cuatro, 4, Urbanización Monte Alina, Pozuelo de Alarcon, 28223 Madrid
DP Coordinator Ana Curbera
Languages English
T: +34 91 352 31 20
W: www.aquinas-american-school.es

Aula Escola Europea
Avinguda Mare de, Déu de Lorda, 34-36, 08034 Barcelona, Catalonia
DP Coordinator Adriana Fasanella Seligrat
Languages Spanish
T: +34 93 203 03 54
W: www.aula-ee.com

Bell-lloc Del Pla
Carrer de Can Pau Birol, 2, 17005 Girona, Catalonia
DP Coordinator Manel Juny Pastells
Languages Spanish
T: +34 972 232 111
W: www.bell-lloc.org/ca

Benjamin Franklin International School
Martorell i Pena 9, 08017 Barcelona, Catalonia
DP Coordinator Laura Blair
Languages English
T: +34 93 434 2380
W: www.bfischool.org

Brains International School, Conde de Orgaz
Calle Frascuelo 2, 28043 Madrid
PYP Coordinator Catherine Roberts
Languages English, Spanish
T: +34 913 889 355
W: www.colegiobrains.com

SPAIN

Brains International School, La Moraleja
Calle Salvia No. 48, 28109 Alcobendas, Madrid
DP Coordinator Michael Harvey
Languages English
T: +34 916 504 300
W: www.colegiobrains.com
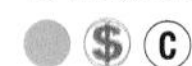

British College of Gava
Carrer de Josep Lluís Sert 32, 08850 Gavà, Barcelona, Catalonia
CP Coordinator Rachel Fenton
DP Coordinator Rachel Fenton
Languages English, Spanish
T: +34 932 777 899
W: www.britishcollegegava.com
 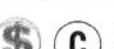

British School of Córdoba
Calle México 4, 14012 Córdoba, Andalusia
DP Coordinator Denise Brown
Languages English, Spanish
T: +34 957 767 048
W: www.colegiobritanicodecordoba.com

C.E. Punta Galea
Urbanización Punta Galea Playa del Sardinero, 1, 28290 Las Rozas, Madrid
DP Coordinator Mercedes Rico Grau
Languages Spanish
T: +34 91 630 26 41
W: www.colegio-puntagalea.com

Canterbury School
San Lorenzo Campus, 35018 San Lorenzo, Las Palmas, Canary Islands
DP Coordinator Pedro Tomás
Languages English, Spanish
T: +34 828 11 34 00
W: www.canterburyschool.com

CASVI INTERNATIONAL AMERICAN SCHOOL
C/ Gavilán, 2, Tres Cantos, 28760 Madrid
DP Coordinator Ana Isabel Domínguez Sánchez
MYP Coordinator Laura Kelly McCutcheon
PYP Coordinator Ryan Posey
Languages English
T: +34 91 804 02 12
E: info@casvitrescantos.es
W: www.casvitrescantos.es
See full details on page 66

Centre Cultural I Esportiu Xaloc
Can Tries, 4-6, L'Hospitalet de Llobregat, 08902 Barcelona, Catalonia
DP Coordinator Martin Curiel
PYP Coordinator Francesc Xavier Dominguez Martín
Languages Spanish
T: +34 93 335 1600
W: www.xaloc.org

Centro de Estudios Ibn Gabirol Colegio Estrella Toledano
Paseo de Alcobendas 7 (La Moraleja), 28109 Alcobendas, Madrid
DP Coordinator Julio Fernando Zapata
Languages English
T: +34 916 50 12 29
W: www.colegiogabiroltoledano.com

Centro Educativo Agave
Camino de la Gloria no 17, 04230 Huercal de Almería, Almería, Andalusia
DP Coordinator Isabel Maria Fenoy Gázquez
Languages English
T: +34 9503 01026
W: www.colegioagave.com

Col·legi Sant Miquel dels Sants
Jaume I, 11, 08500 Vic, Barcelona, Catalonia
DP Coordinator Vanesa Ferrreres Vergés
Languages Catalan, Spanish
T: +34 93 886 12 44
W: www.santmiqueldelssants.cat

Colegio Adharaz
Urb. La Vina. C/ Garnacha 1, 41807 Espartinas, Seville, Andalusia
MYP Coordinator Paloma Valdes Elizalde
PYP Coordinator Marta Campos Fos
Languages English, Spanish
T: +34 955 713 820
W: attendis.com/colegios-sevilla/adharaz

Colegio Alameda de Osuna
Paseo de la Alameda de Osuna, 60, 28042 Madrid
DP Coordinator Diego Corraliza Gil
MYP Coordinator Arantza Carrillo Alonso
PYP Coordinator Sergio Sánchez Moreno
Languages English, Spanish
T: +34 91 742 70 11
W: www.colegio-alameda.com
 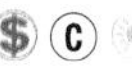

Colegio Alauda
Cerillo 6, 14014 Córdoba, Andalusia
DP Coordinator Laura Paños Díaz
Languages English
T: +34 957 40 55 07
W: www.colegioalauda.org

Colegio Alegra
Calle de Sorolla 4, 28222 Majadahonda, Madrid
DP Coordinator Militza Hernandez
MYP Coordinator Militza Hernandez
Languages English, Spanish
T: +34 916 39 79 03
W: www.alegrabritishschool.com

Colegio Altaduna
Ctra. de Alicún KM. 8, 04740 Roquetas de Mar, Almería, Andalusia
PYP Coordinator Inmaculada Sánchez Tembleque Letamen
Languages English, Spanish
T: +34 950 559 500
W: attendis.com/colegios-almeria/altaduna

Colegio Altasierra
Urb. La Viña. C/ Garnacha 2., 41807 Espartinas, Seville, Andalusia
MYP Coordinator Álvaro Velarde
PYP Coordinator Jesús Hervías Gallardo
Languages English, Spanish
T: +34 954 614 760
W: attendis.com/colegios-sevilla/altasierra

Colegio Antamira
C/ Los Cuadros, 2, Miramadrid, 28860 Paracuellos de Jarama, Madrid
DP Coordinator Pedro Pablo Sacristán Sanz
Languages English, Spanish
T: +34 91 667 27 07
W: www.colegioantamira.com

Colegio Arcangel Rafael
Calle Maqueda no. 4, 28024 Madrid
DP Coordinator Pablo Osma Rodriguez
MYP Coordinator Laura Anton
PYP Coordinator Patricia Veiga
Languages English, Spanish
T: +34 91 711 93 00
W: www.colegio-arcangel.com

Colegio Arenas Atlántico
Paseo San Patricio, No 20, 35413 Trasmontaña, Las Palmas, Canary Islands
DP Coordinator David Arbelo Llorente
MYP Coordinator Encarnación Lorenzo de Armas
Languages Spanish
T: +34 928 629 140
W: www.colegioarenas.es

Colegio Arenas Internacional
Avenida del Mar 37, Lanzarote, 35509 Costa Teguise, Las Palmas, Canary Islands
DP Coordinator Jose Antonio Paz Botana
MYP Coordinator Brian Foster
PYP Coordinator Estela Medina
Languages Spanish
T: +34 928 590 835
W: www.colegioarenas.es

Colegio Arenas Sur
Las Margaritas s/n, 35290 San Agustín, Las Palmas, Canary Islands
DP Coordinator Elias Xerach Rodriguez Manrique de Lara
Languages Spanish
T: +34 928 765 934
W: www.colegioarenassur.com

Colegio Atalaya
Calle Pico Alcazaba 24-28, Urbanización El Marqués, 29680 Estepona, Málaga
DP Coordinator Iraia Manterola Berrueta
Languages English, Spanish
T: +34 952 003 171
W: www.colegioatalaya.es

Colegio Base
Calle del Camino Ancho 10, La Moraleja, 28109 Alcobendas, Madrid
DP Coordinator Victor Acosta Ferreras
MYP Coordinator Helena Pascual Ramirez
Languages Spanish
T: +34 916 500 313
W: www.colegiobase.com
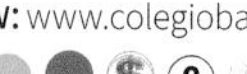

Colegio Bilingüe Villa de Móstoles
Calle Camino de Humanes 40, 28938 Móstoles, Madrid
DP Coordinator Beatriz Muruzábal
Languages Spanish
T: +34 916 453 055
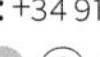

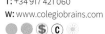

Colegio Brains Maria Lombillo
Calle Maria Lombillo 5, 28027 Madrid
DP Coordinator Linda Keys
PYP Coordinator Daniel Prieto
Languages English, Spanish
T: +34 917 421 060
W: www.colegiobrains.com
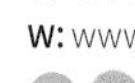

Colegio Camarena Canet
C/ De la Rosa s/n, 46529 Canet d'en Berenguer, Valencia
MYP Coordinator Francisca Martinez Carbonell
PYP Coordinator Amparo Afortunado
Languages English, Spanish
T: +34 960 609 036
W: www.colegiocamarenacanet.es
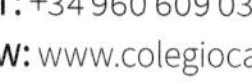

Colegio Camarena Valterna
Calle Carlina s/n 46980, Valterna, Urb. Lloma Llarga, Paterna, Valencia
PYP Coordinator Ángela Meléndez Martín
Languages English, Spanish
T: +34 961 381 898
W: www.colegiovalterna.es

Colegio Cervantes
Avda. de la Fuensanta, 37, 14010 Córdoba, Andalusia
DP Coordinator Manuel Porras García
Languages English
T: +34 957 255150
W: www.maristascordoba.com

Colegio CEU Jesús María Alicante
Calle Deportista Alejandra Quereda 15, 03016 Alicante, Valencia
PYP Coordinator Pablo Jesús Díaz Tenza
Languages Catalan, Valencian, Spanish
T: +34 965 261 400
W: www.colegioceualicante.es

Colegio CEU San Pablo Montepríncipe
Avda. Montepríncipe, s/n, 28668 Boadilla del Monte, Madrid
DP Coordinator Cristina López Mejías
PYP Coordinator Carmen Del Pozo
Languages English, Spanish
T: +34 91 352 05 23
W: www.colegioceumonteprincipe.es

Colegio CEU San Pablo Murcia
Camino San Pablo CEU 16, 30509 Molina de Segura, Murcia
PYP Coordinator Guillermo Naranjo Armas
Languages English, Spanish
T: +34 968 611 905
W: www.colegioceumurcia.es

Colegio CEU San Pablo Sanchinarro
Niceto Alcalá Zamora, 43, 28050 Madrid
DP Coordinator Ruth Jiménez Balboa
Languages English
T: +34 91 392 34 40/41
W: www.colegioceusanchinarro.es

Colegio CEU San Pablo Valencia
Edificio Seminario Metropolitano, 46113 Moncada, Valencia
DP Coordinator Angel Luis Peris Suay
PYP Coordinator Francisco Haro Canet
Languages Spanish
T: +34 961 36 90 14
W: www.colegioceuvalencia.es

Colegio Companía de María - Almería
Rambla Obispo Orberá 35, 04001 Almería, Andalusia
DP Coordinator María del Mar Gómez Bretones
Languages Spanish
T: +34 950 235 422
W: ciamariaalmeria.org

Colegio de San Francisco de Paula
C/ Santa Angela de la Cruz, 11, 41003 Seville, Andalusia
DP Coordinator German Delgado
MYP Coordinator Estela Gonzalez Torres
PYP Coordinator Macarena Vázquez de Cruces
Languages Spanish, English
T: +34 95 422 4382
W: www.sfpaula.com

Colegio del Salvador
Padre Arrupe 13, 50009 Zaragoza, Aragon
DP Coordinator María Laguna MarinYaseli
Languages English, Spanish
T: +34 976 353 400
W: jesuitaszaragoza.es

Colegio Ecos
C/ Velázquez, 7. Urb. Elvira, La Mairena, Ojén, 29612 Marbella, Málaga, Andalusia
MYP Coordinator Ignacio de la Calle Aragón
PYP Coordinator Borja Medina
Languages English, Spanish
T: +34 952 831 027
W: attendis.com/colegios-marbella/ecos

Colegio El Romeral
Calle De Eolo 2, 29010 Málaga, Andalusia
PYP Coordinator Fernando Alba
Languages English, Spanish
T: +34 952 070 370
W: attendis.com/colegios-malaga/el-romeral

Colegio El Valle Alicante
Avda. Condomina 65, 03540 Alicante, Valencia
DP Coordinator Nuria Espinosa Juan
MYP Coordinator José Sánchez Segovia
PYP Coordinator Alberto Fernández de Aguilar
Languages English, Spanish
T: +34 965 155 619
W: www.colegioelvalle.com

Colegio El Valle II - Sanchinarro
Calle Ana De Austria, 60, 28050 Madrid
DP Coordinator Nuria Alvarez Herranz
Languages Spanish
T: +34 91 7188426
W: www.colegioelvalle.com

Colegio Europeo de Madrid
Calle Cólquide 14, Las Rozas de Madrid, 28231 Madrid
PYP Coordinator Melanie McGeever
Languages English, Spanish
T: +34 687 521 151
W: www.colegioeuropeodemadrid.com

Colegio Grazalema
C/ Caracola, 2. Urb. Valdelagrana, 11500 El Puerto de Santa María, Cádiz, Andalusia
PYP Coordinator Leticia Rodriguez Delgado
Languages English, Spanish
T: +34 956 561 542
W: attendis.com/colegios-el-puerto-jerez/grazalema

Colegio Guadalete
C/ Ubrique, 36. Urb. Valdelagrana, 11500 El Puerto de Santa María, Cádiz, Andalusia
PYP Coordinator Alejandro Rincón Jurado
Languages English, Spanish
T: +34 956 561 646
W: attendis.com/colegios-el-puerto-jerez/guadalete

Colegio Heidelberg
Apartado de Correos 248, Barranco Seco 15, 35090 Las Palmas de Gran Canaria, Las Palmas, Can+
DP Coordinator Isis Comas
MYP Coordinator Nacho Santa-María Megía
Languages Spanish
T: +34 928 350 462
W: www.colegioheidelberg.com

Colegio HH. Maristas Sagrado Corazón Alicante
Calle de la Isla de Corfú, 5, 03005 Alicante, Valencia
DP Coordinator Fernando Fuentes Guzmán
Languages Spanish
T: +34 965 130 941
W: www.maristasalicante.com

Colegio Inglés English School of Asturias
Finca La Llosona s/n, 33192 Pruvia, Asturias
DP Coordinator Robert Deuchar
Languages English, Spanish
T: +34 985 237 171
W: asturias.iepgroup.es

Colegio Internacional Ausiàs March
Urbanización Residencial Tancat de l'Alter s/n, 46220 Picassent, Valencia
DP Coordinator María Pérez Galván
Languages Spanish
T: +34 96 123 05 66
W: www.ausiasmarch.com

Colegio Internacional de Levante
Río Jalón 25 Urbanización Calicanto, 46370 Valencia
DP Coordinator Alejandra Mezquida Ferragut
MYP Coordinator Carlos Garcia
Languages Spanish
T: +34 961980650
W: www.colintlev.net

Colegio Internacional Jesuitinas Miralba
Avda Gran Vía 164, 36211 Vigo, Pontevedra, Galicia
DP Coordinator David Fernández Núnez
Languages Spanish, Galician
T: +34 986 213 047
W: www.jesuitinasvigo.es

Colegio Internacional Meres
Carretera Meres, s/n, 33199 Meres, Asturias
DP Coordinator Inés Espiniella Sanmartín
MYP Coordinator Cristina Cuadrado Martínez
PYP Coordinator Carmen González Aller
Languages Spanish
T: +34 985 792 427
W: www.colegiomeres.com

Colegio Internacional Pureza de María Los Realejos
C/ Ciudad Jardín 16. La Montañeta, Los Realejos, 38419 Santa Cruz de Tenerife, Tenerife, Canary Is+
DP Coordinator Eduardo Souto Gross
Languages English, Spanish
T: +34 922 340 550
W: pmaria-losrealejos.org

Colegio Internacional SEK Eiris
C Castaño de Eiris, 1, 15009 A Coruña, Galicia
DP Coordinator Jose Antonio Lopez Fuentes
Languages English, Spanish
T: +34 981 28 44 00
W: www.eiris.edu.es

Spain

Colegio Internacional Torrequebrada
C/ Ronda del Golf Este, 7-11, Urbanización Torrequebrada, 29639 Benalmádena, Málaga, Andalusia
DP Coordinator Guillermo Chaves
MYP Coordinator Fiona Seward
PYP Coordinator Elena Lecertua
Languages English, Spanish
T: +34 952 57 60 65
W: www.colegiotorrequebrada.com
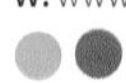  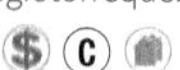

Colegio Las Chapas
Urb. Las Chapas s/n, 29604 Marbella, Málaga, Andalusia
DP Coordinator María Fernanda López-Alcalá Cortinas
MYP Coordinator Maila Piconi
PYP Coordinator Mercedes Cantera Cavestany
Languages English, Spanish
T: +34 952 831 616
W: attendis.com/colegios-marbella/las-chapas

Colegio Legamar
Ctra. Leganés-Fuenlabrada Km. 1.5, 28914 Leganés, Madrid
DP Coordinator Ángel Jiménez Caravaca
Languages English, Spanish
T: +34 916 933 812
W: colegiolegamar.es
 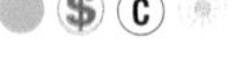

Colegio Lestonnac Barcelona
Pau Claris 131, 08009 Barcelona, Catalonia
DP Coordinator Carlota Aulet i Sol
Languages Spanish, Catalan, Valencian
T: +34 932 159 900
W: lestonnacbcn.org

Colegio Liceo Europeo
C/ Camino Sur 10, 28100 Alcobendas, Madrid
DP Coordinator Esther Arama Ibáñez
MYP Coordinator Rubén Moreno Ferreiro
PYP Coordinator Fatima Rodriguez Vicens
Languages English, Spanish
T: +34 91 650 00 00
W: www.liceo-europeo.es

Colegio Logos
Urbanización Molino de la Hoz c/, Sacre 2, 28232 Las Rozas, Madrid
DP Coordinator Héctor Martínez
Languages English
T: +34 91 630 34 94
W: www.colegiologos.com

Colegio Madrid
Avda. del Comandante Franco 8, 28016 Madrid
DP Coordinator Patricia Gamir Henderson
Languages Spanish
T: +34 910 572 501
W: www.madridcolegio.es

Colegio Manuel Peleteiro
Monte Redondo - Castiñeiriño, 15702 Santiago de Compostela, A Coruña, Galicia
DP Coordinator Rafael Gómez Montero
Languages Spanish
T: +34 98 1591475
W: www.peleteiro.com

Colegio Mater Salvatoris
Calle Valdesquí no. 4, 28023 Madrid
DP Coordinator Almudena Alonso
Languages Spanish
T: +34 91 307 1243
W: matersalvatoris.org

Colegio Monaita
C/ Acequia de la Madraza s/n, 18015 Granada, Andalusia
PYP Coordinator Beatriz Rico Mahuenda
Languages English, Spanish
T: +34 958 806 940
W: attendis.com/colegios-granada/monaita

Colegio Montecalpe
Urb. San García, C/ La Carpa s/n, 11207 Algeciras, Cádiz, Andalusia
PYP Coordinator Alvaro Camacho
Languages English, Spanish
T: +34 956 605 888
W: attendis.com/colegios-algeciras/montecalpe

Colegio Montserrat
Av Vallvidrera, 68, 08017 Barcelona, Catalonia
DP Coordinator Juan Antonio Fernández-Arévalo
MYP Coordinator Olga Casaban
Languages English, Spanish
T: +34 932 038 800
W: www.cmontserrat.org
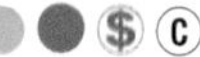

Colegio Mulhacén
Ctra. Pinos Puente 10, 18015 Granada, Andalusia
MYP Coordinator Pablo Calderon
PYP Coordinator Jesús Hervías Gallardo
Languages English, Spanish
T: +34 958 806 800
W: attendis.com/colegios-granada/mulhacen

Colegio Nuestra Señora de Schoenstatt
Camino de Alcorcón 17, 28223 Pozuelo de Alarcón, Madrid
DP Coordinator Fernando De Miguel Losada
Languages English, Spanish
T: +34 917 159 226
W: www.cnsschoenstatt.es

Colegio Nuestra Señora del Recuerdo
Plaza Duque de Pastrana 5, 28036 Madrid
DP Coordinator Gemma Campo
Languages English
T: +34 91 3022640
W: www.recuerdo.net

Colegio Obradoiro
Rua Obradoiro 49, 15190 A Coruña, Galicia
DP Coordinator Fernando Vales Vázquez
MYP Coordinator Consuelo Gajino Cousillas
PYP Coordinator Jorge Muiños Guereca
Languages English, Spanish
T: +34 981 281 888
W: www.colegioobradoiro.es

Colegio Parque
Calle Piamonte, 19 Urbanización Parquelagos, La Navata, 28420 Galapagar, Madrid
DP Coordinator Raul Fernández Pascual
Languages English, Spanish
T: +34 918 590 630
W: www.colegioparque.com

Colegio Puertoblanco
Calle Goleta 2, 11207 Algeciras, Cádiz, Andalusia
PYP Coordinator Leticia De Bedoya Izquierdo
Languages English, Spanish
T: +34 956 604 422
W: attendis.com/colegios-algeciras/puertoblanco
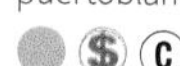

Colegio Retamar
Madrid España, c/ Pajares 22, 28223 Madrid
DP Coordinator Juan Navalpotro
Languages Spanish
T: +34 91 714 10 22
W: www.retamar.com

Colegio Sagrada Familia Jesuitinas
Carretera de Segovia 1, 47012 Valladolid, Castile & León
DP Coordinator María Carmen Martín Arribas
Languages English, Spanish
T: +34 983 230 412
W: www.jesuitinasvalladolid.es

Colegio Saladares
Ctra. de Alicún. KM. 10300, 04721 El Parador de las Hortichuelas, Almería, An+
PYP Coordinator Antonio Manuel Perales Sánchez
Languages English, Spanish
T: +34 950 559 644
W: attendis.com/colegios-almeria/saladares

Colegio San Cayetano
Av. Picasso 21, 07014 Palma De Mallorca, Balearic Islands
DP Coordinator Irene Pascual Sastre
Languages English, Spanish
T: +34 971 220 575
W: www.colegiosancayetano.com

Colegio San Cristóbal
Calle San Jorge del Maestrazgo, 2, 12003 Castellón de la Plana, Castellón, Valencia
DP Coordinator Ana Belen Baldayo
Languages English
T: +34 964 228 758
W: sancristobalsl.com

Colegio San Fernando
Avenida San Agustín, s/n, 33400 Avilés, Asturias
DP Coordinator María Fernández González
MYP Coordinator Lucia Gonzalez
PYP Coordinator Adriana Álvarez
Languages English, Spanish
T: +34 985 565 745
W: www.sanfer.es
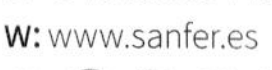

Colegio San Ignacio Jesuitas Oviedo
Avenida Richard Grandío, S/N, 33193 Oviedo, Asturias
DP Coordinator Arnau Pla Novoa
PYP Coordinator María Jesús García-Herrero Suárez
Languages Spanish
T: +34 985 233 300
W: www.colegiosanignacio.es

Colegio San Ignacio Jesuitas Pamplona
C/ Francisco Bergamín 32, 31004 Pamplona, Navarre
DP Coordinator Alejandro Rodríguez Vázquez
Languages English, Spanish
T: +34 948 233 800
W: www.jesuitaspamplona.org

Colegio San Jorge
Soc. Coop. Enseñanza la Alcayna. CIF: F30410328, Avda. Picos de Europa s/n, 30507 Molina de Segura, Murcia
DP Coordinator José Manuel Castro Belmonte
Languages English, Spanish
T: +34 968 430 711
W: colegiosanjorge.es

Colegio San José Estepona
Avd. Litoral 22, 29680 Estepona, Málaga, Andalusia
DP Coordinator Miguel Angel Salazar Troya
Languages Spanish
T: +34 952 800 148
W: www.colegiosanjose.net

COLEGIO SAN PATRICIO EL SOTO
Calle Jazmin 148, El Soto de la Moraleja, 28109 Alcobendas, Madrid
DP Coordinator James Smith
Languages English, Spanish
T: +34 916 500 602
E: infosoto@colegiosanpatricio.es
W: www.colegiosanpatriciomadrid.com
See full details on page 70
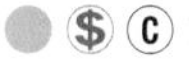

Colegio Santa María del Camino
C/ Peguerinos 13, Puerta de Hierro, 28035 Madrid
DP Coordinator Mary Larrosa
MYP Coordinator Carmen Mosquera Mariño
PYP Coordinator Maria Zavala
Languages English, Spanish
T: +34 913 161 347
W: smc.edu.es

Colegio Sierra Blanca
Avenida de Plutarco 34, 29010 Málaga, Andalusia
PYP Coordinator Carmen Martínez Torres
Languages English, Spanish
T: +34 952 070 650
W: attendis.com/colegios-malaga/sierra-blanca
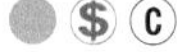

Colegio Valdefuentes
Ana de Austria 6, Sanchinarro, 28050 Madrid
DP Coordinator Sara Escobar
Languages English, Spanish
T: +34 917 188 229
W: www.colegiovaldefuentes.es

COLEGIO VIRGEN DE EUROPA
C/ Valle de Santa Ana No. 1, Las Lomas, 28669 Boadilla del Monte, Madrid
DP Coordinator María Cruz Larrosa
MYP Coordinator Carmen Mosquera Mariño
PYP Coordinator Sarah O'Halloran
Languages English, Spanish
T: +34 91 633 0155
E: mc_larrosa@colegiovirgendeeuropa.edu.es
W: www.colegiovirgendeeuropa.com
See full details on page 71
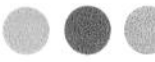
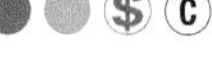

Colegios Ramón Y Cajal
C/ Arturo Soria, 206, 28043 Madrid
DP Coordinator Mariano Sanz Garcia
MYP Coordinator Patricia Martinez Obispo
PYP Coordinator Laura Pérez
Languages English
T: +34 91 413 56 31
W: www.colegiosramonycajal.es

Complejo Educativo Mas Camarena
C/ 1 Urbanización, Mas Camarena, 46117 Bétera, Valencia
CP Coordinator Ana Carrascosa
DP Coordinator Louise Grint
MYP Coordinator John Henry Patton
PYP Coordinator Maite Navarro García
Languages Spanish
T: +34 961687535
W: www.colegios-sigloxxi.com

Cooperativa de Enseñanza San Cernin
Avda. Baranain 3, 31007 Pamplona, Navarre
DP Coordinator Arantxa Hernández
Languages English
T: +34 948176288
W: www.sancernin.es

El Plantío International School of Valencia
Calle 233 No36 Urb El Plantío, La Cañada, 46182 Paterna, Valencia
DP Coordinator Alicia Ocón Crespo
Languages English, Spanish
T: +34 96 132 14 10
W: plantiointernational.com

Elian's British School of La Nucía
Av. El Copet 5, 03530 La Nucía, Alicante, Valencia
DP Coordinator Jorge Sevilla Esclapez
Languages English, Spanish
T: +34 966 877 055
W: lanucia.iepgroup.es

ES AMERICAN SCHOOL
Autovia de Castelldefels C-31 Km 191, El Prat de Llobregat, 08820 Barcelona, Catalonia
PYP Coordinator Lauren Hopkins
Languages English
T: +34 93 479 1611
E: admin@es-school.com
W: www.es-school.com
See full details on page 85

Escola Frederic Mistral Tècnic Eulàlia
Pere II de Montcada 8, 08034 Barcelona, Catalonia
DP Coordinator Jordi Dosaiguas Falcó
Languages English, Spanish
T: +34 932 031 280
W: fredericmistral-tecniceulalia.cat

Escola Internacional del Camp
Salvador Espiriu s/n, 43840 Salou, Tarragona, Catalonia
DP Coordinator Cristina Garcia Bardon
Languages English, Spanish
T: +34 977325620
W: www.escolainternacional.org

Escola Voramar
Passeig de García Fària, 08005 Barcelona, Catalonia
DP Coordinator Mirela Domitrovic
Languages English, Spanish
T: +34 932 251 324
W: www.voramon.cat

ESCUELA IDEO
Highway from Colmenar to Alcobendas, Km. 0.500, 28049 Madrid
DP Coordinator Paloma de Oñate Alguero
Languages Spanish (and English = Language B)
T: +34 917 523 343
E: paloma.deonate@escuelaideo.edu.es
W: www.escuelaideo.edu.es
See full details on page 86

Eurocolegio Casvi Boadilla
C/ Miguel Ángel Cantero Oliva, 13, Boadilla del Monte, Madrid
MYP Coordinator Francisco José Corchero Gómez
PYP Coordinator Álvaro Feijoo Pérez
Languages Spanish
T: +34 91 632 96 53
W: www.casviboadilla.es

EUROCOLEGIO CASVI VILLAVICIOSA
Avenida de Castilla, 27, Villaviciosa de Odón, 28670 Madrid
DP Coordinator Jose Vicente Belizón Collado
MYP Coordinator Félix David Vozmediano León
PYP Coordinator Gema Grañeda
Languages Spanish
T: +34 91 616 22 18
E: casvi@casvi.es
W: www.casvi.es
See full details on page 87

Fundacion Privada Oak House School
Sant Pere Claver 12-18, 08017 Barcelona, Catalonia
DP Coordinator Elaine Sibley
Languages English
T: +34 932 524 020
W: www.oakhouseschool.com

Green Valley School
Cami de la Vileta 210, Son Puig, 07011 Palma De Mallorca, Balearic Islands
DP Coordinator David Méndez Rodríguez
Languages English
T: +34 971 160 817
W: greenvalleyschool.es

GRESOL International-American School
Ctra. Sabadell a Matadepera, (BV-1248) km. 6, 08227 Terrassa, Barcelona, Catalonia
DP Coordinator Eduardo Torrecillas Sanchez
Languages English, Spanish
T: +34 937 870 158
W: www.gresolschool.com

GSD International School Buitrago
Av. de Madrid 16, 28730 Buitrago del Lozoya, Madrid
DP Coordinator Germán Fonseca Marín
Languages English, Spanish
T: +34 918 680 200
W: www.gsdinternationalschool.com/buitrago

GSD Las Rozas
C/ Clara Campoamor 1, 28232 Las Rozas, Madrid
DP Coordinator Jesús Montoro Ruiz
Languages Spanish
T: +34 916 408 923
W: www.gsdeducacion.com/colegios/gsdlasrozas

Hamelin-Laie International School
Ronda 8 de Marc 178-180, 08390 Montgat, Barcelona, Catalonia
DP Coordinator Yolanda Soriano Garcia
Languages English, Spanish, Catalan
T: +34 93 5556717
W: www.hamelininternacionallaie.com

Hastings School
Calle Manuel Maranon 8, 28043 Madrid
DP Coordinator Anna Brickle
Languages English, Spanish
T: +34 918 33 77 90
W: www.hastingsschool.com

I.E.S. Alfonso X 'el Sabio'
Avda D Juan de Borbón 3, 30007 Murcia
DP Coordinator María Dolores Romero Carbonell
Languages Spanish
T: +34 968 232 040
W: www.iesalfonsox.com

I.E.S. Juan de la Cierva y Codorníu
C/San Antonio, 84, 30850 Totana, Murcia
DP Coordinator Vicente Sanz Duart
Languages Spanish
T: +34 968 42 19 19
W: www.murciaeduca.es/iesjuandelacierva/sitio

I.E.S. Maestro Matías Bravo
Avenida Mar Egeo S/N, Valdemoro, 28341 Madrid
DP Coordinator Marta López de la Llana
Languages Spanish
T: +34 91 801 8044
W: www.educa.madrid.org/web/ies.maestromatiasbravo.valdemoro

IES Atenea
Pl. de Santiago de Chuco 1, San Sebastián de los Reyes, 28702 Madrid
DP Coordinator Pedro Lomas Nielfa
Languages English, Spanish
T: +34 916 590 934
W: www.educa2.madrid.org/web/centro.ies.atenea.sansebastian

IES Avenida de los Toreros
Av. de los Toreros 57, 28028 Madrid
DP Coordinator Miryam Martín Martín
Languages English, Spanish
T: +34 913 552 326

IES Bachiller Sabuco
Albacete, Avenida de España 9, 02002 Albacete, Castilla-La Mancha
DP Coordinator María del Mar Buendía Navarro
Languages Spanish
T: +34 967 229 540
W: www.sabuco.com

IES Bilingüe Cervantes
Calle de Embajadores, 70, 28012 Madrid
DP Coordinator Luis Horrillo
Languages English, Spanish
W: external.educa2.madrid.org/web/centro.ies.cervantes.madrid

IES Cañada Real
Calle Carmen Martin Gaite s/n, 28260 Galapagar, Madrid
DP Coordinator Maria del Rosario Sanchez Garcia
Languages English, Spanish
T: +34 918 583 336
W: www.educa2.madrid.org/web/centro.ies.canadareal.galapagar

IES Cardenal López de Mendoza
Plaza Luis Martin Santos s/n, 09002 Burgos, Castile & León
DP Coordinator Olga Barriuso-Merinero
MYP Coordinator Raul Ubierna Hortigüela
Languages Spanish
T: +34 947 257701
W: ieslopezdemendoza.centros.educa.jcyl.es

IES Carlos III de Toledo
Avenida de Francia 5, 45005 Toledo, Castilla-La Mancha
DP Coordinator Ángel Castelló Pola
Languages Spanish
T: +34 925 212 967

IES Castilla
Calle Alonso Velázquez s/n, 42003 Soria, Castile & León
DP Coordinator Ernesto Pastor Lebrero
Languages English
T: +34 975 221 283

IES Celia Vinas
C/ Javier Sanz 15, 04004 Almería, Andalusia
DP Coordinator Juan Diego Estrada Godoy
Languages Spanish
T: +34 950 156 151
W: iescelia.org/web

IES Diego de Guzmán y Quesada
Av. Manuel Siurot 11, 21004 Huelva, Andalusia
DP Coordinator Lorenzo Castilla Mora
Languages Spanish
T: +34 95 952 4835

IES Fernando de Herrera
Paseo de la Palmera 20, 41012 Seville, Andalusia
DP Coordinator Luisa Maria López Gómez
Languages English, Spanish
T: +34 955 622 191
W: www.iesfernandodeherrera.es

IES Francisco Salzillo
C/ Museo de la Huerta 20, 30820 Alcantarilla, Murcia
DP Coordinator Jose Antonio Enrique Jimenez
Languages English, Spanish
W: www.murciaeduca.es/iesfranciscosalzillo/sitio

IES Jorge Manrique
Avda. Republica Argentina s/n, 34002 Palencia, Castile & León
DP Coordinator Miguel Angel Arconada Melero
Languages Spanish
T: +34 979 720 384
W: www.iesjorgemanrique.com

IES Jorge Santayana
Calle Santo Tomás 6, 05003 Ávila, Castile & León
DP Coordinator Ana Rodríguez Pérez
Languages Spanish
T: +34 920 35 21 35
W: iesjorgesantayana.centros.educa.jcyl.es

IES José Saramago
Calle del Maestro 1, Majadahonda, 28220 Madrid
DP Coordinator Gema Muñoz Garcinuño
Languages Spanish
T: +34 916 398 411
W: www.educa2.madrid.org/web/centro.ies.josesaramago.majadahonda

IES Los Castillos
Avd. de Los Castillos No. 5, 28925 Alcorcón, Madrid
DP Coordinator Juan Ignacio Cubero Pérez
Languages English, Spanish
T: +34 916 121 063
W: sites.google.com/iesloscastillos.com/iesloscastillos/inicio

IES Los Cerros
C/ Cronista Juan de la Torre 11, 23400 Úbeda, Jaén, Andalusia
DP Coordinator José María Expósito Garrido
Languages English, Spanish
T: +34 953 779 990
W: loscerros.org
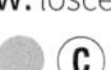

IES Lucas Mallada
C/Torre Mendoza No 2, 22005 Huesca, Aragon
DP Coordinator Laura Domingo Capella
Languages Spanish
T: +34 974 244 834
W: www.ieslucasmallada.com

IES Manacor
c/ Camí de Ses Tapareres, 32, 07500 Manacor, Balearic Islands
DP Coordinator Pilar Caldentey Gomila
Languages Spanish, Catalan, Valencian
T: +34 971 551 489
W: www.iesmanacor.cat

IES María Zambrano
C/ Cipriano Maldonado, 8 Torre del Mar, 29740 Málaga, Andalusia
DP Coordinator Lidia Acosta Gutierrez
Languages Spanish
T: +34 95 128 9559
W: www.iesmariazambrano.org

IES Marqués de Santillana
Avda España, 2, Torrelavega, 39300 Cantabria
DP Coordinator José Manuel Piñeiro Moratinos
Languages Spanish
T: +34 942 88 16 00
W: www.iesmarquesdesantillana.com

IES Martinez Montanes
C/Fernández de Ribera no. 17, 41005 Seville, Andalusia
DP Coordinator Jorge Mejías López
Languages Spanish
T: +34 955 623 877
W: iesmartinezm.es

IES Mateo Sagasta
Glorieta del Doctor Zubia s/n, 26003 Logroño, La Rioja
DP Coordinator Gloria Bernad Pérez
Languages Spanish
T: +34 941 256 500
W: iessagasta.edurioja.org

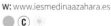

IES Medina Azahara
Av. Gran Vía Parque 2, 14005 Córdoba, Andalusia
DP Coordinator Francisco José Simón Torres
Languages Spanish
T: +34 957 73 46 15
W: www.iesmedinaazahara.es

IES Miguel Catalán
Paseo de Isabel La católica, 3, 50009 Zaragoza, Aragon
DP Coordinator Juan José Carracedo Doval
Languages Spanish
T: +34 976 402 004
W: www.ies-mcatalan.com

IES Navarro Villoslada
Arcadio Mª Larraona, 3, 31008 Pamplona, Navarre
DP Coordinator Elvira Salvador Ercilla
Languages Spanish
T: +34 848 431 150
W: www.iesnavarrovilloslada.com

IES Padre Luis Coloma
Avda. Alcalde Álvaro Domecq, 10, Jerez de la Frontera, 11402 Cádiz, Andalusia
DP Coordinator Isabel Suárez Cachá
Languages Spanish
T: +34 671 565 351
W: www.iescoloma.es

IES Padre Manjón
Gonzalo Gallas s/n, 18003 Granada, Andalusia
DP Coordinator Paloma Soler Celdrán
Languages English, Spanish
T: +34 958 893 493
W: iespm.es
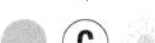

IES Pere Boïl
C/Ceramista Alfons Blat 20, 46940 Manises, Valencia
DP Coordinator Maria José Hellín Méndez
Languages Spanish
T: +34 961 20 62 25
W: www.pereboil.com

IES Príncipe Felipe
Calle de Finisterre No. 60, 28029 Madrid
DP Coordinator Rebeca González Barreiro
Languages Spanish
T: +34 913 14 63 12
W: iespf2014.villatic.org

IES Ramiro de Maeztu
C/ Serrano 127, 28006 Madrid
DP Coordinator Silvia Jiménez Hervás
Languages Spanish
T: +34 91 561 7842
W: www.educa.madrid.org/web/ies.ramirodemaeztu.madrid

IES Real Instituto de Jovellanos
Avenida de la Constitucion s/n, 33071 Gijon, Asturias
DP Coordinator Isabel Hompanera lanzos
Languages Spanish
T: +34 985 38 77 03
W: www.iesjovellanos.com

IES Rosa Chacel
Calle Huertas 68, Colmenar Viejo, 28770 Madrid
DP Coordinator Ignacio Valdés López
Languages Spanish
T: +34 91 846 48 01
W: ies.rosachacel.colmenarviejo.educa.madrid.org

IES Rosalia De Castro
San Clemente 3, Santiago de Compostela, 15705 A Coruña, Galicia
DP Coordinator Arantxa Fuentes
Languages Spanish
T: +34 981 569 650
W: www.iesrosalia.net

IES Salvador Rueda
C/ Corregidor Antonio de Bobadilla 13, 29006 Málaga, Andalusia
DP Coordinator Belén Martinez Uribe
Languages English, Spanish
T: +34 951 298 588
W: www.iessalvadorrueda.es

IES San Isidro
C/ Toledo 39, 28005 Madrid
DP Coordinator Ana Anta Vega
Languages English, Spanish
W: www.educa2.madrid.org/web/centro.ies.sanisidro.madrid

IES Santa Clara
c/ Santa Clara 13, 39001 Santander, Cantabria
DP Coordinator Álvaro Fonseca González
Languages Spanish
T: +34 942 216 550

Institut Arnau Cadell
Avda. Villadelprat 91-93, 08197 Sant Cugat del Vallès, Barcelona, Catalonia
DP Coordinator Laia Gallart Coira
Languages Spanish, Catalan, Valencian
T: +34 936 747 266
W: agora.xtec.cat/iesarnaucadell

Institut d'Educació Secundària Josep Lladonosa
Plaa Maria Rúbies S/N, 25005 Lleida, Catalonia
DP Coordinator Jacint Llauradó
Languages Spanish
T: +34 97 3239531
W: www.insjoseplladonosa.cat

Institut D'Educacio Secundaria Son Pacs
Carretera de Soller 13, 07120 Palma De Mallorca, Balearic Islands
DP Coordinator Antonia Vidal Nicolau
Languages Catalan, Spanish, English
T: +34 97 1292050
W: www.iessonpacs.cat

Institut Dertosa
Av. Estadi, 14, 43500 Tortosa, Tarragona, Catalonia
DP Coordinator Núria Serra Benedicto
Languages Catalan, Valencian, Spanish
T: +34 977 501 310
W: agora.xtec.cat/insdertosa

Institut Forat del Vent
Pizarro, 35, Cerdanyola del Vallès, 08290 Barcelona, Catalonia
DP Coordinator Mavi Climent Savall
Languages Catalan, Valencian, Spanish
T: +34 936 911 200
W: agora.xtec.cat/iesforatdelvent
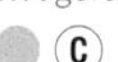

Institut Gabriel Ferrater i Soler
Carretera de Montblanc 5-9, 43206 Reus, Tarragona, Catalonia
DP Coordinator Beatriz Comella Dorda
Languages English
T: +34 977342010
W: institutgabrielferrater.wordpress.com

Institut Jaume Vicens Vives
Isabel la Católica, 17, 17004 Girona, Catalonia
DP Coordinator Farners Brugués Massó
Languages Catalan, Spanish
T: +34 972 200 130
W: ins-jvicensvives.xtec.cat

Institut L'Alzina
Passatge Salvador Riera 2, 08027 Barcelona, Catalonia
DP Coordinator Cristina Sánchez-Guijaldo González
Languages Catalan, Spanish
T: +34 933 409 850
W: www.alzina.cat

Institut Moisès Broggi
Calle Sant Quintí 32-50, 08041 Barcelona, Catalonia
DP Coordinator Jaume Silvestre Llinares
Languages Spanish
T: +34 93 436 89 03
W: www.institutbroggi.org

Institut Sabadell
Carrer de Juvenal 1, 08206 Sabadell, Barcelona, Catalonia
DP Coordinator Raquel López Rodriguez
Languages English, Spanish
T: +34 937 233 905
W: agora.xtec.cat/ies-sabadell

Instituto de Educación Secundaria do Castro
C/Posada Curros 1, 36203 Vigo, Pontevedra, Galicia
DP Coordinator Mercedes Argones Márquez
Languages Spanish
T: +34 986422974
W: centros.edu.xunta.es/iesdocastro

Instituto de Educación Secundaria Lancia
c. Egido Quintín, s/n, 24006 León, Castile & León
DP Coordinator Roberto de la Fuente
Languages Spanish
T: +34 987259800
W: ieslancia.centros.educa.jcyl.es

Instituto Pedralbes
Av. Esplugues 36-42, 08034 Barcelona, Catalonia
DP Coordinator Marta Galindo Casas
Languages Spanish, Catalan
T: +34 932 033 332
W: www.institutpedralbes.cat

Internacional Aravaca
Calle Santa Bernardita 3, 28023 Madrid
MYP Coordinator Alice Pallarés
PYP Coordinator Laura Oran
Languages English, Spanish
T: +34 913 571 256
W: internacionalaravaca.edu.es

International College Spain
C/Vereda Norte, 3, La Moraleja, 28109 Alcobendas, Madrid
DP Coordinator Jeroen Kuipers
MYP Coordinator Kathryn Freeburn
PYP Coordinator Lucy Haddock
Languages English
T: +34 91 650 2398
W: www.nordangliaeducation.com/our-schools/madrid

International School of Barcelona
Passeig Isaac Albeniz s/n, Vallpineda, 08870 Sitges, Barcelona, Catalonia
DP Coordinator Maria Kovac
Languages English
T: +34 93 894 20 40
W: educa4all.com

INTERNATIONAL SCHOOL SAN PATRICIO TOLEDO
Juan de Vergara, 1, Urbanización La Legua, Toledo, Castilla-La Mancha 45005
DP Coordinator Mr. Philip Brotherton
MYP Coordinator Ms. Pilar Molina
PYP Coordinator Ms. Rebeca Albarrán Corroto
Languages English, Spanish
T: +34 925 280 363
E: infotoledo@colegiosanpatricio.es
W: colegiosanpatriciotoledo.com/en
See full details on page 142

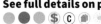

Irabia-Izaga Colegio
Calle Cintruénigo, 31015 Pamplona, Navarre
DP Coordinator Javier Otegui Tellechea
MYP Coordinator Raul Munoz
Languages English, Spanish
T: +34 948 12 62 22
W: www.irabia-izaga.org
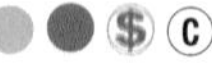

Jesuitinas Donostia, Nuestra Señora de Aranzazu
Paseo de Errondo 121, Aiete, 20009 Donostia-San Sebastian, Gipuzkoa, Basque Co+
DP Coordinator Mikel Gallego
Languages English, Spanish
T: +34 943 212 307
W: www.jesuitinasdonostia.eus

KENSINGTON SCHOOL
Avenida de Bularas No. 2, Pozuelo de Alarcón, 28224 Madrid
DP Coordinator Peter Carlyle
Languages English
T: +34 91 7154 699
E: kensington@kensingtonschool.net
W: www.kensington-school.es
See full details on page 148
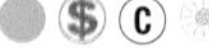

KING'S COLLEGE, THE BRITISH SCHOOL OF ALICANTE
Glorieta del Reino Unido No. 5, 03008 Alicante, Valencia
DP Coordinator Verity Long
Languages English, Spanish
T: +34 96 510 6351
E: info.kca@kingsgroup.com
W: www.alicante.kingscollegeschools.org
See full details on page 152

KING'S COLLEGE, THE BRITISH SCHOOL OF MADRID (SOTO DE VIÑUELAS)
Paseo de los Andes 35, Soto de Viñuelas, 28760 Madrid
DP Coordinator Federica Menon
Languages English
T: +34 918 034 800
E: kc.admissions@kingscollegeschools.org
W: madrid-soto.kingscollegeschools.org
See full details on page 153

KING'S COLLEGE, THE BRITISH SCHOOL OF MURCIA
Calle Pez Volador s/n, Urbanización La Torre Golf Resort, 30709 Roldán, Murcia
DP Coordinator Robert Snowden
Languages English, Spanish
T: +34 968 032 500
E: murcia.info@kings.education
W: www.murcia.kingscollegeschools.org
See full details on page 154

La Dehesa de Humanes
Av. de los Deportes 8, 28970 Humanes de Madrid, Madrid
DP Coordinator Gema Redondo Flores
Languages English, Spanish
T: +34 916 049 002
W: cldh.es

LA MIRANDA THE GLOBAL QUALITY SCHOOL
Carrer del Canigó 15, 08960 Sant Just Desvern, Barcelona, Catalonia
DP Coordinator Berta Vidal Valls
MYP Coordinator Beatriz Olleta
Languages English, Spanish
T: +34 93 371 73 58
E: info@lamiranda.eu
W: www.lamiranda.eu
See full details on page 157

La Salle Bonanova
Passeig de la Bonanova, 8, 08022 Barcelona, Catalonia
DP Coordinator Joan Ferretjans i Marco
Languages English
T: +34 93 254 09 50
W: www.bonanova.lasalle.cat

Laude El Altillo School
C/ Santiago de Chile, s/n, 11407 Jerez de la Frontera, Cádiz, Andalusia
DP Coordinator María Teresa Martos Martos
MYP Coordinator Manuel de la Rosa Marchante
Languages English, Spanish, French
T: +34 956 302 400
W: www.laudealtillo.com

Laude Newton College
Camino Viejo de Elche-Alicante Km, 3, Alicante, Valencia
DP Coordinator Francisco Beltrán Muñoz
MYP Coordinator Abbie Nuttall
Languages Spanish, English
T: +34 96 545 14 28
W: www.laudenewtoncollege.com

Les Alzines
La Creu de Palau 2, 17003 Girona, Catalonia
DP Coordinator Roser Jorba Campo
Languages Spanish
T: +34 972 212162
W: www.institucio.org/lesalzines

Lestonnac L'Ensenyança
Carrer Arc de Sant Llorenç, 2, 43003 Tarragona, Catalonia
DP Coordinator Carmen García Valiente
Languages English
T: +34 977 23 25 19
W: lestonnac-tarragona.net

Liceo Sorolla c
Avda. Bularas 4, 28224 Pozuelo de Alarcón, Madrid
DP Coordinator José Manuel de los Ríos Beca
Languages English
T: +34 91 715 04 99
W: www.colegioliceosorolla.es

Los Sauces La Moraleja
C. del Camino Ancho 83, 28109 Alcobendas, Madrid
DP Coordinator Diego Schillaci
Languages English, Spanish
T: +34 916 501 790
W: colegiolossauces.com/lamoraleja

Los Sauces Pontevedra
Carretera de Campañó a Cabaleiro, 36157 Pontevedra, Galicia
DP Coordinator Isaura María Rivas Gómez
Languages English, Spanish
T: +34 986 870 722
W: colegiolossauces.com/pontevedra

Los Sauces Vigo
As Pereiras Pardellas Cela, 36419 Vigo, Pontevedra, Galicia
DP Coordinator Albino Pombo Rodríguez
Languages English, Spanish
T: +34 986 468 384
W: colegiolossauces.com/vigo
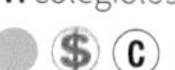

Lycée International Barcelona - Bon Soleil
Camí de la Pava, no. 15, Gavà, 08850 Barcelona, Catalonia
DP Coordinator Eva Grau Mancebo
Languages English, French, Spanish
T: +34 93 633 13 58
W: www.bonsoleil.es

Maristes Sants Les Corts
C/Vallespir 160, 08014 Barcelona, Catalonia
DP Coordinator Isabel Mata Pérez
Languages Catalan, Valencian, Spanish
T: +34 934 908 625
W: www.slc.maristes.cat

MIRABAL INTERNATIONAL SCHOOL
Calle Monte Almenara, s/n, 28660 Boadilla del Monte, Madrid
DP Coordinator Isabel Sargent Busquets
MYP Coordinator Isabel Sargent Busquets
Languages English, Spanish
T: +34 916 331 711
E: mirabal@colegiomirabal.com
W: www.colegiomirabal.com
See full details on page 170
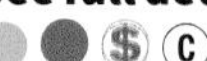

Mirasur School
Calle Pablo Gargallo 1, 28320 Pinto, Madrid
PYP Coordinator Vanesa Mendoza
Languages English, Spanish
T: +34 916 925 089
W: colegiomirasur.com

Princess Margaret School
Passeig de la Fond d'en Fargas 15-17, 8032 Barcelona, Catalonia
MYP Coordinator Renata Djuric
PYP Coordinator Marta García
Languages English, Spanish
T: +34 934 290 313
W: www.princessmargaret.org

Queen's College
Juan de Saridakis 64, 07015 Palma de Mallorca, Balearic Islands
DP Coordinator Ruth Sandler
Languages English, Spanish
T: +34 971 401 011
W: www.queenscollege.es

Salesians Sant Àngel (Salesians de Sarriá)
Rafael Batlle nº 7, 08017 Barcelona, Catalonia
DP Coordinator Carlos Escriche Marco
Languages Spanish
T: +34 932031100
W: sarria.salesians.cat

SEK INTERNATIONAL SCHOOL ALBORÁN
C/ Barlovento 141, Urb. Almerimar, El Ejido, 04711 Almería, Andalusia
DP Coordinator Estefania Sánchez
MYP Coordinator Sebastián Fuentes Valenzuela
PYP Coordinator Natalia López
Languages English, Spanish
T: +34 900 87 87 98
E: sek-alboran@sek.es
W: alboran.sek.es
See full details on page 196

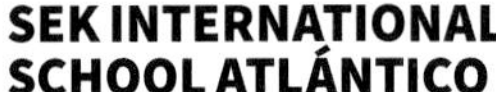

SEK INTERNATIONAL SCHOOL ATLÁNTICO
Rúa Illa de Arousa 4, Boavista. A Caeira, Poio, 36005 Pontevedra, Galicia
DP Coordinator Yolanda Cenamor Montero
MYP Coordinator Mónica Azpilicueta Amorín
PYP Coordinator Sara Bouzada Sanmartin
Languages English, Spanish
T: +34 900 87 87 98
E: sek-atlantico@sek.es
W: atlantico.sek.es
See full details on page 197

SEK INTERNATIONAL SCHOOL CATALUNYA
Av. del Tremolencs, 24, La Garriga, 08530 Barcelona, Catalonia
DP Coordinator Adrià Van Waart
MYP Coordinator Carmen Fernández
PYP Coordinator Concepció Muntada
Languages English, Spanish, Catalan
T: +34 900 87 87 98
E: sek-catalunya@sek.es
W: catalunya.sekinternationalschools.com
See full details on page 198

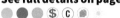

SEK INTERNATIONAL SCHOOL CIUDALCAMPO
Urb. Ciudalcampo, Paseo de las Perdices, 2, San Sebastián de los Reyes, 28707 Madrid
DP Coordinator Dinis Alves Costa
MYP Coordinator James Shaw
PYP Coordinator Marisa Iglesias Lorenzo
Languages English, Spanish
T: +34 900 87 87 98
E: sek-ciudalcampo@sek.es
W: ciudalcampo.sek.es
See full details on page 199

SEK INTERNATIONAL SCHOOL EL CASTILLO
Urb. Villafranca del Castillo, Castillo de Manzanares, s/n, Villanueva de la Cañada, 28692 Madrid
DP Coordinator Ana Karina Cisneros
MYP Coordinator Noemí Taranilla
PYP Coordinator Fátima González
Languages English, Spanish
T: +34 900 87 87 98
E: sek-castillo@sek.es
W: madrid.sekinternationalschools.com
See full details on page 201

SEK INTERNATIONAL SCHOOL SANTA ISABEL
Calle San Ildefonso, 18, 28012 Madrid
PYP Coordinator William Ivey
Languages English, Spanish
T: +34 900 87 87 98
E: sek-santaisabel@sek.es
W: santaisabel.sek.es
See full details on page 204

SOTOGRANDE INTERNATIONAL SCHOOL
Avenida La Reserva SN, Sotogrande, Cádiz, Andalusia 11310
DP Coordinator Hélène Caillet
MYP Coordinator Belén González
PYP Coordinator Andrea Bennett
Languages English
T: +34 956 795 902
E: info@sis.gl
W: www.sis.ac
See full details on page 206

St Peter's School Barcelona
C/Eduard Toldrà, 18, 08034 Barcelona, Catalonia
DP Coordinator Xavier Salvado
MYP Coordinator Teresa Ferrer
PYP Coordinator Agustina Lacarte
Languages English, Spanish
T: +34 93 204 36 12
W: www.stpeters.es

St. George, The British School Madrid
Calle Padres Dominicos 1, 28050 Madrid
DP Coordinator Wyn Morgan
Languages English, Spanish
T: +34 916 508 440
W: stgeorgeinternational.es/madrid

St. George, The British School of Catalunya
Paseo de la Reina Elisenda de Montcada 18, 08034 Barcelona, Catalonia
DP Coordinator Danielle Best
Languages English, Spanish
T: +34 931 293 024
W: stgeorgeinternational.es/barcelona
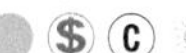

Swans International Secondary School
C/Lago de los Cisnes, s/n, Urb. Sierra Blanca, 29602 Marbella, Málaga, Andalusia
DP Coordinator Leslie Mohally
Languages English
T: +34 952 902 755
W: www.swansschoolinternational.es

Thames British School Madrid Campus
Calle Barbero de Sevilla 16, 28222 Majadahonda, Madrid
DP Coordinator Gareth Finn
Languages English, Spanish
T: +34 915 790 147
W: thamesbritishschool.es

THE ACADEMY INTERNATIONAL SCHOOL
Camí de Son Ametler Vell, 250, 07141 Marratxí, Balearic Islands
DP Coordinator Caroline Foster
Languages English
T: +34 971 605008
E: info@theacademyschool.com
W: www.theacademyschool.com
See full details on page 226

The British School of Aragon
Calle Valencia, KM 8,500, 50410 Cuarte de Huerva, Zaragoza
DP Coordinator Cristina Muñoz
Languages English, Spanish
T: +34 976 50 52 23
W: www.britanico-aragon.edu

The British School of Navarra
Camino Ardanaz 4, 31620 Pamplona, Navarre
DP Coordinator Alex Wreth
Languages English, Spanish
T: +34 948 242 826
W: tbson.es

The Global College
C. de Castellón de la Plana 8, 28006 Madrid
DP Coordinator César Prado Fernández
Languages English, Spanish
T: +34 915 689 937
W: theglobalcollege.com

YAGO SCHOOL
Avda. Antonio Mairena, 54, 41950 Castilleja de la Cuesta, Seville, Andalusia
DP Coordinator Germán Tenorio
Languages English, Spanish, Chinese
T: +34 955 51 1234
E: admissions@yagoschool.com
W: www.yagoschool.com
See full details on page 243

ZÜRICH SCHULE BARCELONA
73 Pearson Avenue, 08034 Barcelona, Catalonia
PYP Coordinator Helena García
Languages German, Spanish
T: +34 932 037 606
E: secretaria@zurichschule.com
W: www.zsbarcelona.com
See full details on page 244

SUDAN

Confluence International School of Khartoum
Greek Community School Campus, Building No.5, Gamhouria Avenue, Khartoum
DP Coordinator Shrikant Landage
MYP Coordinator Doua Abdou
PYP Coordinator Dominika Kawalek
Languages English, Arabic
T: +249 960099970
W: www.confluencesudan.org

Khartoum International Community School
P.O. Box 1840, Madani Street, Khartoum
DP Coordinator Linda Round
PYP Coordinator Darwin Balog-ang
Languages English
T: +249 183 215 000
W: www.kics.org

SWEDEN

Andertorpsgymnasiet Skelleftea
Gymnasievägen 5, 931 57 Skelleftea, Västerbotten
DP Coordinator Maria Hedman
Languages English, Swedish
T: +46 91 0735000
W: skelleftea.se/anderstorpsgymnasiet

Aranäsgymnasiet
Gymnasiegatan 44, 434 42 Kungsbacka, Halland
DP Coordinator Ruth Walton
Languages English
T: +46 300 83 40 00
W: kungsbacka.se/utbildning-och-barnomsorg/gymnasieskola/aranasgymnasiet

Åva Gymnasium
Box 1450, 183 14 Täby, Stockholm
DP Coordinator Jo-Anne Ahlmen
Languages English
T: +46 (0) 855 55 8000
W: www.taby.se/ava

SWEDEN

Bladins International School of Malmö
Box 20093, Själlandstorget 1, 200 74 Malmö, Skåne
MYP Coordinator Valeria Fagiolani
PYP Coordinator Monica Coburn
Languages English
T: +46 40 987970
W: bism.bladins.se

British International School of Stockholm
Östrka Valhallavagen 17, 182 68 Djursholm, Stockholm
DP Coordinator Melanie Stell
Languages English
T: +46 8 755 2375
W: www.bisstockholm.se

Carlforsska gymnasiet
Sångargatan 1, 722 19 Västerås, Västmanland
DP Coordinator Tony Nicolas
Languages English
T: +4621390703
W: www.vasteras.se/carlforsska

Dibber International School Helsingborg
Klostervägen 12, Rydebäck, Helsingborg, Skåne 25732
PYP Coordinator Majken Johansson
Languages English, Swedish
T: +46 0702 760864
W: dibber.se/en/skola/dibber-international-school-helsingborg-2

Dibber International School Sollentuna
Lindvägen 16, 192 70 Sollentuna, Stockholm
MYP Coordinator Jessie Aaron
PYP Coordinator Caroline Darling
Languages English, Swedish
T: +46 73 3350916
W: dibber.se/skola/international-school-sollentuna

Europaskolan in Södermalm
Gotlandsgatan 43, 116 65 Stockholm
MYP Coordinator Julian Bethell
PYP Coordinator Emelie Pettersson
Languages English, Swedish
T: +46 8 335054
W: www.europaskolan.nu

Europaskolan in Vasastan
Luntmakargatan 101, 113 51 Stockholm
MYP Coordinator Katarina Dybeck
PYP Coordinator Maria Angelidou
Languages Swedish
T: +46 8 335095
W: www.europaskolan.nu

Haganässkolan
Box 501, 343 23 Älmhult, Kronoberg
DP Coordinator Ms Karin Elisabet Ringblom
Languages English
T: +46 476 552 22
W: www.almhult.se/haganasskolan

Hvitfeldtska Gymnasiet
Rektorsgatan 2, 411 33 Göteborg, Västra Götaland
DP Coordinator Renée Elfving
Languages English
T: +46 31 36 70 608
W: goteborg.se/hvitfeldtska

International High School of the Gothenburg Region
Molinsgatan 6, 411 33 Göteborg, Västra Götaland
DP Coordinator Tracey Bengtsson-Hopcraft
Languages English
T: +46 31 708 92 00
W: www.ihgr.se

International School of Helsingborg
Östra Vallgatan 9, 254 37 Helsingborg, Skåne
DP Coordinator Daniel Blair
MYP Coordinator Katie Hart
PYP Coordinator Kelly Hodgkinson
Languages English
T: +46 42 105 705
W: www.helsingborg.se/internationalschool

International School of Karlskrona (ISK)
Ekorrvägen 4, 371 42 Karlskrona, Blekinge
PYP Coordinator Mona Persson
Languages English, Swedish
T: +46 45 5305177
W: www.karlskrona.se/skola-och-forskola/Grundskola-och-grundsarskola

International School of Lund - Katedralskolan
Nygatan 21, 222 29 Lund, Skåne
MYP Coordinator Darrell Piper
PYP Coordinator Alison Kruckow
Languages English
T: +46 463 571 24

International School of the Gothenburg Region (ISGR)
Molinsgatan 6, 411 33 Göteborg, Västra Götaland
MYP Coordinator Alexei Gafan
PYP Coordinator Ellen Trelles
Languages English
T: +46 31 708 92 00
W: www.isgr.se

International School of the Stockholm Region
Bohusgatan 24-26, 116 67 Stockholm
DP Coordinator Martin Davidsson
MYP Coordinator Jenny Arvidsson
PYP Coordinator Justina Soewarso Sundström
Languages English
T: +46 8 508 426 50
W: internationalschoolofthe stockholmregion.stockholm.se

Internationella Engelska Gymnasiet
Allhelgonagatan 4, 118 58 Stockholm
DP Coordinator Joseph Hemingway
Languages English
T: +46 8 562 28 700
W: www.engelskagymnasiet.se

IT-Gymnasiet i Skövde
Kylarvägen 1, 541 34 Skövde, Västra Götaland
DP Coordinator Ruth Morrisson Svensson
Languages English
T: +46 500 41 69 90
W: www.it-gymnasiet.se

Katedralskolan in Linköping
Platensgatan 20, 582 20 Linköping, Östergötland
DP Coordinator Jonathan Lowrey
Languages English
T: +46 132 07549
W: www.linkoping.se/katedral

Katedralskolan in Lund
St Södergatan 22, 222 23 Lund, Skåne
DP Coordinator Katarina Flennmark
Languages English
T: +46 4635 76 09
W: www.katte.se

Katedralskolan in Uppsala
Skolgatan 2, 753 12 Uppsala
DP Coordinator Therese Skytt
Languages English
T: +46 18 568100
W: www.katedral.se

Katedralskolan, Skara
Brunsbogatan 1, 532 88 Skara, Västra Götaland
DP Coordinator Thomas Woodgate
Languages English
T: +46 511 326 00
W: www.katedralskolan.nu

Lund International School
Warholmsväg 3, 224 65 Lund, Skåne
MYP Coordinator Lesley Pitman-Lundqvist
PYP Coordinator Jo Moore
Languages English
T: +46737087926
W: www.lundinternationalschool.com

Malmö Borgarskola
Box 17029, 200 10 Malmö, Skåne
CP Coordinator Andreas Lejon
DP Coordinator Anna Ellmark
Languages English
T: +46 4034 1000
W: www.malmoborgarskola.se

Malmö International School
Packhusgatan 2, 205 80 Malmö, Skåne
MYP Coordinator Patrick Kelly
PYP Coordinator Rosa Maria Blanco Macia
Languages English, Spanish, German
T: +46 (0)733 23 70 37

Mora Gymnasium
Kristinebergsgatan 8-10, 792 32 Mora, Dalarna
DP Coordinator Marielle Hjort
Languages English, Swedish
T: +46 250 260 00
W: www.moragymnasium.se

Per Brahegymnasiet
Residensgatan, 553 16 Jönköping
DP Coordinator Janine Bokor
Languages English
T: +46 36 105 472
W: www.pb.edu.jonkoping.se

Rudbecksgymnasiet
Box 31160, 701 35 Örebro
DP Coordinator Anne-Sophie Skalin
Languages English
T: +46 19 21 65 69
W: www.ru.orebro.se

Sigtunaskolan Humanistiska Läroverket
Box 508, 193 28 Sigtunase, Stockholm
CP Coordinator Rebecka Grönstedt
DP Coordinator Adrian Feehan
MYP Coordinator Anna Johansson
Languages English, Swedish
T: +46 8 592 571 00
W: www.sshl.se

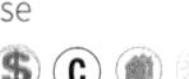

Söderportgymnasiet
Västra Boulevarden 53, 291 31 Kristianstad, Skåne
DP Coordinator Anna Cederlund
Languages English
T: +46 4413 6049
W: www.buf.kristianstad.se/soderport

St Eskils Gymnasium
Smedjegatan 3-5, 631 86 Eskilstuna, Södermanland
DP Coordinator Christopher Thomson-Smith
Languages English
T: +46 16 710 10 00
W: www.eskilstuna.se

Stockholm International School
Johannesgatan 18, 111 38 Stockholm
DP Coordinator Jarno Ampuja
MYP Coordinator Rebecca Gonzalez
Languages English
T: +46 (0)8 412 40 00
W: www.intsch.se

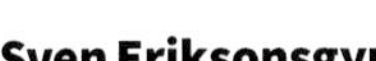

Sven Eriksonsgymnasiet
Sven Eriksonplatsen, 501 80 Borås, Västra Götaland
DP Coordinator Martin Idehall
Languages English
T: +46 33 35 80 48
W: boras.se/svenerikson

Täljegymnasiet
Erik Dahlbergs väg 1-3, 152 40 Södertälje, Stockholm
DP Coordinator Rose-Marie Fallgren
Languages English
T: +46 8 52301336
W: www.sodertalje.se

Teleborg Centrum Skola
Smedsvängen 72, 352 54 Växjö, Kronoberg
MYP Coordinator Erika Glawe
Languages English
T: +46 470 419 34
W: vaxjo.se/teleborgcentrum

The International School of Älmhult
Skolgatan 1, 343 23 Älmhult, Kronoberg
MYP Coordinator Ujjwala Bhatt
PYP Coordinator Lucas Intagliata
Languages English
T: +46 476 55188
W: www.almhult.se/english

Torsbergsgymnasiet
Läroverksgatan 36, 821 33 Bollnäs, Gävleborg
DP Coordinator Margaretta Eriksson
Languages English
T: + 46 278 254 91
W: www.torsbergsgymnasiet.se

Växjö Katedralskola
Samuel Ödmans Väg 1, 352 39 Växjö, Kronoberg
DP Coordinator Gilles Kennedy
Languages English
T: +46 470 41736
W: www.katedralskolan.se

SWITZERLAND

AIGLON COLLEGE
Avenue Centrale 61, 1885 Chesières
DP Coordinator Mrs Laura Hamilton
Languages English
T: +41 (0)24 496 6177
E: admissions@aiglon.ch
W: www.aiglon.ch

See full details on page 48

BKA International School
Gellertstrasse 25, 4052 Basel BS
PYP Coordinator Alexandara Schmid
Languages English, German
T: +41 61 311 76 62
W: www.bkabasel.ch

Collège Alpin Beau Soleil
Route du Village 1, 1884 Villars-sur-Ollon
DP Coordinator Helen Taylor-Cevey
Languages English, French
T: +41 24 496 26 26
W: www.beausoleil.ch

Collège Champittet, Pully
Chemin de Champittet 1, 1009 Pully VD
DP Coordinator David Newsam
Languages English, French
T: +41 21 721 05 05
W: www.champittet.ch

COLLÈGE DU LÉMAN
74, route de Sauverny, 1290 Versoix GE
CP Coordinator Sheena Tandy
DP Coordinator Jana Krainova Samuda
Languages English, French
T: +41 22 775 56 56
E: admissions@cdl.ch
W: www.cdl.ch

See full details on page 72

Collège et Lycée St-Charles
Route de Belfort 10, 2900 Porrentruy JU
DP Coordinator Nicole Pearce
MYP Coordinator Gloria Guerrero
Languages English
T: +41 32 466 11 57
W: www.saint-charles.ch

COPPERFIELD VERBIER
Rue de la Bérarde 10, Le Hameau, 1936 Verbier VS
DP Coordinator Ladislav Burkovic
PYP Coordinator Laura Bickerstaffe
Languages English
T: +41 27 520 61 00
E: info@copperfield.education
W: www.copperfield.education

See full details on page 74

 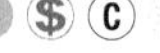

Ecole des Arches
Chemin de Mornex 2-4, PO Box 566, 1001 Lausanne VD
DP Coordinator Didier Curty
Languages French
T: +41 21 311 09 69
W: www.ecoledesarches.ch

Ecole Moser Genève
81 Chemin De-La-Montagne, 1224 Chêne-Bougeries GE
DP Coordinator Carine Marguet-Joly
Languages English, French
T: +41 (0)22 860 80 80
W: www.ecolemoser.ch/geneve

Ecole Moser Nyon
4-6 Avenue Reverdil, 1260 Nyon VD
DP Coordinator Richard Jones-Nerzic
Languages English, French
T: +41 (0)22 593 88 88
W: www.ecolemoser.ch/nyon

ECOLE NOUVELLE DE LA SUISSE ROMANDE - LAUSANNE
Chemin de Rovéréaz 20, CP 161, 1012 Lausanne
DP Coordinator Mr. Gaetan Franzini
Languages French, English
T: +41 21 654 65 00
E: info@ensr.ch
W: www.ensr.ch

See full details on page 82

GYMNASIUM AM MÜNSTERPLATZ
Münsterplatz 15, 4051 Basel BS
DP Coordinator Dr. Manuel Pombo
Languages German, English
T: +41 61 267 88 70
E: gymnasium.muensterplatz@bs.ch
W: www.gmbasel.ch

See full details on page 98

Gymnasium Bäumlihof
Zu den drei Linden 80, 4058 Basel BS
DP Coordinator Isla Ward
Languages English, German
T: +41 61 606 33 11
W: www.gbbasel.ch

HAUT-LAC INTERNATIONAL BILINGUAL SCHOOL
Ch. de Pangires 26, St-Légier-la Chiésaz CH-1806
CP Coordinator Greg Wilson
DP Coordinator Greg Wilson
MYP Coordinator Julien Hernandez
Languages English, French
T: +41 (0)21 555 51 07
E: admissions@haut-lac.ch
W: www.haut-lac.ch

See full details on page 100

Hochalpines Institut Ftan (HIF)
Chalchera 154, 7551 Ftan GR
DP Coordinator Marceline Kelder
Languages English, German
T: +41 81 861 22 11
W: www.hif.ch

Institut auf dem Rosenberg
Hohenweg 60, 9000 St Gallen SG
DP Coordinator Kevin Boyd
Languages English, German
T: +41 71 277 77 77
W: www.instrosenberg.ch

INSTITUT FLORIMONT
37 Avenue du Petit-Lancy, 1213 Petit-Lancy GE
DP Coordinator Noha Benani
Languages English, French
T: +41 22 879 0000
E: admissions@florimont.ch
W: www.florimont.ch

See full details on page 111

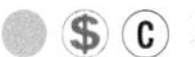

INSTITUT INTERNATIONAL DE LANCY
24, avenue Eugène-Lance, Grand-Lancy CH-1212
DP Coordinator Tania McMahon
Languages English, French
T: +41 22 794 2620
E: info@iil.ch
W: www.iil.ch

See full details on page 114

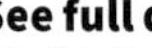

Institut Le Rosey
Château du Rosey, 1180 Rolle VD
DP Coordinator Craig Foreman
Languages English, French
T: +41 21 822 5500
W: www.rosey.ch

INSTITUT MONTANA
Schönfels 5, 6300 Zug ZG
DP Coordinator Michael Meier
Languages English, German
T: +41 41 729 11 77
E: admissions@montana-zug.ch
W: www.montana-zug.ch

See full details on page 115

INTER-COMMUNITY SCHOOL ZURICH
Strubenacher 3, 8126 Zumikon
DP Coordinator Alexandra Carlin
MYP Coordinator Graham Gardner
PYP Coordinator Claire Febrey
Languages English
T: +41 44 919 8300
E: contact@icsz.ch
W: www.icsz.ch

See full details on page 116

 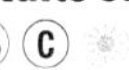

SWITZERLAND

INTERNATIONAL SCHOOL ALTDORF
St. Josefsweg 15, 6460 Altdorf UR
CP Coordinator Francesco Masetti Placci
DP Coordinator Nicoletta Scalabrin
Languages English
T: +41 41 874 0000
E: admission@lisa.swiss
W: www.lisa.swiss
See full details on page 118
   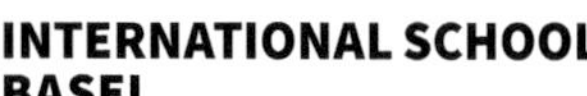

INTERNATIONAL SCHOOL BASEL
Fleischbachstrasse 2, 4153 Reinach
DP Coordinator David Griffiths
MYP Coordinator Siân Thomas
PYP Coordinator Emily McCaughan
Languages English; German (junior School)
T: +41 61 715 33 33
E: info@isbasel.ch
W: www.isbasel.ch
See full details on page 119

International School of Berne
Allmendingenweg 9, 3073 Gümligen, Bern
DP Coordinator Brette Book
MYP Coordinator Kirsty DeWilde
PYP Coordinator Richard Dowse
Languages English
T: +41 (0)31 959 10 00
W: www.isberne.ch

International School of Geneva (Campus des Nations)
11 route des Morillons, 1218 Grand Saconnex GE
CP Coordinator Alexandra Juniper
DP Coordinator Alexandra Juniper
MYP Coordinator Mercy Ikua
PYP Coordinator Nikki Ross
Languages English, French
T: +41 22 770 4700
W: www.ecolint.ch/campus/campus-des-nations

International School of Geneva (La Châtaigneraie Campus)
2 chemin de la Ferme, 1297 Founex VD
DP Coordinator Michael Winter
PYP Coordinator Corine Van Den Wildenberg
Languages English
T: +41 22 960 9111
W: www.ecolint.ch/campus/la-chataigneraie

International School of Geneva (La Grande Boissière Campus)
62, route de Chêne, 1208 Geneva GE
DP Coordinator Jonathan Halden
Languages English, French
T: +41 22 787 2400
W: www.ecolint.ch/campus/la-grande-boissiere
 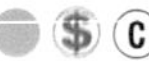

International School of Lausanne
Chemin de la Grangette 2, 1052 Le Mont-sur-Lausanne VD
DP Coordinator Michael Humphrey
MYP Coordinator Darryl Anderson
PYP Coordinator Kyle Hawkins
Languages English
T: +41 21 560 02 02
W: www.isl.ch

International School of Rheinfelden
Zürcherstrasse 9, Drei Könige, 4310 Rheinfelden AG
PYP Coordinator Bryan Murray
Languages German
T: +41 61 831 06 06
W: www.isrh.ch
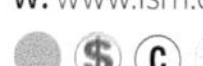

International School of Schaffhausen
Mühlentalstrasse 280, 8200 Schaffhausen SH
DP Coordinator Silke Fox
MYP Coordinator Ebru Guever
PYP Coordinator Mihaela Morello
Languages English
T: +41 52 624 1707
W: www.issh.ch

INTERNATIONAL SCHOOL OF TICINO SA
Via Ponteggia, 23, Cadempino, 6814 Lugano
DP Coordinator Mr. Graeme Wallbank
MYP Coordinator Mrs. Kelly Leagas
PYP Coordinator Mr. Jamie Steele
Languages English, Italian
T: +41 919710344
E: frontoffice@isticino.com
W: www.isticino.com
See full details on page 135

International School of Zug & Luzern, Riverside Campus
Rothustrasse 4b, 6331 Hünenberg ZG
DP Coordinator Kelli Meeker
MYP Coordinator Kelli Meeker
PYP Coordinator Margriet Faber
Languages English
T: +41 41 768 2950
W: www.iszl.ch

INTERNATIONAL SCHOOL RHEINTAL
Werdenbergstrasse 17, 9470 Buchs SG
DP Coordinator Vicki Hayward
MYP Coordinator Andrew Shawcroft
PYP Coordinator Rheannon Elliott (Interim)
Languages English
T: +41 81 750 6300
E: admissions@isr.ch
W: www.isr.ch
See full details on page 137

International School Zurich North
Industriestrasse 50, 8304 Wallisellen ZH
PYP Coordinator Njomza Murtaj
Languages English
T: +41 44 830 7000
W: www.iszn.ch

Kantonsschule am Burggraben St. Gallen
Burggraben 21, 9000 St. Gallen SG
DP Coordinator Peter Litscher
Languages English, German
T: +41 712281414
W: ksbg.ch

Kantonsschule Wettingen
Klosterstrasse 11, 5430 Wettingen AG
DP Coordinator Heinz Anklin
Languages English
T: +41 (0)56 437 24 00
W: www.kanti-wettingen.ch

KV Zürich Die Wirtschaftsschule
Limmatstrasse 310, 8031 Zürich ZH
DP Coordinator Sara Bucher
Languages English, German
T: +41 44 444 66 00
W: www.kvz-schule.ch
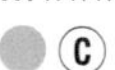

LA CÔTE INTERNATIONAL SCHOOL AUBONNE
Chemin de Clamogne 8, 1170 Aubonne VD
DP Coordinator Alexa Prior
Languages English, French
T: +41 (0)22 823 26 26
E: admissions@lcis.ch
W: www.lcis.ch
See full details on page 155

LA GARENNE INTERNATIONAL SCHOOL
Chemin des Chavasses 23, 1885 Chesières-Villars VD
DP Coordinator Adam Jozef
MYP Coordinator Mischa Mortley
Languages English
T: +41 (0)24 495 24 53
E: admissions@la-garenne.ch
W: www.la-garenne.ch
See full details on page 156
  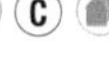 

Le Régent International School
Rue du Zier 4, CH-3963 Crans-Montana
DP Coordinator Jennifer Cogbill
Languages English, French
T: +41 (0)27 480 3201
W: regentschool.ch

Lemania College Lausanne
Chemin de Préville 3, 1003 Lausanne VD
DP Coordinator Giovanna Crisante
Languages English
T: +41 21 320 15 01
W: www.lemania.ch
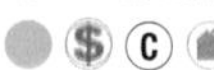

LEYSIN AMERICAN SCHOOL IN SWITZERLAND
3 Chemin de la Source, 1854 Leysin VD
DP Coordinator Ronan Lynch
Languages English
T: +41 24 493 4878
E: admissions@las.ch
W: www.las.ch
See full details on page 160

Literargymnasium Rämibühl
Rämistrasse 56, 8001 Zürich ZH
DP Coordinator Annette Haueter
Languages English
T: +41 1 265 62 11
W: www.lgr.ch

Lyceum Alpinum Zuoz
Lyceum Alpinum 14, 7524 Zuoz GR
CP Coordinator Andrew White
DP Coordinator Dr. Joe Holroyd
Languages English
T: +41 81 851 30 00
W: www.lyceum-alpinum.ch

Mutuelle d'études secondaires
7 bis Boulevard Carl Vogt, 1205 Geneva GE
DP Coordinator Nathalie Rapaille
Languages French
T: +41 (0)22 741 00 01
W: www.ecolemes.ch

Neue Kantonsschule Aarau
Schanzmättelistrasse 32, 5000 Aarau AG
DP Coordinator Kathleen Noreisch
Languages English
T: +41 62 837 94 55
W: www.nksa.ch

Obersee Bilingual School
Eichenstrasse 4C, 8808 Pfaeffikon ZH
DP Coordinator Louise Hoyne-Butler
Languages English, German
T: +41 55 511 38 00
W: www.oberseebilingualschool.ch

Realgymnasium Rämibühl
Rämistrasse 56, 8001 Zürich ZH
DP Coordinator Philipp Wettstein
Languages English
T: +41 44 265 63 12
W: www.rgzh.ch

Rudolf Steiner Schule Oberaargau
Ringstrasse 30, 4900 Langenthal BE
DP Coordinator Philip Pflugbeil
Languages English, German
T: +41 (0)62 922 69 05
W: www.rsso.ch

Scuola Rudolf Steiner ii Lugano Origlio
via ai Magi 4, 6945 Origlio TI
DP Coordinator Mosè Nodari
Languages English, Italian
T: +41 (0)91 966 29 62
W: scuolasteiner-lugano.ch

SIS Swiss International School Basel
Erlenstrasse 15, 4058 Basel BS
DP Coordinator James Brocklehurst
Languages English
T: +41 61 683 71 40
W: www.swissinternationalschool.ch/schulorte/basel
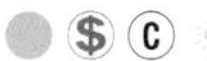

SIS Swiss International School Zürich
Seidenstrasse 2, 8304 Wallisellen ZH
DP Coordinator Shane Peter
Languages English
T: +41 44 388 99 44
W: www.swissinternationalschool.ch/schulorte/zuerich

ST. GEORGE'S INTERNATIONAL SCHOOL, SWITZERLAND
Chemin de St. Georges 19, CH-1815 Clarens/Montreux
DP Coordinator Colin Travis
Languages English, French
T: +41 21 964 3411
E: admissions@stgeorges.ch
W: www.stgeorges.ch
See full details on page 213

Stiftsschule Engelberg
Benediktinerkloster 5, Engelberg 6390
DP Coordinator Dr. Hansueli Flückiger
Languages German, English
T: +41 41 639 61 00
W: www.stiftsschule-engelberg.ch

TASIS THE AMERICAN SCHOOL IN SWITZERLAND
Via Collina d'Oro 15, 6926 Montagnola-Lugano
DP Coordinator Kathy Anderson
Languages English
T: +41 91 960 5151
E: admissions@tasis.ch
W: www.tasis.ch
See full details on page 223

Verbier International School
Route de Verbier Station 88, 1936 Verbier VS
DP Coordinator Frederic Jaccard
Languages English, French
T: +41 27 565 26 56
W: www.lvis.ch

Zurich International School
Steinacherstrasse 140, 8820 Wädenswil ZH
DP Coordinator Sean Maley
Languages English
T: +41 58 750 2500
W: www.zis.ch

TANZANIA

Dar es Salaam International Academy
P.O. Box 23282, Manara Road, Ada Estate, Dar es Salaam
DP Coordinator Linet Edison
MYP Coordinator Susan Ngoye
PYP Coordinator Saviona Furtado
Languages English
T: +255 75 8828300
W: www.diatz.cc

International School of Tanganyika
P.O. Box 2651, Dar es Salaam
DP Coordinator Jason Crook
MYP Coordinator Nicole Payne
PYP Coordinator Tina Fossgreen
Languages English
T: +255 67 7002444
W: www.istafrica.co.tz

The Aga Khan Mzizima Secondary School, Dar es Salaam
P.O. Box 21563, Fire Road, Upanga, Dar es Salaam
DP Coordinator Seema Adlakha
PYP Coordinator Blandina Duwe
Languages English
T: +255 22 2151253
W: www.agakhanschools.org/tanzania/akmssd/index
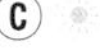

UWC East Africa, Arusha Campus
P.O. Box 2691, Dodoma Road, Kisongo, Arusha
DP Coordinator Nathalie Vignard
MYP Coordinator Anoek van der Vinne
PYP Coordinator Amanda Bowen
Languages English
T: +255 78 4490133
W: www.uwcea.org

UWC East Africa, Moshi Campus
P.O. Box 733, Lema Road, Moshi, Kilimanjaro
DP Coordinator Margaret Brunt
MYP Coordinator Farah Fawaz
PYP Coordinator Deborah Mills
Languages English
T: +255 75 6446777
W: www.uwcea.org
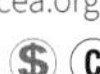

TOGO

Arc-en-Ciel International School
B.P. 2985, Lomé BP: 2985
DP Coordinator Taid Rahimi
MYP Coordinator Taid Rahimi
PYP Coordinator Taid Rahimi
Languages French, English
T: +228 22 22 03 29
W: www.arc-en-ciel.org

Cours Lumière
Rue Alissutin, Agbalépédogan, Lomé
DP Coordinator Komlanvi Ahiakpor
Languages English, French
T: +228 91 77 99 03
W: www.courslumiere.org

The British School of Lomé
B.P. 20050, Résidence du Bénin, Lomé
DP Coordinator Philip Smith
Languages English
T: +228 22 26 46 06
W: www.bsl.tg

TUNISIA

American Cooperative School of Tunis
B.P. 150, Cite Taeib M'hiri, Laouina, 2045 Tunis
DP Coordinator Cory Haugen
Languages English
T: +216 71 760 905
W: www.acst.net

École Canadienne de Tunis
Rue de l'énergie solaire, 2035 Tunis
DP Coordinator Mahmoud Nouaïri
MYP Coordinator Christophe Etienne
PYP Coordinator Meriem Cammoun
Languages French
T: +216 71 206 035
W: www.ec-tunis.com

Groupe Scolaire International Les Nouvelles Générations
Km 5, Route Ajim-Houmt Souk, Bousmayel, 4135 Djerba, Medenine
DP Coordinator Louise d'Aragon
MYP Coordinator Meriem Hathat
PYP Coordinator Siwar Ben Romdhane
Languages French, Arabic
T: +216 70 279 340
W: www.lesnouvellesgenerations.com

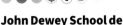

John Dewey School de Sousse
Sahloul, 4054 Sousse
PYP Coordinator Asma Chebil
Languages Arabic, French
T: +216 70 286 900
W: www.johndewey-school.org

Les écoles Idéales
Rue El Akhtal, Dar Châbane Plage, 8075 Nabeul
MYP Coordinator Wissem Ben Abdallah
Languages Arabic, French
T: +216 98 749 402
W: lesecolesideales.com

TURKEY

ABC Okullari Göksu Kampüsü
Göksu Mahallesi 93, Cadde No. 6/1A, Eryaman, Ankara, Central Anatolia
DP Coordinator Nalan Gürakar
PYP Coordinator Rabia Dasdandir
Languages English, Turkish
T: +90 312 444 2221
W: www.abc.k12.tr

Acibadem Schools - Acibadem Campus
Acibadem Mah. Cecen Sok. No:48 Ic Kapi No:1, Üsküdar, 34730 Istanbul, Marmara
PYP Coordinator Hande Özkeskin
Languages Turkish
T: +90 216 510 52 32
W: www.acibadem.k12.tr

TURKEY

Aka School
Radyum Sok No 21 Basin Sitesi, Bahcelievler, Istanbul, Marmara
DP Coordinator Nasstasha Stewart
Languages English
T: +90 212 557 27 72
W: www.akakoleji.k12.tr

ALKEV Schools
Alkent 2000 Mah. Mehmet Yesilgül Cd. No: 7, Büyükcekmece, 34535 Istanbul, Marmara
DP Coordinator Sencer Donmez
Languages English, German
T: +90 212 886 88 40
W: www.alkev.k12.tr
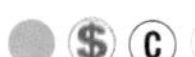

American Collegiate Institute
Inonu Caddesi No. 476, Goztepe, 35290 Izmir, Aegean
DP Coordinator Mine Erim
Languages English
T: +90 232 285 34 01
W: www.aci.k12.tr

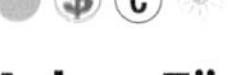

Ankara Türk Telekom Sosyal Bilimler Lisesi
Mutlukent Mah. 1919, Sokak No. 1 Ümitköy, Cankaya, 06810 Ankara, Central Anatolia
DP Coordinator Hülya Temizöz
Languages English
T: +90 312 236 63 77
W: asbl.meb.k12.tr
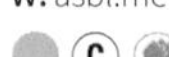

AREL Schools (Kindergarten/Primary/Middle/High)
Merkez Mah, Selahattin Pinar Sok, No:3 Yenibosna , Bahcelievler, 34197 Istanbul, Marmara
MYP Coordinator Dilara Canata
PYP Coordinator Umut Brezina
Languages English, Turkish
T: +90 212 550 49 30
W: www.arel.k12.tr

Balikesir Aci College
Cayirhisar Mah. Yeni Izmir yolu Cad. 3B, 10185 Balikesir, Marmara
DP Coordinator Mertcan Kulavuz
Languages English, Turkish
T: +90 266 239 85 85
W: acikoleji.k12.tr

Batikent ABC Anaokulu
Yenibati Mahallesi 2398, Sok. No. 15, Batikent, Ankara, Central Anatolia
PYP Coordinator Sena Erhan
Languages English, Turkish
T: +90 312 256 12 22
W: www.abc.k12.tr

Besiktas Sakip Sabanci Anadolu Lisesi
Yildiz caddesi No 73, Besiktas, 34359 Istanbul, Marmara
DP Coordinator Senol Selcuk
Languages English, Turkish
T: +90 212 227 46 10
W: sabancilisesi.meb.k12.tr

Beykoz Doga Campus
Fener Yolu Cad. No:6 Dereseki, Akbaba, Beykoz, 81650 Istanbul, Marmara
PYP Coordinator Kadim Can
Languages English
T: +90 216 320 52 00
W: www.dogaokullari.com/eng/schools/beykoz-doga-campus

Bilkent Erzurum Laboratory School
Prof. Dr. Ihsan Dogramaci Bulvari Cat Yolu, Palandöken, 25070 Erzurum, Eastern Anatolia
DP Coordinator Selin Sethi
PYP Coordinator Yunus Emre Özden
Languages English
T: +90 442 342 61 74
W: bels.bilkent.edu.tr

Bilkent Laboratory & International School
East Campus, 06800 Ankara, Central Anatolia
DP Coordinator Feray Ozdemir Gur
MYP Coordinator Tugba Selimoglu
PYP Coordinator Brendan Donnelly
Languages English, Turkish
T: +90 312 290 53 61
W: www.blisankara.org

BJK - Kabatas Vakfi Özel Okullari
Camlica Mahallesi, Seker Maslak Sk. No. 11, Üsküdar, Istanbul, Marmara
DP Coordinator Ismail Aylaz
Languages English, Turkish
T: +90 216 326 19 03
W: bjkkabatasvakfiokullari.k12.tr

Bodrum Marmara Elementary School
Cumhuriyet Avenue No. 2, 48420 Bodrum, Aegean
PYP Coordinator Gul Pasali Yagci
Languages English, Turkish
T: +90 252 358 61 13
W: www.mek.k12.tr
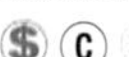

Bodrum Marmara Private College
Cumhuriyet Avenue No. 2, 48420 Bodrum, Aegean
DP Coordinator Renin Öktem
Languages English, Turkish
T: +90 252 358 61 13
W: www.mek.k12.tr

British International School Istanbul - Zekeriyaköy
Zekeriyaköy Mahallesi, Kilyos Caddesi No. 227/12, Sariyer, Istanbul, Marmara
DP Coordinator Seef Eddeen Marsden
Languages English
T: +90 212 202 70 27
W: www.bis.k12.tr

Cakir Schools
Orhaneli Yolu, Egitimciler Cd 15, Nilüfer, Bursa, Marmara
DP Coordinator Ahmet Cihat Yavuz
MYP Coordinator Elif Sen
PYP Coordinator Gamze Sezer
Languages English, Turkish
T: +90 224 451 93 30
W: www.cakir.k12.tr

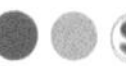

Camlica MBA Primary Schools
Kücük Camlica mah. Libadiye cad. No. 30 Ükudar, 34696 Istanbul, Marmara
PYP Coordinator Sevil Moore
Languages English, Turkish
W: www.mbaokullari.k12.tr/tr/misyonumuz

Çanakkale Özel ilkokulu
Izmir Yolu 12. Km Güzelyali, Güzelyali, 17100 Canakkale, Marmara
PYP Coordinator Pinar Usta
Languages English, Turkish
T: +90 286 232 86 86
W: www.canakkalekoleji.com

Cemberlitas Anadolu Lisesi
Yeniceriler Cad. Evkaf Sok. No 10 Cemberlitas/Fatih, 34130 Istanbul, Marmara
DP Coordinator Gultekin Gocmen
Languages English, Turkish
T: +90 212 516 40 88
W: cemberlitasanadolu.meb.k12.tr

Deutsche Schule Izmir
Kuscular Cad. No. 82, Kuscular Köyü, Urla, 35430 Izmir, Aegean
DP Coordinator Filiz Ünal
Languages English
T: +90 232 234 75 07
W: www.ds-izmir.com
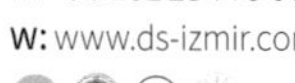

Egitmen Koleji
Istasyon Mah. Fevzi Çakmak Cad. No: 123, Tuzla, 34940 Istanbul, Marmara
PYP Coordinator Ahmet Kilic
Languages Turkish
T: +90 216 446 48 46
W: www.egitmen.k12.tr

Enka Schools - Adapazari Campus
Dagdibi Mahallesi, Enka Yolu Caddesi, No. 66/A, Adapazari, Marmara
MYP Coordinator Samet Cakiroglu
PYP Coordinator Zühal Ergül
Languages English
T: +90 264 323 37 74
W: www.enka.k12.tr/adapazari

Enka Schools - Istanbul Campus
Sadi Gülcelik Spor Sitesi, Istinye, 34460 Istanbul, Marmara
DP Coordinator Natalie Parker
MYP Coordinator Teni Karaman
PYP Coordinator Zeyneb Sengezer
Languages English, Turkish
T: +90 212 705 65 00
W: www.enka.k12.tr/istanbul

Ernst-Reuter-Schule
Tunus Cad 56, Kavaklidere, 06680 Ankara, Central Anatolia
DP Coordinator Suna Ahmad
Languages English
T: +90 312 426 63 82
W: www.ers-ankara.com

Eskisehir Gelisim Okullari
Asagi Sögütönü Mah. 993, Sokak No. 14, Tepebasi, 26200 Eskisehir, Central Anatolia
DP Coordinator Sema Best
Languages English, Turkish
T: +90 222 313 01 01
W: www.gelisimkoleji.k12.tr

Eyüboglu Atasehir Primary School
2 Cadde 59 Ada Manolya 4, Bloklari yani No 6, Atasehir, 34758 Istanbul, Marmara
PYP Coordinator Firuze Vanlioglu
Languages Turkish, English
T: +90 216 522 12 22
W: www.eyuboglu.com

Eyüboglu Kemerburgaz Middle School
Mithatpasa Mah. Pirinccikoy Yolu, 34075 Istanbul, Marmara
MYP Coordinator Arzu Onat Konusmaz
Languages English, Turkish
T: +90 216 522 12 72
W: www.eyuboglu.com

EYÜBOGLU SCHOOLS
Esenevler Mah, Dr Rüstem Eyüboglu sok 3, Ümraniye, 34762 Istanbul, Marmara
DP Coordinator Oguz Günenç
MYP Coordinator Songül Akar & Arzu Onat Konusmaz
PYP Coordinator Ayça Koçer, Firuze Vanlioglu & Meliz Katlav
Languages Turkish, English
T: +90 216 522 12 12
E: eyuboglu@eyuboglu.k12.tr
W: www.eyuboglu.k12.tr
See full details on page 88

Ezgililer Private Primary School
Kusculu Mah. 1728 Sok. No.6, Ilkadim, Samsun, Black Sea
PYP Coordinator Müge Öztürk
Languages English
T: +90 362 233 21 22
W: ezgililer.k12.tr

FMV Ayazaga Isik High School
Maslak Mah. Büyükdere Cad. No:106, Sisli, Sariyer, 34460 Istanbul, Marmara
DP Coordinator Melda Cemal
Languages English
T: +90 212 286 11 30
W: www.fmv.edu.tr

FMV Ayazaga Isik Primary & Middle School
Maslak Mah. Büyükdere Cad. No:106, Sisli, Sariyer, 34460 Istanbul, Marmara
PYP Coordinator Ozlem Mizrahi
Languages English, Turkish
T: +90 212 286 11 30
W: www.fmv.edu.tr

FMV Erenköy Isik High School
Sinan Ercan Cad. No:19, Erenköy, 34736 Istanbul, Marmara
DP Coordinator Sinem Özgöz
Languages English
T: +90 216 385 31 47
W: www.fmv.edu.tr

FMV Erenköy Isik Primary & Middle School
Sinan Ercan Cad. No:19, Erenköy, 34736 Istanbul, Marmara
PYP Coordinator Merve Ünal
Languages English, Turkish
T: +90 216 385 31 47
W: www.fmv.edu.tr

FMV Isik High School
Tesvikiye Cad. No:6 Nisantasi, 34365 Istanbul, Marmara
DP Coordinator Jenny Chavush
Languages English, Turkish
T: +90 212 233 12 03
W: www.fmv.edu.tr

FMV Isik Primary & Middle School
Tesvikiye Cad. No:06, Nisantasi, 34365 Istanbul, Marmara
PYP Coordinator Omer Karabacak
Languages English, Turkish
T: +90 212 233 12 03
W: www.fmv.edu.tr

FMV Ispartakule Isik High School
Tahtakale Mah. Gaffar Okkan Cad. No: 5/7 Blok No: 1, Avcilar, 34325 Istanbul, Marmara
DP Coordinator Erkan Sagnak
Languages English, Turkish
T: +90 212 648 09 75
W: www.fmv.edu.tr

FMV Ispartakule Isik Primary & Middle School
Tahtakale Mah. Gaffar Okkan Cad. No: 5/7 Blok No: 1, Avcilar, 34325 Istanbul, Marmara
PYP Coordinator Gizem Dolu
Languages English, Turkish
T: +90 212 648 09 75
W: www.fmv.edu.tr

Gazi University Foundation Private High School
Ali Suavi Street, Eti Quarter No 15, Maltepe, 06570 Ankara, Central Anatolia
DP Coordinator Asya Geylan
Languages English
T: +90 312 232 28 12
W: www.kolej.gazi.edu.tr

Gaziantep Kolej Vakfi Cemil Alevli College
Guvenevler Mah., Hoca Ahmet Yesevi Caddesi, No. 2, Sehitkamil, 27060 Gaziantep, Southeastern Anatolia
DP Coordinator Ali Pamuk
Languages English
T: +90 342 321 01 00
W: www.gkv.k12.tr

Gökkusagi Koleji - Bahçelievler
Eski Londra Asfalti No: 15 Haznedar, Bahcelievler, 34180 Istanbul, Marmara
DP Coordinator Murat Kotan
Languages English, Turkish
T: +90 212 644 59 00
W: www.gokkusagi.k12.tr

Gökkusagi Koleji - Bahçesehir
Orhan Gazi Mah, 1654 sk. No. 40, Esenyurt, Istanbul, Marmara
PYP Coordinator Zahra Gharnagh
Languages English, Turkish
T: +90 212 672 84 26
W: www.gokkusagi.k12.tr

Gökkusagi Koleji - Ümraniye
Inkilap Mh. Alemdag Cd. Üntel Sk. No. 30, Ümraniye, Istanbul, Marmara
PYP Coordinator Lale Tugba Oral
Languages English
T: +90 216 634 60 60
W: www.gokkusagi.k12.tr

Huseyin Avni Sozen Anatolian High School
Barbaros Mah. Mütevelli Cesme Cad. Sedef Sok., No 5/2 Kosuyolu, Üsküdar, Istanbul, Marmara
DP Coordinator Aysegul Sari
Languages English, Turkish
T: +90 216 651 65 81
W: hasal.meb.k12.tr

IDV Özel Bilkent High School
IDV Özel Bilkent Ilkokulu, Ortaokulu ve Lisesi Universiteler Mah 1600, Cad. No. 6, Dogu Kampus, 06800 Ankara, Central Anatolia
DP Coordinator Elif Günaydin
Languages English, Turkish
T: +90 312 290 89 39
W: www.obl.bilkent.edu.tr

IELEV Private High School
Ensar Cad. No:4/3 Nisantepe Mah. B Blok, Çekmeköy, 34794 Istanbul, Marmara
DP Coordinator Ali Batuhan Bardakci
Languages English, German, Turkish
T: +90 216 304 30 92
W: www.ielev.k12.tr/tr/lise

Irmak School
Cemil Topuzlu Caddesi No. 100, Caddebostan P.K. 34728, Kadiköy, Istanbul, Marmara
DP Coordinator Rabia Yildiran
MYP Coordinator Gamze Kale
PYP Coordinator Ozlem Palaz
Languages Turkish, English
T: +90 216 411 39 23
W: www.irmak.k12.tr

Isikkent Egitim Kampusu
6240/5 Sokak No. 3, Karacaoglan Mah., Yesilova, Bornova, 35070 Izmir, Aegean
DP Coordinator Lyudmyla Boysan
MYP Coordinator Lyudmyla Boysan
PYP Coordinator Evrim Yalcin Onder
Languages Turkish, English
T: +90 232 462 71 00
W: www.isikkent.k12.tr

Istanbul International Community School
Karaagac Koyu Mahallesi, Kahraman Caddesi, 27/1, Buyukcekmece, 34500 Istanbul, Marmara
DP Coordinator Omer Kipmen
MYP Coordinator Ashfaq Esmail
PYP Coordinator Evelyn Galan
Languages English
T: +90 212 857 82 64
W: www.iics.k12.tr

Istanbul Marmara Private College
Marmara Egitim Köyü, Maltepe, 34857 Istanbul, Marmara
DP Coordinator Guzide Pinar Cirpanli
PYP Coordinator Kerem Fındıklı
Languages Turkish, English
T: +90 216 626 10 00
W: www.mek.k12.tr

Istanbul Prof. Dr Mümtaz Turhan Sosyal Bilimler Lisesi
Fevzi Çakmak Cad. Fatih Mah., No. 2 Yenibosna, Bahçelievler, Istanbul, Marmara
DP Coordinator Erdoğan Akar
Languages English
T: +902 1255 161 46
W: www.isbl.k12.tr

ISTEK Acibadem Schools
Acibadem Mah. Bag Sok. No 6, Kadiköy, 34718 Istanbul, Marmara
DP Coordinator Gonca Tasar
PYP Coordinator Özlem Bogahan
Languages English
T: +90 216 325 30 75
W: www.istek.k12.tr/acibadem-kampusu
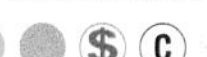

ISTEK Antalya Konyaalti Schools
Uncali Mah. 1257 Sk. No 3, Konyaalti, Antalya, Mediterranean
PYP Coordinator Zeynep Kilic
Languages English, Turkish
T: +90 242 229 30 80
W: antalya.istek.k12.tr

ISTEK Antalya Lara Schools
2421 Sok. No 1 Güzeloba Mah., Muratpasa, Antalya, Mediterranean
DP Coordinator Faden Ceyda Erten
PYP Coordinator Zeynep Kilic
Languages English, Turkish
T: +90 242 502 36 46
W: antalya.istek.k12.tr
 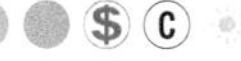

TURKEY

ISTEK Atanur Oguz Schools
Balmumcu Mah. Gazi Umurpasa Sk. No 26, Balmumcu, 34349 Istanbul, Marmara
DP Coordinator Seren Cure
PYP Coordinator Sibel Doğaner
Languages English
T: +90 212 211 34 60
W: www.istek.k12.tr/atanur-oguz-kampusu

ISTEK BARIS SCHOOLS
Bagdat Cad. No. 238/1, Ciftehavuzlar, Kadiköy, 34730 Istanbul, Marmara
PYP Coordinator Nehir Ege
Languages Turkish, English
T: +90 216 360 12 18
E: baris.ilkokulu@istek.k12.tr
W: www.istek.k12.tr
See full details on page 143

ISTEK Belde Schools
Kuzguncuk Mah. Rasimaga Sok. No 7/4, Üsküdar, 34664 Istanbul, Marmara
PYP Coordinator Ebru Salman
Languages English
T: +90 216 495 96 23
W: www.istek.k12.tr/belde-kampusu

ISTEK Bilge Kagan Schools
Senlikköy Mah. Florya Cad. No 2 Florya, Bakirköy, 34153 Istanbul, Marmara
PYP Coordinator Süheyla Dincer
Languages English
T: +90 212 663 29 71
W: www.istek.k12.tr/bilge-kagan-kampusu
 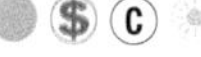

ISTEK Denizli Schools
Selcukbey Mah. 737 Sok. No 13, Merkezefendi, 20030 Denizli, Aegean
PYP Coordinator Ismail Sezen
Languages English, Turkish
T: +90 258 257 19 19
W: www.denizliistekokullari.k12.tr

ISTEK KASGARLI MAHMUT SCHOOLS
Eski Edirne Asfalti No 512, Sultangazi, 34110 Istanbul, Marmara
PYP Coordinator Ayça Özkardes
Languages English, Turkish
T: +90 212 594 26 11/12
E: kasgarlimahmut@istek.k12.tr
W: www.istek.k12.tr/kasgarli-mahmut-kampusu
See full details on page 144

ISTEK KEMAL ATATÜRK SCHOOLS (KINDERGARTEN & PRIMARY SCHOOL)
Tarabya Bayiri Cad. No 60, Tarabya/Sariyer, 34457 Istanbul, Marmara
PYP Coordinator Idil Ayyürek
Languages Turkish
T: +90 212 262 75 75
E: kemalataturk@istek.k12.tr
W: www.istek.k12.tr/kemal-ataturk-kampusu
See full details on page 145

ISTEK Mersin Schools
Gökcebelen Mah. 33195, Sk. No 2, Yenisehir, 33115 Mersin, Mediterranean
PYP Coordinator Gonca Akin
Languages English, Turkish
T: +90 324 473 24 21
W: istekmersinokullari.com

ISTEK Ulugbey Schools
Atalar Mah. Akgün Sok. No 23, Kartal, 34862 Istanbul, Marmara
PYP Coordinator Seray Kok
Languages English, Turkish
T: +90 216 488 13 08
W: www.istek.k12.tr/ulugbey-kampusu

ITÜ ETA Vakfi Doga Koleji
Barbaros Mah. Halk Cad. Kardelen Sok. N.:2 Incity C Blok, Atasehir, Istanbul, Marmara
DP Coordinator Mustafa Abidinoglu
Languages English
T: +90 216 4853580
W: www.dogakoleji.k12.tr

ITU Gelistirme Vakfi Özel Ekrem Elginkan Lisesi
ITU Ayazaga Kampusu, Maslak, 34469 Istanbul, Marmara
DP Coordinator Ahmet Bilaloglu
Languages English
T: +90 212 367 1300
W: www.itugvo.k12.tr/web/default.asp

Jale Tezer Educational Institutions
Jale Tezer Primary & Secondary Schools (Gazi Osman Pasa Campus), Bagcilar Mahallesi Acin Caddesi No:7, Cankaya, 06670 Ankara, Central Anatolia
DP Coordinator Berna Siisli
Languages English, Turkish
T: +90 312 447 49 49
W: www.jaletezer.k12.tr

Kabatas Erkek Lisesi
Ciragan Cad. No. 40, Ortakoy, Besiktas, 34349 Istanbul, Marmara
DP Coordinator Özgen Yildirimtas
Languages English, Turkish
T: +90 212 259 91 12
W: kabataserkeklisesi.meb.k12.tr

Kartal Anadolu Imam Hatip Lisesi
Esentepe Mah. Pamuk Sk. No. 3, Kartal, 34870 Istanbul, Marmara
DP Coordinator Nalan Erdogan
Languages English
T: +90 216 387 15 44
W: kartalaihl.meb.k12.tr

Kirmizi Cizgi Schools
Fener Mah.1964 Sok. Yaliyar Si?t. No : 30/C-D, 07060 Antalya, Mediterranean
DP Coordinator Serpil Acikgöz
Languages English, Turkish
T: +90 242 242 99 98
W: www.kirmizicizgikoleji.com

Kocaeli Marmara Private College
Dumlupinar Mah. Sehit Turgut Cicek Cad. No. 47, 41250 Kartepe, Marmara
DP Coordinator Merve Gürel
Languages English, Turkish
T: +90 262 373 1313
W: en.mek.k12.tr

Kültür2000 College
Karaagac Mah., Sirtköy Bulvari No. 2, Büyükcekmece, 34500 Istanbul, Marmara
DP Coordinator Mrs. Nida Korkmaz
MYP Coordinator Handan Saat
Languages English, Turkish
T: +90 212 850 81 81
W: www.kultur.k12.tr
 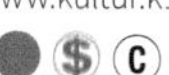

Maya Schools Antalya
Demircikara Mah. 1436. Sk. No:6 Muratpasa, Antalya, Mediterranean 07100
DP Coordinator Janset Aykaya
PYP Coordinator Derya Korkmaz
Languages English, Turkish
T: +90 (242) 242 62 92
W: antalya.maya.k12.tr
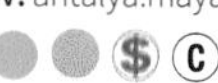

MEF International Schools, Istanbul - Ulus High
Ulus Mah. Leylak Sok. No. 22, Ulus, Besiktas, 34340 Istanbul, Marmara
DP Coordinator Beliz Kearin
Languages English
T: +90 212 362 26 33 (EXT:1360/1332)
W: www.mefis.k12.tr/istanbul

MEF International Schools, Istanbul - Ulus Primary
Ulus Mah. Leylak Sok. No. 22, Ulus, Besiktas, 34340 Istanbul, Marmara
PYP Coordinator Darren Richardson
Languages English
T: +90 212 362 26 33 (EXT:1341/1344)
W: www.mefis.k12.tr/istanbul

MEF International Schools, Izmir
Dokuz Eylül Mah. 699. Sokak No. 2, Gaziemir, Izmir, Aegean
DP Coordinator Malcolm Ringo
Languages English
T: +90 232 274 74 74
W: www.mefis.k12.tr/izmir
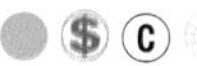

Minecan Okullari
Karsli mah 82064 sok. No. 12-14, Cukurova, 010101 Adana, Mediterranean
PYP Coordinator Aysin Gün
Languages English, Turkish
T: +90 322 233 30 45
W: minecan.com.tr

MURUVVET EVYAP SCHOOLS
Maden District Bakir Street, No. 2A/2B/2C, Sariyer, 34450 Istanbul, Marmara
PYP Coordinator Inci Er
Languages English, Turkish
T: +90 212 342 43 33
E: info@evyapokullari.k12.tr
W: www.evyapokullari.k12.tr
See full details on page 173

Nesibe AYDIN Educational Institutions (Ankara)
Haymana Yolu 5. Km, Karsiyaka Mahallesi 577, Sokak No. 1, Gölbasi, 06830 Ankara, Central Anatolia
DP Coordinator Senol Recber
PYP Coordinator Ebru Hezen
Languages English
T: +90 312 498 25 25
W: nesibeaydin.k12.tr/web/okullarimiz/ankara-okullari

Nesibe AYDIN Educational Institutions (Antalya)
Altinova Sinan Mah. Bilgin Sk. No. 1, Kepez, 07170 Antalya, Mediterranean
PYP Coordinator Fatma Yasemin Aykal
Languages Turkish
T: +90 242 504 12 50
W: nesibeaydin.k12.tr/web/okullarimiz/antalya-kampusu

Nesibe AYDIN Educational Institutions (Gaziantep)
15 Temmuz Mah. 148063, Cadde No. 15, Sehitkamil, 27560 Gaziantep, Southeastern Anatolia
PYP Coordinator Alev Sokucu
Languages Turkish
T: +90 342 999 41 05
W: nesibeaydin.k12.tr/web/okullarimiz/gaziantep-kampusu

Nesibe AYDIN Educational Institutions (Konya)
Beyhekim Mh. Darülhilafet Sk. No. 1, Selcuklu, 42130 Konya, Central Anatolia
PYP Coordinator Bengu Kesen
Languages Turkish
T: +90 332 320 85 11
W: nesibeaydin.k12.tr/web/okullarimiz/konya-kampusu
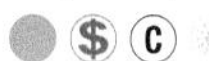 

Nilüfer Anadolu Imam Hatip Lisesi
Nilüfer Hatun Cad., Cumhuriyet, 16140 Nilüfer, Bursa, Marmara
DP Coordinator Saadet Dogan
MYP Coordinator Saadet Dogan
Languages English, Turkish
T: +90 224 453 10 22
W: niluferanadoluihl.meb.k12.tr/tema/iletisim.php

NUN Middle & High School
Elmali Mahallesi, Beykoz Elmali Yolu Sokak No. 5/1, Beykoz, Istanbul, Marmara
DP Coordinator Fatin Bayraktar
MYP Coordinator Ferdi Ünal
Languages English, Turkish
T: +90 216 686 16 86
W: www.nunokullari.com
 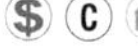 

Özel Antalya Toplum Koleji Anadolu Lisesi
Altinkale, Palmiye Cd. No 10/A, 07192 Dösemealti, Antalya, Mediterranean
DP Coordinator Ceyda Aras Tuncay
Languages English, Turkish
T: +90 242 443 30 80
W: www.antalyatoplumkoleji.com

Özel Ari Anadolu Lisesi
Ögretmenler cad. No. 16/ C 100, Yil Cukurambar, Çankaya, 06530 Ankara, Central Anatolia
DP Coordinator Bülent Inal
PYP Coordinator Tayfun Sen
Languages English
T: +90 312 286 85 85
W: www.ariokullari.k12.tr

Özel Atayurt Ilkokulu
Yukari Sögütönü Mah., Bursa Yolu 10.km. 951 sokak No. 146, 26563 Eskisehir, Central Anatolia
PYP Coordinator Melike Ogut
Languages Turkish
T: +90 222 315 03 60

Özel Ay Egitim Kurumlari
Barbaros Hayrettin Pasa Mahallesi, 1058. Sk. No. 40, Gaziosmanpasa, 34250 Istanbul, Marmara
PYP Coordinator Irem Alacakoc
Languages English, Turkish
T: +90 212 609 26 08
W: www.aykoleji.k12.tr

Özel Egeberk Anaokulu
Özlüce Mah. Hazal Sk. No:3 Nilüfer, 16010 Bursa, Marmara
PYP Coordinator Betul Basturk Oznar
Languages English
T: +90 533 593 92 90
W: www.egeberkanaokulu.com

Ozel Ilk Cizgi Kindergarten
Nilüfer Hatun Caddesi, ilk Cizgi Sokak, No:5, Osmangazi, 16265 Bursa, Marmara
PYP Coordinator Imren Sarisoy
Languages English, Turkish
T: +90 224 244 91 91

Ozel Istanbul Akademik Sistem Okullari
Basaksehir Mah. Yücelen Sok. No. 5, Basaksehir, Istanbul, Marmara
DP Coordinator Rasha Herzalla
Languages English, Turkish
W: ias.school

Özel Kariyer Ilkokulu
Turgut Özal Mh. 2212.Sk No:4, Cakirlarciftligi/Batikent, 06370 Ankara, Central Anatolia
PYP Coordinator Pinar Demirel
Languages Turkish
T: +90 312 566 22 32
W: www.kariyerkoleji.com.tr

Özel Rüzgar Fen Lisesi
Bagcilar Mahallesi 1105, Sokak No. 7 Bagimsiz Bölüm No. 11, Baglar, 21090 Diyarbakir, Southeastern Anatolia
DP Coordinator Ufuk Ozer
Languages English, Turkish
T: +90 412 503 19 79
W: ruzgarfenlisesi.k12.tr

Private ALEV Schools
Kadirova Cad. 52/3, Ömerli Mah. Cekmeköy, 34797 Istanbul, Marmara
DP Coordinator Azize Gökçen Yurttagül
Languages Turkish, German, English
T: +90 216 435 83 50
W: www.alev.k12.tr
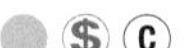

Private Kocaeli Bahcesehir Anatolian High School
Fatih Mah, Demokrasi Cad No.8 B.K.3, Köseköy, 41135 Kartepe, Marmara
DP Coordinator Lale Işıkel Şanlı
Languages English, Turkish
T: +90 262 373 69 69
W: kocaelianadolulisesi.bahcesehir.k12.tr/en/
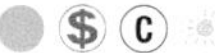

Private Sahin Schools
Prof. Dr. Sabahattin Zaim Bulvari Karaman Yolu 4., Km Karakamis Mah., 54100 Adapazari, Marmara
PYP Coordinator Melike Gürsoy Manav
T: +90 264 777 17 00
W: www.sahinokullari.com

Private Sanko Schools
Pancarli District Kültür Street No. 10, 27060 Sehitkamil, Southeastern Anatolia
PYP Coordinator Mustafa Bagci
Languages English, Turkish
T: +90 342 211 55 00
W: www.sanko.k12.tr

SEV American College
Nisantepe Mah. Kerem Sok. 76, No. 5-9, Cekmeköy, 34794 Istanbul, Marmara
DP Coordinator Isilay Albayrak Zeyrek
Languages English
T: +90 216 625 27 22
W: sevkoleji.k12.tr
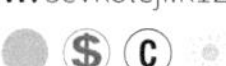

Tarsus American School
Cengiz Topel Caddesi, Caminur Mahallesi No. 66, Tarsus, 33440 Mersin, Mediterranean
DP Coordinator Funda Karaosmanoğlu
Languages English
T: +90 324 241 81 81
W: www.tac.k12.tr

Tas Private Elementary School
Cevizlik Mah. Hallac Hüseyin, Sk. No. 11, Bakirköy, 34142 Istanbul, Marmara
PYP Coordinator Sena Bataklar
Languages Turkish, English
T: +90 212 543 60 00
W: www.taskolej.k12.tr

TED Ankara College Foundation High School
Golbasi Taspinar Koyu Yumrubel, Mevkii No. 310, 06830 Ankara, Central Anatolia
DP Coordinator Serenay Tarhan Guler
Languages English
T: +90 312 586 90 00
W: www.tedankara.k12.tr

TED Bursa College
21 Yüzyil Cad Mürsel, Köyü Mevkii, Bademli, Bursa, Marmara
DP Coordinator Nuray Bayulgen
Languages English
T: +90 224 549 21 00
W: www.tedbursa.k12.tr

Tenzile Erdogan Kiz Imam Hatip Lisesi
Kücüksu Mahallesi Yalniz Selvi Caddesi Asma Sokak No. 8, Rasathane, Üsküdar, Istanbul, Marmara
DP Coordinator Elif Demiryürek
Languages English, Turkish
T: +90 216 332 83 75
W: tenzileerdogankaihl.meb.k12.tr

Terakki Foundation - Levent Campus
Ebulula Mardin Cad. Öztürk Sok No. 2, Levent, 34335 Istanbul, Marmara
DP Coordinator Fulya Müldür Aktürk
PYP Coordinator Sadan Efe
Languages English, Turkish
T: +90 212 351 00 60
W: www.terakki.org.tr

Terakki Foundation - Tepeoren Campus
Medeniyet Blv. No. 55L, Tuzla, 34959 Istanbul, Marmara
DP Coordinator Hasan Ozkaya
PYP Coordinator Yesim Er Özcan
Languages English, Turkish
T: +90 216 709 18 77
W: www.terakki.org.tr

Tev Inanc Turkes High School For Gifted Students
Muallimköy Mah. 4126, Sok. No. 25/A, 41490 Gebze, Marmara
DP Coordinator Joshua Lisi
Languages English
T: +90 262 679 36 36
W: www.tevitol.k12.tr

The Koç School
Tepeören Mahallesi, Eski Ankara Asfalti Caddesi No. 60, 34941 Istanbul, Marmara
DP Coordinator Mick Oneill
Languages Turkish, English
T: +90 216 585 62 00
W: www.kocschool.k12.tr

The Sezin School
Ulubatli Hasan Caddesi No:18, Cekmeköy, 34782 Istanbul, Marmara
DP Coordinator Vahdettin Dogan
Languages English, Turkish
T: +90 216 642 00 10
W: www.sezin.k12.tr

Uluslararasi Murat Hüdavendigar Anadolu Imam Hatip Lisesi
Hamitler, Sht. Saim Tuna Sk. No:6, Osmangazi, 16150 Bursa, Marmara
DP Coordinator Ilkay Capkın
Languages English, Turkish
T: +90 224 242 22 28
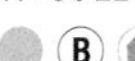  

Üsküdar American Academy
Vakif Sk., No. 1 Baglarbasi, Uskudar, 33664 Istanbul, Marmara
DP Coordinator David Simon Cousens
Languages English
T: +90 216 333 11 00
W: www.uaa.k12.tr

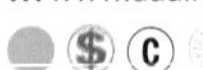

Vefa High School
Kalenderhane Mah. Dede Efendi Cad., No. 5 Sehzadebasi, Fatih, 34134 Istanbul, Marmara
DP Coordinator Evrim Gulec Akova
Languages English, Turkish
T: +90 212 527 38 72
W: vefalisesi.meb.k12.tr

Yeni Yol Schools
Yeniakcayir Mahallesi No. 551, Tepebasi, Eskisehir, Central Anatolia
DP Coordinator Mustafa Yilmazer
PYP Coordinator Elvan Yildirim
Languages English, Turkish
T: +90 222 230 39 00
W: www.yeniyolokullari.com

YUCE Schools
Ozel YUCE Okullari, Zuhtu Tigrel Caddesi, Ismet Eker Sokak No 5, Oran, 06450 Ankara, Central Anatolia
DP Coordinator Özlem Nadiroğlu
MYP Coordinator Özlem Nadiroğlu
PYP Coordinator Sila Derici
Languages English, Turkish
T: +90 312 490 02 02
W: www.yuce.k12.tr

Yusuf Ziya Oner Fen Lisesi
Yesilbayir Mah. Mektep, Sok No. 5, Dösemealti, 07192 Antalya, Mediterranean
DP Coordinator Özge Dönmez Arıkel
Languages English, Turkish
T: +90 242 443 18 56
W: antalyafenlisesi.meb.k12.tr

Zafer Koleji
Eskisehir Yolu, Baglica Kavsagi No. 461, Cayyolu, 06790 Ankara, Central Anatolia
DP Coordinator Andrew Miller
Languages English
T: +90 312 444 55 12
W: zaferkoleji.com.tr

UGANDA

ACORNS INTERNATIONAL SCHOOL (AIS)
Plot 328, Kisota Road, (Along) Northern Bypass, Kisaasi Roundabout, Kampala
DP Coordinator Ken Kanyesigye
MYP Coordinator Sam Weavers
PYP Coordinator Jamal Makki
Languages English
T: +256 393 202 665
E: admissions@ais.ac.ug
W: www.ais.ac.ug
See full details on page 47

International School of Uganda
272 Entebbe Road, Kampala
DP Coordinator Mark Redlich
MYP Coordinator Craig Mcvicar
PYP Coordinator Sarah Ssengendo
Languages English
T: +256 414 200 374
W: www.isu.ac.ug

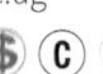

Kampala International School Uganda (KISU)
P.O.Box 34249, Bukoto, Kampala
DP Coordinator Carine Jadot
Languages English
T: +256 752 711 882
W: www.kisu.com

The Aga Khan High School, Kampala
P.O. Box 6837, Muammar Gaddafi Road, Kampala
DP Coordinator Alexander Kakungulu
Languages English
T: +256 414 308 245
W: www.agakhanschools.org/uganda/akhsk/index

UK

ACS Cobham International School
Heywood, Portsmouth Road, Cobham, Surrey KT11 1BL
DP Coordinator Henrietta Knight
Languages English
T: +44 (0) 1932 867251
W: www.acs-schools.com/cobham

ACS Egham International School
London Road, Egham, Surrey TW20 0HS
CP Coordinator Stephanie Leahey
DP Coordinator Anne-Marie Robb
MYP Coordinator Marie MacPhee
PYP Coordinator Caroline MacLean
Languages English
T: +44 (0) 1784 430800
W: www.acs-schools.com/egham

ACS Hillingdon International School
108 Vine Lane, Hillingdon, Uxbridge, Middlesex UB10 0BE
CP Coordinator Sadie Lovell
DP Coordinator Dougal Fergusson
Languages English
T: +44 (0) 1895 259771
W: www.acs-schools.com/hillingdon

ANGLO EUROPEAN SCHOOL
Willow Green, Ingatestone, Essex CM4 0DJ
CP Coordinator Miss Josephine Pickard
DP Coordinator Mrs Susannah Porsz
Languages English
T: 01277 354018
E: admissions@aesessex.co.uk
W: www.aesessex.co.uk
See full details on page 57

Ardingly College
College Road, Ardingly, Haywards Heath, West Sussex RH17 6SQ
DP Coordinator Simon Woodhall
Languages English
T: +44 (0)1444 893320
W: www.ardingly.com

Arts University Plymouth
Tavistock Place, Plymouth, Devon PL4 8AT
CP Coordinator Michelle Lester
Languages English
T: +44 (0)1752 203434
W: www.aup.ac.uk

ASHCROFT TECHNOLOGY ACADEMY
100 West Hill, London SW15 2UT
DP Coordinator Joseph Anson
Languages English
T: +44 (0)208 877 0357
E: joseph.anson@ashcroftacademy.org.uk
W: www.atacademy.org.uk
See full details on page 59

Aylesford School
Teapot Lane, Aylesford, Kent ME20 7JU
CP Coordinator Ria Graham
Languages English
T: 01622 717341
W: www.aylesford.kent.sch.uk

Bearsted Primary Academy
Popesfield Way, Weavering, Maidstone, Kent ME14 5GA
PYP Coordinator Jane Tipple
Languages English
T: 01622 250040
W: bearstedprimaryacademy.org.uk

Bedford Girls' School
Cardington Road, Bedford, Bedfordshire MK42 0BX
DP Coordinator John Gardner
Languages English
T: 01234 361900
W: www.bedfordgirlsschool.co.uk

Bedford School
De Parys Avenue, Bedford, Bedfordshire MK40 2TU
DP Coordinator Mr Adrian Finch MA
Languages English
T: 01234 362200
W: www.bedfordschool.org.uk

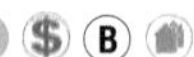

Bedstone College
Bedstone, Bucknell, Shropshire SY7 0BG
CP Coordinator Leonidas Kouniakis
Languages English
T: 01547 530303
W: www.bedstone.org

Bexley Grammar School
Danson Lane, Welling, Kent DA16 2BL
DP Coordinator Tom Martin
Languages English
T: +44 (0)2083 048538
W: www.bexleygs.co.uk

BOX HILL SCHOOL
London Road, Mickleham, Dorking, Surrey RH5 6EA
DP Coordinator Julian Baker
Languages English
T: 01372 373382
E: registrar@BoxHillSchool.com
W: www.boxhillschool.com
See full details on page 63

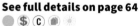

BRADFIELD COLLEGE
Bradfield, Berkshire RG7 6AU
DP Coordinator Colin Irvine
Languages English
T: 0118 964 4516
E: admissions@bradfieldcollege.org.uk
W: www.bradfieldcollege.org.uk
See full details on page 64

Brentwood School
Middleton Hall Lane, Brentwood, Essex CM15 8EE
DP Coordinator Mrs Hollie Carter
Languages English
T: 01277 243243
W: www.brentwoodschool.co.uk

Bridgwater & Taunton College
Bath Road, Bridgwater, Somerset TA6 4PZ
DP Coordinator Rebecca Miller
Languages English
T: 01278 455464
W: www.btc.ac.uk

Bristol Grammar School
University Road, Bristol BS8 1SR
DP Coordinator Ben Schober
Languages English
T: 0117 973 6006
W: www.bristolgrammarschool.co.uk

BROMSGROVE SCHOOL
Worcester Road, Bromsgrove, Worcestershire B61 7DU
DP Coordinator Michael Thompson
Languages English
T: +44 (0)1527 579679
E: admissions@bromsgrove-school.co.uk
W: www.bromsgrove-school.co.uk
See full details on page 65

Bryanston School
Blandford Forum, Dorset DT11 0PX
CP Coordinator Rose Ings
DP Coordinator Ed Pyke
Languages English
T: 01258 484633
W: www.bryanston.co.uk

Buckswood School
Broomham Hall, Rye Road, Guestling, Hastings, East Sussex TN35 4LT
DP Coordinator Carol Richards
Languages English
T: 01424 813 813
W: www.buckswood.co.uk

CHARTERHOUSE
Godalming, Surrey GU7 2DX
DP Coordinator Mr Peter Price
Languages English
T: +44 (0)1483 291501
E: admissions@charterhouse.org.uk
W: www.charterhouse.org.uk
See full details on page 68

CHELTENHAM LADIES' COLLEGE
Bayshill Road, Cheltenham, Gloucestershire GL50 3EP
DP Coordinator Becky Revell
Languages English
T: +44 (0)1242 520691
E: enquiries@cheltladiescollege.org
W: www.cheltladiescollege.org
See full details on page 67

Cherry Orchard Primary Academy
Cherry Orchard, Castle Hill, Ebbsfleet Valley, Kent DA10 1AD
PYP Coordinator Sandra Foxwell
Languages English, Spanish
T: 01322 242 011
W: cherryorchardprimaryacademy.org.uk

Chester International School
Queen's Park Campus, Queen's Park Road, Handbridge, Chester, Cheshire CH4 7AE
CP Coordinator Abbey Peers
DP Coordinator Abbey Peers
MYP Coordinator Abbey Peers
Languages English
T: +44 (0)1244 735610
W: www.chesterinternational.co.uk

Christ's Hospital
Horsham, West Sussex RH13 0LJ
DP Coordinator Martin Stephens
Languages English
T: 01403 211293
W: www.christs-hospital.org.uk

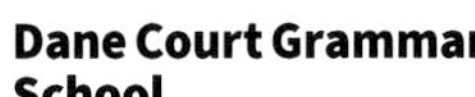

Dane Court Grammar School
Broadstairs Road, Broadstairs, Kent CT10 2RT
CP Coordinator Chris Pleasant
DP Coordinator Chris Pleasant
Languages English
T: +44 (0)1843 864941
W: www.danecourt.kent.sch.uk

Dartford Grammar School
West Hill, Dartford, Kent DA1 2HW
DP Coordinator Edward Crawford
MYP Coordinator Edward Crawford
Languages English
T: 01322 223039
W: www.dartfordgrammarschool.org.uk

Dartford Primary Academy
York Road, Dartford, Kent DA1 1SQ
PYP Coordinator Declan Filsell
Languages English
T: 01322 224453
W: dartfordprimary.org.uk

DEUTSCHE SCHULE LONDON
Douglas House, Petersham Road, Richmond, Surrey TW10 7AH
DP Coordinator Edna Howard
Languages English, German
T: +44 (0)20 8940 2510
E: info@dslondon.org.uk
W: www.dslondon.org.uk
See full details on page 75

Dover Christ Church Academy
Melbourne Avenue, Whitfield, Kent CT16 2EG
CP Coordinator Victoria Wallis
Languages English
T: +44 (0)1304 820126
W: www.dccacademy.org.uk

DWIGHT SCHOOL LONDON
6 Friern Barnet Lane, London N11 3LX
DP Coordinator William Bowry
MYP Coordinator Karine Villatte
PYP Coordinator Waseem Rehman
Languages English
T: 020 8920 0600
E: admissions@dwightlondon.org
W: www.dwightlondon.org
See full details on page 76

Eastcote Primary Academy
Eastcote Road, Welling, Kent DA16 2ST
PYP Coordinator Katie Hall
Languages English
T: 02088 561346
W: eastcoteprimaryacademy.org.uk

École Jeannine Manuel - London
Bloomsbury, London WC1B 3DN
DP Coordinator Jeanne Gonnet
Languages English, French
T: 020 3829 5970
W: www.ecolejeanninemanuel.org.uk

EF Academy Oxford
Pullens Lane, Headington, Oxfordshire OX3 0DT
DP Coordinator Dona Jones
Languages English
T: +41 (0) 43 430 41 00
W: www.efacademy.org

EIFA International School
36 Portland Place, London W1B 1LS
DP Coordinator Mark O'Brien
Languages English, French
T: +44 (0)20 7637 5351
W: www.eifaschool.com

Ellesmere College
Ellesmere, Shropshire SY12 9AB
DP Coordinator Dr Ian Tompkins
Languages English
T: 01691 622321
W: www.ellesmere.com

Eltham Hill School
Eltham Hill, Greenwich, London SE9 5EE
CP Coordinator Rosemary Osborne
Languages English
T: +44 (0)2088 592843
W: www.elthamhill.com

Europa School UK
Thame Lane, Culham, Oxfordshire OX14 3DZ
DP Coordinator Tanya Simpson
MYP Coordinator Rosemary Butcher
Languages English, French
T: +44 (0)1235 524060
W: europaschooluk.org

Exeter College
Hele Road, Exeter, Devon EX4 4JS
DP Coordinator Jan England
Languages English
T: 01392 400500
W: www.exe-coll.ac.uk

FAIRVIEW INTERNATIONAL SCHOOL, BRIDGE OF ALLAN
52 Kenilworth Road, Bridge of Allan, Stirling FK9 4RY
DP Coordinator G. Wilson
MYP Coordinator G. Wilson
PYP Coordinator K. Smith
Languages English
T: +44 (0)1786 231952
E: enquiries@fairviewinternational.uk
W: www.fairviewinternational.uk
See full details on page 89

FELSTED SCHOOL
Felsted, Great Dunmow, Essex CM6 3LL
DP Coordinator Karen Woodhouse
Languages English
T: +44 (0)1371 822600
E: admissions@felsted.org
W: www.felsted.org
See full details on page 91

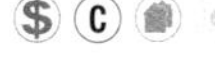

Fettes College
Carrington Road, Edinburgh EH4 1QX
DP Coordinator Mark Henry
Languages English
T: +44 (0)131 332 2281
W: www.fettes.com

GODOLPHIN AND LATYMER SCHOOL
Iffley Road, Hammersmith, London W6 0PG
DP Coordinator Audrey Dubois
Languages English
T: +44 (0)20 8741 1936
E: office@godolphinandlatymer.com
W: www.godolphinandlatymer.com
See full details on page 95

Gresham's Senior School
Cromer Road, Holt, Norfolk NR25 6EA
DP Coordinator Louise Futter
Languages English
T: 01263 714500
W: www.greshams.com

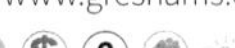

Guernsey Grammar School & Sixth Form Centre
Les Varendes, St Andrews, Guernsey GY8 6TD
CP Coordinator Paul Montague
DP Coordinator Paul Montague
Languages English
T: +44 (0)1481 256571
W: www.grammar.sch.gg

HAILEYBURY
Haileybury, Hertford, Hertfordshire SG13 7NU
DP Coordinator Abigail Mash
Languages English
T: +44 (0)1992 706353
E: admissions@haileybury.com
W: www.haileybury.com
See full details on page 99

Halcyon London International School
33 Seymour Place, London W1H 5AU
DP Coordinator Lori Fritz
MYP Coordinator Kerry Jenkins
Languages English
T: +44 (0)20 7258 1169
W: halcyonschool.com

Hartley Primary Academy
Round Ash Way, Longfield, Kent DA3 8BT
PYP Coordinator Sophie Smith
Languages English
T: 01474 702742
W: hartleyprimaryacademy.org.uk

Hartsdown Academy
George V Avenue, Margate, Kent CT9 5RE
CP Coordinator Stacie Pollard
Languages English
T: +44 (0)1843 227957
W: www.hartsdown.org

Hautlieu School
Wellington Road, St Saviour, Jersey JE2 7TH
CP Coordinator Mandy Campbell
DP Coordinator Mandy Campbell
Languages English
T: +44 (0)1534 736 242
W: www.hautlieu.co.uk

Headington Rye Oxford
Headington Road, Oxford, Oxfordshire OX3 7TD
DP Coordinator Mr James Stephenson
Languages English
T: +44 (0)1865 759100
W: www.headington.org

High Halstow Primary Academy
Harrison Drive, High Halstow, Rochester, Kent ME3 8TF
PYP Coordinator Rachael Heard
Languages English
T: 01634 251098
W: highhalstowprimaryacademy.org.uk

HOCKERILL ANGLO-EUROPEAN COLLEGE
Dunmow Road, Bishops Stortford, Hertfordshire CM23 5HX
DP Coordinator Thea Wilson
MYP Coordinator Michelle Butler
Languages English
T: 01279 658451
E: admissions@hockerill.com
W: www.hockerill.com
See full details on page 103

Horsmonden Primary Academy
Back Lane, Horsmonden, Kent TN12 8NJ
PYP Coordinator Charlotte McLeish
Languages English
T: +44 (0)1892 722529
W: horsmondenprimaryacademy.org.uk

ICS LONDON
7B Wyndham Place, London W1H 1PN
DP Coordinator Vishanu Bhoja
MYP Coordinator Laura Yates
PYP Coordinator Clara Wells
Languages English
T: +44 (0)20 729 88800
E: admissions@ics.uk.net
W: www.icschool.co.uk
See full details on page 107

IMPINGTON INTERNATIONAL COLLEGE
New Road, Impington, Cambridge, Cambridgeshire CB24 9LX
CP Coordinator Leanne Gibbons
DP Coordinator Bronwyn Wilson
MYP Coordinator Christine Incles
Languages English
T: 01223 200402
E: international@ivc.tmet.org.uk
W: www.impingtoninternational.org.uk
See full details on page 110

International School of Aberdeen
Pitfodels House, North Deeside Road, Pitfodels, Cults, Aberdeen AB15 9PN
DP Coordinator Jennifer Grogan
Languages English
T: 01224 730300
W: www.isa.aberdeen.sch.uk

INTERNATIONAL SCHOOL OF LONDON (ISL)
139 Gunnersbury Avenue, London W3 8LG
DP Coordinator Dr El Kahina Meziane
MYP Coordinator Mr David Slaney
PYP Coordinator Ms Emily Loughead
Languages English & Home Language Programme
T: +44 (0)20 8992 5823
E: mail@isllondon.org
W: www.isllondon.org
See full details on page 127

KENT COLLEGE, CANTERBURY
Whitstable Road, Canterbury, Kent CT2 9DT
DP Coordinator Mr Graham Letley
Languages English
T: +44 (0)1227 763 231
E: admissions@kentcollege.co.uk
W: www.kentcollege.com
See full details on page 146

King Edward's School
Edgbaston Park Road, Birmingham, West Midlands B15 2UA
DP Coordinator Andrew Petrie
Languages English
T: 01214 721672
W: www.kes.org.uk

King Ethelbert School
Canterbury Road, Birch ing ton, Kent CT7 9BL
CP Coordinator Rebecca Darch
Languages English
T: 01843 831999
W: www.kingethelbert.com

KING WILLIAM'S COLLEGE
Castletown, Isle of Man IM9 1TP
DP Coordinator Alasdair Ulyett
Languages English
T: +44 (0)1624 820110
E: admissions@kwc.im
W: www.kwc.im
See full details on page 150

KING'S COLLEGE SCHOOL, WIMBLEDON
Southside, Wimbledon Common, London SW19 4TT
DP Coordinator David Cass
Languages English
T: 020 8255 5300
E: admissions@kcs.org.uk
W: www.kcs.org.uk
See full details on page 151

Knole Academy
Bradbourne Vale Road, Sevenoaks, Kent TN13 3LE
CP Coordinator Mrs Jane Elliott
DP Coordinator Mrs Jane Elliott
Languages English
T: 01732 454608
W: www.knoleacademy.org

LANDMARK INTERNATIONAL SCHOOL
The Old Rectory, 9 Church Lane, Fulbourn, Cambridge, Cambridgeshire CB21 5EP
PYP Coordinator Mrs Jenna Fritz
Languages English
T: 01223 755100
E: office@landmarkinternationalschool.co.uk
W: www.landmarkinternationalschool.co.uk
See full details on page 158

Langley Park Primary Academy
Edmett Way, Maidstone, Kent ME17 3FX
PYP Coordinator Jolene Barrett
Languages English
T: 01622 250880
W: langleyparkprimaryacademy.org.uk

Leigh Academy Blackheath
Old Dover Road, Blackheath, London SE3 8SY
CP Coordinator Dean Vaughan
DP Coordinator Dean Vaughan
MYP Coordinator James Cowie
Languages English
T: +44 (0)20 8104 0888
W: leighacademyblackheath.org.uk

LEIGHTON PARK SCHOOL
Shinfield Road, Reading, Berkshire RG2 7ED
DP Coordinator Mrs Helen Taylor
Languages English
T: 0118 987 9600
E: admissions@leightonpark.com
W: www.leightonpark.com
See full details on page 159

LOMOND SCHOOL
10 Stafford Street, Helensburgh, Argyll & Bute G84 9JX
Languages English
T: +44 (0)1436 672476
E: admissions@lomondschool.com
W: www.lomondschool.com
See full details on page 161

Longfield Academy
Main Road, Longfield, Kent DA3 7PH
MYP Coordinator David O'Leary
Languages English
T: +44 (0)1474 700 700
W: longfieldacademy.org.uk

Lycée International de Londres Winston Churchill
54 Forty Lane, Wembley, Middlesex HA9 9LY
DP Coordinator Maaike Kaandorp
Languages English, French
T: +44 (0)203 824 4900
W: www.lyceeinternational.london

MALVERN COLLEGE
College Road, Malvern, Worcestershire WR14 3DF
DP Coordinator Jennifer Akehurst
Languages English
T: +44 (0)1684 581515
E: admissions@malverncollege.org.uk
W: www.malverncollege.org.uk
See full details on page 168

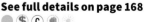

Marymount International School London
George Road, Kingston upon Thames, Surrey KT2 7PE
DP Coordinator Nicholas Marcou
MYP Coordinator Mark Gardner
Languages English
T: +44 (0)20 8949 0571
W: www.marymountlondon.com

Mascalls Academy
Maidstone Road, Paddock Wood, Tonbridge, Kent TN12 6LT
MYP Coordinator Sharon Mahon
Languages English
T: 01892 835366
W: mascallsacademy.org.uk

Molehill Primary Academy
Hereford Road, Maidstone, Kent ME15 7ND
PYP Coordinator Jane Coker
Languages English
T: 01622 751729
W: molehillprimaryacademy.org.uk

MOUNT HOUSE SCHOOL
Camlet Way, Hadley Wood, Barnet, Hertfordshire EN4 0NJ
CP Coordinator Mr Jon Cooper
Languages English
T: 020 8449 6889
E: admissions@mounthouse.org.uk
W: www.mounthouse.org.uk
See full details on page 172

NORTH LONDON COLLEGIATE SCHOOL
Canons, Canons Drive, Edgware, Middlesex HA8 7RJ
DP Coordinator Dr Henry Linscott
Languages English
T: +44 (0)20 8952 0912
E: office@nlcs.org.uk
W: www.nlcs.org.uk
See full details on page 176

 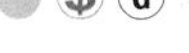

Northfleet School for Girls
Hall Road, Northfleet, Kent DA11 8AQ
CP Coordinator Alison Johnson
Languages English
T: +44 (0)1474 831 020
W: www.nsfg.org.uk

Northfleet Technology College
Colyer Road, Northfleet, Kent DA11 8BG
CP Coordinator Emma Campbell
Languages English
T: 01474 533802
W: ntc.kent.sch.uk

OAKHAM SCHOOL
Chapel Close, Oakham, Rutland LE15 6DT
DP Coordinator Carolyn Fear
MYP Coordinator Dmitriy Ashton
Languages English
T: 01572 758758
E: admissions@oakham.rutland.sch.uk
W: www.oakham.rutland.sch.uk
See full details on page 177

Oaks Primary Academy
Oak Tree Avenue, Maidstone, Kent ME15 9AX
PYP Coordinator Aoife Mehigan
Languages English
T: 01622 755960
W: oaksprimaryacademy.org.uk

Parkside Community College
Parkside, Cambridge, Cambridgeshire CB1 1EH
CP Coordinator Rachel Biltcliffe
DP Coordinator Rachel Biltcliffe
Languages English
T: +44 (0)1223 712600
W: www.parksidecc.org.uk/sixth

Peninsula East Primary Academy
Avery Way, Allhallows, Rochester, Kent ME3 9HR
PYP Coordinator Hannah Penning
Languages English
T: 01634 270428
W: pepa.org.uk

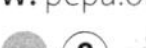 

Redmaids' High School Senior & Sixth Form
Westbury Road, Westbury-on-Trym, Bristol BS9 3AW
DP Coordinator Peter Brealey
Languages English
T: 0117 962 2641
W: www.redmaidshigh.co.uk

Rossall School
Broadway, Fleetwood, Lancashire FY7 8JW
DP Coordinator Lauren Laird
Languages English
T: +44 (0)1253 774201
W: www.rossall.org.uk

ROYAL HIGH SCHOOL BATH, GDST
Lansdown Road, Bath, Bath & North-East Somerset BA1 5SZ
DP Coordinator Ms Jude Taylor
Languages English
T: +44 (0)1225 313877
E: admissions@rhsb.gdst.net
W: www.royalhighbath.gdst.net
See full details on page 190

Rugby School
Lawrence Sheriff Street, Rugby, Warwickshire CV22 5EH
DP Coordinator Natalie Lockhart-Mann
Languages English
T: +44 (0)1788 556216
W: www.rugbyschool.co.uk

RYDE SCHOOL WITH UPPER CHINE
Queen's Road, Ryde, Isle of Wight PO33 3BE
CP Coordinator David Shapland
DP Coordinator David Shapland
Languages English
T: 01983 562229
E: admissions@rydeschool.net
W: www.rydeschool.org.uk
See full details on page 191

 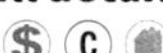 

SCARBOROUGH COLLEGE
Filey Road, Scarborough, North Yorkshire YO11 3BA
DP Coordinator Ms Katie Cooke
Languages English
T: +44 (0)1723 360620
E: admin@scarboroughcollege.co.uk
W: www.scarboroughcollege.co.uk
See full details on page 194

SEVENOAKS SCHOOL
High Street, Sevenoaks, Kent TN13 1HU
DP Coordinator Nigel Haworth
Languages English
T: +44 (0)1732 455133
E: regist@sevenoaksschool.org
W: www.sevenoaksschool.org
See full details on page 205

 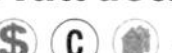

Sidcot School
Oakridge Lane, Winscombe, Somerset BS25 1PD
DP Coordinator Stefania Cauli
Languages English
T: 01934 843102
W: www.sidcot.org.uk

Southbank International School - Hampstead
16 Netherhall Gardens, London NW3 5TH
PYP Coordinator Erika Dingli
Languages English
T: 020 3890 1969
W: www.southbank.org

Southbank International School - Kensington
36-38 Kensington Park Road, London W11 3BU
PYP Coordinator Stefanie Waterman
Languages English
T: 020 3890 1969
W: www.southbank.org

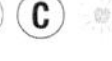

Southbank International School - Westminster
63-65 Portland Place, London W1B 1QR
DP Coordinator Fabienne Fontaine
MYP Coordinator Angela Johnson
Languages English
T: 020 3890 1969
W: www.southbank.org

St Benedict's Catholic High School
Kinwarton Road, Alcester, Warwickshire B49 6PX
DP Coordinator Donna Munford
Languages English
T: +44 (0)1789 762888
W: www.st-benedicts.org

ST CLARE'S, OXFORD
139 Banbury Road, Oxford, Oxfordshire OX2 7AL
DP Coordinator Darrel Ross
Languages English
T: +44 (0)1865 552031
E: admissions@stclares.ac.uk
W: www.stclares.ac.uk
See full details on page 208

ST EDWARD'S, OXFORD
Woodstock Road, Oxford, Oxfordshire OX2 7NN
DP Coordinator Anna Fielding
Languages English
T: +44 (0)1865 319200
E: registrar@stedwardsoxford.org
W: www.stedwardsoxford.org
See full details on page 210

St George's School Windsor Castle
Windsor Castle, Windsor, Berkshire SL4 1QF
PYP Coordinator Emma Adriano
Languages English
T: 01753 865553
W: www.stgwindsor.org

ST LEONARDS SCHOOL
South Street, St Andrews, Fife KY16 9QJ
CP Coordinator Ben Seymour
DP Coordinator Ben Seymour
MYP Coordinator Sharon Moan
PYP Coordinator Catherine Brannen
Languages English
T: 01334 472126
E: registrar@stleonards-fife.org
W: stleonards-fife.org
See full details on page 212

Stationers' Crown Woods Academy
145 Bexley Road, Eltham, London SE9 2PT
MYP Coordinator Jane Elizabeth Barrowcliff
Languages English
T: +44 (0)208 850 7678
W: scwa.org.uk

Stephen Perse Sixth Form
Bateman Street, Cambridge, Cambridgeshire CB2 1NA
DP Coordinator Jacqueline Paris
Languages English
T: 01223 454700 (EXT: 3000)
W: stephenperse.com/sixthform

Stonyhurst College
Stonyhurst, Clitheroe, Lancashire BB7 9PZ
CP Coordinator Emma Walker
DP Coordinator Mrs Deborah Kirkby BSc
Languages English
T: 01254 827073
W: www.stonyhurst.ac.uk

Strood Academy
Carnation Road, Strood, Kent ME2 2SX
CP Coordinator Samira Nasim
MYP Coordinator Nicola Collison
Languages English
T: +44 (0)1634 717121
W: stroodacademy.org.uk

TASIS THE AMERICAN SCHOOL IN ENGLAND
Coldharbour Lane, Thorpe, Surrey TW20 8TE
DP Coordinator Jessica Lee
Languages English
T: +44 (0)1932 582316
E: ukadmissions@tasisengland.org
W: www.tasisengland.org

See full details on page 222

TAUNTON SCHOOL
Staplegrove Road, Taunton, Somerset TA2 6AD
DP Coordinator Adrian Roberts
Languages English
T: +44 (0)1823 703703
E: enquiries@tauntonschool.co.uk
W: www.tauntonschool.co.uk

See full details on page 224

Teikyo School UK
Framewood Road, Wexham, Buckinghamshire SL2 4QS
DP Coordinator Wakako Yachidate
Languages English, Japanese
T: 01753 663711
W: teikyofoundation.com

THE ABBEY SCHOOL
Kendrick Road, Reading, Berkshire RG1 5DZ
DP Coordinator Nicola McDonald
PYP Coordinator Jillian Priestley
Languages English
T: 0118 987 2256
E: admissions@theabbey.co.uk
W: www.theabbey.co.uk

See full details on page 225

The Chalfonts Independent Grammar School
19 London Road, High Wycombe, Buckinghamshire HP11 1BJ
DP Coordinator Alexander Herriott
MYP Coordinator Bart Van Malssen
Languages English
T: +44 (0)1494 875502
W: www.thechalfontsgrammar.co.uk

The Ebbsfleet Academy
Southfleet Road, Ebbsfleet Garden City, Kent DA10 0BZ
CP Coordinator Jonathan Field
Languages English
T: +44 (0)1322 623100
W: theebbsfleetacademy.kent.sch.uk

The Halley Academy
Corelli Road, Blackheath, London SE3 8EP
CP Coordinator Will Burrows
MYP Coordinator Eleanor Parsons
Languages English
T: +44 (0)208 856 2828
W: thehalleyacademy.org.uk

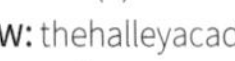

The Hundred of Hoo Academy
Main Road, Hoo St Werburgh, Rochester, Kent ME3 9HH
MYP Coordinator Steven Flower
PYP Coordinator Andrew Bullock
Languages English
T: 01634 251443
W: www.hundredofhooacademy.org.uk

The Leigh Academy
Green Street, Green Road, Dartford, Kent DA1 1QE
CP Coordinator Lee Forcella-Burton
MYP Coordinator Sarah McCabe Knowles
Languages English
T: +44 (0)1322 620400
W: leighacademy.org.uk

The Leigh UTC
The Bridge Development, Brunel Way, Dartford, Kent DA1 5TF
CP Coordinator Syreeta Martin
MYP Coordinator Kieran O'Donnell
Languages English
T: +44 (0)1322 626 600
W: theleighutc.org.uk

The Malling School
Beech Road, East Malling, West Malling, Kent ME19 6DH
CP Coordinator Karen Davey
DP Coordinator Karen Davey
Languages English
T: +44 (0)1732 840995
W: www.themallingschool.kent.sch.uk

The Portsmouth Grammar School
High Street, Portsmouth, Hampshire PO1 2LN
DP Coordinator Simon Taylor
Languages English
T: +44 (0)23 9236 0036
W: www.pgs.org.uk

The Rochester Grammar School
Maidstone Road, Rochester, Kent ME1 3BY
DP Coordinator Karen Hemming
Languages English
T: +44 (0)333 360 2120
W: www.rochestergrammar.org.uk

The Royal Harbour Academy
Newlands Lane, Ramsgate, Kent CT12 6RH
CP Coordinator Josh Stoner
MYP Coordinator Michelle Moss
Languages English
T: 01843 572500
W: www.rha.kent.sch.uk

The Sixth Form College, Colchester
North Hill, Colchester, Essex CO1 1SN
DP Coordinator Karen Burns
Languages English
T: 01206 500700
W: www.colchsfc.ac.uk

The Skinners' Kent Academy
Sandown Park, Tunbridge Wells, Kent TN2 4PY
CP Coordinator David Holl
MYP Coordinator Chi Ribbans-Opara
Languages English
T: +44 (0)1892 534377
W: www.skinnerskentacademy.org.uk

The Whitstable School
Bellevue Road, Whitstable, Kent CT5 1PX
CP Coordinator Luci Brown
Languages English
T: 01227 931300
W: www.thewhitstableschool.org.uk

The Worthgate School
68 New Dover Road, Canterbury, Kent CT1 3LQ
DP Coordinator Jemma Jones
Languages English
T: +44 (0)1227 866540
W: worthgateschool.com

Tonbridge Grammar School
Deakin Leas, Tonbridge, Kent TN9 2JR
DP Coordinator Darryl Barker
MYP Coordinator Caroline Ghali
Languages English
T: +44 (0)1732 365125
W: www.tgs.kent.sch.uk

Torquay Boys' Grammar School
Shiphay Manor Drive, Torquay, Devon TQ2 7EL
DP Coordinator James Hunt
Languages English
T: +44 1803 615 501
W: www.tbgs.co.uk

Tree Tops Primary Academy
Brishing Lane, Maidstone, Kent ME15 9EZ
PYP Coordinator Stefan Bishop
Languages English
T: 01622 754888
W: treetopsprimaryacademy.org.uk

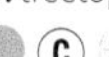

Truro and Penwith College
College Road, Truro, Cornwall TR1 3XX
DP Coordinator Angie Liversedge
Languages English
T: +44 (0)1872 305000
W: www.truro-penwith.ac.uk

UWC Atlantic
St Donat's Castle, St Donat's, Llantwit Major, Vale of Glamorgan CF61 1WF
DP Coordinator Gabor Vincze
Languages English
T: +44 (0)1446 799000
W: www.atlanticcollege.org

Varndean College
Surrenden Road, Brighton, East Sussex BN1 6WQ
DP Coordinator Lee Finlay-Gray
Languages English
T: 01273 508011
W: www.varndean.ac.uk

Warminster School
Church Street, Warminster, Wiltshire BA12 8PJ
CP Coordinator Simon Hall BSc Psychology PGCE
DP Coordinator Simon Hall BSc Psychology PGCE
Languages English
T: +44 (0)1985 210100
W: www.warminsterschool.org.uk

WELLINGTON COLLEGE
Duke's Ride, Crowthorne, Berkshire RG45 7PU
DP Coordinator Dr Robert Cromarty
Languages English
T: +44 (0)1344 444000
E: admissions@wellingtoncollege.org.uk
W: www.wellingtoncollege.org.uk
See full details on page 239

West Buckland School
Barnstaple, Devon EX32 0SX
CP Coordinator Jonathan Wilson
Languages English
T: 01598 760000
W: westbuckland.com

Westbourne School
Hickman Road, Penarth, Glamorgan CF64 2AJ
DP Coordinator Lisa Phillips
Languages English
T: 029 2070 5705
W: www.westbourneschool.com

Westminster Academy
The Naim Dangoor Centre, 255 Harrow Road, London W2 5EZ
CP Coordinator Alex James
DP Coordinator Brian Brackrog
Languages English
T: +44 (0)20 7121 0600
W: www.westminsteracademy.biz

Whitgift School
Haling Park, South Croydon, Surrey CR2 6YT
DP Coordinator Emma Mitchell
Languages English
T: +44 20 8633 9935
W: www.whitgift.co.uk

Wilmington Academy
Common Lane, Wilmington, Dartford, Kent DA2 7DR
CP Coordinator Kathleen Sanders
MYP Coordinator Patrick Lonergan
Languages English
T: +44 (0)1322 272111
W: wilmingtonacademy.org.uk

WINDERMERE SCHOOL
Patterdale Road, Windermere, Cumbria LA23 1NW
CP Coordinator Mrs Theresa Murray
DP Coordinator Mrs Elizabeth Murphy
Languages English
T: 015394 46164
E: admissions@windermereschool.co.uk
W: www.windermereschool.co.uk
See full details on page 241

Worth School
Paddockhurst Road, Turners Hill, Crawley, West Sussex RH10 4SD
DP Coordinator Bruna Gushurst-Moore
Languages English
T: +44 (0)1342 710200
W: worthschool.org.uk

Wotton House International School
Wotton House, Horton Road, Gloucester, Gloucestershire GL1 3PR
MYP Coordinator Daniel Sturdy
Languages English
T: +44 (0)1452 764248
W: www.wottonhouseschool.co.uk

Wrotham School
Borough Green Road, Wrotham, Sevenoaks, Kent TN15 7RD
CP Coordinator Samantha Williams
Languages English
T: +44 (0)1732 905860
W: www.wrothamschool.com

UKRAINE

Gymnasium A+
Berezneva Street 14, Kyiv 02160
DP Coordinator Olga Lytvynova
Languages English, Ukrainian
T: +38 44 363 14 03
W: gymnasiumplus.com.ua

International American School & University (AISU)
Street Dragomanova 1-V, Kyiv 02068
DP Coordinator Olena Tarasenko
Languages English, Ukrainian
T: +38 44 333 88 14
W: aisu.school

Pechersk School International Kyiv
7a Victora Zabily, Kyiv 03039
DP Coordinator Jessica Krueger
MYP Coordinator La Mor
PYP Coordinator Janice Humpleby
Languages English
T: +380 44 377 52 92
W: enrol.psi.kyiv.ua

QSI KYIV INTERNATIONAL SCHOOL
3A Svyatoshinsky Provuluk, Kyiv 03115
DP Coordinator Maria Bizhyk
Languages English
T: +38 (044) 452 27 92
E: kyiv@qsi.org
W: www.qsi.org/kyiv
See full details on page 187

The British International School Ukraine (Pechersk Campus)
1 Dragomirova Street, Kyiv 01103
DP Coordinator Clifford Mace
Languages English
T: +38 44 596 18 28
W: britishschool.ua
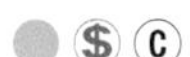

UNITED ARAB EMIRATES

Abu Dhabi International (Pvt) School
Karamah Street, PO Box 25898, Abu Dhabi
DP Coordinator Issam Kobrsi
Languages English
T: +971 2 443 4433
W: aisschools.com

Ajman Academy
Sheikh Ammar Road, Mowaihat 2, Ajman
MYP Coordinator Deborah Vincent
PYP Coordinator Hala Sweilem
Languages English
T: +971 6 731 4444
W: www.ajmanacademy.com

Al Adab Iranian Private School for Boys
Behind Al Bustan Center, Al Nahda 1, Qusais, Dubai
DP Coordinator Naghmeh Dadpanah
Languages English
T: +971 42633405
W: www.adabschool.org

Al Bateen Academy
PO Box 128484, Abu Dhabi
DP Coordinator Samantha Marsden
PYP Coordinator Ninetta Challita
Languages English
T: +971 2 813 2000
W: www.albateenacademy.sch.ae

Al Najah Private School (ANPS)
9 Near Al Safir Mall, Mohammed Bin Zayed City, Abu Dhabi
DP Coordinator Noel Debs
Languages English
T: +971 2 553 0935
W: anps.co

Ambassador International Academy
Al Khail Gate, Al Quoz, Plot No. 3653942, Dubai
MYP Coordinator Lindsay Thomas
PYP Coordinator Talia Lazarus
Languages English
T: +971 4 580 6999
W: aiadubai.com
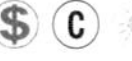

American Community School of Abu Dhabi
P.O. Box 42114, Abu Dhabi
DP Coordinator Jonathan Diaz
Languages English
T: +971 2 681 5115
W: www.acs.sch.ae

American International School in Abu Dhabi
PO Box 5992, Abu Dhabi
DP Coordinator Jodi Styre Yaseen
PYP Coordinator Meghan Dickie
Languages English
T: +971 2 4444 333
W: www.aisa.sch.ae

Aspen Heights British School
P.O. Box 137352, Al Bahya, Abu Dhabi
DP Coordinator Fiona Stewart
Languages English
T: +971 2 564 2229
W: ahbs.ae

Australian International School
PO Box 43364, Sharjah
DP Coordinator Paul Lange
Languages English
T: +971 6 558 9967
W: www.ais.ae

Australian School of Abu Dhabi
Khalifa City B, PO Box 36044, Abu Dhabi
DP Coordinator Mahmoud Dabet
MYP Coordinator Amal Elgamal
PYP Coordinator Ayan Abdullahi
Languages English
T: +971 2 5866980
W: australianschool.ae

Collegiate International School
50 Al Maydar Street, Umm Suqeim 2, P.O. Box: 121306, Dubai
CP Coordinator Purnima Sharma
DP Coordinator Purnima Sharma
MYP Coordinator Weam Ahmed
PYP Coordinator Nicolas Gastaldi
Languages English
T: +971 4 427 1400
W: www.collegiate.sch.ae

Dar Al Marefa Private School
P.O.Box: 112602, Dubai 112602
DP Coordinator Sheugnet Carter
MYP Coordinator Tania Masarwa
PYP Coordinator Habiba Jaballah
Languages English
T: +971 42885782
W: www.daralmarefa.ae

UNITED ARAB EMIRATES

Deira International School
PO Box 79043, Dubai
CP Coordinator Kimberley Shaw
DP Coordinator Helen Wallis
Languages English
T: +9714 2325552
W: www.disdubai.ae

Dubai International Academy, Al Barsha
P.O. Box: 118111, Al Barsha, Dubai
CP Coordinator Abigail Ferrari
DP Coordinator Abigail Ferrari
MYP Coordinator Caterina Marras
PYP Coordinator Andrea Waller
Languages English
T: +971 4 524 4800
W: www.diabarsha.com

Dubai International Academy, Emirates Hills
P.O. Box: 118111, First Al Khail Street, Emirates Hills, Dubai
CP Coordinator Neetu Rathore
DP Coordinator Kanchi Das
MYP Coordinator Ruba Jeshi
PYP Coordinator Ruchika Sachdev
Languages English, Arabic
T: +971 4 368 4111
W: www.diadubai.com

Dunecrest American School
P.O. Box 624265, Wadi Al Safa 3 (next to Al Barari), Dubai
DP Coordinator Eric Barrett
Languages English
T: +971 4 508 7444
W: www.dunecrest.ae

Dwight School Dubai
Umm Sequim Street, Al Barsha South 2, Dubai
DP Coordinator Peter Atkins
MYP Coordinator Jaya Bhavnani
PYP Coordinator Katie Hendry
Languages English
T: +971 800 394448
W: www.dwightschooldubai.ae

Emirates International School - Jumeirah
PO Box 6446, Dubai
CP Coordinator Wissam Yehya
DP Coordinator Nausheen Arif
MYP Coordinator Steve Wellman
PYP Coordinator Scott Kirkland
Languages English
T: +971 4 3489804
W: www.eischools.ae

Emirates International School - Meadows
PO Box 120118, Dubai
DP Coordinator Joanne Branicki-Tolchard
MYP Coordinator Sarah Robson
PYP Coordinator Sumayya Shariff
Languages Arabic, English
T: +971 4 362 9009
W: www.eischools.ae
 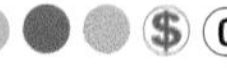

Emirates National School - Abu Dhabi City Campus
P.O. Box 44759, Abu Dhabi
DP Coordinator Sahar Hamade
MYP Coordinator Roula Azzam
Languages English, Arabic
T: +971 2 642 5993
W: www.ens.sch.ae

Emirates National School - Al Ain City Campus
PO Box 69392, Al Ain
DP Coordinator Souha Chebaane
MYP Coordinator Benjamin Smith
PYP Coordinator Dinaulu Neilako
Languages English, Arabic
T: +971 3 761 6888
W: www.ens.sch.ae

Emirates National School - Branch 3
P.O. Box 44759, Khalifa Bin Shakhbout Street, Abu Dhabi
PYP Coordinator Deborah Anitelea
Languages English

Emirates National School - Dubai Campus
Al Khawaneej, Dubai
PYP Coordinator Rola Hallak
Languages English, Arabic
T: +971 4 562 8888
W: www.ens.sch.ae

Emirates National School - Mohammed Bin Zayed Campus
PO Box 44321, Mussafah, Abu Dhabi
DP Coordinator Darine Darwiche
MYP Coordinator Nada Chreim
PYP Coordinator Fiona Finnegan
Languages Arabic, English
T: +971 2 559 00 00
W: www.ens.sch.ae

Emirates National School - Ras Al Khaimah Campus
Ras Al-Khaimah
DP Coordinator George Heusner
MYP Coordinator Roxanne Power
PYP Coordinator Ugo Aimakhu
Languages English
T: +971 7 203 3333
W: www.ens.sch.ae

Emirates National School - Sharjah Campus
Al Rahmaniya, Sharjah
DP Coordinator Shaymaa Alkhatib
MYP Coordinator Princess Lacewell
PYP Coordinator Jillane Strickland
Languages English
T: +971 6 599 0999
W: www.ens.sch.ae
   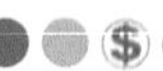

Fairgreen International School
PO Box 392024, The Sustainable City, Dubai
CP Coordinator Lisa Murphy
DP Coordinator Jon Howarth
MYP Coordinator Shannon Johnson
PYP Coordinator David Gerber
Languages English
T: +971 4 875 4999
W: www.fairgreen.ae

GEMS American Academy - Abu Dhabi
Khalifa City A, Abu Dhabi
DP Coordinator John Thompson
PYP Coordinator Tiffany Pulci
Languages English
T: +971 2 201 9555
W: www.gemsaa-abudhabi.com

GEMS Dubai American Academy
Al Barsha, Dubai
DP Coordinator Clare Boyes
Languages English
T: +971 4 704 9777
W: www.gemsaa-dubai.com

GEMS International School - Al Khail
Dubai Hills, Dubai
CP Coordinator Mariona Coderch Lopez
DP Coordinator Burcu Isik Keser
MYP Coordinator Sandy Trull
PYP Coordinator Shannon Garrett
Languages English
T: +971 4 339 6200
W: www.gemsinternationalschool-alkhail.com

GEMS MODERN ACADEMY - DUBAI
PO Box 53663, Nad al Sheeba 3,4, Dubai
DP Coordinator Dr. Sunipa Guha Neogi
MYP Coordinator Hebatallah Tarek
PYP Coordinator Joelle Filfili
Languages English
T: +971 4 326 3339
E: info_mhs@gemsedu.com
W: www.gemsmodernacademy-dubai.com
See full details on page 92
  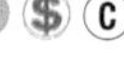 

GEMS Wellington Academy - Silicon Oasis
P.O. Box 49746, Silicon Oasis, Dubai
CP Coordinator Joel Nainie
DP Coordinator Joel Nainie
Languages English
T: +971 4 515 9000
W: www.gemswellingtonacademy-dso.com
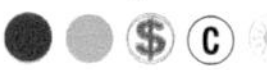

GEMS Wellington International School
Al Sufouh Area, Sheikh Zayed Road, Dubai
CP Coordinator Jacqueline Ronalds
DP Coordinator Kavita Bedi
Languages English
T: +971 4 307 3000
W: www.wellingtoninternationalschool.com

GEMS World Academy - Abu Dhabi
Najmat, Al Reem Island, Abu Dhabi
PYP Coordinator Lynn White
Languages English
T: +971 2 659 5959
W: www.gemsworldacademy-abudhabi.com

GEMS World Academy - Dubai
Al Barsha South, Dubai
CP Coordinator Chris Nitsche
DP Coordinator Chris Nitsche
MYP Coordinator Zunaira Siddiqi
PYP Coordinator Angela Roberts
Languages English
T: +971 4 373 6373
W: www.gemsworldacademy-dubai.com

German International School Sharjah
Al Abar, Sharjah
DP Coordinator Viktoria Rueffer
Languages English
T: +971 6 5676014
W: www.dssharjah.org

Greenfield International School
Dubai Investments Park, Dubai
CP Coordinator George Huteson
DP Coordinator Sarah Atienza
MYP Coordinator Chris Cooke
PYP Coordinator Dr. Sanja Vicevic Ivanovic
Languages English
T: +971 (0)4 885 6600
W: www.gischool.ae
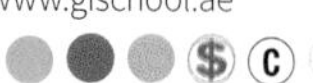

International Community School (ICS) Mushrif
24th Street, Al Mushrif Area, Abu Dhabi 55022
DP Coordinator Abdoul Nasser Abou Adela
Languages English, Arabic
T: +971 2 633 0444
W: mushrif.icschool-uae.com
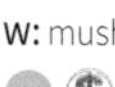 

International Concept for Education (ICE Dubai)
Al meydan Rd, Nad al Sheba1, Near Meydan Hotel, Meydan, Dubai
PYP Coordinator Yasmine Hammoud
Languages English, French
T: +971 4 3377818
W: icedubai.org

Jumeira Baccalaureate School
53 B Street, off Al Wasl Road, Jumeira 1, Dubai
CP Coordinator Michelle Andrews
DP Coordinator Michelle Andrews
MYP Coordinator Emily Coates
PYP Coordinator Gregory Joiner
Languages English
T: +971 (0)4 344 6931
W: www.jbschool.ae
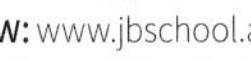

Jumeirah English Speaking School (JESS), Arabian Ranches
Main entrance of Arabian Ranches community, PO Box 24942, Dubai
DP Coordinator Steven Vickers
Languages English
T: +971 4 3619019
W: www.jess.sch.ae

Kent College Dubai
PO Box 334022, Dubai
CP Coordinator Jane Barker
DP Coordinator Arran Elmes
Languages English
T: +971 4343 0987
W: www.kentcollege.ae

Nord Anglia International School, Dubai
off Hessa Street, Dubai
DP Coordinator Louise Brown
Languages English, French
T: +971 (0)4 2199 999
W: www.nasdubai.ae

North London Collegiate School Dubai
Nad Al Sheba, Mohammed Bin Rashid Al Maktoum City, Dubai
DP Coordinator Alaine Christian
MYP Coordinator Jennifer Durston
PYP Coordinator Michaela Carney
Languages Arabic, English
T: +971 (0)4319 0888
W: www.nlcsdubai.ae

Raffles World Academy
Al Marcup Street, Umm Suqeim 3, P.O. Box 122900, Dubai
CP Coordinator Aine O'Donnell
DP Coordinator Stephen Pinto
MYP Coordinator Shagufta Abdul Qdoous
PYP Coordinator Yolanda Maccallum
Languages English
T: +971 4 4271351/2
W: www.rwadubai.com

Raha International School
Khalifa City 'A', Al Raha Gardens, Abu Dhabi
DP Coordinator Andrew Tomlinson
MYP Coordinator Vaughan Kitson
PYP Coordinator Vanessa Keenan
Languages English
T: +971 (0)2 556 1567
W: www.ris.ae

Ras Al Khaimah Academy
PO Box 975, Ras Al Khiamah
DP Coordinator Marc Groenewald
PYP Coordinator Jason Hepokoski
Languages English
T: +971 7 236 2441
W: www.rakaonline.org

Repton Dubai
P.O. Box 300331, Nad Al Sheba 3, Dubai
CP Coordinator Michelle Pomphrett
DP Coordinator John Sayers
Languages English
T: +971 4426 9393
W: www.reptondubai.org

Sunmarke School
District 5 (Behind Limitless Building on Al Khail Road), Jumeirah Village Triangle, Dubai
CP Coordinator Natalie Hadfield
DP Coordinator Thomas Housham
Languages English
T: +971 4 423 8900
W: www.sunmarkedubai.com

Swiss International Scientific School in Dubai
Dubai Healthcare City, Phase 2, Al Jaddaf, PO Box 505002, Dubai
CP Coordinator Lisa Bardin
DP Coordinator Vibha Masand
MYP Coordinator Carolyn Siklos
PYP Coordinator Shona Tait
Languages English, French, German
T: +971 4 375 0600
W: sisd.ae

The British International School, Abu Dhabi
PO Box 60968, Abu Dhabi
DP Coordinator Mrs. Victoria Collinson
Languages English
T: +971 2 510 0176
W: www.bisabudhabi.com

Towheed Iranian School for Boys
Al Qouz 1, Sheikh Zayed Rd, Dubai
DP Coordinator Fereshte Mohammadian Sefat
Languages English
T: +971 4 3389953
W: www.bi-st.com

Universal American School, Dubai
PO Box 79133, Al Rashidiya, Dubai
DP Coordinator Tracey Cummins
PYP Coordinator Nadia Fawzy
Languages English, Arabic
T: +971 4 232 5222
W: www.uasdubai.ae

Uptown International School
Corner of Algeria Road & Tripoli Street, Mirdif, PO Box 78181, Dubai
CP Coordinator Stacey Keeling
DP Coordinator Adrian Duckett
MYP Coordinator Charlotte Daykin
PYP Coordinator Geetha Ashok
Languages English
T: +971 (0)4 2515001
W: www.uischool.ae

Victoria International School of Sharjah
PO Box 68600, Al Mamzar, Sharjah
DP Coordinator Sara Santrampurwala
Languages English
T: +971 6 577 1999
W: www.viss.ae/victoria-international-school
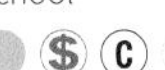

UZBEKISTAN

INVENTO the Uzbek International School
Furqat street 4A, 100021 Tashkent
PYP Coordinator Ranjana Manuel
Languages English, Russian
T: +998 71 210 99 99
W: www.invento.uz

Oxbridge International School
Oymarik Street 10, Mirzo Ulug'bek District, Tashkent
DP Coordinator Alquin Alva
MYP Coordinator Ritika Roy
PYP Coordinator Madhavi Dutt
Languages English, Russian
T: +998 71 263 00 15
W: oxbridgeschool.uz

Smart School
Amir Temur Avenue 33, Mirabad District, Tashkent
DP Coordinator Dilfuza Kodirova
Languages English, Russian
T: +998 71 231 99 55
W: smartschool.uz

Tashkent International School
38 Sarikulskaya Street, Tashkent
DP Coordinator Rana Mneimneh
MYP Coordinator Robert Tate
PYP Coordinator Noah Beaumont
Languages English
T: +998 55 501 96 70
W: www.tashschool.org

Vosiq International School
Domrabad Street, 4th Drive, Chilanzar District, Tashkent
PYP Coordinator Natalya Tsarikova
Languages English, Russian
T: +998 71 207 00 88
W: vosiq.uz

ZAMBIA

American International School of Lusaka
P.O. Box 320176, 487 A/F/3 Leopards Hill Road, Lusaka
DP Coordinator Monica Murphy
MYP Coordinator Ingrid Turner
PYP Coordinator Simone Lieschke
Languages English
T: +26 978 772 600
W: www.aislusaka.org

International School of Lusaka
P.O. Box 50121, Ridgeway, Lusaka
DP Coordinator Silvia Nithyanathan
PYP Coordinator Tasneem Mohmed
Languages English
T: +260 211 252 291
W: islzambia.org

Pestalozzi Education Centre
Off Twin Palm Road, Ibex Hill, Lusaka 10101
DP Coordinator Nash Moonde
Languages English
T: +260 978 950 599
W: enkoeducation.com/pestalozzi

ZIMBABWE

Harare International School
66 Pendennis Road, Mount Pleasant, Harare
DP Coordinator Kate Reeler
MYP Coordinator Kasey Shiver
PYP Coordinator Vinu Kanda
Languages English
T: +263 242 870 514
W: www.harare-international-school.com

IB

ASIA-PACIFIC

Principal
Myles D'Airelle

Vice Principal & PYP Coordinator
Selda Mansur

DP coordinator
Kieran Pascoe

Status Private

Boarding/day Day

Gender Coeducational

Language of instruction
English

Authorised IB programmes
PYP, DP

Age Range 3 - 17 years

Number of pupils enrolled 292

Fees
Day: IDR143,325,000 – IDR340,725,000 per annum

Address
Jl Warung Jati Barat No.19, RW.5,
Jati Padang
Kec. Ps. Minggu, Jakarta Selatan
DKI Jakarta
12540 | INDONESIA

TEL +62 21 2978 0200

WhatsApp
+62 816 297 800

Email
acgjkt@acgedu.com

Website
jakarta.acgedu.com

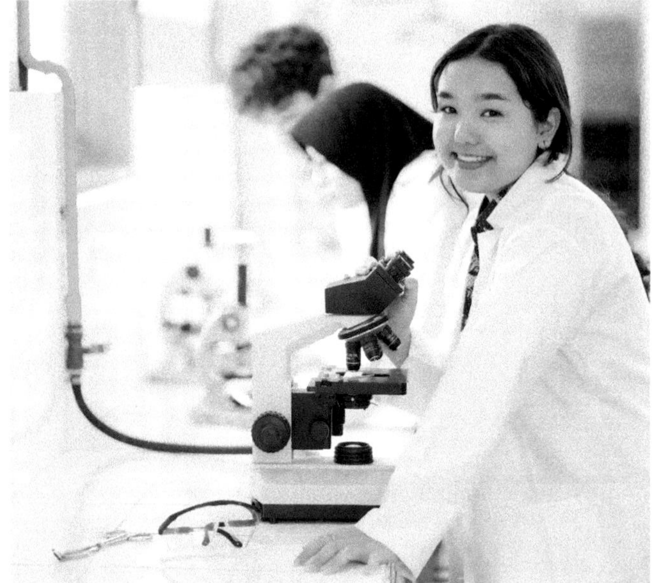

ACG School Jakarta provides an educational pathway from Kindergarten to Year 13 and is regarded as an exceptional option for students seeking a dynamic international education in South Jakarta. We are proud to be an Inspired school. Inspired offers academic excellence to 80,000 students in over 100 schools across 24 countries.

At ACG School Jakarta, our students enjoy the benefits of world-class teaching from specialist educators, and we are committed to ensuring every child is prepared for success. With proven quality and results in a values-driven, inclusive, and diverse environment, we concentrate on the needs of the individual, offering personalised programmes of study that reflect each student's ability and background.

Our globally recognised curricula deliver the best learning outcomes for our students:

- International Baccalaureate Primary Years Programme (IBPYP) and Diploma Programme (IBDP)
- Cambridge International Lower Secondary and IGCSE courses
- Kindergarten programme for students aged three years and up

With our international mindset and emphasis on academic achievement, we encourage students to become innovative problem solvers and advanced critical thinkers. We place a strong focus on inquiry, investigation and experiential discovery, allowing students to be at the forefront of their learning in creative, meaningful and authentic ways.

Additionally, our holistic learning approach and well-established pastoral care system actively supports every student socially, emotionally, and academically. This ensures they reach their full potential during their time with us and are well prepared for life beyond.

Accordingly, ACG School Jakarta students have performed extremely well on the global stage, with ACG graduates accepted to top universities around the world.

Our dedication to developing the individual is also reflected in our co-curricular pursuits, featuring performing and fine arts, sporting and leadership opportunities. Combined with a range of cultural and service activities, this participation equips our students with invaluable life skills such as persistence, commitment, and teamwork, as they contribute to and acquire a wider sense of community.

ACG School Jakarta is uniquely permitted to enrol students who hold passports from Indonesia and other parts of the world. Our central location is ideal for families employed by embassies and multinational corporations. As a private, independent, co-educational school, ACG Jakarta has a non-selective admission policy, serving the needs of expatriate and local communities.

American International School of Guangzhou

(Founded 1981)

Head of School
Kevin Baker

PYP coordinator
Tania Mansfield

DP coordinator
John Kennett

Status Private, Non-Profit

Boarding/day Day

Gender Coeducational

Language of instruction
English

Authorised IB programmes
PYP, DP

Age Range 3 – 18 years

Number of pupils enrolled
1100

Fees
Day: ¥204,000 – ¥270,000 per annum

Address
No 3 Yan Yu Street South
Ersha Island, Yuexiu District
Guangzhou, Guangdong
510105 | CHINA

TEL +86 20 8735 3392

Email
admissions@aisgz.org

Website
www.aisgz.org

The American International School of Guangzhou is a non-profit, co-educational day school for foreign children from Pre-Kindergarten to Grade 12. It is located in Guangzhou, China and has two campuses, one on ErSha Island, Yuexiu District and the other in Science Park, Huangpu District. Founded in 1981, AISG is the oldest and longest established non-profit international school in south China.

AISG is on the path to becoming an International Baccalaureate® Continuum School. It is a Candidate School for the Middle Years Programme(MYP), which is being added to the Primary Years Programme (PYP) and Diploma Programme (DP) that were authorized in 2004. AISG follows the American Education Reaches Out (AERO), Common Core, and Next Generation Science Standards (NGSS). These standards help to guide the curriculum in all phases and allow for a program that is tailored to the specific context and learners at AISG. AISG is a member of EARCOS and ACAMIS.

AISG enrolls over 1,000 international students from Pre-Kindergarten to Grade 12 and our student body demographics reflect our international environment with over 40 nationalities. Our students are guided by faculty who challenge them to achieve, nurtured in an environment where creativity and inquiry are celebrated, and supported by a community who understands the power of a growth mindset.

AISG is a caring community that employs experienced teachers who are passionate and bring their forward-thinking pedagogy along with an empathic approach to enrich each child's learning. More than 75% of our 114 innovative faculty members have attained their master's degrees and more than 70% have over 11 years of experience in education.

Our campuses are designed with the future of learning in mind. Both campuses embrace world-class class learning environments, including open learning spaces to promote collaborative and transparent learning with a green building design and flexible spaces that can evolve with the pedagogical changes that lie ahead.

AISG boasts an extensive athletic program, giving our student athletes the opportunity to participate in a wide variety of sports against other schools both internationally and within China. In addition, AISG offers a diversity of options for our after-school activities program, ranging from academic, sports, arts, music, technology, and social, allowing students to enjoy a current passion or find a new one.

From its volunteer board members to its dedicated faculty, supportive parents, extensive alumni network, and hard-working students, AISG has a sense of connection in working together to fulfill its mission of providing inclusive pathways to empower all learners to make a positive impact.

AOBA

AOBA-JAPAN INTERNATIONAL SCHOOL

Head of School Jake Madden

PYP coordinator Karen Chen

MYP coordinator Chris Radnich

DP coordinator
Preethi Liyanagamage

Status Private

Boarding/day Day

Gender Coeducational

Language of instruction
English

Authorised IB programmes
PYP, MYP, DP

Age Range 2 – 19 years

Number of pupils enrolled 750

Meguro Campus
2-11-5 Aobadai, Meguro-ku,
Tokyo, **153-0042 | JAPAN**

TEL +81 3 4520 2313

Hikarigaoka Campus
7-5-1 Hikarigaoka, Nerima-ku
Tokyo, **179-0072 | JAPAN**

TEL +81 3 4578 8832

Bunkyo Campus
6-18-23 Honkomagome, Bunkyo-ku, Tokyo, **113-0021 | JAPAN**

TEL +81 3 4560 3422

Email
admissions@aobajapan.jp

Website
www.aobajapan.jp

Welcome
Our team is waiting to welcome you at our school either online or in person.

Vision
We are an internationally recognised multi-campus kindergarten through university group, transforming education for learners in Japan and beyond.

Mission statement
In order to achieve our Vision we will continue our emphasis on Aoba's strategic transformative imperatives:

- Group Culture & Leadership to enhance and nurture progressive mindsets and actions.
- Teaching & Learning to ensure continued flexible delivery of internationally relevant curricula connecting to local and global contexts.
- Learning Environment & Capability to facilitate physical & virtual campus design that supports innovative teaching and learning.
- Economic Sustainability & Engagement to ensure sustainable growth and optimal resource alignment with Aoba's identity.

Our Philosophy
We believe that our young people are enabled to reach their full potential as international citizens who are dedicated to learning and who are inspired to succeed in an ever-changing world.

Our 5 Core Values
At Aoba we value the concepts of:

- Global Leadership
- Entrepreneurship and Innovation
- Effective Communication
- Wise Risk Taking
- Effective Problem Solving

Learning at Aoba
Aoba is one of the only full IB World Schools in the Tokyo area and features the typical characteristics expected of an IB school. In recognition of Aoba's expertise in IB curriculum and pedagogy, Aoba has been commissioned by MEXT to lead the IB Consortium in Japan. Aoba has also been selected by the IBO as one of only five schools worldwide to pilot the Online IBDP, leveraging Aoba's innovative teaching methodologies and cutting edge technologies.

What sets Aoba apart from other schools, however, is the innovative, progressive approaches to learning we employ from Kindergarten through Grade 12. Aoba consistently features authentic team-based inquiry in all three IB programmes at the school: PYP, MYP, and DP. We take a multi-age, transdisciplinary approach to the IB that really brings the programmes to life for our students.

Our students co-plan their learning with their teachers and are supported to truly take ownership of their learning whilst developing desirable marketplace skills and dispositions as described in our Core Values. Students move beyond simply solving problems for themselves or even solving them for others. We seek to develop students that can create the conditions to empower others to solve problems for themselves, a more sophisticated and powerful mode of leading positive change in the world.

Executive Principal
Ms Gafiah Dickinson

PYP coordinator
Ms Zawat Souki

MYP coordinator
Mr Kumaravell Sepulohniam

DP coordinator
Ms Naima Keddar

Status Private

Boarding/day Day

Gender Coeducational

Language of instruction
English

Authorised IB programmes
PYP, MYP, DP

Age Range 5 – 18 years

Number of pupils enrolled
1799

Address
Melbourne Senior Campus
56 Bakers Road
North Coburg
VIC 3058 | AUSTRALIA

TEL +61 3 9350 4533

Email
aia@aia.vic.edu.au

Website
aia.vic.edu.au

Educating For The Future
The Australian International Academy of Education is dedicated to providing high-quality education for students from Foundation to Year 12. Australian International Academy of Education is an International Baccalaureate school offering (IB) programmes at all four Melbourne campuses as well as the local Victorian Certificate of Education (VCE). The programmes allow AIAE to enhance its local curriculum and to achieve its mission of developing productive Australian Muslim citizens who will help to create a better and more humane world through intercultural understanding and respect.

At the Australian International Academy of Education, we believe each child is unique. We promote intercultural understanding and a vision to inspire character and leadership. The Academy offers a broad curriculum with global perspectives to primary and secondary school students. We encourage our students to broaden their horizons in a spirit of tolerance, compassion, and cooperation.

Our passionate teaching staff ensures outstanding academic results and inspires and supports students to achieve their highest potential. With small class sizes, we can offer a personalised approach to learning and a diverse range of educational experiences inside and outside the classroom. In addition, our local, national and international learning experiences allow students to develop a greater understanding and appreciation of the world around them.

The Academy also provides a wide range of co-curricular activities that extend and complement the core curriculum, enrich student lives and develop their skills.

Our website includes further information on the IB Diploma at the Australian International Academy of Education, including details of various subjects on offer.

ADVANCEMENT | DETERMINATION | FAITH

Executive Principal
Mr Jon Standen

PYP coordinator
Rebecca Evans

DP coordinator
Anton Luiten

Status Private

Boarding/day Mixed

Gender Coeducational

Language of instruction
English

Authorised IB programmes
PYP, DP

Age Range 18 months – 18 years

Number of pupils enrolled 1250

Fees Day: VND 271,000,000 – 774,000,000 per annum

Thu Thiem Campus (Kindergarten to Year 13)
264 Mai Chi Tho Street
An Phu ward, Thu Duc City
Ho Chi Minh City | **VIETNAM**

Thao Dien Campus (Kindergarten to Year 6)
36 Thao Dien Street,
Thao Dien Ward, Thu Duc City,
Ho Chi Minh City | **VIETNAM**

Xi Campus (Kindergarten)
190 Nguyen Van Huong Street,
Thao Dien Ward, Thu Duc City,
Ho Chi Minh City | **VIETNAM**

TEL +84 28 3742 4040

Email
info@aisvietnam.com

Website
www.aisvietnam.com

Leading to a bright future
At Australian International School (AIS), every action we take is designed to lead our students towards a bright future. Since our establishment in 2006, we have continued to achieve this aim by delivering high-quality international education. We are dedicated to creating an environment where we stimulate inquiry, creativity and innovation, to help our students embrace all opportunities that life brings them and to become global citizens.

Providing the IB curriculum
Understanding the significance of all that the IB curriculum offers, AIS has long identified its ability to foster both academic and personal success while challenging students to excel in their studies and their individual development. AIS was one of the first schools in Vietnam to become an authorised IB World School, and as such, we are now among the most experienced educators in the country to provide this curriculum.

Currently, AIS offers the IB Primary Years Programme (PYP) for both our Kindergarten and Primary School students and the IB Diploma Programme as part of its Senior School education. The University of Cambridge Secondary Programme with the International General Certificate of Secondary Education (IGCSE) is provided for our Lower Secondary School students.

For the IB Diploma, AIS has an extensive background in supporting and preparing students to study this acclaimed curriculum and develop real-world skills that extend beyond the classroom. Consequently, AIS graduates consistently obtain results above the world average, and students have gone on to gain places at leading universities around the globe, many with full or partial scholarships.

Exceptional education with modern facilities
Under the leadership and experience of AIS's Executive Principal, Mr Jon Standen, our team of enthusiastic, internationally-trained and qualified teachers are dedicated to challenging, inspiring, and supporting the individual needs of every student.

We support each child to reach their full academic potential, to nurture a love of arts, to become involved in and passionate about sport and to develop the resilience to overcome challenges. Our Australian values of fairness and a 'have a go' attitude, combined with a world-class curriculum, drive this ambition.

To aid our teaching staff, every classroom and learning environment is spacious, well-resourced, and technologically rich. Additionally, our students have access to an open garden style campus, swimming pools, a double gymnasium, an auditorium, soccer fields, a dedicated IB Centre, and much, much more.

British International School, Phuket

(Founded 1996)

Head of School
Simon Meredith

DP coordinator
Jason Perkins

Status Private

Boarding/day Mixed

Gender Coeducational

Language of instruction
English

Authorised IB programmes
DP

Age Range 2 – 18 years

Number of pupils enrolled
1150

Fees
THB434,700 – THB845,500 per annum

Address
59 Moo 2, Thepkrasattri Road
T. Koh Kaew, A. Muang
Phuket
83000 | THAILAND

TEL +66 (0) 76 335 555

Email
info@bisphuket.ac.th

Website
www.bisphuket.ac.th

British International School, Phuket (BISP) is a co-educational day and boarding school, established in 1996 and set in extensive landscaped grounds. The school aims to deliver the highest standards of teaching and learning to an international community emphasising wellbeing and passion on a modern and well-equipped campus.

Educational Programmes
BISP is structured into Early Years, Primary and Secondary levels, offering a diverse array of academic programs, including the IB Diploma, BTEC, IGCSE, and Cambridge ESOL examinations. BISP also offers an externally assessed programme from London Academy of Music and Dramatic Arts and high-performance academies in Football, Golf, Swimming, Tennis and Aerial Arts.

Mission
Inspire Learning; Nurture Wellbeing; Ignite Passion

A Vibrant Learning Community
In line with our mission, BISP encourages staff and students to develop a deep love for learning. BISP recruits staff who profoundly care about students, are able to share their passion and interest in their subject or role and are deeply invested in a student's education and future. Our staff communicate their excitement, commitment and care for learning through an abundance of pedagogical approaches.

Broad and Contextualised Curriculum
The school is divided into Early Years, Primary and Secondary levels and offers the IB Diploma, BTEC, IGCSE and the Cambridge ESOL examinations. BISP also offers an externally assessed programme from London Academy of Music and Dramatic Arts and high-performance academies in Football, Golf, Swimming, Tennis and Aerial Arts.

Diversity and Active Learning Participation
With over 1,100 students aged 2 to 18, representing 59 nationalities, BISP actively encourages students to be active participants in the learning process.

IB Subjects Offered
BISP offers a comprehensive range of IB subjects, providing students with a well-rounded education that equips them for global challenges. Visit https://www.bisphuket.ac.th/inspire-learning/ib-diploma-programme/ to learn more.

High-Performance Sports Academies
Through the Academy Programme BISP enables student-athletes to realise their full potential and prepare for lifelong success within a safe and supportive athletic structure. High-Performance Academy students receive coaching in the technical, tactical, physical and psychological aspects of their sport at the elite level.

Scholarship Programme
BISP offers scholarships to exceptional students in the areas of academics (at IBDP level), football, tennis, golf, swimming, aerial arts and visual arts. The purpose of the scholarship programme is to maintain and enhance the strong academic, sporting and cultural environment of BISP by attracting outstanding students to the school.

Carey Baptist Grammar School

(Founded 1923)

Principal Mr Jonathan Walter BA, DipEd, MA

DP coordinator Frédérique Petithory BA, PostGradCertEd, MA

Status Private

Boarding/day Day

Gender Coeducational

Language of instruction English

Authorised IB programmes DP

Age Range 3 – 18 years

Number of pupils enrolled 2692

Fees
Day (Local) $24,532 – $37,976 per annum
Day (International) $45,456 – $47,334 per annum

Address
349 Barkers Road, Kew
VIC 3101 | AUSTRALIA

TEL +61 3 9816 1222

Email
admissions@carey.com.au

Website
www.carey.com.au

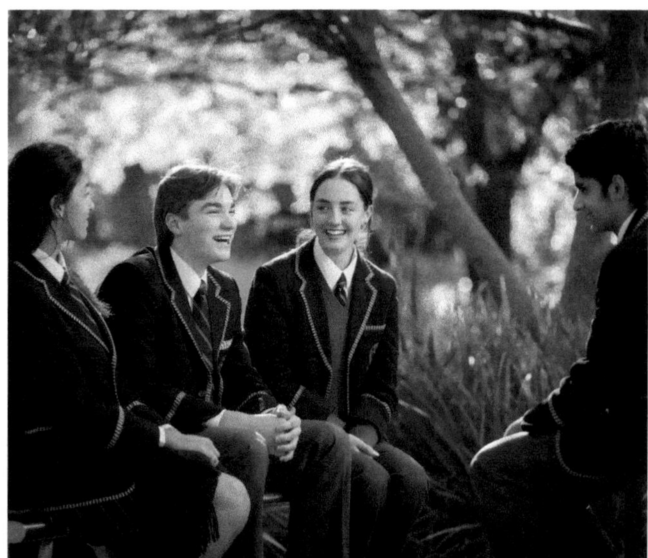

In our complex and ever-changing world, it's clear that today's young people will be faced with a unique set of challenges in the future. To meet these challenges, fulfil their ambitions and contribute to the wider world, students must be equipped with capabilities that will enable them to thrive in a changing environment. At Carey Baptist Grammar School, we believe in adopting a broader expression of success and allowing students to leverage their strengths and follow their passions, whether they be academics, creators, innovators or athletes.

Founded in 1923, Carey is a leading co-educational independent school offering three-year-old Early Learning to Year 12. Carey is situated close to the Central Business District of Melbourne, within easy distance of public transport.

As one of Australia's leading schools, Carey maintains a gender balance, fostering the development of confidence, communication skills and self-esteem in all students. Carey works in partnership with families to develop wise, independent, motivated young people who are inspired and equipped to create positive change. The Senior School offers both IB and VCE and fosters a dynamic and stimulating environment. Our students achieve university entrance scores that place Carey amongst the top schools in Victoria.

The wellbeing of every student is at the heart of everything we do at Carey and our award-winning wellbeing program underpins all our activities, from the very beginning of each student's schooling. Through nurturing student wellbeing and supporting their individual interests, we foster an environment that supports them in achieving their best while also developing individuals with integrity, resilience and a social conscience.

Our IB educators are experts in their fields. With regular professional development and an active engagement with the IB Diploma Co-ordinator's network, we ensure that our program is always at the forefront of IB approaches to teaching and learning. We have a number of workshop leaders within the School. Our educators are committed, passionate and inspiring leaders and mentors for our IB students.

Carey's position as a globally-respected school enhances our students' engagement with the wider world and ensures that when they are applying for tertiary education, whether in Australia or abroad, their applications are looked upon with favour and esteem.

We welcome the cultural diversity that international students bring to our community.

For more information about our programs and purpose built facilities, visit www.carey.com.au or call our Admissions Manager on +61 3 9816 1242, or email admissions@carey.com.au

Head of School
Frederick T. "Ted" Hill

PYP coordinator
Pamela Castillo (Lower Primary) & Nancy Macharia (Upper Primary)

MYP coordinator
Amanda Cooper-Marcon

DP coordinator
Richard Kent

CP coordinator
Gurpreet Kaur

Status Private

Boarding/day Day

Gender Coeducational

Language of instruction
English

Authorised IB programmes
PYP, MYP, DP, CP

Age Range 4 – 18 years

Number of pupils enrolled
1435

Address
45, Art center-daero 97 beon-gil
Yeonsu-gu, Incheon
22002 | REPUBLIC OF KOREA

TEL +82 32 250 5000

Email
songdo-admissions@chadwickschool.org

Website
www.chadwickinternational.org

Chadwick International is a PreK- G12 international school fully equipped with the state-of-the-art facility built in the Songdo International Business District, Incheon, Republic of Korea.

Chadwick International is the sister campus of Chadwick School, a K-12 school in the greater South Bay area of Los Angeles, which was founded by Margaret Lee Chadwick in 1935. The two campuses share the same mission that Chadwick Schools develop global citizens with keen minds, exemplary character, self-knowledge, and the ability to lead.

Chadwick International is an authorized four programme International Baccalaureate (IB) world school, offering PYP, MYP, DP and CP. Chadwick International emphasizes experiential and inquiry-based learning both in and outside the classroom including Outdoor Education and Service Learning programs. The Outdoor Education allows students to develop conflict-resolution abilities and leadership skills through various outdoor experiences. Meanwhile, Service Learning program teaches students how to interact with both their local and international communities and problem solve on a deeper level. These fundamental programs assist students in transferring valuable lessons learned in the classroom and develop them as contributing members and leaders of tomorrow.

Physical Education plays an integral part of the Chadwick curriculum as it focuses on the promotion of good personal health and a holistic lifestyle for our students. Its activity-based program emphasizes the skill development that improves the fitness and well-being of the individual student as well as healthy and safe lifestyles.

Chadwick International has rich and diverse Visual and Performing Arts programs. In these classes, students develop their knowledge, skills, creativity and ability to respond to artistic ideas. Also, students are exposed to a variety of theatrical mediums to express themselves and heighten their awareness of themselves in relation to the people and culture around them.

Chadwick International helps to achieve its educational mission through recruiting and supporting highly experienced, dedicated, and diverse faculty members from around the world. With the support of the faculty, Chadwick International is capable of a low teacher to student ratio of 1:8.

Chadwick International's superior educational facilities include an aquatic center with scuba diving capabilities, two gymnasiums, two performing arts indoor theaters, a television studio that allows production up to eight channels, a working garden, purpose-built science laboratories and three design/maker spaces. These facilities permit the students to cultivate their intellectual, artistic and physical abilities based on Chadwick International's experience-based curriculum.

Chadwick International is accredited by Western Association of Schools and Colleges (WASC) and Council of International Schools (CIS).

Chatsworth International School

(Founded 1995)

Head of School
Dr. Tyler Sherwood

PYP coordinator
Eleri Connor

MYP coordinator
Jonathan Denton

DP coordinator
Iain Hudson

Status Private

Boarding/day Day

Gender Coeducational

Language of instruction
English

Authorised IB programmes
PYP, MYP, DP

Age Range 3 – 18 years

Number of pupils enrolled
800

Address
72 Bukit Tinggi Road
Singapore
289760 | SINGAPORE

TEL +65 6463 3201

Email
admissions.bt@chatsworth.com.sg

Website
www.chatsworth.com.sg

Established in 1995, Chatsworth International School is a community-focussed and diverse K-12 international school in Singapore. As an IB World School, we are authorised to offer the Primary Years Programme (PYP), Middle Years Programme (MYP) and Diploma Programme (DP) of the International Baccalaureate. We pride ourselves on providing top quality international education at exceptional value, guided by our educational philosophy to inspire, educate and enlighten.

We offer the IB PYP for students from Kindergarten to Year 6 (ages 3 to 12). The final year of the PYP culminates in a Year 6 Exhibition, a powerful celebration and showcase of student learning and development. The MYP is offered to students from Years 7 to 11 (ages 12 to 15). The MYP emphasises intellectual challenge, encouraging students to make connections between their studies in traditional subjects and the real world, and sets students up for success in the IB Diploma Programme. In the High School, we offer the two-year IBDP in Years 12 and 13 (ages 16 to 18) and students who have successfully met our graduation requirements also earn our WASC-accredited Chatsworth High School Diploma.

As a non-selective school, we welcome students of all nationalities and abilities. From academics to arts to sports to service learning, our highly qualified and global teachers from over 20 nationalities strive to inspire and challenge the students to bring out their best selves.

Student well-being is at the heart of a Chatsworth education. The established student services team provides a strong pastoral programme and offers the support that students need to thrive academically, personally and socially.

Chatsworth graduates have achieved excellent results in their IB Diploma and consistently scores well above the world average year-on-year. Class of 2023 achieved a school average of 36 points that surpassed the global average of 30.24 points. For the past 5 years, Chatsworth school average score has consistently been 36 points with a high of 39 in 2021. Chatsworth is one of the few international schools in Singapore to offer the full IBMYP eAssessment (includes seven subjects and a personal project) for our Year 11 students.

Loved for our close-knit community, the foundation of a Chatsworth education is more than academic success. The strong relationships that our teachers develop with their students and amongst the different key members of our community underpin the strength of our community. Our supportive Chatsworth Parent Group (CPG), where every parent is a member, contributes to our school culture and ensures families are engaged.

We are honoured to have won a Gold in The Curriculum (IB) Award at Singapore Education Awards 2023, organised by HoneyKids Asia and also the Best IB School Award at the inaugural WhichSchoolAdvisor (Singapore) Best School Award 2022.

CRANBROOK SCHOOL

(Founded 1918)

Headmaster
Nicholas Sampson

PYP coordinator
Genet Erickson Adam

MYP coordinator
Kate Allen

DP coordinator
Nicholas Hanrahan

Status Private

Boarding/day Mixed

Gender Male

Language of instruction
English

Authorised IB programmes
PYP, MYP, DP

Number of pupils enrolled
1685

Fees
Pre-School AUS$9,666 – AUS$24,153 per annum
Junior School AUS$31,188 – AUS$37,956 per annum
Senior School Day Boy AUS$44,733 – AUS$46,497 per annum
Senior School Boarding from Year 7 AUS$85,101 per annum

Address
5 Victoria Road
Bellevue Hill
NSW 2023 | AUSTRALIA

TEL +61 2 9327 9000

Email
Enrol@cranbrook.nsw.edu.au

Website
www.cranbrook.nsw.edu.au

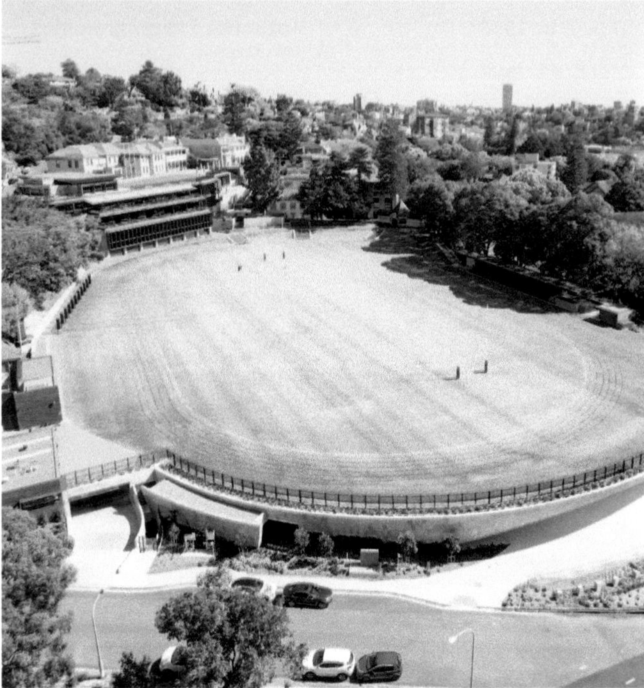

Cranbrook School is a vibrant and inclusive community located in the heart of Sydney. As an IB Continuum School, we offer the Primary Years, Middle Years and IB Diploma programmes. We are excited about our upcoming move to coeducation, welcoming girls to our Senior School in 2026. Our facilities provide the latest in teaching and learning, as well as outstanding performance spaces and sporting venues.

Our motto, 'Esse Quam Videri' – To be rather than to seem to be – anchors and inspires us. We develop the character of the young people in our care, so they can learn to respond to the inevitable challenges of life with optimism and an open mind. Global awareness is a key part of our curriculum.

ACADEMIC EXCELLENCE

We are committed to academic excellence, offering a broad, liberal education. We embrace curiosity and discovery, always experimenting and innovating. We recognise the essential value of great teaching, inspiring our students to achieve beyond their expectations.

THE ARTS: A WORLD CLASS PROGRAMME

We place great importance on cultural and artistic expression. Amongst our alumni we have more than our fair share of gifted painters, architects and sculptors, art curators and gallery owners, digital artists, filmmakers and illustrators.

SPORT: INCLUSIVENESS AND CHALLENGE

Our sports programme is both deep and wide: major sports flourish alongside important minority pursuits. We enjoy truly world class sporting facilities with a state-of-the-art Aquatics and Fitness Centre. We balance the camaraderie of team success with the satisfaction of individual achievement.

CO-CURRICULAR: A HOLISTIC APPROACH TO EDUCATION

Our co-curricular activities are broad, distinctive, holistic and well-rounded. We offer an extensive range of activities, from the arts to the sciences, music to sport, allowing our students to explore their individual interests.

EXPERIENTIAL LEARNING: ESCAPING THE CONSTRAINTS OF CITY LIFE

Experiential learning is at the heart of what we do. We create authentic experiences to make learning interesting, personal and relevant. Our experiential bush campus at Wolgan Valley in the NSW Blue Mountains allows our students to benefit from an enhanced focus on education within the natural environment, free from the distraction of technology and city life.

BOARDING: A BRIDGE TO UNIVERSITY LIFE AND BEYOND

Ever since Cranbrook first opened its gates in 1918, our School has been a home away from home for our boarding students, who thrive in a nurturing community that offers a genuine warmth and an individualised approach.

Delia Memorial School (Glee Path)

(Founded 1972)

Principal
Dr. Chan Kui Pui

DP coordinator
Mr. Paolo Yap

Status State

Boarding/day Day

Gender Coeducational

Language of instruction
Cantonese, English, Mandarin

Authorised IB programmes
DP

Age Range 12 – 18 years

Number of pupils enrolled 711

Fees
Secondary 4-6 HKDSE:
HK$3,000 (US$385)
IBDP Y1 and Y2:
HK$27,180 (US$3,474)

Address
1-3 Glee Path,
Mei Foo Sun Chuen, Kowloon
Hong Kong, SAR |
HONG KONG, CHINA

TEL +852 2741 5239

Email
gp@deliagroup.edu.hk

Website
http://www.deliagp.edu.hk

Delia Memorial School (Glee Path), a member of The Delia Group of Schools, is proud to offer the IB Diploma Programme as a curricular pathway for our students in the last two years of secondary school. Because of its academic rigor, balanced approach, and whole-person focus, the IBDP is an excellent option for our students who seek an internationally-recognized alternative to the local HKDSE curriculum and a thorough preparation for the demands of university education in Hong Kong and abroad.

As a school that affirms and celebrates our students' diverse backgrounds and multicultural identities, Glee Path is especially a committed believer in the IB mission. Our students hail from over 25 countries, with the majority coming from South and Southeast Asia in addition to a growing number of local and overseas Chinese. Together, our students learn in a vibrant, academically rigorous, and English-speaking environment that promotes tolerance, empathy, and understanding. Even before our students graduate, they are already taking their place in the wider world as caring and committed global citizens.

To put into practice our educational belief in equity and equality, Glee Path makes the IBDP available to our students regardless of their financial circumstances. As such, our school offers the lowest tuition fees of any IB World School in Hong Kong, with full need-based scholarships also available to those who qualify. Even learning resources such as laptops, iPads, and course companions, are provided to our students regardless of financial need as are our extracurricular activities and overseas study tours to places like Australia, Canada, Nepal, and Romania. These measures ensure that our students benefit not only from the equitable access to the IBDP but also from being fully included in the learning opportunities enjoyed by the Glee Path community.

Celebrating its 50th Anniversary in 2022, Glee Path has indeed witnessed transformative changes over its five decades, none more so than being fully authorized as an IB World School in 2019. This is truly a testament to the precious trust parents have placed in our school as their community of choice for their children over the years.

As the only IB World School in Hong Kong's Mei Foo neighborhood, our school is easily accessible by public transportation options. So, why not drop by and pay us a visit? We would love to welcome you to Glee Path, where the journey towards excellence and equity begins.

(Founded 1972)

Head of School
Mr. Richard Dyer

DP coordinator
Mr. Dominic O'Shea

Status Private

Boarding/day Day

Gender Coeducational

Language of instruction
English

Authorised IB programmes
DP

Age Range 3 – 18 years

Number of pupils enrolled
1990

Fees
S$25,488 – S$39,843

Address
301 Dover Road
Singapore
139644 | SINGAPORE

TEL +65 6775 7664

Email
admissions@dovercourt.edu.sg

Website
www.dovercourt.edu.sg

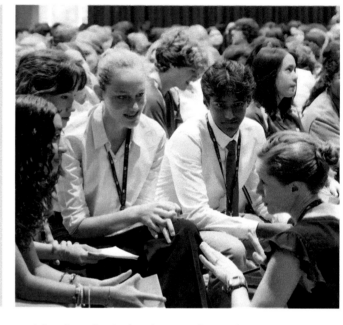

Located in the heart of Singapore, Dover Court International School (DCIS) is an international, multicultural and inclusive school community. Founded in 1972, Dover Court has, over the last 50 years, established a reputation for providing a comprehensive, truly inclusive education underpinned by outstanding teaching and a warm, supportive environment. At Dover Court, success looks different for every student, and diverse curriculum options provide multiple routes to life after school. Here, inclusivity and academic excellence go hand in hand, and we know that students who feel safe and happy can better focus on their learning. We welcome students from 3 to 18 years old, from Nursery to Year 13, with our student body comprising over 60 nationalities.

As part of Nord Anglia Education (NAE) we benefit from the unparalleled opportunities gained from being part of a worldwide network of over 80 schools. At DCIS, we are highly ambitious for our students in all aspects of their academic and personal growth. Our students are energetic, articulate, motivated, confident, and caring, and they are eager to make their mark on the world. One of the great strengths of our British style international education is that such growth involves all aspects of students' moral, physical, emotional, social and academic development focused on each individual's personal best.

At DCIS, this is achieved through superb teaching supported and complemented by a strong pastoral structure. Dover Court is unique in Singapore in welcoming students with diverse needs and talents, and we deliver on our promises, with bespoke programmes that enable every student to thrive, flourish and expand their potential. Education has never succeeded with a "one size fits all" approach but few schools manage to personalise education in the ways that Dover Court does: three pathways, and many qualification routes, blended and customised to each individual.

Students from Nursery to Year 11 follow the National Curriculum for England, adapted for our international context, leading to the IGCSE qualifications. Sixth Form students, Years 12 and 13, complete either the IB Diploma Programme, IB Courses or the International BTEC Diplomas in Business. The diverse cohort of our 2023 IBDP graduates achieved an average score of 35 points; 74% of our students scored above the global average, and our highest score was 43 points. Our graduates are now attending some of the best universities in the world.

Dulwich College (Singapore)

DULWICH COLLEGE

| SINGAPORE |

(Founded 2014)

Headmaster
Mr. Nick Magnus

Head of Senior School
Ms. Melanie Ellis

DP coordinator
Mrs. Lisa Nevers

CP coordinator
Ms. Charlotte Martin

Status Private

Boarding/day Mixed

Gender Coeducational

Language of instruction
English, Mandarin

Authorised IB programmes
DP, CP

Age Range 2 – 18 years

Number of pupils enrolled
2930

Fees
Day: S$18,650 – S$51,730 per annum
Boarding: S$37,800 per annum

Address
71 Bukit Batok West Avenue 8
Singapore
658966 | SINGAPORE

TEL +65 6890 1003

Email
admissions.singapore@dulwich.org

Website
singapore.dulwich.org

Heritage and Tradition

Dulwich College (Singapore) is an international school with a British independent school ethos and values, which draws upon 400 years of excellence and tradition from Dulwich College in London. Our traditions form part of our culture and are firmly embedded in all that we do. Additionally, our collaborations across our family of schools in Asia and London stimulate innovation and encourage an international outlook, which we believe fully prepares students for their futures. The result is a community where academic ability is nourished, creativity is valued, diversity is celebrated, and inspiration is paramount.

Our students go to some of the best universities and colleges in the world and we are proud of our individualised university counselling service and the network of schools which support this.

What is the Dulwich College (Singapore) IB Diploma Programme Difference?

- Embedded enrichment and leadership for all students
- Passionate, highly experienced IB Diploma Programme and IB Career-related Programme teachers who put students first
- Three-year (I)GCSE programme which ensures enriched activities and a focus on skills which enable students to be fully prepared for the IB Diploma Programme and IB Career-related Programme
- Part of a network of schools that truly supports students in terms of opportunities and shared knowledge
- Holistic programme where the arts and sport are a valued and integral part of each student's education
- Smaller class sizes which can focus on personalisation and student wellbeing
- Academically rigorous but holistic at the centre
- Personalised IB Diploma Programme and IB Career-related Programme application process
- Individualised university application process supported by the Dulwich College International network
- An IB Diploma Programme which focuses on feedback and metacognition, so students can independently plan and improve their own learning
- An IB Career-related Programme which focuses on the development of personal and professional skills, allowing students to reflect on their own learning and apply these reflections in both work and academic environments
- True to the "Students come First, Personalised Pathways" learning environment, the IB Career-related Programme (IBCP) offered at the College gives students the opportunity to pursue specialist pathways that include business and sustainability, performance and production arts, and sports
- State-of-the-art facilities for IB students to collaborate, study independently and flourish, including a purpose built IB common room and quiet study areas
- A personalised pathway for every single student

Dulwich College Beijing

DULWICH COLLEGE
| BEIJING |
北京德威英国国际学校

(Founded 2005)

Head of College
Mr. Anthony Coles

DP coordinator
Mr. Anthony Baldwin

Status Private

Boarding/day Day

Gender Coeducational

Language of instruction
English

Authorised IB programmes
DP

Age Range 3 – 18 years

Number of pupils enrolled
1580

Fees
Day: RMB237,000 – RMB347,700 per annum

Address
89 Capital Airport Road
Shunyi District
Beijing
101300 | CHINA

TEL +86 10 6454 9000

Email
admissions.beijing@dulwich.org

Website
beijing.dulwich.org

Our Heritage and Tradition

Dulwich College Beijing is an international school with British independent school ethos and values, which draws upon 400 years of excellence and tradition from Dulwich College, the founding College in London. Established in 2005, Dulwich College Beijing maintains strong ties with Dulwich College. We are proud to share a common heritage across the network of schools in Asia, and equally value the traditions, unique to our school, that we have created since we opened. Dulwich College Beijing was the winner of the Holistic Education and Science and Technology Awards at the British Schools Awards 2021. The College also received the 2022 International School Awards in the Pathways to Continued and University Education category.

Our diverse student body is represented by more than 1,580 students from age 3 to age 18, with over thirty different nationalities. We are extremely proud of our students who achieve excellent academic results while at the same time, engaging in sports, visual and performing arts, science and technology, community service, debating, leadership roles and anything else that they are passionate about. Our graduating classes have consistently achieved IB results and university placements that place the school among the world's best.

Our Curriculum

The primary teaching language is English, with a Dual Language approach in Mandarin and English in Early Years. Children up to age 5 follow the Early Years Foundation Stage, and from Year 1 to Year 9, they follow the National Curriculum of England and Wales, which is enhanced to meet the needs of our international student body.

In Year 10 they begin the IGCSE (International General Certificate of Secondary Education), a rigorous two-year course that requires students to take a broad range of subjects. It culminates in exams at the end of Year 11 and prepares students well for the two-year International Baccalaureate Diploma Programme (IBDP) starting in Year 12.

Extra-Curricular Activities

With 150 extra-curricular activities per term, our students can explore and expand their interests beyond academics. Our extra-curricular activities help develop social, leadership, organisational, creative, technical, speaking and listening skills, among others.

Consistent IB Results

We congratulate our Class of 2023 for their outstanding results and university matriculations:

- Average score of 37.1 points out of 45, significantly above the global average of 30.24 in 2023
- 99% full IBDP pass rate
- 39% of the students scored 40 points and above
- 2 students achieved full score of 45 points
- 83 students received the full Diploma
- University matriculations include Oxbridge and Russell Group universities in the UK, Ivy League in the U.S., as well as top universities in Canada, Europe and Asia.

ELCHK Lutheran Academy

Principal
Patrick Hak Chung LAM

PYP coordinator
Lawrie MACPHERSON

MYP coordinator
Keith HENDERSON

DP coordinator
Julius DRAKE

Status Semi-Government

Boarding/day Day

Gender Coeducational

Language of instruction
English, Mandarin, Cantonese

Authorised IB programmes
PYP, MYP, DP

Age Range 6 – 18 years

Number of pupils enrolled
1146

Fees
IBPYP HK$69,860 –
HK$80,870 per annum
IBMYP HK$72,280 –
HK$78,920 per annum
IBDP HK$80,080 –
HK$98,410 per annum

Address
25 Lam Hau Tsuen Road
Yuen Long, New Territories
Hong Kong, SAR | **HONG KONG, CHINA**

TEL +852 8208 2092

Email info@luac.edu.hk

Website www.luac.edu.hk

ELCHK Lutheran Academy (LA) is a through-train school with its primary and secondary sections at the same location. We gained IB authorization to offer the Diploma Programme (DP) in September 2014, the Primary Years Programme (PYP) in January 2018, and the Middle Years Programme in November 2019 respectively, which marked a great milestone for the Academy.

We offer a wide range of subjects for all the programmes. DP subjects comprise the 6 subject groups: Languages (Chinese, English, and French), Sciences (Physics, Chemistry, and Biology), Individuals and Societies (Economics, Business & Management, and History), Mathematics (Mathematics Analysis & Approaches, and Mathematics Application & Interpretation), and The Arts (Visual Arts and Music). MYP subjects encompass the 8 subject groups such as Languages (Chinese, English), Arts (Visual Arts, Drama, Music), and Design and so on.

The PYP, as the foundation of the curriculum, initiates students to develop ideas contributing to international mindedness. Embracing the Unit of Inquiry (UOI), students are encouraged to question and refine their understanding of individual wellbeing, learning communities, and the world from different perspectives.

Away from the hustle and bustle of city life in Hong Kong, we are dedicated to make a difference in students' lives. Creating a warm and friendly campus, students are nurtured to explore their potentials and develop their talents through diverse experiences.

By offering holistic and balanced Christian education, the professional teaching team with teachers from different cultural backgrounds is committed in nurturing students to strive for excellence and to become global leaders of tomorrow. To maximize the learning opportunities and provide adequate care to individual needs, LA adopts small-class teaching that our overall teacher-student ratio is around 1:8.

We encourage students to explore concepts in manifolds of forms to ensure their whole-person development. Students are exposed to learning from varieties of activities, including field trips, Co-curricular and Extra-Curricular activities. During the EOTC (Education Outside the Classroom) week, students experience the learning outside the classroom and broaden their horizons. After the activities, they showcase to share what they have acquired to their classmates, parents and teachers.

To support programme implementation, Information and Communication Technology (ICT) has been well integrated into education to equip students with ICT skills. With the "Apple One-to-One Program", each secondary student is equipped with a laptop for daily learning. Together with the whole school Wi-Fi coverage, the ICT-infused inquiry-based learning has been effectively and efficiently facilitated.

With the enthusiastic support from the LA community, the school is growing from strength to strength to provide high quality education for the future rising generation.

EtonHouse®
International School • Suzhou
苏州伊顿外籍人员子女学校

(Founded 2003)

Head of School
Murray Fowler

PYP coordinator
Natasha D'Costa

MYP coordinator
Murray Fowler

DP coordinator
Rajesh Kripalani

Status Private

Boarding/day Day

Gender Coeducational

Language of instruction
English

Authorised IB programmes
PYP, MYP, DP

Age Range 2 – 18 years

Number of pupils enrolled
236

Address
102 Kefa Road
Suzhou Science & Technology Town
Suzhou, Jiangsu
215163 | CHINA

TEL +86 512 6825 5666

Email
enquiry-sz@etonhouse.com.cn

Website
www.etonhouse.com.cn/suzhou

EtonHouse International School Suzhou is a small school with a big heart. With class sizes between 10-20 students, only one class per age group and a student to teacher ratio of 6:1, at EtonHouse your child will be much more than a number. Every student can make a difference, no matter how gifted or otherwise.

We are part of the world-renowned EtonHouse International Education Group with more than 120 schools throughout Asia.

We are a well-established IB World Continuum School for students from 5-18 years old. Our PYP was accredited in 2008, MYP in 2011 and DP in 2016. Our Early Years Programme is based on the Regio Emilia approach and blends seamlessly with our Primary Years Programme.

We are an inclusive school that welcomes students of all abilities. We believe that every student can succeed; any student who wishes to pursue the IB Diploma Programme is allowed and encouraged to.

Our student population is highly multicultural. Despite being a small school, we have students from 28 nationalities, and no nationality represents more than 22% of our community.

Despite our small scale, we have all the facilities you would expect from a much larger school, with a heated swimming pool, all-weather sports field, gymnasium, well-stocked library, and assembly hall/theatre. The thoughtfully considered and aesthetically designed campus is set among the hills and trees of SSTT west of downtown Suzhou, a learning environment which provides students with many opportunities for exploration, and provocations that support the rich inquiry-based learning programmes offered at the campus.

European International School HCMC

Acting Head of School
Ms. Jo Roberts

PYP coordinator
Cristy Neves

MYP coordinator
Kevin Alburo

DP coordinator
Erin Tacey

Status Private

Boarding/day Day

Gender Coeducational

Language of instruction
English

Authorised IB programmes
PYP, MYP, DP

Age Range 2 – 18 years

Number of pupils enrolled 730

Fees
VND 255,500,000 – 703,800,000 per annum

Address
730 Le Van Mien Street
Thao Dien Ward, Thu Duc City
Ho Chi Minh City
70000 | VIETNAM

TEL +8428 7300 7257

Email
info@eishcmc.com

Website
www.eishcmc.com

With possibly the most convenient location in Thao Dien, the European International School Ho Chi Minh City (EIS) is the only boutique international school, set in lush garden surroundings, offering the International Baccalaureate (IB) continuum of studies for children aged 2-18.

Our vibrant, unified campus is a place where students, teachers and parents of all grade levels and different backgrounds interact freely with each other within a home-from-home, tranquil village atmosphere. EIS offers a truly diverse 'melting pot' of 40+ nationalities and global cultures, where students are encouraged to find their unique voice, to pursue languages, and to contribute to all aspects of school life.

EIS teachers, with over 13 years' average experience, are well-practiced in individualized learning methods. With a very low student-to-teacher ratio, particularly in the middle-high school sections of the school, students benefit directly from more frequent access to teachers.

Graduating IB Diploma students consistently achieve well-above the world averages, and have achieved acceptances into prestigious universities worldwide, often with significant merit-based scholarships.

EIS provides an outstanding world-class education for students, evidenced by our full accreditation status with the Council of International Schools (CIS).

Being a medium-sized school, we are large enough to offer a wide range of educational opportunities, while also being intimate enough to provide the unique personal attention and care that each child deserves.

Promising Futures

Principal IB
Dr. Tassos Anastasiades

PYP coordinator
Monika Kala

MYP coordinator
Dahlia Atabani

DP coordinator
Rajeev Pargaien

Status Private

Boarding/day Mixed

Gender Coeducational

Language of instruction
English

Authorised IB programmes
PYP, MYP, DP

Age Range 2 years 6 months – 18 years

Address
A1 & A12, Sector 132
Noida Expressway, Uttar Pradesh
201304 | INDIA

TEL +91 9711 000626

Email
info@genesisgs.edu.in

Website
www.genesisglobalschool.edu.in

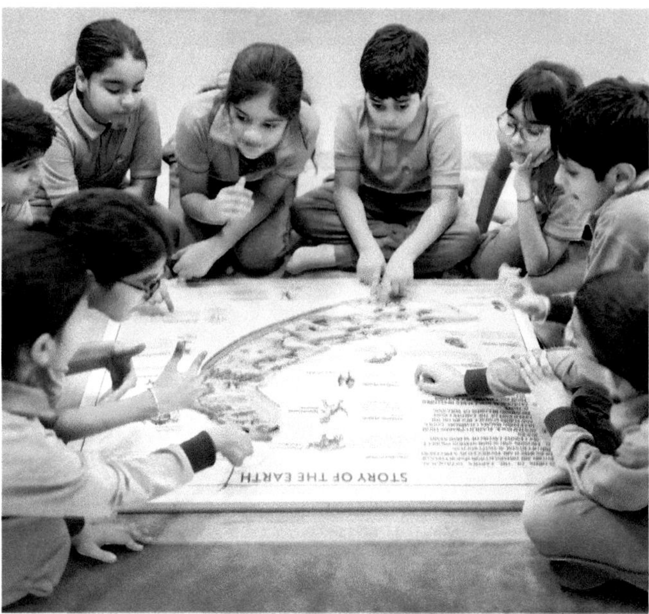

Situated in Noida, a satellite city of Delhi, Genesis Global School is part of the National Capital Region (Delhi NCR). The School is spread over a 30-acre campus, with efficient connectivity via an Expressway. It is an hour's drive from Indira Gandhi International Airport, Delhi and around 25 minutes' drive from cosmopolitan South Delhi. Genesis Global School has become a hub of national and international educational excellence, where every child is important and accepted for who they are. At GGS we ensure that our students have exposure to the best in current global practices, provide them with a truly holistic environment where modern facilities and high-quality teaching and learning practices allow our school ideals to be developed. Our school ideals depicted in the School logo – the hexagon are: Focus on Internationalism, Care for the Environment, Service to Society, Democracy, Leadership and the Spirit of Adventure. These six pillars support our vision of Dream. Inspire. Act – a powerful phrase that encapsulates a motivational and transformative approach to life and education. A GGS education allows students to achieve their potential and take their place in the world. We continuously strive to develop and improve our curriculum to meet the needs of all learners in an ever-changing world both inside and outside the classroom. As an IB World School and a member of the Council of International Schools (CIS) GGS is also part of a community working collaboratively to shape international education. We are committed to incorporating international and intercultural perspectives into our programmes so that students can move forward with the attitudes, knowledge and understanding that will provide them with a solid base wherever their studies or work may take them.

Primary Years Programme (PYP)

The driving force behind the IB Primary Years Programme is a deeply held philosophy about the nature of International Education; to meet the diverse needs of students' physical, social, emotional, intellectual, aesthetic and cultural needs through a rich curriculum. The Primary Years Programme (PYP) approaches learning and teaching through inquiry and play. The learning process is engaging, relevant, challenging and significant, while students delve into explorations driven by their innate curiosity whilst making connections to the world around them. Investigative learning is central to the programme and is a critical element in developing how students view their world both locally and globally.

There is a focus on the pedagogy of play through the primary years as we recognise that young children explore their environment and make sense of the world through play. Powerful provocations though sensory, creative, dramatic and social play are an important part of the PYP curriculum at GGS.

Emotional and social well-being of children is an important area and we have an emotional learning curriculum which helps students understand their emotions and empowers them with strategies to express and harness leading to emotional stability and security. The mentor program

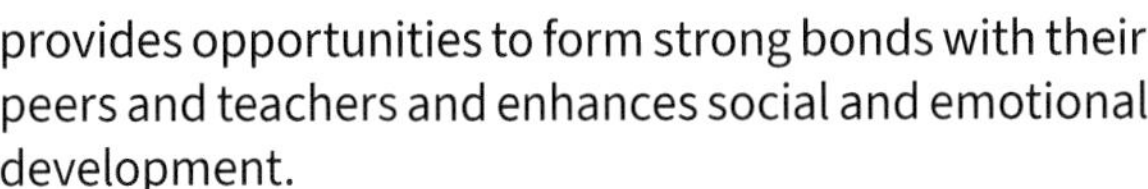

provides opportunities to form strong bonds with their peers and teachers and enhances social and emotional development.

The PYP also focuses on students developing key skills, which are essential in the 21st century – communication, research, thinking and social and self-management skills. This method is experiential, allowing the students to arrive at an understanding through real-life experiences. Inquiries are carefully planned by teachers across levels to provide a complete and coherent curriculum that is of global significance and that also provides an awareness of the local and global context. It creates sensitivity towards the diversity in our world and sustaining the resources of our planet to create a better and more peaceful world. All students from ages 2 years 6 months – 11 years are engaged in the Programme of Inquiry and various subjects are taken through the programme. Each of these trans-disciplinary subjects lead to deepening curiosity and helping students make connections with the real world.

Middle Years Programme (MYP)

The Middle Year Programme is designed for students ages 11 to 16 (grades 6 to 10) following core principles of an IB education and serving as a concept-driven educational framework. The constructive approach towards teaching and learning through inquiry, action, and reflection empowers our learners to develop their own perspectives prompting self-directed, independent learning. The inquiry-based teaching approach which relies on prior knowledge and secures the scaffolding of new learning helps to build student curiosity. This is further enhanced through careful curriculum design and exposure to relevant, challenging, real-world scenarios rooted in global contexts.

Genesis particularly prides itself on a heightened attention to Approaches to Learning. Through the ATL skills framework, students are equipped with 21st-century skills such as critical and creative thinking, research, communication, self-management, and many more, aiding our learners in facing familiar and unfamiliar situations. This also helps the students and teachers to respond to individual learning needs making the programme inclusive. A well-developed student support team helps to reach a student's potential through multiple strategies of teaching and learning. We give students the opportunity to find the area they are strongest in and to grow in it. The teaching and learning approaches ensure that the learners explore and understand what they are learning, how they are learning, and most importantly, why they are learning. With a solid service programme which is a core action component, our learners become principled, open-minded, and caring members of the community. Their responsible action gives us hope for a better and more empathetic world.

Diploma Programme (DP)

At Genesis Global School, the International Baccalaureate Diploma Programme (IB DP) stands as a hallmark of prestigious two-year pre-university education, globally recognized for its excellence. Tailored with utmost care, the program is a comprehensive journey that nurtures both the academic and personal development of our students. Focused on fostering critical thinking, intercultural awareness, and instilling a robust work ethic, the IB DP is a testament to our commitment to providing a world-class education.

At the heart of the IB DP lie three crucial components: Theory of Knowledge (TOK), Extended Essay (EE), and Creativity, Activity, and Service (CAS). In the vibrant environment of Genesis, students engage in independent research, hone critical thinking skills, and actively contribute to their communities. Our diverse range of subjects, spanning languages, individuals and societies, sciences, mathematics, and the arts, is delivered through an inquiry-based, interdisciplinary approach, ensuring a broad knowledge base. Genesis maintains a focus on academic rigor while nurturing well-rounded individuals with a global perspective.

One distinctive feature of the IB DP at Genesis is its unwavering commitment to preparing students for both higher education and future careers. Recognized and highly regarded by prestigious universities worldwide, IB students often receive preferential treatment, including advanced standing and academic credit. Our dedicated University Cell guides Genesis students through the entire admission process, providing continuous support until they successfully secure placements or receive acceptance. The outstanding track record of Genesis students in various universities across the globe reflects our commitment to shaping future leaders.

Guangdong Country Garden School

廣東碧桂園學校
Guangdong Country Garden School

(Founded 1994)

Principal
Jinsheng Cheng

PYP coordinator
Jiuhong Wang

MYP coordinator
Zequn Deng

DP coordinator
Lizhu Zhao

Status Private

Boarding/day Boarding

Gender Coeducational

Language of instruction
Chinese, English

Authorised IB programmes
PYP, MYP, DP

Age Range 2 – 18 years

Number of pupils enrolled
4800

Fees
PYP Kindergarten RMB100,000 – RMB120,000 per annum
IBPYP RMB156,000 per annum
IBMYP RMB156,000 – RMB200,000 per annum
IBDP RMB220,000 per annum

Address
Beijiao Town
Shunde District
Foshan City, Guangdong | **CHINA**

TEL +86 757 2667 7888

Email
cgssao@brightscholar.com

Website
bgy.gd.cn

Guangdong Country Garden School is located in Foshan, Guangdong Province, the central region of the Guangdong-Hong Kong-Macao Greater Bay Area. Founded in 1994, the school was authorized by the International Baccalaureate Organization to run the Middle Years Programme (MYP) and the Diploma Programme (DP) in 2001 and the Primary Years Programme (PYP) in 2011. It is one of the earliest IB world schools in mainland China to implement PYP, MYP and DP programmes simultaneously, with a 15-year CNC&IB integrated curriculum from kindergarten to Year 12. It has more than 4,800 students and 700 teachers from all over the world.

As an IB World School, we focus on lifelong learning and inclusive education by delivering a balanced curriculum that focuses on the well-being of teachers and students, fostering resilience with a growth mindset, and believing that every child can succeed and make a difference. The faculty and staff of the school are committed to preparing students to attain the following ten attributes:

- cultural confidence and dedication
- extensive knowledge and regular reflection
- active exploration and attempts
- thoughtfulness and effective communication
- open-mindedness and responsibility

Covering an area of nearly 200,000m2, the school has a beautiful environment with first-class facilities, such as the STEAM experimental building, two indoor heated swimming pools, opera house, observatory, gym, outward bound spaces, English village and Starmoon garden, etc. The campus is built around a mountain, providing a good ecological environment for students to explore and facilitate the development of various kinds of inquiry courses based on the community.

Our PYP mainly focuses on six transdisciplinary themes. The 42 sub-topics of inquiry "transcend" the boundaries of subjects, helping our kids have a better understanding of the world from different perspectives. The PYP Exhibition for the fifth grade, allows students to choose a topic of their interest from current issues, and work as a group to figure out the potential solutions to the issues. It is a powerful celebration and showcase of student learning and development.

Based on the six global contexts, the MYP programme offers a range of challenging courses and activities to help students think creatively, critically and reflectively. The MYP emphasizes intellectual challenge, and encourages students to make connections between their studies in subjects and with the real world. Additionally, the emphasis on Service and Action and the personal project help to set students up for success in the IB Diploma Programme.

Inquiry-Based Trips

Culture Immersion Trips

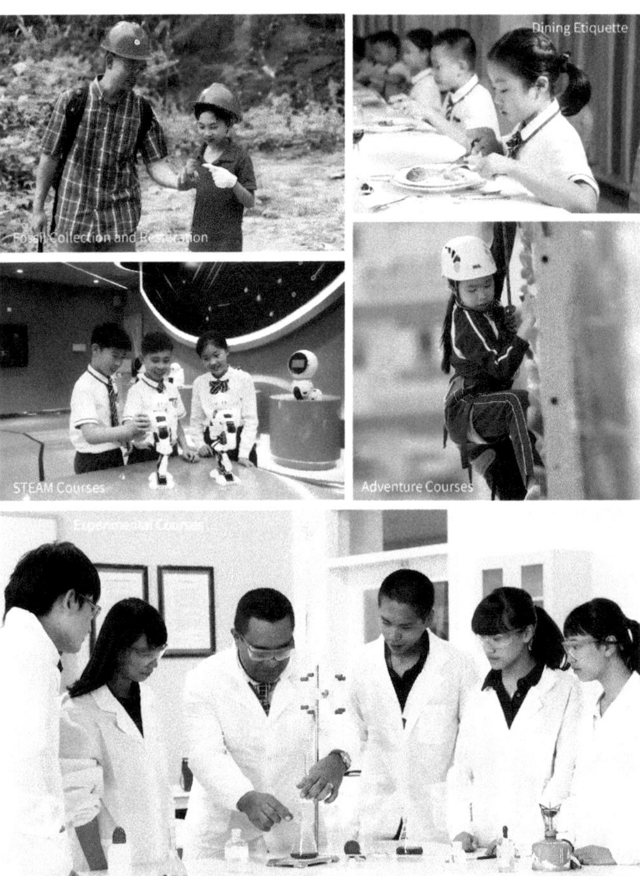

Dining Etiquette

STEAM Courses

Adventure Courses

The six subject groups in DP programme are provided in a balanced way, providing more than 30 subjects to meet the need of personalized learning. The three core elements of TOK, EE and CAS further improve students' thinking skills, research skills, self-management skills and collaboration skills. The IB teachers actively become IBEN members, where 42 of them take the role of the IB examiners and workshop leaders, helping to build a learning community.

The school's signature courses, such as the Leadership courses, the Creativity, Activity, Service (CAS) program, and career planning course, combine elements of action and adventure, service and responsibility, and cross-boundary and cooperation in a fun and challenging way to ensure the balanced academic, mental, social and physical development of students.

Leadership programs are based on student's age and cognitive development. The Research and Hiking Trip in PYP with the topic of "Children of the World, Sharing the Earth" provides students with comprehensive mental, physical and spiritual exercise. In the MYP Culture Immersion Trips in Guangdong Province, nearly 30 categories of Chinese cultural phenomena are deeply experienced and explored, while more than 30 social service activities have been carried out. In the high school section, Cycling the Silk Road, China Week Community Service and The Duke of Edinburgh's International Award further enhance the leadership skills of students. The China Week Community Service initiated by DP students, which started in 2004, has continued for 18 years, spanning 26 provinces and cities, with more than 5,000 students participating and serving more than 360 elementary schools in remote areas. By volunteer teaching, caring for the sick, orphans, the elderly and children, raising funds for libraries situated in mountainous elementary schools, and collaborating with NGOs to make students' voices heard internationally, students truly grow into caring global citizens. In addition, the school offers more than 100 CAS activities on and off campus. Each student is assigned a tutor, with whom the student meets regularly to keep track of their academic progress and engagement in CAS activities.

Our diversified curriculum and dedicated professional teachers assist students develop in a holistic well-rounded way to successfully achieve entrance to prestigious universities around the world. 100% students got the full DP certificate and the average score was far above the world average. Our graduates can be found in Princeton University, The University of Chicago, Columbia University, Cornell University, Johns Hopkins University, University of California-Berkeley, University of Cambridge, University of Oxford, Imperial College London, Tsinghua University, Peking University, the University of Hong Kong, National University of Singapore and many others. We believe that no matter where they are, our students are committed to contributing to a better and more peaceful world.

Guangdong Shunde Desheng School

(Founded 2011)

Head of School
Ms. Chen Qingnian

DP coordinator
Mr. Yu Yue

Status Private

Boarding/day Mixed

Gender Coeducational

Language of instruction
English

Authorised IB programmes
DP

Age Range 12 – 18 years

Number of pupils enrolled 435

Fees
CNY ¥120,000 – ¥170,000 per annum

Address
Minxing Road, New District
Daliang
Shunde, Guangdong
528300 | CHINA

TEL +86 0757 22325121

Email
admin.dsi@desheng-school.com

Website
www.desheng-school.com

At Desheng School (International) (DSI), our outstanding teaching staff includes experienced IB trained teachers, and are integral to the implementation of the curriculum. They are divided into the Studies Wing, the Student Development Wing, and the Student Service Wing, who work together to lead, care, and inspire, ensuring the overall wellbeing of students.

DSI offers a wide range of subject options to cater to varying needs of students in line with the requirements of Cambridge IGCSE, A-Level, and IBDP. From 2017 to 2023, seven cohorts have graduated from DSI. Notably, 90% of the IBDP students have enrolled in top 50 universities in the world, including the University of Oxford, the University of Cambridge, Harvard University, the University of Cornell, the University of Columbia in the United States of America, the University of Toronto in Canada, the Australian National University and the University of Melbourne in Australia, the National University of Singapore and Nanyang Technological University in Singapore, the University of Hong Kong in Hong Kong, China, and several other prestigious institutions worldwide.

An Innovative School

Innovation is ingrained within our learning organization, fostering creative initiatives in organizational structure, program design, pedagogical approaches, and school events. This commitment successfully enhances holistic education in various dimensions. The school has a number of programmes that prepare students for the changing dynamics of the world. These comprise the Champions of Innovation, focusing on Artificial Intelligence, Cyber Safety, 3D Printing, STEM, and other cutting-edge information and communications technology.

Moreover, DSI also places a strong emphasis on language development, critical thinking, and empathy. In addition to the compulsory Super Curriculum subjects such as Philosophy of Disciplines and Research Skills, we offer a wide variety of Co-Curricular Activities. Students gain national and international exposure through platforms such as the Model United Nation conferences, future problem-solving programmes, as well as Experiential Programmes (Local/Overseas/University) which provide students with hands-on experiences to further develop their international mindset. This commitment to international mindedness equips our students with the skills and perspectives needed to thrive in an increasingly interconnected world.

A Caring School

Now more than ever, students need to graduate with more than just a certificate. DSI Student Development Programme and Student Care Programme put emphasis on the continuous growth and all-round development of the students. The House system, Boarding School, Leadership Education system, and Innovative talent development programmes provide platforms for students to excel. The Student Care Guidance Counselling Team, Mentoring System, and Career, Opportunities and Guidance ensure the students are equipped with readiness for university, career, leadership, and life. With a strong emphasis on both academic and student-centric activities, the school is well-positioned to nurture its students to become Scholars, Leaders, and Global Citizens.

Admission

For application enquiries, kindly contact the school directly.

Global Indian International School Pte Ltd

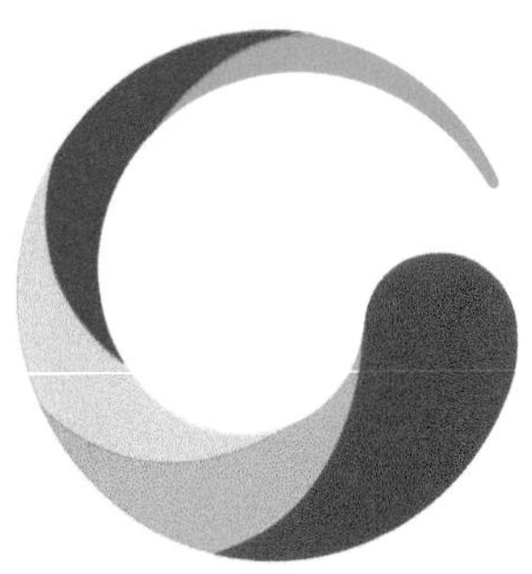

Global Indian International School

(Founded 2002)

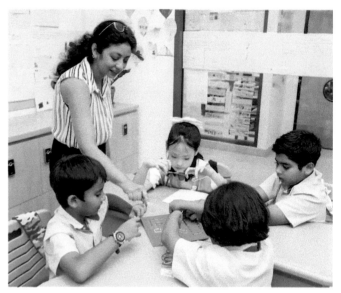

Principal
Melissa Maria

Academic Supervisor
Deepika Sodhi

Chairman and Co-Founder
Atul Temurnikar

PYP coordinator
Manju Nair

DP coordinator
Deepa Chandrasekaran

Status Private

Boarding/day Day

Gender Coeducational

Language of instruction
English

Authorised IB programmes
PYP, DP

Age Range 2.5 – 18 years

Number of pupils enrolled
3300

Address
27 Punggol Field Walk
Singapore
828649 | SINGAPORE

TEL +65 6914 7100

Website
singapore.globalindianschool.org

Global Indian International School (GIIS), operated by the Global Schools Foundation, is a frontrunner in international school education from Nursery to Grade 12, in Asia. The foundation manages a blossoming network of 64 campuses across 11 countries with a vision of becoming the global role model for teaching and learning through its award-winning holistic framework of 9 GEMS.

GIIS has two campuses in Singapore – East Coast Campus and SMART Campus, Punggol, catering to students from ages 2.5 (Nursery) to 18 (Grade 12).

Our flagship campus, GIIS SMART Campus with a capacity of 3.5 K students is a school of the future. The campus offers an innovative learning environment for students with digital classrooms, video conferencing, collaborative learning spaces, data analytics in sports and more than 40 skill-based studios. This learning environment helps to foster creativity in students and allows them to discover and develop their talents.

The school offers complete international curricula – IB Primary Years Programme (IB PYP), Cambridge Lower Secondary Programme, IGCSE and IB Diploma Programme (IB DP). Students begin their educational journey with a strong foundational framework like IB PYP, that sparks curiosity and makes them inquiry-driven. In secondary school from Grades 6 to 10, the Cambridge curriculum offers them analytical skills and a stronghold over diverse subjects, thus preparing them for the challenges of IBDP in Grades 11 and 12.

The IBDP at GIIS is a much sought after course with high achieving students, trained and qualified teachers and modern facilities. In the last 16 years, over 100 of GIIS' IBDP graduates have become World Toppers (with 45/45 points) or near-perfect scorers (with 44/45 points) in the IBDP exams, which is the culmination of the IB Diploma programme.

Close to 250 students graduate every year from the school. The school's unique performance-measuring metrics, called 7S, tracks and monitors each student's academic and all-round progress thus enabling teachers to roll-out a systematic improvement plan.

Our graduates are placed at prestigious universities across the world including the University of Cambridge, University of Oxford, University of California, Cornell University, Imperial College London, National University of Singapore, Nanyang Technological University, and many more.

An amalgamation of great factors including our international curricula, excellent teachers and infrastructure, and holistic education contribute towards making our students well-rounded individuals and global leaders of the 21st-century.

High School Affiliated to Shanghai Jiao Tong University

Head of School
Dr. Wang Jian

DP coordinator
Mr. Sasi Antony

Status State

Boarding/day Mixed

Gender Coeducational

Language of instruction
English, Chinese

Authorised IB programmes
DP

Age Range 15 – 19 years

Address
No 42 Yin Gao Road
Bao Shan District
Shanghai
200439 | CHINA

TEL +86 21 65910979

Email
jdfzib@jdfzib.org

Website
http://fz.sjtu.edu.cn

Founded in 1954, The High School Affiliated to Shanghai Jiao Tong University (known as JDFZ in Chinese Abbreviation) is one of Shanghai's most renowned and competitive public high schools, directly administrated by both Shanghai Municipal Education Commission and Shanghai Jiao Tong University (SJTU).

In 2011, the school started implementing the International Baccalaureate Diploma Programme (IBDP) to enrich curriculum development, emphasizing the integration of localized international education. The school now has four campuses: the main campus is in Baoshan District, the two national curriculum sub-campuses are in Minhang and Jiading District, and the IB Curriculum Center utilizes both the independent campus in Yangpu and the main campus in Baoshan.

JDFZ IBDP students are mainly from Shanghai and the neighbouring provinces across China. The vast majority of them are boarders. They undergo a foundation year at Grade 10 with CAIE IGCSE before being promoted into IBDP. JDFZ also has an excellent IBDP final result in its history as an IB World School. Students achieved the final IBDP grades above the world average in nearly every subject offered at JDFZ. Continuous success comes from the hard work of the students and passionate teachers. Staff are dedicated, enthusiastic, and professional, hailing from China and Overseas. JDFZ IB Curriculum Center is an English medium school, and all lessons are taught in English except Group 1 Chinese A and TOK, which are in Chinese and English. One of the core elements of school ethos is the balance between love for one's mother country and the growth of an international outlook. This thread is woven into all IBDP subjects. The IB Learner Profile is the core of regular discussions, teaching, events, and activities.

Thanks to the excellent students, teaching staff and faculty, the strong support from SJTU, and the advanced education vision, JDFZ has continuously achieved outstanding college matriculation results, achieving a 100% higher education promotion rate. For national curriculum students, 50% of graduates enrol in Tsinghua University, Peking University, Fudan University, and Shanghai Jiao Tong University, and 90% of graduates in Chinese "Double First-Class" Universities. For IBDP students, over 80% of graduate students enrol in the top 30 universities from mainstream world-round university rankings, including the University of Oxford, University of Cambridge, Yale University, Columbia University, University of Chicago, University of Toronto, University of Hong Kong, etc.

Hangzhou Greentown Yuhua School

Head of School
Ma Jinxiu

MYP coordinator
Yan Shujing

Status Private

Boarding/day Mixed

Gender Coeducational

Language of instruction
Chinese, English

Authorised IB programmes
MYP

Address
No. 532 Wenyi West Road
Hangzhou, Zhejiang
310012 | CHINA

TEL +86 571 88477561

Email
greentownedu@163.com

Website
www.hzlcyhcz.cn

Hangzhou Greentown Yuhua School is a fully licensed, private school located at 532 Wenyi West Road, Hangzhou, China. Our mission is to cultivate global citizens with integrity, a rational spirit, cultural literacy and a strong sense of duty; to advocate for professionalism and a healthy lifestyle. We encourage our students to have global literacy, enable them to respect different cultures and beliefs and integrate into multicultural world. The Education Philosophy at Greentown Yuhua provides the students both academic and self-development educational streams, allowing for full cognitive and social development, meeting the requirements and needs of each individual student. Moreover, campus Life at Greentown Yuhua is devoted to improving the quality of student's life on campus. Activities include various student societies and clubs, such as tae kwon do, piano, painting, studios and foreign language courses. The school motto is "Being Benovelent and Tolerant while seeking the Truth". We are dedicated in providing a well-rounded educational experience for our students; both as individuals and as a collective.

Since its foundation in 1992, Greentown Yuhua School has been striving to achieve educational excellence by providing an all-round quality education that will serve the needs for the future development of local community. In previous years, the school was awarded "The National Outstanding Private School" by the Ministry of Education. Since 2000, Zhejiang Greentown Real Estate Group (a national Top 2 real estate company in year 2010) has invested more than 1 billion yuan RMB in the school. And the school now takes up an area of 16.867 hectares, with the construction area about 70,000 square meters. The school is a modern institution with a beautifully landscaped environment and first-class facilities.

We provide Middle Years Programme for students from year 7 to year 9. In this program we are committed to cultivating learners to be inquirers, knowledgeable, thinkers, communicators, principled, open-minded, caring, risk-takers, balanced and reflective. In order to help students achieve these attributes, the school provides English language acquisition, Chinese language and literature, individuals and societies, mathematics, design, drama, music, and visual arts, science, physical and health education. We encourage our students to become active, compassionate and lifelong learners who understand that other people, with their differences, can also be valuable. We participate in the construction of international courses based on the domestic compulsory curriculum to help students adapt to overseas study.

We have a faculty of 280 and 2400 students. All the teachers have the recognized qualifications and are conscientious in their work. They are dedicated to the well-being of each student and have a vacation to provide for the welfare, mentoring of individual students within the harmonious environment of their classes. We also have a beautiful campus, modern teaching facilities, technology and resources. The school has high-standard on-campus rooms for boarding students, along with spacious classrooms, specialized laboratories, a library, lecture halls, auditorium, gymnasium, etc. We have a fully computerized management and monitoring system.

As the only world-wide affiliated boarding school in mainland China, a quality-oriented educationally advanced school in China, a grade-A model school in Zhejiang province, and one of "The most beautiful schools" in Hangzhou, nothing can stop us from constantly improving in warmth, safety, and dignity; both on campus and globally.

(Founded 2000)

Head of School
Stephen Dare

Primary School Principal
Virginia Hunt

Secondary School Principal
Teresa Tung

PYP coordinator Carly Buntin

MYP coordinator
Simon Roberts

DP coordinator Claire Shaffery

Status Private

Boarding/day Day

Gender Coeducational

Language of instruction
English

Authorised IB programmes
PYP, MYP, DP

Age Range 3 – 18 years

Number of pupils enrolled
500

Fees
PreK1-PreK2 HK$109,000 per annum
K-G5 HK$207,300 per annum
G6-G8 HK$228,200 per annum
G9-G10 HK$237,780 per annum
G11-G12 HK$247,460 per annum

Address
33 Wai Man Road
Sai Kung
Hong Kong, SAR | **HONG KONG, CHINA**

TEL +852 2655 1111

Email
admissions@hkacademy.edu.hk

Website
www.hkacademy.edu.hk

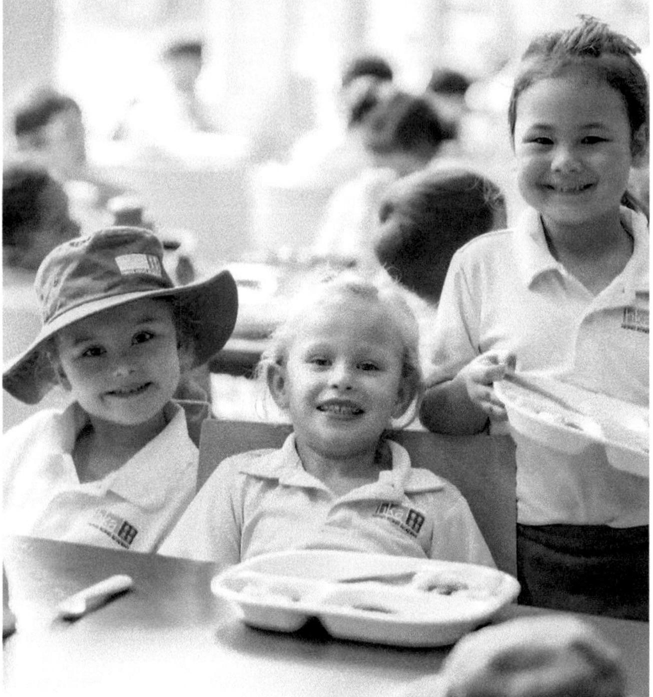

At Hong Kong Academy, we value how children learn as well as what they learn. From Pre-K to Grade 12, we are committed to creating an engaging and supportive learning environment for every student. The unique programmes, exceptional faculty and environmentally-friendly facilities at Hong Kong Academy (HKA) all contribute to the school's rigorous, student-centred education.

Our programmes are designed to challenge students to explore new perspectives, maximise opportunities for growth and develop a strong sense of their own identity. In addition to offering the International Baccalaureate Primary Years, Middle Years and Diploma programmes, all HKA graduates earn an HKA Diploma and the Global Citizen Diploma (GCD) Certificate. HKA is the only school in Hong Kong to offer the GCD and is the host school for the global consortium. We also offer a comprehensive co-curricular programme, including after school activities, clubs, performing arts, sports and mother tongue classes, through which our students build on existing skills, explore new interests, compete, create and grow.

Starting in early childhood, HKA cultivates a commitment in its students to understanding others and making decisions with an awareness of how they affect communities. By studying real-world issues students learn how to analyse information, respect diverse perspectives and positively contribute to society. Starting in middle school students build their Global Citizens Diploma (GCD) portfolio showcasing their unique identity and competencies in the areas of intercultural communication, community engagement, global understanding and academic excellence.

Our whole community is committed to providing a joyful and authentic learning environment for every child. HKA parents are highly engaged, contributing a wide range of backgrounds, expertise, skills and resources which enrich school life on a daily basis. And because we know that strong partnerships between home and school are beneficial to student wellbeing, HKA promotes a culture of thinking, trust and collaboration by hosting regular parent education events, social gatherings and community clubs throughout the year where everyone's voice is valued.

HKA graduates are able to effectively apply research, critical thinking and communication skills precisely, flexibly and intentionally across subject areas and consistently outperform the IB Diploma Programme world pass rate and average total points. Each year HKA alumni are accepted to pursue degrees in a wide variety of professions at competitive universities and colleges all around the world.

Hwa Chong International School

Principal
Ms Linda Lee

DP coordinator
Dr Archana Vijaykumar Kusurkar

Status Private

Boarding/day Mixed

Gender Coeducational

Language of instruction
English

Authorised IB programmes
DP

Age Range 13 – 18 years

Number of pupils enrolled
1000

Fees
Day:
S$28,000 – S$32,000 per annum
Boarding:
from S$27,720 per annum

Address
663 Bukit Timah Road
Singapore
269783 | SINGAPORE

TEL +65 6464 7077

Email
admissions@hcis.edu.sg

Website
www.hcis.edu.sg

Hwa Chong International School (HCIS) is a member of the prestigious Hwa Chong family of schools, drawing its core strengths from a century old tradition of educational excellence and philanthropy.

We offer a six-year integrated curriculum that eventually prepares students for the International Baccalaureate (IB) Diploma at Year 6 (Grade 12). With a vibrant and dynamic learning environment, HCIS is uniquely poised to provide students with positive and enriching learning experiences that stem from its deep traditions and internationally-oriented outlook. The caring school community and plethora of programmes and activities offer support for academic pursuits, leadership and character development of students.

Over the years, HCIS takes great pride in having nurtured many graduates who are talented and successful in their own way. We have set a track record of producing graduands who have gone on to pursue higher education, and our stellar performance in the International Baccalaureate Diploma Programme has provided our students with the springboard for entry into colleges and universities of their choice.

A Premium on Experiential Learning

Experiential learning in HCIS is modelled after Kolb's Learning Cycle and it involves experiencing, reflecting, learning and applying.

Students are exposed to a host of outdoor activities that stretches them and takes them out of their comfort zone. It is through these experiences that critical life skills like communication, teamwork, critical thinking, leadership and resilience are nurtured. More often than not, these experiences provide lasting memories of their school life in HCIS that are talked about in years to come.

On-campus Boarding Residence

As the only local International School with a boarding residence within the school compound, we endeavor to create a conducive and community-oriented environment. Supportive staff and well-equipped facilities promote character development and emphasize diverse competencies of our boarding students beyond just academic success.

At the HCIS Boarding Residence, our mission is to inspire and promote personal growth, while nurturing international-mindedness in our boarders within a safe and caring community. Our boarders are provided with the best quality of care by our Residence Mentors, who take on a close-knit and supportive approach to promote holistic development in students, allowing them to grow into disciplined, responsible and resilient individuals who not only act with integrity and pursue excellence continuously, but also learn to respect and foster lifelong friendships with people of different nationalities through living and sharing together. Find out more about HCIS at www.hcis.edu.sg!

(Founded 1981)

Academic Directors
Dr. Dharshini Jeremiah & Ms. Fiona Edwards

Admissions Manager
Ms. Elaine Yang

Head of HSD
Mr. Kelly Millar

PYP coordinator
Ms. Ariana Rehu

MYP coordinator
Dr. Dharshini Jeremiah

DP coordinator
Mr. Akbar Hussain

Status Private

Boarding/day Day

Gender Coeducational

Language of instruction
English

Authorised IB programmes
PYP, MYP, DP

Age Range 4 – 19 years

Fees
Admission fee (Incl GST) / Registration fee S$3,633 per annum (See www.iss.edu.sg/admissions/school-fees)
School fees for whole year (Incl GST): (See www.iss.edu.sg/admissions/school-fees)

Address
21 Preston Road
109355 | SINGAPORE

TEL +65 6475 4188

Email
admissions@iss.edu.sg

Website
www.iss.edu.sg

Within today's global education landscape, ISS International School stands as a beacon of educational innovation, providing a comprehensive and inclusive education that has made a real difference in students' lives for over four decades. Our unwavering commitment to "Educating to Make a Difference" is deeply embedded in the fabric of our institution.

Nestled in a serene heritage hilltop campus surrounded by nature, ISS is more than a school; it's a community fostering open-minded learners and dedicated educators.

As an authorised K-12 International Baccalaureate (IB) World School, ISS offers the complete IB curriculum, including the IB Certificate and an American-styled High School Diploma for G11 and G12 students. Our school's personalised learning programme, supported by a robust student achievement database, tailors education to diverse student needs and backgrounds.

Central to ISS is "Our Kampong Spirit," embodying a commitment to community togetherness. With intentionally maintained small class sizes, academic excellence is not merely a goal but a journey facilitated by a personalised approach to learning and a nurturing environment.

ISS takes pride in its robust English as an Additional Language (EAL) programme, consistently guiding students from low WIDA scores to success in IBDP and HSD exams. The success is attributed to individualised support, a dedicated team of educators, and a caring culture that cultivates English proficiency, laying the foundation for student success and future pathways.

Students actively participate in developing personalised learning plans in a safe and inclusive environment where confidence thrives. As a school committed to inclusion we believe in being non selective. Notwithstanding, 100% of our HSD students achieved a pass rate and university acceptance, 90% of our IB students achieved bilingual diplomas and the IB class of 2023 scored above global averages in seven IB subjects this year. These achievements underscore our commitment to holistic education and student well-being.

Situated in a space with a rich British colonial history dating back to the late 1930s, ISS cherishes its heritage and architecture, providing students with an escape from technology into a green atmosphere that enhances creativity and overall well-being.

Founded by the late visionary Mr. Chan Chee Seng, ISS remains true to his vision of an inclusive environment with a diverse student population that acts globally, thinks with care, and strives for sustainable change.

At ISS International School, we don't just educate; we educate to make a difference.

(Founded 1989)

Principal
Ms Anne Ford

PYP coordinator
Melissa Cuming & Sheree Zecca

Status Private, Independent

Boarding/day Day

Gender Coeducational

Language of instruction
English

Authorised IB programmes
PYP

Age Range 3 – 18 years

Number of pupils enrolled
1200

Fees
Please see website

Address
Centre Road
Camillo
WA 6111 | AUSTRALIA

TEL +61 (08) 9495 8100

Email
mail@jwacs.wa.edu.au

Website
www.jwacs.wa.edu.au

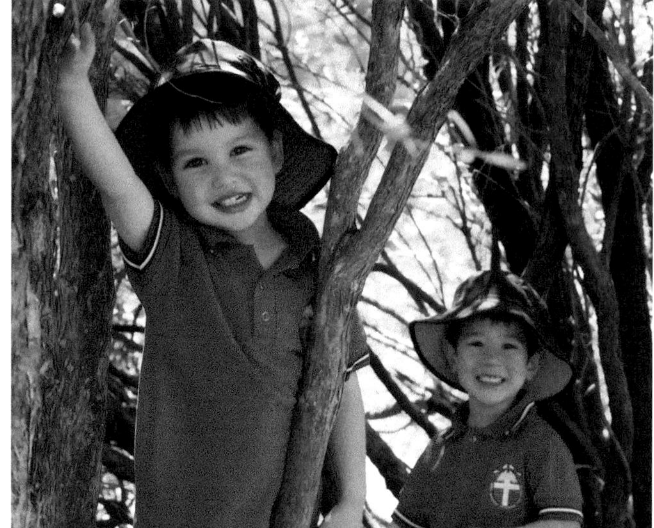

John Wollaston Anglican Community School is a co-educational day School serving families in Perth's south-east for Pre-Kindergarten to Year 12. We are inclusive and welcoming of families from all backgrounds and faiths; a school where every student finds their place in our safe and nurturing environment, where they are free to be and inspired to become.

We are a World School of the International Baccalaureate Primary Years Programme (IB PYP) with a strong academic and pastoral reputation. At John Wollaston, we focus on the development of the whole person, teaching students to be inquirers, knowledgeable thinkers and communicators who are motivated to think for themselves, be courageous and make a difference in the world.

We believe character development is as important as academic progress. Strong relationships underpin the whole school journey. Our students' lives are transformed through connection, creating a positive culture and opportunities to thrive. Our pastoral strategies are designed to embed social and emotional learning across all age groups.

Service Learning and Encounter experiences facilitate character development and personal growth. Students are challenged to be better people who are kind, resilient and confident in their abilities.

The IB PYP encourages students to think critically and creatively through an inquiry-led curriculum. This culminates with the Year 6 PYP Exhibition in which students interrogate a central idea to showcase the depth and breadth of their learning.

Our strong academic and pastoral focus continues in the Secondary School, where John Wollaston provides the foundation for students to develop the knowledge, skills and dispositions for success in further education, work and life. In the 21st century, young people need to be lifelong learners, confident and resilient individuals and responsible change makers. With the world rapidly evolving around us, our teachers are working to 'future-proof' our students' education, providing them with more choice, agency over their learning and inspire innovation for future pathways. We support our students to become innovators, entrepreneurs, collaborators, ethical citizens, effective communicators and creators of technology by offering a range of curriculum and cocurricular opportunities from Years 7 to 10.

Our new approach to Senior Secondary course selection titled 'MYPath' has been designed to help students tailor their learning experience, tapping into their interests and providing flexibility around future pathways. From Year 11, students participate in 'MYPath' choosing from one of six streams of learning including an ATAR pathway, General pathway and one of four Vocational and Education Training pathways.

At John Wollaston, we are committed to making learning as dynamic as the world around us by presenting our students with real world contexts, transforming their knowledge to build a better world. John Wollaston graduates leave our school with a strong foundation for life, valuing personal best and possessing integrity and compassion.

Jerudong International School

(Founded 1997)

Principal
Nicholas Sheehan BSc. Geography, PGCE

DP coordinator
Mr Daniel Roberts

Status Private

Boarding/day Mixed

Gender Coeducational

Language of instruction
English

Authorised IB programmes
DP

Age Range 2 – 18 years
(Boarding from 8 years)

Number of pupils enrolled
1660

Fees
Day:
B$18,084 – B$27,492 per annum
Weekly Boarding:
B$15,420 – B$23,500 per annum
Boarding:
B$21,420 – B$29,500 per annum

Address
Jalan Universiti
Kampong Tungku
Bandar Seri Begawan
BE2119 | BRUNEI DARUSSALAM

TEL +673 241 1000
(Ext: 1206/7100/1214)

Email
admissions@jis.edu.bn

Website
www.jerudonginternationalschool.com

About Jerudong International School

Jerudong International School (JIS) is an outstanding British International, co-educational Day and Boarding School in Brunei with a community of over 1660 students, aged 2-18 years old, from 45 countries. JIS is recognised as one of the best international schools in Asia and is considered the premier school in Brunei Darussalam.

A world-class campus nestled on 120-acres of land with exceptional facilities, qualified teaching staff and excellent pastoral care, plus a large choice of co-curricular activities, enhance the overall learning experience and provide a superior learning environment where JIS students are able to thrive and achieve excellence.

JIS is a leading member of the Federation of British Schools in Asia (FOBISIA), Council of British International Schools (COBIS), an international HMC School, an IB World School, an Eco Schools Green Flag Award recipient and is recognised by the prestigious Good Schools Guide.

In February 2023, JIS was honoured with the COBIS Patron's Accreditation and became the first international school worldwide to receive Beacon Status in three standards: Student Welfare, Boarding and Extracurricular Activities.

Students are encouraged to: Challenge Yourself, Respect Others and Inspire Change by living the school aims of: Communication, Engagement, Integration, Leadership, Resilience and Thinking.

The IB Diploma Programme at JIS

The IB programme at JIS is student centred, designed to enable students to be actively engaged in academic subjects but also thoroughly grounded in world events so they can make a difference. Our IB students are offered 21 subjects across the six IB Group areas. Theory of Knowledge (TOK) lessons include small group discussions and are supplemented by lunchtime lectures from outside speakers, staff and students.

In 2023, 76% of JIS students exceeded the world average score of 30.24. JIS IB students' average score was 34.72; The highest score achieved was 44 points. These results are consistent and continue to build upon the results of the past 12 years of offering the IB Diploma programme.

University Destinations

A specialist team of Higher Education advisors guide and prepare students for their University applications. 2023 graduate destinations include: University of Oxford, Imperial College London, University College London, University of Warwick, University of Bristol, University of Toronto, University of British Columbia, University of Melbourne, Monash University, University of Groningen and the National University of Singapore, to name a few.

Our Campus

JIS provides exceptional facilities, including 27 state-of-the-art science laboratories, an extensive Performing Arts Centre (equipped with a 750 seat theatre, black box theatre,

rehearsal rooms and a dance studio) and an extensive music faculty, as well as art, design and technology studios and traditional classrooms. The sports facilities are second to none, with two swimming pools (Olympic size, 50 metres and 25 metres), three air-conditioned sports halls, three covered netball/ basketball courts and three football/ rugby pitches. A bespoke Racquet Sports Centre includes four squash courts, two championship level tennis courts, and cricket practice nets. The newly enlarged and renovated library provides a comfortable and modern learning space for our students. JIS also has an award-winning Outdoor Discovery Centre – an eco-forestry initiative on the campus that is regularly used for activities and also as an Outdoor Classroom.

Boarding Facilities

The Boarding facilities for students aged 11 to 19 years cater to the needs of our 160 weekly boarders and 60 full boarders. There are two girls' Houses (Osprey and Kingfisher House) and two boys' Houses (Eagle and Ibis House). A programme of weekend activities is arranged for the boarders to fully embrace the wonderful environment of Brunei. Students are cared for by experienced staff, including their Boarding Housemaster or Housemistress and Matrons (qualified nurses).

Houses

All students and teachers in the School are members of a House (a community of about 70 students) which is designed to provide pastoral care, foster competition and promote camaraderie among the students. There are 16 Houses in the Senior School, all named after birds in Borneo, which are single-gendered. The brother and sister Houses collaborate for a range of events and social activities.

Each House has its own leadership team, including a House Captain and Deputy Captain, as well as other students in various unique leadership positions. House competitions take place weekly and include a variety of events such as sports, arts, talent shows, debates, spelling bees and quizzes.

Co-curricular Programme

Creativity, Activity and Service (CAS) builds on an extensive co-curricular programme with almost 300 activities to choose from, including a wide range of sports and arts activities, Eco JIS – a student-led sustainability project, House competitions, the International Award (DoE) programme, the Ivy House Award and the Model United Nations club. The school takes full advantage of the wonderful environment of Brunei to provide students with unique and enriching experiences, helping them to be the very best that they can be.

K.R. Mangalam Global School

Principal
Ms Suman Sharma

Status Private

Boarding/day Day

Gender Coeducational

Language of instruction
English, Hindi

Authorised IB programmes
PYP, MYP, DP, CP

Address
N-Block, Nandi Vithi Road
Greater Kailash-1
New Delhi, Delhi
110048 | INDIA

TEL +91 97 1885 8181

Email
info@krmangalam.global

Website
krmangalam.global

In the words of Nelson Mandela, "Education is the most powerful weapon which you can use to change the world". At K.R Mangalam Global School, we firmly believe that education wields the power to change the world. Rooted in the International Baccalaureate (IB) framework, we transcend conventional teaching methods, cultivating inquisitive, critically thinking lifelong learners. The Primary Years Programme (PYP), Middle Years Programme (MYP), Diploma Programme (DP) and Career Programme (CP) form a comprehensive educational journey, instilling skills vital for success in a rapidly evolving landscape.

Central to our philosophy is embracing each student's uniqueness, fostering diversity and championing inquiry based-learning. We recognize that each student brings a set of talents, interests and perspectives that contribute to the rich tapestry of the learning community. We empower students to question, explore and engage in meaningful research, sparking a genuine passion for exploration. Our commitment extends to creating a wholesome learning environment through well-equipped facilities and collaborative action planning between students and teachers. Whether it's our well-equipped laboratories, advanced robotics equipment, an inviting play area, an expansive performing arts platform or a dedicated fine arts space or libraries, we aim to meet every child's diverse learning needs.

K.R. Mangalam Global School distinguishes itself through its goal-oriented approach, whereby teachers guide students in setting goals, shaping not only academic but also personal and character development. We firmly believe that education is a transformative tool, empowering students to shape their world. Through active engagement in student-driven school projects, students emerge as agents of positive change. It not only enhances their educational journey but also contributes meaningfully to the collective growth of the entire school community.

Furthermore, our co-curricular programs are carefully designed to complement the academic curriculum, providing students with opportunities to explore their passion and interests. Whether involved in a science club, a music ensemble or a community outreach program, students have the freedom to discover and cultivate their talents. With a seamless integration of academics and co-curricular activities, our school strives to ensure that students receive a comprehensive and enriching education, preparing them for success in academic and real-world contexts.

Additionally, we prioritize international mindedness and technological proficiency, preparing students to thrive globally and contribute to a sustainable future. We recognize the demands of the digital era and, as a result, smoothly incorporate technology into the learning process. We are devoted to nurturing individuals who are globally aware and technologically proficient and also equipped with the understanding and adaptability to thrive in diverse cultural settings. These individuals are prepared to contribute to a sustainable future, paving the way as informed and perceptive global citizens.

Kardinia International College

Principal
Catherine Lockhart

PYP coordinator
Geoff Geddes

DP coordinator
Ainslie Howard

Status Private

Boarding/day Day & Homestay

Gender Coeducational

Language of instruction
English

Authorised IB programmes
PYP, DP

Age Range 3 - 18 years

Address
29-31 Kardinia Drive
Bell Post Hill
Geelong
VIC 3215 | AUSTRALIA

TEL +61 3 5278 9999

Email
marketing@kardinia.vic.edu.au

Website
www.kardinia.vic.edu.au

Kardinia International College is a high achieving and highly respected Kindergarten – Year 12 educational institution. The College was established as a symbol of hope for the world, developing knowledgeable and compassionate, globally minded citizens who act as agents of positive and sustainable change.

The College is independent, coeducational, and non-denominational, providing a caring environment for 1900 day and international students.

The College is renowned for the safe, respectful, and inclusive learning environment, which enables students to thrive. We actively encourage our students to develop their social, personal, intercultural, critical thinking, and ethical (SPICE) skills and attributes that enable and inspire them to actively contribute to a more inclusive, respectful and peaceful, and sustainable world. As an IB World school, we offer the Primary Years Programme (PYP) in Kindergarten-6, a vertical curriculum based on the guidelines of the Victorian Curriculum and Assessment Authority to students in Years 7-10 and both the International Baccalaureate Diploma Programme (IB) and the Victorian Certificate of Education (VCE) in Years 11 and 12. In the Senior School, the vertical curriculum offers many advantages, as students' progress at a rate appropriate to their ability, rather than age. Able students can fast track subjects, while other students can allow extra time for consolidation. Some students complete the IB Diploma or VCE in five years, most in six. An extensive range of VCE and IB subjects are available.

The Senior School curriculum is further strengthened by our International Immersion Programs. Our Year 9 students can join our positive, life changing up to eight-week Chiang Mai program in Thailand. Students can also visit our sister schools; Gotemba Nishi High in Japan and Saint Alyre in France. Our world class facilities include Katsumata Centre with our 1500 seat theatre and gymnasium, Goodfellow Aquatic Centre with a 25-metre indoor pool and cafe, School of Performing Arts, Learning Commons, six ovals, six tennis courts, a 1560 seat outdoor Amphitheatre and much more. Our main, 22-hectare campus is in Geelong (near Melbourne), our Year 5, 11-hectare farm campus in Lovely Banks and our 2.5-hectare campus in Chiang Mai, Thailand.

Kardinia International College is renowned for the outstanding results our students achieve in Year 12 examinations every year. We maintain a strong focus on academic excellence, pastoral care and developing globally minded citizens prepared for the challenges of a rapidly changing world.

KiiT International School

Chairperson
Dr. Mona Lisa Bal

Principal & Head of School
Dr. Sanjay Suar

Head of International Curriculum
Mr. Rory McNamara

DP coordinator
Mr. Kartick Chandra Sahoo

Status Private

Boarding/day Mixed

Gender Coeducational

Language of instruction
English

Authorised IB programmes
DP

Age Range 3.5 – 19 years

Number of pupils enrolled
2000+

Fees
Day Boarders:
INR 6 Lakh per annum
Full Boarders:
INR 7 Lakh per annum

Address
KiiT Campus 9
Patia
Bhubaneswar, Odisha
751024 | INDIA

TEL +91 674 2725805

Email
kiitis@kiitis.ac.in
admission@kiitis.ac.in

Website
www.kiitis.ac.in

KiiT International School was the first school in the state of Orissa (India) to offer IBDP. The expansive, lush green campus near to the International Airport offers ample space and infrastructure for sporting, cultural, and leisure activities. Our school prides itself on modern boarding houses and a fully equipped cafeteria that serves nutritious and delicious meals.

In a span of ten years, scores of our alumni have graduated from prestigious universities in the US, Canada, UK, Australia and India, and many more are pursuing various bachelor's programmes in universities across the world.

Apart from strictly adhering to the IB's vision, the school in its mission ensures that a true passion for enquiry and life-long learning is fostered in our students, and that they also develop the necessary skills to be successful in the highly competitive and unpredictable world they are growing into. Our teachers are periodically trained and are totally committed to their profession, and they explore innovative ways to help learners widen their knowledge base and hone the skills required to meet the demands of the future.

We also constantly strive to ensure that our students find pleasure in and are excited about the very process of learning as much as they are anxious about the end results. The teachers and students are dedicated to our mission statement "To lead and Excel by engaging minds, transforming lives and serving the community with compassion and empathy."

The well-coordinated, collective efforts of our management, teaching and non-teaching faculty ensure that our students respect people of all cultures, languages and their ways of life and are also concerned about the well-being of other species of animals, and nature as a whole. They are groomed and transformed into true global citizens.

KiiT International has evolved rapidly to become one of the most reputed schools in Odisha. The Education Today Indian Schools ranking of 2022 placed KiiT International among the top-10 residential schools in India, and No.1 in Odisha.

The school has a well-stocked, ever expanding physical and digital library and well-trained librarians who work closely with our IBDP students. Our labs are state-of-the art and are regularly modernised. As we are growing rapidly, we have started the construction of a separate modern facility exclusively for IBDP, IPYP and MYP programmes with a view to developing a full-fledged IB continuum school in the future.

Kingston International School
京斯敦國際學校

(Founded 1996)

Head of School
Ms. Eliza Wong Ting Fong

PYP coordinator
Ms. Emily Flach (Primary);
Ms. Michelle Chu (Early Years)

Status Private

Boarding/day Day

Gender Coeducational

Language of instruction
English, Mandarin

Authorised IB programmes
PYP

Age Range 1 – 11 years

Number of pupils enrolled 420

Fees
HK$59,400 – HK$159,000 per annum

Kingston International School (Lower Primary Campus)
113 Waterloo Road
Kowloon Tong, Hong Kong, SAR |
HONG KONG, CHINA

Kingston International School (Upper Primary Campus)
105 Waterloo Road,
Kowloon Tong, Hong Kong SAR |
HONG KONG, CHINA

Kingston Children's Centre and Kingston International Kindergarten
12-14 Cumberland Road,
Kowloon Tong, Hong Kong SAR |
HONG KONG, CHINA

TEL +852 2337 9031

Email enquiry@kingston.edu.hk

Website www.kingston.edu.hk

Kingston's mission is to provide a challenging and stimulating environment that nurtures the balanced development of students who, in their own unique way, grow into active and responsible world citizens. Kingston Children's Centre was established in 1996 and quickly grew into a highly successful bilingual Kindergarten using English and Mandarin Chinese as the medium of instruction. With popular demand from our parent community, our Primary School opened in September 2001 as a pathway for our students to continue their education in a bilingual setting and with the Kingston philosophy. The International Baccalaureate Primary Years Programme was introduced at the same time. In 2004, Kingston was the first school in Hong Kong to gain IBPYP authorisation. Since 2010, Kingston has been able to offer our students a through-train to the IBDP through our partnership with ICHK Secondary School.

Our school is spread over three cozy campuses, located very near each other in Kowloon Tong, Hong Kong. Members of the community who take the opportunity to walk the halls and visit the classrooms of Kingston often comment on the fluidity with which our students switch between the two living languages of our school, Mandarin and English. Collaborative teaching practices ensure an ideal environment for native fluency in both of our languages of instruction.

The Kingston community feels like an extended family in which multicultural collaboration has resulted in an excellent, rigorous, bilingual program. We value inclusive learning, which is reinforced by our approach of keeping class numbers low and teacher numbers high. All of our teachers are fully qualified native speakers of their taught languages and come from all over the globe, bringing with them a wide variety of experiences.

For over 25 years, Kingston has successfully provided a bilingual education for learners whose families wanted an international education for their child without foregoing the opportunity for their child to become a bilingual communicator who is confident in using both English and Mandarin. At Kingston we remain committed to the transdisciplinary approach to education, to innovation and to a lifelong learning journey.

Kororoit Creek Primary School

Head of School
Bethany Riseley

PYP coordinator
Drita Demiri

Status State

Boarding/day Day

Gender Coeducational

Language of instruction
English

Authorised IB programmes
PYP

Age Range 3 – 12 years

Number of pupils enrolled
1300

Address
130 Tenterfield Drive
Burnside Heights
VIC 3023 | AUSTRALIA

TEL +61 3 8358 0600

Email
kororoit.creek.ps@education.vic.gov.au

Website
www.kororoitcreekps.vic.edu.au

Kororoit Creek Primary School is a fully authorized PYP school, catering for 3-12-year olds. The school is in Public-Private Partnership, maintained and operated through a connection of government and private sector companies. Established in a high growth area, the school has grown from 260 students in 2011 to over 1600 in 2022. We pride ourselves on being a true representation of our community, with over 50 languages and cultural backgrounds.

The school implements the PYP framework underpinned by the Victorian Curriculum, a transdisciplinary curriculum outlining the key outcomes and expectations of the Victorian Government. The curriculum supports us to unpack the Essential Elements using explicit Scope and Sequence documents, ensuring all students are working within their Zone of Proximal Development.

Being a PYP school, we have a major focus on documented curriculum, assessment and shared pedagogical approaches. We also have a major emphasis on evidence-based school improvement strategies. These strategies include the moderation of common student assessment tasks, data collection and analysis as well as evaluation of student learning growth over time. Timely and effective feedback to its community of learners underpins every student's personal learning goals. Teacher professional practice activities are rigorous and differentiated.

With a whole school approach to health, wellbeing, inclusion and engagement, KCPS supports strong community values that underpin its safe and orderly learning environment. These contribute directly to the school's positive standing and high reputation within the immediate and broader area.

(Founded 1973)

Executive Principal
Mr Mark Wilson

Junior School Principal
Mrs Jayne de la Haye

Middle School Principal
Mrs Kate Pollard

Senior School Principal
Mr David Boardman

PYP coordinator
Ms Sandy Paton

MYP coordinator
Mr John Osborne

DP coordinator
Mrs Debbie Dwyer

Status Private

Boarding/day Day

Gender Coeducational

Language of instruction English

Authorised IB programmes
PYP, MYP, DP

Age Range 6 months – 18 years

Number of pupils enrolled 1800

Address
360 Albany Highway
Albany, Auckland 0632 |
NEW ZEALAND

TEL +64 9 415 9566

Email
admissions@kristin.school.nz

Website www.kristin.school.nz

Kristin School is an independent, modern, co-educational International Baccalaureate (IB) World School located in Albany, Auckland with more than 1800 students aged from six months to 18 years old. Established in 1973, Kristin is non-denominational and welcomes students from all cultures and backgrounds, attracting students from 40 different nationalities.

Based in New Zealand's most dynamic city, all of Kristin's learning environments share the same 50-acre, parklike campus: Little Doves Early Learning Centre, Kristin Kindergarten, Kristin Junior School (for 5-10 year olds), Kristin Middle School (for 10-15 year olds) and Kristin Senior School (for 15-18 year olds).

Kristin was the first IB World School in New Zealand offering the IB Diploma Programme since 1986, and the first school to offer the IB Primary Years Programme, IB Middle Years Programme and IB Diploma Programme (DP) catering for students from Year 0-13. Kristin students regularly achieve at levels well above global averages, with more than 25% achieving scores of 40+ points, placing them in the top 2% of students worldwide. Our students also receive a high quota of scholarships to Oxbridge, Ivy League and top universities in Asia Pacific.

Our small class sizes are critical in providing personalised learning opportunities, and a balanced education at Kristin goes beyond providing a positive school culture. We ensure students are taught skills that will enhance their wellbeing, help them cope with life's challenges, strengthen their relationships with others and enable them to pursue a happy, healthy and prosperous life.

In summary, Kristin offers a:

- Modern, multicultural, co-educational, non-denominational environment with with strong positive values
- Proud record of high academic results and scholarships being awarded locally and internationally
- High level of teaching expertise, with many teachers internationally trained and experienced
- Focus on student wellbeing and developing future-ready citizens
- Choice between the national NCEA or IB Diploma Programme curriculum options for senior students
- Nationally acclaimed performing arts and outdoor education programmes
- Vast range of community service and leadership opportunities
- 30 different popular and specialised sporting codes
- Experiential learning through a wide array of trips and exchanges with more than 15 partner schools overseas
- 50-acre, park-like campus and extensive facilities: two theatres, art, dance and drama studios, a green room/media suite, huge library, numerous sports fields, gyms and courts, technology workshops and more!
- Dedicated bus service travelling 20 routes across Auckland.

For all admission enquiries, please visit kristin.school.nz or call our Admissions Manager on +64 9 415 9566 ext 2324. We look forward to sharing more information with you to help show why Kristin School is the right choice for your child.

Léman International School Chengdu

Principal
Tracy Connor

Head of Secondary
Paul Highdale

Head of Primary
Robert Dolan

MYP coordinator
Patrick Meersman

DP coordinator
Thomas Ainsworth

Status Private

Boarding/day Day

Gender Coeducational

Language of instruction
English

Authorised IB programmes
MYP, DP

Age Range 2 – 18 years

Number of pupils enrolled
400

Fees
Day: RMB153,000 – RMB259,900 per annum

Address
No.1080 Da'an Road,
Zheng Xing County
Tianfu New Area
Chengdu, Sichuan
610218 | CHINA

TEL +86 28 6703 8650

Email
admissions@lis-chengdu.com

Website
www.lis-chengdu.com

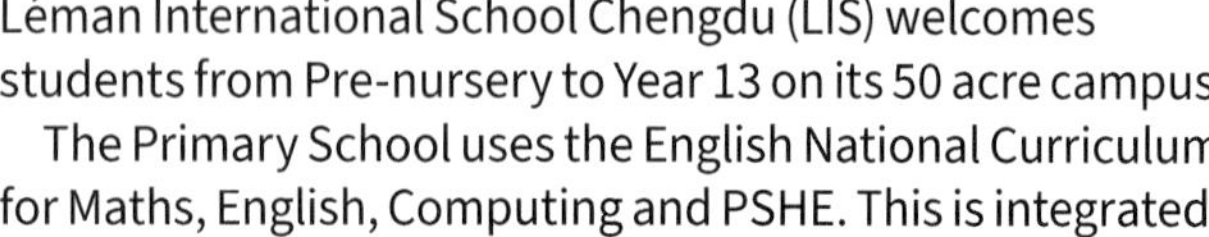

Léman International School Chengdu (LIS) welcomes students from Pre-nursery to Year 13 on its 50 acre campus.

The Primary School uses the English National Curriculum for Maths, English, Computing and PSHE. This is integrated with the International Primary Curriculum (IPC), currently used in over 1000 schools in 65 countries, to give a truly international educational experience throughout the Primary years. The Secondary School, from Years 7 to 11, is based upon the International Baccalaureate Middle Years Programme, with Year 12 and 13 following the International Baccalaureate Diploma Programmme. LIS offers foreign languages including Mandarin and French. Korean and German are also offered to its native speakers.

LIS has world class facilities on an extensive campus, including fully equipped modern classrooms, science laboratories, an art studio, music studios, I.T. rooms, maker spaces, gymnasium, 25-meter indoor swimming pool and further outdoor sports facilities, including two full size football pitches; this allows us to offer an extensive extra-curricular activity program as well as comprehensive sports and arts programs.

We are proud that 3 out of 4 of our graduates have chosen, and been admitted to, the world's top universities (according to the QS World University Rankings 2022). Our graduates attend the very best universities in the world, including Oxford, Tsinghua, UCL, LSE, UBC and NYU. We have graduates attending top Art & Design Institutes, including University of Arts London, the School of Visual Arts, and the Fashion Institute of Technology.

LIS is accredited by the Council of International Schools (CIS), the New England Association of Schools and Colleges (NEASC) and Council of British International Schools (COBIS).

LIS is part of the global Nord Anglia Education family and this gives us a unique link to collaborate with schools and pursue opportunities worldwide. This includes the world leader of performing arts education, The Juilliard School, and the world's top university, MIT, as well as our collaboration with UNICEF, whereby students have their social consciousness raised so they care more deeply about the world and the people in it. Our unique online and classroom collaboration platform, Global Campus, connects more than 80,000 Nord Anglia students, and the Nord Anglia University platform enables the very best professional development for our staff.

Linden Hall High School

Head of School
Ms. Asuka Tsuzuki

DP coordinator
Ms. Karen Hunter

Status Private

Boarding/day Mixed

Gender Coeducational

Language of instruction
English, Japanese

Authorised IB programmes
DP

Age Range 12 – 18 years

Number of pupils enrolled 80

Fees
¥1,518,000

Address
3-10-1 Futsukaichikita
Chikushino, Fukuoka, Kyushu
818-0056 | JAPAN

TEL +81 92 929 4558

Email
hunter@lindenhall.ed.jp

Website
www.lindenhall.ed.jp/highschool

Located approximately 30 minutes from Fukuoka city-centre, Linden Hall High School's goal is to nurture individuals who will play an active role in a rapidly globalizing, dynamic world. Our philosophy, "Develop the individual, instill them with confidence, and send them out into the world" reflects this. In 2013, we became the first Article 1 school (a school recognized as meeting the requirements of the Japanese national Curriculum, guaranteeing that IB graduates are awarded a Japanese High School Diploma as well as the IB Diploma) in Kyushu certified as an International Baccalaureate World School.

In this fast-changing global society, with all its challenges, the need to cultivate open-minded global citizens who can utilise English fluently in various intercultural settings is increasingly apparent. We have therefore adopted an English immersion approach, in which the majority of classes other than Japanese Language classes are conducted in English. Through interacting with teachers and students from around the world, students naturally acquire both English language skills and respect for diversity. Our classroom methods encourage students to engage actively in their learning and discover the joy of unravelling the world's mysteries. Until high school, students progress through a common curriculum before electing, in Year 10, to pursue either the International Baccalaureate Diploma Programme (IBDP) or the Think and Inquire (TI) Course (for students wishing to continue the National Curriculum).

We also provide numerous opportunities for students to study abroad and participate in international exchange and volunteer programmes. In 2018, we became a member of Round Square, an association of approximately 200 private schools from over 50 countries. Founded in 1966 to develop the next generation of international leaders, member schools participate in international exchanges, conferences and various other activities.

The school building is an airy structure, built to make the most of natural light. It is fully air-conditioned with learning facilities such as IT, Art, and Music rooms, a Science laboratory and Wi-Fi in every classroom. The Library houses 12,000 books, one-third of which are in English, and provides subscribed access to many online resources. Next to the school is the cafeteria, where chefs and registered dieticians serve Japan's first year-round organic school meals. The surroundings feature lush greenery and the classrooms offer a panoramic view, including the 60,000m^2 English Garden – an ideal place to relax and observe nature. Our dormitories, one for boys and one for girls, are within easy walking distance.

Marlborough College Malaysia

MARLBOROUGH COLLEGE
MALAYSIA

(Founded 2012)

The Master
Mr Simon Burbury

DP coordinator
Mr Kenton Tomlinson

Status Private

Boarding/day Mixed

Gender Coeducational

Language of instruction
English

Authorised IB programmes
DP

Age Range 3 – 18 years
(boarding from 9)

Number of pupils enrolled
830

Fees
Day: RM45,600 – RM134,400 per annum
Weekly Boarding: RM135,900 – RM182,100 per annum
Boarding: RM159,300 – RM213,600 per annum

Address
Jalan Marlborough
79200 Iskandar Puteri,
Johor | **MALAYSIA**

TEL +60 7 560 2200

Email
admissions@marlboroughcollege.my

Website
www.marlboroughcollegemalaysia.org

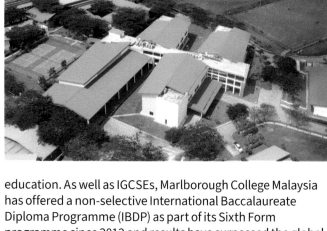

Named as one of the top 125 private schools in the world for three consecutive years by Carfax Education, Marlborough College Malaysia is a co-educational British boarding and day school, conveniently located a short distance from the Singapore border. It is a non-profit, sister school to Marlborough College UK, offering a comprehensive and well-rounded education for pupils aged 3-18 with over 40 nationalities represented among the student body.

Situated on a vast 90-acre site, the College campus features two outdoor swimming pools, a lake for watersports, organic farm, full athletics track, tennis/netball courts, golf driving range and 5 sports pitches, as well as a theatre, indoor climbing wall, gymnastics area and state-of-the-art gym.

Learning broadly follows and extends the British National curriculum with compassion, companionship and conversation at the heart of the College's educational philosophy. A distinctive blend of academic excellence and holistic development gives students a well-rounded education. As well as IGCSEs, Marlborough College Malaysia has offered a non-selective International Baccalaureate Diploma Programme (IBDP) as part of its Sixth Form programme since 2012 and results have surpassed the global average each year. In 2023, 97% of MCM students passed the IBDP with an impressive average points score of 33 points. Over 14% of students in 2023 achieved at an exceptional high level, scoring over 40 points.

Consistently high achievement in the IBDP, along with outstanding university application support has meant that pupils have entered some of the world's leading universities. The University Guidance Department at the College makes every effort to assist pupils with the various international university application platforms with dedicated staff on hand to provide guidance. A comprehensive programme of support with regular visits from many international university representatives throughout the year ensure that students at Marlborough College Malaysia reach their full potential.

Mercedes College

MERCEDES COLLEGE

(Founded 1954)

Principal
Mr Andrew Balkwill

PYP coordinator
Mr Andrew Khabbaz

MYP coordinator
Mr Stuart Wuttke

DP coordinator
Mr Marc Whitehead

Status Private

Boarding/day Day

Gender Coeducational

Language of instruction
English

Authorised IB programmes
PYP, MYP, DP

Age Range 5 – 18 years

Fees
Day: AUS$12,265 – AUS$19,330 per annum

Address
540 Fullarton Road
Springfield
SA 5062 | AUSTRALIA

TEL +61 8 8372 3200

Email
mercedes@mercedes.catholic.edu.au

Website
www.mercedes.catholic.edu.au

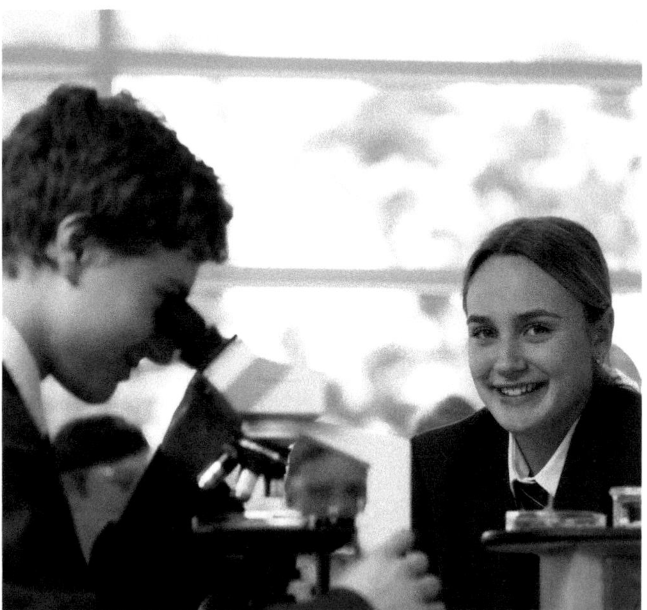

Internationally renowned
Situated in the leafy foothills just 6 kilometres from the city centre, the Mercedes College campus has beautiful gardens, open space and great learning facilities.

A contemporary Reception to Year 12 International Baccalaureate world school, Mercedes College is renowned for providing students with a world class education. Offering all three programmes, the College promotes the education of the whole person, emphasising intellectual, personal, emotional, spiritual, and social growth through all domains of knowledge.

Mercedes College is a learning community in the Mercy tradition, where a strong sense of belonging is fostered and values are lived as we develop creative, caring and critical thinkers who are responsible, compassionate, loyal, show integrity and mutual respect, and have a strong sense of justice.

Achieving success
Through a progressive, internationally focussed curriculum underpinned by values, we prepare our students as future local, national and global community leaders by providing opportunities that enable each of them to reach their full potential.

Success at Mercedes College is measured by academic achievement, plus each student's abilities, breadth of skills and confidence. The wellbeing of our students is deeply intertwined with our curriculum, facilities, approach to teaching and the connection between students and their teachers.

High performance
Set to open in early 2024, the new $25 million Arts and Sports Precinct will be where students refine their performance skills, train and compete in a high performance indoor sports complex, and celebrate achievements in our community plaza.

For more information visit www.mercedes.catholic.edu.au

Merici College

(Founded 1959)

Principal
Anna Masters

MYP coordinator
Jodie Muldoon

DP coordinator
Natalie Fairfax

Status Private

Boarding/day Day

Gender Female

Language of instruction
English

Authorised IB programmes
MYP, DP

Age Range 11 – 18 years

Number of pupils enrolled
850

Fees
Day: AUS$9,235 – AUS$11,418 per annum

Address
Wise Street
Braddon
ACT 2612 | AUSTRALIA

TEL +61 2 6243 4100

Email
info@merici.act.edu.au

Website
www.merici.act.edu.au

Mission
Merici College empowers women to love life, have hope, be faithful and build futures more wondrous than they dare to dream.

Vision
Merici College endeavours to be a vibrant, faithful learning community that fosters excellence, and takes positive action to build a shared global future.

Merici College is a Year 7-12 Catholic girls' college, situated in Braddon in the heart of Canberra. We are very proud to be the oldest established Catholic girls' secondary school in Canberra.

Merici is a vibrant community committed to preparing confident and competent young women well equipped to contribute to the world beyond high school. We create innovative learning environments that meet the needs of individual students and inspire them to strive for the highest levels of personal achievement. We challenge our students to take risks within and beyond the classroom to achieve individual academic excellence.

Merici College is a welcoming community, where authentic relationships are nurtured, and dignity and integrity are affirmed. We seek to foster a life-long love of learning within our students, where each young woman is given the opportunity to grow spiritually and intellectually to make a positive contribution to society. Families also enrich Merici from diverse Christian and other faith traditions.

Academic
We teach the Australian Curriculum in the Junior Years (Years 7-10) delivered through the Middle Years Framework. At the senior level, students choose to study either the IB DP, or our local curriculum. We offer a range of opportunities for gifted and talented students, including differentiated teaching, acceleration, enrichment, and support for students with specific learning needs.

Cocurricular
We believe it's vital that every Merici Girl gets the chance to explore their passion, be creative and try something new. Our co-curricular and enrichment opportunities have something to suit everyone, from our Sustainability at Merici (SAM) group to Art Club and a vast array of sporting teams, including a robust set of Netball teams.

Vertical House System
One of the strengths of our college is the strong House System and excellent pastoral care provided. The seven Pastoral Care (PC) Groups in each House are vertically streamed, and students remain in the same PC group throughout their six years at Merici. This encourages positive relationships and a sense of belonging and continuity for students and their families. It also provides leadership opportunities for older students who support and mentor the younger ones.

(Founded 1886)

Principal
Lisa Moloney

DP coordinator
Olivia Nolan

Status Private

Boarding/day Day

Gender Female

Language of instruction
English

Authorised IB programmes
DP

Number of pupils enrolled
1380

Fees
AU$15,672 (Pre-Kindergarten 3 days per week) – AU$39,648 (Year 12) per annum – Subject to change

Address
Rowley Street
Burwood
Sydney
NSW 2134 | AUSTRALIA

TEL +61 2 9747 1266

Email
enrol@mlcsyd.nsw.edu.au

Website
www.mlcsyd.nsw.edu.au

MLC School is an independent, non-selective Uniting Church school for girls from Pre-Kindergarten to Year 12 in the Inner West of Sydney. From Pre-Kindergarten through to their time as Senior School students, MLC School girls dare to be more.

Led by highly professional staff under the guidance of Principal Lisa Moloney, girls are challenged and encouraged to question traditional perceptions and roles of women and are instilled with the skills and confidence to take their place in an ever-changing society. MLC School prepares girls for a life of learning by motivating them to pursue excellence, demonstrate integrity, celebrate diversity, embrace world citizenship and live with humility. A wide selection of subject choices, as well as an extensive co-curricular program aims to empower girls to be self-reliant and play an active role in their futures.

The award-winning Senior Centre takes classroom practice to a new level and is reflective of modern workplaces. The aim is to equip girls with the skills to be successful in a collaborative, team environment and to be comfortable in open-planned, flexible spaces designed for impromptu group work sessions.

Year 7 to Year 10 are pivotal years where girls experience Immersive Learning journeys that broaden each year. These experiences take place locally, regionally, or abroad; and aim to broaden horizons, encourage resilience and foster a growth mindset to underpin success in their senior years of schooling.

Academically, each girl takes responsibility for her own path in the final years, and this is a crucial stage in her journey towards becoming an independent, fearless and empowered young woman.

Girls choose between the Higher School Certificate (HSC) or the International Baccalaureate (IB) Diploma Programme, with nearly 50 per cent choosing to study the IB. In 2021, the School was named No 1 IB School in Australia and a Top 50 Global IB School. Over 67 MLC School girls have achieved the perfect IB Diploma score of 45 since the programme was introduced here in 2002. All girls consistently score well.

MLC School's Emerging Athlete Program supports talented athletes to navigate through representative sport pathways to achieve their sporting and academic goals, while maintaining a balanced lifestyle. MLC School is one of 32 schools worldwide to be accredited as an Athlete Friendly Education Centre through the World Academy of Sport and athletes can study the IBDP over 3 years.

Visit the campus, meet the girls and professional teaching staff, and experience the benefits of joining the MLC School community.

Newington College

(Founded 1863)

Headmaster
Mr Michael Parker

PYP coordinator
Mr Benjamin Barrington-Higgs

DP coordinator
Ms Cheryl Priest

Status Independent

Boarding/day Mixed

Gender Coeducational

Language of instruction
English

Authorised IB programmes
PYP, DP

Number of pupils enrolled
2129

Fees
Boarding:
AUS$33,651 (inc GST)
Tuition:
AUS$24,390 – AUS$42,201 per annum

Address
200 Stanmore Road
Stanmore
NSW 2048 | AUSTRALIA

TEL +61 2 9568 9333

Email
admissions@newington.nsw.edu.au

Website
www.newington.nsw.edu.au

The hub of Sydney, Australia
Newington College is an International Baccalaureate World School in the heart of Sydney. It includes a Primary Years Programme (PYP) satellite prep school, based in Lindfield on Sydney's upper north shore, and a boarding house for secondary students on the main campus in the inner west suburb of Stanmore.

It's only ten minutes from Sydney International Airport and Central station, and five minutes from the prestigious University of Sydney.

Surrounded by a number of universities, theatres, libraries and museums, the location gives students of all ages the opportunity to access a range of learning and cultural resources, and work with experts from other nearby centres of learning.

The College attracts a diverse range of students from greater Sydney, regional areas, and the Asia-Pacific, with the lush gardens and playing fields creating an oasis of learning within the bustling city.

A tradition of inclusivity and critical thinking
Founded in 1863, the founding fathers realised the need for a quality educational establishment to help students develop into adults that will make a positive difference.

Newington College's holistic approach to education and unique focus on critical and creative thinking, makes it a remarkable place to educate your child.

Its families value the approach of teaching children how to think not want to think, while being open to other student's views and perspectives – a belief espoused by the IB.

The College strives to reaffirm a culture that is vibrant and caring while encouraging their students to be courageous, open-minded, creative, and curious, valuing both independence and teamwork.

Rigorous approach to learning and teaching
Lindfield Preparatory School offers the PYP (Primary Years Programme), while the senior school is the only Greater Public School (GPS) in Sydney that allows students to choose between the Higher School Certificate (HSC) examination and the IB Diploma Programme.

The IB Diploma is a popular option for many at the College and the results achieved are outstanding. Newington is committed to providing an internationally respected education with access to the best teachers, facilities and opportunities. Students are encouraged to take a global perspective to their studies and immerse themselves in their own areas of interest and passion.

The College is equipped with the latest technology and industry level facilities including a modern technology centre, 200-seat drama theatre, light-filled library, lecture theatre and super-labs.

Wellbeing, values, and spirituality
The teachers share a passion for their areas of expertise and build strong connections with their students – tailoring their teaching style to suit each individual.

The students value their teachers and coaches genuine interest in each of their wellbeing, passions, goals and setbacks, something the college is highly committed to.

The staff want to empower them to develop great hearts, inspired minds, and strong wings, who will leave the College ready to make a positive contribution to society and the future.

As a Uniting church school, Christian values are the backbone of the community. This includes welcoming students and families of all faiths and cultural backgrounds.

All students are expected to build a sense of social responsibility, service to others and the development of strong and lasting relationships – not only with teachers and peers but parents, families and past graduates (Old Newingtonians). The College strives for every member of the Newington community to feel welcome, connected and appreciated.

Extensive co-curricular opportunities

Newington encourages all students to experiment and grow through participation in a variety of co-curricular activities and tours in Australia and abroad, to help them discover their unique passion and interests.

These opportunities are a large part of what sets the college apart, with students combining academic life with sports, arts, outdoor education, and hands-on learning activities.

Results

Out of 35 students doing the IB in 2022, 27 received an ATAR rank over 95. For Newington College, the median score was 40/50 which is equivalent to an ATAR of 97.90. The median score was 38/45, compared to a global average of 32/45. Underpinning these results were some exceptional individual performances across all subjects.

NIST
INTERNATIONAL SCHOOL

(Founded 1992)

Head of School Dr James Dalziel

PYP coordinator Bryony Maxted-Miller

MYP coordinator Stuart Donnelly

DP coordinator Robin Wilensky

Status Private

Boarding/day Day

Gender Coeducational

Language of instruction English

Authorised IB programmes PYP, MYP, DP

Age Range 3 – 18 years

Number of pupils enrolled 1760

Fees THB541,700 – THB975,800 per annum

Address
36 Sukhumvit Soi 15
Wattana, Bangkok
10110 | THAILAND

TEL +66 2 017 5888

Email admissions@nist.ac.th

Website www.nist.ac.th

NIST International School in Bangkok is a not-for-profit full IB World School offering a premium international education. The school is committed to building a community of diverse perspectives and experiences and is reflected in its focus on developing students who are ready and ambitious to positively impact their world at NIST and beyond.

Since 1992, NIST has welcomed thousands of internationally-minded students and their families from around the world. Today, our community comprises students aged 3-18 from more than 75 countries. At NIST, holistic education is inspired by our mission of creating inquisitive, lifelong learners and Global Citizens, empowered by world-class teachers and curriculum, and enriched by an environment where everyone feels they belong.

NIST is governed by a parent-elected NIST International School Foundation and was the first school in Thailand to receive triple accreditation through the Council of International Schools (CIS), New England Association of Schools and Colleges (NEASC) and Office for National Education Standards and Quality Assessment (ONESQA).

At NIST, education is more than just an academic programme. While academics are fundamental to the learning experience, we also recognise the importance of wellbeing, activities, service learning and expeditions. These five elements come together to provide a breadth of opportunities for personal, social and cognitive development, helping students to find their interests and reach their full potential.

NIST understands what students gain by playing on a sports team, working with a service group, engaging in a school expedition, participating in a drama production, or looking after their physical and emotional health. These experiences make a lasting and positive impact on the growth of a child.

This is why the NIST Learning Programme has been carefully curated to provide a range of experiences that all work together to deliver a holistic education, every day, from Early Years through to graduation.

Through the experiences that underpin the elements of our Learning Programme, our students develop the skills and dispositions they will need to be successful at NIST and beyond. As a committed IB World School, the NIST Attributes are informed by and align with the IB Learner Profile and Approaches to Learning.

In addition, NIST is a member of an eight school consortium who offer the Global Citizen Diploma (GCD). The GCD provides students with a credential that highlights the qualities of global citizenship, as well as the opportunity to describe their whole education qualitatively through reflection on their learning experiences.

The Global Citizen Diploma (GCD) is a diploma programme designed to complement the rigour of NIST's Learning Programme by recognising a student's comprehensive educational experience – learning that has taken place inside the classroom, within the larger context of school and in the world beyond.

NIST has a proven track record of fostering reflective, principled learners with a passion for making a difference in the lives of others, with its graduates attending the best universities around the world and going on to become community leaders. NIST has become recognised as one of the world's leading international schools.

Nord Anglia International School Shanghai, Pudong

NORD ANGLIA
INTERNATIONAL
SCHOOL
SHANGHAI, PUDONG

(Founded 2002)

Principal
Diane Vaughan

DP coordinator
Hari Raye

Status Private

Boarding/day Day

Gender Coeducational

Language of instruction
English

Authorised IB programmes
DP

Age Range 2 – 18 years

Fees
RMB126,100 – RMB359,870 per annum

Address
2888 Junmin Road
Pudong New District
Shanghai
201315 | CHINA

TEL +86 (0)21 5812 7455 (Ext:1015)

Email
admissions@naispudong.com

Website
naispudong.com

Established in 2002, Nord Anglia International School Shanghai, Pudong (NAIS Pudong) is China's longest-running British international school and the first to be established in the Pudong New District, offering an excellent education by focusing on a personalised learning journey for every child.

The school offers the very best of the British education system in Shanghai for children aged 2 to 18 years. Class sizes are small, with lessons delivered by outstanding academic staff, allowing for a tailored learning journey in which all students are known to staff and where everyone is encouraged to develop and thrive. This is supported by a targeted approach to student and staff wellbeing.

NAIS Pudong provides students with a highly supportive, academic environment, and a warm, welcoming and diverse international community. Its rigorous, contemporary and globally focused curriculum challenges and excites children from their early years through to the International Baccalaureate Diploma Programme (IBDP). Where needed, students have access to an excellent range of EAL support mechanisms which come at no extra cost to families.

To complement classroom teaching, NAIS Pudong offers a broad co-curricular programme that encourages students to take risks, nurture their passions, and serve others. Globally respected curricula are enhanced by innovative collaborations with world leading organisations such as The Juilliard School, Massachusetts Institute of Technology (MIT), UNICEF and IMG Academy to ensure that every student develops the skills and mindset needed to thrive in an ever-changing world.

The school campus provides a range of excellent facilities including a large Performing Arts Centre, natural grass sports pitches, a 25m swimming pool, tennis courts, dojo facility, and two large indoor gymnasia, as well as a range of well-equipped classrooms and outdoor play spaces.

Meanwhile, its Global Campus connects the Nord Anglia Education family of 85+ schools and more than 80,000 students, giving NAIS Pudong students access to a variety of exceptional learning opportunities worldwide. This includes multiple outdoor adventure training camps in its family of schools in Switzerland as well as dedicated community projects in Tanzania.

NAIS Pudong wholeheartedly embraces the educational philosophy and pedagogical principles that underpin all IB programmes. This approach has resulted in the establishment of an optimal learning environment whereby its students are able to achieve outstanding academic results.

Our core values are focused on developing creative, confident, and considerate learners who are prepared for their futures, and at NAIS Pudong we nurture every student to achieve academic success, enabling entry into the world's leading universities.

You want your child to excel, so do we.

Nord Anglia International School, Hong Kong

(Founded 2014)

Principal
Mr Kenny Duncan

DP coordinator
Colin Spanos

Status Private

Boarding/day Day

Gender Coeducational

Language of instruction
English

Authorised IB programmes
DP

Age Range 3 – 18 years

Fees
Pre-school HK$86,770 – HK$182,100 per annum
Primary HK$182,100 per annum
Secondary (Year 7 – 11) HK$203,700 per annum
Secondary (Year 12 – 13) HK$205,700 per annum

Early Years Campus
285 Hong Kin Road,
Tui Min Hoi, Sai Kung, N.T.,
Hong Kong, SAR | **HONG KONG, CHINA**

Primary Campus
11 On Tin Street
Lam Tin, Kowloon
Hong Kong, SAR | **HONG KONG, CHINA**

Secondary Campus
19 Yuet Wah Street,
Kwun Tong, Kowloon,
Hong Kong, SAR | **HONG KONG, CHINA**

TEL +852 3958 1428

Email
admissions@nais.hk

Website
http://www.nais.hk

Nord Anglia International School (NAIS) is part of Nord Anglia Education's (NAE) global family of international schools. A through-train school known for its warm and friendly global community, made up of over 40 nationalities, NAIS nurtures every child to develop a love of learning, enabling them to achieve more than they ever thought possible.

NAE's Global Campus helps students explore the world, learn new skills and set their sights higher, developing a truly international perspective through outstanding online, in-school and worldwide experiences.

NAIS educates children for the future, enhancing its curricula through collaborations with the world's best organisations including MIT and Juilliard. Through opportunities to learn from the best, experiences beyond the ordinary, and the encouragement to achieve more than what they thought possible, NAIS helps students succeed anywhere through a unique global educational offer.

NAIS follows the frameworks of EYFS, IGCSE and IBDP. With a focus on individualised learning, the school's rigorous curricula ensure that students have a creative and challenging learning experience.

(Founded 2011)

Principal
Ms Lynne Oldfield

DP coordinator
Ms Justine Oliver

Status Private

Boarding/day Mixed

Gender Coeducational

Language of instruction
English

Authorised IB programmes
DP

Age Range 4 – 18 years

Number of pupils enrolled
1420

Fees
Day: KRW 34,000,000 – 48,000,000 per annum
Boarding: KRW 11,812,290 – 16,388,510 per annum

Address
33, Global edu-ro 145beon-gil
Daejeong-eup
Seogwipo-si, Jeju-do
63644 | REPUBLIC OF KOREA

TEL +82 64 793 8001

Email
admissions@nlcsjeju.kr

Website
www.nlcsjeju.co.kr

North London Collegiate School Jeju, is an international boarding and day school based in South Korea. The School provides an exceptional education, one in which our students excel academically. They achieve outstanding results and secure places at prestigious universities around the world. Our students are passionate about learning; they are independent thinkers and have an intellectual curiosity that is admirable.

NLCS Jeju provides an environment, which strikes a healthy balance between academics and co-curricular activities; we focus on the whole person. Our programme is designed to inspire confidence, individuality and develop self-esteem. Modelled on our founding school in London, we are a positive and energetic community where both boarders and day students are encouraged to take advantage of the exceptional range of opportunities open to them; academics, sports, the arts, service and much more.

International Outlook

NLCS Jeju students are internationally minded and well informed about the world beyond the School. The IB Diploma resonates with the values of NLCS Jeju, and its international dimension affords students the opportunity to be part of a programme which is recognised throughout the world.

Academic Excellence

We have offered the IB programme since 2011 and have had a consistent record of success. Diploma candidates in the Class of 2023 achieved an average of 36 points and a grade average of 5.7.

Looking to the future

The Class of 2023 showed another outstanding performance. Now they begin their studies at many of the world's top universities – with offers from universities including; the Columbia, Cornell, Carnegie Mellon, New York, Stanford, Oxford, Cambridge and St Andrews. Other destinations around the world are Canada, Hong Kong, Japan and South Korea. The IB Diploma programme offered at NLCS Jeju ensures that students enjoy an exciting and academically stimulating Sixth Form experience, providing them with an excellent preparation for life at university and in the wider world beyond.

(Founded 2008)

Head of School
Mr. Andrew Wyeth

DP coordinators
Ms. Smitha Kumar &
Ms. Selvia Thomas

Status Private

Boarding/day Day

Gender Coeducational

Language of instruction
English

Authorised IB programmes
DP

Age Range 3 – 18 years

Number of pupils enrolled
1400

Fees
Day: S$16,000 –
S$27,000 per annum

Primary School
11 Hillside Drive
Singapore
548296 | SINGAPORE

Secondary School
25 Scotts Road, Singapore
228250 | SINGAPORE

TEL +65 6294 2400

Email
register@npsinternational.edu.sg

Website
npsinternational.com.sg

The school, founded in 2008, is a highly successful IBDP school with strong IB results and cohort averages over several years. The graduates receive offers from some of the top universities worldwide, including Oxford, Cambridge, UPenn, UC Berkeley, Georgia Tech, UIUC, Imperial College etc.

Our Hillside campus in the central Upper Serangoon district, near Kovan MRT, caters to children from the Early Years to Grade VI. The campus has a charming blend of indoor and outdoor spaces to provide the finest learning environment for young learners.

The Secondary campus is a one-of-a-kind large city-centre campus, in the famous Orchard-Scotts district, making it a modern facility that is teaching-learning centred. Our Secondary campus is a sprawling 100,000 square feet of study, collaboration and sports spaces appropriate for our middle school and high school learners.

In 2023, NPS International School students achieved a cohort average score of 38 points, compared to the global average of 30.24 points. 39% of our students received 40 or more points, while another 83% received 35 or more points. Our students received an average of 5.95 points.

The National Public School (NPS) group of educational institutions headquartered in Bangalore, India, has an enviable track record of academic excellence spread over six decades, nurturing 15,000 children each year in over 10 campuses.

NPS International School welcomes students to its child-centred environment, offering Nursery, Kindergarten, Grades I to Grades XII, IBDP and IGCSE programmes. The teacher-student ratio is a healthy 1:13 and the IBDP subjects have an average class size of 16 students. The key difference between NPSI and many other groups of schools is the consistent Top Performing IB results and the founding governors are educationists with vast experience in a wide range of educational contexts. That richness of experience brings a maturity of systems and vision that has been recognised, valued and endorsed by parents.

Join NPS, a Top International IB School located in Singapore. We constantly strive to foster academic excellence and a sense of well-being in our carefully curated positive learning environment. We will encourage your child to blossom into an active, critical learner filled with compassion. Be a part of us and enjoy the impactful educational experience!

Our Vision

Inspiring young minds and empowering them to have a positive impact on the world.

Our Mission

- Providing a child-centred, holistic, and value-based learning experience
- Encouraging creativity, innovation, confidence, and critical thinking in a safe and nurturing environment
- Fostering leadership, empathy and engagement in humanitarian and environment service

NUCB International College

Acting Principal
Robert Chaytor

DP coordinators
Darron Gray & Morgan Veness

Status Private

Boarding/day Boarding

Gender Coeducational

Language of instruction
English, Japanese

Authorised IB programmes
DP

Age Range 15 – 18 years

Number of pupils enrolled 71

Fees
Boarding: ¥3,500,000 – ¥4,000,000 per annum

Address
4-4 Sagamine Komenoki
Nisshin, Aichi,
470-0193 | JAPAN

TEL +81 56 173 8181

Email
info@ic.nucba.ac.jp

Website
ic.nucba.ac.jp

NUCB International College provides a world-class education with excellent facilities and a rich natural environment, on its 200-acre campus, in Nisshin City, Japan.

The school implements leadership education from an early age within an international environment. It is the only boarding school in central Japan accredited by the Ministry of Education, Culture, Sports, Science & Technology (MEXT) to offer two qualifications: the Japanese high school diploma (as an "Article 1" school) and the International Baccalaureate Diploma Programme (IBDP). All subjects apart from language classes are taught in English, and all our students have the opportunity to be awarded the Bilingual IBDP Diploma.

Excellence in Education

Small classes of 25 students enable personalised supervision by multinational faculty members with master's or doctoral degrees and faculty from affiliated top business schools. The learning at NIC is driven by the IB and the Case Method approaches to teaching and learning. After completing the programme, students emerge as well-balanced, internationally-minded and highly-skilled individuals. Furthermore, as part of our early leadership education, we offer a Summer School (July) and the Bridging Programme (April to June), a preparatory programme for prospective students aiming to start their studies in September.

Safe Boarding Environment

The naturally rich and beautiful campus of NUCB International College has been designed for international students, Japanese nationals who have lived overseas for extended periods, and students from domestic schools. In this safe and secure co-educational boarding environment with reference to international boarding standards, each student can work towards their own goals in their studies. 'House Supervisors', who are well versed in psychological and health management, conduct daily life support and regular individual counselling to ensure optimal support and guidance for each student.

Extensive Extracurricular Opportunities

To enrich and enhance the school experience, students engage in various extracurricular activities to foster creativity, autonomy, and cooperation, as well as joint events with our affiliated school and university, including school festivals, sports competitions and art week. House activities include monthly off-campus excursions to nearby attractive spots, such as recreational facilities and tourist destinations where students can learn about history and culture.

One World International School, Nanyang Campus (OWIS Nanyang)

Head of School
James Sweeney

PYP coordinator
Nur Syahdiqin Ismail

DP coordinator
Sanhita Roy

Status Private

Boarding/day Day

Gender Coeducational

Language of instruction
English

Authorised IB programmes
PYP, DP

Age Range 3 – 18 years

Number of pupils enrolled
1300

Fees
Day: S$19,881 – S$22,857 per annum (excluding GST)

Address
21 Jurong West Street 81
Singapore
649075 | SINGAPORE

TEL +65 69146700

Email
admissions.sg@owis.org

Website
owis.org/sg

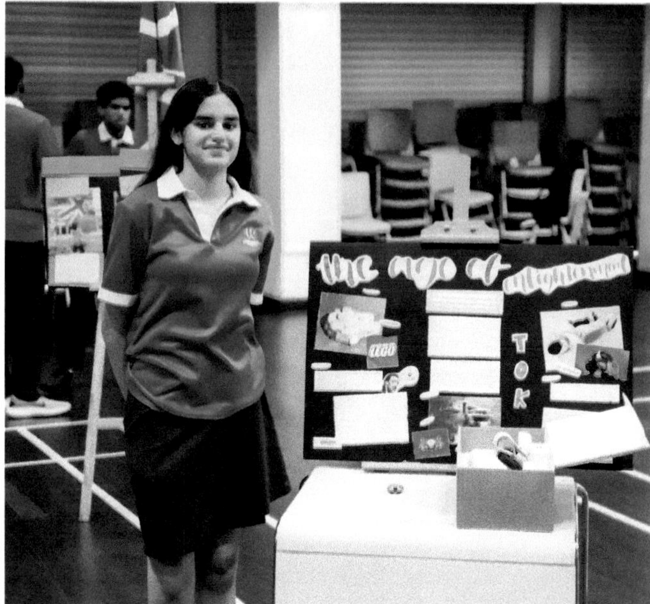

A Thoughtfully-priced Education, A Lifelong Impact
One World International School Nanyang Campus offers a rigorous, developmentally-appropriate IB education at a thoughtfully priced fee structure. Our IB curriculum combines a personalised approach with international standards, focusing on nurturing the natural love of learning within every child. Research has repeatedly demonstrated that for children to thrive academically, they must be engaged and enthused about their learning. At OWIS, our carefully designed curriculum incorporates hands-on learning experiences within a supportive environment to prepare students to become the leaders of tomorrow.

A truly international learning environment
OWIS Nanyang brings together students from over 60 nationalities with a diverse staff. Children have the opportunity to learn and discover in an international environment that prepares them for our global society. As part of our programme, we are committed to providing all students with opportunities to learn other languages with a particular focus on Mandarin across the whole school.

A holistic learning environment
Students at OWIS have access to a future-ready curriculum that not only sets them on the path of academic excellence, but also emphasises the importance of holistic development. Children are nurtured within and outside the classroom environment with rich and varied opportunities to learn sports, perform on stage and work with hands-on projects that stimulate their love of learning.

At OWIS, we understand the importance of personalised learning with each child being given individualised attention and feedback. Our classes, therefore, are capped at 24 students to maintain a small and inclusive environment and ensure that each child receives the attention they need to thrive academically, emotionally and socially. The deep relationships that our teachers develop with their students help to create a welcoming, safe environment for every child to succeed.

Access to the latest in technology and education
Society has rapidly become dominated by digital technology and students today need to be given appropriate opportunities to embrace these technologies. At OWIS, we believe that students should have access to this technology under the guidance of their teachers who carefully consider how and when to incorporate it into the teaching and learning. Our focus is to enhance every child's creativity, communication skills and technical skills. The OWIS values of being "One with the World" provide a balanced, rigorous educational experience that nurtures lifelong learners, unique thinkers and future leaders.

Overseas Family School

Overseas Family School

Head of School Vanessa McConville **MYP coordinator** Adelaida Blat Palacios **DP coordinator** Trapti Trivedi **Status** Private **Boarding/day** Day **Gender** Coeducational **Language of instruction** English **Authorised IB programmes** MYP, DP **Age Range** 2 – 18 years	**Fees** Pre-K1 (Half Day): S$17,200 Pre-K1 (Full Day) & Pre-K2: S$28,400 K1-K2: S$32,400 Grades 1-5: S$35,100 Grades 6-8: S$37,500 Junior High School (Grades 9-10): S$42,500 Senior High School (Grades 11-12): S$44,800 **Address** 81 Pasir Ris Heights Singapore **519292 | SINGAPORE** **TEL** +65 6 738 0211 **Email** enquiry@ofs.edu.sg **Website** www.ofs.edu.sg

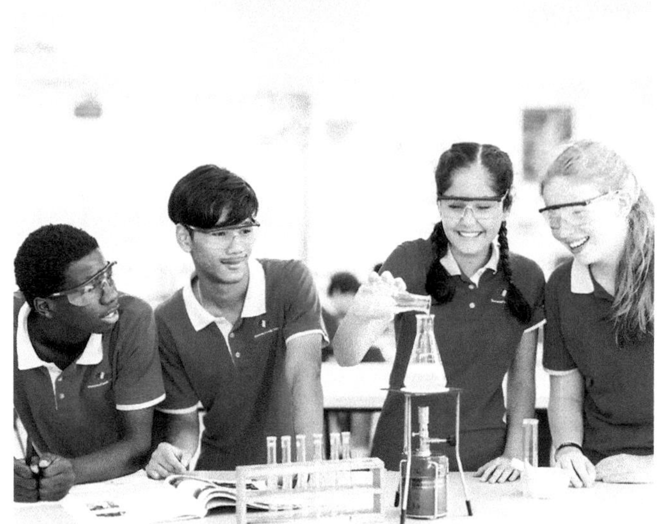

Established in 1991, Overseas Family School (OFS) is a Pre-K to Grade 12 international school that serves a vibrant multicultural community of approximately 65 nationalities. With a beautiful, modern campus located in the eastern part of Singapore, OFS is accredited by Western Association of Schools and Colleges (WASC) and offers the International Early Years Curriculum (IEYC) for Pre-K1 (2 years old) to K2, the International Primary Curriculum (IPC) for Grades 1 to 5, and the International Baccalaureate (IB) for Grades 6 to 12. Students can also pursue the Cambridge International General Certificate of Secondary Education (IGCSE).

At OFS, students learn and grow in a dynamic, diversity rich environment promoting personal initiative, intellectual curiosity and respect for different perspectives. Academic programs at OFS are rigorous and thoughtfully-designed. OFS' highly-acclaimed International Baccalaureate Middle Years and Diploma Programmes (IB MYP and IB DP) immerse students in a wide range of stimulating course offerings designed to help them make practical connections between their learning and the outside world. Because we believe that every student can succeed, OFS students are not preselected into the Diploma programme. Any student who wishes to pursue the IB Diploma programme is allowed and encouraged to do so, making this one of the most inclusive IB Diploma programmes offered in Singapore. We take great pride in our students' academic achievements. With a 98% pass rate, our students' IB results well surpass world averages and the school has consistently produced students scoring a perfect 45 points year after year. Approximately 37% of the diplomas awarded every year are also prestigious IB Bilingual Diplomas, reflecting the exceptional language resources and support available at OFS. The school's extraordinary language acquisition programs support students in their learning journey. Our Study Preparation Program (SPP) is best-in-industry for rapid English language acquisition, while our Mother Tongue Program is the most extensive amongst international schools in Singapore, with 14 different languages on offer. This thoughtful attention and dedicated support, provided at no additional cost, allows many students joining OFS or returning home to quickly progress and join mainstream classes without losing an academic year.

To support the holistic development of students, OFS also encourages broad participation in the arts, sport and other extracurricular activities (ECAs). A wide array of ECAs are open to all students and provide many opportunities to explore interests, join teams and leadership groups, and contribute to the local community. Through our Competitive Sports programme (OFS Tigers) and Enrichment Programme OFS students also enjoy access to an exciting variety of sports ranging from swimming and gymnastics, to badminton, basketball, touch football and sailing at the recreational or competitive skill levels.

QSI International School of Haiphong

(Founded 2005)

Head of School
Dan Owen

DP coordinator
Spencer Sammons

Status Private

Boarding/day Day

Gender Coeducational

Language of instruction
English

Authorised IB programmes
DP

Age Range 2 – 18 years

Address
Lot CC2, Me Linh Village
Anh Dung Ward, Duong Kinh
District
Haiphong | **VIETNAM**

TEL +84 31 381 4258

Email
haiphong@qsi.org

Website
haiphong.qsi.org

QSI International School of Haiphong is nestled in the quiet Me Linh Village, a small residential community in the south of the city of Haiphong. Here, 220 students from Preschool through Graduation gather together to learn daily.

The school, in operation since 2005, has recently moved to its current campus where it offers two new purpose-built buildings that include an Elementary library, a Middle School-Secondary library, a science laboratory, a music exploration room, a black-box theatre, full-service cafeteria, an early childhood center, and classrooms outfitted to provide cutting-edge 21st century learning experiences. In addition to swimming pool and tennis court access, extra-curricular facilities include a turfed soccer field as well as an outdoor court for basketball, volleyball, and badminton.

QSI International School of Haiphong is accredited through the Middle States Association of Colleges and Schools (MSA), an accrediting body from the United States. Last year, the school also received its verification to join the International Baccalaureate Organization.

The school offers students both the opportunity to take the full IB Diploma or certificate courses. Beyond the IB Core classes (Theory of Knowledge, Community Activity Service, and the Extended Essay), we offer Language & Literature, Physics, Mathematics, Theatre, Music, Chinese ab initio, and History. For students who have a desire to take courses that we do not currently offer on campus, we have access to Pamoja online, which provides students with additional IB course options in a distance-learning format. As we continue to grow our program, in addition to our IB team, we will continue to add more course options to be taught in person.

QSI International School of Shenzhen

(Founded 2000)

Director
Claire Berger

Secondary Director of Instruction
Erin Burnett

DP coordinators
Matt Storey & Jeremy Zhang

Status Private

Boarding/day Day

Gender Coeducational

Language of instruction
English

Authorised IB programmes
DP

Age Range 2 – 18 years

Number of pupils enrolled
1100

Address
5th Floor, Bitao Building,
8 Tai Zi Road
Shekou
Shenzhen, Guangdong
518067 | CHINA

TEL +86 755 2667 6031

Email
shenzhen@qsi.org

Website
shenzhen.qsi.org

QSI International School of Shenzhen is a private, nonprofit preschool through Secondary IV co-ed, college-preparatory, day school. It was founded in 2001 to provide a quality education in English for the children of expatriates in Shenzhen. The school is part of Quality Schools International, a consortium of nonprofit international college-preparatory schools with American style curriculum. It is fully accredited by the Middle States Association of Colleges and Schools (MSA) and is a member of the East Asian Council of Overseas Schools (EARCOS) and the Association of China and Mongolia International Schools (ACAMIS).

QSI International School of Shenzhen believes in a personalized approach to instruction leading to mastery of clearly defined objectives within a positive and enjoyable learning environment. It offers a challenging academic curriculum for students age 2 through Secondary IV and utilizes the Mastery Learning model of instruction. This model results in students learning more information compared to traditional school methods in which students receive a percentage grade and then move on. As a Mastery Learning school, we care about our students mastering 100% of their course content because we believe that any gaps in learning, if left unchecked, turn into deficits, difficulties, and frustrations in learning in the future. Therefore, QSI teachers work with students until all course content is mastered and allow students to use time as a resource, instead of a limiting factor, in their classroom.

Success for All is the motto of Quality Schools International. Research indicates that successful people have developed personal orientations that lead to success, and these character traits are at least as important as the knowledge one learns and the competencies one gains through classroom instruction. The Success Orientations are actively encouraged and taught in virtually all areas of the QSI school curriculum with the view of making them a vital part of one's life pattern. QSI promotes trustworthiness, responsibility, aesthetic appreciation, concern for others, kindness and politeness, independent endeavor, and group interaction as character traits that are necessary for personal success beyond the classroom.

QSI International School of Shenzhen is proud to participate in the IB Diploma Programme and continues to offer one of the top IB programs in the area. With scores consistently higher than the world average, our graduates are well-prepared for success at university, and joined with QSI's holistic approach to education our graduates are also prepared for success in life.

Queensland Academy for Science Mathematics and Technology (QASMT)

Queensland Academy for Science Mathematics and Technology

(Founded 2007)

Principal
Ms Kathryn Kayrooz

MYP coordinator
Ms Kirsten Baker

DP coordinator
Dr Esme Hatchell

Status State

Boarding/day Day

Gender Coeducational

Language of instruction
English

Authorised IB programmes
MYP, DP

Age Range 12 – 18 years

Number of pupils enrolled
1258

Address
78 Bywong Street
Toowong
QLD 4066 | AUSTRALIA

TEL +61 7 3377 9333

Email
admin@qasmt.eq.edu.au

Website
qasmt.eq.edu.au

Queensland Academy for Science Mathematics and Technology (QASMT) is located in Brisbane's inner west, and is a Queensland state school for highly capable students in Years 7 to 12. QASMT inspires high achieving students through exclusively offering the International Baccalaureate Middle Years Programme (IB MYP) and Diploma Programme (IB DP).

In conjunction with the University of Queensland and other leading universities, QASMT offers an enriched program to enhance the development of students with an interest and ability in the STEM fields of Science, Mathematics and Technology.

QASMT students achieve outstanding academic results and have a proven record in attaining offers to some of the world's most prestigious universities. Our school consistently has the largest cohort graduating with an IB Diploma in Australia. The QASMT average IB score for 2022 was 38.71, with over 94% of graduates exceeding the world average Diploma score (32.39), and 100% of our students attained an IB Diploma.

Underpinning our academic success is an outstanding pastoral care system which ensures every student feels a part of the QASMT 'family'. Student welfare is implemented through a Mentor Program assisting all students to reach their potential.

We believe in the importance of guiding students to become responsible and caring individuals, who are sensitive, open-minded and respectful of all cultures. QASMT aims to develop tomorrow's leaders; individuals who are internationally minded world citizens.

We develop students' abilities to research, investigate and reflect on local and global matters. The relationship between the students and teachers is based on intellectual challenge and interdependent inquiry.

Our campus and facilities are world standard. Our state-of-the-art STEM and Languages Precincts opened in 2020, and provides dynamic use and enhancement of our learning environments. A central hub of the Academy, our Research Centre, provides innovative learning spaces, such as the Robotics and Digital laboratories and 3D printing Makerspace, quiet individual study nooks and collaborative learning areas with up-to-date e-resources. Students enjoy the benefits of working in wireless learning spaces with computer network access from all work and recreation areas. In addition, we have virtual classrooms, an observatory, and extensive recreational and sporting facilities. Students also enjoy the contemporary university style lecture theatre and large auditorium, plus well equipped music and art rooms.

For more information, please visit our Virtual Academy Tour at: https://qasmt.eq.edu.au/enrolments/virtual-tour

QASMT is located at 78 Bywong Street, Toowong, Brisbane; a convenient ten-minute drive from Brisbane CBD with excellent access to train and bus transport.

Principal
Patrick Gale

DP coordinator
Catherine Brandt

Status State

Boarding/day Day

Gender Coeducational

Language of instruction
English

Authorised IB programmes
DP

Address
564 East Coast Road
Mairangi Bay
Auckland 0753 | NEW ZEALAND

TEL +64 9 477 0150

Email
info@rangitoto.school.nz

Website
www.rangitoto.school.nz

This world-class institution is the largest school in New Zealand with over 3000 students, and is perhaps the most internationally acclaimed New Zealand school. Rangitoto's success is the result of expert teaching in a wide range of academic subjects and extensive extra-curricular opportunities including music, dance, drama and over 40 different sports. The facilities, passionate staff and culture of excellence inspire students to become the best they can be.

Rangitoto has a focus on diversity and has around 50 different nationalities in the school. Our IB students have been accepted into some of the world's best universities, including Cambridge and Oxford in the UK, and Princeton in the USA.

Rangitoto College is located on the beautiful, safe North Shore of Auckland, New Zealand. The school is close to beaches, parks, shops and cinemas, and is about 25 minutes from downtown.

Rangitoto College has some of the best facilities in the Southern Hemisphere including: modern classrooms, a library and information centre featuring senior study and reading rooms, computer access for all students, an auditorium, an Olympic standard all weather hockey turf, three gymnasiums and a weights room, an all-weather athletics track, five sports fields. A purpose built Science block with laboratories for Physics, Chemistry, Biology and Electronics. An English block featuring television and film studios and drama rooms, a music block with practice and performance space. A new dance studio with sprung floor, and a large modern swimming pool and sports institute on the school boundary.

Rangitoto College has been hosting international students for over 15 years and we have developed excellent systems to help students adapt to life in a new country. First language support is available for Korean, Chinese and Spanish speaking students.

A dedicated team of non-teaching and teaching staff, the IB Diploma co-ordinator and a Deputy Principal takes care of our IB students, meeting with them regularly to check they are doing well academically and personally.

(Founded 1901)

Principal
Mrs Anne Johnstone

PYP coordinator
Mrs Anne Gruenewald

DP coordinator
Ms Monique Connor

Status Private

Boarding/day Mixed

Gender Female

Language of instruction
English

Authorised IB programmes
PYP, DP

Number of pupils enrolled
1425

Fees
AUS$22,620 – AUS$37,040 per annum

Address
10 Henry St,
Gordon NSW (Sydney)
NSW 2072 | AUSTRALIA

TEL +612 9498 9898

Email
admin@ravenswood.nsw.edu.au

Website
www.ravenswood.nsw.edu.au

Since its foundation in 1901, Ravenswood has embraced a strong tradition of academic excellence with an emphasis on holistic education. As a proudly non-selective school from Prep to Year 12, we are committed to being at the forefront of education and wellbeing for girls, aiming to ignite the potential of every student – inspiring her passion and purpose to lead her most meaningful life.

Ravenswood is a Uniting Church school, governed by a Christian ethos and our guiding principles of Excellence, Respect, Courage, Optimism and Compassion. Our motto is *semper ad meliora* – Always towards better things.

Ravenswood offers the International Baccalaureate Diploma Programme (IBDP) to students in Years 11 to 12. Ravenswood is also one of few schools in Australia to offer the International Baccalaureate Bilingual Diploma.

Ravenswood's IBDP cohort grows each year and the School's results are always excellent. Our students have achieved perfect scores of 45 for the last six years running. In 2022 alone, four Ravenswood students achieved perfect scores in the International Baccalaureate (IB) Diploma Programme. This is the highest number of perfect scores achieved by a Ravenswood cohort since the commencement of the IB Diploma Programme at the school in 2005.

Ravenswood also launched its innovative new pre-kindergarten offering in 2021, featuring a curriculum infused with the School's own award-winning Positive Education and wellbeing approach, combined with the IB Primary Years Programme (PYP), and the Reggio Emilia philosophy. The result is a Prep learning experience that is student-centred and inquiry-based, encouraging student wonder, empathy, creativity, independence and collaboration.

As one of the first Visible Wellbeing schools in NSW, Ravenswood has embedded evidence-based positive education strategies into the curriculum, recognising that learning and well-being are inextricably linked.

For the last six years, we have been recognised by The Educator as one of Australia's most innovative schools and named 'a school to watch' in the areas of Science, Technology, Engineering and Mathematics (STEM) and Positive Education.

Ravenswood Principal Mrs Anne Johnstone was also selected in 2022 and in 2023 consecutively for *The Educator Hot List* due to her positive impact in the education sector over the past 12 months, her demonstration of expertise in linking theory and practice, and for designing and implementing innovations that provide students with high-quality educational experiences.

In 2023, Mrs Anne Johnstone was named as one of Australia's Most Influential Educators by The Educator. Ravenswood also received four Excellence Awards in the 2022 Australian Education Awards for *Principal of the Year, Boarding School of the Year, Primary School Teacher of the Year,* and, for the second year running, *Best Student Wellbeing Program.*

The innovative Ravenswood Positive Education and wellbeing approach is multi-layered. This runs from the Principal, who is an internationally recognised leader and sought-after speaker in the area of youth wellbeing,

through to class teachers, Mentors, Year Coordinators, the School Chaplain, Psychologists, Health Care unit, the Learning Enrichment team, Head of Positive Education, Head of Senior School, Deputy Principal (Boarding, Wellbeing and Development), and Daisy and Penny, the two therapy dogs – who provide a framework of wellbeing support, guidance and advice for all students. It comprises bespoke curriculum lessons to teach the theory of Positive Education and wellbeing strategies, mentor group sessions, a comprehensive network of student support and wellbeing initiatives, and innovative wellbeing spaces on campus, as well as in the Residential College, Ravenswood's boutique boarding house.

Ravenswood girls have access to more than 100 diverse co-curricular choices designed to extend their development beyond the classroom including gymnastics, snow sports, public speaking and debating, dance and music to name a few. Ravenswood girls also enjoy co-educational opportunities in partnership with our brother school, Knox Grammar School, including army cadets, careers, musical performances and service activities.

Ravenswood girls enjoy the benefits of award-winning world-class facilities including the Mabel Fidler Building, state-of-the-art Learning Resources Centre and Petre Innovation Centre. The Centenary Centre features a performing arts auditorium, music centre, open exhibition space and dance studios. The indoor sports and recreation centre includes a strength and conditioning facility and a 25-metre heated indoor swimming pool and diving apparatus. Ravenswood's beautiful Senior Learning Centre, nominated at the World Architecture Awards for its design and use of colour to create an innovative educational and wellbeing learning space, is a forward-thinking 21st-century learning space designed to provide both flexible academic spaces and relaxation areas for our Years 11-12 students. In 2023, the trailblazing Wellbeing Path, an 800-metre continuous loop within the campus perimeter, was opened. It provides an opportunity for students and staff to enjoy the benefits of exercising in nature which supports physical and mental health.

(Founded 1884)

Principal
Mr Sean Corcoran

DP coordinator
Darren Taylor

Status Private

Boarding/day Day

Gender Coeducational

Language of instruction
English

Authorised IB programmes
DP

Age Range 3 – 19 years

Address
272 Military Road
Cremorne
NSW 2090 | AUSTRALIA

TEL +61 2 9908 6479

Email
dtaylor@redlands.nsw.edu.au
registrar@redlands.nsw.edu.au

Website
www.redlands.nsw.edu.au

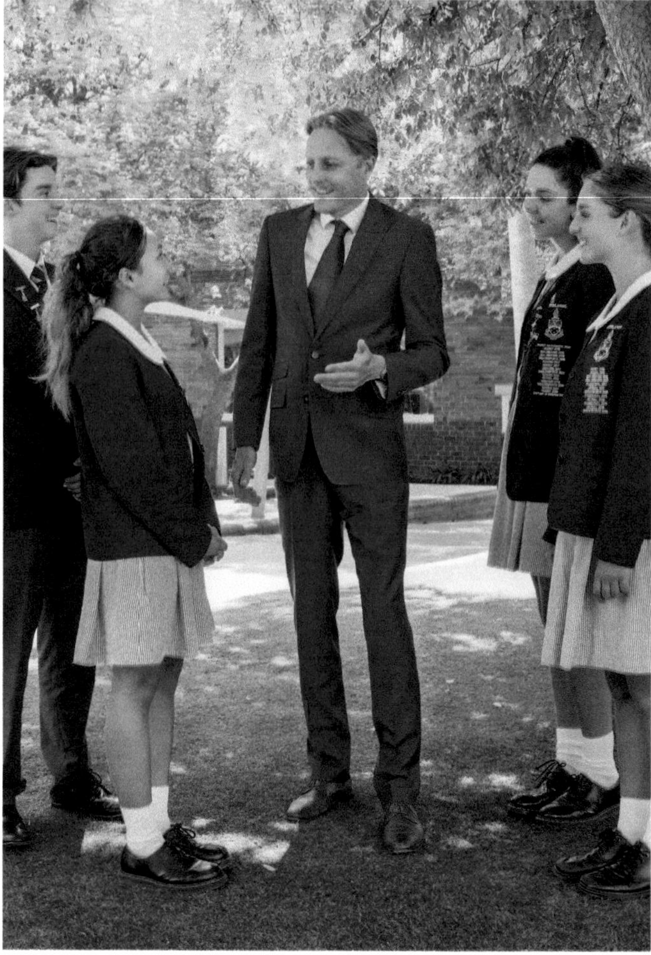

Redlands is a leading Australian independent school that offers a contemporary real world education, fostering academic excellence and confidence for life.

We have offered the International Baccalaureate Diploma Programme for Years 11-12 since 1988, longer than any other school in New South Wales. The 30-year association with the IB has helped the school build its reputation as a leading provider of a well-rounded global education.

Redlands provides an extensive range of opportunities – academic, sports, creative, outdoor education, service – for students to learn, to achieve and to develop their unique skills and talents.

The rich and balanced education programme is aimed at developing well-rounded, confident and compassionate young adults who are prepared for life after school, ready to meet challenges and embrace opportunities and change in the 21st century.

Our students work together within an inclusive, real world, coeducational environment, complemented by a comprehensive leadership and service programme, to develop the knowledge, capability and confidence to let their light shine – at school and beyond.

At Redlands students receive an outstanding academic education as a result of the school's individual approach, committed teachers and world-class learning programmes and resources.

In embarking on the IB Diploma Programme at Redlands, students will commit themselves to:

- a two-year journey of discovery and self-awareness;
- an experience that will be ultimately both rewarding and empowering; and
- an outcome that will enable a smooth transition between school and university.

As a non-selective school, students who come from over 30 different countries have the opportunity to study for the IB Diploma Programme if they so wish. Careful guidance is undertaken in considering course structure and styles of learning to assist students in making the right choice for them. Each year approximately 50% of Redlands students select the IB.

Redlands IB Results

- In recent years, 15 Redlands students have achieved the perfect IB score – 45/45, putting them in the top 0.2% of IB Diploma Programme students worldwide.
- In 2022, 66% of candidates achieved an IB score of 37+, equating to an ATAR of 95 and above.
- Over the past ten years, a number of candidates were awarded rare bilingual diplomas – in French, German, Italian, Chinese, Japanese, Korean, Dutch, Danish, Swedish and Spanish.

At Redlands, all components of the IB Diploma Programme are delivered by a strong team of IB teachers, including moderators in their subject areas, IB trained workshop leaders and experienced teachers.

For more information about Redlands please contact the Registrar or visit our website: www.redlands.nsw.edu.au.

REGENTS INTERNATIONAL SCHOOL
PATTAYA
A NORD ANGLIA EDUCATION SCHOOL

(Founded 1994)

Principal
Ms. Amos Turner-Wardell

Assistant Head of Secondary & Sixth Form
Lauren Hucknall

Status Private

Boarding/day Mixed

Gender Coeducational

Language of instruction
English

Authorised IB programmes
DP

Age Range 2 – 18 years

Number of pupils enrolled
1000+

Fees
THB372,000 per annum

Address
33/3 Moo 1, Pong
Banglamung
Chonburi
20150 | THAILAND

TEL +66 (0)93 135 7736

Email
admissions@regents-pattaya.co.th

Website
regents-pattaya.co.th

About Our School

Regents International School Pattaya is like no other school in Thailand. As part of the global family of more than 80 premium Nord Anglia schools located around the world, we provide unique learning opportunities far beyond the ordinary. We are an exciting, vibrant and inclusive school which has something to offer to every child and every family in our dynamic and diverse community.

We have 1000+ students aged from 2 to 18, spread across our Early Primary, Primary and Secondary schools, including around 50 boarding students. We are an inclusive school that continues to celebrate consistently high academic results in both the IGCSE and IBDP, and cares for the wellbeing of our students so they leave us with everything they need for success, whatever they desire to be or do in life. We are the most successful school on the Eastern Seaboard with a long-established reputation for almost 30 years. Our students are successful because our approach encourages children to think for themselves, how to question, how to learn – skills that will last them for a lifetime.

Regents is the leading school on the Eastern Seaboard for good reason. We have joined forces with the world famous The Juilliard School in New York, and we also collaborate with the prestigious Massachusetts Institute of Technology (MIT) as well as UNICEF. As well as being part of the Nord Anglia family of schools, who provide an outstanding education to over 80,000 students around the world, we are also proud to be a Round Square school, offering unique opportunities for our students to take part in many exciting global projects.

Boarding

We provide a safe, friendly and active boarding community with the emphasis on continued learning. We provide opportunities to collaborate, study independently, have fun, be active and have a sense of adventure. Our boarders develop into confident, independent, resilient and caring individuals who will make the world a better place. The outstanding range of learning opportunities and new environments to discover in Thailand and in South East Asia, make the boarding experience here so much richer and better value-for-money when compared with boarding schools in other parts of the world.

We Invite You to Experience It For Yourself

Choosing the right community and learning environment for your child is an important decision. We hope you agree that Regents is not only a fabulous school but also the right school for you and we look forward to welcoming you into our family.

Ritsumeikan Uji Junior and Senior High School

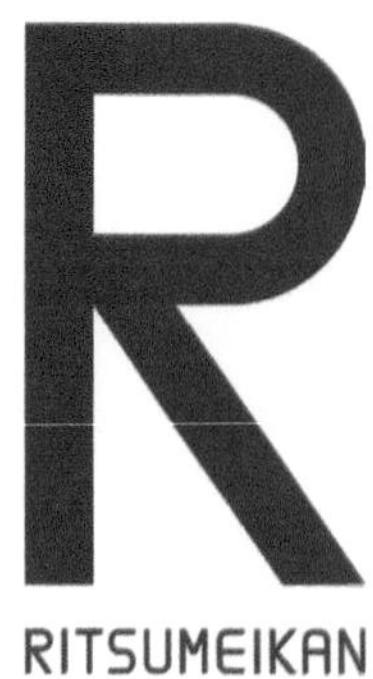

(Founded 1994)

Principal
Ms Noriko Ochi

DP coordinator
Matthew Thomas

Status Private

Boarding/day Mixed

Gender Coeducational

Language of instruction
English, Japanese (IBDP in English)

Authorised IB programmes
DP

Age Range 12 – 17 years

Number of pupils enrolled
1757

Fees
IB course: ¥1,950,000 per annum
IP course: ¥1,300,000 per annum

Address
33-1 Hachikenyadani
Hirono-cho
Uji, Kyoto, Kansai
611-0031 | JAPAN

TEL +81 774 41 3000

Email
ib-info@ujc.ritsumei.ac.jp

Website
en.ritsumei.ac.jp/uji

About

Ritsumeikan Uji Junior and Senior High School is located in scenic Uji City, within a short distance of Kyoto and Osaka. The school is mixed boarding and day, coeducational, and offers an integrated six-year curriculum. Ritsumeikan Uji High School was established in 1994 as an affiliated school of Ritsumeikan University, one of the largest and most prestigious universities in Japan. The school was rebuilt in its current location in 2002 and established a junior high school in 2003.

IP Course

Beginning in April 2021, the IP Course has been designed to provide Japanese returnees and foreign students with an authentic Japanese educational environment, while engaging in a rigorous core of academic subjects taught in English by experienced International Baccalaureate teachers. IPC homerooms are managed by Japanese and English speaking IB staff, where students can enjoy learning a variety of Japanese cultural traditions as well as core IB curricular elements such as the Approaches to Learning. On completion, students will have an intimate understanding of life in Japan, as well as the knowledge, skills and maturity to find success in our senior high school IB Course.

IB Course

Since our authorisation in 2009, Ritsumeikan Uji's English language IB Course has endeavoured to provide the highest levels of guidance and support for the academic and personal growth of our multicultural student body. Our course structure guarantees students the chance to graduate with a bilingual International Baccalaureate diploma, as well as the Japanese high school certificate. Our IB Course prides itself on small class sizes, individualised care, and an inclusive learning community, guided by a team of experienced and committed staff. With their cultural fluency and world class educational backgrounds, our graduates go on to study at top Japanese institutions as well as prestigious schools overseas including Duke University, Imperial College London, Harvard University, the National University of Singapore and many others.

C Building

The Ritsumeikan Uji IB Course recently moved into the new, specially designed C Building on the Uji campus. The new building houses two fully equipped laboratories, an art studio, collaborative and private study spaces, and a large common lounge area. C Building integrates harmoniously with neighbouring parkland to provide students with a peaceful environment for reflection and focused study.

Events

Our community calendar is full of events, including the annual culture and sports days, as well as supervised trips to destinations across Japan and internationally. These shared experiences strengthen our community and enable IBDP students to broaden their world view.

Boarding

High school students are welcome to stay in our dormitory throughout their three years of study. The dormitory provides meals, wireless internet, has a direct bus to campus, and is an easy walk to the city centre of Uji.

Ruamrudee International School

(Founded 1957)

Head of School
Dr. James O'Malley

DP coordinator
Ms. Nicole Sabet

Status Private, Non-Profit

Boarding/day Mixed

Gender Coeducational

Language of instruction
English

Authorised IB programmes
DP

Age Range 3 – 18 years

Number of pupils enrolled
900

Fees
US$16,310 – US$24,330 per annum

Address
6 Ramkhamhaeng 184
Minburi
Bangkok
10510 | THAILAND

TEL +66 (0)2 791 8900

Email
admissions@rism.ac.th

Website
www.rism.ac.th

Ruamrudee International School (RIS), founded in 1957 by Catholic Redemptorist Fathers, is one of the first international schools in Southeast Asia to be accredited by the Western Association of Schools and Colleges (WASC). An IB World School since 1998, RIS offers a rigorous and extremely successful International Baccalaureate Diploma Programme (38 courses) and is one of the region's only schools to simultaneously offer the Advanced Placement program (14 courses).

RIS features a diverse group of experienced teachers who are passionate, supportive, and experts in their fields; most of whom hold master's degrees or higher. From Pre-K 3 through Grade 12, students benefit from small class sizes; relevant and innovative electives; modern languages; a vibrant performing and visual arts program; and a comprehensive extended day program with creative enrichment opportunities.

Located in the Minburi district of Bangkok along the city outskirts, RIS is less than half an hour from Suvarnabhumi International Airport and is surrounded by a thriving local community. Campus highlights include 21st-century learning spaces, a culinary arts center, recording studio, industrial design studio, a makerspace/robotics lab, and a contemporary boarding residence with a warm, familial feel. The school's lush 29-acre campus and facilities also support one of the largest athletic programs of any international school in Southeast Asia.

In the last few years, RIS IB Diploma students have scored an average of 35, far above world averages, with 2021 and 2022 culminating in highs of 37 and 38 respectively. After graduation, RIS students go on to attend the most prestigious universities in the world, and a close-knit alumni community can be found working as government leaders, diplomats, and researchers; in all branches of medicine; as startup entrepreneurs; in the entertainment and film industries; as professional athletes; and in the fields of AI and design technologies.

At RIS, the community is deeply involved in student-led, service learning-based extracurricular clubs, activities, and committees or in organizing events in support of charities and causes. The IB Theory of Knowledge (TOK) and Creativity, Action, Service (CAS) elements at RIS count as a required Values credit, and by the end of a two-year commitment, CAS students will have assessed authentic needs within the community and collaborated with friends and organizations, developing new skills and connections along the way. These CAS experiences are compiled into an annual school publication, written by the students themselves, aptly titled *Reflections*.

Saint Kentigern College

SAINT KENTIGERN

(Founded 1953)

Principal
Damon Anthony Emtage

DP coordinator
Suzie Tornquist

Status Private, Independent

Boarding/day Mixed

Gender Coeducational

Language of instruction
English

Authorised IB programmes
DP

Age Range 11 – 18 years

Number of pupils enrolled
2250

Address
130 Pakuranga Road
Pakuranga, Auckland
1021 | NEW ZEALAND

TEL +64 9 577 0749

Email
skc_admissions@
saintkentigern.com

Website
www.saintkentigern.com

Welcome to Saint Kentigern College
As strong today as the day the College opened in 1953, the Mission of Saint Kentigern is to provide an education that 'Inspires students to strive for excellence in all areas of life for the glory of God and the service of others'.

Saint Kentigern College delivers a world class education for boys and girls from ages 11 to 18 years old in Auckland, New Zealand. The College is located on a leafy 100-acre campus bordering the beautiful Tamaki Estuary in Pakuranga, Auckland.

Curriculum
Academic success is expected of every student at Saint Kentigern and we challenge our young men and women to excel. An unparalleled range of subjects is taught in modern, specialist facilities. In the final two years of school, the International Baccalaureate Diploma programme is taught by talented educators, who are highly qualified and passionate in their areas of expertise. They are committed to creating an environment that encourages, motivates, and challenges every student to realise their personal potential.

Co-Curricular Activities
Our sports facilities and coaches are among New Zealand's best and we enjoy success in regional and national competitions. We are also deeply committed to the performing arts. Our Drama and Dance students learn in dedicated spaces and perform in a purpose-built performance venue. In addition, our separate Music Centre provides superb, soundproofed facilities for our choral and instrumental enthusiasts.

Boarding
Bruce House, with separate houses for boys and girls, is the place our boarders call home. Boarders are involved in every facet of College life and develop lasting friendships and a strong sense of school spirit. Students from as far afield as Germany, Russia, China, Korea, Thailand and the Pacific Islands come to Saint Kentigern to enjoy the many benefits of studying in New Zealand and to enjoy Saint Kentigern's unique learning environment.

Student Wellbeing
Our students receive the best pastoral care. A dedicated team of teachers and personal care specialists monitor the students' progress socially, academically, and emotionally, ensuring they thrive at school.

Enrolment Enquiries Welcome
We look forward to introducing you to 'A World of Opportunity for Boys and Girls' at Saint Kentigern College in clean, green Auckland, New Zealand.

If you would like more information please contact us by email: skc_admissions@saintkentigern.com or phone us: 0064 9 577 0703.

Sanjay Ghodawat International School

Head of School
Mrs. Sasmita Mohanty

Chairman
Mr. Sanjay D. Ghodawat

DP coordinator
Dr. Bonila Sinha

Status Private

Boarding/day Mixed

Gender Coeducational

Language of instruction
English

Authorised IB programmes
DP

Age Range 16 – 18 years
(boarding from 6)

Address
Gat No. 555
Kolhapur – Sangli Highway
Atigre, Maharashtra | INDIA

TEL +91 231 2689700

Email
principal@sgischool.in

Website
http://www.sgischool.in

The Sanjay Ghodawat International School is one such institute which provides world-class education through the IBDP Curriculum in Southern Maharashtra and the North Karnataka region. At the SGIS, education boasts of a blend of high academic challenges, with a unique approach to enrichment and personal development, to create global citizens committed to lifelong learning. We embrace the attributes of the IB learner profile along with our school values of respect, curiosity, integrity, courage, and kindness.

The IBDP strongly emphasizes the holistic development of a student while attempting to offer a global viewpoint that is compatible with SGIS's own education for a life mission and principles. The IBDP curriculum model gives importance to languages, sciences, individuals and societies, mathematics, and the arts. The core components of the IBDP curriculum are Theory of Knowledge, Extended Essay, and Creativity Activity and Services. We at SGIS are proud of our innovation in education and are constantly developing our programme to cater to the needs of the student community.

The school provides modern, high-tech, bright, spacious classrooms; a well-resourced library, state-of-the-art psychology, science, and technology labs and spacious art, music, and dance studios. We offer a variety of indoor and outdoor sports, including horse riding, archery, rifle shooting, table tennis, and lawn tennis. While Multi-Gym is the biggest attraction, the magnanimous stadium can host international sporting events like cricket, football, and volleyball.

SGIS is sincerely concerned about the wellbeing and health of the students and the faculty. Students can develop close relationships with both, their peers and the highly qualified faculty members, thanks to the close-knit school community. Our academic and emotional support systems enable students to think independently and creatively without constraints. We support advancement and imagination in every aspect of the educational plan. In addition to excelling academically, our students also excel in music, visual arts, and sports. Students practice dedication, leadership, and deep self-reflection through a range of activities (field trips, community service-focused CAS projects, and the TOK retreat).

Our philosophy is based on the belief of diversity, cultural exchange, mutual respect and acceptance. Life at the SGIS boarding is a life-changing experience. A boarding experience can alter your life. Our boarders receive the perfect amount of warmth, attention, and discipline, which helps them develop a sense of independence. With spacious and pleasant living quarters and access to a wide range of extracurricular activities, it offers students a home away from home. At SGIS, the boarding houses have study rooms, common lounges, and quad-sharing rooms. There is a fitness centre where round-the-clock medical assistance is available. Students and their daily requirements are taken care of by our dedicated and knowledgeable house parents and service personnel.

Our status, as an important partner and pioneer in international education, is assured by our continued investments in the calibre and expertise of our staff, as well as by the recent upliftment of our infrastructure and technology.

For more information, visit our website – www.sgisib.in

(Founded 1916)

Headmaster
Mr Graeme Yule

Senior School Principal
Mr Christian Zachariassen

Middle School Principal
Mr Will Struthers

Junior School Principal
Mr Richard Kirk

PYP coordinator
Mrs Rosie Roland

MYP coordinator
Ms Kate Bondett

DP coordinator
Mr Mike McKnight

Status Private

Boarding/day Mixed

Gender Coeducational

Language of instruction
English

Authorised IB programmes
PYP, MYP, DP

Age Range 5 – 18 years

Number of pupils enrolled 1104

Address
PO Box 15064, Strathmore, Wellington, 6243 | NEW ZEALAND

TEL +64 4 388 0850

Email enrolments@scotscollege.school.nz

Website
www.scotscollege.school.nz

Scots College was founded in 1916 and provides a world-class, future-focussed education. It is the only co-educational independent school in New Zealand's capital city, Wellington. Scots College's rigorous academic curriculum is supported by a diverse range of sporting, cultural, service and leadership opportunities, enabling each student to reach their potential in all aspects of their lives.

The College is comprised of three schools; Junior, Middle and Senior. It is an authorized IB World School and the IB programmes are an integral part of the school's ethos and curriculum design, developing students prepared to learn for life. The school House system provides another dimension to student life with a Dean and Tutor overseeing an excellent pastoral care system for each student.

Scots Junior School (Years 1-6) provides a safe and caring environment for students to build strong foundations for their future years. The Junior School proudly delivers the IB Primary Years Programme (PYP).

Scots Middle School (Years 7-10) provides a positive and supportive learning environment. Students take specialist classes in science, arts, technology and languages, and are provided opportunities outside the classroom with weekly sporting programmes, service initiatives and an EOTC programme. The Middle School delivers the IB Middle Years Programme (MYP).

Scots Senior School (Years 11-13) prepares students to succeed now and in their futures with the knowledge and skills required for a rapidly evolving workplace. Year 11 students work towards a college-based qualification, the Scots Tohu, which provides a depth and breadth of learning, and is designed to prepare students well for both Level 2 NCEA and the IB Diploma Programme.

A dual pathway is offered in Years 12 and 13 of the IBDP or NCEA qualifications.

Scots College is an internationally minded school with a diverse community which welcomes students from around the globe. An active international services team work closely with the international student community. Language options offered in the curriculum include English, Chinese, French, Spanish and Te Reo Māori.

Outside the classroom Scots is a leader among schools for the quality of its extra-curricular programme. Students are encouraged to try new activities, learn new skills and develop as teams and individuals, and are encouraged to join sports teams and/or cultural activities. In addition, there are a number of specialist academies for high performance athletes including football (soccer), rugby, netball and cricket. The College has a proven track record of assisting top athletes with pathways to US universities.

Scots College is located in Wellington, a harbour city at the heart of government, home to international embassies and renowned for its vibrant city culture and cosmopolitan population of 212,000 centrally, and 500,000 within the region. The campus is located in the suburb of Strathmore, a ten minute drive to the central city. Scots College's boarding house provides accommodation and care for 100 students in a supportive and family orientated environment.

Senior High School at Sakado, University of Tsukuba

Headmaster
Dr. Toshiharu Enomae

DP coordinator
Regina Ver-Santos

Status State

Boarding/day Day

Gender Coeducational

Language of instruction
English, Japanese

Authorised IB programmes
DP

Age Range 15 – 18 years

Number of pupils enrolled
480

Fees
¥800,000

Address
1-24-1 Chiyoda
Sakado, Saitama, Kanto
350-0214 | JAPAN

TEL +81 49 281 1541

Website
www.sakado-s.tsukuba.ac.jp

Senior High School at Sakado, University of Tsukuba (UTSS) is Japan's first "Integrated Course" high school, actively promoting reforms in education and research. In line with the school's mission to provide diverse learning opportunities to students, UTSS is now an IB World School offering the dual language Diploma Programme in Japanese and English.

UTSS is an affiliated Article One high school of the University of Tsukuba. The school campus is located at Sakado, Saitama, approximately an hour from the center of Tokyo, with access through the Tobu Tojo line. Students in the IBDP course of UTSS complete a three-year programme, beginning Year 1 with pre-DP and foundational courses, followed by Years 2 and 3 covering the 6 groups in the IBDP. The high school currently offers the following subjects under the IBDP:

Subjects in Japanese
- Japanese A: Language and Literature (HL)
- History (HL)
- Biology (SL)
- Mathematics AI (SL)

Subjects in English
- English B (HL)
- Economics (SL)
- Theatre (SL)

The core subjects, Creativity, Activity and Service (CAS), Extended Essay (EE) and Theory of Knowledge (TOK) are delivered and supervised in Japanese, however, students have the option to write their EE in English.

The dual-language program requires the students to work in the context of Japanese and English. The curriculum practices and develops reading, speaking, listening and writing skills in both languages, with emphasis on the use of higher order thinking skills.

Students use Japanese and English as a means to understand and express critical and analytical ideas, thus, they are expected to have a solid grasp of both languages.

Even before becoming an IB World School, UTSS has consistently exercised experiential learning through fieldwork, school camps, research, clubs, volunteer work and international student exchange. These activities provide diverse platforms to enrich their learning experiences, and complement the core subjects of the IBDP.

The teachers and staff of UTSS recognize that each student is an individual with unique capabilities and intelligences. The curriculum is designed to encourage and support students in choosing career paths where they will thrive. UTSS graduates are empowered to meet the challenges of a changing world – both local and international.

Scottish High International School

(Founded 2005)

Head of School
Dr Cdr Kartikay Saini

PYP coordinator
Ms Seema Bhati

DP coordinator
Ms Pooja Sharma

Status Private

Boarding/day Mixed

Gender Coeducational

Language of instruction
English

Authorised IB programmes
PYP, DP

Age Range 3 – 17 years

Fees
Fees on request

Address
G-Block, Sector 57
Sushant Lok-II
Gurugram, Haryana
122011 | INDIA

TEL +91 124 4112781-90

Email
avp.admissions@scottishigh.com

Website
www.scottishigh.com

With its distinguished slogan 'Building Personalities, Not Just People', the Scottish High International School, Gurugram, India, stands distinct amidst many. Enterprisingly productive with IB since 2008 (15 Years), Scottish High, the IB World School is going strong with its cosmopolitan vision. Building World Citizens since its inception, it is the institution where the idea of internationalism and inclusiveness has become the way of life.

Housing more than 1600 IB students under one roof, Scottish High International School is a diverse mix of students from across the country and the globe. Looking over the diversity and the infrastructural provisions, one can say that the idea of developing world citizens is rightly justified at Scottish High as the school proudly strives to provide 'one of the best in the world' facilities to the students to foster a consistent and competent climate of international mindedness.

With EOMS ISO 21001:2018 Certification, for Educational Organisation Management System, Scottish High sustains and maintains its proud heritage of quality teaching & learning, occupational health & safety and safe environmental practices through the combined effort of the dedicated students, staff and parents. It is also the first school in India to be associated with this standard to maintain high-quality education.

Curriculum/Examinations offered

Scottish High International School offers:

- IB Primary Years Programme for Nursery to Grade V
- CAIE Secondary I and IGCSE for Grades VI to X
- IB Diploma Programme for Grades XI & XII
- The National Curriculum (ICSE) for Grades VI to X and ISC for Grades XI & XII

Apart from the academic curriculum, Scottish High:

- Has an authorized NCC (National Cadet Corps) wing for boys and girls
- Partners with The Global Education Leadership Foundation (TGELF), which trains young students to cultivate leadership qualities
- Is an authorized centre by CAIE to run the professional development qualifications for teachers
- Is a partner with TAISI, The Association of International Schools of India
- Is associated with Special Olympics, Bharat
- Collaborates with the Govt. of India for research in Autism
- Is an Institutional member of 'The British Council Library', 'The American Center Library', 'The Alliance Francaise De Delhi', 'DELNET' (Developing Library Network)

Facilities:

Structural

- CCTV Secured & Fully Wi-Fi enabled Campus
- A fleet of Air-Conditioned Buses with GPS & CCTV
- 1000 seating air-conditioned dining hall
- 1100 seating air-conditioned auditorium
- Modern medical infirmary with resident doctor and nurses. Fully-equipped with AED, ECG machine, Nebulisers, Inhalers, Ambo Bags, Oxygen Cylinders, and Dental Chair / availability of Emergency Medicines at all times

- Day Care facility handled with professionals
- AV rooms with a seating capacity of 100 people
- IT centre with cutting-edge facilities
- Maximum 25 children in one classroom
- Exclusive 1:12 teacher-student ratio
- Autism research centre
- More than 300 Admin Professionals & Academic staff along with 250 housekeeping, security, drivers & conductors
- Extended Day Boarding – 8:00 am to 4 pm.

Scholastic

- Maths, Science, Social Science, Language, Home Science, IT labs
- Language labs & state-of-the-art activity rooms
- Atal STEM Lab
- CLUBS – Zumba, Photography, Robotics, Astronomy, Bridge Environment
- Special Olympics, MUN, Heritage, Quilling etc.
- State-of-the-art 'Innovation Lab' with hi-tech servers and computers
- Classrooms equipped with audio-visual and computer facilities
- Open shelf library and research centre
- Resource centre for Research & International Curriculum
- Authorized NCC (National Cadet Corps) wing for boys and girls
- Integrated Department for children with special needs
- Spanish, German and French language in addition to English, Hindi & Sanskrit

Sports & Physical Education

- Archery, Gymnastics, Cricket, Soccer, Scuba Diving, Tennis mentored by International level coaches
- Half Olympic size swimming pool / Splash Pool for toddlers

- Highly equipped Indoor Golf Academy with simulators for professional training
- Splash pool with misty sprays for the toddlers
- Badminton, chess, yoga & judo
- Table tennis & Basket Ball
- Skating, Horse-riding Bridge & Taekwondo
- Athletic track and playing field

Admissions open for the next academic year around August/September of the previous year

(Founded 1912)

Head of School
Mr. Colm Flanagan

Elementary School Principal
Damian Prest

Middle School Principal
Justin Smith

High School Principal
Dr. Nancy Le Nezet

PYP coordinator
Michael Lucchesi

MYP coordinator Chris Horan

DP coordinator Piotr Kocyk

Status Private, Non-Profit

Boarding/day Day

Gender Coeducational

Language of instruction
English

Authorised IB programmes
PYP, MYP, DP

Age Range 2 – 18 years

Number of pupils enrolled
1600

Address
39 Yeonhui-ro 22-gil
Seodaemun-gu
Seoul **03723 | REPUBLIC OF KOREA**

TEL +82 2 330 3100

Email
admissions@seoulforeign.org

Website
www.seoulforeign.org

Seoul Foreign School Inspiring Excellence, Building Character – since 1912

Seoul Foreign School is the longest established international school in Korea and one of the first 10 international schools in the world. Founded in 1912, it offers a community of teaching and learning excellence, coming together to educate children at all ages and stages. Seoul Foreign School inspires a passion for learning, pursues academic and creative excellence and is dedicated to the service of others.

An unrivalled legacy is combined with state-of-the-art facilities on our 25 acre campus in central Seoul. With a current population of over 1600 students from more than 55 countries and with many diverse backgrounds, our students are able to learn and grow as truly global citizens.

Four sections, Elementary School, Middle School, High School and the British School, are situated together on a world class campus benefitting from individual space but aligned with one purpose and ethos. Academic, physical and spiritual needs are served across the facilities. Students have the opportunity to participate in various activities – within the school day and in extracurricular time – including many competitive sports, arts, sciences and holistic interests.

Seoul Foreign School is an IB continuum school – a Pre-K to Grade 12 IB World School and additionally Foundation to Year 9 British School. The IB Primary Years Programme and IB Middle Years Programme are offered along with the English National Curriculum and both lead into the IB Diploma Programme. Based on its history of 40 years of IB Diploma Programme, SFS High School provides students an outstanding flexibility allowing 160 combinations of subjects, including unique course offerings in Seoul such as Design & Technology.

Teachers are rigorously selected and their passion, inspiration and academic excellence ensure that students go on to attend prestigious universities and colleges and succeed in all walks of life. Seoul Foreign School is a Christian school for all. Students enjoy an education surrounded by rich heritage in preparation for a future as global contributors.

(Founded 1996)

Director of Schools
Daniel Eschtruth

PYP coordinator
Vincent Lehane

MYP coordinator
Tetsuo Ishii

DP coordinator
Scott Simmons

Status Private

Boarding/day Day

Gender Coeducational

Language of instruction
English

Authorised IB programmes
PYP, MYP, DP

Age Range 2 – 18 years

Number of pupils enrolled
1550

Fees
Day: RMB131,000 – RMB293,000

Hongqiao Campus
1161 Hongqiao Road,
Shanghai **200051 | CHINA**

TEL +86 21 6261 4338

Hongqiao ECE Campus
2212 Hongqiao Road,
Shanghai **200336 | CHINA**

TEL +86 21 6295 1222

Pudong Campus
198 Hengqiao Road,
Zhoupu, Pudong,
Shanghai **201315 | CHINA**

TEL +86 21 5812 9888

Email
admissions@scis-china.org

Website
www.scis-china.org

Established in 1996 as one of Shanghai's first international schools, Shanghai Community International School (SCIS) is a non-profit educational day school, governed by a self-perpetuating board of directors and overseen by the International Schools Foundation.

With over twenty years of rich tradition, SCIS offers a truly unique international experience. The SCIS community is unparalleled, consisting of a diverse mix of outstanding teachers, students, and parents representing over sixty nationalities and thirty-five languages, across six continents. SCIS leverages this unique community to provide a personalized approach to holistic education, ensuring all students have the opportunity to be successful.

SCIS is one of the first international schools in Shanghai to become fully authorized as an International Baccalaureate (IB) Continuum World School, a world class academic program aimed at rigorous critical thinking and global citizenship. This accreditation extends across all SCIS Campuses, including Hongqiao and Pudong, providing a seamless program for students aged 2-18, and comprised of the Primary Years Programme (PYP), Middle Years Programme (MYP), and Diploma Programme (DP).

Primary Years Programme (PYP) prepares students to become active, caring, lifelong learners who demonstrate respect for themselves and others and have the capacity to participate in the world around them. It focuses on the development of the whole child as an inquirer, both within and beyond the classroom. (Age 2-10)

Middle Years Programme (MYP) is a challenging framework that encourages students to make practical connections between their studies and the real world. The MYP is a five-year programme, which can be implemented in a partnership between schools. Students who complete the MYP are well-prepared to undertake the IB Diploma Programme (DP). (Age 11-15)

Diploma Programme (DP) is designed as an academically challenging and balanced program of education with final examinations that prepares students for success at university and life beyond. (Age 16-17)

Shanghai United International School, Gubei/Hongqiao Campus

上海協和双語学校
SHANGHAI UNITED INTERNATIONAL SCHOOL

(Founded 2003)

Principal
Mr David Walsh

PYP coordinator
Jayanthi Nayak

DP coordinator
Ben Griffiths

Status Private

Boarding/day Day

Gender Coeducational

Language of instruction
English

Authorised IB programmes
PYP, DP

Number of pupils enrolled
1985

Gubei Campus
248 Hong Song Road (E),
Gubei,
Minhang District,
Shanghai
201103 | CHINA

Hongqiao Campus
999 Hong Quan Road,
Minhang District,
Shanghai
201103 | CHINA

TEL +8621 51753030

Email
annie.yan@suis.com.cn

Website
www.suis.com.cn

Shanghai United International School was founded in 2003 and was authorized as an IB World School in 2010.

Situated in Shanghai it caters for more than 2,300 students on two campus, Hongqiao and Gubei. Hongqiao Campus offers IB PYP, Gubei Secondary Campus offers Key Stage 3, IGCSE and IBDP.

Students are drawn from more than 40 nationalities, represented across the schools. Close links with nearby Chinese primary and secondary schools allow for rich academic and cultural exchanges leading to the enhancement of the school's signature 'East meets West' characteristic.

At the end of Grade 5, students are bilingual, proficient in both Chinese and English and able to comfortably access the curriculum of their secondary school. Some students use three languages with ease.

Augmenting the academic work of the school is a wide-ranging programme of extracurricular activities catering for the cerebral, the athletic, the artistic and the social aspects of life – hugely supported and enjoyed by the students. The aim of the school is to produce students who are prepared to live life to the full and to contribute to making the world a better place for all.

School facilities include an extensive games field, a 400 seat auditorium, an indoor heated swimming pool, a very large gymnasium and a cultural centre for the benefit of the students (and community at weekends). The range of laboratories and specialist teaching rooms necessary to support the IB programmes are also available.

Staff are recruited from many countries, with the USA, Canada, the UK and Australia being particularly well represented. This staff teaches alongside highly qualified and talented local Chinese teachers to provide a practical cross-cultural pedagogical framework in which students thrive. A comprehensive programme of staff professional development, both locally and internationally, is in place to enhance IB skills and to develop further the expertise of all staff.

Living in Shanghai at the beginning of the 21st century is an extraordinary opportunity for students to be part of a rapidly developing social and economic milieux, with all the benefits and opportunities this possesses. Shanghai United International School is ideally positioned to work with students to maximize their learning in preparation for being truly global citizens.

Introducing Tomorrow's Innovators, Today

SHIV NADAR SCHOOL

Education for Life

(Founded 2012)

Principal Noida: Anju Soni, Gurgaon: Monica Sagar, Faridabad: Anju Wal, Chennai: Padmini Sambasivam

DP coordinator
Noida: Deblina Chakraborty & S R Radhakrishnan, Gurgaon: Sriparna Chakrabarti, Faridabad: Garima Sharma

Status Private

Boarding/day Day

Gender Coeducational

Language of instruction
English

Authorised IB programmes *
DP

Age Range 2.5 – 18 years

Number of pupils enrolled
6000

Noida
Plot No -SS -1, Expressway
Sector 168, Noida, Uttar Pradesh
201305 | INDIA
ibadmissions.noida@sns.edu.in

Gurgaon
DLF City, Phase -1 Block -E,
Pahari Road, Gurugram, Haryana
122011 | INDIA|
ibadmissions.gurugram@sns.edu.in

Faridabad
Sector 82, Neharpar Faridabad,
Faridabad, Haryana **121002 | INDIA**
admissions.faridabad@sns.edu.in

Chennai
Besant Ave Rd, Adyar, Chennai,
Tamil Nadu **600020 | INDIA**
admissions.chennai@sns.edu.in

Website
www.shivnadarschool.edu.in

Introduction:
The Shiv Nadar School (SNS) is an initiative of the Shiv Nadar Foundation in K12 private education, dedicated to delivering educational excellence and offers "Education for Life."
With four campuses in the National Capital Region and one in Chennai, Shiv Nadar School provides students with an environment that challenges them to discover their talents and skills while striving to nurture ethical, respectful, happy, and purposeful citizens of society.

The school follows an experiential pedagogy and integrates technology into its mindful educational practices, keeping the child at the centre of learning while placing significant curricular emphasis on sports, arts, and holistic well-being.
Shiv Nadar School Noida, Gurgaon and Faridabad are IB World Schools accredited for the International Baccalaureate Diploma Programme (IBDP).

Purpose-designed infrastructure: The infrastructure has been purpose-built to reflect Shiv Nadar School's educational ideology, following the best global practices, thus creating a learning architecture to enable students to flourish. Our schools across Noida, Gurgaon and Faridabad have state-of-the-art labs and facilities with dedicated International Curriculum Wings.

Dedicated Career Guidance Centre: Our team of experienced experts specialise in assisting students in selecting career paths that best match their intellect and interests. With diverse initiatives and competent guidance, our students have succeeded in acclaimed universities across 14 countries, including Yale, Cambridge, NYU, Penn State University and many more...

Seasoned and Trained Faculty: Our team of educators delivers exceptional learning experiences with care, knowledge, and passion. All our educators are trained by the International Baccalaureate and attend IB-recognised workshops. Most of them serve as IB examiners and workshop leaders.

Learner-focused pedagogy: Shiv Nadar School offers a rigorous, inquiry-based curriculum that promotes critical thinking and holistic development, including diverse subject combinations. Our initiatives focus on interdisciplinary research to understand and enhance learning mechanisms. We explore motivation, curiosity, knowledge acquisition, retention, mastery, integration, creativity, transfer, and self-efficacy from pre-kindergarten to adulthood. We encourage our students to be intentional about facilitating their purpose, self-understanding, and belonging in the world, preparing them to become well-rounded, responsible global citizens.

**Shiv Nadar Noida and Gurgaon are candidate schools for the Middle Years Programme (IB-MYP). Shiv Nadar School Chennai will be an IB Continuum school in the near future.*

St Andrew's Cathedral School

ST ANDREW'S
CATHEDRAL SCHOOL

(Founded 1885)

Head of School
Dr Julie McGonigle

MYP coordinator
Kathleen Layhe

DP coordinator
Sharon Munro

Status Private

Boarding/day Day

Gender Coeducational

Language of instruction
English

Authorised IB programmes
MYP, DP

Age Range 5 – 18 years

Number of pupils enrolled
1450

Fees
Day: AUS$23,640 – AUS$41,444 per annum

Address
Sydney Square
Sydney
NSW 2000 | AUSTRALIA

TEL +61 2 9286 9500

Email
enrolments@sacs.nsw.edu.au

Website
www.sacs.nsw.edu.au

St Andrew's Cathedral School, an independent Anglican school founded in 1885, has a long history of pursuing excellence in the context of a warm and inclusive community. Our teachers are experts in their chosen fields, deeply committed to the relational nature of teaching and engaged in the character development of every child. Our location, in the heart of Sydney's CBD, enriches our curriculum, allowing students exciting opportunities to engage with significant entrepreneurial and cultural institutions.

Our Academic Programme

We are an International Baccalaureate (IB) World School. Our Middle School students enjoy the real-world richness of being taught the NSW curriculum through the IB Middle Years framework, building critical skills for their later years. Our Senior College students can choose to study either the HSC or the IB Diploma. For schools that offer both IB and HSC the way to measure against other schools is in terms of Australian Tertiary Admission Rank (ATAR). In 2022, our percentage of students with 99+ ATAR was in the top 12 schools, and the percentage with 95+ ATAR was in the top 15 schools. The overwhelming majority of our students pursue university education after graduation, with increasing numbers pursuing overseas study options.

Extracurricular

By secondary school, students can join one of many expeditions offered – hiking from Mount Kosciuszko to the coast, canoeing along the Murray River, mountain biking in New Zealand and back-country skiing and snow camping. Every year, a variety of international tours are offered through various faculties.

You can find out more about us by taking our Virtual tour: https://www.sacs.nsw.edu.au/virtual-tour

Alternatively contact our Enrolments team on +61 2 9286 9579 or by email at enrolments@sacs.nsw.edu.au.

St Andrews International School Bangkok

(Founded 1997)

Head of School
Mr. Paul Schofield

DP coordinator
Mr. William Taylor

CP coordinator
Ms. Faye Wheeler

Status Private

Boarding/day Day

Gender Coeducational

Language of instruction
English

Authorised IB programmes
DP, CP

Age Range 2 – 18 years

Number of pupils enrolled
2200

Fees
Day: THB300,000 – THB800,000 per annum

Primary School
9 Pridi Banomyong 20/1,
Sukhumvit 71,
Phra Khanong Nuea, Vadhana,
Bangkok **10110 | THAILAND**

High School
1020 Sukhumvit Road
Phra Khanong, Khlong Toei
Bangkok **10110 | THAILAND**

TEL +662 056 9555

Email
admissions@standrews.ac.th

Website
www.standrews.ac.th

St Andrews International School Bangkok was founded in 1997 on an attractive, conveniently located site, with excellent facilities and good access to local transportation. Today we are a school of more than 2,200 students representing some 63 nationalities ranging from Nursery (2 years) to Year 13 (18 years). In August 2017 we opened an additional campus at a nearby prime city centre location which delivers state-of-the-art purpose-built learning facilities to our High School.

Our school provides a high-quality, professional, well-resourced learning environment where each child's talents and abilities are recognised and nurtured, and their needs supported. Our teachers are professional and caring, selected for their awareness of the needs of a broad range of children who may come from different social, cultural, religious and educational backgrounds. They are capable educators who take care with their preparation of the curriculum, use a variety of strategies for its delivery and pay close attention to the progression of each individual.

We are an inclusive school that welcomes students of all abilities. To ensure that all our children have an equality of opportunity, we have a professional Learning Support Department. This team works with class teachers to identify and support children in their learning across the school, whether they need extra help with their studies or have been identified as gifted and talented.

The curriculum draws on the best UK practices, adapted to reflect the international context of the school. Students take IGCSE examinations at the end of Year 11 and then follow the Senior Studies Programme in Years 12 and 13. Our school offers the International Baccalaureate Diploma Programme (IBDP), the International Baccalaureate Careers Programme (IBCP), BTEC, alongside an alternative school-based curriculum, all of which leads to graduation and provides the opportunity to apply to prestigious universities all around the world. As part of Nord Anglia Education, the world's leading premium schools organisation, we collaborate with the preeminent performing arts conservatory, The Juilliard School, and one of the world's leading universities, the Massachusetts Institute of Technology (MIT), to bring truly inspiring learning experiences to all of our students.

With high-quality teaching, excellent facilities and small class sizes, St Andrews International School Bangkok offers students the opportunity to fulfil their academic potential in a stimulating, caring and nurturing environment. We are fully accredited by CfBT Education Trust and Thailand's Office for National Education Standards and Quality Assessment (ONESQA), the first school in Thailand to receive this joint accreditation award.

(Founded 1910)

Executive Principal
Mrs Diana Patchett

International Dean
Ms Jo Fogarty

DP coordinator
Ms Beth Rowse

Status Private, Independent

Boarding/day Mixed

Gender Female

Language of instruction
English

Authorised IB programmes
DP

Number of pupils enrolled
850

Fees
International from NZ$46,400 per annum (excluding boarding)

Address
12 Winchester Street
Merivale
Christchurch
8014 | NEW ZEALAND

TEL +64 3 379 2000

Email
enrol@stmargarets.school.nz

Website
www.stmargarets.school.nz

St Margaret's College is one of New Zealand's leading girls' schools with a proud 110-year history of academic, sporting and cultural excellence. An education at St Margaret's College offers a dual academic pathway to leading universities around the world through the International Baccalaureate as well as NCEA, the only girls' school in New Zealand's South Island to do so. Students regularly top both the New Zealand IB and NCEA rankings, opening opportunities at leading international and New Zealand universities.

St Margaret's College values the cultural diversity that students from around the world bring to the school community as they learn to live and lead in a global society. It has played host to thousands of forward-thinking young women and educators over the last century. It leads the way in providing a world-class education in a teaching and learning environment tailored to suit girls while celebrating the traditions of its founding values.

All students are offered a breadth of opportunities where they can shine, unencumbered by gender stereotypes. While academic results are consistently outstanding, it is the variety of curriculum offerings and opportunities available that ensure the interests and learning styles of every girl are catered for. Our international students are completely integrated into school life and, where appropriate, receive additional support in specific areas of the curriculum. Girls come to St Margaret's from many different countries and are actively encouraged to experience and participate in the rich sporting, cultural and social life of the school, Christchurch and Canterbury while studying for the International Baccalaureate Diploma.

The school enjoys the most modern school campus in Christchurch, providing a future-proofed learning environment, including our leading Centre for Innovation and STEM programmes, that attracts high quality teachers and provides students with a safe and inspirational space to learn.

St Margaret's College provides a warm, caring and structured environment in its three boarding houses. The boarding houses are arranged in year groups, tailored to the specific needs of each developmental stage, and provide the opportunity of a first-class education while building strong friendships and learning lifelong values.

St Margaret's College enables girls to make a difference in the world, empowering them to learn, live and lead.

St. Joseph's Institution International

(Founded 2007)

High School Principal
Mr Bradley Bird

Elementary School Principal
Ms Catherine Nicol

DP coordinator
Mr Guy Bromley

Status Private

Boarding/day Mixed

Gender Coeducational

Language of instruction
English

Authorised IB programmes
DP

Age Range 4 – 18 years

Number of pupils enrolled
2000+

Fees
From S$36,686 per annum

Address
490 Thomson Road
Singapore
298191 | SINGAPORE

TEL +65 6353 9383

Email
info@sji-international.com.sg

Website
www.sji-international.com.sg

Established in 2007, St. Joseph's Institution International offers a holistic, values-driven and international educational experience to a diverse student body of over 40 nationalities rooted in the context of Singapore.

As a school with a Lasallian Catholic foundation, our community welcomes students, teachers, parents, friends and supporters of all faiths and cultural backgrounds. We celebrate a community of over 2,000 students across two schools on one campus.

The Elementary School caters to expatriate children from early years Prep 1 – 2 and Grade 1 – 6 (ages 4 – 12), while the High School caters to both Singaporean and international students in Grades 7 – 12 (ages 12 – 18).

As a Lasallian Catholic School, we believe that character education lies at the heart of what we do. On the facade of our main High School building, you will read 'Enter to Learn, Leave to Serve'. That motto describes very clearly the mission of our school: 'Enabling students to learn how to learn and to learn how to live as Lasallian people for others'.

Our core values of Faith, Service, Community, Excellence and Respect are demonstrated daily by all members of the community, be it within the classrooms, playgrounds, theatre, music rooms or sporting facilities.

The IB Diploma Programme

The attributes of the IB Learner profile underpin much of the teaching and learning throughout SJI International with a desire to develop curious, independent and confident learners. The most important principle within the school's educational philosophy is that of active learning. Crucially, active learning is about students doing. This involves a wide range of activities within the programme which will vary according to the subject: research, role plays, simulations, thinking exercises, decision-making exercises, debates, presentations and so on. These provide a stimulating educational environment and one that is intellectually challenging for the students.

Values, education and character-building are achieved through a range of challenging activities in sports, adventure and creativity, with a special emphasis on service, featuring weekly service activities and overseas projects that help students connect with and serve the local and global community.

We are justifiably proud of the outstanding achievements of our IB Diploma students. Many of our graduates have continued their studies at many of the top universities around the world. However, outstanding academic results are only part of what we strive for. Our students leave SJI International ready for lifelong learning.

Stonehill International School

An Embassy Group Education Initiative

(Founded 2008)

Head of School
Joe Lumsden

Primary School Principal
Peter Spartling

Secondary School Principal
Manpreet Kaur

PYP coordinator
Zita Joyce

MYP coordinator
Saba Husain

DP coordinator
Jennifer Browne

Status Private

Boarding/day Mixed

Gender Coeducational

Language of instruction
English

Authorised IB programmes
PYP, MYP, DP

Age Range 3 – 18 years

Number of pupils enrolled 700

Address
Near the International Airport,
No.259/333/334/335
Tarahunise Post, Jala Hobli
Bengaluru, Karnataka
562157 | INDIA

TEL +91 70 2666 6911

Email
admissions@stonehill.in

Website
www.stonehill.in

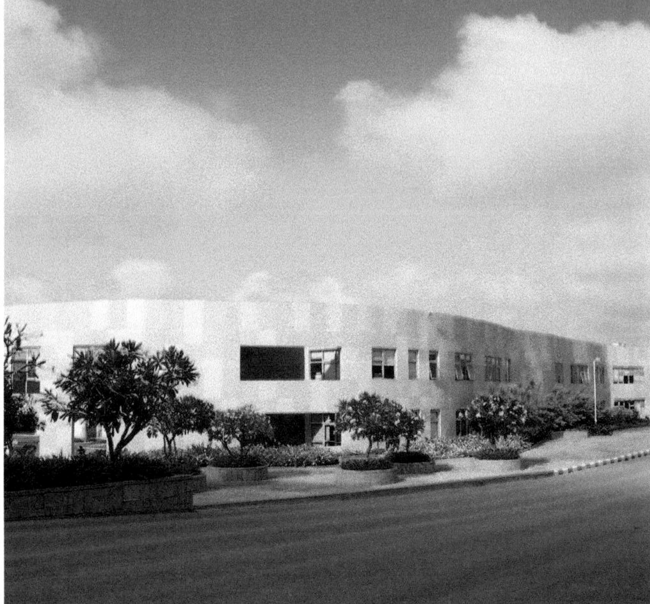

Founded in 2008, Stonehill International School is one of the most widely reputed international schools in Bangalore, India. We are an IB school and are accredited by the Council of International Schools (CIS), and the New England Association of Schools and Colleges (NEASC). Stonehill is also a member of the Australian Boarding Schools Association (ABSA). The expansive 34-acre lush green campus, near the International Airport, offers ample space and infrastructure for sporting, cultural, and leisure activities. Besides state-of-the-art classrooms, the world-class facilities include a 25-metre temperature-controlled swimming pool, synthetic turf football field, tennis and volleyball courts, dedicated buildings for the arts and STEM subjects, a state-of-the-art library, and a multi-purpose sports hall. Stonehill also prides itself on modern boarding houses and a fully equipped cafeteria that serves nutritious and healthy meals.

As a world-class educational institution, Stonehill is a dynamic, inclusive, and friendly day and boarding school. Our students and faculty comprise 35 different nationalities. We are dedicated to our mission statement – "To provide stimulating, engaging academics integrated with enhanced opportunities for technological innovation, sports, and the arts."

University Placement Programme

Our Career and College Counselling Department works with students from Grade 9 onwards to identify their aptitude, understand their interests, and guide them towards colleges that will help them meet their academic and personal goals. Stonehill graduates have been accepted to some of the most prestigious universities across the globe including, Carnegie Mellon University, London School of Economics, UC Berkeley, UCLA, University of Toronto, University of St. Andrews, Imperial College London, Kings College London, University College London (UCL), University of Cambridge, National University of Singapore (NUS), Nanyang Technological University (NTU), University of Amsterdam, Stanford University, MIT, Dartmouth College, NYU, University of Melbourne, University of Michigan Ann Arbor, University of British Columbia, and many more.

English as an additional language (EAL)

Stonehill offers support to non-native English-speaking students. Individual programmes are developed to enable English language acquisition in students. To aid faster learning, EAL students are included in regular classes, as often as possible.

Sports

Through our sports programme, importance is given to not just students' health and fitness, but also to develop skills, learning to work in teams and building leadership and personal growth. Stonehill students also compete regularly with teams from other schools in Bangalore, India, and Asia. Our students have made us proud by demonstrating commitment, great attitude and the spirit of teamwork. Swimming, tennis, equestrian sports, basketball, football, volleyball, and cricket are just a few of our sports offerings.

The Arts

Stonehill prides itself on a committed Arts department with a special focus on Visual Art, Drama, and Music. Stonehill uses the creative arts to promote attitudes such as empathy and appreciation, and skills such as analysis, that help see the uniqueness of each person as well as explore the commonalities that connect each other. We have a dedicated Arts Centre, that has purpose-built spaces for music, visual art, and drama. We also offer private music lessons for instruments such as piano, guitar, drums, violin and cello along with numerous opportunities to perform at concerts, assemblies and other gatherings.

Technology

At Stonehill, we have a 1:1 policy for devices and our students use a wide variety of tools to communicate, collaborate, research, and create. In Primary School, the digital citizenship programme teaches students to be safe and responsible in the online world. They use an all-in-one digital platform for planning, assessments, portfolios, projects, and reports, which they can independently navigate. Learning is supported through the Makerspace where digitally enhanced Lego and robotics work alongside the traditional elements of design, sewing, and construction. Technology in Secondary School is seamlessly integrated into all subjects. Additionally, Product Design, Digital Design, Design Technology, and Computer Science are offered as subjects.

Boarding

Stonehill offers weekly and full-time boarding options to students. The residential programme at Stonehill is for students from Grade 6 onwards, and is designed to extend learning the IB way through academics, extracurricular activities, and the social aspects of boarding. It offers students a home away from home, with spacious and comfortable living areas, and access to a host of extracurricular activities. The small number of boarding students provides a warm atmosphere and creates a sense of community. The boarding houses at Stonehill feature twin and quad-sharing rooms, a common lounge, and a study room. The houses are supported by a cafeteria, a fitness centre, and a 24-hour medical centre. Experienced House Parents, tutors, and service staff take care of children and their individual needs.

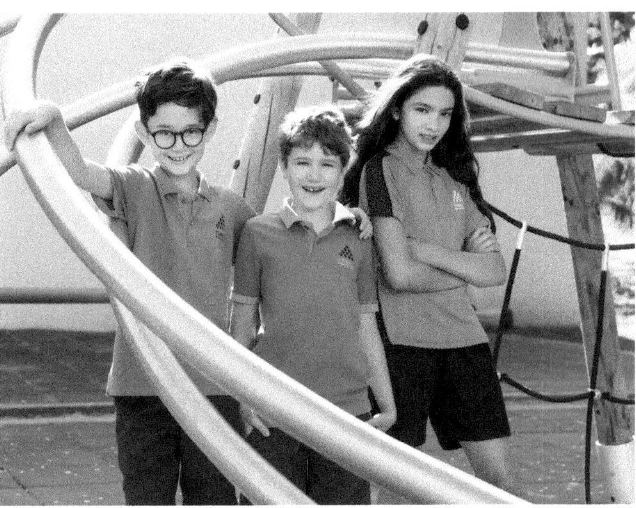

Suzhou Singapore International School

(Founded 1996)

Head of School Samer Khouri

PYP coordinator Katriona Hoskins

MYP coordinator Peter Coats

DP coordinator Dirk van Rooyen

Status Private

Boarding/day Day

Gender Coeducational

Language of instruction English

Authorised IB programmes PYP, MYP, DP

Age Range 2 – 18 years

Number of pupils enrolled 1000+

Address 208 Zhong Nan Street, Suzhou Industrial Park, Jiangsu, **215021 | CHINA**

TEL +86 512 6258 0388

Email information@mail.ssis-suzhou.net

Website www.suzhousinternationalschool.com

Suzhou Singapore International School (SSIS) was founded in 1996 in the Suzhou Singapore Industry Park. It is a fully authorized IB World School as well as the oldest and largest international school in Suzhou, China. Since its establishment, SSIS has grown from 20 students in a few rooms into a school of a 14-hectare campus with 1000+ students from 50 different nationalities.

SSIS offers a challenging curriculum to cultivate global citizens and life-long learners. Everyday students are challenged to actively participate in their education. This produces students that consistently perform well above world averages, and is why SSIS is one of the best schools in China.

Values and Mission

Mission: To provide an excellent international education to the children of expatriate families.

Vision: Encourage and enable students to be self-motivated, lifelong learners, who value other cultures and are responsible, meaningful participants in the international community.

Definition of Learning: Learning is a continuous, transformative, and reflective process, where learners engage with the world and connect meaning to understanding.

Curriculum and Activities

SSIS offers three IB programs including PYP, MYP and DP from preschool to Grade 12 along with a German curriculum in the elementary school. A strong partnership between students, faculty and parents, enables SSIS to maintain a rigorous and challenging education. SSIS offer a wide range of academic, cultural and recreational programs ensuring to deliver the highest quality international education possible. SSIS offers more than 100+ activities, whether it is the visual arts program, showcased by a week-long celebration of the Arts; SSIS Book Week, celebrating global literacy or the much anticipated International Family Day, there is something for everyone. SSIS students also have the opportunity to compete against other peer schools in academics, arts and sports, through its memberships with ACAMIS, SISAC, EARCOS and CISSA.

Accreditations and Affiliations

SSIS is accredited by external agencies including IB (International Baccalaureate Organization), CIS (International Association of Schools), NEASC (New England Association of Schools). SSIS is also a member of the Association of China and Mongolia International Schools (ACAMIS) and the East Asia Regional Council Schools (EARCOS).

Faculty and Staff

SSIS attracts the highest caliber of teachers with masters degrees and doctorates. Faculty is comprised of over 150 dedicated professionals from over 20 countries, each bringing their own unique perspective on teaching and learning.

Campus

Spread across a spacious 14 hectometer campus, the building boasts integrated technology and air purification systems throughout all classrooms and common areas. Art and Performance facilities include 600-seat theater, black box theater, orchestra room, 3 dance studios, individual music practice spaces and art carrels. Recreational facilities include 3 playgrounds, 2 gymnasiums, a new soccer pitch, 400M running track, 25M swimming pool and tennis courts. The Science and Design facilities include fully equipped science, food technology and hard materials labs. The Learning Technology Center includes 500+ ipads, charging stations, green room, podcast facilities and Lego robotics room.

Taipei Kuei Shan School

Head of School
Mr. Erick Cheng

PYP coordinator
Elizabeth Hu

MYP coordinator
Robert Chung

DP coordinator
Steven Hu

Status Private

Boarding/day Day

Gender Coeducational

Language of instruction
Chinese, English

Authorised IB programmes
PYP, MYP, DP

Age Range 4 – 18 years

Number of pupils enrolled 700

Address
200 Mingde Road
Taipei
11280 | TAIWAN

TEL +886 2 2821 2009

Email
info@kss.tp.edu.tw

Website
www.kshs.tp.edu.tw

Taipei Kuei Shan School is an International Baccalaureate World School offering three programmes – PYP, MYP, and DP. It is fully accredited by the Taipei City Government Department of Education and a member of the Association of Christian Schools International.

Kuei Shan was established in 1963 as a K-9 school, founded by Professor Hsiong Hui-Ying as a research project to improve Taiwan Education. Many decades ago, education in Taiwan was a "one-size-fits-all" approach. To allow a holistic development of learners, Professor Hsiong built Kuei Shan as a small school environment with smaller class size to promote active learning, both academically and socially. She practiced the use of unit teaching and theme-based learning to engage students in hands-on and collaborative learning activities. Upon the success of this long-term research, the school continues its commitment to educational research and excellence.

In 2015, the high school program was added, and Kuei Shan's first DP cohort graduated in 2017. As a small private school, we provide a lively campus community for more than 700 students from Pre-Kindergarten to Grade 12 by blending educational excellence and an international perspective with Christian values. About 80% of our student body are Taiwan nationals and 20% are from over 15 other countries.

Our Mission

Kuei Shan's mission is to provide holistic education that is Biblically inspired, academically rigorous, socially friendly, and globally and culturally responsive. Students will be equipped to experience TRUTH:

Transformed: by the renewing of the mind
Rigorous: academic pursuits
United: life-giving community
Twined: heritage with globalization
Holistic: balanced development

Activities and Service

- The school supports students to participate in a Taiwan team sports program which includes basketball, volleyball, soccer, softball, swimming, track & field, and cross-country.
- Students have opportunities to participate in band, string ensemble, choir, worship band, and drama.
- Students have opportunities to conduct a wide range of outreach and community service for underprivileged children and people in need.
- Students participate in student government, scouts, model UN, and Global Issues Network.

Academic Achievement

Our seven cohorts (2017-2023) earned Diploma mean grade and average total points above worldwide average. Students are currently attending four-year universities in various regions – Asia, Australia, Canada, Europe, the U.K., and the U.S.

At Kuei Shan, we celebrate our distinctive place in PreK-12 education – where teaching, learning and faith guide the mind in understanding the complex diversity of God's creation, equip them to experience T.R.U.T.H., and prepare the whole person for service and leadership.

Tanglin Trust School, Singapore

(Founded 1925)

CEO
Mr Craig Considine BA MA

DP coordinator
Joseph Loader

Status Private

Boarding/day Day

Gender Coeducational

Language of instruction
English

Authorised IB programmes
DP

Age Range 3 – 18 years

Number of pupils enrolled
2800

Fees
Nursery to Reception
S$31,695 – S$38,910 per annum
Year 1 to Year 6
S$39,690 – S$41,550 per annum
Year 7 to Year 13
S$46,875 – S$50,865 per annum

Address
95 Portsdown Road
139299 | SINGAPORE

TEL +65 67780771

Email
admissions@tts.edu.sg

Website
www.tts.edu.sg

Established in 1925, Tanglin Trust School is the oldest British international school in Southeast Asia. With over 55 nationalities represented, Tanglin is a vibrant coeducational school that provides British-based learning with an international perspective. Tanglin is the only school in Singapore to offer students the choice to take either A Level or the IBDP programme at Sixth Form, both of which achieve consistently outstanding results. A choice of qualification means each student in Senior School is offered a tailored education. Regular feedback through sharing data and face-to-face parent-teacher meetings are integral to helping students accomplish their academic goals, and for parents to support them on their Sixth Form pathway. Tanglin has an excellent academic reputation. Students' examination results consistently surpass Singapore and global averages, with around 96% of graduates receiving their first or second choice university, which are among the best in the world.

Tanglin believes in providing a holistic education and values the importance of extracurricular activities alongside academic achievement. The co-curricular programme serves as a crucial pathway to broaden students' horizons, presenting them with avenues to explore a diverse range of skills and interests that will support and enhance their studies, and enrich their lives beyond school. Sports and arts are celebrated as part of its extensive CCA programme.

Tanglin's Centenary Building which opened in 2023 is an impressive addition to the school campus, with aspirational facilities designed to benefit the school and wider Tanglin community. Students of all ages now enjoy the Olympic standard gymnasium and swimming pool, 25 metre climbing wall, as well as a state-of-the-art Music Department. Located over two floors, the department is a central music hub for the whole School, where Seniors and Juniors can participate in individual and group lessons, and ensembles and performances can happen. Tanglin recently launched the Centenary Music Scholarship. Open to Senior School students, the scholarship reflects Tanglin's high academic expectations and demonstrates how inspirational learning spaces lead to aspirational learning opportunities. The Centenary Building is also home to The Institute@Tanglin which encourages engagement in meaningful discourse and thought leadership. The forum is designed to promote academic stretch which is required when tackling the challenging IBDP curriculum.

It's no wonder that for the third year in a row, Tanglin was named one of the top 125 private schools globally in the Spear's School Index by Carfax Education and is one of 15 schools selected from the China and Southeast Asia region. All aspects of the school are considered in the selection process. Aside from formal criteria such as academic results and preparation for university entry, schools are selected for their unique ethos, their local and international reputations, and how they prepare future-ready students for the globalised world. The Tanglin 2023 IB cohort is a testament to this award, achieving an average Diploma score of 38.7 points, more than 8.5 points above the world average of 30.2.

The International School of Kuala Lumpur (ISKL)

THE INTERNATIONAL SCHOOL OF KUALA LUMPUR

(Founded 1965)

Head of School
Mr Rami Madani , MA, BSc

DP coordinator
Ms Sarah Mannino, MA, BA

Status Private

Boarding/day Day

Gender Coeducational

Language of instruction
English

Authorised IB programmes
DP

Age Range 3 – 18 years

Number of pupils enrolled
1600

Fees
Day: RM62,500 – RM127,600 per annum

Address
2, Lorong Kelab Polo Di Raja
Ampang Hilir
55000 Kuala Lumpur | **MALAYSIA**

TEL +60 3 4813 5000

Email
admissions@iskl.edu.my

Website
www.iskl.edu.my

The International School of Kuala Lumpur (ISKL) believes that its success today is based on how well it prepares its students for their future. Offering a diverse academic and co-curricular program, ISKL supports learners in exploring and developing the passions, skills, and competencies they need to be future-ready, not only for university and their career but for life itself.

The school is located on a 25-acre, state-of-the-art campus in the heart of Kuala Lumpur and is home to students representing more than 70 nationalities. Students benefit from its robust international curriculum that combines leading North American educational frameworks with global best practices.

ISKL is a fully inclusive school and offers the International Baccalaureate Diploma Programme (IBDP) on a non-selective basis. As the longest-running World IB School in Malaysia, ISKL has seen more than 1,900 students graduate with an IB Diploma over the past 32 years. With IBDP results that are consistently above the world average, ISKL's pass rate of 97% is a testament to the strength of its program and expert international faculty. In 2023, 13% of ISKL students scored 40 or more points, and 23% earned a Bilingual Diploma in Chinese, Dutch, French, Japanese, Korean, and Spanish.

ISKL is one of the only schools in Malaysia offering transdisciplinary pathways that are designed to enable every learner to choose a curriculum best suited to their abilities, interests, and aspirations. In addition to the IBDP, High School options include PRAXIS (Grade 9) and ISKL's Pursuits Program combining individual IB, Advanced Placement, and High School courses for students who want to deep-dive into a specific area. The flexibility of ISKL's academic program enables students to take advantage of higher education opportunities worldwide, as typified by the Class of 2023, which received more than 300 acceptances from over 150 universities in 13 countries.

ISKL is accredited internationally through the Council of International Schools (CIS) and in the United States through the Western Association of Schools and Colleges (WASC). ISKL has a strong focus on service and sustainability across its divisions and is a member of the Eco-Schools organization and the Green Schools Alliance.

The International School of Penang (Uplands)

(Founded 1955)

Principal
Dr Marc Mesich

PYP coordinator
Matthew Holton

DP coordinator
Tanusankar Chakraborty

Status Private

Boarding/day Mixed

Gender Coeducational

Language of instruction
English

Authorised IB programmes
PYP, DP

Age Range 4 – 18 years

Number of pupils enrolled
600

Fees
Day: RM21,500 – RM59,000

Address
Jalan Sungai Satu
Batu Feringgi
Penang **11100** | **MALAYSIA**

TEL +604 8819 777

Email
info@uplands.org

Website
www.uplands.org

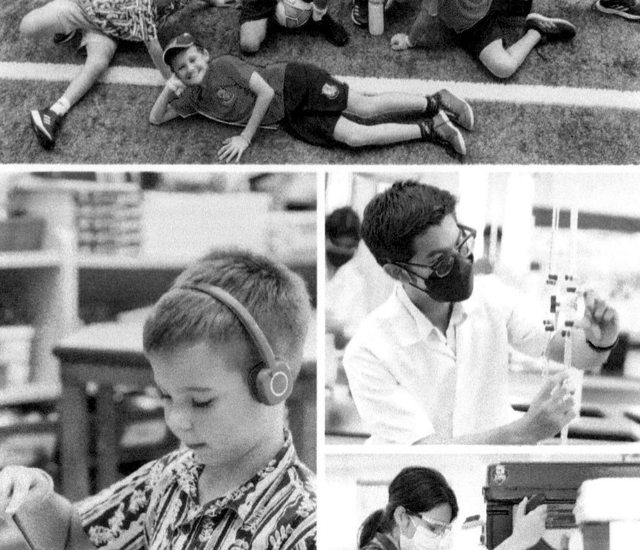

The International School of Penang (Uplands) is a non-profit, co-educational Reception to Primary and Secondary School, open to children aged 4 to 18 years old. It is one of the leading international schools in Malaysia, offering the IB PYP, IB Diploma and IGCSE qualifications.

Since being established in 1955 at the top of Penang Hill we are now established in a modern campus in Batu Feringgi. During our rich history, Uplands has strived to embody a caring community; a school where both international and Malaysian students are happy to learn in with our motto of Respect for Self. Respect for Others.

Students receive a wealth of quality education from an international teaching faculty as well as a range of sporting and extracurricular activities cultivating our values of respect, integrity, inquiry, diversity, collaboration, resilience and balance. Year upon year Uplands students have attained academic results that are consistently higher than global averages, with some achieving perfect scores in the IB Diploma pre-university course and receiving prestigious university scholarships.

Uplands is an IB World School, who are also recognised by the Malaysian Ministry of Education and permitted to admit both foreign and local students. Continuing its long history of excellence in education, Uplands received accreditation by The Council of International Schools (CIS), a global organisation committed to ensuring high-quality international education. Uplands is also accredited by The International Baccalaureate Organisation (IBO), The East Asia Regional Council of Schools (EARCOS) and a member of:

- The Federation of British International Schools in Asia (FOBISIA);
- The Association of International Malaysian Schools (AIMS);

The School is approved to offer external examinations by The International Baccalaureate Organisation (IBO), Cambridge International Examinations (CIE) and Edexcel International Examinations. Uplands has achieved the status of being an MYP Candidate School, marking an important milestone in its educational journey.

Languages offered at the school are English, Bahasa Malaysia, Mandarin, Spanish, French and German. School facilities include air-conditioned and well-resourced classrooms, climbing wall, 25 metre swimming pool, sports field, library, refectory, playground, basketball court, badminton court, IT resource centre, science laboratories, multi-purpose hall, audio/visual room, art rooms, music rooms, drama rooms, design technology workshops and world class boarding facilities. The campus is fully networked with wired and wireless access.

Student support services are also on deck including university guidance counsellors, learning support and school counsellors. Students are able to engage in a wide variety of extracurricular activities using our excellent campus facilities. The International School of Penang (Uplands) is proud to provide an environment for personal and academic challenge, helping our students to achieve, thrive and develop.

The Overseas School of Colombo

(Founded 1957)

Head of School
Dr. Michelle Kleiss

PYP coordinator
Samantha Wood

MYP coordinator
Jake Eagle

DP coordinator
Dr. Philip Leigh

Status Private

Boarding/day Day

Gender Coeducational

Language of instruction
English

Authorised IB programmes
PYP, MYP, DP

Age Range 3 – 18 years

Number of pupils enrolled 320

Fees
Day: US$12,960 – US$27,840 per annum

Address
P.O. Box 9, Pelawatte
Battaramulla **10120 | SRI LANKA**

TEL +94 11 2 784 920-2

Email
admissions@osc.lk

Website
www.osc.lk

Nestled in the vibrant heart of Sri Lanka, The Overseas School of Colombo (OSC) is more than an institution; it's a timeless legacy that traces its roots back to 1957. As the oldest internationally recognised educational institution in Sri Lanka, accredited by both the Council of International Schools (CIS) and the Middle States Association of Colleges and Schools (MSA), OSC proudly stands as the only IB World School in the country, embodying a commitment to providing a truly holistic educational experience.

Our dedication to diversity defines the very essence of OSC. With a tapestry woven from over 40 nationalities, we foster a global family where the principle of 'Unity in Diversity' is not just a slogan but a guiding force. Our educational environment actively cultivates intercultural awareness, understanding, and collaboration among learners, preparing them for a world without borders.

At OSC, the extraordinary teacher-to-student ratio of 1:5 speaks volumes about our commitment to personalised education. Our passionate educators, a diverse cohort drawn from around the world, see teaching as more than a profession; it's a calling to shape future global citizens.

With an unwavering 100% pass rate, OSC adapts and evolves to equip students with the skills and knowledge essential for success. Embracing cutting-edge teaching methods and technologies, we ensure our students are prepared for a world that values not only academic prowess but also creativity, camaraderie, collaboration, and communication.

In pursuit of our mission – Compassion. Courage. Curiosity- OSC has metamorphosed into a vibrant hub of learning, nurturing responsible and accountable adults. Our curriculum spans arts, athletics, design, and co-curricular programmes, offering a versatile and holistic education that goes beyond textbooks.

The self-sufficient OSC campus is a testament to our commitment to excellence, equipped with top-notch facilities – air-conditioned classrooms, libraries, design labs, state-of-the-art science labs, specialist rooms for art, drama, and music, IT labs, counselling offices, a 400-seat auditorium, and a black-box studio theatre. For sports enthusiasts, our expansive football field, 25-metre swimming pool, professional outdoor basketball court, gymnasium with a rock-climbing wall, and various courts and rooms for different sports and fitness activities await.

As an IB World School, OSC stands as a beacon of personalised excellence, virtue, and values, demonstrating an unwavering commitment to experiential learning. Join us in shaping a brighter future for your child; come, be an integral part of the OSC family.

Tokyo Metropolitan Kokusai High School

Head of School
Naoko Saito

DP coordinator
Kazumasa Aoki

Status State

Boarding/day Day

Gender Coeducational

Language of instruction
English

Authorised IB programmes
DP

Age Range 15 – 18 years

Number of pupils enrolled 720

Fees
Annual Fees: ¥118,800 (US800)

Address
2-19-59 Komaba
Meguro-ku
Tokyo
153-0041 | JAPAN

TEL +81 33 468 6811

Website
kokusai-h.metro.ed.jp

Tokyo Metropolitan Kokusai High School is a coeducational public high school that was established in 1989 and is maintained by the Tokyo Metropolitan Government. Located in a leafy suburb not far from the cosmopolitan west side of Tokyo, the school's motto is "Your Wings to the World" and its aim is to provide education to nurture well-balanced students with international mindedness.

In May 2015, Tokyo Metropolitan Kokusai High School was authorised as an International Baccalaureate World School offering the Diploma Programme, the first of which to be offered in a Japanese public high school.

Kokusai High School conducts the IBDP in English with the aim of cultivating internationally-minded students who will study overseas after graduation. The Kokusai IBDP strives to nurture future global leaders, and based on this philosophy, the ideal Kokusai IB student should demonstrate the following attributes.

A Kokusai High School IBDP student should:

1. Demonstrate a clear goal to enter the IBDP, a desire to contribute to a global society, and the willingness to gain entrance into universities overseas.
2. Approach learning with a self-starter mentality by showing a strong sense of inquiry and a willingness to use their own initiative, while having the courage to handle difficult challenges.
3. Exemplify a well-rounded character, being cooperative and considerate of others, and also have the willingness to positively accept and understand different perspectives and opinions.
4. Be motivated to broaden their perspectives, and be able to maintain a healthy mental and physical mindset and actively participate in extracurricular activities.
5. Demonstrate strong academic performances across all subjects, and have a high level of English proficiency.

Kokusai High School offers entrance examinations twice per year: the April enrollment session (held in January) and the September enrollment session (held in July). The April session is for students who will finish Year 9 school education by the end of March, and the September session is for those who will finish Year 9 school education between April and August. The maximum number of successful applicants in 2022 was 25. The ratio of Japanese students to International students for each enrollment session is announced by the Tokyo Metropolitan Board of Education. The assessment methods used in the entrance examinations are the English Language Skills Test, the Mathematics Academic Performance Test, the Essay, the Individual Interview, and the Certificate of Academic Record.

Kokusai High School offers a three-year programme; Year 1 (Grade 10) is the Foundation Year, Year 2 (Grade 11) and Year 3 (Grade 12) are the IBDP. Students also graduate with a Japanese High School Diploma. The subjects we offer are listed below:

Studies in Language and Literature

Year 1: Comprehensive English, English for Academic Purposes, Contemporary Japanese Language, Language Culture.

Year 2 and 3: DP English A: language and literature SL and HL, Japanese A: literature SL and HL.

Language Acquisition

Year 1: Comprehensive English, English for Academic Purposes, Contemporary Japanese Language, Language Culture.

Year 2 and 3: DP English B SL and HL; Japanese B SL and HL.

Individuals and Societies
Year 1: Public, Geography for Cultural Understanding, Modern and Contemporary History.
Year 2 and 3: DP History SL and HL, Economics HL, Geography HL.
Science
Year 1: Basic Physics, Basic Chemistry, Basic Biology.
Year 2 and 3: DP Physics SL and HL, Chemistry HL, Biology SL and HL.
Mathematics
Year 1: Mathematics I
Year 2 and 3: DP Mathematics: analysis and approaches SL and HL, Mathematics: applications and interpretation HL.
Other subjects
Year 1: Physical Education, Health, Art and Design, Basic Home Economics.
Year 2 and 3: Physical Education, Health, Homeroom Activity, Information Study by Scientific Approach, Theory of Knowledge (TOK), Creativity, Activity, Service (CAS).
Creativity, Activity, Service (CAS)
Throughout the two DP years, IB students explore their interests and personal development by setting specific goals and participating in a wide range of experiences in the three areas of creativity, activity and service. Their passions have often led them to get involved locally and globally, including in Tokyo, Hiroshima, Kenya, Nepal, Vietnam, etc. Some exciting experiences that students were actively engaged in the recent past are "3D printer project", "NPO corporation Lion Heart (teaching English to younger students)", "Plogging around Yoyogi Park (jogging and picking up litter as you jog)", etc.

Some universities where students have been accepted
UK: University College London, Imperial College London, University of Edinburgh, King's College London, University of Manchester, London School of Economics. USA: Princeton University, Purdue University, Georgia Institute of Technology, University of California Los Angeles, Williams College. Canada: University of Toronto, University of British Columbia, McGill University. Australia: Australian National University, University of Melbourne, University of Sydney. Germany: Technical University of Munich, Jacobs University. Netherlands: Leiden University, University of Groningen. Singapore: National University of Singapore, Nanyang Technological University.

(Founded 2015)

Head of College
Simon Head

DP coordinator
Christopher Hodachok

Status Private

Boarding/day Boarding

Gender Coeducational

Language of instruction
English

Authorised IB programmes
DP

Age Range 15 – 19 years

Number of pupils enrolled 620

Fees
Two-year fee ¥740,000
(scholarships available)

Address
No. 88 Kunchenghuxi Road
Changshu, Jiangsu
215500 | CHINA

TEL +86 512 5298 2602

Email
info.admissions@uwcchina.org

Website
http://www.uwcchina.org

Introduction
UWC Changshu China, established in 2015, is the first UWC in the mainland of China for students in grades 10, 11, and 12. As part of the UWC movement, the college welcomes students from around the world who share a commitment to peace and a sustainable future.

Learning at UWC Changshu China
At UWC Changshu China, learning is viewed as an iterative process that involves student engagement, inquiry, reflection, and the intentional application of knowledge to enhance personal growth, community development, and global impact. The college offers a Foundation Programme for grade 10 and the IB Diploma Programme for grades 11 and 12. These programmes emphasize experiential learning, critical thinking, self-management skills, community engagement, physical activities, service to others, and creative pursuits. The recently renovated STEAM Innovation Center provides students with state-of-the-art facilities for design thinking and collaborative efforts.

Outside the Classroom
Experiential learning lies at the heart of our educational approach. Students actively participate in a diverse range of cultural, sporting, and social activities. Our Creativity, Activity, Service (CAS) programme, known as Zhi Xing, encourages students to learn by doing and put their knowledge into action. Through Zhi Xing, students have the opportunity to initiate, engage in, or lead various activities and collaborative projects that align with the UWC mission and values.

Campus and Facilities
Situated on a 24-acre island on the northwest side of Kuncheng Lake, the campus design draws inspiration from traditional southern Chinese waterside villages, creating seamless connections between different areas. The campus incorporates cutting-edge technologies to enhance sustainability, and its modern facilities include a multi-function performing arts space, a wellbeing center, a swimming pool, an athletics track, sporting facilities, residential houses for students and faculty, a dining hall, and a library.

Admission
Applicants for the IB Diploma Programme should apply through their respective UWC national committee or the UWC Global Selection Programme. Foundation Programme applicants can directly contact the college for more information.

(Founded 1997)

Head of College
Gaurav Chopra

DP coordinator
Matthew Spall

CP coordinator
Amit Rastogi

Status Private

Boarding/day Boarding

Gender Coeducational

Language of instruction
English

Authorised IB programmes
DP, CP

Age Range 15 – 19 years

Number of pupils enrolled 240

Fees
Two-year fee $61,000 per annum (to be revised) (scholarships available)

Address
Village Khubavali, PO Paud
Taluka Mulshi
Pune, Maharashtra
412108 | INDIA

TEL +91 97644 42751 54

Email
info@muwci.net

Website
http://uwcmahindracollege.org

Introduction
UWC Mahindra College (MUWCI) is a vibrant college for Grades 11 and 12 with a rich tradition of curricular innovation and community engagement. Programmes such as the IB World Studies, Extended Essay were conceived and piloted here. The College also runs the Akshara Foundation which enhances the positive local impact of the College and provide students with numerous opportunities for project-based and service learning.

Inside the Classroom
UWC Mahindra College offers the International Baccalaureate Diploma Programme curriculum. Alongside standard courses, MUWCI offers Visual Arts, Theatre, Film Studies and Philosophy. Additionally, students also benefit from the MUWCI Core – a specially designed curriculum for the college that encompasses the areas of Political Education, Social and Emotional Education, Host Studies and Ecological and Outdoor Education – and regular student-led Global Affairs sessions. UWC Mahindra College has received accreditation to offer the IB Careers Programme, which will begin in the areas of Film and AI.

Outside the Classroom
UWC Mahindra College offers an immense variety of co-curricular activities through its Creativity, Activity, Service program (CAS), referred to as the "Triveni" program, which facilitates project-based learning. Students can choose from a rich diversity of Service Learning opportunities on and off campus spanning areas like menstrual health, organic farming, mental health and rural public education. Students are also active participants in decision-making processes that affect campus life, such as envisioning and executing resource management initiatives on campus. Students benefit from the cultural diversity of the surrounding valley and India at large and have immersive experiences in other parts of the country through Experiential Learning Weeks like Experience India Week and Project Week. MUWCI also conducts short course summer programmes which bring together students from around the world to learn about issues such as sustainability and globalization.

Campus and Facilities
Students live together in five residential clusters known as "wadas", each of which forms a more intimate community. The campus also offers many informal locations for gathering and hiking, and several places on campus are well known among students and faculty for their gorgeous vistas of the valley during sunset. Facilities include a Multi-Purpose Hall, science laboratories, a library, art studios, a dance and music studio, swimming pool, two gymnasiums, basketball and tennis courts and a football field.

Admissions
Students can apply through their UWC national committee or through the UWC Global Selection Programme.

Victorious Kidss Educares

(Founded 6th January 1997)

Founder President
Robbin Ghosh

Vice President & Principal
Saarada Ghosh

Director of Sports
Romen Ghosh

PYP coordinator Pritisha Ahir

MYP coordinator
Vishwajeet Kumar

DP coordinator
Vishwajeet Kumar

EYFP Head Desiree Dhami

EYFP Coordinator Dhara Vyas

PYP Head Ira Ghosh

MYP & DP Head Jaya Kalsy

Status Private

Boarding/day Day

Gender Coeducational

Language of instruction
English

Authorised IB programmes
PYP, MYP, DP

Age Range 6 weeks – 19 years

Number of pupils enrolled 960

Fees
Tuition Fee US$4,326 per annum (average)

Address
Survey No. 53, 54 & 58,
Hissa No. 2/1A
Off. Shreeram Society,
Nagar Road, Kharadi
Pune, Maharashtra
411014 | INDIA

TEL +91 20-67116300/1/2

Email
robbinghosh@victoriouskidsseducares.org

Website
www.victoriouskidsseducares.org

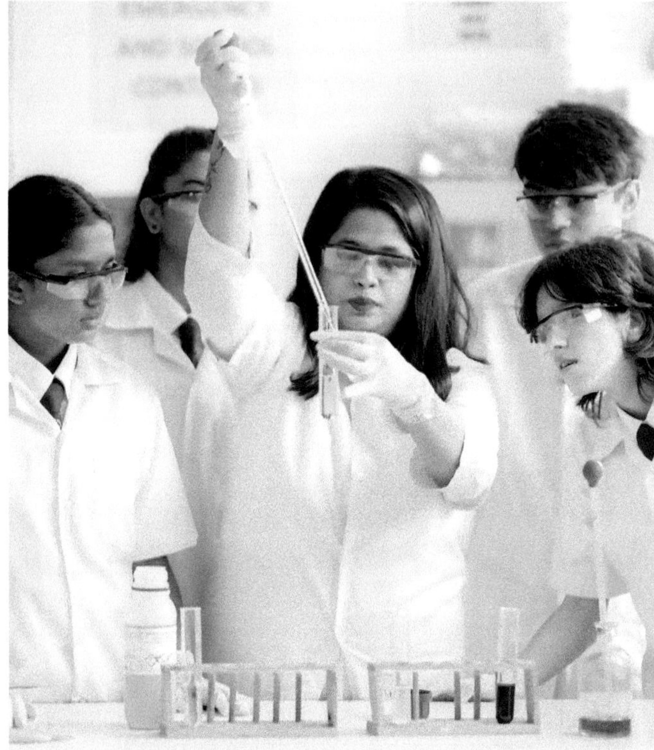

Every Nation, through every school, has a message to deliver, a destiny to create. The vision of education is to guide humanity. We work with the knowledge and rich wisdom, *'Every child has greater potential of intelligence at birth than Leonardo Da Vinci, Isaac Newton, or Albert Einstein ever used'.* We believe that every child is born with a special ability, and the brain of every child has unfathomable potential.

In our pursuit for perfection, we guide every child to fulfil their dreams and reach their goals for life. The deepest desire in every parent's heart is to channelize the potential of their children, to be somebody in this universe, and become a source of pride for the country.

If we teach our children the way we had learnt yesterday, we will rob them of their tomorrow! Discovering the secret power from within the child, is parenting, is schooling.

Victorious Kidss Educares (VKidss), permeates the field of education, with the latest of the world's research-based Teaching and Learning pedagogy of IB, and its standards and practices, is coupled with the rich heritage of Vedanta of India. Thus, enhancing all-round character, leading to attainment of human excellence. Be that as it may, in the subject areas of Academics, Digital literacy, Sports, Virtual Art, Performing Art, Foreign Language skills, Oratory skills, and love for Writing, along with strengthening their Focus, expanding the strength of Mind; amalgamates the best teaching-learning pedagogy.

When IB is coupled with Vedanta – the possibilities of the human child towards spiritual intellectual, and physical growth, become Infinite. They develop an attitude of mindfulness, belongingness, and an awareness of "Learning to Love to Learn". With the standards and practices of IB, we strongly believe that, "If the child has not learnt, it is we who have not taught".

With over 27 years of helping children crystallising their professional and academic dreams, planning their future; we have discovered the presence of an intrinsic power, inherent in all children but have remained unrecognised and sleeping in most.

The philosophy of education, at Victorious Kidss Educares, is to awaken every child, to the immense possibilities and power within their own self. The pedagogical leadership, principles of this school, and education platform involves building character, making the roadmap to their intended academic and lifetime goals.

Achievements:

- Despite the entire Academic Year (2021-22) running Virtual, due to Covid 19; one DP student joined the World Topper Rank – scoring a perfect 45/45. Every other student, whoever had appeared for DP, secured a perfect first division.
- All our DP students have been successfully placed, in their preferred universities, placed across the globe. The majority of which were prestigious ones and a large number of our students received scholarships to aid their academic goals.
- In the Academic Year 2019 – 2020, MYP and DP results were 100 percent, with the highest score being 56/56 – World Topper – in MYP and 44/45 in DP.
- In August 2022 we attained 100% results for MYP and DP, with the highest score being 55/56 in MYP and 43/45 in DP.
- By this balancing power of the best of East and West our school has been blessed by Nature & the Divine Grace with the honour of being, since 2012, a Model IB World School, in Asia.
- On 15 Nov 2019, just four months before the lockdown began (Friday 13 March 2020), we received through an IB Evaluation process, 'accreditation from IB for our excellent standards and practices'. IB has, in addition, requested us to share these standards and practices, through networking.

'Being gifted is primarily a product of the ambience. And by the current definition, the level of intelligence can easily be reached by nearly every child.' (Dr. Neil Harvey). We, at Victorious Kidss Educares, are experiencing this phenomenon, again and again.

Intellectually active engagement of our students, through inquiry, we have been successful in nurturing this power of awareness. With the awareness of their consciousness, understanding, and concept – we crystallise, 'Success for Every Child'.

These children garner and hone their life skills by taking responsibility for their own learning!

As a School Management Core Team, we work with the Wisdom and knowledge that *'Our children are no longer the people as we were in the school. That if we try to teach them, the way we had learnt yesterday, we will rob them of their tomorrow.'*

The VKE team of educators is proud to have a congregation of highly motivated educators. The team comprises three (3) IBEN workshop leaders, one (1) IB consultant, one (1) reader, one (1) IB Senior Team leader, two (2) Quality Curriculum Reviewers and one (1) IBEN leader.

We are a 'Not for Profit' IB World School. VKE thoughtfully offers the following:

- VKE was one of the first schools to onboard virtual classes instantaneously during the Pandemic. We continue to provide the hybrid classroom model to selected students to date.
- Broad-spectrum sporting facilities consist of basketball, volleyball, handball, football, cricket, badminton, tennis, table tennis, swimming, skating, Mallakhamb, gymnastics, yoga, and athletics.
- TED-Ed program for MYP students.
- Career Counselling, Placements, guidance towards scholarships, and Internships.
- Scholarships in top universities for DP Students.
- Vedic Mathematics, Abacus, and Design Technology.
- Visual Art, Performing Art, 3D Digital Arts Lab, and Pottery Studio.
- Diversified Exposure in Performing Arts (Indian Classical, Western, Dance – Bharatanatyam, Hip Hop, Freestyle).
- Concentration Techniques – Pranayama, Yogic breathing exercises, and Mindfulness Meditation.
- Model UN Programme to enhance Communication skills in debating and negotiation.
- Parental Workshops.

The students of VKE march fearlessly and forge ahead on the path of truth, purity, and perseverance and become, *'the torchbearers of the IB learner profile, towards the life they have dreamt for.'*

Every Child Matters

(Founded 1991)

Head of School
Elsa H. Donohue

PYP coordinator
Olwen Millgate

MYP coordinator
Elizabeth England

DP coordinator
Elizabeth England

Status Private

Boarding/day Day

Gender Coeducational

Language of instruction
English

Authorised IB programmes
PYP, MYP, DP

Age Range 3 – 18 years

Number of pupils enrolled
480

Fees
Day: US$11,150 –
US$25,680 per annum

Address
P.O. Box 3180, Phonesavanh Road,
Saphanthong Tai Village,
Sisattanak District
Vientiane | **LAOS**

TEL +856 21 31 8100

Email
contact@vislao.com

Website
www.vislao.com

Mission
We challenge, inspire, and empower our learners to develop their unique potential in our changing world.

Vision
We will lead the way toward a sustainable future.

Values
We value Balance, Respect, Resilience, Innovation, and Courage.

VIS Definition of Learning
We learn when we build and apply new understandings and skills in a variety of contexts

VIS is an independent, non-profit school offering an international-standard curriculum. We are the only school in Laos accredited by the Western Association of Schools and Colleges (WASC) and the Council of International Schools (CIS). We are also the only IB World School in the country, delivering IB Continuum Programme (PYP, MYP, DP). Over the years, VIS has demonstrated consistent improvement in the IB results. Our 2023 Class IB Diploma Average Score was 33, above the world average of 30.24.

The diverse student body of 480 learners draws from 42 nationalities. Most families represent the non-government and diplomatic sectors; international and local businesses are also represented. Our unique VIS Personal and Home Language program currently supports the development and maintenance of 7 different languages. We also offer an English Language Acquisition (ELA) program.

At VIS, we strive to develop empathy, cultural understanding, and global awareness through meaningful interactions with the Lao community. As a Mekong River International Schools Association (MRISA) member, our students participate in sporting and cultural exchanges with schools in neighboring countries.

Our current campus facilities include two swimming pools, two soccer pitches, ample playground spaces, and a collaborative library. Last year we added new buildings with:

- A new multipurpose Performing Arts Center with a capacity of 350+ pax. Retractable seats make space versatile for events and community gatherings;
- An indoor Gymnasium with 2 full-size basketball courts integrated into our sports hub (pool and soccer field);
- A modern administration building with community areas.

Western Australian Primary and High School

Western Australian
International School System

(Founded 2010)

Head of School
Dr. Rung Tran

DP coordinator
Mr. Bao Tran

Status Private

Boarding/day Day

Gender Coeducational

Language of instruction
English

Authorised IB programmes
DP

Age Range 2 – 18 years

Number of pupils enrolled
2500

Address
157 Ly Chinh Thang Street
Vo Thi Sau Ward, District 3
Ho Chi Minh City | **VIETNAM**

TEL +84 28 7109 5077

Email
schooloffice@wass.edu.vn

Website
www.wass.edu.vn/en

Established in 2011, Western Australian International School System (WASS) is proud to be one of only two schools recognized as an Australian Overseas School in Vietnam with the accreditation of the School Curriculum and Standards Authority (SCSA), one of the only 21 international schools in Vietnam licensed to teach by the International Baccalaureate (IB), and is also a member of the Council of International Schools (CIS).

WASS currently offers the Western Australian K-10 Curriculum International – Accredited Program (WA K-10 International) and the Western Australian Curriculum – Partial Integrated Program, which encompass the Australian Curriculum, Assessment and Reporting Authority – ACARA's Australian Curriculum. Moreover, the Western Australian Certificate of Education International Program (WACE International) and the International Baccalaureate Diploma Programme (IBDP) are implemented for Years 11 and 12 students. In the academic year 2023 – 2024, the third generation of IBDP students at WASS will graduate. It is a solid prerequisite for those planning to pursue further education abroad, providing competitive advantages in terms of qualifications and skills when applying for admission to universities around the world.

With the enthusiasm and belief of "A World-Class Education with the World in Your Class", WASS strives to innovate and improve our teaching methods, contributing to offering the most comprehensive academic experiences based on Vietnamese cultural traditions and imbued with an international mindset for students. An excellent academic program built in combination with an international standard learning environment is the foundation for nurturing generations of confident students, contributing positively to the community and inspiring them to become successful lifelong learners.

WASS offers an ideal learning environment with international standards with technologically advanced classrooms, innovative learning centers, specialized function rooms with unique features, and a contemporary library system that contains a wide variety of books. In addition to being strongly committed to the principles of comprehensive development, WASS also organizes a variety of after-school activities that aim to inspire students to develop essential skills and unleash their hidden potential.

The WASS community has become the home of thousands of students from more than 20 different countries around the world, providing diversity in international educational experiences. Students at WASS are educated in a multicultural learning environment in order to become dynamic and enthusiastic global citizens with a solid foundation of knowledge, comprehensive skills, and confidence when entering the world full of challenges in the future.

Western International School of Shanghai (WISS)

Head of School
Mr. David Edwards

PYP coordinator
Vivian Hu

MYP coordinator
Martin Mathieson

DP coordinator
Rajeshree Basu

CP coordinator
Gary Halcrow

Status Private

Boarding/day Day

Gender Coeducational

Language of instruction
English

Authorised IB programmes
PYP, MYP, DP, CP

Age Range 2.5 – 18 years

Number of pupils enrolled 750

Fees
Day:
¥170,500 – ¥275,600 per annum
Early Bird Rate
¥161,975 – ¥261,820 per annum

Address
555 Lian Min Road,
Xujing Town, Qing Pu District,
Shanghai
201702 | CHINA

TEL +86 (21) 69761038/1060

Email
enquiry@wiss.cn

Website
www.wiss.cn

The Western International School of Shanghai (WISS) offers a global education, preparing students to thrive in an interconnected world. With over 17 years of excellence in international education, WISS is a leading educational institution in Shanghai, China.

At WISS, we pride ourselves on providing a comprehensive and balanced academic programme that nurtures the intellectual, social, emotional, and physical development of our students. As a triple-accredited school, holding accreditations from the Council of International Schools (CIS), the Western Association of Schools and Colleges (WASC), and being an IB Continuum World School, we ensure that our students receive a world-class education.

Our commitment to excellence is reflected in our diverse and inclusive community. With students from over 50 nationalities, WISS celebrates multiculturalism, fostering an environment where different perspectives are valued, and intercultural understanding is promoted.

Located in New Hongqiao, our school offers a convenient and strategic location, providing easy access to major commercial and tourist areas. Nestled amidst green residential spaces, WISS provides a peaceful and vibrant learning environment.

As the first and only full continuum International Baccalaureate (IB) World School in Mainland China, WISS offers a range of IB programmes, including the Primary Years Programme (IBPYP), the Middle Years Programme (IBMYP), the Diploma Programme (IBDP), and the Career-related Programme (IBCP). This allows students to embark on personalized pathways that foster critical thinking, creativity, and a lifelong love for learning.

In addition to our strong academic curriculum, WISS offers outstanding athletics, music, arts, and performing arts programmes. Our students have ample opportunities to excel in their chosen fields and develop their talents in a supportive and nurturing environment.

Through our Distinguishing Programs, such as the Global Alliance For Innovative Learning (GAIL) and the International Schools Theatre Association (ISTA), WISS students are encouraged to become leaders, innovators, and compassionate global citizens. We strive to develop skills and qualities that will empower our students to make a positive impact on the world.

If you are seeking an exceptional international school experience for your child, choose the Western International School of Shanghai. Our dedicated faculty, state-of-the-art facilities, and commitment to holistic education make WISS the ideal choice for families who value excellence, diversity, and global citizenship.

Visit our website or contact us today to learn more about the Western International School of Shanghai and discover why we are the preferred choice for families in search of a truly international education.

Directory of schools in the Asia-Pacific region

Key to symbols

- CP
- Diploma
- MYP
- PYP
- Fee Paying School
- Boys' School
- Girls' School
- Coeducational School
- Boarding School
- Day School

AUSTRALIA

Aberfoyle Park High School
36A Taylors Road, East Aberfoyle Park SA 5159
DP Coordinator Ryan Brown
Languages English
T: +61 8 8270 4455
W: intra.aphs.sa.edu.au

Al Zahra College
3-5Wollongong Road, Arncliffe NSW 2205
DP Coordinator Kothar Elrida
MYP Coordinator Maral Bardakjian
PYP Coordinator Michelle Ryan
Languages English
T: +061(002)9599-0161
W: www.azc.nsw.edu.au

Alamanda K-9 College
PO Box 6606, Point Cook VIC 3030
PYP Coordinator Jaymee Stigwood
Languages English
T: +61 3 8376 5200
W: alamandacollege.vic.edu.au

Albert Park College
83 Danks Street, Albert Park, Melbourne VIC 3206
DP Coordinator Jessica Langdon
Languages English
T: +61 3 8695 9000
W: www.albertparkcollege.vic.edu.au

Anglican Church Grammar School
Oaklands Parade, East Brisbane QLD 4169
DP Coordinator Catherine Prosser
PYP Coordinator Larissa Guy
Languages English
T: +61 7 3896 2200
W: www.churchie.com.au

Annesley Junior School
28 Rose Terrace, Wayville SA 5034
PYP Coordinator David Taylor
Languages English
T: +61 8 8422 2288
W: www.annesley.sa.edu.au

Aspendale Gardens Primary School
96 Kearney Drive, Aspendale Gardens VIC 3195
PYP Coordinator Kelly Cornelius
Languages English
T: +61 (03) 9587 0877
W: www.agps.vic.edu.au

Aspendale Primary School
23 Laura Street, Aspendale, Melbourne VIC 3195
PYP Coordinator Tom Pearce
Languages English
T: +61 (0)3 9580 3255
W: www.aspendale.vic.edu.au

Auburn High School
26 Burgess Street, East Hawthorn VIC 3123
DP Coordinator Peter Ryan
Languages English, French
T: +61 3 9822 3247
W: www.auburnhs.vic.edu.au

Auburn South Primary School
419 Tooronga Road, East Hawthorn, Melbourne VIC 3123
PYP Coordinator Benjamin Zonca
Languages English
T: +61 3 9882 2140
W: www.auburnsthps.vic.edu.au

Australian International Academy - Caroline Springs Campus
183-191 Caroline Springs Boulevard, Caroline Springs, Melbourne VIC 3023
DP Coordinator Mahmoud Sammak
PYP Coordinator Zawat Souki
Languages English
T: +61 3 8372 5446
W: cs.aiahome.net

Australian International Academy - Kellyville Campus
57-69 Samantha Riley Drive, Kellyville, Sydney NSW 2155
DP Coordinator Sam Halbouni
MYP Coordinator Lubna Sayed
PYP Coordinator Oznur Aydemir
Languages English
T: +61 02 8801 3100
W: kellyville.aia.nsw.edu.au

Australian International Academy - Sydney Campus
420 Liverpool Road, Strathfield, Sydney NSW 2135
MYP Coordinator Simran Khan
PYP Coordinator Maryam Atalla
Languages English
T: +61 2 9642 0104
W: strathfield.aia.nsw.edu.au

AUSTRALIAN INTERNATIONAL ACADEMY OF EDUCATION
Melbourne Senior Campus, 56 Bakers Road, North Coburg VIC 3058
DP Coordinator Ms Naima Keddar
MYP Coordinator Mr Kumaravell Sepulohniam
PYP Coordinator Ms Zawat Souki
Languages English
T: +61 3 9350 4533
E: aia@aia.vic.edu.au
W: aia.vic.edu.au
See full details on page 314

Ballarat Grammar
201 Forest Street, Wendouree VIC 3355
PYP Coordinator Maria Cahir
Languages English
T: + 61 3 5338 0700
W: www.bgs.vic.edu.au

Balwyn North Primary School
Buchanan Avenue, Balwyn North VIC 3104
PYP Coordinator Nicole McLean
Languages English
T: +61 (0)3 9859 4258
W: balwynnorthps.vic.edu.au

Barker College
91 Pacific Highway, Hornsby NSW 2077
PYP Coordinator Lisa Bonazza
Languages English
T: +61 2 8438 7999
W: www.barker.college

Bayswater South Primary School
Enfield Drive, Bayswater VIC 3153
PYP Coordinator Karyn Georgios
Languages English
T: +61 3 9729 2862
W: www.baysouthps.vic.edu.au

Beaumaris North Primary School
Wood Street, Beaumaris, Melbourne VIC 3193
PYP Coordinator Debbie Murnane
Languages English
T: +61 3 9589 5449
W: www.beaumarisnorthps.vic.edu.au

Belair Primary School
45-83 Main Road, Belair SA 5052
PYP Coordinator Natalie Holmes
Languages English
T: +61 8 8370 3733
W: www.belairps.sa.edu.au

Benowa State High School
PO Box 5733, Gold Coast Mail Centre, Benowa QLD 9726
DP Coordinator Adrian Hays
Languages English
T: +61 (07) 5582 7333
W: www.benowashs.eq.edu.au

Benton Junior College
261 Racecourse Road, Mornington VIC 3931
PYP Coordinator Jodie Brasher
Languages English
T: +61 3 5973 9100
W: www.benton.vic.edu.au

Berwick Primary School
37 Fairholme Boulevard, Berwick VIC 3806
PYP Coordinator Annette Ewing
Languages English
T: +61 03 97071026
W: www.berwickprimary.vic.edu.au

Blackwood High School
4 Seymour Street, Eden Hills SA 5050
MYP Coordinator Lachlan McFarlane
Languages English
T: +61 8 8278 0900
W: www.bhs.sa.edu.au

Blackwood Primary School
4 Seymour Street, Eden Hills SA 5050
PYP Coordinator Natalie Campbell
Languages English
T: +61 8 82785355
W: www.blackwoodps.sa.edu.au

Boronia K-12 College
Albert Avenue, Boronia VIC 3155
PYP Coordinator Cassandra Wright
Languages English
T: +61 3 9760 4900
W: www.boroniak-12.vic.edu.au

Brighton Primary School
59 Wilson Street, Brighton, Melbourne VIC 3186
PYP Coordinator Joel Snowden
Languages English
T: +61 39592 0177
W: www.brighton.vic.edu.au

Brighton Secondary College
120 Marriage Road, Brighton East VIC 3187
DP Coordinator Katherine Perry
Languages English
T: +61 3 9592 7488
W: brightonsc.vic.edu.au

Burwood Heights Primary School & Kindergarten
Cnr Hawthorn & Mahoneys Roads, East Burwood VIC 3151
PYP Coordinator Clare Matthews
Languages English
T: +61 3 9803 8311
W: www.burwoodhps.vic.edu.au

Cairns State High School
PO Box 5643, Cairns QLD 4870
DP Coordinator Stefanie Biancotti
Languages English
T: +61 7 4050 3033
W: www.cairnsshs.eq.edu.au

Calamvale Community College
11 Hamish Street, Calamvale QLD 4116
DP Coordinator Melissa Ellis
PYP Coordinator Alice Pan-Moreau
Languages English
T: +61 (0)7 3712 6333
W: calamvalecc.eq.edu.au

Canberra Girls Grammar School
Melbourne Avenue, Deakin ACT 2600
DP Coordinator Adriaan Van Wijk
PYP Coordinator Alex Galland
Languages English
T: +61 2 6202 6400
W: www.cggs.act.edu.au

Canberra Grammar School
40 Monaro Crescent, Red Hill, Canberra ACT 2603
DP Coordinator Graham Maltby
PYP Coordinator Sarah Dunn
Languages English
T: + 61 2 6260 9700
W: www.cgs.act.edu.au

CAREY BAPTIST GRAMMAR SCHOOL
349 Barkers Road, Kew VIC 3101
DP Coordinator Frédérique Petithory BA, PostGradCertEd, MA
Languages English
T: +61 3 9816 1222
E: admissions@carey.com.au
W: www.carey.com.au
See full details on page 317

Caulfield Grammar School - Caulfield Campus
PO Box 610, 217 Glen Eira Road East, St Kilda VIC 3185
PYP Coordinator Jacinta Crimmins
Languages English
T: +61 3 9524 6300
W: www.caulfieldgs.vic.edu.au

Caulfield Grammar School - Wheelers Hill Campus
74-82 Jells Road, Wheelers Hill VIC 3150
MYP Coordinator Natalie White
PYP Coordinator Jonathan Twigg
Languages English
T: +61 3 8562 5300
W: www.caulfieldgs.vic.edu.au

  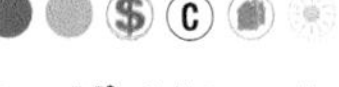

Caulfield South Primary School
Bundeera Road, Caulfield South, Melbourne VIC 3162
PYP Coordinator Andrew McKibbin
Languages English
T: +61 3957 83718
W: www.caulfieldsthps.vic.edu.au

Central West Leadership Academy
8 George Street, Corner Fitzroy & Bultje Streets, Dubbo NSW 2830
DP Coordinator Mandi Randell
Languages English, French
T: +61 2 6882 4216
W: theacademy.nsw.edu.au

Charles Weston School Coombs
80 Woodberry Avenue, Coombs ACT 2611
PYP Coordinator Bianca Bailetti
Languages English
T: +61 2 6142 0404
W: www.charlesweston.act.edu.au

Cleveland District State High School
Russell Street, Cleveland QLD 4163
DP Coordinator Billie Loveday
Languages English
T: +61 (0)7 3824 9222
W: clevelanddistrictshs.eq.edu.au

Coatesville Primary School
21 Mackie Road, East Bentleigh VIC 3165
PYP Coordinator Matthew Cameron
Languages English
T: +61 03 9570 1652
W: www.coatesps.vic.edu.au

Concordia College
24 Winchester St, Highgate SA 5063
MYP Coordinator Emily Johnson
PYP Coordinator Rachel Muldoon
Languages English
T: +61 8 8272 0444
W: www.concordia.sa.edu.au

Cornish College
65 Riverend Rd, Bangholme VIC 3175
PYP Coordinator Alexandra Parrington
Languages English
T: +61 3 9781 9000
W: www.cornishcollege.vic.edu.au

Coromandel Valley Primary School
339 Main Road, Coromandel Valley SA 5051
PYP Coordinator Kate ODriscoll
Languages English
T: +61 8 8278 3693
W: www.coromandps.sa.edu.au

CRANBROOK SCHOOL
5 Victoria Road, Bellevue Hill NSW 2023
DP Coordinator Nicholas Hanrahan
MYP Coordinator Kate Allen
PYP Coordinator Genet Erickson Adam
Languages English
T: +61 2 9327 9000
E: Enrol@cranbrook.nsw.edu.au
W: www.cranbrook.nsw.edu.au
See full details on page 320

Creek Street Christian College
91 Creek Street, Bendigo VIC 3550
DP Coordinator Marie Boulanger
Languages English
T: +61 3 5442 1722
W: www.creekstreet.vic.edu.au

Dingley Primary School
111-115 Centre Dandenong Road, Dingley Village VIC 3172
PYP Coordinator Lauren Thomas
Languages English
T: +61 3 9551 3555
W: www.dingleyps.vic.edu.au

Elonera Montessori School
21 Mount Ousley Road, Mount Ousley NSW 2519
DP Coordinator Carlos Hubbard
Languages English
T: +61 2 4225 1000
W: elonera.nsw.edu.au

Encounter Lutheran College
64 Adelaide Road, Victor Harbor SA 5211
MYP Coordinator Adam Pfeiffer
PYP Coordinator Alicia Puiatti
Languages English
T: +61 8 8552 8880
W: www.encounter.sa.edu.au

Essendon North Primary School
112 Keilor Road, North Essendon VIC 3041
PYP Coordinator Alice Mckenzie
T: +61 (03) 9379 3979
W: www.enps.vic.edu.au

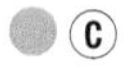

Faith Lutheran College
130 Magnolia Road, Tanunda SA 5352
MYP Coordinator Michelle Schwarz
PYP Coordinator Ashleigh Koch
Languages English
T: +61 8 8561 4200
W: faith.sa.edu.au

Firbank Grammar Junior School - Brighton Campus
51 Outer Crescent, Brighton, Melbourne VIC 3186
PYP Coordinator Michelle Worth
Languages English
T: +61 3 9591 5141
W: www.firbank.vic.edu.au

Firbank Grammar Junior School - Sandringham Campus
45 Royal Avenue, Sandringham VIC 3191
PYP Coordinator Karen Chandler
Languages English
T: +61 3 9533 5711
W: www.firbank.vic.edu.au

Footscray Primary School
PO Box 6019, West Footscray VIC 3012
PYP Coordinator Caroline Donovan
Languages English
T: +61 3 9687 1910
W: www.footscrayps.vic.edu.au

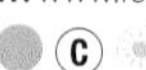

Forrest Primary School
Hobart Avenue, Forrest, Canberra ACT 2603
PYP Coordinator Jemma O'Brien
T: +61 2 6205 5644
W: www.forrestps.act.edu.au

Geelong Grammar School
50 Biddlecombe Avenue, Corio VIC 3214
DP Coordinator Steven Griffiths
PYP Coordinator Lucas Hall
Languages English
T: +61 3 5273 9200
W: www.ggs.vic.edu.au

German International School Sydney
33 Myoora Road, Terrey Hills NSW 2084
DP Coordinator Mrs Annie Thomson
Languages English, German
T: +61 2 9485 1900
W: www.germanschoolsydney.com

Glenferrie Primary School
78-98 Manningtree Road, Hawthorn VIC 3122
PYP Coordinator Ellen Angus
Languages English, Italian
T: +61 3 9818 4338
W: www.glenferrieps.vic.edu.au

Glenroy West Primary School
P.O. Box 547, York Street, Glenroy VIC 3046
PYP Coordinator Lisa Brandecker
Languages English
T: +61 (0)3 9306 8955
W: www.glenroywestps.vic.edu.au

Glenunga International High School
L'Estrange Street, Glenunga SA 5064
DP Coordinator Corin Bone
Languages English
T: +61 88 379 5629
W: www.gihs.sa.edu.au

Gold Creek School
74 Kelleway Avenue, Nicholls, Canberra ACT 2913
MYP Coordinator Nicole Jaggers
PYP Coordinator Kirrally Talbot
Languages English
T: +61 (02) 6205 2955
W: www.goldcreek.act.edu.au

Golden Grove Lutheran Primary School
21-23 Richardson Drive, Wynn Vale SA 5127
PYP Coordinator Jayne Zadow
Languages English
T: +61 8 8282 6000
W: www.goldengrove.sa.edu.au

Good News Lutheran College
580 Tarneit Road, Tarneit VIC 3029
MYP Coordinator Erin Bagot
PYP Coordinator Jessica Clark
Languages English
T: +61 3 8742 9000
W: www.goodnews.vic.edu.au

Good Shepherd Lutheran College - Howard Springs Campus
Corner of Whitewood Road & Kundook Place, Howard Springs NT 0835
MYP Coordinator Shane Rumbold
PYP Coordinator Rebecca Fletcher
Languages English
T: +61 8 8983 0300
W: www.goodshepherd.nt.edu.au

Good Shepherd Lutheran School - Angaston
7 Neldner Avenue, Angaston SA 5353
PYP Coordinator Fiona McDonald
Languages English
T: +61 8 8564 2396
W: www.goodshepherd.sa.edu.au
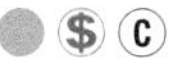

Grace Christian College
20 Kinchington Road, Leneva, Mellboune VIC 3691
DP Coordinator Joel Robotham
Languages English
T: +61 02 6056 2299
W: gcc.vic.edu.au
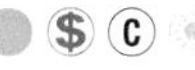

Heany Park Primary School
Buckingham Drive, Rowville VIC 3178
PYP Coordinator Kym Ryan
Languages English
T: +61 (0)3 9764 5533
W: www.heanyparkps.vic.edu.au

Highton Primary School
PO Box 6093, Highton VIC 3216
PYP Coordinator Tracy Thornton
Languages English
T: +61 3 5243 1494
W: www.hightonps.vic.edu.au

Hills International College
105-111 Johanna Street, Jimboomba QLD 4280
PYP Coordinator Stuart Ablitt
Languages English
T: +61 7 5546 0667
W: www.hills.qld.edu.au

Holy Trinity Primary School
18-20 Theodore Street, Curtin ACT 2605
PYP Coordinator Ms Katie Smith
Languages English
T: +61 26281 4811
W: www.holytrinity.act.edu.au

Hunter Valley Grammar School
42 Norfolk Street, Ashtonfield NSW 2323
CP Coordinator Pauliene O'Grady
MYP Coordinator Pauliene O'Grady
PYP Coordinator Madeleine Smith
Languages English
T: +61 2 4934 2444
W: www.hvgs.nsw.edu.au

IES College
495 Boundary Street, Spring Hill QLD 4004
DP Coordinator Cassandra Magar
Languages English
T: +61 7 3832 7699
W: iescollege.com

Immanuel College
32 Morphett Road, Novar Gardens SA 5040
MYP Coordinator Louise Cottell
Languages English
T: +61 08 8294 3588
W: www.immanuel.sa.edu.au

Immanuel Gawler
11 Lyndoch Road, Gawler East SA 5118
PYP Coordinator Andrew Boesch
Languages English
T: +61 8 8522 5740
W: www.ilsg.sa.edu.au

Immanuel Primary School
Saratoga Drive, Novar Gardens SA 5040
PYP Coordinator Katherine Baird
Languages English
T: +61 8 8294 8422
W: www.immanuelps.sa.edu.au

Indooroopilly State High School
PO Box 61, Ward Street, Indooroopilly, Brisbane QLD 4068
DP Coordinator Peter Day
Languages English
T: +61 7 3327 8333
W: www.indooroohs.eq.edu.au

International School of Western Australia
193 St Brigids Terrace, Doubleview, Perth WA 6018
DP Coordinator Mini Balachandran
MYP Coordinator Rachel Garrick
PYP Coordinator Fleur Churton
Languages English
T: +61 8 9285 1144
W: www.iswa.wa.edu.au

Islamic College of Melbourne (ICOM)
83 Wootten Road, Tarneit VIC 3029
DP Coordinator Maha Elsayegh
Languages English
T: +61 3 8742 1739
W: icom.vic.edu.au

Ivanhoe Grammar School
PO Box 91, The Ridgeway, Ivanhoe VIC 3079
DP Coordinator Nicholas Mercer
Languages English
T: +61 3 9490 3501
W: www.ivanhoe.com.au

John Paul College
John Paul Drive, Daisy Hill QLD 4127
PYP Coordinator Kara Ilich
Languages English
T: +61 7 3826 3333
W: www.jpc.qld.edu.au

JOHN WOLLASTON ANGLICAN COMMUNITY SCHOOL
Centre Road, Camillo WA 6111
PYP Coordinator Melissa Cuming & Sheree Zecca
Languages English
T: +61 (08) 9495 8100
E: mail@jwacs.wa.edu.au
W: www.jwacs.wa.edu.au
See full details on page 341
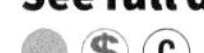

Kambala
794 New South Head Road, Rose Bay, Sydney NSW 2029
DP Coordinator Phillip Bird
Languages English
T: +612 93886777
W: www.kambala.nsw.edu.au

KARDINIA INTERNATIONAL COLLEGE
29-31 Kardinia Drive, Bell Post Hill, Geelong VIC 3215
DP Coordinator Ainslie Howard
PYP Coordinator Geoff Geddes
Languages English
T: +61 3 5278 9999
E: marketing@kardinia.vic.edu.au
W: www.kardinia.vic.edu.au
See full details on page 345

Kew Primary School
Peel Street, Kew, Melbourne VIC 3101
PYP Coordinator Alex Darlington
Languages English, French
T: +61 3 9853 8325
W: www.kewps.vic.edu.au

Kingston Heath Primary School
25 Farm Road, Cheltenham VIC 3192
PYP Coordinator Sue Riley
Languages English
T: +61 3 9584 5805
W: www.khps.vic.edu.au

Kingsville Primary School
58 Bishop Street, Yarraville VIC 3013
PYP Coordinator Samuel Eason
Languages English
T: +61 03 9315 8569
W: www.kingsvilleps.vic.edu.au

Kingswood College
355 Station Street, Box Hill, Melbourne VIC 3128
PYP Coordinator Glen Hayres
Languages English
T: +61 3 9896 1700
W: www.kingswoodcollege.vic.edu.au

KOROROIT CREEK PRIMARY SCHOOL
130 Tenterfield Drive, Burnside Heights VIC 3023
PYP Coordinator Drita Demiri
Languages English
T: +61 3 8358 0600
E: kororoit.creek.ps@education.vic.gov.au
W: www.kororoitcreekps.vic.edu.au
See full details on page 348

Kunyung Primary School
50 Kunyung Road, Mt Eliza VIC 3930
PYP Coordinator Melanie Woodland
Languages English
T: +61 (3) 9787 6102
W: www.kunyung.vic.edu.au/

Launceston Church Grammar School
10 Lyttleton Street, East Launceston TAS 7250
PYP Coordinator Claire Calvert
Languages English
T: +61 3 6336 5900
W: www.lcgs.tas.edu.au

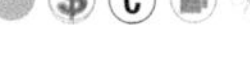

Lauriston Girls' School
38 Huntingtower Road, Armadale VIC 3143
DP Coordinator Sandra Mccowan
Languages English
T: +61 3 9864 7555
W: www.lauriston.vic.edu.au

Le Fevre High School
90 Hart Street, Semaphore South, Adelaide SA 5019
MYP Coordinator Troy Barker
Languages English
T: +61 8 8449 7004
W: www.lefevrehs.sa.edu.au

Linden Park Primary School
14 Hay Road, Linden Park, Adelaide SA 5065
PYP Coordinator Nicole Scrivener
Languages English
T: +61 (0)8 8379 2171
W: www.lindenpkr7.sa.edu.au

Lloyd Street School
Lloyd Street, East Malvern VIC 3145
PYP Coordinator Roshni Amaria
Languages English
T: +61 3 9571 0261
W: www.lloydstps.vic.edu.au

Lycée Condorcet - The International French School of Sydney
758 Anzac Parade, Maroubra, Sydney NSW 2035
DP Coordinator Marcel Hennes
Languages English
T: +61 2 9344 8692
W: www.condorcet.com.au

Macclesfield Primary School
405 Macclesfield Road, Macclesfield VIC 3782
PYP Coordinator Andrea Goodey
Languages English
T: +61 3 5968 4734
W: www.macclesfieldps.vic.edu.au

Mansfield Steiner School
91 Highett Street, Mansfield VIC 3722
DP Coordinator Leith Pierce
Languages English
T: +61 3 57791445
W: mansfieldsteiner.vic.edu.au

Mater Christi College
28 Bayview Road, Belgrave, Melbourne VIC 3160
MYP Coordinator Lisa McLean
Languages English
T: +61 3 9754 6611
W: www.materchristi.edu.au

McKinnon Primary School
253 Tucker Road, Ormond VIC 3204
PYP Coordinator Chris Barker
Languages English
T: +61 3 9578 1851
W: mckinnon-primary.vic.edu.au

Melbourne Montessori School
741 Hawthorn Road, Brighton East VIC 3187
DP Coordinator Casper Buisman
Languages English
T: +61 3 9131 5200
W: melbournemontessori.vic.edu.au

Mentone Girls' Grammar School
11 Mentone Parade, Mentone VIC 3194
PYP Coordinator Karen Chaur
Languages English
T: +61 3 9581 1200
W: www.mentonegirls.vic.edu.au

MERCEDES COLLEGE
540 Fullarton Road, Springfield SA 5062
DP Coordinator Mr Marc Whitehead
MYP Coordinator Mr Stuart Wuttke
PYP Coordinator Mr Andrew Khabbaz
Languages English
T: +61 8 8372 3200
E: mercedes@mercedes.catholic.edu.au
W: www.mercedes.catholic.edu.au
See full details on page 353

MERICI COLLEGE
Wise Street, Braddon ACT 2612
DP Coordinator Natalie Fairfax
MYP Coordinator Jodie Muldoon
Languages English
T: +61 2 6243 4100
E: info@merici.act.edu.au
W: www.merici.act.edu.au
See full details on page 354

Methodist Ladies' College
207 Barkers Road, Kew VIC 3101
DP Coordinator James Prowse
Languages English
T: +61 3 9274 6316
W: www.mlc.vic.edu.au

Mildura West Primary School
Ninth Street, Mildura VIC 3500
PYP Coordinator Rachel Parker
Languages English, Chinese
T: +61 3 50231336
W: mildurawestps.vic.edu.au

Miles Franklin Primary School
Alderman Street, Evatt, Canberra ACT 2617
PYP Coordinator Georgina Sofatzis
Languages English
T: +61 2 6205 7533
W: www.mfps.act.edu.au

Milgate Primary School
96 Landscape Drive, East Doncaster, Melbourne VIC 3109
PYP Coordinator Sarah Brown
Languages English, Mandarin
T: +61 3 9842 7744
W: www.milgateps.vic.edu.au

MLC SCHOOL
Rowley Street, Burwood, Sydney NSW 2134
DP Coordinator Olivia Nolan
Languages English
T: +61 2 9747 1266
E: enrol@mlcsyd.nsw.edu.au
W: www.mlcsyd.nsw.edu.au
See full details on page 355
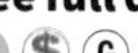

Monte Sant' Angelo Mercy College
PO Box 1064, 128 Miller Street, North Sydney NSW 2059
DP Coordinator Kim Vandervelde
MYP Coordinator Jennifer Symington
Languages English
T: +61 2 9409 6200
W: www.monte.nsw.edu.au

Moreton Bay Boys' College
302 Manly Road, Manly West QLD 4179
PYP Coordinator Paul Dack
Languages English
T: +61 07 3906 9444
W: www.mbbc.qld.edu.au

Moreton Bay College
450 Wondall Rd, Manly West QLD 4179
PYP Coordinator Nicole Bowers
Languages English
T: +61 7 3390 8555
W: www.mbc.qld.edu.au

Mornington Primary School
Vale Street, Mornington VIC 3931
PYP Coordinator Heidi Wittwer
Languages English
T: +61 3 5975 2561
W: www.morningtonps.vic.edu.au

Mount Eliza North Primary School
Moseley Drive, PO Box 219, Mount Eliza VIC 3930
PYP Coordinator Caroline Chilianis
Languages English
T: +61 3 9787 6611
W: www.menps.vic.edu.au

Mount Eliza Secondary College
Canadian Bay Road, Mount Eliza VIC 3930
MYP Coordinator Kylie Russell
Languages English, Indonesian
T: +61 3 9787 6288
W: www.mesc.vic.edu.au

Mount Macedon Primary School
641 Mount Macedon Rd, Mount Macedon VIC 3441
PYP Coordinator Simon Dohler
Languages English
T: +61 3 5426 1446

Mount Scopus Memorial College
245 Burwood Highway, Burwood VIC 3125
MYP Coordinator Sharon Stocker
PYP Coordinator Edna Sackson
Languages English, Hebrew
T: +61 3 9834 0000
W: www.scopus.vic.edu.au

Mount View Primary School
Shepherd Road, Glen Waverley VIC 3150
PYP Coordinator Amanda Petch
Languages English
T: +61 3 9560 0471
W: www.mountviewps.vic.edu.au

Mountain Creek State High School
Lady Musgrave Drive, Mountain Creek QLD 4557
DP Coordinator Adam Duus
Languages English
T: +61 (0)7 5457 8333
W: mountaincreekshs.eq.edu.au
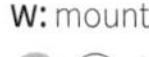

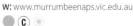

Murrumbeena Primary School
Hobart Road, Murrumbeena VIC 3163
PYP Coordinator Angela Houghton
Languages English
T: +61 3 9568 1300
W: www.murrumbeenaps.vic.edu.au

Narrabundah College
Jerrabomberra Avenue, Narrabundah ACT 2604
DP Coordinator Julie Bauer
Languages English
T: +61 2 6142 3200
W: www.narrabundahc.act.edu.au

Navigator College

PO Box 3199, Port Lincoln SA 5606
MYP Coordinator Helen Hopping
PYP Coordinator Sharyn Williams
Languages English
T: +61 8 86825099
W: www.navigator.sa.edu.au

NEWINGTON COLLEGE - LINDFIELD

26 Northcote Road, Lindfield, New South Wales NSW 2070
PYP Coordinator Benjamin Barrington-Higgs
Languages English
T: +61 2 9416 4280
W: www.newington.nsw.edu.au

See full details on page 356

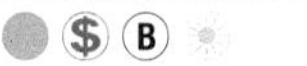

NEWINGTON COLLEGE - STANMORE

200 Stanmore Road, Stanmore NSW 2048
DP Coordinator Ms Cheryl Priest
Languages English
T: +61 2 9568 9333
E: admissions@newington.nsw.edu.au
W: www.newington.nsw.edu.au

See full details on page 356

North Ainslie Primary School

122 Majura Avenue, Ainslie, Canberra ACT 2602
PYP Coordinator Kate Bush
Languages English
T: +61 02 62056533
W: www.nthainslieps.act.edu.au

Oakleigh Grammar

77-81 Willesden Road, Oakleigh VIC 3166
MYP Coordinator Melisa Fitzgerald
Languages English
T: +61 3 9569 6128
W: www.oakleighgrammar.vic.edu.au

Our Lady of the Nativity

29 Fawkner Street, Aberfeldie VIC 3040
PYP Coordinator Catherine Simone
Languages English
T: +61 3 9337 4204
W: www.olnaberfeldie.catholic.edu.au

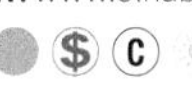

Pedare Christian College

2-30 Surrey Farm Drive, Golden Grove SA 5125
MYP Coordinator Hayley Mayer
PYP Coordinator Marika Brown
Languages English
T: +61 8 8280 1700
W: www.pedarecc.sa.edu.au

Pembroke School

342 The Parade, Kensington Park SA 5068
DP Coordinator Andrew Clark
PYP Coordinator Belinda Reitstatter
Languages English
T: +61 8 8366 6200
W: www.pembroke.sa.edu.au

Presbyterian Ladies' College - Perth

14 McNeil Street, Peppermint Grove, Perth WA 6011
DP Coordinator Rebecca Garbenis
PYP Coordinator Jennifer Rickwood, Paul O'Brien
Languages English
T: +61 8 9424 6444
W: www.plc.wa.edu.au

Presbyterian Ladies' College Melbourne

141 Burwood Highway, Burwood VIC 3125
DP Coordinator Julie Popplestone
Languages English
T: +61 3 9808 5811
W: www.plc.vic.edu.au

Preshil - The Margaret Lyttle Memorial School

395 Barkers Road, Kew, Melbourne VIC 3101
DP Coordinator Caterina Pacitti
MYP Coordinator Natalie Kunst
PYP Coordinator Cressida Batterham-Wilson
Languages English
T: +613 9817 6135
W: www.preshil.vic.edu.au

Prince Alfred College

PO Box 571, Kent Town SA 5071
DP Coordinator James Mower
PYP Coordinator Lisa Foster
Languages English
T: +61 8 8334 1200
W: www.pac.edu.au

  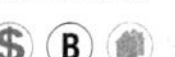

Queensland Academies Creative Industries Campus

61-73 Musk Avenue, Kelvin Grove QLD 4059
DP Coordinator Liam Clifford
Languages English
T: +61 7 3552 9333
W: qaci.eq.edu.au

Queensland Academies Health Sciences Campus

102 Edmund Rice Drive, Southport QLD 4215
DP Coordinator Alan Craig-Ward
Languages English
T: +61 7 5510 1100
W: qahs.eq.edu.au

QUEENSLAND ACADEMY FOR SCIENCE MATHEMATICS AND TECHNOLOGY (QASMT)

78 Bywong Street, Toowong QLD 4066
DP Coordinator Dr Esme Hatchell
MYP Coordinator Ms Kirsten Baker
Languages English
T: +61 7 3377 9333
E: admin@qasmt.eq.edu.au
W: qasmt.eq.edu.au

See full details on page 368

Queenwood

Locked Bag 1, Mosman NSW 2088
DP Coordinator Allison McCulloch & Jennifer Brown
Languages English
T: +61 2 8968 7777
W: www.queenwood.nsw.edu.au

Radford College

College Street, Bruce, Canberra ACT 2617
DP Coordinator Elizabeth Chase
PYP Coordinator Nick Martin
Languages English
T: +61 2 6162 5332
W: www.radford.act.edu.au

RAVENSWOOD

10 Henry Street, Gordon, Sydney NSW 2072
DP Coordinator Ms Monique Connor
PYP Coordinator Mrs Anne Gruenewald
Languages English
T: +612 9498 9898
E: admin@ravenswood.nsw.edu.au
W: www.ravenswood.nsw.edu.au

See full details on page 370

Red Hill School

PO Box 22, Red Hill ACT 2603
PYP Coordinator David Corcoran
Languages English
T: +61 2 6205 7144
W: www.redhillps.act.edu.au

Redeemer Lutheran School, Nuriootpa

Box 397, Nuriootpa SA 5355
PYP Coordinator Petrea Booth
Languages English
T: +61 885 621655
W: www.redeemer.sa.edu.au

REDLANDS

272 Military Road, Cremorne NSW 2090
DP Coordinator Darren Taylor
Languages English
T: +61 2 9908 6479
E: dtaylor@redlands.nsw.edu.au
registrar@redlands.nsw.edu.au
W: www.redlands.nsw.edu.au

See full details on page 372

Rivercrest Christian College

Gate 6, 500 Soldiers Road, Clyde North VIC 3978
DP Coordinator Kristen Dias
MYP Coordinator Elize Kok
PYP Coordinator Sagree Naidu
Languages English
T: +61 3 9703 9777
W: www.rivercrest.vic.edu.au

Rochedale State School

694 Rochedale Road, Rochedale, Brisbane QLD 4123
PYP Coordinator Natasha Ritchie
Languages English
T: +61 733408333
W: www.rochedalss.eq.edu.au

Roma Mitchell Secondary College

Briens Road, Gepps Cross SA 5094
DP Coordinator Kym Willis
MYP Coordinator Kym Willis
Languages English
T: +61 (0)8 8161 4600
W: rmsc.sa.edu.au

Rose Park Primary School

54 Alexandra Avenue, Rose Park, Adelaide SA 5067
PYP Coordinator Ida Capozzi
Languages English
T: +618 8331 7521
W: www.roseparkps.sa.edu.au

Roseville College

Locked Bag 34, 27 Bancroft Avenue, Roseville NSW 2069
PYP Coordinator Jane Sloane
Languages English
T: +61 2 9884 1100
W: www.roseville.nsw.edu.au

Sacred Heart College Geelong

Retreat Road, Newtown VIC 3220
MYP Coordinator Bridget Dunstan
Languages English
T: +61 3 52214211
W: www.shcgeelong.catholic.edu.au

Saltwater P-9 College

15 Kirra Place, Point Cook VIC 3030
PYP Coordinator Michael Nicolaides
Languages English, Spanish
T: +61 3 8366 7700
W: saltwatercollege.vic.edu.au

Santa Maria College

50 Separation Street, Northcote, Melbourne VIC 3070
MYP Coordinator Bradley Denny
Languages English
T: +61 3 9488 1600
W: www.santamaria.vic.edu.au

Santa Sabina College
90 The Boulevarde, Strathfield, Sydney NSW 2135
DP Coordinator Julie Harris
Languages English
T: +61 2 9745 7000
W: www.ssc.nsw.edu.au

Scotch College
76 Shenton Road, Swanbourne, Perth WA 6010
DP Coordinator Brendan Zani
MYP Coordinator Lauren McCormack
PYP Coordinator Warwick Norman
Languages English
T: +61 8 9383 6800
W: www.scotch.wa.edu.au
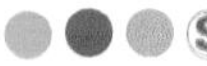

Seabrook Primary School
83-105 Point Cook Road, Seabrook VIC 3028
PYP Coordinator Rima El Souki
Languages English
T: +61 3 9395 1758
W: www.seabrook.vic.edu.au

Seaford North Primary School
81 Hallifax Street, Seaford VIC 3198
PYP Coordinator Chloe Gannon
Languages English
T: +61 3 9786 5674
W: seaford-northps.vic.edu.au

Seymour College
546 Portrush Road, Glen Osmond, Adelaide SA 5064
DP Coordinator Natalie Paelchen
Languages English
T: +61 8 8303 9000
W: seymour.sa.edu.au

Somerset College
Somerset Drive, Mudgeeraba QLD 4213
DP Coordinator Michele Sauer
MYP Coordinator Allison Foster
PYP Coordinator Brenda Millican
Languages English
T: +61 (0)7 5559 7100
W: www.somerset.qld.edu.au

Sophia Mundi Steiner School
St. Mary's Abbotsford Convent, 1 St Heller's Street, Abbotsford, Melbourne VIC 3067
DP Coordinator Melanie Brown
Languages English
T: +61 3 9419 9229
W: www.sophiamundi.vic.edu.au

Southern Christian College
150 Redwood Road, Kingston, Tasmania TAS 7050
MYP Coordinator Todd Barker
PYP Coordinator Jenny Mahoney
Languages English
T: +613 6229 5744
W: www.scc.tas.edu.au

ST ANDREW'S CATHEDRAL SCHOOL
Sydney Square, Sydney NSW 2000
DP Coordinator Sharon Munro
MYP Coordinator Kathleen Layhe
Languages English
T: +61 2 9286 9500
E: enrolments@sacs.nsw.edu.au
W: www.sacs.nsw.edu.au
See full details on page 386

St Andrews Lutheran College
PO Box 2142, Burleigh BC QLD 4220
PYP Coordinator Karen Koehler
Languages English
T: +61 7 5568 5900
W: www.standrewslutheran.qld.edu.au

St Andrew's School
22 Smith Street, Walkerville SA 5081
PYP Coordinator Mary-Anne Muhl
Languages English
T: +61 8 81685555
W: www.standrews.sa.edu.au

St Columba's Primary School
24 Glen Huntly Road, Elwood VIC 3184
PYP Coordinator Claire Van Loon
Languages English
T: +61 3 9531 6560
W: www.stcolumbasprimary.org

St Gregory's College Campbelltown
100 Badgally Road, Gregory Hills NSW 2557
PYP Coordinator Diana Ivancic
Languages English, Spanish
T: +61 2 4629 4222
W: www.stgregs.nsw.edu.au

St John's Anglican College
College Avenue, Forest Lake QLD 4078
PYP Coordinator Martin Brownlow
Languages English
T: +61 (0)7 3372 0111
W: stjohnsanglicancollege.com.au

St John's Lutheran School, Eudunda, Inc.
8 Ward Street, Eudunda SA 5374
PYP Coordinator Josie Wundersitz
Languages English
T: +61 8 8581 1282
W: www.stjohns-eudunda.sa.edu.au

St Leonard's College
163 South Road, Brighton East, Melbourne VIC 3187
DP Coordinator Craig Rodgers
PYP Coordinator Chris Stickman
Languages English
T: +61 3 9909 9300
W: www.stleonards.vic.edu.au

St Margaret's School
27-47 Gloucester Avenue, Berwick, Melbourne VIC 3806
PYP Coordinator Melissa Graham
Languages English
T: +61 3 9703 8111
W: www.stmargarets.vic.edu.au

St Mary Star of the Sea College
15 Harbour St, Wollongong NSW 2500
MYP Coordinator Katrina Wall
Languages English
T: +61 (0)2 4228 6011
W: www.stmarys.nsw.edu.au

St Michael's Lutheran School
6 Balhannah Rd, Hahndorf SA 5250
PYP Coordinator Darlene Hall
Languages English
T: +61 8 8388 7228
W: www.stmichaels.sa.edu.au

St Paul's Grammar School
Locked Bag 8016, Penrith NSW 2751
DP Coordinator Antony Mayrhofer
MYP Coordinator Lauren Cullimore
PYP Coordinator Corinne Harrington
Languages English
T: +61 2 4777 4888
W: www.stpauls.nsw.edu.au

St Peter's Anglican Primary School
Howe Street, Campbelltown NSW 2560
PYP Coordinator Melinda Richardson
Languages English
T: +61 (2) 4627 2990
W: www.stpeters.nsw.edu.au

St Peter's College
Hackney Road, Hackney, Adelaide SA 5069
DP Coordinator Paul Hadfield
Languages English
T: +61 8 8404 0400
W: www.stpeters.sa.edu.au
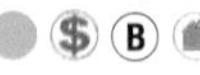

St Peter's Girls' School
Stonyfell Road, Stonyfell SA 5066
DP Coordinator Carolyn Victoria Farr
PYP Coordinator Helen Smith
Languages English
T: +61 88 334 2200
W: www.stpetersgirls.sa.edu.au
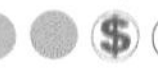 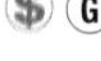

St Peters Lutheran College
66 Harts Road, Indooroopilly QLD 4068
DP Coordinator Roslynne Midgley
PYP Coordinator Simone Mitchell
Languages English
T: +61 7 3377 6222
W: www.stpeters.qld.edu.au

St Peters Lutheran School
71 Cumming Street, Blackwood SA 5051
PYP Coordinator Nicolle Jakube
Languages English
T: +61 8 8278 0800
W: www.stpeterslutheran.sa.edu.au

St Ursula's College Kingsgrove
69 Caroline Street, Kingsgrove NSW 2208
DP Coordinator Heather Jesuadian
Languages English
T: +61 2 9502 3300
W: stursulakingsgrove.syd.catholic.edu.au

Stradbroke School
73 Koonga Avenue, Rostrevor SA 5073
PYP Coordinator Sarah Button
Languages English
T: +61 8 8337 2861
W: www.stradsch.sa.edu.au

Surrey Hills Primary School
2 Beatrice Avenue, Surrey HIlls VIC 3127
PYP Coordinator Marika Smith
Languages English, Chinese
T: +61 3 9890 1560
W: www.surreyhillsps.vic.edu.au

Suzanne Cory High School
225 Hoppers Lane, Werribee VIC 3030
DP Coordinator Jasmine Byrne
Languages English
T: +61 3 8734 2800
W: www.suzannecoryhs.vic.edu.au

Tara Anglican School for Girls
Masons Drive, North Parramatta, Sydney NSW 2151
MYP Coordinator Cassandra Winfield
PYP Coordinator Wendy Abernethy
Languages English
T: +61 2 9630 6655
W: www.tara.nsw.edu.au
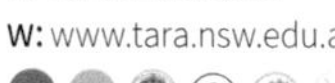

Telopea Park School / Lycée Franco-Australien de Canberra
New South Wales Crescent, Barton ACT 2600
MYP Coordinator Stacey Griffiths
Languages English
T: +61 2 6142 3388
W: www.telopea.act.edu.au

The Armidale School
Locked Bag 3003, 87 Douglas Street, Armidale NSW 2350
MYP Coordinator Rachael Harrison
PYP Coordinator Veronica Waters
Languages English
T: +61 2 6776 5800
W: www.as.edu.au

The Friends' School
23 Commercial Road, North Hobart TAS 7002
DP Coordinator Sarah Walker
PYP Coordinator Wendy Crow
Languages English
T: +61 3 6210 2200
W: www.friends.tas.edu.au

The Illawarra Grammar School
10-12 Western Ave, Wollongong NSW 2500
PYP Coordinator Mrs Karen Wallace
Languages English
T: +61 2 4220 0200
W: www.tigs.nsw.edu.au

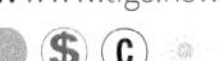

The King's School
87-129 Pennant Hills Road, North Parramatta NSW 2151
PYP Coordinator Shannon O'Dwyer
Languages English
T: +612 9683 8555
W: www.kings.edu.au

The King's School, Tudor House
6480 Illawarra Highway, Moss Vale NSW 2577
PYP Coordinator Caitlin Hayman
Languages English
T: +61 2 4868 0000
W: www.tudorhouse.nsw.edu.au

The Mac.Robertson Girls' High School
350-370 Kings Way, Melbourne VIC 3004
DP Coordinator Shungo Sawaki
Languages English
T: +61 3 9864 7700
W: www.macrob.vic.edu.au

The Montessori School Kingsley
P.O. Box 194, Landsdale WA 6065
CP Coordinator Michael Caldwell
DP Coordinator Katharina Stillitano
Languages English
T: +61 8 9409 9151
W: www.themontessorischool.wa.edu.au

The Norwood Morialta High School
Morialta Road West, Rostrevor SA 5073
MYP Coordinator Jane Pears
Languages English
T: +61 8 83650455
W: www.nmhs.sa.edu.au

The Riverina Anglican College
127 Farrer Road, Wagga Wagga NSW 2650
DP Coordinator Patricia Humble
Languages English
T: +61 (0)2 6933 1811
W: www.trac.nsw.edu.au

The Scots School Albury
393 Perry Street, Albury NSW 2640
PYP Coordinator Georgie Parker
Languages English
T: +61 (0)2 6022 0000
W: www.scotsalbury.nsw.edu.au

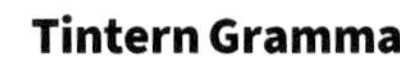

Tintern Grammar
90 Alexandra Road, PO Box 26, Ringwood East VIC 3135
DP Coordinator Nola Joy Brotchie
Languages English
T: +61 3 9845 7777
W: www.tintern.vic.edu.au

Townsville Grammar School
45 Paxton Street, North Ward QLD 4810
DP Coordinator Hein Kamffer
Languages English
T: +61 7 4722 4900
W: www.tgs.qld.edu.au

Treetops Montessori School
PO Box 59, Darlington WA 6076
DP Coordinator Kimberly Steimer
Languages English
T: +61 8 9299 6725
W: www.treetops.wa.edu.au

Trinity Grammar School Preparatory School
115-125 The Boulevarde, Strathfield NSW 2135
PYP Coordinator Fiona Evans
Languages English
T: +61 2 8732 4600
W: www.trinity.nsw.edu.au

Trinity Grammar School, Kew
40 Charles Street, Kew VIC 3101
PYP Coordinator Jonathan Knight
Languages English
T: +61 3 9854 3600
W: www.trinity.vic.edu.au

Trinity Grammar School, Sydney
119 Prospect Road, Summer Hill NSW 2130
DP Coordinator Kai Ikeuchi
PYP Coordinator Merilyn Ormes
Languages English
T: +61 2 9581 6000
W: www.trinity.nsw.edu.au

Trinity Lutheran College
PO Box 322, Ashmore City QLD 4214
PYP Coordinator Melissa O'Shea
Languages English
T: +61 7 5556 8200
W: www.tlc.qld.edu.au

Trinity Lutheran College
920 Fifteenth Street, Mildura VIC 3500
MYP Coordinator Jean Booysen
PYP Coordinator Joanne Botha
Languages English
T: +61 3 5023 7013
W: www.tlc.vic.edu.au

Unity College Murraylands
P.O. Box 5141, Owl Drive, Murray Bridge SA 5253
MYP Coordinator Sophie Cox
PYP Coordinator Rachel Harrip
Languages English
T: +61 8 8532 0100
W: www.unitycollege.sa.edu.au

Unley High School
Kitchener Street, Netherby SA 5062
DP Coordinator Andy inter
Languages English
T: +61 8 8394 5400
W: uhs.sa.edu.au

Urquhart Park Primary School
49 Inkerman Street, Newington, Ballarat VIC 3350
PYP Coordinator Megan Hearn
Languages English, Japanese
T: +61 3 5330 5400
W: urquhartps.vic.edu.au

Wales Street Primary School
Wales Street, Thornbury VIC 3071
PYP Coordinator Luisa Kalenjuk
Languages English
T: +61 (03) 9484 394
W: www.walesstps.vic.edu.au

Walford Anglican School for Girls
316 Unley Road, Hyde Park SA 5061
DP Coordinator Brian Parsons
PYP Coordinator Annabel Howard
Languages English
T: +61 8 8272 6555
W: www.walford.asn.au

Wenona School
176 Walker Street, North Sydney NSW 2060
PYP Coordinator Kate Cameron
Languages English
T: +61 2 9409 4400
W: www.wenona.nsw.edu.au

Werribee Secondary College
PO Box 314, Werribee VIC 3030
DP Coordinator Joanna Sommers
Languages English
T: +61 3 9741 1822
W: www.werribeesc.vic.edu.au

Wesley College Melbourne - Elsternwick Campus
5 Gladstone Parade, Elsternwick VIC 3185
MYP Coordinator Lachlan Morton
PYP Coordinator Michelle Bond
Languages English
T: +61 3 8102 6808
W: www.wesleycollege.net

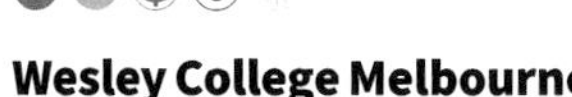

Wesley College Melbourne - Glen Waverley Campus
620 High Street Road, Glen Waverley VIC 3150
MYP Coordinator James Carroll
PYP Coordinator Kathy Saville
Languages English
T: +61 3 8102 6508
W: www.wesleycollege.net

Wesley College Melbourne - St Kilda Road Campus
577 St Kilda Road, Melbourne VIC 3004
DP Coordinator Christopher Marsden
MYP Coordinator Linda Pizzarello
PYP Coordinator Sarah Ho
Languages English
T: +613 8102 6508
W: www.wesleycollege.edu.au

Westbourne College Sydney
Harris Street, Ultimo, Sydney NSW 2007
DP Coordinator Stephen Keegan
Languages English
T: +61 2 8088 0719
W: www.westbournecollege.com.au

Woodcroft College
Bains Road, Morphett Vale SA 5162
PYP Coordinator Karen McCulloch
Languages English
T: +61 8 8322 2333
W: www.woodcroft.sa.edu.au

Woodleigh School
485 Golf Links Road, Langwarrin South VIC 3911
PYP Coordinator Jodie Kirchner
Languages English
T: +61 3 5971 6100
W: www.woodleigh.vic.edu.au

Xavier College, Kostka Hall Campus
47 South Road, Brighton, Melbourne VIC 3186
PYP Coordinator Elena Serraglio
Languages English
T: +61 3 9519 0600
W: www.xavier.vic.edu.au

BANGLADESH

Abdul Kadir Molla International School
16/8 Baghdi (Dhaka-Sylhet Highway), Narsingdi Sadar, Narsingdi 1600, Dhaka
DP Coordinator Md. Tahmidul Haq Ansari
PYP Coordinator Asnaha Farheen
Languages English, Bengali
T: +880 961 750 6070
W: www.akmis.net

American International School, Dhaka
12 United Nations Road, 1212 Dhaka
DP Coordinator Kaitlyn Leach
PYP Coordinator Nancy Snyder
Languages English
T: +880 24 108 1837
W: www.aisdhaka.org

Aurora International School
House NE (A) 3A, Road 74, Gulshan, 1212 Dhaka
PYP Coordinator Mahreen Murad
Languages English
T: +880 222 228 3251
W: www.aurora-intl.org

Australian International School, Dhaka
Joarshahara, Khilkhet, 1229 Dhaka
DP Coordinator Ponny Chacko
MYP Coordinator Rijwana Ameen Chowdhury
PYP Coordinator Shabnam Hossain
Languages English
T: +880 171 156 7236
W: www.ausisdhaka.net

Canadian International School Bangladesh
Senior Campus: Plot No. 110, Road No. 27, Block A, Banani 1213, Dhaka
DP Coordinator Dewan Mehtauddin
Languages English
T: +880 184 146 1999
W: www.canadaeducationbd.com

Crans-Montana International School
Rahaman Housing Family Estate, 1492, C D A Avenue, East Nasirabad, Chittagong
PYP Coordinator Jalal Uddin
Languages English, Bengali
T: +880 163 155 5222
W: cmisbd.com

International School Dhaka (ISD)
Plot 80, Block E, Bashundhara R/A, (Opposite Apollo Hospitals Dhaka), 1229 Dhaka
DP Coordinator Dixon Kibengo
MYP Coordinator Nilanthi Das
PYP Coordinator Towhida Afsar
Languages English
T: +880 2 843 1101
W: www.isdbd.org

Pledge Harbor International School
Singer Dighi, Maona, Gazipur 1741, Dhaka
CP Coordinator Sujata Chowdhury
DP Coordinator Sujata Chowdhury
MYP Coordinator Rajani Roy
PYP Coordinator Babita Sidhu
Languages English
T: +880 967 880 0404
W: pledgeharbor.org

Springdale International School
Road 55, House 11/A, Gulshan 2, 1212 Dhaka
PYP Coordinator Taslima Khatoon
Languages English, Bangla
T: +880 140 707 6610
W: springdaledhaka.org

The Aga Khan School, Dhaka
Road 6A, Sector 4, Uttara Model Town, 1230 Dhaka
DP Coordinator Usha Kasana
Languages English
T: +880 2 4895 9722
W: www.agakhanschools.org/bangladesh/aksd

BRUNEI DARUSSALAM

International School Brunei
Jalan Utama Salambigar, Kampong Sungai Hanching, Berakas 'B' BC2115
DP Coordinator Julia Durston
Languages English
T: +673 233 0608
W: www.isb.edu.bn

JERUDONG INTERNATIONAL SCHOOL
Jalan Universiti, Kampong Tungku, Bandar Seri Begawan BE2119
DP Coordinator Mr Daniel Roberts
Languages English
T: +673 241 1000 (EXT: 1206/7100/1214)
E: admissions@jis.edu.bn
W: www.jerudonginternationalschool.com
See full details on page 342

CAMBODIA

Australian International School Phnom Penh
No. 76 Angkor Boulevard, Sangkat Toul Sangke 2, Khan Russey Keo, Phnom Penh 120707
CP Coordinator Jacob Evans
DP Coordinator Matthew Lloyd
MYP Coordinator Bradley Kremer
PYP Coordinator Wanita Woithe
Languages English, Khmer
T: +855 92 111 136
W: aispp.edu.kh

Canadian International School of Phnom Penh
Koh Pich (Diamond Island), Elite Town Street, Phnom Penh
DP Coordinator Jaclyn George
Languages English, French
T: +855 23 900 399
W: www.cisp.edu.kh

Golden Gate American School
No. 846 Street 1003, Sen Sok District, Phnom Penh 12101
DP Coordinator Rebekah Bell
Languages English
T: +855 99 777 550
W: www.ggas.edu.kh
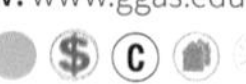

HOPE International School
P.O. Box 2521, Phnom Penh 3 12000
DP Coordinator Sarah Moon
Languages English
T: +855 12 550 522
W: www.hope.edu.kh

International School of Phnom Penh
P.O. Box 138, Hun Neang Boulevard, Phnom Penh
DP Coordinator Lucie Lecocq Otsing
MYP Coordinator Matthew Clouter
PYP Coordinator Rachel Garthe
Languages English
T: +855 23 425 088
W: www.ispp.edu.kh

Northbridge International School Cambodia
Street 2004, Trapang Chhouk Village, Teuk Thlar Commune, Sen Sok District, Phnom Penh 12102
DP Coordinator Kohulan Jeganathan
MYP Coordinator Gillian Presland
PYP Coordinator Donita Bell
Languages English
T: +855 23 900 749
W: www.nisc.edu.kh
 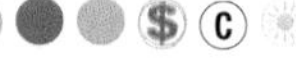

The Giving Tree International School
N4A1, Street 398, Beoung Keng Kang 1, Phnom Penh
PYP Coordinator Daniel Cullinan
Languages English, French
T: +855 17 997 112
W: www.thegivingtreeschool.edu.kh

CHINA

Alcanta International College
14 Guang Sheng Road, Nansha District, Guangzhou City, Guangdong 511458
DP Coordinator David (Jiacun) Dai
Languages English, Mandarin
T: +86 20 8618 3999/3666
W: aicib.org
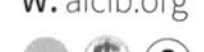

AMERICAN INTERNATIONAL SCHOOL OF GUANGZHOU
No 3 Yan Yu Street South, Ersha Island, Yuexiu District, Guangzhou, Guangdong 510105
DP Coordinator John Kennett
PYP Coordinator Tania Mansfield
Languages English
T: +86 20 8735 3392
E: admissions@aisgz.org
W: www.aisgz.org
See full details on page 312

Bashu Secondary School
No. 51 Bei Qu Road, Yuzhong District, Chongqing 400013
DP Coordinator Yun Liang
Languages English, Chinese
T: +86 23 6300 2371
W: www.bashu.com.cn

Beanstalk International Bilingual School BIBS - Chaoyang Changying Campus
No. 1 Yaojiadian Street, Chaoyang District, Beijing
PYP Coordinator Faith Wyllie
Languages English, Chinese
T: +86 10 8456 2808
W: changying-en.bibs.com.cn

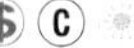

Beanstalk International Bilingual School BIBS - Chengdu Campus
No. 351 Honghe Street, Longquanyi district, Chengdu, Sichuan
DP Coordinator Qianyun Qin
MYP Coordinator Ke Li
PYP Coordinator Ting Long
Languages English, Chinese
T: +86 28 8481 0088
W: www.bibs.com.cn

Beanstalk International Bilingual School BIBS - Kunming Campus
No. 986 Yongzheng Street, Chenggong District, Kunming, Yunnan
DP Coordinator Surika Pienaar
MYP Coordinator Xi Wu
PYP Coordinator Louie Desloge
Languages English, Chinese
T: +86871 6747 8668
W: www.bibs.com.cn

Beanstalk International Bilingual School BIBS - Shunyi Campus
No. 15 Liyuan Jie, TianZhu County, Shunyi District, Beijing 100000
DP Coordinator Keya Mu
MYP Coordinator Phil Rietema
PYP Coordinator Mario Espinal
Languages English
T: +86 10 6456 0618
W: www.bibs.com.cn

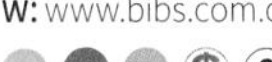

Beanstalk International Bilingual School BIBS - Upper East Side Campus
No.6 North East 4th Ring Rd, Chaoyang District, Beijing 100016
PYP Coordinator Reetika Jain
Languages English
T: +86 10 5130 7951
W: www.bibs.com.cn

Beijing 101 Middle School
11 Summer Palace Road, Haidian District, Beijing
DP Coordinator Eli Walker
Languages English, Chinese
T: +86 10 5163 3264
W: www.beijing101.com

Beijing BISS International School
No 17, Area 4, An Zhen Xi Li, Chaoyang District, Beijing 100029
DP Coordinator Bingxi Li
MYP Coordinator Xiuqi Jin
PYP Coordinator Bingxi Li
Languages English
T: +86 10 64 433151
W: www.biss.com.cn

Beijing Chaoyang KaiWen Academy
No.46 Baoquansan Street, Chaoyang District, Beijing
DP Coordinator John Whitehead
Languages English, Chinese
T: +86 108 302 8199
W: cy.kaiwenacademy.cn

Beijing City International School
77 Baiziwan Nan Er Road, Chaoyang District, Beijing 100022
DP Coordinator David Nguyen
MYP Coordinator Cornel Marais
PYP Coordinator Chantelle Parsons
Languages English
T: +86 10 8771 7171
W: www.bcis.cn

Beijing Enlighten School
No. 300 Shunbai Road, Chaoyang District, Beijing
PYP Coordinator Adrian Gaunt
Languages English, Chinese
T: +86 10 6431 9970
W: www.enlightenschool.cn

Beijing Haidian International School
No.368-2 Hanhe Road, Haidian District, Beijing 100195
DP Coordinator David Eriksen
Languages English
T: +86 10 8843 8003
W: www.bjhdis.com

Beijing Huijia Kindergarten, Beiou Campus
No.80 Maliandao Road, Xicheng District, Beijing 100085
PYP Coordinator Kelly Min Li
Languages Chinese, English
T: +86 10 63354580
W: www.hjkids.com

Beijing Huijia Kindergarten, Xibahe Dongli Campus
No.103 Xibahe Dongli, Chaoyang District, Beijing 100028
PYP Coordinator Melissa Peng
Languages Chinese
T: +86 (10) 64655212
W: www.hjkids.com

Beijing Huijia Private School
157 Changhuai Road, Changping District, Beijing 102200
DP Coordinator Yao Chen
MYP Coordinator Jingyu Li
PYP Coordinator Catherine Ma
Languages Chinese, English
T: +86 (10) 608 49399
W: www.huijia.edu.cn

Beijing Hurston Kindergarten
Room 2-1, Building 2, No. 145, Jiukeshu, Tongzhou District, Beijing
PYP Coordinator Mandy Li
Languages English, Chinese
T: +86 40 0855 1958
W: www.hurston365.com

Beijing International Bilingual Academy
Monet Garden, No 5 Yumin Road, Houshayu, Shunyi, Beijing 101300
DP Coordinator Richa Gupta
MYP Coordinator John Michael Cuepo
Languages English
T: +86 10 80410390
W: www.bibachina.org

Beijing National Day School
No. 66 Yuquan Road, Haidan District, Beijing 100039
DP Coordinator Jhony Arias Vivas
Languages English
T: +86 (10) 88625495
W: www.bndsedu.com

Beijing No 55 High School
12# Xin Zhong Jie Street, Dong Cheng District, Beijing 100027
DP Coordinator Ying Ying Wu
MYP Coordinator Tian Jieping
Languages English, Chinese
T: +86 10 64162247

Beijing No. 80 High School
WangjingBeiluJia 16, Chaoyang District, Beijing 100102
DP Coordinator Jie Song
Languages English
T: +86 10 5804 7300

Beijing Royal Foreign Language School
No. 11, Wangfu Street, Changping District, Beijing 102209
MYP Coordinator Yue Wang
PYP Coordinator Han Zhang
Languages Chinese, English
T: +86 10 81 785 511
W: www.brs.edu.cn

Beijing Royal Kindergarten
No. 11, Wangfu Street, Changping District, Beijing 102209
PYP Coordinator Miao Si
Languages English, Chinese
W: www.brs.edu.cn

Beijing Royal School
No. 11, Wangfu Street, Changping District, Beijing 102209
DP Coordinator Dan Yan
Languages English, Chinese
T: +86 10 81 785 511
W: www.brs.edu.cn

Beijing World Youth Academy
18 Hua Jia Di Bei Li, Chao Yang District, Beijing 100102
DP Coordinator Richard Ambler
MYP Coordinator Juan Xia
Languages English
T: +86 10 6470 6336
W: www.ibwya.net

Beijing Xin Fuxue International Academy
No. 99 Jingshun Road, Shunyi District, Beijing
DP Coordinator Wenjing Luo
MYP Coordinator Yanding Wen
Languages English, Chinese
T: +86 10 8942 0199
W: www.xinfuxue.com

Boston International School
9 Jinghui West Road, New District, Wuxi, Jiangsu 214000
DP Coordinator Matthew Kirk
MYP Coordinator Laura Ward
PYP Coordinator Jerica Claassen
Languages English
T: +86 400 032 8000
W: www.bostonis.org

Boya International Academy - Kindergarten
No. 2756 Qunxian Middle Road, Jinghu New District, Shaoxing, Zhejiang
PYP Coordinator Zeyuan Gao
Languages English, Chinese
W: www.biaintl.com

Bright Academy
Building 39#, ShiFoYing XiLi, Chaoyang District, Beijing 100025
PYP Coordinator Tracie Chen
Languages English, Chinese

IB ASIA-PACIFIC

Brilliant International School

No. 5 Building of Guanyang Mingdi, Chongchuan District, Nantong, Jiangsu 226000
PYP Coordinator Arii Medrano
Languages English

British School of Beijing, Shunyi

South Side, No. 9 An Hua Street, Shunyi District, Beijing 101318
DP Coordinator Sarah Donnelly
Languages English
T: +8610 8047 3558
W: www.bsbshunyi.com

Bubble Kingdom International Kindergarten

No. 431, Linjiang Avenue, Zhujiang New Town, Tianhe District, Guangzhou, Guangdong 510620
PYP Coordinator Lingbo Sun
Languages English, Chinese
T: +86 20 6622 2520
W: www.bkik-kingold.com

Cade International Kindergarten

No. 188 Lianchuang Road, Yuhang District, Hangzhou, Zhejiang
PYP Coordinator Xiaoxi Sun
Languages English, Chinese
T: +86 571 8909 9666
W: www.cadeedu.com

Canada British Columbia International Schools - Hefei

5th Floor, International Department, Hefei No.1 High School, 2356 Xizang Road, Binhu New District, Hefei, Anhui
DP Coordinator Isabelle Mathieu
Languages English, Chinese
T: +86 199 5605 8176
W: www.cbcschools.ca/hefei

Canadian Foreign Language School-Cambridgeshire

Inside Agile Cambridgeshire, Nancun Town, Panyu District, Guangzhou, Guangdong 511442
PYP Coordinator Ting Yi
Languages English, Chinese
T: +86 186 2078 9095
W: en.cls-c.com

Canadian International School Kunshan

555 Chuanshi Road, Kunshan, Jiangsu 215347
DP Coordinator Brice Bomo
MYP Coordinator Keith McCann
PYP Coordinator Linwei Li
Languages English
T: +86 400-828-0084
W: www.ciskunshan.org

Canadian International School of Beijing

38 Liangmaqiao Lu, Chaoyang District, Beijing 100125
DP Coordinator Vishwas Kulkarni
MYP Coordinator Paul Steffan
PYP Coordinator Penny Liu
Languages English
T: +86 10 6465 7788
W: www.cisbeijing.com

Canadian International School of Hefei

Fuxing Rd., High-Tech Zone, Hefei, Anhui 230088
DP Coordinator Ryan Walsh
MYP Coordinator Sean Miller
PYP Coordinator Kathryn Viljoen
Languages English
T: +86 551 6267 6776
W: www.cish.com.cn

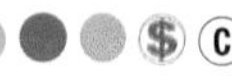

Canadian International School of Shenyang

No.301 Hui Shan Road, Hunnan District, Shenyang, Liaoning 110167
DP Coordinator Michael Coffey
MYP Coordinator Muhammad Ali Asad
PYP Coordinator Don Cox
Languages English, Chinese
T: +86 24 66675379
W: www.cisshenyang.com.cn

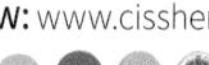

Changchun American International School

2899 Dong Nan Hu Road, Changchun, Jilin 130033
DP Coordinator Santo Kurniawan
MYP Coordinator John Salgado
PYP Coordinator Michael Rylance
Languages English
T: +86 431 8458 1234
W: www.caischina.org

Changjun High School International Department

No. 328 Chazishan Road, Yuelu District, Changsha, Hunan 410023
DP Coordinator Peng Peng
Languages Chinese, English
T: +86 (0)731 85287942
W: changjunap.xhd.cn

Changsha WES (Bilingual) Academy

No. 58 Beidou Road, Changsha National Economic & Technical Development Zone, Changsha, Hunan 410100
PYP Coordinator Yuan Xie
Languages English, Chinese
T: +86 731 8275 8900
W: cwb.wes-cwa.org

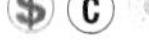

Changsha WES Academy

8 Dongyi Road, Xingsha, Changsha National Economic & Technical Development Zone, Changsha, Hunan 410100
CP Coordinator Yiding Peng
DP Coordinator Yujing Wu
PYP Coordinator Michelle Naidoo
Languages English
T: +86 731 8275 8900
W: www1.wes-cwa.org

Changwai Bilingual School

No.66 Hengshan Road, Changzhou, Jiangsu 213022
DP Coordinator Lei Dong
MYP Coordinator Yuefang Han
PYP Coordinator Yun Ding
Languages English, Chinese
T: +86 519 86921160
W: www.cztis.com

Chengdu Meishi International School

1340 Middle Section of Tianfu Avenue, Chengdu, Sichuan 610042
DP Coordinator Lorry Luo
MYP Coordinator Linda Guo
PYP Coordinator Jing Liu
Languages English, Chinese
T: +86 028 8533 0653
W: www.meishischool.com

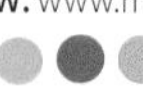

Chengdu Shude High School

No.398, Bairihong West Road, Jinjiang District, Chengdu, Sichuan 610000
DP Coordinator Amy Jingyu Li
Languages English
T: +86 28 86119628/98
W: www.sdgj.com

Chenshan School

QiYunXiDaDao, XiuNing District, Huangshan, Anhui 245400
DP Coordinator Amee Loftis
Languages English, Chinese
T: +86 559 7511878
W: www.chenshanschool.com

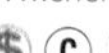

China World Academy Changshu

No.8 Yijia Road, Changshu, Jiangsu 215500
DP Coordinator Hu Yetao
Languages English, Chinese
T: +86 185 0152 9096
W: www.cwacs.cn

Chiway Repton School Xiamen

No. 388 Xibin Road, Jimei District, Xiamen, Fujian 361022
MYP Coordinator Caiyun (Jane) Zhan
PYP Coordinator Qi Wei
Languages English, Chinese
T: +86 59 2210 0886
W: www.chiway-repton.com

Chongqing Nankai Liangjiang Secondary School

No. 209 Yujiang Avenue, Longxing, Yubei District, Chongqing 401135
DP Coordinator Li Wu
Languages English, Chinese
W: www.cqnkljzx.edu.cn/xxcms

Citic Lake Bilingual International School

Citic Lake Community, Lishui Town, Nanhai District, Foshan, Guangdong
PYP Coordinator Spring Li
Languages English
T: +86 (0)757 81008639
W: www.cbis-gd.com

Cogdel Cranleigh School, Changsha

117 Lixin Street, Changsha Economy and Technology Zone, Changsha, Hunan
DP Coordinator Mengjiao Tang
PYP Coordinator Ying Xu
Languages English, Chinese
T: +86 731 8406 1777
W: www.cogdel.com

Country Garden Silver Beach School

Country Garden Silver Beach, Renshan Town, Huidong County, Huizhou, Guangdong 516347
DP Coordinator Miaomiao Song
PYP Coordinator Xin Gao
Languages English, Chinese
T: +86 139 2910 2096
W: sbs.gd.cn

Daystar Academy

No. 2, Shunbai Road, Chaoyang District, Beijing
DP Coordinator Jon Howarth
MYP Coordinator Jon Howarth
PYP Coordinator Yvonne (Vrugtman) Featherer
Languages English
T: +86 (0)10 64337366
W: daystarchina.cn

Daystar Academy Sanlitun

No.13 East 4th Street, Sanlitun, Chaoyang, Beijing 100600
PYP Coordinator Yvonne Horst
Languages English, Chinese

Dehong Beijing International Chinese School

Block #1, Luneng Grassetown, Bifu Road, Tongzhou District, Beijing 101100
DP Coordinator Kevin Chu
Languages English, Chinese
T: +86 10 8083 6983
W: beijing.dehong.cn

Dehong Shanghai International Chinese School
1935 Shuguang Road, Maqiao, Minhang District, Shanghai 201111
DP Coordinator Rebecca Curtin
Languages English, Chinese
T: +86 21 3329 9458
W: shanghai.dehong.cn

Dongguan Hanlin Experimental School
Chuangye Road No.5, Wanjiang District, Dongguan, Guangdong 523000
MYP Coordinator Yan Li
PYP Coordinator Yixiang Liu
Languages English, Chinese
T: +86 769 2277 6456
W: www.hanlinschool.com.cn

DULWICH COLLEGE BEIJING
89 Capital Airport Road, Shunyi District, Beijing 101300
DP Coordinator Mr. Anthony Baldwin
Languages English
T: +86 10 6454 9000
E: admissions.beijing@dulwich.org
W: beijing.dulwich.org
See full details on page 324

Dulwich College Shanghai Pudong
266 Lan An Road, Jinqiao, Pudong, Shanghai 201206
DP Coordinator Anthony Gillett
Languages English, Chinese
T: +8621 3896 1200
W: shanghai-pudong.dulwich.org

Dulwich College Shanghai Puxi
2000 Qianpujing Road, Maqiao, Minhang District, Shanghai 201111
DP Coordinator David Brown
Languages English, Mandarin, Spanish
T: +86 21 3329 9310
W: shanghai-puxi.dulwich.org
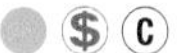

Dulwich College Suzhou
360 Gang Tian Road, Suzhou Industrial Park, Suzhou, Jiangsu 215021
CP Coordinator Stewart Paterson
DP Coordinator Stewart Paterson
Languages English
T: +86 512 6295 9500
W: suzhou.dulwich.org
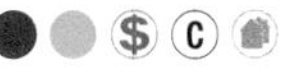

ECNU Affiliated Bilingual
569 Anchi Road, Jiading District, Shanghai 201805
DP Coordinator Ru Wang
Languages English
T: +86 400 920 6698
W: ecnuas.com

ECNU Affiliated Bilingual Kindergarten
221 Rong Ze Road, Shanghai 201805
PYP Coordinator Iuliia Shmatkova
Languages English, Chinese
T: +86 13 5246 94182
W: www.ecnuak.com

EL Genesis Kindergarten
No. 8 Ruichang Road, Hi-Tech Zone, Ningbo, Zhejiang 315048
PYP Coordinator Hangyan Zhang
Languages English, Chinese
T: +86 40 0801 8000
W: en.elgenesis-ece.com

Escola Kao Yip
Avenida Xian Xing Hai, NAPE, Macau SAR
DP Coordinator Darren Lam
MYP Coordinator Ka Wai Leong
PYP Coordinator Liyuan Liu
Languages English, Chinese
T: +853 2875 0013
W: wp.kaoyip.edu.mo/secib
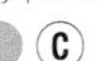

ETONHOUSE INTERNATIONAL SCHOOL SUZHOU
102 Kefa Road, Suzhou Science & Technology Town, Suzhou, Jiangsu 215163
DP Coordinator Rajesh Kripalani
MYP Coordinator Murray Fowler
PYP Coordinator Natasha D'Costa
Languages English
T: +86 512 6825 5666
E: enquiry-sz@etonhouse.com.cn
W: www.etonhouse.com.cn/suzhou
See full details on page 326

EtonHouse International School Times Residence, Chengdu
180 Zhiquan Section, East Avenue, Times Residence, Chengdu, Sichuan 610061
PYP Coordinator Elaine Wang
Languages English
T: +86 28 8477 7977
W: chengdu.etonhouse.com.cn/timesresidence

EtonHouse International School, Dongguan
19 Guangchang North Road, Gaobu, Dongguan, Guangdong 523270
PYP Coordinator Josanne Bally
Languages English
T: +86 769 8878 5333
W: www.etonhouse-dg.com

EtonHouse International School, Foshan
32 Fufeng Square, 1st Foping No.4 Road, Guicheng, Nanhai, Foshan, Guangdong
PYP Coordinator Robert Daws
Languages English
T: +86 757 6668 8333
W: www.foshan.etonhouse.com.cn

EtonHouse International School, Nanjing
10 South Qing'ao Rd, Jianye District, Nanjing, Jiangsu 210019
PYP Coordinator Yuliya Paliukhovich
Languages English
T: +86 25 8669 6778
W: nanjing.etonhouse.com.cn

Etu King's Kindergarten of Wuhan
Building 1, Phase 5, Tongan Home, Houhu Avenue, Houhu Street, Wuhan, Hubei
PYP Coordinator Yiyan Shi
Languages English, Chinese
T: +86 27 8228 6677
W: www.etuking.com

Exploratory Model Primary School
Chongqing BI Academy, No. 766 Konggang East Road, Yubei District, Chongqing 401120
PYP Coordinator Irene Pan Shiyu
Languages English, Chinese
T: +86 186 2076 5920
W: www.biacademy.cn
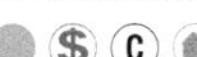

Fettes College Guangzhou
No. 2 Xinxue Road, Phoenix City, Nan'an Village, Xintang Town, Zengcheng District, Guangzhou, Guangdong 511340
MYP Coordinator Wenwen Zhang
Languages English, Chinese
T: +86 20 8299 8816
W: www.fettesgz.com

FLS Personalized Innovative Education Preschool
No. 2 Science Avenue, Science City, Huangpu District, Guangzhou, Guangdong 510665
PYP Coordinator Jing Su
Languages English, Chinese
T: +86 20 8985 2080
W: www.scnufl-piep.com

Fudan International School
No 324 Guoquan Road, Yangpu District, Shanghai 200433
DP Coordinator Yang Gu
Languages English
T: +86 (0) 21 65640560
W: www.fdis.net.cn

Fuzhou International Preschool @ 1 Park Avenue
1 Park Avenue, Jinju Road 826, Jinshan District, Fuzhou, Fujian 350000
PYP Coordinator Junnan Zhang
Languages English, Chinese
T: +86 0591 83505222
W: www.srgedu.com/school/1/

Fuzhou Lakeside International School
No.72 North Meng Shan Road, Gulou District, Fuzhou, Fujian
MYP Coordinator Callum Jackson
Languages English, Chinese
T: +86 591 2806 6277
W: www.flis.cn

Golden Apple International Preschool and Kindergarten
No. 7 Chuangrui Road, Hi-tech District, Chengdu, Sichuan 610041
PYP Coordinator Xuemei Zhong
Languages English, Chinese
T: +86 28 8523 7403
W: www.jpgkids.com

Golden Apple Jincheng No. 1 Secondary School
No. 99 Xianglong 3rd Street, High-tech Zone, Chengdu, Sichuan 610041
DP Coordinator Zoe Yi
Languages English, Chinese
T: +86 28 6010 9299
W: intl.jpgzx.com

Golden Apple New Montessori Kindergarten (Jincheng Lake)
No. 900 Jincheng Avenue, High Tech Zone, Chengdu, Sichuan 610041
PYP Coordinator Robert Brien
Languages Chinese
T: +86 28 8523 1763
W: www.jpgkids.com

Golden Apple Tianfu International Preschool and Kindergarten
No. 187 Shengxing Street, Jiannan Street North, Hi-tech District, Chengdu, Sichuan 610041
PYP Coordinator Yao Chen
Languages English
T: +86 28 8517 1648
W: www.jpgkids.com

GUANGDONG COUNTRY GARDEN SCHOOL

Beijiao Town, Shunde District, Foshan City, Guangdong
DP Coordinator Lizhu Zhao
MYP Coordinator Zequn Deng
PYP Coordinator Jiuhong Wang
Languages Chinese, English
T: +86 757 2667 7888
E: cgssao@brightscholar.com
W: bgy.gd.cn

See full details on page 330

GUANGDONG SHUNDE DESHENG SCHOOL

Minxing Road, New District, Daliang, Shunde, Guangdong 528300
DP Coordinator Mr. Yu Yue
Languages English
T: +86 0757 22325121
E: admin.dsi@desheng-school.com
W: www.desheng-school.com

See full details on page 332

Guangzhou Foreign Language School

No. 102, Fenghuang Avenue, Nansha District, Guangzhou, Guangdong 511455
DP Coordinator Weijia Bo
Languages Chinese, English
T: +86 (0)20 22908716
W: chgzfls.com

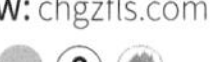

Guangzhou Huamei International School

No. 23 Huamei Road, Tianhe District, Guangzhou, Guangdong 510520
PYP Coordinator Yichun Huang
Languages English, Chinese
T: +86 20 8721 0178
W: en.hm163.com

Guangzhou International Kindergarten Huangpu ZWIE

No. 438 Fengle South Road, Huangpu District, Guangzhou, Guangdong 510700
PYP Coordinator Qin Yuan
Languages Chinese
T: +86 20 6298 6871
W: yey.czwie.com

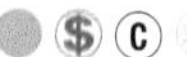

Guangzhou International Middle School Huangpu ZWIE

No. 438 Fengle South Road, Huangpu District, Guangzhou, Guangdong 510700
MYP Coordinator Xiaoming Zhang
Languages English, Chinese
T: +86 40 0780 2003
W: zx.czwie.com

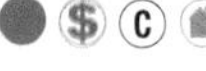

Guangzhou International Primary School Baiyun ZWIE

No. 998 Tonghe Road, Baiyun District, Guangzhou City, Guangdong 510515
PYP Coordinator Wenfang Diao
Languages English, Chinese
T: +86 20 3724 8716
W: wx.czwie.com

Guangzhou International Primary School Huangpu ZWIE

No. 188 Huangpu East Road, Huangpu District, Guangzhou, Guangdong 510700
PYP Coordinator Sharon Xiaolan Lin
Languages English, Chinese
T: +86 40 0780 2003
W: sx.czwie.com

Guangzhou Nanfang International School

No.1 Yu Cui Yuan North, Yinglong Road, Longdong, Tianhe District, Guangzhou, Guangdong
DP Coordinator Lihong Yang
MYP Coordinator Yanyan Jin
PYP Coordinator Xiaoyue Wang
Languages English
T: +86 20 8708 5090
W: www.gnischina.com

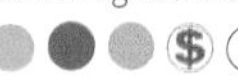

Guangzhou SCA School

No. 2 Ciji Road, China-Singapore Knowledge City, Huangpu District, Guangzhou, Guangdong
DP Coordinator Dennis Ang
Languages English, Chinese
T: +86 16 6020 1230
W: www.singchin.cn

Guiyang Huaxi Country Garden International School

Country Garden Community, Mengguan Town, Huaxi District, Guiyang, Guizhou 550026
PYP Coordinator Rong Gao
Languages English, Chinese
T: +86 (0)851 83651885

Hailiang Foreign Language School

No. 199 West 3rd Ring Road, Taozhu Street, Zhuji, Zhejiang
DP Coordinator Samuel Xin Xiaoming
PYP Coordinator Wanjun Yuan
Languages English, Chinese
T: +86 575 8900 3608
W: www.hailiangeducation.com

Hainan Micro-City Future School

Chengmai County, Hainan 571900
DP Coordinator Dandan Liu
Languages English, Chinese
W: www.ischoolchn.com

Hangzhou Binjiang Wickham Kindergarten

No.525 Weiye Road, Binjiang District, Hangzhou, Zhejiang 31500
PYP Coordinator Yuhuang Huang
Languages English, Chinese

Hangzhou Dipont School of Arts and Science

No. 1 Guowen Road, Hangzhou, Zhejiang 310000
DP Coordinator Mxolisi Valashia
Languages English, Chinese
T: +86 571 5639 5678
W: www.rkcshz.cn

Hangzhou Future Sci-Tech City Wickham Kindergarten

No. 968-8, Gaojiao, Road, Yuhang District, Hangzhou, Zhejiang 311100
PYP Coordinator Hui Chen
Languages English, Chinese
T: +86 571 88665991

Hangzhou Greentown Yuhua Qinqin School

2 Zhujia Road, Yuhang District, Hangzhou, Zhejiang 311112
PYP Coordinator Zhao Bin
Languages English, Chinese

HANGZHOU GREENTOWN YUHUA SCHOOL

No. 532 Wenyi West Road, Hangzhou, Zhejiang 310012
MYP Coordinator Yan Shujing
Languages Chinese, English
T: +86 571 88477561
E: greentownedu@163.com
W: www.hzlcyhcz.cn

See full details on page 336

Hangzhou Huamei Wickham Kindergarten

No. 5, 289 Lane, Daguan Road, Gongshu District, Hangzhou, Zhejiang
PYP Coordinator Li Zhu
Languages English, Chinese
W: mp.weixin.qq.com/s/fxS-TkZ7P6XegqrB3N52vg

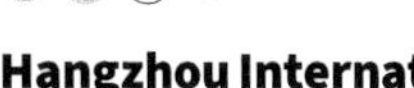

Hangzhou International School

78 Dongxin Street, Bin Jiang District, Hangzhou, Zhejiang 310053
DP Coordinator Mónica Prieto Peris
MYP Coordinator Liam O'Shea
PYP Coordinator Cilla Giannopoulos
Languages English
T: +86 571 8669 0045
W: www.his-china.org

Hangzhou Shanghai World Foreign Language School

167 Li Shui Road, Hangzhou, Zhejiang 310015
PYP Coordinator Frederic (Eric) Thiart
Languages English
T: +86 571 8998 1588

Hangzhou Victoria Kindergarten (Jiarun)

4th Tower, Jiarun Mansion, Jinji Road, Xiaoshan District, Hangzhou, Zhejiang
PYP Coordinator Hu Yue
Languages English, Chinese
T: +86 571 8380 3939
W: www.victoriachina.com

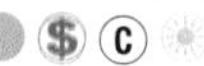

Hangzhou Wesley School (Binjiang Campus)

1426 Wentao Road, Binjiang District, Hangzhou, Zhejiang 310000
PYP Coordinator Bradford Evans
Languages English, Chinese
T: +86 571 8791 6660
W: binjiang.wesleyschool.cn

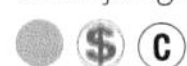

Hangzhou Wesley School (Early Education Center)

269 Gongfa Road, Gongshu District, Hangzhou, Zhejiang 311231
PYP Coordinator Wen Zhang
Languages English, Chinese
T: +86 571 8882 8880
W: www.wesleyschool.cn/index.php/early-education-center-2

Hangzhou Wesley School (Gongshu/Blue Peacock Campus)

60 Chunque Street, Gongshu District, Hangzhou, Zhejiang 310000
PYP Coordinator Li Yu
Languages English, Chinese
T: +86 571 8882 8880
W: gongshu.wesleyschool.cn

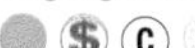

Hangzhou Wesley School (Shangcheng/Jianggan Campus)

162 Yanjia Road, Jianggan District, Hangzhou, Zhejiang 310000
PYP Coordinator Jane Wen Zhang
Languages English, Chinese
T: +86 571 8680 6660
W: wesleyschool.cn

Hangzhou Wickham International School

533 Jingchang Road, Yuhang District, Hangzhou, Zhejiang
PYP Coordinator jun guan
Languages Chinese
T: +86 0571 88665901
W: www.wickham.com.cn

Hangzhou World Foreign Language School
66 Muge Road, Banshan Street, Gongshu District, Hangzhou, Zhejiang 310000
DP Coordinator Wang Yanzhen
Languages English, Chinese
T: +86 189 5814 3128
W: hz.shwfl.edu.cn

Hangzhou Yuhang Xixi Huadongyuan Kindergarten
NO.161 Gaojiao road Xianlin Street, Yuhang District, Hangzhou, Zhejiang 310000
PYP Coordinator Xixi Miao
Languages Chinese

HD Beijing School
No.1 East Jinzhan Forest Park, Chaoyang District, Beijing
DP Coordinator Renee Rehfeldt
Languages English, Chinese
T: +86 10 8539 8568
W: www.hdschools.org/en/beijing

Hefei Run'an Boarding School
292 Fanhua West Road, Economic & Technology Development Zone, Hefei, Anhui 230601
MYP Coordinator Zichang Sun
PYP Coordinator Zichang Sun
Languages Chinese, English
T: +86 551 6982 1861
W: runanid.com
  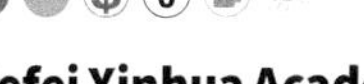

Hefei Xinhua Academy
No.7888 Changjiang West Road, Hefei, Anhui 230088
PYP Coordinator Yi Wan
Languages English, Chinese
T: +86 551 6558 6888
W: en.xhacademy.com
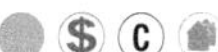 

Henan Jianye Little Harvard Bilingual School
No.31, East Section of Weisi Road, Jinshui District, Zhengzhou, Henan
PYP Coordinator Ian Gu Bo
Languages English, Chinese
T: +86 371 8655 0161
W: www.xiaohafo.cn

Hengyang Royal Kindergarten
No. 8 Changfeng Avenue, Huaxin, Hengyang, Hunan
PYP Coordinator Andrew Lacey
Languages English, Chinese
T: +86 73 4841 7888
W: www.englandroyal.com.cn

High School Affiliated To Nanjing Normal University
37 Chahaer Road, Nanjing, Jiangsu 210003
DP Coordinator Gong Yan
Languages English
T: +86 258 3469000
W: www.nsfz.net

HIGH SCHOOL AFFILIATED TO SHANGHAI JIAO TONG UNIVERSITY
No 42 Yin Gao Road, Bao Shan District, Shanghai 200439
DP Coordinator Mr. Sasi Antony
Languages English, Chinese
T: +86 21 65910979
E: jdfzib@jdfzib.org
W: fz.sjtu.edu.cn
See full details on page 335

High School Attached to Northeast Normal University
No 377 Boxue Road, Jingyue District, Changchun, Jilin 130117
DP Coordinator Mashome Ramotubei
Languages Chinese, English
T: +86 431 85608927

Hong Qiao International School
218 South Yi Li Road, Shanghai 201103
PYP Coordinator Scott Aylwin
Languages English
T: +86 21 62682074
W: www.hqis.org

Huaer Zizhu Lemania College Shanghai
A9, No. 155 Tan Jiatang Road, Min Hang District, Shanghai 200241
DP Coordinator Ning Li
Languages English, Chinese
W: www.hzl-sh.cn

Huanan Country Garden International Kindergarten
Huanan Country Garden, Nancun Town, Panyu District, Guangzhou, Guangdong 511442
PYP Coordinator Fang Wang
Languages English, Chinese
W: hbyey.brightscholar.com

Hübschmann Zhan International School
No. 2-1 Hun He Shi Street, Economic & Technological Development Area, Shenyang, Liaoning 110027
DP Coordinator Christopher J. Dawe
Languages English, German
T: +86 24 3120 0049
W: en.huz-school.com

Huili School Shanghai
No. 235 Linyao Road, Pudong, Shanghai 200126
DP Coordinator Lewis Macdonald
Languages English, Chinese
T: +86 21 3177 5088
W: shanghai.huilieducation.cn

Innova Early Years Center, Yizhuang Campus
Floor 1, Building B, Zhaolin Plaza, Yizhuang, Beijing 100026
PYP Coordinator QiongQiong Wu
Languages English, Chinese
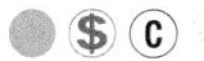

International School of Beijing-Shunyi
No 10 An Hua Street, Shunyi District, Beijing 101318
DP Coordinator Jeffrey Idigo
Languages English
T: +86 10 8149 2345 EXT 1001
W: www.isb.bj.edu.cn

International School of Dongguan
#11 Jin Feng Nan Road, Dongguan, Guangdong 523000
DP Coordinator Manihar Prepto David
Languages English
T: +86 769 2882 5882
W: www.i-s-d.org

International School of Nanshan Shenzhen
11 Longyuan Road, Taoyuan Sub-District, Nanshan District, Shenzhen, Guangdong 518052
DP Coordinator Sean Carroll
MYP Coordinator Ernie Boyd
PYP Coordinator Lauren Dorsey
Languages English
T: +86 755 2666 1000
W: www.isnsz.com

International School of Tianjin
Weishan Road, Shuanggang, Jinnan District, Tianjin 300350
DP Coordinator Hui Ping Chuah
MYP Coordinator Jess Chaudhry
PYP Coordinator Jane Lobsey
Languages English
T: +86 22 2859 2001
W: www.istianjin.org

ISA Science City International School
66 Yushu South Road, Science City, Huangpu District, Guangzhou, Guangdong
DP Coordinator Anne Martin-Bauer
MYP Coordinator Joseph Hamkari
PYP Coordinator Annie Chew
Languages English, Chinese
T: +86 20 3736 2580
W: www.isagzsc.com

ISA Tianhe International School
Block C2-2 Redtory, No.128 Siheng Road, Yuan Village, Tianhe District, Guangzhou, Guangdong 510655
PYP Coordinator Emine Dogan
Languages English
T: +86 20 8890 0909
W: www.isagzth.com

IVY Kindergarten of Tongzhou District, Beijing
Hebin Road No.1, Yongshun Town, Tongzhou District, Beijing 101100
PYP Coordinator Yan Liu
Languages English, Chinese
T: +86 10 8969 6628
W: www.cqtkid.com

Jianye International School
No. 88 Jianye Road, Jinshui District, Zhengzhou, Henan 450000
MYP Coordinator Cui Yujia
Languages English, Chinese
W: www.jianyeedu.net

Jianye Xie He Cheng Bang Kindergarten
Minhang Road, Zhongzhou Avenue, Zhengzhou, Henan 450003
PYP Coordinator Hongyan Li
Languages English, Chinese

Jiaxiang International High School
No. 6, Chenhui North Road, Jinjiang District, Chengdu, Sichuan
DP Coordinator Rihanna Ann
Languages English
T: +86 (0)28 69919908
W: www.cdjxihs.com

Jurong Country Garden School
No.2 Oiuzhi Road, Jurong Economic Development Zone, Zhengjiang City, Jiangsu 212400
DP Coordinator Cuicui Jia
MYP Coordinator Huang Fangfang
PYP Coordinator Daisy Xiaomin Xu
Languages English
T: +86 511 8078 0326
W: www.jrbgy.net

Kang Chiao International School (East China Campus)
No.500, Xihuan Rd., Huaqiao Economic Development Zone, Kunshan City, Jiangsu 215332
DP Coordinator Francis Abdurahman
MYP Coordinator Kate Lin
Languages English, Chinese
T: +86 512 3686 9833
W: en.kcisec.com

Keystone Academy

11 Anfu Street, Houshayu, Hou Sha Yu Town, Shunyi District, Beijing 101318
DP Coordinator Nicholas Daniel
MYP Coordinator Hongwei Gao
Languages English, Chinese
T: +86 10 8049 6008
W: www.keystoneacademy.cn

King's Kindergarten Shenzhen

Jingtian North 5th Street, Lianhua Street, Futian District, Shenzhen, Guangdong
PYP Coordinator Minli Chen
Languages English, Chinese
T: +86 188 2333 5566
W: en.kings-kindergarten.com

Kunming World Youth Academy

Building 2, No.3 High School Dianchixingcheng Campus, Chenggong District, Kunming, Yunnan 650500
DP Coordinator Kyle Gray
Languages English, Chinese
T: +86 871 6745 1511
W: www.kwya.top

Lanzhou Country Garden School

Qingbaishi Street, Chengguan District, Lanzhou, Gansu 730000
DP Coordinator Xiaofan Zhang
PYP Coordinator Zheng Da
Languages English, Chinese
T: +86 931 8790000

LÉMAN INTERNATIONAL SCHOOL CHENGDU

No.1080 Da'an Road, Zheng Xing County, Tianfu New Area, Chengdu, Sichuan 610218
DP Coordinator Thomas Ainsworth
MYP Coordinator Patrick Meersman
Languages English
T: +86 28 6703 8650
E: admissions@lis-chengdu.com
W: www.lis-chengdu.com

See full details on page 350

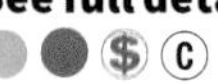

Manila Xiamen International School

No 735 Long Hu Shan Lu, Zeng Cuo An, Si Ming District, Xiamen, Fujian 361005
DP Coordinator Eve Denise Coronel
MYP Coordinator Raymond Ceferino III Meris
Languages English
T: +86 592 2516373
W: www.mxis.org

MOK Kindergarten

Huatang Golf Villa comprehensive Business Building, Yanjiao, Sanhe, Langfang, Hebei 065201
PYP Coordinator Kefan Feng
Languages English, Chinese
W: www.mok2012.com

Morgan Henry Bilingual Kindergarten

567 Jinfeng Road, Huacao Town, Minhang District, Shanghai 201107
PYP Coordinator David graham
Languages English, Chinese
T: +86 21 6091 3366
W: www.shmhkids.com

Nanchang International School

1122 Phoenix Centre Road, Hong Gu Tan District, Nanchang, Jiangxi 330038
PYP Coordinator Luis Hernandez Quintero
Languages English
T: +86 791 83855352
W: www.wes-ncis.org

Nanjing Eternal Sea Kindergarten

No. 8 Huitong Road, Qixia District, Nanjing, Jiangsu 210000
PYP Coordinator Malena Jin
Languages English
T: +852 25 5870 6268
W: www.eternalsea.cn

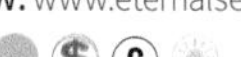 

Nanjing Foreign Language School

No. 35-4 North Taiping Road, Nanjing City, Jiangsu 210018
DP Coordinator Amit Roy
Languages English
T: +86 25 8328 2300
W: www.nfls.com.cn

Nanjing International School

No. 8 Xueheng Road, Nanjing, Jiangsu 210023
DP Coordinator Angela Michaela Fox
MYP Coordinator Jade Bennett
PYP Coordinator Mr. Adam Dodge
Languages English
T: +86 25 85899111
W: www.nischina.org

  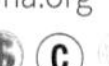

Nantong Stalford International School

No. 46 Hongxing Road, NETDA, Nantong, Jiangsu 226015
DP Coordinator Xian Neng How
Languages English, Chinese
T: +86 4008 4008 63
W: www.ntsis.com

Nanwai King's College School

188 Qingyuan Road, Jingkai District, Wuxi, Jiangsu
DP Coordinator Chaminda Marasinghe
Languages English, Chinese
T: +86 0510 6851 6972
W: www.nkcswx.cn

New Oriental Academy

101 Manbai Road, Machikou Town, Changping District, Beijing 102206
DP Coordinator Yang Cui
Languages English, Chinese
T: +86 40 0688 1000
W: noa.xdf.cn

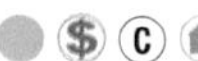

New Oriental Stars Kindergarten

Room 506, 5th Floor, Building F, Phoenix Plaza, No. A5, Shuguangxili, Chaoyang District, Beijing 100028
PYP Coordinator Jana Zhou
Languages English
T: +86 40 0066 5030
W: www.babybrightfuture.cn

Nexus Preschool

No. 1108 Huamu Road, Pudong New Area, Shanghai 201204
PYP Coordinator Yingyi Shang
Languages English, Chinese

Ningbo Huamao International School

No 2 Yinxian dadao (Middle), Ningbo, Zhejiang 31519
DP Coordinator Jonathan Marfleet
MYP Coordinator Keola Johnson
PYP Coordinator Reinette Roberts
Languages English, Chinese
T: +86 574 8821 1160
W: www.nbhis.com

Ningbo Xiaoshi High School

178 Baiyang Street, Ningbo, Zhejiang 315012
DP Coordinator Jacob Miles
Languages English
T: +86 574 8715 9613

Nord Anglia Chinese International School, Shanghai

1399 Jinhui Road, Minhang, Shanghai 201107
DP Coordinator David Jefferson-Gleed
Languages Chinese, English
T: +86 (021) 2403 8800
W: www.nordangliaeducation.com/our-schools/nacis/shanghai

NORD ANGLIA INTERNATIONAL SCHOOL SHANGHAI, PUDONG

2888 Junmin Road, Pudong New District, Shanghai 201315
DP Coordinator Hari Raye
Languages English
T: +86 (0)21 5812 7455 (EXT:1015)
E: admissions@naispudong.com
W: naispudong.com

See full details on page 359

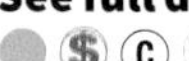

Nord Anglia School Beijing, Fangshan

No. 236 Beiliuzhuang Village, Qinglonghu Town, Fangshan District, Beijing
DP Coordinator David Anthony Burgin
Languages English, Chinese
T: +86 10 8865 8000
W: fangshan.nacis.cn

Nord Anglia School Foshan

No. 55 Dongxi Avenue, West Bank, Xiqiao Town, Nanhai District, Foshan, Guangdong
DP Coordinator Hui (Rainbow) Yuan
Languages English
T: +86 757 8121 7688
W: foshan.nacis.cn

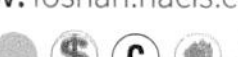

Nord Anglia School Jiaxing

No. 353 Qingze Road, Economic Development Zone, Jiaxing, Zhejiang 314000
DP Coordinator Scott Sloan
Languages English, Chinese
T: +86 189 6734 1988
W: www.nasjiaxing.cn

Nord Anglia School Nantong

No. 99, Jiangcheng Road, Sutong Park, Nantong, Jiangsu 226000
DP Coordinator Samuel Wilson
Languages English, Chinese
T: +86 513 8918 3800
W: nantong.nacis.cn

Nord Anglia School Ningbo, Fenghua

No. 88 Wenbo Road, Xiaowangmiao Street, Fenghua District, Ningbo, Zhejiang 315500
DP Coordinator Alan Jovern Lim
Languages English, Chinese
T: +86 574 8720 3280
W: www.nordangliaeducation.com/schools/asia/china/ningbo

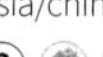 

Nord Anglia School Suzhou, Xiangcheng
No. 8 Liu Jue Road, Xiangcheng District, Suzhou, Jiangsu 215134
DP Coordinator Diwen Shi
Languages English, Chinese
T: +86 512 6580 5800
W: www.nassuzhou.cn
 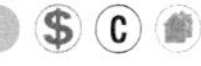

Northeast Yucai School
No.41 Shiji Road, Hunnan New District, Shenyang, Liaoning 110179
DP Coordinator Xun Sun
PYP Coordinator Tianliang Chen
Languages Chinese
T: +86 24 23783945
W: www.neyc.cn
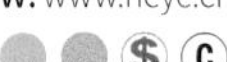 

Olive Tree International Academy, BFSU
No.136 Xincheng Road, Nanyuan Street, Yuhang District, Hangzhou, Zhejiang
MYP Coordinator Ying Yang
PYP Coordinator Ting Zhang
Languages English, Chinese
T: +86 571 8610 0011
W: www.olivedu.com

Oriental Cambridge International School (Shenyang/Benxi Campus)
No 23, Mulan Road, Xihu District, Benxi, Liaoning 117000
DP Coordinator Bo Song
Languages English, Chinese
W: www.oceg.com/en/node/international/690.html

Oriental English College, Shenzhen
No 10 Xuezi Road, Education Town, Bao'an, Shenzhen, Guangdong 518128
DP Coordinator Kongjing Wang
PYP Coordinator Ling Luo (Caroline)
Languages Chinese, English
T: +86 755 2751 2624
W: www.szoec.com.cn

Oujing International Kindergarten
Beicun Road, Yiwu, Zhejiang 322000
PYP Coordinator Rochelle Boshoff
Languages English
T: +86 159 8561 7777
W: www.oujinginternational.com

Overseas Chinese Academy Suzhou
208 Zhong Nan Street, Suzhou Industrial Park, Jiangsu 215021
DP Coordinator James Lau
MYP Coordinator Amanda Yufeng Huang
PYP Coordinator Vivian Gong
Languages Chinese, English
T: +86 (512) 65001600
W: ocac-suzhou.com/zh

Oxstand International School, Shenzhen
No.2040, BuXin Road, Luohu District, Shenzhen, Guangdong
DP Coordinator Swati Nigam
Languages English
T: +86 755 2580 5707
W: www.oxstand.net

PeyJoy Kindergarten
No.7-99 Yayuan Road, Bantian Street, Longgang District, Shenzhen, Guangdong 518000
PYP Coordinator Chen Xiuhong
Languages English, Chinese

Phoenix City International Kindergarten
No. 1 Yaxi Road, Phoenix City, Yongnin Street, Zengcheng District, Guangzhou, Guangdong 511340
PYP Coordinator Rita Fu
Languages English, Chinese
T: +86 20 3298 8186

Phoenix City International School
Xintang Town, Zengcheng City, Guangzhou, Guangdong 511340
MYP Coordinator Max Sumner
PYP Coordinator Yangyi Chen
Languages Chinese, English
T: +86 20 6228 6902
W: www.pcis.com.cn

Princeton SkyLake International Kindergarten
No. 7010 Beihuan Avenue, Futian District, Shenzhen, Guangdong
PYP Coordinator Wing Wu
Languages English, Chinese
T: +86 180 3342 4827
W: www.piclc.com

Qingdao Academy
No 111 Huazhong Road, Gaoxin District, Qingdao, Shandong 266111
DP Coordinator Andie Tong Wang
Languages English, Chinese
T: +86 532 5875 3788
W: www.qdzx.net
 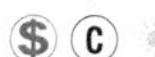

Qingdao Amerasia International School
68 Shandongtou Lu, Qingdao, Shandong 266061
DP Coordinator Kevin Wheeler
MYP Coordinator Kevin Wheeler
PYP Coordinator Consuelo Ravago
Languages English
T: +86 532 8388 9900
W: qingdaoamerasia.org

Qingdao Chaoyin Primary School
No. 2 Zhenjiang Minor Road, Qingdao, Shandong 266000
PYP Coordinator Emily Nie
Languages English, Chinese

Qingdao MINGDE School
No. 111 Gongjian Road, Huangdao District, Qingdao, Shandong
DP Coordinator Richard Woods
Languages English, Chinese
T: +86 532 5558 5997
W: www.qingdaomingdeschool.cn
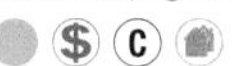

QSI International School of Chengdu
American Garden, 188 South 3rd Ring Road, Chengdu, Sichuan 610041
DP Coordinator Ms. Debbie Nolan
Languages English
T: +86 28 8511 3853
W: chengdu.qsi.org

QSI INTERNATIONAL SCHOOL OF SHENZHEN
5th Floor, Bitao Building, 8 Tai Zi Road, Shekou, Shenzhen, Guangdong 518067
DP Coordinator Matt Storey & Jeremy Zhang
Languages English
T: +86 755 2667 6031
E: shenzhen@qsi.org
W: shenzhen.qsi.org
See full details on page 367

SABIS ULINK International School
No. 559, Laiting South Road, Jiuting Town, Songjiang, Shanghai
DP Coordinator Miranda Lin
Languages English
T: +86 21 5569 8990
W: sabisulink.sabis.net

Sanya Foreign Language School
No. 38 Luhuitou Road, Serenity Coast, Jiyang District, Sanya, Hainan
PYP Coordinator Shi Hui Lin
Languages English, Chinese
T: +86 898 3188 3111
W: www.sls-sanya.com
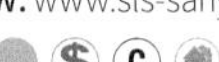

Sanya Foreign Language School Kindergarten (SLSK)
No. 38 Luhuitou Road, Serenity Coast, Jiyang District, Sanya, Hainan
PYP Coordinator Sophia Boller-Caballero
Languages English, Chinese
T: +86 898 3188 0700
W: www.sls-sanya.com

Sanya Overseas Chinese School - Nanxin Campus
Shang Bao Po Road, Lizhi District, Sanya, Hainan
DP Coordinator Yuzhu Wei
Languages English, Chinese
T: +86 89 8886 9023
W: www.sanyaocs.cn

School of the Nations
Rua de Minho, Taipa, Macau SAR
DP Coordinator Gregory Peebles
Languages English
T: +853 2870 1759
W: www.schoolofthenations.com

Seven Star Kindergarten Xiamen
No. 146 Qixing West Road, Siming District, Xiamen, Fujian
PYP Coordinator Joan Hong
Languages English, Chinese
T: +86 59 2766 6678
W: xmsevenstar.com

Shandong Zibo Shiyan High School
No.11 Zhangzhou Rd, Zibo, Shandong
DP Coordinator Sui Shuang
Languages English, Chinese
T: +86 533 2851216
W: www.zsis.cn

Shanghai American School (Pudong Campus)
Shanghai Links Executive Community, 1600 Lingbai Road, Sanjiagang, Pudong, Shanghai 201201
DP Coordinator Josep Capilla
Languages English
T: +86 21 6221 1445 (EXT:2000)
W: www.saschina.org/admission

Shanghai American School (Puxi Campus)
26 Jinfeng Road, Huacao Town, Minhang District, Shanghai 201107
DP Coordinator Gines Bernal
Languages English
T: +86 21 6221 1445
W: www.saschina.org

Shanghai Baoshan Happykids Kindergarten
No. 218, Lane 2488, Wenchuan Road, Baoshan District, Shanghai
PYP Coordinator Danli Luo
Languages English, Chinese
T: +86 21 5678 7887
W: www.happy-bs.com

Shanghai BeiBeiJia Olion Kindergarten

No. 377 Baoju Road, Shanghai
PYP Coordinator Linlin Hong
Languages English, Chinese
T: +86 137 6467 7623
W: www.olion.com.cn

SHANGHAI COMMUNITY INTERNATIONAL SCHOOL - HONGQIAO CAMPUS

1161 Hongqiao Road, Shanghai 200051
DP Coordinator Scott Simmons
MYP Coordinator Tetsuo Ishii
PYP Coordinator Vincent Lehane
Languages English
T: +86 21 6261 4338
E: admissions@scis-china.org
W: www.scis-china.org

See full details on page 383

   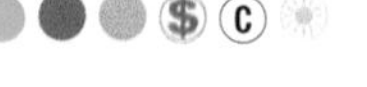

SHANGHAI COMMUNITY INTERNATIONAL SCHOOL - PUDONG CAMPUS

198 Hengqiao Road, Zhoupu, Pudong, Shanghai 201315
DP Coordinator Jill Sculerati
MYP Coordinator Naomi Shanks
PYP Coordinator Heather Knight
Languages English
T: +86 21 5812 9888
W: www.scis-china.org

See full details on page 383

Shanghai Foreign Language School

Zhong Shan Bei Yi Road No. 295, Shanghai 200083
DP Coordinator Jia Zhang
Languages English, Chinese
T: +86 (0)2165 423105
W: www.sfls.cn

Shanghai High School

400 Shangzhong Road, Xuhui, Shanghai 200231
DP Coordinator Hao Jiang
Languages English
T: +86 21 64765516
W: www.shsid.org

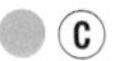

Shanghai Hongwen School

No. 318 Chuanda Road, Pudong, Shanghai
DP Coordinator Fran Chen
Languages English, Chinese
T: +86 189 1784 6368
W: sh-en.hongwenfeh.com

Shanghai Ivy School

No. 816 Xiuyan Road, Pudong New Area, Shanghai 200000
PYP Coordinator Jiang Yuting
Languages English, Chinese
T: +86 40 0050 5553
W: kid.ivy-school.org

Shanghai Jin Cai High School

2788 Mid-Yanggao Road, Pudong New Area, Shanghai 200135
DP Coordinator Angela Ying Zhang
MYP Coordinator Yi Xin Wei
Languages Chinese, English
T: +86 21 6854 1158
W: www.jincai.sh.cn

Shanghai Liaoyuan Bilingual School

No. 150 Pingyang Road, Minhang District, Shanghai
DP Coordinator Zhan Zhu
MYP Coordinator Kevin Fields
PYP Coordinator Jenny Cao
Languages English, Chinese
T: +86 21 6480 6128
W: www.liaoyuanedu.org

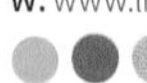

Shanghai Pinghe School

261 Huang Yang Road, Pudong, Shanghai
DP Coordinator Jing Xu
Languages English
T: +86 21 5031 0791
W: www.shphschool.com

Shanghai Qibao Dwight High School

Physical Campus, 3233 Hongxin Road, Minhang District, Shanghai 201101
DP Coordinator Wendy Lin
Languages English
T: +86 21 6461 0367
W: www.qibaodwight.org

Shanghai Qingpu World Foreign Language Kindergarten

639 Panwen Road, Qingpu District, Shanghai 201702
PYP Coordinator German Rincon
Languages English, Chinese
T: +86 21 3988 6958
W: qpwflk.wfl-ischool.cn

Shanghai Qingpu World Foreign Language School

Longlian Road 915, Qingpu District, Shanghai 201700
PYP Coordinator Elaine Wu
Languages English, Chinese
T: +86 21 6928 0977
W: qpwfl.wfl-ischool.cn

Shanghai Shangde Experimental School

No 1688 Xiu Yan Road, Pudong New District, Shanghai 201315
DP Coordinator Ting Feng
MYP Coordinator Honglin Xu
PYP Coordinator Can Li
Languages English
T: +86 21 6818 0001 OR +86 21 6818 0191
W: www.shangdejy.com

Shanghai Shixi High School

404 Yuyuan Rd, Jing'an District, Shanghai 200040
DP Coordinator Lily Hua Su
Languages English
T: +86 21 62521018
W: www.shixi.edu.sh.cn

Shanghai Singapore International School

301 Zhujian Road, Minhang District, Shanghai 201106
CP Coordinator Adam Crossley
DP Coordinator Adam Crossley
Languages English
T: +86 21 62219288
W: www.ssis.asia

SHANGHAI UNITED INTERNATIONAL SCHOOL, GUBEI/ HONGQIAO CAMPUS

248 Hong Song Road (E), Gubei, Minhang District, Shanghai 201103
DP Coordinator Ben Griffiths
PYP Coordinator Jayanthi Nayak
Languages English
T: +8621 51753030
E: annie.yan@suis.com.cn
W: www.suis.com.cn

See full details on page 384

Shanghai Victoria Kindergarten (Gumei)

No. 300 Gumei Road, Minhang District, Shanghai
PYP Coordinator Simon Francis Marginson
Languages English, Chinese
T: +86 21 6401 1084
W: www.victoriachina.com

Shanghai Victoria Kindergarten (Pudong)

38-39 Yinxiao Road, Pudong District, Shanghai
PYP Coordinator Selina Fang
Languages English, Chinese
T: +86 21 5045 9084
W: www.victoriachina.com

Shanghai Victoria Kindergarten (Qibao)

No. 1225 Xinzhen Road, Minhang District, Shanghai
PYP Coordinator Jerry Wong
Languages Chinese, English
T: +86 21 5415 0469
W: www.victoriachina.com

Shanghai Victoria Kindergarten (Xuhui)

71-1 Huating Road, Xuhui District, Shanghai
PYP Coordinator Jeromy Sumner
Languages English, Chinese
T: +86 21 5403 6901
W: www.victoriachina.com

Shanghai Weiyu High School

No 1 Weiyu Road, Xuhui District, Shanghai 200231
DP Coordinator Li Chen
Languages English
T: +86 21 64966996 #8008
W: www.weiyu.sh.cn

Shanghai World Foreign Language Middle School

380 Pu Bei Road, Xu Hui District, Shanghai 200233
DP Coordinator Hector Jiachun Chen
MYP Coordinator Ye Wang
Languages Chinese, English
T: +8621 6436 3556
W: www.wflms.cn

 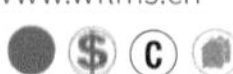

Shanghai World Foreign Language Primary School

No 380 Pubei Road, Xu Hui District, Shanghai 200233
PYP Coordinator Halina Werchiwski
Languages English, Chinese
T: +86 21 5419 2245
W: www.wflps.com

Shekou International School

Jingshan Villas, Nanhai Boulevard, Shekou, Nanshan, Shenzhen, Guangdong
DP Coordinator Erin Garnhum
PYP Coordinator Alice Cheung
Languages English
T: +86 755 2669 3669
W: www.sis-shekou.org

Shen Wai International School

29 Baishi 3rd Road, Nanshan District, Shenzhen, Guangdong 518053
DP Coordinator David Platt
MYP Coordinator Vera Wu
PYP Coordinator Tiffany (Shasha) Xia
Languages English
T: +86 755 8654 1200
W: www.swis.cn

Shenzhen Foreign Languages GBA Academy

No. 30 Xiangtang Road, Bantian Street, Longgang District, Shenzhen, Guangdong
DP Coordinator Iris Tay
MYP Coordinator Stuart Simpson
PYP Coordinator Marilen Guerra
Languages English, Chinese
T: +86 755 2939 5900
W: www.sga-edu.cn

Shenzhen Senior High School
Chuntian Road, Futian District, Shenzhen, Guangdong 518040
DP Coordinator Suzhen Wen
Languages English, Chinese
T: +86 755 8394 8654
W: www.cn-school.com

Shenzhen Shiyan Public School
No. 8 Yucai Rd, Shiyan Street, Baoan District, Shenzhen, Guangdong 518108
DP Coordinator Fangfang Kong
Languages English, Chinese
T: +86 755 2776 6766
W: sygx.baoan.edu.cn
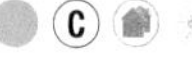

Sias International School
Longhu Middle Ring Road & Chaoyang Road Intersection, Zhengdong New District, Zhengzhou, Henan 450000
PYP Coordinator Juliana Sali
Languages English, Chinese
T: +86 371 8890 8999
W: www.siasinternationalschool.org

SNU-K International Department
Yidu Road Longchengyihao, Chengdu, Sichuan 610101
PYP Coordinator Jian Kang
Languages Chinese, English
T: +86 18428393839

Soochow Foreign Language School
No. 188, Yucheng Road, Xiangcheng District, Suzhou, Jiangsu
DP Coordinator Kaiqiu Jin
PYP Coordinator Lan Zhang
Languages English, Chinese
T: +86 512 8918 0556
W: www.cscfls.com

Springboard International Bilingual School
Gucheng Village, 15 Huosha Road, Houshayu Town, Shunyi District, Beijing 101318
DP Coordinator Shirley Yuan Su
PYP Coordinator Li Jiang
Languages English, Chinese
T: +86 10 80490307
W: www.sibs.com.cn

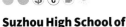

Suzhou High School of Jiangsu Province
699 Renmin Road, Suzhou, Jiangsu 215005
DP Coordinator Ronny Laroche
Languages English, Chinese
T: +86 512 6519 8202
W: www.szzx-intl.cn

Suzhou Industrial Park Foreign Language School
No.89, Suzhou Industrial Park, Suzhou, Jiangsu 215021
DP Coordinator Echo Zuo
Languages English
T: +86 512 6289 7710
W: www.sipfls.com
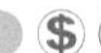

Suzhou Innovation Academy
100 Xiangcheng Ave, Xiangcheng District, Suzhou, Jiangsu
DP Coordinator Cheng Rui Eric Liu
Languages English
T: +86 (0)512 65490211
W: rhodes-ib.com

Suzhou North America High School
268 Tian E Dang Road, Wuzhong District, Suzhou, Jiangsu 215000
DP Coordinator Hongwei Gao
Languages English, Chinese
T: +86 512 6625 8897
W: www.sna-itac.com

Suzhou Science and Technology Town Foreign Language School
No. 180 Jia Ling Jiang Road, Suzhou New District, Suzhou, Jiangsu 215163
PYP Coordinator Vanessa Pfoehler
Languages English, Chinese
T: +86 512 69370111
W: www.ssfls.com.cn

SUZHOU SINGAPORE INTERNATIONAL SCHOOL
208 Zhong Nan Street, Suzhou Industrial Park, Jiangsu 215021
DP Coordinator Dirk van Rooyen
MYP Coordinator Peter Coats
PYP Coordinator Katriona Hoskins
Languages English
T: +86 512 6258 0388
E: information@mail.ssis-suzhou.net
W: www.suzhousinternationalschool.com
See full details on page 392

Suzhou Victoria Kindergarten
Bay Garden Community, Phase 3, 1 Linglong Street, Suzhou Industrial Park, Suzhou, Jiangsu
PYP Coordinator Sian Eatwell
Languages English, Chinese
T: +86 512 8081 1610
W: www.victoriachina.com

The Affiliated Foreign Language School of SCNU
No. 2 Science Avenue, Science City, Huangpu District, Guangzhou, Guangdong 510633
MYP Coordinator Wei Liu
PYP Coordinator Robbie Faninghan
Languages English, Chinese
T: +86 20 3205 1890
W: www.scnufl.com

The British International School Shanghai, Puxi
111 Jinguang Road, Huacao Town, Minhang District, Puxi, Shanghai 201107
DP Coordinator Alexander Cattell
Languages English
T: +86 (0)21 62217542
W: www.bisspuxi.com

The Garden International School
Agile Cambridgeshire, Panyu District, Guangzhou, Guangdong 511400
PYP Coordinator Lovina Pinto
Languages English
T: +86 (0)20 3482 3833
W: www.tgisgz.com

The High School Affiliated to Renmin University of China
No. 37 Zhongguancun Street, Haidian District, Beijing 100080
DP Coordinator Yujie Bai
Languages English
T: +86 10 62513962
W: www.rdfz.cn/en

The International School of Macao
Macau University of Science and Technology (Block K), Avenida Wai Long, Taipa, Macau SAR
DP Coordinator Jody Hubert
Languages English
T: +853 2853 3700
W: www.tis.edu.mo

The Kindergarten of Hefei Run'an Boarding School
No. 268 Cui Wei Road, Economic and Technogical Development Zone, Hefei, Anhui 230601
PYP Coordinator Su Yang
Languages English
T: +86 (0)551 63821888
W: www.hfrayey.com

The MacDuffie School, Shanghai
No. 799 North Hui Feng Road, Fengxian District, Shanghai 201403
DP Coordinator David Scoggins
Languages English
T: +86 21 400 600 2260
W: sh.macduffie.cn/en

The Second Experimental Kindergarten of Jinhua
No.136 Shuanglong South Street, Wucheng District, Jinhua, Zhejiang
PYP Coordinator Lena Wang
Languages English, Chinese
T: +86 579 8916 9590
W: www.tsekjh.com

Tianjin Experimental High School
No 1 Pingshan Road, Hexi District, Tianjin 300074
DP Coordinator Lu Gan
Languages English, Chinese
T: +86 22 2335 4658
W: www.tjsyzx.cn
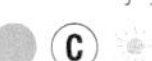

Times College
18 Shennong Road, Qixia District, Nanjing, Jiangsu
DP Coordinator Walter Nagles
MYP Coordinator Gerard Langan
PYP Coordinator Yi Yang
Languages English, Chinese
T: +86 25 85539090
W: www.timescollege.com

Tongwen School, Jiaxing
No. 2339 Huayuan Road, Jiaxing, Zhejiang 314000
PYP Coordinator Graham Wood
Languages English, Chinese

Tungwah Wenzel International School
No. 17 Keyuan Road, Songshan Lake High-Tech Industrial Zone, Dongguan, Guangdong
DP Coordinator Sebastien Gaillard
MYP Coordinator Johnn Paul Montalla
PYP Coordinator Cherie Montalla
Languages English
T: +86 769 2289 0858
W: dgtwis.com

Utahloy International School Guangzhou (UISG)
800 Sha Tai Bei Road, Bai Yun District, Guangzhou, Guangdong 510515
DP Coordinator Anthony kietzmann
MYP Coordinator Matt Phillips
PYP Coordinator Jonathan Harris
Languages English
T: +8620 8720 2019
W: www.utahloy.com

Utahloy International School Zengcheng (UISZ)
San Jiang Town, Zeng Cheng City, Guangdong 511325
DP Coordinator Chunping Lai
MYP Coordinator Jennifer Verontaye
PYP Coordinator Jennifer Verontaye
Languages English
T: +86 20 8291 3201
W: www.utahloy.com
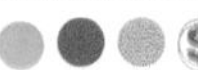 

UWC CHANGSHU CHINA
No. 88 Kunchenghuxi Road, Changshu, Jiangsu 215500
DP Coordinator Christopher Hodachok
Languages English
T: +86 512 5298 2602
E: info.admissions@uwcchina.org
W: www.uwcchina.org
See full details on page 400

Vanke School Pudong
No. 1700-2-4 Kangqiao Road, Pudong, Shanghai
CP Coordinator Jasmine Jiang Xijiao
DP Coordinator Haitao Zhang
MYP Coordinator Tianyu Mao
PYP Coordinator Roise Wang
Languages English, Chinese
T: +86 21 3463 3623
W: vsp.dtd-edu.cn

Victoria Kindergarten Shenzhen (Futian)
No.2135 Fuqiang Road, Futian District, Shenzhen, Guangdong
PYP Coordinator Jane Liu
Languages English, Chinese
T: +86 755 8296 1010
W: www.victoriachina.com

Victoria Kindergarten Shenzhen (Le Parc)
317 Fuzhong Road, Futian District, Shenzhen, Guangdong
PYP Coordinator Lynn Zhang
Languages English, Chinese
T: +86 755 8328 2004
W: www.victoriachina.com

Victoria Kindergarten Shenzhen (Lilin)
7 LongChuanTang Street, DongBin Road, Nanshan District, Shenzhen, Guangdong
PYP Coordinator Vicky Zou
Languages English, Chinese
T: +86 130 5815 8907
W: www.victoriachina.com

Victoria Kindergarten Shenzhen (Shenzhen Bay)
Shenzhen Bay Science & Technology Ecological Park, Building 5, Floor 3, Nanshan District, Shenzhen, Guangdong
PYP Coordinator Amy Yan
Languages English, Chinese
T: +86 755 8653 7070
W: www.victoriachina.com

Wahaha International School
5 Yaojiang Road, Shangcheng District, Hangzhou, Zhejiang 310008
MYP Coordinator Ellen Chai
PYP Coordinator Chaojie Xiang
Languages English, Chinese
T: +86 571 8780 1933
W: www.wischina.org

Wellington College International Shanghai
No.1500 Yao Long Road, Pudong, Shanghai 200124
DP Coordinator Martin OBrien
Languages English
T: +86 21 5185 3866
W: www.wellingtoncollege.cn/shanghai

Western Academy Of Beijing
PO Box 8547, 10 Lai Guang Ying Dong Lu, Chao Yang District, Beijing 100102
DP Coordinator Scott Lindner
MYP Coordinator Jason Reagin
PYP Coordinator Jonathan Mueller
Languages English
T: +86 10 5986 5588
W: www.wab.edu

WESTERN INTERNATIONAL SCHOOL OF SHANGHAI (WISS)
555 Lian Min Road, Xujing Town, Qing Pu District, Shanghai 201702
CP Coordinator Gary Halcrow
DP Coordinator Rajeshree Basu
MYP Coordinator Martin Mathieson
PYP Coordinator Vivian Hu
Languages English
T: +86 (21) 69761038/1060
E: enquiry@wiss.cn
W: www.wiss.cn
See full details on page 406

WHBC of Wuhan Foreign Languages School
7th Floor Administration Building, 48 Wan Song Yuan Road, Wuhan, Hubei 430022
DP Coordinator Yi Zhang
MYP Coordinator Yi Zhang
PYP Coordinator Taylor Bartlett
Languages English
T: +86 27 8555 7389
W: www.whbc2000.com/english

Wuhan Australian International School
No.322 Luoshi Road, Hongshan District, Wuhan, Hubei
PYP Coordinator Xiaoling Xia
Languages Chinese
T: +86 27 8710 5088
W: www.waisedu.com

Wuhan No.6 High School
No. 64 Qiuchang Road, Jiang'an District, Wuhan, Hubei 430010
DP Coordinator Pei Ji
Languages English, Chinese
T: +86 27 8286 8021
W: www.wh6z.com

Wuxi Foreign Language School
1 Xifeng Road, Taihuxincheng, Wuxi, Jiangsu 214131
PYP Coordinator Yixin Chen
Languages Chinese
W: www.wxfls.net

Wuxi United International School
No. 8, Wenjing Road, Xishan District, Xidong New Town, Wuxi, Jiangsu 214104
DP Coordinator Vinod Pokhrel
Languages English
T: +86 510 8853 7700
W: wuxi.suis.com.cn

X.L.X. Kindergarten (Qingcheng Campus)
No.5, Building 7, Lane 2501, Guyang North Road, Songjiang District, Shanghai
PYP Coordinator Yan Liu
Languages English, Chinese
T: +86 21 6029 1140
W: en.ys-edu.com.cn/index.php?m=content&c=index&a=show&catid=45&id=11

X.L.X. Kindergarten (Tangzhen Campus)
No. 58 Hongya Road, Pudong New District, Shanghai
PYP Coordinator Qian Qian Li
Languages English, Chinese
T: +86 21 6070 2623
W: en.ys-edu.com.cn/index.php?m=content&c=index&a=show&catid=45&id=7

Xiamen International School
262 Xing Bei San Lu, Xinglin, Jimei District, Xiamen, Fujian 361022
DP Coordinator James Sutcliffe
MYP Coordinator Laura Bell
PYP Coordinator Mary Collins
Languages English
T: +86 592 625 6581
W: www.xischina.com

Xi'an Hanova International School
188 Yudou Road, Yanta District, Xian, Shaanxi 710077
DP Coordinator Sharon Zhangyu Zhu
MYP Coordinator Rui (Amy) Hou
PYP Coordinator Sandra Venter
Languages English
T: +86 29 88693780
W: www.his-xian.com

Xi'an Liangjiatan International School (XLIS)
International Community, Xi'an, Shaanxi 710100
DP Coordinator Shameek Kumar Ghosh
MYP Coordinator Meng (Emma) Yang
PYP Coordinator Maria Theresa Zialcita
Languages English
T: +86 29 85915100-8000
W: xalis.com

Xiaomiao Kindergarten (Luoxiu Campus)
No. 1977 Luoxiu Road, Minghang District, Shanghai 201104
PYP Coordinator Alisa Zhang
Languages English, Chinese
T: +86 21 5481 6417
W: en.ys-edu.com.cn/index.php?m=content&c=index&a=show&catid=45&id=8

Xiaomiao Kindergarten (Xinsong Campus)
No.47, Lane 499, Xinli Road, Minhang District, Shanghai
PYP Coordinator Pei Ji
Languages English, Chinese
T: +86 21 6492 0495
W: en.ys-edu.com.cn/index.php?m=content&c=index&a=show&catid=45&id=6

Yew Chung International School of Beijing
Honglingjin Park, 5 Houbalizhuang, Chaoyang District, Beijing 100025
DP Coordinator Tanya Nizam
Languages English
T: +86 10 8585 1836
W: www.ycis-bj.com

Yew Chung International School of Chongqing
No 2 Huxia Street, Yuan Yang Town, New Northern Zone, Chongqing 401122
DP Coordinator Jason Bogart
Languages English, Chinese
T: +86 23 8879 1600
W: www.ycef.com

Yew Chung International School of Qingdao
72 Tai Hang Shan Lu, Qingdao West Coast New Area, Huangdao, Shandong 266555
DP Coordinator Kyle Polizotto
Languages English
T: +86 532 8699 5551
W: www.ycis-qd.com

Yew Chung International School of Shanghai - Century Park Campus
1433 Dong Xui Road, Pudong, Shanghai 200127
DP Coordinator Matthew Grady
Languages English
T: +86 21 2226 7666
W: www.ycis-sh.com

Yew Chung International School of Shanghai - Hongqiao Campus
11 Shui Cheng Road, Puxi, Shanghai 200336
DP Coordinator Emma Golden
Languages English, Chinese (mandarin)
T: +86 21 2226 7666
W: www.ycis-sh.com

YK Pao School
1800, Lane 900, North Sanxin Road, Songjiang District, Shanghai 201602
DP Coordinator Helen Lambie-Jones
Languages English
T: +86 21 61671999
W: www.ykpaoschool.cn

Yuwen Princeton Kindergarten
Qingshan Distict, Qingdongdonglu, Baotou, Inner Mongolia AR 014030
PYP Coordinator Jingjing Zhang
Languages English, Chinese

Zhangjiagang Foreign Language School
256 Ji Yang Dong Lu, Zhangjiagang, Jiangsu 215600
DP Coordinator Cathy Zhang
Languages English
T: +86 512 5828 5972
W: www.zjgfls.com

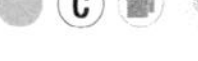

Zhengzhou Middle School
2# Yinghua Street, Hi - Tech Development Zone, Zhengzhou, Henan 450001
MYP Coordinator Judy Zhu
Languages Chinese
T: +86 371 67996825
W: www.zzms.com

Zhuhai International School
Qi ' Ao Island, Tang Jia Wan, Zhuhai, Guangdong 519080
DP Coordinator Nick Atwater
MYP Coordinator Mike Piotrowski
PYP Coordinator Zanda Balode
Languages English
T: +86 756 331 5580
W: www.zischina.com

Ziling Changxing Kindergarten
No. 1099 Qishan Road, Huzhou, Zhejiang
PYP Coordinator Feifei Wu
Languages English, Chinese
T: +86 57 2623 5173
W: mp.weixin.qq.com/s/HKXhpFPt07qoFDqc1BetiA?

DOMINICAN REPUBLIC

Instituto Leonardo Da Vinci
Carretera Don Pedro Km 1, Esq. Calle El Guano, Santiago de los Caballeros
DP Coordinator Freddy Núnez Ureña
Languages English, Spanish
T: +1 809 734 1535
W: www.leonardo-da-vinci.edu.do

EAST TIMOR

Dili International School
14 Rue Avenue de Portugal, Pantai Kelapa, Dili
PYP Coordinator Jordan Harries
Languages English
T: +670 773 39030
W: www.distimor.org

FIJI

International School Nadi
Box 9686 Nadi Airport, Nadi
DP Coordinator Bethan Paterson
MYP Coordinator Shabha Begum
PYP Coordinator Aseri Ratukadreu
Languages English
T: +679 6702 060
W: www.isn.school.fj

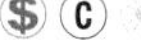

International School Suva
Lot 59, Siga Road, Laucala Beach Estate, Suva
DP Coordinator Yiyuan Chen
MYP Coordinator Katy Hourston
PYP Coordinator Renee Dansey
Languages English
T: +679 339 3300
W: www.international.school.fj

GUAM

St John's School
911 Marine Drive, Tumon Bay 96913
DP Coordinator Ellen Petra
Languages English
T: +1 (671) 646 8080
W: www.stjohnsguam.com

HONG KONG, CHINA

American School Hong Kong
6 Ma Chung Road, Tai Po, New Territories, Hong Kong, SAR
DP Coordinator Amanda Shepherd
Languages English
T: +852 3919 4100
W: www.ashk.edu.hk

Australian International School Hong Kong
3A Norfolk Road, Kowloon Tong, Hong Kong, SAR
DP Coordinator Aileen O'Donnell
Languages English
T: +852 2304 6078
W: www.aishk.edu.hk

Canadian International School of Hong Kong
36 Nam Long Shan Road, Aberdeen, Hong Kong, SAR
DP Coordinator Brian Hull
MYP Coordinator Julie Cook
PYP Coordinator Stephen Brown
Languages English
T: +852 2525 7088
W: www.cdnis.edu.hk

Carmel School
460 Shau Kei Wan Road, Shau Kei Wan, Hong Kong, SAR
DP Coordinator Nick Webber
MYP Coordinator Adam Darell
PYP Coordinator Min Kyung Shin
Languages English
T: +852 3665 5388
W: www.carmel.edu.hk

Causeway Bay Victoria International Kindergarten
32 Hing Fat Street, Causeway Bay, Hong Kong, SAR
PYP Coordinator Charlotte Chong
Languages English, Chinese
T: +852 2578 9998
W: www.cbvictoria.edu.hk

Chinese International School
1 Hau Yuen Path, Braemar Hill, Hong Kong, SAR
DP Coordinator Janelle Codrington
MYP Coordinator Tiffany Hay
Languages English, Mandarin
T: +852 2 510 7288
W: www.cis.edu.hk

Christian Alliance International School
33 King Lam Street, Lai Chi Kok, Kowloon, Hong Kong, SAR
DP Coordinator Benjamin Myers
Languages English, Chinese
T: +852 3699 3899
W: www.caisbv.edu.hk

Creative Primary School
2A Oxford Street, Kowloon Tong, Kowloon, Hong Kong, SAR
PYP Coordinator Bonnie Cheng Mei Wah
Languages Chinese, Englisg
T: +852 2336 0266
W: www.creativeprisch.edu.hk

Creative Secondary School
3 Pung Loi Road, Tseung Kwan O, Sai Kung, NT, Hong Kong, SAR
DP Coordinator Maria Cristina Guevara
MYP Coordinator Sukannya Khan
Languages English, Chinese
T: +852 2336 0233
W: www.css.edu.hk

DELIA MEMORIAL SCHOOL (GLEE PATH)
1-3 Glee Path, Mei Foo Sun Chuen, Kowloon, Hong Kong, SAR
DP Coordinator Mr. Paolo Yap
Languages Cantonese, English, Mandarin
T: +852 2741 5239
E: gp@deliagroup.edu.hk
W: www.deliagp.edu.hk

See full details on page 321

Diocesan Boys' School
131 Argyle Street, Mong Kok, Kowloon, Hong Kong, SAR
DP Coordinator Charles Kar Lun Wu
Languages English
T: +852 2711 5911
W: www.dbs.edu.hk

Discovery Montessori Academy
Block1, Discovery Bay North, Lantau Island, Hong Kong SAR
PYP Coordinator Alia James
Languages English, Chinese
T: +852 2812 9668
W: www.montessori-ami.edu.hk

Hong Kong, China

ELCHK LUTHERAN ACADEMY
25 Lam Hau Tsuen Road, Yuen Long, New Territories, Hong Kong, SAR
DP Coordinator Julius DRAKE
MYP Coordinator Keith HENDERSON
PYP Coordinator Lawrie MACPHERSON
Languages English, Mandarin, Cantonese
T: +852 8208 2092
E: info@luac.edu.hk
W: www.luac.edu.hk

See full details on page 325

ESF Abacus International Kindergarten
Mang Kung Uk Village, Clearwater Bay Road, Hong Kong SAR
PYP Coordinator Ms Fiona Hall
Languages English, Mandarin
T: +852 27195712
W: www.abacus.edu.hk

ESF Beacon Hill School
23 Ede Road, Kowloon Tong, Hong Kong SAR
PYP Coordinator Mr Andy Thompson
Languages English
T: +852 2336 5221
W: www.beaconhill.edu.hk

ESF Bradbury School
43C Stubbs Road, Hong Kong SAR
PYP Coordinator Ms Amanda Bremner
Languages English
T: +852 2574 8249
W: www.bradbury.edu.hk

ESF Clearwater Bay School
DD229, Lot 235, Clearwater Bay Road, New Territories, Hong Kong SAR
PYP Coordinator Ms Helen Read; Ms Chiara Holmes
Languages English
T: +852 2358 3221
W: www.cwbs.edu.hk

ESF Discovery College
38 Siena Avenue, Discovery Bay, Lantau Island, Hong Kong SAR
CP Coordinator Ms Emma Neuprez
DP Coordinator Mr Brian McCann
MYP Coordinator Ms Annette Garnett
PYP Coordinator Ms Kate Agars
Languages English
T: +852 3969 1000
W: www.discovery.edu.hk

ESF Glenealy School
7 Hornsey Road, Mid Levels, Hong Kong SAR
PYP Coordinator Ms Nia Sexton
Languages English
T: +852 2522 1919
W: www.glenealy.edu.hk

ESF Hillside International Kindergarten
43B Stubbs Road, Hong Kong SAR
PYP Coordinator Ms Brenda Yuen
Languages English
T: +852 2540 0066
W: www.hillside.edu.hk

ESF Island School
20 Borrett Road, Hong Kong SAR
CP Coordinator Mr Roger Wilkinson
DP Coordinator Mr Matt Rappel
MYP Coordinator Ms Andrea Walsh
Languages English
T: +852 2524 7135
W: www.island.edu.hk

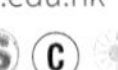

ESF Kennedy School
19 Sha Wan Drive, Pokfulam, Hong Kong SAR
PYP Coordinator Ms Yoon-Ah Lee
Languages English
T: +852 2579 5600
W: www.kennedy.edu.hk

ESF King George V School
2 Tin Kwong Road, Homantin, Kowloon, Hong Kong SAR
CP Coordinator Mr Chris Wightman
DP Coordinator Mr Chris Wightman
MYP Coordinator Mr Rowan Turner
Languages English
T: +852 2711 3029
W: www.kgv.edu.hk

ESF Kowloon Junior School
20 Perth Street, Homantin, Kowloon, Hong Kong SAR
PYP Coordinator Ms Dawn Doucette
Languages English
T: +852 3765 8700
W: www.kjs.edu.hk

ESF Peak School
20 Plunkett's Road, The Peak, Hong Kong SAR
PYP Coordinator Ms Chrissy Etchells-Bailey
Languages English
T: +852 2849 7211
W: www.ps.edu.hk

ESF Quarry Bay School
6 Hau Yuen Path, Braemar Hill, North Point, Hong Kong SAR
PYP Coordinator Miss Ceri Hill
Languages English
T: +852 2566 4242
W: www.qbs.edu.hk

ESF Renaissance College
5 Hang Ming Street, Ma On Shan, New Territories, Hong Kong SAR
CP Coordinator Ms Wilma Shen
DP Coordinator Ms Jess Davey-Peel
MYP Coordinator Ms Brandy Stern
PYP Coordinator Mr Jason Doucette
Languages English
T: +852 3556 3556
W: www.rchk.edu.hk

ESF Sha Tin College
3 Lai Wo Lane, Fo Tan, Sha Tin, New Territories, Hong Kong SAR
CP Coordinator Mr Luke Smetherham
DP Coordinator Ms Kellie Fagan
MYP Coordinator Ms Janice Lee
Languages English
T: +852 2699 1811
W: www.shatincollege.edu.hk

ESF Sha Tin Junior School
3A Lai Wo Lane, Fo Tan, Sha Tin, New Territories, Hong Kong SAR
PYP Coordinator Ms Trudy Mcmillin
Languages English
T: +852 2692 2721
W: www.sjs.edu.hk

ESF South Island School
50 Nam Fung Road, Hong Kong SAR
CP Coordinator Ms Nicola Bosson
DP Coordinator Ms Kelly Diaz
MYP Coordinator Mr Shaine Bushell
Languages English
T: +852 2555 9313
W: www.sis.edu.hk

ESF Tsing Yi International Kindergarten
Maritime Square, 33 Tsing King Road, Tsing Yi, New Territories, Hong Kong SAR
PYP Coordinator Ms Suzannah Large
Languages English
T: +852 2436 3355
W: www.tyk.edu.hk

ESF Tung Chung International Kindergarten
1/F, Commercial Accommodation, The Visionary, 1 Ying Hong Street, Tung Chung, Lantau, New Territories, Hong Kong SAR
PYP Coordinator Ms Cathy Boon
Languages English
T: +852 3742 3500
W: www.tck.edu.hk

ESF West Island School
250 Victoria Road, Pokfulam, Hong Kong SAR
CP Coordinator Ms Emily Buckland
DP Coordinator Mrs Helen Devine Costa
MYP Coordinator Ms Clare Haworth
Languages English
T: +852 2819 1962
W: www.wis.edu.hk

ESF Wu Kai Sha International Kindergarten
599 Sai Sha Road, Ma On Shan, Sha Tin, Hong Kong SAR
PYP Coordinator Ms Aylin Kip
Languages English
T: +852 2435 5291
W: www.wksk.edu.hk

French International School
165 Blue Pool Road, Happy Valley, Hong Kong, SAR
DP Coordinator Pauline Hall
Languages English
T: +852 25776217
W: www.fis.edu.hk

G. T. (Ellen Yeung) College
10, Ling Kong Street, Tiu Keng Leng, Tseung Kwan O, Hong Kong, SAR
DP Coordinator Vincent Tam
Languages English, Chinese
T: +852 2535 6867
W: www.gtcollege.edu.hk

Galilee International School
G/F & 1/F, Peace Garden, 2 Peace Avenue, Ho Man Tin, Kowloon, Hong Kong, SAR
PYP Coordinator Mr Arthur Kenji Noguchi
Languages English, Mandarin, Cantonese
T: +852 2390 3000
W: www.gis.edu.hk

German Swiss International School
11 Guildford Road, The Peak, Hong Kong, SAR
DP Coordinator Sean Wray
Languages English
T: +852 2849 6216
W: www.gsis.edu.hk

Han Academy
G/F - 2/F, 33-35 Wong Chuk Hang Road, Aberdeen, Hong Kong, SAR
DP Coordinator Vahagn Vardanyan
Languages English, Chinese
T: +852 3998 6300
W: www.hanacademy.edu.hk

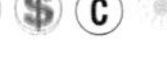

HKCA Po Leung Kuk School
62 Tin Hau Temple Road, Hong Kong, SAR
PYP Coordinator Ms Rose Hopewell-Fong
Languages English, Putonghua
T: +852 3465 8400
W: www.plkis.edu.hk

HONG KONG ACADEMY
33 Wai Man Road, Sai Kung, Hong Kong, SAR
DP Coordinator Claire Shaffery
MYP Coordinator Simon Roberts
PYP Coordinator Carly Buntin
Languages English
T: +852 2655 1111
E: admissions@hkacademy.edu.hk
W: www.hkacademy.edu.hk
See full details on page 338

International College Hong Kong
60 Sha Tau Kok Road, Shek Chung Au, Sha Tau Kok, New Territories, Hong Kong, SAR
DP Coordinator Flora Lai
Languages English
T: +852 2655 9018
W: www.ichk.edu.hk

International College Hong Kong - Hong Lok Yuen
3 Twentieth Street, Hong Lok Yuen, Tai Po, New Territories, Hong Kong, SAR
PYP Coordinator Charlotte Beard
Languages English
T: +852 3955 3000
W: ichkhly.edu.hk

Japanese International School
4663 Tai Po Road, Tai Po, New Territories, Hong Kong, SAR
PYP Coordinator Catherine Wan
Languages English
T: +852 2834 3531
W: www.jis.edu.hk

Kiangsu-Chekiang College, International Section
20 Braemar Hill Road, North Point, Hong Kong, SAR
DP Coordinator Calvin Tse
Languages English
T: +852 2570 1281
W: www.kcis.edu.hk

Kingston International Kindergarten
12-14 Cumberland Road, Kowloon Tong, Hong Kong, SAR
PYP Coordinator Michelle Chu
Languages English
T: +852 2337 9049
W: www.kingston.edu.hk

KINGSTON INTERNATIONAL SCHOOL
113 Waterloo Road, Kowloon Tong, Hong Kong, SAR
PYP Coordinator Ms. Emily Flach (Primary); Ms. Michelle Chu (Early Years)
Languages English, Mandarin
T: +852 2337 9031
E: enquiry@kingston.edu.hk
W: www.kingston.edu.hk
See full details on page 347
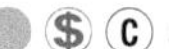

Kornhill Victoria International Kindergarten
2/F., 18 Hong On Street, Kornhill, Quarry Bay, Hong Kong, SAR
PYP Coordinator Ms Vincci Wong
Languages English, Cantonese, Putonghua
T: +852 2885 1888
W: www.victoria.edu.hk

Li Po Chun United World College of Hong Kong
10 Lok Wo Sha Lane, Sai Sha Road, Ma On Shan, Sha Tin, Hong Kong, SAR
DP Coordinator Beta Chau
Languages English
T: +852 2640 0441
W: www.lpcuwc.edu.hk

Logos Academy
1 Kan Hok Lane, Tseung Kwan, Hong Kong, SAR
DP Coordinator Patricia Yeung
Languages English
T: +852-23372123
W: www.logosacademy.edu.hk

Malvern College Hong Kong
3 Fo Chun Road, Pak Shek Kok, Hong Kong, SAR
DP Coordinator Lianne Yu
MYP Coordinator Katrina Englart
PYP Coordinator Benedicte Benoit
Languages English
T: +852 3898 4688
W: www.malverncollege.org.hk

NORD ANGLIA INTERNATIONAL SCHOOL, HONG KONG
11 On Tin Street, Lam Tin, Kowloon, Hong Kong, SAR
DP Coordinator Colin Spanos
Languages English
T: +852 3958 1428
E: admissions@nais.hk
W: www.nais.hk
See full details on page 360

Parkview International Pre-school
Tower 18 Parkview, 88 Tai Tam Reservoir Road, Hong Kong, SAR
PYP Coordinator Joshua Hunter
Languages English
T: +852 2812 6023
W: www.pips.edu.hk

Parkview International Pre-School (Kowloon)
Podium Level, Kowloon Station, 1 Austin Road West, Kowloon, Hong Kong, SAR
PYP Coordinator Don Cruz
Languages English
T: +852 2812 6801
W: www.pips.edu.hk

Po Leung Kuk Choi Kai Yau School
6 Caldecott Road, Piper's Hill, Kowloon, Hong Kong, SAR
DP Coordinator James Kuan
Languages English
T: +852 2148 2052
W: www.cky.edu.hk

Po Leung Kuk Ngan Po Ling College
26 Sung On Street, Tokwawan, Kowloon, Hong Kong, SAR
DP Coordinator Yiu Iu
Languages English
T: +852 2462 3932
W: www.npl.edu.hk
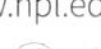

Singapore International School (Hong Kong) - Secondary Section
2 Police School Road, Wong Chuk Hang, Hong Kong, SAR
DP Coordinator Alvin Soon
Languages English, Putonghua
T: +852 2919 6966
W: www.singapore.edu.hk

St. Paul's Co-educational College
33 MacDonnell Road, Central, Hong Kong, SAR
DP Coordinator Belinda Ng
Languages English
T: +852 2523 1187
W: www.spcc.edu.hk

St. Stephen's College
22 Tung Tau Wan Road, Stanley, Hong Kong, SAR
DP Coordinator Derek Barham
Languages English
T: +852 2813 0360
W: www.ssc.edu.hk

Stamford American School Hong Kong
25 Man Fuk Road, Ho Man Tin, Kowloon, Hong Kong, SAR
DP Coordinator Michael Galligan
Languages English
T: +852 3467 4500
W: www.sais.edu.hk

Tai Kwong Hilary College (TKHC)
No. 178 Kam Shan, Tai Po, N.T., Hong Kong SAR
DP Coordinator Juhn Jett Hoo
Languages English, Chinese
W: tkhc.edu.hk

The Independent Schools Foundation Academy
1 Kong Sin Wan Road, Pokfulam, Hong Kong, SAR
DP Coordinator Kevin Hoye
MYP Coordinator Alan Johns
Languages English, Chinese
T: +852 2202 2000
W: www.isf.edu.hk
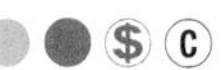

Think International School
117 Boundary Street, Kowloon Tong, Hong Kong, SAR
PYP Coordinator Matthew Green
Languages English
T: +852 2338 3949
W: www.think.edu.hk

Victoria (Belcher) International Kindergarten
Portion of Level 3 (Kindergarten Area), The Westwood, 8 Belchers Street, Hong Kong, SAR
PYP Coordinator Sharon Lui
Languages English, Chinese
T: +852 2542 7001
W: www.victoria.edu.hk

Victoria (Harbour Green) International Kindergarten
8 Sham Mong Road, G/F., Harbour Green, Kowloon, Hong Kong SAR
PYP Coordinator Kit Cheng
Languages English
T: +852 2885 1928
W: www.victoria.edu.hk

Victoria (Homantin) International Nursery
1/F., Carmel-on-the-Hill, 9 Carmel Village Street, Homantin, Kowloon, Hong Kong, SAR
PYP Coordinator Cheng Kar Wai Flora
Languages English
T: +852 2762 9130
W: www.victoria.edu.hk

HONG KONG, CHINA

Victoria (South Horizons) International Kindergarten
Podium Level 2, Phase 2, South Horizons, Ap Lei Chau, Hong Kong, SAR
PYP Coordinator Sau Kei Wendy Lam
Languages Cantonese, English, Mandarin
T: +852 2580 8633
W: www.victoria.edu.hk

Victoria Kindergarten
G/F., 2-8 Hong On Street, Kornhill, Hong Kong, SAR
PYP Coordinator Kathy SIU
Languages English
T: +852 2885 3331
W: www.victoria.edu.hk

Victoria Nursery
Ko Fung Court, Harbour Heights, 5 Fook Yum Road, North Point, Hong Kong, SAR
PYP Coordinator Yu Tina
Languages Cantonese, English, Mandarin
T: +852 2571 7888
W: www.victoria.edu.hk

Victoria Shanghai Academy (VSA)
19 Shum Wan Road, Aberdeen, Hong Kong, SAR
DP Coordinator Chloe Pollack
MYP Coordinator Christopher Wright
PYP Coordinator Yu Sze (Carol) Ng
Languages English, Putonghua
T: +852 3402 1000
W: www.vsa.edu.hk

Yew Chung International School of Hong Kong
3 To Fuk Road, Kowloon, Hong Kong, SAR
DP Coordinator Alan Ramm
Languages English, Mandarin
T: +852 2338 7106
W: www.ycis-hk.com

INDIA

Aarth Universal School
Block 148, Surat-Bhesan-Barbodhan Road, Malgama, Surat, Gujarat 395005
PYP Coordinator Jyothi Nair
Languages English
T: +91 81 5592 2000
W: aarthuniversalschool.org

Adani International School
Opposite Belvedere Golf & Country Club, Shantigram, Near Vaishnodevi Circle, S.G. Highway, Ahmedabad, Gujarat 382421
PYP Coordinator Cheryl Shah
Languages English
T: +91 79 2555 6888
W: www.adaniinternationalschool.org

Aditya Birla World Academy
Vastushilp Annexe, Gamadia Colony, J D Road, Tardeo, Mumbai, Maharashtra 400034
DP Coordinator Shalini John
Languages English
T: +91 22 2352 8400
W: www.adityabirlaworldacademy.com

Aga Khan Academy Hyderabad
Survey No 1/1 Hardware Park, Maheshwaram Mandal, Rangareddy District, Hyderabad, Telangana 501510
DP Coordinator Sudipta Roy
MYP Coordinator Meenakshi Joshi
PYP Coordinator Abhimanyu Das Gupta
Languages English
T: +91 40 66291313
W: www.agakhanacademies.org/hyderabad

Ahlcon Public School
Mayur Vihar Ph 1, New Delhi, Delhi 110091
CP Coordinator Nayna Dhawan
Languages English
T: +91 11 4634 7777
W: www.ahlconpublicschool.com

Ahmedabad International School
Opp Rajpath Row Houses, Behind Kiran Motors, Judges Bungalow Road, Bodakdev, Ahmedabad 380015
DP Coordinator Deepti Shah
PYP Coordinator Jemily Kulkarni
Languages English
T: +91 79 2687 2459
W: www.aischool.net

Ajmera Global School
Yogi Nagar, Eksar Road, Borivali West, Mumbai, Maharashtra 400092
PYP Coordinator Pushpalata Ajit
Languages English
T: +91 22 32401053
W: www.ajmeraglobalschool.com

Akal Academy Baru Sahib
Via Rajgarh, Teh. Pachhad, Distt. Sirmore, Himachal Pradesh 173101
PYP Coordinator P.D Mani
Languages English
T: +91 9816400538
W: www.akalacademybarusahib.com

Akshar Árbol International School - ECR Campus
Bethel Nagar, North 9th Street, Injambakkam, Chennai, Tamil Nadu 600115
PYP Coordinator Latha Muthukrishnan
Languages English
T: +91 94449 73275
W: www.akshararbol.edu.in

Akshar Árbol International School - West Mambalam
The Secondary Space (Grade 6 - 12), 16, Umapathy Street, West Mambalam, Chennai, Tamil Nadu 600033
PYP Coordinator Vinutha Anand
Languages English
T: +91 44248 33275
W: www.akshararbol.edu.in

aLphabet School
178 St. Mary's Road, Alwarpet, Chennai, Tamil Nadu 600018
DP Coordinator Charmaine Jesudoss
MYP Coordinator Suparna Banerjee
PYP Coordinator Minu Simon
Languages English
T: +91 44 4211 2025
W: www.alphabet.school
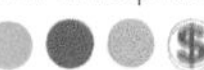 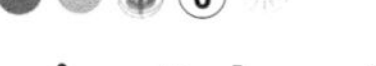

American Embassy School
Chandragupta Marg, Chanakyapuri, New Delhi, Delhi 110021
DP Coordinator Teresa Hjellming
Languages English
T: +91 11 2688 8854
W: aes.ac.in

American International School - Chennai
100 Feet Road, Taramani, Chennai 600113
DP Coordinator Chris Galaty
Languages English
T: +91 44 2254 9000
W: www.aisch.org

American School of Bombay
SF 2, G-Block, Bandra Kurla Complex Road, Bandra East, Mumbai, Maharashtra 400051
DP Coordinator Alistair Nelson
PYP Coordinator Faiza Martin
Languages English
T: SS: +91 22 6772 7272
ES: +91 22 6131 3600
W: www.asbindia.org
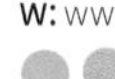  

Amity Global School, Gurgaon
Main Sector Road 4, Sector 46, Gurgaon, Harayana 122002
DP Coordinator Ved Prakash
PYP Coordinator Chandrei Choudhury
Languages English
T: +91 84 4848 1410
W: www.amityglobalschool.com/gurgaon

Amity Global School, Noida
A Block, C Block, Sector 44, Noida, Uttar Pradesh 201301
PYP Coordinator Vishakha Jain
Languages English
T: +91 12 0243 2959
W: amityglobalschool.com/noida

Amrita International Vidyalayam
Choodasandra, Huskur P.O., Bengaluru, Karnataka 560099
PYP Coordinator Ms P Sreeja Nair
Languages English
T: +91 90 1920 2583
W: aiv.edu.in

Apeejay School International, South Delhi
Sheikh Sarai-Phase I, Panchsheel Park, New Delhi, Delhi 110017
DP Coordinator Neha Sharma
MYP Coordinator Pragati Agnihotri
PYP Coordinator Shalini Fate
Languages English
T: +91 11 26016935
W: intl.apeejay.edu
 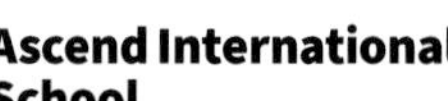

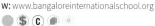

Ascend International School
5 'F' Block, Opp. Govt. Colony, Bandra Kurla Complex (Bandra E), Mumbai, Maharashtra 400051
DP Coordinator Angie Tarun
MYP Coordinator Pooja Agarwal
PYP Coordinator Shilpa Sharma
Languages English
T: +91 22 7122 2000
W: www.ascendinternational.org

Bangalore International School
Geddalahalli, Hennur Bagalur Road, Kothanur Post, Bengaluru, Karnataka 560077
DP Coordinator Deepak Babu
Languages English
T: +91 80 2846 5060/2844 5852
W: www.bangaloreinternationalschool.org

BD Somani International School
625 GD Somani Marg, Cuffe Parade, Mumbai, Maharashtra 400005
DP Coordinator Rupesh Solgaonkar
Languages English
T: +91 22 2216 1355
W: www.bdsomaniinternationalschool.com

BGS International Academia School
BGS Knowledge City, Nityanandha Nagar, K.Gollahalli, Bengaluru, Karnataka 560074
DP Coordinator Sabita Sarma
Languages English
T: +91 96 0626 3332
W: bgsias.school
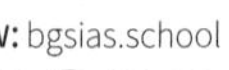 

Birla Open Minds International School
Survey No. 192 & 193, Outer Ring Road, Gachibowli, Kollur, Hyderabad, Telangana 502300
CP Coordinator Aruna Muddana
Languages English
T: +91 84 9999 3928
W: www.openminds-hyderabad.com

BLiSS Edify International School, Pune
38 Phase 1, Rajiv Gandhi Infotech Park, Hinjawadi, Pune, Maharashtra 411057
MYP Coordinator Nihal Ahmed Patel
PYP Coordinator Heena Yera
Languages English
T: +91 77 4185 0000
W: blissedify.org

Bloomingdale International School
Municipal Employee Colony, Main Road, Vijayawada, Andhra Pradesh 520010
DP Coordinator Karn Ragade
MYP Coordinator Hannaneh Hajiaghababa
PYP Coordinator Abha Sharma
Languages English
T: +91 7799787827
W: bloomingdale.edu.in

Bodhi International School
Shikargarh Enclave, Near Mini Market, Jodhpur, Rajasthan 342015
PYP Coordinator Manya Jain
Languages English
T: +91 291 2970100-1
W: www.bodhijodhpur.com

Bombay International School
Gilbert Building, 2nd Cross Lane, Babulnath, Mumbai, Maharashtra 400007
DP Coordinator Disha Sengupta
PYP Coordinator Neha Chheda
Languages English
T: +91 22 2364 8206
W: bis.edu.in

Bunts Sangha's S.M. Shetty International School & Jr. College
Hiranandani Gardens, Powai, Mumbai, Maharashtra 400076
DP Coordinator Snehal Bhortake
Languages English
T: +91 22 61327346
W: smshettyinstitute.org

C P Goenka International School - Juhu
Plot No 44, Gulmohar Cross Road No 1, JVPD, Vile Parle (West), Mumbai, Maharashtra 400049
DP Coordinator Neha Pandit
Languages English
T: +91 93 2259 1709
W: www.cpgoenkainternationalschool.com/international-school-in-juhu

C P Goenka International School - Pune, Wagholi
Behind Hotel Mapple Adhwryou, Gate No. 1347/I, Ubale Nagar, Wagholi, Maharashtra 412207
CP Coordinator Allomy Kadakia
Languages English
T: +91 20 2740 1292
W: www.cpgoenkainternationalschool.com/international-school-in-pune

Calcutta International School
724 Anandapur, E M Bypass, Kolkata, West Bengal 700107
DP Coordinator Tina Servaia
Languages English
T: +91 33 2443 2054
W: www.calcuttais.edu.in

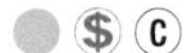

Caledonian International School
Near Power Gym, Saili Road, Pathankot, Punjab 145001
MYP Coordinator Shagun Gupta
PYP Coordinator Srijal Gupta
Languages English
T: +91 98 7883 3613
W: caledonianinternational.com

Calorx Olive International School
Besides Ahmedabad Dental College, Near Arjun Farm, Ranchodpura - Bhadaj Road, Ahmedabad, Gujarat 380058
DP Coordinator Ankur Upadhyay
MYP Coordinator Swini Bagga
PYP Coordinator Sujata Paul
Languages English, French, Hindi
T: +91 90 9993 3804
W: www.cois.edu.in

Cambridge International School
Choti Baradari, Phase II, Jalandhar, Punjab 144001
DP Coordinator Rashmi Saini
PYP Coordinator Meenu Huria
Languages English
T: +91 181 462 3955
W: www.cambridgejalandhar.in

Canadian International School
Survey No 4 & 20, Manchenahalli, Yelahanka, Bengaluru, Karnataka 560064
DP Coordinator Kevin Nielsen
Languages English
T: +91 80 4249 4444
W: www.cisb.org.in

Canary The School
1-110/3/B,Gautami Valley Near Substation Road, Madinaguda, Miyapur, Hyderabad, Telangana 500049
PYP Coordinator Salima Dinani
Languages English
W: www.canaryschool.in

Candor International School
Koppa-harapanhalli Road, Hullahalli, Off, Bannerghatta Main Rd, near Electronic City, Bengaluru, Karnataka 560105
DP Coordinator Gourab Das Sharma
PYP Coordinator Ms. Kiran Singh
Languages English
T: +91 77 6029 9992
W: candorschool.edu.in

Chatrabhuj Narsee School
Valley of Flower, Next to Gundecha Premiere Tower, off. Western Express Highway, Kandivali East, Mumbai, Maharashtra 400101
DP Coordinator Aditi Chakrabarti
Languages English
T: +91 22 2886 6677
W: cns.ac.in

Children's Academy International School
BL Murarka Marg, Bachani Nagar, Malad East, Mumbai, Maharashtra 400097
CP Coordinator Ronit Bhat
Languages English
T: +91 22 2883 5014
W: www.childrens-academy.in

Chinmaya International Residential School
Nallur Vayal Post, Siruvani Road, Coimbatore, Tamil Nadu 641114
DP Coordinator Ganesh Eswaran
Languages English
T: +91 422 261 3300/3303
W: www.cirschool.org

Chinmaya International Vidyalaya
P-125, Warangade, Maan, Taluka and Dist: Palghar, Boisar, Maharashtra 401501
PYP Coordinator Haritha Raghunandanan
Languages English, Hindi
T: +91 73 7848 9121
W: chinmayainternationalvidyalaya.com

CHIREC International
1-55/12C, CHIREC Avenue, Kothaguda, Kondapur, Hyderabad, Telangana 500084
DP Coordinator Sony Sharma
Languages English
T: 91 40 44760999
W: www.chirec.ac.in

Choithram International
Choithram Hospital Campus, 5 Manik Bagh Road, Indore, Madhya Pradesh 452014
DP Coordinator Amit Puranik
MYP Coordinator Kamayani Sharma
PYP Coordinator Meenal Gavlani
Languages English
T: +91 731 2360345/6
W: www.choithraminternational.com

Christ Church School
Clare Road, Byculla, Mumbai, Maharashtra 400008
DP Coordinator Avila Luke
Languages English
T: +91 22 2309 9892
W: www.christchurchschoolmumbai.org

Christ Junior College
29 Hosur Road, Suddagunte Palya, Bengaluru, Karnataka 560029
DP Coordinator Sheela Chacko
Languages English
T: +91 80 40129292
W: www.christjuniorcollege.in

Christ Junior College - Residential
Mysore Road, Kanmanike, Kumbalgodu, Bengaluru, Karnataka 560074
DP Coordinator Nancy Mariyan
Languages English
T: + 91 80 28437915
W: www.cjcib.in

CPS Global School - Anna Nagar Campus
A 80, IIIrd Avenue, Annanagar, Chennai, Tamil Nadu 600102
DP Coordinator Rama Mylavarapu
Languages English
T: +91 44 4351 5121
W: www.cpsglobalschool.com

CPS Global School - Thirumazhisai Campus
SH 50, Thiruvallur High Road, Thirumazhisai, Chennai, Tamil Nadu 600124
DP Coordinator Jayu Ganesh
Languages English
T: +91 44 3500 3800
W: www.cpsglobalschool.com

Crossroads International School
11-12 Modern Complex, Devendra Dham Ki Gali, Opposite Celebration Mall, Udaipur, Rajasthan 313001
PYP Coordinator Shikha Rathore
Languages English, Hindi
T: +91 29 4298 0215
W: crossroadsschool.in

Cygnus World School
Besides Motnath Mahadev Temple, Harni, Vadodara, Gujarat 390022
DP Coordinator Madhusudana Brahma
Languages English, Hindi
T: +91 90 9913 0334
W: www.cygnusworldschool.com

D Y Patil International College
DY Patil Knowledge City, Charholi(BK), Via. Lohegaon, Pune, Maharashtra 412105
DP Coordinator Jovella Dias
Languages English
T: +91 20 30612700/752/753
W: www.dypispune.in

D Y Patil International School, Nerul
Dr D Y Patil Vidhyanagar, Sector 7, Nerul, Navi Mumbai, Maharashtra 400706
DP Coordinator Jhumpa Biswas
Languages English
T: +91 22 47700840
W: www.dypisnerul.in

D Y Patil International School, Worli
Opp MIG Colony A, Worli, Mumbai, Maharashtra 400025
CP Coordinator Vidhi Kanjani
DP Coordinator Suzanne Patel
PYP Coordinator Archana Mehra
Languages English
T: +91-22 69047999
W: www.dypisworli.com

Delhi Public School Bangalore East (DPSBE)
Survey No. 43/1B & 45, Sulikunte Village, Dommasandra Post, Bangalore, Karnataka 562125
CP Coordinator Sarita Farswal
Languages English
T: +91 96 6311 5148
W: east.dpsbangalore.edu.in

Delhi Public School Bangalore North (DPSBN)
Survey No 35/1A, Sathnur Village, Bagalur Post, Off Bellary Road, Jalla Hobli, Bangalore, Karnataka
CP Coordinator Pankaj Ohri
Languages English
T: +91 80 2972 4864
W: north.dpsbangalore.edu.in

Delhi Public School Bangalore South (DPSBS)
11th KM, Bikaspura Main Road, Kanakapura Road, Konanakunte, Bangalore, Karnataka 560062
CP Coordinator Vandana Arora
Languages English
T: +91 80 2666 8581
W: south.dpsbangalore.edu.in

Delhi Public School Ghaziabad (DPSG) International
P.O. Dasna, Hindon Nagar, Dasna, Kallu Garhi, Ghaziabad, Uttar Pradesh 201303
PYP Coordinator Sania Arora
Languages English
T: +91 11 4734 2000
W: www.dpsgs.org/international

Delhi Public School Ghaziabad (DPSG) Meerut Road
Site No. 3, Meerut Road Industrial Area, Ghaziabad, Uttar Pradesh 201001
DP Coordinator Lakshman Sharma
PYP Coordinator Monalisa Sunit Kumar
Languages English
T: +91 11 4734 2000
W: www.dpsgs.org/ghaziabad

Delhi Public School Ghaziabad (DPSG) Palam Vihar
I Block, Palam Vihar, Gurgaon, Haryana 122017
PYP Coordinator Sameeksha Bhatt
Languages English, Hindi
T: +91 11 4734 2000
W: www.dpsgs.org/palam-vihar

Delhi Public School Ghaziabad (DPSG) Vasundhara
Sector 9, Vasundhara, Ghaziabad, Uttar Pradesh 201012
PYP Coordinator Pooja Garg
Languages English
T: +91 11 4734 2000
W: www.dpsgs.org/vasundhara

Dhirubhai Ambani International School
Bandra-Kurla Complex, Bandra (East), Mumbai, Maharashtra 400098
DP Coordinator Soma Basu
PYP Coordinator Pritha Banerjee
Languages English
T: +91 22 3563 7000
W: www.dais.edu.in

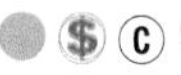

Don Bosco International School
Nathalal Parekh Marg, Matunga (E), Mumbai, Maharashtra 400019
DP Coordinator Aarti Malik
PYP Coordinator Gladys Gonsalves
Languages English
T: +91 22 2412 7474
W: dbis.in

DPS International, Gurgaon
HS-01, Block W, South City II, Gurgaon, Haryana 122001
DP Coordinator Jyotika Singh
MYP Coordinator Ekta Singh
PYP Coordinator Shalini Ranjan
Languages English
T: +91 8377000164
W: www.dpsiedge.edu.in

Dr Pillai Global Academy
Plot No 1, RSC 48, Gorai - II, Borivali (W), Mumbai, Maharashtra 400092
DP Coordinator Roshni Rajan
Languages English
T: +91 22 2868 4467/87
W: www.drpillaiglobalacademy.ac.in

Dr Pillai Global Academy, New Panvel
Sector-7, Khanda Colony, New Panvel, Navi Mumbai, Maharashtra 410206
DP Coordinator Ichha Garg
Languages English
T: +91 22 2748 1737
W: dpgapanvel.ac.in

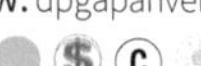

DRS International School
Survey No. 523 Opp.Apparel Park, Gundla Pochampally, Medchal Mandal, Telangana, Hyderabad 500100
DP Coordinator Pushyami Chennupati
PYP Coordinator Shanmugam Paramasivan
Languages English, French, Spanish, Hindi
T: +91 40 237 92123/4/5
W: www.drsinternational.com

DSB International School
Urmi Estate 95, Ganpatrao Kadam Marg, Opposite Peninsula Business Park, Mumbai, Maharashtra 400013
DP Coordinator Angharad Davies
Languages English, German
T: +91 73 0459 7529
W: www.dsbindia.com

Eastern Public School
Ward 1, Abbas Nagar, Bhopal, Madhya Pradesh 462036
DP Coordinator Fraz Ahmed
PYP Coordinator Fozia Mehfooz
Languages English
T: +91 755 2805695
W: www.e-p-s.in

Ebenezer International School Bangalore
Singena Aghara, Via Huskur Road, Near APMC Fruit Yard, Electronic City Phase-I, Bengaluru, Karnataka 560099
DP Coordinator Abhinav Awasthi
PYP Coordinator Jyoti Andrew
Languages English
T: +91 80 67612222
W: www.eisbangalore.edu.in

Ecole Mondiale World School
Gulmohar Cross Road No. 9, J.V.P.D. Scheme, Juhu, Mumbai, Maharashtra 400049
DP Coordinator Dr. Rupesh Solgaonkar
MYP Coordinator Ms. Oyndrida Mukherjee
PYP Coordinator Mr. Jonathan Martin
Languages English
T: +91 22 26237265/66
W: www.ecolemondiale.org

Edubridge International School
Wadilal A. Patel Marg, Grant Road (East), Mumbai, Maharashtra 400007
DP Coordinator Tracy Waller
MYP Coordinator Radha Trivady
PYP Coordinator Chantelle Monteiro
Languages English
T: +91 22 238 999 11
W: www.edubridgeschool.org

Ela Green School
No.1 Karambur Village, Chengalpattu Taluk, Kandchipuram District, Urapakkam, Maraimalai Nagar, Chennai, Tamil Nadu 603209
DP Coordinator Raja Shekhar Reddy Malapati
MYP Coordinator Raja Shekhar Reddy Malapati
PYP Coordinator Sindhuja Balaguru
Languages English
T: +91 89 3995 8989
W: elagreenschool.org

Elpro International School
Elpro compound, Entrance from Shridhar Nagar road, Pimpri-Chinchwad Link Road, Pune, Maharashtra 411033
CP Coordinator Pallavi Mukherjee
DP Coordinator Pallavi Mukherjee
Languages English
T: +91 20 6733 3500
W: www.elproschools.edu.in

Excelsior American School
Sector 43 behind Dell Building, C-2 Block, Sushant Lok, Phase 1, Gurugram, Haryana 122001
DP Coordinator Ruchi Gambhir
Languages English
T: +91 1 124 4049342
W: www.excelsioreducation.org

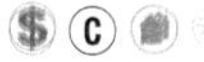

Fazlani L'Académie Globale
Shiv das Chapsi Marg, Opp. Wallace Flour Mills, Mazagaon, Mumbai, Maharashtra 400009
PYP Coordinator Kinjal Shah
Languages English
T: +91 222 373 2730
W: www.flag.org.in

Finland International School (FIS) Thane
Road no. 27, Shreenagar, Wagle Estate, Thane West, Thane, Maharashtra 400604
DP Coordinator Vaishali Phatak
Languages English, Hindi
T: +91 5203 9926
W: fis-thane.com

FirstSteps School
Opp. Blind Girls Hostel, Sector 26, Chandigarh, Punjab 160019
PYP Coordinator Rachanjit Kaur
T: +91 172 2793992
W: firststepsschool.org
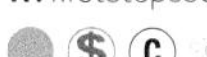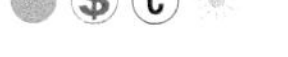

Focus High School
Behind Salar Jung Museum, 22-8-321 Darushifa, Hyderabad, Telangana 500024
MYP Coordinator Vaseema Sultana
PYP Coordinator Amena Imran
Languages English
T: +91 40 2440 4060
W: www.focushighschool.org

Fountainhead School
Opp Ambetha Water Tank, Kunkni, Rander-Dandi Road, Surat, Gujarat 395005
DP Coordinator Bhargavi Bergi
MYP Coordinator Percy Danesh Elavia
PYP Coordinator Nandini Aswani
Languages English
T: +91 800 0130 031
W: www.fountainheadschools.org

G D Goenka Global School
S-3130, DLF 3, Near Neelkanth Hospital, Gurugram, Haryana 122010
PYP Coordinator Mandeep Khaira
Languages English, Hindi
W: gdgoenkaglobal.com

G D Goenka World School
G D Goenka Education City, Sohna-Gurgaon Road, Sohna, Haryana 122103
DP Coordinator Dr Manisha Mehta
PYP Coordinator Poonam Singh
Languages English
T: +91 95 1363 1471
W: gdgws.gdgoenka.com

G Global School
29A, Rajagoundampalayam 2nd Street, Pallipalayam Road, Tiruchengodu, Tamil Nadu 637211
PYP Coordinator Sathyavarthini Gunasekaran
Languages English, Tamil
T: +91 42 8825 0999
W: www.gglobalschool.com

Garodia International Centre for Learning
153, Garodia Nagar, Ghatkopar East, Mumbai, Maharashtra 400077
DP Coordinator Huzefa Kagalwala
Languages English
T: +91 22 25061133/3157
W: www.gicl.edu.in

Gateway International School
TOD Ashram, Jabakadal Street, Padur, Kazhipattur Post, Kelambakkam, Chennai, Tamil Nadu 603103
DP Coordinator Dhivya Nageswari P
MYP Coordinator Dharakeswari G
PYP Coordinator Susan Pramod
Languages English
T: + 91 860 811 7700
W: gatewayschools.edu.in
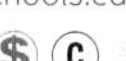

GEMS Modern Academy - Kochi
Plot B1-4, Smart City Kochi, Opp. Infopark Phase II, Brahmapuram, Kochi, Kerala 682303
PYP Coordinator Siba Shekhar
Languages English
T: +91 48 4258 7800
W: www.gemsmodernacademy-kochi.in

GENESIS GLOBAL SCHOOL
A1 & A12, Sector 132, Noida Expressway, Uttar Pradesh 201304
DP Coordinator Rajeev Pargaien
MYP Coordinator Dahlia Atabani
PYP Coordinator Monika Kala
Languages English
T: +91 9711 000626
E: info@genesisgs.edu.in
W: www.genesisglobalschool.edu.in
See full details on page 328

GJR International School
1/1 & 1/2 Chinnappanahalli, Bangalore, Karnataka 560037
PYP Coordinator Neelam Ravi
Languages English
T: +91 96 0648 9500
W: gjrinternationalschool.edu.in

Glendale International School
Plot A, Road No. 20, HMDA Layout, Tellapur, Hyderabad, Telangana 502032
PYP Coordinator Kavitha Sanjeev
Languages English
T: +91 90 3000 1128
W: www.glendale.edu.in/glendale-international-school/ib-pyp-tellapur

Goldcrest International
Sector 29, Plot No: 59, Near Rajiv Gandhi Park, Navi Mumbai, Maharashtra 400703
DP Coordinator Mousumee Mishra
Languages English
T: +91 22 2789 2261
W: www.goldcresthigh.com

Good Shepherd International School
Good Shepherd Knowledge Village, M Palada PO, Ootacamund, Tamil Nadu 643 004
DP Coordinator Suresh Thangarajan
MYP Coordinator Rita Chandran
PYP Coordinator Meera Chhabria
Languages English
T: +91 423 2550371
W: www.gsis.ac.in

GPS Brookes Kochi
P.O, Thiruvaniyoor, Thiruvankulam - Chottanikkara Rd, Kochi, Kerala 682308
DP Coordinator Anuradha Varma
Languages English
T: +91 484 271 3745
W: gpsbrookeskochi.org

Greenwood High International School
No.8-14, Chickkawadayara Pura, Near Heggondahalli, Gunjur Post, Varthur via, Bengaluru, Karnataka 560087
DP Coordinator Nishanth Nagavar
Languages English
T: +91 80 22010500
W: www.greenwoodhigh.edu.in

Harvest International School
Carmalaram post silk farm, Kodathi village, Off sarjapur road, near Kodathi village, Bangalore, Karnataka 560035
PYP Coordinator Jayalakshmy Nambiar
Languages English, Hindi
T: +91 80 6733 1884
W: www.harvestinternationalschool.in

Heritage Xperiential Learning School, Gurgaon
Sector 62, Gurgaon, Haryana 122011
DP Coordinator Poonam Dahiya
PYP Coordinator Meenakshi Gupta
Languages English, Hindi
T: +91 124 2855124
W: www.ths.ac.in

HFS International Powai
Richmond Street, Hiranandani Gardens, Powai, Mumbai, Maharashtra 400076
DP Coordinator Jagruti Joshi
Languages English
T: +91 22 2576 3001
W: www.hfsinternationalpowai.com

Hill Spring International School
C Wing, NSS Educational Complex, MP Mill Compound, Tardeo, Mumbai, Maharashtra 400034
DP Coordinator Prashant Gohil
PYP Coordinator Nisha Vahi
Languages English
T: +91 22 2355 6201
W: www.nsseducation.org

HUS International School
5/63 Old Mahabalipuram Ro, Egattur Village, Padur PO, Kelambakkam, Chennai, Tamil Nadu 600130
DP Coordinator Tejinder Kaur
MYP Coordinator Urvashi Sen
PYP Coordinator Rajarajeswari Thulasiram
Languages English
T: +91 9500 118651
W: www.hus.edu.in

India International School
Kshipra Path, Opp VT Road, Mansarovar, Jaipur, Rajasthan 302020
DP Coordinator Mukta Khandelwal
Languages English
T: +91 141 2786401
W: www.icfia.org

Indus International School (Bangalore)
Billapura Cross, Sarjapur, Bengaluru, Karnataka 562125
CP Coordinator Samuel Dharmendar Gibson
DP Coordinator Lakshmi Chetan
MYP Coordinator Nidhi Beriwal
PYP Coordinator Dominica Ireland
Languages English
T: +91 80 2289 5900
W: www.indusschool.com

IB ASIA-PACIFIC

Indus International School, Hyderabad

Survey No 424 & 425, Kondakal Village, Near Mokila (M), Shankarpally, Hyderabad, Telangana 501203
CP Coordinator Vishaka labar
DP Coordinator Vishaka labar
MYP Coordinator Venu Gopala Swamy Peddinti
PYP Coordinator Sushmita Mohanty
Languages English
T: +91 8417 302100
W: www.indusschoolhyd.com

Indus International School, Pune

576 Bhukum, Near Manas Resort, Tal Mulshi, Pune, Maharashtra 411042
CP Coordinator Manmeeta Sathe Achaarya
DP Coordinator Namita Bansal
MYP Coordinator Achla Kakria
PYP Coordinator Puja Grover
Languages English
T: +91 80 2289 5900
W: www.indusschoolpune.com

International Fateh Academy

Academy Road, Jandiala Guru, Amritsar, Punjab 143001
PYP Coordinator Gurjeet Kaur
Languages English, Punjabi
T: +91 18 3243 0205
W: fatehacademy.com

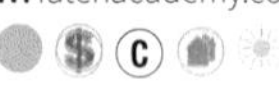

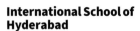

International School of Hyderabad

ICRISAT Main Entrance Gate, Patancheru, Ramachandrapuram, Hyderabad, Telangana 502324
DP Coordinator Vandana Gupta
Languages English
T: +91 4030713865
W: www.ishyd.org

International Village School Chennai

33A, Clasic Farms Road, Sholinganallur, Chennai, Tamil Nadu 600119
PYP Coordinator Dasha Narendra Singh
Languages English
T: +91 44 4860 3757
W: internationalvillage.org

Jain International Residential School

Jakkasandra Post, Kanakpura Road, Ramanagara District, Bengaluru, Karnataka 562112
DP Coordinator Gopalraj Rangaswamy
Languages English
T: +91 80 2757 7750
W: www.jirs.ac.in

Jamnabai Narsee International School

Narsee Monjee Bhavan, N.S. Road No.7, J.V.P.D Scheme, Vile Parle (West), Mumbai, Maharashtra 400049
DP Coordinator Rini Ghosh
MYP Coordinator Sonal Chabria
PYP Coordinator Purti Singh
Languages English
T: +91 (0)22 26187575/ 7676
W: www.jns.ac.in

Jayshree Periwal International School

Mahapura, SEZ Road, Ajmer Road, Jaipur, Rajasthan 302026
DP Coordinator Manisha Razdan
PYP Coordinator Juhi Trivedi
Languages English
T: +91 97827 44444/44445
W: www.jpischool.com

JBCN International School - Chembur

Yogi Tower, Chembur Education Society, CTS No. 1284 (Chembur), R.C. Marg, Chembur (E), Mumbai, Maharashtra 400071
PYP Coordinator Sonia Kedia
Languages English
T: +91 86 5797 6711
W: www.jbcnschool.edu.in/chembur

JBCN International School - Oshiwara

Survey No. 41, CTS No. 1, Off Andheri Link Road, Behind Tarapore Towers, Mhada Colony, Oshiwara, Andher+, Mumbai, Maharashtra 400058
DP Coordinator Harish Hariharan Iyer
PYP Coordinator Sharana Saxena
Languages English
T: +91 22 2630 2398
W: www.jbcnschool.edu.in/oshiwara

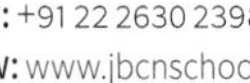

JBCN International School - Parel

Yogi Mansion, CTS No. 244, Dr Vinay Walimbe Road, Off Dr S.S. Rao Marg, Parel East, Mumbai, Maharashtra 400012
DP Coordinator Satish Kumar
PYP Coordinator Manya Jain
Languages English
T: +91 22 2411 4627
W: www.jbcnschool.edu.in/parel

JG International School

JG Campus of Excellence, JG Campus Road, Ahmedabad, Gujarat 380061
DP Coordinator Kavita Sharma
Languages English
T: +91 79 65411315
W: www.jgcampusindia.com

Johnson Grammar School ICSE&IBDP

Street No 3, Kakatiya Nagar, Habsiguda, Hyderabad, Andhra Pradesh 500007
DP Coordinator Vidhya Bhaskar
Languages English
T: +91 81064 72685
W: www.johnsonibdp.org

K.R. MANGALAM GLOBAL SCHOOL

N-Block, Nandi Vithi Road, Greater Kailash-1, New Delhi, Delhi 110048
Languages English, Hindi
T: +91 97 1885 8181
E: info@krmangalam.global
W: krmangalam.global

See full details on page 344

K.R. Mangalam Global School, Gurugram

Opp. D Block, near Patio Club, Block K, South City I, Sector 41, Gurugram, Haryana 122001
PYP Coordinator Neha Nagarsheth
Languages English, Hindi
T: +91 95 1363 2642
W: krmglobalgurgaon.com

Kai Early Years

66/2, 2nd Main Road, Nallurhalli, Whitefield, Bangalore, Karnataka 560066
PYP Coordinator Sharayu Thampi
Languages English, Hindi
T: +91 97 4048 0123
W: kaiearlyyears.com

Kanakia International School Chembur

Ghatkopar - Mankhurd Link Road, ACC Nagar, Chedda Nagar, Mumbai, Maharashtra 400043
DP Coordinator Shuchi Shukla
MYP Coordinator Shreya Mudaliar
PYP Coordinator Mona Chaudhary
Languages English
T: +91 77 3834 9697
W: kanakiaschools.org/our-schools/kis-ib

KC High

12/4, Arunachalam Road, Kotturupuram, Chennai, Tamil Nadu 600085
DP Coordinator Meera Sampath
Languages English
T: +91 (44) 2447 3551
W: www.kchigh.com

KIIT INTERNATIONAL SCHOOL

KiiT Campus 9, Patia, Bhubaneswar, Odisha 751024
DP Coordinator Mr. Kartick Chandra Sahoo
Languages English
T: +91 674 2725805
E: kiitis@kiitis.ac.in
W: www.kiitis.ac.in

See full details on page 346

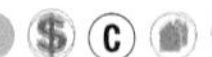

Knowledgeum Academy

44/4 District Fund Road, Jayanagar 9th Block, Bangalore, Karnataka 560069
DP Coordinator Kalai Rajan
Languages English
T: +91 73 5301 2391
W: www.knowledgeumacademy.in

Kodaikanal International School

PO Box 25, Seven Roads Junction, Kodaikanal, Tamil Nadu 624101
DP Coordinator Kirandeep Gour
MYP Coordinator Zita Szigeti
PYP Coordinator Pearlin Joseph
Languages English
T: +91 4542 247500
W: www.kis.in

Lady Andal Venkatasubba Rao Matriculation School

Shenstone Park, No.7 Harrington Road, Chennai, Tamil Nadu 600031
PYP Coordinator Michelle Teresa Noronha
Languages English
T: +91 44 2836 3404
W: www.ladyandalschool.com

Lalaji Memorial Omega International School

79, Omega School Road (Pallavaram Road), Kolapakkam, Kovur Post, Chennai, Tamil Nadu 600128
DP Coordinator Srinivasan P.A.
Languages English
T: +91 44 66241127
W: www.omegaschools.org

Lancers International School

DLF Phase V, Sector 53, Gurgaon, Haryana 122001
CP Coordinator Swati Vats
DP Coordinator Ekta Choudhary
MYP Coordinator Hannaneh Hajiaghababa
PYP Coordinator Prapti Parasher
Languages English
T: +91 124 423 8753
W: www.lis.ac.in

Legacy School, Bangalore
6/1 A, 6/2 Byrathi Village, Bidarahalli Hobli, East Taluk, Bengaluru, Karnataka 560077
DP Coordinator Anthony Gonsalves
Languages English
T: +91 70222 92405
W: lsb.edu.in

M Ct M Chidambaram Chettyar International School
179, Luz Church Road, Mylapore, Chennai, Tamil Nadu 600004
DP Coordinator Sangita Varma
Languages English
T: +91 44 2467 0120
W: www.mctmib.org

Mahatma Gandhi International School
Sheth Motilal Hirabhai Bhavan, Opp. Induben Khakhrawala, Mithakali, Navrangpura, Ahmedabad, Gujarat 380006
CP Coordinator Meenakshi Ganeriwala
DP Coordinator Ravinder Kaur
MYP Coordinator Minoo Joshi
Languages English, Hindi
T: +91 79 2 646 3888
W: www.mgis.in

Mahindra International School
P26, Rajeev Gandhi Infotech park, Phase 1, Hinjewadi, Pune, Maharashtra 411057
DP Coordinator Vijeta Sinha
MYP Coordinator Jose Campillo Campillo
PYP Coordinator Carla Swinehart
Languages English
T: +91 2042954444
W: misp.org

Mainadevi Bajaj International School
Plot No: 23-A, 24-28 Swami Vivekanand Road, Malad (West), Mumbai, Maharashtra 400064
DP Coordinator Husien Burhani Dohadwalla
Languages English
T: +91 22 28733807
W: www.mbis.org.in

Manchester International School
SF 29/3A, Hudco Colony, Vellakinar, Coimbatore, Tamil Nadu 641029
DP Coordinator Ashok Kumar
MYP Coordinator Sayali Joshi
PYP Coordinator Saranya Chandrasekar
Languages English
T: +91 422 655 5551
W: www.manchesters.in

Meluha International School
Adj to Central Forensic Lab, Near VIF College of Engineering & Techno+, Osman Sagar X Roads, Aziz Nagar, Gandipet, Hyderabad, Telangana 500075
CP Coordinator Nyshidha Nekkanti
Languages English
T: +91 81 4237 6666
W: www.meluhaedu.com

Meridian School, Banjara Hills
#8-2-541, Road No.7, Banjara Hills, Hyderabad, Telangana 500034
PYP Coordinator Sailaja Koduri
Languages English, Hindi
T: +91 80 9691 8857
W: meridianschool.in/banjarahills

Meridian School, Madhapur
#11/4 & 11/5, Opp: Hitech City, Kukatpally Bypass Road, Khanamet Village, Sherlingampally Mandal, Hyderabad, Telangana 500081
PYP Coordinator Aparna Vadlamudi
Languages English, Hindi
T: +91 99 4804 3440
W: www.meridianschool.in/madhapur

Modern High School for Girls
78, Syed Amir Ali Avenue, Kolkata, West Bengal 700019
DP Coordinator Sampa Sanyal
Languages English
T: +913322875326
W: www.mhsforgirls.edu.in

Modern Public School
B-Block, Shalimar Bagh, New Delhi, Delhi 110088
PYP Coordinator Naina Nagpal
Languages English, Hindi
T: +91 11 4142 7627
W: www.mpsshalimarbagh.com

Modern School
Sector E, Aliganj, Lucknow, Uttar Pradesh 226024
PYP Coordinator Manisha Rathore
Languages English, Hindi
T: +91 955 493 3337
W: modernschool.org

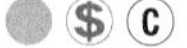

Mount Litera School International
GN Block, Behind Asian Heart Hospital, Near UTI Building, Bandra Kurla Complex, Bandra- East, Mumbai, Maharashtra 400051
DP Coordinator Shivani Fotedar
MYP Coordinator Saolee Roy
PYP Coordinator Chandrani Banerjee
Languages English
T: +91 22 6229 6000
W: www.mlsi.in

Mussoorie International School
Sri Nagar Estate, Polo Ground, Charleville, Mussoorie, Uttarakhand 248179
DP Coordinator Devendra Singh
MYP Coordinator Pravesh Uniyal
PYP Coordinator Deepa Jaiswal
Languages English
T: +91 98 3746 0408
W: www.misindia.net

Nahar International School
Nahar's Amrit Shakti, Chandivali Farm Road, Off Saki Vihar Road, Andheri East, Mumbai, Maharashtra 400072
DP Coordinator Resham Puri
Languages English, Hindi
T: +91 (0)22 6838 5500
W: www.nahar-is.ac.in

National Centre for Excellence - CV Raman Nagar
154/1, Vijay Kiran Knowledge Park, 5th Main, Malleshpalya, Bangalore, Karnataka 560075
CP Coordinator Smitha Menon
Languages English
T: +91 80 6945 5100
W: www.ncfe.ac.in/cv-raman-nagar

Navrachana International School
Vasna Bhayali Road, Bhayali, Vadodara, Gujarat 391410
DP Coordinator Jyoti Nagar
MYP Coordinator Srilakshmi Devi
PYP Coordinator Viraaj Jhaveri
Languages English
T: +91 265 225 3851/2/3/4
W: www.navrachana.ac.in

Neerja Modi School
Shipra Path, Near Building Technology Park, Mansarovar, Jaipur, Rajasthan 302020
DP Coordinator Sarita Nathawat
Languages English
T: +91 141 2785 484
W: www.nmsindia.org

Neev Academy - Yemalur Campus
No. 16, Yemalur-Kempapura Main Road, Opp. Sai Garden Apartments, Yemalur, Bengaluru, Karnataka 560037
DP Coordinator Colin Leslie Kelman
MYP Coordinator Vineet Singh
PYP Coordinator Soumya Anil Venkatram
Languages English
T: +91 80 71101700
W: www.neevacademy.org

NES International School Dombivli
Sankara Nagar, Kalyan-Shil Road, Opp. DNS Bank, Sonarpada, Dombivli (E), Thane, Mumbai, Maharashtra 421203
MYP Coordinator Steffiga D
PYP Coordinator Jyoti Hoskoti
Languages English, Hindi
T: +91 88 2880 1008
W: www.nesisd.org.in

NES International School Mumbai
Malabar Hill Road, Vasant Garden, Mulund(W), Mumbai, Maharashtra 400082
DP Coordinator Ramaswamy Varadarajan
MYP Coordinator Cimmy Ajithkumar
PYP Coordinator Rakhi Vishwakarma
Languages English
T: +91 22 25911478
W: www.nesinternational.org

NEXT School
Park Road, Off Devi Dayal Road, Mulund W, Mumbai, Maharashtra 400080
DP Coordinator Amar Dixit
MYP Coordinator Nikhil Bangera
PYP Coordinator Pragna Kolar
Languages English
T: +91 22 25600036
W: www.nextschool.org

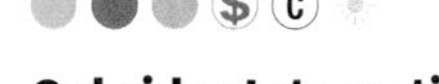

Oakridge International School, Bachupally
Survey No 166/6, Bowrampet Village, Near Bachupally, Hyderabad, Telangana 500043
DP Coordinator Saikrishna Pammi
PYP Coordinator Deepa Devarakonda
Languages English
T: +91 720 764 8111
W: www.oakridge.in/bachupally

Oakridge International School, Bengaluru
Varthur Road, Near Dommassandra Circle, Sarjapur Hobli, Bengaluru, Karnataka 562125
DP Coordinator Ajay Kumar
MYP Coordinator Richa Mehrotra
PYP Coordinator Bindu Thomas
Languages English
T: +91 0802 254 3600
W: www.oakridge.in/bengaluru

IB ASIA-PACIFIC

Oakridge International School, Gachibowli
Khajaguda, Nanakramguda Road, Cyberabad, Hyderabad, Telangana 500008
DP Coordinator Deepalatha Subramanian
MYP Coordinator Savitri Potluri
PYP Coordinator Vasundhara Achanta
Languages English
T: +91 7207 648 111
W: www.oakridge.in/gachibowli

Oakridge International School, Mohali
Next to Thunderzone Amusement Park, Mohali, Punjab 140307
DP Coordinator Balaji Thoppay
PYP Coordinator Thangalakshmi Ramakrishnan
Languages English
T: +91 752 701 3370
W: www.oakridge.in/mohali

Oakridge International School, Visakhapatnam
NH 5 Road, Behind HP Petrol Bunk, Maharajpeta Junction, Tagarapuvalasa, Visakhapatnam, Andhra Pradesh 531162
DP Coordinator Pallavi Joshi
Languages English
T: +91 773 081 6999
W: www.oakridge.in/contact

Oberoi International School
Oberoi Garden City, Off Western Express Highway, Goregaon (E), Mumbai, Maharashtra 400063
DP Coordinator Brian Haynes
MYP Coordinator Rohini Salaskar
PYP Coordinator Neha Minda
Languages English
T: +91 22 4236 3131
W: www.oberoi-is.org

Oberoi International School - JVLR Campus
Jogeshwari Vikroli Link Road, Jogeshwari East, Mumbai, Maharashtra 400060
DP Coordinator Anjali Bhardwaj
MYP Coordinator Barbara Batchelor
PYP Coordinator Archana Gera
Languages English
W: oberoi-is.org/jvlr-campus

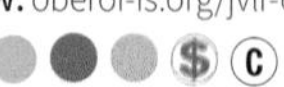

Pathways School Gurgaon
Baliawas, Off Gurgaon Faridabad Road, Gurgaon, Haryana 122003
CP Coordinator Megha Oberoi
DP Coordinator Megha Oberoi
MYP Coordinator Varsha Sinha
PYP Coordinator Geetika Grover
Languages English
T: +91 124 487 2000
W: www.pathways.in/gurgaon/school

  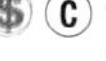

Pathways School Noida
Sector 100, Noida, Uttar Pradesh 201301
DP Coordinator Samuel Osmond
MYP Coordinator Chinki Chhapia
PYP Coordinator Vandana Parashar
Languages English
T: +91 120 461 7000
W: www.pathways.in/noida

Pathways World School, Gurgaon
Aravali Retreat, Off Gurgaon Sohna Road, Gurgaon, Haryana 122102
DP Coordinator Mona Sharma
MYP Coordinator Swati Chhikara
PYP Coordinator Monica Bhimwal
Languages English
T: +91 124 451 3000
W: www.pathways.in/worldschoolgurgaon

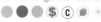

Podar International School
Ramee Emerald Building, Near Shamrao Vithal Bank, S.V.Road, Khar (West), Mumbai, Maharashtra 400052
CP Coordinator Rashmi Talreja
DP Coordinator Hema Rajan
PYP Coordinator Saachi Setpal
Languages English
T: +91 22 2648 7321
W: www.podarinternationalschool.com

Podar O.R.T International School, Worli
PODAR-ORT School Building, 68, Worli Hill Estate, Worli, Mumbai, Maharashtra 400018
DP Coordinator Sreelaxmi Murthy Madhusudan
MYP Coordinator Marsha Joshi
PYP Coordinator Shreya Mahindra
Languages English
T: +91 7506112200
W: www.podareducation.org/school/worli

 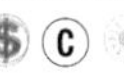

Prometheus School
I-7, Jaypee Wishtown, Sector 131, Noida, Uttar Pradesh 201304
DP Coordinator Jyoti Deveshwar
MYP Coordinator Rashima Vaid Varma
PYP Coordinator Ketaki Kapoor
Languages English, Hindi
T: +91 99 9987 6583
W: prometheusschool.com

Rasbihari International School
Vrindavan, Nashik-Ozar Road, Nashik, Maharashtra 422003
PYP Coordinator Shilpa Ahire
Languages English
T: +91 253 230 4622
W: www.rasbihari.org

 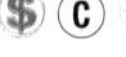

Redbridge International Academy
#114, S Bingipura Village, Hulimangala Post, Begur-Koppa Road, Bangalore, Karnataka 560105
DP Coordinator Karen Kunder
Languages English
T: +91 9620863456
W: www.rbia.in

Rockwell International School
Sy No.160(p), Gandipet Main Rd, Kokapet, Hyderabad, Telangana 500075
DP Coordinator Shruti Sareen
Languages English
T: +91 9618662201
W: rockwellinternationalschool.com

Ruh Continuum School
Sf No. 71/1 Vaigai Nagar, Pattanam Singanallur to Vellalore Road, Coimbatore, Tamil Nadu 641016
CP Coordinator Vishnu Carthi ca Guru Subbaian
DP Coordinator Krushna Pattnaik
Languages English
T: +91 63 8463 1313
W: www.ruh.school

Rungta International School
Near Nandan Van, Veer Savarkar Nagar, Raipur, Chhattisgarh 492099
DP Coordinator Madhuri Paleti
MYP Coordinator Madhuri Paleti
PYP Coordinator Gagandeep Bains
Languages English
T: +91 98261 45333
W: www.rungtainternational.org

Ryan Global School, Andheri
Yamuna Nagar, Near Pizza Hut Circle, Andheri West, Mumbai, Maharashtra 400053
PYP Coordinator Bhavi Furia
Languages English, Hindi
T: +91 22 2632 0205
W: www.ryanglobalschools.com

Ryan Global School, Kharghar
Plot No. 1, 2 & 3, Sector 11 Road, Block G, Sector 11, Kharghar, Navi Mumbai, Maharashtra 410210
CP Coordinator Archana Singh
Languages English, Hindi
T: +91 22 2774 5898
W: www.ryanglobalschools.com

Sai International School
Plot -5A, Infocity, Chandrasekharpur, Bhubaneswar, Odisha 751024
CP Coordinator Subhakanta Jena
Languages English
T: +91 93 3816 9966
W: saiinternational.edu.in

Sanatan High School
D-Block, Ranjeet Nagar, Bharatpur, Rajasthan 321001
PYP Coordinator Ambika Sharma
Languages English, Hindi
T: +91 95 2119 1522
W: www.sanatanschool.co.in

Sancta Maria International School - Faridabad
Sector 93, Faridabad, Haryana 121002
DP Coordinator Ipsa Mohanty
Languages English
T: +91 99991 16900
W: sanctamaria.in

Sangam School of Excellence
N.H. 79, Atun, Bhilwara By Pass, Chittorgarh Highway, Bhilwara, Rajasthan 311001
DP Coordinator Shruti Modi
Languages English
T: +91 1482 249 700
W: www.sangamschoolbhilwara.com

SANJAY GHODAWAT INTERNATIONAL SCHOOL
Gat No. 555, Kolhapur - Sangli Highway, Atigre, Maharashtra
DP Coordinator Dr. Bonila Sinha
Languages English
T: +91 231 2689700
E: principal@sgischool.in
W: www.sgischool.in

See full details on page 377

Sanskar School
117-121, Vishwamitra Marg, Hanuman Nagar Ext., Sirsi Road, Jaipur, Rajasthan 302012
DP Coordinator Manisha Chandra
PYP Coordinator Smita Benuskar
Languages English
T: +91 0141 2246189
W: www.sanskarjaipur.com

Sarala Birla Academy
Bannerghatta PO, Jigni Road, Bengaluru, Karnataka 560083
DP Coordinator Manoj Jaiswal
Languages English
T: +91 80 41348200/03
W: www.saralabirlaacademy.com

Satya School
Block E, South City II, Sector 49, Gurugram, Haryana 122018
PYP Coordinator Hanu Narang
Languages English
T: +91 83 7603 0644
W: satyaschool.com

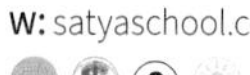 

SCOTTISH HIGH INTERNATIONAL SCHOOL
G-Block, Sector 57, Sushant Lok-II, Gurugram, Haryana 122011
DP Coordinator Ms Pooja Sharma
PYP Coordinator Ms Seema Bhati
Languages English
T: +91 124 4112781-90
E: avp.admissions@scottishigh.com
W: www.scottishigh.com
See full details on page 380

Seedling International Academy
Sector-4, Park Lane, Jawahar Nagar, Jaipur, Rajasthan 302004
DP Coordinator Shruti Kukar
Languages English
T: +91 141 2653377
W: www.seedlingschools.com

Shantiniketan International School
35-25, GKColony, Ramakrishnapuram, Secunderabad, Telangana 500056
PYP Coordinator Madhavi Mutyala
Languages English
T: +91 73311 95555
W: snis.org.in

Sharanya Narayani International School
#232/1, Thoranahalli, Byranahalli post, Near Hoskote, Bengaluru, Karnataka 563130
DP Coordinator Thavamani Thangarathinam
MYP Coordinator Kalyani Ganapathi
PYP Coordinator Kapil Mehrotra
Languages English
T: +91 80 46629500
W: snis.edu.in

SHIV NADAR SCHOOL FARIDABAD
Sector 82, Naharpar, Faridabad, Haryana 121002
DP Coordinator Garima Sharma
Languages English
T: +91 12 9461 5000
W: shivnadarschool.edu.in/faridabad
See full details on page 385

SHIV NADAR SCHOOL GURGAON
DLF City, Phase -1 Block -E, Pahari Road, Gurugram, Haryana 122011
DP Coordinator Sriparna Chakrabarti
Languages English
T: +91 124 4549200
W: shivnadarschool.edu.in/gurgaon
See full details on page 385

SHIV NADAR SCHOOL NOIDA
Plot No -SS -1, Expressway Sector 168, Noida, Uttar Pradesh 201305
DP Coordinator Deblina Chakraborty & S R Radhakrishnan
Languages English
T: +91 8130200199
E: admissions.noida@sns.edu.in
W: www.shivnadarschool.edu.in
See full details on page 385

Silver Oaks International School, Bangalore
Sy No:188/3 & 188/4, Sarjapur Road, Dommasandra village, Bengaluru, Karnataka 562125
DP Coordinator Remya Ramachandran
MYP Coordinator Radha Rani Mishra
PYP Coordinator Chithra Muralidhar
Languages English
T: +91 97394 75900
W: www.silveroaks.co.in/bangalore

Silver Oaks International School, Hyderabad
Miyapur-Dindigal Road, Bachupally, Hyderabad, Telangana 500090
PYP Coordinator Sangeeta Pratti
Languages English
T: +91 40 23047777
W: www.silveroaks.co.in/hyderabad

Silver Oaks International School, Visakhapatnam
Adj Gitam Medical College, Yendada Road, Rushikonda, Visakhapatnam, Andhra Pradesh 530045
PYP Coordinator Kousalya Bozza
Languages English, Telugu
W: www.silveroaks.co.in/visakhapatnam

SilverOaks International School, Whitefield Bangalore
Goravigere Main Road, Whitefield, Bengaluru, Karnataka 560067
PYP Coordinator Lavi Kumar
Languages English
T: +91 80 4716 2062
W: www.silveroaks.co.in/home/whitefield

Singapore International School, Mumbai
On National Highway No. 8, Post Mira Road, Dahisar, Mumbai, Maharashtra 401104
DP Coordinator Shirley Pereira
PYP Coordinator Ann Lindsey
Languages English
T: +91 222 828 5200
W: www.sisindia.net

Skill Stork International School
#55-1-219, SVS Campus, Bheemaram, Hasanparthy(m), Hanamkonda, Warangal, Telangana 506015
PYP Coordinator Hema Konar
Languages English
T: +91 80 0888 0011
W: www.skillstork.org

Smt. Sulochanadevi Singhania School
Pokharan Road No.1, J K Gram, Thane (West), Maharashtra 400606
DP Coordinator Sangeeta Kapur
Languages English
T: +91 22 4036 8410/1
W: www.singhaniaschool.org

Sreenidhi International School
Near Appa Junction, Moinabad, Hyderabad, Telangana 500075
DP Coordinator Sreedevi V
MYP Coordinator Tonderai Mutasa
PYP Coordinator Mary Vinodhini
Languages English
T: +91 9912244409
W: www.sis.edu.in

SRV International School
Marappan Thottam, 4/3 Gandhi Salai, Pattanam Road, Rasipuram, Namakkal, Tamil Nadu 637408
PYP Coordinator Preethi Murugaiyan
Languages English
T: +91 96 5562 4458
W: www.srvisglobal.org
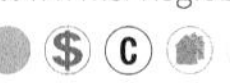

St. Xavier's High School
Rosewood City, Sector-49-50, Main Golf Course, Extension Road, Gurgaon, Haryana
CP Coordinator Swati Rana
Languages English
T: +91 99 1023 8318/19
W: 49.stxaviershighschoolgurgaon.com

Step by Step School
Plot A 10, Sector 132 Taj Expressway, Noida, Uttar Pradesh 201303
DP Coordinator Urmi Debroy
Languages English
T: +91 12 0508 7300
W: www.sbs-school.org

STONEHILL INTERNATIONAL SCHOOL
Near the International Airport, No.259/333/334/335, Tarahunise Post, Jala Hobli, Bengaluru, Karnataka 562157
DP Coordinator Jennifer Browne
MYP Coordinator Saba Husain
PYP Coordinator Zita Joyce
Languages English
T: +91 70 2666 6911
E: admissions@stonehill.in
W: www.stonehill.in
See full details on page 390
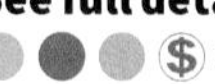 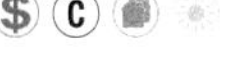

Strawberry Fields High School
Sector 26, Chandigarh, Punjab 160019
DP Coordinator Smita Satyarthi
T: +91 172 279 5903/5904
W: www.strawberryfieldshighschool.com

Suncity School
Suncity Township, Sector 54, Gurgaon, Haryana 122002
DP Coordinator Vivek Mandal
Languages English
T: +91 (0)124 4845300 (EXT:302)
W: www.suncityschool.in

Sunshine Worldwide Secondary School
20/1-B, Bainguinim, Off NH-748 By-pass Kadamba Road, Old Goa. Goa 403402
PYP Coordinator Ashalatha Ravishankar
Languages English, Hindi
T: +91 98 5032 3818
W: www.sunshineworldwideschool.com

SVKM JV Parekh International School
CNM School Campus, Dadabhai Road, Off. S.V. Road, Vile Parle (West), Mumbai, Maharashtra 400056
DP Coordinator Shoma Bhattacharya
Languages English
T: +91 22 4233 3030
W: www.jvparekhintnl.ac.in

Symbiosis International School
Symbiosis Viman nagar Campus, Off. New AirPort road, Viman Nagar, Pune, Maharashtra 411014
DP Coordinator M. Madan Mohan
PYP Coordinator Preethy Sunil
Languages English
T: +91 20 2655 7300
W: www.symbiosisinternationalschool.net

TCIS
Survey no. 215/3, Varthur Sharjapur, Whitefield Main Road, Bangalore, Karnataka
PYP Coordinator Anita Varghese
Languages English, Hindi
T: +91 78 9902 5222
W: tciswhitefield.in
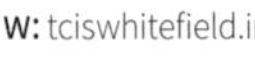

The Bombay Suburban Grain Dealers' Junior College of Commerce, Arts & Science
Road No.1, Bhadran Nagar, S V Road, Malad (W), Mumbai, Maharashtra 400064
CP Coordinator Vasudha Surve
Languages English
T: +91 22 2808 5424
W: www.bsgdjrc.ac.in

The British School
Dr Jose P Rizal Marg, Chanakyapuri, New Delhi, Delhi 110021
DP Coordinator Monisha Singh
Languages English
T: +91 11 4066 4166
W: www.british-school.org

The Cathedral & John Connon School
6 Purshottamdas Thakurdas Marg, Mumbai, Maharashtra 400001
DP Coordinator Vidya Vageesh
Languages English
T: +91 22 2200 1282
W: www.cathedral-school.com

The Doon School
Mall Road, Dehradun, Uttarakhand 248001
DP Coordinator Mohammad Istemdad Ali
Languages English
T: +91-135 2526 400
W: www.doonschool.com

The Galaxy School
SNK Main Building, University Road, Rajkot, Gujarat 360005
DP Coordinator Chirag Jhala
Languages English
T: +91 281 2588391/2588392
W: www.tges.org

The Gaudium School
Survey No. 148, Nanakramguda Village, Serilingampally, Nanakramguda, Hyderabad, Telangana 500008
DP Coordinator Varsha Dillikar
MYP Coordinator Deepa Chhabra
PYP Coordinator Durgesh Jadhav
Languages English, Hindi
T: +91 73370 00200
W: www.thegaudium.com

The Heritage School, Kolkata
994 Maduraha, Chowbaga Road, Anandpur, PO East Kolkata Township, Kolkata, West Bengal 700107
DP Coordinator Seema Sapru
Languages English
T: +91 33 2443 0448
W: www.theheritageschool.org

The International School Bangalore
Whitefield-Sarjapur Road, Near Dommasandra Circle, Bengaluru, Karnataka 562125
DP Coordinator Bimal Ravindranathan
Languages English
T: +91 80 6723 5900
W: tisb.org

The Pupil, Saveetha Eco School
4/68, Thiruverkkadu Road, Behind Saveetha Dental College, Poonamallee, Chennai, Tamil Nadu 600056
PYP Coordinator Suhasini Murali
Languages English, Tamil
T: +91 44 2680 2013
W: www.thepupil.in

The Shri Ram School
Moulsari Avenue DLF Phase-3, Gurgaon, Haryana 122002
DP Coordinator Anjali Sharma
Languages English
W: www.tsrs.org

The Universal School
Plot No. 17, Near Lion's Garden, Tilak Road, Ghatkopar (E), Mumbai, Maharashtra 400077
DP Coordinator Lakshmi Thevar
Languages English, Hindi
T: +91 773 8146 123
W: ghatkopar.universalschool.edu.in

The White School International
HiLITE Knowledge Village, Parammal, Perumanna, Kozhikode, Kerala 673019
DP Coordinator Selvakumari Sankaranarayanan
MYP Coordinator Varaprasad Adidala
PYP Coordinator Venicia Reneesh
Languages English, Malayalam
T: +91 95260 777 78
W: www.thewhiteschool.in

TIPS Chennai
No. 50/51, First Main Road, Perungudi Industrial Estate, Perungudi, Chennai, Tamil Nadu 600069
DP Coordinator Ramya Kumaraswamy
PYP Coordinator Fatima Zaneera Abdulla
Languages English
T: +91 44 7118 8011
W: tipschennai.com

TIPS Coimbatore
193 Sathy Road, S.S.Kulam P.O., Coimbatore, Tamil Nadu 641107
DP Coordinator Ibson T. Arimbur
PYP Coordinator Ruchika Sharma
Languages English
T: +91 42 2236 6666
W: www.tipsglobal.org

TIPS Erode
Chennimalai Road, Senapathipalayam, Goundachi palayam post, Erode, Tamil Nadu 638112
PYP Coordinator Syeda Humera Riyaz
Languages English
T: +91 967745 8888
W: theindianpublicschool.org/location-erode

TIPS Kochi
Edachira, Thengode(Post), Kakkanad, Kochi, Kerala 682030
PYP Coordinator Mridula Vinod
Languages English
T: +91 48 4485 4850
W: www.tipsglobal.org/tips_kochi.php

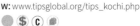

TIPS Salem
No 2, Mangayarkarasi Street, Off Advitha Ashram Road, Fairlands, Salem, Tamil Nadu 636016
PYP Coordinator Renu Koshti
Languages English, Tamil
T: +91 92 8258 8888
W: theindianpublicschool.org/location-salem

Treamis
Hulimangala Post, near Electronics City, Bengaluru, Karnataka 560105
DP Coordinator Jyothis Mathew
PYP Coordinator Vidya Degala
Languages English, Kannada
T: +91 99723 99046
W: www.treamis.org
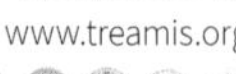

Trio World Academy
3/5 Kodigehalli Main Road, Sahakar Nagar, Bengaluru, Karnataka 560092
DP Coordinator Moinudin Sha
PYP Coordinator Chitra R
Languages English
T: +91 80 40611222
W: trioworldschool.com

Trivandrum International School
Edackcode, PO Korani, Trivandrum, Kerala 695104
DP Coordinator Rachel Jacob
PYP Coordinator Sanjay Prabhakaran
Languages English
T: +91 471 2619051
W: www.trins.org

Udgam School for Children
Opp. Sardar Patel Institute, Thaltej, Ahmedabad, Gujarat 380054
CP Coordinator Jaie Rajeshirke
Languages English
T: +91 79 7101 2345
W: www.udgamschool.com

UNICOSMOS School
Site 2, Sector 55, Off Golf Course Road, Gurugram, Haryana 122011
PYP Coordinator Neelam Oberoi
Languages English, Hindi
T: +91 95 6080 3800
W: www.unicosmos.in

UWC MAHINDRA COLLEGE
Village Khubavali, PO Paud, Taluka Mulshi, Pune, Maharashtra 412108
CP Coordinator Amit Rastogi
DP Coordinator Matthew Spall
Languages English
T: +91 97644 42751 54
E: info@muwci.net
W: uwcmahindracollege.org
See full details on page 401
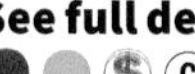

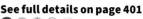

VICTORIOUS KIDSS EDUCARES
Survey No. 53, 54 & 58, Hissa No. 2/1A, Off. Shreeram Society, Nagar Road, Kharadi, Pune, Maharashtra 411014
DP Coordinator Vishwajeet Kumar
MYP Coordinator Vishwajeet Kumar
PYP Coordinator Pritisha Ahir
Languages English
T: +91 20-67116300/1/2
E: robbinghosh@victoriouskidsseducares.org
W: www.victoriouskidsseducares.org
See full details on page 402

Vidya Global School
Vidya Knowledge Park, Baghpat Road, Meerut, Uttar Pradesh 250002
MYP Coordinator Shruti Thukral
PYP Coordinator Tandra Sharma
Languages English
T: +91 121 2439188/89/92
W: vidyaglobalschool.com
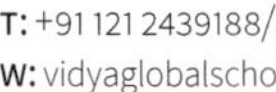

Vishwashanti Gurukul
Rajbaug, off Pune-Solapur Highway, Loni, Pune, Maharashtra 412201
DP Coordinator Arpit Sharma
MYP Coordinator Mandar Gurjar
PYP Coordinator Dimpal Juneja
Languages English
T: +91 20 39210000
W: www.mitgurukul.com

VIVA The School
Beside VVIT college campus, NAMBUR village, Pedakakani Mandal, Nambur, Guntur, Andhra Pradesh 522508
PYP Coordinator Madhavi Ayinada
Languages English, Telugu
T: +91 73 3114 2336
W: www.viva.school

Wockhardt Global School
Dr Habil Khorakiwala Education and Health Foundation, E-1/NP-1, SEZ, Five Star Industrial Estate, MIDC, Shen+, Aurangabad, Maharashtra 431154
DP Coordinator Nirmalendu Tripathy
MYP Coordinator Mahesh Wagh
PYP Coordinator Hetal Ahivasi
Languages English
T: +91 240 6662888
W: wockhardtschools.com
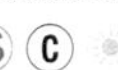

Woodstock School
Mussoorie, Uttarakhand 248179
DP Coordinator Mousumi Basu
MYP Coordinator Imtiaz Rai
Languages English
T: +91 135 263 9000
W: www.woodstock.ac.in

INDONESIA

ACG SCHOOL JAKARTA
Jl Warung Jati Barat No.19, RW.5, Jati Padang, Kec. Ps. Minggu, Jakarta Selatan, Jakarta, DKI 12540
DP Coordinator Kieran Pascoe
PYP Coordinator Selda Mansur
Languages English
T: +62 21 2978 0200
E: acgjkt@acgedu.com
W: jakarta.acgedu.com
See full details on page 311

ACS Jakarta
Jl Bantar Jati, Kelurahan Setu, Jakarta Timur, DKI 13880
DP Coordinator Antony Greg Powell
Languages English
T: +62 21 8459 7175
W: www.acsjakarta.sch.id

Al Firdaus World Class Islamic School
Jl. Al Kautsar, Mendungan, Pabelan, Kec. Kartasura, Kabupaten Sukoharjo, Surakarta, Jateng 57169
MYP Coordinator Rany Maharani
PYP Coordinator Aris Suwastini Ariyanti
Languages English, Indonesian
W: alfirdausina.net

Al Jabr Islamic School
Jl. Bango II No.38, RT.6/RW.3, Pondok Labu, Cilandak, Jakarta Selatan, DKI 12450
CP Coordinator Dina Anggraini
MYP Coordinator Novia Rozet
PYP Coordinator Ryandika Anindra
Languages English, Indonesian
T: +62 21 7591 3675
W: aljabrislamicschool.sch.id

Australian Independent School, Bali
Jl. Imam Bonjol No. 458A, Denpasar, Bali 80119
DP Coordinator Thomas Allan
Languages English
T: +62 36 1845 20000
W: www.ais-indonesia.com

Australian Independent School, Jakarta
Jl. Pejaten Barat No. 68, Jakarta Selatan, DKI 12510
DP Coordinator Jaimin Surani
Languages English
T: +62 21 782 1141
W: www.ais-indonesia.com

Bali Island School
Jl. Danau Buyan IV No. 15, Sanur, Denpasar, Bali 80228
DP Coordinator Klaus Weber
MYP Coordinator Jennifer Jenson
PYP Coordinator Nadia Demolder
Languages English
T: +62 36 128 8770
W: www.baliinternationalschool.com

Bandung Independent School
Jl. Prof. Drg. Surya Sumantri No. 61, Bandung, Jabar 40164
DP Coordinator Kari Brown
MYP Coordinator Sophia Hamilton
PYP Coordinator Katherine Stone
Languages English
T: +62 22 201 4995
W: www.bisedu.or.id

Beacon Academy
Jl. Pegangsaan Dua No. 66, Kelapa Gading, Jakarta Utara, DKI 14250
DP Coordinator Alisher Arstanbek
PYP Coordinator Sheila Canicula
Languages English
T: +62 21 460 3480
W: www.beaconacademy.net

Binus School Simprug
Jl. Sultan Iskandar, Muda Kav G-8, Simprug, Jakarta Selatan, DKI 12220
DP Coordinator Erdolfo L Lardizabal
MYP Coordinator Jyoti Gupta
PYP Coordinator Richel Langit-Dursin
Languages English
T: +62 21 724 3663
W: simprug.binus.sch.id

Blossom International School
Citra Garden 3 Extension Block F No. 1, Kalideres, Jakarta Barat, DKI 11830
PYP Coordinator Meylani Rizki Bangun
Languages English, Chinese
T: +62 21 5595 5756
W: www.blossom-school.com

British School Jakarta
Bintaro Jaya Sektor 9, Jl. Raya Jombang, Ciledug, Pondok Aren, Tangerang, Banten 15427
CP Coordinator Daniel Harbridge
DP Coordinator Jane Kilpatrick
MYP Coordinator Victoria Wicking
Languages English
T: +62 21 745 1670
W: www.bsj.sch.id

BTB School (Sekolah Bina Tunas Bangsa)
Jl. Pluit Tumur Blok MM, Jakarta Utara, DKI 14450
DP Coordinator Christine Macaraig
Languages English
T: +62 21 669 8888
W: www.btbschool.org

Canggu Community School
Jl. Subak Sari, Banjar Tegal Gundul, Tibubeneng, Kuta Utara, Badung, Canggu, Bali 80361
DP Coordinator Heidi Cavanagh
Languages English
T: +62 36 1844 6391
W: www.ccsbali.com

Cita Hati Christian School - East Campus
Jl. Kejawan Putih Barat 28-30, Pakuwon City (Laguna Indah), Surabaya, Jatim 60112
DP Coordinator Ho Peter Troy Holidaya
Languages English
T: +62 3 1742 5470
W: www.bchati.sch.id

Cita Hati Christian School - Samarinda Campus
Aminah Syukur 32, Samarinda, Kaltim 75242
DP Coordinator Dewi Hanna Sri Wahyuli Siahaan
Languages English, Indonesian
T: +62 54 1777 7691
W: www.bchati.sch.id

Cita Hati Christian School - West Campus
Jl. Bukit Golf L2 No. 1, Citra Raya, Surabaya, Jatim 60211
DP Coordinator Sarwanti Purwandari
Languages English
T: +62 812 4901 5181
W: www.bchati.sch.id

Gandhi Memorial Intercontinental School, Bali
Jl. Tukad Yeh Penet No. 8A Renon, Denpasar, Bali 80235
CP Coordinator Emil Macaraig
DP Coordinator Emil Macaraig
MYP Coordinator Meilisa Leonata
PYP Coordinator Sonia Ganguly
Languages English
T: +62 877 5833 2234
W: www.gandhibali.org

Gandhi Memorial Intercontinental School, Jakarta
Jl. HBR Motik No. Kav 1 Block D6, Kemayoran, Jakarta Pusat DKI 14410
CP Coordinator Manish Kumar Semwal
DP Coordinator Manish Kumar Semwal
MYP Coordinator Shalaza Williams
PYP Coordinator Rachna Johar
Languages English
T: +62 21 6586 5667
W: www.gandhijkt.org

Global Jaya School
Emerald Boulevard, Bintaro Jaya Sektor IX, Tangerang, Banten 15224
DP Coordinator Ram Pandey
MYP Coordinator Susan Menand
PYP Coordinator Anindya Hartono
Languages English
T: +62 21 745 7562
W: www.globaljaya.com

Hope Academy
Puri Indah CBD, Jl. Puri Indah Raya Blok U 1, Kembangan Selatan, Jakarta Barat, DKI 11610
PYP Coordinator Putri Adian
Languages English
T: +62 895 4262 88800
W: www.hopeacademy.sch.id

IPEKA Integrated Christian School
Komplek Taman Meruya Ilir, Jalan Batu Mulia Blok K, RT.11/RW.7, Meruya Utara, Kembangan, RT.11/RW.7, Meruya Utara, Kem+, Jakarta Barat, DKI 11620
DP Coordinator Denny Ardian Lie
Languages English, Indonesian
T: +62 21 58905890
W: www.iics.sch.id

Islamic Village School
Jl. Islamic Raya No.1, Komplek Islamic Village, Kelapa Dua, Tangerang, Banten 15810
PYP Coordinator Dupita Ardesi
Languages English, Indonesian
T: +62 21 547 0787
W: www.islamicvillageschool.com

Jakarta Intercultural School
Jalan Terogong Raya No. 33, Cilandak, Jakarta Selatan, DKI 12430
CP Coordinator Darren Seath
DP Coordinator Darren Seath
Languages English
T: +62 21 50989555
W: www.jisedu.or.id

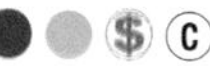

Jakarta Montessori School
Jl. Durian 10, Jagakarsa, Jakarta Selatan, DKI 12620
DP Coordinator Ito Miftahul Jannah
Languages English, Indonesian
T: +62 21 727 2162
W: jakartamontessori.sch.id

Jakarta Multicultural School
Jl. Pisangan Raya No. 99 (Taman Wisata Situ Gintung), Cirendeu, Ciputat Timur, Banten 15419
DP Coordinator Wika Prayogi
Languages English
T: +62 21 744 4864
W: jms.sch.id

Madania
Telaga Kahuripan, Parung, Bogor, Jabar 16330
PYP Coordinator Nida Nidiana
Languages English
T: +62 251 602777
W: www.madania.sch.id

Medan Independent School
Jl. Jamin Ginting Km. 10 / Jl. Tali Air No.5, Medan, North Sumatra 20141
DP Coordinator Karl Sloane
MYP Coordinator Gregory McGuire
PYP Coordinator Sharan Dhami
Languages English
T: +62 61 836 1816
W: www.mismedan.org

Mentari Intercultural School Bintaro
Jalan Perigi Baru No.7A, Tangerang, Pd. Aren, Tangerang Selatan, Banten 15228
DP Coordinator Alquin Alva
Languages English
T: +62 21 745 8418
W: mis.sch.id/w/mis-bintaro.html

Mentari Intercultural School Jakarta
Jl. H. Jian No.2, RT.4/RW.3, North Cipete, Kby. Baru, Jakarta Selatan, DKI 12150
DP Coordinator Joanna Via Teodoro
MYP Coordinator Matthew Roberge
PYP Coordinator Patricia Manning
Languages English
T: 21 727 94 870
W: mis.sch.id/w/mis-jakarta.html

Mt Zaagkam School
Tembagapura Raya Street No. 605, Tembagapura, Papua 99967
PYP Coordinator Raquel Acedo Rubio
Languages English
T: +62 901 408 767
W: www.mzs.sch.id

Mutiara Harapan Islamic School
Jl. Pondok Kacang Raya No. 2, Pondok Kacang Timur, Pondok Aren, Tangerang, Banten 15426
PYP Coordinator Anjali Tewari
Languages English
T: +62 (0)21 74860451
W: mutiaraharapan.sch.id
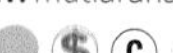

Nassa School
Jl Bojong Nangka II/38, Jati Rahayu-Pondok Melati, Bekasi, Jabar 17414
PYP Coordinator Aryanti Arbian
Languages English, Indonesian
T: +62 21 846 3229
W: nassaschool.sch.id

North Jakarta Intercultural School
PO Box 6759/JKUKP, Jalan Raya Kelapa Nias, Kelapa Gading Permai, Jakarta Utara, DKI 14250
DP Coordinator Warren Wessels
MYP Coordinator Hendriadi Yasir
PYP Coordinator Ezra Alexander
Languages English, Indonesian
T: +62 21 4586 5222; +62 21 36 700 770
W: www.njis.org

Sampoerna Academy, Jakarta Campus
L'Avenue Campus, Jln. Raya Pasar Minggu, Kav. 16 Pancoran, Jakarta 12780
DP Coordinator Devendar Singh Rawat
Languages English, Indonesian
T: +62 (0)21 5022 22 34
W: www.sampoernaacademy.sch.id

Sampoerna Academy, Medan Campus
Jln. Jamin Ginting, Kompleks Citra Garden, Medan
DP Coordinator Sharad Detha
Languages English, Indonesian
T: +62 (0)61 821 27 15
W: www.sampoernaacademy.sch.id/en/medan-campus

SDK BPK Penabur Banda
Jl Bahureksa No 26, Bandung, Jabar 40115
PYP Coordinator Puteri Pamela
Languages English
T: +62 22 4210787
W: www.pissecondary.penabur.sch.id

Sekolah Bogor Raya
Perumahan Danau Bogor Raya, Bogor, Jabar 16143
DP Coordinator Aditya Rao
PYP Coordinator Aninda Rosalia
Languages English
T: +62 251 837 8873
W: www.sekolahbogorraya.com

Sekolah Buin Batu
Sekongkang, Buin Batu, West Sumbawa, NTB
MYP Coordinator Michael Delaney
PYP Coordinator Arief Budiman
Languages English, Indonesian
T: +62 37 2635 318
W: www.sekolahbuinbatu.sch.id

Sekolah Cikal Amri-Setu
Jl. Setu Raya No. 3, Cipayung, Jakarta Timur, DKI
DP Coordinator Anggi Swardhani
MYP Coordinator Mimin Sri Wahyuni
Languages English
T: +62 811 1156 599
W: www.cikal.co.id

Sekolah Cikal Cilandak
Jl. Letjen. TB. Simatupang Kav. 18, Cilandak, Jakarta Timur, DKI
DP Coordinator Evy Verawaty Tarida Sihotang
PYP Coordinator Marsaria Primadonna
Languages English
T: +62 21 7590 2580
W: www.cikal.co.id

Sekolah Cikal Surabaya
Jl. Raya Lontar No. 103, Kelurahan Lontar, Kecamatan Sambikerep, Surabaya, Jatim
PYP Coordinator Putri Isnaini
Languages English
T: +62 815 1550 1010
W: www.cikal.co.id

Sekolah Ciputra, Surabaya
Puri Widya Kencana, Citraland, Surabaya, Jatim 60213
DP Coordinator Simon Bradshaw
MYP Coordinator Stuart Ratcliffe
PYP Coordinator Diana Sumadianti
Languages English
T: +62 31 741 5018
W: www.sekolahciputra.sch.id

Sekolah Global Indo-Asia
Jalan Raya Batam Centre Kav SGIA, Batam Centre, Batam Island, Kepri
DP Coordinator Amit Badola
PYP Coordinator Peggy Ratulangi
Languages English
T: +62 778 467333
W: www.sgiaedu.org

Sekolah Monte Sienna
Jl. Yos Sudarso, Sungai Jodoh, Kecamatan Batu Ampar, Batam, Kepri 29432
PYP Coordinator Berlyn Joy Campomayor
Languages English, Indonesian
T: +62 77 8741 8825
W: montesiennaschool.com

Sekolah Mutiara Nusantara
Jl. Sersan Bajuri - Setiabudi, Km 1.5, RT 3 RW 1, Bandung, Jabar 40559
DP Coordinator Matthew France
Languages English
T: +62 22 201 7773
W: smn.sch.id
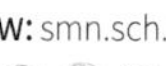

Sekolah Paradisa Cendekia
Jalan Pulo, Leuwinanggung, Kalimanggis, Cibubur, DKI
PYP Coordinator Handayani H
Languages English, Indonesian
T: +62 21 28671700
W: www.spc.sch.id

Sekolah Pelita Harapan, Kemang Village
Jl. Pangeran Antasari 36, Kemang Village, Jakarta Selatan, DKI 12150
DP Coordinator Joseph Chong
Languages English
T: +62 21 290 56 789
W: kemangvillage.sph.edu

Sekolah Pelita Harapan, Lippo Cikarang
Jl. Dago Permai No.1 Komp. Dago Villas, Lippo Cikarang, Bekasi, Jabar 17550
DP Coordinator Sofia Sinaga
Languages English
T: +62 21 897 2786 87
W: lippocikarang.sph.edu

Sekolah Pelita Harapan, Lippo Village
2500 Boulevard Palem Raya, Lippo Village, Tangerang, Banten 15810
DP Coordinator Levi Bollinger
MYP Coordinator Esther McIntyre
PYP Coordinator Ratna Setyowati Putri
Languages English
T: +62 21 546 0234
W: www.sph.edu

Sekolah Pelita Harapan, Sentul City
Jl. Babakan Madang, Sentul City, Bogor, Jabar 16810
DP Coordinator Elisabeth Pristiwi
MYP Coordinator Lisajanti Widjaja
PYP Coordinator Fany Oktavia
Languages English
T: +62 21 8796 0234
W: sentulcity.sph.edu

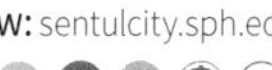

Sekolah Pilar Indonesia
Jl Dewa 9, Ciangsana, Kawasan Cibubur, Bogor, Jabar 16968
PYP Coordinator Martini Sayuti
Languages English
T: +62 21 84936222
W: www.sekolah-pilar-indonesia.sch.id

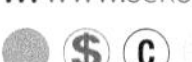

Sekolah Tunas Bangsa
Jalan Arteri Supadio, (Achmad Yani II) Km 2, Pontianak, Kalbar 78391
PYP Coordinator Ronald Sahat Tua Simbolon
Languages English
T: +62 561 725555
W: www.tunasbangsa.sch.id

Sekolah Victory Plus
Jl Kemang Pratama Raya, AN 2-3 Kemang Pratama, Bekasi, Jabar 17116
DP Coordinator Justin Skea
MYP Coordinator Charles Keefe
PYP Coordinator Early Hapsari
Languages English
T: +62 21 8240 3878
W: svp.sch.id

Sinarmas World Academy
Jl TM Pahlawan Seribu, CBD Lot XV, BSD City, Tangerang, Banten 15322
DP Coordinator Andrea Coutinho Bozzetti
MYP Coordinator Haoken Huoermaiti
Languages English
T: +62 21 5316 1400
W: www.swa-jkt.com

SIS Kelapa Gading
Jl. Pegangsaan Dua No. 83, Kelapa Gading, Jakarta Utara, DKI 14250
DP Coordinator Alfredo Iii Garcia
Languages English
T: +62 21 460 8888
W: sisschools.org/sis-kg

SIS Medan
Royal Sumatra Complex, Jl. Letjen Jamin Ginting Km. 8,5, Medan, Sumut
DP Coordinator Eric Manning
Languages English
T: +62 61 836 2880
W: sisschools.org/sis-medan

SIS Pantai Indah Kapuk
Jl. Mandara Indah 4, Pantai Indah Kapuk, Jakarta Utara, DKI 14460
DP Coordinator Callie Shyong
T: +62 21 588 3835
W: sisschools.org/sis-pik

SIS South Jakarta
Jl. Bona Vista Raya, Lebak Bulus, Jakarta Selatan, DKI 12440
DP Coordinator Andi Elisa
Languages English
T: +62 21 759 14414
W: sisschools.org/sis-southjakarta

SMA Islam Al-Azhar 3 Jakarta
Jl. Sisingamangaraja, RT.2/RW.1, Selong, Kec. Kby. Baru, Jakarta Selatan, DKI 12110
DP Coordinator Nazar Rusli
Languages English, Indonesian
T: +62 21 726 9935
W: www.smaialazhar3.sch.id

SMA Pradita Dirgantara
Jl. Cendrawasih No.4. Adi Sumarmo Airport Complex, Surakarta, Jateng 57375
DP Coordinator Oscar Carascalao
Languages English
T: +62 71 7467 569
W: sma.praditadirgantara.sch.id

Stella Maris School
Sektor 8A, Vatican Cluster, Gading Serpong, Tangerang, Banten 15310
DP Coordinator Arsenia Lotivo
Languages English
T: +62 21 54 212 999
W: www.stellamaris.co.id

Surabaya Intercultural School
Citra Raya, Lakarsantri, Tromol Pos 2/ SBDK, Surabaya, Jatim 60225
PYP Coordinator Retno Indrasari
Languages English
T: +62 31 741 4300
W: sis.sch.id

Tunas Muda School Kedoya
Jl Angsana Raya D8/2, Taman Kedoya Baru, Jakarta Barat, DKI 11520
PYP Coordinator Meilianny Jap
Languages English
T: +62 21 581 8766
W: www.sekolahtunasmuda.com

Tunas Muda School Meruya
Jl. Meruya Utara No. 71, Kembangan, Jakarta Barat, DKI 11620
DP Coordinator May Ann Farillon
MYP Coordinator Arniel Defita
PYP Coordinator Maria Imaculata Addelin
Languages English, Bahasa Indonesia
T: +62 (0)21 587 0329
W: www.tunasmuda.sch.id

Tzu Chi School, Pantai Indah Kapuk
Jl. Pantai Indah Kapuk Boulevard, Tzu Chi Centre, Kelurahan Kamal Muara, Kecamatan Penjaringan, Jakarta Utara, DKI 14470
DP Coordinator Kate Siaron
MYP Coordinator Patrick O Sullivan
Languages English
T: +62 21 5055 6668
W: tzuchi.sch.id

Yogyakarta Independent School
Jl. Tegal Mlati No. 1, Jombor Lor, Sinduadi, Mlati, Sleman, Yogyakarta, DIY 55284
DP Coordinator Elia Ekanindita
MYP Coordinator Kencana Candra
PYP Coordinator Veronika Swanti
Languages English
T: +62 274 530 5147
W: www.yis-edu.org

YPJ School Kuala Kencana
Jalan Irian Jaya Barat No.1, Kuala Kencana, Timika, Papua 99910
PYP Coordinator Vini Quamilla
Languages English
W: ypj.sch.id

YPJ School Tembagapura
Jalan Raya Tembagapura No. 605, PO Box 14, Tembagapura, Papua 99910
PYP Coordinator Easter Lusiana
Languages Indonesian
W: ypj.sch.id

JAPAN

Abroad International School - Okayama
Yanagimachi 1-10-9, Kita-ku, Okayama, Chugoku 700-0904
PYP Coordinator Kelly De Jongh
Languages English, Japanese
T: +81 86 221 0144
W: abroadschools.jp/okayama

Abroad International School - Osaka
Being Yotsubashi Bldg 6F, 1-3-2 Kitahorie, Nishi-ku, Osaka, Kansai 550-0014
PYP Coordinator Stacy O'Sullivan
Languages English
T: +81 66 535 0500
W: abroadschools.jp/osaka

AICJ Junior & Senior High School
3-1-15 Gion, Asaminami-ku, Hiroshima, Chugoku 731-0138
DP Coordinator Jesse Green
Languages English
T: +81 82 832 5037
W: www.aicj.ed.jp

AIE International High School
1-48 Hama, Awaji, Hyogo, Kansai 656-2304
DP Coordinator Naoko Watanabe
Languages English
T: +81 79 974 0020
W: www.aie.ed.jp

Angel Kindergarten
80-6 Ojiri Shimonagakubo, Nagaizumi, Shizuoka, Chubu 411-0934
PYP Coordinator Simon Lund
Languages English, Japanese
T: +81 55 987 5323
W: www.angel-kindergarten.com

Aoba-Japan Bilingual Preschool - Harumi Campus
Harumi Triton Square 2F, 1-8-2 Harumi, Chuo-ku, Tokyo, Kanto 104-0053
PYP Coordinator Jeremy Guckert
Languages English, Japanese
T: +81 36 228 1811
W: aoba-bilingual.jp/harumi

IB ASIA-PACIFIC

Aoba-Japan Bilingual Preschool - Mitaka Campus
4-15-41 Shimorenjaku, Mitaka, Tokyo, Kanto 181-0013
PYP Coordinator Nguyen Tran
Languages English, Japanese
T: +81 42 229 8977
W: aoba-bilingual.jp/mitaka

Aoba-Japan Bilingual Preschool - Nakano Campus
3-6-17-2F Minamidai, Nakano-ku, Tokyo, Kanto 164-0014
PYP Coordinator Nguyen Tran
Languages English, Japanese
T: +81 36 380 3218
W: aoba-bilingual.jp/nakano

Aoba-Japan Bilingual Preschool - Waseda Campus
Chiyoda Bldg. 2, 1-14-8 Takadanobaba, Shinjuku-ku, Tokyo, Kanto 169-0075
PYP Coordinator William Chesser
Languages English, Japanese
T: +81 36 385 2818
W: aoba-bilingual.jp/waseda

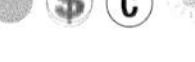

AOBA-JAPAN INTERNATIONAL SCHOOL
7-5-1 Hikarigaoka, Nerima-ku, Tokyo 179-0072
DP Coordinator Preethi Liyanagamage
MYP Coordinator Chris Radnich
PYP Coordinator Karen Chen
Languages English
T: +81 3 4578 8832
E: admissions@aobajapan.jp
W: www.aobajapan.jp

See full details on page 313
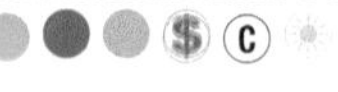

Asahijuku Secondary School
2590 Mitsushitori, Kita-ku, Okayama, Chugoku 709-2136
DP Coordinator Toshitaka Ishiguchi
MYP Coordinator Toshitaka Ishiguchi
Languages English, Japanese
T: +81 86 726 0111
W: m-asahijuku.ed.jp

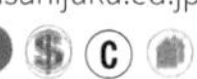

Canadian Academy
4-1 Koyo-Cho Naka, Higashinada-ku, Kobe, Hyogo, Kansai 658-0032
DP Coordinator Toni Hewett
MYP Coordinator Jennifer Johansen
PYP Coordinator Trevor Rehel
Languages English
T: +81 78 857 0100
W: www.canacad.ac.jp

Canadian International School Tokyo
5-8-20 Kitashinagawa, Shinagawa-ku, Tokyo, Kanto 141-0001
PYP Coordinator Peter Cassidy
Languages English
T: +81 35 793 1392
W: www.cisjapan.net

Deutsche Schule Kobe International (DSKI)
3-2-8 Koyochonaka, Higashinada-ku, Kobe, Hyogo, Kansai 658-0032
PYP Coordinator Pia Leah Nepomuceno
Languages English
T: +81 78 857 9777
W: www.dskobe.org

Doshisha International Academy (DIA) Elementary School
7-31-1 Kizugawadai, Kizugawa, Kyoto, Kansai 619-0225
PYP Coordinator Rosemarie Dimal
Languages English
T: +81 77 471 0810
W: www.dia.doshisha.ac.jp

Doshisha International School, Kyoto
7-31-1 Kizugawadai, Kizugawa, Kyoto, Kansai 619-0225
DP Coordinator Vijay Thapliyal
Languages English
T: +81 77 471 0810
W: www.diskyoto.com

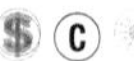

Eisugakkan School
980-1 Hikino-cho, Fukuyama, Hiroshima, Chugoku 721-8502
DP Coordinator Nerissa Momo
PYP Coordinator Andrea Shimizu
Languages English, Japanese
T: +81 84 941 4115
W: www.eisu-ejs.ac.jp

Enishi International School
2-12-32 Kikui Nishi Ward, Nagoya, Aichi 451-0044
DP Coordinator Benjamin Lowe
MYP Coordinator Mahmut Kaya
PYP Coordinator Mark Jones
Languages English, Japanese
T: +81 52 581 0700
W: enishi.ac.jp

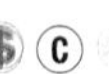

Fukuoka Daiichi High School
22-1 Tamagawa-cho, Minami-ku, Fukuoka, Kyushu 815-0037
DP Coordinator Taiyo Rious
Languages English, Japanese
T: +81 92 541 0165
W: f.f-parama.ed.jp

Fukuoka International School
3-18-50 Momochi, Sawara-ku, Fukuoka, Kyushu 814-0006
DP Coordinator Christian Chiarenza
MYP Coordinator Ken Forde
PYP Coordinator Michelle Jasinska
Languages English
T: +81 92 841 7601
W: www.fis.ed.jp

Global Indian International School (GIIS) Higashi Kasai Campus
9-3-6 Higashikasai, Edogawa-ku, Tokyo, Kanto 134-0084
DP Coordinator Seth Howerton
PYP Coordinator Madhu Khanna
Languages English, Japanese
T: +81 35 676 5081
W: tokyo.globalindianschool.org

Gunma Kokusai Academy
1361-4 Uchigashima-cho, Ota, Gunma, Kanto 373-0813
DP Coordinator James Taylor
MYP Coordinator Shinichiro Takamatsu
Languages English
T: +81 27 647 7711
W: www.gka.jp

Hiroshima Global Academy
3137-2 Okushi, Osakikamijima-cho, Toyota-gun, Hiroshima, Chugoku 725-0303
DP Coordinator Sean Richards
MYP Coordinator Kai Sato
Languages English, Japanese
T: +81 84 667 5581
W: higa-s.jp

Hiroshima International School
3-49-1 Kurakake, Asakita-ku, Hiroshima, Chugoku 739-1743
DP Coordinator Ayako Kurokawa
MYP Coordinator Robert Washington
PYP Coordinator Shefali Lakhina
Languages English
T: +81 82 843 4111
W: www.hiroshima-is.ac.jp

Horizon Academy Sendai Campus
4-2-540 Takamori, Izumi-ku, Sendai, Miyagi, Tohoku 981-3203
PYP Coordinator Tayla Morro
Languages English, Japanese
T: +81 22 739 9622
W: sendai.horizon.ac.jp

Horizon Japan International School
1-24 Onocho, Kanagawa-ku, Yokohama, Kanagawa, Kanto 221-0055
DP Coordinator Rebecca Daum
MYP Coordinator Jennifer Hodge
PYP Coordinator Shailja Jhamb Datt
Languages English
T: +81 45 624 8717
W: www.horizon.ac.jp

Hosei University Kokusai High School
1-13-1 KIshiya, Tsurumi-ku, Yokohama, Kanagawa, Kanto 230-0078
DP Coordinator Andrew Gibbs
Languages English, Japanese
T: +81 45 571 4482
W: kokusai-high.ws.hosei.ac.jp

Ikeda Junior High School Attached to Osaka Kyoiku University
1-5-1 Midorigaoka, Ikeda, Osaka, Kansai 563-0026
MYP Coordinator Atsuko Torii
Languages English, Japanese
T: +81 72 761 8690
W: f.osaka-kyoiku.ac.jp/ikeda-j

Ikuei Nishi Jr. & Sr. High School
4-637-1 Mimatsu, Nara, Kansai 631-0074
MYP Coordinator Isamu Yoshizawa
Languages English, Japanese
T: +81 74 247 0688
W: www.ikuei.ed.jp/ikunishi

India International School in Japan
3-1-4 Sengoku, Koto-ku, Tokyo, Kanto 135-0015
DP Coordinator Suresh Bhakta Shrestha
Languages English
T: +81 35 875 5435
W: www.iisjapan.com

International School of Nagano
7779-1 Shimauchi, Matsumoto, Nagano, Chubu 390-0851
PYP Coordinator Daniel Frisby
Languages English
T: +81 26 387 5971
W: isnedu.org
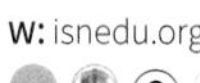

K. International School Tokyo (KIST)
1-5-15 Shirakawa, Koto-ku, Tokyo, Kanto 135-0021
DP Coordinator Hiro Komaki
PYP Coordinator Oliver Sullivan
Languages English
T: +81 33 642 9993
W: www.kist.ed.jp

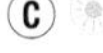

Kagoshima Shugakukan Junior & Senior High School
2-9-1 Nagayoshi, Kagoshima, Kyushu 890-0023
MYP Coordinator Toshifumi Shimmyozu
Languages English, Japanese
T: +81 99 258 2211
W: www.shugakukan.ed.jp

Kaichi Nihonbashi Gakuen Junior & Senior High School
2-7-6 Bakurocho, Nihonbashi, Chuo-ku, Tokyo, Kanto 103-8384
DP Coordinator Jonathan Andreano
MYP Coordinator Jonathan Andreano
Languages English, Japanese
T: +81 33 662 2507
W: www.kng.ed.jp
  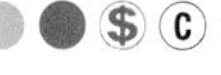

Kaichi Nozomi Primary & Secondary School
3400 Tsutsudoaza-suwa, Tsukubamirai, Ibaraki, Kanto 300-2435
MYP Coordinator Michael Wargon
PYP Coordinator Chikara Okamura
Languages English, Japanese
T: +81 29 738 6000
W: nozomi.kaichigakuen.ed.jp

Kansai International Academy
Abeno Lucius 7F, 1-5-1 Abenosuji, Abeno-ku, Osaka, Kansai 545-0052
DP Coordinator Yoko Homma
MYP Coordinator Solene Matsushita
PYP Coordinator Yoko Morisaki
Languages English, Japanese
W: www.kansai-intlschool.jp

Karugamo English School
987-7 Mimuro, Midori-ku, Saitama, Kanto 336-0911
PYP Coordinator Jordan Long
Languages English
T: +81 48 873 8558
W: www.karugamokids.com

Katoh Gakuen Gyoshu Junior & Senior High School
1361-1 Okanomiya, Numazu, Shizuoka, Chubu 410-0011
DP Coordinator Craig Sutton
MYP Coordinator Geoff Parmenter
Languages English, Japanese
T: +81 55 924 3322
W: bi-lingual.com
 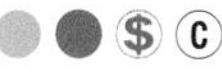

Kids Tairiku Frontown Ikuta
1-1-1 Ikuta, Tama-ku, Kawasaki, Kanagawa, Kanto 214-0038
PYP Coordinator Yukiko Gemma
Languages English, Japanese
T: +81 44 819 6613
W: www.kidstairiku.jp/ikuta

Kindai University High School
5-3-1 Wakaenishishinmachi, Higashiosaka, Osaka, Kansai 578-0944
DP Coordinator Toshikazu Okawa
Languages English, Japanese
T: +81 66 722 1261
W: www.jsh.kindai.ac.jp/hs

Kochi Kokusai Junior & Senior High School
2-5-70 Kamobe, Kochi, Shikoku 780-8052
DP Coordinator Ukyo Ishimaru
MYP Coordinator Miki Igei
Languages English, Japanese
T: +81 88 844 1221
W: www.kochinet.ed.jp/kokusai-jh

Kofu Nishi High School
4-1-1 Shimoiida, Kofu, Yamanashi, Chubu 400-0064
DP Coordinator Yasuko Nozaki
Languages English, Japanese
T: +81 55 228 5161
W: www.nishi.kai.ed.jp

Kohoku Junior High School
892 Mirafu, Kahokucho, Kami, Kochi, Shikoku 781-4212
MYP Coordinator Shu Matsuo
Languages English, Japanese
T: +81 88 759 2135
W: www.kochinet.ed.jp/kahoku-j/index.html

Korea International School
2-13-35 Toyokawa, Ibaraki, Osaka, Kansai 567-0057
DP Coordinator Sea Jin Cho
Languages Korean, Japanese
T: +81 72 643 4200
W: www.kiskorea.ed.jp

Kouhoku School Corporation - Certified Child Center Ainosato
4-jo 6-2-5 Ainosato, Kita-ku, Sapporo, Hokkaido 002-8074
PYP Coordinator Miku Takeuchi
Languages English, Japanese
T: +81 11 778 7272
W: www.kouhoku.ed.jp/ainosato

Kumamoto International School
2-18-8 Nishihara, Higashi-ku, Kumamoto, Kyushu 861-8029
PYP Coordinator Matthew Ohm
Languages English, Japanese
T: +81 96 285 3938
W: kumamotointer.jp

Kyoto International School
317 Kitatawara-cho, Kamigyo-ku, Kyoto, Kansai 602-8247
MYP Coordinator Smita Gangola
PYP Coordinator Arpita Saxena
Languages English
T: +81 75 451 1022
W: www.kis.ac.jp
  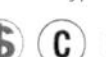

LINDEN HALL HIGH SCHOOL
3-10-1 Futsukaichikita, Chikushino, Fukuoka, Kyushu 818-0056
DP Coordinator Ms. Karen Hunter
Languages English, Japanese
T: +81 92 929 4558
E: hunter@lindenhall.ed.jp
W: www.lindenhall.ed.jp/highschool
See full details on page 351

Machida Kobato Kindergarten
2904 Honmachida, Machida, Tokyo, Kanto 194-0032
PYP Coordinator Toshiko Ishikawa
Languages English, Japanese
T: +81 42 723 1494
W: www.m-kobato.ed.jp

Marist Brothers International School
1-2-1 Chimori-cho, Suma-ku, Kobe, Hyogo, Kansai 654-0072
DP Coordinator Gunseli Yuksel
Languages English
T: +81 78 732 6266
W: www.marist.ac.jp

Matsumoto Kokusai High School
3-6-25 Minami, Murai-cho, Matsumoto, Nagano, Chubu 399-0036
DP Coordinator Sjaak Mintjens
Languages English, Japanese
T: +81 26 388 0033
W: m-kokusai.ac.jp

Meikei High School
1-1 Inarimae, Tsukuba, Ibaraki, Kanto 305-8502
DP Coordinator Hideaki Matsuzaki
Languages English, Japanese
T: +81 29 851 6611
W: www.meikei.ac.jp

Miura Gakuen High School
3-80 Kinugasa-sakaecho, Yokosuka, Kanagawa 238-0031
DP Coordinator Kosaku Tanaka
Languages English, Japanese
T: +81 46 852 0284
W: miura.ed.jp
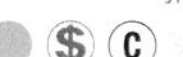

Miyagi Prefectural Sendai Nika Junior & Senior High School
1-4-1 Renbo, Wakabayashi-ku, Sendai, Miyagi, Tohoku 984-0052
DP Coordinator Osamu Jinushi
Languages English, Japanese
T: +81 22 296 8101
W: nika.myswan.ed.jp
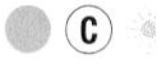

Mizuho School
3-2-25, Shakujiidai, Nerima-ku, Tokyo, Kanto 177-0045
PYP Coordinator Kiyohiko Motohashi
Languages English
T: +81 35 372 1525
W: www.mizuho-edu.co.jp

Musashino University Chiyoda High School
11 Yonbancho, Chiyoda-ku, Tokyo, Kanto 102-0081
DP Coordinator Hiroyuki Nishida
Languages English, Japanese
T: +81 33 263 6551
W: chiyoda.ed.jp

Nagoya International School
2686 Minamihara, Nakashidami, Moriyama-ku, Nagoya, Aichi, Chubu 463-0002
DP Coordinator Ian Radcliffe
MYP Coordinator Peter Goodman
PYP Coordinator Nina Radcliffe
Languages English
T: +81 52 736 2025
W: www.nis.ac.jp
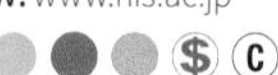

NUCB INTERNATIONAL COLLEGE
4-4 Sagamine Komenoki, Nisshin, Aichi, Chubu 470-0193
DP Coordinator Darron Gray & Morgan Veness
Languages English, Japanese
T: +81 56 173 8181
E: info@ic.nucba.ac.jp
W: ic.nucba.ac.jp
See full details on page 363

NUCB International Junior & Senior High School
1-16 Hiroji Honmachi, Showa-ku, Nagoya, Aichi, Chubu 466-0841
DP Coordinator Emi Watanabe
Languages English
T: +81 52 858 2200
W: www.nihs.ed.jp

Okayama University of Science High School
1-1 Riomachi, Kita-ku, Okayama, Chugoku 700-0005
DP Coordinator Keita Nomura
Languages English, Japanese
T: +81 86 256 8511
W: okayama.ridaifu.net

IB ASIA-PACIFIC

Okinawa International School
143 Tamagusukufusato, Nanjo, Okinawa, Kyushu 901-0611
DP Coordinator Miho Endo
MYP Coordinator Yugo Nakamura
PYP Coordinator Daichi Akiyama
Languages English, Japanese
T: +81 98 948 7711
W: www.ois-edu.com

Okinawa Shogaku School
747 Kokuba, Naha, Okinawa, Kyushu 902-0075
DP Coordinator Noriko Bousckri
Languages English, Japanese
T: +81 98 832 1767
W: www.okisho.ed.jp

Omiya Elementary School
654-1 Birafu, Kahoku, Kami, Kochi, Shikoku 781-4212
PYP Coordinator Sachiyo Okamoto
Languages English, Japanese

Osaka International High School
1-28 Matsushita-cho, Moriguchi-shi, Osaka, Kansai 570-8787
DP Coordinator Eric Baptiste
Languages English, Japanese
T: +81 66 992 5931
W: www.kokusai-h.oiu.ed.jp

Osaka International School of Kwansei Gakuin
4-4-16 Onohara-nishi, Minoh, Osaka, Kansai 562-0032
DP Coordinator Andrew Brown
MYP Coordinator Kelly Deklinski
PYP Coordinator Trevor Jones
Languages English
T: +81 72 727 5050
W: sois.kwansei.ac.jp/osaka-international-school

Osaka Jogakuin Senior High School
2-26-54 Tamatsukuri, Chuo-ku, Osaka, Kansai 540-0004
DP Coordinator Michael Checkley
Languages English, Japanese
T: +81 66 761 4451
W: www.osaka-jogakuin.ed.jp

Osaka Prefectural Suito Kokusai Junior & Senior High School
3-7-13 Nankonaka, Suminoe-ku, Osaka, Kansai 559-0033
DP Coordinator Goro Sato
Languages English, Japanese
T: +81 67 662 9600
W: osaka-city-ib.jp

Osaka YMCA International School
6-7-34 Nakatsu, Kita-ku, Osaka, Kansai 531-0071
DP Coordinator Jamie Riddalls
MYP Coordinator Patrick Anderson
PYP Coordinator Brendan O'Leary
Languages English
T: +81 66 345 1661
W: www.oyis.org

RITSUMEIKAN UJI JUNIOR AND SENIOR HIGH SCHOOL
33-1 Hachikenyadani, Hirono-cho, Uji, Kyoto, Kansai 611-0031
DP Coordinator Matthew Thomas
Languages English, Japanese (ibdp In English)
T: +81 774 41 3000
E: ib-info@ujc.ritsumei.ac.jp
W: en.ritsumei.ac.jp/uji
See full details on page 374

Sai Sishya International School
2-12-8 Naka Kasai, Edogawa-ku, Tokyo, Kanto 134-0083
PYP Coordinator Maria Van Eeden
Languages English, Japanese
T: +81 36 808 9230

Saint Maur International School
83 Yamate-cho, Naka-ku, Yokohama, Kanagawa, Kanto 231-0862
DP Coordinator Oliver Alexander
Languages English
T: +81 45 641 5751
W: www.stmaur.ac.jp

Saitama Municipal Omiya International Secondary School
4-96 Mitsuhashi, Omiya-ku, Mihashi, Saitama, Kanto 330-0856
DP Coordinator Bradley Semans
MYP Coordinator Royal Langer
Languages English, Japanese
T: +81 48 622 8200
W: www.city-saitama.ed.jp/ohmiyakokusai-h

Sapporo Kaisei Secondary School
Kita 22, Higashi 21-chome 1-1, Higashi-ku, Sapporo, Hokkaido 065-8558
DP Coordinator Ken Kuroi
MYP Coordinator Thomas Belshaw
Languages English
T: +81 11 788 6987
W: www.kaisei-s.sapporo-c.ed.jp

Sapporo Nihon University High School
5-7-1 Nijigaoka, Kitahiroshima, Hokkaido 061-1103
DP Coordinator Kentaro Kawai
Languages English, Japanese
T: +81 11 375 5311
W: www.sapporonichidai.ed.jp

Seisen International School
1-12-15 Yoga, Setagaya-ku, Tokyo, Kanto 158-0097
DP Coordinator Dean Bevan
MYP Coordinator Eric Usher
PYP Coordinator Serrin Smyth
Languages English
T: 81 33 704 2661
W: www.seisen.com

Sendai Ikuei Gakuen High School
2-4-1 Miyagino, Miyagino-ku, Sendai, Miyagi, Tohoku 983-0045
DP Coordinator Anthony Sweeney
MYP Coordinator Bryan Stevens
Languages English, Japanese
T: +81 22 256 4141
W: www.sendaiikuei.ed.jp/hs

SENIOR HIGH SCHOOL AT SAKADO, UNIVERSITY OF TSUKUBA
1-24-1 Chiyoda, Sakado, Saitama, Kanto 350-0214
DP Coordinator Regina Ver-Santos
Languages English, Japanese
T: +81 49 281 1541
W: www.sakado-s.tsukuba.ac.jp
See full details on page 379

Shinagawa International School
4-8-8 Higashishinagawa, Shinagawa, Tokyo, Kanto 140-0002
MYP Coordinator Gamze Abis
PYP Coordinator Sandeep Kaur
Languages English
T: +81 36 433 1531
W: sistokyo.jp

Shizuoka Salesio School
3-2-1 Nakanogo, Shimizu-ku, Shizuoka, Chubu 424-8624
DP Coordinator Yasuhiro Mochizuki
MYP Coordinator Akihiro Shimomura
PYP Coordinator Taku Harada
Languages English, Japanese
T: +81 54 345 2296
W: www.ssalesio.ac.jp

Shohei Junior & Senior High School
851 Shimono, Sugito, Saitama, Kanto 345-0044
DP Coordinator Takemi Matsuno
MYP Coordinator Jo Iwase
Languages English, Japanese
T: +81 48 034 3381
W: www.shohei.sugito.saitama.jp

Shukou Junior High School
2-4-1 Miyagino, Miyagino-ku, Sendai, Miyagi, Tohoku 985-0853
MYP Coordinator Bryan Stevens
Languages English, Japanese
T: +81 22 256 4141
W: www.sendaiikuei.ed.jp/shukoh

St. Joseph's Primary School
11-1 Kitadai, Higashiterao, Tsurumi-ku, Yokohama, Kanagawa, Kanto 230-0016
PYP Coordinator Kenichiro Kono
Languages English, Japanese
T: +81 45 581 8808
W: www.st-joseph.ac.jp/primary

St. Mary's International School
1-6-19 Seta, Setagaya-ku, Tokyo, Kanto 158-8668
DP Coordinator Christopher Tihor
Languages English
T: +81 33 709 3411
W: www.smis.ac.jp

Summerhill International School
2-13-8 Moto-Azabu, Minato-ku, Tokyo, Kanto 106-0046
PYP Coordinator Hana Fujishiro
Languages English, Japanese
T: +81 33 453 0811
W: summerhill.jp

Sunnyside International School
4-10-25 Iwai, Gifu, Chubu 501-3101
PYP Coordinator Kanako Morikawa
Languages English, Japanese
T: +81 58 241 1000
W: www.sunnyside-international.jp
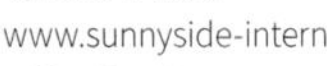

Tamagawa Academy K-12 & University
6-1-1 Tamagawa Gakuen, Machida, Tokyo, Kanto 194-8610
DP Coordinator Richard Beaumont
MYP Coordinator Bronson Chau
Languages English
T: +81 42 739 8111
W: www.tamagawa.jp/en

Teikyo University Kani Junior & Senior High School
1-1 Katsuragaoka, Kani, Gifu, Chubu 509-0237
DP Coordinator Brandon Hune
Languages English, Japanese
T: +81 57 464 3211
W: www.teikyo-kani.ed.jp

Tohoku International School
7-101-1 Yakata, Izumi-ku, Sendai, Miyagi, Tohoku 981-3214
DP Coordinator Robert Zehmke
PYP Coordinator Hiroko Yoshida
Languages English, Japanese
T: +81 22 348 2468
W: www.tisweb.net

Tokyo Gakugei University International Secondary School
5-22-1 Higashi-Oizumi, Nerima-ku, Tokyo, Kanto 178-0063
DP Coordinator Miki Takamatsu
MYP Coordinator Masumi Kobayashi
Languages English, Japanese
T: +81 35 905 1326
W: www.iss.oizumi.u-gakugei.ac.jp

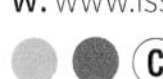

Tokyo Gakugei University Oizumi Elementary School
5-22-1 Higashi-Oizumi, Nerima-ku, Tokyo, Kanto 178-0063
PYP Coordinator Koichi Hosoi
Languages English, Japanese
T: +81 35 905 0200
W: www.es.oizumi.u-gakugei.ac.jp

Tokyo International School
2-13-6 Minami Azabu, Minato-ku, Tokyo, Kanto 106-0047
MYP Coordinator Catherine Dick
PYP Coordinator Kim Engasser
Languages English
T: +81 35 484 1160
W: www.tokyois.com

TOKYO METROPOLITAN KOKUSAI HIGH SCHOOL
2-19-59 Komaba, Meguro-ku, Tokyo, Kanto 153-0041
DP Coordinator Kazumasa Aoki
Languages English
T: +81 33 468 6811
W: kokusai-h.metro.ed.jp

See full details on page 398

Tokyo West International School
185 Umetsubo-machi, Hachioji, Tokyo, Kanto 192-0013
PYP Coordinator Ka Man Luk
Languages English
T: +81 42 691 1441
W: www.tokyowest.jp

Torahime High School
2410 Miyabe-cho, Nagahama, Shiga, Kansai 529-0012
DP Coordinator Mariko Tomioka
Languages English, Japanese
T: +81 74 973 3055
W: www.torahime-h.shiga-ec.ed.jp

Tottori Prefectural Kurayoshi Higashi High School
801 Shimodanakacho, Kurayoshi, Tottori, Chugoku 682-0812
DP Coordinator Chiryon Song
Languages English, Japanese
T: +81 85 822 5205
W: www.torikyo.ed.jp/kurae-h

Tsukinohikari Kokusai Nursery / Moonlight International Preschool
625-1 Tainohara Ohno, Hatsukaichi, Hiroshima, Chugoku 739-0488
PYP Coordinator Winfred Quarshie
Languages English, Japanese
T: +81 82 950 2280
W: tsukinohikari.international

Tsukuba International School
Kamigo 7846-1, Tsukuba, Ibaraki, Kanto 300-2645
DP Coordinator Peter Congreve
MYP Coordinator Vincent Jan Africa
PYP Coordinator Ian Woollard
Languages English
T: +81 29 886 5447
W: www.tis.ac.jp

UPBEAT International School - Atsuta Campus
2-3-18 Hachiban, Atsuta-ku, Nagoya, Aichi, Chubu
PYP Coordinator Rachel Williams
Languages English, Japanese
T: +81 52 661 3155
W: www.upbeatinternationalschool.com

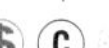

Urawagakuin High School
172 Daiyama, Midori Ward, Saitama City, Saitama, Kanto 336-0975
DP Coordinator Mitsuyo Hoshino
Languages English, Japanese
T: +81 48 878 2101
W: uragaku.ac.jp

UWC ISAK Japan
5827-136 Nagakura, Karuizawa-machi, Kitasaku-gun, Nagano, Chubu 389-0111
DP Coordinator Francis Gonzalez
Languages English
T: +81 26 746 8623
W: uwcisak.jp

Wakakusa Kindergarten
3-15-4 Yoshida, Nagano, Chubu 381-0043
PYP Coordinator Misato Nicoll
Languages English, Japanese
T: +81 26 241 4151
W: wakakusa-kg.net

Willowbrook International School
2-14-28 Moto-azabu, Minato-ku, Tokyo, Kanto 106-0046
PYP Coordinator Louise Boddy
Languages English, Japanese
T: +81 33 449 9030
W: www.willowbrookschool.com

Yamanashi Gakuin School
3-3-1 Sakaori, Kofu, Yamanashi, Chubu 400-0805
DP Coordinator Priw-Prae Litticharoenporn
PYP Coordinator Hidetoshi Horikawa
Languages English, Japanese
T: +81 55 233 1111
W: www.c2c.ac.jp/en/schools

Yamata Kindergarten
351-1 Higashiyamatacho, Tsuzuki-ku, Yokohama, Kanagawa, Kanto 224-0024
PYP Coordinator Manami Nishiyama
Languages Japanese
T: +81 45 592 4850
W: www.yamata-youchien.com

Yokohama International School
2-100-1 Kominato-cho, Naka-ku, Yokohama, Kanagawa, Kanto 231-0802
DP Coordinator Giles Pinto
MYP Coordinator Medeha Zahid
PYP Coordinator Jocelyn Hartley
Languages English
T: +81 45 622 0084
W: www.yis.ac.jp

Yokohama Senior High School of International Studies
1-731 Mutsukawa, Minami-ku, Yokohama, Kanagawa 232-0066
DP Coordinator Kazuhisa Kitazume
Languages English, Japanese
T: +81 45 721 1434
W: www.pen-kanagawa.ed.jp/yokohamakokusai-h

Yoyogi International School
5-67-5 Yoyogi, Shibuya-ku, Tokyo, Kanto 151-0053
PYP Coordinator Mike Mural
Languages English
T: +81 35 478 6714
W: www.yoyogiinternationalschool.com

LAOS

VIENTIANE INTERNATIONAL SCHOOL
P.O. Box 3180, Phonesavanh Road, Saphanthong Tai Village, Sisattanak District, Vientiane
DP Coordinator Elizabeth England
MYP Coordinator Elizabeth England
PYP Coordinator Olwen Millgate
Languages English
T: +856 21 31 8100
E: contact@vislao.com
W: www.vislao.com

See full details on page 404

MALAYSIA

Cempaka International School
No 19, Jalan Setiabakti 1, Damansara Heights, Kuala Lumpur
DP Coordinator Nik Zakiah Nik Kar
Languages English
T: +60 3 2094 0623
W: www.cempaka.edu.my

EtonHouse Malaysia International School
No. 9 Persiaran Stonor, 50450 Kuala Lumpur
PYP Coordinator Shamirah Gafoor
Languages English
T: +60 3 2141 3301/02
W: etonhouse.edu.my

Fairview International School Ipoh (FISI)
Hala Lapangan Suria, Medan Lapangan, Suria, 31350 Ipoh, Perak
MYP Coordinator Vigneswary V
PYP Coordinator Poh Yi Kan
Languages English
T: +60 5 313 6888
W: ipoh.fairview.edu.my

Fairview International School Johor Bahru (FISJB)
Lot PTD 168450, Jalan Dato' Onn Utama, Bandar Dato' Onn, Mukim Tebrau, 81100 Johor Bahru, Johor
MYP Coordinator Adrian Adeel Abader
PYP Coordinator Diya Upadhaya
Languages English
T: +60 7 364 3378
W: johor-bahru.fairview.edu.my

Malaysia

Fairview International School Kuala Lumpur (FISKL)
Lot 4178, Jalan 1/27D, Section 6, Wangsa Maju, 53300 Kuala Lumpur
DP Coordinator Dr. Evan Hui See Chin
MYP Coordinator Dr. Evan Hui See Chin
PYP Coordinator Ms. Elaine Wong
Languages English, Mandarin
T: +60 3 4142 0888
W: kuala-lumpur.fairview.edu.my

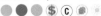

Fairview International School Penang (FISP)
Tingkat Bukit Jambul 1, Bukit Jambul Indah, 11900 Bayan Lepas, Penang
MYP Coordinator Eswari Subramaniam
PYP Coordinator Samantha Leong
Languages English
T: +60 4 640 6633
W: penang.fairview.edu.my

Fairview International School Subang Jaya (FISJ)
2A, Jalan TP 2, Sime UEP Industrial Park, 47600 Subang Jaya, Selangor
MYP Coordinator Cynthia Patricia Nicholas
PYP Coordinator Elaine Wong
Languages English
T: +60 3 8023 7777
W: subang-jaya.fairview.edu.my

 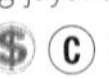

IGB International School
Jalan Sierramas Utama, Sungai Buloh, Kuala Lumpur, Selangor 47000
CP Coordinator Magnus Drechsler
DP Coordinator Magnus Drechsler
MYP Coordinator Lennan MacDonald
PYP Coordinator Aga Chojnacka
Languages English
T: +60 3 6145 4688
W: www.igbis.edu.my

  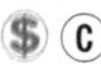

Kolej MARA Banting
Bukit Changgang, 42700 Banting, Selangor
DP Coordinator Rosmaria Abdullah
Languages English
T: +60 3 3149 1318
W: www.kmb.edu.my

Kolej Tunku Kurshiah
Kompleks Pendidikan Nilai, Bandar Enstek, 71760 Seremban, Negeri Sembilan
DP Coordinator Noraini Ishak
Languages English
T: +60 6 7979800
W: www.tkc.edu.my

Malay College Kuala Kangsar
Jalan Tun Abdul Razak, 33000 Kuala Kangsar, Perak
DP Coordinator Norsafaliza Ibrahim
Languages English
T: +60 5 7761400
W: www.mckk.edu.my

MARLBOROUGH COLLEGE MALAYSIA
Jalan Marlborough, 79200 Iskandar Puteri, Johor
DP Coordinator Mr Kenton Tomlinson
Languages English
T: +60 7 560 2200
E: admissions@marlboroughcollege.my
W: www.marlboroughcollegemalaysia.org

See full details on page 352

Mont'Kiara International School
22 Jalan Kiara, Mont'Kiara, 50480 Kuala Lumpur
DP Coordinator Kenneth Tuttle Wilhelm
MYP Coordinator Kenneth Tuttle Wilhelm
PYP Coordinator Sarah Herbert
Languages English
T: +60 3 2093 8604
W: www.mkis.edu.my

MRSM Balik Pulau (Mara Junior Science College)
Jalan Pondok Upeh, Kampung Shee Tan, 11000 Balik Pulau, Penang
MYP Coordinator Noor Haziah Abdul Halin
Languages English
T: +60 4 8669499
W: bpulau.mrsm.edu.my

MRSM Tun Dr Ismail, Pontian
Jalan Benut Jelutong, 82100 Pontian, Johor
MYP Coordinator Mohd Yusof Zaki Che Amat
Languages English
T: +60 7 6933744
W: mrsmpontian.edu.my

MRSM Tun Mohammad Fuad Stephens Sandakan
Education Hub, Batu 10, Jalan Sungai Batang, 90000 Sandakan, Sabah
MYP Coordinator Hariza Abd Halim
Languages English
T: +60 8 9225609
W: tmfs.mrsm.edu.my/cms

Nexus International School Malaysia
No 1 Jalan Diplomatik 3/6, Presint 15, 62050 Putrajaya
DP Coordinator Amanda O'Hara
Languages English
T: +60 3 8889 3868
W: www.nexus.edu.my

Raffles American School
Raffles K12 Sdn Bhd, Jalan Raffles, 79050 Iskandar Puteri, Johor
DP Coordinator Gisou Ravanbaksh
Languages English
T: +60 7 509 8750
W: www.raffles-american-school.edu.my

Repton International School Malaysia
No. 8, Jalan Purnama, Bandar Seri Alam, 81750 Johor Bahru, Johor
DP Coordinator Joan Malabuyoc
Languages English
T: +60 7 888 999
W: www.repton.edu.my

Sekolah Menengah Kebangsaan Dato' Sheikh Ahmad
Jalan Besar Arau, 02600 Arau, Perlis
MYP Coordinator Shaharom Bakar
Languages English
T: +60 4 9861239
W: www.smkdsaperlis.edu.my

Sekolah Menengah Kebangsaan Sultanah Bahiyah
Lebuhraya Sultanah Bahiyah, 05350 Alor Star, Kedah
MYP Coordinator Noor Afiza Salleh
Languages English
T: +60 4 7331531
W: www.smksultanahbahiyah.edu.my

SMK Pantai, W.P Labuan
Jalan Pohon Batu, 87027 Labuan
MYP Coordinator Maureen Imang Jau
Languages English
T: +60 8 7410863
W: www.smkpantaiwpl.webs.com

SMK Putrajaya Presint 9(2)
Jalan P9A, Presint 9, Wilayah Persekutuan, 62250 Putrajaya
MYP Coordinator Syafini Ismail
Languages English
T: +60 3 8881 1207
W: www.smkpp92.com

SMK Seri Tualang
28000 Temerloh, Pahang
MYP Coordinator Nur Amalina Mazlan
Languages English
T: +60 9 290 1061
W: www.smkseritualang.com

SMK Sungai Tapang
KM 13, Jalan Penrissen, 93250 Kuching, Sarawak
MYP Coordinator Angelina Suzie Anak Rinyod
Languages English
T: +60 8 2612851
W: www.smksungaitapang.edu.my

SMKA Sheikh Abdul Malek
20400 Kuala Terengganu
MYP Coordinator Huzzaimah Basir
Languages English
T: +60 96235155
W: www.shams.edu.my

SMS Tengku Muhammad Faris Petra
Taman Orkid, Kota Bharu, 16100 Pengkalan Chepa
MYP Coordinator Roziah Mohd Ali
T: +60 9 773 8277
W: www.smstmfp.edu.my

Sri KDU International School (Kota Damansara)
No. 3, Jalan Teknologi 2/1, Kota Damansara, 47810 Daerah Petaling, Selangor
DP Coordinator Barnaby Everett
Languages English
T: +60 3 6145 3888
W: www.srikdu.edu.my

St. Joseph's Institution International School Malaysia (Tropicana PJ Campus)
No. 1, Jalan PJU 3/13, 47410 Petaling Jaya, Selangor
DP Coordinator Sarah Cole
Languages English
T: +60 3 8605 3605
W: www.sji-international.edu.my

Stella Maris Medan Damansara
7, Lorong Setiabistari 2, Bukit Damansara, 50490 Kuala Lumpur
DP Coordinator Madhu Singh
Languages English
T: +60 3 20830025
W: stellamaris.edu.my/home

Sunway International School, Bandar Sunway
No. 3, Jalan Universiti, Bandar Sunway, 47500 Selangor
DP Coordinator Mark Milberg
T: +60 3 7491 8070
W: sis.sunway.edu.my
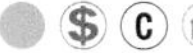

Sunway International School, Sunway Iskandar
Jalan Persiaran Medini 3, Sunway Iskandar, 79250 Johor
CP Coordinator Patric Elder
DP Coordinator Patric Elder
MYP Coordinator Kimberly Percy
Languages English
T: +60 7 533 8070
W: sis.sunway.edu.my

THE INTERNATIONAL SCHOOL OF KUALA LUMPUR (ISKL)
2, Lorong Kelab Polo Di Raja, Ampang Hilir, 55000 Kuala Lumpur
DP Coordinator Ms Sarah Mannino, MA, BA
Languages English
T: +60 3 4813 5000
E: admissions@iskl.edu.my
W: www.iskl.edu.my
See full details on page 395

THE INTERNATIONAL SCHOOL OF PENANG (UPLANDS)
Jalan Sungai Satu, Batu Feringgi, 11100 Penang
DP Coordinator Tanusankar Chakraborty
PYP Coordinator Matthew Holton
Languages English
T: +604 8819 777
E: info@uplands.org
W: www.uplands.org
See full details on page 396

UCSI International School
1 Persiaran UCSI International School, 71010 Port Dickson, Negeri Sembalan
DP Coordinator John Harvey
MYP Coordinator Peter Vinoj
PYP Coordinator Peter Vinoj
Languages English
T: +60 6653 6888
W: www.uis.edu.my

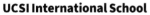

MONGOLIA

International School of Ulaanbaatar
P.O. Box 36/10, Four Seasons Garden, Khan-Uul District, 18 Khoroo, Ulaanbaatar 17032
DP Coordinator Jonathan Armitage
MYP Coordinator David Gates
PYP Coordinator Jeanne Peloquin
Languages English
T: +976 7 0160010
W: www.isumongolia.edu.mn

Olonlog Academy
Capital Circle Avenue Street No. 363, Bayanzurkh District No. 26, Ulaanbaatar 13312
DP Coordinator Dulguun Bayasgalan
Languages English, Mongolian
T: +976 9 4999125
W: olonlogacademy.mn

Shine Ue School
UNESCO Street 12, Khoroo 1, Sukhbaatar District, Ulaanbaatar 14220
DP Coordinator Bulgan Ganbaatar
Languages English, Mongolian
T: +976 7 0128044
W: shineue.edu.mn

The English School of Mongolia
Tokyo-89, 1st Khoroo, Bayanzurkh District, Ulaanbaatar 13380
DP Coordinator Erdene Tulga
PYP Coordinator Connor Vinnicombe
Languages English, Mongolian
T: +976 1 1451230
W: esm.edu.mn

MYANMAR

Bahan International Science Academy
No. 25 Po Sein Road, Bahan Township, Yangon
DP Coordinator Saumya Pandit
Languages English
T: +95 1 548452
W: www.bisa.edu.mm

Brainworks Total International Schools Yangon
No. 1 Thumingalar Street, 16/4 Quarter, Thingangyun Township, Yangon
DP Coordinator Garrett Tuck
Languages English, Burmese
T: +95 1 855 1360
W: www.brainworks-total.com

SKT International College
No. 235 Shu Khinn Thar Myo Pat Road, Thaketa Township, Yangon
DP Coordinator Saumya Pandit
Languages English
T: +95 145 0396
W: www.sktcollege.edu.mm

Taunggyi International School
24/12 Kan Baw Za Street (Wun Gyi Street), Yae Aye Quin Quarter, Taunggyi
DP Coordinator Mohan Aiyer
Languages English, Burmese
T: +95 8 120 6765
W: taunggyiinternational.school

The International School Yangon
20 Shwe Taungyar Street, Bahan Township, Yangon
DP Coordinator Nicolas Lapoujade
Languages English
T: +95 9 880 441 040
W: www.isyedu.org

Yangon American International School
No. 2A Yangon-Insein Road, Building (2), No. 9 Ward, Hlaing Township, Yangon
PYP Coordinator Shannon Keane
Languages English, Burmese
T: +95 997 701 2100
W: yangonamerican.edu.mm

Yangon International School
No. 117 Thumingalar Housing, Thingangyun Township, Yangon
DP Coordinator Tshering L
Languages English
T: +95 1 578171
W: www.yismyanmar.com

NEPAL

Genius School Lalitpur
Mahalaxmi Municipality, Lubhu, Lalitpur 44700
PYP Coordinator Nehru Joshi
Languages English
T: +977 1 5582 564
W: www.geniusschool.edu.np

Machhapuchchhre School
Lalitpur Metropolitan-13, Lalitpur
PYP Coordinator Sampurna Dewapatey Dewapatey
Languages English, Nepali
T: +977 1 5193 144
W: www.machhapuchchhreschool.edu.np

Premier International School
Khumaltar Height, Satdobato, Lalitpur
DP Coordinator Sharmistha Mukherjee
MYP Coordinator Rhandy Jermia
PYP Coordinator Durgesh Jadhav
Languages English, Nepali
T: +977 1 5528 032
W: www.premier.edu.np

Swostishree Gurukul
Sanobharyang, Kathmandu
PYP Coordinator Maksud Alam
Languages English, Nepali
T: +977 1 4890 314
W: swostishreegurukul.edu.np

Ullens School
G.P.O. Box 8975, Khumaltar, Lalitpur 15, Kathmandu 1477
DP Coordinator Raisa Pandey
Languages English
T: +977 1 5230 944
W: www.ullens.edu.np

NEW ZEALAND

ACG Parnell College
2 Titoki Street, Parnell, Auckland 1052
DP Coordinator Alex Marshall
Languages English
T: +64 9 308 1666
W: www.parnellcollege.acgedu.com

Auckland Normal Intermediate School
Poronui Street, Mt Eden, Auckland 1024
PYP Coordinator Shane Devery
Languages English
T: +64 96 301109
W: ani.school.nz

Bay of Islands International Academy
935 Purerua Road, Kerikeri, Northland 0294
PYP Coordinator Chris Bell
Languages English
T: +64 9 407 9749
W: www.boi.ac.nz

Bucklands Beach Intermediate School
247 Bucklands Beach Road, Bucklands Beach, Auckland 2012
PYP Coordinator Anita Leeuw
Languages English
T: +64 9 534 2896
W: www.bbi.school.nz

Diocesan School for Girls
Clyde Street, Epsom, Auckland 1051
DP Coordinator Susan Marriott
PYP Coordinator Nicole Lewis
Languages English
T: +64 9 520 0221
W: www.diocesan.school.nz

Glendowie College
21 Crossfield Road, Glendowie, Auckland 1071
MYP Coordinator Sharon Hewetson
Languages English
T: +64 9 575 9128
W: www.gdc.school.nz

IB ASIA-PACIFIC

NEW ZEALAND

Glendowie Primary School
217 Riddell Road, Glendowie, Auckland 1071
PYP Coordinator Christine Matos
Languages English
T: +64 9 575 7374
W: www.glendowieprimary.school.nz

John McGlashan College
2 Pilkington Street, Maori Hill, Dunedin 9010
DP Coordinator Brendan Porter
Languages English
T: +64 3 467 6620
W: www.mcglashan.school.nz

KRISTIN SCHOOL
360 Albany Highway, Albany, Auckland 0632
DP Coordinator Mrs Debbie Dwyer
MYP Coordinator Mr John Osborne
PYP Coordinator Ms Sandy Paton
Languages English
T: +64 9 415 9566
E: admissions@kristin.school.nz
W: www.kristin.school.nz
See full details on page 349

Milford School
34 Shakespeare Road, Milford, Auckland 0620
PYP Coordinator Sara Baker
Languages English
T: +64 9 489 7216
W: www.milford.school.nz

Mt Pleasant Primary School
82 Major Hornbrook Road, Mt Pleasant, Christchurch 8081
PYP Coordinator Maria Arneil
Languages English
T: +64 03 384 3994
W: www.mtpleasant.school.nz

Queen Margaret College
53 Hobson Street, PO Box 12274, Thorndon, Wellington 6011
DP Coordinator Emma Birch
MYP Coordinator Camille Le Prou
PYP Coordinator Jan Treeby
Languages English
T: +64 4 473 7160
W: www.qmc.school.nz

RANGITOTO COLLEGE
564 East Coast Road, Mairangi Bay, Auckland 0753
DP Coordinator Catherine Brandt
Languages English
T: +64 9 477 0150
E: info@rangitoto.school.nz
W: www.rangitoto.school.nz
See full details on page 369

SAINT KENTIGERN COLLEGE
130 Pakuranga Road, Pakuranga, Auckland 1021
DP Coordinator Suzie Tornquist
Languages English
T: +64 9 577 0749
E: skc_admissions@saintkentigern.com
W: www.saintkentigern.com
See full details on page 376

SCOTS COLLEGE
PO Box 15064, Strathmore, Wellington 6243
DP Coordinator Mr Mike McKnight
MYP Coordinator Ms Kate Bondett
PYP Coordinator Mrs Rosie Roland
Languages English
T: +64 4 388 0850
E: enrolments@scotscollege.school.nz
W: www.scotscollege.school.nz
See full details on page 378
 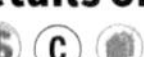

Selwyn House School
PO Box 25049, 122 Merivale Lane, Christchurch 8014
PYP Coordinator Gregory Pearce
Languages English
T: +64 3 3557299
W: www.selwynhouse.school.nz
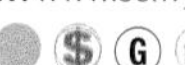

St Cuthbert's College
122 Market Road, Epsom, Auckland 1051
DP Coordinator Buino Vink
Languages English
T: +64 9 520 4159
W: www.stcuthberts.school.nz

ST MARGARET'S COLLEGE
12 Winchester Street, Merivale, Christchurch 8014
DP Coordinator Ms Beth Rowse
Languages English
T: +64 3 379 2000
E: enrol@stmargarets.school.nz
W: www.stmargarets.school.nz
See full details on page 388

St Mark's Church School
13 Dufferin Street, PO Box 7445, Wellington 6021
PYP Coordinator Angelee Jarrett
Languages English
T: +64 4 385 9489
W: www.st-marks.school.nz

St Peter's School, Cambridge
1716 Hamilton Road, Private Bag 884, Cambridge 3450
DP Coordinator Toni Foley
Languages English
T: +64 7 827 9899
W: www.stpeters.school.nz

Takapuna Grammar School
PO Box 33-1096, Takapuna, Auckland 0740
DP Coordinator Jack Chapman
Languages English
T: +64 94894167
W: www.takapuna.school.nz

Takapuna Normal Intermediate School
54B Taharoto Road, Takapuna, Auckland 1309
PYP Coordinator Kathy O'Meara
Languages English
T: +64 9 489 3940
W: www.tnis.school.nz

Te Hihi School
767 Linwood Rd, Karaka, Auckland
PYP Coordinator Charlotte Stoppard
Languages English
T: +64 9 292 7706
W: www.tehihi.school.nz

PAPUA NEW GUINEA

Port Moresby International School
PO Box 276, Boroko
DP Coordinator Ronan Moore
Languages English
T: +675 325 6690
W: ieapng.net

PHILIPPINES

Assumption College San Lorenzo
San Lorenzo Drive, San Lorenzo Village, 1223 Makati City, Metro Manila
DP Coordinator Anthere Paul Bunales
Languages English, Filipino
T: +63 2 8817 0757
W: www.assumption.edu.ph

Bannister Academy
Circulo Verde, Calle Industria, Bagumbayan, Quezon City, Metro Manila
DP Coordinator Neil Paolo Reblando
Languages English, Pilipino
T: +63 0998 575 7448
W: bannister.edu.ph

Brent International School Baguio
Brent Road, 2600 Baguio City, Cordillera
DP Coordinator Paul Engler
Languages English
T: +63 74 442 4050
W: www.brentbaguio.edu.ph

Brent International School Manila
Brentville Subdivision, Mamplasan, 4024 Biñan, Calabarzon
DP Coordinator Maria Cristina Pozon
Languages English
T: +63 2 8779 5140
W: www.brent.edu.ph

Brent International School Subic
Building 6601 Binictican Drive, Subic Bay Freeport Zone, Zambales, 2222 Subic, Central Luzon
DP Coordinator Sheila Marie Griarte
Languages English
T: +63 47 252 6871/72
W: www.brentsubic.edu.ph

British School Manila
36th Street, University Park, Bonifacio Global City, 1634 Taguig City, Metro Manila
DP Coordinator Kate Gleaves
Languages English
T: +63 2 8860 4800
W: www.britishschoolmanila.org

Cebu International School
Pit-os, 6000 Cebu City, Central Visayas
DP Coordinator Emily Cornet
MYP Coordinator Jonathan Denton
PYP Coordinator Maureen Juanson
Languages English
T: +63 32 342 7788
W: www.cis.edu.ph
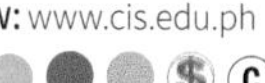

Chiang Kai Shek College
1274 Padre Algue Street, Tondo, 1012 Manila, Metro Manila
DP Coordinator Glicerio Manalo
MYP Coordinator Diane Lee
PYP Coordinator Hannah-Mae De Jesus
Languages English, Pilipino
T: +63 2 252 6161
W: www.cksc.edu.ph

Chinese International School Manila
Upper McKinley Road, McKinley Hill, Fort Bonifacio, 1634 Taguig City, Metro Manila
DP Coordinator Jourdan Shanley Gan
Languages English
T: +63 2 8743 8134
W: www.cismanila.org

Domuschola International School
#13 J. Cruz Street, Ugong, 1609 Pasig City, Metro Manila
DP Coordinator Mary Grace Rosas
PYP Coordinator Ginalyn Delizo
Languages English, Filipino
T: +63 2 8635 2002
W: domuschola.edu.ph
 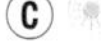

German European School Manila
75 Swaziland Street, Better Living Subdivision, 1711 Paranaque City, Metro Manila
CP Coordinator Santanu Bhowmik
DP Coordinator Santanu Bhowmik
PYP Coordinator Viola Buck
Languages English
T: +63 2 8776 1000
W: www.gesm.org

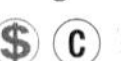

Hope Christian High School
1242 Benavidez Street, Santa Cruz, 1003 Manila, Metro Manila
PYP Coordinator Jan Laurice Ong
Languages English, Chinese
T: +63 2 5310 8071
W: www.hchs.edu.ph

Immaculate Conception Academy
10 Grant Street, Greenhills, San Juan, Metro Manila
DP Coordinator Mary An Olaveja
Languages English, Tagalog
T: +63 2 8723 7041
W: www.icagh.edu.ph

International School Manila
University Parkway, Fort Bonifacio Global City, 1634 Taguig City, Metro Manila
DP Coordinator Patrick Hillman
Languages English
T: +63 2 8840 8400
W: www.ismanila.org

Keys School Manila
951 Luna Mencias Street, corner Araullo Street, Addition Hills, 1550 Mandaluyong City, Metro Manila
DP Coordinator Girard Immanuel Crudo
Languages English
T: +63 2 8727 9357
W: www.ksm.ph

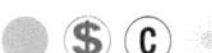

Life Academy International
CCF Center, Ortigas East, Ortigas Avenue cor. C-5 Road, Ugong, Pasig City, Metro Manila
DP Coordinator Joanne Miranda
Languages English
T: +63 917 777 5433
W: lifeacademy.edu.ph

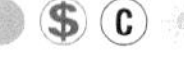

Mother Goose Lipa
City Park Avenue, corner of Gladiola Street, City Park Subd., Sabang, 4217 Lipa City, Calabarzon
PYP Coordinator Bernadette Beria
Languages English, Pilipino
T: +63 43 702 9630
W: www.mgplipa.org

Noblesse International School
Circumferential Road, Friendship Highway, Cutcut, Santo Domingo, 2009 Angeles City, Central Luzon
DP Coordinator Alyssa Fry
MYP Coordinator Katrina Musni
PYP Coordinator James McKone
Languages English
T: +63 45 459 9000
W: www.nis.com.ph

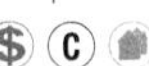

Our Lady of Victories Catholic School of Quezon City
6 Cannon Road Street, 1112 Quezon City, Metro Manila
PYP Coordinator Virginia Ala
Languages English, Pilipino
T: +63 2 998 886 5809
W: www.olvcs.edu.ph

Saint Jude Catholic School
327 Ycaza Street, San Miguel, 1005 Manila, Metro Manila
DP Coordinator Genalyn Alfonso
Languages English
T: +63 2 8735 6386
W: www.sjcs.edu.ph

Singapore School Cebu
Zuellig Avenue, North Reclamation Area, Mandaue City, 6014 Cebu, Central Visayas
DP Coordinator Barbara Magallona
Languages Chinese, English
T: +63 32 236 5772
W: www.singaporeschoolcebu.com

Singapore School Manila
Lots 1 & 40, Block 2 East Street, East District, Asena City, Paranaque City, Metro Manila
DP Coordinator Denise Villegas
Languages English
T: +63 2 7500 4672
W: www.singaporeschoolmanila.com.ph

Southville International School & Colleges (SISC)
1281 Luxembourg Street, corner Tropical Avenue, B.F. Homes International, 1740 Las Pinas City, Metro Manila
DP Coordinator Armie Ababa
Languages English
T: +63 2 8825 6374
W: www.southville.edu.ph

The Beacon Academy
Cecilia Araneta Parkway, 4024 Binan, Calabarzon
DP Coordinator Iris Morga
MYP Coordinator Roy Aldrin Villegas
Languages English
T: +63 2 425 1326
W: www.beaconacademy.ph

The Beacon School
PCPD Building, 2332 Chino Roces Avenue Extension, Taguig City 1630
MYP Coordinator Erica Gancayco
PYP Coordinator DJ Leonardia
Languages English
T: +632 840 5040 LOC 105
W: www.beaconschool.ph

The Manila Times College of Subic
George Dewey Complex, Subic Bay Gateway District II, Subic Bay Freeport Zone, Zambales, 2222 Subic, Central Luzon
PYP Coordinator Jonille Pimentel
Languages English, Pilipino
T: +63 927 365 8270
W: tmtc.edu.ph

Xavier School
64 Xavier Street, Greenhills West, 1500 San Juan, Metro Manila
DP Coordinator Paolo Suapengco
Languages English
T: +63 2 8723 0481
W: www.xs.edu.ph

REPUBLIC OF KOREA

Branksome Hall Asia
234 Global edu-ro, Daejeong-eup, Seogwipo-si, Jeju-do 63644
DP Coordinator Mr. Edward Cabrelli
MYP Coordinator Dr. Paula Swartz
PYP Coordinator Ms. Jennifer Kesler
Languages English
T: +82 64 902 5000
W: www.branksome.asia

British International Academy
24, Deokpo 3-gil, Geoje 53213
DP Coordinator Angela Walker
MYP Coordinator Tara Dhital
PYP Coordinator Tara Dhital
Languages English
T: +82 055 688 5154
W: www.biakorea.org

CHADWICK INTERNATIONAL
45, Art center-daero 97 beon-gil, Yeonsu-gu, Incheon 22002
CP Coordinator Gurpreet Kaur
DP Coordinator Richard Kent
MYP Coordinator Amanda Cooper-Marcon
PYP Coordinator Pamela Castillo (Lower Primary) & Nancy Macharia (Upper Primary)
Languages English
T: +82 32 250 5000
E: songdo-admissions@chadwickschool.org
W: www.chadwickinternational.org

See full details on page 318

Chung Nam Samsung Academy
77 Samseong-ro, Tangjeong-myeon, Asan-si, Chungcheongnam-do
DP Coordinator Nikki Birdsall
Languages English, Korean
T: +82 41 339 3000
W: www.cnsa.hs.kr/hpwEng

Daegu Deokin Elementary School
66 Daemyeongcheon-ro 43-gil, Dalseo-gu, Daegu, North Gyeongsang 42694
PYP Coordinator Seong Kyu Kim
Languages English, Korean
T: +82 53 234 2274
W: www.dukin.es.kr

Daegu Dongduk Elementary School
20 Dongdeok-ro 26-gil, Daegu, North Gyeongsang 41948
PYP Coordinator Mina Kwon
Languages English, Korean
W: sites.google.com/dongduk.es.kr/discover

Daegu Hyenpung Elementary School
167-6 Biseul-ro 134-gil, Hyeonpung-eup, Dalseong-gun, Daegu, North Gyeongsang 42997
PYP Coordinator Won Ho Cho
Languages English, Korean
T: +82 53 235 0589
W: www.hyenpung.es.kr/index.do

Daegu Joong Ang Middle School
496 Sincheondong-ro, Suseong-gu, Daegu, North Gyeongsang 42000
MYP Coordinator Seung Min Lee
Languages English, Korean
T: +82 82 770 0001

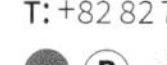

Daegu Jungri Elementary School
135 Gukchaebosang-ro, Seo-gu, Daegu, North Gyeongsang 41759
PYP Coordinator Seungyeop Shin
Languages English, Korean
T: +82 53 233 0750
W: jungri.dge.es.kr/jungrie/main.do?sysId=jungrie

Daegu Namdong Elementary School
258 Nongong-ro, Nongong-eup, Dalseong-gun, Daegu, North Gyeongsang 42985
PYP Coordinator Miryoung Lee
Languages English, Korean
W: www.tgnamdong.es.kr/index.do

Republic of Korea

Daegu Samyoung Elementary School
Naegok-ro 63, Sasu-dong Buk-gu, Daegu, North Gyeongsang
PYP Coordinator Hyunjo Kim
Languages English, Korean
T: +82 53 233 4950
W: www.ensamyoung.com

Daegu Wolbae Elementary School
131 Wolbae-ro, Dalseo-gu, Daegu, North Gyeongsang 42784
PYP Coordinator Codi Wolbae
Languages English, Korean
T: +82 53 234 1406
W: wolbae.dge.es.kr/wolbaee/sso/index.do

Daegu Youngsun Elementary School
Daegu Namgu Icheondong Youngsungil 96, Daegu, North Gyeongsang 42423
PYP Coordinator Gyunsuk Kim
Languages English, Korean
T: +82 10 500 63324

Dulwich College Seoul
6 Sinbanpo-ro 15-gil, Seocho-gu, Seoul 06504
DP Coordinator Rebecca Gardner
Languages English
T: +82 2 3015 8500
W: seoul.dulwich.org

Dwight School Seoul
21 World Cup Buk-ro 62-gil, Mapo-gu, Seoul 03919
DP Coordinator Terence Mitchell
MYP Coordinator Cameron Forbes
PYP Coordinator Sarah Gouge
Languages English
T: +82 2 6920 8600
W: www.dwight.or.kr

Gyeonggi Academy of Foreign Languages
30, Gosan-ro 105 Beon-gil, Uiwang-si, Gyeonggi-do 16075
DP Coordinator Anthony Cartmel
Languages English
T: +82 (0)31 361 0500
W: www.gafl.hs.kr

Gyeonggi Suwon International School
451 YeongTong-Ro, YeongTong-Gu, Suwon City, Gyeonggi-Do 16706
DP Coordinator Hoin Kim
MYP Coordinator Nishtha Daniel
PYP Coordinator Jabbie Rosario
Languages English
T: +82 31 695 2800
W: www.gsis.sc.kr

Gyeongnam International Foreign School
49-22, Jodong-gil, Sanam-myeon, Sacheon-si, Gyeongnam 52533
DP Coordinator Samuel Kuntz
MYP Coordinator Darrell Hardman
PYP Coordinator Timothy Balaz
Languages English
T: +82 (0)55 853 5125
W: www.gifs.or.kr

International School of Busan
50 Gijang-daero, Gijang-eup, Gijang-gun, Busan 46081
DP Coordinator Merriss Shenstone
MYP Coordinator Jennifer Montague
PYP Coordinator Jennifer Fenton
Languages English
T: +82 51 742 3332
W: www.bifskorea.org

Korea Foreign School
7-16, Nambusunhwan-ro 364-gil, Seocho-gu, Seoul 06739
PYP Coordinator Marwa Koujan
Languages English
T: +82 2 571 2917/18
W: koreaforeign.org

Kyungpook National University Elementary School
2150 Dalgubeol-daero, Jung-gu, Daegu, North Gyeongsang 41959
PYP Coordinator Jee Hyeon Park
Languages English, Korean
T: +82 53 232 5804
W: www.ksadae.es.kr/index.do

Kyungpook National University High School
2178 Dalgubeol-daero, Jung-gu, Daegu, North Gyeongsang 41950
DP Coordinator Unah Lyu
Languages English, Korean
T: +82 53 231 9410
W: www.knu.hs.kr/index.do

Kyungpook National University Middle School
2178 Dalgubeol-daero, Jung-gu, Daegu, North Gyeongsang 41950
MYP Coordinator Eunyoung Kim
Languages English, Korean
T: +82 53 232 8234
W: ivy.knu.ac.kr/index.do

NORTH LONDON COLLEGIATE SCHOOL JEJU
33, Global edu-ro 145beon-gil, Daejeong-eup, Seogwipo-si, Jeju-do 63644
DP Coordinator Ms Justine Oliver
Languages English
T: +82 64 793 8001
E: admissions@nlcsjeju.kr
W: www.nlcsjeju.co.kr
See full details on page 361

Posan High School
556-13 Biseul-ro, Hyeonpung-eup, Dalseong-gun, Daegu, North Gyeongsang 43005
DP Coordinator Sangwook Park
Languages English, Korean
T: +82 53 231 5300
W: www.posan.hs.kr/index.do

Posan Middle School
10 Technobuk-ro 6-gil, Yuga-eup, Dalseong-gun, Daegu, North Gyeongsang 43015
MYP Coordinator Aekyung Lee
Languages Korean
T: +82 53 235 2900
W: www.posan.ms.kr

Pyoseon Elementary School
293 Pyoseondongseo-ro, Pyoseon-myeon, Seogwipo-si, Jeju 63629
PYP Coordinator Sunyoung Moon
Languages English, Korean
T: +82 64 786 4800
W: pyoseon.jje.es.kr

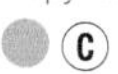

Pyoseon High School
22-15 Pyoseonjungang-ro, Pyoseon-myeon, Seogwipo-si, Jeju 63629
DP Coordinator Young Kim
Languages Korean
T: +82 64 786 5560
W: jjps.jje.hs.kr

Pyoseon Middle School
Pyoseon Jungang-ro 31, Pyoseon-myeon, Seogwipo-si, Jeju 63629
MYP Coordinator Eunrim Kang
Languages English, Korean
T: +82 64 780 7400
W: pyoseon.jje.ms.kr

Seodong Middle School
11-11, Seojae-ro 12-gil, Dasa-eup, Dalseong-gun, Daegu, North Gyeongsang 42928
MYP Coordinator Juyeon Kim
Languages Korean
T: +82 53 233 9801

SEOUL FOREIGN SCHOOL
39 Yeonhui-ro 22-gil, Seodaemun-gu, Seoul 03723
DP Coordinator Piotr Kocyk
MYP Coordinator Chris Horan
PYP Coordinator Michael Lucchesi
Languages English
T: +82 2 330 3100
E: admissions@seoulforeign.org
W: www.seoulforeign.org
See full details on page 382

Taegu Foreign Language High School
21 Seonwon-ro 11-gil, (1675 Sindang-dong), Dalseo-gu, Daegu, North Gyeongsang 42603
DP Coordinator Soojin Baek
Languages English, Korean
T: +82 53 231 7777
W: www.taegu-fh.hs.kr/index.do

Taejon Christian International School
77 Yongsan 2 Ro, Yuseong Gu, Daejeon 305-500
DP Coordinator Minsoo Cho
MYP Coordinator Jonathan Hayhoe
PYP Coordinator Jodi Deuth
Languages English
T: +82 42 620 9000
W: www.tcis.or.kr

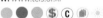

Tosan Elementary School
68-9 Tosanjoongang-ro, Tosanri Pyosun-myun, Seogwipo-si, Jeju 63626
PYP Coordinator Gyeongmi Jeong
Languages English, Korean

SINGAPORE

ACS (International), Singapore
61 Jalan Hitam Manis, Singapore 278475
DP Coordinator Carol Ling
Languages English
T: +658 6472 1477
W: www.acsinternational.com.sg

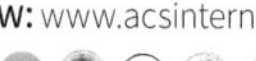

Anglo-Chinese School (Independent)
121 Dover Road, Singapore 139650
DP Coordinator Siew Hwa Chock
Languages English
T: +65 6773 1633
W: www.acs.sch.edu.sg/acs_indep

Ascensia International School
Blk 106A Henderson Crescent, #01-01 Henderson Area Office, Singapore 151106
DP Coordinator Nikko Hsiang
PYP Coordinator Danica Castelino
Languages English
T: +65 6466 5505
W: www.aais.edu.sg
 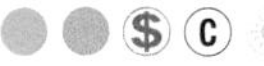

Australian International School, Singapore
1 Lorong Chuan 556818
DP Coordinator Ruth Williams
PYP Coordinator Emma McAulay
Languages English
T: +65 6653 7906
W: www.ais.com.sg
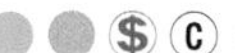

Barker Road Methodist Church Kindergarten
70 Barker Road, Singapore 309936
PYP Coordinator Jummy Laurentius
Languages English, Chinese
T: +65 6255 8430
W: www.brmck.edu.sg

Canadian International School, Lakeside Campus
7 Jurong West Street 41, Singapore 659414
DP Coordinator Elsa Baptista
MYP Coordinator Rebecca Hosick
PYP Coordinator Austin Wellman
Languages English
T: +65 6743 8088
W: www.cis.edu.sg

CHATSWORTH INTERNATIONAL SCHOOL
72 Bukit Tinggi Road, Singapore 289760
DP Coordinator Iain Hudson
MYP Coordinator Jonathan Denton
PYP Coordinator Eleri Connor
Languages English
T: +65 6463 3201
E: admissions.bt@chatsworth.com.sg
W: www.chatsworth.com.sg
See full details on page 319

DOVER COURT INTERNATIONAL SCHOOL SINGAPORE
301 Dover Road, Singapore 139644
DP Coordinator Mr. Dominic O'Shea
Languages English
T: +65 6775 7664
E: admissions@dovercourt.edu.sg
W: www.dovercourt.edu.sg
See full details on page 322

DULWICH COLLEGE (SINGAPORE)
71 Bukit Batok West Avenue 8, Singapore 658966
CP Coordinator Ms. Charlotte Martin
DP Coordinator Mrs. Lisa Nevers
Languages English, Mandarin
T: +65 6890 1003
E: admissions.singapore@dulwich.org
W: singapore.dulwich.org
See full details on page 323

EtonHouse International School, Broadrick
51 Broadrick Road, Singapore 439501
PYP Coordinator Mr Peter Dart
Languages English
T: +65 6346 6922
W: www.etonhouse.edu.sg/school/broadrick

EtonHouse International School, Mountbatten 718
718 Mountbatten Road, Singapore 437738
PYP Coordinator Hannah Sim
Languages English
T: +65 6846 3322
W: www.etonhouse.edu.sg/school/mountbatten718
 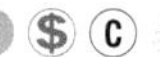

EtonHouse International School, Newton
39 Newton Road, Singapore 307966
PYP Coordinator Asmita Sharma
Languages English
T: +65 6352 3322
W: www.etonhouse.edu.sg/school/newton

EtonHouse International School, Orchard
10 Tanglin Road, Singapore 247908
DP Coordinator Silvie Edwards
PYP Coordinator Maggie Dawson
Languages English, Spanish
T: +65 6513 1155
W: www.etonhouse.edu.sg/school/orchard

GESS International School
2 Dairy Farm Lane, Singapore 677621
DP Coordinator Jason Graham
MYP Coordinator Rebecca Scrivener
PYP Coordinator Kristyn Holland
Languages English, German
T: +65 6461 0881
W: www.gess.sg

GLOBAL INDIAN INTERNATIONAL SCHOOL (GIIS) EAST COAST CAMPUS
82 Cheviot Hill, Singapore 459663
DP Coordinator Rashida Paghdiwala
PYP Coordinator Odaia Ranido
Languages English
T: +65 6914 7100
W: singapore.globalindianschool.org
See full details on page 334

GLOBAL INDIAN INTERNATIONAL SCHOOL (GIIS) SMART CAMPUS
27 Punggol Field Walk, Singapore 828649
DP Coordinator Deepa Chandrasekaran
PYP Coordinator Manju Nair
Languages English
T: +65 6914 7100
W: singapore.globalindianschool.org
See full details on page 334

HWA CHONG INTERNATIONAL SCHOOL
663 Bukit Timah Road, Singapore 269783
DP Coordinator Dr Archana Vijaykumar Kusurkar
Languages English
T: +65 6464 7077
E: admissions@hcis.edu.sg
W: www.hcis.edu.sg
See full details on page 339

HWA International School
6 Raffles Boulevard, Marina Square #02-100/101, Singapore 039594
DP Coordinator Xiaoxia Huang
MYP Coordinator Wenjing Yang
PYP Coordinator Marilyn Lim
Languages English, Chinese
T: +65 6254 0200
W: www.hwa.edu.sg

ISS INTERNATIONAL SCHOOL
21 Preston Road 109355
DP Coordinator Mr. Akbar Hussain
MYP Coordinator Dr. Dharshini Jeremiah
PYP Coordinator Ms. Ariana Rehu
Languages English
T: +65 6475 4188
E: admissions@iss.edu.sg
W: www.iss.edu.sg
See full details on page 340

Madrasah Aljunied Al-Islamiah
30 Victoria Lane, Singapore 198424
DP Coordinator Khalidah Abdullah
Languages English, Malay
T: +65 6391 5970/1
W: www.aljunied.edu.sg

Nexus International School (Singapore)
1 Aljunied Walk, Singapore 387293
DP Coordinator Vicky Holdcroft
PYP Coordinator Paul Rimmer
Languages English
T: +65 6536 6566
W: www.nexus.edu.sg

North London Collegiate School Singapore
130 Depot Road, Singapore 109708
DP Coordinator Emma Graham
MYP Coordinator Alison Dangerfield
Languages English
T: +65 6989 3000
W: nlcssingapore.sg

NPS INTERNATIONAL SCHOOL
11 Hillside Drive, Singapore 548296
DP Coordinator Ms. Smitha Kumar & Ms. Selvia Thomas
Languages English
T: +65 6294 2400
E: register@npsinternational.edu.sg
W: npsinternational.com.sg
See full details on page 362
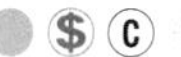

Odyssey The Global Preschool - Fourth Avenue Campus
20 Fourth Avenue, Singapore 268669
PYP Coordinator Melise Wang
Languages English, Chinese
T: +65 6781 8800
W: theodyssey.sg

Odyssey The Global Preschool - Loyang Campus
191 Jalan Loyang Besar, Singapore 506996
PYP Coordinator Nor Faizah
Languages English, Chinese
T: +65 6781 8800
W: theodyssey.sg

Odyssey The Global Preschool - Wilkinson Campus
101 Wilkinson Road, Singapore 436559
PYP Coordinator Vanessa Lee
Languages English, Chinese
T: +65 6781 8800
W: theodyssey.sg

ONE WORLD INTERNATIONAL SCHOOL, NANYANG CAMPUS (OWIS NANYANG)
21 Jurong West Street 81, Singapore 649075
DP Coordinator Sanhita Roy
PYP Coordinator Nur Syahdiqin Ismail
Languages English
T: +65 69146700
E: admissions.sg@owis.org
W: owis.org/sg
See full details on page 364
 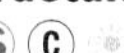

OVERSEAS FAMILY SCHOOL
81 Pasir Ris Heights, Singapore 519292
DP Coordinator Trapti Trivedi
MYP Coordinator Adelaida Blat Palacios
Languages English
T: +65 6 738 0211
E: enquiry@ofs.edu.sg
W: www.ofs.edu.sg
See full details on page 365

School of the Arts, Singapore
1 Zubir Said Drive, Administration Office #05-01, Singapore 227968
CP Coordinator Cheryl Lim
DP Coordinator Ronald Lim
Languages English
T: +65 63389663
W: www.sota.edu.sg

Singapore Sports School
1 Champions Way, Woodlands 737913
DP Coordinator Damien Chiang
Languages English
T: +65 6766 0100
W: www.sportsschool.edu.sg

St Francis Methodist School
492 Upper Bukit Timah Road 678095
DP Coordinator Choon Lee Chong
Languages English
T: +65 6760 0889
W: www.sfms.edu.sg

St. Joseph's Institution
21 Bishan Street 14, Singapore 579781
DP Coordinator Woh Un Tang
Languages English
T: +65 62500022
W: www.sji.edu.sg

ST. JOSEPH'S INSTITUTION INTERNATIONAL
490 Thomson Road, Singapore 298191
DP Coordinator Mr Guy Bromley
Languages English
T: +65 6353 9383
E: info@sji-international.com.sg
W: www.sji-international.com.sg
See full details on page 389

Stamford American International School
1 Woodleigh Lane 357684
DP Coordinator Amit Khanna
MYP Coordinator Rhonda Weins & Natalie Martin
PYP Coordinator Michael Hughes
Languages English
T: +65 6653 2949
W: www.sais.edu.sg

TANGLIN TRUST SCHOOL, SINGAPORE
95 Portsdown Road 139299
DP Coordinator Joseph Loader
Languages English
T: +65 67780771
E: admissions@tts.edu.sg
W: www.tts.edu.sg
See full details on page 394
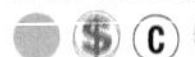

The Little Skool-House International (By-the-Vista)
170 Ghim Moh Road, Ulu Pandan Community Club, #03-01, Singapore 279621
PYP Coordinator Nurazura Binte Mohamed Amran
Languages English
T: +65 6468 3725
W: www.littleskoolhouse.com

UWC South East Asia, Dover Campus
1207 Dover Road 139654
DP Coordinator Andrew McCarthy
Languages English
T: +65 6775 5344
W: www.uwcsea.edu.sg

UWC South East Asia, East Campus
1 Tampines Street 73 528704
DP Coordinator Gemma Elford Dawson
Languages English
T: +65 6305 5344
W: www.uwcsea.edu.sg
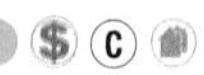

Westbourne College Singapore
491B River Valley Road, No. 16-03 Valley Point, Singapore 248371
DP Coordinator Edmund Ng
Languages English, Chinese
T: +65 6235 1538
W: westbournecollege.com.sg

XCL World Academy
2 Yishun Street 42, Singapore 768039
DP Coordinator Michael Fletcher
MYP Coordinator Rachel Satralkar
PYP Coordinator Lisa George
Languages English
T: +65 6871 8835
W: www.xwa.edu.sg
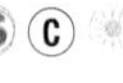

SOLOMON ISLANDS

Woodford International School
Prince Philip Highway, P.O. Box R44, Kukum, Honiara
PYP Coordinator Vivienne Wallace
Languages English
T: +677 30186
W: www.wis.edu.sb

SRI LANKA

THE OVERSEAS SCHOOL OF COLOMBO
P.O. Box 9, Pelawatte, Battaramulla 10120
DP Coordinator Dr. Philip Leigh
MYP Coordinator Jake Eagle
PYP Coordinator Samantha Wood
Languages English
T: +94 11 2 784 920-2
E: admissions@osc.lk
W: www.osc.lk
See full details on page 397

TAIWAN

Dayuan International Senior High School
No. 8, Section 2, Dacheng Road, Dayuan District, Taoyuan 337
DP Coordinator Glen Johnston
Languages English, Chinese
T: +886 3 381 3001
W: www.dysh.tyc.edu.tw

I-Shou International School
No 6, Sec 1, Xuecheng Road, Dashu District, Kaohsiung 840302
DP Coordinator William Tolley
MYP Coordinator Taryn Smith
PYP Coordinator John Osmar
Languages English, Chinese
T: +886 7 657 7115
W: www.iis.kh.edu.tw

Juntou International School
No. 48 Shuitou Road, Puli
PYP Coordinator Pierre-Paul Therrien
Languages English, Chinese
T: +886 4 9242 0272
W: www.jtis.org.tw

Kang Chiao International School, Xiugang Campus
No. 800 Huacheng Road, Xindian District, New Taipei City 231308
DP Coordinator Steven Bates
MYP Coordinator Joseph Sun
Languages Chinese, English
T: +886 2 2216 6000
W: www.kcis.com.tw

Kaohsiung American School
889 Cueihua Road, Zuoying District, Kaohsiung 81354
DP Coordinator Claudia Fidalgo
MYP Coordinator Kolas Yang
Languages English
T: +886 7 586 3300
W: www.kas.tw

Mingdao High School
497 Sec. 1, Zhongshan Road, Wuri District, Taichung 41401
CP Coordinator Kurt Chen
DP Coordinator Alexandra Lopez
MYP Coordinator Feon Chau
Languages English, Chinese
T: +886 4 2337 2101
W: www3.mingdao.edu.tw

Starlight International Kindergarten - Feng Yuan Campus
No. 569, Section 7, Fengyuan Boulevard, Shengang District, Taichung
PYP Coordinator Eric Chang
Languages English, Chinese
T: +886 4 2520 8466
W: www.facebook.com/starlight.fengyuankindergarten

Starlight International Kindergarten - Hui Wen Campus
No. 8, Section 1, Huilai Road, Nantun District, Taichung
PYP Coordinator Yung-I Fu
Languages English, Chinese
T: +886 4 2251 4007
W: www.facebook.com/StarlightHuiWen
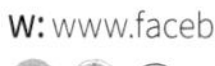

Taichung City Starlight Experimental Education
No. 23 Daguan Road, Nantun District, Taichung 408
MYP Coordinator Shui-Chin (Nina) Chen
PYP Coordinator Isabel Yuan
Languages English, Chinese
T: +886 4 2389 1626

Taipei American School
800 Zhongshan North Road, Section 6, Taipei 11152
DP Coordinator Meagan Frazier
Languages English
T: +886 2 7750 9900
W: www.tas.edu.tw

Taipei European School
Swire European Campus, 31 Jian Ye Road, Yang Ming Shan, Shihlin District, Taipei 11193
CP Coordinator Fabrice Laureti
DP Coordinator Ian Stewart
Languages English
T: +886 2 8145 9007
W: www.tes.tp.edu.tw

IB ASIA-PACIFIC

TAIPEI KUEI SHAN SCHOOL
200 Mingde Road, Taipei 11280
DP Coordinator Steven Hu
MYP Coordinator Robert Chung
PYP Coordinator Elizabeth Hu
Languages Chinese, English
T: +886 2 2821 2009
E: info@kss.tp.edu.tw
W: www.kshs.tp.edu.tw

See full details on page 393

Taipei Municipal Binjiang Experimental Junior High School
No. 262 Lequn 2nd Road, Zhongshan District, Taipei 104353
MYP Coordinator Risa Chen
Languages English, Chinese
T: +886 2 8502 0126
W: www.bjjh.tp.edu.tw

Taipei Municipal Xisong High School
No. 7, Lane 325, Jian Kang Road, Taipei
DP Coordinator Hyeseong Ahn
Languages English, Chinese
T: +886 2 2528 6618
W: www.hssh.tp.edu.tw

Taipei Municipal Zhong Zheng Senior High School
No. 77 Wenlin North Road, Beitou District, Taipei 112046
CP Coordinator Yi-ming Lee
DP Coordinator Tanya Kao
Languages English, Chinese
T: +886 2 2823 4811
W: www.ccsh.tp.edu.tw

  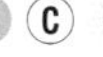

Victoria Academy
1110 Jhen-Nan Road, Douliu, Yun-Lin 640
DP Coordinator Nerissa Puntawe
Languages Chinese, English
T: +886 5 5378 899 (EXT: 2202)
W: www.victoria.ylc.edu.tw

THAILAND

American Pacific International School
158/1 Moo 3, Hangdong-Samoeng Road, Banpong, Hangdong, Chiang Mai 50230
DP Coordinator Alisa Cooper
MYP Coordinator Stefanie Ammirata
PYP Coordinator Erika Vargas
Languages English
T: +66 53 365 303/5
W: www.apis.ac.th

Ascot International School
80/82 Ramkhamhaeng Soi 118, Sapansung, Bangkok 10240
DP Coordinator James Guthrie
PYP Coordinator Nicola Holloway
Languages English
T: +66 2 373 4400
W: www.ascot.ac.th

Bangkok Patana School
643 Lasalle Road (Sukhumvit 105), Bangna Tai, Bangna, Bangkok 10260
DP Coordinator Andrew Roff
Languages English
T: +66 2 785 2200
W: www.patana.ac.th

BRITISH INTERNATIONAL SCHOOL, PHUKET
59 Moo 2, Thepkrasattri Road, T. Koh Kaew, A. Muang, Phuket 83000
DP Coordinator Jason Perkins
Languages English
T: +66 (0) 76 335 555
E: info@bisphuket.ac.th
W: www.bisphuket.ac.th

See full details on page 316

Canadian International School of Thailand
1001 Charan Sanitwong 46, Bangyeekhan, Bang Phlat, Bangkok 10700
MYP Coordinator Nolan Harvey
PYP Coordinator Heather Burtch
Languages English, Thai
T: +66 02 886 9464
W: www.canadianschool.com

Concordian International School
918 Moo 8, Bangna-Trad Highway Km 7, Bangkaew, Bangplee Samutprakarn 10540
DP Coordinator Markus Mattila
MYP Coordinator Rachel Samson
PYP Coordinator Ariel Wang
Languages English
T: +66 2 706 9000
W: www.concordian.ac.th

D-PREP International School
38, 38/1-3, 39, Moo 6, Bangna Trad Rd., Km. 8, Bang Kaeo, Bang Phli District, Samut Prakan 10540
PYP Coordinator Maricar Dorego
Languages English, Thai
T: +66 95 879 4944
W: www.dprep.ac.th

Garden International School (Rayong Campus)
188/24 Moo 4, Pala-Ban Chang Road, Tambol Pala, Ban Chang, Rayong 21130
DP Coordinator Jo Childs
Languages English
T: +66 3803 0808
W: www.gardenrayong.com

Hua Hin International School
549 Moo 7, Hin Lek Fai, Hua Hin, Prachuap Khiri Khan 77110
DP Coordinator David Coulson
Languages English, Thai
T: +66 32 900 632
W: www.huahinschool.com

International School Bangkok
39/7 Soi Nichada Thani, Samakee Road, Pakkret, Nonthaburi 11120
DP Coordinator Justyna McMillan
Languages English
T: +66 2 963 5800
W: www.isb.ac.th

International School Eastern Seaboard
282 Moo 5 T. Bowin, SriRacha, Chonburi 20230
DP Coordinator Richard Kennedy
Languages English
T: +66 38 372 591
W: www.ise.ac.th

KIS International School
999/123-124 Pracha Utit Road, Samsennok, Huay Kwang, Bangkok 10310
CP Coordinator François de Ryckel
DP Coordinator Daniel Trump
MYP Coordinator Alison Ya-Wen Yang
PYP Coordinator Jennifer Jaques
Languages English
T: +66 (0)2 2743444
W: www.kis.ac.th

Magic Years International School
22/122, Moo 3, Soi Prasoet Islam, Bang Talat, Pakkret, Nonthaburri 11120
PYP Coordinator Tahireh Thampi
Languages English
T: +66 2156 6222
W: www.magicyears.ac.th

NIST INTERNATIONAL SCHOOL
36 Sukhumvit Soi 15, Wattana, Bangkok 10110
DP Coordinator Robin Wilensky
MYP Coordinator Stuart Donnelly
PYP Coordinator Bryony Maxted-Miller
Languages English
T: +66 2 017 5888
E: admissions@nist.ac.th
W: www.nist.ac.th

See full details on page 358

Pan-Asia International School
100 Moo 3, Charaemprakiat, Rama 9 St, Soi 67, Kwang Dokmai Prawet District, Bangkok 10250
DP Coordinator Amani Naiem Ahmad Saleh
MYP Coordinator Jacob Conger
Languages English
T: +66 2 726 6273-4
W: www.pais.ac.th

Panyaden International School
218 Moo 2, T.Namprae, A.Hang Dong, Chiang Mai 50230
DP Coordinator Paul Sebastian
Languages English
T: +66 80 078 5115
W: www.panyaden.ac.th

Phuket Thaihua ASEAN Wittaya School
103/5 Wichitsongkram Road, Talad Nuea, Mueang, Phuket 83000
MYP Coordinator Girana Boongoysin
Languages English, Chinese
T: +66 7 652 2567
W: www.phuketthaihua.ac.th

Prem Tinsulanonda International School
234 Moo 3, Huay Sai, Mae Rim, Chiang Mai 50180
CP Coordinator Emma Shaw
DP Coordinator Abbie Neall
MYP Coordinator Luke Ramsdale
PYP Coordinator Mary Ann Van De Weerd
Languages English
T: +66 53 301 500
W: www.ptis.ac.th

REGENTS INTERNATIONAL SCHOOL PATTAYA
33/3 Moo 1, Pong, Banglamung, Chonburi 20150
Languages English
T: +66 (0)93 135 7736
E: admissions@regents-pattaya.co.th
W: regents-pattaya.co.th

See full details on page 373

THAILAND

Roong Aroon International School
391/5 Soi 33 Rama 2 Road (Soi Wat Yai Rom), Bang Khunthien, Bangkok 10150
CP Coordinator Vijay Singh
MYP Coordinator Stacey Jones
Languages English, Thai
T: +66 (0)2 870 7512 3
W: www.roongaroonis.ac.th

RUAMRUDEE INTERNATIONAL SCHOOL
6 Ramkhamhaeng 184, Minburi, Bangkok 10510
DP Coordinator Ms. Nicole Sabet
Languages English
T: +66 (0)2 791 8900
E: admissions@rism.ac.th
W: www.rism.ac.th
See full details on page 375

Satit Bilingual School of Rangsit University
52/347 Muang Ake, Phahonyothin Road., Lak Hok, Mueang, Pathum Thani 12000
PYP Coordinator Babita Seth
Languages English
T: +66 2 792 7500 4
W: bkk.sbs.ac.th

Silver Fern International School
16 Moo 21 Airport Road, Tambon Neua Muang, Amphoe Muang, Roi-Et 45000
PYP Coordinator Grzegorz Slowinski
Languages English
T: +66 994 671 222
W: silverfern.ac.th

Singapore International School of Bangkok
Pracha Utit Campus, 498/11 Soi Ramkhamhaeng 39 (Tepleela 1), Wangthonglang, Bangkok 10310
DP Coordinator Eleora Irene Pua
Languages English, Chinese, Thai
T: +66 2 158 9191
W: www.sisb.ac.th

ST ANDREWS INTERNATIONAL SCHOOL BANGKOK
1020 Sukhumvit Road, Phra Khanong, Khlong Toei, Bangkok 10110
CP Coordinator Ms. Faye Wheeler
DP Coordinator Mr. William Taylor
Languages English
T: +662 056 9555
E: admissions@standrews.ac.th
W: www.standrews.ac.th
See full details on page 387
 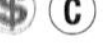

St Andrews International School, Green Valley Campus
Moo 7, Ban Chang-Makham Koo Road, Ban Chang, Rayong 21130
DP Coordinator Andrew Emery
PYP Coordinator Faye Wood
Languages English
T: +66 38 030611
W: www.standrewsgreenvalley.com

St Andrews International School, Sukhumvit Campus
7 Sukhumvit 107 Road, Bangna, Bangkok 10260
CP Coordinator Deepa Patel
DP Coordinator Dave Brundage
Languages English
T: +66 2 393 3883
W: www.standrewssukhumvit.com

The American School of Bangkok - Green Valley Campus
900 Moo 3 Bangna-Trad Road Km. 15 Bangplee, Samutprakarn, Bangkok 10540
DP Coordinator Lester Lin
Languages English
T: +66 (0)2026 3518
W: asbgv.ac.th

The Regent's School, Bangkok
601/99 Pracha-Uthit Road, Wangthonglang, Bangkok 10310
DP Coordinator Alan Perkins
Languages English
T: +66 (0)2 957 5777
W: www.regents.ac.th

Udon Thani International School (UDIS)
222/2 Moo. 2 Mittrapab Road, Tumbonkudsra, Aumpearmuang, Udon Thani 41000
MYP Coordinator Jay Randall
PYP Coordinator Charlotte Trufit
Languages English
T: +66 (0)42 110 379
W: www.udoninternationalschool.com

UWC Thailand International School
115/15 Moo 7 Thepkasattri Road, Thepkasattri, Thalang, Phuket 83110
DP Coordinator Katharine Feather
MYP Coordinator Emma Neuprez
PYP Coordinator Jen Friske
Languages English
T: +66 76 336 076
W: uwcthailand.ac.th

Wells International School - Bang Na Campus
10 Srinakarin Soi 62, Nong Bon, Prawet, Bangkok 10250
PYP Coordinator Sunee Steyn
Languages English, Thai
T: +66 02 746 6060 1
W: www.wells-school.com

Wells International School - On Nut Campus
2209 Sukhumvit Road, Bangchak, Prakanong, Bangkok 10260
DP Coordinator Katherine Caouette
Languages English
T: +66 097 920 8511
W: www.wells-school.com

VIETNAM

American International School of Vietnam
220 Nguyen Van Tao, Nha Be District, Ho Chi Minh City
DP Coordinator Elizabeth Tinnon
MYP Coordinator Emma Burns
PYP Coordinator Karin Tellis
Languages English
T: +84 28378 00808
W: www.ais.edu.vn

AUSTRALIAN INTERNATIONAL SCHOOL (AIS)
264 Mai Chi Tho Street, An Phu ward, Thu Duc City, Ho Chi Minh City
DP Coordinator Anton Luiten
PYP Coordinator Rebecca Evans
Languages English
T: +84 28 3742 4040
E: info@aisvietnam.com
W: www.aisvietnam.com
See full details on page 315

British International School Ho Chi Minh City
246 Nguyen Van Huong Street, Thao Dien, Thu Duc City, Ho Chi Minh City
DP Coordinator Danielle Fountain
Languages English
T: +84 (0)28 3744 2335
W: www.bisvietnam.com

British International School, Hanoi
Hoa Lan Road, Vinhomes Riverside, Long Bien District, Hanoi 100000
DP Coordinator Gemma Archer
Languages English
T: +84 24 3946 0435
W: www.bishanoi.com

Canadian International School - Vietnam
No. 86, Road 23, Phu My Hung, Tan Phu Ward, District 7, Binh Chanh District, Ho Chi Minh City
DP Coordinator Alex Raffle
Languages English
T: +84 94 295 8557
W: www.cis.edu.vn
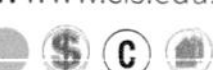

EUROPEAN INTERNATIONAL SCHOOL HCMC
730 Le Van Mien Street, Thao Dien Ward, Thu Duc City, Ho Chi Minh City 70000
DP Coordinator Erin Tacey
MYP Coordinator Kevin Alburo
PYP Coordinator Cristy Neves
Languages English
T: +8428 7300 7257
E: info@eishcmc.com
W: www.eishcmc.com
See full details on page 327

Hanoi International School
48 Lieu Giai Street, Ba Dinh District, Hanoi
DP Coordinator Heather Anne Neill
MYP Coordinator Jeffrey Joseph Araula
PYP Coordinator Lara Johnston
Languages English
T: +84 4 3832 8140
W: www.hisvietnam.com

International German School HCMC
12 Vo Truong Toan, An Phu Ward, District 2, Ho Chi Minh City
DP Coordinator Tim Reisdorf
Languages English, German
T: +84 (0)28 37 44 63 44
W: igs-hcmc.org
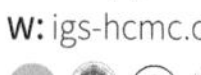

International School Ho Chi Minh City (ISHCMC)
28 Vo Truong Toan St., An Phu ward, Thu Duc City, Ho Chi Minh City
DP Coordinator Ms. Laney Rweyemamu
MYP Coordinator Mr. Simon Scoones
PYP Coordinator Ms. Ishbel How & Mr. Daniel Barker
Languages English
T: +84 28 3898 9100
W: www.ishcmc.com

International School of Vietnam
No. 6-7 Nguyen Cong Thai Street, Dai Kim Urban area, Hoang Mai, Hanoi
DP Coordinator Gita Gemuts
PYP Coordinator Nicola Farrar
Languages English
T: +84 (0)435 409 183
W: www.isvietnam.edu.vn

International School Saigon Pearl
92 Nguyen Huu Canh Street, Ward 22, Binh Thanh District, Ho Chi Minh City
PYP Coordinator Jason Barton
Languages English, Vietnamese
T: +84 282 222 7788
W: www.issp.edu.vn

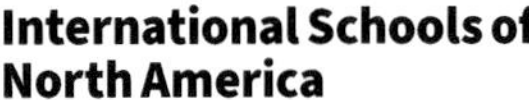

International Schools of North America
Street 20, Him Lam Residential Area, Binh Chanh District, Ho Chi Minh City
DP Coordinator Sergio Jose Chiri Espejo
MYP Coordinator Archana Singh
PYP Coordinator Harvinjitt Kaur
Languages English
T: +84 28 730 197 99
W: sna.edu.vn

QSI INTERNATIONAL SCHOOL OF HAIPHONG
Lot CC2, Me Linh Village, Anh Dung Ward, Duong Kinh District, Haiphong
DP Coordinator Spencer Sammons
Languages English
T: +84 31 381 4258
E: haiphong@qsi.org
W: haiphong.qsi.org
See full details on page 366

Renaissance International School Saigon
74 Nguyen Thi Thap Street, Binh Thuan Ward, District 7, Ho Chi Minh City
DP Coordinator Richard Fluit
Languages English
T: +84 283 7733 171
W: www.renaissance.edu.vn

Saigon South International School
78 Nguyen Duc Canh, Tan Phong Ward, District 7, Ho Chi Minh City 70000
DP Coordinator Tucker Barrows
Languages English
T: +84 28 5413 0901
W: www.ssis.edu.vn

Tesla Education - Tan Binh Campus
171B Hoang Hoa Tham Street, Ward 13, Tan Binh District, Ho Chi Minh City
PYP Coordinator Yen To
Languages English, Vietnamese
T: +84 98 494 8080
W: tesla.edu.vn

The Olympia Schools
Trung Van New urban area, South Tu Liem, Hanoi
DP Coordinator Le Thuy Pham
Languages English, Vietnamese
T: +84 24 6267 7999
W: theolympiaschools.edu.vn

United Nations International School of Hanoi
G9 Ciputra, Tay Ho, Hanoi
DP Coordinator Elliott Cannell
MYP Coordinator Tanay Naik
PYP Coordinator Kay Strenio Anagnost
Languages English
T: +84 24 7300 4500
W: www.unishanoi.org

Vietnam-Finland International School
01, D1 Street, Tan Phong Ward, District 7, Ho Chi Minh City
DP Coordinator Catherine Symes-Matheus
Languages English, Vietnamese
T: +84 28 37 755 110
W: vfis.tdtu.edu.vn
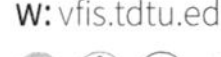

WESTERN AUSTRALIAN PRIMARY AND HIGH SCHOOL
157 Ly Chinh Thang Street, Vo Thi Sau Ward, District 3, Ho Chi Minh City
DP Coordinator Mr. Bao Tran
Languages English
T: +84 28 7109 5077
E: schooloffice@wass.edu.vn
W: www.wass.edu.vn/en
See full details on page 405

Wisdomland Diamond Island
Block Hawaii, Diamond Island, Binh Trung Tay Ward, Thu Duc City, Ho Chi Minh City
PYP Coordinator Editha Agustin
Languages English, Vietnamese
T: +84 28 6287 19 74
W: www.wisdomlandpreschool.com

IB
AMERICAS

Atlanta International School

(Founded 1984)

Head of School
Kevin Glass

PYP coordinator
Leonie Ley-Mitchell

MYP coordinator
Carmen Samanes

DP coordinator
Adam Lapish

Status Private, Non-Profit

Boarding/day Day

Gender Coeducational

Language of instruction
English, Chinese, French, German, Spanish

Authorised IB programmes
PYP, MYP, DP

Age Range 3 – 18 years

Number of pupils enrolled
1330

Address
2890 North Fulton Drive
Atlanta
GA 30305 | USA

TEL +1 404 841 3840

Email
admission@aischool.org

Website
www.aischool.org

Atlanta International School. Developing Courageous Leaders Who Shape Their World For The Better

Founded over thirty years ago by people who wanted a different sort of school in Atlanta, Atlanta International School offers a comprehensive and challenging International Baccalaureate (IB) curriculum from 3K to Grade 12, enhanced with a world-class language acquisition program.

At Atlanta International School (AIS) students are focused on developing the skills to creatively collaborate on the challenges of the future and are equipped to become changemakers.

Offering an authentic, nurturing, learning community, AIS values curiosity, empathy and a passion to create a world with environmental, economic and social well-being for everyone.

Faculty from around the world are focused on genuinely getting to know, value and nurture each and every student, and his or her unique skills and strengths. The result is a spirit of community and a celebration of the diversity of perspectives that come from students, families, faculty and staff representing 90 nationalities and over 65 languages.

A full immersion preschool program for children ages three and four is offered in German, French, Chinese and Spanish. From 5K through Grade 5, the inquiry-based IB curriculum is taught in two languages. All faculty are mother tongue speakers of the language they teach.

Students not only learn at least one other language, they learn through language, developing so much more than linguistic proficiency. At AIS students are taught to develop 'intercultural competence', the ability to easily navigate and flow between and among different nationalities and complex cultural situations – and to do so with tremendous empathy, diplomacy and tact.

Students entering Secondary School have varied language backgrounds and a wide range of options to develop their language proficiency, from beginner to taking both Language & Literature and Humanities courses at an advanced level, many choosing to pursue dual language IB Diplomas.

The curriculum is complemented by an extensive range of age-appropriate activities to enhance students' learning experiences beyond the classroom.

The athletics department is home to more than 40 teams pursuing 12 different sports. Theatrical and musical talent is showcased via regular performances alongside frequent art exhibitions.

In Secondary School, in addition to internships that students complete as part of a STEM or STEAM Diploma Endorsement, students participate in many other activities including service projects, Model United Nations, Mock Trial, the AIS Space Program, Robotics and educational international trips.

Parents, alumni, faculty, staff and students actively participate in the growth and sustainability of the school, with community firmly at the centre of all activities. The result is a pioneering and courageous spirit built upon local impact and global reach.

Blue Valley School

An **inspired** school

(Founded 1989)

General Director
Kathryn Scanlan

DP coordinator
Gisele Cordero

Status Private

Boarding/day Day

Gender Coeducational

Language of instruction
English, Spanish

Authorised IB programmes
DP

Age Range 3 – 18 years

Number of pupils enrolled
806

Address
From Multiplaza,
1.2 Km. northwest
right hand side of the road,
Guachipelín,
Escazú
San José | **COSTA RICA**

TEL +506 2215 2204

Email
admissions@bluevalley.ed.cr

Website
www.bluevalley.ed.cr

School, Community and Students

Founded in 1989, BVS is a private, co-educational, bilingual Pre-K to 12th grade school which offers a challenging integrated curriculum of Costa Rican and International curricula. Student Nationalities: 68% are Costa Rican and 32% are international. While English is the language of instruction for the majority of the curriculum, Spanish is the social language and our students switch effortlessly between the two.

In 2018, Blue Valley joined INSPIRED, a leading global premium schools group educating over 80,000 students across an international network of over 100 schools on 5 continents. All the Inspired schools are individually developed and designed in response to their environment and location, delivering an excellent education to their respective communities.

Definition of Learning

Learning at BVS encourages curiosity. Students have opportunities to actively engage in learning through choice, hands-on activities and reflection. Learners demonstrate mastery by linking concepts and knowledge to real-world applications. Students take pride in becoming inquisitive, well-rounded, conscious citizens of the world.

Vision

Become the school of choice for parents who expect and appreciate an excellent bilingual, holistic education for their children.

Mission

To offer cutting-edge academic preparation and ensure that our students become individuals guided by a strong moral compass. A proper balance between the Humanities and the Sciences will support our academic goals, guided by the principle of "a sound mind in a sound body." Blue Valley School models and teaches students to become architects of their destiny, wise decision makers, prudent risk takers, and active participants in local and global communities, safeguarding individual and collective rights and responsibilities inherent to a free society.

Headmaster
Mr Ben Holman

DP coordinator
Adrian Everitt

Status Private

Boarding/day Day

Gender Coeducational

Language of instruction
English, Spanish

Authorised IB programmes
DP

Age Range 2 – 18 years

Number of pupils enrolled
1108

Fees
Entry Fee:
US$16,000
Reception to V Form:
PEN 3,016 per month
IB Diploma (VI Form):
PEN 3,798 per month

Address
Av. Alameda de los Molinos
728-730
La Encantada de Villa, Chorrillos
Lima 15067 | **PERU**

TEL +51 12 540107

Email
office@cambridge.edu.pe

Website
cambridge.edu.pe

Located in La Encantada de Villa, far from the noise and pollution of the city, our school occupies a privileged position in a protected environment, offering ample green spaces for sports and outdoor activities.

Cambridge College offers a balanced approach to education, placing value not only on an internationally recognised education of academic excellence but also on achievements in sports and the arts. Additionally, we take pride in nurturing individuals who are attuned to matters of social responsibility and the environment.

The educational philosophy, which is shared by the Inspired group of schools and has been pursued by Cambridge College Lima since its inception, is grounded in a commitment to excellence that permeates every facet of the school. This commitment is reflected in our integration of innovative, challenging, and enriching academic, performing arts, and sports programmes-the three pillars of an Inspired education.

Since 2017, we have been part of Inspired, a leading global group of premium schools dedicated to delivering educational excellence to more than 80,000 students ranging from infants to 18 years of age. With a network of over 111 schools across 25 countries spanning five continents, Inspired draws upon the best practices and methodologies from around the world, ensuring a world-class education.

(Founded 1995)

Head of School
Eleonor Prescott

PYP coordinator
Sandra Nicoli

MYP coordinator
Paloma Krüger

DP coordinator
Yolanda Meneses

Status Private

Boarding/day Day

Gender Coeducational

Language of instruction
Spanish, English

Authorised IB programmes
PYP, MYP, DP

Age Range 2 – 18 years

Number of pupils enrolled
900

Fees
Day: Monthly fee from S/15,880 to 30,290 per annum.

Address
Av. La Arboleda 385
Urb. Sirius, La Molina
Lima 15024 | **PERU**

TEL +51 13 650298

Email
admision@altair.pe

Website
www.altair.edu.pe

Colegio Altair, one of the leading international schools located in Lima, Peru, is proud to offer a modern and sophisticated curriculum that prepares students for a demanding and ever-changing world. As one of only six private schools in Peru with three of the four International Baccalaureate programmes, we are committed to providing our students with a comprehensive and holistic education.

Colegio Altair is recognised for its holistic and humanistic educational model, where the student is at the centre of everything we do. We believe in nurturing each student's individual talents, interests, and aspirations, enabling them to reach their full potential. Our dedicated faculty and staff are passionate about creating a supportive and inclusive learning environment that fosters intellectual growth, personal development, and character building. We respect and value the individuality of our students. Our dedicated faculty and staff are passionate about fostering a sense of belonging and providing personalised attention to each student. We believe that by recognising and embracing their uniqueness, we can inspire them to become confident, compassionate, and well-rounded.

Since 2017, Colegio Altair has been a proud member of the Inspired group, a global educational network comprising more than 111 schools worldwide. This affiliation with Inspired not only grants us access to global experts in education, wellness, and safety but also enhances our commitment to excellence.

At Altair, we believe in the power of experiential learning, which allows our students to gain valuable life experiences beyond the classroom. Colegio Altair is a distinguished institution that offers arts, sports, and academic excellence as the three pillars of a first-rate education. Our commitment to personalised education, along with our membership in the Inspired group, ensures that our students receive a complete and exceptional educational experience.

Cultural Arts Academy Charter School at Spring Creek

Founding Principal/Head of School
Dr Laurie B. Midgette

PYP coordinator
Esther Hong

Status State

Boarding/day Day

Gender Coeducational

Language of instruction
English, Spanish

Authorised IB programmes
PYP

Age Range 5 – 10 years

Number of pupils enrolled
280

Address
1400 Linden Blvd
Brooklyn
NY 11212 | USA

TEL +1 718 683 3300

Email
caacs@caa-ny.org

Website
www.culturalartsacademy.org

Cultural Arts Academy Charter School offers a dynamic elementary education of both the mind and heart, focusing on developing the whole child. Our mission is to provide a college preparatory education, with exemplary cultural arts proficiency, to young leaders who will profoundly impact the human condition.

Established over twelve years ago, CAACS boasts two global recognitions; The prestigious Franklin Covey Lighthouse School designation, attained in 2017, and authorization as an International Baccalaureate (IB) World School, attained in 2019. Through these two designations, CAACS operates one synergistic learning model, rooting in student-lead learning and leadership.

Our goal is to fully prepare our scholars for college, career, and citizenship, starting with instilling the foundational principles of open-mindedness, problem-solving, strong character, and intrinsic motivation. Establishing 21st century skills through project-based learning across all grade levels equips our scholars with the necessary tools for success.

At the core of our school, of course, is culture and the arts. All scholars, from Kindergarten through 5th grade, receive extensive education through the arts, including Dance, Drama, Music, and the Visual Arts. Learning through multiple forms of expression provides our scholars with a deep appreciation and passion for the arts across time periods and cultures, as well as an ownership of self-expression.

True evidence of student learning, mastery, and success comes not only from their research-backed presentations, artistic performances, and creative projects, but through their ability to identify problems within the world around them and construct reasonable and effective solutions. Recently, the strength of their character is seen in the resiliency they exhibit amongst all the changes happening within their school and home life, given the nature of the state of the world. This has been the value of the International Baccalaureate Primary Years Programme for our students. CAACS is proud of the self-motivation and agency our students have developed and exercised in their own learning experiences.

In June of 2024 our 5th grade students will graduate as open-minded and principled thinkers, ready for the next level in their educational journey and beyond.

(Founded 1872)

Chancellor
Stephen H. Spahn

Vice Chancellor
Blake Spahn

Head of School
Dianne Drew

PYP coordinator
Alex White

MYP coordinator
Beth Billard

DP coordinator
Mike Paul

Status Private

Boarding/day Day

Gender Coeducational

Language of instruction
English

Authorised IB programmes
PYP, MYP, DP

Age Range 2 – 18 years

Number of pupils enrolled
946

Fees
Kindergarten
US$57,860 per annum
Grades 1-12
US$60,185 per annum

Address
291 Central Park West
New York
NY 10024 | USA

TEL +1 212 724 6360

Email
admissions@dwight.edu

Website
dwight.edu/newyork

Founded in 1872, Dwight School is an internationally renowned college preparatory school with a rich tradition of academic excellence and igniting the "spark of genius" in every child. Dwight's exceptional education rests on three pillars: personalized learning, community, and global vision. The School's diverse faculty and student body represent over 55 countries, deepening the internationally minded, innovative learning environment.

A leader in global education, Dwight is the first school in the Americas to offer the comprehensive International Baccalaureate (IB) curriculum for students from preschool through grade 12. It is also the first school in New York City to offer the PYP. The rigorous IB is recognized as the "gold standard" in pre-university preparation. Through the IB, Dwight is educating students to become caring, open-minded and critical-thinking global leaders. Foreign language instruction is extensive and begins in preschool.

Through Spark Tank, Dwight's unique incubator designed to nurture innovation, entrepreneurship, and leadership skills beyond the classroom, K-12 students develop their own ideas for new businesses, non-profits, and products.

Dwight School in New York is the flagship campus of a global network, which includes schools in London, Seoul, Shanghai, Dubai, and (starting in 2024) Hanoi. Dwight Global Online School – a campus in the cloud ranked the #2 best online high school in the U.S. – extends a world-class Dwight education everywhere. Dwight students benefit from a wide range of exciting cross-campus academic, leadership, and creative collaborations.

Dwight School has a comprehensive college guidance program beginning early in grade 9. Graduates attend the finest colleges and universities in the world, including Harvard, Yale, Princeton, MIT, Stanford, Oxford, St. Andrew's, and the University of Edinburgh, among many others. Upon graduation, they join an extensive global network of alumni leaders – all dedicated to making our world a better place.

Dwight is accredited by the Council of International Schools, the International Baccalaureate, the Middle States Association of Colleges and Secondary Schools, and the World Academy of Sport. Financial aid is granted on the basis of need.

Edgewood High School

Principal
Kimberly Cabrera Ed.D

MYP coordinator
Manny Co

DP coordinator
Veronica Perez

CP coordinator
Veronica Perez

Status State

Boarding/day Day

Gender Coeducational

Language of instruction
English

Authorised IB programmes
MYP, DP, CP

Age Range 14 – 18 years

Number of pupils enrolled 792

Address
1625 W Durness
West Covina
CA 91790 | USA

TEL +1 626 939 4600

Email
vperez@wcusd.org

Website
edgewoodib.wcusd.org

Edgewood High School is a public high school located in the city of West Covina, 19 miles east of Los Angeles. Edgewood is an International Baccalaureate World School authorized to offer the Middle Years Programme, Diploma Programme, and Career-related Programme. Edgewood serves a diverse population of 792 students. Edgewood reopened as a high school in 2010 with our first graduation class in May of 2014. In addition to being an IB World School since 2011, Edgewood has been accredited by the Western Association of Schools and Colleges.

Edgewood offers a smaller learning community focused on preparing creative, inquiring, and caring students prepared for college and career. This can be seen in our Mission Statement, *"Edgewood, an IB World School, is committed to building a globally aware community of lifelong learners who achieve high academic standards. Edgewood provides a diverse, challenging curriculum that is student-centered and develops inquisitive, knowledgeable, and empathetic students who actively engage in and contribute to their family, community, and the world around them."*

Edgewood offers a variety of courses to meet our diverse student needs. The curriculum includes: honors courses in 9th and 10th grade, both standard level and higher level IB courses, a world language program, a fine arts department offering visual arts, music, and drama, a health and physical education program, career and technical education pathways in athletic training, game design, public safety, performance dance, CISCO, and video production, and support services for special education and English learner students. Students at Edgewood learn in state of the art facilities including a new Event Center. The Event Center features a 350-seat auditorium and freestanding seats and houses the IB Career Programme courses in Game Design and Video Production.

Students at Edgewood are also provided personal and social development opportunities created by participation in extracurricular activities such as ASB, clubs, yearbook, dances, study trips, performances, cheer, athletics, and service opportunities. Edgewood offers CIF sports in cross country, baseball, softball, tennis, basketball, volleyball, water polo, soccer, wrestling, track, and swim. The new Edgewood Sports Complex features an Olympic-size swimming pool, updated locker rooms, two digital scoreboards capable of video playback, a high-quality sound system, and updated basketball courts.

Edgewood Middle School

Principal
Kimberly Cabrera Ed.D

MYP coordinator
Manny Co

Status State

Boarding/day Day

Gender Coeducational

Language of instruction
English, Spanish

Authorised IB programmes
MYP

Age Range 11 – 14 years

Number of pupils enrolled 595

Address
1625 W. Durness St.
West Covina
CA 91790 | USA

TEL +1 626 939 4600

Email
kcabrera@wcusd.org

Website
edgewoodib.wcusd.org

Edgewood, an International Baccalaureate World School, is committed to building a globally-aware community of lifelong learners who achieve high academic standards.

Edgewood provides a diverse, challenging curriculum that is student-centered and develops inquisitive, knowledgeable, and empathetic students who actively engage in and contribute to their family, community, and the world around them.

Edgewood Middle School is a public school located in the city of West Covina, 19 miles east of Los Angeles. Edgewood received the IB Middle Years Programme authorization in December 2018 and is authorized to offer the International Baccalaureate Middle Years Programme. Edgewood is a school of choice serving a diverse population of 595 students in grades 6-8. Edgewood provides a smaller learning community focused on preparing creative, inquiring, and caring students. Edgewood IB students are ready to make connections between subjects studied and the real world as well as develop critical and reflective thinking skills.

EMS offers a variety of courses to meet our diverse student needs. The curriculum includes: honors courses in 7th and 8th grade, a Dual Language program, a world language program offering both Mandarin and Spanish, a fine arts department offering visual arts, music, theater, a health and physical education program, dance, yearbook, and services for special education and English learner students.

Edgewood Middle School offers outstanding student support through committed, compassionate teachers that provide multi-tiered systems of interventions and enrichment opportunities. Edgewood students are holistically taught in diverse learning environments that prepare students for a global workplace. Partnerships with community, local agencies, and organizations provide opportunities for students to participate in activities for service. Students at Edgewood get to learn in our modern, newly constructed state-of-the-art Event Center. The Event Center features a multi-purpose auditorium with a 350-seat capacity, and houses the IB Career Programme courses in Game Design, Athletic Training, Performance and professional Dance, and Video Production. The new Edgewood Sports Complex features an Olympic-size swimming pool, updated locker rooms, two digital scoreboards capable of video playback, a high-quality sound system, and updated basketball courts. Students at EMS are provided personal and social development opportunities created by participation in extracurricular activities such as WEB, 40+ clubs, dances, performances, cheer and athletics. Edgewood offers sports in track and field, flag football, tennis, softball, basketball, volleyball, and soccer.

(Founded 1937)

Head of School
Dr. Nigel J. Winnard

Gávea Campus Principals
Ms. Doreen Garrigan (Lower) & Mr. Steve Spanning (Upper)

Barra Campus Principals
Ms. Kirstin White (Lower) & Mr. Scott Little (Upper)

PYP coordinator
Ms. Anna Cottrell (Barra) & Ms. Susan Loafmann (Gávea)

MYP coordinator
Ms. Mary-Jo Rawleigh (Barra) & Ms. Teresa Araújo (Gávea)

DP coordinator
Ms. Flavia DiLuccio (Gávea) & Mr. Gregory Sipp (Barra)

Status Private

Boarding/day Day

Gender Coeducational

Language of instruction
English

Authorised IB programmes
PYP, MYP, DP

Age Range 3 – 18 years

Number of pupils enrolled
1300

Gávea Campus
Estrada da Gávea 132
Gávea@data:
Rio de Janeiro
RJ 22451-263 | BRAZIL

TEL +55 21 2125 9000

Email
admissions.gavea@earj.com.br

Barra Campus
Rua Colbert Coelho 155,
Barra da Tijuca,
Rio de Janeiro
RJ 22793-313 | BRAZIL

TEL +55 21 3747 2000

Email
admissions.barra@earj.com.br

Website
www.earj.com.br

EARJ – Escola Americana do Rio de Janeiro is one of the America's most respected international teaching institutions. Established in 1937, and an IB World School since 1982, EARJ is a non-profit school, providing an American international education to the expatriate and Brazilian communities of Rio de Janeiro. It blends a rigorous academic program with rich co-curricular opportunities.

EARJ occupies two campuses in different parts of the city, each offering programs from Preschool to the IB Diploma. EARJ is distinctive in that its 1,300 students can work towards graduating with three Diplomas concurrently: the IB Diploma, the US High School Diploma, and the Brazilian Diploma. Every year, EARJ graduates are accepted to the world's leading universities, and we pride ourselves on each student finding the institution that is best for them. Whilst a few graduates remain to study in Brazil, the vast majority head abroad to the USA, Canada and Europe for university.

EARJ is proud to offer a holistic education that, through the philosophy and practices of the IB, inspires creativity, critical thinking, collaboration, communication, and the confidence to lead and excel in an ever-changing global community.

Since 1982, EARJ has offered the International Baccalaureate® (IB) Diploma Programme, in addition to American and Brazilian diplomas, contributing to making our institution one of the most respected international educational institutions in Latin America.

More recently, we've reached a fantastic new milestone in our school's history – EARJ has been awarded PYP School and MYP School status. This means that we can offer the Primary Years Programme and the Middle Years Programme, as a Full IB Continuum School.

EARJ is a diverse international community of learners. Across our two campuses, our student body comprises 77% Brazilian and 23% International students. Our faculty demographic is composed of 39% international and 61% national. The past years have seen tremendous growth in our enrollment, with further growth expected in the coming years. Our community is spread far and wide, via our Panther Alumni network, who keeps us connected to our past as we work towards an even brighter future.

Escola Canadense de Brasilia

ESCOLA
CANADENSE
DE BRASÍLIA
we love • we care • we share

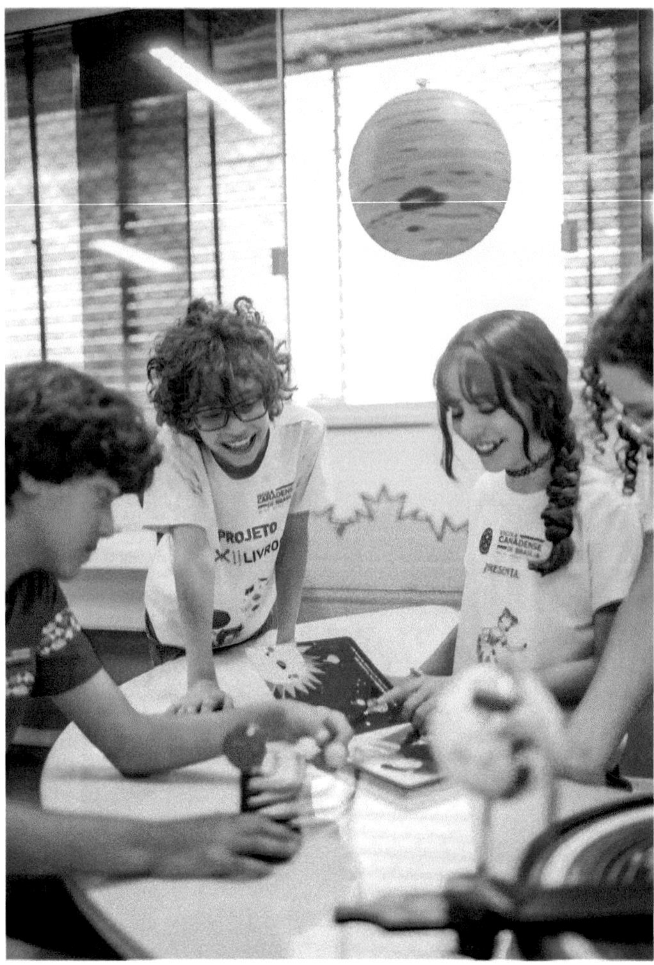

(Founded 2005)

Headmaster
André Sobreira

PYP coordinator
Amanda Salles

Status Private

Boarding/day Mixed

Gender Coeducational

Language of instruction
English, Portuguese

Authorised IB programmes
PYP

Age Range 2 – 18 years

Sudoeste Campus
SIG Quadra 8,
Lote 2225,
Parte F
Brasília
DF 70610-480 | BRAZIL

TEL +55 61 3961 4350

Águas Claras Campus
QS 05 Av. Areal,
Lote 04,
Águas Claras
DF 71955-000 | BRAZIL

TEL +55 61 3247 1130

Website
www.escolacanadensedebrasilia.com.br

The Canadian School of Brasilia is a Brazilian bilingual school (Portuguese/English) that has two campuses in the Brazilian capital city, Brasília, Sudoeste campus and Águas Claras campus. Our mission is to encourage active learning, with a strong focus on individual and group needs and development. Our main curricular focus is in respect to the Brazilian curriculum aligned with the best educational practices. We foster a culture of collaborative learning, empathy and respect of individual differences, while aiming to develop global values and the full academic potential of each student that we are supporting and making them better global citizens.

We are aligned with strong Canadian educational teaching practices. Our dedicated educational staff embeds these practices in their teaching. These practices focus on hands-on experiences as well as the importance of group interaction which supports and develops the academic, social and emotional strengths of the student. The Canadian School of Brasilia is committed to offer a holistic educational approach.

We are an IB PYP programme authorized school, and in High School we work in partnership with Columbia International College for a dual degree program.

We are a bilingual school, Portuguese/English, and we believe that solid language skills are the basis for educational achievement. As part of our co-curricular offering and, according to the age of the student, we provide music, drama, arts, advanced Math, Spanish language, concert band, among others interactive clubs.

Established in 2005, the school has grown significantly over time. In 2022 we started our High School program at Sudoeste Campus.

Extracurricular activities

At both campuses, students have the opportunity to join in a wide range of extracurricular activities. These include soccer, ballet, jazz dance, judo, musical theater, music (violin, guitar, choir), cooking, chess, robotics, basketball, and French language. All of these opportunities continue to foster the development of the whole child which supports the respect, cooperation and positive interaction of students in a non academic environment.

As our school motto exemplifies: *We Love, We Care, We Share*

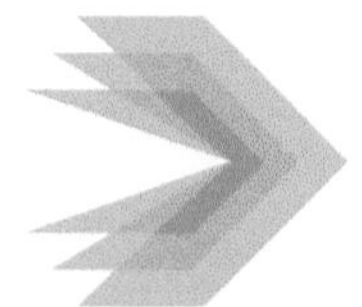

ESCOLA **Eleva**

BARRA DA TIJUCA

Principal
Maíra Timbó

DP coordinator
Barbara Furtado

Status Private

Boarding/day Day

Gender Coeducational

Language of instruction
English, Portuguese

Authorised IB programmes
DP

Age Range 2 – 18 years

Number of pupils enrolled
1200

Address
Av. José Silva de Azevedo Neto
309, Barra da Tijuca
Rio de Janeiro
RJ 22775-056 | BRAZIL

TEL +55 21 3094 5020

Email
admissoes@escolaeleva.com.br

Website
www.escolaeleva.com.br

Escola Eleva is a Brazilian bilingual school that has six campuses in Brazil. Three of those are in Rio de Janeiro: one in Barra da Tijuca, a second one in Botafogo and a third one in Urca. It also has campuses in Recife, in the Northeast of Brazil, in Brasília, our capital city, and is opening the sixth school unit in São Paulo, Brazil's major city both for business and finance, in 2024. Across all sites, Escola Eleva students attend a nurturing school committed to academic excellence and are proud to celebrate the diversity of Brazilian culture. Our mission is to form a new generation of leaders capable of making a difference in their lives and contributing to a better world.

Located in Av José Silva de Azevedo Neto, in front of the Peninsula Condominium, with an area of 16,000m2, Escola Eleva Barra da Tijuca was intentionally built to stimulate creativity and the pleasure of learning, following the world's trends in education. The sports areas are made up of 3 sports courts, an AstroTurf soccer field, an athletics track, and a 640m2 covered gymnasium. Among the internal learning spaces, you can find a Maker Space with a Media Lab, a Dance Studio, a matted Martial Arts Studio, 2 libraries, Visual Arts Studios, Physics, Chemistry and Biology labs, and an auditorium. In addition, the site has an exclusive space for Early Childhood Education, with more than 800m2 of parks, terraced classrooms, a Reggio-Inspired Atelier, and a music class.

We educate students aged 2 to 19 offering a bilingual academic environment that enables our learners to exceed their goals and to become successful, well-rounded individuals, while positively contributing to a better world.

Our highly qualified educators are dedicated to each and every child, ensuring they receive the best possible opportunities to achieve their full potential, while at school and beyond graduation. Internationally-recognized IB-accredited qualifications, exciting extracurricular activities, and a unique socio-emotional programme place our children in a prime position to thrive.

Students learn in cutting-edge facilities and access resources that offer outstanding modern technology to support STEAM, Sports, Humanities, and Arts classes. Additionally, each learner receives excellent pastoral care and advice from specialist University Counsellors over an extended period, aiming to provide the support they need to proceed to the best universities and opportunities in the world.

Today the IB curriculum is available on the Urca and Barra campuses, as these are the school sites that currently offer High School education.

Since May 2022, Escola Eleva has been proud to be part of the Inspired Education Group, the leading global group of premium schools. We have since been adapting our curriculum and activities to achieve even higher standards, bringing Inspired's best practices and experience from more than 100 schools in over 20 countries to our grounds.

ESCOLA **Eleva**

URCA

Principal
Fabiano Franklin

T&L Coordinator
Renato Coimbra Frias

DP coordinator
Fabiano Franklin

Status Private

Boarding/day Day

Gender Coeducational

Language of instruction
English, Portuguese

Authorised IB programmes
DP

Age Range 14 – 18 years

Number of pupils enrolled 241

Address
Alameda Floriano Peixoto 13
Urca
Rio de Janeiro
RJ 22291-090 | BRAZIL

TEL +55 21 3528 4370

Email
admissoes.urca@escolaeleva.com.br

Website
www.escolaeleva.com.br

Escola Eleva is a Brazilian bilingual school that has six campuses in Brazil. Three of those are in Rio de Janeiro: one in Barra da Tijuca, a second one in Botafogo and a third one in Urca. It also has campuses in Recife, in the Northeast of Brazil, in Brasília, our capital city, and is opening the sixth school unit in São Paulo, Brazil's major city both for business and finance, in 2024. Across all sites, Escola Eleva students attend a nurturing school committed to academic excellence and are proud to celebrate the diversity of Brazilian culture. Our mission is to form a new generation of leaders capable of making a difference in their lives and contributing to a better world.

Currently Escola Eleva offers the IB Diploma for high school students at two campuses, Urca and Barra da Tijuca, both in Rio de Janeiro.

Eleva Urca School is located at a traditional address in the city of Rio de Janeiro, on Urca beach, in a century-old historic building that we are proud to preserve and occupy. Our spaces encourage creativity, autonomy and constant exchange between students, staff, and other members of our community.

The building housed the Urca Casino in the 1930s and was later the headquarters of TV Tupi until the 1980s.In 2006 the building was occupied by the European Institute of Design (IED), which carried out a partial restoration of the building for the installation of the institute, which opened in 2014. After seven years of operation, the IED gave way to the Eleva School, which, with a complete restoration, returned the building to its former glory. To transform the site into the Eleva School, we balanced tradition and innovation: we kept the architectural details, the beauty and grandeur of the building, giving it the innovative characteristics of our way of educating. The internal learning spaces include an Innovation Lab, two Visual Arts rooms, a library, drama room, music room and the iconic theatre.

Escola Eleva Urca is a campus exclusive for high school students, offering a bilingual academic environment that enables our learners to exceed their goals and to become successful, well-rounded individuals, while positively contributing to a better world.

In high school, our focus is on consolidating student autonomy and protagonism, balanced with academic rigor. We work on ethical training and intellectual curiosity, preparing students for admission to universities in Brazil and abroad. We provide support and encouragement, self-knowledge, organization, perspectives and the ability to choose.

Our teaching staff is made up of a team dedicated both to the national curriculum – with exclusive preparation for the country's main entrance exams – and for students who wants to study the international curriculum (Full DP).

Since May 2022, Eleva is proud to be part of the Inspired Education Group, the leading global group of premium schools. We have since been adapting our curriculum and activities to achieve even higher standards, bringing Inspired's best practices and experience from more than 80 schools in over 20 countries.

Foxcroft Academy

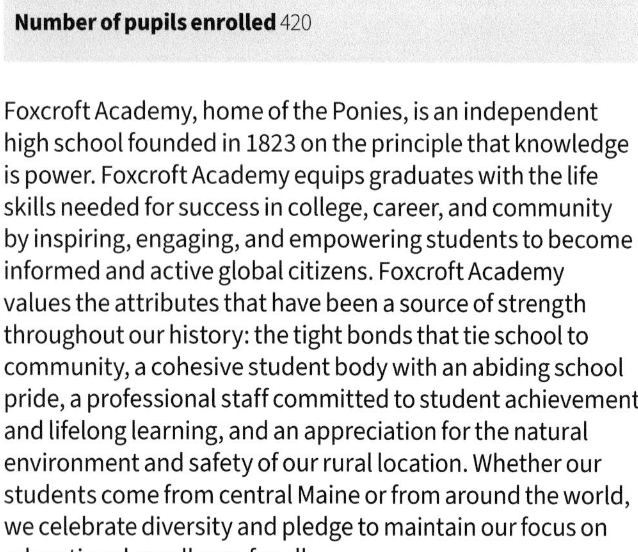

Head of School
Mr. Arnold Shorey

Director of Admissions
Mr. Jason Tardy

DP coordinator
Brian Krause

Status Private

Boarding/day Mixed

Gender Coeducational

Language of instruction
English

Authorised IB programmes
DP

Age Range 14 – 18 years

Number of pupils enrolled 420

Address
975 West Main Street
Dover-Foxcroft
ME 04426 | USA

TEL +1 207 564 8351

Email
admissions@foxcroftacademy.org

Website
www.foxcroftacademy.org

Foxcroft Academy, home of the Ponies, is an independent high school founded in 1823 on the principle that knowledge is power. Foxcroft Academy equips graduates with the life skills needed for success in college, career, and community by inspiring, engaging, and empowering students to become informed and active global citizens. Foxcroft Academy values the attributes that have been a source of strength throughout our history: the tight bonds that tie school to community, a cohesive student body with an abiding school pride, a professional staff committed to student achievement and lifelong learning, and an appreciation for the natural environment and safety of our rural location. Whether our students come from central Maine or from around the world, we celebrate diversity and pledge to maintain our focus on educational excellence for all.

As we celebrate our bicentennial (1823-2023), Foxcroft Academy exists as one of only nine remaining private academies (from an original 122) that serve the public trust as part of its mission. Today, Foxcroft Academy is proud to have an enrollment of more than 400 day and boarding students from 16 Maine communities and over 20 different nations. Students at Foxcroft Academy can choose from more than 150 different course offerings, including college preparatory, Advanced Placement (AP), International Baccalaureate (IB), and more. This extensive curriculum represents the core liberal arts requirements, college preparatory courses, advanced placement courses, vocational/technical courses, and an alternative education program.

Your success as a student is paramount to our mission and vision as an independent school. In addition to inside-the-classroom learning, Foxcroft Academy has plenty of co-curricular activities that you can be a part of. We offer over 20 interscholastic varsity sports playing under the auspices of the Maine Principals Association consisting of sports such as football, field hockey, soccer (boys & girls), golf, cross-country, basketball (boys & girls), wrestling, track & field, baseball, softball, and more. We have dozens of clubs and organizations for students to work with and belong to, such as Key Club, Spanish Club, National Honor Society, Latin Club, Student Council, and so much more!

Foxcroft Academy has a 125-acre campus consisting of a main academic building, gymnasium, an art center, an industrial technology building, several athletic fields (football field with track, soccer, field hockey, baseball, and softball), two weight//fitness rooms, a full-size indoor field house, and an indoor ice arena, all within walking distance of the dormitories. We also have access to an indoor pool at the local YMCA. All of our facilities are well-maintained, and our students have access to them multiple times a week.

Being a boarding student at Foxcroft Academy means you have access to a world-class curriculum, a wide variety of offerings, and a caring and supportive faculty and staff, all in the safe environment Northern New England offers.

Learn more about Foxcroft Academy at www.foxcroftacademy.org. Together, we will ride on.

French-American School of New York

(Founded 1980)

Head of School
Mr. Francis Gianni

DP coordinator
Fred Ondiko

Status Private

Boarding/day Day

Gender Coeducational

Language of instruction
English, French

Authorised IB programmes
DP

Age Range 3 – 18 years

Number of pupils enrolled 750

Fees
Tuition US$34,290 –
US$40,640 per annum

Address
320 East Boston Post Road
Mamaroneck
NY 10543 | USA

TEL +1 914 250 0000

Email
admissions@fasny.org

Website
www.fasny.org

The French-American School of New York (FASNY) is an international and bilingual independent coeducational day school providing an international education to approximately 750 students in Nursery through Grade 12. FASNY develops globally literate, multicultural lifelong learners through a unique program that integrates French, American, and international curricula.

A unique location

FASNY is located in Westchester County, New York, 20 miles north of Manhattan (35 minutes from Grand Central Station by rail) and 9 miles south of Greenwich, Connecticut. Most families choose to enjoy the space and quiet that this peaceful yet active area has to offer with a convenient commute to Manhattan.

Stellar academics

FASNY is the only school in the New York metropolitan area to be accredited by the International Baccalaureate Organisation and by the French Ministry of Education (AEFE). They are also accredited by the New York State Association of Independent Schools. Students enjoy the unique privilege of graduating with either the IBDP or the French Baccalaureate (with or without the International Option) and a New York State High School Diploma.

The school offers a bilingual immersion program in Nursery through Kindergarten, bringing children of all cultural and linguistic backgrounds to academic fluency in French and English. In grades 1 through 8, students have the option to continue with the French-American Track or a new International Track. New in 2020, FASNY offers a predominantly English speaking curriculum for students in grades 1 through 8. With little to no french required, students study roughly 70% of their subjects in English, with the remaining 30% in French, at the individual level and pace of each child's language skills. This lower and middle school International Track naturally leads students to our current 9-12 international curriculum, creating a cohesive 1-12 learning environment.

Each year FASNY sends students to top colleges and universities. Our acceptance list includes: Columbia, Harvard, MIT, Princeton, Stanford, and Yale in the United States, and Cambridge, Imperial College, LSE, Oxford, and UCL in the United Kingdom. Many students also choose to study in Canada, France, and other fine European institutions.

A vast array of co-curricular activities

FASNY's strong STEM, Arts, Music, and Athletics programs along with our many clubs ensure a well-rounded education and encourage leadership. Strong Community Service, educational trips, and a large choice of clubs all contribute to the development of balanced and caring individuals.

A diverse and welcoming community

The community of teachers and students represents over 50 nationalities, and the fabric of our school is one of tolerance, acceptance, and appreciation of our diversity. FASNY mix French and American school-life traditions, creating a warm and engaging experience for our students.

(Founded 1893)

Head of School
Sam Houser

DP coordinator
Kim McGlynn

Status Private

Boarding/day Mixed

Gender Coeducational

Language of instruction
English

Authorised IB programmes
DP

Age Range 13 – 19 years

Address
1690 Newtown Langhorne Rd
Newtown
PA 18940-2414 | USA

TEL +1 215 579 6500

Email
admission@georgeschool.org

Website
www.georgeschool.org

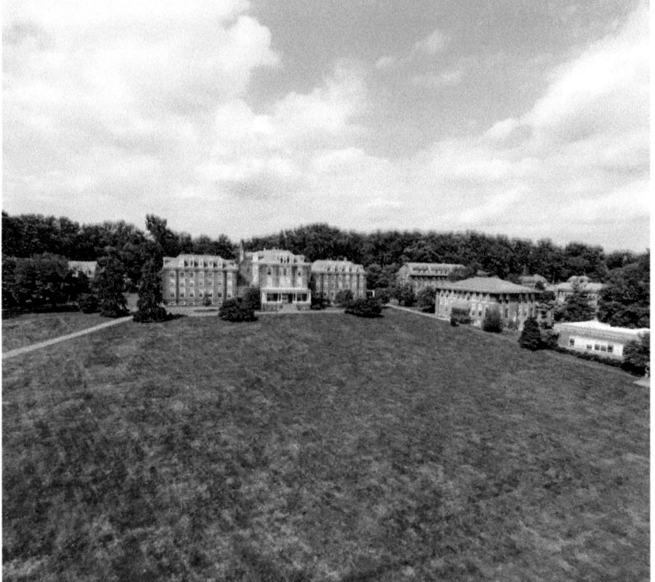

Founded in 1893, George School is a Quaker, co-ed boarding and day school for students in grades 9 to 12 located in Newtown, PA. The school is close to major cities on a picturesque, expansive 240-acre campus of open lawns and beautiful woods. Students arrive from nearly fifty countries and more than twenty states.

George School is an experienced leader in education, offering the International Baccalaureate (IB) Diploma Programme for more than thirty-five years and boasting a diploma success rate in the mid-ninetieth percentile over the past ten years. In addition to the IB diploma, George School offers nearly 20 Advanced Placement (AP) courses.

Experiential learning across disciplines is a hallmark of a George School education. Students gain practical experience in subjects such as film, artificial intelligence, robotics, human geography, stagecraft, and more. Local and global service-learning opportunities are also an integral part of the curriculum and student life at George School. The chance to freely explore new passions, as well as dive deep into existing ones, makes for a journey of discovery and preparation for life beyond George School.

Understanding that knowledge and character go hand in hand is at the foundation of the George School community. Graduates enter the world confident and capable leaders rooted in self-awareness, self sufficiency, and the ability to listen deeply to others while letting their lives speak. They attend the most selective colleges and universities worldwide.

Greenville
International School
Understanding is Greatness

(Founded 2011)

Head of School
María Isabel Zapata Vásquez

PYP coordinator
Iris Torres (early years) & Silvia González (elementary years)

MYP coordinator
Sara Pérez

DP coordinator
Alma Ruíz

Status Private

Boarding/day Day

Gender Coeducational

Language of instruction
English

Authorised IB programmes
PYP, MYP, DP

Age Range 2 – 18 years

Number of pupils enrolled 926

Fees Please call
+52 (993) 310 8060 Ext. 113

Address
Prolongación Avenida Paseo
Usumacinta 2122
Ría. Lázaro Cárdenas 2a Sección
Villahermosa, Tabasco
C.P. 86287 | MÉXICO

TEL +52 (993) 310 8060

Email info@greenville.edu.mx

Website
www.greenville.edu.mx

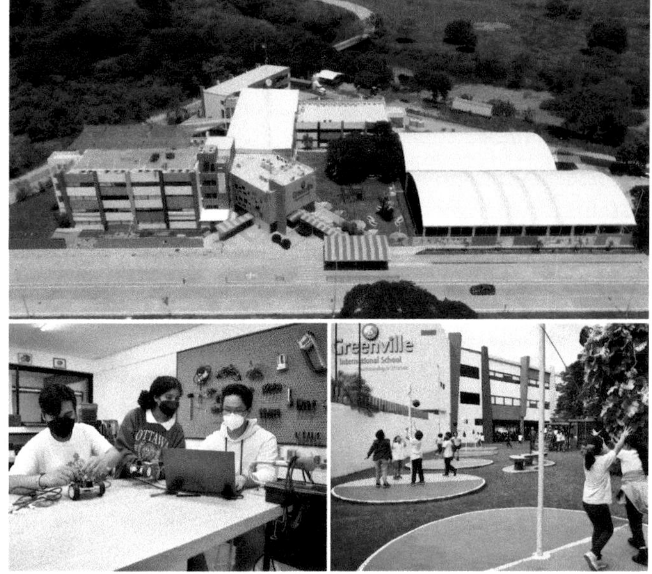

Founded in 2011 in Villahermosa, Tabasco, Mexico Greenville is an international school with an avant-garde and holistic educational model. 845 students between 2 and 18 years representing 20 nationalities find themselves in a multilingual and multicultural environment, where we prepare them to be global citizens and face the challenges of today's world. We are an excellent alternative for the local and foreign community.

We have been a member of the IB World Schools since May 2016. In all our activities we encourage a philosophy of respect and appreciation of diversity. We provide the necessary environment, tools and skills that allow our students to think globally and to take responsibility for their own life-long learning.

Thanks to our certification as an International Baccalaureate (IB) World School: Diploma Program (DP), Middle Years Program (MYP) and Primary Years Program (PYP), our evaluation system is approved with both, international and national criteria, which makes it easier to integrate into any educational system around the world.

Since the beginning, we have built a reputation as an inclusive and green school. We promote ecological awareness that is fostered through the study plans and the environmentally friendly facilities. At Greenville, we seek that our students achieve personal growth, which is why, in addition to our exceptional academic offer, we provide various extra-curricular artistic and sports disciplines.

While most classes are delivered in English, all students in Grades K1-12 receive language instruction in Spanish and French. Greenville is an ETS (Educational Testing Service) and Alliance Française authorized center for the application of the TOEFL (junior/ITP) and DELF (junior) certifications.

We are proud of the community we have formed, where children and young people feel valued and happy.

(Founded 1951)

General Director
Eamonn Mullally

DP coordinator
David Grant

Status Private

Boarding/day Day

Gender Coeducational

Language of instruction
English

Authorised IB programmes
DP

Age Range 3 – 18 years

Number of pupils enrolled
1100

Fees
Please contact the school

Address
Av. Circunvalación Pte. 102
Balcones de San Mateo
Naucalpan, Estado de México
C.P. 53200 | MÉXICO

TEL +52 55 5373 0088

Email
admissions@greengates.edu.mx

Website
www.greengates.edu.mx

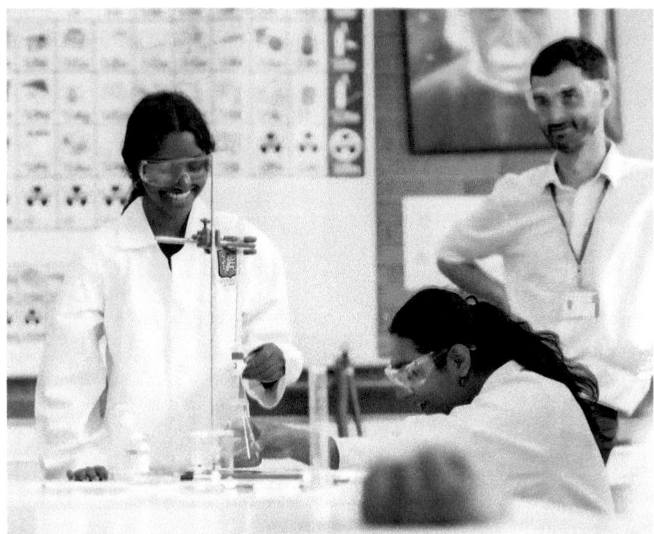

Greengates School, founded in 1951, is the premier British international school of Mexico with nearly 1100 students. The school is private, selective, K-12 and coeducational. It is the most international school by percentage of students and the highest scoring IB Diploma Programme school in the country. As a member of the Nord Anglia Education family of schools, we are committed to providing an exceptional educational experience that fosters character development, self-discipline, respect, and reflection within a challenging learning environment.

At Greengates, we prioritise academic excellence on the world stage. Our team of highly qualified teachers brings together the best of British and international academics, ensuring that our students receive an exceptional standard of education. Through the world-renowned International Baccalaureate Diploma Programme (IBDP), we equip our students with the necessary skills and knowledge to thrive in their future. Whether they aspire to attend the best universities or pursue promising career paths, our students are prepared to excel on a global scale.

We take pride in the achievements of our multicultural community, which resonates around the world. Our international curriculum opens doors to a myriad of opportunities for growth and accomplishment, laying a strong foundation for success in a globally connected future. By embracing diversity and promoting a global perspective, we empower our students to broaden their horizons and develop a deep understanding of different cultures and viewpoints.

Greengates has been held in high esteem for over 70 years. It is recognised in Mexico and the world for its high academic standards, respectful treatment of all and for being a truly international and multi-cultural community. It is a self-sustained day school set in the metropolitan area of Mexico City just 20 minutes away from the prestigious Polanco neighbourhood. The campus covers an area of over 20,000 square metres, with purpose-built facilities that include state-of-the-art library, nine science laboratories, computer media centres, four art studios, a theatre, a spacious and modern 700-seat auditorium, a large multi-purpose gymnasium, basketball and volleyball courts, an indoor swimming pool, an organic learning garden, a new STEAM Makerspace, a cafeteria, an all-weather field and an adventure playground.

At Greengates we act with integrity and seek to motivate our students to become socially responsible citizens while achieving academic excellence. Most of our students come from the diplomatic and business communities in Mexico City. Over 50 different nationalities are represented, and we receive students from different educational systems and academic calendars year-round and while there is a significant population of long-term locally based students, newcomers are ever present and warmly embraced.

The faculty at Greengates is comprised of almost 120 teachers from a wide variety of backgrounds. Alongside the many British teachers, highly qualified and experienced educators come from around the world; Australia, Brazil, Canada, France, Ireland, Mexico, South Africa, and the USA. Teachers bring an array of different skills and modern methods to the classroom and beyond.

As a British International school, our language of

instruction is English, though all students from the age of six study Spanish at the appropriate level, and some +50 percent of students who require Mexican educational qualifications take a limited number of courses in Spanish. Support in both languages is given as required. Furthermore, French is taught in the Secondary School and can be taken at IGCSE and IB Diploma. Korean and Japanese are also available as options of the Diploma Programme.

The Primary School is the first fully accredited International Early Years Curriculum (IEYC) and International Primary Curriculum (IPC) School in Latin America with aspects of mastering in its practice. Learning with the IEYC and IPC means that children focus on a combination of academic, personal and international learning that is exciting, engaging and challenging.

The Secondary School prepares students for the International General Certificate of Secondary Education (IGCSE) administered by Cambridge Assessment International Education. We offer a wide range of IGCSE subjects. Our IGCSE results are always above the world average. The IGCSE two-year course is studied prior to embarking on the IB Diploma Programme.

In Years 12 and 13 all students follow the International Baccalaureate Diploma Programme (IBDP) with cohorts between 45 to 60 students. Greengates is the only school in Mexico to require all these students to complete and graduate with the IBDP and not an alternate pathway. We expect the highest standard of academic excellence from our students and prepare them for the rigour of the IBDP. The Secondary School has been accredited to offer the Diploma Programme since 1986, obtaining a pass rate of 98-100 percent during each of the last five years, with overall points scores consistently well above the world average. Greengates is the highest IBDP scoring school in Mexico. Whilst the world average for academic year 23/24 dropped by nearly 2 points, Greengates maintained its high average.

Greengates has a remarkable track record of sending students to prestigious colleges and universities worldwide, while also securing an extraordinary sum of over 6 million USD in scholarships and financial aid within the past 5 years supported by a comprehensive and personalised university counselling programme. This achievement stands as a testament to our exceptional educational standards, ensuring our students are well-prepared to thrive and succeed at recognised and esteemed institutions globally. The academic excellence and international diversity of Greengates make us both unique in Mexico and renowned worldwide.

International School Nido de Aguilas

(Founded 1934)

Head of School
Mr. Ken Kunin

DP coordinator
Kurt Supplee

Status Private

Boarding/day Day

Gender Coeducational

Language of instruction
English, Spanish

Authorised IB programmes
DP

Age Range 3 – 18 years

Number of pupils enrolled
1550

Address
Av. El Rodeo 14200
Lo Barnechea
Santiago | **CHILE**

TEL +56 2 2339 8100

Email
admissions@nido.cl

Website
www.nido.cl

Founded in 1934, Nido de Aguilas is a private, co-educational, non-sectarian, non-profit day school rooted in the best traditions of Chilean and North American education. Today, Nido has over 1500 students from 45 countries and offers a comprehensive liberal arts college preparatory educational program from Early Years (age three) through Grade 12. Nido serves the international business and diplomatic community of Santiago, as well as local students seeking an English-language, U.S.-style education.

Nido has offered the IB Diploma since 1982, and today, over 50% of our Grade 11 and 12 students enroll in the full IB Diploma Programme. Their IB Diploma scores are above the worldwide average, and our IB Coordinator ensures that students are provided the opportunities to succeed across all aspects of their IB courses. IB Diploma candidates are examined internally at Nido and externally by the IB Organization to award IB Diploma results.

Toward the end of the first semester of Grade 10, the course registration process for the following school year starts. During this process, students and parents are informed on the IB programme and evaluated to determine if it fits their academic pathway. Admission to the program is based on a student's academic record, including having a record of academic honesty. Students transferring from IB programmes with good standing may continue in the IB programme at Nido. In the case of English language learners, they must meet English language proficiency requirements to participate in the full IB Diploma.

IB courses are also open to non-Diploma students. All Nido HS students are exposed to the IB curriculum during their academic career, as many upper-level courses are taught at the IB level. It is possible to earn the IB Diploma simultaneously with the Nido/US diploma and the Chilean National Plan Diploma.

Nido's high school faculty includes 34 IB teachers recruited from the best schools in the world. They have an average IB teaching experience of over nine years, and all attend official workshops in their subject group. In addition, Nido has a robust mentoring program for teachers new to the IB.

International School of Boston

(Founded 1962)

Head of School
Mr. Richard Ulffers

Secondary School Director
Mr. Philippe Caron-Audet

DP coordinator
Mr. Robert Wilson

Status Private

Boarding/day Day

Gender Coeducational

Language of instruction
English, French, Spanish, Chinese

Authorised IB programmes
DP

Age Range 2 – 18 years

Number of pupils enrolled 570

Fees
Day: US$31,560 – US$43,870 per annum

Address
45 Matignon Road
Cambridge
MA 02140 | USA

TEL +1 617 499 1451

Email
admissions@isbos.org

Website
www.isbos.org

The International School of Boston (ISB) opens a world of possibilities for students from preschool through Grade 12. ISB provides a rigorous multilingual education, inclusive cultural experiences, and a fearless global mindset needed to learn and lead, both today and in the future.

At ISB, students are immersed in a dynamic learning environment. Classes are taught in English and French, equipping students with not only the ability to fluently speak at least two languages, but also empowering them to think in at least two languages. Their minds will be forever opened to the diverse ideas, insights, and innovations of peoples, countries, and societies that they will discover at ISB and beyond.

Academic Excellence Meets Individual Flexibility
Our integrated school-wide curriculum balances age-appropriate academic challenge and rigor with individual choice. Students immerse themselves in an academic program rooted in decades of proven results, culminating with the choice between our two internationally respected Upper School programs, including the International Baccalaureate.

Enable Your Child to Connect with Anyone, Anywhere
Students acquire and refine the critical thinking skills to make sound decisions, the intellect to navigate different languages, and the social awareness to assimilate diverse cultures, ultimately enabling them to reason, communicate, and connect with anyone, anywhere, about virtually anything.

A Global Community Close to Home
As students and parents make their way around campus each day, our hallways ring with "Hi!", "Bonjour!", "Nǐhǎo!", and the joyful greetings of peers from 50 countries, a reminder of you and your child's once-in-a-lifetime opportunity to meet, learn alongside, and befriend families from around the world.

World-class Faculty from Around the World
Our faculty are extraordinarily skilled in engaging each student, regardless of their native language, country, or educational background, and supporting them closely to achieve the high standards of ISB's challenging curriculum.

In the ISB Upper School program, students become knowledgeable, critical thinkers – prepared to thrive in universities across every continent and willing to embrace the unique challenges and boundless opportunities of an interconnected world. As International Baccalaureate students at ISB, they graduate as skillful communicators, effective collaborators, creative problem solvers, critical thinkers, and confident global citizens.

At ISB, the IB programme is split into two phases: the International Programme (Grades 9-10) and the International Baccalaureate Diploma Programme (Grades 11-12). The foundational work students undertake in the International Programme (IP) will set them up for success in the Diploma Programme (DP).

At ISB, we are Teaching the World. We invite you to contact the ISB Admissions Office at admissions@isbos.org.

International School of Los Angeles

(Founded 1978)

Head of School
Mr Michael Maniska

DP coordinator
Donald Buer

Status Private

Boarding/day Day

Gender Coeducational

Language of instruction
English, French

Authorised IB programmes
DP

Age Range 3 – 18 years

Number of pupils enrolled
1080

Fees
Day: $21,100 – $27,400 per annum

Address
1105 W. Riverside Drive
Burbank
CA 91506 | USA

TEL +1 626 695 5159

Email
admissions@lilaschool.com

Website
www.internationalschool.la

The International School of Los Angeles is an independent, international, high-quality school that offers both a French immersion track from preschool through 12th grade and a separate international high school track that prepares students for the International Baccalaureate® Diploma Programme in grades 11 – 12.

Students study a common bilingual program from preschool through 8th grade, after which they choose one of two rigorous programs that culminates in the International Baccalaureate® Diploma (taught in English) or the French baccalauréat (taught in French). With an education delivered in an intimate, nurturing and diverse environment, our students become caring global citizens prepared to thrive in a changing world.

The School has offered the IB Diploma Programme for more than 20 years. Possessing such a robust bilingual background, many of its students pursue the prestigious Bilingual Diploma, demonstrating their proficiency by completing the requirements in both English and French at Literature level. This highly sought-after credential has become another mark of distinction for the International School of Los Angeles' IB students.

In the 2019-2020 school year, the School extended its international track to the beginning of 9th grade, thereby realigning its entry points to reflect the US educational model, further internationalizing its curriculum, and providing students an additional year of preparation ahead of the IB Diploma Programme. Students entering the international track in 9th grade are not required to demonstrate proficiency in French but should display an openness to learning another language.

With multiple Los Angeles-area campuses (Burbank, Los Feliz, Pasadena, and West Valley), and more than 1,000 students, the International School of Los Angeles holds accreditation from the French Ministry of Education, the Western Association of Schools and Colleges (WASC), the California Association of Independent Schools (CAIS), and the International Baccalaureate® (IB). The School is also a member of the National Association of Independent Schools (NAIS) and the National Honor Society (NHS) networks.

The International School of Los Angeles is committed to the values of respect, excellence, and diversity, and to preparing students of all backgrounds to excel in and contribute to a global world. Since 1978, the School has been instilling the love of learning in all its students through small classes and low student-to-teacher ratios. With over 65 nationalities and 40 spoken languages represented on the campuses, students study and live in a diverse global community every day.

Principal
Prof. Estela María Irrera de Pallaro

DP coordinator
Clotilde Alleva

Status Private

Boarding/day Day

Gender Coeducational

Language of instruction
Spanish, English, Italian, Portuguese

Authorised IB programmes
DP

Age Range 2 – 18 years

Address
Amenábar St. 1840
1428 Ciudad de Buenos Aires |
ARGENTINA

TEL +54 11 4787 2294

Website
www.intschools.org/school/islands

Working together with Southern International School and Northern International School.

In 1981 Mrs. Estela María Irrera de Pallaro and her husband Andrés Pallaro founded a kindergarten in a lovely house situated in O'Higgins St. in Belgrano, which was later to become Islands International School. Some years later, as a result of hard work, clear objectives and true commitment, a primary school was opened in a spacious building situated in Virrey del Pino and Arcos St. In 1988, a secondary school was opened with a curriculum based on the latest, most prestigious syllabi in Argentina and the whole world. The new building situated in Amenábar St. offered our students appropriate facilities and modern equipment to meet the highest educational standards.

From the beginning, our aim has been to present our students with a demanding curriculum while emphasizing the values of hard work, effort and commitment. The outstanding achievements of our alumni both in college and later on in their jobs are irrefutable proof of our success.

In 1990 Islands embraced a new challenge by joining the International Baccalaureate Organization, a well known association of schools seeded in Geneva, Switzerland whose main objective is to foster the students' skills so that they can perform successfully in an increasingly demanding academic world and expanding job market. Furthermore, it is essential that our students should acquire full command of the languages taught at our school: Spanish, English and Italian.

By getting an IB diploma our students can also get the "Maturità Linguistica o Scientifica", which is a diploma issued by the Government of Italy at the end of secondary school and which grants students admission to European Universities.

Our school emphasizes the values of respect and hard work as the main tools, which will enable our students to achieve success. Islands International School provides students with quality education, which comprises the latest technological breakthroughs and the practice of human and social values.

King's College School Panama

(Founded 2012)

Headteacher
Oliver Proctor

DP coordinator
Warren Green

Status Private

Boarding/day Day

Gender Coeducational

Language of instruction
English, Spanish

Authorised IB programmes
DP

Age Range 2 – 18 years

Address
Av. Demetrio B. Lakas
Clayton
Panama City | **PANAMA**

TEL +507 282 3300

Email
ana.mantovani@kings.education

Website
www.panama.kingscollegeschools.org

King's College School Panama, established in 2012, is a world-class premium international school, bordered by the Panamanian rainforest and situated on a brand-new, state-of-the-art campus, conveniently located within easy access to the vibrant city centre. We proudly stand as the sole accredited British school in Panama, offering a distinguished education enriched with British values and global perspectives. With an extraordinary 2023 BSO inspection, earning the accolade of "Outstanding In Every Category," our commitment to excellence is underscored.

Comprising a faculty of 90% native English speakers, King's is a beacon of British education in the Americas. We became the first school in the region to join the esteemed Fellowship of World Class High-Performance Learning Schools. Our students are trailblazers, embracing British education and High-Performance Learning, setting the standard for educational innovation in the region.

As a diverse and inclusive British international school, we nurture a multicultural community with 450 students aged 2 to 18, representing over 47 nationalities. Our commitment to holistic education is recognized with the 2023 Wellbeing Award for Schools.

At the heart of our educational ethos is a distinctive blended curriculum, marrying the UK National curriculum with the rigorous IB Diploma programme. This approach offers extensive coverage and in-depth learning opportunities, serving as a gateway to prestigious universities worldwide.

We emphasise firsthand experiences over textbook reliance. Our students are encouraged to foster creativity, embrace independence, and cultivate critical thinking, exhibiting unwavering dedication to academic pursuits. Transitioning to the IB Diploma programme in Years 12 and 13, our students gain a globally recognised qualification, fostering confidence, independence, and a curious mindset.

The blended curriculum at King's College School Panama, provides a unique advantage, combining academic rigour and subject depth through the acclaimed International GCSEs. This approach embeds the transformative qualities of the global learner profile inherent in the IB Diploma Programme, ensuring our students are well-prepared for success in leading universities worldwide. King's College School Panama is not just a school; it's a nurturing community dedicated to shaping future leaders with a global perspective.

La Scuola d'Italia Guglielmo Marconi

LA SCUOLA D'ITALIA GUGLIELMO MARCONI

www.lascuoladitalia.org

(Founded 1977)

Head of School
Dr. Michael Cascianelli

DP coordinator
Dr. Beatrice Paladini

Status Private

Boarding/day Day

Gender Coeducational

Language of instruction
English, Italian

Authorised IB programmes
DP

Age Range 2 – 18 years

Number of pupils enrolled 143

Fees
Preschool US$26,000
Elementary US$29,000
Middle & High School US$37,000

Address
12 East 96th Street
New York
NY 10128 | USA

TEL +1 212 369 3290

Email
admissions@lascuoladitalia.org

Website
www.lascuoladitalia.org

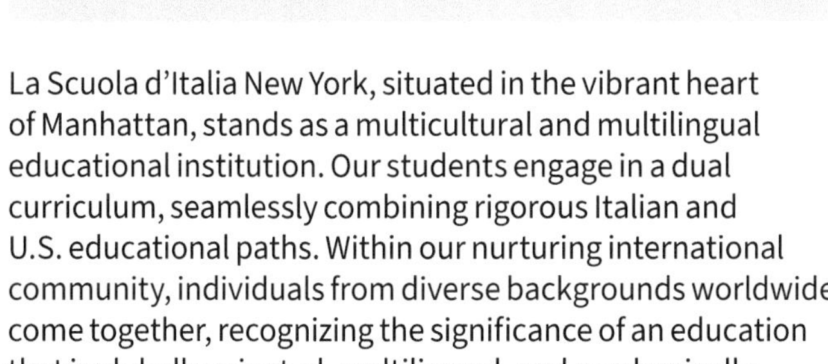

La Scuola d'Italia New York, situated in the vibrant heart of Manhattan, stands as a multicultural and multilingual educational institution. Our students engage in a dual curriculum, seamlessly combining rigorous Italian and U.S. educational paths. Within our nurturing international community, individuals from diverse backgrounds worldwide come together, recognizing the significance of an education that is globally oriented, multilingual, and academically demanding.

Acknowledged by the Italian Ministry of Education, La Scuola holds a charter from the Regents of the University of the State of New York and accreditation from the New York State Association of Independent Schools (NYSAIS). Underscoring the excellence of our educational approach, we have proudly offered the International Baccalaureate (IB) Diploma Programme to students in grades 11 and 12 since 2018.

This distinctive feature enables La Scuola students to graduate with a high school diploma universally recognized by universities across Europe, the United States, and beyond. Committed to integrating various disciplines, cultures, and languages into our thoughtfully crafted K-12 curriculum, our institution boasts an outstanding faculty dedicated to refining the curriculum regularly, maintaining a low teacher-student ratio.

At La Scuola, our mission is to equip students for the challenges of a globalized world, not only academically but also professionally, socially, culturally, and ethically. Our educational approach is designed to instill the skills and knowledge necessary for success in higher education and beyond. We strive to cultivate a profound understanding of our students' future roles as thoughtful, respectful, caring, and principled individuals within an ever-expanding global community.

Head of School
Valentina Imbeni Ph.D.

Director of Admissions
Nichole Leon & Paola Barberi

PYP coordinator
Leticia O'Sullivan

MYP coordinator
Yarrow Ulehman

Status Private, Non-Profit

Boarding/day Day

Gender Coeducational

Language of instruction
English, Italian and Spanish

Authorised IB programmes
PYP, MYP

Age Range 2 – 14 years

Number of pupils enrolled 410

Fees
US$32,900 –
US$43,675 per annum

San Francisco Preschool Campus
728 20th Street, San Francisco,
CA 94107 | USA

San Francisco K-8 Campus
3250 18th Street, San Francisco
CA 94110 | USA

Silicon Valley Preschool & Elementary School Campus
2086 Clarke Ave, East Palo Alto,
CA 94303 | USA

TEL +1 415 551 0000

Email
admissions@lascuolasf.org

Website
www.lascuolasf.org

San Francisco's only International Baccalaureate Primary and Middle School Programme, and the only Reggio Emilia inspired IB PYP and MYP, and Italian Language immersion school in the world! At La Scuola International School we've been inspiring brave learners to shape the future for more than 20 years.

It's the students at La Scuola who ask the challenging questions… they lead and embrace their own ability to learn across languages, cultures, and subject areas. Because when children are open to the world and protagonists in their own education, there's no limit to their ability to learn, find beauty in life, and discover extraordinary answers. We believe children are innately curious. The challenging questions they ask ignite a process of arriving at answers with peers and teachers, not an opportunity for us to tell them the answer.

Our role as a community is to nurture the child intellectually, physically, emotionally, and to always do so with joy. Children learn meaningful experiences and exploration of the world, and doing so in a beautiful environment leads to a love of learning for life.

- The International Baccalaureate framework provides a rigorous and globally minded curriculum that prepares students for academic excellence and a lifelong love of learning.
- We offer an inquiry based, immersive Italian language curriculum for Preschool – Grade 8 students. Students learn in multiple languages – Spanish is introduced as a third language in Grade 4 up through Middle School – extending the students' ability to thrive in a multicultural world.
- With inquiry as the leading tool of our education, students foster critical and creative thinking skills, confidence, collaboration, and empathy.
- The Reggio Emilia-inspired approach puts students at the center of their learning process by nurturing collaboration and inquiry, while immersing students in a warm, beautiful, and joyful environment.
- In our diverse, multicultural and multilingual school – 34 languages spoken by La Scuola families – students grow in a community that balances academic rigor with creativity and real-life tools like cultural awareness and global citizenship.
- La Scuola students attend and thrive at selective boarding, and local private, parochial, and public high schools in the Bay Area and abroad.
- La Scuola is also recognized by the Italian Ministry of Education as a Scuola Paritaria.

Children do not need to speak Italian to attend La Scuola!

Nothing Without Joy!
Niente Senza Gioia!
!Nada Sin Alegria!

Lincoln Park High School

(Founded 1899)

Principal
Dr. Eric Steinmiller

MYP coordinator
Theresa McCormick

DP coordinator
Mary Enda Tookey

CP coordinator
James Conzen

Status State

Boarding/day Day

Gender Coeducational

Language of instruction
English

Authorised IB programmes
MYP, DP, CP

Age Range 13 – 19 years

Number of pupils enrolled
2055

Address
2001 North Orchard Street
Chicago
IL 60614 | USA

TEL +1 773 534 8149

Email
lpibprogram@aol.com

Website
www.lincolnparkhs.org

Lincoln Park High School, founded in 1899, is a Chicago public high school that offers very successful IB Diploma, MYP & CP Programmes within the context of a college preparatory school for students of all ability levels. Students living in our attendance area or anywhere within the Chicago city limits can make application to Lincoln Park's Magnet Programs, which include the IB Diploma Programme, the IBCP (Performance Music, ROTC, Sports & Health, Theatre, Computer Science, and Visual & Digital Arts), an Advanced College Prep (Honors/Double Honors/AP) Program, and a Performing/Fine Arts Program with concentrations available in drama, band, strings or visual arts. After admission, any student may elect music or visual arts. Special consideration for admission is extended to students from other IB schools and to international students from the business and diplomatic communities.

Fluent/bilingual French students can participate in a special program (EFAC) that can include preparation for DELF or the French Baccalaureate in addition to college prep, AP, and/or IB classes. All students with special needs are supported in their IB and college preparatory classes by a full special services program.

Newsweek magazine has ranked Lincoln Park as one of the top 100 high schools in the US and, for the last fourteen years, *US News & World Report* awarded the school gold and silver medal rankings.

Its staff places high value on rigor, mutual respect and creativity, while encouraging students in both their academic and extracurricular activities to develop their talents and interests to the full. Personal excellence, a willingness to challenge oneself, inventiveness, and a can-do spirit are at the core of Lincoln Park's culture.

Students come from over 80 countries and speak more than 60 different languages at home. A significant number of students in the IB Diploma Programme were born in other countries, are first-generation in this country, or the children of internationals. Within this diverse urban context students acquire insight into others and the leadership skills needed in a global society.

A wide variety of extracurricular activities (62) and interscholastic sports opportunities (currently 31) are available for all students. IB students are active in sports, drama, music, art, school clubs, and local organizations. Many do community service beyond the CAS requirement and are active in their individual churches, synagogues, and mosques. In addition to their work in their classes, all Lincoln Park students participate in a number of academic competitions in writing, history, experimental science, literature, social issues, world languages, and the fine and performing arts; many have gone on to the national and international levels of these competitions. Every year, the boys' and girls' athletic teams win division and sectional championships. The music program regularly earns superior ratings in competitions and is currently ranked among the top music programs in the state of Illinois.

Since 1984 approximately 80% of the IB students have gained the IB diploma on completion of the IB Diploma Programme. Lincoln Park enjoys an outstanding record of university acceptances both in the US and internationally.

London International Academy

Head of School
Linda Thomas

DP coordinator
Abeera Atique

Status Private

Boarding/day Mixed

Gender Coeducational

Language of instruction
English, Spanish, Mandarin

Authorised IB programmes
DP

Age Range 13 – 18 years

Number of pupils enrolled
200

Fees
Day: CAD$36,000 per annum (scholarships available)
International Boarders CAD$56,000 per annum (all inclusive)

Address
361-365 Richmond Street
London, ON
N6A 3C2 | CANADA

TEL +1 519 433 3388

Email
admissions@lia-edu.ca

Website
www.lia-edu.ca

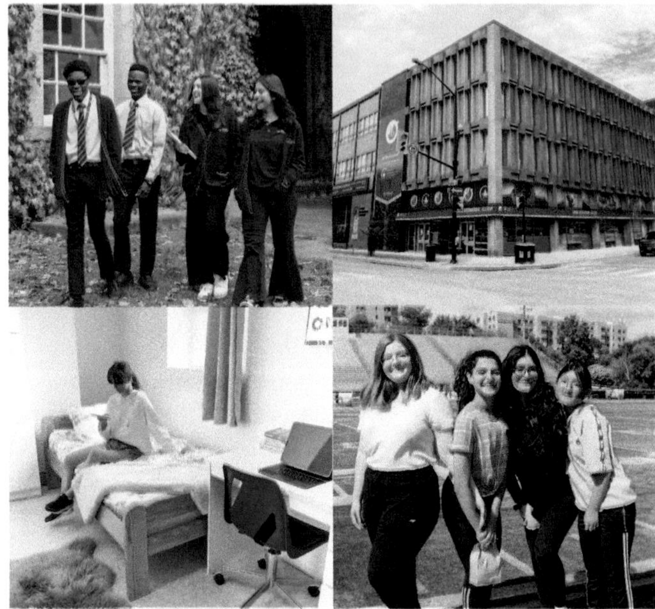

London International Academy (LIA) is a private, co-educational day and boarding school located in the beautiful "forest city" of London, Ontario, Canada.

LIA is an International Baccalaureate (IB) authorized world school with programme offerings from 9th to 12th grade in the Ontario Secondary School program (OSSD) as well as the IB Diploma Programme (11th and 12th grade). LIA offers small classes with sizes averaging 10-15 students per class.

The goal of LIA is to prepare and graduate our students for admissions to the top universities in Canada, United Kingdom, Southeast Asia, and the United States.

Our graduates are our greatest resource, and their successes are our greatest achievements.

LIA is in a privileged position to have established University Pathway Programmes with some of the finest universities in the country, our graduates are heavily favoured in the universities in which they apply to. In some cases, our senior students can earn university credits while in their senior year of high school.

In addition to the highest-level academic standards, the school offers numerous leadership development options such as The Duke of Edinburgh Awards Society, The Circle Round Society, Model United Nations, and Student Prefects.

LIA's IB students continue to excel each year achieving excellent admission results. The 2023 IB cohort achieved 100% graduation rate with the highest grade achieved being 43. LIA is also known for their highly academic and hands on STEM program and is recognized for being amongst the top competitors in mathematics, robotics, artificial intelligence, coding, and science competitions across Canada.

In addition to exceptional academics and student leadership opportunities the school well understands the mental health and emotional needs of our students. All staff are trained in "Wellness" approaches to student counselling and support. In addition, we have on site counsellors trained to assist and support our students.

The school provides both boarding and homestay options. The boarding facility offers 24/7 supervision and meals provided by several local restaurants offering a variety of international cuisine. Its main campus, located in the heart of the city of London (Ontario), is a vibrant hub for activities and student innovation.

Student services takes an individualized approach to university admissions and applications having recently placed students at the University of Toronto, University of Waterloo, University of British Columbia, Carnegie Melon, Imperial College, University of Manchester, Kings College, London School of Economics, University College of London, New York University, University of Amsterdam, University of Melbourne, Australia National University, Hong Kong University, Chinese University of Hong Kong.

LIA looks to educate young, bright minds while providing exceptional opportunities that allow students to stand out amongst the crowd, worldwide.

Madison Campus Monterrey

(Founded 1978)

Head of School
Lic. Lucía Ma. Guzmán

PYP coordinator
Ricardo Domínguez Gámez

MYP coordinator
Perla Priscila Vargas Andrade

Status Private

Boarding/day Day

Gender Coeducational

Language of instruction
English, Spanish

Authorised IB programmes
PYP, MYP

Age Range 2 – 15 years

Fees
PYP Programme US$4,900 per annum
MYP Programme US$5,800 per annum

Address
Marsella #3055, Col. Alta Vista
Monterrey, Nuevo León
C.P. 64840 | MÉXICO

TEL +52 81 8359 0627

Email contacto@colegiosmadison.edu.mx

Website
madisonmonterrey.edu.mx

Madison schools have been nurturing minds and creating successful learning experiences for more than 45 years in our community. We have been fulfilling internationally certified academic standards through collaborative work, positive attitudes and core values. These are highly regarded in our schools.

Madison Campus Monterrey was the first school founded in the Madison Group of Schools, which are located in different Mexican states: Nuevo León, Yucatán, and Chihuahua.

Monterrey is a modern and industrial city, known as one of the three most industrious and important cities in Mexico.

Monterrey has at least four well-known universities with important international exchange programs and several smaller ones.

Madison Campus Monterrey became bilingual in 1994. Since then, it has had a strong emphasis on the English language.

The school has programs that nurture its students' development:

- "Ruta de Independencia" School Trip: 5th-grade students spent five days travelling throughout different places in Mexico where the Independence Movement took place. This program enriches what they had learned in their classes, so they can live, themselves, a real learning experience.
- United Nations Model: Academic simulation of the United Nations that aims to educate participants about civics, effective communication, globalization, and multilateral diplomacy.
- Youth Leader Explorer exhibition: organized by one of the most important high schools in Mexico where students develop different scientific skills.
- French Immersion Program: a week program held in Quebec, Canada.
- International trips: Every year we offer a complete Educational Travel Program to reinforce our main objective, that is to educate citizens of the world.

In 1999 the school decided to become part of the IB and began working towards its authorization. The school achieved authorization to offer the International Baccalaureate Primary Years Programme (PYP) in 2003 and the International Baccalaureate Middle Years Programme (MYP) in 2007.

We have had students from Russia, Argentina, Venezuela, Canada, Nicaragua, Colombia, United States, Philippines, Lebanon, Poland, Switzerland, Germany, Spain, India, and Japan.

One of Madison Group of Schools' greatest strengths is an International Teachers Program that enhances our students' abilities to interact with foreign cultures and learn from them.

For the last fifteen years, we have had instructors from Canada, China, Costa Rica, Croatia, Cuba, England, Ireland, Lebanon, Scotland, Poland, and the United States, teaching at our schools. Students and graduates from our school are well appreciated by the community and by the high schools they attend. Our well-articulated, inquisitive, mature and responsible graduates and students have already made a difference here in Mexico.

Madison Campus Monterrey is a certified school by SEP, an active member of FEP as well as IBAMEX.

Madison International School

(Founded 2007)

Head of School
Samanta Galvan

PYP coordinator
Rolando De La Torre

MYP coordinator
Anna Carstens

Status Private

Boarding/day Day

Gender Coeducational

Language of instruction
English, Spanish

Authorised IB programmes
PYP, MYP

Age Range 1 – 15 years

Number of pupils enrolled
938

Fees
PYP US$8,700 per annum
MYP US$10,500 per annum

Address
Camino Real #100
Col. El Uro
Monterrey, Nuevo León
C.P. 64986 | MÉXICO

TEL +52 81 8218 7909

Email
admisiones@mis.edu.mx

Website
www.mis.edu.mx

We belong to the Madison Group of Schools, which has more than 40 years of educational experience.

On a national level, we have campuses in the cities of Chihuahua and Mérida•. Locally, we have the Madison International School (MIS), Instituto Anglo Británico, and Madison Monterrey.

Our particular campus opened its doors in 2007 in the south of Monterrey, in the area of El Uro, and we offer Nursery, Kindergarten, Primary and Secondary levels of schooling.

MIS is located in Monterrey, an industrial and modern city in Northeastern Mexico. The city is anchor to the third-largest metropolitan area in Mexico. Its economic, cultural and social influence makes it one of Mexico's most developed cities with the highest per capita income in the nation.

MIS provides a first-class education for students and gives children a head start in the modern world by taking their English skills to a higher level. Madison's superb bilingual program teaches children English beginning in their most formative years.

Madison International School uses the constructivist educational method and is also based on inquiry, reflexion, and active participation of our students.

As part of our international profile we encourage our students to participate in different programmes that nurture their development, such as:

- Destination Imagination: engage participants in project-based challenges that are designed to build confidence and develop extraordinary creativity, critical thinking, communication, and teamwork skills.
- Model United Nations: academic simulation of this international organization, which aims to educate participants about effective communication, globalization and multilateral diplomacy.

Madison International School proudly boasts some of the best student facilities in Monterrey such as computer and science labs, video and conference halls, library, cafeteria, music and art rooms, and substantial sports fields that are all staffed by teachers committed to creating a fun and interesting learning environment for the children. The school offers extracurricular classes ranging from guitar, piano, robotics, to sports teams. Madison's dedication to students' safety and wellbeing is the most important element, which is why we provide excellent security features that will give every parent and child peace of mind.

We encourage diversity and internationalism and therefore we welcome students, teachers and families from any religion, race, and nationality.

(Founded 1946)

Head of School
Mrs. Judy Cooper

DP coordinator
Dr. Guinevere Dyker

Status Private, Non-Profit

Boarding/day Day

Gender Coeducational

Language of instruction
English, Spanish

Authorised IB programmes
DP

Age Range 3 – 18 years

Number of pupils enrolled
2000

Fees
Day: US$12,200 –
US$15,250 per annum

Address
Calle Augusto Angulo 291
San Antonio, Miraflores
Lima 15048 | **PERU**

TEL +51 13 156750 (Ext: 1325)

Email
admissions@markham.edu.pe

Website
www.markham.edu.pe

Established in 1946, Markham College is a regional influence in South America for educational leadership and academic excellence. We are an independent school that provides bilingual education to children from 3-18 years of age at our Miraflores and Surco campuses in Lima, Peru.

Markham has a British heritage and international perspective. We have an adapted British Curriculum that respects our distinct Peruvian setting. Our Early Years bilingual programme starts at 3 years old, and we are in the process of adopting the PYP-IB. Our IB Diploma programme, with over 27 subjects, gives students the tools to succeed in universities worldwide. We encourage diversity and support passion by allowing our students to choose from over 100 different extracurricular activities and sports.

Our mission is to support children to become leaders in their chosen fields and be agents of change in Peru and the world. The pillars of academic and creative endeavour, character development and service learning underpin our curriculum. Our outdoor education programme and social programmes are our special and unique features. They ensure that students receive a balanced and rounded education, focusing on how they can make a difference in society. Furthermore, our student leadership programme means that students are central to the decision-making process concerning their learning experiences. We are members of the CIS and are in the process of achieving accreditation.

Our teachers are also tutors and integral to our children's pastoral care. Supporting our students' emotional, psychological, and physical development and academic growth is central to our educational philosophy throughout their Markham journey.

Peru's rich cultural history and fantastic territory offer many opportunities for unforgettable experiences. Over 3000 km of Pacific Ocean coastline through the majestic Andean high peaks to the vast Amazon rainforest provide infinite places, sports and adventures. Numerous field trips ensure that the IB curriculum is enriched by the geographic and demographic variety Peru offers. International exchanges, debates and Model United Nations ensure that IB students receive an education steeped in logical and global contexts.

New world-class primary facilities have been built in Monterrico's 27,778 m2 campus, opened in 2024. It is a state-of-the-art educational facility reflecting the school's advanced pedagogic approach.

Markham is moving away from the traditional four-wall classroom, developing flexible learning spaces that encourage independent learning in different environments. Teachers are developing new ways of working and collaborating across groups and disciplines in our 'Learning Communities'. Architect Rosan Bosch has worked with the school to show how breakout spaces and rooms for immersion give students at Markham more autonomy and choices in planning and executing their learning journey.

Maryland International School

(Founded 2017)

Head of School
Rebekah Ghosh

Assistant Head of School
Kylea Goree

PYP coordinator
Kylea Goree

MYP coordinator
Pauline Boiser

DP coordinator
Jason Schmidt

Status Private

Boarding/day Day

Gender Coeducational

Language of instruction
English

Authorised IB programmes
PYP, MYP, DP

Age Range 6 – 18 years

Number of pupils enrolled 200

Fees
Domestic Students: US$12,850 – US$19,250 per annum
International Students: US$24,450 – US$32,000 per annum

Address
6135 Old Washington Road
Elkridge
MD 21075 | USA

TEL +1 410 220 3792

Email
info@maryland internationalschool.org

Website
www.maryland internationalschool.org

The future belongs to the curious. The ones who are not afraid to try something, explore it, poke at it, question it and turn it inside out.

About

Maryland International School (MDIS) is an independent, private school in Howard County, Maryland, conveniently located in the Baltimore-Washington metropolitan area. MDIS is the first school in the state of Maryland, and the second in the mid-Atlantic region, to offer three International Baccalaureate (IB) programmes: Primary Years Programme (PYP), Middle Years Programme (MYP), and Diploma Programme (DP).

Our beautiful 9 acre campus serves students from grades 1-12. Our mission and vision is to provide an academically rigorous and supportive college-preparatory education with an interdisciplinary and applied focus on the Science, Technology, Engineering, and Mathematics (STEM) disciplines in order to prepare students to become creative problem solvers, effective communicators, and tomorrow's leaders who think ethically, independently, and globally.

IB & STEM

Our curriculum integrates the International Baccalaureate curriculum with STEM specific programs and pathways. Our STEM-integrated curriculum was developed taking into account the principles of Universal Design for Learning (UDL), technology standards, disciplinary literacy standards, Next Generation Science Standards (NGSS), and transdisciplinary core content lessons. Our curriculum is designed to promote critical thinking, collaboration, and innovation in order to develop the academic, emotional and social skills that students will need to live and work in a globalized world. Our after school STEM programs include, but are not limited to: Robotics Club, Science Olympiad, FIRST Lego League, Coding Club, and a Drone Club.

Signature Programs & Events

MDIS highlights the IB philosophy of building international-mindedness through our Global Ambassadors Program (GAP), Mother Language Day, and Celebration of Nations. GAP, our study abroad immersion program with a service-learning component builds leadership beyond the classroom. It includes an international student program bringing students together from around the world to study at MDIS. We celebrate the cultures, languages, and traditions of countries around the world with our Celebration of Nations and our Mother Language day. These events showcase the diversity of our students by giving them a day to share their experiences, teach their language and to build connections through the use of the 10 learner profiles.

Admissions

Our admissions process operates on a rolling basis and so we welcome student applications year-round. When considering an applicant, we recognize that every child is unique. We evaluate a student's overall academic and developmental readiness and whether they will thrive in, and benefit from, the academic challenges of our curriculum. For additional information, please reach out by phone or email to learn more about the MDIS admission process.

Mott Hall Science and Technology Academy

Principal
Mrs. Miriam Ruiz

Assistant Principals
Ms. Marcia Thomas &
Ms. Jaymie Hernandez

MYP coordinator
Mr. Thomas Moore

Status State

Boarding/day Day

Gender Coeducational

Language of instruction
English, Spanish

Authorised IB programmes
MYP

Age Range 11 – 14 years

Number of pupils enrolled
382

Address
250 East 164th Street
Bronx, New York
NY 10456 | USA

TEL +1 718 293 4017

Email
MHSTAIB@motthallsta.org

Website
www.motthallsta.org

Mott Hall Science and Technology Academy is a rigorous math, science, and technology focused middle school. We offer families the opportunity for their children to meet the highest academic expectations and standards, to make smooth transitions to selective high schools, to compete successfully for admission to top public and private colleges and to succeed as a global citizen. Our school culture is characterized by a shared vision for academic excellence, the healthy personal growth of all students, and a commitment to our strong belief that all students can and will succeed in their endeavours.

At Mott Hall, students, faculty, and staff members have a shared vision of the individual's ability to achieve personal success each day as preparation to become active members of our global society. The journey our students embark on when they enter our doors is marked by continuous support and guidance academically, emotionally, and physically, to ensure the holistic development of our young people. Students enter a community that embraces them while challenging them.

Instruction in our school is rooted in collaboration and inquiry, which leads to deeper individual understanding of content and application of this content to real life. Our curriculum remains driven by conceptual learning, using digital activities and personalized differentiation to meet the needs of our students. We aim to provide an equitable education that allows each student to discover and utilize their full potential, while finding joy in learning.

Along with strong support in our classrooms, we create a safe learning environment for our students, nurturing and supporting them as they grow. Students are equipped with tools to overcome obstacles they may face and to help them become understanding and respectful of different identities and cultures. To do so, we focus on our school's core values: respect, responsibility, integrity, compassion, and honesty, along with the International Baccalaureate learner profile traits. With these tools, our students become lifelong learners ready to actively participate in the world.

In 2014, our school became the first New York City public middle school to be certified as an International Baccalaureate Middle Years programme. In addition, we have been a certified Advancement Via Individual Determination (AVID) model school since 2013. After over a decade of service to our students and families, we look forward to our continued growth as a community.

(Founded 1926)

Principal Tom Rinke

President Joseph J. Haas

DP coordinator Paul Cancilla

Status Private

Boarding/day Mixed

Gender Coeducational

Language of instruction English

Authorised IB programmes DP

Age Range 13 – 18 years

Number of pupils enrolled 441

Address
538 East Grandview Boulevard
Erie **PA 16504 | USA**

TEL +1 814 824 2323

Email aorlando@mpslakers.com

Website www.mpslakers.com

Mission
Mercyhurst Preparatory School (MPS) is a four year coeducational Catholic secondary school founded by the Sisters of Mercy to prepare students from all religious and ethnic backgrounds for a successful, productive, and compassionate life in an ever-changing and interdependent world. A Mercyhurst Prep education is based upon the teachings of Jesus Christ, the Mercy charism, and a modeling of Judeo Christian values. We strive for excellence in academic and co-curricular programs, promote service to our local and global communities, and foster the dedication and active support of the students, parents, faculty, staff, and alumni of the Mercyhurst community.

Community
Mercyhurst Prep is located on the beautiful shores of Lake Erie in the USA where students experience seasonal change and access to numerous outdoor activities in this safe community of 200,000. Erie, Pennsylvania has easy access to major US cities – Cleveland, Buffalo, and Pittsburgh – as well as Toronto, Canada.

Curriculum
As a college preparatory school, the curriculum is rigorous. 98% of graduates matriculate to post-secondary institutions. The school offers a wide range of courses at the college prep, honors, and International Baccalaureate (IB) levels. Implemented in 1985, the International Baccalaureate programme is geared towards knowledgeable and caring students who are motivated to succeed in a well-rounded interdisciplinary curriculum, which leads to IB certificates or the IB diploma.

Students take eight courses in each of the school's three terms. Our block schedule classes are ninety minutes long. We encourage every student to study at least one IB course.

STEAM (Science, Technology, Engineering, Arts, and Math in the Classroom)
One-to-one iPad deployment provides a tremendous blending of cutting-edge classroom technology with best educational practice. MPS faculty receives extensive ongoing training. Faculty and students are supported by two full-time technology experts. Technology integration occurs across the curriculum.

Creative Arts
The school offers 54 courses in the performing and visual arts taught by a faculty of active award-winning artists. Students exhibit and perform year-round in the school's nationally recognized musical theatre, dance, and choral groups.

Collaboration with Local Universities
Academically advanced students may begin college course work or pursue a subject in greater depth at Mercyhurst University. Some students may complete freshman year of college and senior year of high school simultaneously. The two schools are adjoined by a walkway, making each easily accessible to the other. Students also earn college credit at Gannon University and Penn State Behrend.

Athletics, Activities, and Clubs
A wide variety of extracurricular programs meets the interests of our students and helps them develop time management skills, hone their ability to prioritize, assume responsibility for learning and social events, and compete in ventures that highlight their talents. Athletic teams include football, soccer, tennis, golf, volleyball, basketball, swimming, softball, cheerleading, baseball, rowing, cross country, track, and bowling. MPS teams regularly win district, regional, and state titles with a program philosophy that emphasizes dedication, teamwork, and good sportsmanship.

Boarding Opportunities

While 95% of the students are day students, the school also serves international students from countries such as China, Vietnam, Taiwan, India, Brazil, Canada, Mexico, and Russia. A partnership Christian Boarding provide dormitory housing for international and American students who board full-time as well as weekdays. Visit mpslakers.com/boarding for more information.

A small sampling of colleges attended by Mercyhurst Prep grads includes:

- Boston University
- Brandeis University
- Carnegie Mellon University
- Case Western University
- Dartmouth University
- New York University
- Penn State University
- Rochester Institute of Technology
- Rutgers University
- Swarthmore College
- University of Notre Dame
- Wake Forest University
- Villanova University

Faculty

60% of our faculty/administration hold postgraduate degrees. The student to faculty ratio is 11:1. Besides in-depth expertise in their specific fields, our faculty embody the Mercy charism, an attribute that makes them unique and exceedingly qualified to work with teens. Many teachers travel extensively during breaks and summer vacation, bringing an international mindset to instruction.

Admissions Policy

Mercyhurst Prep admits students of any race, creed, color, or national origin without discrimination. When any student applies for admission, every effort is made to determine whether the school offers an educational program which will allow that student to develop intellectually, socially, spiritually, emotionally, and physically.

Future Ready and Engaging

The Bill and Audrey Hirt DREAM Lab and Room 201 serve as learning environments where the infusion of new digital tools and technology can enhance the learning process. Teachers utilize proven and emerging teaching strategies while students learn fundamental concepts like communication, collaboration, critical thinking, and creativity.

Examples of our technology include: 9 Touchscreens, 2 Video Walls, 40 Lenovo Intel Laptops, 16 Makerbot 3D Printers, 3 Workstations with Touchscreens, Drones, 3 Oculus Rift Immersive Virtual Reality Systems, 12 zSpace Combined Virtual Reality and Augmented Reality Systems, 12 Oculus Quest 2, 5 DJI Robomaster S-1, 15 Sphero Bolts, 10 Lego Mindstorm Expansion Kits, 8 Lego Spike Expansion Kits, 24 Lenovo Laptops, 15 Raspberry Pi 4 Desktop Kits, 6 HP Omen Gaming Computers.

Performing Arts Center (PAC)

Our-newly renovated PAC boasts a cutting-edge flying system, acoustics, lighting, and climate control. These improvements will help prepare our students for the creative endeavors of a 21st century actor, dancer, vocalist, musician, lighting designer and technician.

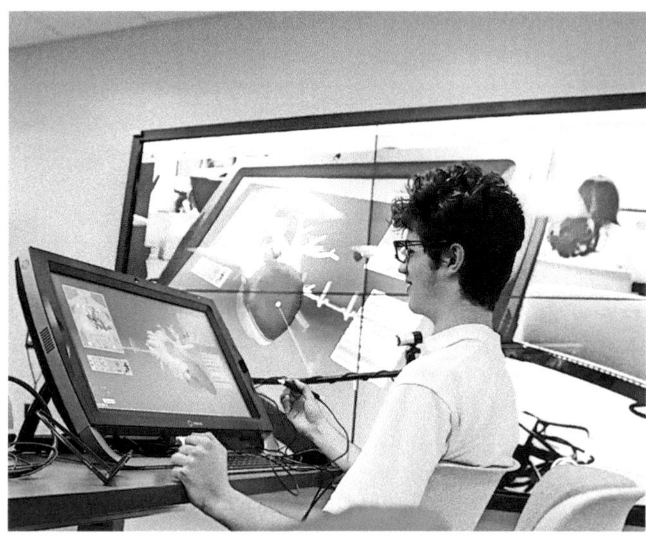

METROPOLITAN SCHOOL OF PANAMA

A NORD ANGLIA EDUCATION SCHOOL

(Founded 2011)

Headteacher Dr. Mark Starbuck

PYP coordinator Ms. Olivia McKevett

MYP coordinator Mr. Ryan Manary

DP coordinator Ms. Lori Guerra

Status Private

Boarding/day Day

Gender Coeducational

Language of instruction English

Authorised IB programmes PYP, MYP, DP

Age Range 3 – 18 years

Number of pupils enrolled 800

Fees Day: $10,758 – $21,379 per annum

Address Green Valley, Panama Norte Panama City | **PANAMA**

TEL +507 317 1130

Email admissions@themetropolitanschool.com

Website www.nordanglia education.com/met-panama

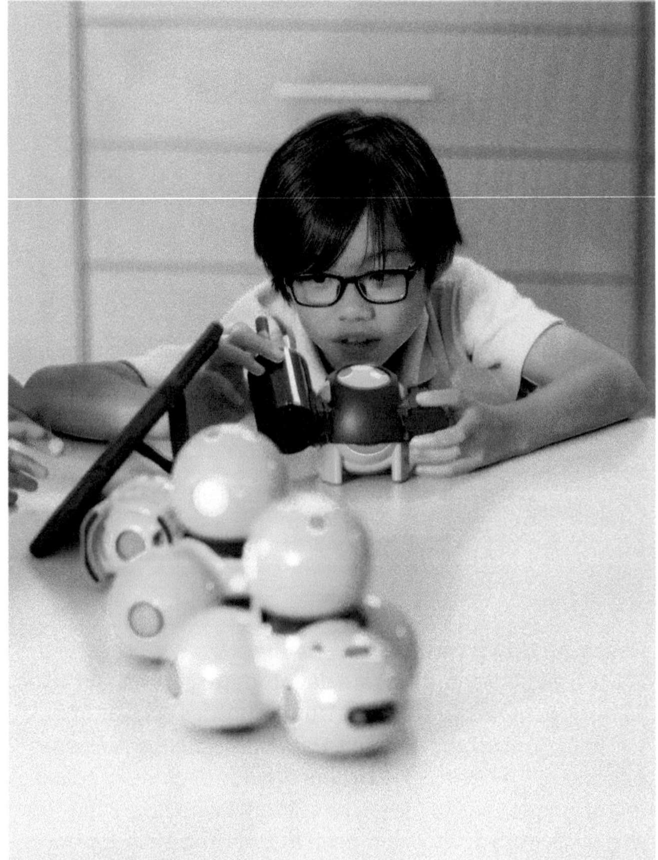

The Metropolitan School of Panama (MET), is an International Baccalaureate (IB) World School for students aged 3-18, and the only IB continuum school in Panama authorized to offer the PYP, MYP and DP programmes in Panama.

Celebrating 12 years of world-class academics, the MET offers Preschool through 12th grade programs, with 800 students hailing from 45 nationalities.

Our school is committed to each child reaching their personal level of excellence through a balanced academic program. Your child will develop all the skills they need to thrive, no matter what they want to do or be in life. Our teachers are highly experienced in delivering the IB Continuum and, most importantly, encourage students' talents and love for learning.

The MET is proud to form part of Nord Anglia Education, the world's leading premium schools organization, uniting with more than 80 other outstanding schools in 30+ countries worldwide. NAE's global family of schools share a common philosophy that there is no limit to what its students can achieve. Our students benefit from collaborations with world renowned institutions through our Juilliard-Nord Anglia Performing Arts Programme, preparing them for the world's stage. Our MIT STEAM curriculum focuses on transferable skills in an evolving world. Our global scale enables us to recruit and retain the best teachers in the world, offering a quality education in Panama.

A campus built for the future

The MET's 5-hectare purpose built campus offers unparalleled educational facilities, not just in Panama but in Central America.

MET students discover a world beyond the traditional classroom with modern learning spaces designed for collaborative learning; including 7 fully-equipped science labs, a STEAM lab, black box theater, FIFA sized soccer field, a 25 meter pool and specialized areas for design, technology and music.

We are a school committed to the education of the future and are proud to offer a 1-to-1 technology program for all students, implementing Apple technology throughout the school. MET students are encouraged to use technology strategically and mindfully, reinforcing their responsibility through our Digital Citizenship Program.

Our goal is to educate your child for the future, enhancing learning through collaborations with the world's best organizations. No two children learn the same way, which is why we personalise learning to what works best for your child. Our approach enables each child to achieve the best academic results while developing the skills, resilience and mind-set to thrive in an ever-changing world.

The MET's excellent results and acceptances at the world's leading universities are a testament to our excellent execution of the IB Programmes and our experienced teachers. The 2023 MET class achieved an excellent 90% IBDP pass rate, and a very high proportion of our Senior class (79%) studied for and achieved the IBDP. Our highest IB score was 43 points and 68% of our cohort earned a bilingual IB Diploma. MET graduates attend some of the most prestigious colleges and universities worldwide. Our 2023 graduating class received scholarship offers totalling $2.3M USD.

Come and learn more about the Metropolitan School of Panama. **Enrolment is open throughout the year and we always welcome enquiries and visits from prospective families.** To explore the MET difference take a virtual tour: https://guiap.com/360/met/ or contact: admissions@themetropolitanschool.com

Mulgrave School, The International School of Vancouver

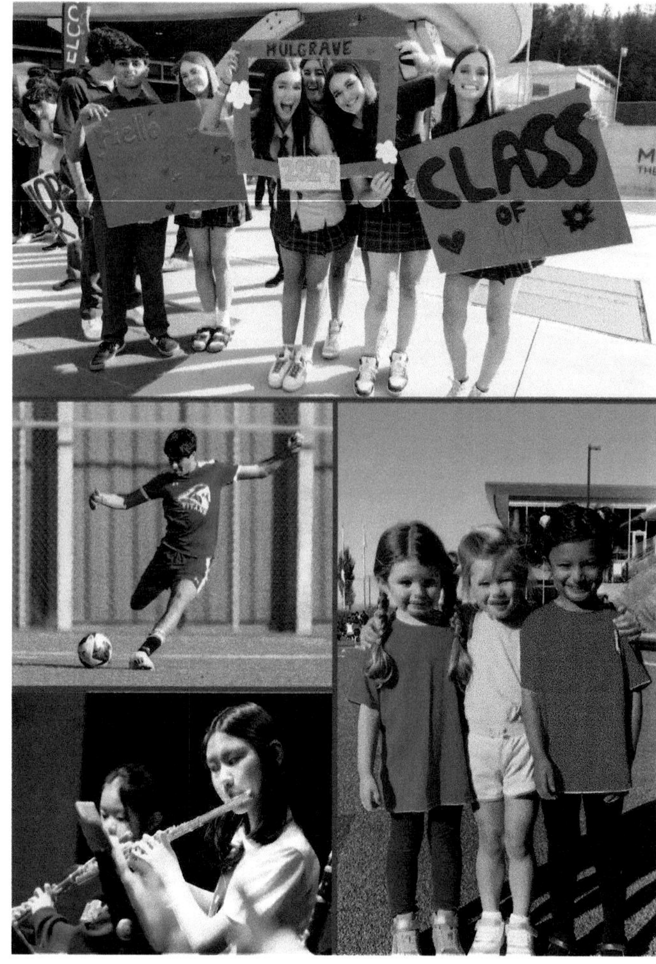

(Founded 1993)	**Authorised IB programmes** PYP, MYP, DP
Head of School Craig Davis	**Age Range** 3 – 18 years
PYP coordinators Janet Hicks & Shanaz Ramji	**Number of pupils enrolled** 1030
MYP coordinator Mike Olynyk	**Fees** Day: CND$26,850 – CND$30,290 per annum
DP coordinator Aziz Batada	**Address** 2330 Cypress Bowl Lane West Vancouver BC V7S 3H9 | CANADA
Status Private	**TEL** +1 604 922 3223
Boarding/day Day	**Email** admissions@mulgrave.com
Gender Coeducational	**Website** www.mulgrave.com
Language of instruction English	

Mulgrave, The International School of Vancouver is a gender-inclusive, multicultural International Baccalaureate World School offering Preschool to Grade 12. Our campus is located at the base of Cypress Mountain, providing our students and faculty with breathtaking ocean views and access to nature. The purpose-built spaces on our stunning campus inspire our diverse community to develop interpersonal and intercultural skills, attitudes, and values that allow our students to thrive and be happy anywhere in the world. Our graduates have been accepted at post-secondary institutions around the globe, including UBC and McGill in Canada, NYU and UC Berkeley in the United States, and Maastricht and Cambridge internationally.

Our Mission: Inspiring Excellence in Education and Life

Through the continuous pursuit of personal best, Mulgrave strives to equip lifelong learners to thrive in a culturally diverse and interdependent world. Our goal is for students to embrace, with passion and confidence, their responsibility to make a difference by serving their communities, locally and in the world at large.

Our Culture: A warm, vibrant, supportive community

Developing a strong aptitude for learning, service, and leadership is inherent to our school's ethos, as is a strong culture of caring and support. Mulgrave is highly valued for our positive community spirit, enriched by the diversity of families from around 40 countries, and its vibrant learning atmosphere. Experienced teachers from around the world provide a comprehensive, appropriately challenging, and personalised IB curriculum to an equally ambitious and capable student body.

Our Strategic Plan: Weaving Our Future, Common Threads

It is our intention, while being true to our school's guiding statements, to build on our success from our previous strategic plan and to ensure that we continue to provide an outstanding future-oriented education for the students in our care. We will engage student agency and technology to continue to support increased personalisation of learning, curriculum and support. We will focus on student health and wellbeing with more emphasis on social and emotional learning and the use of outdoor educational experiences. And we will focus on students' skill development with special emphasis on creativity, global citizenship, and social entrepreneurship.

Accreditations

Mulgrave is proud to be an accredited member of the Council of International Schools (CIS), the Independent Schools Association of British Columbia (ISABC), and Canadian Accredited Independent Schools (CAIS), and is also authorised by the International Baccalaureate Organization as an IB Continuum School.

(Founded 1821)

Head of School
Joe Williams

DP coordinator
Jennifer McMahon

Status Private

Boarding/day Mixed

Gender Coeducational

Language of instruction
English

Authorised IB programmes
DP

Age Range 14 – 19 years

Number of pupils enrolled
340

Fees
Day: US$41,000 per annum
Boarding: US$68,900 per annum

Address
70 Main Street
New Hampton
NH 03256 | USA

TEL +1 603-677-3400

Email
admission@newhampton.org

Website
www.newhampton.org

Lifelong Learners and Active Global Citizens
New Hampton School is an independent, coeducational, college preparatory school for boarding and day students, grades 9 through 12, and postgraduate. Nestled in the foothills of New Hampshire's White Mountains and the heart of the beautiful Lakes Region, yet just 90 minutes from Boston, Massachusetts, the 350-acre campus features six contemporary classroom buildings. On-campus housing includes 13 dormitories, varying in size, each with resident dorm parents/family and complementary dorm life programming activities throughout the year.

Sharing the whole world
Our school's mission is to cultivate lifelong learners who will serve as active global citizens. Core values of respect and responsibility provide an essential foundation, while our inclusive community immerses students in diverse cultures, travel opportunities and a worldwide network of alumni, families, and friends. By allowing classroom conversations to represent more points of view, expertise from outside sources, and intellectual links to coursework, we introduce students to a full range of insights. Ours is a conscious curriculum built on an interconnected understanding of the world.

The student body includes representation from 28 states and 30 different countries. Twenty-five percent of students are international. New Hampton routinely sends students to top colleges and universities, including Harvard University, Massachusetts Institute of Technology, Dartmouth College, University of Michigan, Brown University, University of Wisconsin, Madison, UCLA, and the University of Chicago.

Empowering Technology
New Hampton School is considered a leader in technology integration and is recognized by Apple for continuous innovation in learning, teaching, and the school environment. Students benefit from a 1:1 iPad Program, used to individualize the learning process and expand ideas, and are well-versed in the promise of technology in their futures.

Enlivened Learning
Our school is proud of its programmatic variety, spirited athletics, robust art offerings, including Animation by the Walt Disney Family Museum, a new Entrepreneurial Studies curriculum, student leadership opportunities, clubs, and activities. International Baccalaureate classes begin in eleventh grade and can be taken as part of the full Diploma Programme or as certificate courses. The IB philosophy permeates the curriculum and prepares ninth and tenth graders to embrace its challenges. Equally prominent is the School's commitment to delivering durable skills using relevant content, emphasizing experiential education and career partnerships. The average class size is 11, and the academic rigor is well-balanced with project-based learning modules and dynamic, supportive educators. Students preparing to meet the demands of the IB Diploma Programme may take advantage of our Academic Support Program tutorials or International Support classes to better understand their learning styles and build confidence.

Weekend activities on and off campus include dances, dinner trips, shopping, hikes, concerts, day trips to Boston, and student-designed outings.

Northern International School

Principal
Prof. Estela María Irrera de Pallaro

DP coordinator
Clotilde Alleva

Status Private

Boarding/day Day

Gender Coeducational

Language of instruction
Spanish, English, Italian, Portuguese

Authorised IB programmes
DP

Age Range 2 – 18 years

Address
Ruote 8 Km 61.5.
1633. Pilar,
Buenos Aires
| ARGENTINA

TEL +54 2322 49 1208

Website
www.intschools.org/school/northern

Together with Islands International School and Southern International School.

Northern International School opened its doors in 1997 in a site of 8 hectares in Pilar.

Its founder, Prof. Estela María Irrera de Pallaro, has as an aim to offer a demanding educational quality for families looking for a better lifestyle for their children. With the benefits that contact with nature offers, Northern International School develops all its regular activities in a bright and cheerful environment.

The International Baccalaureate, of which we have been members since 1997, is key in this institution; that is why teachers and heads are trained regularly.

The school has all the facilities needed to comply with this modern and demanding programme: science and IT labs, a library for research, a multi-purpose hall as well as comfortable and bright classrooms.

Our three schools have fully equipped laboratories for the experimental sciences; they are an essential facility for classes in Physics, Chemistry and Biology. Our laboratory provisions are not only for demonstration classes but also for students to become personally acquainted with different research techniques and apply them in practice in experiments ranging from the simple to the more complex. Our students learn to handle laboratory materials safely and efficiently and make full use of them in different pieces of research.

At primary level, research projects include: photosynthesis, animal nutrition, the ill effects of tobacco, analysis of animal movements, electrical resistance, the structure of materials, magnetism, the human body, heat energy, ecosystems, soil, water, cells, life process in vegetables and diet in humans.

At secondary level, research projects include: coefficients of contact, genetics, physical and chemical properties of hydrocarbons, evolutionary theory, population growth, biodiversity, pollution of the environment, ecosystems, and health and human physiology.

Year after year, our students take part in different events and competitions, among these Physics and Biology Olympiads, science fairs organized by ESSARP (English Speaking Scholastic Association of the River Plate), local representative of the University of Cambridge, and Mathematics Olympiads organized by OMA (Argentine Mathematics Olympiads). In recent years the schools have taken part in the worldwide NASA projects and one of our schools has on three occasions won the regional competition and taken part in the world finals in Houston in the United States.

(Founded 1920)

Head of School
Lucila Minvielle PhD

PYP coordinator
Maria Ines Martinez Beccar Varela & Natalia Torlaschi

DP coordinator
Alicia Rodriguez Loredo

Status Private

Boarding/day Day

Gender Coeducational

Language of instruction
English, Spanish

Authorised IB programmes
PYP, DP

Age Range 2 – 18 years

Number of pupils enrolled
1828

Olivos Site
Roma 1248, Olivos,
Buenos Aires
| ARGENTINA

TEL +54 11 4711 8400

Email admissionsolivos@northlands.edu.ar

Nordelta site
Av de los Colegios 680 Nordelta,
Provincia de Buenos Aires
| ARGENTINA

TEL +54 11 4871 2668/9

Email admissionsnordelta@northlands.edu.ar

Website www.northlands.edu.ar

NORTHLANDS is a coeducational, bilingual IB World School that, through caring and innovative teaching, educates young people to the full extent of their individual potential. It is a school that values its Anglo-Argentine roots, while respecting all cultures, religions and nationalities. It offers an all-encompassing friendly environment reflected in its motto: Friendship & Service.

We aim to strengthen our position as leaders in education and innovation by focusing on our students' wellbeing and helping them discover their individual learning paths. We are expanding project based learning, Design and Technology and Education for Sustainable Development, instilling a culture of healthy lifestyle choices. We keep developing our campuses to meet the needs of our highly demanding programmes, and continue to develop a closely knit community influenced by the diversity of our families. We appreciate the richness of diversity and promote international mindedness as we currently have 11% of international families in Olivos and 19% in Nordelta.

Kindergarten Education

An all-embracing curriculum that works on physical, social, emotional, intellectual, ethical and aesthetic aspects through teaching and learning strategies focused on encouraging curiosity and the desire to know in children.

Primary Education

Our integral curriculum is based on inquiry and research as the ideal vehicles for learning. We provide a caring and stimulating environment where children enjoy doing their work and develop positive academic and interpersonal attitudes, self-confidence and self-discipline.

Secondary Education

During this phase students develop critical thinking skills, creativity and autonomy. Individual talents and personal interests are nurtured so that students can make satisfactory career choices at the end of their school life.

While we constantly pursue academic excellence, NORTHLANDS embraces many different programmes where students can develop a variety of skills. We consider Physical Education as an integral part of education as the well being of our students is accomplished through physical, mental and emotional balance. The Visual & Performing Arts Programme stimulates children to find alternative ways to express themselves. As students mature, they have the opportunity to explore visual arts, music and drama through a variety of techniques, instruments and cultures. Our Design & Technology Programme seeks to build a culture of innovation through the implementation of different techno-educational abilities such as construction, designing, programming and robotics, where students apply them to the real world by investigating digital solutions. Finally, our Personal & Social Education Programme is a central part of the comprehensive education that NORTHLANDS aims for its students. We help develop the values of integrity based on high moral standards enabling our children to freely choose what is right.

Orangewood Elementary

Principal
Ms. Janet Shirley

PYP coordinator
Mrs. Candice Hernandez

Status State

Boarding/day Day

Gender Coeducational

Language of instruction
English, Spanish, Mandarin

Authorised IB programmes
PYP

Age Range 4 – 11 years

Number of pupils enrolled
600

Address
1440 S. Orange Avenue
West Covina
CA 91790 | USA

TEL +1 626 939 4820

Website
orangewood.wcusd.org

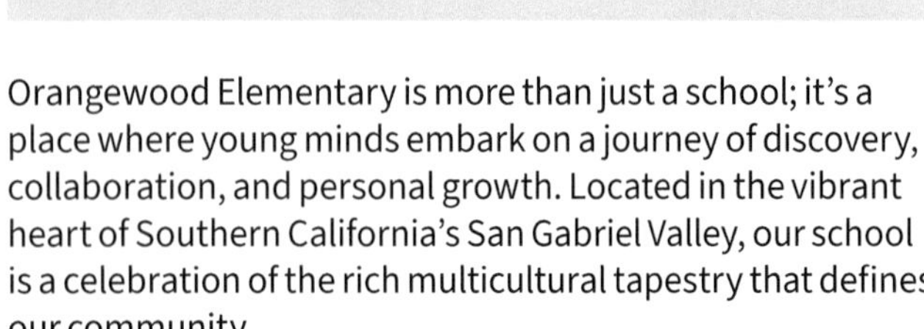

Orangewood Elementary is more than just a school; it's a place where young minds embark on a journey of discovery, collaboration, and personal growth. Located in the vibrant heart of Southern California's San Gabriel Valley, our school is a celebration of the rich multicultural tapestry that defines our community.

Orangewood's mission is clear: we are dedicated to developing globally-minded problem solvers. Our approach is all about empowering students to inquire and take action through transdisciplinary units. We believe in cultivating a love for learning that extends beyond the classroom.

Orangewood Elementary is proud to be the starting point for the West Covina Unified School District's International Baccalaureate (IB) continuum. Our students become part of a journey that extends through the Middle Years Programme and into the Diploma and Career Pathways programs in high school, offering them a seamless and enriching educational experience.

In an increasingly interconnected world, bilingualism is a powerful asset. Orangewood embraces the power of dual immersion, offering students the opportunity to learn in both Spanish and Mandarin. This not only provides the advantage of bi-literacy but also fosters cognitive flexibility and international mindedness.

In a digital age, we equip our students with 21st-century skills. Beginning with kindergarten, we introduce 1:1 tech devices, ensuring they are well-prepared for the future. Our Specials classes, including coding and robotics, promote engineering design and perseverance, while dance lessons allow students to express their creativity. Additionally, our students engage in music, dance, theater, and visual arts through West Covina Unified School District's Visual and Performing Arts (VAPA) program during and after the school day.

At Orangewood, we believe in nurturing the whole child. Our school is a principled and caring community that values the uniqueness of each child. Our staff actively works to promote the health and well-being of our students, and our learning garden encourages cooperative skills, individual responsibility, and scientific curiosity.

Collaboration is at the heart of what we do. Our students, families, and staff come together to create a supportive and inclusive environment. Together, we embark on numerous collaborative projects and events, both within our campus and in the broader community.

Orangewood Elementary is not just a school; it's a launchpad for lifelong learning, global citizenship, and personal growth. We take pride in preparing our students to become the innovative problem solvers of the future while fostering a sense of community that extends far beyond the classroom. Here at Orangewood, we believe in the boundless potential of every child and are committed to helping them achieve it.

Parkland Secondary School

Head of School
Kal Russell

DP coordinator
Erin Stinson

Status State

Boarding/day Day

Gender Coeducational

Language of instruction
English

Authorised IB programmes
DP

Number of pupils enrolled 515

Fees
Day: CND$250 deposit + $150 per IB course to a maximum of $500 CAN per year

Address
10640 McDonald Park Road
North Saanich BC
V8L 5S7 | CANADA

TEL +1 250 655 2700

Email
krussell@saanichschools.ca

Website
parkland.saanichschools.ca

Parkland Secondary School is located on the northern tip of the Saanich peninsula on beautiful Vancouver Island in British Columbia, Canada. We are within kilometers of the Victoria International Airport and the Schwartz Bay Ferry Terminal making for easy access to students and visitors. Parkland Secondary is mere steps from the Pacific Ocean creating fantastic opportunities for students in our Outdoor Education programs and our Sailing Academy. The school's catchment area includes Sidney, North Saanich and the Indigenous communities of Tseycum, Pauquachin and Tsawout. Every year Parkland hosts a number of International students from around the world-attracted to our school and community for the beautiful location and the myriad of programs offered for students.

Parkland Secondary is proud of its innovative, inspiring and inclusive learning environment on which it's built a solid reputation for unique programs. Parkland has a diverse selection of courses offerings including its renowned Marine Academy complementing the region's rich coastal geography. Students can also choose from courses in Trades, Technology, Visual and Performing Arts, and Athletics including a Hockey Academy and Canada's only Judo Academy.

Our International Baccalaureate Diploma Programme makes Parkland the only English speaking public school on Vancouver Island to offer the IB Diploma Programme for students in their final two years of high school. The IB Diploma Programme prepares students for participation in a rapidly evolving and increasingly global society as they develop intellectually, emotionally, physically and ethically while acquiring skills that will prepare them for further education and life in the 21st century.

Students and families interested in finding out more about Parkland Secondary and the IB Diploma Programme can visit the Parkland website https://parkland.saanichschools.ca/ and the Parkland IB website https://parkland.saanichschools.ca/parkland-ib. If you are an international student you can visit the Saanich International Student Program website https://studyinsaanich.ca/. To find out more information about Parkland Secondary School and our IB Diploma Programme you are also welcome to contact Kal Russell, the principal, at krussell@saanichschools.ca or Erin Stinson, the IB Diploma Programme Coordinator, at estinson@saanichschools.ca.

RIDLEY COLLEGE

SINCE 1889

(Founded 1889)

Headmaster
Mr. J. Edward Kidd

PYP coordinator
Marcie Lewis

MYP coordinator
Paul O'Rourke

DP coordinator
Saralyn Covent

Status Independent

Boarding/day Mixed

Gender Coeducational

Language of instruction
English

Authorised IB programmes
PYP, MYP, DP

Age Range 4 – 18 years

Number of pupils enrolled 797

Fees
Day: CAD$25,875 – CAD$39,500 per annum
Domestic Boarders: CAD$69,950 – CAD$73,250 per annum
International Boarders: CAD$79,250 – CAD$82,500 per annum

Address
PO Box 3013
2 Ridley Road
St Catharines ON
L2R 7C3 | CANADA

TEL +1 905 684 1889

Email
admissions@ridleycollege.com

Website
www.ridleycollege.com

Ridley College is focused on educating the whole child and provides students with tools that will help them lead flourishing lives. Our coeducational boarding programme was established in 1889, making Ridley one of Canada's oldest and most prestigious schools.

- Located on a beautiful 90-acre campus in St. Catharines, Ontario
- Canada's leader in positive education
- Easily accessible from Toronto Pearson and Buffalo Niagara International Airport
- Largest CAIS boarding programme in Ontario with 375+ boarding students from 59 countries
- Kindergarten to Grade 12

"World Prep" is what you will find here: a forward-looking, rigorous programme that prepares students for university and a promising future. Ridley is one of only four International Baccalaureate (IB) Continuum boarding schools in North America which offer the Primary Years Programme, Middle Years Programme, and Diploma Programme.

In addition to the IB Programme, Ridley offers the Ontario Secondary School Diploma and a wide range of summer programmes, including an EAL credit course. Together with its impressive academics, students experience a diverse co-curricular programme comprised of arts, athletics, leadership development and community service.

Ridley graduates matriculate to some of the most prestigious universities in the world, including:

- Berklee College of Music
- Carnegie Mellon University
- Johns Hopkins University
- New York University
- Princeton University
- Royal College of Surgeons in Ireland
- University of British Columbia
- University of Cambridge
- University of Hong Kong
- University of Oxford
- University of Toronto
- University of Waterloo
- Yale University

For more than 134 years, Ridley College has held to its motto, *Terar Dum Prosim*, which translates to "May I be consumed in service." Students have plenty of opportunities year-round to give back to their communities, explore new interests, cultivate passions, and reach their potential in a challenging and supportive environment.

One of the school's defining features is its traditional House system, which integrates boarding and day students into ten boarding houses on campus, each with its own distinctive identity and sense of community. By incorporating local day students into its boarding programme, Ridley provides each member with the opportunity to learn more about global cultures while enjoying a uniquely Canadian experience.

Rochambeau, The French International School

Head of School
Mr Xavier Jacquenet

DP coordinator
Sandra Percy

Status Private

Boarding/day Day

Gender Coeducational

Language of instruction
English, French

Authorised IB programmes
DP

Age Range 2 – 18 years

Number of pupils enrolled
1215

Fees
Grade 5
US$24,705 per annum
Grades 6-9
US$25,510 per annum
Grades 10-12
US$29,865 per annum

Address
9600 Forest Rd
Bethesda
MD 20814 | USA

TEL +1 301 530 8260

Email
admissions@rochambeau.org

Website
www.rochambeau.org

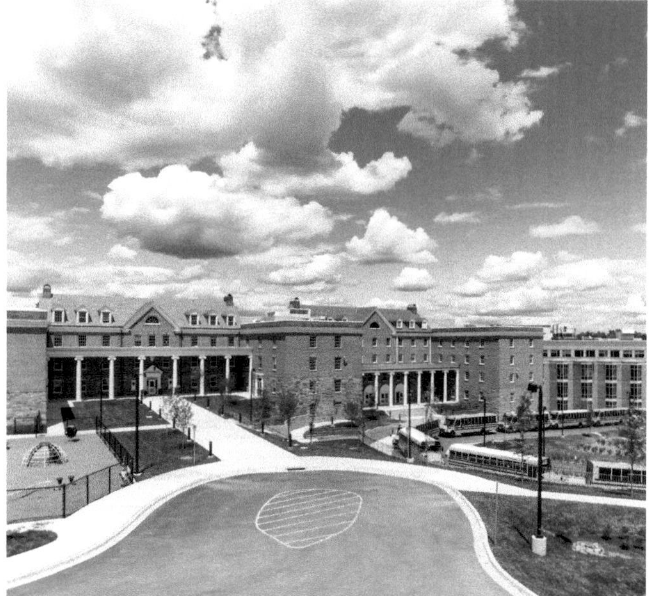

Founded in 1955, Rochambeau, The French International School of Washington DC provides a safe and caring environment that welcomes students of all backgrounds and nationalities, nurturing them to become plurilingual, confident, and open-minded critical thinkers. Our multicultural students graduate with the French Baccalauréat or International Baccalaureate, two academically balanced and challenging curricula with schools all over the world. Rochambeau belongs to the AEFE Network of French Schools Abroad, the Mission Laique Française network and is an International Baccalaureate school. Rochambeau is also accredited by the AIMS, the Association of Independent Schools in Maryland and by The Maryland State Department of Education.

Our beautiful two campuses in Bethesda, Maryland, located a short distance from one another, are the home to a vibrant international community representing more than 80 nationalities. Students can start as young as age 2, acquiring proficiency in both French and English. The maternelle (preschool) program, noted as the "crown jewel of the French school system," emphasizes play, written and oral skills, and learning to live in a community. Students appreciate the holistic approach implemented in this well-balanced comprehensive program. French beginners can enroll in the school until the 3rd grade through a specially designed immersion program. In addition to French, students have the option of learning a number of languages, including Arabic, German, Latin, and Spanish, some starting as early as 4th grade.

Field trips are an important part of their academic enrichment and students actively engage in a number of extracurricular activities, including, Model UN, soccer, theater, volleyball, or rock climbing. In 9th grade (3e), Rochambeau students can continue with the French curriculum, culminating in the French International Baccalauréat, or can switch to the International Baccalaureate track in 9th and 10th grade. This gives our students the distinct advantage to select a diploma program that best suits their learning styles and goals. Rochambeau is one of three schools in North America to offer the IB Advanced Bilingual Diploma, another option of the IDBP in 11th and 12th grade. Students can also receive their US high school diploma at the end of 11th grade. Graduates of Rochambeau go on to study in both the US and internationally, attending some of the top universities around the world.

For more information, please see Rochambeau's website: www.rochambeau.org.

Santiago College

(Founded 1880)

Director
Ms Lorna Prado Scott

PYP coordinator
Mónika Naranjo

MYP coordinator
Angel Girano

DP coordinator
Renato Hamel

Status Private

Boarding/day Day

Gender Coeducational

Language of instruction
Spanish, English

Authorised IB programmes
PYP, MYP, DP

Age Range 3 years 9 months – 18 years

Number of pupils enrolled
1970

Address
Av. Camino Los Trapenses 4007
Lo Barnechea
Santiago | **CHILE**

TEL +56 2 27338800

Email
master@scollege.cl

Website
www.scollege.cl/index.php/es/

Santiago College is a bilingual, independent, co-educational day school, founded as a non-sectarian institution in 1880 with support from the US Methodist Church.

The educational programme at Santiago College meets the requirements of the Chilean Ministry of Education and is authorized to offer three of the IB Programmes: PYP, MYP and DP. Santiago College is accredited by CIS and NEASC.

Students normally enter Santiago College at PK level and stay until they graduate from 12th Grade. Students applying for admission to PK must be four years old by December 31st of the year prior to school entry. Santiago College accepts students without regard to gender, colour, creed, or ethnic, nationality or social origin. The selection process includes an interview with prospective students and their parents. Although most students are Chilean, a considerable number of students come from other countries and priority admission is given to overseas applicants. Approximately 90% of the graduating class enters Chilean universities and the remainder pursues studies in the USA or Europe.

The school operates a 180-day minimum calendar starting in early March and ending in mid-December. PK and kindergarten children have a half-day schedule. All other grades have a full school day beginning at 7:55am and ending between 3:30 and 5:10 pm. The school campus of 11 hectares is located in Lo Barnechea, 30 minutes drive from the city centre. Facilities include a library of 40,000 volumes, 98 classrooms, AV rooms, an auditorium, gymnasium, swimming pool, playing fields, science and computing labs, music and art studios and one cafeteria. All classrooms are equipped with interactive projectors, and numerous devices are available for student use at all grade levels, to support the integration of technology into learning.

Southern International School

Principal
Prof. Estela María Irrera de Pallaro

DP coordinator
Clotilde Alleva

Status Private

Boarding/day Day

Gender Coeducational

Language of instruction
Spanish, English, Italian, Portuguese

Authorised IB programmes
DP

Age Range 2 – 18 years

Address
Freeway Buenos Aires – La Plata Km 34.
1884 Hudson, Buenos Aires | ARGENTINA

TEL +54 11 4215 3636

Website
www.intschools.org/school/southern

Working together with Islands International School and Northern International School.

A community committed to education

In 1999 Mrs. Estela María Irrera de Pallaro, backed up and encouraged by her experience in founding and developing a comprehensive educational project, creates a new school with the aim of improving the institution objectives in a place where families can not only find peace and privacy but also a space in contact with nature.

The school mission is to teach students to interact and adapt to a complex social environment in which they need numerous tools to be able to succeed, accompanied by a teaching staff permanently trained. For this purpose, with a history of more than three decades, the school provides a demanding education that not only abides by academic aspects but expects to educate upright people as well.

Southern International School develops the students' capacities through different activities so that they can interact with full independence and freedom in today's society.

International Baccalaureate Programme

International Schools want their students to complete their studies hand in hand with this organization. Born in Geneva, Switzerland, these programmes, which demand a strong commitment from teachers and heads, are worldwide recognized by their excellent quality.

To belong to or to be a member of this organization implies meeting certain requirements such as having fully equipped experimental sciences laboratories, where the students acquire and handle different research techniques in order to apply them in class in a practical manner, which will help them achieve a better understanding of all kinds of topics, easy or complex.

Southpointe
ACADEMY

(Founded 2000)

Head of School
Gordon MacIntyre

Sr. School Principal
Gordon Cogan

Middle School Principal
Cori Kusel

Jr. School Principal
Coralie MacIntyre

PYP coordinator
J. Roxanne Young

MYP coordinator
Samantha Goodard

DP coordinator
Theresa Kwan

Status Private, Independent

Boarding/day Day

Gender Coeducational

Language of instruction
English

Authorised IB programmes
PYP, MYP, DP

Fees
Kindergarten – Grade 12
CND$21,600 – CND$24,200 per annum
International CND$42,825 per annum

Address
1900 56th Street
Tsawwassen BC
V4L 2B1 | CANADA

TEL +1 604 948 8826

Email
admissions@southpointe.ca

Website
www.southpointe.ca

Southpointe Academy is situated between the mountains and the sea, providing expansive views of the surrounding region, including Boundary Bay, Centennial Beach, the Salish Sea, and the panoramas of the North Shore mountains. A short 40-minute drive from Vancouver, Tsawwassen is known for its community atmosphere and beachside living, which is commonly integrated into our student curriculum through beach cleanups, wildlife and environmental advocacy, and collaborations with local businesses.

Southpointe is an International Baccalaureate (IB) Continuum World School authorized to deliver the complete Primary Years Programme (K-5), Middle Years Programme (Grades 6-10), and Diploma Programme (Grades 11-12). As an IB Continuum World School offering a continuum of IB programmes, Southpointe embraces the philosophy of the IB "to develop inquiring, knowledgeable and caring young people, who help to create a better and more peaceful world through intercultural understanding and respect." At Southpointe, we aim to develop young people of character who will make a positive difference in the world.

With a foundation built on community, Southpointe has grown into an internationally recognized school, seeking to expand the boundaries of what is possible while staying committed to its founding mandate. Shaped by experienced faculty and staff who bring diverse perspectives and extensive knowledge to every department, an internationally recognized curriculum framework, and a state-of-the-art campus, Southpointe looks ahead to a bright future while continuing to provide a world-leading education for our students to learn, lead and succeed.

Our Future

Southpointe Academy is in the development stage of our Master Campus Plan expansion. We are expanding and enriching our curricular and co-curricular offerings for students and families with additional specialist classrooms and amenities. Southpointe will be able to offer more courses from Kindergarten to Grade 12 as Delta's only International Baccalaureate (IB) Continuum School and enrich the strength of its athletics, arts, outdoor education and service-learning programs. The growth of Southpointe will serve local families' needs, enhance the local economy, and enrich the overall community development of South Delta.

St. Francis College, Brazil

ST. FRANCIS COLLEGE

(Founded 2003)

College Principal
Mrs Shirley Hazell

Head of Early Years & Primary
Jefferson Smith

Head of Secondary
Carolina Giannetto

PYP coordinator
Benedict Bowler

MYP coordinator
Thomas Holesgrove

DP coordinator
Antonia Zanotto

Status Private

Boarding/day Day

Gender Coeducational

Language of instruction
English, Portuguese

Authorised IB programmes
PYP, MYP, DP

Age Range 3 – 18 years

Number of pupils enrolled
904

Fees
Day: US$21,000 – US$25,000 per annum

Address
Rua Joaquim Antunes 678
Pinheiros
São Paulo
SP 05415-001 | BRAZIL

TEL +55 11 3728 8053

Email
office@stfrancis.com.br

Website
www.stfrancis.com.br

St. Francis College is an international school which strives for excellence providing a warm and friendly community committed to the IB Philosophy. We offer a challenging educational programme with rigorous assessment through inquiry-based instruction.

We empower pupils to be passionate lifelong learners, achieve academic and personal excellence and be committed to impact the world positively.

Curriculum

The international curriculum offered is taught in English. The formal curriculum is guided by the Brazilian and British National Curriculum and the IB Programmes. A broad approach of concept-based learning encompasses the humanities, arts, sciences, mathematics, and information technology. An important element in the curriculum are the Portuguese language subjects, which include Brazilian literature, Portuguese language as well as the history and geography of Brazil. The College provides pupils with academic challenge and key life skills in a flexible and transdisciplinary programme. We are a continuum school and offer three of the IB Programmes. Throughout the primary school we offer the IB PYP, in the secondary school we offer the IB MYP and the IB DP in the last two years.

IGCSE exams are taken in the main subjects in MYP 5. Pupils will conclude their secondary education having obtained their Brazilian and IB diploma.

A wide range of physical activities and sports are offered to students as well as outstanding programmes in visual arts, drama and music, from Early Years through Secondary Years. Once our students graduate from St. Francis College they go on to both Brazilian and international universities and continue to excel academically, personally and professionally.

Extracurricular activities

Extracurricular activities offered include football, basketball, volleyball, dance, skateboarding, martial arts, cooking, drama, music, arts, MUN (Model United Nations), Duke of Edinburgh Award and more.

Members of

We are members of the IBO, Cambridge Assessment Centre, LAHC, BAIBS, College Board SAT and PSAT10.

St. John's School

Head of School
Mr. Blayne Addley

PYP coordinator
Leslie Morden

MYP coordinator
Daniel Ahn

DP coordinator
Christine Miklitz

Status Private, Independent

Boarding/day Day

Gender Coeducational

Language of instruction
English

Authorised IB programmes
PYP, MYP, DP

Age Range 3 – 18 years

Number of pupils enrolled 570

Fees
Day: CAD$11,950 – CAD$30,450 per annum

Address
2215 West 10th Avenue
Vancouver BC
V6K 2J1 | CANADA

TEL +1 604 732 4434

Email
admissions@sjs.ca

Website
www.sjs.ca

St. John's School At A Glance
Established over 35 years ago, St. John's School (SJS) is located in the heart of beautiful Vancouver, British Columbia. It is a non-denominational, co-educational, IB World School. Our graduates go on to attend Universities across the globe in North America, Europe and Asia.

SJS is known first and foremost as a tight-knit community of teachers, students, staff and parents who work together to ensure everyone is healthy, safe and thriving. An SJS education is shaped by small class sizes, individual attention and a culture of collaboration.

Our Students
SJS students are challenged and encouraged by the rigour of the IB curriculum. Every member of the SJS community explores their talents, skills and interests so they can make a difference in the world in their own way.

Outside academics, SJS aims to provide its students with a real-world grounding. Just like real-life SJS is co-educational. In the classroom, the gym, theatre and art studio, SJS boys and girls use their individual and combined strengths to work and play together. Plus, being based in the heart of Vancouver means students are never far away from the city's cultural and civic delights.

Above all, SJS students are interesting. They are artists, public speakers, chess players, basketball stars, designers and so much more. Whatever their passion, they can explore it at St. John's School.

Our Mission & Values
St. John's aims to develop confident, lifelong learners who make a difference in their communities. Each student embraces and celebrates their unique abilities.

To achieve this, SJS students work hard to cultivate five key values.

- Respect: SJS is a warm, caring and inclusive community. A culture of kindness, empathy and service to others is encouraged.
- Curiosity: SJS promotes critical thinking and stringent inquiry into the nature of things.
- Integrity: Honesty is rewarded. SJS students strive to do the right thing.
- Courage: Students embrace new ideas that challenge them to improve themselves and the communities they are a part of.
- Wellness: SJS cares deeply about personal and environmental health. Students are encouraged to be mindful of their emotions and to nurture personal relationships.

St. Nicholas School – Alphaville

St. Nicholas

Head of School
Simon Lee

Head of Early Years
Jennifer Fletcher

Heads of Primary School
Cristina Prado & Katrina Fabbri

Head of Secondary School
Gudrun Bjorg Ingimundardottir

PYP coordinator
Katrina Fabbri

MYP coordinator
Gudrun Bjorg Ingimundardottir

Status Private

Boarding/day Day

Gender Coeducational

Language of instruction
English, Portuguese

Authorised IB programmes
PYP, MYP

Age Range 18 months – 16 years

Number of pupils enrolled 474

Fees
Tiny Tots I, Tiny Tots II & Nursery (08:00-12:00): R$ 7,070 per month
Kindergarten 1 to Grade 5: R$ 9,696 per month
Grade 6 to Year 12: R$ 12,020 per month

Address
Av. Honório Álvares Penteado 5463
Tamboré, Santana de Parnaíba
SP 06543-320 | BRAZIL

TEL +55 11 3465 9658; +55 11 3465 9697

Email
office.al@stnicholas.com.br

WhatsApp
+55 11 96408 6838

Website
www.stnicholas.com.br

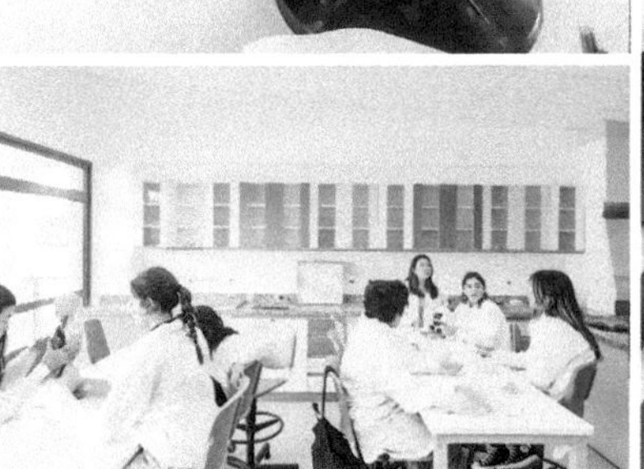

St Nicholas School Alphaville serves families who primarily live in the Alphaville or Tamboré residential neighbourhoods, seeking a personal and purposeful learning experience: a unique learning adventure following the programmes of the International Baccalaureate.

As an IB World School offering the PYP and MYP (currently a candidate school for DP, with the first cohort expected to begin in August 2024), communication, collaboration, and reflection are highly valued. We are extremely proud to call ourselves a truly inclusive school, with strong Personalised Learning and Wellbeing teams to support individual students and their needs.

As an international school, we strive to nurture students who are global citizens and internationally-minded young people, where cultural diversity is celebrated, valued, and respected. St Nicholas students connect their learning with local, national, and global communities. Learning is led through inquiry and agency, and by activating creative and critical thinking skills, developing their passion for learning. Students discover and use their voices, engage in service learning opportunities, and take purposeful action to make an impact.

Our beautiful, purpose-built campus is situated in a semi-rural area, surrounded by nature, and still only 35 minutes from the dynamic city of Sao Paulo. With a community composed of approximately 20 nationalities, we learn from each other, building our appreciation for the languages, cultures, and backgrounds represented on campus.

Our excellent, dedicated, and qualified teachers who are passionate about excellence in teaching and learning, allow us to prepare St Nicholas graduates for their onward learning journey for a life in Brazil or overseas. A caring culture with a belief in every child and a commitment to holistic education, provides a truly enriching learning experience for all St Nicholas Alphaville students.

St. Nicholas School – Pinheiros

Head of School
Andrew VanderMeulen

Head of Early Years
Penelope Cardoso

Head of Primary School
Stephen Eagles

Head of Secondary School
Victor Calzada

PYP coordinators
Juliana Peluzzi, Samantha Waller & Jucileia Oliveira

DP coordinator
Saulo Vianna

Status Private

Boarding/day Day

Gender Coeducational

Language of instruction
English, Portuguese

Authorised IB programmes
PYP, DP

Age Range 18 months – 18 years

Number of pupils enrolled
665

Fees
Tiny Tots I, Tiny Tots II & Nursery (08:00-12:00): R$ 7,070 per month
Kindergarten 1 to Grade 5: R$ 9,696 per month
Grade 6 to Year 12: R$ 12,020 per month

Address
Rua do Emissário 333
Pinheiros
São Paulo
SP 05423-070 | BRAZIL

TEL +55 11 3465 9650; +55 11 3465 9666

Email
admin.pin@stnicholas.com.br

WhatsApp
+55 11 97224 1033

Website
www.stnicholas.com.br

St. Nicholas School serves families who live in São Paulo, seeking a personal and purposeful learning experience: a unique learning adventure following the programmes of the International Baccalaureate.

As an IB World School, communication, collaboration, and reflection are highly valued. As an inclusive school, all members of the St Nicholas community are valued and provided with opportunities to access the learning experience – we meet students where they are and help them to strive for their very best.

As an international school, our goal is to guide children to be global, internationally-minded citizens who understand that the whole world is their place and that there is a place for everyone. Cultural diversity is celebrated and with it, values of respect, citizenship, curiosity, and caring are developed.

As a priority, St Nicholas students connect their learning with their school and local, national, and global communities. Learning is led through inquiry, generating questions, and activating creative and critical thinking skills, developing their passion for learning. Students discover and use their voices, engage in their communities, and take purposeful action to make an impact.

In our international setting in the dynamic city of Sao Paulo, we use all of the advantages of our cultural and linguistic diversity to enrich learning. With numerous nationalities together each day, we learn from each other, building our appreciation for the languages and backgrounds represented on campus.

What distinguishes us and allows us to send St. Nicholas graduates into their onward learning journey with confidence? The answer is found in excellent teachers who are dedicated to excellence in teaching and learning, a caring culture with a belief in every child, and a commitment to the education of the whole child through meaningful, purposeful, and enriching learning experiences on and off campus.

St. Paul's School

(Founded 1926)

Head Teacher
Mr Titus Edge

DP coordinator
Mr Sam Bishop

Status Private

Boarding/day Day

Gender Coeducational

Language of instruction
English

Authorised IB programmes
DP

Age Range 3 – 18 years

Address
Rua Juquiá 166
Jardim Paulistano
São Paulo
SP 01440-903 | BRAZIL

TEL +55 11 3087 3399

Email
head@stpauls.br

Website
www.stpauls.br

St. Paul's School was the first British School to be established in São Paulo (Brazil) and continues to offer an Anglo-Brazilian curriculum, embracing the best of both cultures. As an all-through (ages 3-18) co-educational school, offering the IGCSE and IB courses to pupils, we are affiliated to a global network of top UK Schools through our membership of HMC (Headmaster's Conference) and COBIS (Council of British International Schools). Almost 100 years old, we draw on our proud heritage as the first British school in Latin America to be recognised as a British School Overseas (BSO) by the UK government. Yet, we look forward with creativity and confidence.

At St. Paul's we always strive to be our better selves. We have the courage of our convictions, essential values, freedom to imagine and create. This is achieved through our high quality British and Brazilian holistic education which drives the personal and academic development of pupils, within a framework of a caring, inclusive and united community.

It is our aim to discover the passion and talents of every pupil, and create the right environment to develop these. The school prides itself on an excellent enrichment programme ranging from MUN to Duke of Edinburgh, from knitting classes to a robotics programme, from mathematical Olympiads to outstanding drama and music. We have been awarded as a Microsoft Showcase School and an Apple Distinguished School in recognition for our excellence in transforming and enhancing our physical and online learning environment to deliver more personalised education to our pupils.

The school is a positive agent of change, helping its pupils to be caring individuals ready to inspire and mobilise those around them to impact the world for the best. Our commitment to broad educational experiences opens many opportunities for pupils who go on to leading universities in the United Kingdom, America and Brazil.

We believe in helping our pupils achieve their full intellectual, emotional, social, physical, artistic, creative and spiritual potential. An innovative, structured curriculum, combined with excellent teaching, state of the art facilities, and the best in pastoral care, equip pupils to flourish.

(Founded 2000)

Head of School
Richard Kassissieh

Senior School Principal
Hazel Chee

PYP coordinator
Amanda Lempriere

MYP coordinator
Mark Pulfer

DP coordinator
Hazel Chee

Status Private

Boarding/day Day

Gender Coeducational

Language of instruction
English

Authorised IB programmes
PYP, MYP, DP

Age Range 5 – 18 years

Number of pupils enrolled
545

Fees
Day: CAD$26,750 – CAD$31,250 per annum

Address
3000 Commercial Drive
Vancouver BC
V5N 4E2 | CANADA

TEL +1 604 436 0608

Email
info@stratfordhall.ca

Website www.stratfordhall.ca

Stratford Hall is an independent, gender-inclusive, non-denominational, university preparatory day school with a student population of 545 ranging from Kindergarten to Grade 12. Our location in a vibrant, urban setting in East Vancouver, British Columbia reflects our diverse community of students. Through the continuum of International Baccalaureate (IB) programmes, the Primary Years Programme (Kindergarten – Grade 5), Middle Years Programme (Grade 6 – 10) and Diploma Programme (Grade 11 & 12), the School provides a level of individual challenge and academic rigour beyond the norm. Equally important is our commitment to the IB Learner Profile as a guide, fostering international-mindedness in students and adults alike.

At Stratford Hall, every child is given the opportunity to learn and to thrive; to discover their unique strengths, and to explore the diverse opportunities our rapidly changing world offers. Under the guidance of our staff and faculty, they will grow and mature, while equipping themselves with intellectual tools, strength of character, and a global perspective.

Stratford Hall is a not-for-profit school operating under the authority of the Ministry of Education of British Columbia.

Our Mission

Stratford Hall educates students to the highest global standards through the programmes of the International Baccalaureate. Excellence and confidence are developed through a challenging academic curriculum with further emphasis on creativity, activity and service. We foster a strong pluralistic community built on integrity and respect.

Our Vision

Stratford Hall strives to be a global leader in the International Baccalaureate community. Our students will gain a deep understanding of the world around them, and they will act on their connections to the outside community. They will excel to the best of their abilities, and graduates will be equipped to achieve their chosen goals. This is accomplished by acquiring and retaining the best teachers, and by a commitment to a balanced and enriched curriculum. The success of Stratford Hall is deeply rooted in the establishment of a supportive, knowledgeable and committed community.

Stratford Hall is proud to be an accredited member of the Independent Schools Association of British Columbia (ISABC), Canadian Accredited Independent Schools (CAIS), National Association of Independent Schools (NAIS), and is authorized by the International Baccalaureate Organization as an IB Continuum School.

CANADA'S INTERNATIONAL SCHOOL | L'ÉCOLE INTERNATIONALE DU CANADA

(Founded 1962)

Head of School
Norman Gaudet

PYP coordinator
Emna Beji

MYP coordinator
Julie Rouette

DP coordinator
Dr. Jennifer Elliott

Status Private

Boarding/day Day

Gender Coeducational

Language of instruction
French, English

Authorised IB programmes
PYP, MYP, DP

Age Range 2 – 18 years

Number of pupils enrolled
1500

Fees
Day: CAD$23,070 – CAD$39,020 per annu

Address
306 Lawrence Avenue East
Toronto ON
M4N 1T7 | CANADA

1293 Meredith Avenue,
Mississauga, ON
L5E 2E6 | CANADA

TEL +1 416 484 6533

Email
admissions@tfs.ca

Website
www.tfs.ca

GENERATIONS

"TFS has always been, and remains, the French school with an international outlook."

Andrew '93 and Françoise '93 with Irene

TFS | CANADA'S INTERNATIONAL SCHOOL | L'ÉCOLE INTERNATIONALE DU CANADA

TFS.CA

Bilingual and co-educational since 1962, TFS is renowned as Canada's leading bilingual International Baccalaureate (IB) school, providing an internationally focused education with high academic standards to over 1,500 students. Teaching the curricula of France and Ontario through the framework established by the IB programmes, we offer our students an education that is rich in academic excellence, diversity and opportunity.

Authorized to offer the PYP, MYP and IB Diploma, TFS is an IB World School and the only full continuum bilingual IB school in Canada.

We welcome boys and girls from age two to university entrance. No prior knowledge of French is required for entry up to and including Grade 7. Thanks to our Introductory Program, we successfully integrate students with no background in French. While 90% of TFS students have little or no knowledge of French when they enrol, they graduate fully bilingual with an international outlook that sets them on a path to a bright future.

TFS' mission is to develop multilingual, critical thinkers who celebrate difference, transcend borders and strive for the betterment of humankind.

Our educators come from around the world to teach at either our Toronto or West Campus in Mississauga, and provide a caring and supportive learning environment that encourages students of diverse backgrounds to become individuals who reflect, and citizens who act.

We demonstrate our commitment to the development of the whole child through stimulating academic and co-curricular programs that include recreational and competitive sports, music, visual and dramatic arts.

In addition to being authorized by the IB, TFS is accredited by the Ministry of Education of Ontario, the French Ministry of Education, and Canadian Accredited Independent Schools (CAIS). TFS is also a member of the Conference of Independent Schools of Ontario (CIS), the Council of International Schools, and Agence pour l'enseignement français à l'étranger (AEFE).

Please visit us at www.tfs.ca.

The Baldwin School of Puerto Rico

(Founded 1968)

Head of School
Mr. Greg MacGilpin, Jr

PYP coordinator
Ms. Janelle Méndez

MYP coordinator
Mr. Gregorio Vázquez

DP coordinator
Mrs. Laura Maristany

Status Private

Boarding/day Day

Gender Coeducational

Language of instruction
English

Authorised IB programmes
PYP, MYP, DP

Age Range 3 – 18 years

Number of pupils enrolled 820

Fees
US$9,646 – US$15,895 per annum

Address
PO Box 1827
Bayamón 00960-1827
| **PUERTO RICO**

TEL +1 787 720 2421

Email
admissions@baldwin-school.org

Website
www.baldwin-school.org

The Baldwin School of Puerto Rico, located in the greater San Juan metropolitan area, is the premier independent, PPK-12, college preparatory English language day school in Puerto Rico. It is the first school on the Caribbean island to offer the Primary, Middle and Diploma levels of the International Baccalaureate (IB) program. "What is most congruent with our mission and the IB, is how both are focused on the type of environment that optimizes student learning," says Head of School, Mr. Greg MacGilpin. "We grow with the IB as it challenges us to reflect and act iteratively because of the diversity of our learners' experiences."

At Baldwin School, technology is broadly integrated in the classroom. Students use a range of platforms, applications and web-based software; to research, organize and create content. A fully modern, wireless digital mainframe allows students to leverage the world's resources and conceive original content. Touchscreen technology supports literacy and numeracy across all grades. Interior and exterior laboratories combine hands-on and digital learning. "We were fortunate and deliberate in the transition to online platforms during our pandemic response. Our students and adults have innovated in both, grand and simple ways to share learning," says Mr. MacGilpin.

Baldwin offers a beautiful and spacious twenty-three acre campus, which is also a Certified Wildlife Habitat. Its location means that students can take part in a range of outdoor activities. Spectacular facilities include a swimming pool, tennis courts, field house, outdoor courts, soccer field, and a rainforest biological field station. Indoor facilities include science and computer labs, a performing arts center, a recording studio, multiple art studios, a dance studio, and music rooms.

Baldwin's student body very much reflects Puerto Rico's diverse population. Students participate in dozens of co-curricular activities. Athletes compete at mini, youth, junior varsity, and varsity levels. Math, Science and Model United Nations teams also compete at the national level. Campus life includes opportunities to participate in many clubs and organizations, most of which serve the broader community through both service and donations. All of Baldwin's graduates go on to study at university, mostly abroad, including the United States' most prestigious colleges and universities.

Baldwin School is committed to the belief that every child can flourish if they are given the right combination of time, opportunity, and support.

Established 1926

(Founded 1926)

Principal
Gina C. Duarte-Romero M.Ed.

Assistant Principal
Ana V. Seoane

PYP coordinator
Sofia C. Romero

Status Private

Boarding/day Day

Gender Coeducational

Language of instruction
English

Authorised IB programmes
PYP

Age Range 1 – 14 years

Number of pupils enrolled
200

Fees
US$10,300 – US$22,300 per annum

Address
1600 S. Red Road
Miami
FL 33155 | USA

TEL +1 305 266 4666

Email
info@biltmoreschool.com

Website
www.biltmoreschool.com

Originally founded in Coral Gables in 1926, The Biltmore School is one of the oldest schools in Miami Dade County. Our school enjoys a tradition of educational excellence that has provided guidance to children for the past 90 years.

Our Principal, Gina Romero and our Biltmore Staff members are actively involved in the "Project Zero" research initiative, sponsored by Harvard University that promotes creative thinking, encourages children to be self-reliant, and empowers them to think "outside the box" through a challenging curriculum that incorporates instruction that maximizes the multiple intelligences, individual learning styles and modalities. Through participation in ongoing professional development workshops in partnership with Florida International University, our staff actively explores "Visible Thinking" strategies that promote the highest levels of abstract and critical thinking in children of all ages.

During the 2007-2008 school year our school was awarded accreditation by AISF (Association of Independent Schools of Florida), NIPSA (National Independent Private School Association), COGNIA, MSA-CESS (Middle States Association Commisions on Elementary and Secondary Schools).

The Biltmore School has also been an IB World School since March 2012 and offers the IB Primary Years Programme and is currently considering the IB Middle Years Programme.

The Biltmore School believes that students are capable and knowledgeable agents of their learning. We feel that it is the responsibility of the educator to be both the partner and guide in the growth and development of the child. It is through much research and collaboration that our school has embraced and synthesized diverse educational views and practices to best benefit our students.

The Biltmore School offers a comprehensive program for students from age one through eighth grade.

The British College of Brazil

THE BRITISH
COLLEGE
OF BRAZIL

A NORD ANGLIA EDUCATION SCHOOL

Headteacher
Mr. Nick West

DP coordinator
Mr. Timothy Jones

Status Private

Boarding/day Day

Gender Coeducational

Language of instruction
English

Authorised IB programmes
DP

Age Range 2 – 18 years

Number of pupils enrolled
540

Fees
R$ 88,000 – 120,000 per annum

Address
Rua Álvares de Azevedo, 50
Chácara Flora
São Paulo
SP 04671-040 | BRAZIL

TEL +55 11 5547 3030

Email
info@britishcollegebrazil.org

Website
www.britishcollegebrazil.org

The British College of Brazil (BCB), a Nord Anglia Education school, is São Paulo's school of choice for expatriate families looking to provide their children with an international education. We offer engaging learning environments to students in Early Years, Primary and Secondary school in a warm and supportive atmosphere where they can thrive. Our schools and the one-of-a-kind opportunities we create inside and outside the classroom enrich learning, instil lifelong memories and a deep sense of achievement. We welcome your family to become a valued member of our community.

At the British College of Brazil, we teach the English National Curriculum adapted to an international environment, the International Primary Curriculum, the IGCSE in Year 10 and 11 followed by the IB Diploma Programme in Years 12 and 13. Throughout our core curricula and programs we help your child to develop a global mindset and nurture essential skills such as creativity, collaboration, and resilience. We want every student to become lifelong learners, to try something new and, above all, to be ambitious.

We are part of the Nord Anglia Education family of 86 international schools. Together we can enrich your child's learning experience with opportunities beyond the ordinary.

From online debates and challenges, Global Campus connects our students around the world to learn together every day. Our unique international programs provide our students a great opportunity to broaden their horizons, expand cultural knowledge and foster connections. They can either opt for summer camps in exciting locations from Oxford to Florida, to Switzerland, or choose spending a year in one of our boarding schools – Windermere Preparatory School, The Village School, or North Broward Preparatory School, through our Study Abroad Program.

Through our Global expeditions in Tanzania and Switzerland, or participating in our Performing Arts Festival in Miami or in the Global Games in Orlando, Nord Anglia's students grow up with a well-rounded view of the world, a passion for learning and discovery, and life-long memories of achievement and leadership.

Additionally, our collaborations with world leading institutions such as The Juilliard School, The Massachusetts Institute of Technology (MIT) and UNICEF enhance the curriculum and offer exceptional professional development for teachers. This approach results in high academic outcomes and equips students with the skills that are essential to thrive in the 21st century.

We believe that there is no limit to what our students, our people, and our communities can achieve. We encourage your child to set their sights higher by fostering a global perspective together with our school's personalised approach to learning – helping every child to succeed, thrive and love learning.

The British School, Rio de Janeiro

A caring community, striving for excellence, where every individual matters.

(Founded 1924)

Directors
Jeremy Wong (interim), Fernanda Reis & Isadora Guise

DP coordinator
Guy Smith & André Filho

Status Private

Boarding/day Day

Gender Coeducational

Language of instruction
English

Authorised IB programmes
DP

Age Range 2 – 18 years

Number of pupils enrolled
2300

Fees
Day: R90,000 approx per annum

Address
Rua Real Grandeza 99
Botafogo
Rio de Janeiro
RJ 22281-030 | BRAZIL

TEL +55 21 2539 2717

Email
edu@britishschool.g12.br

Website
www.britishschool.g12.br

Founded in 1924, we are a non-profit, independent and coeducational day school offering a complete and coherent curriculum for students of all nationalities from ages 2-18. Our school aims to give students a broad, balanced and relevant educational experience. The educational philosophy and practice are primarily British in nature with international and Brazilian elements incorporated. Programmes of study are: Early Years Foundation Stage (EYFS) and International.

Primary Curriculum (IPC) for 2 to 11 year olds; Key Stage 3 (Middle Years) of the UK National Curriculum for 11 to 14 year olds; Cambridge IGCSE for 14 to 16 year olds; and the International Baccalaureate (IB) Diploma for 16 to 18 year olds. Over 80% of our students are Brazilian and the remainder are from over 30 different countries, with British and other European students being the biggest proportion.

English is the main language of instruction with Portuguese, French and Spanish also being taught. We are an IB World School accredited by the Council of International Schools (CIS). The director is a member of the Latin American Heads Conference (LAHC). There are 2200 students located on three sites. The Zona Sul Unit is split into two Sites: Botafogo Site (primary school) and Urca Site (secondary school). The Barra Unit caters for students from age 2 (Pre- Nursery) to age 18.

Classes are small and school environment is pleasant, well-resourced and stimulating, with a strong focus on health, safety and security. Performing arts, sports, Model United Nations, Duke of Edinburgh's Award Scheme and work experience provide a wide range of co-curricular opportunities. There are numerous local day visits, national or international residential trips for most year groups. Our teachers are well-qualified (some 30% being recruited from overseas) and supported by a robust and effective programme of continuing professional development.

Our school provides a caring and friendly, yet demanding, learning environment and makes every effort to ensure that each individual has the opportunity to develop their particular abilities and talents to the full. Emphasis on academic achievement is also balanced by our concern to meet our students' physical, emotional and social needs. We place a high value on good social behaviour and ethical standards, with respect for the individual and the environment.

We want our students to be happy in school and we hope that their school experience will be fondly and warmly remembered for life. We believe that this can be achieved through high expectations; clear guidelines and limits; constant encouragement; and addressing individual needs.

Extracurricular Activities

Football, capoeira, volleyball, basketball, ballet, artistic gymnastics, judo, choir, music (instruments and singing), cooking, drama and arts are available.

Facilities

Air-conditioned classrooms, interactive whiteboards, computers, laptops, tablets, science and computer & technology & robotics labs, libraries, gymnasiums and open spaces for sports and games, playgrounds with a variety of toys, Music suites, auditoriums for Drama classes, presentations and art exhibitions, sickbays (first-aid – nurses), and dining halls.

The Newman School

(Founded 1945)

Head of School
Michael Schafer

MYP coordinator
Elizabeth Esposito

DP coordinator
Rachel Ollagnon

Status Private

Boarding/day Mixed

Gender Coeducational

Language of instruction
English

Authorised IB programmes
MYP, DP

Age Range 12 – 19 years

Number of pupils enrolled
250

Fees
Domestic tuition: US$32,000 per annum
International tuition: US$42,500 + Boarding $28,000 per annum

Address
247 Marlborough Street
Boston
MA 02116 | USA

TEL +1 617 267 4530

Email
admissions@newmanboston.org

Website
www.newmanboston.org

At The Newman School, we live our motto, "Heart Speaks to Heart." Faculty relationships are the foundation of students' intellectual exploration and personal growth. Our International Baccalaureate curriculum cultivates students' abilities to think critically, ask questions, learn across disciplines, and develop research skills to thrive in college and become global contributors.

Founded in 1945, located on Marlborough Street, in the heart of Boston's Back Bay neighborhood, The Newman School serves students from grades 7-12 from Boston, surrounding towns, and 40 countries.

We offer the only comprehensive boarding program in the city. Our students participate in activities and sports, pursuing their passions in the "education city," and embrace Boston as their campus to engage in meaningful community service and countless activities.

Students develop a global and community mindedness that enriches their ability to make an impact in the world. The warm and caring environment and small class sizes make Newman a place where students are seen and valued. Integral at Newman are programs in service, leadership, sports, arts, and activities that build skills and friendships with the support of teachers who care, are passionate about learning, and provide ways for each student to demonstrate their capability for success in colleges and universities.

Currently, Newman alumni are enrolled at schools such as Boston College, Boston University, Brandeis, Brown, College of the Holy Cross, Columbia, Connecticut College, Cornell, Duke, Massachusetts Institute of Technology, McGill University, Tufts, University of Michigan, University of Southern California, and Worcester Polytechnic Institute.

THE VILLAGE SCHOOL
A NORD ANGLIA EDUCATION SCHOOL
THE VILLAGE SCHOOL
EST. 1966

(Founded 1966)

Head of School
Mr. Bill Delbrugge

DP coordinator
Kerri Peters

Status Private

Boarding/day Mixed

Gender Coeducational

Language of instruction
English

Authorised IB programmes
DP

Age Range 2 – 18 years

Number of pupils enrolled
1700

Fees
Day: US$19,425 – US$32,675 per annum
Boarding: US$57,850 – US$76,850 per annum

Address
13051 Whittington Drive
Houston
TX 77077 | USA

TEL +1 281 496 7900

Email
admissions@thevillageschool.com

Website
www.thevillageschool.com

One World. One Village.
The Village School, a pre-k through 12th grade private day and boarding school in Houston, delivers a global perspective, exceptional learning experiences, and access to world-class teachers. Voted the #1 most diverse private school in Houston, Village is home to a collaborative, supportive and global community. Recognized for our excellence in STEAM education, world-class internships and differentiated programs, we offer a rigorous but nurturing individualized environment. The Village School provides a rich selection of academic, arts, and athletics to help our students prepare for future success at the best colleges and universities around the world.

Exceptional Learning Experiences
At Village, we offer a unique and enriched approach inclusive of entrepreneurship, internships, and experiential learning, along with collaborations with world-leading institutions. Our visionary teachers inspire your child to excel and foster a thirst for knowledge. This unique approach to teaching and learning enables our students to gain a better grasp of concepts, think more creatively, and allows for greater reflection on experiences.

Four Diploma Options
Village is proud to offer four rigorous diploma options: the International Baccalaureate Diploma Program, Pre-Medical Science Diploma, Entrepreneurship Diploma, and The Village School U.S. Diploma. To prepare for their college of choice, students can also take Advanced Placement (AP) courses.

Cultivating a Global Perspective
The Village School student body represents over 80 different countries across six continents, offering our students the opportunity to interact with and learn from students across the globe. This culturally rich environment helps cultivate a global perspective and awareness and provides access to people from other ethnicities, cultures, schools of thought, and viewpoints.

Preparing for the Future
We offer our students access to experienced college advisors who know the complexities of the application process and university requirements for schools both nationally and abroad. Our advisors have a proven track record for helping Village students gain acceptance into the top colleges and universities. In addition, our recent graduating class earned more than $18M in scholarships toward higher education institutions around the world.

Premier Collaborations
Village students benefit from our collaborations with esteemed institutions such as Massachusetts Institute of Technology (MIT), The Juilliard School, UNICEF, and Space Center Houston.

Visit Village!
Schedule a tour online at www.thevillageschool.com or find out more by emailing our Admissions Team at admissions@thevillageschool.com or by calling (281) 491-7900. Take a virtual tour at https://www.nordangliaeducation.com/village-houston/virtual-tour.

Interim Head of School
Mr. David Friedrich

PYP coordinator
Jane Lu

Status Private

Boarding/day Day

Gender Coeducational

Language of instruction
English, Chinese

Authorised IB programmes
PYP

Age Range 18 months – 13 years

Number of pupils enrolled 98

Fees
Day: US$18,000 – US$27,900 per annum

Mapleton Campus
75 Mapleton Road
Princeton
NJ 08540 | USA

Laurel Campus
25 Laurel Avenue in Kingston
NJ 08528 | USA

TEL +1 609 375 8015

Email
admissions@yhis.org

Website
yhis.org

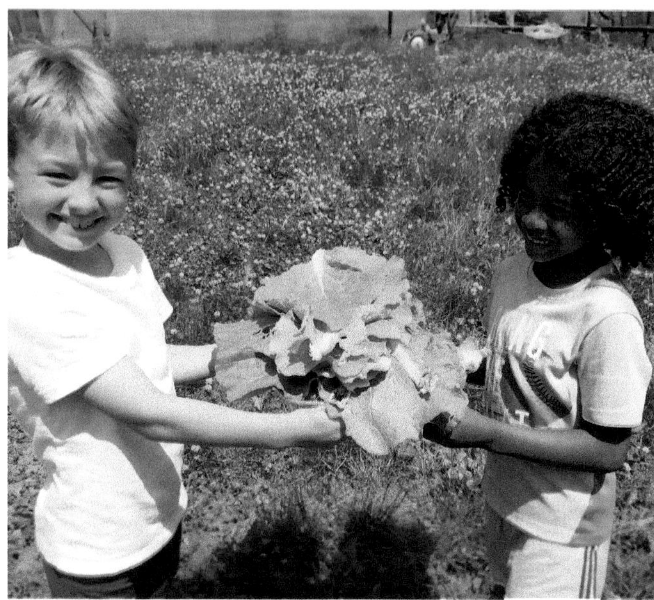

Nestled in the outskirts of Princeton, New Jersey, YingHua International School (YHIS) is the only not-for-profit, independent school in the greater Princeton area that offers English-Chinese dual language education with an internationally-focused, inquiry-based curriculum. YHIS is also the only school in the Eastern United States that offers the IB Primary Years Programme with whole-school Chinese immersion.

YingHua International School (YHIS) was founded in 2007 with a mission to enable academic excellence and prepare students for compassionate, effective, and ethical global citizenship through English and Chinese language acquisition and instilling a passion for lifelong learning. A hidden gem in Central New Jersey, YHIS accomplishes its mission by combining total Chinese Immersion with IB inquiry-based learning.

Through this unique approach, YHIS enables ethnically diverse students from as young as 18 months old through 8th grade, to develop the skills and mindset needed to become leaders in an increasingly global world. Through exposure at an early age to a language-immersive environment combined with IB inquiry-based learning, YHIS students gain deeply rooted cognitive benefits that stay with them well into adulthood.

At YHIS this approach is further characterized by small, nurturing, and inclusive classes led by passionate, dedicated teachers. The results are students who consistently outperform their suburban and private school peers on the local and national stage and in standardized testing. While many parents are initially drawn to YHIS for Chinese immersion, they often stay because of its ability to foster independence and self-reliance while instilling critical thinking skills and academic excellence in students.

Much of YHIS' success can be attributed to its core values of Excellence, Diversity, Integrity and Compassion. Excellence is striving for and being the best that we can be. It means high standards of teaching, learning, and all that we do. It includes well-rounded development in addition to intellectual curiosity and rigor. It requires teamwork, community service and leadership. Diversity is embracing difference and building on the best of all worlds. It embraces equity among cultures and peoples, and suggests respect for the natural world including its animal and plant inhabitants. Integrity is excellence of character and Compassion is caring for diverse others: both integrity and compassion are essential for guiding how we relate to and treat one another and are critical cornerstones for what YHIS stands for.

YHIS welcomes all into its warm and nurturing community!

Directory of schools in the Americas region

Key to symbols

- CP
- Diploma
- MYP
- PYP
- Fee Paying School
- Boys' School
- Girls' School
- Coeducational School
- Boarding School
- Day School

ANGUILLA

Omololu International School
P.O Box 703, The Valley BWI, AI2640
PYP Coordinator Barbara Franks-Rolle
Languages English
T: +1 264 497 5430
W: www.omololuschool.org

ANTIGUA

Island Academy International School
Oliver's Estate, PO Box W1884, St John's
DP Coordinator Mckala Fleming
Languages English
T: +1 268 460 1094
W: www.islandacademy.com

ARGENTINA

Asociación Cultural Pestalozzi
R Freire 1882, 1428 Ciudad de Buenos Aires
DP Coordinator Mariel Santarelli
Languages Spanish
T: +54 11 4555 3688
W: www.pestalozzi.edu.ar
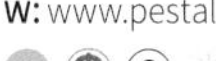

Asociación Escuelas Lincoln
Andres Ferreyra 4073, 1637 La Lucila, Buenos Aires
DP Coordinator Sarah Fang
Languages English
T: +54 11 4851 1700
W: www.lincoln.edu.ar
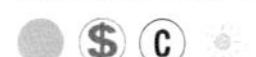

Austin Eco Bilingual School (Austin EBS) Argentina
Porto 463, Campana, Buenos Aires
DP Coordinator Jessica Gino
Languages Spanish, English
T: +54 3489 462203/4
W: www.austin-ebs.com.ar

Colegio 4 DE 9 Nicolás Avellaneda
El Salvador 5228, 1414 Ciudad de Buenos Aires
DP Coordinator Veronica Converti
Languages English
T: +54 11 4771 4022
W: colegio4de9.wixsite.com/nicolasavellaneda

Colegio Alemán Córdoba
Recta Martinoli 6230 (Esq. Neper), 5021 Argüello, Córdoba
DP Coordinator Silvina Martinez
Languages Spanish
T: +54 35 4342 0834
W: www.colegioalemancba.edu.ar

Colegio De La Salle
Ayacucho 665, 1025 Ciudad de Buenos Aires
DP Coordinator Laura Simonotto
Languages Spanish
T: +54 011 4374 6449
W: www.lasalleba.edu.ar

Colegio de Todos Los Santos
Thames 798, Villa Adelina, 1607 San Isidro, Buenos Aires
DP Coordinator Araceli Fangi
Languages English, Spanish
T: +54 114 766 3878
W: www.tls.edu.ar

Colegio Lincoln
Olleros 2283, Belgrano, Ciudad de Buenos Aires
DP Coordinator Andrea García
Languages Spanish, English
T: +54 11 4772 0108
W: www.lincoln.esc.edu.ar

Colegio Mark Twain
José Roque Funes 1525, 5009 Córdoba
DP Coordinator Pablo Esteban Cedro
Languages Spanish
T: +543 514 830 664
W: www.marktwaincba.com.ar

Colegio Montessori de Luján
Mitre 1247, Lujan, Buenos Aires
DP Coordinator Estefanía Fusco
Languages English, Spanish
T: +51 23 2343 3981
W: colegio-montessori.com.ar

Colegio Palermo Chico
Thames 2037/41, 1425 Ciudad de Buenos Aires
DP Coordinator Nora Cavuto
Languages Spanish
T: +54 114 774 3975
W: www.colegiopalermochico.edu.ar

Colegio San Ignacio
Guardias Nacionales 1400, 5806 Río Cuarto, Córdoba
DP Coordinator Horacio Toledo Carranza
Languages English, Spanish
T: +54 (358) 464 8484/0802
W: www.colegiosanignacio.edu.ar

Colegio San Jorge
Godoy Cruz, Pedro J Godoy 1191, 5547 Mendoza
DP Coordinator Patricia Arias
Languages Spanish
T: +54 2 614 287 247
W: colegiosanjorge.com.ar

Colegio San Marcos
Nivel Secundario, Jorge Miles 153, 1842 Monte Grande, Buenos Aires
DP Coordinator Gustavo Junco
Languages Spanish
T: +54 11 4296 3138
W: www.stmarks.com.ar

Colegio San Patricio
Moreno y Las Higueritas, 4107 Yerba Buena, Tucumán
DP Coordinator Mauro Juliano
Languages Spanish
T: +54 381 4250 708
W: www.sanpatriciotucuman.edu.ar

Colegio San Patricio de Luján
Acceso Oeste 2145, Lujan, Buenos Aires
DP Coordinator Maria Belen Mastellone
Languages Spanish
T: +54 23 2343 7998
W: www.sanpatriciodelujan.com

Colegio Santa María
Coronel Suárez 453, 4400 Salta
DP Coordinator Florencia Rovaletti
Languages Spanish
T: +54 387 421 3127
W: www.colegiosantamariasalta.com

Colegio Tarbut
Rosales 3019, 1636 Olivos, Buenos Aires
DP Coordinator Andrea Lichtensztein
Languages Spanish
T: +54 11 4794 3444
W: www.tarbut.edu.ar

Deutsche Schule Temperley
Av. Fernández 27, 1834 Temperley, Buenos Aires
DP Coordinator Cecilia Quarleri
Languages English, Spanish
T: +54 114244 2832
W: www.temperleyschule.edu.ar

Dover High School
San Martín y Ruta 26, 1623 Maschwitz, Buenos Aires
DP Coordinator Rodrigo Negro
Languages English, Spanish
T: +54 93488 441106
W: www.dover.edu.ar

Escuela Goethe Rosario
España 440, 2000 Rosario, Santa Fe
DP Coordinator Eduardo Palandri
Languages Spanish
T: +54 34 1426 3024
W: goetherosario.org

Escuela Municipal Paula Albarracin de Sarmiento
Juan Bautista Alberdi 1227, Olivos, Buenos Aires
DP Coordinator Romina Biga
Languages Spanish
T: +54 11 4513 9873
W: escuelas.mvl.edu.ar/empas
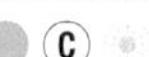

Escuela Normal Superior en Lenguas Vivas
Av. Córdoba 1951, 1120 Ciudad de Buenos Aires
DP Coordinator Fernando Grisi
Languages English
W: www.ens1caba.edu.ar

Escuela Normal Superior en LV 'Sofia Broquen de Spangenberg'
Juncal 3251, 1425 Ciudad de Buenos Aires
DP Coordinator Pablo Scolaro
Languages Spanish
T: +54 114 807 2967/2966

Escuela Tecnica 32 DE 14 - Gral. Jose de San Martin
Teodoro Garcia 3899, 1427 Ciudad de Buenos Aires
DP Coordinator Marisa Casares
Languages Spanish
T: +54 11 4551 9121
W: escuelatecnica32.com.ar

Escuela Técnica N°24 D.E. 17- Defensa de Buenos Aires
Ricardo Gutierrez 3246, 1417 Ciudad de Buenos Aires
DP Coordinator Marcelo Saporito
Languages Spanish
T: +54 11 45019251
W: www.et24debsas.blogspot.com.ar

Escuela Técnica N°28 D.E. 10 República Francesa
Cuba 2410, 1428 Ciudad de Buenos Aires
DP Coordinator Daniel Vena
Languages English
T: +54 11 47816881/31
W: www.et28.net

Escuela Técnica N°29 D.E. 6 - Reconquista de Buenos Aires
Av. Boedo 760, 1218 Ciudad de Buenos Aires
DP Coordinator Dario Balbuena
Languages Spanish
W: www.tecnica29.org

Escuela Técnica N° 9 D.E. 7 Ingeniero Luis A. Huergo
Martín de Gainza 1060, 1405 Ciudad de Buenos Aires
DP Coordinator Luciano Cocciro
Languages Spanish
T: +54 11 4582 6690
W: www.et9huergo.edu.ar

ARGENTINA

Holmberg Schule
Sarmiento 679, Quilmes, Buenos Aires
DP Coordinator Natalia Montini
Languages German, Spanish
T: +54 11 4254 8583
W: www.holmbergschule.edu.ar

Holy Trinity College
Gascón 544, 7600 Mar del Plata, Buenos Aires
DP Coordinator Ana Beatriz Ranero Celius
Languages English, Spanish
T: +54 223 486 3471
W: www.trinity.esc.edu.ar

Instituto Ballester
Calle 69 N° 5140 (ex San Martín 444), 1653 Villa Ballester, Buenos Aires
DP Coordinator Sergio García
Languages Spanish
T: +54 11 4768 0760
W: iballester.edu.ar

Instituto Santa Brígida
Av Gaona 2068, 1416 Ciudad de Buenos Aires
DP Coordinator Gladys Lesmi Dallas
Languages Spanish
T: +54 1 145 811 268
W: www.santabrigida.esc.edu.ar

Instituto Wolfsohn
2972, AEB, Amenábar, 1429 Ciudad de Buenos Aires
DP Coordinator Florencia Silva
Languages English, Spanish
T: +54 11 4545 6020
W: wolfsohn.edu.ar

ISLANDS INTERNATIONAL SCHOOL
Amenábar St. 1840, 1428 Ciudad de Buenos Aires
DP Coordinator Clotilde Alleva
Languages Spanish, English, Italian, Portuguese
T: +54 11 4787 2294
W: www.intschools.org/school/islands
See full details on page 481

NORTHERN INTERNATIONAL SCHOOL
Ruote 8 Km 61.5., 1633. Pilar, Buenos Aires
DP Coordinator Clotilde Alleva
Languages Spanish, English, Italian, Portuguese
T: +54 2322 49 1208
W: www.intschools.org/school/northern
See full details on page 498

NORTHLANDS SCHOOL
Olivos Site: Roma 1248, Olivos, Buenos Aires
DP Coordinator Alicia Rodriguez Loredo
PYP Coordinator Maria Ines Martinez Beccar Varela & Natalia Torlaschi
Languages English, Spanish
T: +54 11 4711 8400
E: admissionsolivos@northlands.edu.ar
W: www.northlands.edu.ar
See full details on page 499

Northlands School Nordelta
Nordelta site: Av de los Colegios 590, Nordelta, Buenos Aires B1670NNN
DP Coordinator Alicia Rodriguez Loredo
PYP Coordinator Natalia Torlaschi
Languages English
T: +54 11 4871 2668/9
W: www.northlands.edu.ar

Orange Day School
Av. San Martín 1651/7, 1657 Ramos Mejia, Buenos Aires
DP Coordinator María Penén Ramirez
Languages English, Spanish
T: +54 11 4464 7014
W: www.orangeschool.com.ar

Poplars School
Estrada 335, 9400 Río Gallegos, Santa Cruz
DP Coordinator Nicolás Mayorga
Languages English, Spanish
T: +54 29 6642 5703
W: poplarsschool.edu.ar

Saint Mary of the Hills School
Xul Solar 6650, 1646 San Fernando, Buenos Aires
DP Coordinator Gastón Arana
Languages Spanish
T: +54 11 4714 0330
W: www.stmary.edu.ar

Saint Mary of the Hills School Sede Pilar
Ruta 25 y Caamaño, 1644 Pilar, Buenos Aires
DP Coordinator Mariana Xanthopoulos
Languages Spanish
T: +54 2304 458181
W: www.stmary.edu.ar

Saint Patrick College
Av. Maipú 3187, Corrientes
DP Coordinator Maria Veronica Sellares
Languages English, Spanish
W: www.saintpatrick.edu.ar

SOUTHERN INTERNATIONAL SCHOOL
Freeway Buenos Aires - La Plata Km 34., 1884 Hudson, Buenos Aires
DP Coordinator Clotilde Alleva
Languages Spanish, English, Italian, Portuguese
T: +54 11 4215 3636
W: www.intschools.org/school/southern
See full details on page 505

St George's College
Guido 800, 1878 Quilmes, Buenos Aires
DP Coordinator María Soledad Texidó
PYP Coordinator Mabel Orlando
Languages English, Spanish
T: +54 (11) 4350 7900
W: www.stgeorges.edu.ar/quilmes

St George's College North
Mosconi 3500 y Don Bosco s/n, 1613 Los Polvorines, Buenos Aires
DP Coordinator Candelaria Durruty
PYP Coordinator Noelia Zago
Languages English, Spanish
T: +54 (11) 4663 2494
W: www.stgeorges.edu.ar/north

St Mary's International College
Martin Garcia 1435/1236/1501, 1804 Ezeiza, Buenos Aires
DP Coordinator María Eugenia Aramendi
Languages English, Spanish
T: +54 11 5075 0370
W: www.stmarys.edu.ar

St Matthew's College - Sede Fundadora
Moldes 1469, 1426 Ciudad de Buenos Aires
DP Coordinator Patricia Capecce
Languages Spanish, English
T: +54 11 4783 1110
W: www.smc.edu.ar
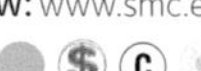

St Matthew's College - Sede Norte
Caamano 493, 1631 Pilar, Buenos Aires
DP Coordinator Graciela Mouzo
Languages Spanish
T: +54 230 4693600
W: www.smcn.edu.ar

St Xavier's College
José Antonio Cabrera 5901, 1414 Ciudad de Buenos Aires
DP Coordinator Karla Fohl
Languages English
T: +54 114 777 5011/14
W: www.colegiosanjavier.com.ar

St. Andrew's Scots School
Roque Saenz Peña 601, 1636 Olivos, Buenos Aires
DP Coordinator Analia Heidenreich
Languages English
T: +54 11 4846 6500
W: www1.sanandres.esc.edu.ar

St. Catherine's Moorlands - Belgrano
Carbajal 3250, 1426 Ciudad de Buenos Aires
DP Coordinator Ana Figueroa
MYP Coordinator Agustina Sangiacomo
Languages English, Spanish
T: +54 11 4552 4353
W: www.scms.edu.ar/es/belgrano
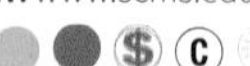

St. Catherine's Moorlands - Tortuguitas
Ruta Panamericana Km 38 Ramal Pilar, 1667 Tortuguitas, Buenos Aires
MYP Coordinator Alejandro Elia
Languages English
T: +54 348 463 9001/2
W: www.scms.edu.ar/es/tortuguitas

St. Francis School
Av. Benavidez 1326, 1621 Benavidez, Buenos Aires
DP Coordinator Silvina Massa
Languages English
T: +54 11 2078 4200
W: www.saintfrancis.edu.ar

St. John's School - Beccar
España 348/370, 1643 Beccar, Buenos Aires
DP Coordinator Santiago Olcese
Languages English, Spanish
T: +54 11 4513 4400
W: www.stjohns.edu.ar

St. John's School - Pilar
Panamericana Km. 48.800, 1629 Pilar, Buenos Aires
DP Coordinator Juan Pablo Varela
Languages English, Spanish
T: +54 23 0466 7667
W: www.stjohns.edu.ar
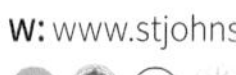

Sunrise School
Chacra 116 Colonia Lucinda, 8324 Cipolletti, Río Negro
DP Coordinator Juan Manuel Ginez
Languages Spanish
T: +54 299 4786590
W: www.sunriseschoolpatagonia.com

Villa Devoto School
Pedro Morán 4441, 1419 Ciudad de Buenos Aires
DP Coordinator Roberto Mancuso
Languages English
T: +54 114 501 9419
W: vds.edu.ar

Washington School
Av. Federico Lacroze 1973/2012, 1426 Ciudad de Buenos Aires
DP Coordinator Sonia Pino
Languages English, Spanish
T: +54 11 4772 8131
W: www.washingtonschool.edu.ar

Woodville School
Av. Los Pioneros km 2,900, 8400 San Carlos de Bariloche, Río Negro
DP Coordinator Andrew Schwartz
Languages Spanish, English
T: +54 2944 44 11 33
W: www.woodville.org

BAHAMAS

Lucaya International School
Chesapeake Drive, Freeport
DP Coordinator Kerry Gray
PYP Coordinator Erin Cordes
Languages English
T: +1 242 373 4004
W: www.lisbahamas.com

Lyford Cay International School
Lyford Cay Drive, PO Box N-7776, Nassau NB
CP Coordinator Timothy Connolly
DP Coordinator Michèle (Scullion) Mindorff
MYP Coordinator Harry Almond
PYP Coordinator Katina Seymour
Languages English
T: +1 242 362 4774
W: www.lcis.bs

St Andrew's International School
PO Box EE 17340, Yamacraw Hill Road, Nassau, NP
DP Coordinator Ashish Bowen
PYP Coordinator Vashni Carey
Languages English
T: +1 242 677 7800
W: www.standrewsbahamas.com

BARBADOS

The Codrington School
St John BB 20008
DP Coordinator Kirsty Thomas
MYP Coordinator Nicola Leedham
PYP Coordinator Susanne Fischer
Languages English
T: +1 246 423 2570
W: www.codrington.edu.bb

BERMUDA

Bermuda High School
19 Richmond Road, Pembroke HM08
DP Coordinator Sarah Wheddon
Languages English
T: +441 295 6153
W: www.bhs.bm

Somersfield Academy
107 Middle Road, Devonshire DV 06
DP Coordinator Anne-Laure Bazin
MYP Coordinator Summer Wood, Brice Pursell
Languages English
T: +1 441 236 9797
W: www.somersfield.bm

Warwick Academy
117 Middle Road, Warwick PG01
CP Coordinator Sara Jackson
DP Coordinator Sara Jackson
Languages English
T: +1 441 236 1917/239 9452
W: www.warwick.bm

BOLIVIA

American International School of Bolivia
Casilla 5309, Cochabamba
DP Coordinator Ximena Aguilera
Languages English
T: +591 4 428 8577
W: www.aisb.edu.bo

Colegio Alemán Santa Cruz
Casilla 624, Av San Martin s/n, Santa Cruz
DP Coordinator Romina Ortiz Torres
MYP Coordinator Juan Martin Arteaga
Languages Spanish
T: +591 3 3326820
W: ds-santacruz.bo

Saint Andrew's School
Casilla 1679, Av Las Retamas s/n La Florida, La Paz
DP Coordinator Eduardo Blanco
PYP Coordinator Mónica Villarreal
Languages English, Spanish
T: +591 22 79 24 84
W: www.saintandrews.edu.bo

BRAZIL

ABA Global School
Av. Rosa e Silva, 1510, Aflitos, Recife, Pernambuco PE 52050-245
PYP Coordinator Maria do Rozario Botelho
Languages English
T: +55 81 3427 8800
W: www.estudenaaba.com

American School of Brasilia
SGAS 605, Conjunto E, Lotes 34/37, Brasília DF 70200-650
DP Coordinator Maria Sieve
Languages English
T: +55 61 3442 9700
W: www.eabdf.br

American School of Campinas - Escola Americana de Campinas
Rua Cajamar, #35, Campinas, São Paulo SP 13090-860
DP Coordinator Erika Bonet
PYP Coordinator Alyssa Wakely
Languages English
T: +55 19 21021006
W: www.eac.com.br

Associação Educacional Luterana Bom Jesus / IELUSC
Rua Princesa Isabel, 438, Joinville, Santa Catarina SC 89201-270
DP Coordinator Marcelli Mazzei Ramalho
Languages English
T: +55 47 3026 8000
W: www.ielusc.br

Beacon School
Rua Berlioz 245, Alto de Pinheiros, São Paulo SP 05467-000
DP Coordinator Karine Vairo
MYP Coordinator Felipe Pregnolatto
PYP Coordinator Maiara Terra
Languages English, Portuguese
T: +55 11 3021 0262
W: www.beaconschool.com.br
 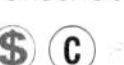

Bright School
R. Anfrisio Lobao 2024, Sao Cristovao, Teresina, Piaui PI 64051-152
DP Coordinator Otavio Menezes
MYP Coordinator Thalita Arre
Languages English, Portuguese
T: +55 86 3233 1839
W: www.brightschools.com.br
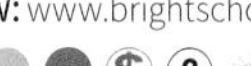

Centro Internacional de Educacao Integrada
Estrada do Pontal 2093, Recreio dos Bandeirantes, Rio de Janeiro RJ 22790-877
DP Coordinator Pedro Fernandes
PYP Coordinator Vanessa Vianna
Languages English
T: +55 21 2490 1673
W: www.ciei.g12.br

Chapel School - The American International School of Brazil
Rua Vigário João de Pontes, 537, Chácara Flora, São Paulo SP 04748-000
DP Coordinator Donald Campbell
Languages English
T: +55 11 2101 7400
W: www.chapelschool.com

Colégio 7 de Setembro
R. Henriqueta Galeno, 1011, Dionísio Torres, Fortaleza, Ceará CE 60135-420
DP Coordinator Janaina Façanha
Languages English, Portuguese
T: +55 85 4006 7777
W: www.c7s.com.br

Colégio Miguel de Cervantes
Avenida Jorge João Saad, 905, São Paulo, Morumbí SP 05618-001
DP Coordinator Katia Pupo
Languages Portuguese, Spanish, English
T: +55 11 3779 1800
W: cmc.com.br

Colegio Positivo Internacional
Professor Pedro Viriato de Souza St 5300, Curitiba, Paraná PR 81280-330
DP Coordinator Juliana Lazari
MYP Coordinator Maria Fernanda Caneparo
PYP Coordinator Michelline Ramos
Languages Portuguese, English
T: +55 (41) 3335 3535
W: www.colegiopositivo.com.br

Colegio Sao Luis
Av. Dr. Dante Pazzanese, 295, Vila Mariana, São Paulo SP 04012-180
DP Coordinator Andrea Rodrigues
Languages English, Portuguese
W: www.saoluis.org
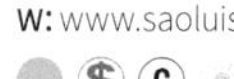

Colégio Soka do Brasil
Avenida Cursino, 362, Saúde SP 04132-000
DP Coordinator Juraci Alcantara dos Santos
Languages English, Portuguese
T: +55 11 5060 3300
W: www.colegiosoka.org.br

Colégio Suíço-Brasileiro de Curitiba
Rua Wanda dos Santos Mallmann, 537, Jardim Pinhais, Pinhais, Paraná PR 83323-400
DP Coordinator Carlos Machado
Languages English
T: +55 41 3525 9100
W: www.chpr.com.br

Coree International School
R. Gothard Kaesemodel 961, Anita Garibaldi, Joinville, Santa Catarina SC 89203-522
DP Coordinator Rebeca Alonso Saeta
PYP Coordinator Dorota Szczepanska Oliveira
Languages English
T: +55 47 3121 6700
W: coree.org.br/home-coree/international-school

Escola Americana de Belo Horizonte
Av. Professor Mario Werneck, 3002, Bairro Buritis, Belo Horizonte, Minas Gerais MG 30575-180
MYP Coordinator Leonardo Botaro
PYP Coordinator Judy Imamudeen
Languages English, Portuguese
T: +55 31 3378 6700
W: www.eabh.com.br

ESCOLA AMERICANA DO RIO DE JANEIRO - BARRA DA TIJUCA
Rua Colbert Coelho 155, Barra da Tijuca, Rio de Janeiro RJ 22793-313
DP Coordinator Mr. Gregory Sipp
MYP Coordinator Ms. Mary Jo Rawleigh
PYP Coordinator Ms. Anna Cottrell
Languages English
T: +55 21 3747 2000
W: www.earj.com.br
See full details on page 467

ESCOLA AMERICANA DO RIO DE JANEIRO - GÁVEA
Estrada da Gávea 132, Gávea, Rio de Janeiro RJ 22451-263
DP Coordinator Ms. Flavia DiLuccio
MYP Coordinator Ms. Teresa Araújo
PYP Coordinator Ms. Susan Loafmann
Languages English
T: +55 21 2125 9000
E: admissions.gavea@earj.com.br
W: www.earj.com.br
See full details on page 467

Escola Beit Yaacov
Av Marques de Sao Vicente no 1748, Barra Funda, São Paulo SP 01139-002
DP Coordinator Raphael Silva
PYP Coordinator Alexandra Cunha
Languages English, Hebrew, Portuguese
T: +55 11 3611 0600
W: www.beityaacov.com.br

Escola Bilíngue Pueri Domus - Aclimação Campus
Rua Muniz de Sousa 1051, Aclimação, São Paulo SP 01534-020
DP Coordinator Cintia Etsuko Yamashita
Languages English, Portuguese
T: +55 11 3478 7701
W: www.pueridomus.com.br

Escola Bilíngue Pueri Domus - Itaim Campus
Rua Itacema 214, Itaim Bibi, São Paulo SP 04530-050
DP Coordinator Ricardo Lourenco
Languages English, Portuguese
T: +55 11 3078 6999
W: www.pueridomus.com.br

Escola Bilíngue Pueri Domus - Perdizes Campus
Rua Ministro Godói 1697, Perdizes, São Paulo SP 05015-001
DP Coordinator Igor Souza
Languages English, Portuguese
T: +55 11 3803 4240
W: www.pueridomus.com.br

Escola Bilíngue Pueri Domus - Verbo Divino Campus
Rua Verbo Divino 993-A, Chacara Sto. Antonio, São Paulo SP 04719-001
DP Coordinator Ms Cindy Obi
Languages English, Portuguese
T: +55 11 3512 2222
W: www.pueridomus.com.br

ESCOLA CANADENSE DE BRASILIA
SIG Quadra 8, Lote 2225, Parte F, Brasília DF 70610-480
PYP Coordinator Amanda Salles
Languages English, Portuguese
T: +55 61 3961 4350
W: www.escolacanadensedebrasilia.com.br
See full details on page 468

Escola Castanheiras
Alameda Castanheiras, 250, Res. Tres (Tambore), Santana de Parnaíba, São Paulo SP 06543-510
DP Coordinator Airton Pretini Junior
Languages English
T: +55 114 152 4600
W: www.escolacastanheiras.com.br

ESCOLA ELEVA - BARRA DA TIJUCA
Av. José Silva de Azevedo Neto 309, Barra da Tijuca, Rio de Janeiro RJ 22775-056
DP Coordinator Barbara Furtado
Languages English, Portuguese
T: +55 21 3094 5020
E: admissoes@escolaeleva.com.br
W: www.escolaeleva.com.br/colegios/escola-barra-da-tijuca
See full details on page 470

ESCOLA ELEVA - URCA
Alameda Floriano Peixoto 13, Urca, Rio de Janeiro RJ 22291-090
DP Coordinator Fabiano Franklin
Languages English, Portuguese
T: +55 21 3528 4370
E: admissoes.urca@escolaeleva.com.br
W: www.escolaeleva.com.br
See full details on page 471

Escola Internacional de Alphaville
Av. Copacabana, 624, Cond. Empresarial 18 do Forte, Alphaville, Barueri SP 06472-001
DP Coordinator Peter Rifaat
MYP Coordinator Juliana Nico
PYP Coordinator Roberta Deliberato
Languages English
T: +55 11 4134 6686
W: www.escolainternacional.com.br

Escola Internacional UniSociesc Blumenau
Rua Pandiá Calógeras 272, Jardim Blumenau, Blumenau, Santa Catarina SC 89010-350
DP Coordinator Lawrence Soderstrom
PYP Coordinator Juliane Chicatto
Languages English, Portuguese
T: +55 47 2111 2966
W: www.eiublumenau.com.br

Escola Internacional UniSociesc Florianopolis
Rua Salvatina Feliciana dos Santos 525, Itacorubi, Florianópolis, Santa Catarina SC 88034-600
DP Coordinator Leonardo Gomes Oliveira
PYP Coordinator Ana Paula Costa
Languages English, Portuguese
T: +55 48 3239 4757
W: www.eiufloripa.com.br
 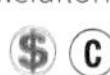

Escola Lourenco Castanho
Rua Fiandeiras 77, Vila Olímpia, São Paulo SP 04545-000
DP Coordinator Maria Cecília R. Palma T. Pastorelli
Languages English, Portuguese
T: +55 11 3047 0099
W: www.lourencocastanho.com.br

Escola Nova
Rua Major Rubens Vaz, 392, Gávea, Rio de Janeiro RJ 22470-070
DP Coordinator Gustavo Paiva
Languages English, Portuguese
T: +55 21 3875 9899
W: www.escolanova.com.br

Escola Suíço-Brasileira (ESB) by SIS Swiss International School
Rua Corréa de Araújo 81, Barra da Tijuca, Rio de Janeiro RJ 22611-060
DP Coordinator Maurício Da Silva Drumond Costa
MYP Coordinator Aline Costa
PYP Coordinator Giulia Souto da Costa Schneider
Languages English
T: +55 21 33 89 20 89
W: www.swissinternationalschool.com.br/school-locations/esb-rio-de-janeiro

Escola Suíço-Brasileira de São Paulo
Rua Visconde de Porto Seguro 391, Alto da Boa Vista, São Paulo SP 04642-000
DP Coordinator Andreas Panse
Languages English
T: +55 11 5682 2140
W: www.esbsp.com.br

GIS SP - The International School of São Paulo
Alameda dos Jurupis 485, Moema, São Paulo SP 04088-000
PYP Coordinator Selma Moura
Languages English, Portuguese
T: +55 11 3900 8931
W: www.issaopaulo.com.br

Graded - The American School of São Paulo
Av. José Galante, 425, São Paulo SP 05642-000
DP Coordinator Justin Morris
Languages English
T: +55 11 3747 4800
W: www.graded.br

Great International School
Av. Nossa Senhora de Fátima 1000, Jóquei, Teresina, Piaui PI 64048-185
DP Coordinator Graciela Coracini
Languages English, Portuguese
T: +55 86 2222 4000
W: greatschool.com.br

Gurilândia International School
Av. Cardeal Da Silva 1433, Federacao, Salvador, Bahia BA 40231-250
PYP Coordinator Luciana Pinho Teixeira Araujo
Languages English, Portuguese
T: +55 71 3336 6595
W: www.gurilandia.com.br

International School of Curitiba
Ave. Eugenio Bertolli, 3900, Sta. Felicidade, Curitiba, Paraná PR 82410-530
DP Coordinator Fritz O'Brien
Languages English
T: +55 41 3525 7400
W: www.iscbrazil.com

Land School
Av. Cardeal da Silva, No. 136, Federacao, Salvador, Bahia BA 40231-250
DP Coordinator Reygar Bernal
MYP Coordinator Jessica Carvalho
Languages English, Portuguese
T: +55 71 3021 2550
W: www.landschool.com.br
   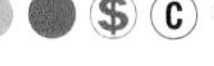

Liceu Albert Sabin
Rua José Curvelo da Silveira Jr. 110, Ribeirão Preto, São Paulo
DP Coordinator Débora Alcalde
Languages English, Portuguese
T: +55 16 3602 8200
W: liceuasabin.br
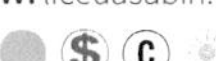 

Maple Bear Barra da Tijuca
Rua Martinho de Mesquita 136, Barra da Tijuca, Rio de Janeiro RJ 22630-220
DP Coordinator Flavia Rosa Costa
Languages English, Portuguese
T: +55 21 3486 6466
W: barradatijuca.maplebear.com.br

Pan American School of Bahia
Av Ibirapitanga, Loteamento Patamares, s/n, Salvador, Bahia BA 41680-060
DP Coordinator Roberta Rodrigues
PYP Coordinator Sam Whitney
Languages English
T: +55 71 3368 8400
W: www.escolapanamericana.com

Pan American School of Porto Alegre
Av. João Obino 110, Petrópolis, Porto Alegre, Rio Grande do Sul RS 90470-150
MYP Coordinator Bruno Britto
PYP Coordinator Otto Neitzel Neto
Languages English, Portuguese
T: +55 513 334 5866
W: www.panamerican.com.br

Red House International School
Rua Engenheiro Edgar Egidio de Souza 444, Pacaembu SP 01233-020
PYP Coordinator Henrique Oliveira
Languages English
T: +55 11 2309 7999
W: www.redhouseschool.com.br

SIS Swiss International School Brasília
SGA/SUL, Quadra 905, cj B, Brasília DF 70390-050
MYP Coordinator Mikke Marttinen
PYP Coordinator Hayley Waghorn
Languages English
T: +55 61 34 43 41 45
W: www.swissinternationalschool.com.br/school-locations/brasilia

Sphere International School
Av Anchieta, 908 - Jardim Nova Europa, Sao José dos Campos, São Paulo SP 12242-280
DP Coordinator Rafael Seckler
MYP Coordinator Rafael Seckler
PYP Coordinator Melissa Therriault Zaramella
Languages English, Portuguese
T: +55 11 9 7279 4340
W: sphereinternationalschool.com.br

ST. FRANCIS COLLEGE, BRAZIL
Rua Joaquim Antunes 678, Pinheiros, São Paulo SP 05415-001
DP Coordinator Antonia Zanotto
MYP Coordinator Thomas Holesgrove
PYP Coordinator Benedict Bowler
Languages English, Portuguese
T: +55 11 3728 8053
E: office@stfrancis.com.br
W: www.stfrancis.com.br
See full details on page 507

ST. NICHOLAS SCHOOL - ALPHAVILLE
Av. Honório Álvares Penteado 5463, Tamboré, Santana de Parnaíba SP 06543-320
MYP Coordinator Gudrun Bjorg Ingimundardottir
PYP Coordinator Katrina Fabbri
Languages English, Portuguese
T: +55 11 3465 9658; +55 11 3465 9697
E: office.al@stnicholas.com.br
W: www.stnicholas.com.br
See full details on page 509

ST. NICHOLAS SCHOOL - PINHEIROS
Rua do Emissário 333, Pinheiros, São Paulo SP 05423-070
DP Coordinator Saulo Vianna
PYP Coordinator Juliana Peluzzi, Samantha Waller & Jucileia Oliveira
Languages English, Portuguese
T: +55 11 3465 9650; +55 11 3465 9666
E: admin.pin@stnicholas.com.br
W: www.stnicholas.com.br
See full details on page 510

ST. PAUL'S SCHOOL
Rua Juquiá 166, Jardim Paulistano, São Paulo SP 01440-903
DP Coordinator Mr Sam Bishop
Languages English
T: +55 11 3087 3399
E: head@stpauls.br
W: www.stpauls.br
See full details on page 511

THE BRITISH COLLEGE OF BRAZIL
Rua Álvares de Azevedo, 50, Chácara Flora, São Paulo SP 04671-040
DP Coordinator Mr. Timothy Jones
Languages English
T: +55 11 5547 3030
E: info@britishcollegebrazil.org
W: www.britishcollegebrazil.org
See full details on page 516

THE BRITISH SCHOOL, RIO DE JANEIRO
Rua Real Grandeza 99, Botafogo, Rio de Janeiro RJ 22281-030
DP Coordinator Guy Smith & André Filho
Languages English
T: +55 21 2539 2717
E: edu@britishschool.g12.br
W: www.britishschool.g12.br
See full details on page 517

The British School, Rio de Janeiro - Barra Site
Rua Mario Autuori, 100, Barra da Tijuca RJ 22793
DP Coordinator André Filho
Languages English
T: +55 21 3329 2854
W: www.britishschool.g12.br

Valley International School
Av. Osvaldo Reis, 2000 Praia Brava, Itajai, Santa Catarina SC 88306-600
PYP Coordinator Virginia Nichele
Languages English, Portuguese
T: +55 47 3349 0969
W: valleyschool.com.br

Villa Global Education
Avenida Luis Viana 7731, Salvador, Bahia BA 41745-130
DP Coordinator Iruska Garboggini
Languages English, Portuguese
T: +55 71 3281 1000
W: www.campusvilla.com.br

BRITISH VIRGIN ISLANDS

Cedar International School
Waterfront Drive, Kingston
DP Coordinator Thibaud Guenegou
MYP Coordinator Enrica Rymer
PYP Coordinator Lesley Bayles
Languages English
T: +1 284 494 5262
W: cedar.vg

CANADA

Alberta

Annunciation
9325-165 Street, Edmonton AB T5R 2S5
PYP Coordinator Christine Szaszkiewicz
Languages English
T: +1 780 484 4319
W: www.ecsd.net/8001

Archbishop Macdonald
14219-109 Avenue, Edmonton AB T5N 1H5
DP Coordinator Jennifer Vandendooren
Languages English
T: +1 780 451 1470
W: www.ecsd.net/8403

Bellerose Composite High School
49 Giroux Road, St Albert AB T8N 6N4
DP Coordinator Clayton Wowk
Languages English
T: +1 780 460 8490

Bishop David Motiuk Elementary/Junior High School
855 Lewis Greens Drive NW, Edmonton AB T5T 4B2
MYP Coordinator Lyndsy Panizzon
PYP Coordinator Andrea Olivieri
Languages English, French
T: +1 780 409 2603
W: www.ecsd.net/1967

Bishop O'Byrne High School
Suite 500, 333 Shawville Blvd SE, Calgary AB T2Y 4H3
DP Coordinator Brendan Bulger
Languages English
T: +1 403 500 2103
W: www.cssd.ab.ca/schools/bishopobyrne

CANADA

Calgary French and International School
700-77th Street SW, Calgary AB T3H 5R1
DP Coordinator Christian Legault
Languages English, French
T: +1 403 240 1500
W: www.cfis.com

Coronation School
10925-139 Street, Edmonton AB T5M 1P8
PYP Coordinator Rachel Mcouat
Languages English
T: +1 780 455 2008
W: coronation.epsb.ca

Glenora School
13520-102 Avenue, Edmonton AB T5N 0N7
MYP Coordinator Laura Johnson
Languages English
T: +1 780 452 4740

Grande Prairie Composite High School
11202 - 104 Street, Grande Prairie AB T8V 2Z1
DP Coordinator Lee Brentnell
Languages English
T: +1 780 532 7721
W: www.gppsd.ab.ca/school/gpcomposite

Harry Ainlay High School
4350 111 Street NW, Edmonton AB T6J 1E8
DP Coordinator Dean Zuberbuhler
Languages English
T: +1 780 413 2700
W: harryainlay.epsb.ca

Henry Wise Wood High School
910 - 75th Avenue SW, Calgary AB T2V 0S6
DP Coordinator Glenn Finockio
Languages English
T: +1 403 253 2261
W: school.cbe.ab.ca/school/henrywisewood

Holy Trinity High School
7007-28th Avenue, Edmonton AB T6K 4A5
DP Coordinator Richard Downing
Languages English
T: +1 780 462 5777
W: www.holytrinity.ecsd.net
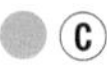

John G Diefenbaker High School
6620 - 4th Street NW, Calgary AB T2K 1C2
DP Coordinator Tamara Ulanicki
Languages English
T: +1 403 274 2240
W: school.cbe.ab.ca/school/johngdiefenbaker

Lester B Pearson High School
3020 52nd Street NE, Calgary AB T1Y 5P4
CP Coordinator Tammy Lock
DP Coordinator Pawanbir Minhas
Languages English
T: +1 403 244 2278
W: www.schools.cbe.ab.ca

Lillian Osborne High School
2019 Leger Road NW, Edmonton AB T6R 0R9
DP Coordinator Wendy Foote
Languages English
T: +1 780 970 5249
W: lillianosborne.epsb.ca

Lindsay Thurber Comprehensive High School
4204-58th Street, Red Deer AB T4N 2L6
DP Coordinator Jackie Shukin
Languages English
T: +1 403 347 1171
W: lindsaythurber.rdpsd.ab.ca

M.E. LaZerte School
6804 144 Ave, Edmonton AB T5C 3C7
DP Coordinator Craig Korte
Languages English
T: +1 780 408 9800
W: www.melazerte.com

McNally High School
8440-105 Avenue, Edmonton AB T6A 1B6
DP Coordinator Omneya Khamis
Languages English
T: +1 780 469 0442
W: mcnally.epsb.ca

Millarville Community School
130 Millarville Rd, Millarville AB T0L 1K0
PYP Coordinator Karla Davis
Languages English
T: +1 403 938 7832
W: millarville.fsd38.ab.ca

Old Scona Academic High School
10523-84th Avenue, Edmonton AB T6E 2H5
DP Coordinator Jeff Karas
Languages English
T: +1 780 433 0627
W: oldscona.epsb.ca

Prairie Waters Elementary School
201 Invermere Drive, Chestermere AB T1X 1M6
PYP Coordinator Breanna Baxter
Languages English
T: +1 403 285 6969
W: prairiewaters.rockyview.ab.ca

Ross Sheppard High School
13546-111th Avenue, Edmonton AB T5M 2P2
DP Coordinator Jennifer Gross
Languages English
T: +1 780 448 5000
W: shep.epsb.ca

Salisbury Composite High School
#20 Festival Way, Sherwood Park AB T8A 4Y1
DP Coordinator Michelle Wyman
Languages English
T: +1 780 467 8816
W: www.salcomp.ca

Sir Winston Churchill High School, Calgary
5220 Northland Drive NW, Calgary AB T2L 2J6
DP Coordinator Arlene Lee
Languages English
T: +1 403 289 9241
W: school.cbe.ab.ca/school/sirwinstonchurchill

St Albert Catholic High School
33 Malmo Drive, St Albert AB T8N 1L5
DP Coordinator Damon Clayton
Languages English
T: +1 780 459 7781
W: www.sachs.gsacrd.ab.ca

St Clement Catholic Elementary/Junior High School
7620 Mill Woods Road South, Edmonton AB T6K 2P7
MYP Coordinator Meaghan Jenny
PYP Coordinator Meaghan Jenny
Languages English
T: +1 780 462 3806
W: www.stclement.ecsd.net

St. Edmund IB World School
11712-130 Avenue, Edmonton AB T5E 0V2
MYP Coordinator Laura Manucci
PYP Coordinator Laura Manucci
Languages English
T: +1 780 453 1596
W: www.ecsd.net/8215

St. Mary's High School
111-18th Avenue SW, Calgary Catholic, Calgary AB T2S 0B8
DP Coordinator Cathy Harradence
Languages English
T: +1 403 500 2024
W: www.cssd.ab.ca/schools/stmarys

Strathcona-Tweedsmuir School
RR 2, Okotoks AB T1S 1A2
DP Coordinator Chris Ruskay
MYP Coordinator Gabe Kemp
PYP Coordinator Shannon Taggart
Languages English
T: +1 403 938 4431
W: www.sts.ab.ca

Victoria School of the Arts
10210 - 108 Avenue, Edmonton AB T5H 1A8
CP Coordinator Joanne Lowry
DP Coordinator Joanne Lowry
MYP Coordinator Tanya Vanderven
PYP Coordinator Tanya Vanderven
Languages English
T: +1 780 426 3010
W: www.victoria-school.ca

Western Canada High School
641 17 Avenue S.W., Calgary AB T2S 0B5
DP Coordinator Susan Rivers
Languages English
T: +1 403 228 5363
W: school.cbe.ab.ca/school/westerncanada

Westglen School
10950-127 Street, Edmonton AB T5M 0S7
MYP Coordinator Laura Johnson
Languages English
T: +1 780 454 3449
W: westglen.epsb.ca

Westminster School
13712-102 Avenue, Edmonton AB T5N 0W4
MYP Coordinator Laura Johnson
Languages English
T: +1 780 452 4343
 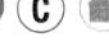

Winston Churchill High School
1605-15th Avenue North, Lethbridge AB T1H 1W4
DP Coordinator Aaron Fitchett
Languages English
T: +1 403 328 4723
W: wchs.lethsd.ab.ca

British Columbia

Abbotsford Middle School
33231 Bevan Avenue, Abbotsford BC V2S 0A9
MYP Coordinator Laura Inglis
Languages English
T: +1 604 859 7125
W: abbymiddle.abbyschools.ca

Abbotsford Senior Secondary School
33355 Bevan Avenue, Abbotsford BC V2S 0E7
DP Coordinator Michael Keeley
Languages English
T: +1 604 853 3367
W: abbysenior.sd34.bc.ca

Alexander Academy
200-688 West Hastings Street, Vancouver BC V6B 1P1
DP Coordinator Spencer Todd
Languages English, French
T: +1 604 687 8832
W: www.alexanderacademy.ca

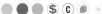

Aspengrove School
7660 Clark Drive, Lantzville BC V0R 2H0
DP Coordinator Robert Ohly
MYP Coordinator Carrie Turunen
PYP Coordinator Susan Riordan
Languages English
T: +1 250 390 2201
W: www.aspengroveschool.ca

Bodwell High School
955 Harbourside Drive North, Vancouver BC V7P 3S4
MYP Coordinator Cathy Lee
Languages English
T: +1 604 998 1000
W: bodwell.edu

Britannia Secondary School
1001 Cotton Drive, Vancouver BC V5L 3T4
DP Coordinator Hubert Wong
Languages English
T: +1 604 713 8266
W: britannia.vsb.bc.ca

Brockton School
3467 Duval Road, North Vancouver BC V7J 3E8
CP Coordinator Noble Kelly
DP Coordinator Svetlana Catia
MYP Coordinator Nichole Carrigan
PYP Coordinator Christina Miller
Languages English
T: +1 604 929 9201
W: www.brocktonschool.com

Brookes Westshore
1939 Sooke Road, Victoria BC V9B 1W2
DP Coordinator Rui Li
MYP Coordinator Melanie Moroz
Languages English
W: westshore.brookes.org

Capilano Elementary School
1230 West 20th Street, North Vancouver BC V7P 2B9
PYP Coordinator Arash Kaboli
Languages English
T: +1 604 903 3370
W: www.sd44.ca/school/capilano/Pages/default.aspx

Carson Graham Secondary School
2145 Jones Avenue, North Vancouver BC V7M 2W7
DP Coordinator Liz Thornhill
MYP Coordinator Cora Pross
Languages English
T: +1 604 903 3555
W: carsongraham.ca

Cypress Park Primary School
4355 Marine Drive, West Vancouver BC V7V 1P2
PYP Coordinator Andrea Anderson
Languages English
T: +1 604 981 1330
W: westvancouverschools.ca/cypresspark-primary

École Andre-Piolat
380 West Kings Road, North Vancouver BC V7L 2L9
DP Coordinator Audrey Coquery
MYP Coordinator Trâm Tran
Languages English
T: +1 604 980 6040
W: andrepiolat.csf.bc.ca

Ecole Cedardale Elementary
595 Burley Drive, West Vancouver BC V7T 1Z3
PYP Coordinator Kristina Hayes
Languages English
T: +1 604 981 1390
W: westvancouverschools.ca/ecole-cedardale-elementary

École des Pionniers Port Coquitlam
1618 Patricia Ave, Port Coquitlam BC V3B 4A8
DP Coordinator Richard Hoole
MYP Coordinator Karine De Serres
Languages French
T: +1 604 552 7915
W: pionniers.csf.bc.ca

École Gabrielle-Roy
6887, 132 Rue, Surrey BC V3W 4L9
DP Coordinator Jean-Philippe Schall
Languages French, English
T: +1 604 599 6688
W: gabrielleroy.csf.bc.ca

École Jules-Verne
5445 rue Baillie, Vancouver BC V5Z 3M6
DP Coordinator Jessika Girard
Languages French
T: +1 604 731 8378
W: julesverne.csf.bc.ca

École Victor-Brodeur
637 Head Street, Victoria BC V9A 5S9
DP Coordinator Elizabeth Rush
Languages French
T: +1 250 220 6010
W: brodeur.csf.bc.ca

Elsie Roy Elementary School
150 Drake Street, Vancouver BC V6Z 2X1
MYP Coordinator Erica Sullivan
Languages English
T: +1 604 7135890

English Bluff Elementary
402 English Bluff Road, Delta BC V4M 2N2
PYP Coordinator Jessica Elkin
Languages English
T: +1 604 943 0201
W: eb.deltasd.bc.ca

Fraser Valley School
19533 64th Avenue, Surrey BC V3S 4J3
PYP Coordinator Natalie Morris
Languages English
T: +1 604 427 2282
W: fraservalleyschool.ca

Garibaldi Secondary School
24789 Dewdney Trunk Road, Maple Ridge BC V4R 1X2
DP Coordinator Kyle Ludeman
MYP Coordinator Assunta Budd
Languages English
T: +1 604 463 6287
W: gss.sd42.ca

Glenlyon Norfolk School
801 Bank Street, Victoria BC V8S 4A8
DP Coordinator Mme. Angela Girard
MYP Coordinator Mrs. Gina Simpson
PYP Coordinator Mrs. Leanne Giommi
Languages English
T: +1 250 370 6801
W: www.mygns.ca

Hugh Boyd Secondary School
9200 No. 1 Road, Richmond BC V7E 6L5
MYP Coordinator Michelle Korber
Languages English
T: +1 604 668 6615
W: boyd.sd38.bc.ca

Island Pacific School
671 Carter Road, Box 128, Bowen Island BC V0N 1G0
MYP Coordinator Amanda Szabo
Languages English
T: +1 604 947 9311
W: www.islandpacific.org

Johnston Heights Secondary School
15350-99 Avenue, Surrey BC V3R 0R9
DP Coordinator Emily Hayler
MYP Coordinator Alana Douglas
Languages English
T: +1 604 581 5500
W: www.surreyschools.ca

King George Secondary School
1755 Barclay Street, Vancouver BC V6G 1K6
MYP Coordinator Erin Stacey
Languages English
T: +1 604 713 8999
W: kinggeorge.vsb.bc.ca

Lord Roberts Elementary School
1100 Bidwell Street, Vancouver BC V6G 2K4
MYP Coordinator Kay Shetty
Languages English
T: +1 604 713 5055
W: lordroberts.vsb.bc.ca

Lowell High School
750 Hamilton Street, Suite 210, Vancouver BC V6B 2R5
DP Coordinator Priyam Sagar
Languages English, Chinese
T: +1 604 336 0456
W: www.lowellhighschool.ca

Meadowridge School
12224 240th Street, Maple Ridge BC V4R 1N1
DP Coordinator Ms. Kristal Bereza
MYP Coordinator Mr. Scott Rinn
PYP Coordinator Mrs. Heather Nicholson
Languages English
T: +1 604 467 4444
W: www.meadowridge.bc.ca

Mountain Secondary School
7755-202 A Street, Langley BC V2Y 1W4
DP Coordinator Tina Costopoulos
Languages English
T: +1 604 888 3033
W: www.msssd35.bc.ca

MULGRAVE SCHOOL, THE INTERNATIONAL SCHOOL OF VANCOUVER
2330 Cypress Bowl Lane, West Vancouver BC V7S 3H9
DP Coordinator Aziz Batada
MYP Coordinator Mike Olynyk
PYP Coordinator Janet Hicks & Shanaz Ramji
Languages English
T: +1 604 922 3223
E: admissions@mulgrave.com
W: www.mulgrave.com
See full details on page 496

New Westminster Secondary School
835 Eighth Street, New Westminster BC V3M 3S9
DP Coordinator Pawel Korczyk
Languages English
T: +1 604 517 6220
W: nwss.ca

NorKam Senior Secondary School
730 12th Street, Kamloops BC V2B 3C1
DP Coordinator Susan Kabotoff
Languages English
T: +1 250 376 1272
W: nkss.sd73.bc.ca

Pacific Academy
10238 168th Street, Surrey BC V4N 1Z4
DP Coordinator David Rosborough
Languages English
T: +1 604 581 5353
W: www.pacificacademy.net

PARKLAND SECONDARY SCHOOL
10640 McDonald Park Road, North Saanich BC V8L 5S7
DP Coordinator Erin Stinson
Languages English
T: +1 250 655 2700
E: krussell@saanichschools.ca
W: parkland.saanichschools.ca
See full details on page 501

Pearson College UWC
650 Pearson College Drive, Victoria BC V9C 4H7
CP Coordinator Emily Coolidge
DP Coordinator Sherry Crowther
Languages English
T: +1 250 391 2411
W: www.pearsoncollege.ca

Port Moody Secondary School
300 Albert Street, Port Moody BC V3H 2M5
DP Coordinator Sean Lenihan
Languages English
T: +1 604 939 6656
W: www.sd43.bc.ca/secondary/portmoody

Princess Margaret Secondary High School
120 Green Avenue W., Penticton, BC V2A 3T1
MYP Coordinator Karla Kirmis
Languages English, French
T: +1 250 770 7620
W: www.sd67.bc.ca/school/princessmargaretsecondary

Queen Mary Community School
230 West Keith Road, North Vancouver BC V7M 1L8
PYP Coordinator Jen Aragon
Languages English
T: +1 604 903 3720
W: www.queenmary.ca

Richmond Secondary School
7171 Minoru Boulevard, Richmond BC V6Y 1Z3
DP Coordinator David Miller
Languages English
T: +1 604 668 6400
W: rhs.sd38.bc.ca

Rockridge Secondary School
5350 Headland Drive, West Vancouver BC V7W 3H2
MYP Coordinator Rhonette Millare
Languages English
T: +1 604 981 1300
W: westvancouverschools.ca/rockridge-secondary

Seaquam Secondary School
11584 Lyon Road, Delta BC V4E 2K4
DP Coordinator Dhana Matthews
Languages English
T: +1 604 591 6166
W: se.deltasd.bc.ca

Semiahmoo Secondary School
1785 - 148th Street, Surrey BC V4A 4M6
DP Coordinator David Kenny
Languages English
T: +1 604 536 6174
W: www.surreyschools.ca/schools/semi

SenPokChin School
1156 SenPokChin Boulevard, Oliver BC V0H 1T8
PYP Coordinator Mubeen Safura
Languages English, Nsyilxcen
T: +1 250 498 2019
W: www.senpokchin.ca

Sir Winston Churchill Secondary School, Vancouver
7055 Heather Street, Vancouver BC V6P 3P7
DP Coordinator Karen Puzio
Languages English
T: +1 604 713 8189
W: churchill.vsb.bc.ca

Southlands Elementary School
5351 Camosun Street, Vancouver BC V6N 2C4
PYP Coordinator Joanna Wood
Languages English
T: +1 604 713 5414
W: www.vsb.bc.ca/schools/southlands

SOUTHPOINTE ACADEMY
1900 56th Street, Tsawwassen BC V4L 2B1
DP Coordinator Theresa Kwan
MYP Coordinator Samantha Goodard
PYP Coordinator J. Roxanne Young
Languages English
T: +1 604 948 8826
E: admissions@southpointe.ca
W: www.southpointe.ca
See full details on page 506

Southridge School
2656 160th Street, Surrey BC V3S 0B7
MYP Coordinator Alison Ito
PYP Coordinator Jo-Ann Murchie
Languages English
T: +1 604 535 5056
W: www.southridge.bc.ca

St. John's Academy Shawnigan Lake
2371 Shawnigan Lake Road, Shawnigan Lake BC V0R 2W5
DP Coordinator Kristine Greenlaw
MYP Coordinator Bradley Myrholm
Languages English
T: +1 250 220 4888
W: stjohnsacademy.ca/shawniganlake

ST. JOHN'S SCHOOL
2215 West 10th Avenue, Vancouver BC V6K 2J1
DP Coordinator Christine Miklitz
MYP Coordinator Daniel Ahn
PYP Coordinator Leslie Morden
Languages English
T: +1 604 732 4434
E: admissions@sjs.ca
W: www.sjs.ca
See full details on page 508

St. Margaret's School
1080 Lucas Avenue, Victoria BC V8X 3P7
DP Coordinator Sean Murray
Languages English
T: +1 250 479 7171
W: www.stmarg.ca

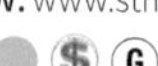

STRATFORD HALL
3000 Commercial Drive, Vancouver BC V5N 4E2
DP Coordinator Hazel Chee
MYP Coordinator Mark Pulfer
PYP Coordinator Amanda Lempriere
Languages English
T: +1 604 436 0608
E: info@stratfordhall.ca
W: www.stratfordhall.ca
See full details on page 512

The High School at Vancouver Island University
Nanaimo (Main Campus), 900 Fifth Street, Nanaimo BC V9R 5S5
DP Coordinator Tricia Young
Languages English
T: +1 250 753 3245
W: ths.viu.ca

Unisus Junior School
7808 Pierre Dr, Summerland BC V0H 1Z2
PYP Coordinator Tara Avenia
Languages English, Spanish
T: +1 250 404 3232
W: www.unisus.ca

Unisus School
7808 Pierre Dr, Summerland BC V0H 1Z2
DP Coordinator Tracey Hobbs
Languages English
T: +1 250 404 3232
W: www.unisus.ca

West Bay School
3175 Thompson Place, West Vancouver BC V7V 3E3
PYP Coordinator Morikke Espenhain
Languages English
T: +1 604 981 1260
W: westvancouverschools.ca/westbay-elementary

West Vancouver Secondary School
1750 Mathers Avenue, West Vancouver BC V7V 2G7
DP Coordinator Joanne Pohn
Languages English
T: +1 604 981 1100
W: www.sd45.bc.ca

White Rock Christian Academy
2265 -152nd Street, Surrey BC V4A 4P1
DP Coordinator Jeff Weichel
MYP Coordinator Natalie Poirier
PYP Coordinator Emily Berry
Languages English
T: +1 604 531 9186
W: www.wrca.ca

Manitoba

Balmoral Hall School
630 Westminster Ave, Winnipeg MB R3C 3S1
PYP Coordinator Cathy Doerksen
Languages English
T: +1 204 784 1600
W: www.balmoralhall.com

Collège Louis-Riel
585 rue Saint-Jean-Baptiste, Winnipeg MB R2H 2Y2
DP Coordinator Dave Rondeau
Languages French
T: +1 204 237 8927
W: www.louis-riel.mb.ca

Collège Sturgeon Heights Collegiate
2665 Ness Ave, Winnipeg MB R3J 1A5
DP Coordinator Jennifer Peters
Languages English
T: +1 204 888 0684
W: www.sjasd.ca/school/sturgeonheights
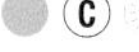

Kelvin High School
155 Kingsway, Winnipeg MB R3M 0G3
DP Coordinator Melani Decelles
Languages English
T: +1 204 474 1492
W: www.winnipegsd.ca/schools/kelvin

Miles MacDonell Collegiate
757 Roch Street, Winnipeg MB R2K 2R1
DP Coordinator Laura McMaster
Languages English
T: +1 204 667 1103
W: www.retsd.mb.ca/school/miles

River Heights School
1350 Grosvenor Ave., Winnipeg MB R3M 0P2
MYP Coordinator Amanda Tetrault
Languages English, French
T: +1 204 488 7090
W: www.winnipegsd.ca/riverheights

Westwood Collegiate
360 Rouge Road, Winnipeg MB R3K 1K3
DP Coordinator Art Penning
Languages English
T: +1 204 888 7650
W: www.sjasd.ca/school/westwood

New Brunswick

Ecole Mathieu-Martin
511 rue Champlain, Dieppe, Nouveau-Brunswick NB E1A 1P2
DP Coordinator Daniel Bourgeois
Languages French
T: +1 506 856 2791

École Sainte-Anne
715 rue Priestman, Fredericton NB E3B 5W7
DP Coordinator Michelle Foreman
Languages English
T: +1 506 453 3991
W: esa.nbed.nb.ca

Rothesay Netherwood School
40 College Hill Road, Rothesay NB E2E 5H1
DP Coordinator Tammy Earle
Languages English
T: +1 506 847 8224
W: www.rns.cc

St John High School
170-200 Prince William Street, #8, Saint John NB E2L 2B7
DP Coordinator Tracy Lutz
Languages English
T: +1 506 658 5358
W: www.sjhigh.ca

Newfoundland and Labrador

Holy Heart of Mary High School
55 Bonaventure Avenue, St. John's NL A1C 3Z3
DP Coordinator Michelle O'Connell
Languages English
T: +1 709 754 1600
W: www.holyheart.ca

Lakecrest Independent School
58 Patrick Street, St. John's NL A1E 2S7
PYP Coordinator Lisa Dove Major
Languages English
T: +1 709 738 1212
W: www.lakecrest.ca
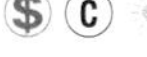

Nova Scotia

Charles P. Allen High School
200 Innovation Dr., Bedford NS B4B 0G4
DP Coordinator Christopher Hall
Languages English
T: +1 902 832 8964
W: cpa.hrce.ca

Citadel High School
1855 Trollope Street, Halifax NS B3H 0A4
DP Coordinator Heather Michael
Languages English
T: +1 902 491 4444
W: www.qeh.ednet.ns.ca

Cobequid Educational Centre
34 Lorne Street, Truro NS B2N 3K3
DP Coordinator Taunya Pynn Crowe
Languages English
T: +1 902 896 5700
W: cec.ccrsb.ca

Cole Harbour District High School
2 Chameau Cresent, Dartmouth NS B2W 4X4
DP Coordinator Michael Jean
Languages English
T: +1 902 464 5220
W: chd.hrce.ca

Dr. John Hugh Gillis Regional High School
105 Braemore Avenue, Antigonish NS B2G 1L3
DP Coordinator Lindsay MacInnis
Languages English
T: +1 902 863 1620
W: drjhg.srce.ca

École du Carrefour
201A Avenue du Portage, Dartmouth NS B2X 3T4
DP Coordinator Pauline André
Languages French
T: +1 902 433 7000
W: carrefour.ednet.ns.ca

Halifax Grammar School
945 Tower Road, Halifax NS B3H 2Y2
DP Coordinator Laura Brock
Languages English
T: +1 902 423 9312
W: www.hgs.ns.ca
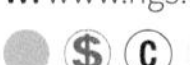

Halifax West High School
283 Thomas Raddall Drive, Halifax NS B3S 1R1
DP Coordinator Jackie Adamski
Languages English
T: +1 902 457 8900
W: www.hwhs.ednet.ns.ca

Horton High School
75 Greenwich Road S, Greenwich NS B4P 2R2
DP Coordinator Jason Fuller
Languages English
T: +1 902 542 6060
W: hortonhighschool.ca

King's-Edgehill School
11 King's-Edgehill Lane, Windsor NS B0N 2T0
DP Coordinator Derek Bouwman
Languages English
T: +1 902 798 2278
W: www.kes.ns.ca
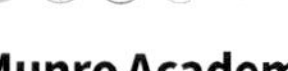

Munro Academy
2 School Street, Sydney Mines NS B1V 1R3
CP Coordinator Sarah Barrett
Languages English, French
T: +1 902 241 5090
W: www.munroacademy.org

Northumberland Regional High School
104 Alma Road, Westville NS B0K 2A0
DP Coordinator Christina Cameron
Languages English
T: +1 902 396 2750
W: nrhs.ccrsb.ca

Park View Education Centre
1485 King Street, Bridgewater NS B4V 1C4
DP Coordinator Charlotte Brooks
Languages English
T: +1 902 541 8200
W: www.pvec.ednet.ns.ca

Prince Andrew High School
31 Woodlawn Road, Dartmouth NS B2W 2R7
DP Coordinator Kristen Amiro
Languages English
T: +1 902 435 8452
W: www.pahs.ednet.ns.ca

Sydney Academy
49 Terrace Street, Sydney NS B1P 2L4
DP Coordinator Heather Urquhart
Languages English
T: +1 902 562 5464
W: sites.google.com/gnspes.ca/sydneyacademy

Yarmouth Consolidated Memorial High School
146 Forest Street, Yarmouth NS B5A 0B3
DP Coordinator Colleen Daley
Languages English
T: +1 902 749 2810
W: www.ycmhs.com

Ontario

Académie de la Capitale
1010 Morrison Dr Suite 200, Ottawa ON K2H 8K7
PYP Coordinator Shannon Neill
Languages English, French
T: +1 613 721 3872
W: www.acadecap.org

Académie Ste Cécile International School
925 Cousineau Road, Windsor ON N9G 1V8
DP Coordinator Laurie Bruce
MYP Coordinator Loranda Burton
Languages English, French
T: +1 519 969 1291
W: www.stececile.ca
  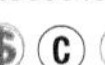

Alexander Mackenzie High School
300 Major Mackenzie Dr. W., Richmond Hill ON L4C 3S3
DP Coordinator Keith Auyeung
Languages English
T: +1 905 884 0554
W: www.yrdsb.ca/schools/alexandermackenzie.hs

Ancaster High School
374 Jerseyville Road West, Ancaster ON L9G 3K8
DP Coordinator Del Taylor
Languages English
T: +1 905 648 4468
W: www.hwdsb.on.ca/ancasterhigh
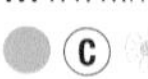

Ashbury College
362 Mariposa Avenue, Ottawa ON K1M 0T3
DP Coordinator Shannon Howlett
Languages English
T: +1 613 749 5954
W: www.ashbury.ca

Assumption College Catholic High School
1100 Huron Church Road, Windsor ON N9C 2K7
DP Coordinator Brianne Trudell
MYP Coordinator Janet Gursoy
Languages English
T: +1 519 256 7801 EXT:278
W: sites.google.com/a/catholicboard.ca/acs-website

Bayview Secondary School
10077 Bayview Avenue, Richmond Hill ON L4C 2L4
DP Coordinator Lara Joffe
Languages English
T: +1 905 884 4453
W: www.yrdsb.ca/schools/bayview.ss

Bishop Macdonell Catholic High School
200 Clair Road West, Guelph ON N1L 1G1
DP Coordinator Amy Wilson
Languages English
T: +1 519 822 8502
W: www.wellingtoncdsb.ca/school/bishopmacdonell/Pages/default.aspx

Branksome Hall
10 Elm Avenue, Toronto ON M4W 1N4
DP Coordinator Leslie Miller
MYP Coordinator Owen Williams
PYP Coordinator Andrea Mills
Languages English
T: +1 416 920 9741
W: www.branksome.on.ca

Bristol Road Middle School
210 Bristol Rd E, Mississauga ON L4Z 3V5
MYP Coordinator Sarah Rowsell
Languages English
T: +1 905 755 9809

Bronte College
88 Bronte College Court, 1444 Dundas Cres, Mississauga ON L5C 1E9
DP Coordinator Wynn Looi
Languages English
T: +1 905 270 7788
W: www.brontecollege.ca

Cameron Heights Collegiate Institute
301 Charles St. E., Kitchener ON N2G 2P8
DP Coordinator Julie Clancy
Languages English
T: +1 519 578 8330
W: chc.wrdsb.ca

Cardinal Carter Catholic High School
210 Bloomington Rd. W., Aurora ON L4G 0P9
DP Coordinator Andrea Steele
Languages English
T: +1 905 727 2455
W: www.ycdsb.ca/cch

Cardinal Carter Catholic Secondary School
120 Ellison Ave., Leamington ON N8H 5C7
DP Coordinator Elisa Houston
MYP Coordinator Paula Cinicolo
Languages English, French
T: +1 519 322 2804
W: sites.google.com/site/cougarscardinalcarter

Catholic Central High School
450 Dundas Street, London ON N6B 3K3
CP Coordinator Carla Mascherin Walton
DP Coordinator Carla Mascherin Walton
Languages English
T: +1 519 675 4431
W: www.ldcsb.on.ca

Chippewa Secondary School
539 Chippewa St. West, North Bay ON P1B 4R4
DP Coordinator Kim Larivee
Languages English
T: +1 705 475 2341
W: www.nearnorthschools.ca/chippewa

Cobourg Collegiate Institute
335 King Street East, Cobourg ON K9A 1M2
DP Coordinator Scott Caister
Languages English
T: +1 905 372 2271
W: cci.kprdsb.ca

Collège Catholique Franco-Ouest
411 promenade Seyton, Nepean ON K2H 8X1
DP Coordinator Natalie Beaucaire
MYP Coordinator Karl Todd
Languages French
T: +1 613 820 2920
W: franco-ouest.ecolecatholique.ca

Collège catholique Mer Bleue
6401 chemin Renaud, Orléans ON K1W 0H8
DP Coordinator Sylvain Miette
MYP Coordinator Marie-Pier Parisien
Languages French
T: +1 613 744 4022
W: mer-bleue.ecolecatholique.ca

Colonel By Secondary School
2381 Ogilvie Road, Ottawa ON K1J 7N4
DP Coordinator Lewis Harthun
Languages English
T: +1 613 745 9411
W: www.colonelby.com

Craig Kielburger Secondary School
1151 Ferguson Dr., Milton ON L9T 7V8
DP Coordinator Jude Miranda
Languages English, French
T: +1 905 878 0575
W: cks.hdsb.ca

Dr. G.W. Williams Secondary School
39 Dunning Ave., Aurora ON L4G 1A2
DP Coordinator Hailey King
Languages English
T: +1 905 727 3131
W: drgwwilliams.ss.yrdsb.ca
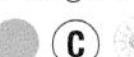

Eastside Secondary School
275 Farley Avenue, Belleville ON K8N 4M2
DP Coordinator Mary Reuvekamp
Languages English
T: +1 613 962 8668
W: ess.hpedsb.on.ca

École élémentaire catholique Au Coeur d'Ottawa
88 rue Main, Ottawa ON K1S 1C2
PYP Coordinator Isabelle Gauthier-Cossette
Languages English, French
T: +1 613 216 0017
W: aucoeurdottawa.ecolecatholique.ca

École élémentaire catholique Corpus Christi
362, avenue Hillside, Oshawa ON L1J 6L7
PYP Coordinator Epiphane Dohou
Languages English
T: +1 905 728 0491
W: cc.cscmonavenir.ca

École élémentaire catholique Jean-Paul II
1001 avenue Hutchison, Whitby ON L1N 2A3
PYP Coordinator Caroline Rivest
Languages French
T: +1 905 665 5393
W: jpii.cscmonavenir.ca

École élémentaire publique L'Odyssée
1770, promenade Grey Nuns, Orléans ON K1C 1C3
PYP Coordinator Jacinthe Chapdelaine
Languages French
T: +1 613 834 2097
W: www.odyssee.cepeo.on.ca/Ecole

École élémentaire publique Michaëlle-Jean
11 chemin Claridge, Ottawa ON K2J 5A3
PYP Coordinator Pauline Mpouma
Languages English
T: +1 613 823 2288
W: www.michaelle-jean.cepeo.on.ca

École élémentaire publique Rose des Vents
1650, 2e Rue Est, Cornwall ON K6H 2C3
PYP Coordinator Samantha Sabourin
Languages French
T: +1 613 932 4183
W: www.rose-des-vents.cepeo.on.ca

École secondaire catholique l'Essor
13605, St Gregory's Road, Windsor ON N8N 3E4
DP Coordinator Jason Defoe
Languages French
T: +1 519 735 4115
W: vibe.cscprovidence.ca/lessor

École secondaire catholique Monseigneur-de-Charbonnel
110, avenue Drewry, Toronto ON M2M 1C8
DP Coordinator Florence Kulnieks
Languages French
T: +1 416 393 5537
W: esmdc.cscmonavenir.ca

École secondaire catholique Monseigneur-Jamot
2350 boulevard Woodglade, Peterborough ON K9K 2L1
DP Coordinator Maryssa Credger-Blackwell
Languages English, French
T: +1 705 742 7571
W: mj.cscmonavenir.ca

École secondaire catholique Père-Philippe-Lamarche
2850 Eglinton Ave E., Scarborough ON M1J 2C8
DP Coordinator Johanne Joly
Languages English, French
T: +1 416 986 6414
W: esppl.cscmonavenir.ca

École secondaire catholique Père-René-de-Galinée
450, chemin Maple Grove, Cambridge ON N3H 4R7
MYP Coordinator Danica Lalich
Languages French
T: +1 519 650 9444
W: esprdg.cscmonavenir.ca
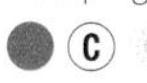

École secondaire catholique Renaissance
700, chemin Bloomington, Aurora ON L4G 0E1
DP Coordinator Zinta Anna Amolins
MYP Coordinator Adam Constantineau
Languages French
T: +1 905 727 4631
W: esr.cscmonavenir.ca

École secondaire catholique Saint Frère André
330, avenue Lansdowne, Toronto ON M6H 3Y1
DP Coordinator Dumitru Trinca-Costica
Languages French
T: +1 416 393 5324
W: essfa.cscmonavenir.ca

École secondaire catholique Saint-Charles-Garnier
4101, rue Baldwin Sud, Whitby ON L1R 2W6
MYP Coordinator Natalie Desgroseilliers
Languages French
T: +1 905 655 5635
W: esscg.cscmonavenir.ca

École secondaire catholique Sainte-Famille
1780, boulevard Meadowvale, Mississauga ON L5N 7K8
CP Coordinator Christine Guindy
DP Coordinator Emmanuel Sincennes
MYP Coordinator Henriette Tebit Nwabang
Languages French
T: +1 905 814 0318
W: essf.cscmonavenir.ca

École secondaire catholique Sainte-Trinité
2600, Grand Oak Trail, Oakville ON L6M 0R4
DP Coordinator Emmanuel Denou
MYP Coordinator Paul Courville
Languages French
T: +1 905 339 0812
W: esst.cscmonavenir.ca

École secondaire Gaétan-Gervais
1075, McCraney Street East, Oakville ON L6H 1H9
DP Coordinator Aboubacar Sanogo
Languages English, French
T: +1 289 529 0065
W: gaetangervais.csviamonde.ca

École secondaire Hanmer
4800, Ave Notre-Dame, Hanmer ON P3P 1X5
DP Coordinator Michelle Jobin-Quenville
Languages French
T: +1 705 969 4402
W: esh.cspgno.ca
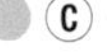 

École secondaire Jeunes sans frontières
7585 promenade Financial, Brampton ON L6Y 5P4
DP Coordinator Beatrice Khemiss
Languages French
T: +1 905 450 1106
W: csviamonde.ca/ecoles/jeunessansfrontieres

École secondaire publique Gisèle-Lalonde
500 Boulevard Millenium, Orléans ON K4A 4X3
DP Coordinator Caroline Joly
MYP Coordinator Francine Foisy
Languages English, French
T: +1 613 833 0018
W: www.gisele-lalonde.cepeo.on.ca

École secondaire publique L'Héritage
1111 chemin Montréal, Cornwall ON K6H 1E1
DP Coordinator Jasmine Bernier
MYP Coordinator Jasmine Bernier
Languages English
T: +1 613 933 3318

École secondaire publique Le Sommet
894, boul. Cécile, Hawkesbury ON K6A 3R5
DP Coordinator Chantal Lalonde
MYP Coordinator Chantal Lalonde
Languages French
T: +1 613 632 6059
W: lesommet.cepeo.on.ca

École Secondaire Publique Mille-Îles
72 Gilmour Avenue, Kingston ON K7M 9G6
DP Coordinator Louis Nguenang
MYP Coordinator Michèle Guitard
Languages French
T: +1 613 547 2556
W: www.mille-iles.cepeo.on.ca

École Secondaire Publique Omer-Deslauriers
159 Chesterton Dr, Nepean ON K2E 7E6
DP Coordinator Sophie Tchu-Ut-Gnon
MYP Coordinator Tej Kouraichi
Languages French
T: +1 613 820 0992
W: omer-deslauriers.cepeo.on.ca

École secondaire publique Pierre-de-Blois
1310 Promenade Chapman Mills, Ottawa ON K2J 6L9
DP Coordinator Michelle Goulet
MYP Coordinator Lise Gravelle
Languages French
T: +1 613 825 4232
W: pierre-de-blois.cepeo.on.ca

École secondaire Toronto Ouest
330, Avenue Lansdowne, Toronto ON M6H 3Y1
DP Coordinator Amy Morris
Languages French
T: +1 416 532 6592
W: ecolesecondairetorontoouest.csviamonde.ca

Elmwood School
261 Buena Vista Road, Ottawa ON K1M 0V9
DP Coordinator Jason Levesque
MYP Coordinator Alyson Bartlett
PYP Coordinator Kate Meadowcroft
Languages English
T: +1 613 749 6761
W: www.elmwood.ca

Erindale Secondary School
2021 Dundas Street West, Mississauga ON L5K 1R2
DP Coordinator Carolyn LaRoche
Languages English
T: +1 905 828 7206
W: schools.peelschools.org/sec/erindale

Father Michael McGivney Catholic Academy
5300 Fourteenth Avenue, Markham ON L3S 3K8
DP Coordinator Christine Gomes
Languages English
T: +1 905 472 4961
W: fmmh.ycdsb.ca
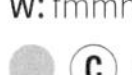

Georgetown District High School
70 Guelph Street, Georgetown ON L7G 3Z5
DP Coordinator Kyle Stewart
Languages English
T: +1 905 877 6966
W: geo.hdsb.ca
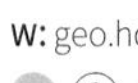

Glenforest Secondary School
3575 Fieldgate Drive, Mississauga ON L4X 2J6
DP Coordinator Daphne Habib
MYP Coordinator Diana Wang-Martin
Languages English
T: +1 905 625 7731
W: schools.peelschools.org/sec/glenforest

IB AMERICAS

Glenview Park Secondary School
55 McKay Street, Cambridge ON N1R 4G6
DP Coordinator Colleen Caplin
Languages English
T: +1 519 621 9510
W: gps.wrdsb.on.ca

Glenwood Public School
1601 Norfolk Street, Windsor ON N9E 1H6
PYP Coordinator Darryl Dinham
Languages English, French
T: +1 519 969 3990
W: www.publicboard.ca/en/glenwood/index.aspx

Harold M. Brathwaite Secondary School
415 Great Lakes Drive, Brampton ON L6R 2Z4
DP Coordinator Bluky Ng
Languages English
T: +1 905 793 2155
W: www.hmbss.com

Holy Cross Catholic Academy
7501 Martin Grove Road, Woodbridge ON L4L 9E4
DP Coordinator Dina Monaco
Languages English
T: +1 905 851 6699
W: hocr.ycdsb.ca

I E Weldon Secondary School
24 Weldon Road, Lindsay ON K9V 4R6
DP Coordinator Erin Matthew
Languages English
T: +1 705 324 3585
W: www.tldsb.on.ca/schools/iewss
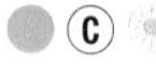

Kenner CVI & Intermediate School
633 Monaghan Road South, Peterborough ON K9J 5J2
DP Coordinator Peter Mullins
Languages English
T: +1 705 743 2181
W: www.kenner.kprdsb.ca

Khalsa Community School
69 Maitland Street, Brampton ON L6S 3B5
MYP Coordinator Kiran Bedi
Languages English
T: +1 905 791 1750
W: khalsacommunityschool.com

Khalsa School Malton
7280 Airport Rd., Mississauga ON L4T 2H3
MYP Coordinator Neha Paul
Languages English
T: +1 905 671 2010
W: www.khalsaschoolmalton.com

King Heights Academy
28 Roytec Road, Woodbridge ON L4L 8E4
PYP Coordinator Kirti Pankaj
Languages English
T: +1 905 652 1234
W: kingheightsacademy.com

Kingston Collegiate & Vocational Institute
235 Frontenac Street, Kingston ON K7L3S7
DP Coordinator Adam Watson
Languages English
T: +1 613 544 4811

Korah Collegiate and Vocational School
636 Goulais Avenue, Sault Ste Marie ON P6C 5A7
DP Coordinator Kathryn Johnstone
Languages English
T: +1 705 945 7180
W: www.korahcvs.com

La Citadelle International Academy of Arts & Science
36 Scarsdale Road, North York, Toronto ON M3B 2R7
MYP Coordinator Denise Voinica
Languages English, French
T: +1 416 385 9685
W: www.lacitadelleacademy.com

Le Collège Français
100 rue Carlton, Toronto ON M5B 1M3
DP Coordinator Odin Cabrera
MYP Coordinator Christina Campisi
Languages French
T: +1 416 393 0175

Leamington District Secondary School
80 Oak St. W., Leamington ON N8H 2B3
DP Coordinator Lisa Jeffery
Languages English, French
T: +1 519 326 6191
W: www.publicboard.ca/school/ldss

Lo-Ellen Park Secondary School
275 Loach's Road, Sudbury ON P3E 2P8
DP Coordinator Julie Wuorinen
Languages English
T: +1 705 522 2320

LONDON INTERNATIONAL ACADEMY
361-365 Richmond Street, London, ON N6A 3C2
DP Coordinator Abeera Atique
Languages English, Spanish, Mandarin
T: +1 519 433 3388
E: admissions@lia-edu.ca
W: www.lia-edu.ca
See full details on page 486

Lynn-Rose Heights Private School
7215 Millcreek Drive, Mississauga ON L5N 3R3
MYP Coordinator Farah Kiblawi
PYP Coordinator Lina Mosawy
Languages English
T: +1 905 567 3553
W: www.lynnroseheights.com

MacLachlan College
337 Trafalgar Road, Oakville ON L6J 3H3
PYP Coordinator Ashleigh Woodward
Languages English
T: +1 905 844 0372
W: www.maclachlan.ca

Maple High School
50 Springside Rd., Maple ON L6A 2W5
DP Coordinator Jacqueline Sandercock
Languages English
T: +1 905 417 9444
W: maple.hs.yrdsb.ca
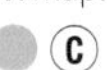

Margaret D. Bennie Public School
259 Sherk Street, Leamington ON N8H 3K8
PYP Coordinator Sherry Wiper
Languages English, French
T: +1 519 326 6603
W: www.publicboard.ca/en/mdbennie/index.aspx

Merivale High School
1755 Merivale Road, Nepean ON K2G 1E2
DP Coordinator Lewis Harthun
Languages English, French
T: +1 613 224 1807
W: merivalehs.ocdsb.ca

Michael Power - St Joseph High School
105 Eringate Drive, Toronto ON M9C 3Z7
DP Coordinator Claudia Grilo
Languages English
T: +1 416 393 5529

Milliken Mills High School
7522 Kennedy Rd, Unionville ON L3R 9S5
DP Coordinator Natalie White
Languages English
T: +1 905 477 0072
W: www.yrdsb.ca/schools/millikenmills.hs

Monarch Park Collegiate
1 Hanson Street, Toronto ON M4J 1G6
DP Coordinator Karen Doherty Ross
Languages English
T: +1 416 393 0190
W: www.monarchparkcollegiate.ca

Nicholson Catholic College
301 Church Street, Belleville ON K8N 3C7
DP Coordinator Justin Walsh
Languages English
T: +1 613 967 0404
W: www.nccschool.org

NOIC Academy
50 Featherstone Avenue, Markham ON L3S 2H4
DP Coordinator Michael Bales
Languages English
T: +1 905 472 2002
W: noic.ca
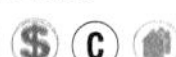

Notre Dame Secondary School
2 Notre Dame Avenue, Brampton ON L6Z 4L5
DP Coordinator Lorian Feres
Languages English
T: +1 905 840 2802
W: www.dpcdsb.org/ndame

Oakridge Secondary School
1040 Oxford Street West, London ON N6H 1V4
DP Coordinator Jeff Kunder
Languages English
T: +1 519 452 2750
W: oakridge.tvdsb.ca

Parkdale Collegiate Institute
209 Jameson Avenue, Toronto ON M6K 2Y3
DP Coordinator Miro Bartnik
Languages English
T: +1 416 393 9000
W: schools.tdsb.on.ca/parkdale

Regiopolis-Notre Dame Catholic High School
130 Russell Street, Kingston ON K7K 2E9
DP Coordinator James David
Languages English
T: +1 613 545 1902
W: alcdsb.on.ca/school/regi

Richland Academy
11570 Yonge Street, Richmond Hill, ON L4E 3N7
PYP Coordinator Joanne Pace
Languages English, French
T: +1 905 224 5600
W: www.richlandacademy.ca

RIDLEY COLLEGE
PO Box 3013, 2 Ridley Road, St Catharines ON L2R 7C3
DP Coordinator Saralyn Covent
MYP Coordinator Paul O'Rourke
PYP Coordinator Marcie Lewis
Languages English
T: +1 905 684 1889
E: admissions@ridleycollege.com
W: www.ridleycollege.com
See full details on page 502

Riverside Secondary School
8465 Jerome Street, Windsor ON N8S 1W8
DP Coordinator Derek Tomkins
Languages English, French
T: +1 519 948 4116

Robert Bateman High School
5151 New Street, Burlington ON L7L 1V3
DP Coordinator Jennifer Bright
Languages English
T: +1 905 632 5151
W: www.rbh.hdsb.ca

Sacred Heart Catholic School
125 Huron Street, Guelph ON N1E 5L5
PYP Coordinator Natasha Finoro
Languages English, French
T: +1 519 824 2751

Sir Wilfrid Laurier Collegiate Institute
145 Guildwood Parkway, Scarborough ON M1E 1P5
DP Coordinator Charis Kelso
Languages English
T: +1 416 396 6820
W: www.sirwilfridlaurierci.ca

St Francis Xavier Secondary School
50 Bristol Road West, Mississauga ON L5R 3K3
DP Coordinator Eugene Ladna
Languages English
T: +1 905 507 6666
W: www.dpcdsb.org/STFXS

St John's - Kilmarnock School
2201 Shantz Station Road, Box 179, Breslau (Waterloo Region) ON N0B 1M0
DP Coordinator Jordan Grant
MYP Coordinator Rebecca Dufour
PYP Coordinator Jennifer Wilkinson
Languages English
T: +1 519 648 2183
W: www.sjkschool.org

St Jude's Academy
2150 Torquay Mews, Mississauga ON L5N 2M6
DP Coordinator Leslie Roe-Etter
MYP Coordinator Kawaljit Kaur
PYP Coordinator Marijana Haag
Languages English
T: +1 905 814 0202
W: www.stjudesacademy.com

St Robert Catholic High School
8101 Leslie Street, Thornhill ON L3T 7P4
DP Coordinator Sheri Burke
Languages English
T: +1 905 889 4982
W: www.strobertchs.com

St Thomas Aquinas Roman Catholic Secondary School
124 Dorval Drive, Oakville ON L6K 2W1
DP Coordinator Antonia Montanari
Languages English
T: +1 905 842 9494
W: secondary.hcdsb.org/sta

St. Basil-the-Great College School
20 Starview Lane, North York ON M9M 3B2
DP Coordinator Melissa Ammendolia
Languages English
T: +1 416 393 5513
W: stbasilthegreat.tcdsb.org

St. James Catholic Global Learning Centre
98 Wanita Rd, Mississauga ON L5G1B8
MYP Coordinator Steven Kelenc
PYP Coordinator Nicola Hughes
Languages English
T: +1 905 891 7619
W: dpcdsb.org/jamee

St. John Paul II Catholic Secondary School
685 Military Trail, Scarborough ON M1E 4P6
DP Coordinator Suzanne Regimbal
Languages English
T: +1 416 393 5531
W: www.tcdsb.org/schools/stjohnpaulii

St. Mary Catholic Academy
66 Dufferin Park Avenue, Toronto ON M6H 1J6
DP Coordinator Judi Calado Costa
Languages English
T: +1 416 393 5528
W: www.tcdsb.org/schools/stmarycatholicacademy

St. Paul Secondary School
815 Atwater Avenue, Mississauga ON L5E 1L8
DP Coordinator Anne Marie Miki
Languages English, French
T: +1 905 278 3994
W: www3.dpcdsb.org/pauls

Sunnybrook School
469 Merton Street, Toronto ON M4S 1B4
PYP Coordinator Michael Rossiter
Languages English
T: +1 416 487 5308
W: www.sunnybrookschool.com

Superior Collegiate & Vocational Institute
333 N. High Street, Thunder Bay ON P7A 5S3
DP Coordinator Karen Watt
Languages English
T: +1 807 768 7284
W: superior.lakeheadschools.ca

Tall Pines School
8525 Torbram Road, Brampton ON L6T 5K4
MYP Coordinator Tima Nisbet
PYP Coordinator Tima Nisbet
Languages English, French
T: +2 905 458 6770
W: tallpinesschool.com

TFS - CANADA'S INTERNATIONAL SCHOOL
306 Lawrence Avenue East, Toronto ON M4N 1T7
DP Coordinator Dr. Jennifer Elliott
MYP Coordinator Julie Rouette
PYP Coordinator Emna Beji
Languages French, English
T: +1 416 484 6533
E: admissions@tfs.ca
W: www.tfs.ca
See full details on page 513

The Guelph Collegiate Vocational Institute
155 Paisley Street, Guelph ON N1H 2P3
DP Coordinator Alexandra Zahnd
Languages English
T: +1 519 824 9800
W: www.ugdsb.on.ca/gcvi

The Leo Baeck Day School
36 Atkinson Avenue, Thornhill ON L4J 8C9
MYP Coordinator Sheryl Faith
PYP Coordinator Sheryl Faith
Languages English
T: +1 905 709 3636
W: www.leobaeck.ca

The York School
1320 Yonge Street, Toronto ON M4T 1X2
DP Coordinator Marie Aragona
MYP Coordinator Fabio Biagiarelli
PYP Coordinator Yochabel De Giorgio
Languages English
T: ADMISSIONS: +1 416 646 5275
SWITCHBOARD: +1 416 926 1325
W: www.yorkschool.com

TMS School
500 Elgin Mills Road East, Richmond Hill ON L4C 5G1
DP Coordinator Shane Small
MYP Coordinator Jessica Wong
Languages English
T: +1 905 889 6882
W: www.tmsschool.ca

Town Centre Montessori Private Schools
155 Clayton Drive, Markham ON L3R 7P3
DP Coordinator Kenneth Huber
MYP Coordinator Christine Lau
PYP Coordinator Magdalena Therrien
Languages English
T: +1 905 470 1200
W: tcmps.com

Turner Fenton Secondary School
7935 Kennedy Road South, Brampton ON L6V 3N2
DP Coordinator Angela De Jong
MYP Coordinator Michael Langford
Languages English
T: +1 905 453 9220
W: www.turnerfenton.com

Upper Canada College
200 Lonsdale Road, Toronto ON M4V 1W6
DP Coordinator Colleen Ferguson
MYP Coordinator Gillian Levene
PYP Coordinator Dianne Jojic
Languages English
T: +1 416 488 1125
W: www.ucc.on.ca

Victoria Park Collegiate Institute
15 Wallingford Road, North York ON M3A 2V1
DP Coordinator Deana Ho Yan
Languages English
T: +1 416 395 3310
W: victoriaparkci.ca

Walden International School
1030 Queen Street West, Brampton ON L6X 0B2
MYP Coordinator Cindy Tom
PYP Coordinator Shelley Charanduk
Languages English, French
T: +1 905 338 6236
W: www.waldeninternationalschool.com
 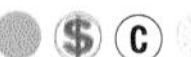

Westdale Secondary School
700 Main Street West, Hamilton ON L8S 1A5
DP Coordinator Kim Parkes-Hallmark
Languages English
T: +1 905 522 1387
W: www.hwdsb.on.ca/westdale

Weston Collegiate Institute
100 Pine Street, York, Toronto ON M9N 2Y9
DP Coordinator Anne Dale
Languages English
T: +1 416 394 3250
W: www.westonci.ca

Wheatley School
497 Scott Street, St Catharines ON L2M 3X3
MYP Coordinator Isabel N. Machinandiarena
Languages English
T: +1 905 641 3012
W: www.wheatleyschool.com

White Oaks Secondary School
1330 Montclair Drive, Oakville ON L6K 1Z5
DP Coordinator Erin Davidson
Languages English
T: +1 905 845 5200
W: www.wossweb.com

William Grenville Davis Senior Public School
491 Bartley Bull Parkway, Brampton ON L6W 2M7
MYP Coordinator Mandi Borek
Languages English
T: +1 905 459 3661
W: www.wgdavis.com

Prince Edward Island

Charlottetown Rural High School
100 Raiders Road, Charlottetown PE C1E 1K6
DP Coordinator Kevin Scully
Languages English
T: +1 902 368 6905
W: therural.ca

Colonel Gray High School
175 Spring Park Road, Charlottetown PE C1A 3Y8
DP Coordinator Angela MacCorquodale
Languages English
T: +1 902 368 6860
W:

Quebec

Académie François-Labelle
1227 rue Notre Dame, Repentigny QC J5Y 3H2
PYP Coordinator Maryse Cadieux
Languages French
T: +1 450 582 2020
W: www.academiefrancoislabelle.qc.ca

Bishop's College School
80 Moulton Hill Road, PO Box 5001, Station Lennoxville, Sherbrooke QC J1M 1Z8
DP Coordinator Amber Rommens
Languages English
T: +1 819 566 0227
W: www.bishopscollegeschool.com

Carlyle Elementary School
109 Carlyle Avenue, Mount Royal QC H3R 1S8
PYP Coordinator Aspasia Tzovanis-Manolias
Languages English
T: +1 514 738 1256
W: www.emsb.qc.ca/carlyle

Cégep André-Laurendeau
1111 rue Lapierre, Lasalle QC H8N 2J4
DP Coordinator Mehran Kabraelian
Languages French
T: +1 514 364 3320
W: www.claurendeau.qc.ca

Cégep de Rivière-du-Loup
80, rue Frontenac, Rivière-du-Loup QC G5R 1R1
DP Coordinator Martine Riou
Languages English
T: +1 418 862 6903
W: www.cegeprdl.ca

Cégep Garneau
1660 boulevard de l'Entente, Québec QC G1S 4S3
DP Coordinator Annie Jacques
Languages French
T: +1 418 688 8310 EXT:2372
W: www.cegepgarneau.ca

Children's World Academy
2241 Ménard, LaSalle QC H8N 1J4
PYP Coordinator Guy Walker
Languages English, French
T: +1 514 595 2043
W: cwa.lbpsb.qc.ca

Clearpoint Elementary School
17 Cedar Avenue, Pointe-Claire QC H9S 4X9
PYP Coordinator Layla Barroca
Languages English, French
T: +1 514 798 0792
W: clearpoint.lbpsb.qc.ca

Collège Charlemagne
5000 rue Pilon, Pierrefonds, Montréal QC H9K 1G4
MYP Coordinator Luc Fortin
Languages French
T: +1 514 626 7060

Collège Charles-Lemoyne - Campus Longueuil
901, chemin Tiffin, Longueuil QC J4P 3G6
MYP Coordinator Karine Savoie
PYP Coordinator Audrey Cantin
Languages English, French
T: +1 514 875 0505
W: www.monccl.com

Collège de l'Assomption
270 boulevard de l'Ange-Gardien, L'Assomption, Montréal QC J5Y 3R7
MYP Coordinator Hélène Pelland
Languages French
T: +1 450 589 5621
W: www.classomption.qc.ca

Collège Esther-Blondin
101 rue Sainte-Anne, Saint-Jacques QC J0K 2R0
MYP Coordinator Jessica Demers Lavigne
Languages French
T: +1 450 839 3672
W: collegeestherblondin.qc.ca
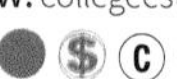

Collège Jean-de-Brebeuf
3200, chemin de la Côte-Sainte-Catherine, Montréal QC H3T 1C1
DP Coordinator David Pilon
MYP Coordinator Lyne Harvey
Languages French
T: +1 514 342 9342
W: www.brebeuf.qc.ca

Collège Jésus-Marie de Sillery
2047 chemin Saint-Louis, Québec City QC G1T 1P3
MYP Coordinator Isabelle Cloutier
Languages French
T: +1 418 687 9250
W: www.collegejesusmarie.com
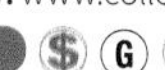

Collège Mont Notre-Dame de Sherbrooke
114 rue Cathédrale, Sherbrooke QC J1H 4M1
MYP Coordinator Nathalie Arès
Languages French
T: +1 819 563 4104
W: www.mont-notre-dame.qc.ca

Collège Notre-Dame-de-Lourdes
845 chemin Tiffin, Longueuil QC J4P 3G5
MYP Coordinator Marie-Josée Bellemare
Languages French
T: +1 450 670 4740
W: www.ndl.qc.ca

Collège Saint-Louis
275 36e Avenue, Lachine QC H8T 2A4
MYP Coordinator Denis Cadieux
Languages French
T: +1 514 855 4198
W: collegesaintlouis.ecolelachine.com

Collège Saint-Maurice
630 rue Girouard Ouest, Saint-Hyacinthe QC J2S 2Y3
MYP Coordinator Elsa Würtele
Languages French
T: +1 450 773 7478 EXT:222
W: www.csm.qc.ca

Collège Ville-Marie
2850 rue Sherbrooke Est, Montréal QC H2K 1H3
MYP Coordinator Odie Miller-Maboungou
Languages French
T: +1 514 525 2516
W: www.cvmarie.qc.ca
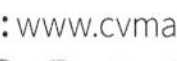

Courtland Park International School
1075 Wolfe, St-Bruno QC J3V 3K6
PYP Coordinator Grace Palmieri
Languages English
T: +1 450 550 2514
W: www.rsb.qc.ca

École Bois-Joli Sacré-Coeur
775 Rue du Sacré-Coeur Ouest, Saint-Hyacinthe QC J2S 1V2
PYP Coordinator Julie Bessette
Languages French
T: +1 450 774 5130
W: www.cssh.qc.ca/ecole-bois-joli-sacre-coeur

École Centrale
682 Rue Principale, Saint-Joachim de Shefford QC J0E 2G0
PYP Coordinator Claude Boisseau
Languages French
T: +1 450 539 1816

École Chabot et du l'Oasis
1666 Avenue De Lozère, Charlesbourg QC G1G 3L4
PYP Coordinator Caroline Giguère
Languages French
T: +1 418 624 3752

Ecole de la Baie Saint Francois
70 rue Louis VI Major, Salaberry De Valleyfield QC J6T 3G2
MYP Coordinator Daniel Hébert
Languages French
T: +1 450 371 2004

École de la Magdeleine
1100 boulevard Taschereau, La Prairie QC J5R 1W8
MYP Coordinator Maude Lemieux
Languages French
T: +1 514 380 8899
W: www.lamag.qc.ca

École de la Synergie
2255 Cavendish Boulevard, Montréal QC H4B 2L4
MYP Coordinator Khelidja Ait Ouali
Languages English, French
T: +1 514 484 5084
W: esynergie.ca

École de l'Équinoxe
2949 boulevard de la Renaissance, Laval, QC H7L 0H3
PYP Coordinator Karine Bouffard
Languages English, French
T: +1 450 662 7000
W: delequinoxe.cslaval.qc.ca

École d'éducation internationale
720 rue Morin, McMasterville QC J3G 1H1
MYP Coordinator François Brophy
Languages French
T: +1 450 467 4222
W: eei.csp.qc.ca

École d'éducation internationale de Laval
5075 boul du souvenir, Laval QC H7W 1E1
MYP Coordinator Élise Lalonde
Languages French
T: +1 450 662 7000 4300
W: eeil.cslaval.qc.ca

École d'éducation internationale Filteau-St-Mathieu
830 rue de Saurel, Sainte Foy QC G1X 3P6
PYP Coordinator Susie Goulet
Languages French
T: +1 418 652 2152
W: www.csdecou.qc.ca/filteau

École d'éducation internationale Notre-Dame-des-Neiges
4140, boulevard Gastonguay, Québec QC G2B 1M7
PYP Coordinator Gabrielle Prévost
Languages French
T: +1 418 686 4040
W: cscapitale-ecole-notre-dame-des-neiges.ca

École du Petit-Collège
9343 Rue Jean-Milot, LaSalle QC H8R 1Y7
PYP Coordinator Julie Masson
Languages English, French
T: +1 514 748 4661

École du Sentier
1225 rue Victorin, Drummondville, QC J2C 7Z9
PYP Coordinator Marylène Bienvenue
Languages French
T: +1 819 850 1632
W: www.dusentier.com

École Guy-Drummond
1475 avenue La Joie, Outremont QC H2V 1P9
PYP Coordinator Fanie Perras
Languages French
T: +1 514 270 4866

École internationale de Montréal
11 chemin Côte St-Antoine, Westmount, Montréal QC H3Y 2H7
MYP Coordinator Annie Beauchamp
PYP Coordinator Charlie Brière-Couture
Languages French
T: +1 514 596 7240
W: ecole-internationale.csdm.ca

École Internationale de Saint-Sacrement
1430 chemin Ste-Foy, Québec QC G1S 2N8
PYP Coordinator Sonya Fiset
Languages French
T: +1 418 686 4040
W: cscapitale-ecole-dest-sacrement.ca

École Internationale des Apprenants
4505 Boul Henri-Bourassa O, Saint-Laurent QC H4L 1A5
PYP Coordinator Adela Vintila
Languages French
T: +1 514 334 4153
W: ecoleia.ca

École internationale du Mont-Bleu
45 rue Boucher, Gatineau QC J8Y 6G2
PYP Coordinator Léticia Sanchez
Languages French
T: +1 819 777 5921
W: internationaledumontbleu.cspo.qc.ca

École internationale du Phare
405, rue Sara, Sherbrooke QC J1H 5S6
MYP Coordinator Stéphanie Dussault
Languages French
T: +1 819 822 5455
W: www.csrs.qc.ca/fr/internationale-du-phare

École internationale du Vieux-Longueuil
2301 boulevard Fernand-Lafontaine, Longueuil QC J4N 1N7
PYP Coordinator Claude Coupal
Languages English, French
T: +1 450 670 9494

École Internationale du Village
19, rue Symmes, Gatineau QC J9H 3J3
PYP Coordinator Mélanie Bazinet
Languages French
T: +1 819 685 2611
W: internationaleduvillage.cspo.qc.ca

École internationale Lucille-Teasdale
8350 boulevard Pelletier, Brossard QC J4X 1M8
MYP Coordinator Martin Laplante
Languages French
T: +1 450 465 6290

École internationale primaire de Greenfield Park
776 Cambell, Greenfield Park QC J4V 1YZ
PYP Coordinator Grace Palmieri
Languages French
T: +1 450 672 0042

École internationale Saint-François-Xavier
8-A, rue Pouliot, Rivière-du-Loup QC G5R 3R8
PYP Coordinator Julie Nadeau
Languages French, English, Spanish
T: +1 418 862 6901
W: web.cskamloup.qc.ca/sfx

École Internationale Wilfrid-Pelletier
8301 boulevard Wilfrid-Pelletier, Montréal (Anjou) QC H1K 1M2
PYP Coordinator Nathalie Fortier
Languages French
T: +1 514 352 7300
W: www.wilfrid-pelletier.ca

École Jeanne-Mance
4240 rue de Bordeaux, Montréal QC H2H 1Z5
MYP Coordinator Adeline Roy
Languages English
T: +1 514 596 5815
W: jeanne-mance.csdm.ca

École Joseph François Perrault
7540 rue François Perrault, Montréal QC H2A 1L9
MYP Coordinator Sylvie Durocher
Languages French
T: +1 514 596 4620

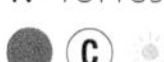

École La Vérendrye
3055, rue Mousseau, Montréal QC H1L 4W1
PYP Coordinator Vicky Desaulniers
Languages French
T: +1 514 596 4845
W: la-verendrye.csdm.ca

École Le tandem
605 rue Notre-dame Ouest, Victoriaville QC G6P 6Y9
MYP Coordinator Caroline Bilodeau
Languages French
T: +1 819 758 1534

École l'Envolée
549 rue Fournier, Granby QC J2J 2K5
MYP Coordinator Martin Nadeau
Languages French
T: +1 450 777 7536
W: lenvolee.csvdc.qc.ca

École Les Mélèzes
393 de Lanaudière, Joliette QC J6E3L9
PYP Coordinator Caroline Beaulieu
Languages French
T: +1 450 752 4433
W: www.lesmelezes.qc.ca

École Marie-Clarac
3530 Boul Gouin Est, Montréal-Nord QC H1H 1B7
MYP Coordinator Annie Frenette
Languages French
T: +1 514 322 1160
W: www.ecolemarie-clarac.qc.ca

École Monseigneur Robert
769 rue de lEducation, Québec QC G1E 1J2
PYP Coordinator Julie Duplain
Languages French
T: +1 418 666 4490

École Paul-Hubert
250, boulevard Arthur-Buies Ouest, Rimouski QC G5L 7A7
MYP Coordinator Martin Cote
Languages French
T: +1 418 724 3439
W: paulhubert.csphares.qc.ca

École Père-Marquette
6030 rue Marquette, Montréal QC H2G 2Y2
MYP Coordinator Priscilla Houde
Languages French
T: +1 514 596 4128
W: pere-marquette.csdm.qc.ca

École Plein Soleil (Association Coopérative)
300, rue de Montréal, Sherbrooke QC J1H 1E5
PYP Coordinator François Normandeau
Languages French
T: +1 819 569 8359
W: www.pleinsoleil.qc.ca

École Pointe-Lévy
55 Rue des Commandeurs, Levis QC G6V 1P5
MYP Coordinator Harold Pouliot
Languages French
T: +1 418 838 8402
W: www.pointe-levy.qc.ca

École Polyvalente Le Carrefour
125 Rue Self, Val d'Òr, Québec QC J9P 3N2
MYP Coordinator Dominic Ruel
Languages French
T: +1 819 825 4670

École Polyvalente Saint-Jérôme
535 rue Filion, Saint-Jérôme QC J7Z 1J6
MYP Coordinator Chantal Dion
Languages French
T: +1 450 436 4330
W: epsjcsrdn.ca

École primaire d'éducation internationale
2750,boulevard des Forges, Trois-Rivières QC G8Z 1V2
PYP Coordinator Maryse Gélinas
Languages French
T: +1 819 379 6565
W: www.ecolepei.com

École primaire d'éducation internationale du secteur Est
175, rue Saint-Alphonse, Trois-Rivières QC G8T 7R8
PYP Coordinator Maryse Gélinas
Languages French
T: +1 819 840 4358
W: www.ecolepei.com

École primaire Terre des jeunes
128 25e Avenue, St-Eustache QC J7P 2V2
PYP Coordinator Suzanne Allard
Languages French
T: +1 450 473 9219
W: terre-des-jeunes.cssmi.qc.ca

École Saint-Barthélemy
7081 avenue des Érables, Montréal QC H2E 2R1
PYP Coordinator Renée Martineau
Languages French
T: +1 514 596 4877
W: st-barthelemy.csdm.ca

École Saint-Jean
245, 2e Rue Ouest, Rimouski QC G5L 4Y1
MYP Coordinator Caroline Michaud
Languages French
T: +1 418 724 3381
W: stjean.csphares.qc.ca

École Saint-Pierre et des Sentiers
1090 chemin de Château-Bigot, Charlesbourg QC G2L 1G1
MYP Coordinator Melanie Tremblay
Languages French
T: +1 418 624 3757
W: www.sentiers.csdps.qc.ca

École Saint-Rémi
16 avenue Neveu, Beaconsfield QC H9W 5B4
PYP Coordinator Martine Gagnon
Languages English, French
T: +1 514 855 4206
W: saintremi.ecoleouest.com

École secondaire André-Laurendeau
7450 boulevard Cousineau, St-Hubert QC J3Y 3L4
MYP Coordinator Carole St-Amant
Languages French
T: +1 450 678 2080
W: andre-laurendeau.ecoles.csmv.qc.ca

Ecole Secondaire Armand-Corbeil
795 JF Kennedy Ouest, Terrebonne QC J6W 1X2
MYP Coordinator Annie Fournier
Languages French
T: +1 450 492 3619 EXT:1112

École secondaire Bernard-Gariépy
2800 boulevard des Érables, Sorel-Tracy QC J3R 2W4
MYP Coordinator Patrick Péloquin
Languages French
T: +1 450 742 5601

École secondaire Camille-Lavoie
500 avenue des Métiers, Alma QC G8B 3C4
MYP Coordinator Dominique Fortin
Languages French
T: +1 418 669 6062
W: www.ecolecamillelavoie.com

École Secondaire Cavelier-De LaSalle
9199 rue Centrale, LaSalle QC H8R 2J6
MYP Coordinator Terez Kai Lawson
Languages French
T: +1 514 595 2044

École secondaire Charles-Gravel
350 rue Saint-Gérard, Chicoutimi QC G7G 1J2
MYP Coordinator Audrey Morin
Languages French
T: +1 418 541 4343
W: charlesgravel.csrsaguenay.qc.ca

École secondaire de l'Île
255 rue Saint-Rédempteur, Gatineau QC J8X 2T4
MYP Coordinator Jean-François Simard
Languages French
T: +1 819 771 6126

École secondaire De Mortagne
955 boulevard de Montarville, Boucherville QC J4B 1Z6
MYP Coordinator Amélie Charron
Languages French
T: +1 450 655 7311
W: demortagne.csp.qc.ca

École secondaire de Neufchâtel
3600 avenue Chauveau, Neufchâtel QC G2C 1A1
MYP Coordinator Martine Vadeboncoeur
Languages French
T: +1 418 847 7300
W: www.cscapitale.qc.ca/neufchatel
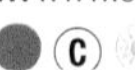

École secondaire de Rivière-du-Loup
464 rue Lafontaine, C.P. 910, Rivière du Loup QC G5R 3Z5
MYP Coordinator Valérie Bélanger
Languages French
T: +1 418 862 8201
W: www.cskamloup.qc.ca

École secondaire de Rochebelle
1095 de Rochebelle, Sainte Foy QC G1V 4P8
MYP Coordinator Karine Mercier
Languages French
T: +1 418 652 2167
W: www.derochebelle.qc.ca

École secondaire des Pionniers
1725, boulevard du Carmel, Trois-Rivières QC G8Z 3R8
MYP Coordinator Sylvie Gour
Languages French
T: +1 819 379 5822
W: despionniers.csduroy.qc.ca

École secondaire des Sources
2900 chemin Lake, Dollard-des-Ormeaux QC H9B 2P1
MYP Coordinator Inas Mourad
Languages French
T: +1 514 855 4208
W: www2.csmb.qc.ca/dessources/

École secondaire d'Oka
1700 Chemin Oka, Oka QC J0N 1E0
MYP Coordinator Mélanie Corneau
Languages French
T: +1 450 491 8410

École secondaire Dorval Jean XXIII
1301 avenue Dawson, Dorval QC H9S 1Y3
MYP Coordinator Bouchra Rhazi
Languages French
T: +1 514 855 4244

École secondaire Fernand-Lefebvre
265 rue de Ramezay, Sorel-Tracy QC J3P 4A5
MYP Coordinator Patrick Péloquin
Languages French
T: +1 450 742 5901
W: esfl.cs-soreltracy.qc.ca

École secondaire Grande-Rivière
100 rue Broad, Gatineau QC J9H 6A9
MYP Coordinator Annie Lavigne
Languages French
T: +1 819 682 8222
W: esgr.cspo.qc.ca

École secondaire Guillaume-Couture
70 Rue Philippe-Boucher, Levis QC G6V 1M5
MYP Coordinator Marianne Rhéaume
Languages French
T: +1 418 838 8550

École secondaire Henri-Bourassa
6051 boul Maurice-Duplessis, Montréal-Nord QC H1G 1Y6
MYP Coordinator Francine Lalonde
Languages French
T: +1 514 328 3200 EXT:3210

École secondaire Hormisdas-Gamelin
580 rue Maclaren Est, Gatineau QC J8L 2W2
MYP Coordinator Marie-France Bastien
Languages French
T: +1 819 986 8511
W: eshg.csscv.gouv.qc.ca

École secondaire Hubert-Maisonneuve
364 Rue Académie, Rosemère QC J7A 1ZA
MYP Coordinator Isabelle Bois
Languages French
T: +1 450 621 2003
W: hubert-maisonneuve.cssmi.qc.ca

École secondaire Jacques-Rousseau
444 rue Gentilly est, Longueuil QC J4H 3X7
MYP Coordinator Nathalie Hosson
Languages French
T: +1 450 651 6800 EXT:467

École secondaire Jean-Baptiste-Meilleur
777 boul d`Iberville, Repentigny QC J5Y 1A2
MYP Coordinator Genevieve Fournier
Languages French
T: +1 450 492 3777
W: www.csaffluents.qc.ca/etablissements/secondaire/jean-baptiste-meilleur

École secondaire Jean-Jacques-Bertrand
255 rue Saint-André Sud, Farnham QC J2N 2B8
MYP Coordinator Julie Filion
Languages French
T: +1 450 293 3181 EXT:223

École secondaire Jeanne-Mance
45 avenue des Freres, Drummondville QC J2B 6A2
MYP Coordinator Mélanie Flamand
Languages French
T: +1 819 474 0753

École secondaire Joseph-François-Perrault
140 chemin Ste-Foy, Québec QC G1R 1T2
MYP Coordinator Audrey Cook
Languages French
T: +1 418 686 4040 EXT:6011
W: www.cscapitale.qc.ca/jfperrault

École secondaire Kénogami
1954 Boulevard des Etudiants, Jonquière, Québec QC G7X 4B1
MYP Coordinator Andrée Ménard
Languages French
T: +1 418 5423571

École secondaire La Courvilloise
2265 avenue Larue, Beauport QC G1C 1J9
MYP Coordinator François Couillard
Languages French
T: +1 418 821 4220
W: www.courvilloise.ca

École secondaire La Voie
6755 rue Lavoie, Montréal QC H3W 2K8
MYP Coordinator Karine Laroche
Languages French
T: +1 514 736 3500
W: la-voie.csdm.ca

École secondaire Le tandem boisé
605 rue Notre-dame Est, Victoriaville QC G6P 6Y9
MYP Coordinator Marie-Eve Jutras
Languages French
T: +1 819 758 1534

École secondaire Louis-Joseph-Papineau
378, rue Papineau, Papineauville QC J0V 1R0
MYP Coordinator Véronique Cloutier
Languages French
T: +1 819 427 6258
W: ljp.csscv.gouv.qc.ca

École secondaire Louis-Philippe-Paré
235 boulevard Brisebois, Châteauguay QC J6K 3X4
MYP Coordinator Mélanie Bissonnette
Languages French
T: +1 514 380 8899 EXT:5480
W: lpp.csdgs.qc.ca

École secondaire Louis-Riel
5850 avenue de Carignan, Montréal QC H1M 2V4
MYP Coordinator Nathalie Lacroix
Languages French
T: +1 514 596 4134
W: www.louis-riel.csdm.qc.ca

École secondaire Monseigneur Euclide-Théberge
677 rue Desjardins, Marieville QC J3M 1R1
MYP Coordinator Patrick Mullen
Languages French
T: +1 450 460 4491
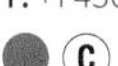

École secondaire Mont Saint-Sacrement
200 boulevard Saint-Sacrement, Saint-Gabriel-de-Valcartier QC G0A 4S0
MYP Coordinator Jocelyne Boivin
Languages French
T: +1 418 844 3771 P35
W: www.mss.qc.ca

École secondaire Mont-Royal
50 avenue Montgomery, Ville Mont-Royal QC H3R 2B3
MYP Coordinator Mounira Aouf
Languages French
T: +1 514 731 2761
W: www.ecolesecondairemontroyal.ca

École secondaire Ozias-Leduc
525 rue Jolliet, Mont-Saint-Hilaire QC J3H 3N2
MYP Coordinator Anne-Marie Bellemare
Languages French
T: +1 450 467 0261

École secondaire Paul-Gérin-Lajoie-d'Outremont
475, avenue Bloomfield, Outremont, QC H2V 3R9
MYP Coordinator Christian Girouard
Languages French
T: +1 514 276 3746
W: www.paul-gerin-lajoie-doutremont.ca

École secondaire polyvalente de l'Ancienne-Lorette
1801 rue Notre-Dame, L'Ancienne-Lorette QC G2E 3C6
MYP Coordinator Mylène Bellavance
Languages French
T: +1 418 872 9836
W: pal.csdecou.qc.ca

École secondaire Rive-Nord
400 rue Joseph-Paquette, Bois des Filions QC J6Z 4P7
MYP Coordinator Pascale Gauthier
Languages French
T: +1 450 621 3686
W: rive-nord.cssmi.qc.ca

École secondaire Roger-Comtois
158 boulevard des Étudiants, Loretteville QC G2A 1N8
MYP Coordinator Jean-François Beaumont
Languages French
T: +1 418 847 7201

École secondaire Saint-Joseph de Saint-Hyacinthe
2875 avenue Bourdages Nord, Saint-Hyacinthe QC J2S 5S3
MYP Coordinator Michèle Lemelin
Languages French
T: +1 450 774 3775
W: www.essj.qc.ca

École secondaire Saint-Luc
6300, chemin de la Côte, Saint-Luc, Montréal QC H3X 2H4
MYP Coordinator Véronique Patry
Languages French
T: +1 514 596 5920
W: st-luc.csdm.ca

École secondaire Serge-Bouchard
640 boulevard Blanche, Baie-Comeau QC G5C 2B3
MYP Coordinator Chantal Bérubé
Languages French
T: +1 418 589 1301
W: www.csestuaire.qc.ca/ecoles-secondaires

IB AMERICAS

École secondaire St-Gabriel
8 Rue Tassé, Ste Thérèse QC J7E 1V3
MYP Coordinator Isabelle Miron
Languages French
T: +1 450 433 5445
W: st-gabriel.cssmi.qc.ca

École St-Noël
993 8e Avenue, Thetford Mines QC G6G 2E3
PYP Coordinator Lisa Vachon
Languages French
T: +1 418 335 9826
W: www.csappalaches.qc.ca/fr/ecoles-et-centres/ecoles-primaires/ecole-saint-noel
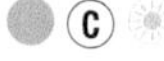

École Val-des-Ormes
199 chemin de la Grande-Côte, Rosemère QC J7A 1H6
PYP Coordinator Nancy Prézeau
Languages French
T: +1 450 437 5770
W: www6.cssmi.qc.ca/vdo

Heritage Regional High School
7445 Chambly Road, St Hubert QC J3Y 3S3
MYP Coordinator Angela Cavaliere
Languages English
T: +1 450 678 1070

Howard S Billings High School
210 McLeod, Chateauguay QC J6J 2H4
MYP Coordinator Paul Couture
Languages English
T: +1 450 691 3230
W: www.hsbillingsib.ca

JPPS-Bialik High School
6500 Kildare Road, Montreal QC H4W 3B8
MYP Coordinator Andrea Mendell
PYP Coordinator Elizabeth Doss
Languages English
T: +1 514 731 6456
W: www.jppsbialik.ca

Lakeside Academy
5050 Sherbrooke, Lachine QC H8T 1H8
MYP Coordinator Andrew Stepancic
Languages English
T: +1 514 637 2505
W: lakesideacademy.lbpsb.qc.ca
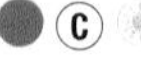

LaSalle Community Comprehensive High School
240-9th Avenue, LaSalle QC H8P 2N9
MYP Coordinator Julie Canty-Homier
Languages English
T: +1 514 595 2050
W: lcchs.lbpsb.qc.ca

Laurier Macdonald High School
7355 Boulevard Viau, St Leonard QC H1S 3C2
MYP Coordinator Valérie Barnabé
Languages English, French
T: +1 514 374 6000
W: www.lauriermacdonald.ca

Le Carrefour École Polyvalente
50 chemin de la Savane, Gatineau QC J8T 3N2
MYP Coordinator Sindy Poirier
PYP Coordinator Sindy Poirier
Languages French
T: +1 819 568 9012
W: www.csdraveurs.qc.ca/carrefour

Le Collège Saint-Bernard
25 avenue des Frères, Drummondville QC J2B 6A2
MYP Coordinator Marie-Eve Poulin
Languages French
T: +1 819 478 3330

L'École des Ursulines de Québec
4 rue du Parloir, CP 820, Haute - Ville, Québec QC G1R 4S7
PYP Coordinator Veronique Dussault
Languages French
T: +1 418 692 2612
 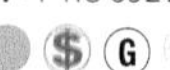

L'Externat Saint-Jean-Eudes
650 avenue du Bourg-Royal, Charlesbourg, Québec City QC G2L 1M8
MYP Coordinator Isabelle Therrien
Languages French
T: +1 418 627 1550
W: www.sje.qc.ca

Lower Canada College
4090, avenue Royal, Montréal QC H4A 2M5
DP Coordinator Brian Moore
MYP Coordinator Nathalie Lemelin
Languages English, French
T: +1 514 482 9916
W: www.lcc.ca

Marymount Academy
5100 Côte St-Luc Road, Montréal QC H3W 2G9
MYP Coordinator Ramin Khodaie
Languages English
T: +1 514 488 8144
W: www.emsb.qc.ca/marymount/

Michelangelo International Elementary School
9360 5e rue, Montréal QC H1E 1K1
PYP Coordinator Suzanne Fortin
Languages English, French
T: +1 514 648 1218
W: www.michelangelo.emsb.qc.ca

Pensionnat du Saint-Nom-de-Marie
628 chemin de la Côte, St Catherine, Outremont QC H2V 2C5
MYP Coordinator Chantal Gobeil
Languages French
T: +1 514 735 5261
W: www.psnm.qc.ca

Pierrefonds Comprehensive High School
13800 Pierrefonds Boulevard, Pierrefonds QC H9A 1A7
MYP Coordinator Caroline Clarke
Languages English
T: +1 514 626 9610

Polyvalente Chanoine-Armand-Racicot
940 boulevard de Normandie, St Jean-Sur-Richelieu QC J3A 1A7
MYP Coordinator Valérie Gosselin
Languages French
T: +1 450 348 6134

Polyvalente de Charlesbourg
900, rue de la Sorbonne, Québec QC G1H 1H1
MYP Coordinator Cynthia Turcotte
Languages English, French
T: +1 418 622 7820
W: polyvalentedecharlesbourg.csdps.qc.ca

Polyvalente de Thetford Mines
561 rue St-Patrick, Thetford Mines QC G6G 5W1
MYP Coordinator Nathalie Houle
Languages French
T: +1 418 338 7832 EXT:1514

Polyvalente des Quatre-Vents
1099 Boulevard Hamel, St-Félicien QC G8K 2R4
MYP Coordinator Catherine Langlais
Languages French
T: +1 418 275 4585

Polyvalente Deux-Montagnes
500 chemin des Anciens, Deux-Montagnes QC J7R 6A7
MYP Coordinator Marie-France Rochon
Languages French
T: +1 450 472 3070

Polyvalente Hyacinthe-Delorme
2700 Avenue T D Bouchard, Saint-Hyacinthe QC J2S 7G2
MYP Coordinator Isabelle Guertin
Languages French
T: +1 450 773 8401

Polyvalente Marcel-Landry
365 Avenue Landry, Saint-Jean-sur-Richelieu QC J2X 2P6
MYP Coordinator Annie Bédard
Languages French
T: +1 450 347 1225

Polyvalente Saint Francois
228 Avenue Lambert, Beauceville QC G5X 3N9
MYP Coordinator Lina Carrier
Languages French
T: +1 418 228 5541

Saint Anthony Elementary School
17750 Rue Meloche, Pierrefonds QC H9J 3P9
PYP Coordinator Lucie Vinet
Languages English, French
T: +1 514 624 6614
W: stanthony.lbpsb.qc.ca

Saint Lambert International High School
675 Green Street, St Lambert QC J4P 1V9
MYP Coordinator Kristen Witczak
Languages English
T: +1 450 671 5534
W: www.saintlambertinternational.ca

St Thomas High School
120 Ambassador, Pointe-Claire QC H9R 1S8
MYP Coordinator Amber Carlon
Languages English
T: +1 514 694 3770

Saskatchewan

Aden Bowman Collegiate Institute
1904 Clarence Ave S, Saskatoon SK S7J 1L3
DP Coordinator Jeff Speir
Languages English
T: +1 306 683 7600
W: www.spsd.sk.ca

Bedford Road Collegiate
722 Bedford Road, Saskatoon SK S7L 0G2
DP Coordinator Kim Buglass
Languages English
T: +1 306 683 7650
W: www.spsd.sk.ca/school/bedfordroad

Luther College High School

1500 Royal Street, Regina SK S4T 5A5
DP Coordinator Derek Frostad
Languages English
T: +1 306 791 9150
W: www.luthercollege.edu

North Battleford Comprehensive High School

1791-110th Street, North Battleford SK S9A 2Y2
DP Coordinator Joshua Radchenko
Languages English
T: +1 306 445 6101
W: www.nbchs.north-battleford.sk.ca

CAYMAN ISLANDS

Cayman International School

P.O. Box 31364, 95 Minerva Drive, Camana Bay, Grand Cayman KY1-1206
DP Coordinator Sarah Dyer
Languages English
T: +1 345 945 4664
W: www.caymaninternationalschool.org

Prospect Primary School

169 Poindexter Road, P.O. Box 910, Grand Cayman KY1-1103
PYP Coordinator Rachel Samaroo
Languages English
T: +1 345 947 8889
W: schools.edu.ky/pps/Pages/Home.aspx

Savannah Primary School

1659 Shamrock Road, P.O. Box 435, Grand Cayman KY1-1500
PYP Coordinator Kiimia Hemmings
Languages English
T: +1 345 947 1344
W: schools.edu.ky/sav/Pages/Home.aspx

Sir John A. Cumber Primary School

44 Fountain Road, P.O. Box 405, Grand Cayman KY1-1302
PYP Coordinator Charmaine Bravo
Languages English
T: +1 345 949 3314
W: schools.edu.ky/jac/Pages/Home.aspx

CHILE

Bradford School

Avada Luis Pateur 6335, Vitacura, Santiago
DP Coordinator Ximena Long Arriagada
Languages English
T: +56 (2) 29 12 31 40
W: www.bradfordschool.cl

Colegio Alemán Chicureo

Av. Alemania 170, Piedra Roja, Chicureo, Santiago
DP Coordinator Alvaro Javier Fuentealba Jara
MYP Coordinator Javier Silva
PYP Coordinator Belén Cáceres
Languages Spanish
T: +56 223078962
W: www.dsch.cl

 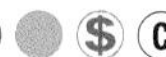

Colegio Alemán de Concepción

Camino El Venado 1075, Andalué, San Pedro de la Paz, Concepción, Biobío
DP Coordinator Cristian Muñoz
Languages Spanish
T: +56 41 2140000
W: www.dsc.cl

Colegio Alemán de San Felipe de Aconcagua

60 CH N° 501 Panquehue, San Felipe, Valparaíso
DP Coordinator Miriam Ramirez
Languages English, Spanish
T: +56 34 2 59 11 71
W: www.dssanfelipe.cl

Colegio Alemán de Temuco

Avenida Holandesa 0855, Temuco, Araucanía
DP Coordinator Leonardo Hernández Zapata
Languages Spanish
T: +56 45 963000
W: www.dstemuco.cl

Colegio Alemán de Valparaiso

Alvarez 2950, El Salto, Viña del Mar, Valparaíso
DP Coordinator Rafael Yanez
Languages Spanish
T: +56 32 216 1531
W: www.dsvalpo.cl

Colegio Alemán La Serena

Avda. Cuatro Esquinas s/n, El Milagro, 401346 La Serena, Coquimbo
DP Coordinator Natalia Salas Tapia
Languages German, Spanish
T: +56 512 294 703
W: www.dsls.cl

Colegio Alemán Los Angeles

Casilla 367, Av. Gabriela Mistral 1360 (ex 1751), Los Ángeles, Biobío
DP Coordinator Claudio Ibacache Soto
Languages Spanish
T: +56 43 2521111
W: www.dsla.cl

Colegio Alemán Puerto Varas

KM1, 4 Camino Ensenada, Puerto Varas, Los Lagos
MYP Coordinator Susana Carrillo Castillo
PYP Coordinator Natalia Federici Maggi
Languages Spanish, German
T: +56 65 223 0450
W: www.dspuertovaras.com

Colegio Alemán St Thomas Morus

Avenida Pedro de Valdivia 320, Providencia, Santiago
DP Coordinator Matthias Waldow
Languages Spanish
T: +56 2 2729 1600
W: www.dsmorus.cl

Colegio Internacional SEK Chile

Avd Los Militares 6640, Las Condes, Santiago
DP Coordinator Marcela Gangas
Languages Spanish
T: +56 2 2127116
W: www.sekchile.com

Colegio Internacional SEK Pacifico

San Estanislao 50 Lomas de Montemar, Concón, Valparaíso
DP Coordinator Paola de la Fuente Estay
PYP Coordinator Paulette Larrea Wachtendorff
Languages English, Spanish
T: +56 32 2275700
W: www.sekpacifico.com

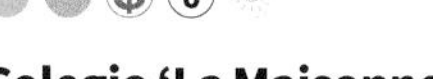

Colegio 'La Maisonnette'

Avda Luis Pasteur 6076, Vitacura, Santiago
DP Coordinator Oriana Martínez
Languages Spanish
T: +56 2 228162945
W: www.lamaisonnette.cl

Craighouse School

Casilla 20 007, Correo 20., Santiago
DP Coordinator Fernanda Silva
MYP Coordinator Leonora Cardemil
PYP Coordinator Barbara Atkinson
Languages English, Spanish
T: +56 2 227560218
W: www.craighouseschool.cl

Instituto Alemán Carlos Anwandter

Los Laureles 050, Casilla 2-D, Valdivia, Los Ríos
DP Coordinator Sonia Marcela Videla Perez
Languages Spanish
T: +56 63 2471100
W: www.dsv.cl

Instituto Alemán de Osorno

Los Carreras 818, Osorno, Los Lagos
DP Coordinator Carla Sommer
MYP Coordinator Jaime Serón
PYP Coordinator Leonardo Jara Adad
Languages Spanish
T: +56 64 233 1800/1805
W: www.dso.cl

Instituto Alemán Puerto Montt

Bernardo Phillipi #350, Sector Seminario, 5480000 Puerto Montt, Los Lagos
PYP Coordinator Pilar Portaluppi Kupfer
Languages Spanish
T: +56 65 2 252560
W: www.ialeman.cl

INTERNATIONAL SCHOOL NIDO DE AGUILAS

Av. El Rodeo 14200, Lo Barnechea, Santiago
DP Coordinator Kurt Supplee
Languages English, Spanish
T: +56 2 2339 8100
E: admissions@nido.cl
W: www.nido.cl

See full details on page 478

Liceo A 43 'Liceo Siete'

Monseñor Sótero Sanz 060, Santiago
DP Coordinator Isabel Villarroel
Languages Spanish
T: +56 2 2235 7921
W: www.liceosiete.cl

Mackay School

Vicuña Mackenna 700, Viña del Mar, Valparaíso
DP Coordinator Silvio Bermudez Salas
MYP Coordinator Sebastián Díaz
PYP Coordinator Evangelina Di Girolamo
Languages English
T: +56 32 2386614
W: www.mackay.cl

Redland School

Camino El Alba 11357, Las Condes, 7600022 Santiago
DP Coordinator Ruth Guzmán
MYP Coordinator Pablo Loayza
PYP Coordinator Miguel Ramos
Languages Spanish
T: +56 2 29598500
W: www.redland.cl

Saint Gabriel's School

Avda Fco Bilbao 3070, Providencia, Santiago
DP Coordinator Laura Schiaffino
Languages Spanish
T: +56 22 462 5400
W: www.sangabriel.cl

CHILE

SANTIAGO COLLEGE
Av. Camino Los Trapenses 4007, Lo Barnechea, Santiago
DP Coordinator Renato Hamel
MYP Coordinator Angel Girano
PYP Coordinator Mónika Naranjo
Languages Spanish, English
T: +56 2 27338800
E: master@scollege.cl
W: www.scollege.cl/index.php/es/

See full details on page 504

St John's School
Fundo el Venado, San Pedro de la Paz, Concepción, Biobío
DP Coordinator Gloria Soledad Guerrero Pastene
MYP Coordinator Patricia Uribe
PYP Coordinator Alexandra Krumm
Languages English, Spanish
T: +56 41 2466440
W: www.stjohns.cl

St Margaret's British School For Girls
Casilla 392, Viña del Mar, Valparaíso
DP Coordinator Andrea Villalobos Danessi
Languages Spanish
T: +56 32 245 1700
W: www.stmargarets.cl

St Paul's School
Merced Oriente 54, Viña del Mar, Valparaíso
PYP Coordinator Mónica Pavez von Martens
Languages English, Spanish
T: (56 32) 314 2200
W: www.stpaul.cl

The Antofagasta British School
Pedro León Gallo 723, Antofagasta
DP Coordinator Maria Alicia Paz
MYP Coordinator Giselle Rojas
PYP Coordinator M.Ignacia Brieba
Languages English, Spanish
T: +55 2 598931
W: abs.school

The British School - Punta Arenas
Waldo Seguel 454, Punta Arenas, Magallanes
DP Coordinator José Antonio Vergara Rodríguez
MYP Coordinator Ximena Morales Trabazo
PYP Coordinator Cristian Barrera
Languages Spanish, English
T: +56 61 2 22 33 81
W: www.britishschool.cl

The Mayflower School
Avda Las Condes 12 167, Las Condes, Santiago
DP Coordinator Andrea Edwards Neut
MYP Coordinator Ricardo Quiroga Cortes
PYP Coordinator Constanza Postigo Gaete
Languages Spanish
T: +56 22 3523100
W: www.mayflower.cl

Wenlock School
Casilla 27169, Correo 27, Santiago
DP Coordinator Marta Poblete
Languages Spanish
T: +56 223631803
W: www.wenlock.cl

COLOMBIA

Aspaen Gimnasio Iragua
Av. Calle 170, No. 76-55, Barrio San José de Bavaria, Bogotá, D.C.
DP Coordinator Yamid Guerra Pedroza
Languages Spanish
T: +57 (1) 667 95 00
W: www.iragua.edu.co

British International School
Apartado Aéreo 4368, Barranquilla, Atlántico
DP Coordinator Jose Donado Coronell
MYP Coordinator Guisella Pilonieta
Languages English
T: +57 (5) 359 92 43
W: www.britishschool.edu.co

Buckingham School
Cra 52 No 214 - 55, Bogotá, D.C.
DP Coordinator Aramis Vega arias
MYP Coordinator Elena Rokhas
PYP Coordinator Julieta Galeano León
Languages English, Spanish
T: +57 (1) 676 08 12
W: cbk.edu.co

Bureche School
Troncal del Caribe Km2 vía Gaira, Santa Marta, Magdalena
DP Coordinator Patrick Bauch
Languages English, Spanish
T: +57 315 389 98 77
W: colegiobureche.edu.co

CAS Colombo American School
Carrera 73 No. 214-53, Bogotá, D.C.
DP Coordinator Leslie Herrera
PYP Coordinator Vanessa Buzeta
Languages English, Spanish
W: www.colegiocolomboamericano.edu.co

CIEDI - Colegio Internacional de Educación Integral
Km 3 vía Suba-Cota, Bogotá, D.C.
DP Coordinator Ernesto Campos
MYP Coordinator Andrea Barrera Rico
PYP Coordinator Lilia Gonzalez
Languages Spanish, English
T: +57 (1) 683 06 04
W: www.ciedi.edu.co

Colegio Abraham Lincoln
Av. Calle 170 # 65 31, Bogotá, D.C.
DP Coordinator Glenda Liliana Buitrago Ramirez
Languages Spanish
T: +57 (1) 742 31 66
W: www.abrahamlincoln.edu.co

Colegio Albania
Calle 15 3-00, Campamento de Mushaisa, Cerrejón La Mina, La Guajira
DP Coordinator Juan Carlos Tarazona Bautista
MYP Coordinator Juan Carlos Tarazona Bautista
PYP Coordinator Rubys Chinchia
Languages English, Spanish
T: +57 (5) 350 56 48
W: www.colegioalbania.edu.co

Colegio Alemán
Autopista al Mar poste 89 Electricaribe, Baranquilla, Atlántico
DP Coordinator Heidys María Navarro Escorcia
Languages Spanish
T: +57 (5) 359 85 20
W: www.colegioaleman.edu.co

Colegio Anglo-Colombiano
Apartado Aéreo 253393, Avenida 19 N° 152A-48, Santa Fé, Bogotá, D.C.
DP Coordinator Peter O'Reilly
MYP Coordinator Rusbel Martinez Rodriguez
PYP Coordinator Christianne Cowie
Languages English, Spanish
T: +57 (1) 259 57 00
W: www.anglocolombiano.edu.co

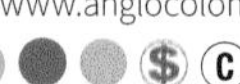

Colegio Berchmans
Carrera 120A No. 16-86, El Retiro, Pance, Cali, Valle del Cauca
DP Coordinator Eliana Herrera
Languages English, Spanish
T: +57 2 321 10 00
W: berchmans.edu.co

Colegio Británico - The British School
Call 18 # 142-255 (Esquina), La Viga, Pance, Cali, Valle del Cauca
DP Coordinator Edilson Sánchez Buitrago
Languages Spanish
T: +57 (2) 555 75 45
W: www.thebritishschoolcali.edu.co

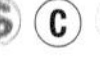

Colegio Británico de Cartagena
Anillo Vial Km. 12, 130001 Cartagena, Bolívar
DP Coordinator Alexandra Martinez
Languages English, Spanish
T: +57 5 693 0982 83 84
W: www.colbritanico.edu.co/newcbc

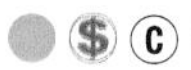

Colegio Británico de Montería
Calle 65 No. 9-100, Montería
PYP Coordinator Hiole Cecilia Gonzalez
Languages English, Spanish
T: +57 3 227 71 82 91
W: britanicomonteria.edu.co

Colegio Cambridge
Sede Cajicá, Kilómetro 2 Vía Cajicá, Chía Vereda El Canelón, Cajicá, Cundinamarca
DP Coordinator Juan Carlos Villamizar
Languages English, Spanish
T: +1 601 746 4737
W: colegiocambridge.edu.co

Colegio Colombo Británico
Avenida La Maria 69, Pance, Cali, Valle del Cauca
DP Coordinator Reynaldo Muñoz
MYP Coordinator Eleanor Alicia Cosh Lacouture
PYP Coordinator Claudia Fayad
Languages English, Spanish
T: +57 2 555 53 85
W: www.colombobritanico.edu.co

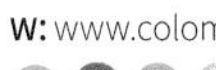

Colegio Colombo Gales
Avenida Guaymaral, Costado sur Aeropuerto, Bogotá, D.C.
DP Coordinator Nidia Elvira Gallego Vargas
PYP Coordinator Tilcia Ruth Melo Lugo
Languages Spanish
T: +57 (1) 668 49 10
W: www.colegiocolombogales.edu.co

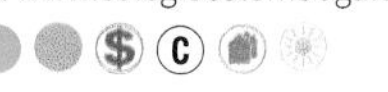

Colegio de Cambridge (Cambridge International School)
Vereda La Aurora, Municipio La Calera, Bogotá, D.C.
DP Coordinator Claudia Patricia Torres Bojacá
Languages Spanish
T: +57 (1) 593 18 90
W: www.colegiocambridge.edu.co

Colegio de Inglaterra - The English School

Calle 170 #15-68, Bogotá, D.C.
CP Coordinator Álvaro Rodríguez Vásquez
DP Coordinator Álvaro Rodríguez Vásquez
MYP Coordinator Lizbeth Santana
PYP Coordinator Andrea Vanegas Bonilla
Languages English, Spanish
T: +57 601 676 77 00
W: www.englishschool.edu.co

Colegio Domingo Savio

Calle 24 Sur #24 f-16, Bogotá, D.C.
MYP Coordinator Andrea Guiovanna Sanchez Waltero
Languages English, Spanish
T: +57 366 61 63
W: www.domingosaviobilingualschool.edu.co

Colegio El Minuto de Dios Siglo XXI

Transversal 74 No 81 C - 05, Bogotá, D.C.
DP Coordinator Jimmy Damian Vozmediano Pinchao
Languages Spanish
T: +57 (1) 508 22 30
W: colegiosminutodedios.edu.co/sigloxxi

Colegio Gimnasio Internacional de Medellín

Calle 73 sur #64-23, La Estrella, 055468 Medellín, Antioquia
DP Coordinator Juan Carlos Pizano Sotomayor
Languages English, Spanish
W: gim.edu.co

 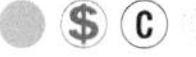

Colegio Gran Bretaña

Carrera 51 No 215-20, Bogotá, D.C.
DP Coordinator Monica Woodward
Languages English
T: +57 (1) 676 03 91
W: www.cgb.edu.co

Colegio Internacional Los Cañaverales

Carrera 29 No 10-500, Arroyohonfo, Vía Dapa Km 1 Yumbo, Yumbo, Valle del Cauca
DP Coordinator Carolina Avendaño Rodríguez
Languages English
T: +57 (2) 658 28 18
W: www.canaverales.edu.co

Colegio Jordán de Sajonia

Cra. 1 Nro 68-50 Rosales, Bogotá, D.C.
DP Coordinator Marjorie Zambrano
Languages English, Spanish
T: +57 1 756 10 11
W: www.jordandesajonia.edu.co

Colegio La Arboleda

Carrera 125 No. 2, Avenida La Maria 80, Pance, Cali, Valle del Cauca
DP Coordinator Marian Aponte
Languages English, Spanish
T: +57 2 555 34 05
W: laarboleda.edu.co

Colegio Los Ángeles Tunja

Calle 73A No. 2-02 E, Altos de la Arboleda, Tunja, Boyacá
DP Coordinator Nicolas Enrique Romero Murillo
Languages English, Spanish
T: +57 304 380 8353
W: colegiolosangelestunja.com

Colegio Los Tréboles

Vereda cerca de Piedra, Finca Santa Elena, Chía, Cundinamarca
DP Coordinator Clara Inés Díaz Rodríguez
Languages English, Spanish
T: +57 (1) 862 48 30
W: www.clt.edu.co

Colegio Mayor de los Andes

Kilómetro 3 vía Chía, Cajicá, Cundinamarca
DP Coordinator Adelina Nuñez Rojas
Languages Spanish
T: +57 (1) 866 29 56
W: www.colegiomayordelosandes.edu.co

Colegio Nueva Inglaterra (New England School)

Calle 218, No. 50-60, Bogotá, D.C.
DP Coordinator Adolfo De La Cruz Celis
Languages Spanish
T: +57 (1) 676 07 88
W: www.colegionuevainglaterra.edu.co

Colegio Nueva York

Calle 227, No. 49-64 Urbanización El Jardín, Bogotá, D.C.
DP Coordinator Andres Verano
PYP Coordinator Deisy Liliana Pérez
Languages English, Spanish
T: +57 1 668 48 90
W: colegionuevayork.edu.co

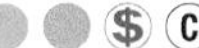

Colegio San Viator - Sede Bogotá

Autopista Norte 209-51, Bogotá, D.C.
DP Coordinator Luis Fernando Peña Paladines
MYP Coordinator Erika Martínez Torres
PYP Coordinator Yineth Luz Dary Tausa Montoya
Languages English
T: +57 (1) 676 09 97
W: www.sanviator.edu.co

Colegio San Viator - Sede Tunja

Av Universitaria 62 - 100, Tunja, Boyacá
DP Coordinator Steffany Contreras Moreno
Languages English, Spanish
W: www.sanviatortunja.edu.co

Colegio Santa Francisca Romana

Calle 151 No. 16 - 40, Bogotá, D.C.
DP Coordinator Ángel Orlando Valderrama Ramos
Languages English, Spanish
T: +57 1 580 44 44
W: www.csfr.edu.co

Colegio Tilatá

Kilómetro 9 vía La Calera, Bogotá, D.C.
DP Coordinator Paulo Lopez-Orellana
MYP Coordinator Diana Olivos Suarez
PYP Coordinator Marcela Castañeda
Languages English, Spanish
T: +57 (1) 592 14 14
W: www.colegiotilata.edu.co

Deutsche Schule - Cali / Kolumbien

Avenida Gualí N° 31, Barrio Ciudad Jardín, Cali, Valle del Cauca
DP Coordinator Carlos Rojas Padilla
Languages German, Spanish
T: +57 (2) 685 89 00
W: www.dscali.edu.co

Deutsche Schule Medellín

Cra 61, No. 34-62, Itagüi, Antioquia
DP Coordinator Mitja Lüderwaldt
Languages Spanish
T: +57 (604) 2818811 (EXT:100)
W: www.dsmedellin.edu.co

Fundacion Gimnasio Ingles de Armenia (GI SCHOOL)

KM.3 Via Armenia-Circasia, 630007 Salento, Quindío
DP Coordinator Milagros Zapata
PYP Coordinator Lina Marcela Africano Moreno
Languages English, Spanish
T: +57 6 749 51 11
W: gi.edu.co

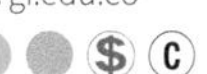

Fundación Gimnasio Los Portales

Calle 212 No. 77- 20, Bogotá, D.C.
DP Coordinator Juan Pulido
MYP Coordinator Alirio Sneider Saavedra
PYP Coordinator Caroll Marulanda Guzmán
Languages English, Spanish
T: +57 (1) 676 40 55
W: www.losportales.edu.co

Fundación Nuevo Marymount

Calle 169B, No 74A-02, Bogotá, D.C.
DP Coordinator Liliana Manzanera
Languages English
T: +57 (1) 669 90 77
W: www.marymountschool.edu.co

GCB - Bilingüe Internacional

Costado Sur - Occidental Aeropuerto Guaymaral, Bogotá, D.C.
DP Coordinator Jorge Eduardo Baquero Cañas
Languages English, Spanish
T: +57 1 668 39 99
W: www.gcb.edu.co

Gimnasio Británico

Calle 21 No 9A-58, Avenida Chilacos, Chía, Cundinamarca
DP Coordinator Gabriel Alfredo Piraquive García
Languages English, Spanish, French
T: +57 (1) 861 50 84
W: www.gimnasio-britanico.edu.co

Gimnasio Campestre la Fontana

Km 4 Vereda El Amor, Vía Multf. Centauros, Villavicencio, Meta
DP Coordinator Yadira Cruz García
Languages English, Spanish
T: +57 314 279 7928
W: www.lafontana.edu.co

Gimnasio Campestre Los Cerezos

Vereda Canelón, Cajicá, Cundinamarca
DP Coordinator Marcia Malpica Ortiz
PYP Coordinator Ingrid Mogollón
Languages Spanish
T: +57 866 26 79
W: www.gimnasioloscerezos.edu.co

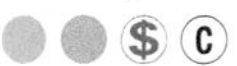

Gimnasio Campestre San Rafael

Sede Campestre, Km 6 vía Siberia, Tenjo, Cundinamarca
DP Coordinator Alba Orozco Bernal
Languages Spanish
T: +57 593 30 40
W: colegiosminutodedios.edu.co/sanrafael

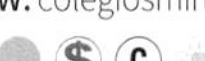

Gimnasio Contemporaneo

Cra. 6 #29 Norte-648 a 29 Norte-1034, Salento, Quindío
DP Coordinator Maria Camila Quiceno Henao
Languages English, Spanish
T: +57 310 4322191
W: www.gimnasiocontemporaneo.edu.co

 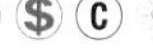

Gimnasio de Los Cerros
Calle 119 N° 0-68, Usaquén, Santa Fé, Bogotá, D.C.
DP Coordinator Jorge Arango
Languages Spanish
T: +57 (1) 657 60 00
W: www.loscerros.edu.co

Gimnasio del Norte
Calle 207 N° 70 - 50, Bogotá, D.C.
DP Coordinator Mary Ortiz
MYP Coordinator Adriana Rodríguez
PYP Coordinator Patricia Gonzalez
Languages Spanish, English
T: +57 (1) 668 39 39
W: www.gimnasiodelnorte.edu.co

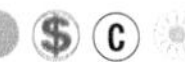

Gimnasio El Hontanar
Cra. 76 No. 150-26, Bogotá, D.C.
DP Coordinator Edwin Rueda Acosta
Languages English, Spanish
T: +57 (1) 681 52 87
W: www.gimnasiohontanar.edu.co

Gimnasio Femenino
K7 #128-40, Bogotá, D.C.
DP Coordinator Fernando Rueda
MYP Coordinator Xiomara Grande
PYP Coordinator Gisela Toro López
Languages Spanish, English
T: +57 (1) 657 84 20
W: www.gimnasiofemenino.edu.co

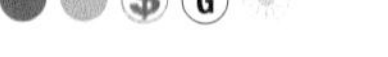

Gimnasio Los Alcázares
Calle 63 Sur No 41-05 Sabaneta, Medellín, Antioquia
DP Coordinator Carlos Mejía
Languages Spanish
T: +57 (4) 305 40 00
W: www.alcazares.edu.co

Gimnasio Los Pinos
Calle 193 #38-20, Bogotá, D.C.
DP Coordinator Andrés Palomino Ortega
MYP Coordinator German Barbosa
PYP Coordinator Ángela Marí Romero Carvajal
Languages English, Spanish
T: +57 1 670 00 08
W: gimnasiolospinos.edu.co

Gimnasio Vermont
Cl 195 No 54-75, Bogotá, D.C.
DP Coordinator Claudia Aguirre
Languages Spanish
T: +57 (1) 674 80 70
W: www.gimnasiovermont.edu.co

International Berckley School
Km 5 - Vía al Mar, Poste 115, Barranquilla, Atlántico
DP Coordinator Denys Coronell Vargas
Languages Spanish
T: +575 354 81 31
W: ibs.edu.co

Jardín Infantil Tía Nora y Liceo Los Alpes
Av 8 Norte, No. 66-05 Urbanización Menga, Cali, Valle del Cauca
DP Coordinator Judy Roja Garcia
MYP Coordinator David García
PYP Coordinator Claudia Salazar
Languages Spanish, English
T: +57 (2) 665 41 20
W: www.jardintianorayliceolosalpes.edu.co

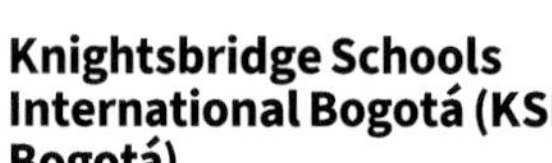

Knightsbridge Schools International Bogotá (KSI Bogotá)
Calle 221 No. 115-51, Vereda Recodo de Guaymaral, 111176 Bogotá, D.C.
DP Coordinator Michael Mackenna
PYP Coordinator Andrea Roa
Languages English, Spanish
T: +57 60 1 745 62 15
W: www.ksi-bogota.com

Liceo Pino Verde
Vereda Los Planes kilometro, 5 Vía Cerritos Entrada 16, El Tigre, Pereira, Risaralda
DP Coordinator Rosa Damian Mesa
PYP Coordinator Catalina Gutierrez
Languages English
T: +57 (6) 313 26 68
W: www.liceopinoverde.edu.co

Neil Armstrong School
Dir. Cr 44 Cl 14 El Buque, Villavicencio
DP Coordinator Andres Flantermesk Escobar
Languages English, Spanish
W: www.nas.edu.co

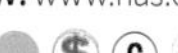

New Cambridge School Bucaramanga - Sede Cabecera
Cra. 39 No. 44-72, Bucaramanga, Santander
DP Coordinator Lia Vanessa Buzeta De La Fuente
Languages English, Spanish
T: +57 7 638 61 52
W: cambridge.edu.co

New Cambridge School Bucaramanga - Sede Cañaveral
Calle 32 No. 22-140, Floridablanca, Bucaramanga, Santander
DP Coordinator Maria Cristina Martin Ceballos
Languages English, Spanish
T: +57 7 638 61 52
W: cambridge.edu.co

Nuevo Gimnasio School
Kilometro 1 Autopista, Villavicencio, Meta
DP Coordinator Orlando Aguirre Urrutia
Languages English, Spanish
T: +57 310 801 52 83
W: www.nuevogimnasioschool.edu.co

The Victoria School
Calle 215 N° 50-60, Bogotá, D.C.
DP Coordinator María Bernal Baracaldo
MYP Coordinator Maria del Pilar Robles
PYP Coordinator Luis Prieto Serrato
Languages English, Spanish
T: +57 (1) 676 15 03
W: www.tvs.edu.co

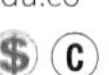

Vermont School Medellín
Avenida Las Palmas Indiana Mall Km. 2 Vía La Fe, El Retiro, Antioquia
DP Coordinator Mauricio Ruíz Vahos
Languages English, Spanish
T: +57 (4) 520 60 60
W: vermontmedellin.edu.co

COSTA RICA

Academia Teocali
2.5 Km Norte de la Entrada Principal de Liberia, Carretera Interamericana Norte, Liberia, Guanacaste
DP Coordinator César Gabriel Lara Vanegas
Languages English
T: +506 2666 8780
W: www.academiateocali.ed.cr

Anglo American School
La Unión, 1 Km al norte de Sub Estación Eléctrica del ICE, Provincia de Cartago, Tres Rios, San Jose
DP Coordinator Bernal Villalobos Calvo
Languages Spanish
T: +506 2279 2626
W: anglo.ed.cr

BLUE VALLEY SCHOOL
From Multiplaza, 1.2 Km. northwest, right hand side of the road, Guachipelín, Escazú, San José
DP Coordinator Gisele Cordero
Languages English, Spanish
T: +506 2215 2204
E: admissions@bluevalley.ed.cr
W: www.bluevalley.ed.cr
See full details on page 460

Centro Educativo Futuro Verde
1 km este del Banco Nacional, Cóbano, Puntarenas 60111
DP Coordinator Karol Segura
Languages English, Spanish
T: +506 2642 0291
W: www.futuro-verde.org

Centro Educativo Nueva Generacion
Sn Rafael de Heredia Del parqu 1 km al norte, Heredia 24-3015
DP Coordinator Nataly Campos
Languages English
T: +506 2237 8927
W: nuevageneracion.ed.cr/web

Colegio Bilingüe de Palmares
50 Metros sur Banco Popular, Palmares, Alajuela 215-4300
DP Coordinator Kendrich Vargas Vásquez
Languages Spanish
T: +506 2452 0157

Colegio de Bagaces
Contiguo al Gimnasio Municipal, Bag aces, Guanacaste
DP Coordinator Lelia Pineda Laguna
Languages Spanish
T: 506 2671 1116

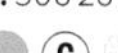

Colegio de Santa Ana
300 oeste de la Cruz Roja, Uruca, Santa Ana, San José
DP Coordinator Francisco Javier Cortés González
Languages English, Spanish
T: +506 2282 2636

Colegio Internacional SEK Costa Rica
Cipreses de Curridabat, San José 963 2050
DP Coordinator Geovanny Cordero Gutiérrez
Languages English, Spanish
T: +506 2 272 5464
W: www.sekcostarica.com

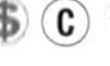

Colegio Iribó
Lomas de Ayarco sur, segunda entrada, 800 mts. sur, Curridabat, San José
DP Coordinator Beatriz Vinueza
Languages Spanish
T: +506 4000 8989
W: colegiosadec.org/iribo

Colegio Los Ángeles
Calle Luisa, San José
DP Coordinator Carlos Darío Quirós Morales
Languages English, Spanish
T: +506 2232 0122
W: www.colegiolosangeles.ed.cr

Colegio Miravalle
800m al sur de la esquina sureste de los Tribunales de Justicia, Cartago
DP Coordinator Susana Víquez Madrigal
Languages English, Spanish
T: +506 2552 7378
W: colegiomiravalle.com

Colegio Saint Francis
San Vicente, Moravia, San José
DP Coordinator María Laura Fernández Soto
Languages English, Spanish
T: +506 2430 7639
W: www.saintfranciscr.org

Colegio Yorkín
Lomas de Ayarco sur, segunda entrada, 800 mts. sur y 200 mts. este, Curridabat, San José
DP Coordinator Harold Molina Venegas
Languages Spanish
T: +506 4000 8900
W: colegiosadec.org/yorkin

Del Mar Academy
P.O. Box: 130, Nosara, Nicoya, Guanacaste 5233
DP Coordinator Monica Marin
Languages English
T: +506 2682 1211
W: www.delmaracademy.com

European School
Heredia, San Pablo, P.O. Box: 177, Heredia
DP Coordinator Karen A Bye
Languages English
T: +506 2261 0717
W: www.europeanschool.com

Franz Liszt Schule
800 metros al sur de la gasolinera, Hermanos Montes a mano izq, Santa Ana, San José 10901
DP Coordinator Varela Valeri
Languages English, German
T: +506 2203 8128
W: www.fls.ed.cr

Golden Valley School
Del Lubricentro San Francisco 800 mts. Suroeste, Portones azules grandes a mano derecha, San Isidro, Heredia 40604
DP Coordinator Carlos Vega
Languages English, Spanish
T: +506 2268 9114
W: www.goldenvalleyschool.com

Instituto Dr. Jaim Weizman
100 norte, 100 oeste Compañía Nacional de Fuerza y Luz, Carretera Anonos, Mata Redonda, San José 4114-100
DP Coordinator Maria Alfaro Barrios
MYP Coordinator Helly Nunez van Eyl
PYP Coordinator Sarahi Paz
Languages English, Spanish
T: +506 2220 1050

Instituto de Educación Dr. Clodomiro Picado Twight
De la Universidad de Costa Rica, Sede del Atlántico 150 metros al oeste, Turrialba, Cartago
DP Coordinator Jesús Alonso Quirós Paniagua
Languages Spanish
T: +506 25560025

International Christian School
San Miguel de Santo Domingo, Heredia
DP Coordinator Chelsea McGill
Languages English, Spanish
T: +506 22411445
W: ics.ed.cr

La Paz Community School
500 metros sur de la ferreteria, Buenaventura, Flamingo, Guanacaste 50309
DP Coordinator Martha Ortega
Languages English
T: +506 2654 4532
W: www.lapazschool.org

Liceo de Atenas Martha Mirambell Umaña
Atenas, Alajuela
DP Coordinator Ivannia María Campos Carranza
Languages English, Spanish
T: +506 2446 5124
W: liceoatenasbi.wixsite.com/info

Liceo de Cariari
1Km al Norte de la Agencia del Banco Nacional de Costa Rica, Mano izquierda, carretera a Semillero, Pococí, Limón 70205
DP Coordinator Edgar Ruiz Contreras
Languages Spanish
T: +506 27677180

Liceo de Costa Rica
Calle 9, Avenida 18 y 20, San José
DP Coordinator Lucas Peraza Orellana
Languages Spanish
T: +506 221 3792

Liceo de Cot
100 mts norte y 500 este de Palí de Cot, Cot, Oreamuno, Cartago 30702
DP Coordinator Sandra Córdoba Cortés
Languages Spanish
T: +506 2536 6509
W: www.liceodecot.com

Liceo de Miramar
Costado Oeste del Cementerio Municipal, Miramar de Montes de Oro, Puntarenas 6-01-04
DP Coordinator Dilana Ramirez
T: +506 26 39 90 69
W: liceomiramar.com

Liceo de Moravia
San Rafael de Moravia, San José
DP Coordinator Mario Sanchez Ugalde
Languages English
T: +506 22351336

Liceo de Poás
500 m Norte del Templo Católico, de San Pedro de Poás, Alajuela 24059
DP Coordinator Karol Ledezma Céspedes
Languages Spanish
T: +506 2448 50 27
W: www.liceodepoas.ed.cr

Liceo de Puriscal
Costado oeste del nuevo, Templo Católico, Santiago de Puriscal, San José 214-6000
DP Coordinator Sally Sánchez Jiménez
Languages Spanish
T: +506 2416 5424 /6163
W: www.liceodepuriscal.ed.cr

Liceo de Tarrazú
Carretera a San Pablo de León Cortés, Barrio Santa Cecilia,, 200 metros este de Coopesantos R. L., San Marcos de Tarrazú, San José 8055
DP Coordinator Leonardo Vinicio Fonseca Hernández
Languages English
T: +506 25 46 60 12
W: tarrazu.edupage8.org
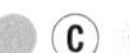

Liceo de Villarreal
200 metros Sur del centro de salud de Villarreal, Santa Cruz, Villarreal, Guanacaste 50309
DP Coordinator Siviany Piña Soto
Languages Spanish
T: +506 26530716

Liceo Gregorio José Ramirez Castro
200 m norte del plantel de MOPT, Montecillos de Alajuela, Alajuela
DP Coordinator Elenilzon Arroyo Bolaños
Languages Spanish
T: +506 2430 02 72
W: colegiogregoriojoseramirez.jimdo.com

Liceo Nuevo de Limón
Barrio La Colina, Contiguo a la Universidad de Costa Rica, Limón
DP Coordinator Andra Joyce Edwards Loban
Languages Spanish
T: +506 2758 09 80

Liceo Pacífico Sur
Principal hacia la Municipalidad de Osa, Cortés, Puntarenas
DP Coordinator Zaida Porras Santamaría
Languages Spanish
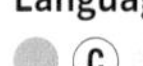

Liceo San Carlos
1 kilómetro al norte del parque de Ciudad Quesada, Quesada, Alajuela 21001
DP Coordinator Danny Gaitán Rodríguez
Languages English
T: +506 2460 0332

Liceo Santo Domingo
De la Clínica Dr. Hugo Fonseca, 150 Norte, San Vicente de Santo Domingo, Heredia 40302
DP Coordinator Osvaldo Molina Zamora
T: +506 2244 9549
W: www.liceosantodomingo.ed.cr

Liceo Sinaí
100 m E, de la Universidad Nacional, Sede Regional Brunca, San Isidro, Pérez Zeledón, San José
DP Coordinator Xédric Ureña Carvajal
Languages Spanish
T: +506 2770 66 69
W: www.liceosinai.com

Lighthouse International School
1 km north of the Guachipelin Tunnel, Escazú, San José 29028
DP Coordinator Fiorella Fuster
Languages English, Spanish
T: +506 2215 2390
W: www.lighthouse.ed.cr

IB AMERICAS

Costa Rica

Lincoln School
Barrio Socorro, Santo Domingo de Heredia
DP Coordinator Ellen King
Languages English
T: +506 2247 6600
W: www.lincoln.ed.cr

Marian Baker School
PO Box 4269-1000, San José 1000
DP Coordinator Carolina Vargas
Languages English, Spanish
T: +506 2273 0024
W: www.mbs.ed.cr

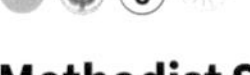

Methodist School of Costa Rica
Sabanilla, Montes de Oca, San José 11502
DP Coordinator Guillermo Fernandez
Languages English, Spanish
T: +506 2280 1230
W: www.metodista.ed.cr

Mount View School
Guachipelín de Escazú, De ConstruPlaza 2kms al norte, San José 10203
DP Coordinator Andres Lacayo Alvarado
Languages English, Spanish
T: +506 2215 1154
W: www.mountviewcr.com

Pan-American School
632-4005 San Antonio de Belen, Heredia
DP Coordinator Henry Gutierrez
MYP Coordinator Christopher Brodie
PYP Coordinator Nikki Merval
Languages English, Spanish
T: +506 2298 5700
W: www.panam.ed.cr

Saint Gregory School
San Juan de La Unión, Cartago
DP Coordinator Ivannia Brenes Flores
Languages English, Spanish
T: +1 506 2279 4444
W: www.saintgregory.cr

Saint Mary School
Apartado 1471, Escazu 1250, San José ESCAZÚ 1250
DP Coordinator Adriana Calvo Barrantes
Languages Spanish
T: +506 2215 2133
W: www.saintmary.ed.cr

Saint Paul College
San Rafael, Alajuela
DP Coordinator Mauricio Jurado
Languages English, Spanish
T: +506 2438 0824 (EXT:108)
W: www.saintpaul.ed.cr

St. Jude School
1.5 Kilometros al Oeste de Davivienda, Santa Ana, San José 488-6150
DP Coordinator Paula Forero
Languages Spanish
T: +506 2203 6474
W: www.stjude.ed.cr

The British School of Costa Rica
PO Box 8184, San José 1000
DP Coordinator Sundey Christensen
Languages English
T: +506 2220 0131
W: www.thebritishschoolofcostarica.com

UWC Costa Rica
De la esquina sureste de la Iglesia Católica, 400m al norte, Santa Ana, San José 10901
DP Coordinator Zoe Bullock
Languages Spanish, English
T: +506 22825609
W: www.uwccostarica.org

CURAÇAO

International School of Curaçao
PO Box 3090, Koninginnelaan z/n, Emmastad
DP Coordinator Suhasini Iyengar
MYP Coordinator Ulises Franco
Languages English
T: +599 9 737 3633
W: www.isc.cw

DOMINICAN REPUBLIC

Babeque Secundaria
Roberto Pastoriza #329, Ens. Naco, Distrito Nacional, Santo Domingo 10124
DP Coordinator Grace Baez
Languages Spanish
T: +1 809 567 9647
W: babequesecundaria.edu.do

Comunidad Educativa Conexus
Máximo Avilés Blonda 34, Evaristo, Santo Domingo
DP Coordinator Victor Hidalgo
Languages English, Spanish
T: +1 809 334 5634
W: www.conexus.edu.do

Comunidad Educativa Lux Mundi
Av. Gustavo Mejía Ricart No. 87, Ens. Piantini, Santo Domingo
DP Coordinator Luis Pena
Languages English, Spanish
T: +1 829 520 7947
W: www.luxmundi.edu.do

Instituto Iberia
José Giménez Miralles 12, Santiago De Los Caballeros 51054
DP Coordinator Jorge Hernández Valiente
Languages English, Spanish
T: +1 809 736 9111
W: www.iberia.edu.do

Saint George School
C/ Porfirio Herrera #6, Ens. Piantini, Santo Domingo
DP Coordinator Rhayza Baptista de Hurtado
Languages English, Spanish
T: +1 809 562 5262
W: www.stgeorge.do

DUTCH CARIBBEAN

St Dominic High School
LB Scot Road # 209, South Reward, St Maarten
DP Coordinator Marie Richardson
Languages English
T: +1 721 548 4277
W: www.stdominichigh.com

ECUADOR

Academia Cotopaxi American International School
PO Box 17-11-6510, Quito, Pichincha
DP Coordinator Susan Galle
PYP Coordinator Paul Cheevers
Languages English
T: +593 (0)2 382 3270
W: www.cotopaxi.k12.ec

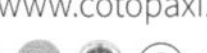

Academia Naval Almirante Illingworth
Ave José Gómez Gault KM 8 1/2, Vía Daule, Guayaquil, Guayas
DP Coordinator Betsy Medina
Languages Spanish
T: +593 (0)4 3703300
W: www.anai.edu.ec

APC Unidad Educativa
Imbabura 156-09 y Sucre, Loja
DP Coordinator Maria Angelina Orellana Aguilar
Languages Spanish
T: +593 7 257 3081
W: www.apc.edu.ec

Atenas Unidad Educativa
Calle Gabriel Roman y Av. Pedro Vasconez, Yacupamba, Izamba, Ambato, Tungurahua EC 180156
DP Coordinator Belén Quintana
Languages English, Spanish
T: +593 3 285 4297
W: www.atenas.edu.ec

Centro Educativo La Moderna
Km 2,5 Vía a Samborondón, Guayaquil, Guayas
DP Coordinator Alexandra Alexandre
Languages English, Spanish
T: +593 42830581
W: www.lamoderna.edu.ec

Centro Educativo Naciones Unidas
Samborondón Km. 1 detrás del C.C. La Piazza, Samborondón, Guayas EC 092301
DP Coordinator Johanna Catalina Guachichullca Bohorquez
MYP Coordinator Carmen Cornejo Robelly
PYP Coordinator Heydy Lara Rodriguez
Languages English, Spanish
T: +593 (0)4 6018560
W: www.cenu.edu.ec

Colegio Alemán Humboldt - DS Samborondón
Av. Ing. León Febres-Cordero #4571, Ciudad Celeste, Samborondón, Guayas EC 090902
DP Coordinator Paola Gomez
Languages Spanish, German
T: +593 (4) 259 7800
W: www.alemanhumboldt.edu.ec

Colegio Alemán Humboldt de Guayaquil
Ciudadela Los Ceibos, Dr. Héctor Romero 216 y Av. Dr. José M. García Moreno, Guayaquil, Guayas EC 090904
DP Coordinator Nataniela Barreiro
Languages Spanish, German, English
T: +593 (0)4 2850260
W: www.cahgye.edu.ec

Colegio Alemán Stiehle Cuenca Ecuador
Autopista Cuenca - Azogues, Km 11,5, Sector Challuabamba, Cuenca, Azuay
DP Coordinator Susanna Wehner
Languages Spanish
T: +593 (0)7 4075646
W: www.casc.edu.ec

Colegio Americano De Guayaquil
Direccion General, Casilla 3304, Guayaquil, Guayas
DP Coordinator Whymper León Kuffó
Languages Spanish, English
T: +593 (0)4 3082 020
W: www.colegioamericano.edu.ec

Colegio Americano de Quito
Casilla 17-01-157, Quito, Pichincha
DP Coordinator David Weaver
MYP Coordinator Ana Maria Ricaurte
PYP Coordinator Estela Proaño
Languages English
T: +593 (0)2 3976 300
W: www.fcaq.k12.ec

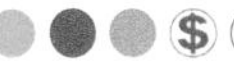

Colegio Balandra Cruz del Sur
Perimeter Road, The Prosperina, Guayaquil, Guayas
DP Coordinator Margarita Guillén Jiménez
Languages Spanish
T: +593 (0)4 285 0020
W: www.balandra.edu.ec

Colegio Becquerel
Tulipanes E12-50 y Los Rosales, Quito, Pichincha
DP Coordinator Ximena Del Pozo Espinosa
Languages Spanish
T: +593 (0)2 2257896
W: www.becquerel.edu.ec

Colegio Católico José Engling
Calle Juan Montalvo s/n, Barrio La Dolorosa, Tumbaco, Quito, Pichincha EC 17172010
DP Coordinator Raúl Alejandro Enríquez Delgado
Languages English, Spanish
T: +593 (0)2 237 4329
W: www.jengling.org

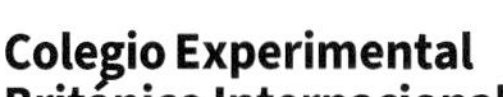

Colegio Experimental Británico Internacional
Amagasí del Inca, Calle de las Nueces E18-21, y Las Camelias, Quito, Pichincha
DP Coordinator Martín Fernández
MYP Coordinator Maria Brioso Augustin
PYP Coordinator Gabriela Gonzalez
Languages English, Spanish
T: +593 (0)2 3261254
W: www.colegiobritanico.edu.ec

Colegio Internacional Rudolf Steiner
Calle Francisco Montalvo Nro 212, y Av Mariscal Sucre, (Av Occidental), Sector Cochabampa, Quito, Pichincha
DP Coordinator Edmundo Burgos Cevallos
MYP Coordinator Luis Franco
PYP Coordinator Oscar Tapia
Languages Spanish
T: +593 2244 3315
W: www.colegiorudolfsteiner.edu.ec

Colegio Internacional SEK Ecuador
De los Guayacanes N51-69 y Carmen Olmo Mancebo, San Isidro de El Inca, Quito, Pichincha
DP Coordinator Marcelo Pérez
MYP Coordinator Carla Flores Dulce
PYP Coordinator Teresa Piedra
Languages English, Spanish
T: +593 2 2401 896
W: www.sekquito.com

Colegio Internacional SEK Guayaquil
Vía Salinas Km. 20.5, Guayaquil, Guayas EC 11373
DP Coordinator Hoover Mora
PYP Coordinator Carolina Castro
Languages Spanish, English
T: +593 4 3904794
W: www.sekguayaquil.com

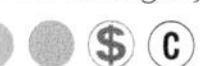

Colegio Internacional SEK Los Valles
Eloy Alfaro S8-48 y De los Rosales, San Juan de Cumbayá, Quito, Pichincha EC 1717933
DP Coordinator Diana Bazurto Vergara
PYP Coordinator Mercedes Flores
Languages Spanish
T: +593 2 3566220
W: www.seklosvalles.ec

Colegio Intisana
Avenida Occidental 5329, y Marcos Joffre, Quito, Pichincha
DP Coordinator Diego Astudillo Cervantes
Languages Spanish
T: +593 2 2440 128
W: www.intisana.com

Colegio Letort
Los Guayabos Nro E 13-05 y Farsalias, San Isidro del Inca, Quito, Pichincha
DP Coordinator Lucía Carolina Pinzón Posada
MYP Coordinator Jose Hidalgo Carrillo
PYP Coordinator Gabriela Gonzalez
Languages Spanish
T: +593 2 326 0202
W: www.colegioletort.edu.ec

Colegio Los Pinos
Calle Agustín Zambrano entre Vicente Pajuelo y Tomás Chariove, Quito, Pichincha EC 170104
DP Coordinator Idanelys Beltrán
Languages Spanish
T: +593 2 246 3189
W: www.colegiolospinos.ec

Colegio Municipal Experimental 'Sebastián de Benalcázar'
RECTORADO, Irlanda E10-77 y Av 6 de Diciembre, Apartado Postal 17-01-25-37, Quito, Pichincha
DP Coordinator Ramón Humberto Flores Pozo
Languages Spanish
T: +593 2 243 5313

Colegio Pachamama
Via Ilalo S/N, San José de Rumihuaico-Tumbaco, Quito, Pichincha EC 170157
DP Coordinator Ana Karina Herrera Alvarez
Languages English, Spanish
T: +593 2 382 3210
W: pachamama.edu.ec

Colegio Séneca
Calle Juan Díaz y Paseo de la Universidad # 20, Urb. Iñaquito Alto, Quito, Pichincha EC 170523
DP Coordinator Paola Jaramillo
T: +593 22 922 544
W: www.seneca.edu.ec

Colegio Stella Maris
Avenida 6 y Calle 14, Manta, Manabí
DP Coordinator Valeria Sandoval Santacruz
Languages Spanish
T: +593 5 2611352
W: smaris.edu.ec

EducaMundo
Km 12 Av. León Febres-Cordero, Urb. Villa Club, entre las etapas Aura y Doral, Guayaquil, Guayas
DP Coordinator Alberto Ulises Ottati Baquero
Languages English, Spanish
T: +593 4372 5860
W: www.educamundo.edu.ec

El Sauce School
Via Interoceánica Km. 12, Junto al Club El Nacional, Tumbaco, Quito, Pichincha EC 170184
DP Coordinator Rosy De Labastida
Languages English, Spanish
T: +593 237 4684/5/6
W: elsauce.edu.ec

EMDI School
EMDI sector B, Parroquia Alangasi, Valle de los Chilos, Quito, Pichincha
DP Coordinator Enrique Segovia
Languages English, Spanish
T: +593 2278 8652
W: www.emdischool.edu.ec/pags/inicio/inicio.html

Escuela Particular Liceo Panamericano - Sede Centenario
Dolores Sucre 302 y Nicolás Augusto González, Guayaquil
MYP Coordinator Denisse Ruiz Moran
PYP Coordinator María de los Ángeles Mendoza Giler
Languages English, Spanish
T: +593 (0)4 3707888
W: liceopanamericano.edu.ec

ISM Academy Quito
San Miguel de Anagaes, Quito, Pichincha EC 170124
DP Coordinator Sandra Acosta
MYP Coordinator Lucia Guevara Espinosa
Languages Spanish
T: +593 2 2414 198
W: www.ism.edu.ec

ISM International Academy
Calle Unión 886 y Ave Geovanny Calle, Sector Calderon, Quito, Pichincha
DP Coordinator Julio Quinteros
MYP Coordinator Miguel Márquez Carrillo
PYP Coordinator Rebeca Polo
Languages English, Spanish
T: +593 2 282 0549
W: www.ism.edu.ec

JESSS - International Christian Academy
Pasaje E18 No 52-120 y, De los Nogales, Quito, Pichincha EC 170124
PYP Coordinator Merci Pallo Vaca
Languages English, Spanish
T: +593 9 9901 9696
W: www.jesss.edu.ec

Johannes Kepler
Av. Simón Bolívar s/n Vía a Nayón, Sector Bosque Protector Bellavista, Quito, Pichincha EC 170511
DP Coordinator Fernando Torres Usechi
Languages Spanish
T: +593 2 394 4180
W: www.jkepler.edu.ec

La Salle Conocoto
Av. Abdón Calderón S18 - 104, Conocoto, Quito, Pichincha EC 170156
DP Coordinator Adriana Carolina Ruiz Báez
Languages English, Spanish
T: +593 2 234 2115
W: www.lasalleconocoto.edu.ec

La Salle Latacunga
Calle Quijano y Ordoñez 532, Y Av. General Maldonado, Latacunga, Cotopaxi EC 050104
DP Coordinator Consuelo Acosta
Languages English
T: +593 32 807 884 / +593 32 801 333
W: www.lasallelatacunga.edu.ec

Liceo del Valle
km 1 vía a Pintag, Valle de los Chillos, Quito, Pichincha
DP Coordinator María de Lourdes Ochoa Delgado
MYP Coordinator Marta Salomé Moscoso Sánchez
PYP Coordinator Ma. Belén Arroyo
Languages Spanish
T: +593 2 2330703
W: www.liceodelvalle.edu.ec

Liceo José Ortega y Gasset
Calle de los Cipreses N64-332 y Manuel Ambrosi, Quito, Pichincha EC 170309
DP Coordinator Geovanna Salazar
Languages Spanish
T: +593 22482976
W: www.gasset.edu.ec

Liceo Panamericano Internacional
Km 3.5 vía Samborondón, Samborondon, Guayas
DP Coordinator Fatima Andrade
MYP Coordinator Claudia Perez
PYP Coordinator Erika Arguello
Languages English, Spanish
T: +593 04 3707888
W: www.liceopanamericano.edu.ec

Logos Academy
Km 14.5 Via a la Costa, Guayaquil, Guayas
DP Coordinator Mariella Coral
Languages Spanish
T: +59 34 390 0125
W: www.logosacademy.edu.ec

Ludoteca Elementary & High School, Padre Victor Grados
Av Simón Bolívar y Camino de los Incas # 5-6, Nueva Vía Oriental, Quito, Pichincha
DP Coordinator Roberto Rojas
MYP Coordinator Amparo de Jesus Albán Grados
PYP Coordinator Gloria Rebeca Bedon Criollo
Languages English, Spanish
T: +593 2 268 8142
W: ludoteca.edu.ec

Martim Cererê Unidad Educativa Particular Bilingüe
De Los Guayacanes N51-01, y Los Álamos, Quito, Pichincha EC 170150
DP Coordinator Zoili Noboa
Languages English, Spanish
T: +593 2 380 2980
W: www.martimcerere.edu.ec

The British School Quito
Via Cununyacu, Km 2.5 Tumbaco, PO Box 17-21-52, Quito, Pichincha
DP Coordinator Paola Montenegro
Languages English
T: +593 2 2 374 649
W: www.britishschoolquito.edu.ec

Uk School
Campus Macasto, Calle Sn y Av. Teniente Hugo Ortiz, Ambato
DP Coordinator Jenny Sánchez Naranjo
MYP Coordinator Heidi Sánchez
Languages English, Spanish
T: +593 3 370 0820
W: ukschool.edu.ec

Unidad Educativa Alberto Einstein
Av Diego Vásquez de Cepeda N77-157 y Alberto Einstein, Casilla Postal 17-11-5018, Quito, Pichincha
DP Coordinator Leonor Alvarez Herrera
MYP Coordinator Carolina Munchmeyer
PYP Coordinator Ana Maldonado
Languages Spanish, English
T: +593 2 393 2570
W: www.einstein.k12.ec

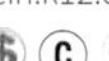

Unidad Educativa Bilingüe Delta
Kilómetro 12.5 Vía Puntilla-Samborondón, Guayaquil, Guayas
DP Coordinator Monica Macchiavello
Languages English, Spanish
T: +593 4 251 1266
W: www.uedelta.k12.ec

Unidad Educativa Bilingüe Hontanar
Calle El Canelo E17-121 y Las Nueces, Sector Amagasí del Inca., Quito
DP Coordinator Alba Marlene Toledo Delgado
Languages English, Spanish
T: +593 2 3261 264
W: www.hontanar.edu.ec

Unidad Educativa Bilingüe Mixta Sagrados Corazones
El Oro 1219 y Avenida Quito, Guayaquil, Guayas
DP Coordinator Neyla Mora Rosales
MYP Coordinator Maria Isabel Gárate Célleri
Languages Spanish
T: +593 04 2440087
W: www.sscc.edu.ec

Unidad Educativa Bilingüe Nueva Semilla
Barrio Centenario Calle D and Argüelles, Guayaquil, Guayas
DP Coordinator Carolina Aldaz
Languages English
T: +593 4 2441174
W: www.nuevasemilla.com.ec

Unidad Educativa Bilingüe Nuevo Mundo
Calle Celeste Blacio de Rendón #112, y Km. 2,5 Vía Samborondón, Guayaquil, Guayas
DP Coordinator Fernando Castro
MYP Coordinator Mónica Aragundi
Languages English, Spanish
T: +593 4 2 830 095
W: www.nuevomundo.edu.ec

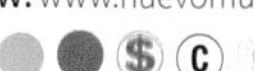

Unidad Educativa Bilingüe William Caxton College
Moises Luna Andrade y Calle 6, Quito, Pichincha EC 170144
DP Coordinator Paola Maldonado Sánchez
Languages English, Spanish
T: +593 2 340 6309
W: www.williamcaxton.edu.ec

Unidad Educativa Cristo Rey
Calle Cristo Rey entre Sucre y Baquerizo Moreno, Portoviejo, Manabí EC 13010014
DP Coordinator Carlos Orozco
Languages Spanish
T: +593 052632558
W: www.cristorey.edu.ec

Unidad Educativa 'Émile Jaques-Dalcroze'
Av. Ilaló y Río Pastaza No. 777, Valle de Los Chillos, Quito, Pichincha
DP Coordinator Sara Arroba Benítez
MYP Coordinator Andrea Torres Ramos
Languages Spanish
T: +593 2 2861 500
W: ejd.edu.ec

Unidad Educativa Internacional Pensionado Atahualpa
El Milagro, San Jose de Cananvalle S/N, Ibarra, Imbabura EC 100150
DP Coordinator Geovanna del Rocío Andrade Tapia
Languages Spanish
T: +593 6 2 542 115

Unidad Educativa Isaac Newton
Guayabos N50-120 y Los Álamos, Quito, Pichincha EC 170149
DP Coordinator Rosario Llerena
Languages Spanish
T: +593 22405001
W: www.isaacnewton.edu.ec

Unidad Educativa 'Julio Verne'
De Los Nopales #58 Y De Los Helechos, Quito, Pichincha EC 170150
DP Coordinator Lucia del Carmen Aguinaga Cáceres
Languages English, Spanish
T: +593 2280 7117
W: www.julioverne.edu.ec

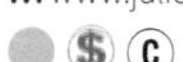

Unidad Educativa Maurice Ravel
Av. Cantabria OE2-18 y Av. Cacha (Sector San José de Morán), Quito, Pichincha EC 170155
DP Coordinator América Apolo
Languages Spanish
T: +593 2 202 3508
W: mauriceravel.edu.ec

Unidad Educativa Monte Tabor Nazaret
Km 13.5 Via Samborondón, Guayaquil, Guayas
DP Coordinator Lorena Arriaga
MYP Coordinator María Puyol Pino
PYP Coordinator Virginia Lozada
Languages English, Spanish
T: +593 4 259 0370
W: www.montetabornazaret.edu.ec

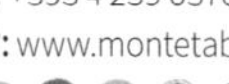

Unidad Educativa Municipal del Milenio Bicentenario
Av. El Beaterio y Calle E2D, Quito, Pichincha EC 170150
DP Coordinator Maribel Jessenia Coello Almagro
Languages English
T: +593 2269 8620
W: www.educacion.quito.gob.ec/unidades/bicentenario

Unidad Educativa Particular Bilingüe Ecomundo
Av. Juan Tanca Marengo Km 2, Guayaquil, Guayas EC 90112
DP Coordinator Jorge Balseca
MYP Coordinator Karrie Orellana
Languages English
T: +593 4 3703700 (EXT:115-118)
W: www.ecomundo.edu.ec

Unidad Educativa Particular Bilingüe Leonardo da Vinci
Vía a San Mateo Km. 2.4, a 100 metros de la Urbanización Ciudad del Mar, Manta, Manabí EC 130802
DP Coordinator Rubén Muñoz Pérez
Languages Spanish
T: +593 5 3 700 865
W: www.ueldv.edu.ec

Unidad Educativa Particular Bilingüe Principito y Marcel Laniado de Wind
Avenida Luis Ángel León Roman y 1era Avenida 5ta, Machala, El Oro EC 0701835
DP Coordinator Diego Ayala Anzoátegui
Languages English
T: +593 72981881
W: www.ueprim.edu.ec

Unidad Educativa Particular Bilingüe Santiago Mayor
Urb. Torres del Salado Km 11.5 vía a la costa, Guayaquil, Guayas
DP Coordinator Juan Gabriel Rodriguez Bernal
Languages English, Spanish
T: +593 4 380 3770
W: www.uesm.edu.ec

Unidad Educativa Particular Bilingüe Santo Domingo de Guzmán
Calle 5ta # 608 y Las Monjas (URDESA), Guayaquil, Guayas
DP Coordinator Isaac Augusto Caicedo Vera
Languages Spanish
T: +593 2 882 561
W: www.stodomingo.edu.ec

Unidad Educativa Particular Hermano Miguel De La Salle
Av. Solano 7-01 y Luis Moreno Mora, Cuenca, Azuay
DP Coordinator Christian Lata Reino
Languages English, Spanish
T: +593 7 281 0349
W: www.delasallecuenca.edu.ec

Unidad Educativa Particular Javier
Km 5.5 vía a la Costa, Guayaquil, Guayas
DP Coordinator Natalia Patino
Languages Spanish
T: +593 4 2001590/3520/0724
W: www.uejavier.com

Unidad Educativa Particular Politécnico
Campus Politécnico 'Gustavo Galindo Velasco', Km. 30.5 vía Perimetral, contiguo a Ceibos Norte, Guayaquil, Guayas
DP Coordinator Linda García Muñoz
MYP Coordinator Roxana Mariuxi Guamanquispe Intriago
PYP Coordinator Mónica Lasso Gallo
Languages Spanish
T: +593 4 226 9654
W: www.copol.edu.ec

Unidad Educativa Particular Redemptio
10 de Agosto 701 entre Colón y Juan Montalvo, Jipijapa, Manabí
DP Coordinator Gustavo Bykovsky Cañarte Gutiérrez
Languages English, Spanish
T: +593 5 2 600 475
W: www.redemptio.edu.ec

Unidad Educativa Particular 'Rosa de Jesús Cordero'
Parroquia Ricaurte, Sector el Tablón, Cuenca, Azuay EC 010162
DP Coordinator María José González
Languages Spanish
T: +593 7 2890503
W: www.catalinas.edu.ec
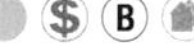

Unidad Educativa Paul Dirac
Av. Pedro Vicente Maldonado y la Cocha, Quito, Pichincha EC 170146
DP Coordinator Carmen Ramirez
Languages English, Spanish
T: +593 2 691 241 (EXT:1)
W: www.pauldirac.edu.ec
 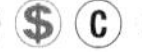

Unidad Educativa Sagrados Corazones de Rumipamba
Av. Atahualpa Oe1-20 y Av. 10 de Agosto, Quito, Pichincha EC 170521
DP Coordinator Marco Vinicio Duque Romero
Languages Spanish
T: +593 22 442 242
W: rumipamba.edu.ec

Unidad Educativa Saint Dominic School
César Davila N10-222 y Charles Darwin, Quito, Pichincha
DP Coordinator Jorge Peralta
Languages Spanish
T: +593 (0)2 3959960
W: www.saintdominic.edu.ec

Unidad Educativa Salesiana Cardenal Spellman
Mercadillo OE340 y Ulloa, Quito, Pichincha EC 1703125
DP Coordinator Alejandro Vinces
MYP Coordinator Helen Jara Bolaños
Languages Spanish
T: +593 2 3560 001/2/3
W: www.spellman.edu.ec

Unidad Educativa San Francisco de Sales
Av. Cristobal Colón E10-07 y Tamayo, Quito, Pichincha
DP Coordinator Hugo Eduardo Ortiz Guerra
Languages English, Spanish
T: +593 2903 861
W: frasales.edu.ec

Unidad Educativa San Jose La Salle
Tomás Martínez 501 y Baquerizo Moreno, Guayaquil, Guayas EC 090150
DP Coordinator Luiggi Saenz de Viteri
Languages Spanish
T: +593 4 25 631 37
W: lasalleguayaquil.edu.ec
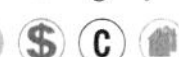

Unidad Educativa San Martín
Calle Sigsipamba S-2159 y Picoazá, Quito, Pichincha EC 170613
DP Coordinator Miriam Zambrano Macías
Languages Spanish
T: +593 (0)2 3080979
W: www.sanmartin.edu.ec

Unidad Educativa Santana
Av. los Cerezos S/N y vía a Racar, Cuenca, Azuay
DP Coordinator Diana Dominguez
Languages Spanish
T: +593 7 4121879
W: www.santana.edu.ec

Unidad Educativa Terranova
Calle De Los Rieles 507, y Ave Simón Bolívar, San Juan Alto de Cumbayá, Quito, Pichincha
DP Coordinator Farah Jalile Mahauad Wittmer
MYP Coordinator Farah Jalile Mahauad Wittmer
PYP Coordinator Yohaina Younes
Languages English, Spanish, French
T: +593 2 356 4000
W: www.colegioterranova.com.ec

Unidad Educativa Tomás Moro
Av De Las Orquideas E13-120, y De Los Guayacanes, Quito, Pichincha
DP Coordinator Jacqueline Rivadeneira Jaramillo
MYP Coordinator Ligia Rosales
PYP Coordinator Daniela Valdez
Languages Spanish
T: +593 2 2405357
W: www.tomasmoro.ec

Unidad Educativo Bilingüe CEBI
Calle Modesto Chacón y Av. Pedro Vásconez Sevilla, Parroquia Izamba, Ambato, Tungurahua
DP Coordinator Rodrigo Naranjo
MYP Coordinator David Jiménez
PYP Coordinator Stefania Solis
Languages Spanish, English
T: +593 3 373 0370
W: www.cebi.edu.ec
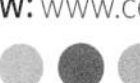 

Victoria Bilingual Christian Academy
Melchor de Valdez Oe-9240, Pbx: 253-6116, Quito, Pichincha EC 170528
DP Coordinator Sarah Catalina Ingman Bastidas
Languages Spanish
T: +593 (0)2 2536116
W: victoriaacademy.edu.ec

Young Living Academy
Km. 24 vía a la Costa, Chongoncito, Guayaquil, Guayas
DP Coordinator Verónica Alexandra Piguave Ruiz
Languages English, Spanish
T: +593 9965 4897
W: www.younglivingacademy.edu.ec

EL SALVADOR

Academia Britanica Cuscatleca
KM 10.5 Carretera a Santa Tecla, Santa Tecla, La Libertad
DP Coordinator Sarah Diebelius
MYP Coordinator Helen Kinder
Languages English, Spanish
T: +503 2201 6200
W: www.abc.edu.sv

Colegio La Floresta
Estamos en el Km. 13 1/2, Carretera al Puerto de La Libertad
DP Coordinator Laura Calderón
Languages English
T: +503 2534 8800
W: www.lafloresta.edu.sv

El Salvador

Colegio Lamatepec
Carretera al Puerto de La Libertad Km 12.5, Calle Nueva a Comasauga Santa Tecla, La Libertad, San Salvador
DP Coordinator Alfonso Humberto Castillo Mejía
Languages English, Spanish
T: +503 2534 8900
W: www.lamatepec.edu.sv

Deutsche Schule - Escuela Alemana San Salvador
Calle del Mediterráneo, Jardines de Guadalupe, Antiguo Cuscatlán, San Salvador CA
DP Coordinator Beatriz Dreyer
Languages Spanish
T: +503 2243 4898
W: www.ds.edu.sv

Escuela Bilingüe Maquilishuat
Boulevard del Hipodromo No. 540, Colonia San Benito, San Salvador
PYP Coordinator José Guzmán
Languages English, Spanish
T: +503 2132 8700
W: www.ebm.edu.sv

GUATEMALA

Centro Escolar Campoalegre
35 Calle and 12 Av Final, Zona 11, Código 01011
DP Coordinator Angela María Gabriela Martínez Orti
Languages English, Spanish
T: +502 2380 3900
W: www.campoalegre.edu.gt

Centro Escolar 'El Roble'
11 Avenida Sur Final Zona 11, Guatemala City 01011
DP Coordinator Luis Fernando Micheo Hernández
Languages Spanish
T: +502 2387 7000
W: www.ceroble.edu.gt

Centro Escolar Entrevalles
Km. 16.8 Antigua Carretera a El Salvador, Santa Catarina Pinula
DP Coordinator Aida Camacho
Languages Spanish, English
T: +502 6685 4700
W: www.entrevalles.edu.gt

Centro Escolar Solalto
Km. 22.5 Carretera a Fraijanes, Fraijanes
DP Coordinator Juan Carlos Velásquez Valladares
Languages English, Spanish
T: +502 6686 0500
W: www.solalto.edu.gt

HONDURAS

The American School of Tegucigalpa
P.O. Box 2134, Tegucigalpa
DP Coordinator Daniel Dobbe
Languages English
T: +504 2276 8400
W: www.amschool.org

JAMAICA

American International School of Kingston
2 College Green Avenue, Kingston
DP Coordinator Sophie Kropman
Languages English
T: +1 876 702 2070
W: www.aisk.com

Hillel Academy
PO Box 2687, 51 Upper Mark Way, Kingston 8
DP Coordinator Pauladene Steele
Languages English
T: +1 876 925 1980
W: hillelacademyjm.com/

MÉXICO

Alexander Bain Colegio
Barranca de Pilares 29, Colonia Tlacopac, San Angel, México D.F. C.P. 01040
PYP Coordinator Loren Karam Karam
Languages Spanish
T: +52 55 5595 0493
W: www.colegioab.mx

American School Foundation of Chiapas
Blvd. Belisario Dominguez 5588-F, Fraccion Las Cinco Plumas, Terán, Tuxtla Gutierrez, Chiapas C.P. 29052
PYP Coordinator Gabriela Princivil
Languages English, Spanish
T: +52 961 346 4840
W: www.americanschool.edu.mx

Avalon International School
Av. San Jerónimo 1135, San Jerónimo de Lídice La Magdalena Contreras, Mexico D.F. C.P. 10200
PYP Coordinator Silvia Diaz Salinas
Languages English, Spanish
T: +52 555 595 5582
W: avalon-school.mx

Bachillerato 5 de Mayo
Ave. del Trabajo # 6, Cuautlancingo, Puebla C.P. 72700
DP Coordinator María Del Rosario Ayala Rojas
Languages English
T: +52 222 2295500 EXT:2770
W: cmas.siu.buap.mx/portal_pprd/wb/b5mayo/inicio

Bachillerato Alexander Bain, SC
Las Flores 497, Tlacopac, San Ángel, Ciudad de México C.P. 01049
DP Coordinator Ana Elia Hernández
MYP Coordinator Loxa Tamayo
Languages Spanish, English, French
T: +52 (55) 5683 2911
W: www.bab.edu.mx

Bachillerato UPAEP Atlixco
Camino a la Uvera #2004, Ex-Hacienda La Blanca, 74365 Atlixco, Puebla
CP Coordinator Marco Emilio Domínguez Chánez
Languages English, Spanish
T: +52 244 445 1991
W: upaep.mx//prepa/atlixco
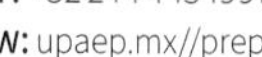

Bachillerato UPAEP San Martín
C/ Lardizabal s/n Col. La Purisima, San Martín Texmelucan, Puebla C.P. 74030
CP Coordinator Maria Del Rosario Rojas Rojas
Languages English, Spanish
W: upaep.mx/prepa/san-martin
 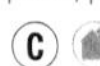

Bachillerato UPAEP Santa Ana
Avenida Tecpanxochitl 52 A, San Pedro Tlalcuapan, Chiautempan, Tlaxcala C.P. 90845
CP Coordinator Elia Zempoaltecatl Ramírez
Languages English, Spanish
T: +52 246 46 496 33
W: upaep.mx/prepa/santa-ana

British American School S.C.
Fuente del Niño #16 Col. Tecamachalco, Naucalpan de Juárez, Estado de México C.P. 53950
PYP Coordinator María Guadalupe Antimo Rivera
Languages English
T: +55 52 94 37 21
W: www.british.edu.mx

Centro de Educación Media de la Universidad Autónoma de Aguascalientes
Av de la Convencion Esq, Con Av Independencia S/N Fraccionamiento Norte, Aguascalientes C.P. 20020
DP Coordinator Diana Cecilia Diaz Dena
Languages Spanish
T: +52 01 449 9 147708
W: www.uaa.mx/centros/cem/

Centro de Enseñanza Técnica y Superior - Campus Mexicali
Calzada del Cetys S/N, Colonia Rivera, Mexicali, Baja California C.P. 21259
DP Coordinator Gerardo Jesús López Verdugo
Languages Spanish
T: +52 686 567 3704
W: www.cetys.mx

Centro de Ensenanza Tecnica y Superior - Campus Tijuana
Av. CETYS Universidad, No. 4 Fracc. El Lago, Tijuana, Baja California C.P. 22210
DP Coordinator Paulina Bueno
Languages Spanish
T: +52 664 903 1800
W: www.cetys.mx

Centro de Investigación y Desarrollo de Educación Bilingüe
Lázaro Cárdenas Al Ote, Sin Número, Unidad Mederos, Monterrey, Nuevo León C.P. 64930
DP Coordinator Jorge Jesús López Castro
Languages Spanish
T: +52 818 3294180
W: cideb.uanl.mx

Centro Educativo Alexander Bain Irapuato
Enrique del Moral Domínguez 335, Ejido Lo de Juárez, 36630, Irapuato, Guanajuato
DP Coordinator María Elena Victoria Jardón
MYP Coordinator Martha Elisa Baqueiro Lespron
PYP Coordinator Atala Gamboa Ruiz
Languages Spanish, English
T: +52 462 114 2246
W: www.alexbain.edu.mx
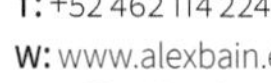

Centro Educativo CRECER AC
Calle del Vecino No 3, Atlihuetzia, Yahuquehmecan, Tlaxcala C.P. 90459
MYP Coordinator Erika López Temoltzin
PYP Coordinator Lucero Getzany Rodríguez Ovando
Languages English, Spanish
T: +52 24 646 13 148
W: www.crecer.edu.mx
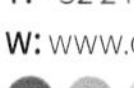   

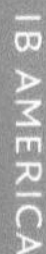

Centro Escolar Instituto La Paz, SC
Av Plan de San Luis 445, Col Nueva Santa María, Ciudad de México C.P. 02800
MYP Coordinator Maribel Sánchez
PYP Coordinator Maribel Sánchez
Languages Spanish, English
T: +52 55 55 56 66 46
W: www.institutolapaz.edu.mx

Churchill College
Moctezuma 125, Colonia San Pablo Tepetlapa, Ciudad de México C.P. 04620
DP Coordinator Tanya Weston
Languages English
T: +52 55 56 19 82 43
W: www.cc.edu.mx

Colegio Álamos
Acceso al Aeropuerto 1000, Colonia Arboledas, Santiago de Querétaro, Querétaro C.P. 76940
DP Coordinator Kevin Coll
Languages English, Spanish
T: +52 442 182 0222
W: www.colegioalamos.edu.mx

Colegio Alemán de Guadalajara
Av Bosques de los Cedros No. 32, Las Cañadas, Zapopan, Jalisco C.P. 45132
DP Coordinator Patrick Weilandt
Languages Spanish
T: +52 33 3685 0136
W: alemangdl.edu.mx

Colegio Alerce
Blvd. Juan Navarrete No. 631, Col. Obispos Residencial, Hermosillo, Sonora C.P. 83210
PYP Coordinator Isabel Vargas Padilla
Languages English, Spanish
T: +52 66 2260 7770
W: alerce.edu.mx
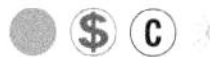

Colegio Americano de San Carlos
Blvd. Luis Encinas S/N, esquina Faustino Félix, Colonia Miramar, Guaymas, Sonora C.P. 85450
MYP Coordinator Elda Fabiola Rascon Flores
PYP Coordinator Martha Corina Zaragoza Farfán
Languages English, Spanish
T: +52 622 221 2551
W: casc.edu.mx

Colegio Anglo de las Américas
Av. 5 de Febrero 1007, Valle del Tecnológico, Lázaro Cárdenas, Michoacán C.P. 60950
PYP Coordinator Perla Ríos Ramos
Languages English, Spanish
T: +52 753 537 7274
W: www.colegioanglo.mx

Colegio Arji
Avenida México # 2, esquina Periférico, Colonia del Bosque, Villahermosa, Tabasco C.P. 86160
DP Coordinator Andrea Tellaeche Merino
MYP Coordinator Nancy Guadalupe De Alba Bellizzia
PYP Coordinator Ligia Teresa Balcázar Avilés
Languages English, Spanish
T: +52 993 3 510 250
W: www.arji.edu.mx

Colegio Atid AC
Av. Carlos Echanove #224, Col. Vista Hermosa Cuajimalpa, Ciudad de México C.P. 05100
CP Coordinator Sandra Mejia
DP Coordinator Laura Aida Reyes Flores
MYP Coordinator Diana Dichi Salame
PYP Coordinator Gustavo Mejía
Languages English, Spanish
T: +52 55 5814 0800
W: www.atid.edu.mx

Colegio Bilingüe Carson de Ciudad Delicias
Ave 50 Aniversario 1709, Delicias, Chihuahua C.P. 33058
PYP Coordinator Sandra Rosales Escamilla
Languages Spanish
T: +52 (639) 472 9340
W: www.colegiocarson.com

Colegio Bosques
Prol. Zaragoza No. 701, Fracc. Valle de las Trojes, Aguascalientes C.P. 20115
MYP Coordinator Aldo García
PYP Coordinator Manuel Macías Flores
Languages English, Spanish
T: +52 449 162 04 05
W: www.colegiobosques.edu.mx

Colegio Británico
Calle Pargo # 24, S.M. 3, Cancun, Quintana Roo C.P. 77500
DP Coordinator Silvia Ivette Luna Barra
PYP Coordinator Maria Del Carmen Zorrilla Velázquez
Languages English
T: +52 (998) 884 1295
W: www.cbritanico.edu.mx
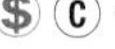

Colegio Celta Internacional
Libramiento Sur-Poniente Km 4+200, Colonia Los Olvera, Villa Corregidora, Querétaro C.P. 76902
CP Coordinator María Mayela Sosa Rodriguez
MYP Coordinator Antonio Ayala Simonin
PYP Coordinator Ma Flora del Piar Lavin Alvarez
Languages English, Spanish
T: +52 442 227 36 00
W: www.celta.edu.mx

Colegio Ciudad de México
Campos Elíseos # 139, Col Polanco, Ciudad de México C.P. 11560
DP Coordinator Sergio Morales
MYP Coordinator Sergio Morales
PYP Coordinator Maruja Esperante
Languages Spanish
T: +52 55 5254 4053
W: www.colegiociudad.edu.mx

Colegio Ciudad de Mexico - Plantel Contadero
Calle de la Bolsa 456, El Contadero, Cuajimalpa, Ciudad de México C.P. 05500
PYP Coordinator Ana Lilia Rueda Moreno
Languages Spanish
T: +52 58 12 06 10
W: www.colegiociudad.edu.mx/contadero.html

Colegio Discovery
Circuito Interior Norte Socorro Romero, Sánchez, No. 3525, Col. San Lorenzo, Tehuacán, Puebla
DP Coordinator Violeta Juárez
Languages English, Spanish
T: +52 238 3820005
W: colegiodiscovery.edu.mx

Colegio El Camino
Callejon del Jornongo #210, Colonia El Pedregal, Cabo San Lucas, B.C.S. C.P. 23453
DP Coordinator Isaac Esteban Perez Bolado
MYP Coordinator Ginger Fell
PYP Coordinator María Inés Mayaudon
Languages English, Spanish
T: +52 624 143 2100 (EXT:112)
W: elcamino.edu.mx

Colegio Fontanar
Camino al Fraccionamiento, Vista Real 119, Corregidora, Querétaro C.P. 76900
DP Coordinator Erika Duhne
Languages Spanish
T: +52 442 228 13 65
W: www.fontanar.edu.mx

Colegio Hebreo Maguen David
Antiguo Camino a Tecamachalco #370, Lomas de Vista Hermosa, Ciudad de México
DP Coordinator Shely Finkelbrand
MYP Coordinator Lorena Herrera Delgado
PYP Coordinator Mónica Hernández
Languages Spanish, Hebrew, English
T: +52 (55) 52 46 26 00
W: www.chmd.edu.mx
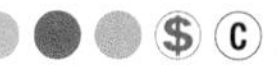

Colegio Hebreo Monte Sinai AC
Av Loma de la Palma 133, Col Vista Hermosa, Cuajimalpa, Ciudad de México C.P. 05109
DP Coordinator Denisse Caram
MYP Coordinator Denisse Caram
PYP Coordinator Tania Navarro Elizalde
Languages Spanish, English
T: +52 55 52 53 01 68
W: www.chms.edu.mx

Colegio Internacional de México
Río Magdalena 263, Colonia Tizapan San Ángel, Álvaro Obregón, Ciudad de México D.P. 01090
MYP Coordinator Susana Valenzuela Esquivel
PYP Coordinator Andrea Pimentel Matute
Languages English, Spanish
T: +52 55 55 50 01 01
W: www.colegiointernacional.edu.mx

Colegio Internacional SEK Guadalajara
Daniel Comboni #850, Colonia Jardines de Guadalupe, Zapopan Jalisco C.P 45030
DP Coordinator Elvia Patricia Gallegos Teran
Languages English, Spanish
T: +52 33 36202423
W: www.sekmexico.com

Colegio Internacional Terranova
Av Palmira No. 705, Privadas del Pedregal, San Luis Potosí C.P. 78295
DP Coordinator Enriqueta Pérez
MYP Coordinator Enrique Freeman Rubio
PYP Coordinator María Covarrubias Gómez
Languages Spanish
T: +52 444 8 41 64 22
W: www.terranova.edu.mx
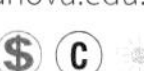

México

Colegio La Paz de Chiapas
Carretera Tuxtla, Villaflores N° 1170, Tuxtla Gutiérrez, Chiapas C.P. 29089
DP Coordinator Alejandra Fraguas Castañón
MYP Coordinator Ana Cecilia Toledo Palacio
Languages Spanish
T: +52 961 663 7000
W: www.colegio-lapaz.edu.mx

Colegio Laureles Chiapas
Blvd. Paso Limón No. 1581, Zona Sin Asignación de Nombre de Col 24, Tuxtla Gutiérrez, Chiapas C.P. 29049
DP Coordinator David Gomez
Languages English, Spanish
T: +52 55 5852 9002
W: colegiolaureleschiapas.mx

Colegio Linares AC
Marina Silva de Rodriguez 1301 Pte, Colonia centro Linares, Nuevo León C.P. 67700
DP Coordinator Margarita María Leal Tamez
Languages Spanish
T: +52 821 212 0269
W: www.colegiolinares.edu.mx

Colegio Madison Chihuahua
Fuente Trevi #7001, Fracc. Puerta de Hierro, Chihuahua C.P. 31205
MYP Coordinator Arantxa Hernández García
PYP Coordinator Rossana Ortegón Alvarez
Languages English, Spanish
T: +52 614 430 1464
W: www.colegiosmadison.edu.mx/colegios-madison-chihuahua.htm

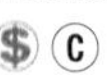

Colegio Maria Montessori de Monclova
Blvd Harold R Pape Nro 2002, Col Jardines del Valle, Monclova, Coahuila C.P. 25730
DP Coordinator Sara Aimee Montes de Oca Nolla
Languages Spanish
T: +52 866 633 2993
W: www.montessorimonclova.com

Colegio Monteverde
Av Santa Lucia No 260, Col Prados de la Montaña, Cualjimalpa, Ciudad de México C.P. 05610
DP Coordinator Fernanda Sanemeterio
Languages Spanish
T: +52 55 50819700
W: www.colegiomonteverde.edu.mx

Colegio Nuevo Continente
Nicolás San Juan 1141, Colonia Del Valle, Ciudad de México C.P. 03100
DP Coordinator Elisa Aizpuru González
Languages English, Spanish
T: +52 55 5575 4066
W: www.nuevocontinente.edu.mx

Colegio Suizo de México - Campus Cuernavaca
Calle Amates s/n, Col. Lomas de Ahuatlán, Cuernavaca, Morelos C.P. 62130
DP Coordinator Dilip Verma
Languages English, Spanish
T: +52 777 323 5252
W: www.csm.edu.mx

Colegio Suizo de México - Campus México DF
Nicolás San Juan 917, Col del Valle, Ciudad de México C.P. 03100
DP Coordinator Aurelio Reyes
Languages English, Spanish
T: +52 55 55 43 78 62
W: www.csm.edu.mx

Colegio Suizo de México - Campus Querétaro
Circ. La Cima 901, Fracc. La Cima, Santiago de Querétaro, Querétaro C.P. 76146
DP Coordinator Pilar Eugenia Carrión Fajardo
Languages Spanish, German, English
T: +52 442 254 3390
W: www.csm.edu.mx

Colegio Vista Hermosa
Bachillerato, Av Loma de Vista Hermosa 221, Cuajimalpa, Ciudad de México C.P. 05100
DP Coordinator Ramón García Govea
MYP Coordinator Viviana Calleja
Languages Spanish
T: +52 55 50914630
W: www.cvh.edu.mx

Colegio Williams
Mixcoac Campus, Empresa 8, Col Mixcoac, Alcaldía Benito Juárez, Ciudad de México C.P. 03910
DP Coordinator Laura Silva Rico
MYP Coordinator Erika Daniela Mendoza Pineda
PYP Coordinator María del Pilar González Mata
Languages Spanish
T: +52 55 1087 9797
W: www.colegiowilliams.edu.mx

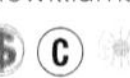

Colegio Williams de Cuernavaca
Luna #32, Jardines de Cuernavaca, Cuernavaca, Morelos C.P. 62360
DP Coordinator Martha Nocetti Vilchis
MYP Coordinator Alicia Martinez Lara
PYP Coordinator María López Covarrubias
Languages English, Spanish
T: +52 (777) 3223640
W: www.cwc.edu.mx

Colegio Xail
Calle Xail No 10, Col. Lázaro Cárdenas, San Francisco de Campeche, Campeche C.P. 24520
MYP Coordinator Balbina Guadalupe Sosa Bautista
PYP Coordinator Susana Gómez Rodríguez
Languages Spanish
T: +52 981 813 0322
W: www.xail.edu.mx

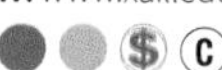

Discovery School
Chilpancingo No 102, Colonia Vista Hermosa, Cuernavaca, Morelos C.P. 62290
PYP Coordinator Luz Gabriela Briseño Tellez
Languages English, Spanish
T: +52 777 318 5721
W: www.discovery.edu.mx

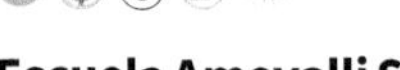

Escuela Ameyalli SC
Calzada de las Águilas 1972, Axomiatla, Ciudad de México C.P. 01820
MYP Coordinator Analía Zarate
PYP Coordinator Paula Lara
Languages English, Spanish
T: +52 55 12 85 70 20
W: www.ameyalli.edu.mx

Escuela John F. Kennedy
Av Sabinos 272, Jurica, Querétaro C.P. 76100
DP Coordinator Alejandra Galindo
MYP Coordinator Laura Davis
PYP Coordinator Christine Scharf
Languages English, Spanish
T: +52 442 218 0075
W: www.jfk.edu.mx

Escuela Lomas Altas S.C.
Montañas Calizas #305, Lomas de Chapultepec, Ciudad de México C.P. 11000
PYP Coordinator Humberto Rodriguez Vega
Languages English
T: +52 55 55 20 53 75/20 37 25
W: www.lomasaltas.edu.mx

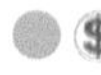

Escuela Mexicana Americana, A. C.
Gabriel Mancera 1611, Col. Del Valle, Ciudad de México C.P. 03100
DP Coordinator Adriana Cruz
Languages English, Spanish
T: +52 55 240214
W: mexicanaamericana.edu.mx

Escuela Preparatoria Federal 'Lázaro Cárdenas'
Paseo de los Héroes #11161, Zona Rio, Tijuana, Baja California C.P. 22010
DP Coordinator Alejandro Valdez Vega
Languages Spanish
T: +52 664 686 12 97
W: www.lazarocardenas.edu.mx

Eton, SC
Domingo García Ramos s/n, Col. Prados de la Montaña, Santa Fe, Cuajimalpa, Ciudad de México C.P. 05619
DP Coordinator Laura Alicia Salazar
MYP Coordinator Rosa María Olmos
Languages English, Spanish
T: +52 5 261 5800
W: www.eton.edu.mx

Foresta International School
Calle Publico los Gallos #3, Rancho Blanco, Espiritu Santo, Jilotzingo, Estado de México C.P. 54570
PYP Coordinator Maricarmen Ugalde
Languages English, Spanish
T: +52 55 5308 4236
W: www.fis.edu.mx

Formus
Cañón de la Mesa 6745, Monterrey, Nuevo León C.P. 64898
MYP Coordinator Aracely Garza Montes
Languages Spanish
T: +52 8317 8560
W: www.formus.edu.mx

Fundación Colegio Americano de Puebla
Av 9 Pte 2709, La Paz, Puebla C.P. 72160
CP Coordinator Xavier Enrique Cordero Mendez
DP Coordinator Emily Ueland
MYP Coordinator Christopher Collupy
PYP Coordinator Vita Enrich Urrea
Languages English, Spanish
T: +52 22 2303 0400
W: www.cap.edu.mx

GREENGATES SCHOOL
Av. Circunvalación Pte. 102, Balcones de San Mateo, Naucalpan, Estado de México C.P. 53200
DP Coordinator David Grant
Languages English
T: +52 55 5373 0088
E: admissions@greengates.edu.mx
W: www.greengates.edu.mx
See full details on page 476

GREENVILLE INTERNATIONAL SCHOOL
Prolongación Avenida Paseo Usumacinta 2122, Ría. Lázaro Cárdenas 2a Sección, Villahermosa, Tabasco C.P. 86287
DP Coordinator Alma Ruíz
MYP Coordinator Sara Pérez
PYP Coordinator Iris Torres (early years) & Silvia González (elementary years)
Languages English
T: +52 (993) 310 8060
E: info@greenville.edu.mx
W: www.greenville.edu.mx
See full details on page 475

Harmony School
Mariano Narváez 414, Col. Los Alpes Norte, Saltillo, Coahuila C.P 25253
PYP Coordinator Perla Patricia Rubio
Languages English, Spanish
T: +52 84 4485 5598
W: www.harmonyschool.mx

Humanitree
725 Sierra Madre, Lomas de Chapultepec, Miguel Hidalgo, Ciudad de México C.P. 11000
DP Coordinator Sue Ellingham
Languages English, Spanish
T: +52 55 8620 7301
W: www.humanitree.edu.mx

Instituto Alexander Bain SC
Cascada 320, Jardines del Pedregal, Ciudad de México
MYP Coordinator Loxá Tamayo Márquez
PYP Coordinator Pamela Suárez
Languages Spanish, English
T: +52 55 5595 6579
W: www.alexanderbain.edu.mx

Instituto Anglo Británico Campus Cumbres
Paseo de los leones 7001, Avenida Bosque de las Lomas, Valle de Cumbres, García, Nuevo León C.P. 66035
MYP Coordinator Esther de Keratry
PYP Coordinator Mrs Alejandra Tijerina Reyna
Languages English, Spanish
T: +52 81 8526 2222
W: www.colegiosmadison.edu.mx/instituto-anglo-britanico-campus-cumbres.htm

Instituto Anglo Británico Campus La Fe
Av. Isidoro Sepúlveda #555, Col. La Encarnación, Apodaca, Nuevo León C.P. 66633
MYP Coordinator Hiram Cisneros R
PYP Coordinator Brunhi Gebauer
Languages English, Spanish
T: +52 8183 21 5000
W: www.iab.edu.mx

Instituto Bilingüe Rudyard Kipling
Cruz de Valle Verde No 25, Santa Cruz del Monte, Naucalpan, Estado de México C.P. 53110
DP Coordinator Magali Guerrero Olvera
MYP Coordinator Sandra Lorena Padró Torres
PYP Coordinator Silvia Garcia
Languages Spanish, English
T: +52 55 5572 6282
W: www.kipling.edu.mx

Instituto Cervantes, A.C.
Prol. León García # 2355, Col. General I. Martínez, San Luis Potosí C.P. 78360
MYP Coordinator Marcela Robles Espinosa
PYP Coordinator inglise castillo martínez
Languages Spanish
T: +52 444 815 91 50
W: www.apostolica.mx

Instituto D'Amicis, AC
Camino a Morillotla s/n, Colonia Bello Horizonte, Puebla C.P. 72170
CP Coordinator Luis Jahir Mendoza
DP Coordinator Luis Jahir Mendoza
MYP Coordinator Adriana Cruz Hernández
PYP Coordinator Ma. Eugenia Tanus Diego
Languages English, Spanish
T: +52 222 303 2618
W: www.damicis.edu.mx

Instituto Educativo Olinca
Periférico Sur 5170, Col Pedregal de Carrasco, Delegación Coyoacán, Ciudad de México C.P. 04700
DP Coordinator Julieta López Olalde
MYP Coordinator Adriana Noguez Reyes
PYP Coordinator Claudia Ghigliazza Lopez
Languages Spanish, English, French
T: +52 55 5606 3113/4197
W: www.olinca.edu.mx

Instituto Internacional Octavio Paz
Calle Internacional 63 Fracc. Las Brisas el Jaguey, Col. Las Redes, Chapala, Jalisco C.P. 45903
DP Coordinator Fátima Flores
Languages English
T: +52 376 766 0903
W: www.iiop.edu.mx

Instituto Kipling de Irapuato
Villa Mirador 5724, Villas de Irapuato, Irapuato, Guanajuato C.P. 36670
MYP Coordinator Sara Patricia Juárez Sánchez
PYP Coordinator Diana Muttio Limas
Languages English, Spanish
T: +52 462 6230165
W: www.kiplingirapuato.edu.mx

Instituto Ovalle Monday - Plantel Secundaria
Guillermo Massieu Helguera 265, Col. Residencial La Escalera, Del. Gustavo A. Madero, Ciudad de México C.P. 07320
MYP Coordinator Maiella Gerardina Martínez Jiménez
Languages Spanish
T: +52 5586 0316 (EXT:101)
W: www.ovallemonday.edu.mx

Instituto Piaget
Nubes 413, Col Jardines del Pedregal, Ciudad de México C.P. 01900
PYP Coordinator Mariana Mejía Fonseca
Languages English, Spanish
T: +52 555568 8881
W: www.institutopiaget.edu.mx

Instituto Tecnológico Sanmiguelense de Estudios Superiores
Calle Escuadrón 201, No. 10 Palmita de Landeta Km. 0.5, San Miguel de Allende, Guanajuato C.P. 37748
DP Coordinator Mayra Vianey Álvarez Soria
Languages Spanish
T: +52 415 154 8484
W: www.itses.edu.mx

Instituto Thomas Jefferson, Campus Santa Monica
Gardenia 5, Ex-hacienda de Santa Monica, Tlalnepantla de Baz, Ciudad de México C.P. 54050
DP Coordinator Sara Beatriz Yeo Canela
Languages English, Spanish
T: +52 55 4160 2000
W: www.itj.edu.mx/santamonica

Instituto Thomas Jefferson, Campus Zona Esmeralda
Av. Jorge Jiménez Cantu 1, Hacienda de Valle Escondido, 52937 Ciudad López Mateos, Estado de México
DP Coordinator Nina Covarrubias Cardenas
Languages English, Spanish
T: +52 55 4162 2100
W: www.itj.edu.mx/zonaesmeralda

Kipling Esmeralda
Av. Parque de los Ciervos No.1, Hacienda de Valle Escondido, Zona Esmeralda, Atizapan de Zaragoza, EEstado de México C.P. 52937
DP Coordinator Ariana Grimaldo Cardenas
MYP Coordinator Claudia García Ybarra
PYP Coordinator Irma Liliana Morales Lozano
Languages Spanish, English
T: +52 55 55726282
W: www.kiplingesmeralda.edu.mx

La Escuela de Lancaster A.C.
Av Insurgentes sur 3838, Tlalpan, Ciudad de México C.P. 14000
DP Coordinator Susan Mann
PYP Coordinator Laura Montes
Languages English, Spanish
T: +52 5556 6697 96
W: www.lancaster.edu.mx
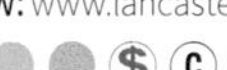

Liceo de Apodaca Centro Educativo
Ave. Virrey de Velazco No. 500, Apodaca, Nuevo León C.P. 66606
MYP Coordinator Guadalupe Nájera Rodríguez
PYP Coordinator Monica Estrada
Languages English
T: +52 81 83862089
W: www.liceodeapodaca.edu.mx

Liceo de Monterrey
Humberto Junco Voigt #400, Col. Valle Oriente, San Pedro Garza García, Nuevo León C.P. 66269
DP Coordinator Cecilia Leal
Languages English, Spanish
T: +52 (81) 8748 4146
W: www.liceodemonterrey.edu.mx

Liceo de Monterrey - Centro Educativo
Col Sendero San Jeronimo, Monterrey, Nuevo Leon C.P. 64659
DP Coordinator Mario Sanchez Monroy
MYP Coordinator Alfonso Alderete de la Cruz
Languages English, Spanish
T: +1 8122 8900
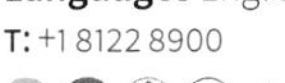

Liceo Federico Froebel de Oaxaca
Ajusco No. 100, Colonia Volcanes, Oaxaca C.P. 68020
DP Coordinator Nancy Villanueva Castillo
Languages Spanish
T: +52 951 5200 675
W: www.federicofroebel.edu.mx

Lomas Hill
Av. Veracruz 158, Cuajimalpa, Ciudad de México C.P. 05000
PYP Coordinator Mariana Resa Romo
Languages English, Spanish
T: +52 55 5812 0818
W: lomashill.edu.mx

MADISON CAMPUS MONTERREY
Marsella #3055, Col. Alta Vista, Monterrey, Nuevo León C.P. 64840
MYP Coordinator Perla Priscila Vargas Andrade
PYP Coordinator Ricardo Domínguez Gámez
Languages English, Spanish
T: +52 81 8359 0627
E: contacto@colegiosmadison.edu.mx
W: madisonmonterrey.edu.mx
See full details on page 487

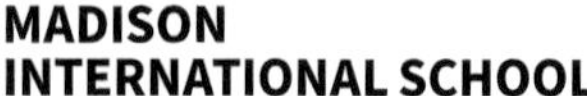

MADISON INTERNATIONAL SCHOOL
Camino Real #100, Col. El Uro, Monterrey, Nuevo León C.P. 64986
MYP Coordinator Anna Carstens
PYP Coordinator Rolando De La Torre
Languages English, Spanish
T: +52 81 8218 7909
E: admisiones@mis.edu.mx
W: www.mis.edu.mx
See full details on page 488

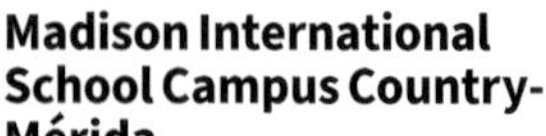

Madison International School Campus Country-Mérida
Calle 24776 s/n, Chablekal, Merida, Yucatán C.P. 97300
DP Coordinator Jhon Mariño Vargas
MYP Coordinator Annabelle Bossard
PYP Coordinator Kate Wade
Languages English, Spanish
T: +52 99 9611 9053
W: www.colegiosmadison.edu.mx/colegios-madison-merida.htm

Noordwijk International College
Blvd. del Mar #491, Fracc. Costa de Oro, Boca del Río, Veracruz C.P. 94299
MYP Coordinator Carolina Zuluaga Moreno
PYP Coordinator Sandra Gamboa
Languages English, Spanish
T: +52 229 130 0714
W: www.noordwijk.com.mx

Peterson School - Lomas
Monte Himalaya 615, Lomas de Chapultepec, Miguel Hidalgo, México D.F. C.P. 11000
DP Coordinator Bella Cherem Picciotto
Languages Spanish
T: +52 5520 2213
W: www.peterson.edu.mx/lomas

Prepa UNI
Carretera Panamerican Km 269, Celaya, Guanajuato C.P. 38080
DP Coordinator Alejandra Nuñez
Languages Spanish
T: +52 461 61 39099
W: www.udec.edu.mx

Prepa UPAEP Angelópolis
Av. del Sol No. 5, Col. Concepción La Cruz, San Andrés Cholula, Puebla C.P. 72160
CP Coordinator Laura Mariana Hernández De la Torre
DP Coordinator Laura Mariana Hernández de la Torre
Languages Spanish
T: +52 222 225 2291
W: upaep.mx/prepa/angelopolis

Prepa UPAEP Cholula
Av. Forjadores No. 1804, Col Barrio de Jesús, San Pedro Cholula, Puebla C.P. 72760
CP Coordinator Claudia Yamilet Lomas Mendoza
DP Coordinator Claudia Yamilet Lomas Mendoza
Languages Spanish
T: +52 222 403 7373
W: upaep.mx/prepa/cholula

Prepa UPAEP Huamantla
Carr. Lib. Carr. México-Veracruz Kilómetro 147.5, Santa Clara, Huamantla, Tlaxcala C.P. 90500
CP Coordinator Yolanda Sánchez Flores
Languages Spanish
T: +52 247 472 2550
W: upaep.mx/prepa/huamantla

Prepa UPAEP Lomas
Circuito Mario Molina No. 15, Lomas de Angelópolis, San Andrés Cholula, Puebla C.P. 72828
CP Coordinator Alejandra Paola Anaya Salas
DP Coordinator Alejandra Paola Anaya Salas
Languages English, Spanish
T: +52 (0)1 222 5822102
W: upaep.mx/prepa/lomas
  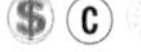

Prepa UPAEP Santiago
Av 9 Pte 1508, Barrio de Santiago, Puebla C.P. 72160
CP Coordinator Ulises Alarcón
DP Coordinator Ulises Alarcón
Languages Spanish
T: +52 222 246 8264
W: upaep.mx/prepa/santiago

Prepa UPAEP Sur
Calle Independencia No. 6339, Col. Patrimonio, Puebla C.P. 72470
CP Coordinator Rafael Vazquez Salamanca
DP Coordinator Agueda Martinez Epinosa
Languages Spanish
T: +52 222 233 1342
W: upaep.mx/prepa/sur

Prepa UPAEP Tehuacán
Boulevard Tehuacán San Marcos No. 1700, Col. El Humilladero, Tehuacán, Puebla
CP Coordinator Francisco Javier Martínez Orea
Languages English, Spanish
T: +52 238 383 7800
W: upaep.mx/prepa/tehuacan

Rootland School
Hortensia 6, Florida, Álvaro Obregón, Ciudad de México C.P. 01030
PYP Coordinator Ana Rocha Jove
Languages English, Spanish
T: +52 55 2096 3660
W: www.rootland.edu.mx

Tecnológico de Monterrey - PrepaTec Ciudad de México
Calle del Puente #222, Col. Ejidos de Huipulco, Tlalpan, Distrito Federal C.P. 14380
DP Coordinator César Akim Erives Chaparro
Languages Spanish
T: +52 (55) 5483 2110
W: miPrepaTec.ccm.itesm.mx

Tecnológico de Monterrey - PrepaTec Cumbres
Linces #1000, Col. Cumbres Elite, Monterrey, Nuevo León C.P. 64639
DP Coordinator Ada Verónica Chavarría Treviño
Languages Spanish, English
T: +52 (81) 8158 4622
W: www.prepatec.mty.itesm.mx

Tecnológico de Monterrey - PrepaTec Esmeralda
Fracc. Conjunto Urbano, Col. Bosque Esmeralda, Manzana 7 Lote 1 y 2, Atizapán de Zaragoza, Estado de México C.P. 52930
DP Coordinator David Lee
Languages Spanish
T: +52 (55) 5864 5370 (EXT:2903)
W: www.itesm.mx/wps/wcm/connect/PrepaTec/esm/esmeralda

Tecnológico de Monterrey - PrepaTec Estado de México
Carretera Lago de Guadalupe, Km 3.5, Col. Margarita Maza de Juárez, Atizapán de Zaragoza, Estado de México C.P. 52926
DP Coordinator Andrea Fabiola Rodríguez Iniesta
Languages Spanish, English
T: +52 (55) 5864 5714
W: www.cem.itesm.mx
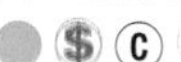

Tecnológico de Monterrey - PrepaTec Eugenio Garza Lagüera
Topolobampo #4603, Valle de las Brisas, Monterrey, Nuevo León C.P. 64790
DP Coordinator Ana Isabel López
Languages Spanish
T: +52 (81) 8155 4490
W: www.prepatec.mty.itesm.mx

Tecnológico de Monterrey - PrepaTec Eugenio Garza Sada
Dinamarca #451 Sur Col Del Carmen, Monterrey, Nuevo León C.P. 64710
DP Coordinator Mónica Otálora
Languages Spanish, English
T: +52 (81) 8151 4264
W: admisionprepatec.itesm.mx

Tecnológico de Monterrey - PrepaTec Metepec
Av. Las Torres 1957 Ote., San Salvador Tizatlali, Metepec C.P. 52172
DP Coordinator Marina Villazón
Languages Spanish, English
T: +52 (722) 271 5977
W: www.tol.itesm.mx

Tecnológico de Monterrey - PrepaTec Querétaro
Av. Epigmenio González #500, Fracc. San Pablo, Santiago de Querétaro C.P. 76130
DP Coordinator Christina Norris-González
Languages Spanish
T: +52 (442) 238 3208
W: www.qro.itesm.mx

Tecnológico de Monterrey - PrepaTec Santa Catarina
Morones Prieto No 290 Pte., Col Jesús M. Garza, Santa Catarina, Nuevo León C.P. 66180
DP Coordinator Rosalba Serrano
Languages Spanish, English
T: +52 (81) 8153 4045
W: www.prepatec.mty.itesm.mx

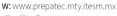

Tecnológico de Monterrey - PrepaTec Santa Fe
Av Carlos Lazo #100, Santa Fe, Delegación Alvaro Obregón C.P. 01389
DP Coordinator Karla Franceli Villagrán Guadarrama
Languages Spanish, English
T: +52 (55) 9177 8130
W: miPrepaTec.csf.itesm.mx

Tecnológico de Monterrey - PrepaTec Valle Alto
Carretera Nacional #8002 Km. 267.7, Col. La Estanzuela, Monterrey, N.L C.P. 64986
DP Coordinator Marcela Valero Cervantes
Languages English, Spanish
T: +52 (81)8228 5310
W: www.prepatec.mty.itesm.mx
 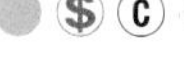

The American School Foundation, A.C.
Calle Sur 136-135, Colonia Las Americas, México D.F. C.P. 01120
DP Coordinator Rafael Vazquez
PYP Coordinator Michael Herndon
Languages English, Spanish
T: +52 55 5227 4900
W: www.asf.edu.mx

The Churchill School
Felipe Villanueva No. 24, Col. Guadalupe Inn, Mexico City
MYP Coordinator Itzel Nava
PYP Coordinator Maria Garza Caligaris
Languages English
T: +52 55 50288800
W: www.churchill.edu.mx

The Edron Academy
Calz. Desierto de los Leones #5578, Col Olivar de Los Padres, Ciudad de México C.P. 1740
DP Coordinator Lorna Villasana
Languages English
T: +52 55 5585 1920
W: www.edron.edu.mx

Tomás Alva Edison
Heriberto Frías 1401 Colonia del Valle, Benito Juárez, Ciudad de México C.P. 03100
DP Coordinator Mara Urinda Quiroga Guillén
Languages English, Spanish
T: +52 55 5604 0314
W: www.tae.edu.mx

Universidad de Monterrey Unidad Fundadores
Nova Scotia 109, between Av. Newfoundland and Av. General Mariano Escob+, Escobedo, Nuevo Leon C.P. 66054
CP Coordinator Homero Treviño
DP Coordinator Homero de Jesús Treviño Villagómez
Languages Spanish
T: +52 (81) 8215 4151
W: www.udem.edu.mx

Universidad de Monterrey Unidad Valle Alto
Carretera Nacionala Salida Valle Alto Km1, Colonia Valle Alto, Monterrey, NL C.P. 64989
CP Coordinator Claudia Gabriela De La Pena Sepúlveda
DP Coordinator María Adriana Rodríguez De la Garza
Languages English, Spanish
W: www.udem.edu.mx/Esp/Preparatoria/Pages/Unidad-Valle-Alto.aspx

Universidad Internacional Jefferson
Boulevard Jefferson No 666, Morelia, Michoacán C.P. 58090
DP Coordinator Ana Yunnuen Avila Villegas
Languages Spanish
T: +52 44 3680 5333
W: jefferson.edu.mx

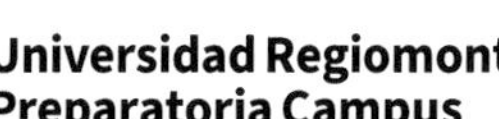

Universidad Regiomontana Preparatoria Campus Centro
Matamoros # 430 Pte., Col. Centro, Monterrey, NL C.P. 64000
DP Coordinator Guillermo Acosta Cazares
Languages Spanish
T: +52 81 8220 4830
W: u-erre.mx

University of Monterrey
Av. Ignacio Morones Prieto 4500, Pte., 66238, San Pedro Garza García, Nuevo León C.P. 66238
CP Coordinator Nabor Rodríguez Loera
DP Coordinator Patricia Menendez Aguilar
Languages Spanish
T: +52 81 8215 1010
W: www.udem.edu.mx/prepaudem

Westhill Institute
Domingo Garcia Ramos No. 56, Col. Prados de la Montaña, Santa Fe, Cuajimalpa, Mexico City C.P. 05610
DP Coordinator Ana Isabel Almeida Leñero
MYP Coordinator Mónica Flórez
PYP Coordinator Erika Leonor Pérez
Languages English, Spanish, French
T: +52 55 8851 7000
W: www.westhillinstitute.edu.mx

Winpenny School
José María Castorena 318, Colonia Cuajimalpa, México D. F. C.P. 05000
DP Coordinator Zachary Rubin
Languages English, Spanish
T: +52 55 8000 6100
W: www.winpenny.edu.mx

NICARAGUA

Colegio Alemán Nicaragüense
Apartado 1636, Managua
DP Coordinator Hubert Luna Palacios
Languages Spanish, English
T: +505 2265 8449
W: www.coalnic.edu.ni/index.php/en/

Notre Dame International School
Km 8.5 Carretera a Masaya, Managua
DP Coordinator Carlos Ordoñez Mondragon
MYP Coordinator Alejandra Mendoza
PYP Coordinator Silvia Vallecillo
Languages English
T: +505 2276 0353 54
W: notredame.edu.ni
 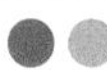 

PANAMA

Academia Panamá Para El Futuro
Ciudad del Saber, Ancón, Panama City
DP Coordinator Angel Sánchez
Languages English, Spanish
T: +507 678 13594

Boston School International
Ave. Arnulfo Arias Madrid Building. #727, Balboa, Ancón, Panama City
DP Coordinator Ruth Mendoza
PYP Coordinator Bronwyn Gordon-Bennett
Languages English
T: +507 833 8888
W: www.bostonschool.edu.pa

Colegio Isaac Rabin
Edificio 130, Ciudad del Saber
DP Coordinator Reina Laura Companioni
MYP Coordinator Sonia Martínez Robles
PYP Coordinator Marissa Rocha De Medina
Languages Spanish
T: +507 3170059
W: www.isaacrabin.com

International School of Panama
P.O. Box 0819-02588, Cerro Viento Rural, Panama City
DP Coordinator Gray Galloway
Languages English
T: +507 293 3000
W: www.isp.edu.pa

KING'S COLLEGE SCHOOL PANAMA
Av. Demetrio B. Lakas, Clayton, Panama City
DP Coordinator Warren Green
Languages English, Spanish
T: +507 282 3300
E: ana.mantovani@kings.education
W: www.panama.kingscollegeschools.org
See full details on page 482

METROPOLITAN SCHOOL OF PANAMA
Green Valley, Panama Norte, Panama City
DP Coordinator Ms. Lori Guerra
MYP Coordinator Mr. Ryan Manary
PYP Coordinator Ms. Olivia McKevett
Languages English
T: +507 317 1130
E: admissions@themetropolitanschool.com
W: www.nordangliaeducation.com/met-panama
See full details on page 494

PARAGUAY

Centro Educativo Arambé
Santísima Trinidad No 3.211, c/ Avda. Ita Ybaté (Zona Brítez Cue), Luque, Asunción
DP Coordinator Carolina Susana Bianco Wehrli
Languages Spanish
T: +595 21 694 662
W: www.arambe.edu.py

Colegio Goethe Asunción
Cnl Silva esq Tte Rocholl, Asuncion 232
DP Coordinator Gustavo González
Languages Spanish
T: +595 21 606860
W: www.goethe.edu.py

Faith Christian School
Del Maestro 3471 c/ Soriano González, Barrio Herrera, Asunción
DP Coordinator Marisa Vaesken de Ramos
Languages English, Spanish
T: +595 21 620 5024
W: www.faith.edu.py

IB AMERICAS

St Anne's School

Tte. Manuel Pino Gonzalez y Eulalio Facetti, Asunción
DP Coordinator Mirko Zayas
Languages English
T: +595 21 295649
W: www.sas.edu.py

PERU

American School

Av. Larco Nro 288, Urb. San Andrés, Trujillo, La Libertad 13008
DP Coordinator Alana Lam Peña
Languages English, Spanish
T: +51 44 612370
W: www.americanschooltrujillo.com

Andino Cusco International School

Km 10.5 Carretera, Chinchero Distrito de Cachimayo, Cusco
DP Coordinator Bruno Vázquez Molinero
PYP Coordinator Emperatriz Yepez
Languages English, Spanish
T: +51 84 275135
W: www.andinoschool.edu.pe

CAMBRIDGE COLLEGE LIMA

Av. Alameda de los Molinos 728-730, La Encantada de Villa, Chorrillos, Lima 15067
DP Coordinator Adrian Everitt
Languages English, Spanish
T: +51 12 540107
E: office@cambridge.edu.pe
W: cambridge.edu.pe

See full details on page 461

Casuarinas International College

Av Jacarandá 391, Valle Hermoso, Monterrico, Santiago de Surco, Lima 15023
CP Coordinator Verónica Herrera
DP Coordinator Verónica Herrera
MYP Coordinator Luis Eduardo Camelo Roa
PYP Coordinator Carmen del Rosario Linares Gamarra
Languages Spanish, English, French, Portuguese, Mandarin
T: +51 13 444040
W: www.casuarinas.edu.pe

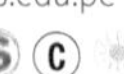

Clemente Althaus

Prolongación Jirón Cuzco 360, San Miguel - Alt. Cdra. 12 Av. La Marina, Lima 15086
DP Coordinator Katherine Fernandez Alvarez
Languages Spanish
T: +51 14 194700
W: clementealthaus.edu.pe

Colegio Alpamayo

Calle Bucaramanga 145, Urb Mayorazgo, Lima 15026
DP Coordinator Johan Fripp Anicama
Languages Spanish
T: +51 13 490111
W: www.alpamayo.edu.pe

COLEGIO ALTAIR

Av. La Arboleda 385, Urb. Sirius, La Molina, Lima 15024
DP Coordinator Yolanda Meneses
MYP Coordinator Paloma Krüger
PYP Coordinator Sandra Nicoli
Languages Spanish, English
T: +51 13 650298
E: admision@altair.pe
W: www.altair.edu.pe

See full details on page 462

Colegio Champagnat

Paseo de la República 7930, Santiago de Surco, Lima 15049
DP Coordinator Humberto Lara Ceroni
MYP Coordinator Karen Quinto Loa
PYP Coordinator Ana Elizabeth Gálvez Calderón
Languages Spanish
T: +51 15 1905000
W: www.champagnat.edu.pe

Colegio de Alto Rendimiento de Amazonas

Jirón Amazonas 120, Chachapoyas, Amazonas
DP Coordinator Ever Gustavo Marín Chávez
Languages Spanish
W: www.minedu.gob.pe/coar

Colegio de Alto Rendimiento de Ancash

Sector Llacshahuanca, Recuay, Ancash
DP Coordinator Giomar Sotomayor Aquino
Languages Spanish
W: www.minedu.gob.pe/coar

Colegio de Alto Rendimiento de Apurímac

Jiron Tupac Amaru S/N, Pairaca, Chalhuanca, Apurímac
DP Coordinator Alejandro Sanchez Pomalaza
Languages Spanish
W: www.minedu.gob.pe/coar

Colegio de Alto Rendimiento de Arequipa

Ca. Federico Barreto Nª 148, CEBA Nuestra Señora del Pilar, Arequipa
DP Coordinator Mauro Ronal Ramos Valdivia
Languages Spanish
W: www.minedu.gob.pe/coar

Colegio de Alto Rendimiento de Ayacucho

Jr. Mariano Ruiz de Castilla N° 150, Alameda Valdelirios, Ayacucho
DP Coordinator Cosme Gerardo Palomino Cárdenas
Languages Spanish
W: www.minedu.gob.pe/coar

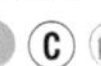

Colegio de Alto Rendimiento de Cajamarca

Jirón José Pardo No 103, Distrito Jesús, Cajamarca
DP Coordinator Julio Trigoso Mori
Languages Spanish
W: www.minedu.gob.pe/coar

Colegio de Alto Rendimiento de Cusco

Sector Bellavista a 6 Km. del distrito de Anta, Pucyura, Cusco
DP Coordinator Gregory Enrique Hernández Borja
Languages Spanish
W: www.minedu.gob.pe/coar

Colegio de Alto Rendimiento de Huancavelica

Jr. José Gabriel Condorcanqui S/N, CP Santa Ana, Huancavelica
DP Coordinator Jaime Artica
Languages Spanish
W: www.minedu.gob.pe/coar

Colegio de Alto Rendimiento de Huánuco

Centro Poblado Canchán, a 12 km de Huánuco, Huánuco
DP Coordinator Saúl Mejía Ortíz
Languages Spanish
W: www.minedu.gob.pe/coar

Colegio de Alto Rendimiento de Ica

Calle José María Mejía S/N, Nazca, Ica
DP Coordinator Luisa Angélica Loredo Valdéz
Languages Spanish
W: www.minedu.gob.pe/coar

Colegio de Alto Rendimiento de Junín

Ca. Huayna Capac, Cdra. 4 IESTP Jaime Cerrón Palomino, Chongos Bajo, Chupaca, Junín
DP Coordinator Edith Alexandra Yalle Taboada
Languages Spanish
W: www.minedu.gob.pe/coar

Colegio de Alto Rendimiento de La Libertad

Campamento San José Carretera Trujillo, Chimbote, Virú, La Libertad
DP Coordinator Diana Rosales Murga
Languages Spanish
W: www.minedu.gob.pe/coar

Colegio de Alto Rendimiento de Lambayeque

Prolongación Bolognesi S/N, A media cuadra de la Av. José Leonardo Ortiz, Chiclayo, Lambayeque
DP Coordinator Mike Hamilton Hernández Girón
Languages Spanish
W: www.minedu.gob.pe/coar

Colegio de Alto Rendimiento de Lima-Provincias

Av. 5 de Diciembre s/n Santa María, Huaura, Lima
DP Coordinator Jose Wilder Tarrillo Vasquez
Languages Spanish
W: www.minedu.gob.pe/coar

Colegio de Alto Rendimiento de Loreto

Avenida Mariscal Cáceres con Pasaje Jorge Chávez S/N, Iquitos, Loreto
DP Coordinator Luis Alberto Tulumba Villacrez
Languages Spanish
W: www.minedu.gob.pe/coar

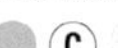

Colegio de Alto Rendimiento de Madre de Dios

Av. Madre de Dios cuadra 4 esquina con, Madre de Dios
DP Coordinator Miguel Antonio Arrelucea Del Pozo
Languages Spanish
W: www.minedu.gob.pe/coar

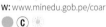

Colegio de Alto Rendimiento de Moquegua

Prlg. Av. Mariano Lino Urquieta S/N, CP San Antonio, Moquegua
DP Coordinator Reynaldo Arteta Ávila
Languages Spanish
W: www.minedu.gob.pe/coar

Colegio de Alto Rendimiento de Pasco

Jr. Joseph Albert Walijewski Szydlo Nro 201, Oxapampa, Pasco
DP Coordinator Eduardo Verastegui Borja
Languages Spanish
W: www.minedu.gob.pe/coar

Colegio de Alto Rendimiento de Piura
Ca. Juan Velasco Alvarado S/N, AAHH Nueva Esperanza, CETPRO Bosconia, Piura
DP Coordinator Maritza Quintana Carlin
Languages Spanish
W: www.minedu.gob.pe/coar

Colegio de Alto Rendimiento de Puno
Av. Panamericana Nª943, a 17 km. de Puno- Carretera Chucuito, Seminario Ntra Señora de Guadalupe, Puno
DP Coordinator Osmar Loza
Languages Spanish
W: www.minedu.gob.pe/coar

Colegio de Alto Rendimiento de San Martin
Jr. Pedro Pascasio Noriega Nª 061, IESPP Generalísimo José de San Martín, San Martín
DP Coordinator Mario Campos
Languages Spanish
W: www.minedu.gob.pe/coar

Colegio de Alto Rendimiento de Tacna
Sector Irrigación Copare, por la carretera Panamericana Sur, IE Norah Flores Tor+, Tacna
DP Coordinator Freddy Edinson Jimenez Paredes
Languages Spanish
W: www.minedu.gob.pe/coar

Colegio de Alto Rendimiento de Tumbes
San Juan de la Vírgen s/n, Tumbes
DP Coordinator Efraín Villacorta Zárate
Languages Spanish
W: www.minedu.gob.pe/coar

Colegio de Alto Rendimiento de Ucayali
Psje. Huáscar S/N, PPJJ Micaela Bastidas, Calleria 61, Coronel Portillo, Ucayali
DP Coordinator Gianina Gil Rengifo
Languages Spanish
W: www.minedu.gob.pe/coar

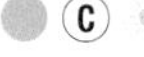

Colegio Franklin Delano Roosevelt
Av. Las Palmeras 325, Camacho, Lima 15023
DP Coordinator Robert Allan
Languages English, Spanish
T: +51 14 350890
W: www.amersol.edu.pe

Colegio Hipólito Unanue
Sector 2, Grupo 25, Mz M Lote 3, Villa el Salvador, Lima
DP Coordinator Rebeca Amelia Palomino Sanchez
Languages English, Spanish
T: +51 947 242115
W: www.hu.edu.pe

Colegio La Unión
Av. Cipriano Dulanto 1950, Pueblo Libre, Lima 15084
DP Coordinator Miriam Palacios Velasquez
Languages English
T: +51 12 610533
W: www.launion.edu.pe

Colegio León Pinelo
Calle Maimónides 610 (ex Los Manzanos), San Isidro, Lima 15076
DP Coordinator Yoana Kaliksztein Fihman
MYP Coordinator Diego Kierzner
PYP Coordinator María Pía Iglesias Denegri
Languages Spanish
T: +51 12 183040
W: www.lp.edu.pe

Colegio Los Álamos
Calle Estados Unidos 731, Jesús María, Lima 15701
DP Coordinator César Chora Chamochumbi
Languages Spanish
T: +51 14 631044
W: www.losalamos.edu.pe

Colegio Magister
Calle Francisco de Cuéllar 686, Monterrico, Santiago de Surco, Lima
DP Coordinator Edwin James Vargas Haro
Languages English, Spanish
T: +51 14 363063
W: www.magister.edu.pe

Colegio Mater Admirabilis
Av. Arica 898, San Miguel, Lima
MYP Coordinator Roxana Calderón
Languages Spanish
W: www.maternet.edu.pe

Colegio Max Uhle
Av. Fernandini s/n, Sachaca, Arequipa 04013
DP Coordinator Alejandro Gutiérrez Osorio
Languages Spanish
T: +51 54 232921
W: www.maxuhle.edu.pe

Colegio Mayor Secundario Presidente del Perú
Centro Vacacional de Huampaní, Carretera Central, Km 24.5, Chaclacayo, Lima
DP Coordinator Alcides Roman Rivas
Languages Spanish
T: +51 14 971278
W: www.colegiomayor.edu.pe

Colegio Montealto
Los Eucaliptos 491, San Isidro, Lima
DP Coordinator Tania Gonzales Sanez
Languages Spanish
T: +51 441 2685
W: montealto.edu.pe

Colegio Nuestra Señora del Pilar
Av. Virgen del Pilar 1711, Cercado, Arequipa
DP Coordinator Ricardo Enríquez Cáceres
Languages Spanish
T: +51 54 226262
W: www.cnspilar.edu.pe

Colegio Peruano - Alemán Reina del Mundo
Avenida Rinconada del Lago 675, La Molina, Lima
DP Coordinator Luis Ernesto Gutierrez
Languages Spanish
T: +51 14 792191
W: www.rdm.edu.pe

Colegio Peruano Alemán Beata Imelda
Carretera Central Km 29 s/n, Lurigancho-Chosica, Lima
DP Coordinator Martin Heinrich
Languages Spanish
T: +51 13 603119
W: www.cbi.edu.pe

Colegio Peruano Británico
Av. Vía Láctea 445, Monterrico, Santiago de Surco, Lima 15023
DP Coordinator María Del Pilar Vildoso
Languages English
T: +51 14 360151
W: www.britishschool.edu.pe

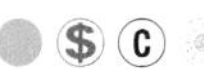

Colegio Peruano Norteamericano Abraham Lincoln
Av. José Antonio 475, Urb. Parque de Monterico, La Molina, Lima 15023
DP Coordinator Brenda Yohana Caycho Avalos
MYP Coordinator Eliana Alcalde
PYP Coordinator Karla Puente Garcia
Languages Spanish, English
T: +51 16 174500
W: www.abrahamlincoln.edu.pe

Colegio Pestalozzi (Colegio Suizo del Peru)
Casilla 18-1027, Aurora-Miraflores, Lima
DP Coordinator Karen Coral
Languages Spanish
T: +51 16 178600
W: www.pestalozzi.edu.pe

Colegio Sagrados Corazones 'Recoleta'
Av. Circunvalación del Golf 368, La Molina, Lima 15023
DP Coordinator Erick Joel Huaman Licas
Languages Spanish
T: +51 17 022500
W: www.recoleta.edu.pe

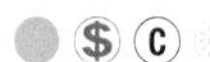

Colegio Salcantay
Av. Pío XII 261, Monterrico, Santiago de Surco, Lima 15023
DP Coordinator Rosa Elena Galagarza
Languages Spanish
T: +51 14 359224
W: www.salcantay.edu.pe

Colegio San Agustín
Av. Javier Prado Este 980, Urb. El Palomar, San Isidro, Lima
DP Coordinator Germán Ramos Ibias
PYP Coordinator Oscar Raúl Medina Ycaza
Languages Spanish
T: +51 16 164242
W: www.sanagustin.edu.pe

Colegio San Agustín de Chiclayo
Km. 8 Carretera Pimentel S/N, Pimentel, Chiclayo, Lambayeque
DP Coordinator Rocio Moza Chávarry
Languages Spanish
T: +51 74 208173
W: www.sanagustinchiclayo.edu.pe

Colegio San Ignacio de Recalde
Calle Géminis 251, San Borja, Lima 15037
DP Coordinator Patricia Loo Salas
PYP Coordinator Norma Pagaza Sotelo
Languages English
T: +51 12 119430
W: www.sir.edu.pe

Colegio San Pedro
Calle Hurón 409, Rinconada del Lago, La Molina, Lima 15026
DP Coordinator Ella Tenorio
Languages English, Spanish
T: +51 16 149500
W: sanpedro.edu.pe

Colegio Santa Úrsula
Av. Nicolas de Rivera 132, San Isidro, Lima 15073
DP Coordinator Ana María Reyes Fajardo
Languages Spanish
T: +51 12 027430
W: www.santaursula.edu.pe

Colegio Santísimo Nombre de Jesús
Urbanización Chacarilla del Estanque Calle Mayorazgo 176, San Borja, Lima
DP Coordinator Edwin Borda Meza
Languages English, Spanish
T: +51 13 721655

Colegio Villa Caritas
Calle Hurón 409, Rinconada del Lago, La Molina, Lima 15026
DP Coordinator Fairuz Saba
Languages English, Spanish
T: +51 16 149500
W: villacaritas.edu.pe

Colegio Virgen Inmaculada de Monterrico
Av. Morro Solar No. 110, Santiago de Surco, Lima 15039
DP Coordinator Martin Ponce Guillen
Languages English, Spanish
T: +51 13 726499
W: virgeninmaculada.edu.pe

Collège André Malraux
Calle Batallón Concepción 245, Urb. Sta. Teresa, Santiago de Surco, Lima
DP Coordinator Veronica Bringas
Languages English
T: +51 12 754937
W: www.andremalraux.edu.pe

Davy College
Av. Hoyos Rubio 2684, Cajamarca 06001
DP Coordinator Cecilia Kanashiro
Languages English, Spanish, French
T: +51 76 367501
W: www.davycollege.edu.pe

Euroamerican College
Fundo Casablanca, Pachacamac, Lima
DP Coordinator Carla Gloria Piscoya Salinas
PYP Coordinator Karina Munoz
Languages Spanish, English
T: +51 12 311617
W: www.euroamericancollege.edu.pe

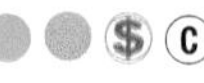

Fleming College
Av América Sur 3701, Trujillo, La Libertad 13008
DP Coordinator Andrés Navárro
PYP Coordinator Alba Morales
Languages English, Spanish
T: +51 44 284440
W: www.fleming.edu.pe

Hiram Bingham, The British International School of Lima
Av. Paseo la Castellana 919, Urbanización La Castellana, Santiago de Surco, Lima 15048
DP Coordinator Martha Marengo
MYP Coordinator Rosa Luz Yamamoto Parasi
PYP Coordinator Cinthya Estremadoyro
Languages English, Spanish
T: +51 27 19880
W: www.hirambingham.edu.pe/hiram

IE Fuerza Aérea Peruana José Quiñones
Av. Evitamiento S/N-Urb, Camacho, La Molina, Lima
DP Coordinator Patricia Aparicio Vargas
Languages Spanish
W: www.cased.edu.pe/?cat=41

IE Pedro Ruiz Gallo
Av. Cdra 2 S/N Costado de la Clinica Maison de Sante Chorrillos, Chorrillos, Lima
DP Coordinator Sandra Villanueva Sánchez
MYP Coordinator Luz Rosas
Languages Spanish
T: +51 16 802673
W: prg.edu.pe

Institución Educativa Particular San Antonio de Padua
Av. Estados Unidos 569, Jesús Maria, Lima
DP Coordinator Jenny Polo Churrango
Languages Spanish
T: +51 16 143600
W: www.sanantoniodepadua.edu.pe

Institución Educativa Privada Lord Byron
Calle Grande 250, Sr. de la Caña, Cayma, Arequipa
DP Coordinator Jeffrey Dagmar Fernández Castillo
Languages Spanish
T: +51 54 255038
W: www.lordbyron.edu.pe

Liceo Naval 'Almirante Guise'
Calle Monti 350, San Borja, Lima 15037
DP Coordinator Carito Ayala Delgado
Languages Spanish
T: +51 14 758055
W: www.lnag.edu.pe

Lord Byron School
Jr. Viña del Mar 375 - 379, Sol de la Molina, Lima 15026
DP Coordinator Joselito Vallejos Avalos
MYP Coordinator Ysabel Martínez Lora
PYP Coordinator Karolina Cueva
Languages English, Spanish
T: +51 14 791717
W: www.byron.edu.pe

MARKHAM COLLEGE - PERU
Calle Augusto Angulo 291, San Antonio, Miraflores, Lima 15048
DP Coordinator Dr. Guinevere Dyker
Languages English, Spanish
T: +51 13 156750 (EXT: 1325)
E: admissions@markham.edu.pe
W: www.markham.edu.pe
See full details on page 489

Montessori International College
Maz. A Sub Lote 01A, Urb. Tecsup, Distrito Víctor Larco Herrera, Trujillo, La Libertad 13009
DP Coordinator Tatjana Merzyn
PYP Coordinator Inés Gabriela Velásquez Ramos
Languages Spanish, English
T: +51 44 340000
W: www.montessoricollege.edu.pe

Newton College
Av. Ricardo Elías Aparicio 240, Lima 15026
DP Coordinator Constanza Beck
MYP Coordinator Jimena La Rosa Massa
PYP Coordinator Daniel Kasnick
Languages English
T: +51 12 079900
W: www.newton.edu.pe

Prescott
Avenida Alfonso Ugarte No. 565, Arequipa 04000
DP Coordinator Patricio González Luna
MYP Coordinator Romina Ramos Solis
PYP Coordinator Katia Aita Fuentes
Languages English, Spanish
T: +51 54 232540
W: www.prescott.edu.pe

San Francisco College
Urb. El Oasis II, Calle Costa del Sol Mz 'D' Lote 14, (Pista Camino a Huacachina), Ica 11004
DP Coordinator Gabriela Cabrejas Hernandez
PYP Coordinator Guadalupe Khairel Márquez Larreátegui
Languages English, Spanish
T: +51 95 6298110
W: sanfranciscocollege.edu.pe

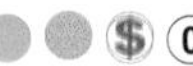

San Silvestre School
Av. Santa Cruz 1251, Miraflores, Lima 15074
DP Coordinator Rafaela Antezana
Languages English
T: +51 12 413334
W: www.sansilvestre.edu.pe

St George's College - Sede Miraflores
Av. General Ernesto Montagne No.360, Miraflores, Lima 15048
CP Coordinator Luis Sifuentes Maldonado
DP Coordinator Luis Sifuentes Maldonado
Languages English, Spanish
T: +51 14 458147
W: www.stgeorgescollege.edu.pe

Villa Alarife School
Jr. Alameda Don Augusto Mz. D Lt. 5, Urb. Los Huertos de Villa, Chorrillos, Lima 15067
DP Coordinator María Luz Rojas Bonilla
T: +51 12 346969
W: villaalarife.edu.pe

Weberbauer School
Calle Pio XII 123, Santiago de Surco, Lima 15023
DP Coordinator Maria Inés Prado
Languages German, Spanish
T: +51 14 366212
W: weberbauer.edu.pe

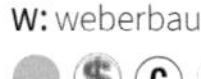

PUERTO RICO

Robinson School
5 Nairn Street, San Juan 00907
DP Coordinator Enid Camacho
MYP Coordinator Carine Poinson Simon
PYP Coordinator María Turner
Languages English
T: +1 787 999 4600
W: www.robinsonschool.org

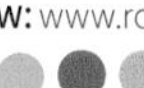
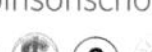

IB AMERICAS

THE BALDWIN SCHOOL OF PUERTO RICO
PO Box 1827, Bayamón 00960-1827
DP Coordinator Mrs. Laura Maristany
MYP Coordinator Mr. Gregorio Vázquez
PYP Coordinator Ms. Janelle Méndez
Languages English
T: +1 787 720 2421
E: admissions@baldwin-school.org
W: www.baldwin-school.org
See full details on page 514

TRINIDAD & TOBAGO

The International School of Port of Spain
1 International Drive, Westmoorings, Port of Spain
MYP Coordinator Angela Shahien
PYP Coordinator Angela Shahien
Languages English
T: +1 868 633 4777
W: www.isps.edu.tt

URUGUAY

Colegio Stella Maris
Máximo Tajes 7357/7359, CP 11500 Montevideo 11500
DP Coordinator Maria Brossard Hitta
Languages English, Spanish
T: +598 2 600 0702
W: www.stellamaris.edu.uy
 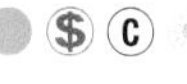

Escuela Integral Hebreo Uruguaya
Jose Benito Lamas 2835, Montevideo 11300
DP Coordinator Rosana Erosa
PYP Coordinator Victoria Soria
Languages Spanish
T: +598 2 708 1712
W: www.escuelaintegral.edu.uy

Escuela y Liceo Elbio Fernandez
Maldonado 1381, Montevideo 11200
DP Coordinator Leticia Santos Bentos
MYP Coordinator Stella Arrieta
Languages English, Spanish
T: +598 2901 1254
W: www.elbiofernandez.edu.uy
  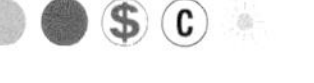

International College
Blvr Artigas y Avda del Mar, Punta del Este, Maldonado
DP Coordinator Alicia Olea
Languages English, Spanish
T: +598 42 228 888
W: www.ic.edu.uy
 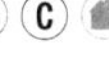

St Brendan's School
Av Rivera 2314, Montevideo CP 11200
CP Coordinator Maria del Rosario Rodríguez
DP Coordinator Maria del Rosario Rodríguez
MYP Coordinator Helena Sastre Abreu
PYP Coordinator Claudia Ourthe-Cabalè
Languages English, Spanish
T: +598 2409 4939
W: www.stbrendan.edu.uy

St Clare's College
California y los Médanos, Punta del Este, San Rafael 20000
DP Coordinator Josué Naranjo
Languages Spanish, English
T: +598 42 490200
W: www.scc.edu.uy

St Patrick's College
Camino Gigantes 2735, Montevideo 12100
MYP Coordinator José Antonio Padilla Agrafojo
Languages Spanish
T: +598 2 601 3474
W: www.stpatrick.edu.uy

The British Schools, Montevideo
Máximo Tajes 6400, esq Havre, Montevideo 11500
DP Coordinator Florencia Paullier
PYP Coordinator Maria Fernanda Sobral
Languages English, Spanish
T: +598 2 600 3421
W: www.british.edu.uy

Uruguayan American School
Saldún de Rodríguez 2375, Montevideo 11500
DP Coordinator Gabriel Amaral
Languages English
T: + (598) 2600 7681
W: www.uas.edu.uy

Woodlands School
San Carlos de Bolivar s/n entre Havre y Cooper, Montevideo 11500
MYP Coordinator Fanny Bozzo Aldecosea
Languages Spanish
T: +59 82 604 27 14
W: www.woodlands.edu.uy

Woodside School
Mercedes y Louvre. Barrio Cantegril, 20100 Punta del Este, Maldonado
DP Coordinator Ximena Indarte
Languages English, Spanish
T: +598 4223 2298
W: www.woodsideschool.edu.uy

USA

Alabama

Auburn High School
405 South Dean Road, Auburn AL 36830
DP Coordinator Davis Thompson
Languages English
T: +1 334 887 4970
W: www.auburnschools.org/ahs

Central High School, Tuscaloosa
905 15th Street, Tuscaloosa AL 35401
DP Coordinator Jennifer Hines
MYP Coordinator Jennifer Hines
Languages English
T: +1 205 759 3720
W: www.tuscaloosacityschools.com/domain/10

Charles A. Brown Elementary School
4811 Court J, Birmingham AL 35208
PYP Coordinator Vieshell Tatum
Languages English
T: +1 205 231 6860
W: www.bhamcityschools.org/page/67

Columbia High School
300 Explorer Boulevard, Huntsville AL 35806
MYP Coordinator Morgan McCants
Languages English
T: +1 256 428 7576
W: www.columbiahigh.org

Columbia High School
300 Explorer Boulevard, Huntsville AL 35806
CP Coordinator Karli LeCompte
DP Coordinator Karli LeCompte
Languages English
T: +1 256 428 7576
W: www.columbiahigh.org

Cornerstone Schools of Alabama
118 55th Street North, Birmingham AL 35212
PYP Coordinator Rebecca Stivender
Languages English
T: +1 205 591 7600
W: www.csalabama.org

Daphne High School
9300 Lawson Road, Daphne AL 36526
DP Coordinator Deborah Few
Languages English
T: +1 251 626 8787
W: www.daphnehs.com

Fairhope High School
One Pirate Drive, Fairhope AL 36532
DP Coordinator Darla Litaker
Languages English
T: +1 251 928 8309
W: www.fairhopehs.com

Hoover High School
1000 Buccaneer Drive, Hoover AL 35244
DP Coordinator Melissa Hamley
Languages English
T: +1 205 439 1200
W: www.hoovercityschools.net/hhs

Jefferson County IB School
6100 Old Leeds Road, Birmingham AL 35210
DP Coordinator April Miller
MYP Coordinator Lauren Brown
Languages English
T: +1 205 379 5356
W: jcib.jefcoed.com

John Herbert Phillips Academy
2316 7th Avenue North, Birmingham AL 35203
MYP Coordinator Jessica Jones Wedgeworth
PYP Coordinator Tamara Sharpe
Languages English
T: +1 205 231 9500
W: www.bhamcityschools.org/Domain/31

MacMillan International Academy
4015 McInnis Road, Montgomery AL 36116
PYP Coordinator Emily Baldwin
Languages English
T: +1 334 284 7137
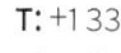

Murphy High School
100 South Carlen Street, Mobile AL 36606
CP Coordinator Sarah Woltring
DP Coordinator Rebecca Mullins
Languages English
T: +1 251 221 3186
W: www.mhspanthers.com

Phillips Preparatory School
3255 Old Shell Road, Mobile AL 36607
MYP Coordinator Jennifer Morgan
Languages English
T: +1 251 221 2286
W: phillipsprep.com

Providence Elementary School
10 Chalkstone Street, Huntsville AL 35806
PYP Coordinator Kim Davidson
T: +1 256 428 7125
W: www.huntsvillecityschools.org/schools/providence-elementary

Ramsay Alternative High School
1800 13th Avenue South AL 35205
DP Coordinator Jonathan Barr
MYP Coordinator Carolyn Russell-Walker
Languages English
T: +1 205 231 7000
W: www.bhamcityschools.org/ramsay

The Academy for Science and Foreign Language
3221 Mastin Lake Road, Huntsville AL 35810
MYP Coordinator Adam Landingham
PYP Coordinator Kim Davidson
Languages English
T: +1 256 428 7000
W: www.huntsvillecityschools.org/schools/academies-science-foreign-language

Tuscaloosa Magnet Elementary School
315 McFarland Blvd. East, Tuscaloosa AL 35404
PYP Coordinator Kathryn Busby
Languages English
T: +1 205 759 3655
W: www.tuscaloosacityschools.com/tmse

Tuscaloosa Magnet Middle School
315 McFarland Blvd. East, Tuscaloosa AL 35404
MYP Coordinator Lavanda Wagenheim
Languages English
T: +1 205 759 3653
W: www.tuscaloosacityschools.com/Domain/25

W H Council Traditional School
751 Wilkinson Street, Mobile AL 36603-1397
PYP Coordinator Mrs. E Danae Bowman
Languages English
T: +1 251 221 1139

W P Davidson High School
3900 Pleasant Valley Road, Mobile AL 36609
DP Coordinator Ashley Cauley
Languages English
T: +1 251 221 3084
W: www.wpdavidson.org

Williams School
155 Barren Fork Blvd SW, Huntsville AL 35824
MYP Coordinator Fisher Hedgeman
PYP Coordinator Kim Davidson
Languages English
T: +1 256 428 7540/5
W: www.huntsvillecityschools.org/schools/williams-middle

Alaska

Inlet View Elementary School
1219 N Street, Anchorage AK 99501
PYP Coordinator Beth Daly-Gamble
Languages English, Spanish
T: +1 907 742 7630
W: www.asdk12.org/inletview

Palmer High School
1170 West Arctic Avenue, Ma -Su Borough School District, Palmer AK 99645
DP Coordinator Kelsey Kraemer
Languages English
T: +1 907 746 8408

West Anchorage High School
1700 Hillcrest Drive, Anchorage AK 99517
DP Coordinator John Ruhlin
Languages English
T: +1 907 742 2610
W: www.asdk12.org/domain/3104

Arizona

Anasazi Elementary School
12121 N. 124th Street, Scottsdale AZ 85259
PYP Coordinator Sara Armstrong
Languages English, Spanish
T: +1 480 484 7300
W: www.susd.org/anasazi

Anthem K-8 School
2700 N Anthem Way, Florence AZ 85132
MYP Coordinator Melissa Haugen
Languages English
T: +1 520 723 6400
W: www.fusdaz.com/anthem

Barry Goldwater High School
2820 West Rose Garden Lane, Deer Valley United School Dist, Phoenix AZ 85027
DP Coordinator Bridget Romero
MYP Coordinator Bridget Romero
Languages English
T: +1 623 445 3000
W: www.dvusd.org/domain/39

Betty H Fairfax High School
8225 South 59th Avenue, Laveen AZ 85339
DP Coordinator Elana Payton
Languages English
T: +1 602 764 9020
W: www.bettyfairfaxhs.org

Buckeye Union High School
1000 E. Narramore, Buckeye AZ 85326
DP Coordinator Joshua Stringham
Languages English, Spanish
T: +1 623 386 4423
W: www.buhsd.org/buckeye

Cactus Shadows High School
PO Box 426, Cave Creek AZ 85327-0426
DP Coordinator Angela Thomas
Languages English
T: +1 480 575 2400
W: www.ccusd93.org/cshs

Canyon del Oro High School
25 West Calle Concordia, Oro Valley AZ 85704
DP Coordinator Amy Bomke
Languages English
T: +1 520 696 5560
W: www.amphi.com/cdo

Chandler High School
350 N. Arizona Ave., Chandler AZ 85225
CP Coordinator Courtney Kemp
DP Coordinator Jacqueline Hartrick
MYP Coordinator Laura Helt
Languages English
T: +1 480 812 7700
W: www.cusd80.com/chs

Cholla High Magnet School
2001 West Starr Pass Blvd, Tucson AZ 85713
DP Coordinator Teresa Green
Languages English
T: +1 520 225 4000
W: www.tusd1.org/Cholla

Coconino High School
2801 N Izabel St, Flagstaff AZ 86004
DP Coordinator Chelsea Drey
Languages English, Spanish
T: +1 928 773 8200
W: www.fusd1.org/chs

Desert Garden Montessori
5130 E. Warner Rd., Phoenix AZ 85044
MYP Coordinator Krista John
Languages English
T: +1 480 496 9833
W: desertgardenmontessori.org

Desert Mountain High School
12575 E Via Linda, Scottsdale Unified, Scottsdale AZ 85259
DP Coordinator Laura Kamka
MYP Coordinator Kevin Sheh
Languages English
T: +1 480 484 7009
W: www.susd.org/Domain/19

EDUPRIZE Schools
580 W Melody Ave., Gilbert AZ 85233
DP Coordinator Amy Smith
Languages English
T: +1 480 888 1610
W: www.eduprizeschools.net

Estrella Foothills Global Academy
5400 W. Carver Road, Laveen AZ 85339
MYP Coordinator Erin Lebish
Languages English
T: +1 602 304 2050
W: estrellafoothills.laveenschools.org

Estrella Mountain Elementary School
10301 S. San Miguel Road, Goodyear AZ 85338
MYP Coordinator Michele Bove
PYP Coordinator Zuzana Finn
Languages English
T: +1 623 386 3001

Florence High School
1000 S. Main St, Florence AZ 85232
DP Coordinator Dawn Waggoner
MYP Coordinator Dawn Waggoner
Languages English
T: +1 520 866 3560
W: fhs.fusdaz.com

Gilbert High School
1101 East Elliot Road, Gilbert AZ 85234
CP Coordinator Meghan Gray
DP Coordinator Meghan Gray
Languages English
T: +1 480 497 0177
W: www.gilbertschools.net/gilberthigh

Global Academy of Phoenix
6615 N. 39th Avenue, Phoenix AZ 85019
MYP Coordinator Melody Hodges
PYP Coordinator Melody Hodges
Languages English, Spanish
T: +1 602 336 2202
W: www.alhambraesd.org/gap

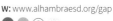

Ironwood High School
6051 W. Sweetwater Ave, Glendale AZ 85304
DP Coordinator Ian Curtis
Languages English
T: +1 623 486 6400
W: www.peoriaunified.org/ironwood
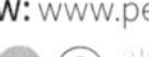

Kyrene Middle School
1050 E Carver Rd, Tempe AZ 85284
MYP Coordinator Kathie Cigich
Languages English
T: +1 480 541 6600
W: www.kyrene.org/kyr

Madison Meadows Middle School
225 W. Ocotillo Rd, Phoenix AZ 85013
MYP Coordinator Claire Vacanti
Languages English
T: +1 602 664 7610
W: madisonaz.org/meadows-middle-school/home

Madison Simis Elementary School
7302 N. 10th Street, Phoenix AZ 85020
PYP Coordinator Melissa Powers
Languages English
T: +1 602 664 7300
W: madisonaz.org/simis-elementary-school/home

Marc T. Atkinson Middle School
4315 N. Maryvale Parkway, Phoenix AZ 85031
MYP Coordinator Suzi Brown
Languages English, Spanish
T: +1 623 691 1700
W: www.atkinson.csd83.org

Mesa Academy of Advanced Studies
6919 East Brown Road, Mesa AZ 85217
MYP Coordinator Angela Shults
Languages English
T: +1 480 308 7400
W: www.mpsaz.org/academy

Millennium High School
14802 W Wigwam Blvd, Goodyear AZ 85395
DP Coordinator Monique Winfield
Languages English
T: +1 623 932 7200
W: www.aguafria.org/Domain/10

Mountain View Preparatory School
2939 Del Rio Drive, Cottonwood AZ 86326
PYP Coordinator Heather Langley
Languages English
T: +1 928 649 8144
W: mvp.cocsd.us

Mountainside Middle School
11256 N 128th Street, Scottsdale AZ 85259
MYP Coordinator Kate Hillman
Languages English
T: +1 480 484 5500
W: www.susd.org/mountainside

Nogales High School
1905 N. Apache Blvd., Nogales AZ 85621
DP Coordinator Jennifer Valenzuela
Languages English
T: +1 520 377 2021

Norterra Canyon School
2200 W Maya Way, Phoenix AZ 85085
MYP Coordinator Bridget Romero
Languages English, French
T: +1 623 445 8200
W: www.dvusd.org/Domain/119

North Canyon High School
1700 East Union Hills Drive, Phoenix AZ 85024
DP Coordinator Matt Case
Languages English
T: +1 623 780 4200
W: www.pvschools.net/schools/north-canyon-high/home

North High School
1101 E. Thomas Rd., Phoenix AZ 85014
DP Coordinator Estaban Flemons
Languages English
T: +1 602 826 4702
W: www.northhs.com

Puente de Hózhó Elementary School
3401 N 4th Street, Flagstaff AZ 86004
PYP Coordinator Jillian Hernandez
Languages English, Spanish
T: +1 928 773 4090
W: www.fusd1.org/pdh

Quail Run Elementary School
3303 E. Utopia Rd., Phoenix AZ 85050
PYP Coordinator Dianna Rubey
Languages English
T: +1 602 449 4400
W: www.pvschools.net/qres

Rancho Solano Preparatory School
9180 E. Via de Ventura, Scottsdale AZ 85258
DP Coordinator Marco Garbarino
Languages English
T: +1 480 646 8200
W: www.ranchosolano.com

Sinagua Middle School
3950 E Butler Avenue, Flagstaff AZ 86004
MYP Coordinator Chelsea Drey
Languages English, Spanish
T: +1 928 527 5500
W: www.fusd1.org/domain/725

Summit Academy (7-8 Campus)
1550 Wets Summit Place, Chandler AZ 85224
MYP Coordinator Angela Shults
Languages English
T: +1 480 472 3430
W: www.mpsaz.org/summitacademy

Summit Academy (K-6 Campus)
1560 W Summit Place, Chandler AZ 85224
PYP Coordinator Angela Shults
Languages English
T: +1 480 472 3500
W: www.mpsaz.org/summitacademy

Tempe Academy of International Studies
3205 S. Rural Road, Tempe AZ 85282
MYP Coordinator Kathy Gannon
Languages English
T: +1 480 730 7101
W: www.tempeschools.org

Tempe High School
1730 S Mill Avenue, Tempe AZ 85281
DP Coordinator James Michael Cooper
Languages English
T: +1 480 967 1661
W: www.tempeunion.org

The Odyssey Institute High School
1495 S Verrado Way, Buckeye AZ 85326
DP Coordinator Randy Hiatt
MYP Coordinator Randy Hiatt
Languages English
T: +1 623 327 1757
W: odyprep.com/oi

Verde Valley School
3511 Verde Valley School Road, Sedona AZ 86351
DP Coordinator Andy Gill
Languages English
T: +1 928 284 2272
W: www.vvsaz.org

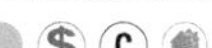

Vista Verde Middle School
2826 E. Grovers Ave., Phoenix AZ 85032
MYP Coordinator Cassy Lough
Languages English
T: +1 602 449 5300
W: www.pvschools.net/domain/44

Westwood High School
945 West 8th Street, Mesa AZ 85201
CP Coordinator Jennifer Keller
DP Coordinator Jacob Davis
MYP Coordinator Brian Buck
Languages English
T: +1 480 472 4400
W: www.mpsaz.org/westwood

Willow Canyon High School
17901 West Lundberg St, Surprise AZ 85388
CP Coordinator Jason Ward
DP Coordinator Jason Ward
Languages English
T: +1 623 523 8000
W: www.dysart.org/schoolsite/?schoolid=210

Arkansas

Bentonville High School
1801 SE J Street, Bentonville AR 72712
DP Coordinator Trista McGinley
Languages English
T: +1 479 254 5100
W: bhs.bentonvillek12.org/pages/bentonville_hs

Hot Springs High School
701 Emory Street, Hot Springs AR 71913
CP Coordinator Shannon Geoffrion
DP Coordinator Shannon Geoffrion
MYP Coordinator Kate Neighbors
Languages English
T: +1 501 624 5286

Hot Springs Middle School
701 Main Street, Hot Springs AR 71913
MYP Coordinator Kate Neighbors
Languages English
T: +1 501 624 5228

Park International Magnet School
617 Main Street, Hot Springs AR 71913
PYP Coordinator Marissa Burton
Languages English
T: +1 501 623 5661

 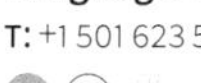

Springdale High School
1103 West Emma Avenue, Springdale AR 72764
DP Coordinator Shannon Green
Languages English
T: +1 479 750 8832
W: www.sdale.org/o/springdale-high-school

California

32nd Street/LAUSD USC Magnet School
822 W 32nd Street, Los Angeles CA 90007
MYP Coordinator Margarita Clark
Languages English, Spanish
T: +1 213 748 0126
W: 32ndstreet-uscmagnet.schoolloop.com

Academia Moderna Charter
2410 Broadway, Walnut Park CA 90255
PYP Coordinator Miram Choi
Languages English
T: +1 323 923 0383
W: www.academiamoderna.org

USA

ACE Charter High School
570 Airport Way, Camarillo CA 93010
CP Coordinator Marina Morales
Languages English, Spanish
T: +1 805 437 1410
W: www.acecharterhigh.org

Agoura High School
28545 W Driver Avenue, Agoura Hills CA 91301
DP Coordinator Jennifer Correia
Languages English
T: +1 818 889 1262
W: www.agourahighschool.net

Al-Arqam Islamic School & College Preparatory
6990 65th Street, Sacramento CA 95823
DP Coordinator Leena Jamaleddin
Languages English
T: +1 916 391 3333
W: www.alarqamislamicschool.org

Albert Einstein Academy Charter School
3035 Ash Street, San Diego CA 92102
MYP Coordinator Corie Julius
PYP Coordinator Corie Julius
Languages English
T: +1 619 795 1190
W: www.aeacs.org

Alice Birney Elementary School
4345 Campus Ave., San Diego CA 92103
PYP Coordinator Jennifer Sims
Languages English
T: +1 619 497 3500
W: www.sandi.net/birney

Alto International School
475 Pope St, Menlo Park CA 94025
DP Coordinator Richard Goulding
MYP Coordinator Veronique Merckling
PYP Coordinator Stephanie Wafzig
Languages English, German
T: +1 650 324 8617
W: www.altoschool.org

Amelia Earhart Elementary School of International Studies
45-250 Dune Palms Road, Indio CA 92201
PYP Coordinator Jennifer Lindsay
Languages English
T: +1 760 200 3720
W: sites.google.com/desertsands.us/amelia-earhart-elementary

American Lakes School
2800 Stonecreek Drive, Sacramento CA 95833
PYP Coordinator Mary Rimbey
Languages English
T: +1 916 567 5500

Anahuacalmecac International University Prep High School
4736 Huntington Drive South, Los Angeles CA 90032
MYP Coordinator Minnie Ferguson
PYP Coordinator Minnie Ferguson
Languages English
T: +1 323 225 4549 EXT:100
W: www.dignidad.org

Andrew P Hill High School
3200 Senter Road, San Jose CA 95111-1399
DP Coordinator Michael Winsatt
MYP Coordinator John Estrela
Languages English
T: +1 408 347 4100
W: andrewphill.esuhsd.org

Armijo High School
824 Washington Street, Fairfield CA 94533
DP Coordinator Tessa Pryor
Languages English
T: +1 707 422 7500
W: www.fsusd.org/armijo

Arroyo Elementary School
1700 E. 7th Street, Ontario CA 91764
PYP Coordinator Silvia Bustamante
Languages English
T: +1 909 985 1012
W: www.omsd.net/Arroyo

Arroyo Valley High School
1881 W Base Line, San Bernardino CA 92411
DP Coordinator Erik Sanchez
MYP Coordinator Dimitrios Chronopoulos
Languages English
T: +1 909 381 4295

Azusa High School
240 North Cerritos Avenue, Azusa CA 91702
DP Coordinator Robert Colera
Languages English
T: +1 626 815 3400
W: www.ahs-ausd-ca.schoolloop.com

Beechwood School
780 Beechwood Avenue, Fullerton CA 92835
MYP Coordinator Jason Lee
Languages English
T: +1 714 447 2850
W: beechwood.fullertonsd.org

Bel Aire Park Magnet School
3580 Beckworth Drive, Napa CA 94558
PYP Coordinator Stacey Abeyta
Languages English
T: +1 707 253 3775
W: bape-nvusd-ca.schoolloop.com

Benjamin Franklin Elementary School
77-800 Calle Tampico, La Quinta CA 92253
PYP Coordinator Christina Winchester
Languages English
T: +1 760 238 9424
W: sites.google.com/a/desertsands.us/franklin-elem

Berkeley High School
1980 Allston Way, Berkeley CA 94704
DP Coordinator Keldon Clegg
Languages English
T: +1 510 644 6120
W: www.berkeleyschools.net/schools/high-schools/berkeley-high-school

Bishop Amat Memorial High School
14301 Fairgrove Avenue, La Puente CA 91746
DP Coordinator Jolene Joseph Pudvan
Languages English
T: +1 626 962 2495
W: www.bishopamat.org

Blair High School
1135 S. Euclid Avenue, Pasadena CA 91106
CP Coordinator Karen Favor
DP Coordinator Karen Law
MYP Coordinator Christine McLaughlin
Languages English
T: +1 626 396 5820
W: blair.pasadenausd.org
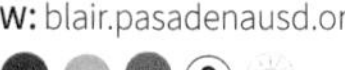

Bob Holcomb Elementary School
1345 W 48th St, San Bernardino CA 92407
PYP Coordinator Krista Bjur
Languages English
T: +1 909 887 2505

Bon View Elementary School
2121 S. Bon View Avenue, Ontario CA 91761
PYP Coordinator Shawnna Viramontes
Languages English
T: +1 909 947 3932
W: www.omsd.net/bonview

Bonita Vista High School
751 Otay Lakes Road, Chula Vista CA 91913
DP Coordinator Jared Phelps
Languages English
T: +1 619 397 2000
W: bvh.sweetwaterschools.org

Cajon High School
1200 Hill Drive, San Bernardino CA 92407
DP Coordinator Matthew Reisenhofer
MYP Coordinator Matthew Reisenhofer
Languages English
T: +1 909 881 8120

Caleb Greenwood Elementary School
5457 Carlson Drive, Sacramento CA 95819
PYP Coordinator Kelly Cordero Cordero
Languages English
T: +1 916 277 6266
W: www.scusd.edu/calebgreenwood

Camerado Springs Middle School
2480 Merrychase Drive, Cameron Park CA 95682
MYP Coordinator Amy Gargani
Languages English, Spanish
T: +1 530 677 1658
W: www.buckeyeusd.org/csms

Canyon High School
220 S Imperial Highway, Anaheim Hills CA 92807
DP Coordinator Nancy Belinge
Languages English
T: +1 714 532 8000
W: www.canyonhighschool.org

Canyon Springs High School
23100 Cougar Canyon Rd., Moreno Valley CA 92557
DP Coordinator Amanda Tornero
T: +1 951 571 4760
W: canyonsprings.mvusd.net
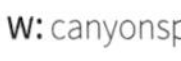

Capistrano Valley High School
26301 Via Escolar, Mission Viejo CA 92692
DP Coordinator Dina Kubba
Languages English
T: +1 949 364 6100
W: www.cvhs.com/

Capuchino High School
1501 Magnolia Avenue, San Bruno CA 94066
DP Coordinator Martee Lopez-Schmitt
Languages English
T: +1 650 558 2700
W: www.smuhsd.org/capuchinohigh

Carl Hankey K-8 School
27252 Nubles, Mission Viejo CA 92692
MYP Coordinator Kathy Beitz
PYP Coordinator Stacy Rumpf
Languages English
T: +1 949 234 5315
W: chhawks.schoolloop.com

Carpenter Elementary School
9439 Foster Road, Downey CA 90242
PYP Coordinator Shirley Barrera
Languages English, Spanish
T: +1 562 904 3588

Casita Center for Technology, Science & Math
260 Cedar Rd., Vista CA 92083
PYP Coordinator Elizabeth Weiser
Languages English
T: +1 760 724 8442

Castle Park High School
1395 Hilltop Drive, Chula Vista CA 91911
DP Coordinator Robert Manroe
Languages English
T: +1 619 585 2000
W: cph.sweetwaterschools.org

Castle Rock Elementary School
2975 Castle Rock Road, Diamond Bar CA 91765
PYP Coordinator Kelly Howard
Languages English
T: +1 909 598 5006
W: www.castlerockknights.org

Cathedral City High School
69250 Dinah Shore Drive, Cathedral City CA 92234
DP Coordinator Ed Perry
Languages English
T: +1 760 770 0100
W: catcityhigh.com

Centennial High School
1820 Rimpau Avenue, Corona CA 92881
DP Coordinator Colleen Lum
MYP Coordinator Sheila Nguyen
Languages English
T: +1 951 739 5670

Cesar E Chavez Middle School
6650 N Magnolia Avenue, San Bernardino CA 92407
MYP Coordinator Natasha Flores Naranjo
Languages English
T: +1 909 886 2050

Charter Oak High School
1430 E. Covina BLVD, Covina CA 91724
DP Coordinator Kathy Archer
Languages English
T: +1 626 915 5841
W: www.cousd.net/Domain/14

Citrus Hill High School
18150 Wood Rd., Perris CA 92570
DP Coordinator Andrea Williamson
Languages English
T: +1 951 460 0400
W: citrushill.valverde.edu

Claremont High School
1601 North Indian Hill Blvd, Claremont CA 91711
DP Coordinator Natalie Sieg
Languages English
T: +1 909 624 9053
W: chs-claremont-ca.schoolloop.com

Colfax High School
24995 Ben Taylor Rd, Colfax CA 95713
DP Coordinator Kara Diederichs
Languages English
T: +1 530 346 2284
W: sites.google.com/a/puhsd.k12.ca.us/colfax

Competitive Edge Charter Academy
34450 Stonewood Drive, Yucaipa CA 92399
MYP Coordinator Kristin Bernier
PYP Coordinator Jennifer Stahl
Languages English
T: +1 909 790 3207
W: ceca.yucaipaschools.com

Cook Elementary School
875 Cuyamaca Ave., Chula Vista CA 91911
PYP Coordinator Anthony Morales
Languages English
T: +1 619 422 8381
W: schools.cvesd.org/schools/cook

Cooper Academy
2277 W. Bellaire Way, Fresno CA 93705
MYP Coordinator Jayne Day
Languages English
T: +1 559 248 7050
W: www.fresnounified.org/schools/cooper

Cordova High School
2239 Chase Drive, Rancho Cordova CA 95670
CP Coordinator Chris Mahaffey
DP Coordinator Zandi Llanos
MYP Coordinator Grace Martinez
Languages English
T: +1 916 294 2450
W: www.fcusd.org/chs

Corona Fundamental Intermediate
1230 South Main Street, Corona CA 92882
MYP Coordinator Karen White
Languages English
T: +1 909 736 3321

Cypress Elementary School
4200 Kimber Drive, Newbury Park CA 91320
PYP Coordinator Danielle Barra
Languages English
T: +1 805 498 6683
W: www.conejousd.org/domain/289

Cyrus J Morris Elementary School
91785 E Calle Baja, Walnut CA 91789
PYP Coordinator Kelly Howard
Languages English
T: +1 909 594 0053
W: cjmorris.wvusd.k12.ca.us

Dailey Elementary Charter School
3135 N. Harrison Ave, Fresno CA 93704
PYP Coordinator Julia Cabrera
Languages English
T: +1 559 248 7060
W: fics.us/dailey

Damien High School
2280 Damien Avenue, La Verne CA 91750
CP Coordinator Angela Curry
Languages English
T: +1 909 596 1946
W: www.damien-hs.edu

David Starr Jordan High School
6500 Atlantic Avenue, Long Beach CA 90805
DP Coordinator Heather Banks
Languages English
T: +1 562 423 1471
W: www.lbjordan.schoolloop.com

Del Mar High School
1224 Del Mar Avenue, San Jose CA 95128
DP Coordinator Jessica Olamit
Languages English
T: +1 408 626 3403
W: www.delmar.cuhsd.org

Diamond Bar High School
21400 East Pathfinder Rd, Diamond Bar CA 91765
DP Coordinator Margaret Ku
Languages English
T: +1 909 594 1405
W: dbhs.wvusd.k12.ca.us

Dolores Huerta International Academy
17777 Merrill Avenue, Fontana CA 92335
PYP Coordinator Maria Dolores Delgado
Languages English, Spanish
T: +1 909 357 5070
W: www.fusd.net/dhia

Dos Pueblos High School
7266 Alameda Avenue, Goleta CA 93117
DP Coordinator Matt Moran
Languages English
T: +1 805 968 2541

Downtown Magnets High School
1081 W. Temple St, Los Angeles CA 90012
DP Coordinator Marilyn Watt
Languages English
T: +1 213 481 0371
W: www.downtownmagnets.org

Eagle Rock Junior/Senior High School
1750 Yosemite Drive, Los Angeles CA 90041
DP Coordinator Jonathan Malmed
MYP Coordinator Benjamin Elizondo
Languages English
T: +1 323 340 3500
W: www.erhs.la

East Bay German International School
1070 41st Street, Emeryville CA 94608
DP Coordinator Neil Hetrick
Languages English, German
T: +1 510 380 0301
W: www.ebgis.org

EDGEWOOD HIGH SCHOOL
1625 W Durness, West Covina CA 91790
CP Coordinator Veronica Perez
DP Coordinator Veronica Perez
MYP Coordinator Manny Co
Languages English
T: +1 626 939 4600
E: vperez@wcusd.org
W: edgewoodib.wcusd.org
See full details on page 465

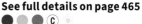

EDGEWOOD MIDDLE SCHOOL
1625 W. Durness St., West Covina CA 91790
MYP Coordinator Manny Co
Languages English, Spanish
T: +1 626 939 4600
E: kcabrera@wcusd.org
W: edgewoodib.wcusd.org
See full details on page 466

El Rancho High School
6501 S. Passons Blvd., Pico Rivera CA 90660
DP Coordinator Parvin Qureshi
Languages English, Spanish
T: +1 562 801 7500
W: www.erusd.k12.ca.us/elrancho

El Segundo Middle School
332 Center St., El Segundo CA 90245
MYP Coordinator Crystal Winner
Languages English, Spanish
T: +1 310 615 2690 EXT:1102
W: www.elsegundomiddleschool.org

El Sereno Middle School
2839 North Eastern Avenue, Los Angeles CA 90032
MYP Coordinator Jeannette Castro
Languages English
T: +1 323 224 4700
W: www.elserenoms.org

Ellen Ochoa Prep Academy
8110 Paramount Boulevard, Pico Rivera CA 90660
DP Coordinator Esmeralda Montoya
Languages English, Spanish
T: +1 562 801 7560
W: ochoaprep.erusd.org

Empowering Possibilities International Charter School
2945 Ramco Street, Ste. 200, West Sacramento CA 95691
MYP Coordinator Micah Hancock
PYP Coordinator Nina Semeryuk
Languages English, Russian
T: +1 916 286 1960
W: www.gccharters.org/epics
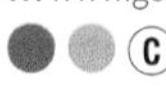

Escuela Bilingüe Internacional
410 Alcatraz Avenue, Oakland CA 94609
MYP Coordinator Jeniffer Cals
PYP Coordinator Talia Romero
Languages English
T: +1 510 653 3324
W: www.ebinternacional.org

Fairfax Senior High School
7850 Melrose Avenue, Los Angeles CA 90046
DP Coordinator Ariana Barker
Languages English, Spanish
T: +1 323 370 1200
W: www.fairfaxhs.org

Fairmont Private School of Fresno
435 W. Fairmont, Fresno CA 93705
PYP Coordinator Lydia Medina
Languages English, Spanish
T: +1 559 226 2347
W: www.fairmontprivateschool.com

Fairmont Private Schools - Historic Anaheim Campus
1557 W. Mable Street, Anaheim CA 92805
MYP Coordinator Karen O'Hanlon
PYP Coordinator Karen O'Hanlon
Languages English
T: +1 714 563 4050
W: www.fairmontschools.com/historic-anaheim-campus

Fairmont Private Schools - Preparatory Academy
2200 West Sequoia Avenue, Anaheim CA 92801
DP Coordinator Michael Wheeler
Languages English
T: +1 714 999 5055
W: www.fairmontprepacademy.com

Fallbrook High School
2400 S Stage Coach Lane, Fallbrook CA 92028
CP Coordinator George Herring
DP Coordinator George Herring
Languages English, Spanish
T: +1 760 723 6300
W: www.fallbrookhs.org

Farmdale Elementary School
2660 Ruth Swiggett Drive, Los Angeles CA 90032
PYP Coordinator Christina Dominguez
Languages English
T: +1 323 222 6659
W: farmdalees-lausd-ca.schoolloop.com

Foothill High School
19251 Dodge Avenue, Santa Ana CA 92705
DP Coordinator Katie Montgomery
Languages English
T: +1 714 730 7464
W: www.tustin.k12.ca.us/foothill

Frances E Willard Elementary Magnet School
301 South Madre Street, Pasadena CA 91107
PYP Coordinator Linda Wittry
Languages English
T: +1 626 793 6163
W: www.pusd.us/site/Default.aspx?PageID=41

Franklin High School
4600 E Fremont St, Stockton CA 95215
DP Coordinator Evelyn Reyes
MYP Coordinator Evelyn Reyes
Languages English
T: +1 209 933 7435
W: www.stocktonusd.net/franklin

French American International School & International High School
150 Oak Street, San Francisco CA 94102-5812
DP Coordinator Tessa Dalmedo
Languages English
T: +1 415 558 2000
W: www.internationalsf.org

Fresno High School
1839 N Echo Avenue, Fresno CA 93704
CP Coordinator Shabazz Keisha
DP Coordinator Kyra Orgill
MYP Coordinator Kyra Orgill
Languages English
T: +1 559 457 2793
W: go.fresnounified.org/fresno

Fullerton Union High School
201 E. Chapman Ave, Fullerton CA 92832
DP Coordinator Mark Henderson
Languages English
T: +1 714 626 3800
W: www.fullertonhigh.org

Gateway International School
900 Morse Avenue, Sacramento CA 95864
MYP Coordinator Dara Patel
PYP Coordinator Adrian Peer
Languages English
T: +1 916 286 1985
W: gischarter.org

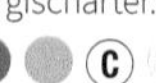

George Sargeant Elementary
1200 Ridgecrest Way, Roseville CA 95661
PYP Coordinator Regina DeArcos
Languages English
T: +1 916 771 1800
W: sargeant.rcsdk8.org

Glen A Wilson High School
16455 East Wedgeworth Drive, Hacienda Heights CA 91745
DP Coordinator Christina Rouw
Languages English
T: +1 626 934 4401

Goethe International Charter School
12500 Braddock Dr, Los Angeles CA 90066
PYP Coordinator Angel Truong
Languages English, German
T: +1 310 306 3484
W: goethecharterschool.org

Granada High School
400 Wall Street, Livermore CA 94550
DP Coordinator Jon Cariveau
Languages English
T: +1 925 606 4800
W: www.granadahigh.com

Granada Hills Charter High School
10535 Zelzah Avenue, Granada Hills CA 91344
DP Coordinator Sean Lewis
MYP Coordinator Victoria Marzouk
PYP Coordinator Laura Hanley
Languages English
T: +1 818 360 2361
W: www.ghchs.com

Granada Preparatory School
10400 Zelzah Avenue, Northridge CA 91326
MYP Coordinator Erica Berg Fonvergne
PYP Coordinator Paulette Collins
Languages English
T: +1 818 368 7254
W: www.gpsschool.org
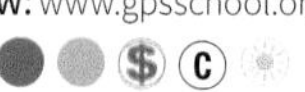

Granite Bay High School
1 Grizzly Way, Granite Bay CA 95746
DP Coordinator Bernadette Cranmer
Languages English
T: +1 916 786 8676
W: granitebayhigh.org

Granite Hills High School
1719 East Madison Avenue, El Cajon CA 92021
DP Coordinator Matthew Davis
Languages English
T: +1 619 593 5500

Great Oak High School
32555 Deer Hollow Road, Temecula CA 92592
DP Coordinator Melissa Casady
Languages English
T: +1 951 294 6450
W: gohs.tvusd.k12.ca.us

IB AMERICAS

Grover Beach Elementary School
365 South Tenth Street, Grover Beach CA 93433
PYP Coordinator Alissa Mohr
Languages English
T: +1 805 474 3770
W: groverbeach.luciamarschools.org

Guajome Park Academy
2000 North Santa Fe Avenue, Vista Unified School District, Vista CA 92083
CP Coordinator Melissa Ritchie
DP Coordinator Juan Solano
Languages English
T: +1 760 631 5000
W: www.guajome.net/gppa

Guide Academy
121 S. Citron Street, Anaheim CA 92805
MYP Coordinator Mina Hosseini
Languages English, Arabic
T: +1 714 603 7811
W: guideacademy.org

H. Allen Hight Elementary School
3200 North Park Dr., Sacramento CA 95835
PYP Coordinator Cody Worrall
Languages English
T: +1 916 567 5700
W: www.natomasunified.org/hah

H. Clarke Powers Elementary School
3296 Humphrey Road, Loomis CA 95650
MYP Coordinator Rebecca Connolly
PYP Coordinator Rebecca Connolly
Languages English
T: +1 916 652 2635
W: www.powers.loomis-usd.k12.ca.us

Harbor High School
300 La Fonda Ave., Santa Cruz CA 95062
DP Coordinator Kim Lenz
Languages English
T: +1 831 429 3810

Harding University Partnership School
1625 Robbins Street, Santa Barbara CA 93101
PYP Coordinator Mikaela Burkett
Languages English
T: +1 805 965 8994
W: harding.sbunified.org

Harriet G. Eddy Middle School
9329 Soaring Oaks Drive, Elk Grove CA 95758
MYP Coordinator Carolynn Puccioni
Languages English
T: +1 916 683 1302

Hawthorne Elementary School
705 W. Hawthorne, Ontario CA 91762
PYP Coordinator Elizabeth Alapizco
Languages English
T: +1 909 986 6582
W: www.omsd.net/Hawthorne

Horace Mann School
55 North 7th Street, San Jose CA 95112
PYP Coordinator Sophia Rueda
Languages English
T: +1 408 535 6237
W: mann.sjusd.org

Hubert Howe Bancroft Middle School
323 N. Las Palmas Avenue, Los Angeles CA 90023
MYP Coordinator Ryan Sutton
Languages English
T: +1 323 993 3400
W: bancroftmiddleschool.org

iLEAD Agua Dulce
11311 Frascati Street, Agua Dulce CA 91390
CP Coordinator Angie Nastovska
Languages English, Spanish
T: +1 661 268 6386
W: ileadaguadulce.org

Imperial Middle School
1450 S. Schoolwood Drive, La Habra CA 90631
MYP Coordinator Carole Mortl
Languages English
T: +1 562 690 2344
W: www.lahabraschools.org/imperial

Inderkum High School
2500 New Market Drive, Sacramento CA 95835
DP Coordinator Jessica Downing
MYP Coordinator Theresa Quinby
Languages English
T: +1 916 567 5640
W: natomasunified.org/ihs

INTERNATIONAL SCHOOL OF LOS ANGELES
1105 W. Riverside Drive, Burbank CA 91506
DP Coordinator Donald Buer
Languages English, French
T: +1 626 695 5159
E: admissions@lilaschool.com
W: www.internationalschool.la
See full details on page 480

International School of Monterey
1720 Yosemite Street, Seaside CA 93955
MYP Coordinator Rick Barlow
PYP Coordinator Rick Barlow
Languages English
T: +1 831 583 2165
W: ISMonterey.org

James A Foshay Learning Center
3751 S. Harvard Blvd., Los Angeles CA 90018
MYP Coordinator Esther Lee
PYP Coordinator Danielle Mabry
Languages English
T: +1 323 373 2700
W: www.foshaylc.org

Jefferson Elementary School
3743 Jefferson Street, Carlsbad CA 92009
PYP Coordinator Christy Haeberlein
Languages English
T: +1 760 331 5500
W: jefferson.schoolloop.com

Jefferson School
2001 Pebblewood Drive, Sacramento CA 95833
PYP Coordinator Mary Rimbey
Languages English, Spanish
T: +1 916 567 5580
W: natomasunified.org/jfs

Joe Michell K-8 School
1001 Elaine Ave, Livermore CA 94550
MYP Coordinator Ezgi Booth
PYP Coordinator Ezgi Booth
Languages English
T: +1 925 606 4738
W: www.livermoreschools.org/michell

John F Kennedy High School
8281 Walker Street, La Palma CA 90623
DP Coordinator Caylin Ledterman
Languages English
T: +1 714 220 4118

John Glenn Middle School
79-655 Miles Avenue, DSUSD, Indio CA 92201
MYP Coordinator James Harper
Languages English
T: +1 760 200 3700
W: www.dsusd.k12.ca.us/schools/JGMS

John W. North High School
1550 Third St., Riverside CA 92507
DP Coordinator Christine Schive
Languages English
T: +1 951 788 7311

Jurupa Hills High School
10700 Oleander Avenue, Fontana CA 92337
DP Coordinator Kelly Navas
MYP Coordinator Denise Kohler
Languages English
T: +1 909 357 6300
W: www.jhills.org

Kate Sessions Elementary School
2150 Beryl Street, San Diego CA 92109
PYP Coordinator Dianne Bermudez
Languages English
T: +1 858 273 3111
W: www.sandiegounified.org/sessions

Kavod Charter School
6991 Balboa Ave., San Diego CA 92111
MYP Coordinator Todd McKeown
Languages English, Hebrew
T: +1 858 386 0887
W: kavodelementary.org

Kit Carson Middle School
5301 N Street, Sacramento CA 95819
DP Coordinator Shawn D'Alesandro
MYP Coordinator Shawn D'Alesandro
Languages English
T: +1 916 277 6750
W: www.kitcarson.scusd.edu

La Costa Canyon High School
1 Maverick Way, Carlsbad CA 92009
DP Coordinator Cindi Schildhouse
Languages English
T: +1 760 436 6136
W: lc.sduhsd.net

La Quinta High School
79-255 Westward Ho Drive, La Quinta CA 92253
DP Coordinator Elizabeth Van Dorn
Languages English
T: +1 760 772 4150
W: www.dsusd.k12.ca.us/schools/LQHS/

LA SCUOLA INTERNATIONAL SCHOOL
3250 18th Street, San Francisco CA 94110
MYP Coordinator Yarrow Ulehman
PYP Coordinator Leticia O'Sullivan
Languages English, Italian And Spanish
T: +1 415 551 0000
E: admissions@lascuolasf.org
W: www.lascuolasf.org
See full details on page 484

Laguna Creek High School
9050 Vicino Drive, Elk Grove CA 95758
DP Coordinator Rod De Luca
MYP Coordinator Jose Oseguera
Languages English
T: +1 916 683 1339
W: www.egusd.net/schools/high-schools/laguna-creek-high-school

Laguna Hills High School
25401 Paseo de Valencia, Laguna Hills CA 92653
DP Coordinator Laurel Crossett
Languages English
T: +1 949 770 5447
W: www.svusd.org/schools/high-schools/laguna-hills

Las Positas Elementary School
1400 S. Schoolwood Drive, La Habra CA 90631
PYP Coordinator Dana Riggs
Languages English
T: +1 562 690 2356
W: www.lahabraschools.org/laspositas

Letha Raney Intermediate
1010 West Citron Street, Corona CA 92882
MYP Coordinator Bronya Martinez
Languages English
T: +1 951 736 3221

Lexington Elementary School
19700 Old Santa Cruz Highway, Los Gatos CA 95033
PYP Coordinator Kristin Johnson
Languages English
T: +1 408 335 2150
W: lex.lgusd.org

Linda Vista Magnet Elementary School
25222 Pericia Drive, Mission Viejo CA 92691
PYP Coordinator Tricia Gray
Languages English, Spanish
T: +1 949 830 0970
W: www.svusd.org/schools/elementary-a-l/linda-vista

Loomis Basin Charter School
5438 Laird Road, Loomis CA 95650
MYP Coordinator Karen Long
PYP Coordinator Karen Long
Languages English
T: +1 916 652 2642
W: www.loomischarter.org

Luther Burbank High School
3500 Florin Road, Sacramento CA 95823
DP Coordinator Katherine Bell
Languages English
W: lutherburbank.scusd.edu

Marco Antonio Firebaugh High School
5246 Martin Luther King Jr. Blvd, Lynwood CA 90262
DP Coordinator Dayrin Flores
Languages English
T: +1 310 886 5200
W: fhs.lynwood.k12.ca.us

Maxwell Academy
733 Euclid Avenue, Duarte CA 91010
MYP Coordinator Johna Stienstra
PYP Coordinator Johna Stienstra
Languages English
T: +1 626 599 5302
W: www.duarteusd.org/page/156

Mira Loma High School
4000 Edison Avenue, Sacramento CA 95821
CP Coordinator Marcy Alexander
DP Coordinator Rochelle Jacks
MYP Coordinator Rachel Volzer
Languages English
T: +1 916 971 7465
W: miraloma.sanjuan.edu

Mission Bay High School
2475 Grand Ave., San Diego CA 92109
DP Coordinator Tracy Borg
Languages English
T: +1 858 273 1313
W: www.sandi.net/missionbay

Mission Viejo High School
25025 Chrisanta Drive, Mission Viejo CA 9269
DP Coordinator Sandra Hanneman
Languages English
T: +1 949 837 7722
W: www.svusd.org/schools/high-schools/mission-viejo

Modesto High School
First & H Street, Modesto City Schools, Modesto CA 95351
DP Coordinator Kerry Castellani
Languages English
T: +1 209 576 4404

Monte Vista Christian School
2 School Way, Watsonville CA 95076
DP Coordinator Laramie Holtzclaw
MYP Coordinator Amber West
Languages English
T: +1 831 722 8178
W: www.mvcs.org

Monterey High School
101 Herrmann Drive, Monterey CA 93940
DP Coordinator Nikki Ahrenstorff
MYP Coordinator Nikki Ahrenstorff
Languages English, Spanish
T: +1 831 392 3801
W: montereyhigh.mpusd.net
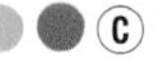

Montgomery High School
1250 Hahman Drive, Santa Rosa CA 95405
DP Coordinator Jim Rudesill
Languages English
T: +1 707 528 5512
W: www.montgomeryhighschool.com

Murrieta Valley High School
42200 Nighthawk Way, Murrieta CA 92562
DP Coordinator Alanna Fields
Languages English
T: +1 951 696 1408
W: www.murrieta.k12.ca.us/Domain/1416

Muwekma Ohlone Middle School
850 North Second Street, San Jose CA 95112
MYP Coordinator April Gaylord
Languages English
T: +1 408 535 6267
W: ohlone.sjusd.org

Natomas Middle School
3200 North Park Drive, Sacramento CA 95835
MYP Coordinator Cody Worrall
Languages English
T: +1 916 567 5540
W: natomasunified.org/nms

New Covenant Academy
3119 W 6th Street, Los Angeles CA 90020
DP Coordinator Salvador Torres
Languages English
T: +1 213 487 5437
W: www.e-nca.org

Newbury Park High School
456 Reino Road, Newbury Park CA 91320
DP Coordinator Deborah Dogançay
Languages English
T: +1 805 498 3676
W: dev.nphs.org

Newport Harbor High School
600 Irvine Avenue, Newport Beach CA 92663
DP Coordinator Alma Di Giorgio
Languages English
T: +1 949 515 6300
W: nhhs.schoolloop.com

Nogales High School
401 Nogales Street, Rowland Unified School Distric, La Puente CA 91744
DP Coordinator Clay Woodside
Languages English
T: +1 626 965 3437

Norte Vista High School
6585 Crest Avenue, Riverside CA 92503
DP Coordinator Shawn Marshall
Languages English
T: +1 951 351 9316
W: www.alvord.k12.ca.us/nortevista

Northcoast Preparatory Academy
285 Bayside Rd, 1761 11th St., Arcata CA 95521
DP Coordinator Amy Bazemore
MYP Coordinator Amy Bazemore
Languages English
T: +1 707 822 0861

Oakmont High School
1710 Cirby Way, Roseville CA 95661
DP Coordinator Jolie Geluk
Languages English
T: +1 916 782 3781
W: ohs.rjuhsd.us

Ocean Knoll Elementary School
910 Melba Road, Encinitas CA 92024
PYP Coordinator Sanjana Bryant
Languages English
T: +1 760 944 4351
W: www.eusd.net/ok

Ocean View High School
17071 Gothard St., Huntington Beach CA 92647
DP Coordinator Brenda Mcdonough
Languages English
T: +1 714 848 0656
W: www.ovhs.info

ORANGEWOOD ELEMENTARY
1440 S. Orange Avenue, West Covina CA 91790
PYP Coordinator Mrs. Candice Hernandez
Languages English, Spanish, Mandarin
T: +1 626 939 4820
W: orangewood.wcusd.org
See full details on page 500

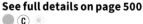

Pacific Beach Middle School
4676 Ingraham Street, San Diego CA 92109
MYP Coordinator Ashley Hensen
Languages English
T: +1 858 273 9070
W: www.sandiegounified.org/schools/pacific-beach-middle

Palmdale Learning Plaza
38043 Division Street, Palmdale CA 93551
MYP Coordinator Wynne May
PYP Coordinator Wynne May
Languages English
T: +1 661 538 9034
W: www.palmdalesd.org/Page/4471

Paso Verde School
3800 Del Paso Rd, Sacramento CA 95834
MYP Coordinator Kristen Martin
PYP Coordinator Kristen Martin
Languages English, Spanish
T: +1 916 567 5810
W: natomasunified.org/pvs

Pinole Valley High School
2900 Pinole Valley Rd, Pinole CA 94564
DP Coordinator Dayna Dibble
Languages English
T: +1 510 231 1442
W: www.wccusd.net/pinolevalley

Prepa Tec Middle School
6005 Stafford Ave., Huntington Park CA 90255
MYP Coordinator Vanessa Garcia
Languages English
T: +1 323 800 2738
W: altapublicschools.org

Primary Years Academy
1540 N.Lincoln St, Stockton CA 95204
PYP Coordinator Hina Lee
Languages English
T: +1 209 933 7355
W: www.stocktonusd.net/PYA

Quarry Lane School
6363 Tassajara Road, Dublin CA 94568
DP Coordinator Jyothi Kiran Hoskere
Languages English
T: +1 925 829 8000
W: www.quarrylane.org

Quartz Hill High School
6040 West Avenue L, Quartz Hill CA 93536
DP Coordinator Jeff Cassady
Languages English
T: +1 661 718 3100

Rancho Buena Vista High School
1601 Longhorn Drive, Vista CA 92081
DP Coordinator Melissa Neumann
Languages English
T: +1 760 727 7284

Ray Wiltsey Middle School
1450 E., Ontario CA 91764
MYP Coordinator Terri Bradley
Languages English
T: +1 909 986 5838
W: www.omsd.net/Wiltsey

Rio Mesa High School
545 Central Avenue, Oxnard CA 93030
CP Coordinator Ingrid Brennan
DP Coordinator Rano Sidhu
MYP Coordinator Marleen Gracom
Languages English
T: +1 805 278 5500
W: www.riomesahigh.us

Roosevelt Middle School
3366 Park Blvd., San Diego CA 92103
MYP Coordinator Deborah Christensen
Languages English
T: +1 619 293 4450
W: www.sandiegounified.org/roosevelt

Rowland High School
2000 S Otterbein Avenue, Rowland Heights CA 91748
DP Coordinator Stephen Ludlam
Languages English
T: +1 626 965 3448
W: www.rowlandhs.org

Royal High School
1402 Royal Avenue, Simi Valley CA 93065
DP Coordinator Kari Lev
Languages English
T: +1 805 306 4875 EXT:1
W: www.rhs.simi.k12.ca.us

Running Springs Academy
8670 E. Running Springs Drive, Anaheim CA 92808
PYP Coordinator Brandi Gower
Languages English
T: +1 714 281 4512
W: www.orangeusd.org/running-springs

Saddleback High School
2802 South Flower Street, Santa Ana CA 92707
DP Coordinator Heather LaBare
Languages English
T: +1 714 569 6300
W: www.sausd.us/saddleback

San Clemente High School
700 Avenida Pico, San Clemente CA 92673
DP Coordinator Allison Shick
Languages English
T: +1 949 492 4165

San Diego High School of International Studies
1405 Park Boulevard, San Diego CA 92101
DP Coordinator Nirit Cohen-Vardi
Languages English
T: +1 619 525 7455
W: www.sandiegounified.org/sdhsis

San Jacinto Elementary
136 N. Ramona Blvd., San Jacinto CA 92583
PYP Coordinator Stacy Ward
Languages English
T: +1 951 654 7349
W: sjes.sanjacinto.k12.ca.us

San Jacinto High School
500 Idyllwild Drive, San Jacinto CA 92583
DP Coordinator Matthew Corum
Languages English
T: +1 951 654 7374
W: sjhs.sanjacinto.k12.ca.us

San Jacinto Valley Academy
480 N San Jacinto Avenue, San Jacinto CA 92583
DP Coordinator Marissa Espinosa
PYP Coordinator Kelly Perez
Languages English
T: +1 951 654 6113
W: www.sjva.net

San Jose High School
275 North 24th St., San Jose CA 95116-1109
CP Coordinator Ryan Jahrman
DP Coordinator Ryan Jahrman
MYP Coordinator Ryan Jahrman
Languages English
T: +1 408 535 6320
W: sjhs.sjusd.org

  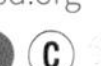

Santa Clarita Valley International School
28060 Hasley Canyon, Castaic CA 91384
DP Coordinator Matthew Wayne
Languages English
T: +1 661 705 4820
W: www.scvcharterschool.org

Santa Margarita Catholic High School
22062 Antonio Parkway, Rancho Santa Margarita CA 92688
DP Coordinator Maria D.S. Andrade Johnson
Languages English
T: +1 949 766 6000
W: www.smhs.org

Schools of the Sacred Heart
2222 Broadway, San Francisco CA 94115
DP Coordinator Devin DeMartini
Languages English
T: +1 415 563 2900
W: www.sacredsf.org

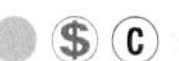

Scotts Valley High School
Principal, 555 Glenwood Drive, Scotts Valley CA 95066
DP Coordinator John Postovit
Languages English
T: +1 831 439 9555

Sequoia Elementary School
277 Boyd Road, Pleasant Hill CA 94523
PYP Coordinator Aline Lee
Languages English, Chinese
T: +1 925 935 5721
W: sees-mdusd-ca.schoolloop.com

Sequoia High School
1201 Brewster Avenue, Redwood City CA 94062
DP Coordinator Lisa McCahon
Languages English
T: +1 650 369 1411
W: www.sequoiahs.org

Short Avenue Elementary School
12814 Maxella Ave, Los Angeles CA 90066
PYP Coordinator Rachel Burris
Languages English, Spanish
T: +1 310 397 4234
W: www.shortavenue.org

Shu Ren International School
2125 Jefferson Avenue, Berkeley CA 94703
PYP Coordinator Alexandra Ditchey
Languages English, Mandarin
T: +1 510 841 8899
W: shurenschool.org

Sierra Elementary School
6811 Camborne Way, Rocklin CA 95677
PYP Coordinator Lisa Johnson
Languages English
T: +1 916 788 7141
W: ses.rocklinusd.org

IB AMERICAS

Sonora High School
401 South Palm Street, Fullerton Joint Union, La Habra CA 90631
DP Coordinator Shannon Appenrodt
Languages English
T: +1 562 266 2013

South Hills High School
645 S. Barranca Street, West Covina CA 91791
DP Coordinator Marisol Marquez
Languages English
T: +1 626 974 6200
W: www.southhillshigh.com

Southridge Tech Middle School
14500 Live Oak Avenue, Fontana CA 92337
MYP Coordinator Monysa Pollard
Languages English, Spanish
T: +1 909 357 5420
W: www.fusd.net/Southridgetech

Southwest High School
2001 Ocotillo Drive, El Centro CA 92243
DP Coordinator Marina Corral
Languages English
T: +1 760 336 4100
W: www.eaglesnet.net

St. Francis of Assisi Elementary School
2500 K Street, Sacramento CA 95816
MYP Coordinator Sharon Pressburg-Nevans
PYP Coordinator Isabel Garcia
Languages English
T: +1 916 442 5494
W: www.stfranciselem.org

St. Mary's School
7 Pursuit, Aliso Viejo CA 92656
MYP Coordinator Jillian Kearney
PYP Coordinator Lauren Sterner
Languages English
T: +1 949 448 9027
W: www.smaa.org

Stanley G Oswalt Academy
19501 Shadow Oak Drive, Walnut CA 91789
PYP Coordinator Raquel Bahena
Languages English
T: +1 626 810 4109
W: oswalt.rowlandschools.org

Stockton Collegiate International Elementary School
321 E. Weber Ave, Stockton CA 95202
PYP Coordinator John Piasecki
Languages English
T: +1 209 390 9861
W: www.stocktoncollegiate.org

Stockton Collegiate International Secondary School
PO Box 2286, Stockton CA 95201
DP Coordinator Manuel Aguilar
MYP Coordinator Hauna Zaich
Languages English
T: +1 209 464 7108
W: www.stocktoncollegiate.org

Stowers Magnet School of International Studies
13350 Beach Street, Cerritos CA 90703
PYP Coordinator Sharie Tom
Languages English
T: +1 562 229 7905
W: www.stowerses.us

Summit Charter Academy
1509 Lombardi Street, Porterville CA 93257
PYP Coordinator Shana Watson
Languages English
T: +1 559 788 6445
W: www.summitlombardi.org

Summit Charter Collegiate Academy
15550 Redwood Drive, Porterville CA 93257
MYP Coordinator Jenifer Sanders
Languages English, Spanish
T: +1 559 788 6440
W: www.summitcollegiate.org

Sunny Hills High School
1801 Warburton Way, Fullerton CA 92833
DP Coordinator Brian Wall
Languages English
T: +1 714 626 4213
W: www.sunnyhills.net

Temescal Canyon High School
28755 El Toro Road, Lake Elsinore CA 92532
DP Coordinator Jason Garrison
Languages English
T: +1 951 253 7250
W: tch.leusd.k12.ca.us

The Healdsburg School
33H Healdsburg Avenue, Healdsburg CA 95448
PYP Coordinator Jami Trinidad
Languages English
T: +1 707 433 4847
W: www.thehealdsburgschool.org

Thomas Jefferson Elementary School
3770 Utah Street, San Diego CA 92104
PYP Coordinator Erin Knight
Languages English
T: +1 619 344 3300
W: www.sandiegounified.org/jefferson

Thomas Kelly Elementary School
6301 Moraga Drive, Carmichael CA 95608
PYP Coordinator Deb Olivarria-Matson
Languages English
T: +1 916 867 2401
W: www.sanjuan.edu/kelly

Trabuco Hills High School
27501 Mustang Run, Mission Viejo CA 92691
DP Coordinator Lindsay Casserly
Languages English
T: +1 949 768 1934

Tracy Joint Union High School
315 East 11th Street, Tracy Public Schools, Tracy CA 95376
DP Coordinator Jeff Alexandre
Languages English
T: +1 209 830 3360
W: tracyhigh.tracy.k12.ca.us

Troy High School
2200 East Dorothy Lane, Fullerton CA 92831
DP Coordinator Charlotte Kirkpatrick
Languages English
T: +1 714 626 4401
W: www.troyhigh.com

Valencia High School
500 N Bradford Avenue, Placentia CA 92870
DP Coordinator Fred Jenkins
Languages English
T: +1 714 996 4970

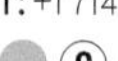

Valley Preparatory School
1605 Ford Street, Redlands CA 92373
PYP Coordinator Melanie Whitenack
Languages English, Spanish
T: +1 909 793 3063
W: www.valleyprepredlands.org

Valley View Charter Montessori
1665 Blackstone Parkway, El Dorado Hills CA 95762
MYP Coordinator Amy Gargani
Languages English, Spanish
T: +1 916 939 9640
W: www.buckeyeusd.org/vvcm

Villanova Preparatory School
12096 N. Ventura Avenue, Ojai CA 93023
DP Coordinator Brian Roney
Languages English
T: +1 805 646 1464
W: www.villanovaprep.org

Vista Academy of Visual and Performing Arts
600 N. Santa Fe Avenue, Vista CA 92083
PYP Coordinator Sharon Scott-Gonzalez
Languages English
T: +1 760 941 0880

Vista Heights Middle School
23049 Old Lake Drive, Moreno Valley CA 92557
MYP Coordinator Jill Dayton
Languages English, Spanish
T: +1 951 571 4300
W: vistaheights.mvusd.net

Vista High School
1 Panther Way, Vista CA 92084
DP Coordinator Michael Pink
Languages English
T: +1 760 726 5611
W: vhs.vistausd.org

Vista Magnet Middle School
151 Civic Center Dr, Vista CA 92084
MYP Coordinator Amy Sapau
Languages English
T: +1 760 726 5766

W.E. Mitchell Middle School
2100 Zinfandel Drive, Rancho Cordova CA 95670
MYP Coordinator Suzanne Titchenal
Languages English
T: +1 916 635 8460
W: www.fcusd.org/mitchell

Walnut High School
400 N Pierre Rd, Walnut CA 91789
CP Coordinator Manette Idris
DP Coordinator Manette Idris
Languages English
T: +1 909 594 1333

Walter Colton Middle School
100 Toda Vista, Monterey CA 93940
MYP Coordinator Anne Davis
Languages English
T: +1 831 649 1951
W: wcms.mpusd.net

Warren T. Eich Middle School
1509 Sierra Gardens Drive, Roseville CA 95661-4804
MYP Coordinator Lisa Shrider
Languages English
T: +1 916 771 1770
W: eich.rcsdk8.org

West County Mandarin School
1575 Mann Drive, Pinole CA 94564
PYP Coordinator Leixia Liu
Languages English, Chinese
T: +1 510 307 4523
W: wcmspta.org

West Valley High School
3401 Mustang Way, Hemet CA 92545
DP Coordinator Ahmed El-Sayad
Languages English, Spanish
T: +1 951 765 1600
W: www.wvhsmustangs.net

Will Rogers Learning Community
2401 14th Street, Santa Monica CA 90405
PYP Coordinator Laura Simon
Languages English, Spanish
T: +1 310 452 2364
W: www.smmusd.org/rogers

William F McKinley Elementary School
3045 Felton Street, San Diego CA 92104
PYP Coordinator Roni Greenwood
Languages English
T: +1 619 282 7694
W: www.sandiegounified.org/mckinley

Winston Churchill Middle School
4900 Whitney Avenue, Carmicheal CA 95608
MYP Coordinator Kristen Manchester
Languages English
T: +1 916 971 7324

Woodrow Wilson High School
4500 Multnomah Street, Los Angeles CA 90032
DP Coordinator Erica Welsh-Westfall
MYP Coordinator Ashley Englander
Languages English
T: +1 323 276 1600
W: www.ibwilsonmules.com

Ybarra Academy of the Arts & Technology
1300 Brea Canyon Cut-off Road, Walnut CA 91789
PYP Coordinator Jacquie Robinson
Languages English, Spanish
T: +1 909 598 3744
W: ybarra.rowlandschools.org

Ygnacio Valley High School
755 Oak Grove Road, Concord CA 94518
DP Coordinator Carissa Weintraub
Languages English
T: +1 925 685 8414
W: yvhs.mdusd.org

Yosemite High School
50200 Road 427, Oakhurst CA 93644
DP Coordinator Arlene Aoki
Languages English
T: +1 559 683 4667
W: www.yosemiteusd.com/yosemite

Colorado

Academy International Elementary School
8550 Charity Drive, Colorado Springs CO 80920
PYP Coordinator Katherine Scott
Languages English
T: +1 719 234 4000
W: academyinternational.asd20.org/Pages/default.aspx

Alameda International High School
1255 S. Wadsworth Blvd., Lakewood CO 80232
CP Coordinator Steve Houwen
DP Coordinator Merinda Sautel
MYP Coordinator Erin Murphy
Languages English
T: +1 303 982 8160

Alpine Elementary School
2005 Alpine Street, Longmont CO 80504
PYP Coordinator Robert Roy
Languages English
T: +1 720 652 8140
W: aes.svvsd.org

Antelope Trails Elementary
15280 Jessie Drive, Colorado Springs CO 80921
PYP Coordinator Tia Guillan
Languages English
T: +1 719 234 4100
W: antelopetrails.asd20.org

Aspen High School
235 High School Road, Aspen CO 81611
DP Coordinator Eileen Knapp
MYP Coordinator Sarah After
Languages English
T: +1 970 925 3760
W: ahs.aspenk12.net

Aspen Middle School
235 High School Road, Aspen CO 81611
MYP Coordinator Sarah After
Languages English
T: +1 970 925 3760
W: ams.aspenk12.net

Aurora Hills Middle School
1009 S Uvalda, Aurora CO 80012
MYP Coordinator Sue Wagoner
Languages English
T: +1 303 341 7450
W: ahills.aurorak12.org

Bear Valley International School
3005 South Golden Way, Denver CO 80227
MYP Coordinator Alberto Martinez
Languages English
T: +1 720 423 9600

Bennett Elementary School
1125 Bennett Road, Fort Collins CO 80521
PYP Coordinator Kurt Woolner
Languages English
T: +1 970 488 4750
W: ben.psdschools.org

Boulder Country Day School
4820 Nautilus Court North, Boulder CO 80301
MYP Coordinator Gwynn Reback
Languages English
T: +1 303 527 4931
W: www.bouldercountryday.org

Bradley International School
3051 S. Elm St., Denver CO 80222
PYP Coordinator Jodie Leatherman
Languages English
T: +1 720 424 9468

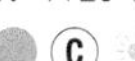

Breckenridge Elementary School
312 S. Harris Street, PO Box 1213, Breckenridge CO 80424
PYP Coordinator Kelley Fletcher
Languages English, Spanish
T: +1 970 368 1300
W: bre.summitk12.org

Brentwood Middle School
2600 24th Avenue Court, Greeley CO 80634
MYP Coordinator Lisa McGee
T: +1 970 348 3000
W: www.greeleyschools.org/domain/24

Brown International Academy
2550 Lowell Boulevard, Denver CO 80211
PYP Coordinator Melissa Capozza
Languages English
T: +1 720 424 9287

Cache La Poudre Elementary School
3511 W. County Rd., Laporte CO 80535
PYP Coordinator Mandy Parton
Languages English
T: +1 970 488 7600
W: cpe.psdschools.org

Cache La Poudre Middle School
3511 W. County Rd. 54 G, La Porte CO 80535
MYP Coordinator Delhia Mahaney
Languages English
T: +1 970 488 7400
W: clp.psdschools.org

Centaurus High School
10300 E South Boulder Road, Lafayette CO 80026
DP Coordinator Johanna Wintergerst
Languages English
T: +1 720 561 7500
W: www.centaurushs.org

Central Elementary School
1020 4th Avenue, Longmont CO 80501
PYP Coordinator Hillary Simonson
Languages English
T: +1 303 776 3236
W: centrales.svvsd.org

Century Middle School
13000 Lafayette Street, Thornton CO 80241
MYP Coordinator Jennifer Viers
Languages English
T: +1 720 972 5240
W: century.adams12.org

Charles Hay World School
3195 S Layfayette Street, Englewood CO 80113
PYP Coordinator Leah Meier
Languages English
T: +1 303 761 2433
W: www.englewoodschools.net/schools/charles-hay-world-school

Cherokee Trail High School
25901 E Arapahoe Road, Aurora CO 80016
DP Coordinator Karen Slusher
Languages English
T: +1 720 886 1900
W: www.cherrycreekschools.org/cherokeetrail

Corwin International Magnet School
1500 Lakeview Ave., Pueblo CO 81004
MYP Coordinator Cassie Pate
PYP Coordinator Jaime Quinn
Languages English
T: +1 719 549 7400
W: cims.pueblocityschools.us

Coyote Ridge Elementary School
7115 Avondale Road, Fort Collins CO 80525
PYP Coordinator Jennifer Bozic
Languages English
T: +1 970 679 9400
W: www.thompsonschools.org/coyoteridge

Dakota Ridge High School
13399 West Coal Mine Avenue, Littleton CO 80127
DP Coordinator Holly Davis
Languages English
T: +1 303 982 1970

Dillon Valley Elementary School
P.O. Box 4788, 0108 Deerpath, Dillon CO 80435
PYP Coordinator Jaime Levi
Languages English
T: +1 970 368 1400
W: dve.summitk12.org

Discovery Canyon Campus
1810 North Gate Blvd, Colorado Springs CO 80921
CP Coordinator Melissa Knight
DP Coordinator Melissa Knight
MYP Coordinator Alisa Schleder
PYP Coordinator Autumn Cave-Crosby
Languages English
T: +1 719 234 1800
W: dccelementary.asd20.org/Pages/default.aspx

Dos Rios Elementary School
2201 34th Street, Evans CO 80620
PYP Coordinator Katherine Dickinson
Languages English
T: +1 970 348 1309
W: www.greeleyschools.org/dosrios

Douglas County High School
2842 Front Street, Castle Rock CO 80104
DP Coordinator Steven Fleet
MYP Coordinator Christine Veto
Languages English
T: +1 303 387 1004

Dunn Elementary School
501 South Washington, Fort Collins CO 80521
PYP Coordinator Esther Croak
Languages English
T: +1 970 482 0450

Eagle Valley Elementary School
PO Box 780, Eagle CO 81631
PYP Coordinator Anita ortiz
Languages English, Spanish
T: +1 970 328 6981
W: www.eagleschools.net/schools/eagle-valley-elementary

East Middle School
1275 Fraser Street, Aurora CO 80011
MYP Coordinator Dale Krueger
Languages English
T: +1 303 340 0660
W: east.aurorak12.org

Elkhart Elementary School
1020 Eagle Street, Aurora CO 80011
PYP Coordinator Michelle Karp
Languages English
T: +1 303 340 3050
W: elkhart.aurorak12.org

Fairview High School
1515 Greenbriar Blvd., Boulder CO 80305-7043
DP Coordinator Christopher Weber
Languages English
T: +1 720 561 3100
W: www.fairviewhs.org

Fountain International Magnet School
925 North Glendale Avenue, Pueblo CO 81001
PYP Coordinator Stephanie Burke
Languages English
T: +1 719 423 3050
W: fims.pueblocityschools.us

Frisco Elementary
PO Box 4820, Frisco CO 80443
PYP Coordinator Amy Hume
Languages English
T: +1 970 368 1500
W: fre.summitk12.org

George Washington High School
655 S Monaco Pkwy, Denver CO 80224
DP Coordinator Lorraine Stark
Languages English
T: +1 303 394 8620

Global Leadership Academy
7480 North Broadway, Denver CO 80221
MYP Coordinator Jessica Sullivan
Languages English
T: +1 303 853 1930
W: www.mapleton.us/globalleadershipacademy

Greeley West High School
2401 35th Avenue, Greeley CO 80634
DP Coordinator Bridget Koehler
MYP Coordinator Kaylyn Kingman
Languages English
T: +1 970 348 5400
W: www.west.greeleyschools.org

Hamilton Middle School
8600 East Dartmouth Avenue, Denver CO 80231
MYP Coordinator Christine Manzanares
Languages English, Spanish
T: +1 720 423 9500
W: hamilton.dpsk12.org

Harrison High School
2755 Janitell Road, Colorado Springs CO 80906
DP Coordinator Kathia Molina
MYP Coordinator Miranda Schaelling
Languages English
T: +1 719 579 2080
W: www.hsd2.org/hhs

Hinkley High School
1250 Chambers Road, Aurora CO 80011
CP Coordinator Matthew Brown
DP Coordinator Matthew Brown
MYP Coordinator David Nickoloff
Languages English
T: +1 303 340 1500
W: hinkley.aurorak12.org

International Academy of Denver at Harrington
2401 E. 37th Avenue, Denver CO 80205
PYP Coordinator Anne Witwer
Languages English, Spanish
T: +1 720 424 6420
W: www.internationalacademyofdenver.com

International School of Denver
7701 E. 1st Pl, Unit C, Denver CO 80230
MYP Coordinator Lauren Cantor
PYP Coordinator Helene Hernandez-Caudron
Languages Chinese, English, French, Spanish
T: +1 303 340 3647
W: www.isdenver.org

John F. Kennedy High School
2855 S. Lamar St., Denver CO 80227
DP Coordinator Alissa Warren
Languages English
T: +1 720 423 4300

Lakewood High School
9700 W. 8th Ave., Lakewood CO 80215
DP Coordinator Joellen Kramer
Languages English
T: +1 303 982 7096

Lesher Middle School
1400 Stover Street, Fort Collins CO 80524
MYP Coordinator Beth Wilms
Languages English
T: +1 970 472 3800
W: les.psdschools.org

Liberty Point International School
484 S. Maher Dr., Pueblo West CO 81007
MYP Coordinator Kelly Jackson
Languages English
T: +1 719 547 3752
W: lpi.district70.org

Lincoln Middle School
1600 Lancer Drive, Fort Collins CO 80521
MYP Coordinator Julie Israelson
Languages English
T: +1 970 488 5700
W: lin.psdschools.org

Littleton High School
199 East Littleton Boulevard, Littleton CO 80121
DP Coordinator Claudia Anderson
MYP Coordinator Margaret Chen
Languages English
T: +1 303 347 7700
W: www.littleton.littletonpublicschools.net

Loveland High School
920 W 29th Street, Loveland CO 80538
DP Coordinator Michelle Ray
MYP Coordinator Tané Leach
Languages English
T: +1 970 613 5209
W: www.thompsonschools.org/loveland

Lucile Erwin Middle School
4700 Lucerne Ave., Loveland CO 80538
MYP Coordinator Jill Prindiville
Languages English
T: +1 970 613 7600
W: www.thompsonschools.org/erwin

Mackintosh Academy Boulder
6717 S. Boulder Road, Boulder CO 80303
MYP Coordinator Libbi Peterson
PYP Coordinator Maggie Bendicksen
Languages English
T: +1 303 554 2011
W: www.mackboulder.com

Mackintosh Academy Littleton
7018 S. Prince Street, Littleton CO 80120
MYP Coordinator Sharon Muench
PYP Coordinator Sharon Muench
Languages English
T: +1 303 794 6222
W: www.mackintoshacademy.com

Mandalay Middle School
9651 Pierce Street, Westminster CO 80021
MYP Coordinator April Tompkins
Languages English
T: +1 303 982 9802

McAuliffe International School
2540 Holly Street, Denver CO 80207
MYP Coordinator Becky Middleton
Languages English
T: +1 720 424 1540
W: mcauliffe.dpsk12.org

McGraw Elementary School
4800 Hinsdale drive, Fort Collins CO 80526
PYP Coordinator Paul Schkade
Languages English
T: +1 970 223 0137
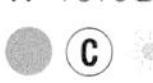

Mesa Middle School
365 North Mitchell Street, Castle Rock CO 80104
MYP Coordinator Rita Yokell
Languages English
T: +1 303 387 4750

Mountain Ridge Middle School
9150 Lexington Drive, Colorado Springs CO 80920
MYP Coordinator Laura Clibor
Languages English
T: +1 719 234 3200
W: mountainridge.asd20.org

Niwot High School
8989 E Niwot Road, Niwot CO 80503
DP Coordinator Elzbieta Towlen
Languages English
T: +1 303 652 2550
W: nhs.svvsd.org

North Middle School
301 North Nevada Avenue, Colorado Springs CO 80903
MYP Coordinator Adam Millman
Languages English
T: +1 719 328 5078

Northfield High School
5500 Central Park Blvd, Denver CO 80238
DP Coordinator Peter Wright
Languages English
T: +1 720 423 8000

Overland Trail Middle School
455 North 19th Ave., Brighton CO 80601
MYP Coordinator Christy Meredith
Languages English, Spanish
T: +1 303 655 4000
W: www.sd27j.org/domain/21

Palisade High School
3679 G Road, Palisade CO 81526
DP Coordinator Kimberly Popick
MYP Coordinator Matthew Borgmann
Languages English
T: +1 970 254 4800

Patterson International School
1263 S Dudley St., Lakewood CO 80232
PYP Coordinator Penny Strait
Languages English
T: +1 303 982 8470

Poudre High School
201 Impala Drive, Fort Collins CO 80521
DP Coordinator Cori Hixon
MYP Coordinator Marcia Lewis
Languages English
T: +1 970 488 6000
W: phs.psdschools.org

Pueblo East High School
9 MacNeil Road, Pueblo CO 81001
DP Coordinator Dora Davis
MYP Coordinator Dora Davis
Languages English
T: +1 719 549 7222
W: east.pueblocityschools.us

Pueblo West High School
661 Capitstrano Drive, Pueblo West CO 81007
DP Coordinator Kati Wilson
MYP Coordinator Kati Wilson
Languages English
T: +1 719 547 8050
W: pwh.district70.org

Rampart High School
8250 Lexington Drive, Colorado Springs CO 80920
DP Coordinator Avalon Manly
MYP Coordinator Avalon Manly
Languages English
T: +1 719 234 2000
W: rampart.asd20.org

Ranch Creek Elementary School
9155 Tutt Blvd, Colorado Springs CO 80924
PYP Coordinator Teresa Mulholland
Languages English
T: +1 719 234 5500
W: ranchcreek.asd20.org/Pages/default.aspx

Ranch View Middle School
1731 Wildcat Reserve Parkway, Highlands Ranch CO 80129
MYP Coordinator Erin Isley
Languages English
T: +1 303 387 2300
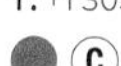

Range View Elementary School
700 Ponderosa Drive, Severance CO 80550
PYP Coordinator Tracy Ryberg
Languages English
T: +1 970 674 6000
W: rv.weldre4.k12.co.us

Riffenburgh Elementary School
1320 East Stuart Street, Fort Collins CO 80525
PYP Coordinator Jennifer McCoy
Languages English
T: +1 970 488 7935
W: rif.psdschools.org

Rifle High School
1350 Prefontaine Avenue, Rifle CO 81650
DP Coordinator Nathaniel Miller
Languages English
T: +1 970 665 7725

Rock Ridge Elementary School
400 N Heritage Road, Castle Rock CO 80104
PYP Coordinator Pam Gutierrez
Languages English
T: +1 303 387 5150

Rockrimmon Elementary School
194 W Mikado Drive, Colorado Springs CO 80919
PYP Coordinator Leigh Ann Lawrentz
Languages English
T: +1 719 234 5200
W: rockrimmon.asd20.org/Pages/default.aspx

Rose Stein Elementary School
80 S Teller Street, Lakewood CO 80226
PYP Coordinator Kaitlyn Campbell
Languages English
T: +1 303 982 9144

Roxborough Primary and Intermediate School
8000 Village Circle West, Littleton CO 80125
PYP Coordinator Laura Maestas
Languages English
T: +1 303 387 6000

Sabin World Elementary School
3050 S Vrain Street, Denver CO 80236
PYP Coordinator Carrie Hartman
Languages English
T: +1 720 424 4520
W: sabin.dpsk12.org

Sand Creek Elementary School
550 Sand Creek Drive, Colorado Springs CO 80916
MYP Coordinator April Pratt
PYP Coordinator Marika Gillis
Languages English
T: +1 719 579 3760
W: www.hsd2.org/Domain/15

Semper Elementary School
7575 W 96th Ave., Westminster CO 80021
PYP Coordinator Stacy Heller
Languages English, Spanish
T: +1 303 982 6460

Silverthorne Elementary School
PO Box 1039, Silverthorne CO 80498
PYP Coordinator Madeline Johnson
Languages English
T: +1 970 368 1600
W: sve.summitk12.org

Smoky Hill High School
16100 E. Smoky Hill Rd., Aurora CO 80015
DP Coordinator Michael Ady
MYP Coordinator Kathleen Fitzgerald
Languages English
T: +1 720 886 5300
W: smokyhill.cherrycreekschools.org

South Ridge Elementary School
1100 South Street, Castle Rock CO 80104
PYP Coordinator Marne Katsanis
Languages English
T: +1 303 387 5075

Standley Lake High School
9300 W 104th Avenue, Westminster CO 80021
DP Coordinator Benjamin Thompson
MYP Coordinator April Tompkins
Languages English
T: +1 303 982 3311

Summit Cove Elementary School
727 Cove Boulevard, Dillon CO 80435
PYP Coordinator Lesley Gregory
Languages English
T: +1 970 368 1700
W: sce.summitk12.org

Summit High School
PO Box 7, Frisco CO 80443
DP Coordinator Jotwan Daniels
MYP Coordinator Douglas Blake
Languages English
T: +1 970 368 1100
W: shs.summitk12.org

Summit Middle School
PO Box 7, Frisco CO 80443
MYP Coordinator Nelle Biggs
Languages English
T: +1 970 368 1100
W: sms.summitk12.org

Summit Ridge Middle School
11809 W Coal Mine Ave., Littleton CO 80127
MYP Coordinator Brittany Svaldi
Languages English
T: +1 303 982 9013

Sunset Middle School
1300 S. Sunset Street, Longmont CO 80501
MYP Coordinator Alex Armstrong
Languages English
T: +1 303 776 3963
W: sms.svvsd.org

Swigert International School
3480 Syracuse Street, Denver CO 80238
PYP Coordinator Caroline Dane
Languages English
T: +1 720 424 4800

Telluride Mountain School
Lawson Hill, 200 San Miguel River Dr., Telluride CO 81435
DP Coordinator Emily Durkin
Languages English
T: +1 970 728 1969
W: telluridemtnschool.org

Thornton High School
9351 North Washington Street, Thornton CO 80229
DP Coordinator Kathleen Fuller
Languages English
T: +1 720 972 4803

Thunder Ridge High School
1991 West Wildcat Reserve Pkwy, Highlands Ranch CO 80129
DP Coordinator Kelse Risner
MYP Coordinator Cristina Berrett-Braun
Languages English
T: +1 303 387 2000

Upper Blue Elementary School
PO Box 1255, 1200 Airport Road, Breckenbridge CO 80424
PYP Coordinator Toni Napolitano
Languages English
T: +1 970 368 1800
W: ube.summitk12.org

Westminster High School
6933 Raleigh Street, Westminster CO 80030
CP Coordinator Jeff Dennis
DP Coordinator Jeff Dennis
Languages English
T: +1 720 542 5085
W: www.westminsterpublicschools.org/westminsterhs

Whittier International Elementary School
2008 Pine Street, Boulder CO 80302
PYP Coordinator Alysia Hayas
Languages English
T: +1 303 442 2282
W: whittier.mpls.k12.mn.us

William J Palmer High School
301 N. Nevada Ave., Colorado Springs CO 80903
CP Coordinator Karen Owens
DP Coordinator Karen Owens
MYP Coordinator Anton Schulzki
Languages English
T: +1 719 328 5000
W: www.d11.org/palmer

Woodmen-Roberts Elementary School
8365 Orchard Path Road, Colorado Springs CO 80919
PYP Coordinator Jordan Zettek
Languages English
T: +1 719 234 5300
W: woodmenroberts.asd20.org

Connecticut

Brien McMahon High School
300 Highland Ave, Norwalk CT 06854
CP Coordinator Stephanie Tom
DP Coordinator Laura Bassler
MYP Coordinator Laura Quagliata
Languages English
T: +1 203 852 9488
W: bmhs.norwalkps.org

Charter Oak International Academy
425 Oakwood Avenue, West Hartford CT 06110
PYP Coordinator Elizabete Nascimento
Languages English
T: +1 860 233 8506
W: charteroak.whps.org

Cheshire Academy
10 Main Street, Cheshire CT 06410
DP Coordinator Marc Aronson
Languages English
T: +1 203 272 5396
W: www.cheshireacademy.org

Connecticut IB Academy
857 Forbes Street, East Hartford CT 06118
DP Coordinator Travis Marciniak
MYP Coordinator Travis Marciniak
Languages English
T: +1 860 622 5590
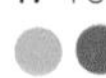

Dr. Thomas S. O Connell Elementary School
301 May Rd, East Hartford CT 06118
PYP Coordinator Laurie Stock
Languages English
T: +1 860 622 5460

Global Communications Academy
85 Edwards Street, Hartford CT 06120
PYP Coordinator Ashley Lyman
Languages English
T: +1 860 695 6020
W: www.hartfordschools.org

Groton Middle School
35 Groton Long Point Road, Groton CT 06340
MYP Coordinator Kathleen Wilson
Languages English
T: +1 860 446 4200
W: www.grotonschools.org/gms

Guilford High School
605 New England Road, Guilford CT 06437
DP Coordinator Kevin Buno
Languages English
T: +1 203 453 2741
W: ghs.guilfordps.org

International Magnet School for Global Citizenship
625 Chapel Road, South Windsor CT 06074
PYP Coordinator Katy Twyman
Languages English
T: +1 860 291 6001
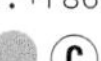

King/Robinson Inter-District Magnet School
150 Fournier Street, New Haven CT 06511
MYP Coordinator Caterina Salamone
PYP Coordinator Caterina Salamone
Languages English
T: +1 203 691 2700

Lawrence Elementary
Kaplan Drive, Middletown CT 06457
PYP Coordinator Denise Kraft
Languages English, Spanish
T: +1 860 632 2158
W: lawrence.middletownschools.org/o/les

New Lebanon School
25 Mead Avenue, Greenwich CT 06830
PYP Coordinator Cheri Amster
Languages English
T: +1 203 531 9139
W: www.greenwichschools.org/NLS

Notre Dame High School
One Notre Dame Way, West Haven CT 06516
DP Coordinator Kim Butz
Languages English, Spanish
T: +1 203 933 1673
W: www.notredamehs.com

Regional Multicultural Magnet School
1 Bulkeley Pl, New London CT 06320
PYP Coordinator Amy Rios
Languages English, Spanish
T: +1 860 437 7775

Robert E Fitch Senior High School
101 Groton Long Point Road, Groton CT 06340
CP Coordinator Anne Keefe-Forbotnick
DP Coordinator Kelley Donovan
MYP Coordinator Kelley Donovan
Languages English
T: +1 860 449 7200 EXT. 4507
W: www.grotonschools.org/fitch

Rogers International School
202 Blachley Road, Stamford CT 06902
MYP Coordinator Virginia Maher
PYP Coordinator Virginia Maher
Languages English
T: +1 203 977 4562
W: www.stamfordpublicschools.org/rogers-international-school

Stamford High School
55 Strawberry Hill Avenue, Stamford CT 06902
DP Coordinator Tiffany Flynn
Languages English
T: +1 203 977 4223
W: www.stamfordhigh.org

Sunset Ridge Middle School
450 Forbes St, East Hartford CT 06118
MYP Coordinator Alexandra Turner
Languages English
T: +1 860 622 5800

The International School at Dundee
55 Florence Road, Riverside CT 06878
PYP Coordinator Rosanna Sangermano
Languages English
T: +1 203 637 3800
W: www.greenwichschools.org/isd

The Metropolitan Learning Center Interdistrict Magnet School
1551 Blue Hills Avenue, Bloomfield CT 06002
DP Coordinator Stacey Pagliaro
MYP Coordinator Emily Wright
Languages English
T: +1 860 242 7834
W: choosemlc.com

Valley Regional High School
256 Kelsey Hill Rd, Deep River CT 06417
DP Coordinator Maria Ehrhardt
Languages English
T: +1 860 526 5328

Whitby School
969 Lake Avenue, Greenwich CT 06831
MYP Coordinator Shelley Castro
PYP Coordinator Diana Ljepoja
Languages English
T: +1 203 302 3900
W: www.whitbyschool.org

Delaware

John Dickinson High School
1801 Milltown Road, Wilmington DE 19808
DP Coordinator Geoffrey Ott
MYP Coordinator Valerie Morano
Languages English
T: +1 302 992 5500
W: www.redclayschools.com/dickinson

Mount Pleasant High School
5201 Washington St Extension, Wilmington DE 19809
DP Coordinator Leslie Carlson
MYP Coordinator Jeanne Beadle
Languages English
T: +1 302 762 7054
W: www.brandywineschools.org/mphs

Sussex Academy
21150 Airport Road, Georgetown DE 19947
DP Coordinator Janet Owens
Languages English
T: +1 302 856 3636
W: www.sussexacademy.org

Sussex Central High School
26026 Patriots Way, Georgetown DE 19947
DP Coordinator Kelly Deleon
Languages English
T: +1 302 934 3166
W: schs.irsd.net

Talley Middle School
1110 Cypress Road, Wilmington DE 19810
MYP Coordinator Jeanne Beadle
Languages English
T: +1 302 475 3976
W: www.brandywineschools.org/talley

Wilmington Friends School
101 School Road, Wilmington DE 19803
DP Coordinator Ed Gallagher
Languages English
T: +1 302 576 2900
W: www.wilmingtonfriends.org

District of Columbia

Alexander R. Shepherd Elementary School
7800 14th Street NW, Washington DC 20012
PYP Coordinator Avani Mack
Languages English
T: +1 202 576 6140
W: www.shepherd-elementary.org

Alice Deal Middle School
3815 Fort Drive, NW, Washington DC 20016
MYP Coordinator Caitlin Daniels
Languages English
T: +1 202 939 2010
W: www.alicedealmiddleschool.org

Benjamin A Banneker Academic High School
800 Euclid Street NW, Washington DC 20001
DP Coordinator Jesse Nickelson
Languages English
T: +1 202 673 7325
W: www.benjaminbanneker.org

British International School of Washington
2001 Wisconsin Avenue NW, Washington DC 20007
DP Coordinator Catherine Yates
Languages English
T: +1 202 829 3700
W: www.biswashington.org

DC International School
1400 Main Drive NW, Washington DC 20012
CP Coordinator Shane Donovan
DP Coordinator Ezra Miller
MYP Coordinator Dean Harris
Languages English, Spanish
T: +1 202 459 4790
W: www.dcinternationalschool.org

Eliot-Hine Middle School
1830 Constitution Ave NE, Washington DC 20002
MYP Coordinator Jeffrey Lynn
Languages English
T: +1 202 939 5380

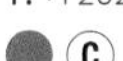

Elsie Whitlow Stokes Community Freedom Public Charter School
Brookland Campus, 3700 Oakview Terrace NE, Washington DC 20017
PYP Coordinator Rebecca Courouble
Languages English
T: +1 202 265 7237
W: www.ewstokes.org

Friendship Public Charter School - Woodridge Campus
2959 Carlton Ave. NE, Washington DC 20018
PYP Coordinator Chastity Shipp
Languages English
T: +1 202 635 6500
W: www.friendshipschools.org/schools/woodridge

Girls Global Academy
733 8th Street NW, Washington DC 20001
CP Coordinator Shayne Swift
Languages English
T: +1 202 600 4822
W: girlsglobalacademy.org

Mary McLeod Bethune Day Academy PCS
1404 Jackson Street NE, Washington DC 20017
PYP Coordinator Linda McKay
Languages English
T: +1 202 459 4710
W: www.mmbethune.org

National Collegiate Preparatory Public Charter High School
4600 Livingston Road SE, Washington DC 20032
DP Coordinator Thmaine S. Morgan
Languages English
T: +1 202 832 7737
W: www.nationalprepdc.org

Strong John Thomson Elementary School
1200 L Street NW, Washington DC 20005
PYP Coordinator Maria Sparkman
Languages English
T: +1 202 898 4660
W: www.thomsondcps.org

Turner at Green Elementary School
1500 Mississippi Avenue SE, Washington DC 20032
PYP Coordinator Marian Horton
Languages English
T: +1 202 645 3470
W: sites.google.com/a/dc.gov/turner-at-green-elementary-school

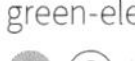

Washington International School
3100 Macomb Street NW, Washington DC 20008
DP Coordinator Neil MacDonald
PYP Coordinator Stephanie Sneed
Languages English
T: +1 202 243 1800
W: www.wis.edu

Washington Yu Ying Public Charter School
220 Taylor St. NE, Washington DC 20017
PYP Coordinator Rebecca J Rosenberg
Languages English, Mandarin
T: +1 202 635 1950; +1 202 635 1960
W: www.washingtonyuying.org

Florida

Ada Merritt K-8 Center
660 SW 3 Street, Miami FL 33130
MYP Coordinator Yosvany Hernandez
PYP Coordinator Jackeline Sanchez Jimenez
Languages English
T: +1 305 326 0791
W: adamerrittk-8center.org

Allen D Nease High School
10550 Ray Road, Ponte Vedra FL 32081
DP Coordinator Missy Kennedy
Languages English
T: +1 904 547 8300
W: www-nhs.stjohns.k12.fl.us

Alonso High School
8302 Montague Street, Tampa FL 33635
DP Coordinator Yung Romano
Languages English
T: +1 813 356 1525
W: www.hillsboroughschools.org/alonso

American Youth Academy
5905 E. 130th Ave, Tampa FL 33617
DP Coordinator Omar Abed
Languages English
T: +1 813 987 9282
W: www.ayatampa.org

Annabel C. Perry PK-8
6850 SW 34th Street, Miramar FL 33023
PYP Coordinator Jacqueline Foster
Languages English
T: +1 754 323 7050
W: www.browardschools.com/perryelem

Arthur I. Meyer Jewish Academy
5225 Hood Rd, Palm Beach Gardens FL 33418
MYP Coordinator Judy Edelman
Languages English
T: +1 561 686 6520
W: www.meyeracademy.org

Atlantic Community High School
2455 West Atlantic Ave, Palm Beach County, Delray Beach FL 33445
CP Coordinator Jill Meadow
DP Coordinator Jackie Boileau
MYP Coordinator Jill Meadow
Languages English
T: +1 561 243 1502
W: ahs.palmbeachschools.org

Bhaktivedanta Academy
17414 NW 112th Blvd, Alachua FL 32615
MYP Coordinator Jaya Kaseder
Languages English
T: +1 386 462 2886
W: www.bhaktischool.org

Biscayne Elementary Community School
800 77th Street, Miami Beach FL 33141
PYP Coordinator Iris Garcia
Languages English, Spanish
T: +1 305 868 7727
W: api.dadeschools.net/schoolwebsite/#!/?schoolId=0321

Boca Prep International School
10333 Diego Drive South, Boca Raton FL 33428
DP Coordinator Maria Starkand
MYP Coordinator Tylar Tracy
PYP Coordinator Cristina Swanson
Languages English
T: +1 561 852 1410
W: www.bocaprep.net

Boyd H. Anderson High School
3050 NW 41st Street, Lauderdale Lakes FL 33309
DP Coordinator Clara Gonzalez
MYP Coordinator Clara Gonzalez
Languages English
T: +1 754 322 0200
W: www.browardschools1.com/boydanderson

Brigham Academy
601 Avenue C SE, Winter Haven FL 33880
PYP Coordinator Susie Kallan
Languages English, Spanish
T: +1 863 291 5300
W: brighamacademy.polk-fl.net

Brookside Middle School
3636 South Shade Avenue, Sarasota FL 34239
MYP Coordinator Holly Dewitt
Languages English
T: +1 941 361 6472
W: www.sarasotacountyschools.net/schools/brookside

C Leon King High School
6815 North 56th Street, Tampa FL 33610
DP Coordinator Joyce Hoehn-Parish
Languages English
T: +1 813 744 8333
W: king.mysdhc.org

Cape Coral High School
2300 Santa Barbara Blvd, Cape Coral FL 33991
DP Coordinator Katelyn Uhler
Languages English
T: +1 239 574 6766

Cardinal Newman High School
512 Spencer Drive, West Palm Beach FL 33409
DP Coordinator Scott Powell
Languages English
T: +1 561 683 6266
W: www.cardinalnewman.com
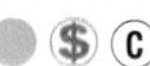

Carrollton School of the Sacred Heart
3747 Main Highway, Miami FL 33133
DP Coordinator Caroline Gillingham-Varela
Languages English
T: +1 305 446 5673
W: www.carrollton.org

Carrollwood Day School
1515 W. Bearss Avenue, Tampa FL 33613
DP Coordinator Nancy Hsu
MYP Coordinator Sabrina McCartney
PYP Coordinator Lisa Vicencio
Languages English
T: +1 813 920 2288
W: www.carrollwooddayschool.org

Carver Middle School
101 Barwick Road, Delray Beach FL 33445
MYP Coordinator Nadia Stewart
Languages English
T: +1 561 638 2100
W: crvm.palmbeachschools.org

Carver Middle School
4500 W Columbia Street, Orlando FL 32811
MYP Coordinator Debbie Villar
Languages English
T: +1 407 296 5110
W: www.carvermiddle.ocps.net

Celebration High School
1809 Celebration Boulevard, Celebration FL 34747
DP Coordinator Alissa Petersen
Languages English
T: +1 321 939 6600
W: www.osceolaschools.net/clhs

Choctawhatchee Senior High School
110 Racetrack Road NW, Fort Walton Beach FL 32547
DP Coordinator Katherine White
Languages English
T: +1 850 833 3614
W: www.okaloosaschools.com/choctaw

Clearwater Central Catholic High School
2750 Haines Bayshore Road, Clearwater FL 33760
DP Coordinator Alan Hamacher
Languages English
T: +1 727 531 1449
W: www.ccchs.org

Cocoa Beach Junior/Senior High School
1500 Minutemen Causeway, Cocoa Beach FL 32931
DP Coordinator Matt Kellam
MYP Coordinator Matt Kellam
Languages English
T: +1 321 783 1776
W: www.brevardschools.org/CocoaBeachJRSR
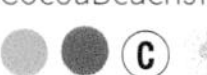

College Park Middle School
1201 Maury Road, Orlando FL 32804-3541
MYP Coordinator Debbie Villar
Languages English
T: +1 407 245 1800
W: collegeparkms.ocps.net

Conniston Community Middle School
673 Conniston Road, West Palm Beach FL 33405
MYP Coordinator Rebekah Majava
Languages English
T: +1 561 802 5477
W: cntm.palmbeachschools.org

Coral Gables Senior High School
450 Bird Road, Coral Gables FL 33146
DP Coordinator Diana Van Wyk
Languages English
T: +1 305 443 4871
W: www.coralgablescavaliers.org

Coral Reef High School
10101 SW 152 Street, Miami FL 33157
DP Coordinator Kelli Wise
Languages English
T: +1 305 232 2044
W: coralreef.dadeschools.net

Corbett Preparatory School of IDS
12015 Orange Grove Drive, Tampa FL 33618
MYP Coordinator Jennifer Jagdmann
PYP Coordinator Linda Wenzel
Languages English
T: +1 813 961 3087
W: www.corbettprep.com

Cornerstone Learning Community
2524 Hartsfield Road, Tallahassee FL 32303
MYP Coordinator Karen Metcalf
Languages English
T: +1 850 386 5550
W: www.cornerstonelc.com

Creation Village Preparatory School
599 Celebration Place, Celebration FL 34747
MYP Coordinator Chris Stephenson
PYP Coordinator Sagrario Argüelles
Languages English
T: +1 407 900 7708
W: creationvillage.com

Cypress Creek High School
1101 Bear Crossing Drive, Orange County, Orlando FL 32824
DP Coordinator Helen Philpot
Languages English
T: +1 407 852 3400

Deerfield Beach High School
910 Buck Pride Way, Deerfield Beach FL 33441
DP Coordinator Kelly Caputo
MYP Coordinator Kelly Caputo
Languages English
T: +1 754 322 0650
W: www.deerfieldbeachhigh.net

Deerfield Beach Middle School
701 SE 6th Avenue, Deerfield Beach FL 33441
MYP Coordinator MJ Caputo
Languages English
T: +1 754 322 3300
W: www.browardschools.com/deerfieldbeachmiddle

Deland High School
800 North Hill Avenue, Volusia, Deland FL 32724
DP Coordinator Lisa Nehrig
Languages English
T: +1 386 822 6909
W: www.delandhs.org

Doral Academy Preparatory - High School
11100 NW 27th Street, Doral FL 33172
DP Coordinator Sophie Perez
Languages English, Spanish
T: +1 305 597 9950
W: www.doralacademyprep.org

Doral Performing Arts and Entertainment Academy
11100 NW 27th Street, Doral FL 33172
DP Coordinator Sophie Perez
Languages English, Spanish
W: www.doralacademyprep.org

Downtown Doral Charter Upper School
7905 NW 53 Street, Doral FL 33166
DP Coordinator Jessica Chavez
MYP Coordinator Jessica Chavez
Languages English, Spanish
T: +1 305 513 3013
W: ddcus.org

Dr Mary McLeod Bethune Elementary School
1501 Avenue 'U', Riviera Beach FL 33404
PYP Coordinator Sherrita Crummell
Languages English
T: +1 561 882 7600
W: mmbe.palmbeachschools.org

Dunbar High School
3800 E. Edison Avenue, Ft. Myers FL 33916
CP Coordinator Gayle Baisch
DP Coordinator Gayle Baisch
Languages English
T: +1 239 461 5322

Dundee Elementary Academy
415 E Frederick Ave, Dundee FL 33838
PYP Coordinator Phillip Daniels
Languages English
T: +1 863 421 3316

Dundee Ridge Academy
5555 Lake Trask Rd, Dundee FL 33838
MYP Coordinator Kerri Collins
Languages English
T: +1 863 419 3088

Earlington Heights Elementary School
4750 NW 22nd Avenue, Miami FL 33142
PYP Coordinator Leanna Zuccarelli
Languages English
T: +1 305 635 7505
W: earlingtonheightselem.dadeschools.net

Eastside High School
1201 South East 43rd Street, Gainesville FL 32641-7698
DP Coordinator Anne Koon
Languages English
T: +1 352 955 6704
W: www.ehs.sbac.edu

Fienberg-Fisher K-8 Center
1420 Washington Ave, Miami Beach FL 33139
MYP Coordinator Pierrela JeanBaptiste
PYP Coordinator Pierrela Jeanbaptiste
Languages English
T: +1 305 351 0419
W: www.fienbergfisherk8.com

Flagler Palm Coast High School
3265 Highway 100 East, Palm Coast FL 32164
DP Coordinator Jacqueline McKeown
Languages English
T: +1 386 437 7540
W: www.flagler.k12.fl.us
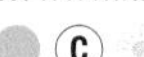

Forest Hill Community High School
3340 Forest Hill Boulevard, West Palm Beach FL 33405
CP Coordinator Shannon Deere
DP Coordinator Shannon Deere
MYP Coordinator Justin Boruch
Languages English
T: +1 561 540 2400

Forest Park Elementary School
1201 SW 3rd Street, Boynton Beach FL 33435
PYP Coordinator Simone Green
Languages English
T: +1 561 292 6900
W: www.edline.net/pages/forest_park_es

Fort Myers High School
2635 Cortez Boulevard, Fort Myers FL 33901
DP Coordinator Susan Postma
Languages English
T: +1 239 334 2167
W: www.lee.k12.fl.us/schools/fmh/home.asp

Fox Chapel Middle School
9412 Fox Chapel Lane, Spring Hill FL 34606
MYP Coordinator Brandy Enders
Languages English
T: +1 352 797 7025
W: www.hernandoschools.org/schools/fox-chapel-middle-school

Frank C Martin Elementary School
14250 Boggs Drive, Miami FL 33176
MYP Coordinator Katheryn Capodiferro
PYP Coordinator Katheryn Capodiferro
Languages English
T: +1 305 238 3688
W: fcmartin.dadeschools.net

Franklin Academy - Boynton Beach
7882 S. Military Trail, Boynton Beach FL 33463
PYP Coordinator Yamile Francese
Languages English, Spanish
T: +1 561 767 4700
W: bb.franklin-academy.org

Franklin Academy - Cooper City Campus
6301 S. Flamingo Road, Cooper City FL 33330
MYP Coordinator Eileen Olmedo
Languages English
T: +1 954 780 5533
W: cc.franklin-academy.org

Franklin Academy - Palm Beach Gardens
5651 Hood Road, Palm Beach Gardens FL 33418
MYP Coordinator Leah Hanza
PYP Coordinator Leah Hanza
Languages English
T: +1 561 348 2525
W: pbg.franklin-academy.org

Franklin Academy - Pembroke Pines (K-12) Campus
5000 SW 207th Terrace, Pembroke Pines FL 33332
DP Coordinator Astrid Rivera-Ortiz
MYP Coordinator Eileen Olmedo
Languages English
T: +1 954 315 0770
W: pphs.franklin-academy.org

Franklin Academy - Pembroke Pines (K-8) Campus
18800 Pines Blvd, Pembroke Pines FL 33029
MYP Coordinator Kathy Ross
Languages English, Spanish
T: +1 954 703 2294
W: pp.franklin-academy.org
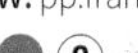

Franklin Academy - Sunrise Campus
4500 NW 103 Ave, Sunrise FL 33351
MYP Coordinator Callie Scott
Languages English, Spanish
T: +1 754 206 0850
W: sun.franklin-academy.org

Freedom 7 Elementary School of International Studies
400 4th Street South, Cocoa Beach FL 32931
PYP Coordinator Jennifer Noe
Languages English
T: +1 321 868 6610
W: www.brevardschools.org/Freedom7ES

Gateway High School
93 Panther Paws Trail, Osceola School District, Kissimmee FL 34744
DP Coordinator Kathryn Stubbs
Languages English
T: +1 407 935 3600

Glenridge Middle School
2900 Upper Park Road, Orlando FL 32814
MYP Coordinator Matthew Astone
Languages English
T: +1 407 623 1415
W: glenridgems.ocps.net

Grove Park Elementary School
8330 N. Military Trail, Palm Beach Gardens FL 33410
PYP Coordinator Whitney Lloyd
Languages English
T: +1 561 904 7700
W: gpes.palmbeachschools.org

G-Star School of the Arts for Motion Pictures & Broadcasting
2065 Prairie Road, Building J, Palm Springs FL 33406
DP Coordinator Emily Snedeker
Languages English
T: +1 561 967 2023
W: www.gstarschool.org

Gulf High School
5355 School Road, New Port Richey FL 34652
DP Coordinator Cheryl Macri
Languages English
T: +1 727 774 3300
W: ghs.pasco.k12.fl.us

Gulf Middle School
6419 Louisiana Avenue, New Port Richey FL 34653
MYP Coordinator Kimberly Fox
Languages English, Spanish
T: +1 727 774 8000
W: gms.pasco.k12.fl.us

Gulliver Academy Middle School
12595 Red Road, Coral Gables FL 33156
MYP Coordinator Tiffany Medina
Languages English
T: +1 305 665 3593
W: www.gulliverschools.org

Gulliver Preparatory School
6575 North Kendall Drive, Miami FL 33156
DP Coordinator Jan Patterson
Languages English
T: +1 305 666 6333
W: www.gulliverprep.org

Haines City High School
2800 Hornet Drive, Haines City FL 33844
DP Coordinator Crystal Young
Languages English
T: +1 863 421 3281

Heights Elementary School
15200 Alexandria Court, Fort Myers FL 33908
PYP Coordinator Lacey Davis
Languages English
T: +1 239 481 1761

Herbert A Ammons Middle School
17990 SW 142 Avenue, Miami FL 33177
MYP Coordinator David Wilson
Languages English
T: +1 305 971 0158
W: www.ammonseagles.com

Hillsborough High School
5000 Central Avenue, Tampa FL 33603
DP Coordinator Lisa Sigmon
Languages English
T: +1 813 276 5620
W: hillsborough.mysdhc.org

Homestead Middle School
650 N.W. 2nd Avenue, Homestead FL 33030
MYP Coordinator Claudia Davis
Languages English
T: +1 305 247 4221
W: homesteadmiddle.org

Howard Middle School
1655 NW 10th Street, Ocala FL 34475
MYP Coordinator Helen Hamel
Languages English
T: +1 352 671 7225
W: www.marionschools.net/hms

Howell L. Watkins Middle School
9480 Mac Arthur Blvd, Palm Beach Gardens FL 33403
MYP Coordinator Shari Alexios
Languages English, Spanish
T: +1 561 776 3600
W: hlwm.palmbeachschools.org

Idyllwilde Elementary School
430 Vihlen Road, Sanford FL 32771
PYP Coordinator Julie Biggs
Languages English, Spanish
T: +1 407 320 3750
W: www.idyllwilde.scps.k12.fl.us

International Baccalaureate School at Bartow High School
1270 South Broadway Avenue, Bartow FL 33830
DP Coordinator Katherine Marsh
Languages English
T: +1 863 534 0194

J. Colin English Elementary School
120 Pine Island Rd., North Fort Myers FL 33903
PYP Coordinator Erica Littman
Languages English
T: +1 239 995 2258

J.H. Workman Middle School
6299 Lanier Avenue, Penacola FL 32504
MYP Coordinator Michael Burton
Languages English
T: +1 850 494 5665
W: jhwms-ecsd-fl.schoolloop.com

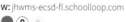

Jackson Middle School
6000 Stonewall Jackson Road, Orlando FL 32807
MYP Coordinator Lynne Newsom Newsom
Languages English
T: +1 407 249 6430
W: www.stonewalljackson.ocps.net

James B. Sanderlin PK-8
2350 22nd Avenue South, St Petersburg FL 33712
MYP Coordinator Gina villano
PYP Coordinator Kristen Herman
Languages English
T: +1 727 552 1700
W: www.pcsb.org/sanderlinib
 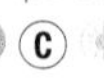

James S Rickards High School
3013 Jim Lee Road, Leon District Schools, Tallahassee FL 32301-7057
DP Coordinator Joe Williams
Languages English
T: +1 850 488 1783

Jewett Middle Academy
601 Ave T NE, Winter Haven FL 33881
MYP Coordinator Paulette Jacobs
Languages English
T: +1 863 291 5320

John A Ferguson Senior High School
15900 SW 56th Street, Miami FL 33185
DP Coordinator Denise Graham
Languages English
T: +1 305 408 2700
W: www.fergusonhs.org

John F Kennedy Middle School
1901 Avenue 'S', Riviera Beach FL 33404
MYP Coordinator Patreka Mckelton
Languages English
T: +1 561 845 4502
W: jfkm.palmbeachschools.org

Jones High School
801 South Rio Grande Avenue, Orlando FL 32805
DP Coordinator Nicole Blackmon
MYP Coordinator Nicole Blackmon
Languages English
T: +1 407 835 2300
W: www.jones.ocps.net

Kids Community College Southeast Campus
11519 McMullen Road, Riverview FL 33569
MYP Coordinator Stacey O'Neill
PYP Coordinator Diana Davila-Gonzalez
Languages English
T: +1 813 699 4600
W: www.kidscc.org

Lake Wales High School
1 Highlander Way, Lake Wales FL 33853
DP Coordinator Chance Cook
Languages English
T: +1 863 678 4222
W: www.lakewaleshigh.com

Lake Weir High School
10351 SE Maricamp Road, Ocala FL 34472
DP Coordinator Cassandra Bonnett
Languages English
T: +1 352 671 4820
W: www.marionschools.net/lwh

Lamar Louise Curry Middle School
15750 SW 47th Street, Miami FL 33185
MYP Coordinator Iran Miranda
Languages English
T: +1 305 222 2775

Land O'Lakes High School
20325 Gator Lane, Land O'Lakes FL 34639
DP Coordinator Marc Jarke
Languages English
T: +1 813 794 9400

Largo High School
410 Missouri Ave N, Largo FL 33770
DP Coordinator Michael Vasallo
Languages English
T: +1 727 588 9158
W: www.largo-hs.pcsb.org

Largo Middle School
155 8th Avenue SE, Largo FL 33771
MYP Coordinator Olivia Crawford
Languages English
T: +1 727 588 4600
W: www.pcsb.org/largo-ms

Lauderdale Lakes Middle School
3911 Northwest 30 th Avenue, Lauderdale Lakes FL 33309
MYP Coordinator Jeana Louis
Languages English
T: +1 954) 497 3900

Lawton Chiles Middle Academy
400 North Florida Avenue, Lakeland FL 33801
MYP Coordinator Angela Price
Languages English
T: +1 863 499 2742

Lecanto High School
3810 W Educational Path, Lecanto FL 34461
DP Coordinator Jessica Price
Languages English
T: +1 352 746 2334

Lexington Middle School
16351 Summerlin Road, Fort Myers FL 33908
MYP Coordinator James Kroll
Languages English
T: +1 239 454 6130

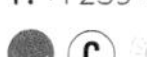

Liberty Magnet Elementary School
6850 81st Street, Vero Beach FL 32967
PYP Coordinator Jamie Lunsford
Languages English
T: +1 772 564 5300

Lincoln Avenue Academy
1330 North Lincoln Avenue, Lakeland FL 33805
PYP Coordinator Diane Lokey
Languages English
T: +1 863 499 2955
W: lincolnavenuejaguars.weebly.com

Lincoln Elementary Magnet School
1207 E Renfro Street, Plant City FL 33563
PYP Coordinator Sarah Keel
Languages English
T: +1 813 757 9329
W: lincoln.mysdhc.org

Lincoln Park Academy
1806 Avenue I, St Lucie County, Fort Pierce FL 34950
DP Coordinator Carol Kuhn
MYP Coordinator Carol Kuhn
Languages English
T: +1 772 468 5474
W: schools.stlucie.k12.fl.us/lpa

Louise R Johnson Middle School
2121 26th Avenue East, Bradenton FL 34208
MYP Coordinator Christine Clem
Languages English
T: +1 941 741 3344
W: www.edline.net/pages/sdmcjohnsonms

Macfarlane Park Elementary Magnet School
1721 North MacDill Avenue, Tampa FL 33607
PYP Coordinator Angela Hartle
Languages English
T: +1 813 356 1760
W: macfarlanepark.mysdhc.org

Mariner Middle School
425 Chiquita Blvd N., Cape Coral FL 33993
MYP Coordinator Tiffany Hightower
Languages English
T: +1 239 772 1848

Marshall Middle Magnet School
18 South Maryland Avenue, Plant City FL 33563
MYP Coordinator Kathy Webb
Languages English
T: +1 813 757 9360
W: www.hillsboroughschools.org/marshall

Maynard Evans High School
4949 Silver Star Road, Orlando FL 32808
DP Coordinator John Harrell
Languages English
T: +1 407 522 3400
W: www.evanshs.ocps.net

Melbourne High School
74 Bulldog Boulevard, Melbourne FL 32901
CP Coordinator Lesley Cosgrove
DP Coordinator Jennifer Mason
Languages English
T: +1 321 952 5880
W: www.brevardschools.org/MelbourneHS

Memorial Middle School
2220 W 29th Street, Orlando FL 32805
MYP Coordinator Alicia Morris
Languages English
T: +1 407 245 1810
W: www.memorial.ocps.net

Miami Beach Senior High School
2231 Prairie Avenue, Miami Beach FL 33139
DP Coordinator Jason Jackson
Languages English
T: +1 305 532 4515
W: miamibeachhigh.schoolwires.com

Mildred Helms Elementary School
561 S. Clearwater-Largo Rd., Largo FL 33770-3294
PYP Coordinator Jennifer Kelly
Languages English, Spanish
T: +1 727 588 3569
W: www.pcsb.org/mildred-es

Miramar High School
3601 SW 89th Avenue, Miramar FL 33025
DP Coordinator John Lamb
Languages English
T: +1 754 323 1350
W: www.browardschools.com/miramarhigh

Morikami Park Elementary School
6201 Morikami Park Road, Delray Beach FL 33484
PYP Coordinator Amy Mercier
Languages English
T: +1 561 865 3960

Nautilus Middle School
4301 N. Michigan Ave., Miami Beach FL 33140
MYP Coordinator Rick Fernandez
Languages English
T: +1 305 532 3481
W: nautilus.dadeschools.net

New Gate School
5237 Ashton Road, Sarasota FL 34233
DP Coordinator Lydia Dumais
Languages English
T: +1 941 922 4949
W: www.newgate.edu

New Renaissance Middle School
10701 Miramar Blvd., Miramar FL 33025
MYP Coordinator Ermina Pierre
Languages English, Spanish
T: +1 754 323 3500
W: www.browardschools.com/newrenaissance

North Beach Elementary School
4100 Prairie Avenue, Miami Beach FL 33140
PYP Coordinator Lourdes Figarola
Languages English
T: +1 305 531 7666
W: northbeachelementary.com

North Broward Preparatory School
7600 Lyons Road, Coconut Creek FL 33073
DP Coordinator Tamara Wolpowitz
Languages English
T: +1 954.247.0011
W: www.nbps.org

North Dade Middle School
1840 NW 157th Street, Miami Gardens FL 33054
MYP Coordinator Diana Antoine
Languages English
T: +1 305 624 8415
W: northdademiddleschool.com

North Miami Middle School
700 NE 137th St, North Miami FL 33161
MYP Coordinator Melissa Ortiz
Languages English
T: +1 305 891 3680
W: northmiamims.net

North Miami Senior High School
13110 NE 8 Avenue, North Miami FL 33161
DP Coordinator Rose Weintraub
Languages English
T: +1 305 891 6590
W: schoolsites.schoolworld.com/schools/NMSH

Oak Hammock Middle School
5321 Tice Street, Fort Myers FL 33905
MYP Coordinator Brandie Della-Luna
Languages English, Spanish
T: +1 239 693 0469

Pahokee Elementary School
560 E Main Place, Pahokee FL 33476
PYP Coordinator Cassandra Moreland
Languages English
T: +1 561 924 9705
W: pes.palmbeachschools.org

Pahokee Middle Senior High School
900 Larrimore Road, Pahokee FL 33476
DP Coordinator Aya Hasegawa
MYP Coordinator Iolanthe Brown
Languages English
T: +1 561 924 6400
W: pmsh.palmbeachschools.org

Palm Harbor University High School
1900 Omaha Street, Palm Harbor FL 34683
DP Coordinator Evette Striblen
Languages English
T: +1 727 669 1131

Palmer Trinity School
7900 SW 176th Street, Miami FL 33157
DP Coordinator Orlando Sarduy
Languages English
T: +1 305 251 2230
W: www.palmertrinity.org

Palmetto Elementary School
5801 Parker Ave., West Palm Beach FL33405
PYP Coordinator Whitney Fisher
Languages English, Spanish
T: +1 561 202 0400
W: pmte.palmbeachschools.org

Parkway Middle School
857 Florida Parkway, Kissimmee FL 34743
MYP Coordinator Katalina Dasilva
Languages English
T: +1 407 344 7000
W: www.osceolaschools.net/pwms

Paxon School for Advanced Studies
3239 Norman E Thagard Blvd., Jacksonville FL 32254-1796
DP Coordinator Krystal Culpepper
Languages English
T: +1 904 693 7583
W: www.duvalschools.org/psas

Pedro Menendez High School
600 State Road 206 West, St Augustine FL 32086
CP Coordinator Tim Davidson
DP Coordinator Carolie Schultz
Languages English
T: +1 904 547 8660
W: www-pmhs.stjohns.k12.fl.us

Pensacola High School
A and Maxwell Streets, Pensacola FL 32501
DP Coordinator Colleen Boyett
Languages English
T: +1 850 595 1500
W: phs-ecsd-fl.schoolloop.com

Phillippi Shores Elementary School
4747 South Tamiami Trail, Sarasota FL 34231
PYP Coordinator Suzette Trapani
Languages English
T: +1 941 361 6424
W: www.sarasotacountyschools.net/phillippi

Pine View Elementary School
5333 Parkway Boulevard, Land O' Lakes FL 34639
PYP Coordinator Erin Greco
Languages English, Spanish
T: +1 813 794 0600
W: pves.pasco.k12.fl.us

Pine View Middle School
5334 Parkway Boulevard, Land O' Lakes FL 34639
MYP Coordinator Rebecca Cardinale
Languages English
T: +1 813 794 4800
W: pvms.pasco.k12.fl.us

Plantation High School
6901 NW 16th Street, Plantation FL 33313
DP Coordinator Catherine Gonzalez
Languages English
T: +1 754 322 1850
W: www.browardschools.com/plantationhigh

Plantation Middle School
6600 West Sunrise Blvd, Plantation FL 33313
MYP Coordinator Coniell Bursac
Languages English
T: +1 754 322 4100
W: browardschools.com/plantationmid

Ponce de Leon Middle School
5801 Augusto Street, Coral Gables FL 33146
MYP Coordinator Marlene Ramos
Languages English
T: +1 305 661 1611 EXT:2212
W: ponce.dadeschools.net

Port St Lucie High School
1201 S E Jaguar Lane, Port St Lucie FL 34952
DP Coordinator Jamie Malone
Languages English
T: +1 772 337 6770
W: www.stlucie.k12.fl.us/our-schools/profile/?sch=phs

Richey Elementary School
6850 Adams Street, New Port Richey FL 34652
PYP Coordinator Shaun Burr
Languages English, Spanish
T: +1 727 774 3500
W: res.pasco.k12.fl.us

Ridgeview High School Academy for Advanced Studies
466 Madison Avenue, Clay County, Orange Park FL 32065
DP Coordinator Angela Randall
Languages English
T: +1 904 213 5203
W: rhsibacademyofadvancedstudies.weebly.com

Riverdale High School
2600 Buckingham Road, Fort Myers FL 33905
DP Coordinator Traci Budmayr
Languages English
T: +1 239 694 4141

Riverhills Elementary Magnet
405 S. Riverhills Drive, Temple Terrace FL 33617
PYP Coordinator LaGretta Snowden
Languages English
T: +1 813 987 6911
W: riverhills.mysdhc.org

Riverview High School
One Ram Way, Sarasota FL 34231
CP Coordinator Jessica Bies
DP Coordinator James R Minor
Languages English
T: +1 941 923 1484
W: www.riverviewib.com

Robinson High School
6311 S Lois Avenue, Tampa FL 33616-1617
DP Coordinator Eduardo Escudero
Languages English
T: +1 813 272 3006
W: robinsonhs.mysdhc.org

Robinswood Middle School
6305 Balboa Drive, Orlando FL 32818
MYP Coordinator Vernalee Bickerstaff
Languages English
T: +1 407 296 5140
W: robinswoodms.ocps.net

Roland Park K-8 Magnet School
1510 N. Manhattan Ave, Tampa FL 33607
MYP Coordinator Adrienne Rundle
PYP Coordinator Adrienne Rundle
Languages English
T: +1 813 872 5212
W: rolandpark.mysdhc.org

Royal Palm Beach High School
10600 Okeechobee Blvd., Royal Palm Beach FL 33411
DP Coordinator Daniel Dicurcio
Languages English
T: +1 561 753 4000

Rutherford High School
1000 School Avenue, Springfield FL 32401
CP Coordinator Catherine Rutland
DP Coordinator Catherine Rutland
Languages English
T: +1 850 767 4500
W: www.bayschools.com/rhs

Saint John Paul II Catholic School
4341 W Homosassa Trail, Lecanto FL 34461
MYP Coordinator Wes Park
Languages English
T: +1 352 746 2020
W: www.sjp2.us

Samuel W. Wolfson High School
7000 Powers Ave., Jacksonville FL 32217-3398
DP Coordinator Brandi Benga
Languages English
T: +1 904 739 5265
W: www.duvalschools.org/wolfson

Sebastian River High School
9001 Shark Blvd, Sebastian FL 32958
DP Coordinator Jaime Sturgeon
Languages English
T: +1 772 564 4170

Sebastian River Middle School
9400 Fellsmere Rd, Sebastian FL 32958
MYP Coordinator Christine Sturgeon
Languages English
T: +1 772 564 5111

Sebring High School
3514 Kenilworth Boulevard, Sebring FL 33870
DP Coordinator Jo Anna Cochlin
Languages English
T: +1 863 471 5500
W: www.highlands.k12.fl.us/~shs

Seminole High School
2701 Ridgewood Avenue, Seminole, Sanford FL 32773-4916
DP Coordinator Benjamin Ellis
Languages English
T: +1 407 320 5100
W: www.seminolehs.scps.k12.fl.us

South Dade Senior High School
28401 SW 167 Ave., Homestead FL 33030
DP Coordinator Karina Papili
Languages English
T: +1 305 247 4244
W: sdshs.net

South Fork High School
10000 SW Bulldog Way, Stuart FL 34997-2799
DP Coordinator Joseph Shewmaker
Languages English
T: +1 772 219 1840
W: sfhs.martinschools.org/pages/south_fork_high_school

South Pointe Elementary School
1050 4th Street, Miami Beach FL 33139
PYP Coordinator Carolyn Greene
Languages English
T: +1 305 531 5437

Southeast High School
1200 37th Avenue East, Bradenton FL 34208
DP Coordinator Kathleen Grim
Languages English
T: +1 941 741 3366
W: www.manateeschools.net/southeast

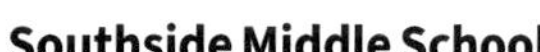

Southside Middle School
2948 Knights Lane E, Jacksonville FL 32216-5697
MYP Coordinator Kassandra Kieffer
Languages English
T: +1 904 739 5238
W: www.duvalschools.org/southside

Spring Park Elementary School
2250 Spring Park Road, Jacksonville FL 32207
PYP Coordinator Charita Penny
Languages English
T: +1 904 346 5640
W: www.duvalschools.org/springpark

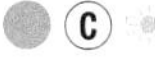

Springstead High School
3300 Mariner Boulevard, Spring Hill FL 34609
DP Coordinator John Imhof
Languages English
T: +1 352 797 7010
W: www.hernandoschools.org/Domain/29

Spruce Creek High School
801 Taylor Road, Port Orange FL 32127
DP Coordinator Karie Cappiello
Languages English
T: +1 386 322 6272
W: www.sprucecreekhigh.com

St Andrew's School
3900 Jog Road, Boca Raton FL 33434
DP Coordinator Charles Pawlik
MYP Coordinator Kimberly Yash
PYP Coordinator Veronica Steffen
Languages English
T: +1 561 210 2000
W: www.saintandrews.net

St Ann Catholic School
324 North Olive Avenue, West Palm Beach FL 33401
MYP Coordinator David Farley
PYP Coordinator Susan Demes
Languages English
T: +1 561 832 3676
W: www.stannwpb.org

St John Vianney Catholic School
500 84th Avenue, St Pete Beach FL 33706
MYP Coordinator Sarah Fortier
Languages English
T: +1 727 360 1113
W: www.sjvcs.org

St Petersburg High School
2501 Fifth Avenue North, St Petersburg FL 33713
DP Coordinator Shahlaine Kaur Barrett
Languages English
T: +1 727 893 1842
W: www.pcsb.org/stpete-hs

St. Cecelia Interparochial Catholic School
1350 Court Street, Clearwater FL 33756
MYP Coordinator Staci Benson
PYP Coordinator Staci Benson
Languages English
T: +1 727 461 1200
W: www.st-cecelia.org

Stanton College Preparatory School
1149 West 13th Street, Jacksonville FL 32209
DP Coordinator Tamla Simmons
Languages English
T: +1 904 630 6760
W: www.duvalschools.org/stanton

Strawberry Crest High School
4691 Gallagher Road, Dover FL 33527
DP Coordinator Jamie Ferrario
Languages English
T: +1 813 707 7522
W: strawberrycrest.mysdhc.org

Suncoast Community High School
1717 Avenue S, Riviera Beach FL 33404
CP Coordinator Clarence Walker
DP Coordinator Maria Edgar
MYP Coordinator Brett Stubbs
Languages English
T: +1 561 882 3401
W: suh.palmbeachschools.org

Tavares High School
603 N. New Hampshire Avenue, Tavares FL 32778
DP Coordinator Bonnie Watkins
Languages English
T: +1 352 343 3007
W: ths.lake.k12.fl.us

Terry Parker High School
7301 Parker School Road, Jacksonville FL 32211
DP Coordinator MaryBeth Weaver
Languages English
T: +1 904 720 1650
W: www.duvalschools.org/tphs

Thacker Avenue Elementary School for International Studies
301 N. Thacker Avenue, Kissimmee FL 34741
PYP Coordinator Jodie Wiseman Livingston
Languages English
T: +1 407 935 3540
W: www.osceolaschools.net/taes

THE BILTMORE SCHOOL
1600 S. Red Road, Miami FL 33155
PYP Coordinator Sofia C. Romero
Languages English
T: +1 305 266 4666
E: info@biltmoreschool.com
W: www.biltmoreschool.com
See full details on page 515

The Discovery School
102 15th Street South, Jacksonville Beach FL 32250
PYP Coordinator Lauren John
Languages English
T: +1 904 247 4577
W: thediscoveryschool.org

The French American School of Tampa Bay
2100 62nd Avenue N, St. Petersburg FL 33702
PYP Coordinator Emmy Decker
Languages English, French
T: +1 727 800 2159
W: fastb.org

The Rock School
Suite B, 9818 SW 24th Avenue, Gainesville FL 32607
DP Coordinator Erica Littauer
Languages English
T: +1 352 331 7625
W: therocklions.com

The Roig Academy
8000 SW 112 St, Miami FL 33156
PYP Coordinator Gustavo Roig
Languages English, Spanish
T: +1 305 235 1313
W: www.roigacademy.com

Treasure Island Elementary School
7540 East Treasure Drive, North Bay Village FL 33141
PYP Coordinator Tarese Joseph
Languages English
T: +1 305 865 3141
W: www.treasureislandschool.com

Trinity Catholic School
706 E. Brevard Street, Tallahassee FL 32308
MYP Coordinator Allie Lattner
Languages English, Spanish
T: +1 850 222 0444
W: www.trinityknights.org

Union Academy Magnet School
1795 East Wabash Street, Bartow FL 33830
MYP Coordinator Deborah Draper
Languages English
T: +1 863 534 7435

University High School
11501 Eastwood Drive, Orange County, Orlando FL 32817
DP Coordinator Wanda Alvarado
Languages English
T: +1 407 482 8700

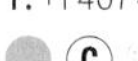

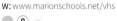

Vanguard High School
7 NW 28th Street, Ocala FL 34475
DP Coordinator Stephanie DeVilling
Languages English
T: +1 352 671 4900
W: www.marionschools.net/vhs

Venice High School
1 Indian Ave., Venice FL 34285
CP Coordinator Gretchen Myers
DP Coordinator Kathleen Jones
Languages English
T: +1 941 488 6726
W: sarasotacountyschools.net/schools/venicehigh

Walker Middle Magnet School
8282 North Mobley Road, Odessa FL 33556
MYP Coordinator Josephine Corder
Languages English
T: +1 813 631 4726
W: walker.mysdhc.org

Westward Elementary School
1101 Golf Avenue, Palm Beach, West Palm Beach FL 33401
PYP Coordinator Bernadette Beneby-Coleman
Languages English
T: +1 561 802 2130
W: wses.palmbeachschools.org

Wicklow Elementary School
100 Placid Lake Drive, Sanford FL 32773
PYP Coordinator Ann Glass
Languages English, Spanish
T: +1 407 320 1250
W: www.wicklow.scps.k12.fl.us

William T Dwyer High School
13601 N Military Trail, Palm Beach Gardens FL 33418
DP Coordinator Deanna Schneider
Languages English
T: +1 561 625 7858
W: wtdh.palmbeachschools.org

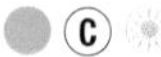

Williams Middle Magnet School for International Studies
5020 N 47th Street, Tampa FL 33610
MYP Coordinator Michelle Weedon-Zimmerman
Languages English
T: +1 813 744 8600
W: www.williams.mysdhc.org/

Wilton Manors Elementary School
2401 NE 3rd Avenue, Wilton Manors FL 33305
PYP Coordinator Gina Pineda
Languages English
T: +1 754 322 8950
W: www.browardschools.com/wiltonmanors

Windermere Preparatory School
6189 Winter Garden Vineland Road, Windermere FL 34786
DP Coordinator Anne Lyng
Languages English
T: +1 407 905 7737
W: www.windermereprep.com

Winter Park High School
2100 Summerfield Road, Winter Park FL 32792
CP Coordinator Donald Blackmon
DP Coordinator Donald Blackmon
Languages English
T: +1 407 622 3212

Winter Springs High School
130 Tuskawilla Road, Winter Park FL 32708
DP Coordinator Sean Loomis
Languages English
T: +1 407 320 8750
W: www.winterspringshs.scps.k12.fl.us

Georgia

4/5 Academy at Fifth Avenue
101 5th Avenue, Decatur GA 30030
PYP Coordinator Shannon Stewart
Languages English
T: +1 404 371 6680
W: fifthavenue.csdecatur.net

A. Philip Randolph Elementary School
5320 Campbellton Road SW, Atlanta GA 30331
PYP Coordinator Shena Small
Languages English
T: +1 470 254 6520
W: www.fultonschools.org/aphiliprandolphes

A.L. Burruss School
325 Manning Road, Marietta GA 30064
PYP Coordinator Candace Torrence
Languages English
T: +1 770 429 3144
W: alburruss.marietta-city.org

Academy of Richmond County
910 Russell Street, Augusta GA 30904
CP Coordinator Carson Thompson
DP Coordinator Carson Thompson
Languages English
T: +1 706 737 7152
W: www.rcboe.org/arc

Alpharetta High School
3595 Webb Bridge Road, Alpharetta GA 30005
DP Coordinator Frank Fortunato
Languages English
T: +1 470 254 7640
W: school.fultonschools.org/hs/alpharetta

ATLANTA INTERNATIONAL SCHOOL
2890 North Fulton Drive, Atlanta GA 30305
DP Coordinator Adam Lapish
MYP Coordinator Carmen Samanes
PYP Coordinator Leonie Ley-Mitchell
Languages English, Chinese, French, German, Spanish
T: +1 404 841 3840
E: admission@aischool.org
W: www.aischool.org

See full details on page 459

Atlanta Neighborhood Charter School
820 Essie Ave, Atlanta GA 30316
MYP Coordinator Dale Scott
Languages English
T: +1 678 904 0051
W: atlncs.org

Avondale Elementary School
10 Lakeshore Drive, Avondale Estates GA 30052
PYP Coordinator Lisa Bonner
Languages English
T: +1 678 676 5202
W: www.avondalees.dekalb.k12.ga.us

Beecher Hills Elementary School
2257 Bollingbrook Drive, SW, Atlanta GA 30311
PYP Coordinator Tiffany Harvey
Languages English
T: +1 404 802 8300
W: www.atlanta.k12.ga.us/Domain/316

Benjamin E. Mays High School
3450 Benjamin E. Mays Dr. SW, Atlanta GA 30331
CP Coordinator Akil Mason
Languages English
T: +1 404 802 5100
W: www.atlantapublicschools.us/domain/3246

Benjamin H Hardaway High School
2901 College Drive, Columbus GA 31906
CP Coordinator Ashley Snow
DP Coordinator Ashley Snow
Languages English
T: +1 706 649 0748

Benteen Elementary School
200 Cassanova Street SE, Atlanta GA 30315
PYP Coordinator Samuel Jones
Languages English, Spanish
T: +1 404 802 7300
W: www.atlantapublicschools.us/Domain/942

Bolton Academy Elementary School
2268 Adams Dr., Atlanta GA 30318
PYP Coordinator Sandy White
Languages English
T: +1 404 802 8350
W: www.atlanta.k12.ga.us/domain/1979

Brandon Hall School
1701 Brandon Hall Drive, Atlanta GA 30350
DP Coordinator Nicole Chapman
Languages English
T: +1 770 394 8177
W: www.brandonhall.org

Burgess-Peterson Academy
480 Clifton Street, Atlanta GA 30316
PYP Coordinator Melanie Searcy
Languages English
T: +1 404 802 3400
W: www.atlantapublicschools.us/Domain/1407

Burke County High School
1057 Burke Veterans Parkway, Waynesboro GA 30830
CP Coordinator LaChonna Avery
Languages English
T: +1 706 554 6691
W: bchs.burke.k12.ga.us

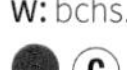

Campbell High School
5265 Ward Street, Cobb County, Smyrna GA 30080
DP Coordinator Lisha Wood
Languages English
T: +1 678 842 6850
W: www.cobbk12.org/campbellhs

Campbell Middle School
3295 South Atlanta Road, Smyrna GA 30080
MYP Coordinator Candace Ellis
Languages English
T: +1 678 842 6873
W: www.cobbk12.org/campbellms/

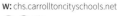

Carrollton High School
202 Trojan Drive, Carrollton GA 30117
DP Coordinator Noah Brewer
Languages English
T: +1 770 834 7726
W: chs.carrolltoncityschools.net

Cascade Elementary School
2326 Venetian Drive SW, Atlanta GA 30311
PYP Coordinator Tiffany Proctor
Languages English, Spanish
T: +1 404 802 8100
W: www.atlantapublicschools.us/cascade

Centennial High School
9310 Scott Road, Roswell GA 30076
DP Coordinator T Lee
Languages English
T: +1 470 254 4230
W: school.fultonschools.org/hs/centennial

Central High School, Macon
2155 Napier Avenue, Macon GA 31204
CP Coordinator Joshua McCorkle
DP Coordinator Joshua McCorkle
Languages English
T: +1 478 779 2300

Clubview Elementary School
2836 Edgewood Road, Columbus GA 31906
PYP Coordinator Kaylee Brooks
Languages English
T: +1 706 565 3017
W: sites.muscogee.k12.ga.us/clubview

Coastal Middle School
4595 US Highway 80 East, Savannah GA 31410
MYP Coordinator Deborah Looye
Languages English
T: +1 912 395 3950

Continental Colony Elementary School
3181 Hogan Rd SW, Atlanta GA 30331
PYP Coordinator Annette Mitchell
Languages English, Spanish
T: +1 404 802 8000
W: www.atlantapublicschools.us/domain/457

Copeland Elementary School
1440 Jackson Road, Augusta GA 30909
PYP Coordinator Joseph Cordova
Languages English, Spanish
T: +1 706 737 7228
W: www.rcboe.org/copeland

D. M. Therrell High School
3099 Panther Trail SW, Atlanta GA 30311
CP Coordinator Sarah Talluri
DP Coordinator Sarah Talluri
MYP Coordinator Ollienia Holloway
Languages English
T: +1 404 802 5300
W: www.atlantapublicschools.us/domain/1327

Dalton High School
1500 Manly Street, Dalton GA 30720
DP Coordinator Marybeth Meadows
Languages English
T: +1 706 278 8757
W: dhs.daltonpublicschools.com

Decatur High School
310 N. McDonough St., Decatur GA 30030
CP Coordinator Duane Sprull
DP Coordinator Karina Green
MYP Coordinator Jessica Miller
Languages English
T: +1 404 370 4170
W: dhs.csdecatur.net

Deerwood Academy
3070 Fairburn Road, Atlanta GA 30331
PYP Coordinator Demiris Gates
Languages English
T: +1 404 802 3300
W: www.atlantapublicschools.us/deerwood

Douglas County High School
8705 Campbellton Street, Douglasville GA 30134
DP Coordinator Robert Bennett
Languages English
T: +1 770 651 6500

Druid Hills High School
1798 Haygood Drive NE, Atlanta GA 30307
DP Coordinator Anne Bracewell
Languages English
T: +1 678 874 6300
W: www.druidhillshs.dekalb.k12.ga.us

Druid Hills Middle School
3100 Mount Olive Drive, Decatur GA 30033
MYP Coordinator Kim Colossale
Languages English
T: +1 678 874 7602
W: www.druidhillsms.dekalb.k12.ga.us

Dublin High School
1127 Hillcrest Parkway, Dublin GA 31021
DP Coordinator Heather Hartley
Languages English
T: +1 478 277 4107
W: www.dublinschools.net/dublinscioto_home.aspx

Dunbar Elementary School
500 Whitehall Terrace, Atlanta GA 30312
PYP Coordinator Keith Tennyson
Languages English
T: +1 404 802 7950
W: www.atlantapublicschools.us/domain/1036

E Rivers Elementary School
8 Peachtree Battle Avenue, Atlanta GA 30305
PYP Coordinator Paul Hulsing
Languages English
T: +1 404 802 7050
W: www.atlantapublicschools.us/rivers

Endeavor International School
48 Perimeter Center East, Atlanta GA 30346
MYP Coordinator Carmen Serghi
Languages English, Spanish
T: +1 770 637 4737
W: endeavorinternationalschool.com

Fernbank Elementary School
157 Heaton Park Dr, Atlanta GA 30307
PYP Coordinator Kelly Taylor
Languages English
T: +1 678 874 9302
W: www.fernbankes.dekalb.k12.ga.us

Fred A. Toomer Elementary School
65 Rogers Street, Atlanta GA 30317
PYP Coordinator JaBria Cooper
Languages English
T: +1 404 802 3450
W: www.atlantapublicschools.us/domain/1631

Garden Hills Elementary School
285 Sheridan Drive, Atlanta GA 30305
PYP Coordinator Melissa Gilbert
Languages English
T: +1 404 842 3103
W: www.gardenhillselementary.com

Heards Ferry Elementary School
6151 Powers Ferry Road, Sandy Springs GA 30339
PYP Coordinator Allie Yancey
Languages English
T: +1 470 254 6190
W: school.fultonschools.org/es/heardsferry

Hephzibah Elementary School
2542 Hwy 88, Hephzibah GA 30815
PYP Coordinator Jennifer Williams
Languages English, Spanish
T: +1 706 592 4561
W: www.rcboe.org/hes

Hephzibah High School
4558 Brothersville Road, Hephzibah GA 30815
MYP Coordinator Tabatha Tucker
Languages English, Spanish
T: +1 706 592 2089
W: www.rcboe.org/hhs

Hephzibah Middle School
2427 Mims Road, Hephzibah GA 30815
MYP Coordinator Stephanie Smith
Languages English, Spanish
T: +1 706 592 4534
W: www.rcboe.org/HMS

High Meadows School
1055 Willeo Road, Roswell GA 30188
PYP Coordinator Danielle Wright
Languages English
T: +1 770 993 2940
W: www.highmeadows.org

High Point Elementary School
520 Greenland Rd NE, Sandy Springs GA 30342
PYP Coordinator Riana Kidder
Languages English
T: +1 470 254 7716
W: school.fultonschools.org/es/highpoint

International Charter School of Atlanta
1335 Northmeadow Parkway, Suite 100, Roswell GA 30076
MYP Coordinator Nicole Bomeli
PYP Coordinator Severine Plesnarski
Languages English, French
T: +1 470 222 7420
W: www.icsatlanta.org

International Community School
2418 Wood Trail Lane, Decatur GA 30033
PYP Coordinator Alexsandra Bermudez
Languages English
T: +1 404 499 8969
W: www.intcomschool.org

International Studies Elementary Charter School
2237 Cutts Drive, Albany GA 31705
PYP Coordinator Amber Davis
Languages English
T: +1 229 431 3384

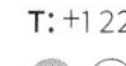

Jackson County Comprehensive High School
1668 Winder Highway, Jefferson GA 30549
DP Coordinator Alex Nichols
Languages English
T: +1 706 367 5003
W: jcchs.jacksonschoolsga.org

Johnson High School
3305 Poplar Springs Road, Gainesville GA 30507
DP Coordinator Holly Wilson
Languages English
T: +1 770 536 2394
W: jhs.hallco.org/web

Jonesboro Middle School
1308 Arnold Street, Jonesboro GA 30236
MYP Coordinator Tracy King
Languages English, Spanish
T: +1 678 610 4331
W: 014.clayton.k12.ga.us

LaGrange High School
North Greenwood Street, LaGrange GA 30240
DP Coordinator Randolph Hardigree
Languages English, Spanish
T: +1 706 883 1590
W: www.troup.org/lhs

Lake Forest Elementary School
5920 Sandy Springs Circle, Sandy Springs GA 30328
PYP Coordinator Stephanie Soldo
Languages English
T: +1 470 254 8740
W: school.fultonschools.org/es/lakeforest
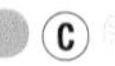

Lake Forest Hills Elementary School
3140 Lake Forest Drive, Augusta GA 30909
PYP Coordinator Crystal Coleman
Languages English
T: +1 706 737 7317
W: www.rcboe.org/lakeforesthills

Lakeside High School
533 Blue Ridge Drive, Evans GA 30809
DP Coordinator Stacey Brown
Languages English
T: +1 706 863 0027
W: lakesidehs.ccboe.net

Langford Middle School
3019 Walton Way, Augusta GA 30909
MYP Coordinator Thaddeaus Mohler
Languages English
T: +1 706 737 7301
W: www.rcboe.org/langford

Lee Street Elementary
178 Lee Street, Jonesboro GA 30236
PYP Coordinator Kizzy Oweregbulem
Languages English
T: +1 770 473 2815
W: 114.clayton.k12.ga.us

Marietta High School
1171 Whitlock Avenue, Marietta GA 30064
CP Coordinator Jose Gonzalez
DP Coordinator Jose Gonzalez
MYP Coordinator Pamela Holman
Languages English
T: +1 770 428 2631
W: www.marietta-city.k12.ga.us/mhs

Marietta Middle School
121 Winn Street, Marietta GA 30064
MYP Coordinator Jill Sims
Languages English
T: +1 770 422 0311
W: www.marietta-city.k12.ga.us/mms

Marietta Sixth Grade Academy
340 Aviation Road, Marietta GA 30060
MYP Coordinator Tamara Edwards
Languages English
T: +1 770 429 3115
W: www.marietta-city.k12.ga.us

Martin Luther King Jr High School
3991 Snapfinger Road, Lithonia GA 30038
DP Coordinator Hanifah Ali
Languages English
T: +1 678 874 5402
W: www.mlkinghs.dekalb.k12.ga.us

Martin Luther King, Jr. Middle School (GA)
545 Hill Street SE, Atlanta GA 30312
MYP Coordinator Tanesha Calhoun
Languages English
T: +1 404 802 5400
W: www.atlantapublicschools.us/page/8440

Maynard Holbrook Jackson High School
801 Glenwood Ave SE, Atlanta GA 30316
CP Coordinator Yusef King
DP Coordinator Yusef King
MYP Coordinator Emily Galloway
Languages English
T: +1 404 802 5200
W: www.atlanta.k12.ga.us/domain/3508

Midvale Elementary School
3836 Midvale Road, Tucker GA 30084
PYP Coordinator Ashley Little
Languages English
T: +1 678 874 3402
W: midvalees.dekalb.k12.ga.us

Montessori Academy Sharon Springs
2830 Old Atlanta Road, Cumming GA 30041
DP Coordinator Carmen Serghi
Languages English, Spanish
T: +1 770 205 6277
W: montessoriacademysharonsprings.com

Morgan County High School
1231 College Drive, Madison GA 30650
DP Coordinator Lisa Hamilton
Languages English
T: +1 706 342 2336
W: www.morgan.k12.ga.us/mchs

Morris Brandon Elementary School
2741 Howell Mill Road, Atlanta GA 30327
PYP Coordinator Samuel De Carlo
Languages English
T: +1 770 350 2153
W: www.morrisbrandon.com

Norcross High School
5041 Staverly Lane, Norcross GA 30092
DP Coordinator Dan Byrne
MYP Coordinator Katherine Kaiser
Languages English
T: +1 770 448 3674
W: www.gcpsk12.org/norcrosshs

North Atlanta High School
4111 Northside Parkway, Atlanta GA 30327
CP Coordinator Danielle Costarides
DP Coordinator Danielle Costarides
MYP Coordinator Nikia Showers
Languages English
T: +1 404 802 4700
W: www.atlanta.k12.ga.us/domain/3377

North Hall High School
4885 Mt Vernon Road, Gainesville GA 30506
DP Coordinator Lori Barrett
Languages English
T: +1 770 534 1080
W: nhhs.hallco.org

Notre Dame Academy, GA
4635 River Green Parkway, Duluth GA 30096
DP Coordinator Marisol Lopez
MYP Coordinator Catherine Rossi
PYP Coordinator Patricia Miletello
Languages English
T: +1 678 387 9385
W: www.ndacademy.org

Parkside Elementary School
685 Mercer Street SE, Atlanta GA 30312
PYP Coordinator Ramia Lowe
Languages English, Spanish
T: +1 404 802 4100
W: www.atlantapublicschools.us/parkside

Peachtree Elementary School
5995 Crooked Creek Road, Peachtree Corners GA 30092
PYP Coordinator Brian Ginley
Languages English
T: +1 770 448 8710
W: www.peachtreees.org

Pinckneyville Middle School
5440 West Jones Bridge Road, Norcross GA 30092
MYP Coordinator Varonica Donham
Languages English
T: +1 770 263 0860
W: www.pinckneyvillemiddle.org

R.N. Fickett Elementary School
3935 Rux Road SW GA 30331
PYP Coordinator Jacqueline Varnado
Languages English, French
T: +1 404 802 7850
W: www.atlantapublicschools.us/fickett

Ralph J. Bunche Middle School
1925 Niskey Lake Rd SW, Atlanta GA 30331
MYP Coordinator Akouvi Nakou
Languages English
T: +1 404 802 6700
W: www.atlantapublicschools.us/bunche

Renfroe Middle School
220 W. College Ave., Decatur GA 30030
MYP Coordinator Julie McFaddin
Languages English
T: +1 404 370 4440
W: renfroe.csdecatur.net

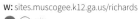

Richards Middle School
2892 Edgewood Road, Columbus GA 31906
MYP Coordinator Kimberly M. Casleton
Languages English
T: +1 706 569 3697
W: sites.muscogee.k12.ga.us/richards

Ridgeview Middle School
5340 S Trimble Road, Atlanta GA 30342
MYP Coordinator Kathleen McCaffrey
Languages English
T: +1 404 843 7710
W: www.fultonschools.org/ridgeviewms

Riverwood International Charter School
5900 Heards Drive NW, Atlanta GA 30328
DP Coordinator Diane Kopkas
MYP Coordinator Beverly Brown
Languages English
T: +1 404 847 1980
W: www.riverwoodics.org

Salem Middle School
5333 Salem Road, Lithonia GA 30058
MYP Coordinator Anne Marion
Languages English
T: +1 678 676 9402
W: www.salemms.dekalb.k12.ga.us

Sandy Creek High School
360 Jenkins Road, Tyrone GA 30290
DP Coordinator Karina Grewe
Languages English
T: +1 770 969 2840
W: www.fcboe.org/Page/45

Sarah Smith Elementary School
4141 Wieuca Road, NE, Atlanta GA 30342
PYP Coordinator Karla Lamar
Languages English
T: +1 404 802 3880
W: www.sarahsmithelementary.com

Sawyer Road Elementary School
840 Sawyer Road, Marietta GA 30062
PYP Coordinator Summer Davis
Languages English
T: +1 770 429 9923
W: www.marietta-city.org/sawyerroad

Shiloh High School
4210 Shiloh Road, Snellville GA 30039
DP Coordinator Kirsten Menosky
Languages English
T: +1 770 972 8471
W: www.shilohhighschool.org

Shiloh Middle School
4285 Shiloh Road, Snellville GA 30039-6146
MYP Coordinator Stacee Brown
Languages English
T: +1 770 972 3224
W: shilohms.com

Sol C Johnson High School
3012 Sunset Blvd, Savannah GA 31404
CP Coordinator Amanda Fanelli
DP Coordinator Amanda Fanelli
Languages English
T: +1 912 395 6400
W: internet.savannah.chatham.k12.ga.us/schools/jhs

South Forsyth High School
585 Peachtree Parkway, Forsyth County, Cumming GA 30041
CP Coordinator Tera Graham
DP Coordinator Kevin Denney
Languages English
T: +1 770 781 2264
W: www.forsyth.k12.ga.us/site/Default.aspx?PageID=22248

Southwest Middle School
6030 Ogeechee Road, Savannah GA 31419
MYP Coordinator Lakisha Gilford
Languages English
T: +1 912 395 3540
W: swms.sccpss.com

St Andrew's School
601 Penn Waller Road, Savannah GA 31410
DP Coordinator Tiffany Phillips
Languages English
T: +1 912 897 4941
W: www.saintschool.com

Stonewall Tell Elementary School
3310 Stonewall Tell Road, College Park GA 30349
PYP Coordinator Karriteshia Hooks
Languages English
T: +1 470 254 3500
W: www.fultonschools.org/stonewalltelles

Summerour Middle School
585 Mitchell Road, Norcross GA 30071
MYP Coordinator Rhonda Perry
Languages English
T: +1 770 448 3045
W: www.gwinnett.k12.ga.us/summerourms

Sutton Middle School
2875 Northside Drive NW, Atlanta GA 30305
MYP Coordinator Colette Minnifield
Languages English
T: +1 404 802 5600
W: www.suttonmiddleschool.org

Teasley Elementary School
3640 Spring Hill Parkway, Smyrna GA 30080
PYP Coordinator Alice Maclellan
Languages English, Spanish
T: +1 770 437 5945
W: www.cobbk12.org/teasley

Tucker High School
5036 Lavista Road, Tucker GA 30084
CP Coordinator Stephanie Willocks
DP Coordinator Stephanie Willocks
Languages English
T: +1 678 874 3702
W: www.tuckerhs.dekalb.k12.ga.us

Tucker Middle School
2160 Idlewood Road, Tucker GA 30084
MYP Coordinator Deborah Mau
Languages English
T: +1 678 875 0902
W: www.tuckerms.dekalb.k12.ga.us

Valdosta High School
3101 N Forrest Street, Valdosta GA 31601
DP Coordinator Betsy McTier
Languages English
T: +1 229 333 8540
W: vhs.gocats.org

Warren T Jackson Elementary School
1325 Mt Paran Road, Atlanta GA 30327
PYP Coordinator Bria Pete
Languages English
T: +1 404 802 8800
W: www.wtjackson.org

Wesley International Academy
211 Memorial Drive, Atlanta GA 30312
MYP Coordinator Anthony Chung
PYP Coordinator Teri Swain
Languages English
T: +1 678 904 9137
W: www.wesleyacademy.org

West Hall High School
5500 McEver Road, Oakwood GA 30566
CP Coordinator Julie Pritchard
DP Coordinator Julie Pritchard
Languages English
T: +1 770 967 9826
W: whhs.hallco.org/web

West Manor Elementary School
570 Lynhurst Dr SW, Atlanta GA 3031
PYP Coordinator Azuree Walker
Languages English, Spanish
T: +1 404 802 3350
W: www.atlantapublicschools.us/westmanor

Westlake High School, Atlanta
2400 Union Road, Atlanta GA 30331
DP Coordinator Alanna Johnson
Languages English
T: +1 470 254 6400
W: www.westlakehs.org

Hawaii

Aina Haina Elementary School
801 W. Hind Drive, Honolulu HI 96821
PYP Coordinator Brendan Burns
Languages English
T: +1 808 377 2419
W: www.ainahaina.k12.hi.us
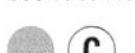

Haha`ione Elementary School
595 Pepeekeo Street, Honolulu HI 96825
PYP Coordinator Denise Kealoha
Languages English
T: +1 808 397 5822
W: www.hahaionees.org

Henry J Kaiser High School
511 Lunalilo Home Road, Honolulu HI 96825
CP Coordinator Shareen Murayama
DP Coordinator Bradley Bogard
MYP Coordinator Kristie Yamamoto
Languages English
T: +1 808 394 1200
W: www.kaiserhighschoolhawaii.org

Island Pacific Academy
909 Haumea Street, Kapolei HI 96707
DP Coordinator Susan Goya
Languages English
T: +1 808 674 3523
W: www.ipahawaii.org
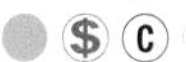

James Campbell High School
91-980 North Road, Ewa Beach HI 96706
DP Coordinator Jo-Hannah Liz Valdez
Languages English
T: +1 808 689 1200
W: www.campbellhigh.org

Kamiloiki Elementary School
7788 Hawaii Kai Drive, Honolulu HI 96825
PYP Coordinator Amber Stanley
Languages English
T: +1 808 397 5800
W: www.kamiloikielementary.org

Koko Head Elementary School
189 Lunalilo Home Road, Honolulu HI 96825
PYP Coordinator Jared Kagihara
Languages English
T: +1 808 397 5811
W: kokoheadschool.org

Le Jardin Academy
917 Kalanianaole Highway, Kailua HI 96734
DP Coordinator Lindsey Schiffler
MYP Coordinator Rachel Domenic
PYP Coordinator Robert Marsden
Languages English
T: +1 808 261 0707
W: www.lejardinacademy.org

Mid-Pacific Institute
2445 Kaala Street, Honolulu HI 96822
DP Coordinator Kymbal Roley
Languages English
T: +1 808 973 5020
W: www.midpac.edu

Niu Valley Middle School
310 Halemaumau Street, Honolulu HI 96821
MYP Coordinator Jennifer Fung
Languages English
T: +1 808 377 2440
W: niuvalleymiddle.org

Idaho

Alturas International Academy
151 N Ridge Avenue, Idaho Falls ID 83402
DP Coordinator Jennifer Radford
MYP Coordinator Jennifer Radford
PYP Coordinator Deana Peoples
Languages English
T: +1 208 522 5145
W: www.alturasacademy.org

 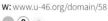

Forge International School
208 S Hartley Lane, Middleton ID 83644
PYP Coordinator Nora Strauch
Languages English, Spanish
T: +1 208 244 0577

North Star Charter School
1400 N Park Lane, Eagle ID 83616
DP Coordinator Danica Holladay
Languages English
T: +1 208 939 9600
W: www.northstarcharter.org

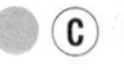

Renaissance High School
1307 East Central Drive, Meredian ID 83642
CP Coordinator Michelle Farrell
DP Coordinator Michelle Farrell
Languages English
T: +1 208 350 4380
W: www.westada.org/domain/58

Riverstone International School
5521 Warm Springs Avenue, Boise ID 83716
DP Coordinator Brittany Roper
MYP Coordinator Jennifer Bistritz
PYP Coordinator Jessica Waugh
Languages English
T: +1 208 424 5000
W: www.riverstoneschool.org

Sage International School of Boise
457 E Parkcenter Blvd, Boise ID 83706
CP Coordinator Guy Falconer
DP Coordinator Andrea Blythe
MYP Coordinator Lainey McGrady
PYP Coordinator Danyelle Davis
Languages English
T: +1 208 343 7243

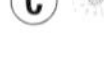

Illinois

Academy for Global Citizenship
4647 West 47th Street, Chicago IL 60632
MYP Coordinator Meredith McNamara
PYP Coordinator Meredith McNamara
Languages English
T: +1 312 316 7373
W: www.agcchicago.org

Agassiz Elementary School
2851 N. Seminary Ave., Chicago IL 60657
MYP Coordinator Jennifer Vincent
PYP Coordinator Freeda Pirillis
Languages English
T: +1 773 534 5725
W: agassizschool.org

Andrew Carnegie Elementary School
1414 East 61st Place, Chicago IL 60637
MYP Coordinator Franci Boateng
Languages English
T: +1 773 535 0882
W: www.carnegie.cps.edu

Back of the Yards College Preparatory High School
2111 West 47th Street, Chicago IL 60609
CP Coordinator Neha Jotwani
DP Coordinator Neha Jotwani
MYP Coordinator Barbara Manjarrez
Languages English
T: +1 773 520 1774
W: www.boycp.org

Barnard Elementary School
10354 S. Charles Street, Chicago IL 60643
MYP Coordinator Madeline Lee
Languages English
T: +1 773 535 2625

Beacon Academy
622 Davis St., Evanston IL 60201
DP Coordinator Hayley Ropiequet
Languages English
T: +1 224 999 1177
W: www.beaconacademyil.org

Belding Elementary School
4257 North Tripp Ave., Chicago IL 60641
MYP Coordinator Michele Stefl
Languages English, Spanish
T: +1 773 534 3590
W: beldingelementary.com

Benito Juarez Community Academy
1450 - 1510 W Cermak Rd, Chicago IL 60608
DP Coordinator Fadwa Fino Rantisi
MYP Coordinator Fadwa Fino Rantisi
Languages English
T: +1 773 534 7030
W: www.benitojuarez.net

Bogan Computer Technical High School
3939 West 79th Street, Chicago IL 60652
DP Coordinator Nora Dandurand
MYP Coordinator John Boggs
Languages English
T: +1 773535 8138
W: www.boganhs.org

British International School of Chicago, South Loop
161 W. 9th Street, Chicago IL 60605
DP Coordinator Jennifer Taylor
Languages English
T: +1 773 599 2472
W: www.bischicagosl.org

Bronzeville Scholastic Institute
4934 South Wabash Avenue, Chicago IL 60615
DP Coordinator Sarah Collins
MYP Coordinator Sarah Collins
Languages English
T: +1 773 535 1101
W: www.bronzevillescholastic.org

Carl Schurz High School
3601 N. Milwaukee Ave, Chicago IL 60641
DP Coordinator Lori Kingen-Gardner
MYP Coordinator Lori Kingen-Gardner
Languages English
T: +1 773 534 3420
W: www.schurzhs.org

Christian Ebinger Elementary School
7350 West Pratt Avenue, Chicago IL 60631
MYP Coordinator Leslie Rector
Languages English
T: +1 773 534 1070
W: ebingerschool.org

Coretta Scott King Magnet School
1009 Blackhawk Drive, University Park IL 60484
PYP Coordinator Shannon Bruns
Languages English
T: +1 708 672 2651

Crete-Monee Middle School
635 Olmstead Ln, University Park IL 60484
MYP Coordinator Kristen Shreffler
Languages English, Spanish
T: +1 708 367 2400

David G. Farragut Career Academy High School
2345 S. Christiana Avenue, Chicago IL 60623
CP Coordinator Andrea Kulas
DP Coordinator Emily Brightwell
MYP Coordinator Emily Brightwell
Languages English
T: +1 773 534 1300
W: www.farragutcareeracademy.org

Daystar Academy
1550 S. State St., Chicago IL 60605
DP Coordinator Alison Good
MYP Coordinator Alison Good
PYP Coordinator Vanessa Espinosa
Languages English, Spanish
T: +1 312 791 0001
W: www.daystaracademy.org

DePaul College Prep
3633 North California Avenue, Chicago IL 60618
DP Coordinator Heidi Bojorges
Languages English
T: +1 773 539 3600
W: www.depaulprep.org

Dr. Edward Alexander Bouchet International Academy
7355 S. Jeffery Boulevard, Chicago IL 60649
MYP Coordinator Franchesca Little
PYP Coordinator Tina Franklin-Bertrand
Languages English, Spanish
T: +1 773 535 0501
W: www.bouchet-brynmawr.cps.edu

Edward K. Duke Ellington Elementary School
243 N Parkside Ave, Chicago IL 60644
MYP Coordinator Anna Baskin-Tines
Languages English
T: +1 773 534 6361
W: www.ellingtoncps.weebly.com

Elgin High School
1200 Maroon Drive, Elgin IL 60120
DP Coordinator Keleigh Foreman
Languages English, Spanish
T: +1 847 888 5100
W: www.u-46.org/domain/58

Elizabeth Sutherland Elementary School
10015 South Leavitt Avenue, Chicago IL 60643
MYP Coordinator Meredith Parker
Languages English
T: +1 773 535 2580

Esmond Elementary School
1865 W Montvale Avenue, Chicago IL 60643
MYP Coordinator Bernika Green
Languages English
T: +1 773 535 2650
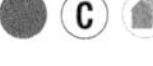

Francisco I Madero Middle School
3202 West 28th Street, Chicago IL 60623
MYP Coordinator Wendy Preciado
Languages English
T: +1 773 535 4466

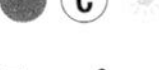

Frazier International Magnet School
4027 West Grenshaw Street, Chicago IL 60624
MYP Coordinator Qiana Wiley-Ruffin
PYP Coordinator Qiana Wiley-Ruffin
Languages English
T: +1 773 534 6880
W: fraziermagnet.cps.edu

GEMS World Academy Chicago
350 E. South Water Street, Chicago IL 60601
DP Coordinator Justin Christensen
MYP Coordinator Sarah Lawrence
PYP Coordinator Taneal Sanders
Languages English
T: +1 312 809 8900
W: www.gemschicago.org

George Washington High School
3535 East 114th Street, Chicago IL 60617
DP Coordinator Mike Pestich
MYP Coordinator Karolina Walkosz
Languages English
T: +1 773 535 6430

German International School Chicago
1447 West Montrose Ave, Chicago IL 60613
PYP Coordinator Katharina Koch
Languages English
T: +1 773 880 8812
W: www.germanschoolchicago.com
 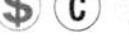

Gwendolyn Brooks Middle School
325 S Kenilworth Ave, Oak Park IL 60302
MYP Coordinator Veena Rajashekar
Languages English
T: +1 708 524 3050
W: www.op97.org/brooks

Hansberry College Prep
8748 S. Aberdeen St., Chicago IL 60620
DP Coordinator Hannah Specht
Languages English
T: +1 773 729 3400
W: nobleschools.org/hansberry

Helen C. Peirce School of International Studies
1423 W. Bryn Mawr, Chicago IL 60660
MYP Coordinator Samuel Lee
PYP Coordinator Kimberly Lebovitz
Languages English
T: +1 773 534 2440
W: peirce.cps.edu

Henry R Clissold School
2350 West 110th Place, Chicago IL 60643
MYP Coordinator Teena Van Dyke
Languages English
T: +1 773 535 2560
W: www.clissold-school.org

Holy Family Catholic Academy
2515 Palatine Road, Inverness IL 60067
PYP Coordinator Laura Clark
Languages English
T: +1 847 907 3452
W: holyfamilycatholicacademy.net

Homewood-Flossmoor High School District 233
999 Kedzie Avenue, Flossmoor IL 60422
DP Coordinator Krystal Davis
Languages English
T: +1 708 799 3000
W: www.hfhighschool.org

Hubbard High School
6200 South Hamlin Avenue, Chicago IL 60629
DP Coordinator Jean Brown
Languages English
T: +1 773 535 2403
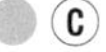

Hyde Park Academy
6220 South Stoney Island Ave, Chicago IL 60637
CP Coordinator Meghan Hoff
DP Coordinator Meghan Hoff
MYP Coordinator Meghan Hoff
Languages English
T: +1 773 535 0882

Ida B Wells Preparatory Elementary Academy
249 E 37TH St, Chicago IL 60653
MYP Coordinator Rozetta Toney
Languages English
T: +1 773 535 1204
W: wellsprepelementary.com

Iles School
1700 South 15th Street, Springfield IL 62703
PYP Coordinator Carolyn Korza
Languages English
T: +1 217 525 3226
W: www.springfield.k12.il.us/schools/iles

Irvin C. Mollison Elementary
4415 South King Drive, Chicago IL 60653
MYP Coordinator Adele Wright
Languages English
T: +1 773 535 1804

James B McPherson Elementary School
4728 N Wolcott, Chicago IL 60640
MYP Coordinator Marianne Turk
Languages English
T: +1 773 534 2625

John F. Kennedy High School
6325 West 56th Street, Chicago IL 60638
CP Coordinator James Clarke
DP Coordinator James Clarke
MYP Coordinator James Clarke
Languages English
T: +1 773 535 2325
W: www.kennedyhschicago.org

John Fiske Elementary
6020 S Langley Avenue, Chicago IL 60637
MYP Coordinator Joi Tillman
Languages English
T: +1 773 535 0990
W: fiskeelementary.org

John H. Kinzie Elementary School
5625 S. Mobile Ave., Chicago IL 60638
MYP Coordinator Lorraine O'Malley
Languages English, Spanish
T: +1 773 535 2425
W: kinzie.cps.edu

John L Marsh Elementary School
9810 South Exchange Avenue, Chicago IL 60617
MYP Coordinator Armando Avila
Languages English
T: +1 773 535 6430

John M Smyth Magnet School
1059 West 13th Street, Chicago IL 60608
MYP Coordinator Kiyana Grayer
PYP Coordinator Debra Ellis
Languages English
T: +1 773 534 7180

Jones-Farrar Magnet School
1386 South Kiwanis Drive, Freeport IL 61032
PYP Coordinator Laura Stocker
Languages English
T: +1 815 232 0610
W: www.fsd145.org/Domain/11

Jose de Diego Community Academy
1313 N Claremont, Chicago IL 60622
MYP Coordinator Angie Field
Languages English
T: +1 773 534 4451
W: josedediego.org

Joshua D Kershaw Elementary
6450 S Lowe Avenue, Chicago IL 60621
MYP Coordinator Aileen Lopez
PYP Coordinator Aileen Lopez
Languages English
T: +1 773 535 3050
W: www.kershawmagnet.org

Kate Starr Kellogg Elementary School
9241 S Leavitt Street, Chicago IL 60643
MYP Coordinator Mary Blake
Languages English
T: +1 773 535 2590
W: kellogg.cps.edu

Legacy Academy of Excellence Charter School
4029 Prairie Road, Rockford IL 61102
MYP Coordinator Lynn Victorov
Languages English
T: +1 815 961 1100
W: www.legacy-academy.com

LINCOLN PARK HIGH SCHOOL
2001 North Orchard Street, Chicago IL 60614
CP Coordinator James Conzen
DP Coordinator Mary Enda Tookey
MYP Coordinator Theresa McCormick
Languages English
T: +1 773 534 8149
E: lpibprogram@aol.com
W: www.lincolnparkhs.org
See full details on page 485

IB AMERICAS

Little Village Elementary School

2620 South Lawndale Avenue, Chicago IL 60623
MYP Coordinator Ivette Loza
Languages English, Spanish
T: +1 773 534 1880
W: lva.cps.edu

Locke Elementary School

2828 North Oak Park Avenue, Chicago IL 60634
MYP Coordinator Edgar Valentin
PYP Coordinator Casey McLeod
Languages English
T: +1 773 534 3300
W: www.lockeschool.org

Lycée Français de Chicago

1929 W Wilson Ave, Chicago IL 60640
DP Coordinator Sebastien Tourlouse
MYP Coordinator Sebastien Tourlouse
Languages English, French
T: +1 773 665 0066
W: www.lyceechicago.org

Mansueto High School

2911 W. 47th Street, Chicago IL 60632
DP Coordinator Thomas Evans
Languages English
T: +1 773 349 8200
W: nobleschools.org/mansueto

Marie Sklodowska Curie Metropolitan High School

4959 South Archer Avenue, Chicago IL 60632
CP Coordinator Alexandra Rake
DP Coordinator Sharyl Barnes
MYP Coordinator Maria Chavez
Languages English
T: +1 773 535 2100
W: www.curiehs.org

Marquette Elementary School

3939 West 79th Street, Chicago IL 60652
MYP Coordinator Dray Patterson
Languages English
T: +1 773 535 2174

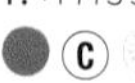

Michael M. Byrne Elementary School

5329 S. Oak Park Avenue, Chicago IL 60638
MYP Coordinator Anyine Galvan-Rodriguez
Languages English, Spanish
T: +1 773 535 2170
W: www.byrnecps.org

Michele Clark Academic Prep Magnet High School

5101 West Harrison Street, Chicago IL 60644
MYP Coordinator Rishawd Watson
Languages English
T: +1 773 534 6250
W: micheleclark.org

Mildred I. Lavizzo Elementary School

138 West 109th Street, Chicago IL 60628
MYP Coordinator Tracey Turner
Languages English, Spanish
T: +1 773 535 5300
W: lavizzo.cps.edu

Moos Elementary School

1711 N. California Ave, Chicago IL 60647
MYP Coordinator Tiffany Frayer
PYP Coordinator Rachel Sweeney
Languages English
T: +1 773 534 4340
W: www.mooselementary.org

Morgan Park High School

1744 West Pryor, Chicago IL 60643
CP Coordinator Bethany Kaufmann
DP Coordinator Bethany Kaufmann
MYP Coordinator Ebony Jones
Languages English
T: +1 773 535 2550
W: www.morganparkcps.org

Nicholas Senn High School

5900 Glenwood Avenue, Chicago IL 60660
CP Coordinator David Gregg
DP Coordinator Claire Saura
MYP Coordinator Lauren Lucchesi
Languages English
T: +1 773 534 2365

Oscar DePriest Elementary School

139 South Parkside Avenue, Chicago IL 60644
MYP Coordinator Tanya Bateson
Languages English
T: +1 773 534 6800
W: depriestschool.org

Oscar F Mayer Elementary School

2250 N Clifton Avenue, Chicago IL 60614
MYP Coordinator Jill Kittinger
Languages English
T: +1 773 534 5535
W: mayermagnet.org

Peoria Academy

2711 West Willow Knolls Drive, Peoria IL 61614
MYP Coordinator Holly Rocke
PYP Coordinator Kay Kellenberger
Languages English, Spanish
T: +1 309 692 7570
W: www.peoriaacademy.org

Percy Julian Middle School

416 S Ridgeland Ave, Oak Park IL 60302
MYP Coordinator Casey Leiby
Languages French, Spanish
T: +1 708 524 3040
W: www.op97.org/julian

Pickard Elementary School

2301 West 21st Place, Chicago IL 60608
MYP Coordinator Jennifer McSurley
Languages English, Spanish
T: +1 773 535 7280
W: www.pickard.cps.edu

Prosser Career Academy

2148 N Long Avenue, Chicago IL 60639
CP Coordinator Jessica Stephenson
DP Coordinator Jessica Stephenson
Languages English
T: +1 773 534 3200
W: www.prosseracademy.org

Proviso East High School

807 S. 1st Avenue, Maywood IL 60153
DP Coordinator Rebecca Tanaka
Languages English
T: +1 708 344 7000
W: www.pths209.org/east

Proviso Mathematics & Science Academy

8601 W. Roosevelt Rd, Forest Park IL 60130
DP Coordinator Rebecca Tanaka
Languages English
T: +1 708 338 4100
W: www.pths209.org/pmsa

Proviso West High School

4701 West Harrison, Hillside IL 60162
CP Coordinator Rebecca Tanaka
DP Coordinator Rebecca Tanaka
Languages English, Spanish
T: +1 708 449 6400
W: www.pths209.org/west

Pulaski International School of Chicago

2230 W McLean Ave, Chicago IL 60647
MYP Coordinator Catherine Green
PYP Coordinator Catherine Green
Languages English
T: +1 773 534 4390
W: www.pulaskischool.org

Rich Township High School

Fine Arts and Communications Campus, 5000 Sauk Trail, Richton Park IL 60471
DP Coordinator Maureen Waters
Languages English, Spanish
T: +1 708 679 3000
W: www.rich227.org

Richard Edwards School

4815 S Karlov Avenue, Chicago IL 60632
MYP Coordinator Elpidio Pintor
Languages English
T: +1 773 535 4878
W: edwardsib.org

Richwoods High School

6301 N. University Street, Peoria IL 61614
DP Coordinator Thomas Hayes
Languages English
T: +1 309 693 4400
W: www.peoriapublicschools.org/richwoods

Roald Amundsen High School

5110 N Damen Avenue, Chicago IL 60625
CP Coordinator Colleen Murray
DP Coordinator Colleen Murray
MYP Coordinator Irwin Lim
Languages English
T: +1 773 534 2320

Roberto Clemente Community Academy

1147 N. Western Avenue, Chicago IL 60622
CP Coordinator Ashten Cales
DP Coordinator Ashten Cales
MYP Coordinator Gillian Dryjanski
Languages English
T: +1 773 534 4000
W: www.rccachicago.org

Sayre Language Academy

1850 N. Newland Avenue, Chicago IL 60707
MYP Coordinator Tara Exarhos
Languages English
T: +1 773 534 3351
W: www.sayre.cps.edu

South Shore International College Prep

1955 E. 75th Street, Chicago IL 60649
CP Coordinator Donna Delmonico
DP Coordinator Donna Delmonico
MYP Coordinator Elsa Rottenberg
Languages English
T: +1 773 535 8350
W: www.southshoreinternational.org

St. Laurence High School
5556 West 77th Street, Burbank IL 60459
DP Coordinator Pete Lotus
Languages English, Spanish
T: +1 708 458 6900
W: www.stlaurence.com

St. Matthias School
4910 N. Claremont Ave, Chicago IL 60625
MYP Coordinator Hope Zollars
PYP Coordinator Jennifer Snell
Languages English
T: +1 773 784 0999
W: www.stmatthiasschool.org

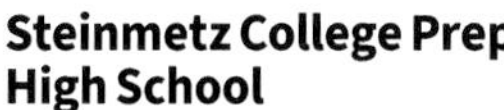

Steinmetz College Prep High School
3030 North Mobile Avenue, Chicago IL 60634
DP Coordinator Rachel Rezny
MYP Coordinator Rachel Rezny
Languages English
T: +1 773 534 3030
W: steinmetzcollegeprep.org

The Ogden International School of Chicago
1250 W Erie, Chicago IL 60642
DP Coordinator John McGinnis
MYP Coordinator Erin Romo
PYP Coordinator Sara Schneeberg
Languages English
T: +1 773 534 0866
W: ogden.cps.edu

Thomas Kelly College Preparatory
4136 South California Avenue, Chicago IL 60632
DP Coordinator Carolyn Brown
Languages English
T: +1 773 535 4915
W: www.kellycollegeprep.org

Thornridge High School
15000 Cottage Grove, Dolton IL 60419
DP Coordinator Jason Curl
Languages English
T: +1 708 271 4403
W: www.district205.net/thornridge

Thornton Township High School
15001 S. Broadway, Harvey IL 60426
DP Coordinator Bradley Ablin
Languages English
T: +1 708 225 4102
W: www.district205.net/thornton

Thornwood High School
17101 South Park Avenue, South Holland IL 60473
DP Coordinator Jennifer Merwald
Languages English
T: +1 708 225 4700
W: www.district205.net/thornwood

Trinity College Preparatory High School
7574 West Division Street, River Forest IL 60305
DP Coordinator Rose Crnkovich
Languages English
T: +1 708 771 8383
W: www.trinityhs.org

Wildwood IB World Magnet School
6950 N Hiawatha, Chicago IL 60646
MYP Coordinator Tammy Guerra
PYP Coordinator Tammy Guerra
Languages English
T: +1 773 534 1187
W: www.wildwoodworldmagnet.org

William H. Seward Communication Arts Academy
4600 S. Hermitage, Chicago IL 60609
MYP Coordinator Lorel Madden
Languages English
T: +1 773 535 4890
W: seward.cps.edu

William Howard Taft High School
6530 West Bryn Mawr Avenue, Region 1 Area 19, Chicago IL 60631
CP Coordinator David Fingado
DP Coordinator Irene Kondos
MYP Coordinator Sarah Gomez
Languages English
T: +1 773 534 1000

Indiana

Carmel High School
520 East Main Street, Carmel IN 46032
DP Coordinator Kathleen Overbeck
Languages English
T: +1 317 846 7721
W: www.ccs.k12.in.us/chs

Cathedral High School
5225 East 56th Street, Indianapolis IN 46226
DP Coordinator Lizabeth Bradshaw
Languages English
T: +1 317 542 1481
W: www.gocathedral.com

Center for Inquiry School 2
725 N. New Jersey Street, Indianapolis IN 46202
MYP Coordinator Christine Snow
PYP Coordinator Christine Snow
Languages English
T: +1 317 226 4202
W: myips.org/cfischools/cfi-school-2

Center for Inquiry School 27
545 E. 19th Street, Indianapolis IN 46202
MYP Coordinator Chad Hyatt
PYP Coordinator Chad Hyatt
Languages English
T: +1 317 226 4227
W: myips.org/cfischools/cfi-school-27

Center for Inquiry School 70
510 46th Street, Indianapolis IN 46205
MYP Coordinator Karla Reilly
PYP Coordinator Karla Reilly
Languages English, Spanish
T: +1 317 226 4270
W: myips.org/cfischools/cfi-school-70

Center for Inquiry School 84
440 E. 57th Street, Indianapolis IN 46220
MYP Coordinator Rachel Green Sharpe
PYP Coordinator Rachel Green Sharpe
Languages English
T: +1 317 226 4284
W: myips.org/cfischools/cfi-school-84

Central Middle School
303 E. Superior St, Kokomo IN 46901
MYP Coordinator Mary Page
Languages English
T: +1 765 454 7000
W: www.kokomoschools.com

Chesterton High School
2125 S 11th Street, Chesterton IN 46304
DP Coordinator Cassie Wallace
Languages English
T: +1 219 983 3730
W: www.duneland.k12.in.us/chs

Childs Elementary School
2211 S. High Street, Bloomington IN 47401
PYP Coordinator Kris Stewart
Languages English
T: +1 812 330 7756
W: www.mccsc.edu/childs

Fishers High School
13000 Promise Road, Fishers IN 46038
DP Coordinator Jennifer Gabbard
Languages English
T: +1 317 915 4290
W: hse.k12.in.us/fhs

Floyd Central High School
6575 Old Vincennes Road, Floyd Knobs IN 47119
DP Coordinator Karen Mayer-Sebastian
Languages English
T: +1 812 542 3005
W: fchs.nafcs.k12.in.us

Goshen High School
401 Lincolnway East, Goshen IN 46526
DP Coordinator Chris Weaver
Languages English
T: +1 574 533 8651

Goshen Middle School
1216 S Indiana Ave., Goshen IN 46526
MYP Coordinator Lisa Carpenter
Languages English, Spanish
T: +1 574 533 0391

Guerin Catholic High School
15300 Gray Road, Noblesville IN 46062
DP Coordinator Meaghan Neman
Languages English
T: +1 317 582 0120
W: www.guerincatholic.org

International School of Indiana
4330 N. Michigan Road, Indianapolis IN 46208
DP Coordinator Jane Bramhill
MYP Coordinator Marithe Benavente-Llamas
PYP Coordinator Lasin Ilbay
Languages English
T: +1 317 923 1951
W: www.isind.org

John Adams High School
808 South Twyckenham Blvd, South Bend IN 46615
DP Coordinator Stacee Fischer Gehring
Languages English
T: +1 574 283 7700

Kokomo High School
2501 S. Berkley Road, Kokomo IN 46902
CP Coordinator Christa Jordan
DP Coordinator Brittany Troyer
MYP Coordinator Lori Magnuson
Languages English
T: +1 765 455 8040
W: www.kokomoschools.com

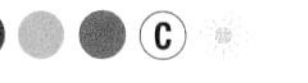

Lafayette Park Elementary School
919 N. Korby, Kokomo IN 46901
PYP Coordinator Nicole Geary
Languages English
T: +1 765 454 7060
W: www.kokomoschools.com

Lawrence Central High School
7300 East 56th Street, Indianapolis IN 46226
DP Coordinator Kathleen Legge
Languages English
T: +1 317 454 5301

Lawrence North High School
7802 Hague Road, Indianapolis IN 46256
DP Coordinator Rebecca Cash
Languages English
T: +1 317 964 7700
W: lawrencenorth.ltschools.org

North Central High School
1801 E 86th St., Indianapolis IN 46240
DP Coordinator Andrew Hodson
Languages English
T: +1 317 259 5301
W: www.nchs.cc

Northridge High School
57697-1 Northridge Drive, Middlebury IN 46540
DP Coordinator Savanna Kimmerling Troyer
Languages English
T: +1 574 825 2142
W: www.mcsin-k12.org/nhs

Pike High School
5401 West 71th street, Indianapolis IN 46268
DP Coordinator Danielle D. Vohland
Languages English
T: +1 317387 2600
W: www.pike.k12.in.us/4/home

Shortridge High School
3401 N. Meridian Street, Indianapolis IN 46208
CP Coordinator Rebecca Huehls
DP Coordinator Jessica Carlson
MYP Coordinator Chloe Richardson
Languages English
T: +1 317 226 2810
W: www.myips.org/shs

Signature School
610 Main Street, Evansville IN 47708
DP Coordinator Shannon Hughes
Languages English
T: +1 812 421 1820
W: www.signature.edu

South Side High School, Fort Wayne
3601 S Calhoun St., Fort Wayne IN 46807
DP Coordinator Kara Fultz
Languages English
T: +1 260 467 2600
W: www.fortwayneschools.org/SouthSide

Sycamore Elementary School
1600 E. Sycamore St., Kokomo IN 46901
PYP Coordinator Laura Yates
Languages English
T: +1 765 454 7090
W: www.kokomoschools.com

Templeton Elementary
1400 S. Brenda Lane, Bloomington IN 47401
PYP Coordinator Amie Easton
Languages English
T: +1 812 330 7735
W: www.mccsc.edu/templeton

University Elementary School
1111 N. Russell Road, Bloomington IN 47408
PYP Coordinator Mary D'Eliso
Languages English
T: +1 812 330 7753
W: www.mccsc.edu/domain/21

Valparaiso High School
2727 North Campbell Street, Valparaiso IN 46383
DP Coordinator Lauren Pickett
Languages English
T: +1 219 531 3070
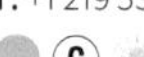

Iowa

Brody Middle School
2501 Park Avenue, Des Moines IA 50321
MYP Coordinator Timm Pilcher
Languages English
T: +1 515 242 8443
W: brody.dmschools.org

Carter Lake Elementary
1000 Willow Dr, Carter Lake IA 51510
PYP Coordinator Erin Schoening
Languages English
T: +1 712 347 5876
W: www.cb-schools.org/Domain/110

College View Elementary School
1225 College Road, Council Bluffs IA 51503
PYP Coordinator Erin Schoening
Languages English
T: +1 712 328 6452
W: www.cb-schools.org/domain/111

East High School
214 High Street, Waterloo IA 50703
DP Coordinator Ellen Shay
Languages English
T: +1 319 433 1800
W: www.waterlooschools.org/schoolsites/easthigh

Goodrell Middle School
3300 East 29th Street, Des Moines IA 50317
MYP Coordinator Lori Bonnstetter
Languages English
T: +1 515 242 8444

Hoover High School
4800 Aurora Ave., Des Moines IA 50310
MYP Coordinator Megan Austin
Languages English
T: +1 515 242 7300
W: hoover.dmschools.org

Hubbell Elementary School
800 42nd Street, Des Moines IA 50312
PYP Coordinator Kati Medick
Languages English
T: +1 515 242 8414
W: hubbell.dmschools.org

Kirn Middle School
1751 Madison Avenue, Council Bluffs IA 51503
MYP Coordinator Debora Masker
Languages English, Spanish
T: +1 712 328 6454
W: www.cb-schools.org/Domain/116

Meredith Middle School
4827 Madison Ave., Des Moines IA 50310
MYP Coordinator Olivia Howe
Languages English
T: +1 515 242 7250
W: meredith.dmschools.org

Merrill Middle School
5301 Grand Avenue, Des Moines IA 50312
MYP Coordinator Danielle Taylor
Languages English
T: +1 515 242 8448
W: merrill.dmschools.org

Moore Elementary School
3716 50th Street, Des Moines IA 50310
PYP Coordinator Laura Manroe
Languages English
T: +1 515 242 8426
W: moore.dmschools.org

Perry Creek Elementary School
3601 Country Club Boulevard, Sioux City IA 51104
PYP Coordinator Tina Brennan
Languages English, Spanish
T: +1 712 279 6836
W: perry-creek.siouxcityschools.org

Stowe Elementary School
1411 East 33rd Street, Des Moines IA 50317
PYP Coordinator Tricia McCarty
Languages English
T: +1 515 242 8435
W: stowe.dmschools.org

Walnut Street School
901 Walnut Street, Des Moines IA 50309
PYP Coordinator Leslie Barnhizer
Languages English
T: +1 515 242 8438
W: walnutstreet.dmschools.org

West High School
425 E. Ridgeway Avenue, Waterloo IA 50702
DP Coordinator Ellen Shay
Languages English
T: +1 319 433 1800
W: www.waterlooschools.org/schoolsites/westhigh
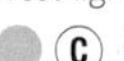

Wilson Middle School
715 N 21st Street, Council Bluffs IA 51501
MYP Coordinator Erin Eckholt
Languages English, Spanish
T: +1 712 328 6476
W: www.cb-schools.org/Domain/123
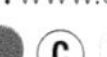

Kansas

Campus High School
2100 W. 55th St. South, Wichita KS 67217
DP Coordinator Casey Meier
Languages English
T: +1 316 554 2236
W: usd261.com/Campus

Hutchinson High School
810 East 13th St, Hutchinson KS 67501
CP Coordinator Cheri Horyna
DP Coordinator Cheri Horyna
Languages English
T: +1 620 615 4100
W: www.usd308.com/node/14

Shawnee Mission East High School
7500 Mission Road, Shawnee Mission KS 66208-4298
DP Coordinator Meredith Sternberg Sternberg
Languages English
T: +1 913 993 6600
W: smeast.smsd.org

Shawnee Mission North High School
7401 Johnson Drive, Overland Park KS 66202
DP Coordinator Jonathan Durham
Languages English
T: +1 913 993 6900
W: smnorth.smsd.org

Shawnee Mission Northwest High School
12701 West 67th Street, Shawnee KS 66216
DP Coordinator Amy Walker
Languages English
T: +1 913 993 7200
W: smnorthwest.smsd.org

Sumner Academy of Arts and Science
1610 N 8th Street, Kansas City KS 66101
CP Coordinator Edward Gunter
DP Coordinator Paula Biggar
Languages English
T: +1 913 627 7200
W: sumner.schools.kckps.org

Washburn Rural High School
5900 SW 61st Street, Topeka KS 66619
DP Coordinator Nick Bowling
Languages English
T: +1 785 339 4100
W: www.wrhs.net

Wichita High School East
2301 East Douglas, Wichita KS 67211
DP Coordinator Michael Boykins
Languages English
T: +1 316 973 7289
W: www.usd259.org/East

Kentucky

Atherton High School
3000 Dundee Road, Louisville KY 40205
DP Coordinator Theresa Beckley
Languages English
T: +1 502 485 8202
W: schools.jefferson.kyschools.us/high/atherton

Highland Middle School
1700 Norris Place, Louisville KY 40205
MYP Coordinator Todd Stanis
Languages English
T: +1 502 485 8266
W: highlandmiddle.com

Holmes High School
2500 Madison Ave., Covington KY 41014
DP Coordinator Ashley Lorenz
Languages English
T: +1 859 655 9545
W: www.covington.kyschools.us/1/home

Sacred Heart Academy
3175 Lexington Road, Louisville KY 40206
DP Coordinator Candace Kresse
MYP Coordinator Tricia Forde
Languages English
T: +1 502 897 6097
W: sha.shslou.org

Tates Creek High School
1111 Centre Parkway, Lexington KY 40517
DP Coordinator John Hatfield
Languages English
T: +1 859 381 3620
W: www.tchs.fcps.net

Tates Creek Middle School
1105 Centre Parkway, Lexington KY 40517
MYP Coordinator Jayme Gill
Languages English
T: +1 859 381 3052
W: www.tcms.fcps.net

Whitney M Young Elementary School
3526 West Muhammad Ali Boulevard, Louisville KY 40212
PYP Coordinator Heidi Cantrell
Languages English
T: +1 502 485 8354
W: www.jefferson.kyschools.us/schools/profiles/young-elementary

Louisiana

Hammond Eastside Elementary Magnet School
45050 River Road, Hammond LA 70401
MYP Coordinator Stephanie Ciresi
PYP Coordinator Katherine Johnson
Languages English
T: +1 985 474 8660
W: www.tangischools.org/heems

Hammond High Magnet School
45168 River Road, Hammond LA 70401
CP Coordinator Deirdra Disher
DP Coordinator Deirdra Disher
Languages English
T: +1 985 345 7235
W: www.tangischools.org/hhms

International High School of New Orleans
727 Carondelet Street, New Orleans LA 70130
DP Coordinator Cody Bourque
Languages English
T: +1 504 613 5703
W: www.ihsnola.org

John Ehret High School
4300 Patriot Street, Marrero LA 70072
DP Coordinator Milena Cajina-Axinn
Languages English
T: +1 504 340 7651
W: www.jpschools.org/Domain/29

Kehoe-France Northshore
25 Patricia Drive, Covington LA 70433
MYP Coordinator Brandy Calato
PYP Coordinator Brandy Calato
Languages English, Spanish
T: +1 985 892 4415
W: www.kf-ns.com

Kehoe-France School
720 Elise Avenue, Metairie LA 70003
MYP Coordinator Alexandra Nichols
PYP Coordinator Samantha Gammon
Languages English, Spanish
T: +1 504 733 0472
W: www.kehoe-france.com

Louisiana State University Laboratory School
45 Dalrymple Drive, Baton Rouge LA 70803-0501
DP Coordinator Candence Robillard
Languages English
T: +1 225 578 9147
W: www.uhigh.lsu.edu

Morris Jeff Community School
3368 Esplanade Ave, New Orleans LA 70119
DP Coordinator Carmen Mack
MYP Coordinator Billie Holmes
PYP Coordinator Michaela Gibboni
Languages English
T: +1 504 373 6200
W: www.morrisjeffschool.org

Riverdale High School
240 Riverdale Drive, Jefferson LA 70121
DP Coordinator David Lindberg
Languages English
T: +1 504 833 7288
W: www.jpschools.org/Domain/67

Maine

FOXCROFT ACADEMY
975 West Main Street, Dover-Foxcroft ME 04426
DP Coordinator Brian Krause
Languages English
T: +1 207 564 8351
E: admissions@foxcroftacademy.org
W: www.foxcroftacademy.org
See full details on page 472

Gray-New Gloucester High School
10 Libby Hill Road, Gray ME 04039
DP Coordinator Bobbie-Jo Thibodeau
Languages English
T: +1 207 657 9306
W: msad15.org/gray-new-gloucester-high-school

Greely High School
303 Main Street, Cumberland ME 04021
DP Coordinator Kimberly MacDonald
Languages English
T: +1 207 829 4805
W: sites.google.com/a/msad51.org/greely_high_school

Kennebunk High School
89 Fletcher Street, Kennebunk ME 04043
DP Coordinator William Putnam
Languages English
T: +1 207 985 1110
W: www.rsu21.net/khs

L'Ecole Francaise du Maine
P.O. Box 737, 99 South Freeport Road, South Freeport ME 04078
PYP Coordinator Elise Le Bihan
Languages English, French
T: +1 207 865 3308
W: efdm.org

Ocean Avenue Elementary School
150 Ocean Avenue, Portland ME 04103
PYP Coordinator Patricia Sprague
Languages English
T: +1 207 874 8180
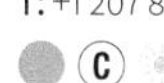

Maryland

Albert Einstein High School
11135 Newport Mill Road, Kensington MD 20895
DP Coordinator Lynette O'Reggio
Languages English
T: +1 301 929 2200

Annapolis High School
2700 Riva Road, Annapolis MD 21401
CP Coordinator Mary Abdo
DP Coordinator Mary Abdo
MYP Coordinator Jay Koller
Languages English
T: +1 410 266 5240
W: www.annapolishighschool.org

Annapolis Middle School
1399 Forest Drive, Annapolis MD 21403
MYP Coordinator Jeanne Aman
Languages English
T: +1 410 267 8658
W: www.aacps.org/Page/3949

Archbishop Spalding High School
8080 New Cut Road, Severn MD 21144
DP Coordinator Angela Bentzley
Languages English
T: +1 410 969 9105
W: www.archbishopspalding.org

Baltimore City College
3220 The Alameda, Baltimore MD 21218
DP Coordinator Ndaneh Smart-Smith
MYP Coordinator Sarah Jeanblanc
Languages English
T: +1 410 396 6557
W: www.baltimorecitycollege.us

Baltimore International Academy
4410 Frankford Avenue, Baltimore MD 21206
MYP Coordinator Henriette Sindjui
PYP Coordinator Beatrice Tchapda
Languages Spanish, Mandarin, Arabic, Russian, French
T: +1 410 426 3650
W: www.baltimoreinternationalacademy.org

Bethesda Chevy Chase High School
4301 East West Highway, Bethesda MD 20814
DP Coordinator Christine Smithson
MYP Coordinator Tony Louis
Languages English
T: +1 240 497 6300
W: www2.montgomeryschoolsmd.org/schools/bcchs

Central High School
200 Cabin Branch Road, Capitol Heights MD 20743
DP Coordinator Corrine Goldt
Languages English
T: +1 301 499 7080
W: www.pgcps.org/central

College Gardens Elementary School
1700 Yale Place, Rockville MD 20850
PYP Coordinator Michael Dushel
Languages English
T: +1 301 279 8470
W: www.mcps.k12.md.us/schools/collegegardenses

Crossland High School
6901 Temple Hill Road, Temple Hills MD 20748
DP Coordinator Melissa Boyd
Languages English
T: +1 301 449 4800
W: www.pgcps.org/crossland
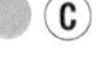

Dwight D Eisenhower Middle School
13725 Briarwood Drive, Laurel MD 20708
MYP Coordinator Steve Mellen
Languages English
T: +1 301 497 3620
W: www.pgcps.org/dwightdeisenhower

Eastport Elementary School
420 Fifth Street, Annapolis MD 21403
PYP Coordinator Corinne Codjoe
T: +1 410 222 1605
W: www.aacps.org/Page/4283

Edgewood High School
2415 Willoughby Beach Road, Edgewood MD 21040
DP Coordinator Jamie Childs
Languages English
T: +1 410 612 1500
W: www.hcps.org

Francis Scott Key Middle School
910 Schindler Drive, Silver Spring MD 20903
MYP Coordinator Beth Hester
Languages English
T: +1 301 422 5600
W: www.mcps.k12.md.us/schools/fskms

Frank Hebron-Harman Elementary School
7660 Ridge Chapel Road, Hanover MD 21076
PYP Coordinator Lacey Gandy
Languages English
T: +1 410 859 4510
W: www.aacps.org/Page/4463

Frederick Douglass High School
8000 Croom Road, Upper Marlboro MD 20772
DP Coordinator Kim Watson
MYP Coordinator Letty Maxwell
Languages English
T: +1 301 952 2400
W: www.pgcps.org/douglass

Germantown Elementary School
1411 Cedar Park Road, Annapolis MD 21401
PYP Coordinator Erika Boltz
Languages English
T: +1 410 222 1615
W: www.aacps.org/Page/4448

Jacobsville Elementary
3801 Mountain Road, Pasadena MD 21122
PYP Coordinator Chelsea Wenzel
Languages English, Spanish
T: +1 410 222 6460
W: www.aacps.org/page/4523

James Madison Middle School
7300 Woodyard Road, Upper Marlboro MD 20772
MYP Coordinator Dana Blair
Languages English
T: +1 301 599 2422
W: www.pgcps.org/jamesmadison

John F Kennedy High School
1901 Randolph Road, Silver Spring MD 20902
DP Coordinator Kia Patrice Davis
MYP Coordinator Erin Radebe
Languages English, Spanish
T: +1 301 929 2100
W: www.mcps.k12.md.us/schools/kennedyhs

Julius West Middle School
651 Great Falls Road, Rockville MD 20850
MYP Coordinator Krista Fiabane
Languages English
T: +1 301 279 3979
W: www.montgomeryschoolsmd.org/schools/westms

Kenwood High School
501 Stemmers Run Road, Essex MD 21221
DP Coordinator Lacey Williams
MYP Coordinator Angela Single
Languages English
T: +1 410 887 0153

Laurel High School
8000 Cherry Lane, Laurel MD 20707
DP Coordinator Allen Diewald
Languages English
T: +1 301 497 2050
W: www.pgcps.org/laurelhs
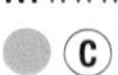

MacArthur Middle School
3500 Rockenbach Road, Fort Meade MD 20755
MYP Coordinator Donna McCallister
Languages English
T: +1 410 679 0032
W: www.aacps.org/Page/6091

Manor View Elementary School
2900 Macarthur Road, Fort Meade MD 20755
PYP Coordinator Marcia Ross
Languages English
T: +1 410 518 6473
W: www.aacps.org/Page/4613

Martin Luther King, Jr. Middle School (MD)
13737 Wisteria Dr., Germantown MD 20874
MYP Coordinator Sarah Day
Languages English
T: +1 301 353 8080
W: www.montgomeryschoolsmd.org/schools/mlkms

MARYLAND INTERNATIONAL SCHOOL
6135 Old Washington Road, Elkridge MD 21075
DP Coordinator Jason Schmidt
MYP Coordinator Pauline Boiser
PYP Coordinator Kylea Goree
Languages English
T: +1 410 220 3792
E: info@marylandinternationalschool.org
W: www.marylandinternationalschool.org
See full details on page 490

Maya Angelou French Immersion School
2000 Callaway Street, Temple Hills MD 20748
PYP Coordinator Alphonse Talon
Languages English
T: +1 301 702 3950
W: www.pgcps.org/mayaangelou

Meade Senior High School
1100 Clark Road, Ft Meade MD 20755
CP Coordinator Jennifer Quinn
DP Coordinator Jennifer Quinn
MYP Coordinator Codie Chaudoin
Languages English
T: +1 410 674 7710
W: www.aacps.org/Page/7917

Melwood Elementary School
7100 Woodyard Road, Upper Marlboro MD 20772
PYP Coordinator Stephanie Major
Languages English
T: +1 301 599 2500
W: www.pgcps.org/melwood

Mercy High School Baltimore
1300 E. Northern Parkway, Baltimore MD 21239
MYP Coordinator Samantha Pomplon
Languages English, Spanish
T: +1 410 433 8880
W: mercyhighschool.com
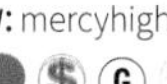

Middle River Middle School
800 Middle River Road, Middle River MD 21220
MYP Coordinator Carey Schuler
Languages English
T: +1 443 809 0165

Monarch Academy Annapolis
2000 Capital Drive, Annapolis MD 21401
PYP Coordinator Annaliese Rudis
Languages English, Spanish
T: +1 410 934 1444
W: monarchacademy.org/annapolis

Monarch Global Academy
430 Brock Bridge Road, Laurel MD 20724
PYP Coordinator Beth Matthews
Languages English
T: 301-886-8648
W: www.monarchacademy.org/global

Montgomery Village Middle School
19300 Watkins Mill Road, Germantown MD 20886
MYP Coordinator Wendy Farmer
Languages English
T: +1 301 840 4660
W: montgomeryschoolsmd.org/schools/mvms

Mount Washington School
1801 Sulgrave Avenue, Baltimore MD 21209
MYP Coordinator Sarah Martin
Languages English
T: +1 410 396 6354
W: mountwashingtonschool.org

Neelsville Middle School
11700 Neelsville Church Road, Germantown MD 20876
MYP Coordinator Daisy Peay
Languages English
T: +1 301 353 8064
W: montgomeryschoolsmd.org/schools/neelsvillems

New Town High School
4931 New Town Blvd, Owings Mills MD 21117
CP Coordinator Chanell Johnson
DP Coordinator Chanell Johnson
MYP Coordinator Molly Muller
Languages English
T: +1 443 809 1614

Newport Mill Middle School
11311 Newport Mill Road, Kensington MD 20895
MYP Coordinator Courtney Osborne
Languages English
T: +1 301 929 2244
W: www.montgomeryschoolsmd.org/schools/newportmillms

North Hagerstown High School
1200 Pennsylvania Ave, Hagerstown MD 21742
CP Coordinator Chris Downs
DP Coordinator Chris Downs
MYP Coordinator Crystal Olszeski
Languages English
T: +1 301 766 8238
W: wcpsmd.com/schools/high-schools/north-hagerstown-high

Northern Middle School
701 Northern Avenue, Hagerstown MD 21742
MYP Coordinator James Rossi
Languages English
T: +1 301 766 8258
W: wcpsmd.com/schools/middle-schools/northern-middle

Old Mill High School
600 Patriot Lane, Millersville MD 21108
CP Coordinator Virginia Sutherin
DP Coordinator Virginia Sutherin
MYP Coordinator Monica Meerman
Languages English
T: +1 410 969 9010
W: www.oldmillhs.org

Old Mill Middle School North
610 Patriot Lane, Millersville MD 21108
MYP Coordinator Diana Christadore
Languages English
T: +1 410 969 5950
W: www.aacps.org/Page/5264

Our Lady of Good Counsel High School
17301 Old Vic Boulevard, Olney MD 20832
DP Coordinator Megan Dean
Languages English
T: +1 240 283 3200
W: www.olgchs.org

Overlook Elementary
401 Hampton Road, Linthicum MD 21090
PYP Coordinator Marcia Ross
Languages English
T: +1 410 222 6585
W: www.aacps.org/Page/4793

Parkdale High School
6001 Good Luck Road, Riverdale MD 20737
DP Coordinator Eric Pavlat
Languages English
T: +1 301 513 5700

Richard Montgomery High School
250 Richard Montgomery Drive, Rockville MD 20852
DP Coordinator Amanda Trivers
MYP Coordinator Molly Clarkson
Languages English
T: +1 301 279 8400
W: montgomeryschoolsmd.org/schools/rmhs

Roberto Clemente Middle School
18808 Waring Station Road, Germantown MD 20874
MYP Coordinator Liz Gall
Languages English
T: +1 301 284 4750
W: montgomeryschoolsmd.org/schools/clementems

ROCHAMBEAU, THE FRENCH INTERNATIONAL SCHOOL
9600 Forest Rd, Bethesda MD 20814
DP Coordinator Sandra Percy
Languages English, French
T: +1 301 530 8260
E: admissions@rochambeau.org
W: www.rochambeau.org
See full details on page 503

Rockville High School
2100 Baltimore Road, Rockville MD 21805
CP Coordinator Laurie Ainsworth
DP Coordinator Laurie Ainsworth
Languages English
T: +1 301 517 8105
W: www.montgomeryschoolsmd.org/schools/rockvillehs

Seneca Academy
15601 Germantown Road, Darnestown MD 20874
PYP Coordinator Melissa Karasek
Languages English
T: +1 301 869 3728
W: www.senecaacademy.org

Seneca Valley High School
19401 Crystal Rock Drive, Germantown MD 20874
CP Coordinator Natasha Ezerski
DP Coordinator Natasha Ezerski
MYP Coordinator Kimberly Becraft
Languages English
T: +1 301 353 8000
W: www.senecavalleyhighschool.com

Silver Creek Middle School
3701 Saul Road, Kensington MD 20895
MYP Coordinator Renee Hill
Languages English
T: +1 240 740 2200
W: www.montgomeryschoolsmd.org/schools/silvercreekms

Silver Spring International Middle School
313 Wayne Avenue, Silver Spring MD 20910
MYP Coordinator Molly Kuhn
Languages English
T: +1 301 650 6544
W: www.mcps.k12.md.us/schools/ssims

South Shore Elementary School
1376 Fairfield Loop Rd, Crownsville MD 21032
PYP Coordinator Erika Boltz
Languages English
T: +1 410 222 3865
W: www.aacps.org/Page/5063

Southgate Elementary School
290 Shetlands Ln, Glen Burnie MD 21061
PYP Coordinator Allison Fleck
Languages English
T: +1 410 222 6445
W: www.aacps.org/Page/5078

Springbrook High School
201 Valley Brook Drive, Silver Spring MD 20904
DP Coordinator Christopher Knocke
MYP Coordinator Lindsey Lipinski
Languages English
T: +1 301 989 5700
W: www.mcps.k12.md.us/schools/springbrookhs

Springdale Preparatory School
1000 Green Valley Rd, New Windsor MD 21776
DP Coordinator Daniele Tellish
Languages English
T: +1 443 671 0072
W: springdaleprep.org

St. Francis of Assisi
3617 Harford Rd, Baltimore MD 21218
MYP Coordinator Catherine Thibault
Languages English
T: +1 410 467 1683
W: www.sfa-school.org

St. Timothy's School
8400 Greenspring Ave, Stevenson MD 21153
DP Coordinator Ghada Jaber
MYP Coordinator Ghada Jaber
Languages English
T: +1 410 486 7400
W: www.stt.org

Stemmers Run Middle School
201 Stemmers Run Rd, Essex MD 21221
MYP Coordinator Nicole Boyd
Languages English
T: +1 443 809 0177

Suitland High School
5200 Silver Hill Road, Forestville MD 20747
DP Coordinator Kamilah Williams
Languages English
T: +1 301 817 0500
W: www1.pgcps.org/suitlandhs

Sunset Elementary School
8572 Ft. Smallwood Road, Pasadena MD 21122
PYP Coordinator Allison Fleck
Languages English
T: +1 410 222 6478
W: www.aacps.org/Page/5093

Tarbiyah Academy
6785 Business Pky, Elkridge MD 21075
PYP Coordinator Shabana Ahmed
Languages English
T: +1 844 827 2492
W: www.tarbiyahacademy.com

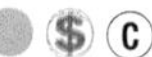

The Boys' School of St Paul's Parish
PO Box 8100, Brooklandville MD 21022-8100
DP Coordinator Andrew Mezeske
Languages English
T: +1 410 825 4400
W: www.stpaulsschool.org

The Calverton School
300 Calverton School Rd, Huntingtown MD 20639
DP Coordinator Susan Dice
Languages English
T: +1 410 535 0216
W: www.calvertonschool.org

Tracey's Elementary School
20 Deale Road, Tracys Landing MD 20779
PYP Coordinator Corinne Codjoe
Languages English
T: +1 410 222 1633
W: www.aacps.org/Page/5108

Urbana High School
3471 Campus Drive, Ijamsville MD 21754
DP Coordinator Jessica McBroom
Languages English
T: +1 240 236 7600

Watkins Mill High School
10301 Apple Ridge Road, Gaithersburg MD 20879
CP Coordinator Reina Flores Sesnich
DP Coordinator Reina Flores Sesnich
MYP Coordinator Richard Courtot Iii
Languages English
T: +1 301 840 3959

Waugh Chapel
840 Sunflower Drive, Odenton MD 21113
PYP Coordinator Lacey Gandy
Languages English
T: +1 410 222 6542
W: www.aacps.org/page/5153

Wellwood International School
2901 Smith Ave, Baltimore MD 21208
PYP Coordinator Katherine Lugli
Languages English, French
T: +1 410 887 1212

Westland Middle School
5511 Massachusetts Avenue, Bethesda MD 20816
MYP Coordinator Rachel Johns
Languages English
T: +1 301 320 6515

Windsor Mill Middle School
8300 Windsor Mill Rd, Milford Mill MD 21244
MYP Coordinator Rebecca Macri
Languages English
T: +1 443 809 0618

Woodmoor Elementary School
3200 Elba Drive, Baltimore MD 21207
PYP Coordinator Cecelia Saunders
Languages English, Spanish
T: +1 410 887 1318

Massachusetts

Abby Kelley Foster Charter Public School
10 New Bond Street, Worcester MA 01606
DP Coordinator Kelly Davila
Languages English
T: +1 508 854 8400
W: www.akfcs.org

British International School of Boston
416 Pond Street, Boston MA 02130
DP Coordinator Karen McWilliam
Languages English
T: +1 617 522 2261
W: www.bisboston.org

Brockton High School
470 Forest Ave, Brockton MA 02301
DP Coordinator Julia Baker
Languages English
T: +1 508 580 7633
W: www.bpsma.org/schools/brockton-high-school

Eagle Hill School
242 Old Petersham Road, P.O. Box 116, Hardwick MA 01037
DP Coordinator Jason Przypek
Languages English
T: +1 413 477 6000
W: www.eaglehill.school

INTERNATIONAL SCHOOL OF BOSTON
45 Matignon Road, Cambridge MA 02140
DP Coordinator Mr. Robert Wilson
Languages English, French, Spanish, Chinese
T: +1 617 499 1451
E: admissions@isbos.org
W: www.isbos.org
See full details on page 479

Joseph F Plouffe Academy
150 Clinton Street, Brockton MA 02302
MYP Coordinator Bonnie Brady
Languages English
T: +1 508 894 4301
W: www.bpsma.org/schools/middle-schools/plouffe-academy

Josiah Quincy Elementary School
885 Washington Street, Boston MA 02111
PYP Coordinator Matthew Lydon
Languages English
T: +1 617 635 8497
W: www.jqes.org

Josiah Quincy Upper School
152 Arlington Street, Boston MA 02116
DP Coordinator Kristina Danahy
MYP Coordinator Jessica Tsai
Languages English
T: +1 617 635 8940
W: bostonpublicschools.org/jqus

Kensington International School
31 Kensington Avenue, Springfield MA 01108
PYP Coordinator Sheree Nolley
Languages English
T: +1 413 787 7522
W: kensington.springfieldpublicschools.com

Marthas Vineyard Public Charter School
P.O. Box 1150, 424 State Road, West Tisbury MA 02575
CP Coordinator Scott Goldin
DP Coordinator Hillary Smith
Languages English
T: +1 508 693 9900
W: mvpcs.org

Mystic Valley Regional Charter School
770 Salem Street, Malden MA 02148
DP Coordinator Jonathan Keating
Languages English
T: +1 781 388 0222
W: www.mvrcs.org

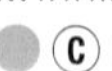

Nauset Regional High School
100 Cable Road, Eastham MA 02642
DP Coordinator Amy Roberts
Languages English
T: +1 508 255 1505
W: www.nausetschools.org/page/537

New Bedford High School
230 Hathaway Boulevard, New Bedford MA 02740
DP Coordinator Donna Guay
Languages English
T: +1 508 997 4511 (EXT: 20559)
W: nbhs.newbedfordschools.org

Pioneer Valley Chinese Immersion Charter School
317 Russell Street, Hadley MA 01035
DP Coordinator Mary MacPherson
Languages English
T: +1 413 582 7040
W: www.pvcics.org

Provincetown Schools
12 Winslow Street, Provincetown MA 2657
MYP Coordinator Richard Gifford
PYP Coordinator Elizabeth Francis
Languages English
T: +1 508 487 5000
W: www.provincetownschools.com

Quabbin Regional High School
800 South Street, Barre MA 01005
DP Coordinator Carrie Vasseur
Languages English
T: +1 978 355 4651

Snowden International School
150 Newbury Street, Boston MA 02116
DP Coordinator Denise Bylaska
Languages English
T: +1 617 635 9989
W: www.snowdeninternational.net

Stoneleigh-Burnham School
574 Bernardston Road, Greenfield MA 01301
DP Coordinator Rose Chaffee-Cohen
Languages English
T: +1 413 774 2711
W: www.sbschool.org

Sturgis Charter School
Administration, 427 Main Street, Hyannis MA 02601
DP Coordinator Camille Manrique
Languages English
T: +1 508 778 1782
W: www.sturgischarterschool.com

THE NEWMAN SCHOOL
247 Marlborough Street, Boston MA 02116
DP Coordinator Rachel Ollagnon
MYP Coordinator Elizabeth Esposito
Languages English
T: +1 617 267 4530
E: admissions@newmanboston.org
W: www.newmanboston.org
See full details on page 518

Wareham High School
7 Viking Drive, Wareham MA 02571
DP Coordinator Ashlie Yates-Paquin
Languages English
T: +1 508 291 3510
W: www.warehamps.org/domain/34

Woodrow Wilson Elementary School
169 Leland St, Framingham MA 01702
PYP Coordinator Heather Flugrad
Languages English, Portuguese
T: +1 508 626 9164
W: www.framingham.k12.ma.us/wilson

Michigan

Adams Elementary School
1005 Adams Drive, Midland MI 48642
PYP Coordinator Melissa Ahearn
Languages English
T: +1 989 923 6037
W: ade.midlandps.org

Adrian High School
785 Riverside Avenue, Adrian MI 49221
DP Coordinator Marie Lucius
Languages English
T: +1 517 263 2115
W: www.adrianmaples.org/schools/adrian-high-school.php

Algonac High School
5200 Taft Road, Clay Township MI 48001
DP Coordinator Miechelle Landrum
Languages English
T: +1 810 794 4911 EXT:1202
W: www.acsk12.us/schools/algonac_jr_sr_high/index.php

Bloomfield Hills High School
3456 Lahser Road, Bloomfield Hills MI 48302
DP Coordinator Amy Merchant
MYP Coordinator Amy Merchant
Languages English
T: +1 248 341 5700
W: www.bloomfield.org/schools/bloomfield-hills-high-school

Bloomfield Hills Middle School
4200 W Quarton Road, Bloomfield Hills MI 48304
MYP Coordinator Kathy Janelle
Languages English
T: +1 248 341 6000
W: www.bloomfield.org/schools/bloomfield-hills-middle-school

Cass Technical High School
2501 Second Ave., Detroit MI 48201
DP Coordinator Sherise Hedgespeth
Languages English
T: +1 313 263 2079
W: www.detroitk12.org/casstech

Central Academy
2459 South Industrial Hwy, Ann Arbor MI 48104
PYP Coordinator Mandy Kaufman
Languages English
T: +1 734 822 1100
W: centralacademy.net

Central Park Elementary School
1400 Rodd Street, Midland MI 48640
PYP Coordinator Whitney Jacobs
Languages English, Spanish
T: +1 989 923 6836
W: www.cpe.midlandps.org

Charyl Stockwell Preparatory Academy
1032 Karl Greimel Drive, Brighton MI 48116
DP Coordinator Elizabeth Holland
T: +1 810 225 9940
W: www.csaschool.org/schools/csa-elementary

Chestnut Hill Elementary School
3900 Chestnut Hill Drive, Midland MI 48642
PYP Coordinator Sarah Westervelt
Languages English
T: +1 989 923 6634
W: che.midlandps.org

City High Middle School
1400 Fuller Avenue NE, Grand Rapids MI 49505
DP Coordinator Jesse Antuma
MYP Coordinator Jesse Antuma
Languages English
T: +1 616 819 2380
W: www.grpublicschools.org/city/

Clarkston High School
6093 Flemings Lake Road, Clarkston MI 48346
DP Coordinator Rebecca Kroll
Languages English
T: +1 248 623 3600
W: chs.clarkston.k12.mi.us

Clear Lake Elementary School
2085 W Drahner Rd, Oxford MI 48371
PYP Coordinator Stephanie Niemi
Languages English
T: +1 248 969 5200

Coit Creative Arts Academy
617 Coit Ave NE, Grand Rapids MI 49503
PYP Coordinator Anne E. Crylen
Languages English
T: +1 616 819 2390
W: www.grps.org/coit

Conant Elementary School
4100 West Quarton Road, Bloomfield Hills MI 48302
PYP Coordinator Stephanie Olson
Languages English
T: +1 248 341 7000
W: www.bloomfield.org/schools/conant-elementary-school

Daniel Axford Elementary School
74 Mechanic Street, Oxford MI 48371
PYP Coordinator Courtney Morin
Languages English
T: +1 248 969 5050

Detroit Country Day School
22305 West 13 Mile Road, Beverly Hills MI 48025
DP Coordinator Celeste Mahabir
Languages English
T: +1 248 646 7717
W: www.dcds.edu

Detroit Edison Public School Academy
1903 Wilkins Street, Detroit MI 48207
DP Coordinator Kimberly Bland
MYP Coordinator Kimberly Bland
Languages English
T: +1 313 833 1100

Dexter High School
2200 North Parker Road, Dexter MI 48130
DP Coordinator Debora Marsh
Languages English
T: +1 734 424 4240
W: dexterschools.org

East Grand Rapids High School
2211 Lake Drive SE, Grand Rapids MI 49506
DP Coordinator Jeff Webb
Languages English
T: +1 616 235 7555
W: egrhs.egrps.org

East Hills Middle School
2800 Kensington Road, Bloomfield Hills MI 48304
MYP Coordinator Julia Beattie
Languages English
T: +1 248 341 6200
W: www.bloomfield.org/schools/east-hills-middle-school

Farmington High School
32000 Shiawassee St., Farmington MI 48336
CP Coordinator Janet Cadeau
DP Coordinator Kevin Miesner
Languages English
T: +1 248 489 3455
W: www.farmington.k12.mi.us/fhs

Fenton High School
3200 W Shiawassee Avenue, Fenton MI 48430
DP Coordinator Mark Suchowski
Languages English
T: +1 810 591 2600
W: www.fentonschools.org

Fremont International Academy
115 East Emmett Street, Battle Creek MI 49017
PYP Coordinator Lena Oliver
Languages English
T: +1 269 965 9715
W: www.battlecreekpublicschools.org/schools/fremont-international

Genesee Academy
9447 Corunna Road, Swartz Creek MI 48473
MYP Coordinator Hana Sankari
Languages English
T: +1 810 250 7557
W: www.gaflint.org

Handley Elementary School
224 N Elm Street, Saginaw MI 48602
PYP Coordinator Kathy Gonzales
Languages English
T: +1 989 399 4250
W: www.spsd.net/handley

Helen Keller Elementary School
1505 N Campbell Road, Royal Oak MI 48067
PYP Coordinator Kara Daunt
Languages English
T: +1 248 542 6500
W: www.royaloakschools.org/elementary/keller

Herbert Henry Dow High School
3901 North Saginaw Road, Midland MI 48640
DP Coordinator Sarah Pancost
Languages English
T: +1 989 923 5382
W: www.dhs.midlandps.org

Hillside Middle School
774 N. Center St., Northville MI 48167
MYP Coordinator William Lambdin
Languages English
T: +1 248 344 8493
W: hillside.northvilleschools.org

Huda School and Montessori
32220 Franklin Road, Franklin MI 48025
MYP Coordinator Aamna Saleem
Languages English
T: +1 248 626 0900
W: www.hudaschool.org

Huron High School
2727 Fuller Road, Ann Arbor MI 48105
CP Coordinator Carrie James
DP Coordinator Carrie James
MYP Coordinator Todd Newell
Languages English
T: +1 734 994 2040
W: www.a2schools.org/huron

International Academy
1020 East Square Lake Road, Bloomfield Hills MI 48304
DP Coordinator Joanne Juco
MYP Coordinator Joanne Juco
Languages English
T: +1 248 341 5900
W: www.iatoday.org
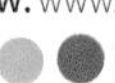 

International Academy of Macomb
42755 Romeo Plank Road, Clinton Township MI 48038
DP Coordinator John Samonie
MYP Coordinator Kyle Kilpatrick
Languages English
T: +1 586 723 7200
W: www.iamacomb.org

Lakeville Elementary School
1400 E Lakeville Rd, Oxford MI 48371
PYP Coordinator Rita Flynn
Languages English
T: +1 248 969 1850

Lansing Eastern High School
220 North Pennsylvania Ave, Lansing MI 48912
DP Coordinator Symantha Outwater
Languages English
T: +1 517 325 6500

Leland Public School
200 N. Grand Ave, Leland MI 49654
PYP Coordinator Ellen Keen
Languages English
T: +1 231 256 9857

Leonard Elementary School
335 East Elmwood, Leonard MI 48367
PYP Coordinator Rita Flynn
Languages English
T: +1 248 969 5300

Lone Pine Elementary
3100 Lone Pine Road, Orchard Lake MI 48323
PYP Coordinator Stephanie Olson
Languages English
T: +1 248 341 7300
W: www.bloomfield.org/schools/lone-pine-elementary-school

Meads Mill Middle School
16700 Franklin Rd., Northville MI 48168
MYP Coordinator Sandra Brock
Languages English
T: +1 248 344 8435
W: meadsmill.northvilleschools.org

Midland High School
1301 Eastlawn Drive, Midland MI 48642
DP Coordinator Amy Rankin
Languages English
T: +1 989 923 5181
W: mhs.midlandps.org

Mitchell Elementary School
3550 Pittsview Dr., Ann Arbor MI 48108
PYP Coordinator Wendy Rothman
Languages English
T: +1 734 997 1216
W: www.a2schools.org/mitchell

Northville High School
45700 Six Mile Road, Northville MI 48168
DP Coordinator James Davis
MYP Coordinator Sandra Brock
Languages English
T: +1 248 344 3800
W: nhs.northvilleschools.org

Notre Dame Preparatory School & Marist Academy
1300 Giddings Road, Pontiac MI 48340
DP Coordinator Katrina Sagert
MYP Coordinator Katherine Thomas
PYP Coordinator Paul Frank
Languages English
T: +1 248 373 5300
W: www.ndpma.org

Novi High School
24062 Taft Road, Novi MI 48375
CP Coordinator Sarah Lephart
DP Coordinator Alaina Brown
Languages English
T: +1 248 449 1500
W: hs.novi.k12.mi.us

Owosso High School
765 East North Street, Owosso MI 48867
MYP Coordinator Lance Little
Languages English
T: +1 989 723 8231
W: www.owosso.k12.mi.us

Owosso Middle School
219 North Water Street, Owosso MI 48867
MYP Coordinator Lance Little
Languages English
T: +1 989 723 3460
W: owossomiddle.mi.opm.schoolinsites.com

Oxford Elementary School
109 Pontiac Street, Oxford MI 48371
PYP Coordinator Courtney Morin
Languages English
T: +1 248 969 1850

Oxford High School
745 North Oxford Road, Oxford MI 48371
DP Coordinator Nicole Barnett
MYP Coordinator Molly Darnell
Languages English
T: +1 248 969 5101

Oxford Middle School
1420 Lakeville Road, Oxford MI 48371
MYP Coordinator Molly Darnell
Languages English
T: +1 248 969 1800

Plymouth Elementary School
1105 East Sugnet Rd, Midland MI 48642
PYP Coordinator Whitney Jacobs
Languages English
T: +1 989 923 7616
W: pme.midlandps.org

Plymouth High School
8400 Beck Road, Canton MI 48187
DP Coordinator Casey Swanson
Languages English
T: +1 734 582 6936
W: www.pccsk12.com/our-schools/plymouth-canton-educational-park

Portage Central High School
8135 South Westnedge Avenue, Portage MI 49002
DP Coordinator Jason Frink
Languages English
T: +1 269 323 5255
W: portageps.org/chs

Portage Northern High School
1000 Idaho Avenue, Portage MI 49024-1233
DP Coordinator Rick Searing
Languages English
T: +1 269 323 5455
W: portageps.org/nhs
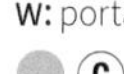

Post Oak Magnet School
2320 Post Oak Lane, Lansing MI 48912
PYP Coordinator Sarah Latty
Languages English
T: +1 517 755 1610

Raisinville Elementary School
2300 North Raisinville Road, Monroe MI 48162
PYP Coordinator Kelly Davis
Languages English
T: +1 734 265 4800
W: www.monroe.k12.mi.us/res

Renaissance High School
6565 W. Outer Drive, Detroit MI 48235
DP Coordinator Melissa Jones
Languages English
T: +1 313 416 4600
W: www.detroitk12.org/renaissance

Royal Oak High School
1500 Lexington Blvd., Royal Oak MI 48073
DP Coordinator Leah Barnett
MYP Coordinator Angela Mallory
Languages English
T: +1 248 435 8500
W: www.royaloakschools.org/high-school

Royal Oak Middle School
709 N. Washington Ave, Royal Oak MI 48067
MYP Coordinator Angela Mallory
Languages English
T: +1 248 541 7100
W: www.royaloakschools.org/middle-school

Scarlett Middle School
3300 Lorraine St, Ann Arbor MI 48108
MYP Coordinator Ryan Soupal
Languages English
T: +1 734 997 1220
W: www.a2schools.org/scarlett

Sherwood Park Global Studies Academy
3859 Chamberlain Ave. SE, Grand Rapids MI 49508
PYP Coordinator Linda Lorenz
Languages English, Spanish
T: +1 616 819 3095
W: www.grps.org/sherwood

Siebert Elementary School
5700 Siebert Street, Midland MI 48640
PYP Coordinator Melissa Ahearn
Languages English
T: +1 989 923 7835
W: sbe.midlandps.org

Southfield High School for the Arts and Technology
24675 Lahser Road, Southfield MI 48033
DP Coordinator Angela Mallory
Languages English
T: +1 248 746 8600
W: www.southfieldk12.org/schools/hs/southfield-high-school

Spring Lake High School
16140 148th Avenue, Spring Lake MI 49456
DP Coordinator Ann Henke
Languages English
T: +1 616 846 5500
W: springlakeschools.org/high

Thompson K-8 International Academy
16300 Lincoln Drive, Southfield MI 48076
MYP Coordinator Angela Mallory
PYP Coordinator Angela Mallory
Languages English
T: +1 248 746 7400
W: www.southfieldk12.org/schools/elem/thompson-k-8-international-academy

Utica Academy for International Studies
37400 Dodge Park Road, Sterling Heights MI 48312
DP Coordinator Christopher Layson
Languages English
T: +1 586 797 3100
W: uais.uticak12.org

Walled Lake Western High School
600 Beck Road, Walled Lake MI 48390
DP Coordinator Ami Friedman
Languages English
T: +1 248 956 4400
W: www.wlcsd.org/Western.cfm

Washtenaw International High School
510 Emerick, Ypsilanti MI 48198
DP Coordinator Daniel Giddings
MYP Coordinator Rachel Hervey
Languages English
T: +1 734 994 8100 EXT:1263
W: www.wihi.org

West Hills Middle School
2601 Lone Pine Road, West Bloomfield MI 28323
MYP Coordinator Kristen Vigier
PYP Coordinator Kristen Vigier
Languages English
T: +1 248 341 6100
W: www.bloomfield.org/schools/west-hills-middle-school

West Ottawa High School
3685 Butternut Drive, Holland MI 49424
DP Coordinator Kate Farney
Languages English
T: +1 616 994 5001
W: www.westottawa.net

Wood Creek Elementary
28400 Harwich Drive, Farmington Hills MI 48334
PYP Coordinator Melissa Wiercinski
Languages English, Spanish
T: +1 248 785 2077
W: www.farmington.k12.mi.us/wck

Woodcrest Elementary School
5500 Drake Street, Midland MI 48640
PYP Coordinator Robin Harshman-Rogers
Languages English
T: +1 989 923 7940
W: wce.midlandps.org

Ypsilanti International Elementary School
503 Oak Street, Ypsilanti MI 48198
PYP Coordinator Sarah Flott
Languages English, Spanish
T: +1 734 221 2400
W: www.ycschools.us

Minnesota

Annunciation Catholic School
525 W 54th St, Minneapolis MN 55419
PYP Coordinator Sheila Loschy
Languages English
T: +1 612 823 4394
W: annunciationmsp.org/school

Anwatin Middle School
256 Upton Ave. S., Minneapolis MN 55405-1997
MYP Coordinator Sarah Wernimont
Languages English, Spanish
T: +1 612 668 2450
W: anwatin.mpls.k12.mn.us

Aquila Elementary School
8500 W 31st Street, St Louis Park MN 55426
PYP Coordinator Olivia Tolzin
Languages English
T: +1 952 928 6500
W: www.slpschools.org/aq

Bancroft Elementary School
3829 13th Ave So, Minneapolis MN 55407
PYP Coordinator Susan Francis
Languages English
T: +1 612 668 3550
W: bancroft.mpls.k12.mn.us

Benjamin E. Mays Magnet School
560 Concordia Ave., St Paul MN 55103
PYP Coordinator Andrea George
Languages English
T: +1 651 325 2400
W: benmays.spps.org

Central High School, St Paul
275 Lexington Pkwy N, St Paul MN 55105
DP Coordinator Ethan Cherin
MYP Coordinator Joleen Armstrong
Languages English
T: +1 651 744 4900
W: central.spps.org

Champlin Park High School
6025 109th Avenue North, Champlin MN 55316
CP Coordinator Georgia Larson
DP Coordinator Ashley Brown
Languages English
T: +1 763 506 6800
W: www.anoka.k12.mn.us/cphs

Fridley High School
6000 West Moore Lake Drive, Fridley MN 55432
CP Coordinator Timothy Leistikow
DP Coordinator Timothy Leistikow
MYP Coordinator Kari Reiter
Languages English
T: +1 763 502 5600
W: fhs.fridleyschools.org

Fridley Middle School
6100 West Moore Lake Drive, Fridley MN 55432
MYP Coordinator Kari Reiter
Languages English
T: +1 763 502 5400
W: fms.fridleyschools.org

Fridley Preschool
6085 7th St NE, Fridley MN 55432
PYP Coordinator Karin Beckstrand
Languages English
T: +1 763 502 5117
W: www.fridleyschools.org/our-schools/fridley-preschool

Global Academy
4065 Central Ave NE, Columbia Heights MN 55421
PYP Coordinator Melissa Storbakken
Languages English
T: +1 763 404 8200
W: www.globalacademy.us

Grand Rapids Senior High School
800 Conifer Drive, Grand Rapids MN 55744
DP Coordinator Dale Christy
Languages English
T: +1 218 327 5760
W: www.isd318.org

Great River School
1326 Energy Park Drive, St Paul MN 55108
DP Coordinator Lindsey Weaver
Languages English
T: +1 651 305 2780
W: www.greatriverschool.org

Harding High School
1540 E. Sixth Street, St Paul MN 55106
CP Coordinator Daniel Weyandt
DP Coordinator Daniel Weyandt
MYP Coordinator Tara Dobbelaere
Languages English
T: +1 651 793 4700
W: harding.spps.org

Hayes Elementary School
615 Mississippi Street NE, Fridley MN 55432
PYP Coordinator Cara Claggett
Languages English
T: +1 763 502 5200
W: www.fridley.k12.mn.us

Hazel Park Preparatory Academy
1140 White Bear Avenue, St. Paul MN 55106
MYP Coordinator Monica Johnson
PYP Coordinator Duane Dutrieuille
Languages English
T: +1 651 293 8970
W: hppa.spps.org

Highland Park Elementary School
1700 Saunders Ave., St Paul MN 55116
PYP Coordinator Michelle Strecker
Languages English
T: +1 651 293 8770
W: highlandel.spps.org

Highland Park Middle School
975 S Snelling Ave., St Paul MN 55116
MYP Coordinator Linda Jones
Languages English
T: +1 651 293 8950
W: highlandms.spps.org

Highland Park Senior High School
1015 Snelling Ave S, Saint Paul MN 55116
DP Coordinator Randolph Stagg
MYP Coordinator Marissa Bonk
Languages English
T: +1 651 293 8940
W: highlandsr.spps.org

Hopkins North Junior High School
10700 Cedar Lake Rd., Minnetonka MN 55305
MYP Coordinator Angela Wilcox
Languages English, French, German, Spanish
T: +1 952 988 4800
W: www.hopkinsschools.org/schools/hopkins-north-junior-high

Hopkins West Junior High School
3830 Baker Road, Hopkins MN 55305
MYP Coordinator Jennifer Poncelet
Languages English
T: +1 952 988 4401
W: www.hopkinsschools.org/schools/hopkins-west-junior-high

International Spanish Language Academy
5959 Shady Oak Road, Minnetonka MN 55343
PYP Coordinator Karen Speich
Languages English, Spanish
T: +1 952 746 6020
W: isla-academy.org

Kaposia Education Center
1225 First Avenue South, South St Paul MN 55075
PYP Coordinator Kim Laska
Languages English
T: +1 651 451 9260
W: kaposia.sspps.schoolfusion.us

Lakes International Language Academy
246 11th Avenue SE, Forest Lake MN 55025
DP Coordinator Gina Graham
MYP Coordinator Natalie Kainz
PYP Coordinator Amy Mueller
Languages Spanish, Mandarin
T: +1 651 464 0771
W: www.mylila.org

Lakeview Elementary School
4110 Lake Drive North, Robbinsdale MN 55422
PYP Coordinator Molly James
Languages English
T: +1 763 504 4100
W: lve.rdale.org

Lincoln Center Elementary School
357 9th Avenue North, South St Paul MN 55075
PYP Coordinator Diane Tiffany
Languages English
T: +1 651 457 9426
W: lincoln.sspps.schoolfusion.us

Matoska International
2530 Spruce Place, White Bear Lake MN 55110
PYP Coordinator Julie Stonehouse
Languages English
T: +1 651 653 2847
W: www.whitebear.k12.mn.us/mis/index.html

Minnetonka High School
18301 Highway 7, Minnetonka MN 55345
DP Coordinator Laura Herbst
Languages English
T: +1 952 401 5703
W: www.minnetonka.k12.mn.us/mhs

Northeast Middle School
2955 Hayes Street North East, Minneapolis MN 55418
MYP Coordinator Angela Evenson
Languages English
T: +1 612 668 1500
W: northeast.mpls.k12.mn.us

Olson Middle School
1607 51st Ave. N., Minneapolis MN 55430
MYP Coordinator Kate Andrews Van-Horne
Languages English
T: +1 612 668 1640
W: olson.mpls.k12.mn.us

Park Center Senior High School
7300 Brooklyn Boulevard, Brooklyn Park MN 55443
DP Coordinator Jon Eversoll
MYP Coordinator Arthur Wachholz
Languages English
T: +1 763 569 7600
W: schools.district279.org/pcsh

Park High School
8040 80th Street South, Cottage Grove MN 55016
DP Coordinator Lisa Martineau
Languages English
T: +1 651 768 3701
W: phs.sowashco.org

Patrick Henry Senior High School
4320 Newton Ave N, Minneapolis MN 55412
CP Coordinator Dale Sedgwick
DP Coordinator Chad Owen
MYP Coordinator Chad Owen
Languages English
T: +1 612 668 2000
W: henry.mpls.k12.mn.us

Peter Hobart Elementary School
6500 West 26th Street, St Louis Park MN 55416
PYP Coordinator Anne LaLonde-Laux
Languages English
T: +1 952 928 6600
W: www.slpschools.org

Ramsey Middle School
1700 Summit Ave., St Paul MN 55105
MYP Coordinator Elisabeth Fontana
Languages English
T: +1 651 293 8860
W: ramsey.spps.org

Rice Elementary
200 NE Third Avenue, Rice MN 56367
PYP Coordinator Nancy Davis
Languages English
T: +1 320 393 2177
W: www.isd47.org/rice

Robbinsdale Cooper High School
8230-47th Avenue North, New Hope MN 55428
DP Coordinator Kari Christensen
MYP Coordinator Kari Christensen
Languages English
T: +1 763 504 8501
W: chs.rdale.org

Robbinsdale Middle School
3730 Toledo Ave. N., Robbinsdale MN 55422
MYP Coordinator Casey Strecker
Languages English
T: +1 763 504 4801
W: rms.rdale.org

Robert Louis Stevenson Elementary School
6080 East River Road, Fridley MN 55432
PYP Coordinator Katherine Talafous
Languages English
T: +1 763 502 5300
W: www.fridley.k12.mn.us/page.cfm?p=2558

Rochester Arts and Sciences Academy
400 5th Avenue SW, Rochester MN 55902
PYP Coordinator Brianna Zabel
Languages English
T: +1 507 206 4646
W: www.rasamn.org

Rochester Montessori School
5099 7th Street NW, Rochester MN 55901
MYP Coordinator Kelley Flanders
Languages English
T: +1 507 288 8725
W: www.rmschool.org

Rockford High School
7600 County Road 50, Rockford MN 55373
CP Coordinator Jill Gordee
DP Coordinator Jill Gordee
MYP Coordinator Jill Gordee
Languages English
T: +1 763 477 5846
W: www.rockford.k12.mn.us/Domain/158
  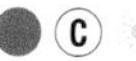

Roosevelt High School
4029 28th Avenue South, Minneapolis MN 55406
CP Coordinator Nicole Lamb
DP Coordinator Christopher Baker-Raivo
MYP Coordinator Nicole Lamb
Languages English
T: +1 612 668 4800
W: roosevelt.mpls.k12.mn.us

Saint John's Preparatory School
1857 Watertower Road, Collegeville MN 56321
DP Coordinator Martina Talic
Languages English
T: +1 320 363 3315
W: www.sjprep.net

Sanford Middle School
3524 42nd Avenue S., Minneapolis MN 55406
MYP Coordinator Elizabeth O'Connell
Languages English
T: +1 612 668 4900
W: sanford.mpls.k12.mn.us

Scandia Elementary School
14351 Scandia Trail North, Scandia MN 55073
PYP Coordinator Anthony Hansen
Languages English
T: +1 651 982 3301
W: sc.forestlake.k12.mn.us

Sejong Academy of Minnesota
1885 University Ave W., Saint Paul MN 55104
MYP Coordinator Lisa Thompson
Languages English, Korean
T: +1 651 301 8722
W: www.sejongacademy.org

South St. Paul Secondary
700 North Second Street, South St Paul MN 55075
DP Coordinator Conrad Anderson
MYP Coordinator Melissa Miller
Languages English
T: +1 651 457 9408
W: southp.schoolwires.net/domain/8

Southwest High School
3414 West 47th Street, Minneapolis MN 55410
CP Coordinator Maria Kimmes
DP Coordinator James Lipps
MYP Coordinator Margaret Berg
Languages English
T: +1 612 668 3036
W: southwest.mpls.k12.mn.us

St Louis Park Middle School
2025 Texas Avenue North, St. Louis Park MN 55426
MYP Coordinator Mia Waldera
Languages English
T: +1 952 928 6300
W: www.slpschools.org/domain/12

St Louis Park Senior High School
6425 W 33nd Street, St Louis Park MN 55426
DP Coordinator Alissa Case
Languages English
T: +1 952 928 6107
W: www.slpschools.org

Susan B Anthony Middle School
5757 Irving Avenue South, Minneapolis MN 55419
MYP Coordinator Joy Misselt
Languages English
T: +1 612 668 3240
W: anthony.mpls.k12.mn.us

Susan Lindgren Elementary School
4801 West 41st Street, St Louis Park MN 55416
PYP Coordinator Nancy Litvack
Languages English
T: +1 952 928 6700
W: www.slpschools.org/sl

Thomas Edison High School
700 22nd Ave. NE, Minneapolis MN 55418
DP Coordinator Sarah Gregg
MYP Coordinator Sharon Cormany
Languages English
T: +1 612 668 1300
W: edison.mpls.k12.mn.us

Washburn High School
201 West 49th St., Minneapolis MN 55419
DP Coordinator Aaron Percy
Languages English
T: +1 612 668 3400
W: washburn.mpls.k12.mn.us

Whittier International Elementary School
315 West 26th Street, Minneapolis MN 55404
PYP Coordinator Libby Dominguez
Languages English
T: +1 612 668 4170
W: whittier.mpls.k12.mn.us

Mississippi

Barack H. Obama Magnet
750 N. Congress Street, Jackson MS 39202
PYP Coordinator Beth West Roach
Languages English
T: +1 601 960 5333
W: www.jackson.k12.ms.us/obama

Jim Hill High School
2185 Coach Fred Harris Drive, Jackson MS 39204
DP Coordinator Felicia Jennings-Wolfe
MYP Coordinator Felicia Jennings-Wolfe
Languages English
T: +1 601 960 5354
W: jimhill.jpsms.org

Northwest Magnet Middle School
7020 Highway 49N, Jackson MS 39213
MYP Coordinator Lakeisha Holmes
Languages English
T: +1 601 960 8700

Ocean Springs High School
PO Box 7002, Ocean Springs MS 39566
DP Coordinator Nell Driggers
Languages English
T: +1 228 875 0333
W: oshs.ossdms.org

Missouri

Academie Lafayette
6903 Oak Street, Kansas City MO 64113
DP Coordinator Katy Wilson
MYP Coordinator Katy Wilson
Languages French
T: +1 816 361 7735
W: www.academielafayette.org

Boyd Elementary School
1409 N. Washington Ave., Springfield MO 65802
PYP Coordinator Shannon Benne
Languages English
T: +1 417 523 1500
W: boyd.spsk12.org

Camdenton High School
662 Laker Pride Road, Camdenton MO 65020
DP Coordinator Melissa Jackson
Languages English
T: +1 573 346 9232
W: camdentonschools.schoolwires.net/chs

Central High School, Springfield
423 E. Central St., Springfield MO 65802
CP Coordinator Donita Cox
DP Coordinator Molly Gray
MYP Coordinator Gretchen Teague
Languages English
T: +1 417 523 9600
W: central.spsk12.org

Eugene Field Elementary School
2120 E. Barataria, Springfield MO 65804
PYP Coordinator Jamie Quirk
Languages English
T: +1 417 523 4800
W: field.spsk12.org

Foreign Language Academy
3450 Warwick Blvd., Kansas City MO 64111
MYP Coordinator Kayla Barnes
PYP Coordinator Michelle Aguirre-Hill
Languages English, Spanish
T: +1 816 418 6000
W: www.kcpublicschools.org/foreignlanguage

Lee's Summit High School
400 Blue Parkway, Lee's Summit MO 64063
CP Coordinator Michelle Edwards
DP Coordinator Michelle Edwards
Languages English
T: +1 816 986 2000
W: lshs.lsr7.org

Lee's Summit North High School
901 NE Douglas, Lee's Summit MO 64086
CP Coordinator Robert Rossiter
DP Coordinator Robert Rossiter
Languages English
T: +1 816 986 3005
W: lsnhs.lsr7.org
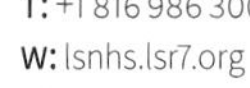

Lee's Summit West High School
2600 SW Ward Road, Lee's Summit MO 64082
CP Coordinator Christy Dabalos
DP Coordinator Christy Dabalos
Languages English
T: +1 816 986 4000

Lincoln College Preparatory Academy
2111 Woodland Ave., Kansas City MO 64108
DP Coordinator Christopher Jennens
Languages English
T: +1 816 418 3000
W: www.kcpublicschools.org/domain/10

Lindbergh High School
5000 S. Lindbergh Blvd., St Louis MO 63126
DP Coordinator Miranda Gelven
Languages English
T: +1 314 729 2410
W: go.lindberghschools.ws/domain/8
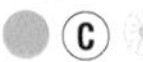

MAP St. Louis
3840 Washington Boulevard, St. Louis MO 63108
DP Coordinator Jennifer Bavaconti
Languages English
T: +1 314 391 2994
W: www.mapstlouis.org

Metro Academic & Classical High School
4015 McPherson Avenue, St Louis MO 63108
DP Coordinator Jeremy VanPelt
Languages English
T: +1 314 534 3894

North Kansas City High School
620 East 23rd Avenue, North Kansas City School Distr, North Kansas City MO 64116
CP Coordinator Chad Lower
DP Coordinator Mitsi Nessa
Languages English
T: +1 816 413 5900
W: www.nkcschools.org/Domain/35

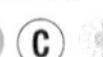

Ozark High School
1350 West Bluff Drive, Ozark MO 65721
DP Coordinator Stacie Wood
Languages English
T: +1 417 582 5701
W: www.ozarktigers.org/Domain/14

Pipkin Middle School
1215 N. Boonville, Springfield MO 65802
MYP Coordinator Michelle Caffey
Languages English
T: +1 417 523 6000
W: www.sps.org/pipkin

Raymore-Peculiar High School
PO Box 789, Peculiar MO 64078
DP Coordinator Kevin Crean
Languages English
T: +1 816 892 1400
W: www.raypec.k12.mo.us/102/Raymore-Peculiar-High-School

Rountree Elementary School
333 E. Grand St., Springfield MO 65804
PYP Coordinator Nicki Foltz
Languages English
T: +1 417 523 4900
W: www.sps.org/rountree

STEAM Academy at McCluer South-Berkeley High
201 Brotherton Lane, Ferguson MO 63135
CP Coordinator Byron Crawford
Languages English
T: +1 314 506 9800
W: www.fergflor.org/mccluer-south-berkeley-high

Montana

Big Sky High School
3100 South Ave. West, Missoula MT 59804
DP Coordinator Cameron Johnson
Languages English
T: +1 406 728 2401
W: www.mcpsmt.org/bigsky

Flathead High School
644 4th Avenue West, Kalispell Public Schools, Kalispell MT 59901
DP Coordinator Kelli Higgins
Languages English
T: +1 406 751 3462
W: www.sd5.k12.mt.us

Hellgate High School
900 South Higgins Avenue, Missoula MT 59801
DP Coordinator Britt Hanford
Languages English
T: +1 406 728 2402
W: www.mcpsmt.org/hellgate

Lone Peak High School
45465 Gallatin Road, Gallatin Gateway MT 59730
DP Coordinator Tim Sullivan
Languages English
T: +1 406 995 4281
W: www.bssd72.org/lone-peak-high-school

McCluer North High School
705 Waterford Drive, Florissant MO 63033
DP Coordinator Byron Crawford
Languages English
T: +1 314 506 9200
W: www.fergflor.org/mccluer-north-high

Missoula International School
1100 Harrison Street, Missoula MT 59802
MYP Coordinator Jeffrey Kessler
PYP Coordinator Julie Lennox
Languages Spanish, English
T: +1 406 542 9924
W: www.mismt.org

Ophir Elementary School
45465 Gallatin Road, Gallatin Gateway MT 59730
PYP Coordinator Brittany Shirley
Languages English
T: +1 406 995 4281
W: www.bssd72.org/ophir-elementary

Nebraska

Bess Streeter Aldrich Elementary
506 N 162nd Avenue, Omaha NE 68118
PYP Coordinator Jodi Fidone
Languages English
T: +1 402 715 2020
W: aldrich.mpsomaha.org

Black Elk Elementary
6708 S 161st Ave, Omaha NE 68135
PYP Coordinator Nicole Beins
Languages English, Spanish
T: +1 402 715 6200
W: blackelk.mpsomaha.org

Central High School
124 North 20th Street, Omaha NE 68102
DP Coordinator Paul Nielson
Languages English
T: +1 531 299 2660

Lewis and Clark Middle School
6901 Burt Street, Omaha NE 68132
MYP Coordinator Philip LaFleur
Languages English
T: +1 402 557 4300

Lincoln High School
2229 J Street, Lincoln NE 68510
DP Coordinator J.P. Caruso
Languages English
T: +1 402 436 1301
W: lhs.lps.org

Millard North High School
1010 S 144th Street, Millard Public Schools, Omaha NE 68154
DP Coordinator Rhonda Betzold
MYP Coordinator Leslie Irwin
Languages English
T: +1 402 715 1411
W: mnhs.mpsomaha.org

Millard North Middle School
2828 South 139th Plaza, Omaha NE 68144
MYP Coordinator Melissa Betts
Languages English
T: +1 402 715 1280
W: nms.mpsomaha.org

Nevada

Basic Academy of International Studies
400 N. Palo Verde Dr., Henderson NV 89015
CP Coordinator James Mitchell
DP Coordinator Cylia Lagunas
MYP Coordinator James Mitchell
Languages English
T: +1 702 799 8000
W: www.basicacademy.org

Brown Junior High School
307 N. Cannes St, Henderson NV 89015
MYP Coordinator Erika Benedict
Languages English
T: +1 702 799 8900
W: www.brownjhs.org

Clarence A. Piggott Academy of International Studies
9601 Red Hills Drive, Las Vegas NV 89117
PYP Coordinator Robert Mitchell
Languages English
T: +1 702 799 4450
W: www.clarencepiggott.org

Earl Wooster High School
1331 East Plumb Lane, Reno NV 89502
CP Coordinator Dustin Coli
DP Coordinator Jennifer Lienau
MYP Coordinator Zeynep Evenson
Languages English
T: +1 775 333 5100
W: www.woostercolts.com

Green Valley High School
460 Arroyo Grande Blvd., Henderson NV 89014
DP Coordinator Angelique Callicoat
Languages English
T: +1 702 799 0950
W: greenvalleyhs.org

Palo Verde High School
333 Pavilion Center Drive, Las Vegas NV 89144
CP Coordinator Amy Reed
DP Coordinator Amy Reed
Languages English
T: +1 702 799 1450
W: www.paloverde.org

Roy W. Martin Middle School
200 N. 28th St., Las Vegas NV 89101
MYP Coordinator Jennifer Cain
Languages English
T: +1 702 799 7922
W: roymartinms.org

Sandy Searles Miller Academy for International Studies
4851 East Lake Mead Blvd, Las Vegas NV 89115
PYP Coordinator Lynn Tyrell
Languages English
T: +1 702 799 8830
W: www.sandymilleracademy.com

Sheila Tarr Academy of International Studies
9400 W. Gilmore Ave., Las Vegas NV 89129
PYP Coordinator Tracy Baldwin
Languages English, Spanish
T: +1 702 799 6710
W: tarracademy.weebly.com

Spring Valley High School
3750 Buffalo Drive, Las Vegas NV 89147
CP Coordinator Anthony Gebbia
DP Coordinator Anthony Gebbia
MYP Coordinator Tiffany Hemberger
Languages English
T: +1 702 799 2580
W: www.springvalleyhs.com

Valley High School
2839 S Burnham Ave., Las Vegas NV 89169
DP Coordinator Andrew Magness
MYP Coordinator Sara Hupp
Languages English
T: +1 702 799 5450
W: www.valleyhs.vegas

Vaughn Middle School
1200 Bresson Avenue, Reno NV 89502
MYP Coordinator Reid Johnson
Languages English
T: +1 775 333 5160
W: www.washoeschools.net/vaughn

Walter Johnson Academy of International Studies
7701 Ducharme Ave, Las Vegas NV 89145-4937
MYP Coordinator Kirsten Lewis
Languages English
T: +1 702 799 4480

New Hampshire

Bedford High School
47 Nashua Road, Bedford NH 03110
DP Coordinator Stephanie Nichols
Languages English
T: +1 603 310 9000
W: www.sau25.net/highschool/BHShome.htm

NEW HAMPTON SCHOOL
70 Main Street, New Hampton NH 03256
DP Coordinator Jennifer McMahon
Languages English
T: +1 603-677-3400
E: admission@newhampton.org
W: www.newhampton.org

See full details on page 497

New Jersey

All Saints Episcopal Day School
707 Washington Street, Hoboken NJ 07030
MYP Coordinator Elizabeth Vino
PYP Coordinator Kim Giammarino
Languages English
T: +1 201 792 0736
W: www.allsaintsdayschool.org

Bergen County Academies
200 Hackensack Avenue, Hackensack NJ 07601
DP Coordinator Michelle Pinke
Languages English
T: +1 201 343 6000 EXT:3385
W: www.bergen.org

Biotechnology High School
5000 Kozloski Road, Freehold NJ 07728
DP Coordinator Linda Rogers
Languages English
T: +1 732 431 7208
W: www.bths.mcvsd.org

Donovan Catholic
711 Hooper Ave, Toms River NJ 08753
DP Coordinator Kimberly Gleinig
Languages English
T: +1 732 349 8801
W: donovancatholic.org

Dr. Orlando Edreira Academy, School 26
631-657 Westminster Avenue, Elizabeth NJ 07208
MYP Coordinator William Clark
PYP Coordinator Diane Bliss
Languages English
T: +1 908 436 5970
W: edreira.epsnj.org/pages/dr__orlando_edreira_academy_no

East Side High School
238 Van Buren St, Newark NJ 07105
DP Coordinator Matthew Ramsay
Languages English
T: +1 973 465 4900
W: www.nps.k12.nj.us/EAS

Fort Lee High School
3000 Lemoine Ave, Fort Lee NJ 07024
DP Coordinator Brandon Barron
Languages English
T: +1 201 585 4675

Freehold Township High School
281 Elton Adelphia Rd, Freehold NJ 07728
DP Coordinator David Fusco
Languages English
T: 732-431-8460
W: www.frhsd.com/freeholdtwp

Hatikvah International Academy Charter School
7 Lexington Avenue, East Brunswick NJ 08816
MYP Coordinator Jeffrey Villanueva
Languages English
T: +1 732 254 8300
W: hatikvahcharterschool.com

Howell High School
405 Squankum-Yellowbrook Road, Farmingdale NJ 07727
DP Coordinator Kristine Jenner
Languages English
T: +1 732 919 2131
W: www.frhsd.com/Domain/13

International High School
200 Grand Street, Paterson NJ 07501
CP Coordinator Catherine Forfia-Dion
DP Coordinator Catherine Forfia-Dion
Languages English
T: +1 973 321 2280
W: ihs-pps-nj.schoolloop.com

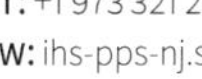

Learning Ladders
35 Hudson Street, Jersey City NJ 07302
PYP Coordinator Zenaida Rivera
Languages English
T: +1 201 885 2960
W: www.learningladdersnj.com

Linden High School
121 W St Georges Avenue, Georges Avenue, Linden NJ 07036
DP Coordinator Anthony Fischetti
Languages English
T: +1 908 486 5432

Morris Knolls High School
50 Knoll Drive, Rockaway NJ 07866
DP Coordinator Scott Gambale
Languages English
T: +1 973 664 2200
W: www.mhrd.org/mkhs

Newark Academy
91 South Orange Avenue, Livingston NJ 07039
DP Coordinator Neil Stourton
Languages English
T: +1 973 992 7000
W: www.newarka.edu

Princeton Junior School
90 Fackler Road, Princeton NJ 08540
PYP Coordinator Courtney Shannon
Languages English
T: +1 609 924 8126
W: www.princetonjuniorschool.org

Princeton Montessori School
487 Cherry Valley Road, Princeton NJ 08540
MYP Coordinator Nuria Perez
Languages English
T: +1 609 924 4594
W: www.princetonmontessori.org

Red Bank Regional High School
101 Ridge Road, Little Silver NJ 07739
DP Coordinator Lisa Boyle
Languages English
T: +1 732 842 8000
W: www.rbrhs.org

Rosa International Middle School
485 Browning Lane, Cherry Hill NJ 08003
MYP Coordinator Al Morales
Languages English
T: +1 856 616 8787
W: rosa.chclc.org

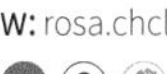

Salem High School
219 Walnut St, Salem NJ 08079
DP Coordinator Jordan Pla
Languages English
T: +1 856 935 3900

Science Park High School
260 Norfolk Street, Newark NJ 10703
DP Coordinator Randolph Mitchell
Languages English
T: +1 973 733 8787
W: www.nps.k12.nj.us/SCI

Shore Regional High School
132 Monmouth Park Highway, West Long Branch NJ 07764
DP Coordinator Vanessa Miano
Languages English
T: +1 732 222 9300 EXT 210
W: www.shoreregional.org

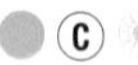

Solomon Schechter Day School of Bergen County
275 McKinley Ave, New Milford NJ 07646
MYP Coordinator Jennifer Coxe
Languages English
T: +1 201 262 9898
W: www.ssdsbergen.org

Tessa International School
720 Monroe Street, Hoboken NJ 07030
PYP Coordinator Amelie Moyaerts Tareen
Languages French, Spanish
T: +1 201 755 5585
W: tessais.org

The Red Oaks School
340 Speedwell Ave., Morristown NJ 07960
MYP Coordinator Benjamin Wagor
Languages English
T: +1 973 998 9424
W: www.redoaksschool.org

Waterfront Montessori
150 Warren St., Suite 108, Jersey City NJ 7302
MYP Coordinator Sarah Woodruff
Languages English
T: +1 201 333 5600
W: www.waterfrontmontessori.com

West Morris Central High School
259 Bartley Road, Chester NJ 07930
CP Coordinator Erin Feltmann
DP Coordinator Debbie Gonzalez
Languages English
T: +1 908 879 5212

West Morris Mendham High School
65 East Main Street, Mendham NJ 07945
CP Coordinator Lindsay Schartner
DP Coordinator Laura Pereira
Languages English
T: +1 973 543 2501
W: www.wmmhs.org

World of ABC
159 2nd St, Jersey City NJ 07302
PYP Coordinator Courtney Bode
Languages English
T: +1 201 963 5555
W: www.worldofabc.com

YINGHUA INTERNATIONAL SCHOOL
75 Mapleton Road, Princeton NJ 08540
PYP Coordinator Jane Lu
Languages English, Chinese
T: +1 609 375 8015
E: admissions@yhis.org
W: yhis.org
See full details on page 520

New Mexico

Corrales International School
5500 Wilshire Ave NE, Albuquerque NM 87113
MYP Coordinator Ana Perea
PYP Coordinator Ana Perea
Languages English
T: +1 505 344 9733
W: corralesis.org

Cottonwood Classical Preparatory School
1776 Montano Road NW, Building 3, Los Ranchos de Albuquerque NM 87107
DP Coordinator Meghan Lowe
Languages English
T: +1 505 998 1021
W: www.cottonwoodclassical.org

Mandela International Magnet School
1720 Llano St, Santa Fe NM 87505
DP Coordinator Jessie Gac
MYP Coordinator Holly Call
Languages English
T: +1 505 467 3370

Navajo Preparatory School
1220 West Apache Street, Farmington NM 87401
DP Coordinator Donna Fernandez
Languages English
T: +1 505 326 6571
W: www.navajoprep.com

New Mexico International School
8650 Alameda Blvd NE, Albuquerque NM 87122
PYP Coordinator Cynthia Pedrotty
Languages English
T: +1 505 503 7670
W: nmis.org

Sandia High School
7801 Candelaria NE, Albuquerque NM 87110
DP Coordinator Derek Maestas
Languages English
T: +1 505 294 1511
W: sandia.aps.edu

Taos International School
Diamond Plaza, 118 Este Es Road, Taos NM 87571
MYP Coordinator Nadine Vigil
PYP Coordinator Yvett Driskell
Languages English, Spanish
T: +1 575 751 7115
W: taosinternationalschool.weebly.com

The International School at Mesa del Sol
2660 Eastman Crossing SE, Albuquerque NM 87106
MYP Coordinator Bonnie Jackson
PYP Coordinator Bonnie Jackson
Languages English
T: +1 505 508 3295
W: www.tisnm.org

UWC-USA
State Rte 65, Montezuma NM 87731
DP Coordinator Alexis Mamaux
Languages English
T: +1 505 454 4252
W: www.uwc-usa.org

New York

Albany High School
700 Washington Avenue, Albany NY 12203
DP Coordinator Leah Evans
Languages English
T: +1 518 475 6200
W: ahs.albany.k12.ny.us

Alverta B. Gray Schultz Middle School
70 Greenwich Street, Hempstead NY 11550
MYP Coordinator Linda St John
Languages English, Spanish
T: +1 516 434 4000
W: www.hempsteadschools.org/site/default.aspx?pageid=23

Archbishop Walsh Academy
208 North 24th Street, Olean NY 14760
DP Coordinator Liselle Esposito
Languages English
T: +1 716 372 8122
W: www.stcswalsh.org

Baccalaureate School for Global Education
34-12 36th Avenue, Astoria NY 11106
DP Coordinator Jaime Meisler
Languages English
T: +1 718 361 5275
W: www.bsge.org

Ballston Spa High School
220 Ballston Avenue, Ballston Spa NY 12020
DP Coordinator Nicole Stehle
Languages English
T: +1 518 884 7150
W: www.bscsd.org/domain/87

Barack Obama Elementary School
176 William Street, Hempstead NY 11550
PYP Coordinator Vicki McMillan
Languages English, Spanish
T: +1 516 434 4400
W: www.hempsteadschools.org/domain/12

Bay Shore High School
155 Third Avenue, Bay Shore NY 11706
DP Coordinator Jonathan Nelson
Languages English
T: +1 631 968 1157
W: www.bayshore.k12.ny.us/SeniorHigh.cfm

BELA Charter School
125 Stuyvesant Ave., Brooklyn NY 11221
DP Coordinator David Boone
Languages English
T: +1 347 473 8830
W: www.belahs.org

Binghamton High School
31 Main Street, Binghamton NY 13905
CP Coordinator Steve McGovern
DP Coordinator James Gill
MYP Coordinator Mark Ward
Languages English
T: +1 607 762 8200

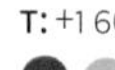

Bishop Ludden Junior Senior High School
815 Fay Road, Syracuse NY 13219
DP Coordinator Heidi Busa
Languages English
T: +1 315 468 2591
W: www.bishopludden.org

Bloomfield Elementary School
45 Maple Avenue, Suite B, Bloomfield NY 14469
PYP Coordinator Kathryn Taylor
Languages English
T: +1 585 657 6121
W: bloomfieldcsd.org

Bloomfield High School
PO Box 250, Oakmount Avenue, East Bloomfield NY 14469
DP Coordinator Melissa Arber
Languages English
T: +1 585 657 6121
W: www.bloomfieldcsd.org

Boerum Hill School for International Studies
284 Baltic Street, Brooklyn NY 11201
DP Coordinator Lindsay Zackman
MYP Coordinator Emily Brandt
Languages English
T: +1 718 330 9390
W: www.K497.org

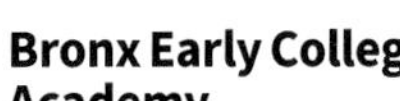

Bronx Early College Academy
250 East 164th Street, Bronx NY 10456
CP Coordinator Theodore Ramey
DP Coordinator Theodore Ramey
Languages English
T: +1 718 681 8287
W: www.beca324.org

Brooklyn Friends School
375 Pearl Street, Brooklyn, New York NY 11201
DP Coordinator Daniel Paccione
Languages English
T: +1 718 852 1029
W: www.brooklynfriends.org

Brooklyn Prospect Charter School
80 Willoughby Street, Brooklyn NY 11201
DP Coordinator Jamie Vaughan
Languages English
T: +1 718 722 7634
W: www.brooklynprospect.org

Buffalo Academy of the Sacred Heart
3860 Main Street, Buffalo NY 14226
DP Coordinator Meghan D'Andrea
Languages English
T: +1 716 834 2101
W: www.sacredheartacademy.org

Canandaigua Academy
1 Academy Circle, Canandaigua NY 14424
DP Coordinator Dave Gioseffi
Languages English
T: +1 585 396 3802

Center Moriches High School
311 Frowein Road, Center Moriches NY 11934
DP Coordinator Richard Roberts
Languages English
T: +1 631 878 0540

Center Moriches Middle School
311 Frowein Road, Center Moriches NY 11934
MYP Coordinator Teresa Horoszewski
Languages English, French
T: +1 631 878 2519

Chestnut Ridge Middle School
892 Chestnut Ridge Road, Chestnut Ridge NY 10977
MYP Coordinator Yolanda Gardner
Languages English
T: +1 845 577 6300
W: www.ercsd.org/chestnutridge

Churchville-Chili Senior High School
5786 Buffalo Road, Churchville NY 14428
DP Coordinator Kelley Fahy
Languages English
T: +1 585 293 4540
W: www.cccsd.org/seniorhighschool_home.aspx

City Honors School
186 E North Street, Buffalo NY 14204
DP Coordinator Elissa Morganti Banas
MYP Coordinator James Moses
Languages English
T: +1 716 816 4230
W: www.cityhonors.org

Clarkstown High School North
151 Congers Road, New City NY 10956-6272
DP Coordinator Andrea Miranda
Languages English
T: +1 845 639 6500
W: www.ccsd.edu/Domain/19

Clarkstown Senior High School South
31 Demarest Mill Road, West Nyack NY 10994
DP Coordinator Melina Balducci-Flugger
Languages English
T: +1 845 624 3400
W: www.ccsd.edu/south

Clary Middle School
100 Amidon Drive, Syracuse NY 13205
MYP Coordinator Jessica Stagnitta
Languages English
T: +1 315 435 4411

Clayton Huey Elementary School
511 Main Street Center, Moriches NY 11934
PYP Coordinator Michelle Craig
Languages English, Spanish
T: +1 631 878 9780
W: www.cmschools.org/schools/claytonhuey

Commack High School
1 Scholar Lane, Commack NY 11725-1297
CP Coordinator Eric Biagi
DP Coordinator Eric Biagi
Languages English
T: +1 631 912 2106
W: www.commack.k12.ny.us/commackhighschool_home.aspx

Commack Middle School
700 Vanderbilt Parkway, Commack NY 11725
MYP Coordinator Kristen Kornweiss
Languages English
T: +1 631 858 3500
W: www.commack.k12.ny.us/commackmiddleschool_home.aspx

Corning-Painted Post High School
201 Cantigney St., Corning NY 14830
DP Coordinator Kristie Radford
MYP Coordinator Tammie Edinger
Languages English
T: +1 607 654 2988
W: www.corningareaschools.com/1/home

Corning-Painted Post Middle School
35 Victory Highway, Painted Post NY 14870
MYP Coordinator Tammie Edinger
Languages English
T: +1 607 654 2966
W: www.corningareaschools.com/2/home

CULTURAL ARTS ACADEMY CHARTER SCHOOL AT SPRING CREEK
1400 Linden Blvd, Brooklyn NY 11212
PYP Coordinator Esther Hong
Languages English, Spanish
T: +1 718 683 3300
E: caacs@caa-ny.org
W: www.culturalartsacademy.org
See full details on page 463

Curtis High School
105 Hamilton Avenue, Staten Island NY 10301
CP Coordinator Alicia Isasi-Endress
DP Coordinator Kathleen Francis
Languages English
T: +1 718 390 1800
W: www.curtishs.org

Cypress Hills Collegiate Prep
999 Jamaica Avenue, Brooklyn NY 11208
DP Coordinator Anthony Stipanov
Languages English, Spanish
T: +1 718 647 1672
W: chcpschool.org

David Paterson Elementary School
40 Fulton Street, Hempstead NY 11550
PYP Coordinator Elyse Amos
Languages English, Spanish
T: +1 516 434 4450
W: www.hempsteadschools.org/domain/11

Dobbs Ferry High School
505 Broadway, Dobbs Ferry NY 10522
DP Coordinator Michelle Haggerty
MYP Coordinator Jennifer Hickey
Languages English
T: +1 914 693 7645
W: www.dfsd.org/hs

Dobbs Ferry Middle School
505 Broadway, Dobbs Ferry NY 10522
MYP Coordinator Jennifer Hickey
Languages English
T: +1 914 693 7640
W: www.dfsd.org/ms

DWIGHT SCHOOL
291 Central Park West, New York NY 10024
DP Coordinator Mike Paul
MYP Coordinator Beth Billard
PYP Coordinator Alex White
Languages English
T: +1 212 724 6360
E: admissions@dwight.edu
W: dwight.edu/newyork
See full details on page 464

East Middle School
167 E Frederick Street, Binghamton NY 13904
MYP Coordinator Mark Ward
Languages English
T: +1 607 762 8300

Eastridge High School
2350 East Ridge Road, Rochester NY 14622
CP Coordinator Andrew Walter
DP Coordinator Terry Reynolds
Languages English
T: +1 585 339 1450
W: www.eastiron.org/Domain/9

EF Academy New York
582 Columbus Avenue, Thornwood NY 10594
DP Coordinator Amy Park
Languages English
T: +1 914 495 6056
W: www.efacademy.org

FRENCH-AMERICAN SCHOOL OF NEW YORK
320 East Boston Post Road, Mamaroneck NY 10543
DP Coordinator Fred Ondiko
Languages English, French
T: +1 914 250 0000
E: admissions@fasny.org
W: www.fasny.org
See full details on page 473

Global Community Charter School
2350 Fifth Avenue, New York NY 10037
PYP Coordinator Jasmin Candelario
Languages English
T: +1 646 360 2363
W: www.globalcommunitycs.org

Greenville Central School District
Route 81, PO Box 129, Greenville NY 12083
DP Coordinator Kendall Fritze
Languages English
T: +1 518 966 5190
W: www.greenville.k12.ny.us

Harlem Village Academies High
35 West 124th Street, New York NY 10027
DP Coordinator David Quinn
Languages English
T: +1 646 812 9200
W: www.harlemvillageacademies.org/high-school

Harrison High School
255 Union Avenue, Harrison NY 10528
DP Coordinator Christopher Tyler
MYP Coordinator Shari Heyen
Languages English
T: +1 914 630 3095
W: www.harrisoncsd.org

Hauppauge High School
PO Box 6006, Hauppauge NY 11788
DP Coordinator Kelly Barry
Languages English
T: +1 631 761 8302
W: www.hauppauge.k12.ny.us/site/Default.aspx?PageID=9

Highview School
200 North Central Avenue, Hartsdale NY 10530
PYP Coordinator Sharon Harris
Languages English
T: +1 914 946 6946
W: www.greenburghcsd.org/domain/154

Hilton High School
400 East Avenue, Hilton NY 14468
DP Coordinator Tim Ackroyd
MYP Coordinator Steve Cudzilo
Languages English
T: +1 585 392 1000

Horizons-on-the-Hudson Magnet School
137 Montgomery Street, Newburgh NY 12550
PYP Coordinator Robert Glowacki
Languages English
T: +1 845 563 3725
W: www.newburghschools.org/horizons.php

International School of Brooklyn
477 Court Street, Brooklyn, New York NY 11231
MYP Coordinator Brenna DiCola
PYP Coordinator Selena Lynn
Languages English, French, Spanish
T: +1 718 369 3023
W: www.isbrooklyn.org

J. T. Roberts PreK-8 School
715 Glenwood Avenue, Syracuse NY 13207
MYP Coordinator Brooke Thomas
Languages English
T: +1 315 435 4635

Jackson Main School
451 Jackson Street, Hempstead NY 11550
PYP Coordinator Saritha Perez
Languages English, Spanish
T: +1 516 434 4650
W: www.hempsteadschools.org/site/Default.aspx?PageID=21

James A Beneway High School
6200 Ontario Center Road, Ontario Center NY 14520
DP Coordinator Ryan VanAllen
Languages English
T: +1 315 524 1050
W: wh.waynecsd.org

John Adams High School
101-01 Rockaway Blvd, Ozone Park NY 11417
DP Coordinator Jagroop Singh
Languages English
T: +1 718 322 0500
W: www.johnadamsnyc.org

Jordan-Elbridge Middle School
19 N. Chappell Street, Jordan NY 13080
MYP Coordinator Alexis Farnsworth
Languages English
T: +1 315 689 8520

Joseph A. McNeil Elementary School
335 South Franklin Street, Hempstead NY 11550
PYP Coordinator Juanita Winfield
Languages English, Spanish
T: +1 516 434 4500
W: www.hempsteadschools.org/domain/10

Joseph C Wilson Foundation Academy
200 Genesee Street NY 14611
MYP Coordinator Rhonda Neal
PYP Coordinator Katherine Chinappi
Languages English
T: +1 585 463 4100
W: www.rcsdk12.org/wilsonfoundation
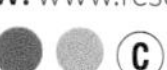

Joseph C Wilson Magnet High School
501 Genesee Street, Rochester NY 14611
DP Coordinator Lori Locker
Languages English
T: +1 585 328 3440
W: www.rcsdk12.org/wilsoncommencement

Kenmore East High School
350 Fries Road, Tonawanda NY 14150
DP Coordinator Denise Carr
Languages English
T: +1 716 874 8402
W: www.kenton.k12.ny.us/kentonkehs

Kenmore West High School
33 Highland Parkway, Buffalo NY 14223
DP Coordinator Mary White
Languages English
T: +1 716 874 8401
W: www.kenton.k12.ny.us/kentonkwhs

Khalil Gibran International Academy
362 Schermerhorn Street, Brooklyn NY 11217
DP Coordinator Maria Huliaris
Languages English
T: +1 718 237 2502
W: www.khalilgibranhs.org

Knowledge & Power Preparatory Academy (KAPPA) International
500 East Fordham Road, Bronx, New York NY 10458
DP Coordinator Elizabeth Calvert-Kilbane
Languages English
T: +1 718 933 1247

LA SCUOLA D'ITALIA GUGLIELMO MARCONI
12 East 96th Street, New York NY 10128
DP Coordinator Dr. Beatrice Paladini
Languages English, Italian
T: +1 212 369 3290
E: admissions@lascuoladitalia.org
W: www.lascuoladitalia.org
See full details on page 483

Lee F Jackson Elementary School
2 Saratoga Road, White Plains NY 10607
PYP Coordinator Valarie Williams
Languages English
T: +1 914 948 2992
W: www.greenburghcsd.org/domain/153

Léman Manhattan Preparatory School
41 Broad Street, New York NY 10004
DP Coordinator Luz Garcelon
Languages English
T: +1 212 232 0266
W: www.lemanmanhattan.org

Link IB World School
51 Red Hill Road, New City NY 10956
PYP Coordinator Lauren Haugh
Languages English
T: +1 845 6243494
W: www.ccsd.edu/Domain/11

Locust Valley High School
99 Horse Hollow Road, Locust Valley NY 11560
DP Coordinator Angela Manzo
Languages English
T: +1 516 277 5105
W: www.lvcsd.k12.ny.us/our_schools/high_school
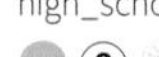

Long Beach High School
322 Lagoon Drive West, Lido Beach NY 11561
DP Coordinator Christine Graham
Languages English
T: +1 516 897 2013
W: www.lbeach.org/schools/long_beach_high_school

Long Beach Middle School
239 Lido Boulevard, Lido Beach NY 11561
MYP Coordinator Eliot Lewin
Languages English
T: +1 516 897 2162
W: www.lbeach.org/schools/long_beach_middle_school

Louis M. Klein Middle School
50 Union Ave., Harrison NY 10528
MYP Coordinator Joanna Venditto
Languages English
T: +1 914 630 3033
W: lmk.harrisoncsd.org

Lyceum Kennedy French American School
225 East 43rd Street, New York NY 10017
DP Coordinator Dr. Vera Pohland
Languages French, English
T: +1 212 681 1877
W: www.LyceumKennedy.org

Massena Central High School
84 Nightengale Avenue, Massena NY 13662
DP Coordinator Jan Normile
Languages English
T: +1 315 764 3710
W: mhs.mcs.k12.ny.us

Merton Williams Middle School
200 School Lane, Hilton NY 14468
MYP Coordinator Steve Cudzilo
Languages English
T: +1 585 392 1000 (EXT: 30)
W: www.hilton.k12.ny.us/MertonMiddle.cfm

Millbrook High School
70 Church Street, Millbrook NY 12545
DP Coordinator Georgia Herring
Languages English
T: +1 845 677 2510
W: www.millbrookcsd.org/domain/91

Mott Hall Bronx High School
1595 Bathgate Avenue, Bronx, New York NY 10457
DP Coordinator Catherine Friesen
Languages English
T: +1 718 466 6800

MOTT HALL SCIENCE AND TECHNOLOGY ACADEMY
250 East 164th Street, Bronx, New York NY 10456
MYP Coordinator Mr. Thomas Moore
Languages English, Spanish
T: +1 718 293 4017
E: MHSTAIB@motthallsta.org
W: www.motthallsta.org

See full details on page 491

Mount Vernon High School
100 California Road, Mount Vernon NY 10552
DP Coordinator Daphne Platt
Languages English, Spanish
T: +1 914 665 5300
W: ny01913181.schoolwires.net/Domain/21

North Shore High School
450 Glen Cove Avenue, Glen Head NY 11545
DP Coordinator Kerri Titone
Languages English
T: +1 516 277 7801

Northport High School
154 Laurel Hill Road, Northport NY 11768
DP Coordinator Anna Kessler
Languages English
T: +1 631 262 6654
W: northport.k12.ny.us/schools/northport_high_school

Northwood Elementary School
433 North Greece Road, Hilton NY 14468
MYP Coordinator Steve Cudzilo
Languages English
T: +1 585 392 1000 EXT:45
W: www.hilton.k12.ny.us/NorthwoodElementary.cfm

Odyssey Academy
750 Maiden Lane, Rochester NY 14615
DP Coordinator Jonathan Ivers
Languages English
T: +1 585 966 5200
W: www.greececsd.org/Domain/13

Our World Neighborhood Charter School
36-12 35th Avenue, Astoria NY 11106
MYP Coordinator Eileen Lepetit
PYP Coordinator Gina Patino
Languages English
T: +1 718 392 3405
W: www.owncs.org

P.S. 316 Elijah G. Stroud Elementary School
750 Classon Avenue, Brooklyn NY 11238
PYP Coordinator Alissa Porto
Languages English
T: +1 718 638 4043
W: www.ps316brooklyn.org

Palmyra-Macedon High School
151 Hyde Parkway, Palmyra NY 14522
DP Coordinator Pamela Wagner
MYP Coordinator Pamela Wagner
Languages English
T: +1 315 597 3420
W: www.palmaccsd.org/1/home

Palmyra-Macedon Middle School
163 Hyde Parkway, Palmyra NY 14522
MYP Coordinator Pamela Wagner
Languages English
T: +1 315 597 3450
W: www.palmaccsd.org/2/home

Palmyra-Macedon Primary School
120 Canandaigua Street, Palmyra NY 14522
PYP Coordinator Katie HerrGesell
Languages English, Spanish
T: +1 315 597 3475
W: www.palmaccsd.org/4/home

Pelham Middle School
28 Franklin Place, Pelham NY 10803
MYP Coordinator Sean Llewellyn
Languages English
T: +1 914 738 8190
W: pms.pelhamschools.org

Pierson High School
200 Jermain Avenue, Sag Harbor NY 11963
DP Coordinator Michael Edward Guinan
Languages English
T: +1 631 725 5302
W: www.sagharborschools.org/o/pierson-high-school

Pine Street School
25 Pine Street, New York NY 10005
PYP Coordinator Lauren Angarola
Languages English, Spanish, Mandarin
T: +1 212 235 2325
W: www.pinestreetschool.com

Port Chester High School
One Tamarack Road, Port Chester NY 10573
DP Coordinator Rich Laconi
Languages English
T: +1 914 934 7950
W: shs.portchesterschools.org

Portledge School
355 Duck Pond Road, Locust Valley NY 11560-2499
DP Coordinator Trish Rigg
Languages English
T: +1 516 750 3100
W: www.portledge.org

Prospect School
185 Peninsula Boulevard, Hempstead NY 11550
PYP Coordinator Rhonda Chung
Languages English, Spanish
T: +1 516 434 4000
W: www.hempsteadschools.org

Putnam Valley High School
146 Peekskill Hollow Road, Putnam Valley NY 10579
DP Coordinator Vincent DeGregorio
Languages English
T: +1 845 526 7847
W: pvcsd.org/index.php/hs

Queensbury High School
409 Aviation Rd, Queensbury NY 12804
DP Coordinator Marnie DeJohn
Languages English
T: +1 518 824 4601
W: www.queensburyschool.org

Quest Elementary School
225 West Ave, Hilton NY 14468
PYP Coordinator Gregory Booth
Languages English
T: +1 585 392 1000 (6100)
W: www.hilton.k12.ny.us/QuestElementary.cfm

Red Hook Central High School
103 West Market Street, Red Hook NY 12571
DP Coordinator Michael McCrudden
Languages English
T: +1 845 758 2241 EXT3247
W: www.redhookcentralschools.org

Rhodes Academy
270 Washington Street, Hempstead NY 11550
PYP Coordinator Lavern Lariosa
Languages English, Spanish
T: +1 516 434 4800
W: www.hempsteadschools.org/rhodesacademy

Richard J Bailey Elementary School
33 West Hillside Avenue, White Plains NY 10607
PYP Coordinator Lenore Rotanelli
Languages English
T: +1 914 948 2992
W: www.greenburghcsd.org/domain/155

Saint Edmund Preparatory High School
2474 Ocean Avenue, Brooklyn, New York NY 11229
DP Coordinator Crissa Kostadaras
Languages English
T: +1 718 743 6100
W: www.stedmundprep.org

Schenectady High School
1445 The Plaza, Schenectady NY 12308
DP Coordinator Wendy Ausfeld
Languages English
T: +1 518 370 8190

School for Global Leaders
145 Stanton Street, New York NY 10002
MYP Coordinator Cheryl Campos
Languages English, Chinese
T: +1 212 260 5375
W: www.sgl378.org

Somers High School
PO Box 620, 120 Primrose Street, Lincolndale NY 10540
DP Coordinator Alison Scanlon
Languages English
T: +1 914 248 8585
W: www.somersschools.org/domain/8

Somers Middle School
250 Route 202, Somers NY 10589
MYP Coordinator Jenna Schettino
Languages English
T: +1 914 277 3399
W: www.somersschools.org/domain/9

South Side High School
140 Shepherd Street, Rockville Centre NY 11570
DP Coordinator Elizabeth Nisler
Languages English
T: +1 516 255 8834
W: sshs.rvcschools.org
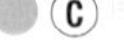

South Side Middle School
67 Hillside Avenue, Rockville Centre NY 11570
MYP Coordinator Kristen Carroll
Languages English
T: +1 516 255 8978

Stanley Makowski Early Childhood Center
1095 Jefferson Avenue, Buffalo NY 14208
PYP Coordinator Natasha Marciano
Languages English
T: +1 716 816 4180

The British International School of New York
20 Waterside Plaza, New York NY 10010
MYP Coordinator Ann Marie Hourigan
PYP Coordinator Amy Simmons
Languages English
T: +1 212 481 2700
W: www.bis-ny.org

The Brooklyn Latin School
325 Bushwick Ave, 4th floor, Brooklyn, New York NY 11206
DP Coordinator Daniel Lao
Languages English
T: +1 718 366 0154
W: www.brooklynlatin.org

The Clinton School
10 East 15th Street, New York NY 10003
DP Coordinator Lauren Jabara
Languages English
T: +1 212 524 4360
W: theclintonschool.net

The High School for Enterprise, Business, and Technology
850 Grand St, Brooklyn NY 11211
DP Coordinator Erwin Lara
Languages English, Spanish
T: +1 718 387 2800
W: www.ebtbrooklyn.com

Thomas J Corcoran High School
919 Glenwood Avenue, Syracuse NY 13207
CP Coordinator Ryan Terpening
DP Coordinator Carrianne Kirby
MYP Coordinator Cassandra Malley-Donovan
Languages English
T: +1 315 435 4321

United Nations International School
24-50 Franklin D Roosevelt Drive, New York NY 10010
DP Coordinator Anthony Staccone
Languages English
T: +1 212 684 7400
W: www.unis.org

Vestal High School
205 Woodlawn Drive, Vestal NY 13850
DP Coordinator Jeffrey Dunham
Languages English
T: +1 607 757 2281
W: www.vestal.stier.org/highschool_home.aspx/

Village Elementary School
100 School Lane, Hilton NY 14468
MYP Coordinator Steve Cudzilo
Languages English
T: +1 585 392 1000 (EXT: 51)
W: www.hilton.k12.ny.us

Walton Avenue School
1425 Walton Avenue, Bronx NY 10452
PYP Coordinator Taisha Rodriguez
Languages English, Spanish
T: +1 718 293 5970
W: www.ps294.org

West Islip High School
1 Lions Path, West Islip NY 11795
DP Coordinator James Gilmartin
Languages English
T: +1 631 893 3250
W: www.wi.k12.ny.us

West Middle School
West Middle Avenue, Binghamton NY 13905
MYP Coordinator Mark Ward
Languages English
T: +1 607 763 8400

Westlake Middle School
825 West Lake Drive, Thornwood NY 10594
MYP Coordinator Anthony Mungioli
Languages English
T: +1 914 769 8540
W: wms.mtplcsd.org

Woodlands Middle/High School
475 West Hartsdale Avenue, Hartsdale NY 10570
MYP Coordinator Susana Torres
Languages English
T: +1 914 761 6052
W: www.greenburghcsd.org/domain/157

Yonkers Middle/High School
150 Rockland Avenue, Yonkers NY 10705
DP Coordinator Marcella Lentine
Languages English
T: +1 914 376 8191
W: www.yonkerspublicschools.org/ymhs

Young Diplomats Magnet Academy
134 West 122nd Street, New York NY 10473
PYP Coordinator Iffat Hossain
Languages English, French
T: +1 212 678 2908
W: www.ps242.com

North Carolina

Albemarle Road Middle School
6900 Democracy Drive, Charlotte NC 28212
MYP Coordinator Kimberly Lynch
Languages English
T: +1 980 343 6420
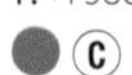

Ben L Smith High School
2407 South Holden Road, Greensboro NC 27407
DP Coordinator Steven Atchison
Languages English
T: +1 336 294 7300
W: www.gcsnc.com/Smith_High

Billingsville Elementary School
124 Skyland Avenue, Charlotte NC 28205
PYP Coordinator Tonya Pointer
Languages English
T: +1 980 343 5520
W: schools.cms.k12.nc.us/billingsvillees

Broughton Magnet High School
723 St Mary's Street, Raleigh NC 27605
DP Coordinator David Brooks
Languages English
T: +1 919 856 7810
W: www.wcpss.net/broughtonhs

Burton Magnet Elementary School
1500 Mathison Street, Durham NC 27701
PYP Coordinator Amy Sanchez
Languages English
T: +1 919 560 3908
W: burton.dpsnc.net

Cedar Ridge High School
1125 New Grady Brown School Rd, Hillsborough NC 27278
DP Coordinator Tabitha Campbell
Languages English
T: +1 919 245 4000
W: www.orangecountyfirst.com/crhs
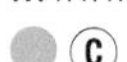

Charlotte Country Day School
1440 Carmel Road, Charlotte NC 28226
DP Coordinator Stewart Peery
Languages English
T: 0017049434500
W: www.charlottecountryday.org

Cloverleaf Elementary School
300 James Farm Road, Statesville NC 28625
PYP Coordinator Alison Whitaker
Languages English
T: +1 704 978 2111
W: cloverleaf.issnc.org
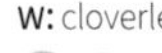

Coddle Creek Elementary School
141 Frank's Crossing Loop, Mooresville NC 28115
PYP Coordinator Lindsey Mehall
Languages English
T: +1 704 439 4077
W: coddlecreek.issnc.org

Concord High School
481 Burrage Road NE, Concord NC 28025
CP Coordinator Marie Deal
DP Coordinator Marie Deal
MYP Coordinator Megan Wingfield
Languages English
T: +1 704 786 4161
W: www.cabarrus.k12.nc.us/concordhs

Cotswold Elementary School
300 Greenwich Road, Charlotte NC 28211
PYP Coordinator Tonya Pointer
Languages English
T: +1 980 343 6720
W: schools.cms.k12.nc.us/cotswoldes

East Garner Magnet Middle School
6301 Jones Sausage Road, Garner NC 27529
MYP Coordinator Joanne Edwards
Languages English
T: +1 919 662 2339
W: www.wcpss.net/eastgarnerms

East Mecklenburg High School
6800 Monroe Road, Charlotte NC 28212
CP Coordinator Heather Hays
DP Coordinator Heather Hays
MYP Coordinator Erika Flanagan
Languages English
T: +1 980 343 6430
W: schools.cms.k12.nc.us/eastmecklenburghs

Enloe Magnet High School
128 Clarendon Crescent, Raleigh NC 27610
DP Coordinator April Ellis
Languages English
T: +1 919 856 7918
W: www.wcpss.net/enloehs

Farmington Woods Elementary School
1413 Hampton Valley Road, Cary NC 27511
PYP Coordinator Anna Norris Goodrum
Languages English
T: +1 919 460 3469
W: www.wcpss.net/farmingtonwoodses

Ferndale Middle School
701 Ferndale Blvd, High Point NC 27262
MYP Coordinator Bryant Thompson
Languages English
T: +1 336 819 2855
W: www.gcsnc.com/Ferndale_Middle

Fox Road Magnet Elementary School
7101 Fox Road, Raleigh NC 27616
PYP Coordinator Megan Peterson
Languages English
T: +1 919 850 8845
W: www.wcpss.net/foxroades

Garner Magnet High School
2101 Spring Drive, Garner NC 27529
CP Coordinator Gerald Siemering
DP Coordinator Jon Sherwin
MYP Coordinator Amy Bennett
Languages English
T: +1 919 662 2379
W: www.wcpss.net/garnerhs

Grimsley High School
801 Westover Terrace, Greensboro NC 27408
DP Coordinator Ben Barnard
Languages English
T: +1 336 370 8184

Hairston Middle School
3911 Naco Road, Greensboro NC 27401
MYP Coordinator Karen Martin-Jones
Languages English
T: +1 336 378 8280
W: www.gcsnc.com/Hairston_Middle

Harding University High School
2001 Alleghany Street, Charlotte NC 28208
DP Coordinator Falisa Hankins
MYP Coordinator Falisa Hankins
Languages English
T: +1 980 343 6007
W: schools.cms.k12.nc.us/hardinguniversityHS

Harold E. Winkler Middle School
4501 Weddington Road, Concord NC 28027
MYP Coordinator Andrea Kiser
Languages English
T: +1 704 260 6450
W: www.cabarrus.k12.nc.us/winkler

Hickory Day School
2535 21st Ave NE, Hickory NC 28601
PYP Coordinator Alison Tompkins
Languages English
T: +1 828 256 9492
W: www.hickoryday.org

High Point Central High School
801 Ferndale Blvd., High Point NC 27262
DP Coordinator David Williams
Languages English
T: +1 336 819 2825
W: www.gcsnc.com/high_point_central_high

Hillside High School
3727 Fayetteville Street, Durham NC 27707
DP Coordinator Angelia Euba McKoy
MYP Coordinator Keshetta Henderson
Languages English
T: +1 919 560 3925
W: www.hillside.dpsnc.net

Huntingtowne Farms Elementary School
2520 Huntingtowne Farms Lane, Charlotte NC 28210
PYP Coordinator Nancy Bullard
Languages English
T: +1 980 343 3625
W: schools.cms.k12.nc.us/huntingtownefarmsES

J. N. Fries Magnet Middle School
133 Stonecrest Circle, Concord NC 28027
MYP Coordinator Laurie Taylor
Languages English
T: +1 704 788 4140
W: www.cabarrus.k12.nc.us/fries

J.Y. Joyner Magnet Elementary School
2300 Lowden Street, Raleigh NC 27608
PYP Coordinator Sheryl Davis
Languages English, Spanish
T: +1 919 856 7650
W: www.wcpss.net/joyneres

Jacksonville High School
1021 Henderson Drive, Jacksonville NC 28540
CP Coordinator Amber Lumley
DP Coordinator Amber Lumley
Languages English
T: +1 910 989 2048
W: www.onslow.k12.nc.us/jacksonvillehs

James E. Shepard Magnet Middle
2401 Dakota Street, Durham NC 27707
MYP Coordinator Patrice Fletcher
Languages English
T: +1 919 560 3938
W: www.dpsnc.net/shepard

JM Alexander Middle School
12010 Hambright Road, Huntersville NC 28078
MYP Coordinator Mary Kendrick
Languages English
T: +1 980 343 3830
W: schools.cms.k12.nc.us/jmalexanderms

John T. Hoggard High School
4305 Shipyard Boulevard, Wilmington NC 28403
DP Coordinator Mary Lillge
Languages English
T: +1 910 350 2072
W: www.nhcs.net/hoggard

Kinston High School
2601 North Queen Street, Kinston NC 28501
DP Coordinator Joshua Bridges
Languages English
T: +1 252 527 8067

Lansdowne Elementary School
6400 Prett Court, Charlotte NC 28270
PYP Coordinator Laura Bentley
Languages English
T: +1 980 343 6733
W: schools.cms.k12.nc.us/lansdownees

Lee County High School
1708 Nash Street, Sanford NC 27330
DP Coordinator Katherine Brown
Languages English
T: +1 919 776 7541
W: www.lee.k12.nc.us/Domain/17

Legette Blythe Elementary School
12202 Hambright Rd, Huntersville NC 28078
PYP Coordinator Erik Hoover
Languages English
T: +1 980 343 5770
W: schools.cms.k12.nc.us/blythees

Marie G. Davis K-8 School
3351 W Griffith St., Charlotte NC 28203
MYP Coordinator Kirsten Rodgers
PYP Coordinator Kirsten Rodgers
Languages English
T: +1 980 343 0006
W: schools.cms.k12.nc.us/mariegdavisES

Marvin Ridge High School
2825 Crane Road, Waxhaw NC 28173
DP Coordinator Lindsey Arant
Languages English
T: +1 704 290 1520
W: mrhs.ucps.k12.nc.us

Millbrook High School
2201 Spring Forest Road, Raleigh NC 27615
DP Coordinator Loren Baron
MYP Coordinator Lashonda Haddock
Languages English
T: +1 919 850 8787
W: mhs.wcpss.net

Morganton Day School
305 West Concord Street, Morganton NC 28655
PYP Coordinator Teresa Cape
Languages English
T: +1 828 437 6782
W: www.morgantondayschool.com

Mount Mourne School
1431 Mecklenburg Highway, Mooresville NC 28115
MYP Coordinator Elisabeth White
Languages English
T: +1 704 892 4711
W: www.iss.k12.nc.us/domain/1964

Myers Park High School
2400 Colony Road, Charlotte NC 28209
DP Coordinator Katie Willett
MYP Coordinator Katie Willett
Languages English
T: +1 704 343 5800
W: schools.cms.k12.nc.us/myersparkHS

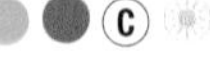

North Mecklenburg High School
11201 Old Statesville Road, Huntersville NC 28078
CP Coordinator Amy Pasko
DP Coordinator Amy Pasko
MYP Coordinator Amy Pasko
Languages English
T: +1 980 343 3840

Northview School
625 Carolina Avenue, Statesville NC 28677
MYP Coordinator Elisabeth White
Languages English
T: +1 704 873 7354
W: www.iss.k12.nc.us/domain/1227

Northwood Elementary School
818 W Lexington Avenue, High Point NC 27262
PYP Coordinator Sara Carter
Languages English
T: +1 336 819 2920
W: www.gcsnc.com/Domain/80

Paisley Magnet School
1400 Grant Street, Winston-Salem NC 27105
MYP Coordinator Erin Knapp
Languages English
T: +1 336 727 2775
W: www.wsfcs.k12.nc.us/paisley

Parkland High School
1600 Brewer Road, Winston-Salem NC 27127
CP Coordinator Margaret Powers
DP Coordinator Margaret Powers
MYP Coordinator Tara Pidgeon
Languages English
T: +1 336 771 4700
W: www.wsfcs.k12.nc.us/Domain/1012

Piedmont Open Middle School
1241 East 10th Street, Charlotte NC 28204
MYP Coordinator Maranda Thornburg
Languages English
T: +1 980 343 5435
W: schools.cms.k12.nc.us/piedmontMS

Ralph L Fike High School
500 Harrison Drive, Wilson NC 27893
DP Coordinator Jill Wheeler
Languages English
T: +1 252 399 7905
W: fike.wilsonschoolsnc.net

Randolph Middle School
4400 Water Oak Road, Charlotte NC 28211
MYP Coordinator Leah Clawson
Languages English
T: +1 980 343 6700
W: schools.cms.k12.nc.us/randolphMS

Ranson Middle School
5850 Statesville Road, Charlotte NC 28269
MYP Coordinator Michelle Fox
Languages English
T: +1 980 343 6800
W: schools.cms.k12.nc.us/ransonMS

Reidsville High School
1901 South Park Drive, Reidsville NC 27320
DP Coordinator Wayne Knight
Languages English
T: +1 336 349 6361
W: www.rock.k12.nc.us

Rocky Mount High School
1400 Bethlehem Road, Rocky Mount NC 27803
DP Coordinator Jeffrey Pageau
Languages English
T: +1 252 977 3085
W: www.nrms.k12.nc.us/Domain/32

Smith Magnet Elementary School
1101 Maxwell Drive, Raleigh NC 27603
PYP Coordinator Megan Flynn
Languages English
T: +1 919 662 2458
W: smithes.wcpss.net

Smithfield Middle School
1455 Buffalo Road, Smithfield NC 27577
MYP Coordinator Allison Beadle
Languages English
T: +1 919 934 4696
W: www.johnston.k12.nc.us/smms

Smithfield-Selma High School
700 Booker Dairy Rd., Smithfield NC 27577
CP Coordinator Carlos Sousa
DP Coordinator Cynthia Hutchings
MYP Coordinator Rhett Smith
Languages English
T: +1 919 934 5191
W: johnston.k12.nc.us/sss

South Iredell High School
299 Old Mountain Road, Statesville NC 28677
CP Coordinator Latonia Bostic
DP Coordinator Latonia Bostic
MYP Coordinator Latonia Bostic
Languages English
T: +1 704 528 4536
W: southhigh.issnc.org

South View High School
4184 Elk Road, Cumberland County, Hope Mills NC 28348
CP Coordinator W Oxendine
DP Coordinator Dawn Curle
Languages English
T: +1 910 425 8181

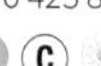

Southeast Raleigh Magnet High School
2600 Rock Quarry Road, Raleigh NC 27610
DP Coordinator Hunter Thane
Languages English
T: +1 919 856 2800
W: www.wcpss.net/southeastraleighhs

Speas Global Elementary School
2000 W. Polo Road, Winston-Salem NC 27106
PYP Coordinator Katryna Jacober
Languages English, Spanish
T: +1 336 703 4135
W: www.wsfcs.k12.nc.us/domain/5628

Statesville Road Elementary
5833 Milhaven Road, Charlotte NC 28213
PYP Coordinator Mary Farrell
Languages English
T: +1 980 343 6815
W: schools.cms.k12.nc.us/statesvilleroadES

The British International School of Charlotte
7000 Endhaven Lane, Charlotte NC 28277
DP Coordinator Julie Tombs
Languages English
T: +1 704 341 3236
W: www.britishschoolofcharlotte.org

The Montessori School of Raleigh
408 Andrews Chapel Road, Durham NC 27703
DP Coordinator Michelle Miller
Languages English, Spanish
T: +1 919 848 1545
W: msr.org

Union Day School
3000 Tilley Morris Road, Weddington NC 28104
MYP Coordinator Patricia Davalos
Languages English
T: +1 704 256 1494
W: www.uniondayschool.com

Waldo C Falkener IB Elementary School
3931 Naco Road, Greensboro NC 27401
PYP Coordinator Keaira Price
Languages English
T: +1 336 370 8150
W: www.gcsnc.com/Domain/29

Walter Hines Page High School
201 Alma Pinnix Drive, Greensboro NC 27405
DP Coordinator Elizabeth Hackney
Languages English
T: +1 336 370 8200
W: www.gcsnc.com/Domain/84

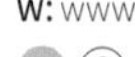

Walter M. Williams High School
1307 South Church Street, Burlington NC 27215-4919
DP Coordinator Patrick Stokes
Languages English, Spanish
T: +1 336 570 6161
W: www.abss.k12.nc.us/wwh

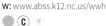

Weddington Hills Elementary School
4401 Weddington Rd, Concord NC 28027
PYP Coordinator Mary Hooks
Languages English
T: +1 704 795 9385
W: www.cabarrus.k12.nc.us/Domain/22

West Cabarrus High School
4100 Weddington Road, Concord NC 28027
CP Coordinator Jennifer Ward
DP Coordinator Jennifer Ward
Languages English
T: +1 704 260 5970
W: www.cabarrus.k12.nc.us/wchs

West Charlotte High School
2219 Senior Drive, Charlotte NC 28216
DP Coordinator LaDawna Robinson
MYP Coordinator LaDawna Robinson
Languages English
T: +1 980 343 6060
W: schools.cms.k12.nc.us/westcharlotteHS

West Millbrook Middle School
8115 Strickland Road, Raleigh NC 27615
MYP Coordinator James Bollenbacher
Languages English
T: +1 919 870 4050
W: www.wcpss.net/westmillbrookms

Ohio

Alliance Middle School
3205 S. Union Ave., Alliance OH 44601
MYP Coordinator Andy Toth
Languages English
T: +1 330 829 2254
W: www.alliancecityschools.org/o/middle-school

Beaumont School
3301 North Park Boulevard, Cleveland Heights OH 44118
DP Coordinator Simon Masters
Languages English
T: +1 216 321 2954
W: www.beaumontschool.org

Boulevard Elementary School
14900 Drexmore Road, Shaker Heights OH 44120
PYP Coordinator Jennifer Goulden
Languages English
T: +1 216 295 4020
W: www.shaker.org/boulevardschool_home.aspx

Campus International High School
3100 Chester Ave, Cleveland OH 44114
DP Coordinator Amy Brodsky
MYP Coordinator Sarah Schwab
Languages English
T: +1 216 838 8100
W: www.clevelandmetroschools.org/cihs

Campus International School
3000 Euclid Ave, Cleveland OH 44115
MYP Coordinator Sheila Orourke
PYP Coordinator Sheila Orourke
Languages English
T: +1 216 431 2225
W: www.clevelandmetroschools.org/CIS

Canterbury Elementary School
2530 Canterbury Road, Cleveland Heights OH 44118
PYP Coordinator Melissa Garcar Garcar
T: +1 216 371 7470
W: www.chuh.org/canterburyelementary_home.aspx

Case Elementary School
400 W. Market St., Akron OH 44303
PYP Coordinator Jennifer Victor
Languages English
T: +1 330 873 3350

Columbus Alternative High School
2632 McGuffey Road, Columbus OH 43211
DP Coordinator Alice Webb
Languages English
T: +1 614 365 6006
W: www.ccsoh.us/CAHS

Discovery School
855 Millsboro Rd, Mansfield OH 44903
PYP Coordinator Simon Clark
Languages English
T: +1 419 756 8880
W: www.discovery-school.net

Dublin Coffman High School
6780 Coffman Road, Dublin OH 43107-1099
DP Coordinator Eric Bringardner
Languages English
T: +1 614 764 5900
W: www.dublinschools.net/dublincoffman_home.aspx

Dublin Jerome High School
8300 Hyland-Croy Road, Dublin OH 43016
DP Coordinator Ann Tiefenthaler
Languages English
T: +1 614 873 7377
W: www.dublinschools.net/dublinjerome_home.aspx

Dublin Scioto High School
400 Hard Road, Dublin OH 43016-8349
DP Coordinator Eric Bringardner
Languages English
T: +1 614 718 8300
W: www.dublinschools.net/dublinscioto_home.aspx

Eastwood Elementary School
198 East College Street, Oberlin OH 44074
PYP Coordinator Maureen Freda
Languages English
T: +1 440 775 3473
W: eastwood.oberlinschools.net

Fairfax Elementary School
3150 Fairfax Road, Cleveland Heights OH 44118
PYP Coordinator Leslie Garrett
Languages English
T: +1 216 371 7480
W: www.chuh.org/fairfaxelementary_home.aspx
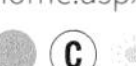

Fairmont High School
3301 Shroyer Road, Kettering OH 45429
DP Coordinator Darren McGarvey
Languages English
T: +1 937 499 1601
W: www.ketteringschools.org/1/Home

Fernway Elementary School
17420 Fernway Road, Shaker Heights OH 44120
PYP Coordinator Jean Reinhold
Languages English
T: +1 216 295 4040
W: www.shaker.org/fernwayschool_home.aspx

Firestone High School
333 Rampart Avenue, Akron OH 44313
DP Coordinator Jennifer Beaven
Languages English
T: +1 330 873 3315

GlenOak High School
1801 Schneider Street NE, Canton OH 44721
DP Coordinator Jennifer Austin
Languages English
T: +1 330 491 3800
W: www.plainlocal.org/17/home

Kent State University Child Development Center
775 Loop Rd., Kent OH 44242
PYP Coordinator Adonia Porto
Languages English
T: +1 330 672 2559
W: www.kent.edu/ehhs/centers/cdc

King Community Learning Center
805 Memorial Parkway, Akron OH 44303
PYP Coordinator Janet Lippincott
Languages English
T: +1 330 761 7962

Lakewood Catholic Academy
14808 Lake Avenue, Lakewood OH 44107
MYP Coordinator Eileen Murphy
Languages English
T: +1 216 521 0559
W: www.lakewoodcatholicacademy.com

Langston Middle School
150 North Pleasant Street, Oberlin OH 44074
MYP Coordinator Maureen Freda
Languages English, Spanish, Mandarin
T: +1 440 775 7961
W: langston.oberlinschools.net

Litchfield Middle School
470 Castle Blvd, Akron OH 44313
MYP Coordinator Sandra Cline
Languages English
T: +1 330 761 2775
W: www.akronschools.com

Lomond Elementary School
17917 Lomond Boulevard, Shaker Heights OH 44122
PYP Coordinator Shifa Isaacs
Languages English
T: +1 216 295 4050
W: www.shaker.org/lomondschool_home.aspx

McKinley Elementary School
602 Plum Street, Fairport Harbor OH 44077
PYP Coordinator Candace Vahcic
Languages English
T: +1 440 354 5400
W: www.fhevs.org/mckinley
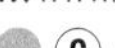

USA

Mercer Elementary School
23325 Wimbledon Road, Shaker Heights OH 44122
PYP Coordinator Maria Baker
Languages English
T: +1 216 295 4070
W: www.shaker.org/mercerschool_home.aspx

Monticello Middle School
3665 Monticello Blvd., Cleveland Heights OH 44121
MYP Coordinator Leslie Garrett
Languages English
T: +1 216 371 6520
W: www.chuh.org/monticellomiddle_home.aspx

Notre Dame Academy, OH
3535 W Sylvania Avenue, Toledo OH 43623
DP Coordinator Angela Joseph
Languages English
T: +1 419 475 9359
W: www.nda.org

Oberlin High School
281 North Pleasant Street, Oberlin OH 44074
DP Coordinator Rebecca Lahetta
MYP Coordinator Kristin Miller
Languages English
T: +1 440 774 1295
W: ohs.oberlinschools.net

Onaway Elementary School
15600 Parkland Boulevard, Shaker Heights OH 44120
PYP Coordinator Denise Brown
Languages English
T: +1 216 295 4080
W: www.shaker.org/onawayschool_home.aspx
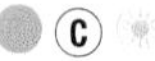

Portage Path Community Learning Center
55 S Portage Path, Akron OH 44303
PYP Coordinator Jill Holcomb
Languages English
T: +1 330 761 2795

Princeton High School
11080 Chester Road, Princeton City Schools, Cincinnati OH 45246
DP Coordinator Michele Ritzie
Languages English
T: +1 513 864 1500
W: www.princetonschools.net/Domain/8
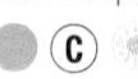

Purcell Marian High School
2935 Hackberry Street, Cincinnati OH 45206
DP Coordinator Bob Herring
Languages English
T: +1 513 751 1230
W: www.purcellmarian.org

Resnik Community Learning Center
65 N. Meadowcroft Dr., Akron OH 44313
PYP Coordinator Lori Wammes
Languages English, French
T: +1 330 873 3370

Roxboro Elementary School
2405 Roxboro Road, Cleveland Heights OH 44106
PYP Coordinator Melissa Garcar Garcar
Languages English
T: +1 216 371 7115
W: www.chuh.org/roxboroelementary_home.aspx

Roxboro Middle School
2400 Roxboro Road, Cleveland Heights OH 44106
MYP Coordinator Melissa Garcar Garcar
Languages English
T: +1 216 320 3500
W: www.chuh.org/heightsmiddle.aspx

Shaker Heights High School
15911 Aldersyde Drive, Shaker Heights OH 44120
DP Coordinator Laura Hartel
MYP Coordinator Molly Miles
Languages English
T: +1 216 295 4200
W: www.shaker.org/highschool_home.aspx

Shaker Heights Middle School
20600 Shaker Blvd, Shaker Heights OH 44122
MYP Coordinator Addie Tobey
Languages English
T: +1 216 295 4100
W: www.shaker.org/middleschool_home.aspx

Springfield High School
701 East Home Road, Springfield OH 45504
DP Coordinator Beth Biester
Languages English
T: +1 937 342 4100
W: www.scsdoh.org/Domain/2242

St Edward High School
13500 Detroit Avenue, Lakewood OH 44107
DP Coordinator Nicholas Kuhar
MYP Coordinator Nicholas Kuhar
Languages English
T: +1 216 221 3776
W: sehs.net

Tri-County International Academy
c/o Wooster H.S., 515 Oldman Road, Wooster OH 44691
DP Coordinator Victoria Birk
Languages English
T: +1 330 345 4000 EXT:3004

Upper Arlington High School
1650 Ridgeview Road, Upper Arlington OH 43221
CP Coordinator Cynthia Ballheim
DP Coordinator Cynthia Ballheim
Languages English
T: +1 614 487 5200
W: www.uaschools.org/upperarlingtonhighschool_home.aspx

Westerville South High School
303 South Otterbein Avenue, Westerville OH 43081
DP Coordinator Bill Heinmiller
Languages English
T: +1 614 797 6000
W: www.westerville.k12.oh.us/31/Home

Westlake High School
27200 Hilliard Blvd., Westlake OH 44145
DP Coordinator Matthew Planisek
Languages English
T: +1 440 250 1260
W: www.wlake.org/our-schools/westlake-high

Woodbury Elementary School
15400 South Woodland Road, Shaker Heights OH 44120
MYP Coordinator Addie Tobey
Languages English
T: +1 216 295 4150
W: www.shaker.org/woodburyschool_home.aspx

Worthington Kilbourne High School
1499 Hard Road, Columbus OH 43235
DP Coordinator Jeannie Goodwin
Languages English
T: +1 614 883 2550
W: www.worthington.k12.oh.us/Domain/9

Oklahoma

Booker T Washington High School
1514 E. Zion St., Tulsa OK 74106
DP Coordinator Sharon Lazdins
MYP Coordinator Joyelle Payne
Languages English
T: +1 918 925 1000
W: btw.tulsaschools.org

Classen School of Advanced Studies
1901 North Elison Street, Oklahoma City OK 73106
DP Coordinator Mitch McIntosh
Languages English
T: +1 405 587 5400
W: www.okcps.org/domain/80

George Washington Carver Magnet Middle School
624 E Oklahoma Place, Tulsa OK 74106
MYP Coordinator Emily Baker
Languages English
T: +1 918 595 2939

Jenks West Elementary School
205 East B. Street, Jenks OK 74037
PYP Coordinator Stephanie Collins
Languages English
T: +1 918 299 4415
W: www.jenksps.org

Oregon

Bend Senior High School
230 NE 6th Street, Bend OR 97701
DP Coordinator Paul Hutter
Languages English
T: +1 541 383 6293
W: www.bend.k12.or.us/bendhigh

Cedar Park Middle School
11100 SW Park Way, Portland OR 97225
MYP Coordinator Amy Hattendorf
Languages English
T: +1 503 672 3620
W: cedarpark.beaverton.k12.or.us

Cleveland High School
3400 SE 26 Ave, Portland OR 97202
DP Coordinator Jennifer Wiandt Owens
Languages English
T: +1 503 916 5120

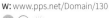

Dr Martin Luther King Jr Elementary School
4906 NE 6th Avenue, Portland OR 97211
PYP Coordinator Paige Thomas
Languages English
T: +1 503 916 6155
W: www.pps.net/Domain/130

Eugene International High School
400 East 19th Avenue, Eugene OR 97401
DP Coordinator Steven Smith
Languages English
T: +1 541 687 3196
W: www.schools.4j.lane.edu/ihs/

French International School of Oregon
8500 NW Johnson Street, Portland OR 97229
MYP Coordinator Anne Prouty
PYP Coordinator Kathlin Gabaldon
Languages English, French
T: +1 503 292 7776
W: www.fisoregon.org

German International School of Portland
3900 SW Murray Blvd, Beaverton OR 97005
PYP Coordinator Michelle Bahr
Languages German, English
T: +1 503 626 9089
W: www.gspdx.org

Gresham High School
1200 North Main Street, Gresham OR 97030-3899
DP Coordinator Alan Simpson
Languages English
T: +1 503 674 5500
W: www.gresham.k12.or.us/ghs

Hillsboro High School
3285 SE Rood Bridge Road, Hillsboro OR 97123
DP Coordinator Ashley Clemens
Languages English
T: +1 503 844 1980
W: schools.hsd.k12.or.us/hilhi

International School of Beaverton
17770 SW Blanton Street, Beaverton OR 97007
DP Coordinator Amy Schuff
MYP Coordinator Gina Velasco
Languages English
T: +1 503 259 3800
W: isb.beaverton.k12.or.us

Le Monde French Immersion Public Charter School
2044 E. Burnside Street, Portland OR 97214
PYP Coordinator Genevieve Maull
Languages English, French
T: +1 503 467 7529
W: lemondeimmersion.org

Lincoln High School
1600 SW Salmon St., Portland OR 97205
DP Coordinator Kim Bliss
Languages English
T: +1 503 916 5200
W: www.pps.net/domain/136

Meadow Park Middle School
14100 SW Downing Street, Beaverton OR 97006
MYP Coordinator Megan Poole
Languages English, Spanish
T: +1 503 672 3660
W: meadowpark.beaverton.k12.or.us

Mountainside High School
12500 SW 175th Avenue, Beaverton OR 97007
DP Coordinator Juveria Khan
MYP Coordinator Jeremiah Hubbard
Languages English
T: +1 503 356 3500
W: mountainside.beaverton.k12.or.us

Newport High School
322 NE Eads Street, Newport OR 97365
DP Coordinator Jody Hanna
Languages English
T: +1 541 265 9281

North Eugene High School
200 Silver Lane, Eugene OR 97404
CP Coordinator Kara Walter
DP Coordinator Kendall Lawless
Languages English
T: +1 541 790 4500
W: nehs.4j.lane.edu

North Salem High School
765 14th Street NE, Salem OR 97301
CP Coordinator Amy Green
DP Coordinator Amy Green
Languages English
T: +1 503 399 3241
W: north.salkeiz.k12.or.us

Oregon Trail Academy
36520 SE Proctor Rd, Boring OR 97009
PYP Coordinator Megan Durst
Languages English
T: +1 503 668 4133
W: oregontrailschools.com/ota

Pilot Butte Middle School
1501 N.E. Neff Road, Bend OR 97701
MYP Coordinator Lyndsey Hendrix
Languages English
T: +1 541 355 7520
W: www.bend.k12.or.us/pilotbutte

Rex Putnam High School
4950 SE Roethe Road, Milwaukie OR 97267
DP Coordinator Traci Clarke
Languages English
T: +1 503 353 5860
W: www.nclack.k12.or.us/phs

Sabin School
4013 NE 18 Avenue, Portland OR 97212
PYP Coordinator Michael Diltz
Languages English
T: +1 503 916 6181
W: www.pps.k12.or.us/schools/sabin

Seven Peaks School
19660 SW Mountaineer Way, Bend OR 97702
MYP Coordinator Hope Royes
PYP Coordinator Samantha Lyke
Languages English
T: +1 541 382 7755
W: www.sevenpeaksschool.org

Skyline School
11536 NW Skyline Blvd, Portland OR 97231
MYP Coordinator Sharon Morgan
PYP Coordinator Bradley Manker
Languages English
T: +1 503 916 5412
W: www.pps.k12.or.us/schools/skyline

South Salem High School
1910 Church Street SE, Salem OR 97302
DP Coordinator Jennifer Harris-Clippinger
Languages English
T: +1 503 399 3252
W: www.southsaxons.com

Southridge High School
9625 SW 125th Street, Beaverton OR 97008
CP Coordinator Wayne Grimm
DP Coordinator Natalie Ballard Strauhal
Languages English
T: +1 503 259 5400
W: southridge.beaverton.k12.or.us

Sunset High School
13840 NW Cornell Road, Portland OR 97229
DP Coordinator Jill Boeschenstein
Languages English
T: +1 503 259 5050

The International School
025 SW Sherman Street, Portland OR 97210
PYP Coordinator Paula Cano
Languages Chinese, Japanese, Spanish
T: +1 503 226 2496
W: www.intlschool.org

Tigard High School
9000 SW Durham Rd., Tigard OR 97224
DP Coordinator Michael Savage
Languages English
T: +1 503 431 5400
W: www.ttsdschools.org/ths

Tualatin High School
22300 SW Boones Ferry Rd, Tualatin OR 97062
DP Coordinator Lisa Lacy
Languages English
T: +1 503 431 5600
W: www.ttsdschools.org/tuhs

Valley Inquiry Charter School
5774 Hazel Green Road, Salem OR 97305
PYP Coordinator Taylor Tuepker
Languages English
T: +1 503 399 3150

Vernon School
2044 N.E. Killingsworth Street, Portland OR 97211
MYP Coordinator Lyndsey Mackenzie
PYP Coordinator Lyndsey Mackenzie
Languages English
T: +1 503 916 6415
W: www.pps.net/Domain/158

Willamette High School
1801 Echo Hollow Road, Eugene OR 97402
DP Coordinator Jade Starr
Languages English
T: +1 541 689 0731

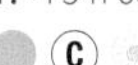

Woodburn High School
1785 N Front Street, Woodburn OR 97071
DP Coordinator Doug Peterson
Languages English
T: +1 503 981 2600

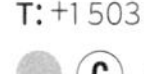

Pennsylvania

Barack Obama Academy of International Studies
515 N. Highland Avenue, Pittsburg PA 15206
DP Coordinator Joseph Ehman
MYP Coordinator Michael Chapman
Languages English
T: +1 412 622 5980
W: www.pghschools.org/ibworld2

Boyce Middle School
1500 Boyce Road, Upper St Clair PA 15241
MYP Coordinator Christina Caragein
Languages English
T: +1 412 833 1600

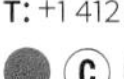

Central High School
1700 W Olney Avenue, Philadelphia PA 19141
DP Coordinator Aviva Hockfield
Languages English
T: +1 215 276 5262
W: centralhs.philasd.org

Chambersburg Area Senior High School
511 South Sixth Street, Chambersburg PA 17201
DP Coordinator Kristofer Cole
Languages English
T: +1 717 261 3324
W: www.casdonline.org/Domain/224

Cumberland Valley High School
6746 Carlisle Pike, Mechanicsburg PA 17050
DP Coordinator Amy Miller
Languages English
T: +1 717 506 3454

Downingtown STEM Academy
335 Manor Avenue, Downingtown PA 19335
DP Coordinator Michael Sheehan
Languages English
T: +1 610 269 8460
W: www.dasd.org

Fort Couch Middle School
515 Ft Couch Road, Upper St Clair PA 15241
MYP Coordinator Andrew Bowers
Languages English
T: +1 412 833 1600

GEORGE SCHOOL
1690 Newtown Langhorne Rd, Newtown PA 18940-2414
DP Coordinator Kim McGlynn
Languages English
T: +1 215 579 6500
E: admission@georgeschool.org
W: www.georgeschool.org
See full details on page 474

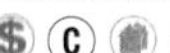

George Washington High School
10175 Bustleton Avenue, Philadelphia PA 19116
DP Coordinator Maria Pacheco
Languages English
T: +1 215 961 2001
W: gwhs.philasd.org

Harrisburg Academy
10 Erford Road, Wormleysburg PA 17043
DP Coordinator Maureen Smith
PYP Coordinator Leyla Goldfinger
Languages English
T: +1 717 763 7811
W: www.harrisburgacademy.org

Harriton High School
600 North Ithan Avenue, Rosemont PA 19010
DP Coordinator Thomas O'Brien
Languages English
T: +1 610 658 3970
W: www.lmsd.org

Hill-Freedman World Academy
6200 Crittenden Street, Philadelphia PA 19138
DP Coordinator Thomas Emerson
MYP Coordinator Katherine Lauher
Languages English
T: +1 215 276 5260
W: hfwa.philasd.org

J P McCaskey High School
445 North Reservoir St, Lancaster PA 17602
CP Coordinator Kelly White
DP Coordinator Benjamin Deardorff
Languages English
T: +1 717 291 6211
W: www.lancaster.k12.pa.us

Lehigh Valley Academy Regional Charter School
1560 Valley Center Parkway, Suite 200, Bethlehem PA 18017
CP Coordinator Andrew Hall
DP Coordinator Andrew Hall
MYP Coordinator Lisa Simmers
PYP Coordinator Kelly Eddinger
Languages English
T: +1 610 866 9660

Lincoln Middle School
1001 Lehigh Avenue, Lancaster PA 17602
MYP Coordinator Ann Fesenmyer
Languages English
T: +1 717 291 6187
W: sdlancaster.org/explore-our-schools/middle/lincoln-ms

Manheim Township High School
PO Box 5134, School Road, Lancaster PA 17606
DP Coordinator Larry Penner
Languages English
T: +1 717 560 3097

Mayfair Elementary School
3001 Princeton Avenue, Philadelphia PA 19149
MYP Coordinator Jenna Fell
PYP Coordinator Jessica O'Neill
Languages English
T: +1 215 400 3280
W: mayfair.philasd.org

MERCYHURST PREPARATORY SCHOOL
538 East Grandview Boulevard, Erie PA 16504
DP Coordinator Paul Cancilla
Languages English
T: +1 814 824 2323
E: aorlando@mpslakers.com
W: www.mpslakers.com
See full details on page 492

Northeast High School
Cottman & Algon Avenues, Philadelphia PA 19111
DP Coordinator Marie Herrick
Languages English
T: +1 215 728 5018
W: nehs.philasd.org

Owen J. Roberts High School
901 Ridge Road, Pottstown PA 19465
CP Coordinator Kevin Kirby
Languages English, Spanish
T: +1 610 469 5100
W: www.ojrsd.com/Domain/14

Pan American Academy Charter School
2830 North American Street, Philadelphia PA 19133
MYP Coordinator Laura Higgins Di Vito
PYP Coordinator Constance Malone
Languages English, Spanish
T: +1 215 425 1212
W: www.panamcs.org

Philadelphia High School for Girls
1400 West Olney Avenue, Philadelphia PA 19141-2398
DP Coordinator Megan McNamara
Languages English
T: +1 215 276 5258
W: girlshs.philasd.org

Pittsburgh Linden PreK-5
725 S Linden Avenue, Pittsburgh PA 15208
PYP Coordinator Derek Fuchs
Languages English, Chinese
T: +1 412 665 3996
W: www.pghschools.org/linden
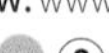

Plymouth Whitemarsh High School
201 East Germantown Pike, Plymouth Meeting PA 19462
CP Coordinator Rebecca Duffy
Languages English
T: +1 610 825 1500
W: www.colonialsd.org/our-schools/plymouth-whitemarsh-high

Reynolds Middle School
605 West Walnut Street, Lancaster PA 17603
MYP Coordinator Amanda Funk
Languages English
T: +1 717 291 6257
W: sdlancaster.org/explore-our-schools/middle/reynolds-ms

School Lane Charter School
2400 Bristol Pike, Bensalem PA 19020
DP Coordinator Katherine Hewitt
MYP Coordinator Karen Schade
Languages English
T: +1 215 245 6055
W: www.schoollane.org

State College Area High School, Pennsylvania
650 Westerly Parkway, State College PA 16801
CP Coordinator Jennifer Schreiber
DP Coordinator Jennifer Schreiber
Languages English
T: +1 814 231 1111
W: www.scasd.org/schighschool

Streams Elementary School
1560 Ashlawn Avenue, Upper St Clair PA 15241
PYP Coordinator Katie Hendrickson
Languages English
T: +1 412 833 1600
W: www.uscsd.k12.pa.us/Domain/542
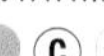

Upper St. Clair High School
1825 McLaughlin Run Road, Upper St. Clair PA 15241
DP Coordinator Tanya Chothani
MYP Coordinator Gordon Mathews
Languages English
T: +1 412 833 1600
W: uscsd.k12.pa.us/Domain/59

William W Bodine High School for International Affairs
1101 North 4th Street, Philadelphia PA 19123
DP Coordinator Kelli Mackay
Languages English
T: +1 215 351 7332
W: bodine.philasd.org

Woodrow Wilson Middle School
1800 Cottman Ave., Philadelphia PA 19111
MYP Coordinator Ryan Smith
Languages English
T: +1 215 728 5015
W: wwilson.philasd.org

York Academy Regional Charter School
32 West North Street, PO Box 1787, York PA 17401
MYP Coordinator Alina Henninger
PYP Coordinator Julia Ross
Languages English
T: +1 717 801 3900

York County School of Technology
2179 S. Queen St., York PA 17402
CP Coordinator Brandon May
Languages English
T: +1 717 741 0820

Young Scholars of Central PA Charter School
1530 Westerly Parkway, State College PA 16801
MYP Coordinator Baris Yilmaz
PYP Coordinator Crystal Confer
Languages English
T: +1 814 237 9727
W: www.yscp.org

Rhode Island

Prout School
4640 Tower Hill Road, Wakefield RI 02879
DP Coordinator Christopher Bromley
Languages English
T: +1 401 789 9262
W: www.theproutschool.org

St. Andrew's School (RI)
63 Federal Road, Barrington RI 02806
DP Coordinator Ryan Alescio
MYP Coordinator Alexandra McMullen
Languages English
T: +1 401 246 1230
W: www.standrews-ri.org
 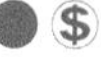 

South Carolina

A C Flora High School
1 Falcon Drive, Columbia SC 29204
DP Coordinator Stephen Keller
Languages English
T: +1 803 738 7300
W: flora.richlandone.org

Aynor High School
201 Jordanville Road, Aynor SC 29511
DP Coordinator Renee Atkinson
Languages English
T: +1 843 488 7100
W: www.horrycountyschools.net/aynor_high_school

Beechwood Middle School
1340 Highway #378, Lexington SC 29072
MYP Coordinator Lauren LaVenia
Languages English
T: +1 803 821 5700
W: schools.lexington1.net/bms

Buist Academy for Advanced Studies
103 Calhoun Street, Charleston SC 29401
MYP Coordinator Sara Lyle
PYP Coordinator Sara Lyle
Languages English
T: +1 843 724 7750
W: buist.ccsdschools.com

Christ Church Episcopal School
245 Cavalier Drive, Greenville SC 29607
DP Coordinator Amanda Beckrich
PYP Coordinator Stephanie Morgan
Languages English
T: +1 864 299 1522
W: www.cces.org

E. L. Wright Middle School
2740 Alpine Road, Columbia SC 29223
MYP Coordinator Latoya Young
Languages English
T: +1 803 736 8740
W: www.richland2.org/elwm

Fork Shoals Elementary School
916 McKelvey Road, Pelzer SC 29669
PYP Coordinator Amy Giles
Languages English
T: +1 864 243 5680
W: www.greenville.k12.sc.us/forksh

Fort Dorchester High School
8500 Patriot Boulevard, North Charleston SC 29420
DP Coordinator Janel Raquet
Languages English
T: +1 843 760 4450

Greer High School
3032 East Gap Creek Road, Greer SC 29651
DP Coordinator Mary Smith
Languages English
T: +1 864 355 5819
W: www.greenville.k12.sc.us/greerhs

Hartsville High School
701 Lewellyn Avenue, Hartsville SC 29550
DP Coordinator Paula Alvarez
Languages English
T: +1 843 857 3700

Hendrix Elementary School
1084 Springfield Road, Boiling Springs SC 29316
PYP Coordinator Allison Watson
Languages English
T: +1 864 216 4000
W: hes.spart2.org

Hilton Head Elementary School
30 School Road, Hilton Head Island SC 29926
PYP Coordinator Karen Perdue
Languages English
T: +1 843 342 4100

Hilton Head High School
70 Wilborn Road, Beaufort, Hilton Head Island SC 29926
DP Coordinator Mary Beth White
MYP Coordinator Mary Beth White
Languages English
T: +1 843 689 4801

Hilton Head Island Middle School
55 Wilborn Road, Hilton Head Island SC 29926
MYP Coordinator Amy Prior
Languages English
T: +1 843 689 4500
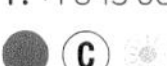

Hopkins Middle School
1601 Clarkson Road, Hopkins SC 29061
MYP Coordinator Michelle Peay
Languages English
T: +1 803 695 3331
W: www.richlandone.org/Domain/40

Irmo High School
6671 St Andrews Road, Columbia SC 29212
CP Coordinator Tamara Jones
DP Coordinator Hazel Walker
Languages English
T: +1 803 732 8100
W: www.lexrich5.org/ihs

James Island High School
1000 Fort Johnson Road, Charleston SC 29412
DP Coordinator Gregory Webster
Languages English
T: +1 843 762 2754
W: jichs.ccsdschools.com

Jesse Boyd Elementary School
1505 Fernwood Glendale Road, Spartanburg SC 29307
PYP Coordinator Jennifer Squires
Languages English
T: +1 864 594 4430
W: boyd.spartanburg7.org

Latta High School
618 N. Richardson St., Latta SC 29565
DP Coordinator Christy Berry
Languages English
T: +1 843 752 5751
W: www.dillon3.k12.sc.us/lhs

Lexington High School
2463 Augusta Highway, Lexington SC 29072
DP Coordinator Derek Allison
Languages English
T: +1 803 821 3400
W: sites.google.com/lexington1.net/lhswebsite/home

Lower Richland High School
2615 Lower Richland Blvd, Hopkins SC 29061
CP Coordinator Elvionna White
DP Coordinator Atonce Joseph
MYP Coordinator Constantina Green
Languages English
T: +1 803 695 3000
W: www.richlandone.org/Domain/52
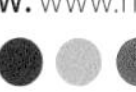 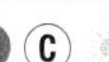

Memminger Elementary School
20 Beaufain Street, Charleston SC 29401
PYP Coordinator Maggie McClary
Languages English
T: +1 843 724 7778
W: memminger.ccsdschools.com

Northwestern High School
2503 West Main Street, Rock Hill SC 29732
DP Coordinator Katie Tinker
Languages English
T: +1 803 981 1200
W: www.rock-hill.k12.sc.us/domain/31

Richland Northeast High School
7500 Brookfield Road, Columbia SC 29223
CP Coordinator Aleksandria Rhodes
DP Coordinator Sonja Merriwether-Hawki
MYP Coordinator Sonja Merriwether-Hawkins
Languages English
T: +1 803 699 2800
W: www.richland2.org/rnh

Rock Hill High School
320 West Springdale Road, Rock Hill SC 29730
DP Coordinator Ian Young
Languages English
T: +1 803 981 1300
W: www.rock-hill.k12.sc.us/Domain/32

Socastee High School
4900 Socastee Boulevard, Myrtle Beach SC 29588
DP Coordinator Danny Wilson
Languages English
T: +1 843 293 2513
W: www.horrycountyschools.net/Socastee_High_School

South Pointe High School
806 Neely Road, Rock Hill SC 29730
DP Coordinator Laura Hall
Languages English
T: +1 803 984 3558
W: www.rock-hill.k12.sc.us/Domain/33

Southeast Middle School
731 Horrell Hill Road, Hopkins SC 29061
MYP Coordinator Michelle Peay
Languages English
T: +1 803 695 5700
W: www.richlandone.org/Domain/43

Southside High School
6630 Frontage Rd, Greenville SC 29605
DP Coordinator Julie McGaha
Languages English
T: +1 864 355 8700
W: www.greenville.k12.sc.us/shs

Spartanburg Day School
1701 Skylyn Drive, Spartanburg SC 29307
PYP Coordinator Katie Clayton
Languages English
T: +1 864 582 8380
W: www.spartanburgdayschool.org

Sullivan Middle School
1825 Eden Terrace, Rock Hill SC 29730
MYP Coordinator Kallie Cromer
Languages English
T: +1 803 981 1450
W: www.rock-hill.k12.sc.us/Domain/29

Sumter High School
2580 McCray's Mill Road, School District 17, Sumter SC 29154-6098
DP Coordinator Marie Broadway
Languages English
T: +1 803 481 4480

Travelers Rest High School
301 North Main Street, Travelers Rest SC 29690
DP Coordinator Robert Giles
Languages English
T: +1 864 355 0000
W: www.greenville.k12.sc.us/trest

Williams Middle School
1119 North Irby Street, Florence SC 29501
MYP Coordinator Joe Anderson
Languages English
T: +1 843 664 8162
W: f1s.org/Domain/26

Wilson High School
1411 Old Marion Highway, Florence SC 29506
DP Coordinator Brian Howell
MYP Coordinator C. Danielle Pressley
Languages English
T: +1 843 664 8440
W: www.f1s.org/Wilson

Woodmont High School
2831 West Georgia Road, Piedmont SC 29673
DP Coordinator Emily Styer
Languages English
T: +1 864 355 8600

Tennessee

Antioch High School
1900 Hobson Pike, Antioch TN 37013
CP Coordinator Andrew Price
DP Coordinator Tosha Mannings
Languages English
T: +1 615 641 5400
W: schools.mnps.org/antioch-high-school

Avery Trace Middle School
230 Raider Drive, Cookeville TN 38501
MYP Coordinator Amber Campbell
Languages English
T: +1 931 520 2200

Balmoral Ridgeway Elementary
5905 Grosvenor Avenue, Memphis TN 38119
PYP Coordinator Lanna Byrd
Languages English
T: +1 901 416 2128
W: schools.scsk12.org/balmoralridgeway-es

Bearden Middle School
1000 Francis Road, Knoxville TN 37909
MYP Coordinator Bahar Hill
Languages English
T: +1 865 539 7839
W: www.knoxschools.org/beardenms

Bellevue Middle School
655 Colice Jeanne Road, Nashville TN 37221
MYP Coordinator Anna Bernstein
Languages English
T: +1 615 662 3000
W: schools.mnps.org/bellevue-middle-prep

Bolton High School
7323 Brunswick Road, Arlington TN 38002
DP Coordinator Ebony Johnson
Languages English
T: +1 901 873 8150
W: www.boltonhigh.org

Cookeville High School
1 Cavalier Drive, Cookeville TN 38506
DP Coordinator Emily Chambers
Languages English
T: +1 931 520 2287
W: www.cookevillecavaliers.com

Eakin Elementary School
2500 Fairfax Avenue, Nashville TN 37212
PYP Coordinator Kirsten Clark
Languages English
T: +1 615 298 8076
W: schools.mnps.org/eakin-elementary-school

East Nashville Magnet High School
110 Gallatin Ave., Nashville TN 37206
DP Coordinator Scott Wofford
MYP Coordinator Scott Wofford
Languages English

East Nashville Magnet Middle School
110 Gallatin Ave., Nashville TN 37206
MYP Coordinator Scott Wofford
Languages English, Spanish
T: +1 615 262 6670

Franklin High School
810 Hillsboro Road, Franklin TN 37064
DP Coordinator Lindsey McEwen
Languages English
T: +1 615 472 4468

Germantown High School
7653 Old Poplar Pike, Germantown TN 38138
DP Coordinator Kimberly Tucker
Languages English
T: +1 901 756 2350
W: www.germantownreddevils.org

Goodlettsville Middle School
1460 McGavock Pike, Nashville TN 37216
MYP Coordinator Felicia Agee
Languages English
T: +1 615 227 1042
W: schools.mnps.org/goodlettsville-middle-prep

Hillsboro Comprehensive High School
3812 Hillsboro Road, Nashville TN 37215
CP Coordinator Sharon Humphrey
DP Coordinator Sharon Humphrey
MYP Coordinator Matthew King
Languages English
T: +1 615 298 8400

Hunters Lane High School
1150 Hunters Lane, Nashville TN 37207
DP Coordinator Angela Scott
MYP Coordinator Olivia Roller
Languages English
T: +1 615 860 1401
W: schools.mnps.org/hunters-lane-high-school

J T Moore Middle School
4425 Granny White Pike, Nashville TN 37204
MYP Coordinator David Myers
Languages English
T: +1 615 298 8095
W: www.jtmoore.org

Julia Green Elementary School
3500 Hobbs Road, Nashville TN 37215
PYP Coordinator Shannon Meadows
Languages English
T: +1 615 298 8082
W: www.juliagreen.org

Lausanne Collegiate School
1381 West Massey Road, Memphis TN 38120
DP Coordinator Wade Linebaugh
MYP Coordinator Michelle Spain
PYP Coordinator Erica McBride
Languages English
T: +1 901 474 1001
W: www.lausanneschool.com

Oak Forest Elementary
7440 Nonconnah View Cove, Memphis TN 38119
PYP Coordinator Timkia Bryant
Languages English
T: +1 901 416 2257
W: schools.scsk12.org/oakforest-es

Oakland High School
2225 Patriot Drive, Murfreesboro TN 37130
DP Coordinator Ann Borombozin
Languages English
T: +1 615 904 3780
W: ohs.rcschools.net
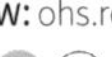

Ooltewah High School
6123 Mountain View Road, Ooltewah TN 37363
DP Coordinator Andrea McGuirt
Languages English
T: +1 423 498 6920
W: ohs.hcde.org

Ridgeway High School
2009 Ridgeway Road, Memphis TN 38119
DP Coordinator Amy Dorsey
Languages English
T: +1 901 416 8820
W: www.ridgewayhigh.org

Ridgeway Middle School
6333 Quince Road, Memphis TN 38119
MYP Coordinator Patrice Carter
Languages English
T: +1 901 416 1588
W: schools.scsk12.org/ridgeway-ms

Signal Mountain Middle/High School
2650 Sam Powell Trail, Signal Mountain TN 37377
DP Coordinator Tara Tharp
MYP Coordinator Tara Tharp
Languages English
T: +1 423 886 0880
W: smmhs.hcde.org

West End Middle School
3529 West End Avenue, Nashville TN 37205
MYP Coordinator Adam Warner
Languages English
T: +1 615 298 8425
W: westendptso.org

West High School
3300 Sutherland Avenue, Knoxville TN 37919
CP Coordinator Nathan Kenner
DP Coordinator Valerie Schmidt-Gardner
MYP Coordinator Valerie Schmidt-Gardner
Languages English
T: +1 865 594 4477
W: www.knoxschools.org/wesths

Texas

Alcuin School
6144 Churchill Way, Dallas TX 75230
DP Coordinator Margaret Davis
MYP Coordinator Matthew Lundberg
Languages English
T: +1 972 239 1745
W: www.alcuinschool.org

Allen High School
300 Rivercrest Boulevard, Allen TX 75002
DP Coordinator Lauren Cammack
Languages English
T: +1 972 727 0400
W: www.allenisd.org/allenhs

Alonzo De Leon Middle School
4201 North 29th St, McAllen TX 78504
MYP Coordinator Kimberly Alaniz
Languages English
T: +1 956 632 8800
W: deleon.mcallenisd.org

Amarillo High School/AISD
4225 Danbury Drive, Amarillo TX 79109
DP Coordinator Phillip Miller
Languages English
T: +1 806 326 2000

Anderson Mill Elementary School
10610 Salt Mill Hollow, Austin TX 78750
PYP Coordinator Jennifer Foster
Languages English
T: +1 512 428 3700
W: andersonmill.roundrockisd.org

Andress High School
5400 Sun Valley Dr., El Paso TX 79924
DP Coordinator Frances Morales
Languages English
T: +1 915 236 4000
W: www.episd.org/andress

Arlington High School
818 W Park Row, Arlington TX 76013
DP Coordinator Christine Boutilier
Languages English
T: +1 682 867 8100

Arthur Kramer Elementary IB World School
7131 Midbury Drive, Dallas TX 75230
PYP Coordinator Kim West
Languages English
T: +1 972 794 8300
W: www.dallasisd.org/domain/540

Austin Eco Bilingual School (Austin EBS) USA
8707 Mountain Crest Dr, Austin TX 78735
PYP Coordinator Adriana Rodriguez
Languages English
T: +1 512 299 5731
W: www.austinbilingualschool.com

Austin Elementary
700 E Austin Ave, Harlingen TX 78550
PYP Coordinator Magda Gonzalez
Languages English, Spanish
T: +1 956 427 3060
W: hcisd-austin.edlioschool.com

Baker Middle School
3445 Pecan Street, Corpus Christi TX 78411
MYP Coordinator Marlo Bazan
Languages English
T: +1 361 878 4600
W: baker.ccisd.us

Barbara Bush Middle School
515 Cowboys Parkway, Irving TX 75063
MYP Coordinator Christina Flatt
Languages English
T: +1 972 968 3700
W: bush.cfbisd.edu

Bellaire High School
5100 Maple Street, Houston ISD, Bellaire TX 77401
DP Coordinator Ann Linsley
Languages English
T: +1 713 295 3704
W: www.houstonisd.org/bellairehigh

Benjamin Franklin International Exploratory Academy
6920 Meadow Road, Dallas TX 75230
MYP Coordinator Dan Roberts
Languages English
T: +1 972 502 7100
W: www.dallasisd.org/franklin

Berta Palacios Elementary
801 E. Thomas Road, Pharr TX 78577
PYP Coordinator Jeanette Mijares
Languages English, Spanish
T: +1 956 354 2930
W: www.psjaisd.us/palacios

Bluebonnet Trail Elementary
11316 Farmhaven Road, Austin TX 78754
PYP Coordinator Callista Janosky
Languages English, Spanish
T: +1 512 278 4125
W: www.manorisd.net/domain/9

Borman Elementary School
1201 Parvin St., Denton TX 76205
PYP Coordinator Angeles Muñoz
Languages English
T: +1 940 369 2500
W: www.dentonisd.org/bormanes

Bramlette STEAM Academy
111 Tupelo Drive, Longview TX 75601
PYP Coordinator Dara Brazile
Languages English, Spanish
T: +1 903 803 5600
W: sites.google.com/lisd.org/bramlette

Briargrove Elementary School
6145 San Felipe, Houston TX 77057
PYP Coordinator Quinetta Sampy
Languages English, Spanish
T: +1 713 917 3600
W: www.houstonisd.org/briargrovees

Briarmeadow Charter School
3601 Dunvale Rd, Houston TX 77063-5707
PYP Coordinator Tondelyn Johnson
Languages English
T: +1 713 458 5500
W: www.houstonisd.org/briarmeadow

Bright Academy
7600 Woodstream Drive, Frisco TX 75034
PYP Coordinator Christina McLain
Languages English, Spanish
T: +1 469 633 2700

Brighter Horizons Academy
3145 Medical Plaza Dr., Garland TX 75044
PYP Coordinator Nadia Elatrash
Languages English
T: +1 972 675 2062
W: www.bhaprep.org

Briscoe Elementary School
2015 S. Flores St., San Antonio TX 78204
PYP Coordinator Cari Richter
Languages English, Spanish
T: +1 210 228 3305
W: schools.saisd.net/page/112.homepage

British International School of Houston
2203 North Westgreen Boulevard, Katy TX 77449
CP Coordinator Ashley Thorpe
DP Coordinator Ashley Thorpe
Languages English
T: +1 713 290 9025
W: www.bishouston.org
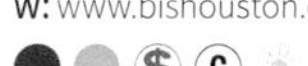

Bryan High School
3450 Campus Drive, Bryan TX 77802
DP Coordinator Sarah Patterson
Languages English
T: +1 979 209 2400
W: bryanhs.bryanisd.org

Caldwell Heights Elementary
4010 Eagles Nest, Round Rock TX 78665
PYP Coordinator Macy Lane
Languages English
T: +1 512 428 7300
W: caldwellheights.roundrockisd.org

Calhoun Middle School
709 Congress Street, Denton TX 76201
MYP Coordinator Ashly Sharp
Languages English
T: +1 940 369 2400
W: www.dentonisd.org/calhounms

CC Mason Elementary
1501 N. Lakeline Blvd, Cedar Park TX 78613
PYP Coordinator Janat Blackmon
Languages English
T: +1 512 570 5500
W: mason.leanderisd.org

Cesar E. Chavez High School
8501 Howard Dr., Houston TX 77017
CP Coordinator Liana Silva
DP Coordinator Liana Silva
Languages English
T: +1 713 495 6950
W: www.houstonisd.org/chavez

Chandler Oaks Elementary
3800 Stone Oak Drive, Round Rock TX 78681
PYP Coordinator Elizabeth Hall
Languages English
T: +1 512 704 0400
W: chandleroaks.roundrockisd.org
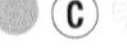

Clarence W. Bailey Elementary
1011 S. Mobberly, Longview TX 75602
PYP Coordinator Sandra Gonzalez
Languages English, Spanish
T: +1 903 803 5200
W: sites.google.com/lisd.org/south-ward-campus

Coppell High School
185 West Parkway Blvd, Coppell TX 75019
DP Coordinator Michael Brock
Languages English
T: +1 214 496 6100
W: www.coppellisd.com/chs

Coronado High School, El Paso
100 Champions Place, El Paso TX 79912
DP Coordinator Leslie Harris
Languages English
T: +1 915 236 2000
W: www.episd.org/coronado
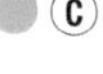

Coronado High School, Lubbock
4910 29th Drive, Lubbock TX 79410
CP Coordinator Dana Gustafson
Languages English
T: +1 806 219 1100
W: www.lubbockisd.org/chs

Crow Leadership Academy
1201 Coke Drive, Arlington TX 76010
PYP Coordinator Jen Ruby
Languages English, Spanish
T: +1 682 867 1850
W: www.aisd.net/crow-academy

Cullen Middle School
6900 Scott, Houston TX 77021-4899
MYP Coordinator Nora Lemon
Languages English, Spanish
T: +1 713 746 8180
W: www.houstonisd.org/domain/7203

Cunae International School LLC
5655 Creekside Forest Drive, Spring TX 77389
DP Coordinator Maria Jose Ferrer Garay
PYP Coordinator Maria Jose Ferrer Garay
Languages English
T: +1 281 516 3770
W: www.doortomyschool.com

Dallas International School
17811 Waterview Pkwy, Dallas TX 75252
DP Coordinator Robert Reese
Languages English
T: +1 469 250 0001
W: www.dallasinternationalschool.org

Daniel Ortiz Middle School
6767 Telephone Road, Houston TX 77061-2056
MYP Coordinator Olivia Holub
Languages English
T: +1 713 845 5650
W: www.houstonisd.org/page/79424

Denton High School
1007 Fulton Street, Denton TX 76201
DP Coordinator Crystal Sullivan
MYP Coordinator Crystal Sullivan
Languages English
T: +1 940 369 2000
W: www.dentonisd.org/dentonhs

Dr. Pablo Perez Elementary School
7801 N. Main Street, Mc Allen TX 78504
PYP Coordinator Laura Garcia
Languages English
T: +1 956 971 1125
W: perez.mcallenisd.org

Durham Elementary School
4803 Brinkman Street, Houston TX 77018
PYP Coordinator Anne Baumgarten
Languages English, Spanish
T: +1 713 613 2527
W: www.houstonisd.org/Domain/12141

Dwight D Eisenhower High School
7922 Antoine Drive, Houston TX 77088
DP Coordinator Mary Williams
MYP Coordinator Mary Williams
Languages English
T: +1 281 878 0900

E A Murchison Middle School
3700 North Hills Drive, Austin TX 78731
MYP Coordinator Kevin Gaffney
Languages English
T: +1 512 414 3254

East Texas Montessori Prep Academy
400 North Eastman Road, Longview TX 75601
PYP Coordinator Brenda Bell
Languages English, Spanish
T: +1 903 803 5000
W: sites.google.com/lisd.org/etmpa

Edgar Allan Poe Elementary School
5100 Hazard Street, Houston TX 77098
PYP Coordinator Carol clayton
Languages English
T: +1 713 535 3780
W: www.houstonisd.org/poees

Eisenhower Ninth Grade School
3550 W Gulf Bank Road, Houston TX 77088
MYP Coordinator Shameka Garner
Languages English
T: +1 281 878 7700
W: eisenhower9.aldineisd.org

El Dorado High School
12401 Edgemere, El Paso TX 79938
DP Coordinator Rosa Harding
Languages English
T: +1 915 937 3200
W: www.sisd.net/eldoradohs

Esprit International School
4890 W Panther Creek Dr, The Woodlands TX 77381
PYP Coordinator Rosemary Brumbelow
Languages English
T: +1 281 298 9200
W: www.espritinternationalschool.com

Fondren Middle School
6333 South Braeswood Blvd, Houston TX 77096
MYP Coordinator Melodye Montgomery
Languages English
T: +1 713 778 3360
W: www.houstonisd.org/fondrenms

Forest Park Middle School
1644 North Eastman Road, Longview TX 75601
MYP Coordinator Sonya Taylor
Languages English
T: +1 903 446 2510
W: www.lisd.org/forestpark/fpjump.htm

Foster Middle School
1504 MLK Boulevard, Longview TX 75602
MYP Coordinator Christi Shobert
Languages English
T: +1 903 446 2710
W: sites.google.com/lisd.org/fms

Francisca Alvarez Elementary School
2606 Gumwood Avenue, McAllen TX 78501
PYP Coordinator Melissa Leo
Languages English
T: +1 956 971 4471
W: alvarez.mcallenisd.org

Frisco High School
6401 Parkwood Blvd, Frisco TX 75034
DP Coordinator Jenna Gates
Languages English

Garland High School
310 S. Garland Ave., Garland TX 75040
DP Coordinator Timothy Schmidt
Languages English
T: +1 972 494 8492
W: www.garlandisdschools.net/ghs

Geneva Heights Elementary School
2911 Delmar Avenue, Dallas TX 75206
PYP Coordinator Rhonda Barnwell
Languages English
T: +1 972 749 7400
W: www.dallasisd.org/relee

Graciela Garcia Elementary School
1002 W. Juan Balli Road, Pharr TX 78577
PYP Coordinator Fernanda Sanchez
Languages English, Spanish
T: +1 956 354 2790
W: www.psjaisd.us/garcia

Grandview Hills Elementary
12024 Vista Parke Drive, Austin TX 78726
PYP Coordinator Erin Carroll
Languages English
T: +1 512 434 7266

Grisham Middle School
10805 School House Lane, Austin TX 78750
MYP Coordinator Rosalinda Bedolla
Languages English
T: +1 512 428 2650
W: grisham.roundrockisd.org

Harry Stone Montessori Academy
4747 Veterans Dr., Dallas TX 75216
MYP Coordinator Reneice Reed
Languages English
T: +1 972 794 3400
W: www.dallasisd.org/stone

Harvard Elementary School
810 Harvard Street, Houston TX 77007-1607
PYP Coordinator John Pacheco
Languages English
T: +1 713 867 5210
W: www.houstonisd.org/harvardes

Headwaters School
801 Rio Grande, Austin TX 78701
DP Coordinator Stephanie Roach
Languages English
T: +1 512 480 8142
W: headwaters.org

Heights High School
413 East 13th Street, Houston TX 77008-7021
CP Coordinator Cristina Bagos
DP Coordinator Anne Nelson
MYP Coordinator Natalie Martinez
Languages English
T: +1 713 865 4400
W: www.houstonisd.org/heights

Hernandez Middle School
1901 Sunrise Road, Round Rock TX 78664
MYP Coordinator Emilee Hinegardner
Languages English
T: +1 512 424 8800
W: hernandez.roundrockisd.org

Herrera Elementary School
525 Bennington, Houston 77511
PYP Coordinator Melody Vizi
Languages English, Spanish
T: +1 713 696 2800
W: www.houstonisd.org/herreraelem

Hillcrest High School
9924 Hillcrest Road, Dallas TX 75230
DP Coordinator Jeri Smith
Languages English
T: +1 972 502 6800
W: www.dallasisd.org/hillcrest

Hirschi High School
3106 Borton Lane, Wichita Falls TX 76306-6952
DP Coordinator Henri Naylor
Languages English
T: +1 940 716 2800
W: www.wfisd.net/hirschi

Hudson PEP Elementary School
1311 Lilly Street, Longview TX 75602
PYP Coordinator Sue Wilson
Languages English
T: +1 903 803 5100
W: sites.google.com/lisd.org/hudsonpep

Huffman Elementary School
5510 Channel Isle Drive, Plano TX 75093
PYP Coordinator Callie Anthony
Languages English, Spanish
T: +1 469 752 1900
W: www.pisd.edu/huffman

Humble High School
1700 Wilson Road, Humble TX 77338
DP Coordinator Sherrill Rene Lane
Languages English
T: +1 281 641 8129
W: www.humbleisd.net/hhs

Hutchinson Middle School
3102 Canton Ave, Lubbock TX 79410
MYP Coordinator Toby Klameth
Languages English
T: +1 806 219 3800
W: www.lubbockisd.org/hutchinson

IDEA College Prep Brownsville
4395 Paredes Line Road, Brownsville TX 78526
DP Coordinator Norma Jimenez Cerda
T: +1 956 832 5150
W: ideapublicschools.org/our-schools/idea-brownsville

IDEA College Preparatory McAllen
201 N. Bentsen Rd., McAllen TX 78501
DP Coordinator Leticia Silva
Languages English
T: +1 956 429 4100
W: ideapublicschools.org/our-schools/idea-mcallen

IDEA College Preparatory South Flores
6919 South Flores Street, San Antonio TX 78221
DP Coordinator Caitlin McCloskey
Languages English, Spanish
T: +1 210 239 4150
W: www.ideapublicschools.org/our-schools/idea-south-flores

IDEA Donna
401 S. 1st St., Donna TX 78537
DP Coordinator Dikla Medina
Languages English
T: +1 956 464 0203
W: www.ideapublicschools.org/our-schools/idea-donna

IDEA Frontier
2800 S. Dakota Ave, Brownsville TX 78521
DP Coordinator Hermelinda Kaney
Languages English
T: +1 956 541 2002
W: ideapublicschools.org/our-schools/idea-frontier

Imagine International Academy of North Texas
2860 Virginia Parkway, McKinney TX 75071
DP Coordinator Hannah Nayakanti
MYP Coordinator Kendra Cooper
PYP Coordinator Kim Wood
Languages English
T: +1 214 491 1500
W: www.imaginenorthtexas.org

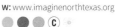

Imagine Lone Star International Academy
5301 Democracy Drive, Plano TX 75024
PYP Coordinator Julie King
Languages English
T: +1 972 244 7220
W: www.lonestartx.org

International School of Texas
4402 Hudson Bend, Austin TX 78734
MYP Coordinator Lyn Osburne
PYP Coordinator Ashley Swindle
Languages English, Spanish
T: +1 512 351 3403
W: www.internationalschooloftexas.com

J. L. Everhart Elementary
2919 Tryon Rd, Longview TX 75602
PYP Coordinator Carol Pruitt
Languages English
T: +1 903 758 5622
W: w3.lisd.org/our-schools/everhart-elementary

J.L. Long Middle School
6116 Reiger Avenue, Dallas TX 75214
MYP Coordinator Kymberle Allen
Languages English
T: +1 972 502 4700
W: www.dallasisd.org/Long

Jack Yates High School
3650 Alabama St., Houston TX 77004
DP Coordinator April LaSalle
Languages English
T: +1 713 748 5400
W: www.houstonisd.org/yates

James Bowie High School
2101 Highbank Drive, Arlington TX 76018
DP Coordinator Amy Hayes
Languages English
T: +1 682 867 4500

James S Hogg Middle School
1100 Merrill Street, Houston TX 77009
MYP Coordinator Lynn Graham
Languages English
T: +1 713 802 4700
W: www.houstonisd.org/hogg

Joel C. Harris Middle School
325 Pruitt Ave., San Antonio TX 78204
MYP Coordinator Amanda McKay
Languages English, Spanish
T: +1 210 228 1220
W: schools.saisd.net/page/047.homepage

Johnston-McQueen Elementary
422 Farm-to-Market 2751, Longview TX 75605
PYP Coordinator Brandi Patterson
Languages English, Spanish
T: +1 903 803 5300
W: w3.lisd.org/schools/johnston-mcqueen-elementary

Judson High School
9142 FM Road 78, Converse TX 78109
DP Coordinator Alexis Mcjilton
Languages English
T: +1 210 945 1100
W: www.judsonisd.org/Domain/36

Judson STEAM Academy
5745 Judson Road, Longview TX 75605
MYP Coordinator Tracey Fernandez
Languages English
T: +1 903 446 2610
W: w3.lisd.org/schools/judson-middle

Killeen High School
500 N. 38th Street, Killeen TX 76543-4161
DP Coordinator Keina Cook
Languages English
T: +1 254 336 7208
W: tx02205734.schoolwires.net/Page/99

KIPP University Prep
4343 W. Commerce Street, San Antonio TX 78237
DP Coordinator Jonathan Villegas-Caine
Languages English
T: +1 210 290 8720
W: kipptexas.org/school/kipp-university-prep

Klein Oak High School
22603 Northcrest Drive, Spring TX 77389
DP Coordinator Elizabeth Bowling
Languages English, Spanish
T: +1 834 484 5000
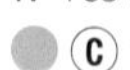

Kujawa EC/PK/K School
7111 Fallbrook Dr., Houston TX 77086
PYP Coordinator Jodi Angen
Languages English
T: +1 281 878 1514
W: kujawaec.aldineisd.org

L C Anderson High School
8403 Mesa Drive, Austin TX 78759
DP Coordinator Jill Spencer
Languages English
T: +1 512 414 2538
W: www.andersononline.org

L.D. Bell High School
1601 Brown Trail, Hurst TX 76054
DP Coordinator Nancy Shane
Languages English
T: +1 817 282 2551
W: www.hebisd.edu/Domain/33

Lamar Academy
1009 N 10th Street, McAllen TX 78501
DP Coordinator Rachelle Downey
MYP Coordinator Rachelle Downey
Languages English
T: +1 956 632 3222
W: lamar.mcallenisd.org

Lamar High School
3325 Westheimer Road, Houston TX 77098-1003
CP Coordinator David Munoz
DP Coordinator Suzanne Acord
MYP Coordinator Dennis Gillespie
Languages English
T: +1 713 522 5960
W: www.houstonisd.org/lamarhs

Lamar High School
1400 Lamar Blvd West, Arlington TX 76012
DP Coordinator Abby Rosenthal
Languages English
T: +1 682 867 8300
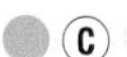

Lanier Middle School
2600 Woodhead, Houston TX 77098-1534
MYP Coordinator Rodrigus Graham
Languages English
T: +1 713 942 1900
W: www.houstonisd.org/domain/3518

Las Colinas Elementary
2200 Kinwest Parkway, Irving TX 75063
PYP Coordinator Kristen Schroder
Languages English
T: +1 972 968 2200
W: lascolinas.cfbisd.edu

Leander High School
3301 South Bagdad Road, Leander TX 78641
DP Coordinator Shawn Doctor
Languages English
T: +1 512 435 8000

Liberty Middle School
1212 S Fir Street, Pharr TX 78577
MYP Coordinator Emma Saenz
Languages English
T: +1 956 354 2610
W: liberty.psjaisd.us

Lincoln Middle School
500 Mulberry Ave., El Paso TX 79932
MYP Coordinator Karen Reid
Languages English, Spanish
T: +1 915 236 3400
W: www.episd.org/lincoln

Longfellow Middle School
1130 E Sunshine Dr, San Antonio TX 78228
MYP Coordinator Jacqueline Carter
Languages English, Spanish
T: +1 210 438 6520
W: schools.saisd.net/page/050.homepage

Longview High School
PO Box 3268, Longview TX 75606
DP Coordinator Beverly Coker
MYP Coordinator Nastascia Horton
Languages English
T: +1 903 663 1301
W: www.lisd.org/lhs

Lubbock High School
2004 19th Street, Lubbock TX 79401
DP Coordinator Erin Castle
Languages English
T: +1 806 766 1444
W: www.lubbockisd.org/lhs

Luther Burbank High School
1002 Edwards Street, San Antonio TX 78204
DP Coordinator Erin McKee
MYP Coordinator Jaeger Tate
Languages English
T: +1 210 532 4241 EXT:103

Lycée International de Houston
15950 Park Row, Houston TX 77084
DP Coordinator Margaret Combs
Languages English, French
T: +1 832 474 1013
W: www.lihouston.org

Magellan International School
7938 Great Northern Boulevard, Austin TX 78757
MYP Coordinator Nicolas Puga
PYP Coordinator Julieta Carrillo
Languages English, Spanish
T: +1 512 782 2327
W: www.magellanschool.org

Magnolia High School
14350 FM 1488, Magnolia TX 77354
DP Coordinator Derek Parsons
Languages English
T: +1 281 356 3572
W: mhs.magnoliaisd.org

Magnolia West High School
42202 FM 1774, Magnolia TX 77354-0426
DP Coordinator Jeremy Day
Languages English
T: +1 281 252 2550
W: mwhs.magnoliaisd.org

Manara Leadership Academy
8001 Jetstar Dr #100, Irving TX 75063
DP Coordinator Laura Bectarte
Languages English
T: +1 972 304 1155

Marcellus Elliot Foster Elementary
3919 Ward Street, Houston TX 77021
PYP Coordinator D'Arnisha Allen
Languages English
T: +1 713 746 8260
W: www.houstonisd.org/page/6956

Marin B. Fenwick Academy
1930 Waverly Ave., San Antonio TX 78228
MYP Coordinator Erica Guerra
PYP Coordinator Christina Sims
Languages English, Spanish
T: +1 210 438 6540
W: schools.saisd.net/page/123.homepage

Mark Twain Elementary School
7500 Braes Blvd, Houston TX 77025
PYP Coordinator Kathleen Blakeslee
Languages English
T: +1 713 295 5230

Mary Huppertz Elementary School
247 Bangor Drive, San Antonio TX 78228
PYP Coordinator Veronika Gutierrez
Languages English, Spanish
T: +1 210 438 6580
W: schools.saisd.net/page/139.homepage

Meridian School
2555 North IH-35, Round Rock TX 78664
DP Coordinator Charles Ryder
MYP Coordinator Kristen Machczynski
PYP Coordinator Leah Lieurance
Languages English
T: +1 512 660 5232
W: www.mwschool.org

Morehead Middle School
5625 Confetti Dr., El Paso TX 79912
MYP Coordinator Francisco Vasquez
Languages English, Spanish
T: +1 915 236 3500
W: morehead.episd.org

Ned E. Williams Magnet STEAM Academy
5230 Estes Parkway, Longview TX 75603
PYP Coordinator Christina Eagan
Languages English, Spanish
T: +1 903 803 5500
W: sites.google.com/lisd.org/nedwilliams

Newton Rayzor Elementary School
1400 Malone Street, Denton TX 76201
PYP Coordinator Linda Marquez-Gavilanes
Languages English
T: +1 940 369 3700
W: www.dentonisd.org/Domain/4079
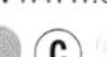

Nolan Richardson Middle School
11350 Loma Franklin Dr., El Paso TX 79934
MYP Coordinator Deena Roberts
Languages English, Spanish
T: +1 915 236 6650
W: www.episd.org/richardson

Northline Elementary
821 E Witcher Ln, Houston TX 77076-4818
PYP Coordinator Jenn Martinez
Languages English
T: +1 713 696 2890
W: www.houstonisd.org/northline

Odessa High School
1301 Dotsy Ave., Odessa TX 79763
DP Coordinator Melissa Roth
Languages English
T: +1 432 456 0029
W: www.ectorcountyisd.org/Domain/40

Patterson Dual Language Literature Magnet School
5302 Allendale Road, Houston TX 77017-6214
PYP Coordinator Karlie Signor
Languages English, Spanish
T: +1 713 943 5750
W: www.houstonisd.org/pattersones

Pinkerton Elementary
260 Southwestern Blvd., Coppell TX 75019
PYP Coordinator Marnie Ward
Languages English
T: +1 214 496 6800
W: www.coppellisd.com/pinkerton

Plano East Senior High School
3000 Los Rios Boulevard, Plano TX 75074
DP Coordinator Karen Stanton
Languages English
T: +1 469 752 9000
W: www.pisd.edu/pesh

Presidential Meadows Elementary
13252 George Bush Street, Manor TX 78653
PYP Coordinator Rebecca Garcia
Languages English, Spanish
T: +1 512 278 4225
W: pme.manorisd.net

Preston Hollow Elementary School
6423 Walnut Hill Lane, Dallas TX 75230
PYP Coordinator Araceli Hernandez
Languages English
T: +1 972 794 8500
W: www.dallasisd.org/prestonhollow

R E Good Elementary School
1012 Study Lane, Carrollton TX 75006
PYP Coordinator Kristen Schroder
Languages English
T: +1 972 968 1900
W: cfbisd.edu/schools/elementary-schools/good-elementary

Ramirez Elementary School
702 Ave. T, Lubbock TX 79401
PYP Coordinator Amber Faske
Languages English
T: +1 806 219 6500
W: ramirez.lubbockisd.org

River Oaks Elementary School
2008 Kirby Drive, Houston TX 77019
PYP Coordinator Bryant Johnson
Languages English
T: +1 713 942 1460
W: www.houstonisd.org/riveroakseib

Roberts Elementary School
6000 Greenbriar Drive, Houston TX 77030
PYP Coordinator Kristina Tran
Languages English
T: +1 713 295 5272
W: www.houstonisd.org/robertselem

Rockwall High School
901 Yellowjacket Lane, Rockwall TX 75087
DP Coordinator Michelle Ghormley
Languages English
T: +1 972 771 7339
W: www.rockwallisd.com/Domain/8

Rockwall-Heath High School
801 Laurence Drive, Heath TX 75032
DP Coordinator Gretchen Kimpel
Languages English
T: +1 972 772 2474
W: www.rockwallisd.com/Domain/9

Roscoe Wilson Elementary School
2807 25th Street, Lubbock TX 79410
PYP Coordinator Amber Faske
Languages English
T: +1 806 766 0922
W: rwilson.lubbockisd.org

Sam Houston Elementary Dual Language Academy
301 E Taft Street, Harlingen TX 78550
PYP Coordinator Vanessa Garcia
Languages English, Spanish
T: +1 956 427 3110
W: hcisd-houston.edlioschool.com

Sam Houston High School
2000 Sam Houston Drive, Arlington TX 76014
DP Coordinator Poppy Moore
Languages English
T: +1 682 867 8200

Sam Houston Math, Science, and Technology Center
9400 Irvington Blvd., Houston TX 77076-5224
MYP Coordinator Bryan White
Languages English, Spanish
T: +1 713 696 0200
W: www.houstonisd.org/Domain/648

Samuel Clemens High School
1001 Elbel Road, Schertz TX 78154
DP Coordinator Lauren Rollins
Languages English
T: +1 210 945 6100
W: www.scuc.txed.net/Domain/2065

Sci-Tech High School
10704 Bradshaw Road, Austin TX 78747
DP Coordinator Krissy Ford
Languages English
T: +1 512 220 9104
W: waysideschools.org/stp

Scott Elementary School
2301 West Ave. P, Temple TX 76504
PYP Coordinator Carlinda Rex
Languages English
T: +1 254 215 6222
W: scott.tisd.org

Sharpstown International School
8330 Triola Lane, Houston TX 77036-6310
DP Coordinator Alexander Brahm
MYP Coordinator Robin Bissell
Languages English, Spanish
T: +1 713 778 3440
W: www.houstonisd.org/sis

Shotwell Middle School
6515 Trail Valley Way, Houston TX 77086
MYP Coordinator Sharnell Nelms
Languages English
T: +1 281 878 0960
W: shotwellms.aldineisd.org

South Texas Business Education & Technology Academy
510 S. Sugar Road, Edinburg TX 78539
DP Coordinator Erika Sarabia
Languages English
T: +1 956 383 1684

Spicewood Elementary School
11601 Olson Drive, Austin TX 78750
PYP Coordinator Nicole Cimo
Languages English
T: +1 512 428 3600
W: spicewood.roundrockisd.org

Springwoods Village Middle School
1120 Crossgate Blvd., Spring TX 77373
MYP Coordinator Melissa Lynch
Languages English, Spanish
T: +1 281 891 8100
W: www.springisd.org/springwoods

St Anthony Academy
3732 Myrtle Street, Dallas TX 75215
PYP Coordinator Kimberly Stephens
Languages English
T: +1 214 421 3645
W: www.stanthonydallas.org

Stony Point High School
1801 Tiger Trail, Round Rock TX 78664
DP Coordinator Andi Brosché
Languages English
T: +1 512 428 7000
W: stonypoint.roundrockisd.org

Sylvan Rodriguez Elementary
5858 Chimney Rock, Houston TX 77081
PYP Coordinator Minerva Gonzalez
Languages English
T: +1 713 295 3870
W: www.houstonisd.org/rodriguezes

Tanglewood Middle School
5215 San Felipe, Houston TX 77056-3605
MYP Coordinator Tal Gribbins
Languages English
T: +1 713 625 1411
W: www.houstonisd.org/grady

Temple Emanu-El
8500 Hillcrest Road, Dallas TX 75225
PYP Coordinator Kelsey Winocour
Languages English
T: +1 214 706 0000
W: www.tedallas.org

Temple High School
415 North 31st Street, Temple TX 76504
DP Coordinator Kaleigh Verett
Languages English
T: +1 254 215 7000
W: ths.tisd.org

The Awty International School
7455 Awty School Lane, Houston TX 77055-7222
DP Coordinator Lucas Anderson
Languages English
T: +1 713 686 4850
W: www.awty.org

IB AMERICAS

The Post Oak School
4600 Bissonnet Street, Bellaire TX 77401
DP Coordinator Kim Harrison
Languages English
T: +1 713 661 6688
W: www.postoakschool.org

The School at St. George Place
5430 Hidalgo St., Houston TX 77056
PYP Coordinator Lauren Kussmaul
Languages English
T: +1 713 625 1499
W: www.houstonisd.org/stgeorge

THE VILLAGE SCHOOL
13051 Whittington Drive, Houston TX 77077
DP Coordinator Kerri Peters
Languages English
T: +1 281 496 7900
E: admissions@thevillageschool.com
W: www.thevillageschool.com
See full details on page 519

The Westwood School
14340 Proton Road, Dallas TX 75244
DP Coordinator Gail Macalik
Languages English
T: +1 972 239 8598
W: www.westwoodschool.org

Theodore Roosevelt Elementary School
4801 S 26th St, McAllen TX 78503
PYP Coordinator Rosa Solis
Languages English, Spanish
T: +1 956 971 4424
W: roosevelt.mcallenisd.org

Thomas Jefferson High School
723 Donaldson Ave., San Antonio TX 78201
DP Coordinator Yareli Melendez
MYP Coordinator Jennifer Love
Languages English, Spanish
T: +1 210 438 6570
W: schools.saisd.net/page/007.homepage
 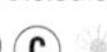

Travis Science Academy
1551 S. 25th Street, Temple TX 76504
MYP Coordinator Kathy Cook
Languages English
T: +1 254 215 6300
W: travis.tisd.org

Trinity High School
500 North Industrial, Euless TX 76039
DP Coordinator William Wells
Languages English
T: +1 817 571 0271
W: www.hebisd.edu/Domain/34

Uplift Atlas Preparatory
4600 Bryan Street, Dallas TX 75204
DP Coordinator Brooke Parsons
MYP Coordinator Sarah Boykins
PYP Coordinator Denitra Sanders
Languages English
T: +1 214 276 0879
W: www.upliftedudcation.org/domain/322

Uplift Grand Preparatory
300 E Church Street, Grand Prairie TX 75050
DP Coordinator Grace Kirkland
MYP Coordinator Elizabeth Coughenour
PYP Coordinator Mary Merrifield
Languages English, Spanish
T: +1 972 854 0600
W: www.upliftedudcation.org/domain/1994

Uplift Hampton Preparatory
8915 S. Hampton Road, Dallas TX 75232
DP Coordinator Shaun Thompson
MYP Coordinator Charelle Calloway
PYP Coordinator Brittany Murrell
Languages English
T: +1 972 421 1982
W: www.upliftedudcation.org/domain/47
 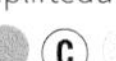

Uplift Heights Preparatory
2650 Canada Drive, Dallas TX 75212
DP Coordinator Jeffrey Fuller
MYP Coordinator Zakyla Dickerson
PYP Coordinator Michael Mason
Languages English
T: +1 214 442 7094
W: www.upliftedudcation.org/domain/729

Uplift Infinity Preparatory
1401 S. MacArthur Street, Irving TX 75060
DP Coordinator Jesus Sesma
MYP Coordinator Jennifer Buysman
PYP Coordinator Samantha Newman
Languages English
T: +1 469 621 9200
W: www.upliftedudcation.org/domain/884

Uplift Luna Preparatory
2020 N. Lamar Street, Dallas TX 75202
DP Coordinator Frank Wu
MYP Coordinator Austin Cadle
PYP Coordinator Sydney celestin
Languages English
T: +1 214 442 7882
W: www.upliftedudcation.org/domain/787

Uplift Meridian Preparatory
1801 South Beach Street, Fort Worth TX 76105
PYP Coordinator Ann Wilson
Languages English
T: +1 817 288 1700
W: www.upliftedudcation.org/domain/932

Uplift Mighty Preparatory
3700 Mighty Mite Drive, Fort Worth TX 76105
DP Coordinator Te Taime Green
MYP Coordinator Carla allen
PYP Coordinator Sonja Sherrer
Languages English
T: +1 817 288 3800
W: www.upliftedudcation.org/domain/930

Uplift North Hills Preparatory
606 East Royal Lane, Irving TX 75039
DP Coordinator Katherine Biela
MYP Coordinator Nicolau Pereira
PYP Coordinator Julie Hills
Languages English
T: +1 972 501 0645
W: www.upliftedudcation.org/domain/147

Uplift Pinnacle Preparatory
2510 South Vernon Ave, Dallas TX 75224
PYP Coordinator Leah Malone
Languages English
T: +1 21 444 26100
W: www.upliftedudcation.org/domain/841

Uplift Summit International Preparatory
1305 North Center Street, Arlington TX 76011
DP Coordinator Tobias Rather
MYP Coordinator Tamara Phillips
PYP Coordinator Danielle Erbert
Languages English
T: +1 817 287 5121
W: www.upliftedudcation.org/domain/449

Uplift Triumph Preparatory
9411 Hargrove Drive, Dallas TX 75220
PYP Coordinator Louis Bertenshaw
Languages English, Spanish
T: +1 972 590 5100
W: www.upliftedudcation.org/domain/1427

Uplift Williams Preparatory
1750 Viceroy Drive, Dallas TX 75235
DP Coordinator Jessica Staggs
MYP Coordinator Mildred Miller
PYP Coordinator Yamid Barraza
Languages English
T: +1 214 276 0352
W: www.upliftedudcation.org/domain/606

Uplift Wisdom High School
301 W Camp Wisdom Road, Dallas TX 75232
DP Coordinator Ciara Rucker
Languages English, Spanish
T: +1 214 453 6900
W: www.upliftedudcation.org/domain/3380

Vandegrift High School
9500 McNeil Dr., Austin TX 78750
DP Coordinator Sherilyn Green
Languages English
T: +1 512 570 2300
W: vhs.leanderisd.org

Vernon Middle School World Languages Academy
125 S 13th Street, Harlingen TX 78550
MYP Coordinator Jessica Saldivar
Languages English, Spanish
T: +1 956 427 3040
W: vernon.hcisd.org

W B Ray High School
1002 Texan Trail, Corpus Christi TX 78411
DP Coordinator Lorinda Hamilton
MYP Coordinator Lorinda Hamilton
Languages English
T: +1 361 878 7300
W: ray.ccisd.us

Ware East Texas Montessori Academy
601 W. Garfield, Longview TX 75602
PYP Coordinator Nastascia Horton
Languages English, Spanish
T: +1 903 803 5700
W: sites.google.com/lisd.org/wareelementary

Westchester Academy for International Studies
901 Yorkchester, Houston TX 77079
CP Coordinator Sara Sebesta-Camano
DP Coordinator Sara Guillory
MYP Coordinator Cheryl Wegscheid
Languages English
T: +1 713 251 1800
W: wais.springbranchisd.com

Western Hills High School
3600 Boston Avenue, Fort Worth TX 76133
DP Coordinator Jane Card
Languages English
T: +1 817 871 2000
W: www.fwisd.org/WesternHills

Westlake Academy
2600 J.T. Ottinger Road, Westlake TX 76262
DP Coordinator Dr. James Owen
MYP Coordinator Terri Watson
PYP Coordinator Alison Schneider
Languages English
T: +1 817 4905757
W: www.westlakeacademy.org

Westwood High School
12400 Mellow Meadow, Austin TX 78750
DP Coordinator Christin Key
Languages English
T: +1 512 464 4000
W: westwood.roundrockisd.org

William B. Lipscomb Elementary School
5801 Worth Street, Dallas TX 75214
PYP Coordinator Torrian Timms
Languages English
T: +1 972 794 7300
W: www.dallasisd.org/lipscomb

William Wharton K-8 Dual Language Academy
900 West Gray Street, Houston TX 77019
PYP Coordinator Ana Silva
Languages English, Spanish
T: +1 713 535 3771
W: www.houstonisd.org/whartondla

Windsor Park Elementary School
4525 South Alameda Street, Corpus Christi TX 78412
PYP Coordinator Rachel Beavers
Languages English
T: +1 361 994 3664
W: windsorpark.ccisd.us

Woodlawn Academy
1717 W. Magnolia Ave, San Antonio TX 78201
MYP Coordinator Xochitl Gonzalez
PYP Coordinator Ana Femath
Languages English
T: +1 210 438 6560
W: schools.saisd.net/page/175.homepage

Woodlawn Hills Elementary School
110 W. Quill Drive, San Antonio TX 78228
PYP Coordinator Sharon Franco
Languages English, Spanish
T: +1 210 438 6565
W: schools.saisd.net/page/176.homepage

Woodrow Wilson High School
100 S Glasgow, Dallas TX 75214
DP Coordinator Mary Ochoa
Languages English
T: +1 972 502 4400
W: www.woodrowwildcats.org

Worthing Early College High School
9215 Scott Street, Houston TX 77051-3302
CP Coordinator Nina Jolivet
Languages English
T: +1 713 733 3433
W: www.houstonisd.org/worthing

Utah

Bountiful High School
695 South Orchard Drive, Bountiful UT 84010
DP Coordinator Luisa (Vickie) Ludwig
Languages English
T: +1 801 402 3900
W: www.davis.k12.ut.us/Domain/7221

Channing Hall
13515 South 150 East, Draper UT 84020
MYP Coordinator Aaron Webb
PYP Coordinator Aaron Webb
Languages English
T: +1 801 572 2709
W: www.channinghall.org

Clearfield High School
931 South 1000 East, Clearfield UT 84015
DP Coordinator Layne Carter
Languages English
T: +1 801 408 8200
W: www.davis.k12.ut.us/domain/7356

Highland High School
2166 South 1700 East, Salt Lake City UT 84106
DP Coordinator Kyle Bracken
Languages English
T: +1 801 484 4343
W: highland.slcschools.org

Hillcrest High School
7350 South 900 East, Midvale UT 84047
CP Coordinator John Olsen
DP Coordinator John Olsen
Languages English
T: +1 801 256 5484

Midvale Middle School
7852 S Pioneer St, Midvale UT 84047
MYP Coordinator Shelley Allen
Languages English
T: +1 801 826 7300
W: www.canyonsdistrict.org/midvale-middle

Ogden High School
2828 Harrison Blvd, Ogden UT 84403
CP Coordinator Tim Dunn
DP Coordinator Tim Dunn
Languages English
T: +1 801 737 8700
W: ogdenhigh.ogdensd.org

Providence Hall Charter School
4557 West Patriot Ridge Drive, Herriman UT 84096
PYP Coordinator Kim Randall
Languages English
T: +1 801 727 8260
W: www.providencehall.com

Skyline High School
3251 East 3760 South, Salt Lake City UT 84109
DP Coordinator Jill thackeray
Languages English
T: +1 385 646 5420
W: schools.graniteschools.org/skylinehigh

Walden School of Liberal Arts
4266 N University Avenue, Provo UT 84604
DP Coordinator Diana West
Languages English
T: +1 801 623 1388
W: www.waldenschool.us

Weber High School
430 West Weber High Drive, Pleasant View UT 84414
DP Coordinator Marcia Kloempken
Languages English
T: +1 801 476 3700
W: whs.wsd.net

West High School
241 North 300 West, Salt Lake City UT 84103
CP Coordinator Jennifer Nicholas
DP Coordinator Jennifer Nicholas
Languages English
T: +1 801 578 8500
W: west.slcschools.org

West Jordan High School
8136 South 2700 West, West Jordan UT 84088
DP Coordinator Chandler Bishop
Languages English
T: +1 801 256 5600
W: www.westjordanhigh.org

Vermont

Bridport Central School
3442 Vt Route 22a, Bridport VT 05734
PYP Coordinator C.Joy Dobson
Languages English
T: +1 802 758 2331
W: www.acsdvt.org/bridport

Cornwall School
112 School Road, Cornwall VT 05753
PYP Coordinator C.Joy Dobson
Languages English
T: +1 802 462 2463
W: www.acsdvt.org/cornwall

Long Trail School
1045 Kirby Hollow Road, Dorset VT 05251
DP Coordinator Kelley Swarthout
Languages English
T: +1 802 867 5717
W: www.longtrailschool.org

Mary Hogan Elementary School
201 Mary Hogan Drive, Middlebury VT 05753
PYP Coordinator C. Joy Dobson
Languages English
T: +1 802 388 4421
W: www.acsdvt.org/maryhogan

Middlebury Union High School
73 Charles Avenue, Middlebury VT 05753
DP Coordinator Cindy Atkins
MYP Coordinator Eileen Sears
Languages English
T: +1 802 382 1500
W: www.acsdvt.org/muhs

Middlebury Union Middle School
48 Deerfield Lane, Middlebury VT 05753
MYP Coordinator Pam Quinn
Languages English
T: +1 802 382 1600
W: www.acsdvt.org/mums

Ripton Elementary School
753 Lincoln Rd, Ripton VT 05766
PYP Coordinator C.Joy Dobson
Languages English
T: +1 802 388 2208
W: www.acsdvt.org/ripton

Salisbury Community School
286 Kelly Cross Road, Salisbury VT 05769
PYP Coordinator C. Joy Dobson
Languages English
T: +1 802 352 4291
W: www.acsdvt.org/salisbur

Shoreham Elementary School
130 School Road, Shoreham VT 05770
PYP Coordinator C.Joy Dobson
Languages English
T: +1 802 897 7181
W: www.acsdvt.org/shoreham

The Dover School
9 Schoolhouse Road, East Dover VT 05341
PYP Coordinator Susan Neuman
Languages English
T: +1 802 464 5386
W: www.doverschool.net

Weybridge Elementary School
210 Quaker Village Road, Weybridge VT 05753
PYP Coordinator C.Joy Dobson
Languages English
T: +1 802 545 2113
W: www.acsdvt.org/weybridge

Virginia

Academy for Discovery at Lakewood
1701 Alsace Avenue, Norfolk VA 23509
MYP Coordinator Judy Gulledge
Languages English
T: +1 757 628 2477
W: www.npsk12.com/afdl

Annandale High School
4700 Medford Drive, Annandale VA 22003
DP Coordinator Linda Bradshaw
MYP Coordinator Jeniva Miller
Languages English
T: +1 703 642 4100
W: annandalehs.fcps.edu

Antietam Elementary School
12000 Antietam Rd, Woodbridge VA 22192
PYP Coordinator Melissa Bloomrose
Languages English
T: +1 703 497 7619

Atlee High School
9414 Atlee Station Road, Mechanicsville VA 23116
DP Coordinator Wendy Edelman
Languages English
T: +1 804 723 2100

Belvedere Elementary School
6540 Columbia Pike, Falls Church VA 22101
PYP Coordinator Ellen Rogers
Languages English
T: +1 703 916 6800
W: belvederees.fcps.edu

Brooke Point High School
1700 Courthouse Road, Stafford VA 22554
DP Coordinator Meghan Stone
Languages English
T: +1 540 658 6080
W: www.staffordschools.net/BP

Buckland Mills Elementary School
10511 Wharfdale Place, Gainesville VA 20155
PYP Coordinator Amy Hardt
Languages English
T: +1 703 530 1560
W: bucklandmillses.pwcs.edu

Chimborazo Elementary School
3000 East Marshall Street, Richmond VA 23223
PYP Coordinator Andrea Stewart
Languages English
T: +1 804 780 8392
W: web.richmond.k12.va.us/ces/Home.aspx

Clarke County High School
627 Mosby Blvd, Berryville VA 22611
DP Coordinator Thom Potts
Languages English
T: +1 540 955 6130
W: cchs.clarke.k12.va.us

Dogwood Elementary School
12300 Glade Drive, Reston VA 20191
PYP Coordinator Adrienne Schumer
Languages English, Spanish
T: +1 703 262 3100
W: dogwoodes.fcps.edu

Edgar Allen Poe Middle School
7000 Cindy Lane, Annandale VA 2203
MYP Coordinator Darcy Hood
Languages English
T: +1 703 813 3800
W: poems.fcps.edu

Ellen Glasgow Middle School
4101 Fairfax Parkway, Alexandria VA 22312
MYP Coordinator Chinoyerem (Nonye) Oladimeji
Languages English
T: +1 703 813 8700
W: glasgowms.fcps.edu

Ellis Elementary School
10400 Kim Graham Lane, Manassas VA 20109
PYP Coordinator Rebecca Lucas
Languages English
T: +1 703 365 0287
W: ellises.pwcs.edu

Fairfield Middle School
5121 Nine Mile Road, Henrico VA 23223
MYP Coordinator Kashira Turner
Languages English
T: +1 804 328 4020
W: fairfield.henricoschools.us

Fred M. Lynn Middle School
1650 Prince William Parkway, Woodbridge VA 22191
MYP Coordinator Greg Patterson
Languages English
T: +1 703 494 5157
W: lynnms.pwcs.edu

Galileo Magnet High School
230 South Ridge Road, Danville VA 24541
DP Coordinator Johnny Cressell
Languages English
T: +1 434 773 8186

Gar-Field High School
14000 Smoketown Road, Woodbridge VA 22192
CP Coordinator Michelle Schneider
DP Coordinator Brian Bassett
MYP Coordinator Della Gordon
Languages English
T: +1 703 730 7000
W: gar-fieldhs.pwcs.edu

George C Marshall High School
7731 Leesburg Pike, Falls Church VA 22043
DP Coordinator Matthew Axelrod
Languages English
T: +1 703 714 5402
W: marshallhs.fcps.edu

George H Moody Middle School
7800 Woodman Road, Richmond VA 23228
MYP Coordinator April Craver
Languages English
T: +1 804 261 5015
W: schools.henrico.k12.va.us/moody
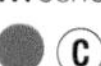

George M. Hampton Middle School
14800 Darbydale Avenue, Woodbridge VA 22193
MYP Coordinator Ryan Koontz
Languages English
T: +1 703 670 6166
W: hamptonms.pwcs.edu

Granby High School
7101 Granby Street, Norfolk VA 23505
DP Coordinator Rebecca Gardner
Languages English
T: +1 757 451 4110
W: www.npsk12.com/ghs

Green Run Collegiate
1700 Dahlia Drive, Virginia Beach VA 23456
CP Coordinator Rianne Patricio
DP Coordinator Rianne Patricio
MYP Coordinator Tonia Waters
Languages English
T: +1 757 648 5350
W: greenruncollegiate.vbschools.com

Hampton High School
1491 W Queen Street, Hampton City Schools, Hampton VA 23669
DP Coordinator Haneef Majied
Languages English
T: +1 757 825 4430
W: www.sbo.hampton.k12.va.us

Hanover High School
10307 Chamberlayne Road, Mechanicsville VA 23116
DP Coordinator Jessica Orth
Languages English
T: +1 804 723 3700

Henrico High School
302 Azalea Avenue, Richmond VA 23227
CP Coordinator Gregory Lyndaker
DP Coordinator Gregory Lyndaker
MYP Coordinator Gregory Lyndaker
Languages English
T: +1 804 228 2700
W: henrico.henricoschools.us

Holmes Middle School
6525 Montrose Street, Alexandria VA 22312
MYP Coordinator Alex Anderson
Languages English
T: +1 703 658 5900
W: holmesms.fcps.edu

James Monroe High School
2300 Washington Ave, Fredericksburg VA 22401
DP Coordinator Stephanie Teri
Languages English
T: +1 540 372 1100
W: www.cityschools.com/jamesmonroehighschool

James W Robinson, Jr Secondary School
5035 Sideburn Road, Fairfax County Public Schools, Fairfax VA 22032
DP Coordinator Wendy Vu
MYP Coordinator Kristin Webster
Languages English
T: +1 703 426 2100
W: www.fcps.edu/RobinsonSS

Jefferson Houston PreK-8 School
1501 Cameron Street, Alexandria VA 22314
MYP Coordinator Melissa Bouldin
PYP Coordinator Melissa Bouldin
Languages English, Spanish
T: +1 703 706 4400
W: www.acps.k12.va.us/Domain/15

John Randolph Tucker High School
2910 North Parham Road, Henrico VA 23294
DP Coordinator Katherine Snow
MYP Coordinator Katherine Snow
Languages English
T: +1 804 527 4600
W: tucker.henricoschools.us

Justice High School
3301 Peace Valley Lane, Falls Church VA 22044
DP Coordinator Stephanie Bilimoria
MYP Coordinator Katherine Naughton
Languages English
T: +1 703 824 3900
W: justicehs.fcps.edu

Key Middle School
6402 Franconia Road, Springfield VA 22150
MYP Coordinator Danielle Danz
Languages English
T: +1 703 313 3900
W: keyms.fcps.edu

King Abdullah Academy
2949 Education Dr, Herndon VA 20171
DP Coordinator Jalaika Hasan
MYP Coordinator Deborah Mohammed
PYP Coordinator Sumaya Jaghlit
Languages Arabic, English
T: +1 571 351 5520
W: www.kaa-herndon.com

King's Fork High School
351 King's Fork Road, Suffolk VA 23434
DP Coordinator Shawn Barnard
Languages English
T: +1 757 923 5240
W: kfhs.spsk12.net

Langston Hughes Middle School
11401 Ridge Heights Road, Reston VA 20191
MYP Coordinator Chris Delgrosso
Languages English
T: +1 703 715 3600
 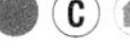

Lee High School
6540 Franconia Road, Fairfax county, Springfield VA 22150
DP Coordinator Mariano Acevedo
MYP Coordinator Mariano Acevedo
Languages English
T: +1 703 924 8300
W: www.fcps.edu/LeeHS

Lee-Davis High School
7052 Mechanicsville Pike, Hanover County, Mechanicsville VA 23111-3629
DP Coordinator Lesa Berlinghoff
Languages English
T: +1 804 723 2200

Lucille Brown Middle School
6300 Jahnke Road, Richmond VA 23225
MYP Coordinator Tracy S. Cady
Languages English
T: +1 804 319 3013
W: www.rvaschools.net/Domain/27

Mark Twain Middle School
4700 Franconia Road, Alexandria VA 22310
MYP Coordinator Angela Ramacci
Languages English
T: +1 703 313 3700
W: twainms.fcps.edu

Mary Ellen Henderson Middle School
7130 Leesburg Pike, Falls Church VA 22043
MYP Coordinator Rory Dippold
Languages English
T: +1 703 720 5702
W: www.fccps.org/o/meh

Meadowbrook High School
4901 Cogbill Road, North Chesterfield VA 23234
DP Coordinator Jelani Lynch
Languages English
T: +1 804 743 3675
W: sites.google.com/a/ccpsnet.net/mbkhs

Meridian High School
121 Mustang Alley, Falls Church VA 22043
CP Coordinator William Snyder
DP Coordinator Josh Singer
MYP Coordinator Rory Dippold
Languages English
T: +1 703 248 5500
W: mhs.fccps.org

Midlothian High School
401 Charter Colony Parkway, Chesterfield County, Midlothian VA 23114
DP Coordinator Stuart Jones
Languages English
T: +1 804 378 2440
W: sites.google.com/a/ccpsnet.net/mdhs

Mount Vernon High School
8515 Old Mount Vernon Road, Alexandria VA 22309
CP Coordinator Sarah Freeland
DP Coordinator Sarah Freeland
MYP Coordinator Nikolas Short
Languages English
T: +1 703 619 3103
W: www.fcps.edu/MtVernonHS

Mountain View High School
2135 Mountain View Road, Stafford VA 22556
DP Coordinator Jeanne Mills
Languages English
T: +1 540 658 6840
W: www.staffordschools.net/MVHS

Mullen Elementary School
8000 Rodes Drive, Manassas VA 20109
PYP Coordinator Elizabeth Hooker
Languages English
T: +1 703 330 0427

Murray High School
1200 Forest Street, Charlottesville VA 22903
DP Coordinator Rebecca Hostetter
Languages English
T: +1 434 296 3090
W: mcs.k12albemarle.org

Oscar F Smith High School
1994 Tiger Drive, Chesapeake VA 23320
DP Coordinator Cristina Foss
Languages English
T: +1 757 548 0696
W: cpschools.com/osh
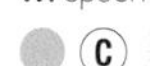

Patrick Henry High School
12449 West Patrick Henry Road, Ashland VA 23005
DP Coordinator Luke Kupscznk
Languages English
T: +1 804 365 8011
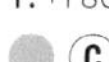

Plaza Middle School
3080 South Lynnhaven Road, Virginia Beach VA 23452
MYP Coordinator Catherine Susewind
Languages English
T: +1 757 431 4060
W: www.plazams.vbschools.com

Princess Anne High School
4400 Virginia Beach Boulevard, Virginia Beach VA 23462-3198
DP Coordinator Jamie LaCava-Owen
MYP Coordinator Jamie LaCava-Owen
Languages English
T: +1 757 473 5000
W: www.princessannehs.vbschools.com

Randolph Elementary School
1306 S Quincy Street, Arlington VA 22204
PYP Coordinator Shannon Quinn
Languages English
T: +1 703 228 5830

Rosa Parks Elementary School
13446 Princedale Drive, Woodbridge VA 22193
PYP Coordinator Alicia Strahan
Languages English
T: +1 703 580 9665

Saint Mary's Catholic School
9501 Gayton Road, Richmond VA 23229
MYP Coordinator Carole Forkey
Languages English
T: +1 804 740 1048
W: www.saintmary.org

Salem High School
400 Spartan Drive, Salem VA 24153
DP Coordinator Sara Epperly
Languages English
T: +1 540 387 2437
W: shs.salem.k12.va.us

South Lakes High School
11400 South Lakes Drive, Reston VA 20191
CP Coordinator Charo Tomlin
DP Coordinator Marie Turner
MYP Coordinator Desiree Satterfield
Languages English
T: +1 703 715 4500

Spotsylvania High School
6975 Courthouse Road, Spotsylvania VA 22551
DP Coordinator Catherine Larocco
Languages English
T: +1 540 582 3882
W: www.spotsyschools.us/shs

Stonewall Jackson High School
8820 Rixlew Lane, Manassas VA 20109
CP Coordinator Herman Hruska
DP Coordinator Katie Hodgson
MYP Coordinator Alaina Lynard
Languages English
T: +1 703 365 2900

Stonewall Middle School
10100 Lomond Drive, Manassas VA 20109
MYP Coordinator Jeanine Fox
Languages English
T: +1 703 361 3185
W: stonewallms.pwcs.edu

Strelitz International Academy
5000 Corporate Woods Driv, Suite 180, Virginia Beach VA 23462
PYP Coordinator Alicia Pahl-Cornelius
Languages English, Hebrew
T: +1 757 424 4327
W: strelitzinternationalacademy.org

Stuart M Beville Middle School
4901 Dale Boulevard, Woodbridge VA 22193-4700
MYP Coordinator Patricia Kramolisch
Languages English
T: +1 703 878 2593

The Hague School
739 Yarmouth St., Norfolk VA 23510
DP Coordinator Bonnie Schneider
Languages English, French
T: +1 757 317 3033
W: www.thehagueschool.org

Thomas Alva Edison High School
5801 Franconia Road, Alexandria VA 22310
DP Coordinator Sabra Devers
MYP Coordinator Corinne Nuttall
Languages English
T: +1 703 924 8007
W: edisonhs.fcps.edu

Thomas Jefferson Elementary
601 South Oak Street, Falls Church VA 22046
PYP Coordinator Carrie Checca
Languages English
T: +1 703 248 5661
W: www.fccps.org/o/tje

Thomas Jefferson High School
4100 West Grace Street, Richmond VA 23230
DP Coordinator Melissa Johnston
MYP Coordinator Tracy S. Cady
Languages English
T: +1 804 780 6028
W: www.rvaschools.net/Domain/14

Thomas Jefferson Middle School
125 S Old Glebe Road, Arlington VA 22204
MYP Coordinator Christopher "Kip" Malinosky
Languages English
T: +1 703 228 5900
W: www.apsva.us/jefferson

Trinity Episcopal School
3850 Pittaway Road, Richmond VA 23235
DP Coordinator Elizabeth Kelley
Languages English
T: +1 804 272 5864
W: www.trinityes.org

Tuckahoe Middle School
9000 Three Chopt Road, Henrico VA 23229
MYP Coordinator Marie Wilcox
Languages English
T: +1 804 673 3720
W: tuckahoems.henricoschools.us

Walt Whitman Middle School
2500 Parkers Lane, Alexandria VA 22306
MYP Coordinator Michelle Johnson
Languages English
T: +1 703 660 2400

Warwick High School
51 Copeland Lane, Newport News VA 23601
DP Coordinator Maranda Hall
Languages English
T: +1 757 591 4700
W: warwick.nn.k12.va.us

Washington-Liberty High School
1301 N Stafford St, Arlington VA 22201
DP Coordinator Julie Cantor
Languages English
T: +1 703 228 6200
W: washingtonlee.apsva.us

Williamsburg Christian Academy
101 School House Lane, Williamsburg VA 23188
DP Coordinator Chelsea Meisinger
MYP Coordinator Chelsea Meisinger
PYP Coordinator Noelle Rennolds
Languages English, Spanish
T: +1 757 568 9322
W: private-christian-school.williamsburgchristian.org

York High School
9300 George Washington, Memorial Highway, Yorktown VA 23692
DP Coordinator Kevin Valliant
Languages English
T: +1 757 898 0354
W: ycsd.yorkcountyschools.org/YHS

Washington

A C Davis High School
212 South 6th Avenue, Yakima WA 98902
DP Coordinator Beth Dallman
Languages English
T: +1 509 573 2501
W: www.yakimaschools.org/davis

Alderwood Elementary School
3400 Hollywood Avenue, Bellingham WA 98225
PYP Coordinator Gretchen Stiteler
Languages English
T: +1 360 676 6404
W: alderwood.bellinghamschools.org

Annie Wright Schools
827 N Tacoma Avenue, Tacoma WA 98403
DP Coordinator Emily Lynn
MYP Coordinator Briana Samuelson
PYP Coordinator Jennifer Bills
Languages English
T: +1 253 272 2216
W: www.aw.org

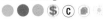

Bellevue Children's Academy
14600 NE 24th St., Bellevue WA 98007
PYP Coordinator Britt Dougherty
Languages English
T: +1 425 649 0791
W: www.bcacademy.com

Birchwood Elementary School
3200 Pinewood Avenue, Bellingham WA 98225
PYP Coordinator Cori Stothart
Languages English
T: +1 360 676 6466
W: birchwood.bellinghamschools.org

Capital High School
2707 Conger Avenue, Olympia WA 98502
DP Coordinator Amelia Young
Languages English
T: +1 360 753 8880
W: capital.osd.wednet.edu

Carl Cozier Elementary School
1330 Lincoln St., Bellingham WA 98229
PYP Coordinator Monica Savory
Languages English
T: +1 360 676 6410
W: carlcozier.bellinghamschools.org

Cedar Heights Middle School
2220 Pottery Ave, Port Orchard WA 98366
MYP Coordinator Jennifer Knowles
Languages English
T: +1 360 874 6020
W: www.kent.k12.wa.us/Domain/9

Chief Sealth International High School
2600 SW Thistle, Seattle WA 98126
CP Coordinator Allison Hays
DP Coordinator Allison Hays
Languages English
T: +1 206 252 8550
W: chiefsealthhs.seattleschools.org

Columbia Elementary School
2508 Utter Street, Bellingham WA 98225
PYP Coordinator April O'Halloran
Languages English, Spanish
T: +1 360 676 6413
W: columbia.bellinghamschools.org

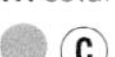

Columbia River High School
800 North West 99th Street, Vancouver WA 98665
CP Coordinator Morgan Parker
DP Coordinator Julie A Nygaard
Languages English
T: +1 360 313 3900
W: river.vansd.org

Discovery Middle School
800 E. 40th Street, Vancouver WA 98663
MYP Coordinator Mark Phelan
Languages English
T: +1 360 313 3300
W: disco.vansd.org

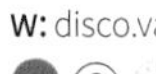

Eastern Senior High School
1700 East Capitol Street NE, Washington DC 20003
DP Coordinator Danielle Imhoff
Languages English
T: +1 202 698 4500
W: www.easternhighschooldc.org

Edmonds-Woodway High School
7600 212th St South West, Edmonds WA 98026
DP Coordinator Nick Wellington
Languages English
T: +1 425 431 7900

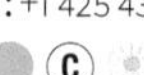

Giaudrone Middle School
4902 S Alaska Street, Tacoma WA 98408
MYP Coordinator Ulrike Puryear
Languages English
T: +1 253 571 5810
W: www.tacomaschools.org/giaudrone

Harrison Preparatory School
9103 Lakewood DR SW, Lakewood WA 98499
DP Coordinator Erika Cox
MYP Coordinator Erika Cox
Languages English
T: +1 253 583 5419
W: www.cloverpark.k12.wa.us

Henry Foss High School
2112 South Tyler Street, Tacoma WA 98405
CP Coordinator Casey Church
DP Coordinator Casey Church
MYP Coordinator Casey Church
Languages English
T: +1 253 571 7300
W: www.tacoma.k12.wa.us/foss

Idlewild Elementary School
10806 Idlewild Rd. SW, Lakewood WA 98499
PYP Coordinator Shanee Kettell
Languages English
T: +1 253 583 5290
W: www.cloverpark.k12.wa.us

Inglemoor High School
15500 Simonds Rd NE, Kenmore WA 98028
DP Coordinator Christopher McQueen
Languages English
T: +1 425 408 7200
W: www.nsd.org/inglemoor

Ingraham High School
1819 North 135th Street, Seattle WA 98133-7709
DP Coordinator Guy Thomas
Languages English
T: +1 206 252 3923
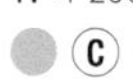

Interlake High School
16245 NE 24th St., Bellevue WA 98008
DP Coordinator Megan Bennett
Languages English
T: +1 425 456 7200
W: bsd405.org/interlake

Kennewick High School
500 S. Dayton Street, Kennewick WA 99336
DP Coordinator David Piper
Languages English
T: +1 509) 222-7100
W: kennewick.ksd.org

Kent-Meridian High School
10020 SE 256th Street, Kent WA 98031
DP Coordinator Beth Shoemaker
Languages English
T: +1 253 373 7405

Kilo Middle School
4400 S. 308th St, Auburn WA 98001
MYP Coordinator Theresa Lee
Languages English
T: +1 253 945 4700
W: www.fwps.org/Domain/32

Liberty Bell Junior-Senior High School
24 Twin Lakes Rd, Winthrop WA 98862
MYP Coordinator Matt Hinckley
Languages English
T: +1 509 996 2215
W: methow.org/schools/liberty-bell-jr-sr-high

McCarver Elementary
2111 S. J St, Tacoma WA 98405
PYP Coordinator Kendra Hartman
Languages English
T: +1 253 571 4900
W: www.tacomaschools.org/mccarver/Pages

Methow Valley Elementary
18 Twin Lakes Rd, Winthrop WA 98862
PYP Coordinator Kelly Wiest
Languages English
T: +1 509 996 2186
W: methow.org/methow-valley-elementary-school

Mount Rainier High School
22450 19th Avenue S, Des Moines WA 98198
DP Coordinator Veronica Fairchild
MYP Coordinator Jim Dyer
Languages English
T: +1 206 631 7000
W: mrhs.highlineschools.org

Northern Heights Elementary
4000 Magrath Road, Bellingham WA 98226
PYP Coordinator Kacey EMerson
Languages English
T: +1 360 647 6820
W: northernheights.bellinghamschools.org

PRIDE Schools
811 E Sprague Ave, Spokane WA 99202
DP Coordinator Hayden Fairley
Languages English, Spanish
T: +1 509 309 7680
W: www.prideschools.org

Rainier Beach High School
8815 Seward Park Avenue S WA 98118
CP Coordinator Steven Miller
DP Coordinator Steven Miller
Languages English
T: +1 206 252 6350
W: rainierbeachhs.seattleschools.org

Renton High School
400 S Second Street, Renton WA 98057
CP Coordinator Joseph Bento
DP Coordinator Malcolm Collie
Languages English
T: +1 425 204 3400
W: rentonhs.rentonschools.us

Saint George's School
2929 W. Waikiki Road, Spokane WA 99208
DP Coordinator Elizabeth Tender
Languages English
T: +1 509 466 1636 EXT:331
W: www.sgs.org

Skyline High School
1122 228th Avenue SE, Issaquah School District, Sammamish WA 98075-6914
CP Coordinator Stephania Gullikson
DP Coordinator Chris Wilder
Languages English
T: +1 425 837 7700
W: www.issaquah.wednet.edu/skylinehs

Soundview School
6515 196th Street SW, Lynnwood WA 98036
MYP Coordinator Chrissy Sinclair
PYP Coordinator Chrissy Sinclair
Languages English
T: +1 425 778 8572
W: www.soundview.org

South Charleston High School
One Eagle Way, South Charleston WA 25309
DP Coordinator Sarah Carroll
Languages English
T: +1 304 766 0352
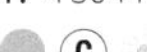

St. Luke School
17533 St Luke Place N, Shoreline WA 98133
MYP Coordinator Kathi Hand
PYP Coordinator Meaghan Roach
Languages English
T: +1 206 542 1133
W: www.stlukeshoreline.net

Sumner High School
1707 Main Street, Sumner WA 98390
DP Coordinator Monica Swigart
Languages English
T: +1 253 891 5500
W: www.sumner.wednet.edu

Thomas Jefferson High School
4248 S. 288th Street, Auburn WA 98001
CP Coordinator Jaclyn Fisher
DP Coordinator Kailey Harem
MYP Coordinator Shari Winslow
Languages English
T: +1 253 945 5600
W: www.fwps.org/tjhs

Totem Middle School
26630 40th Avenue S., Kent WA 98032
MYP Coordinator Liz Andrade
Languages English
T: +1 253 945 5100
W: www.fwps.org/Domain/37

Wade King Elementary School
2155 Yew Street Road, Bellingham WA 98229
PYP Coordinator Hana Anderson
Languages English
T: +1 360 647 6840
W: wadeking.bellinghamschools.org

Wainwright Intermediate School
130 Alameda Avenue, Fircrest WA 98466
MYP Coordinator Cheryl Steighner
PYP Coordinator Donna Basil
Languages English, Spanish
T: +1 253 571 2100
W: wainwright.tacomaschools.org

Washington Preparatory School
18323 Bothell-Everett Highway, Suite 220, Bothell WA 98012
DP Coordinator Janelle Brin
Languages English
T: +1 425 892 8669
W: waprep.org

West Sound Academy
16571 Creative Drive NE, Poulsbo WA 98370
DP Coordinator Catherine Freeman
Languages English
T: +1 360 598 5954
W: www.westsoundacademy.org

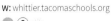

Whittier Elementary School
777 Elmtree Lane, Fircrest WA 98466
PYP Coordinator Traci Frank
Languages English, Spanish
T: +1 253 571 7500
W: whittier.tacomaschools.org

Willows Preparatory School
12280 NE Woodinville-Redmond Rd, Redmond WA 98052
DP Coordinator Mary Ewart
MYP Coordinator Mary Ewart
Languages English
T: +1 425 649 0791
W: www.willowsprep.com

Wisconsin

Academia de Lenguaje y Bellas Artes (ALBA)
1712 S 32nd Street, Milwaukee WI 53215
PYP Coordinator Keelin Eggleston
Languages English

Academy of Accelerated Learning
3727 South 78th Street, Milwaukee WI 53220
PYP Coordinator Renee Bast
Languages English
T: +1 414 604 7300
W: www2.milwaukee.k12.wi.us/aal

Bay Port High School
2710 Lineville Road, Green Bay WI 54313
DP Coordinator Chad McAllister
Languages English
T: +1 920 662 7000
W: bayporthssd.weebly.com

Casimir Pulaski High School
2500 W Oklahoma Ave, Milwaukee WI 53215
CP Coordinator Robin Harris
DP Coordinator Christine Lemon
MYP Coordinator Christine Lemon
Languages English, Spanish
T: +1 414 902 8900
W: www5.milwaukee.k12.wi.us/school/pulaski

Catholic Memorial High School
601 East College Avenue, Waukesha WI 53186
CP Coordinator Nicholas Doyle
DP Coordinator Nicholas Doyle
Languages English
T: +1 262 542 7101
W: www.catholicmemorial.net

Chappell Elementary School
205 N Fisk Street, Green Bay WI 54303
PYP Coordinator Jackie Brosteau
Languages English
T: +1 920 492 2630
W: chappell.gbaps.org

Darrell Lynn Hines College Preparatory Academy of Excellence
7151 North 86th Street, Milwaukee WI 53224
PYP Coordinator Monica Carrington
Languages English
T: +1 414 358 3542

Franklin Middle School
1233 Lore Lane, Green Bay WI 54303
MYP Coordinator Jennifer Burgraff
Languages English
T: +1 920 492 2670
W: franklin.gbaps.org

Green Bay West High School
966 Shawano Avenue, Green Bay WI 54303
DP Coordinator Stephane Bielen
MYP Coordinator Andrew Evenson
Languages English
T: +1 920 492 2730
W: west.gbaps.org

Green Lake School
612 Mill Street, PO Box 369, Green Lake WI 54941
DP Coordinator Joshua LeGreve
MYP Coordinator Mary Hunter
PYP Coordinator Katie James
Languages English
T: +1 920 294 6411
W: www.glsd.k12.wi.us

Holy Family School
1204 S. Fisk Street, Green Bay WI 54304
MYP Coordinator Taylor Lepak
Languages English
T: +1 920 494 1931
W: holyfamilygreenbay.com

Isthmus Montessori Academy
1802 Pankratz Street, Madison WI 53704
DP Coordinator Caleb Wilson
Languages English, Spanish
T: +1 608 661 8200
W: isthmusmontessoriacademy.org

Jefferson Lighthouse Elementary
1722 West Sixth Street, Racine WI 53404
PYP Coordinator Colleen Strain
Languages English
T: +1 262 664 6900
W: www.rusd.org/jefferson

Jerome I Case High School
7345 Washington Avenue, Racine WI 53406
CP Coordinator Rebecca Madsen
DP Coordinator Nicola Malacara
Languages English
T: +1 262 619 4200
W: www.rusd.org/case

Lincoln High School
1433 South Eighth Street, Manitowoc WI 54220
DP Coordinator Lee Thennes
Languages English
T: +1 920 663 9602
W: www.manitowocpublicschools.org

Lowell Elementary School
4360 S. 20th Street, Milwaukee WI 53221
PYP Coordinator Amrit Kaur
Languages English
T: +1 414 304 6600
W: www5.milwaukee.k12.wi.us/school/lowell.html

MacDowell Montessori School
6415 W Mount Vernon Avenue, Milwaukee WI 53213
DP Coordinator Aaron Spiering
MYP Coordinator Stacey Geiger
Languages English
T: +1 414 935 1400

Madison Country Day School
5606 River Road, Waunakee WI 53597
DP Coordinator Mark Childs
MYP Coordinator Mark Childs
PYP Coordinator Kristina Luedtke
Languages English, Spanish
T: +1 608 850 6000
W: www.madisoncountryday.org
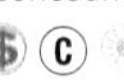

Marvin E. Pratt Elementary School
5131 N Green Bay Avenue, Milwaukee WI 53209
PYP Coordinator Michael Gaatz
Languages English, Spanish
T: +1 414 247 7300
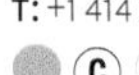

McKinley Middle School
2340 Mohr Avenue, Racine WI 53405
MYP Coordinator Stephanie Skaarnes
Languages English
T: +1 262 664 6150
W: www.rusd.org/mckinley/welcome

North Woods International School
2541 Sablewood Road, La Crosse WI 54601
PYP Coordinator Sara DePaolo
Languages English, Spanish
T: +1 608 789 7000
W: www.lacrosseschools.org/northwoods-international

Notre Dame de la Baie Academy
610 Maryhill Drive, Green Bay WI 54303
CP Coordinator Christian Dory
DP Coordinator Matthew Schultz
Languages English
T: +1 920 429 6100
W: www.NotreDameAcademy.com

Oconomowoc High School
641 East Forest Street, Oconomowoc WI 53066-3888
CP Coordinator Carrie Schultz
DP Coordinator Carrie Schultz
Languages English
T: +1 262 560 3100
W: www.oasd.k12.wi.us/page.cfm?p=6767

Ronald Reagan High School
4965 South 20 Street, Milwaukee WI 53221
CP Coordinator Jamie Gonzalez
DP Coordinator Jamie Gonzalez
MYP Coordinator Cassandra Christensen
Languages English
T: +1 414 304 6100
W: www.milwaukee.k12.wi.us/pages/mps/school/highs/reagan

Rufus King International School - High School Campus
1801 West Olive Street, Milwaukee WI 53209
DP Coordinator Daniel Gatewood
MYP Coordinator Laura Lewandowski
Languages English
T: +1 414 267 0705
W: www.rkhs.org

Rufus King International School - Middle School Campus
121 E Hadley St, Milwaukee WI 53212
MYP Coordinator Vernita Phillips
Languages English
T: +1 414 616 5200
W: www5.milwaukee.k12.wi.us/school/rkims

Stuart Elementary School
7001 N 86th Street, Milwaukee WI 53224
PYP Coordinator Sharonda Robinson
Languages English
T: +1 414 393 3700
W: mps.milwaukee.k12.wi.us/schools/stuart-school.htm

Wausau East High School
2607 N 18th Street, Wausau WI 54403
DP Coordinator Darlene Beattie
Languages English
T: +1 715 261 0650
W: www.wausau.k12.wi.us/east/

Wedgewood Park International School
6506 W Warnimont Avenue, Milwaukee WI 53220
MYP Coordinator Jeannette Bahr
Languages English
T: +1 414 604 7800

West Ridge Elementary School
1347 S. Emmertsen Road, Racine WI 53406
PYP Coordinator Michael Maxwell
T: +1 262 664 6200
W: www.rusd.org/westridge

Wyoming

Cheyenne East High School
2800 E Pershing Blvd, Cheyenne WY 82001
DP Coordinator Jonathon Lever
Languages English
T: +1 307 771 2663 EXT 108
W: www.east.laramie1.org/

Mountain Academy
700 Coyote Canyon Road, Jackson WY 83001
DP Coordinator David Porter
Languages English
T: +1 307 733 3729
W: www.tetonscience.org/programs/mountain-academy

Natrona County High School
930 Elm Street, Casper WY 82601
DP Coordinator Brandi Ramage
Languages English
T: +1 307 253 1700

VENEZUELA

Colegio Guayamuri
Av. Luisa Cáceres de Arismendi, Atamo Norte, La Asunción 6311
DP Coordinator Alexandra De Fina
Languages English, Spanish
T: +58 295 2423048
W: guayamuri.com

Colegio Integral El Avila
Centro de Artes Integradas, Urb. Terrazas del Avila, La Urbina Norte, Caracas 1073
DP Coordinator Carmen Winkler
Languages Spanish
T: +58 500 3528452
W: www.elavila.org

Colegio Integral El Manglar
Carrera No. 41 S/N Sector Nueva Barcelona, Barcelona 6001
DP Coordinator Maria Eugenia Behrens
Languages English, Spanish
T: +58 281 3172170
W: elmanglar.org.ve

Colegio Internacional de Caracas
Calle el Colegio Americano Entre Samanes y Minas, Baruta, Caracas 1080
DP Coordinator Mike East
MYP Coordinator Mike East
Languages English, Spanish
T: +58 212 9450708
W: www.cic-caracas.com

Colegio Los Arcos
Calle Los Arcos, Caracas 1080
DP Coordinator Pedro Domingo Carrillo Carrillo
Languages English, Spanish
T: +58 212 9453344
W: www.losarcos.edu.ve

Colegio Los Campitos
Urbanización Los Campitos, Ruta C, Caracas 1080
DP Coordinator Margot Peña
Languages Spanish
T: +58 212 9771695
W: colegioloscampitosweb.com

Colegio Moral y Luces 'Herzl-Bialik'
Final Av. Principal de Los Chorros, Caracas 1071
DP Coordinator Naily Gamboa
Languages English
T: +58 212 2736894
W: www.secmyl.edu.ve

Escuela Bella Vista
67th Street between Av. 3D and 3E, La Lago sector, Maracaibo 4001
DP Coordinator Gregg Sipp
Languages English
T: +58 261 7940000
W: www.ebv.org.ve

Escuela Campo Alegre
Final Calle La Cinta, Las Mercedes, Caracas 1080
DP Coordinator Cynthia Adballah
Languages English
T: +58 212 9933922
W: www.ecak12.com

Instituto Educacional Juan XXIII
Calle San Enrique No 85-70, Trigal Centro, Valencia 2002
CP Coordinator Jorge Bolivar Manzano
DP Coordinator Elkys Sequera
Languages English, Spanish
T: +58 241 8425732
W: www.juanxxiii.e12.ve

Liceo Los Robles
Urb. El Doral Norte, Calle 34. Esquina con Avenida Fuerzas Armadas, Edificio Liceo Los Robles, Maracaibo
DP Coordinator Jesús Antonio Vilchez Chávez
Languages Spanish
T: +58 261 7421833
W: losroblesenlinea.com.ve

The British School Caracas
Transversal 9 Este Av. Luis Roche, Quinta DAMI Urbanización Altamira, Caracas 1060
DP Coordinator Stephanie Mitchell
Languages English
T: +58 212 6271000
W: www.tbscaracas.com

Washington Academy
Calle C, Urb. Colinas de Valle Arriba, Caracas 1080
DP Coordinator Prof. Yajaira Graterol
MYP Coordinator Prof. Gianna De Sena
Languages Spanish, English
T: +58 212 9757077
W: washington.academy

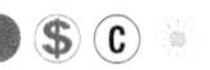

VIRGIN ISLANDS (US)

Virgin Islands Montessori School & Peter Gruber International Academy
6936 Vessup Lane, St Thomas VI 00802
DP Coordinator Bennett Ott
MYP Coordinator Bennett Ott
Languages English
T: +1 340 775 6360
W: www.vimsia.org

IB AMERICAS

Appendices

1. Addresses of all IB Offices
2. Location of IB World Schools
3. Diploma Programme Subjects Offered in 2024 (May and November sessions)
4. Associations of IB World Schools

1. Addresses of all IB Offices

IB FOUNDATION OFFICE

International Baccalaureate
Route des Morillons 15
Grand–Saconnex, Genève
CH – 1218
SWITZERLAND

IB GLOBAL CENTRES

Africa, Europe, Middle East

IB Global Centre, The Hague
Churchillplein 6
2517 JW
The Hague
The Netherlands

IB Global Centre, Cardiff
Peterson House, Malthouse Avenue
Cardiff Gate
Cardiff, Wales
CF23 8GL
United Kingdom

Americas

IB Global Centre, Washington DC
International Baccalaureate,
3950 Wisconsin Avenue NW,
Washington, DC 20016.
USA

Asia – Pacific

IB Global Centre, Singapore
600 North Bridge Road,
#21 – 01 Parkview Square,
Singapore 188778
Republic of Singapore

2. Location of IB World Schools

Location (as of 15 September 2023)	IB World Schools	Number of Programmes				Total number of Programmes
		PYP	MYP	CP	DP	
ALBANIA	3	2	2		3	7
ANDORRA	4			1	3	4
ANGOLA	1	1	1		1	3
ANGUILLA	1	1				1
ANTIGUA AND BARBUDA	1				1	1
ARGENTINA	53	4	2		52	58
ARMENIA	4	2	1		3	6
AUSTRALIA	207	148	43	2	80	273
AUSTRIA	18	5	6	1	17	29
AZERBAIJAN	9	5	3		8	16
BAHAMAS	3	3	1	1	3	8
BAHRAIN	15	2	2	1	15	20
BANGLADESH	11	9	3	1	7	20
BARBADOS	1	1	1		1	3
BELARUS	1				1	1
BELGIUM	12	5	7	3	12	27
BERMUDA	3		1	1	3	5
BOLIVIA	3	1	1		3	5
BOSNIA AND HERZEGOVINA	4		1		4	5
BOTSWANA	3	2	1		2	5
BRAZIL	56	26	11		46	83
BRITISH VIRGIN ISLANDS	1	1	1		1	3
BRUNEI DARUSSALAM	2				2	2
BULGARIA	11	1	3	1	9	14
BURKINA FASO	2				2	2
BURUNDI	1				1	1
CAMBODIA	7	4	3	1	6	14
CAMEROON	5	1	1		5	7
CANADA	374	98	158	7	186	449
CAYMAN ISLANDS	4	3			1	4
CHILE	30	14	11		27	52
CHINA	278	169	71	5	163	408
COLOMBIA	63	20	15	1	61	97
COSTA RICA	49	2	3		49	54
CÔTE D'IVOIRE	2		1		2	3
CROATIA	7	1	2		6	9

CUBA	1				1	1
CURACAO	1		1		1	2
CYPRUS	4				4	4
CZECHIA	15	2	1	2	15	20
DENMARK	20	5	5		17	27
DOMINICAN REPUBLIC	6				6	6
ECUADOR	80	21	23		78	122
EGYPT	47	23	14	1	39	77
EL SALVADOR	5	1	1		4	6
ESTONIA	6	5	4		5	14
ESWATINI	2		1		1	2
ETHIOPIA	3	1			3	4
FIJI	2	2	2		2	6
FINLAND	20	3	4	1	16	24
FRANCE	22	8	6	1	20	35
GABON	2	2	1		2	5
GEORGIA	4	3	3	1	4	11
GERMANY	81	27	18	5	76	126
GHANA	13	8	5	1	9	23
GREECE	19	8	6		15	29
GUAM	1				1	1
GUATEMALA	4				4	4
GUERNSEY	1			1	1	2
HONDURAS	1				1	1
HONG KONG	71	41	16	7	38	102
HUNGARY	10	1	2		10	13
ICELAND	2		1		1	2
INDIA	223	137	59	26	155	377
INDONESIA	69	40	20	5	49	114
IRAQ	7	6	3		3	12
IRELAND	5	2	2		4	8
ISLAMIC REPUBLIC OF IRAN	6	3	3		3	9
ISLE OF MAN	1				1	1
ISRAEL	5		1		5	6
ITALY	43	23	17		35	75
JAMAICA	2				2	2
JAPAN	107	55	35		67	157
JERSEY	1			1	1	2
JORDAN	19	11	14	2	18	45
KAZAKHSTAN	13	9	10		6	25
KENYA	11	4	3	2	9	18
KOSOVO	1	1	1		1	3
KUWAIT	5	4	2		2	8

KYRGYZSTAN	2	1	1		2	4
LATVIA	10	3	4	1	7	15
LEBANON	26	7	4		25	36
LESOTHO	1				1	1
LITHUANIA	16	3	4		13	20
LUXEMBOURG	5	1	1		4	6
MACAU	3	1	1		3	5
MADAGASCAR	1	1			1	2
MALAWI	1	1	1		1	3
MALAYSIA	22	10	9	2	17	38
MALI	1				1	1
MALTA	2			1	2	3
MAURITIUS	5	2	2	1	3	8
MEXICO	122	59	45	17	79	200
MONACO	1			1	1	2
MONGOLIA	4	2	1		4	7
MONTENEGRO	2	1	1		2	4
MOROCCO	13	2	6		5	13
MOZAMBIQUE	4	3	2		3	8
MYANMAR	6	1			5	6
NAMIBIA	1	1			1	2
NEPAL	5	4	1		2	7
NEW ZEALAND	23	14	4		12	30
NICARAGUA	3	1	1		2	4
NIGER	1				1	1
NIGERIA	5	2			3	5
NORWAY	43	21	21	1	25	68
OMAN	7	6	5		5	16
PAKISTAN	32	26	14	1	14	55
PALESTINE, STATE OF	3	1	1		2	4
PANAMA	6	3	2		6	11
PAPUA NEW GUINEA	1				1	1
PARAGUAY	4				4	4
PEOPLE'S DEMOCRATIC REPUBLIC LAO	1	1	1		1	3
PERU	78	16	11	2	77	106
PHILIPPINES	27	10	4	1	22	37
POLAND	68	13	17		60	90
PORTUGAL	14	4	4		13	21
PUERTO RICO	2	2	2		2	6
QATAR	18	13	9	1	14	37
REPUBLIC OF KOREA	34	21	14	1	17	53
REPUBLIC OF NORTH MACEDONIA	6	4	3		4	11
ROMANIA	12	5	3		11	19

RUSSIAN FEDERATION	36	23	15		25	63
RWANDA	1	1	1	1	4	1
SAUDI ARABIA	29	21	10		15	46
SENEGAL	6	1	2		6	9
SERBIA	7	2	2		7	11
SINGAPORE	40	22	9	2	31	64
SINT MAARTEN	1				1	1
SLOVAKIA	9	5	3		7	15
SLOVENIA	7	1	2		6	9
SOLOMON ISLANDS	1	1				1
SOUTH AFRICA	12	10	2		3	15
SPAIN	219	61	46	2	193	302
SRI LANKA	1	1	1		1	3
SUDAN	2	2	1		2	5
SWEDEN	39	13	13	2	28	56
SWITZERLAND	54	14	11	5	51	81
TAIWAN	16	6	7	2	11	26
THAILAND	33	15	11	5	24	55
THE DEMOCRATIC REPUBLIC OF THE CONGO	4	3	2		3	8
THE NETHERLANDS	33	11	19	6	26	62
TIMOR-LESTE	1	1				1
TOGO	3	1	1		3	5
TRINIDAD AND TOBAGO	1	1	1			2
TUNISIA	5	3	3		3	9
TÜRKIYE	115	65	14		73	152
UGANDA	4	2	2		4	8
UKRAINE	5	1	1		5	7
UNITED ARAB EMIRATES	55	33	26	18	50	127
UNITED KINGDOM	133	26	29	39	90	184
UNITED REPUBLIC OF TANZANIA	5	5	4		5	14
UNITED STATES	1901	643	589	167	930	2329
UNITED STATES VIRGIN ISLANDS	1		1		1	2
URUGUAY	11	3	4	1	9	17
UZBEKISTAN	5	4	2		3	9
VENEZUELA	13		2	1	13	16
VIETNAM	21	11	6		18	35
ZAMBIA	3	2	1		3	6
ZIMBABWE	1	1	1		1	3
Grand Total	**5684**	**2268**	**1683**	**363**	**3651**	**7965**

*Programme count does not include European Platform or MYP Partner Schools
**School count does not include European Platform, includes MYP Partner Schools

3. Diploma Programme Subjects offered in 2024 (May and November sessions)

Language and literature
Language A: literature HL
Language A: literature SL
Language A: language and literature HL
Literature and performance SL

Language acquisition
Language B HL
Language B SL
Language *ab initio* SL
Classical languages HL
Classical languages SL

Individuals and societies
Business management HL
Business management SL
Digital society HL
Digital society SL
Economics HL
Economics SL
Geography HL
Geography SL
Global politics HL
Global politics SL
History HL
History SL
Philosophy HL
Philosophy SL
Psychology HL
Psychology SL
Social and cultural anthropology HL
Social and cultural anthropology SL
World religions SL

Sciences
Biology HL
Biology SL
Chemistry HL
Chemistry SL
Computer science HL
Computer science SL
Design technology HL
Design technology SL
Physics HL
Physics SL
Sports, exercise and health science HL
Sports, exercise and health science SL

Mathematics
Mathematics: analysis and approaches HL
Mathematics: analysis and approaches SL
Mathematics: applications and interpretation HL
Mathematics: applications and interpretation SL

The arts
Dance HL
Dance SL
Film HL
Film SL
Music HL
Music SL
Theatre HL
Theatre SL
Visual arts HL
Visual arts SL

Core requirements
Creativity, activity, service
Extended essay
Theory of knowledge

Interdisciplinary subjects
Environmental systems and societies SL
Literature and performance SL

School based syllabuses

Art history
Astronomy
Brazilian social studies
(also examined in November session)
Classical Greek & Roman studies
Food science and technology
Literary arts
Marine science
Modern history of Kazakhstan
Political thought
Turkey in the 20th century
World arts and cultures

Languages offered in studies in language and literature

Language A: literature

Afrikaans A (Nov only)
Albanian A (May only)
Amharic A (May only)
Arabic A (May only)
Armenian A (May only)
Azerbaijani A (May only)
Bengali A (May only)
Bosnian A (May only)
Bulgarian A (May only)
Catalan A (May only)
Chinese A
Croatian A (May only)
Czech A (May only)
Danish A (May only)
Dutch A (May only)
English A
Estonian A (May only)
Filipino A (May only)
Finnish A (May only)
French A
Georgian A (May only)
German A
Hebrew A (May only)
Hindi A (May only)
Hungarian A (May only)
Icelandic A (May only)
Indonesian A
Italian A (May only)
Japanese A
Khmer A (May only)
Korean A
Latvian A (May only)
Lithuanian A (May only)
Macedonian A (May only)
Malay A (May only)
Modern Greek A (May only)
Mongolian A (May only)
Nepali A (May only)
Norwegian A (May only)
Persian A (May only)
Polish A (May only)
Portuguese A
Romanian A (May only)
Russian A (May only)
Serbian A (May only)
Sesotho A (May only)
Siswati A (November only)
Slovak A (May only)
Slovene A (May only)
Spanish A
Swahili A (May only)
Swedish A (May only)
Thai A (May only)
Turkish A
Ukrainian A (May only)
Urdu A (May only)
Vietnamese A (May only)

Language A: language and literature

Arabic A (May only)
Chinese A
Dutch A (May only)
English A
French A
German A
Indonesian A (May only)
Italian A (May only)
Japanese A
Korean A (May only)
Modern Greek A (May only)
Norwegian A (May only)
Portuguese A
Russian A (May only)
Spanish A
Swedish A (May only)
Thai A (May only)

Literature and performance

English
Spanish

Language B

Arabic B (May only)
Chinese B – Cantonese (May only)
Chinese B – Mandarin
Danish B (May only)
Dutch B (May only)
English B
Finnish B (May only)
French B
German B
Hebrew B (SL only, May only)
Hindi B (May only)
Indonesian B
Italian B (May only)
Japanese B
Korean B (May only)
Malay B (SL only, Nov only)
Norwegian B (May only)
Portuguese B (May only)
Russian B (May only)
Spanish B
Swahili B (May only)
Swedish B (May only)
Tamil B (Nov only, SL only)

Language *ab initio*

Arabic *ab initio* (May only)
Danish *ab initio* (May only)
Dutch *ab initio* (May only)
English *ab initio*
French *ab initio*
German *ab initio* (May only)
Indonesian *ab initio* (Nov only)
Italian *ab initio* (May only)
Japanese *ab initio*
Mandarin *ab initio*
Russian *ab initio* (May only)
Spanish *ab initio*
Swahili *ab initio* (May only)
Swedish *ab initio* (May only)

Classical languages

Classical Greek (English) May only
Latin (English and Spanish)

Language B Notes:
Malay SL and Tamil SL are available only in the November session. Therefore, any candidate registered for a May session wishing to take Malay SL or Tamil SL must be additionally registered for a November session C1.6 Availability of subjects for 2023 and 2024 examination sessions Diploma Programme Assessment procedures 2021 51 (usually, but not necessarily, in the preceding year). They must take all Malay SL or Tamil SL assessment components (IA, paper 1 and paper 2) in that November session. Note: Italian B and Portuguese B were withdrawn from the November session after the November 2019 session. Note: The Chinese B – Cantonese (May session only) and Chinese B – Mandarin (both May and November sessions) examination papers will continue to be produced in both traditional and simplified characters.

Language *ab initio* Notes:
Indonesian is not available in the May session. Therefore, any candidate registered for a May session wishing to take Indonesian must be additionally registered for a November session (usually, but not necessarily, in the preceding year). They must take all Indonesian assessment components (IA, paper 1 and paper 2) in that November session. There is no special request service for language *ab initio*.

4. Associations of IB World Schools

Associations of IB World Schools (AIBWS) are groups of IB World Schools, who come together in order to provide mutual support to the community of IB World Schools. AIBWS are organized in various ways, sizes and constituencies, depending on their local circumstances and provide a forum for school collaboration, hold periodic meetings, deliver professional development and share best practice among members.

Each AIBWS is an independent entity that is not run or managed by the IB, but in order to formalize its relationship with the IB, they must meet certain criteria, by means of a recognition agreement and licence. They have their own constitution that describes their structure, membership and financial responsibilities. The IB works closely with all the recognized AIBWS.

Associations are often an indispensable resource for schools discovering the IB for the first time, offer a wealth of IB experience and support, and are often active at district, state or government level raising awareness of all IB programmes within their area of representation. They may also, working closely with their regional IB office, assist in negotiations with governments for acceptance of all IB programmes and with universities for recognition for the Diploma Programme.

Association of IB World Schools benefits

The IB raises the profile of the AIBWS by featuring them on its website, IBWS yearbook, inviting their representatives to regional meetings, as well to dedicated IB Associations' events at IB Conferences. AIBWS have access to IB materials the same way as IBWS, permitting their use of a specially created logo for use under licence on their websites and in publicity to denote their status, and have multiple communication channels with IB.

Establishing an Association of IB World Schools

Groups of schools who wish to be recognized by the IB as an AIBWS should ensure that they can meet IB criteria for recognition. Full overview of the criteria, as well as detailed guideline on how to form an AIBWS is available on the IB website.

More information is available on AIBWS website: www.ibo.org/contact-the-ib/associations-of-ib-schools

List of recognized Associations of IB World Schools

AIBWS family is growing and there are 67 recognized AIBWS globally, that cover 73 countries, 54 states and provinces on six continents.

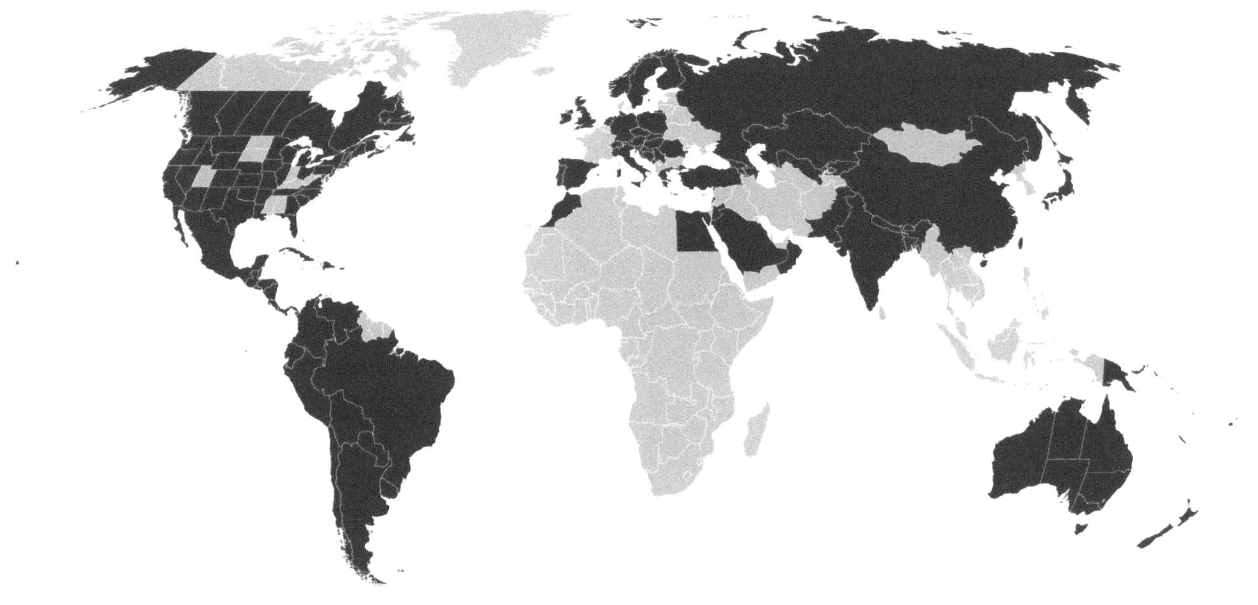

Associations of IB World Schools in Africa

Country/region	Name	Contact	Website
Morocco	Association des Ecoles du BI du Maroc	cherrouk@madina.ma +212 6 61 30 88 96	www.aebim-ma.org

Associations of IB World Schools in Europe

Country/region	Name	Contact	Website
Andorra, Portugal and Spain (Iberian Peninsula)	Asociación Ibérica de Colegios de BI	comunicacion@asibi.org +34 645 851 604	asibi.org
Andorra, Spain	Asociación de Centros del BI de España	jvarela@colegioobradoiro.es +34 667 534 647	
Austria, Bosnia and Herzegovina, Croatia, Czech Republic, Hungary, Kosovo, North Macedonia, Poland, Romania, Serbia, Slovakia, Slovenia	Association of Central European IB Schools	coordinator@aces-ib.org +420 739 021 601	www.aces-ib.org
Azerbaijan, Georgia, Kazakhstan, Kyrgyzstan, Uzbekistan	Caucasus and Central Asia Association of IB World Schools (CCAAIBWS)	info@ccaaibws.org +994 51 777 28 79	http://www.ccaaibws.org/
Commonwealth of Independent States CIS	IB Schools Association of Commonwealth Independent States (IBSA)	natalyab@mes.ru +7 499 255 0070	https://ibsa.su/
Finland	The Association of Finnish IB Schools (AFIB)	mats.borgmastars@abo.fi +358 (0) 46 923 6574	sites.google.com/eduespoo.fi/afib/home
Germany	Association of German International Schools (AGIS) *	julia@agis-schools.org +49 17610224981	agis-schools.org
Greece	IB Schools in Greece Association (IBSIGA)	zgeitona@cgs.edu.gr +30 210 6663930	ibsiga.wordpress.com
Italy	Association of IB World Schools in Italy (AIBWSI)	l.pazzi@isturin.it	www.aibwsi.it
Norway	Norwegian IB Schools (NIBS)	larsjo@innlandetfylke.no +47 404 495 77	norwegianibschoolsnibs.org
Poland	The Association of Polish IB Schools	jrosiek@kopernik.edu.pl	iberse.wixsite.com/ssib
Sweden	Association of Swedish IB Schools (ASIB)	tony.nicolas@vasteras.se 021 390765 / 0765 693 663 +46 8 5925721	www.swedishibschools.se
Switzerland	Swiss Group of International Schools (ISA)SGIS)	denise.coates@isberne.ch	www.sgischools.com
The Netherlands	The Dutch International Secondary Schools (DISS)	secondary@ dutchinternationalschools.nl	www. dutchinternationalschools.nl
Turkey	Turkish IB Schools Association (TIBSA)	merim@aci.k12.tr +90 532 6532 575	www.sgischools.com
United Kingdom and Ireland, Channel Islands and Isle of Man	IB Schools and Colleges Association (IBSCA)	ibsca@ oxfordcoursemanagers.org +44 1865 636 400	www.ibsca.org.uk

Associations of IB World Schools in Middle East

Country/region	Name	Contact	Website
Egypt	IB Schools in Egypt Association (IBSEA)	Ghada Dajani GDajani@mescairo.com + 20 2 26189600	www.ibsea.org
Jordan	Jordan Association of IB World Schools	alice.abboud@ ahliyyahmutran.edu.jo +962 79 559 9357	
Kingdom of Saudi Arabia	Saudi IB Association (SIBA)	Randa Dahshe rdahshe@kfs.sch.sa +966 595912912	
Lebanon	The Association of IB World Schools in Lebanon	+961 3906597 Rania Jibai rania@outlook.com	
Oman	The Oman Association of IB World Schools (OAIBWS)	Craig Williamson +968 - 7151 8846	
Qatar	Qatar IB World Schools Association (QIBA)	Ghada Maalouf g.maalouf@aia.qa 97430804701	
United Arab Emirates	UAE Association of IB Schools	RDrew@jbschool.ae +971 50 6806583	

Associations of IB World Schools in Canada

Province	Name	Contact	Website
Alberta	Alberta Association of International Baccalaureate World Schools (ABIBS)	abibspresident@gmail.com +1 403-938-4431, ext. 271	www.abibs.ca
Bermuda, New Brunswick, Newfoundland & Labrador, Nova Scotia and Prince Edward Island	Atlantic Canadian Association of IB World Schools	acaibws@gmail.com +1 902 957 1314	sites.google.com/view/ acaibws
British Columbia	British Columbia Association of International Baccalaureate World Schools	rohly@aspengroveschool. com +1 250 933 8029	bcaibws.ca/
Manitoba, Saskatchewan	Prairie Association of IB World Schools	lmcmaster@retsd.mb.ca +1 204 667 1103	www.paibws.org
Ontario	IB Schools of Ontario	director@ibso.ca	www.ibschoolsofontario.ca
Quebec	Société des écoles du monde du BI du Québec et de la francophonie (SÉBIQ)	sec@sebiq.ca +1 450 593 33 93	www.sebiq.ca

Associations of IB World Schools in Latin America

Country	Name	Contact	Website
Costa Rica, Central America and Caribbean	Asociación de Colegios del Mundo IB Costa Rica, Centro America y El Caribe	info@ibcompass.org +506 2267 1880	http://www.ibcompass.org/
Argentina	Asociación de Colegios del Bachillerato Internacional del Rio de la Plata	accbirp.cd@gmail.com +54 114 772-6256	

Brazil	Associação Brasileira de IB Schools	deivis.pothin@pueridomus.com.br +55 11 3512 2222	www.baibs.org.br
Chile	Asociación Chilena del Bachillerato Internacional	karla@achbi.cl +569 9331 5395	www.achbi.cl
Colombia	Asociación Andina de Colegios de Bachillerato Internacional	presidenciaaacbi@gmail.com +573124578603	www.aacbi.org.com
Ecuador	Asociación Ecuatoriana de Colegios con Bachillerato Internacional	coordinacion@aseccbi.edu.ec +593 987673197	www.aseccbi.edu.ec
Mexico	Asociación de colegios IB de México	enlace@ibamex.mx +52 55 43 23 10 11	www.ibamex.com
Peru	Asociación de Colegios IB Perú	ascibp@gmail.com +511 957 222 090	ascibp.pe
Uruguay	Uruguay AIBWS	aucbiuruguay@gmail.com +59 898 123 510	www.aucbi.edu.uy
Venezuela	Asociación de Colegios Del Mundo BI de Venezuela	juan@juanxxiii.e12.ve +58 4124 883 254	

Associations of IB World Schools in the United States of America

State(s)	Name	Contact	Website
Alaska, Idaho, Montana, Oregon, Washington	Northwest Association of IB World Schools	nwaibws1992@gmail.com	www.northwestibassociation.com
Arizona	Arizona AIBWS International Baccalaureate Schools (AZIBS)	jadavis@mpsaz.org +1 480 472 4419	www.azibs.org
Arkansas, Iowa, Kansas, Missouri, Nebraska, Oklahoma	Midwest IB Schools (MIBS)	christy.dabalos@lsr7.net +1 816-986-4061	sites.google.com/view/midwestibschools/home
California	California Association of IB World Schools (CAWS)	cawsedir@gmail.com +1 909 896 9557	cawsib.org
Colorado, Wyoming	Rocky Mountain Association of IB World Schools (IBARMS)	director@ibarms.org +1 720 878 7430	www.ibarms.org/ib
Connecticut, Maine, Massachusetts, New Hampshire, New Jersey, New York, Pennsylvania (east), Rhode Island, Vermont	Guild of IB Schools of the Northeast (GIBS)	gibsnortheast@gmail.com +1 212-724-6360 x318	gibs.wildapricot.org
Delaware, DC, Maryland, Pennsylvania, Virginia	Mid-Atlantic Association of IB World Schools	johnLday@mac.com +1 608 238 1284	www.ibmidatlantic.org
Florida	The Florida Association of IB World Schools FLIBS	info@flibs.org +1 850-228-8044	flibs.org
Georgia	Association of IB World Schools of Georgia	Kdenney@forsyth.k12.ga.us	www.ibgeorgia.com
Illinois	Illinois International Baccalaureate Schools	akulas@cps.edu+1 312 945 8240	ilibschools.org
Louisiana	Louisiana IB Schools	cherissa.vitter@selu.edu	sites.google.com/a/selu.edu/libs/
Michigan	IB Schools of Michigan	ibsom@icloud.com	www.ibsom.org

Minnesota	Minnesota Association of IB World Schools	director@mnibschools.org +1 612 483 3749	www.mnibschools.org
Nevada	Nevada Association of International Baccalaureate World Schools	feinsbc@nv.ccsd.net +1 702 799 2580	www.naibws.org
North Carolina	IB Schools of North Carolina	ibschoolsofnc@gmail.com +1 980 239 7547	ibsnc.org
Ohio	Ohio Association of IB World Schools	OhioIBWorldSchools@gmail.com + 1 937 475 5177	www.ohioib.org/index.html
South Carolina	South Carolina IB Schools	karen.perdue@beaufort.k12.sc.us	www.facebook.com/SouthCarolinaIB
Tennessee	Tennessee IB Association of World Schools	Emily.munn.seibert@gmail.com +1 615-333-5175 ext. 858009	sites.google.com/site/tennesseeibschools
Texas	Texas IB Schools	karen@texasibschools.org 972-834-8934	www.texasibschools.org
Utah	IB World Schools of Utah	aibwsu@gmail.com +1 801-578-8500	www.ibschoolsofutah.org
Wisconsin	Wisconsin Association of IB World Schools	walkerd5@milwaukee.k12.wi.us +1 414 688 5889	ibwisconsin.org

Associations of IB World Schools in Asia – Pacific region

Country	Name	Contact	Website
Australia, Fiji, New Zealand and Papua New Guinea and the South-West Pacific	IB Schools Australasia	office@ibaustralasia.org +61(0) 457 490 500	ibaustralasia.org
India	The Association of International Schools of India *	info@taisi-india.org +91 997118852	www.taisi-india.org
South Asia and India	Association for Heads Of IB World Schools in India & South Asia	President@ibheadsassociationindia.com	http://www.ibheadsassociationindia.com/
Japan	IB Association of Japan	chair@ibaj.or.jp	ibaj.or.jp
Mainland China, Hong Kong(SAR), Macau(SAR) Taiwan	Chong Wa International Baccalaureate Schools Association	cisa_2020@163.com	ibcisa.net/lxcisa
Pakistan	Association of IB World Schools in Pakistan (IBPAK)	info@ibpak.pk farah.masood@learningalliance.edu.pk +92 21 3583 5805-6 +92 42 111-66-66-33 Ext.: 355	ibpak.pk

Cooperation with other groups of schools

In addition to the work with the AIBWS and in order to support IB World Schools, the IB communicates and collaborates with other groups of schools and international school associations on an informal basis. These International Schools Associations are marked with an asterisk (*)

5. University Recognition

IB Diploma Programme

The IB Diploma Programme is an excellent passport to higher education. Universities around the world welcome the unique characteristics of IB Diploma Programme students and recognize the way in which the programme helps to prepare students for higher education.

Each year the IB is asked by students and their schools to send transcripts to over 4,500 different universities and colleges, in over 100 different countries. The most popular destinations include the United States (40%), United Kingdom (17%), Australia (10%), Canada (10%) and Netherlands (4%).

IB students routinely gain admission to some of the best universities and colleges in the world. Every year the IB sends significant numbers of transcripts to the university members of:

- the Ivy League in the United States
- the Russell Group in the United Kingdom
- the U15 group in Canada
- the Group of Eight in Australia
- the RU11 group in Japan
- the U15 group in Germany

As well as other academically elite universities across the globe.

The IB has established strong relationships with universities who have granted recognition of the IB Diploma programme in a number of different ways. It is recommended that schools, students and parents visit the individual university websites in order to gain the most up to date information regarding recognition.

Admission

The IBDP is widely accepted as a valid qualification for entry into higher education, without the need for other tests or qualifications. Note that this does not guarantee admission to a particular university, rather provides the opportunity to compete for a place at the institution.

Students wishing to be admitted for certain degree programmes may be required to study certain subjects, which may be specified at either standard or higher level. Students may also be required to achieve a particular number of points for the Diploma and may be required to gain a certain number of points in individual subjects.

The IBDP also acts of proof of English Language proficiency for admission into university in a number of countries.

A number of universities also accept students who are not completing the full IBDP, but are instead studying for one or more IB DP Courses.

Credit and Advanced Placement

Many universities, particularly in the United States, will offer students Credit and/or Advanced Placement on their chosen university degree programme. This may reduce the overall tuition cost, or the time required to complete their degree.

Scholarship

A number of universities have established scholarships specifically for IB graduates. The value and nature of these awards will vary from university to university and are aimed to support the student during their time in higher education.

IB Career-Related Programme

Since its launch in 2014, the IBCP has grown its reputation with universities as a valid route for students to progress to higher education, as well as the world of employment.

CP students have requested that their transcripts be sent to universities and colleges in 35 countries, across North America, Africa, Europe, the Middle East, Asia, and Australasia. They have requested that their transcripts be sent to over 1,000 universities around the world, including more than 750 institutions in the United States and more than 130 in the United Kingdom.

The IB continues to work with universities to improve the knowledge and understanding of the CP, as well as its recognition.

For more information regarding recognition or both the DP and CP, please see the University Admissions section of the IB website www.ibo.org/university-admission/

Index

An index of all IB World Schools listed alphabetically.

B

C

D

E

F

G

H

I

J

K

M

N

O

P

Q

R

S

T

U

V

W

X

Y

Z